BRITISH POETRY
AND
THE AMERICAN REVOLUTION

BRITISH POETRY
AND
THE AMERICAN REVOLUTION

A Bibliographical Survey of
Books and Pamphlets,
Journals and Magazines,
Newspapers, and Prints

1755-1800


by

Martin Kallich


Volume II


The Whitston Publishing Company
Troy, New York
1988

Copyright 1988
Martin Kallich

Library of Congress Catalog Card Number 86-50943

ISBN for set of two volumes 0-87875-318-4
ISBN for Volume II 0-87875-364-8

Printed in the United States of America

1778  Books & Pamphlets

78-1.  America Lost.  A Poem of Condolence, Addressed to Britannia.
London:  Lewis, 1778.

Notices:  CR 46 (Jul 1778), 72;  MR 58 (Jun 1778), 469;  LR 8 (Jul 1778), 62.

Sabin 1026.

Copies:  none located.  (This poem may really be The Complaint, 76-5.)


78-2.  [Atkinson, Joseph]
Congratulatory Ode, to General Sir William Howe, on his Return from America.
Dublin:  Hoey, 1778.  iii-iv + 5-15p.

"From all the cares of high command."  (144)

Copies:  BL 11632.bb.52.

Regular Horatian ode in sixains.  In dedication, Atkinson declares that he has tried "to rescue, from ungrateful and malicious censure," the injured military character of Howe.  In the poem, he insists that Howe deserves applause although he did not pacify rebel America.  His leadership was acknowledged by his veterans:  Howe, "with mild heroic care,/ Conquer'd to save,--and fought to spare."  Atkinson praises Howe's friendly and patriot military policy and regrets that it did not succeed in restoring loyalty.  The poet refers to "The guilty Congress," "the republican faction" pushing for independence, and "Puritanic rage" and fanaticism fanning discord and sedition.  Handwritten on the title page of the BL copy is the author's name:  "Cap[n]. Joseph Atkinson.  46 Foot."


78-3.  Bellona;  Or, The Genius of Britain;  A Poetical Vision:  Inscribed to John Dunning, Esq. of Lincoln's-Inn.
London:  Greenlaw & Christie, [1778].  25p.

"As pensive on my tear-stain'd couch I lay."  (c. 240)

Notices:  CR 46 (Jul 1778), 71-2;  MR 59 (Oct 1778), 311;  LR 8 (Appendix 1778), 466.

Copies:  NUC  IU, OCU.

HC.  A patriotic reaction to the menace of France.  The poet recalls the triumphs of Caractacus, Alfred, Edward at Cressy and Poitiers, Henry at Agincourt, Drake and

Raleigh, Cromwell, William of Nassau, Anne and Marlborough, Chatham under George II, and the achievements of Hawke, Granby, Boscawen, Blackney, Townshend, Wolfe, and Amherst in the Seven Years War. Although Chatham has died, a patriot group remains to guard the land. Britannia mourns the lost opportunity to rescue Corsica, then rouses Britons to "fight against a perjur'd land," France, and seeks revenge under the leadership of Keppel: "Again we combat half the world in arms." The poet wants Britain to free Corsica.

78-4. [Bertie, Willoughby, Fourth Earl of Abingdon, pseud.]
  *An Adieu to the Turf: A Poetical Epistle from the E[ar]l of A[bingdo]n to His Grace the A[rchbisho]p of Y[or]k.*
  London: Smith, 1778. vii + 24p.

  "Great Prelate! Thou whose bloody Birch." (c. 290)

  Notices: CR 45 (May 1778), 395-6; MR 58 (Jun 1778), 470.

  Copies: BL 11630.d.11 (12); NUC CtY, DFo, NjP, OCU.

  Stanzas in sixains. Ironic satire on Tory Markham, Archbishop of York, through the persona of Abingdon. But the peer is not treated gently either: his aristocratic education is belittled as well as his fascination for horse racing. But then Abingdon takes up politics and America. His persona begs Markham's forgiveness for engaging in treason, for fostering the American rebellion, and remarking on his exchange with Burke admits "In foul Rebellion's paths I trod,/ And Burke himself surpass'd there," which pleased Wilkes, Sawbridge, Townsend, and Glynn, City leaders in the opposition. Now he asks Markham to counsel him as he turns over a new leaf. He promises to "Raise high the Right divine of Kings, / Damn Liberty, and such mean things," and to "shew America a vast Trick," and "cut Prince Washington in two,/ Give Silas Deane, and Franklin too,/ A new Electric stroke." So the persona bids adieu to the turf and turns to Lord North, whom he ironically praises for his fame in directing the ship of state. (The source for this satire may be George Chalmers' *Second Thoughts: Or, Observations Upon Lord Abingdon's Thoughts On the Letter of Edmund Burke, Esq. To the Sheriffs of Bristol* [1777].)

78-5. *Caledonia, A Poem.*
  London: Cadell, 1778. [vii] + 63p.

  "Through rugged mountains clad in gloomy heath." (c. 950)

  Notices: CR 47 (Apr 1779), 311-12; MR 60 (May 1779), 397.

  Copies: BL 164.n.73, 1346.f.56; NUC CtY, MB, MH, NN.

  Blank verse. A romantic topographical and social poem about Scots Highland customs, larded with notes. Discusses emigrations from Scotland, causes and effects, and "colonizing the boundless regions of the American continent." The poet asks the state to relax the penal law prohibiting the Highland dress, because the Scots are now loyal and approved. Taking up the problem of Highland emigrations, he declares (p. 48) that the British empire in America is a disadvantage, "a cumbrous load," and a source of weakness. The depopulation of the Highlands had reached proportions of "epidemic rage": "Had not the American rebellion put a stop to it, God knows where it would have ended" (p. 49). He speculates that Britain, so badly weakened, would become a province of France! Should the rebellion end happily for Britain, he advises against land grants and colonization because the descendants will be inevitably alienated. Concludes with advice that the Highlanders be treated humanely, in accord with constructive economic policies, so they will not emigrate to America.

78-6. Captain Parolles at M[i]nden: A Rough Sketch for the Royal Academy. Most Respectfully Dedicated to Temple Luttrell, Esq; In Honour of his Spirited Speech on the 26th of May last. By the Author of Royal Perseverance, Tyranny the Worst Taxation, Epistle to L[or]d M[ans]f[iel]d, &c.
London: Bew, 1778. 5-28p.

"Awake, ye Bards! and with Pindaric Fire." (c. 320)

Notices: CR 46 (Sep 1778), 236; MR 59 (Oct 1778), 312; LR 8 (Oct 1778), 279.

Copies: BL 643.k.20; Bod 4° W 71 Jur; NUC CtY, DFo, InU.

HC. Satire on Lord George Germain (Sackville), Secretary of State for the American Department, for his cowardice at the Battle of Minden; contrasts his shameful conduct there with his failure to convey orders to Burgoyne, thereby dooming the British general to defeat at Saratoga, despite his bravery. Believes he is not qualified to plan military strategy from the safety of his office "Three Thousand Leagues beyond the Cannon's Reach." Temple Luttrell, MP from Milborne Port, was a vociferous opponent of the ministry's American War.


78-7. [Chandler, Daniel ?]
An Apology for the Times: A Poem, Addressed to the King.
London: J. F. and C. Rivington; Oxford: Prince, 1778. 72p.

"In this tremendous Hour, when gloomy Fate." (c. 1500)

Notices: CR 45 (Apr 1778), 313-14; MR 58 (May 1778), 397; GA, Jul 8, Dec 14, 1778; G Eve Post, Jun 18, 1778; GM 48 (Jun 1778), 288; Lloyd's Eve Post 42 (Mar 23, 1778), 284; L Eve Post, Jun 16, Jul 4, 1778; L Mag 47 (Apr 1778), 182; MP, Oct 1, 1779.

Sabin 1766.

Copies: BL 11630.d.11 (11); Bod Godwyn Pamph 1734 (15); NUC CtY, DLC, IU, RPJCB.

HC. A Tory satire. In the beginning, the poet versifies Price's arguments as developed in his Civil Liberty (1776), which he totally rejects. Mourns the corrupt, slothful country in which the "manly spirit" is extinct. Statesmen such as Chatham, Rockingham, Burke, Bertie (Abingdon) support faction and rebellion. False patriots and demagogues, like the old Puritan republicans, will bring England to ruin. Nevertheless, England is blessed, and "Yankee Doodle" an "ungrateful son." England still has some men of spirit--North, the King, Mansfield, Beaufort, Howe, Bathurst, Burgoyne, Sandwich. Urges unanimity (under the present ministry) and the banishment of the treacherous faction to America ("Let Washington and Putnam disunite,/ Hancock and Adams jar"), the forgetting of party feuds and discord, the checking of lawless rebellion. Then England will be great again. Incidentally, blames Rockingham for "the Stamp Act's rash Repeal," fatal to Britain and the source of all her trouble. Mason, Wilkes, Percy, and Burke appear.--Attributed to "Jack Chandler of New College" (Oxford) in a copy at MH.

78-8. [Combe, William]
An Heroic Epistle to An Unfortunate Monarch, By Peregrine the Elder. Enriched with Explanatory Notes. The Second Edition.
London: Benson, 1778. 14p.

"Whilst you, dread Sir, Tegean chains provide." (210)

Notices: CR 45 (Apr 1778), 312; MR 58 (May 1778), 399; G Apr 20, 1778; GM 48 (Jun 1778), 288; LR 7 (Appendix 1778), 498.

Copies: BL 840.1.17 (13); Bod Vet A5d.256 (18); NUC CSmH, DFo, MH, MiU-C.

HC. Satire on George III. Plainly addresses (unlike Macpherson, Johnson, and Shebbeare) the King and warns him against treacherous Scots who would divorce King's from people's interest. Then ironically reminds him of the (presumed) triumphs of Burgoyne over Gates, Gage over the ragamuffin Yankees; of the glories of British arts and sciences in the figure of Pinchbeck, and of a bankrupt commerce--i.e., paper credit. Concludes straightforwardly with observation that just as one Revolution (the Glorious) raised him to the English throne, another (presumably the American) will dethrone him. Cited are Benedict Arnold, Bunker's Hill, the Howe brothers, Bute, the tea tax, and Hampden. The first edition has the same title.

78-9. [-----]
Perfection. A Poetical Epistle, Calmly Addressed to the Greatest Hypocrite in England.
London: Bew, 1778. 5-36p.

"When first the Spirit urg'd you to the chace." (358)

Notices: CR 45 (Jan 1778), 75; MR 58 (Apr 1778), 305; G Eve Post Feb 21, 1778; GM 48 (Feb 1778), 85; LR 7 (May 1778), 377-8.

Sabin 60919.

Copies: BL 164.n.44; NUC CtY, ICN, IU, MH, NN, RPJCB.

HC. Satire on Wesley and the Methodists for hypocrisy and self-interest, particularly Wesley's Calm Address to our American Colonies (1775) and Calm Address to the Inhabitants of England (1777). Wesley will serve under North or Hancock, Christ or Pope, so long as he gains. But most damnable is his support of coercive measures against America. Combe notes that Wesley's second Calm Address "whets his sacred Knife" at "Arch-Fiend and Rebel" Hancock. He takes Wesley to task for making "earthly Kings co-equal with thy God," which he labels "sycophantic Blasphemy" and an "impious Piece of Pagan Flattery." Thus he objects to Wesley's Tory politics which deifies kings, who are really "Creatures of Man's Choice!" Concludes with a summary of his objections to Wesley, for encouraging tyranny and the suppression of the American rebels: "Stir up Revenge to shed a Nation's Blood/ . . . And massacre Mankind with CALM ADDRESS." (Combe repeats this attack in an incidental allusion in another satire, The Love Feast [1778], p. 33: "He who on Canting lays so great a Stress,/ Cou'd drink hot blood, yet write a Calm Address.")

78-10. [-----]
The Saints, A Satire.
London: Bew, 1778. 30p.

"Is there a Tribe who boast peculiar Light." (c. 450)

Notices: CR 44 (Dec 1777), 473; MR 58 (Jan 1778), 73; GM 48 (Feb 1778), 95; L Mag 47 (Feb 1778), 88; LP Jan 28 & Feb 9, 1778; LR 6 (Appendix 1777), 523.

Copies: BL 163.1.20, 11602.gg.25 (16), 11630.d.8 (7); Bod Godwyn Pamph 1731; NUC CtY, ICN, IU, MH, NN.

HC. Satire on the Methodists, Wesley and Whitefield, with some comments on Wesley's politics. Objects to Wesley's support of the American War, and berates him for entering politics: "On passive Slav'ry hear this Tool insist,/ Beating his Drum for Murd'rers to enlist" (p. 23). Also, "Hear him . . . Intestine Broils with 'Calm Address' inflame" and note how he "Out-lies Sam. J---s-n" (p. 24). Combe also declares Wesley "never could get any firm Footing in America [because of George Whitefield's success]. And at the very Time he pyrated the Pamphlet entitled Taxation No Tyranny, a celebrated Preacher of George's Party had the Honour of being Preceptor to General Washington's Son" (p. 23). (A subsequent edition is entitled The Fanatic Saints; A Satire, with explanatory Notes, and References to the Writings of the Methodists [London: Bew, 1778].)

78-11. [-----]
Sketches for Tabernacle-Frames. A Poem. By the Author of The Saints, a Satire; Perfection, &c. &c.
London: Bew, 1778. 6-36p.

"Where Quack'ry, Pray'r, and Grubstreet Arts combine." (c. 675)

Notices: CR 45 (Apr 1778), 314;  MR 59 (Aug 1778), 156;  LR 7 (May 1778), 378-80.

Copies: BL 163.1.21, 11630.e.6 (3);  NUC  CSmH, CtY, ICN, ICU.

HC. Satire on the Methodists, "fanatical Enthusiasts," especially Wesley as a medical, religious quack. A short section focuses on Wesley's political tracts, one of which "America bely'd, and Johnson minc'd"--his Calm Address to our American Colonies (1775), a notorious plagiary of Johnson's Taxation No Tyranny. Damns Wesley for being a dupe to corruption and undermining liberty in his "sycophantic Calm Address" (to the Inhabitants of England [1777]), a "sacrifice to North." Combe believes Wesley was bribed by the administration.


78-12. The Conquerors. A Poem. Displaying the Glorious Campaigns of 1775, 1776, 1777, &c. &c. &c. &c.
London: Setchel, Fielding & Walker, [1778]. 5-72p.

"Pursue thy fav'rite scheme, great ---- proceed." (c. 1400)

Notices: CR 45 (Feb 1778), 150;  MR 58 (Mar 1778), 237;  Freeman's J Feb 24, 1778; GA Feb 16, Oct 24, 1778;  GM 48 (Mar 1778), 144;  L Eve Post Feb 12, 14, Mar 21, 1778; LR 7 (Mar 1778), 225.

Sabin 15885.

Copies: BL 162.1.47;  NUC  DLC, MB, MiU-C, NN, RPJCB.

HC. Satire on the King and ministry, responsible for the unjust American War, a civil war. Blasts the King's stubborn, disastrous policies wronging America, but praises Pitt and Camden for their temperate, reasonable views. Defends the minority--Manchester, Rockingham, Shelburne, Effingham, Bishop of Peterborough--and the American position on its rights, and believes the Americans were provoked to declare independence. Criticizes North, Germain, Sandwich, Mansfield, Bute, bribery, and corruption. Correcting the lies of the ministry at every turn, the poet gives a realistic view of the several military campaigns mounted in the first three years of the war in an attempt to subdue the rebel Americans: Lexington, Bunker's Hill;  the episodes in Boston, at Quebec (Montgomery), at Sullivan's Island, Charleston, June 28, 1776;  the defeat of the provincials at Long Island, August 27, 1776;  Washington's capture of three Hessian mercenary regiments at Trenton, December 26, 1776;  the Rhode Island action in early 1777; and Burgoyne's campaign (versifies Burgoyne's proclamation) and defeat at Saratoga by

Gates and Arnold. Concludes that only justice and a change in administration will end this mad and wasteful war. Incidentally, savagely criticizes the Scotch whenever he can.

78-13. An Epistle from the Earl of Chatham to the King. Written during his last Illness.
  Oxford and London: Goldsmith, 1778.

  Notices: CR 46 (Aug 1778), 153; MR 59 (Jul 1778), 155; LR 8 (Sep 1778), 212.

  Copies: none located.

78-14. An Epistle to the Right Honourable Lord G[eorge] G[ermaine].
  London: Almon, 1778. 13p.

  "He comes, his sword yet reeking with the gore." (162)

  Notices: MR 58 (Mar 1778), 237; GM 48 (Apr 1778), 192; LR 7 (May 1778), 382.

  Copies: BL 164.n.47; NUC CtY, DFo, DLC, MH.

HC. Satire on Germaine as a minister, his "country's foe, and vile oppression's friend." Blames him for waging bloody war (against America), citing such victims as Fraser and Acland. Objects to the shameful employment of the Indians in the war, condemning their savage warfare "against a guiltless race." But this was not always so, for under Chatham and Amherst the Indians submitted to British law. Blames him for Burgoyne's defeat. Sympathizes with Burgoyne, who obeyed his command, but "'Twas by a [coward] this command was given." Praises the conqueror Gates for treating Burgoyne's surrendering forces humanely. The poet asks Germaine to resign and concludes with praise for the minority opposition--Savile, Burke, Abingdon, Richmond, Portland, Bishop of St. Asaph, Camden, Rockingham; hopes the King (?) will be restored to reason and "vile" Germaine be executed, receiving "the traitor's fate."

78-15. An Epistle to W[illia]m, E[ar]l of M[ans]f[iel]d, The most <u>unpopular</u> Man in the Kingdom, Except His [Majesty] and L[or]d B[ute]. By the Author of Royal Perseverance and Tyranny the Worst Taxation.
  London: Bew, 1778. 5-25p.

  "How can the Man who serves <u>despotic</u> <u>Ends</u>." (c. 340)

  Notices: CR 46 (Aug 1778), 153; MR 59 (Aug 1778), 157; GA Dec 1, 1778; LR 8 (Sep 1778), 213.

Copies: BL 841.k.12; Bod 4° W 71 Jur (4), Godwyn Pamph 1728; NUC TxU.

First printed in The Crisis (May 13, 1775), pp. 109-16; this is a revision. HC. Satire on Mansfield for being hated Bute's proxy, carrying on Bute's work and serving despotic ends. Contrasting Mansfield with Chatham, the poet wishes for the latter's wise counsels to check Mansfield's crimes at Boston and Quebec. Mansfield, with other sycophantic Scotch Jacobites at court, gives poisonous advice to the King, especially regarding America; eventually, the nation will judge his crimes--unless he advises the King properly, to "bend Prerogative to Public Good." Cited is the Boston Port Bill (the "Famine-Bill").

78-16. The Favourite; A Character from the Life. Addressed to the Sovereign Minion of the Times, On the much-lamented Death of the patriotic Earl of Chatham. Dedicated to that rare Society of [Caledonian] Gentlemen, the Critical Reviewers. . . .
London: Bew, 1778. 5-42p.

"Preferr'd to quench a Messalina's Rage." (c. 400)

Notices: CR 46 (Oct 1778), 315; MR 59 (Nov 1778), 394; LR 8 (Nov 1778), 360.

Copies: BL 643.k.27; NUC DFo, OCU.

HC. Scurrilous lampoon on Bute and satire on the Scotch and administration. In a patriotic Whig review of history, attacks Bute for the forced resignation of Pitt and the poor peace ending the Seven Years War, the persecution of Wilkes for publishing North Briton No. 45, the education in tyranny given the young King, and other Scots (Thurloe) for the St. George's Fields Massacre. Mansfield is blamed for the war against America and for losing the colonies; Bute is blamed for trying to import popery there and for draining the British treasury with pensions for his countrymen, also for the atrocities in the Battle of Lexington, seen as a massacre of American innocents. The poet defends Burgoyne for his bravery and blames Germain for the defeat at Saratoga; criticizes Sandwich for the unprepared state of the fleet, making Keppel's failure inevitable. Bute and traitors rule; the state faces ruin. Also derided are Johnson, Taxation No Tyranny, and the Carlisle Peace Commission.

The Genius of America to General Carleton, An Ode. See 78-46 and 78-47.

78-17. [Greene, Edward Burnaby]
The Conciliation: A Poem. By the Author of Juvenal's Satires Paraphrastically Imitated.
London: Almon, 1778. iii + 12p.

"Strange, that the heart with deep revenge should glow." (c. 240)

Notices: CR 46 (Sep 1778), 236; MR 58 (May 1778), 398; LR 8 (Oct 1778), 279.

Copies: Bod Vet A5.d.976 (4).

HC. Satire on the administration. A difficult and highly elusive poem satirizing the several cities--Birmingham, Manchester, Liverpool, et al.--that have subscribed their support to the war, now that Franklin has secured the assistance of France. Sir George Savile is complimented.


78-18. Hastings, Thomas.
The Tears of Britannia; A Poem, On the Much-Lamented Death of William Earl of Chatham.
London: Bew, Williams, et al., [1778]. 18p.

"Thy fate, O Chatham, myriads now deplore." (c. 300)

Notices: CR 45 (May 1778), 394-5; MR 58 (May 1778), 397; LR 7 (May 1778), 371-3.

Copies: BL 1346.k.27; NUC DLC.

HC. Hastings mourns Chatham's death at this critical time when France is preparing for war and Britain's "glory 'cross th'Atlantic shore" is lost. His leadership gone, Britannia mourns that no one can "bid my wayward sons rebel no more," or unite the now-divided nation, even unable to join in mourning Chatham's death. His oratory was superb, with but one object--"To save the western world . . . [to see] America restor'd." Britannia thereupon begs that America be restored to the King, that France not be allowed to dispose of America, "what belongs to Brunswick's sacred race." Britannia recalls the last war and Wolfe's great victory at Quebec, when Chatham was premier. Finally, just before Chatham's apotheosis, Britannia asks America to weep, for its firmest friend has died, and begs America to end the war: "Return, return, and all our joys renew,/ The Patriot in his death still harp'd on you."


78-19. Henvill, Philip.
A Poem on the American War. Wherein the fatal Consequences thereof, are impartially consider'd and illustrated by fictitious Example. To Which Is Prefix'd, A Humorous Dedication; Address'd To The Right Honourable Lord ------ -------- One of His Majesty's principal Secretaries of State.
Plymouth: Weatherley, [1778]. [5]-44p.

"Forbear my muse! of civil-wars to sing." (c. 400)

Copies: NUC RPJCB.

In verse dedication to Germain, dated March 10, 1778, Henvill takes Tory Germain to task for the blunders of Burgoyne's campaign, and complains of taxes and corruption.
In the poem, he announces his theme: the tragic civil war between Britain and America, which he portrays poignantly, and then proceeds to trace the cause through a rapid historical review of American colonial development until Britain tries to force a tax tribute. But when France enters the war, Henvill wants to see unanimity and concord among the British political leaders so that, no longer guided by self-interest, they will support [their] country's cause, . . . and protect her laws," and, regarding

"haughty France, compel them to repent/ Their base alliance."

78-20. [Huddesford, George]
  Warley: A Satire. Addressed to the First Artist in Europe. Part the First.
  London: Brown, 1778. 25p.

  "For thee, whom Minerva, St. Luke and Apelles." (c. 360)

  Notices: CR 46 (Dec 1778), 472; MR 59 (Nov 1778), 394, & (Dec 1778), 473 [Pt. 2]; LR 8 (Dec 1778), 428, & 9 (Jan 1779), 72 [Pt. 2]; M Chron Nov 30, 1778.

  Copies: BL 840.k.33; NUC CtY, DFo, ICN, IU, MH, NN.

Hexameter couplets. Satire on the military review at Warley camp. Included are verses on a hypocritical parson taking an opportunistic position on the American War. When poor and at the bottom of the clerical ladder, he incessantly baits King, Lords, and Commons; but when rich and advanced, this "Clerical Scavenger Vicar of Bray" sides with the administration. The point is clear: the well-paid higher clergy support administration policy in America. Cited are rebels, Gen. Clinton, Howe, Washington, and corruption. (Part 2, added in December 1778, is not relevant.)

78-21. The Indian Scalp, Or Canadian Tale, A Poem.
  London: Folingsby, 1778. 32p.

  "Near Hudson's Banks, unknown to public View." (c. 500)

  Notices: CR 45 (Mar 1778), 227-8; MR 58 (Apr 1778), 308; GM 48 (Apr 1778), 192; LR 7 (May 1778), 380-1.

  Sabin 34475.

  Copies: BL 11630.d.17 (18); NUC MH, NN.

HC. A narrative blackening the reputation of Britain for employing Indian savages to fight American rebels. Indian atrocities are emphasized. An American family lived a blissful, simple, virtuous life close to nature near the Hudson River; but, because the British sought Indian allies in this war, life became dangerous: in an act of friendship, the father exposes himself to danger from the Indians, and is killed. The friend returns with the terrible news, shocking the mother to death. This exemplary tale is meant to shame Britain for its infamous use of savage Indians "To murder Rebels"--"A savage crew employ'd in England's Cause/ To havock Nature and break down her Laws" (pp. 15, 23). The author is John Reynolds, 19 years old, older brother of Frederick Reynolds: see The Life and Times of Frederick Reynolds (London: H. Colburn, 1827), I, 43-50 (sec. ed.).

78-22. John and Susan; Or, The Intermeddler Rewarded: A Tale, Addressed to the French King.
   Bath: Hazard et al.; London: Wilkie,& Robson, 1778. 11p.

"A simple tale in simple dress." (c. 125)

Notices: CR 45 (Jun 1778), 472; MR 58 (May 1778), 397; LR 8 (Jul 1778), 64.

Copies: BL 164.n.50; NUC MH.

Octosyllabic couplets, a fable. John and Susan are set against each other by lies. But when Ralph invites Susan to leave John for him, both turn upon Ralph in anger and are reconciled. The moral is clear: America and Britain are kindred souls despite their quarrel, the war. What they share in common will spark love, "kindle Friendship's smother'd flame." And should France intervene, America and Britain will turn "their united powers" against Britons' "bitt'rest foes."

78-23. Liberty and Patriotism: A Miscellaneous Ode, With Explanatory Notes, and Anecdotes.
   London: Fielding & Walker, 1778. [i] + ii +12p.

"Sweet Liberty! coelestial maid." (144)

Notices: CR 45 (Apr 1778), 312; MR 58 (Apr 1778), 306-7; GM 48 (Jun 1778), 288; LR 7 (May 1778), 380.

Sabin 40936.

Copies: BL 164.n.48; Bod Godwyn Pamph 1732 (16); NUC CtY, InU.

Regular Horatian ode in sixains. This Tory poet ironically invokes Liberty ("Thy Massachusett plumage bring"), and with ironic praise satirizes "modern patriots" like Horne, Wilkes, Dr. Price (who "foretells New England's glory"). Asks North whether he cannot stop such "patriot mouths" and "mollify their spleen." Cited are Catharine Macaulay, Barré, Burke (st. 8), Rockingham, Chatham, Camden--all "patriots" opposed to the American War. Also refers to the "flaming" periodical The Crisis (st. 19).

78-24. Lucas, Henry.
   A Visit from the Shades; or Earl Chatham's Adieu to his Friend Lord Cambden. To which is added an Epitaphial Inscription to the Memory of William Pitt, Earl of Chatham; and A proposed Sketch of a Monument suitable thereto. By Henry Lucas, Esq. of the Middle Temple. Author of the Tears of Alnwick, &c. &c.
   London: Hooper & Davis, [1778]. 31 + iip.

"By Heav'n's decree, releas'd from worldly care." (c. 400)

Notices: CR 46 (Jul 1778), 68; MR 59 (Aug 1778), 155; L Chron 43 (Jun 20, 1778), 593; LR 8 (Sep 1778), 213.

Copies: BL 11630.b.1 (8); NUC MH.

Pindaric. Panegyric on Chatham. Dedication to Lord Cambden is dated June 2, 1778. Cambden envisions Chatham returning from the shades to warn the nation and express his fears of Britain's decline, because "Revolted Provinces have ever been/ The sure forerunners of this aweful scene"--the end of "Grandeur." (William Pitt, Earl of Chatham, died May 11, 1778.)

78-25. Matrimonial Overtures, From An Enamour'd Lady, To Lord G[eorge] G[e]rm[ai]ne.
London: Bew, 1778. 20p.

"Much-lov'd G-rm---ne, with kind attention view." (c. 360)

Notices: CR 45 (Apr 1778), 312; MR 58 (May 1778), 398; GA Apr 20 & 24, 1778; LR 7 (Appendix 1778), 504.

Copies: BL 11630.e.4 (6); Bod Godwyn Pamph 1697 (8); NUC IU, MH, MiU-C, RPJCB.

HC. Satire on the administration, particularly Germain. "An enamour'd lady" (Madamoiselle D'Eon, a notorious hermaphrodite) confesses love for Germain and says their marriage would be a happy union for Britain: Germain could retreat from the battlefield, she could do the fighting, and her arms could shield him from a nation's hate. Their marriage would delight the age: Johnson would praise it, as would Bute, North, and Sandwich. Concludes by offering what Germain adores, "a safe retreat" in her arms. Cited also are Arnold, the Howe brothers, Carlisle, Scots and Scotland, King George, St. George's Fields, Burgoyne and Saratoga, and Mansfield.

78-26. [Murray, James]
The New Maid of the Oaks: A Tragedy, As Lately acted near Saratoga, By a Company of Tragedians; Under the Direction of the Author of The Maid of the Oaks, a Comedy.
By Ahab Salem.
London: n.p., 1778. 64p.

Prologue. "Perhaps it can't be found upon record." (24)

Epilogue. "I mean not now to wipe your tears away." (50)

Sabin 51508.

Copies: BL 11777.f.69; NUC IU, MiU-C, NN, RPJCB.

Blank verse tragedy in four acts on Burgoyne's defeat by Gates at Saratoga, including the scalping of Jane McCrea, an Indian atrocity for which Burgoyne was blamed. The play puts Burgoyne and the struggle against America in a poor light, the author sympathizing with the rebel cause. The Prologue admits courtiers will say "that it is a damn'd rebellious play." The Epilogue expresses the need for caution about telling the truth about the war against America because those presently in power will deem it a crime--the Tories and the Scots. "Rebellion now is quite a different word," as contrasted with the year 1745.

78-27. An Ode, addressed to the Scotch Junto, and their American Commission, on the late Quarrel between Commissioner Ed[e]n and Commissioner J[o]hnst[o]ne: With some digressive Stanzas on the late political Conduct of certain ministerial Dependents and their Feeders.
London: Bew, 1778. 22p.

"Hail, sov'reign Thane!--All hail, Macbeth." (282)

Notices: CR 46 (Oct 1778), 315; MR 59 (Nov 1778), 395; L Mag 47 (Oct 1778), 471; LR 8 (Nov 1778), 358.

Copies: BL 643.k.14 (1); NUC NN, OCU.

Regular Horatian ode in sixains. Satire on the Scotch Junto, the secret cabinet influencing King George. It includes "the omnipotent Laird B-te," Mansfield, and Charles Jenkinson; William Eden was Under-Secretary to the Junto. The Carlisle Commission sent by the Junto to negotiate with the Americans on the basis of North's Conciliatory Proposals is rendered absurd by the poet, who describes a supposed quarrel between Eden and George Johnstone of "this ridiculous Commission," caused by Eden who was ordered to make "secret Overtures in Obedience to private Instructions from the Scotch Junto." Eden is scurrilously attacked as a tool of Bute; the commission is ridiculed because, though sent to make peace, it could not keep peace itself. Cited are Sandwich, belittled because the fleet was unprepared, making it impossible for Admiral Keppel to operate effectively; the poor Peace of 1763 made by Bute and "all his Tory crew." Blames Britain for oppressing the colonial Americans, "three injured Millions," because--as Johnson explained in "his vile Tory-Treatise," Taxation No Tyranny--government "did not contend for the Point of Right, but for Power." Condemns the Earl of Suffolk for advocating the use of savage Indians against America. Concludes with a request for Bute's assassination, for he lost America and dismembered the British empire.

78-28. An Ode to Mars.
London: Millar, 1778. [5-8] + 9-17p.

"O for a Muse, whose matchless fire." (c. 110)

Notices: MR 60 (Jan 1779), 65-7.

Copies: Bod Godwyn Pamph 1746 (11).

Irregular Pindaric ode. In the dedication to Burgoyne, dated Nov. 10, 1778, the poet blames his defeat upon the "infatuated counsels" of the present ministry. In the Advertisement, he criticizes the poor leadership of North's administration and Carlisle's peace commission.

In the poem, Mars stalks battle scenes of terror, death, despair. In the past, at Cressy and Agincourt, and in Germany, Britain was protected by the god of war, but not now in the civil war with America. Mars should assuage his wrath and bid civil fury cease, or let it be diverted to the real enemy France, "Freedom's foe," tyrant of Corsica.

78-29. On the Present War.
London: Baldwin, 1778.

Notices: GM 48 (Feb 1778), 96.

Copies: none located.

78-30. The Patriot Minister: A Poem.
London: Flexney, 1778. iv + 17p.

"Accept my friend, versed in the muses flights." (c. 270)

Notices: CR 46 (Jul 1778), 69-70; MR 59 (Jul 1778), 72; L Chron 44 (Aug 6, 1778), 132; LR 8 (Aug 1778), 143.

Copies: BL 643.k.26; NUC DLC.

Advertisement (preface) is dated May 13, 1778. HC. The poet defends the political character of Chatham, despite disagreement with Chatham's advice to the nation concerning the colonies. He presents Chatham as a political leader of incorruptible integrity, a genuine patriot. But Chatham's policies are not discussed, or even mentioned.

78-31. The Patriot Vision. A Poem. Dedicated To The Memory Of The Earl of Chatham.
London: Bew, 1778. 48p.

"On Vecta's woody Shore a Bard resides." (c. 850)

Notices: CR 46 (Jul 1778), 69-70; MR 59 (Oct 1778), 308-10; LR 8 (Jul 1778), 67-8.

Copies: BL 163.m.28, 643.k.25; NUC CtY, DFo, MiU-C.

HC. A patriotic poem. The poet mourns Chatham, who just died, and then dreams of the numerous British Worthies--Alfred, Henry II, Edward III, the Black Prince, Henry V, Elizabeth, "virtuous" Charles I, William III, Anne, the three Georges, Freedom, Newton, Bacon, Locke, Hampden, Russel, Sydney, Marlborough, Addison, Spenser, Milton, and others; of the last war--Wolfe, Howe, Townshend, Granby, Boscawen, concluding with Chatham and praise of his message to turn to war with France, "the just War" (implying, perhaps, that the American War is unjust).

78-32. Peace, A Poem. By M----r P-----t.
London: Bew, 1778. 33p.

"Where great Atlantic rears his ruffled head." (c. 650)

Notices: CR 46 (Oct 1778), 316; MR 59 (Nov 1778), 394; LR 8 (Sep 1778), 202-5.

Copies: BL recent acquisition; NUC RPJCB.

HC. The theme of peace is framed in classical mythology. The ghost of General Wolfe is sent down from Olympus by Jupiter Ammon to warn Sir William Howe not to fight the American rebels.

78-33. [Peart, Joseph]
A Continuation of Hudibras in Two Cantos. Written in the Time of the Unhappy Contest between Great Britain and America, In 1777 and 1778.
London: n. p., 1778. 76p.

"When Hudibras's cause of Dudgeon." (1015 + 851)

Sabin 16169.

Copies: BL 1078.f.23; NUC CtY, MH, MiU C, RPJCB.

Hudibrastics, octosyllabic couplets. I. The present Americans originated in the Presbyterian Puritan movement, and so they learned to be hypocritical rebels who hated England. Their hypocrisy can only explain their alliance with France, who had threatened them in the last war.
II. The Patriot Opposition is likewise hypocritical in its support of America and in encouraging the Americans to declare their independence. (The Declaration is versified!) Thus France sees its opportunity to intervene in the American War. But this eventuality may bring back the colonists to the English fold. (Handwritten on a blank leaf at the beginning of the BL copy is "The author I believe is a Sollicitor, it was never published only given to his friends." This copy also has four pages of MS notes at the end.)

78-34. A Poetical Epistle, Addressed to William, Earl of Mansfield. By the Author of the Ciceroniad.
   London: Bew, 1778. 12p.

"No more, ye Muses! I invoke your Aid." (c. 150)

Notices: CR 45 (Apr 1778), 312-13; MR 58 (Apr 1778), 308; GM 48 (Jun 1778), 288.

Copies: BL 164.n.49.

HC. Panegyric on Lord Mansfield and attack on his enemies. Only "Knaves and Fools" fail to revere him; it suggests Fox and Barré are among those not recognizing his virtues. This poem does not definitely discuss politics, though simply to stress Mansfield's virtuous character may be a political gesture. In the conclusion, the writer declares he will be pleased if North and others like the premier approve this poem.


78-35. [Polwhele, Richard]
   The Spirit of Frazer, To General Burgoyne. An Ode. To Which Is Added, The Death of Hilda; An American Tale. Inscribed to Mrs. Macaulay.
   Bath: Cruttwell; London: Goldsmith, 1778. 18p.

"Silence held the midnight gloom." (90)

Notices: CR 45 (Jun 1778), 471-2; MR 58 (Jun 1778), 472-3; LR 8 (Jul 1778), 63.

Sabin 89476.

Copies: NUC  DLC, MiU-C, RPJCB.

The Spirit of Frazer, subtitled on the first page of verse "The Night before his Capitulation with Gates, the General of the Continental Army." The ghost of Gen. Frazer, killed in the Saratoga fighting, warns Burgoyne to listen to reason and yield, to ask that Britain stop the war against America--"Freedom's ravag'd land,/ Where soon a glorious Empire shall arise"--and to allow peace to be restored, as Chatham has urged.
   The Death of Hilda, a sentimental ballad, is neither relevant nor especially "American."


78-36. Royal Perseverance. A Poem. Humbly Dedicated to That Prince, Whose Piety, Clemency, Moderation, Magnanimity, and other Christian and Patriotic Virtues, Are the Admiration of All Mankind.
   London: Bew, 1778. 7-27p.

"In Realms, not bless'd like ours, what Evil springs." (c. 300)

Notices: CR 45 (Apr 1778), 312-13;  MR 58 (May 1778), 399;  GM 48 (Jun 1778), 288; LR 7 (Appendix 1778), 497.

Sabin 73804.

Copies: BL 1600/499;  NUC  CSmH, DFo, IU, MH, RPJCB.

HC. Satire on King George. Ironically contrasts one ideal and three real characters of persevering tyrants--Augustus Caesar, Charles XII of Sweden, and Philip II of Spain with George as the ideal. Incidentally objects to the savage Indians as British allies in the American War. Defends independence on the principles of Locke, Sidney, Price, and others.

Salem, Ahab. See 78-26.

78-37. Second Thought is Best. An Opera in Two Acts . . . in which is introduced the Song rejected by the Lord Chamberlain.
   London: Murray, Greenlaw, 1778.

Song. By Conrad. "The nation is in ruin, Sir." (16)  pp. 10-11.

Notices: CR 45 (Jun 1778), 473;  MR 58 (Jun 1778), 473.

Copies: NUC  CtY.

The opera is not relevant, but the censored song is. The lyric declares that "the nation is in ruin" and that "the Constitution is at stake."

78-38. The Seducers. A Poem. Dedicated to the Right Honourable the Earl of M[ansfiel]d.
   London: Kearsly, 1778. vii + 36p.

"Seducers! hah--why startle at the sound." (649)

Notices: CR 46 (Jul 1778), 68;  MR 59 (Oct 1778), 308;  L Chron 43 (Jun 27, 1778), 621;  LR 8 (Sep 1778), 211.

Copies: NUC  NN.

HC. Social satire. Seduction occurs at all levels of life--everyone engages in it, and it is of all types, even seduction "from bad to GOOD," as illustrated by Mansfield and North. We follow Mansfield's judgment and North's leadership. North deserves praise for effectively bribing MP's to do right! Burke and Fox are demeaned, as well as Barré; there is hope North will triumph over Americans and restore peace in the west. Only relatively few lines (36-65) are relevant; they are about North, a "high seducer." The rest concerns common seducers, who are sexually motivated.

78-39. [Stevenson, William]
An Ode to Peace; Occasioned by the Present Crisis of the British Empire. Blessed are the Peace-Makers, For they shall be called the children of God. The Bible.
London: Almon, 1778. iv + 17p.

"Hail Peace! thou daughter of the skies." (c. 600)

Notices: CR 45 (Feb 1778), 152-3; MR 58 (Mar 1778), 237; GM 48 (May 1778), 144; LR 7 (Feb 1778), 141-3.

Sabin 56708.

Copies: BL 162.m.68; NUC PHi, PPL.

Irregular Pindaric ode. The Preface argues for peace and objects to the American War. Stevenson hopes that his remarks may enlighten "the unhappy dispute between Great-Britain and America" and determine its outcome. He asks for the Christian spirit of forgiveness to guide present counsels, and denounces the established clergy for their "hostile and bloody addresses" supporting the sovereignty of Great Britain "in all cases whatsoever" (referring to the Declaratory Act of March 16, 1766, to which Price also objected in his Civil Liberty). To him, in this war God is not on the side of the ministry. He denounces North as responsible for the war--"the present horrid and most unnatural civil war." He believes that Britons attacked and subdued in America is a prelude to Britons being attacked and subdued in Britain.

The poem invokes the spirit of Peace to end discord, terror, and devastation, and to restore the social compact, order, and trade. Britain is destroying herself in this shameful fratricidal, parricidal, suicidal war, from which only France and Spain can gain. The King must relent and forgive; he does not rule by arbitrary divine right, but for the common good and safety. This war denies all past history, for in it Britain is not on the side of freedom and virtue, or fighting a just war. A senator must be corrupt to wish to fight such a war: "Pow'r, gold, his being's aim and end," really a vicious traitor! See 76-33 and 82-25 for other editions of this poem.


78-40. [Tasker, William]
An Ode to the Warlike Genius of Great Britain.
London: Bew, Richardson & Urquhart, et al., 1778. 21p.

"Immortal Power! to whom by Heaven." (258)

Notices: CR 46 (Jul 1778), 70-1; MR 59 (Jul 1778), 72; L Mag 47 (Sep 1778), 422; LR 8 (Jul 1778), 61; M Chron Jul 22, 1778; MP Jul 22, 1778; PA Jul 23, 1778; St J's Chron Jul 21, 1778.

Copies: BL 164.n.46, 1346.k.23; Bod Godwyn Pamph 1488 (3); NUC CtY, DFo, ICN, NjP.

Irregular Pindaric ode. Patriotic poem. Celebrates the martial spirit of Great

Britain upon the beginning of the war with France. He addresses the "Warlike Genius" and envisions the victories of the past--Edward at Cressy, Henry at Agincourt; he receives inspiration from the vision of the martial forces at Cox-Heath Camp led by Amherst as well as the fleet led by Keppel, the success of Marlborough at Blenheim. He also invokes the Druid bards of Stonehenge, where the military camp of Wilton is. Concludes with mourning for "Immortal Chatham," for he, too, could give inspiration to the British forces who will make France tremble.

In lines 274-80 of the later editions, he alludes to Col. John Dyke Acland, who had just died. (Incidentally, it is interesting to note the poet's criticism of the use of German mercenaries, in lines 74-6.)


78-41. [-----]
-----. The 2d. ed. with considerable additions.
London: Dodsley, 1778.

"Immortal Power! to whom by Heaven." (319)

Notices: CR 47 (Jan 1779), 75-6; MR 60 (Jan 1779), 66; GM 49 (Jul 1779), 357-8; L Chron 45 (Feb 16, 1779), 161; L Eve Post Apr 1, 1779; MP Jan 8, 1779.

Copies: NUC DFo, NN.

See 78-40. Also in Tasker's Select Odes of Pindar and Horace, translated (1781), I.


78-42. [-----]
-----. The 3d edition with additions.

"Immortal Power! to whom by Heaven." (319)

In his Poems (London: Dodsley, 1779).

Notices: CR 47 (Feb 1779), 155-6; MR 60 (Feb 1779), 162 & 61 (Sep 1779), 235.

Copies: BL 1346.k.22, 11630.c.11 (7); NUC DFo, ICN.

See 78-40.


78-43. [Tickell, Richard]
The Project. A Poem. Dedicated to Dean Tucker.
London: Becket, 1778. ii + 12p.

"Since sage philosophers aver." (230)

Notices: CR 45 (May 1778), 228-30; MR 58 (Apr 1778), 303-5; GM 48 (Apr 1778), 192; L Chron 43 (Apr 16, 1778), 369; L Mag 47 (Apr 1778), 182-3; LR 7 (Apr 1778), 319-20; SM 40 (Sep 1778), 504.

Copies: BL 163.m.40 & T.669 (3) (1st ed), 11630.e.17 (12) (2nd ed), 11630.c.3 (4) (3rd ed), 11630.d.7 (10) (4th ed), 11630.d.11 (15) (6th ed); Bod Godwyn Pamph 1493 (2nd & 6th eds); NUC CtY, DFo, ICN, & MH (1st ed), CtY & NN (2nd ed), CtY, MH, NN, & PU (3rd ed), CtY & IU (4th ed), InU & PPL (6th ed).

Octosyllabic couplets. Humorous satire on parliamentary politics. Applying Montesquieu's principle that "climate forms character" to Parliament, Tickell declares that in winter, when the cold produces a love of liberty, the English grow wild and fierce, and the Lords and Commons are scenes of wild debate. So he proposes heating the parliament buildings with a big stove fueled by the inflammatory press--by Almon who can supply libels, Junius, Tucker, Johnson, Shebbeare. Thus faction, mollified, will die, opposition cease, and politicians become civil to each other--Chatham and Sandwich, Shelburne and Bute, Camden and Mansfield, Richmond and Denbigh, Abingdon and Markham. In the Commons, Burke is uninfluenced ("For party zeal is Burke's religion"), but others do become civil--Barré, Wilkes, Sawbridge. Chatham is made to agree "America has gone too far;/ We must support so just a war." (Also in New Foundling Hospital for Wit [1786], I, 307-17.)

78-44. Tyranny the Worst Taxation; A Poetical Epistle to the Right Honourable Lord N[orth], Ostensible Prime M[iniste]r. By the Author of Royal Perseverance.
London: Bew, 1778. [5]-28p.

"To you, my Lord, these honest Lines I send." (c. 300)

Notices: CR 45 (Jun 1778), 471; MR 58 (Jun 1778), 470; LR 8 (Jul 1778), 63.

Sabin 97634.

Copies: BL 1346.k.26; Bod 4° W 71 Jur (3); NUC DLC, MiU-C, RPJCB.

HC. This satire is an extensive revision of "Casca's Epistle to Lord North," The Crisis No. 18 (May 20, 1775), 117-22. Attacks Tory principles of government and the present Tory ministry under North. Charges him with the death of the empire because of his support of tyranny, the divine right theory, and his corrupt administration, with Bute, Mansfield, and the hated Scots. Parliament is powerless because of Bute and the King's friends, despite resistance of patriots like the late Beckford. Defends the Whig system of government by consent (thus the Americans are justified in resisting tyranny). Certainly the ministry is wrong to require their unconditional submission. North's despotism is defended by Samuel Johnson's false tenets and lies, while others who publish are suppressed. Implores North to tell King George the truth that Americans, aided by France and Spain, will spurn "Conciliation's Plan" and will triumph. Cited also are Mrs. Macaulay, Algernon Sidney, St. George's Fields, Wesley, Germaine, and Sandwich.

78-45. The Voice of the Minority: Being an Expostulatory Address to an Unpopular Minister, On Occasion of an Impolitic War. An Original Poem, never before publish'd.
London: Fielding & Walker; York: Frobisher, 1778. 42p.

"Say, N[or]th, obsequious, forward man." (c. 350)

"Deaf to th'advice of those." (150)

Notices: CR 46 (Aug 1778), 153; MR 59 (Sep 1778), 227-32; LR 8 (Nov 1778), 359-60.

Sabin 100671.

Copies: NUC InU.

Octosyllabic couplets. Two political poems. The first, The Voice of the Minority, was written soon after the action at Bunker's Hill and only published in the summer of 1778 "to celebrate the sound policy and wisdom of a slighted though patriotic MINORITY" (Advertisement). The second has a separate half title: A Second Address to the Same M-n--r, Written when certain United Colonies declared themselves Independent (pp. 29-42).
The Voice of the Minority. North's policies are questioned, and the minority's are defended. The principle of taxation only with consent is insisted upon, a view validated by Locke, Coke, Camden, Chatham, and Price. So, because America never consented through delegated representatives, the war against her is unjust, cruel, and oppressive, resulting in great loss of life and wealth, leaving Britain exposed to attack from its "natural enemies." Americans are not rebels; they resist lawless tyranny. Nothing can be gained from a war that cannot be won. The author derives many of his arguments from Price, Abingdon, Congress, and Arthur Lee's Appeal to the Justice and Interests of the People of Great Britain (1774).
A Second Address argues that North, since he refused leniency but chose coercion, drove the colonies away and forced them to release their ties and declare independence. Price and Abingdon are quoted to illustrate this argument. The poet still hopes that Americans may wish to remain united with Britain, citing as evidence Gates' humane treatment of Burgoyne's captured army.


78-46. The Watch, An Ode, Humbly inscribed to the Rt. Hon. the Earl of M[ans]f[iel]d. To Which Is Added, The Genius of America to General Carleton, An Ode.
London: Bew, 1778. 23p.

"When low-born, base Plebeians send." (120)

"Scarce had Carleton's sword atchiev'd." (192)

See 78-47.

78-47. The Watch, An Ode, Suggested to the Author by a late Present of a superb Watch from the King of France to his Majesty of Great-Britain. Humbly Inscribed to The Rt. Hon. the Earl of M[ans]f[iel]d. Revised by the Author, and re-published, together with 25 additional Stanzas. To Which Is Added, The Genius of America to Gen. Carleton, An Ode. The Second Edition.
London: Bew, 1778. 39p.

"If low-born, base Plebeians send." (270)

"Scarce had Carleton's Sword atchiev'd." (192)

Notices: CR 45 (Feb 1778), 150-1, & (May 1778), 395; MR 58 (Apr 1778), 308; GM 48 (Mar 1778), 144; LR 7 (Mar 1778), 224. Also G Eve Post, Mar 26, 1778.

Sabin 26946, 102041, 102042.

Copies: BL 164.n.45 (1st ed); Bod Godwyn Pamph 1725 (2nd ed); NUC DLC, ICN, MH, & MiU-C (1st ed), MB, MiU-C, PHi, & RPJCB (2nd ed).

The Watch. Regular Horatian ode in sixains. Satire on the ministry. France insulted England with a gift of a watch signifying that domestic policies are failing, as demonstrated by a growing national debt and burdensome taxes. Likewise, the military campaigns of Carleton, Burgoyne, and the Howes fail, delighting France. Concludes that Mansfield, instead of bringing back a watch from France, would do better to cross the Atlantic and bring home a peace. (Despite the additional stanzas, there is no substantial difference between the two editions.)
The Genius of America. Quatrains. Carelton, recalled to Britain, dreams that the Genius tells him virtue and glory cannot be achieved by "beating down Freedom," that the clergy (Wesley included) should be condemned for sanctioning slaughter, that America will be the "Mart of the Commercial World" and a pure nation supported by all the people, incapable (being virtuous) of being overcome, that Britain is wrong and the despotic King will be awakened from his dream of conquest. "Freedom in resistance stands"--the American rebellion is justified, and this is Chatham's view. Incidentally, objects to the use of mercenary troops.

Serials

78-48. An Account of the Battle off Ushant, in a Letter to a Friend.

"I have sent you these lines, but I'm forc'd to be short." (28)

L Eve Post, Sep 22, 1778.

Anapest tetrameter couplets. On the inconclusive battle between the naval forces of Keppel and Chartres.


78-49. The Address from Glasgow, presented by R. D. the Provost and the Convener, to the King, in Rhyme.

"We the Provost, the Magistrates, Council, and all." (42)

PA, Jan 23, 1778.

Hexameter couplets. Ironic satire on the Scotch, who urge greater militancy against America than Howe is using and declare they are willing to deliver a regiment or two to the King to defeat the American rebels.


78-50. An Address from the Inhabitants of White Lackington, Somerset, to Lord North, on his Arrival at Dillington, in the said parish, to celebrate his son's birth-day with Fire Works, &c.

"O Thou, that in squibs from the Treasury Bench." (34)

GA, Sep 25, 1778; L Eve Post, Sep 22, 1778.

Hexameter couplets. Satire on North for corruption and chicanery -- selfishness and hypocrisy.


78-51. Address intended to have been spoken at the Mischianza by a Herald, holding in his Hand a Laurel Wreath with the following Inscription.

"Mars, conquest plum'd, the Cyprian Queen disarms." (46)

Cal Merc, Jul 15, 1778; LP, Jul 3, 1778; RWM, Jul 22, 1778.

From the Pennsylvania Ledger, May 23, 1778. These verses, by John Andre, appear in a report of the homage paid to Howe by his officers in Philadelphia, May 18, 1778, before passing on the command of the army to Clinton and departing for England.
See Andre, "Verses intended for the Mischianza," 79-504, for additional lines.

78-52.  Admiral Keppel's Letter to Stephens Versified.

"Sir, By the message I sent you before it appears."  (23)

Freeman's J, Aug 29, 1778;  L Chron 44 (Aug 20, 1778), 180;  LP, Aug 19, 1778; MP, Aug 20, 1778;  St J's C, Aug 18, 1778;  SM 40 (Sep 1778), 507-8;  UM 63 (Aug 1778), 92;  W Eve Post, Aug 18, 1778.

Anapest tetrameter couplets.  Satire on Keppel, whose persona confesses, in a letter to the Secretary of the Admiralty, Philip Stephens, to evidence of poor command performance regarding the attack on the French fleet.  (SM also prints "A Poetical Paraphrase of the Supplement to the Gazette of France," the French view of the episode.)

78-53.  [The aid of my Parliament gives me great pleasure.]

"The aid of my Parliament gives me great pleasure."  (17)

Freeman's J, Jan 17, 1778.

Anapest tetrameter couplets.  Satire on the King's speech concerning American policy.  The speech is versified.  The persona of the King expresses hope for the reclamation of the colonies.

78-54.  Air.  March in Rinaldo.  On their Majesties Approach to Portsmouth, By Jemmy Twitcher and his Boat's Crew.

"Let us take the road."  (8)

G, May 20, 1778;  GA, May 21, 1778.

Quatrains.  Ironic satire on the Secretary of the Admiralty, Sandwich, for arranging the naval review, thereby responding effectively to the criticism of ineptitude charged by the opposition Patriots.

78-55.  [Alas! false Ministers of Peace.]

"Alas! false Ministers of Peace."  (4)

GA, Feb 11, 1778;  L Eve Post, Feb 7, 1778.

Quatrain.  Extempore.  Satire on the court for its peace proposals.

78-56.  Alexander's Feast Parodied;  or, The Grand Portsmouth Puppet-Shew.

"'Twas at the royal show, and grand display." (c. 150)

GA, May 15, 1778; New Foundling Hospital for Wit (1786), IV, 220-8; Jeffrey Dunstan, Fugitive Pieces (1789), pp. 65-73.

Parody of Dryden's great Pindaric, Alexander's Feast, an oratorio, ironically assigned to William Whitehead. Satire on the Portsmouth Naval Review and the Scotch, especially Bute, the King, and Sandwich.
A complaint that Britain was led to ruin and destruction by Scotchmen, that the King still seeks Bute's poisonous counsel, and that British troops and Burgoyne are captured. North and Bute are blamed for the ills Britain now suffers.
This poem fills two columns and a little more in GA!

78-57. All in the Wrong.

"When first the Squabble Transatlantic." (12)

LM 47 (Jun 1778), 281; PA, May 13, 1778; W Eve Post, May 12, 1778.

Quatrains. Both America and Britain are in the wrong in "the Squabble Transatlantic."

78-58. America's Reflections on the Conciliatory Acts.

"Submissive to a Mother's will." (8)

G, Mar 17, 1778.

Quatrains. Ironic reflections on America's rejection of Lord North's Conciliatory Proposals: America has matured, while Mother England has become a child.

78-59. Anthem Performed at Boston.

"Strike, strike the trembling strings." (40)

GA, Feb 27, 1778.

Quatrains. An American song celebrating Gates's victory over Burgoyne at Saratoga.

78-60. An Apostrophe.

"Pensive the Genius of Britannia stood." (33)

G Eve Post, May 28, 1778; MP, May 29, 1778.

Blank verse. The Prince (of Wales?) rededicates himself to virtue and his country upon the death of Chatham. France cannot win, for England fights a just war.

78-61. [Arise, my soul, and tune the charming lyre.]

"Arise, my soul, and tune the charming lyre." (18)

M Chron, Jun 20, 1778.

HC. A panegyric on Lord North, virtuous and generous friend, innocent and great, despite the criticism of his enemies.

78-62. An Attempt to versify the Substance of Certain Late Dispatches from Philadelphia, as published in the last Gazette Extraordinary.

"'Tis with pleasure, my Lord, the good news I report." (40)

Freeman's J, Jan 29, 1778; L Eve Post, Jan 15, 1778; PA, Jan 17, 1778.

Ballad. A satiric narrative of Howe's seizure of the forts (Red Bank and Mud Fort) blocking the Delaware approach to Philadelphia. Howe succeeded, but the Yankee troops escaped, leaving their supplies as booty.

78-63. [Attend, Britannia's Sons, attend to Heaven's Decree.]

"Attend, Britannia's Sons, attend to Heaven's Decree." (8)

PA, Jul 28, 1778.

Hexameter couplets. A prophecy of doom. Because the thirteen colonies have been unjustly attacked, Britain is guilty of a terrible crime. No matter what -- if Britain wins or loses -- it will perish; the colonies shall rise and be independent.

78-64. The Audience's Answer to Punch's Speech, as inserted, in this Paper, on the Commencement of the present Session of Parliament.

"In humble Submission, with Reverence meet." (42)

PA, Jan 20, 1778.

Anapest tetrameter couplets. An ironic answer to "Punch's Speech" (to Parliament), Nov. 24, 1777, regarding the difficulties of the British armies under Howe and Burgoyne. Cited are Burke, Abingdon, Arnold, North, and Germain. See 77-258.

78-65. A Ballad.

"Should Monsieur come." (46)

L Mag 47 (Appendix 1778), 604; MP, Sep 22, 1778.

Song in sixains. Anti-gallican "ballad" inspired by the threat of a French invasion. Cited are King Louis, Keppel, King George, and the unity of political parties. The French threats "unite" and "reconcile" British parties. See 79-229.

78-66. A Ballad. To an Irish Tune called The Dargle.

"Oh! dear Mamma-Country, why were you so cruel." (90)

M Chron, Oct 2, 1778; PA, Oct 1, 1778.

An American song that reviews the contest between the colonies and Britain from the time of the Stamp Tax to the surrender of Burgoyne's army. The point is made that the Yankees do not trust the English, including the Patriots, some who simply wish to get in place (Richmond, Camden, Shelburne), others who have no property (Burke, Barre, Fox). The Americans are independent, possess Cromwellian canniness, and pride themselves on their invincibility. Cited also are tea, petitions, Declaratory Act, Yankee Doodle, Otis, Hancock, Sam Adams, and Cushing.

78-67. The Battle of Brest. A New Song.

"Some say that we wan, and some say that they wan." (56)

GA, Sep 26, 1778.

A ballad narrating Keppel's inconclusive engagement with the French Chartres off Ushant, in which Palliser participated.

The Battle of the Kegs. See Francis Hopkinson, 78-236.

Berkeley, George. Verses on the Prospect of Planting Arts and Learning in America. GA, Mar 23 & Dec 8, 1778. See 75-41.

78-68. A Birth Day Ode.

"Britons once hail'd this glorious day." (c. 150)

GA, Jun 12, 1778; L Eve Post, Jun 9, 1778.

Irregular Pindaric ode. Satire on the King for allowing the nation to suffer the loss of America and a disastrous decline in power. Cited are the naval review, Whitehead, Burgoyne, the Howes, the ministers, and the Scotch.

78-69. A Birth-Day Ode. Written, as it is supposed, by one of the Sybils, on the Emperor Nero.

"Oh speak! What honest bosom can resist the strain." (38)

GA, Jun 6, 1778.

Irregular Pindaric ode. Satire on Whitehead's birthday odes for the King. By implication, the King is compared with cruel Nero.

78-70. [The blessed Peace-makers, it may be presumed.]

"The blessed Peace-makers, it may be presumed." (4)

W Eve Post, Mar 19, 1778.

Epigram. Satire on the Commissioners. The Commissioners sent to America (with North's Conciliatory Proposals) will be tarred and feathered.

78-71. [A Bonny Lad: A Scotch Ballad.]

"A bonny lad frae yont the Tweed." (28)

L Eve Post, Jul 4, 1778.

Ballad: triplets with tail as chorus. Satire on the Scotch eager for the war. A Scotch view of the Battle of Bunker's Hill, ironically presented. Cited are Yankees and German mercenaries.

78-72. Bonum Publicum; or a Word to honest Britons.

"Patriots of old, when out of place." (16)

St J's C, Mar 3, 1778; West M 6 (Mar 1778), 161-2; W Eve Post, Mar 10, 1778.

Quatrains. Satire on the Whig patriots, as partisan as the Tories. Both Whig and Tory are self-interested. But "An Honest Man no Party knows," and is concerned only for the public welfare.

78-73. Brackenridge, Hugh H. and Philip Freneau.

The Rising Glory of America.

"No more of Memphis and her mighty Kings." (c. 240)

GA, Feb 14, 1778.

First delivered at Commencement Exercises, College of New Jersey, Sept. 25, 1771. A substantial excerpt from this prophetic poem, reprinted after the defeat of Burgoyne's army gives many of the British second thoughts about coercing the colonies.

Blank verse. A prophecy of the future greatness of "this Western world" that will be superior to the great cultures and empires of the past: Egypt, Greece, Rome, Britain. America will be the new Jerusalem, the seat of empire and freedom, settled by those in Europe who fled persecution and "Popish cruelty" to a safe retreat. Cited are Wolfe, Braddock, Washington, Franklin; New York, Philadelphia, Boston. Eventually America will produce its Homer, Milton, and Hampden. See 72-14, 89-2.

78-74. The Brest Fight.

G, Aug 20, 1778.

A poem of 42 lines. Because the newsprint was unclear, I could not read this poem.

78-75. Britain's Disgrace.

"When mighty Pitt had humbled England's Foes." (45)

St J's C, May 30, 1778.

Blank verse. Satire on the Tory leaders. Ignorant and stupid Tories are ruining the country with their ineptitude and also losing the colonies. France and Spain, Sandwich's Royal Regatta, and bribery are cited.

78-76. Britannia to Admiral Keppel.

"Droop not, my son, thy laurels cannot fade." (10)

GA, Dec 18, 1778.

HC. An expression of support for Keppel, who is being criticized for his naval command, his failure to defeat the French fleet.

78-77. The British Tars.

"Now my jolly Boys be ready." (28)

G Eve Post, Oct 24, 1778; LM 47 (Nov 1778), 520; MP, Oct 29, 1778; PA, Oct 24, 1778.

Song. A ballad that narrates the technique of privateering, which should make fortunes for British sailors. Also entitled "Privateering. A New Ballad."

Burgoyne's Defeat on the Plains of Saratoga. See Freeth, "Scale of Talent," 78-213.

78-78. [Buxom Joan. Chorus.]

"To conquer in our Country's Cause." (4)

St J's C, Jun 25, 1778.

The chorus in this burletta of Buxom Joan emphasizes the country's patriotic determination to win the fight.

78-79. By a Lady in America to her Husband in England.

"To thee, whom Albion's distant Shore detains." (34)

AM 1 (Dec 1778), 596-7.

HC. A sentimental non-political poem in John Wesley's journal. An American lady expresses sorrow over her enforced separation from her husband. She takes no pleasure in the scene at home because of his absence. (We can only infer that the prolonged separation is caused by the war.)

78-80. Camp on Coxheath.

"Tho' the dog-star inflames, and the heat is intense." (30)

Freeman's J, Aug 29, 1778; Lloyd's 43 (Aug 17, 1778), 180; L Chron 44 (Aug 18, 1778), 168; LP, Aug 19, 1778; UM 63 (Aug 1778), 92-3.

Song. Quatrains with chorus. Everyone goes to Coxheath Camp, especially women.

78-81. A Certain Speech Versified.

"My Lords, if I must tell you true." (34)

GA, Dec 1, 1778.

OC. The persona of the King speaks to Parliament about the present situation -- French aid for America, the rejection of North's conciliatory proposals by Congress, the threat of a French invasion, the militia camps and his pleasure in reviews, and the need to carry on with more money. Everyone seems to enjoy the prospect of war.

78-82. [Characters from Shakespeare.]

GA, Feb 26 & Apr 9, 1778; L Eve Post, Apr 25, 1778.

Negative "characters," with lines by Shakespeare, on the Earl of Bute, Archbishop of York, Lord North, Burgoyne, Samuel Johnson, and General Howe.

78-83. [Characters from Shakespeare.] Lord Cornwallis. Lord Advocate for Scotland.

GA, Apr 30, 1778.

Quotations from Coriolanus and Macbeth, supported by notes, on the character of Lord Cornwallis, who leads his troops bravely in America, and Henry "Starvation" Dundas, who is extremely belligerent towards America.

78-84. Characters from Thomson's Seasons. General Burgoyne's Army, Lord Amherst, Administration, the British Empire, Lord and General Howe.

GA, Jul 9, 1778.

These excerpts are like the "characters" from Shakespeare's plays that are adapted to the present times.

78-85. [Chatham, be gone! with thee may faction's fire.]

"Chatham, be gone! with thee may faction's fire." (50)

M Chron, May 30, 1778.

HC. An attack on Chatham, promoter of faction.

78-86. Chatham to Germaine.

"Since I rejoic'd they did resist." (8)

W Eve Post, Feb 21, 1778.

OC. Satire on Administration, i.e., Germain. Chatham is made to say he will humble the French and the rebels -- even in the buff!

78-87. The Chathamania.

"When a ship's under sail." (24)

MP, May 26, 1778.

Regular ode in sixains. The death of Lord Chatham diverts the nation from attending to its real trouble -- the opposition of the whole world.

78-88. The Citizens of London Dedicate this Monument as a grateful tribute, to the memory of that virtuous Statesman, William Pitt, Earl of Chatham.

"Infinite success dignified the Counsels of his enlightened mind." (2)

GA, Sep 26, 1778.

Inscription honoring Chatham -- when he was removed from power, the empire declined.

78-89. Coach-Makers Hall. Martha Mark'em to Kitty Curious.

"Dear Kitty Curious, I sent you a Sketch, tho' imperfect and small." (44)

PA, Jan 15, 1778.

Anapest tetrameter couplets. A visit to Parliament to hear the debate on the American prisoners, concluding with an agreement to donate to their welfare. See 77-168.

78-90. Columbia and Ivor. An American Tale.

"If beauty and innocence please." (120)

T&C 10 (Jan 1778), 45-6.

Ballad. A sentimental tale of Columbia and Ivor, young Americans, whose idyllic romance is interrupted by the war. Indians savagely murder the girl, her lover, and her father. Britain should pray for peace, and the patriots exert all their skill to end the war. May their eloquence meet with success!

78-91. A Comparison.

"Of Old, great Fabius, in Rome's gloomiest Days." (4)

PA, Jul 22, 1778; W Eve Post, Jul 21, 1778.

HC. Howe's delays have lost the colonies.

78-92. The Comparison.

"In George the Second's glorious Days." (12)

PA, Apr 15, 1778; W Eve Post, Apr 14, 1778.

Quatrains. In the present reign, unlike that of George II, France is abusing Britain. "The fatal Cause" is the war with America.

78-93. The Congratulation.

"Says North to Burgoyne, I give you much joy." (8)

PA, May 16, 1778.

Quatrains. Epigram. North congratulates Burgoyne on his victories; but Burgoyne says the premier is asleep.

78-94. Congratulatory Ode.

"Great H---, so thick the Laurels grow." (72)

M Chron, Jul 20, 1778; PA, Jul 18, 1778; W Eve Post, Jul 21, 1778.

Regular (Horatian) ode in sixains. Satire on Howe because of his poor and overcautious strategy in several important battles -- Bunker's Hill, the retreat from Boston, Staten Island, Long Island, Brooklyn, White Plains, Trenton, and Mud Island.

78-95. The Conqueror and Captive. A Fable.

"Success intoxicates the brain." (c. 100)

L Chron 44 (Jul 28, 1778), 101; SM 40 (Jul 1778), 380.

OC. A moral fable that teaches this lesson: Empires rise and fall; "life is but a varying round." Kings will get more pleasure from being loved than from being feared. Conquest or power is absurd. (Is the moral applicable to the American War?)

78-96. The Contrast. A Supplement to the Verses in Memory of Lord Chatham.

"While Chatham liv'd, first glorious name." (132)

GA, Jun 3, 1778; L Eve Post, May 30, 1778.

Regular ode in sixains. Chides the present blundering ministry for thrusting this leader aside and losing America. The King, too, is criticized. (A supplement to the verses "To the Memory of Lord Chatham," 78-503.)

78-97. The Contrast: -- On the Arrival of a certain General.

"In the last George's famous Days." (16)

L Chron 43 (May 19, 1778), 488; PA, May 20, 1778.

Quatrains. When Pitt led the nation, Wolfe heroically conquered Canada, and the Court and the army cooperated effectively. But now we fight for years and cannot win. Defeated Burgoyne returns to tell the tale. (He appeared before Commons on May 23.)

78-98. Cox-Heath Camp.

"Ye Madcaps of London, who frolicksome be." (25)

W Eve Post, July 4, 1778.

Song. The Cox-Heath training camp is ready for the French. Note the new tactics being taught -- "The manner of fighting thro' bushes and briers."

78-99. Coxheath Camp. Sung by Mrs. Wrighten at Vauxhall. The Music of this Song by Mr. Hook.

"Ye Beaus and ye Belles, pray attend to my Song." (23)

G, Aug 8, 1778; G Eve Post, Aug 6, 1778; Lloyd's 43 (Aug 7, 1778), 139; L Chron 44 (Aug 6, 1778), 136; L Eve Post, Aug 6, 1778; LM 47 (Sep 1778), 423; LP, Aug 5, 1778; MP, Aug 10, 1778; Vocal Mag (1778), Song 888, p. 242; West M 6 (Aug 1778), 438.

A favorite song on the pleasures of visiting a military camp. Coxheath Camp is a delightful, "merry" place. Indeed, the war is "charming"!

78-100. The Crisis.

"[This] dread suspence around! -- A solemn pause." (31)

L Eve Post, Jul 14, 1778.

Blank verse. Prophetic lines on the destruction of the empire caused by the King's advisers who were responsible for the American War.

78-101. The Crisis. With Advice to the best of P-----.

"The Colonies are gone, the Nation's boast." (8)

GA, Aug 26, 1778.

HC. A criticism of the ministry. The country is in a state crisis -- the colonies are lost, the fleet blockaded by the French; an army is lost. The ministry must resign. (The King too?)

78-102. Dawes, Matthew.
   The War in America. By Mr. Dawes.

"Thro' the dull Waste by savage Warriors made." (230)

PA, Jul 4, 8, 11, 14, 21, 23, 1778; W Eve Post, Jul 7, 11, 30, 1778.

Printed in six installments in PA; W Eve Post prints only three installments.
   HC. Protests the American War, but blames both Whigs and Tories, and asks for a patriot king to bring freedom. Also criticizes the Scotch for the war and protests the oppression of America caused by "the King's Friends" at a court motivated by self-interest. Praises Pitt and Camden.
   Dawes wrote The Prospect from Malvern-hill (1777): 77-7. "The War in America" had apparently not been published independently of the newspapers.
   Mr. M. Dawes is referred to as the author of "The War in America" in M Chron, Sep 9, 1779.

78-103. [Dear Twitcher, is this fit Amusement for Age.]

"Dear Twitcher, is this fit Amusement for Age." (12)

LP, Jul 24, 1778; PA, Jul 25, 1778.

Quatrains in couplets. Satire on Sandwich, old and inept manager of the navy. Here he is fishing while France rules the ocean.

78-104. Death and Taxes.

"The King of Terrors ne'er relaxes." (8)

W Eve Post, Mar 19, 1778.

Epigram. The colonists brave death in order to avoid taxes.

78-105. The Deplorable Case of Poor Britannia. Addressed to Apollo.

"Britannia once, unequall'd for her sway." (32)

GA, Apr 27, 1778.

HC. Britain is ill and weak; she must get rid of the quacks who are mistreating her.

78-106. A Desperate Case.

"That nation must be sick, in ev'ry part." (2)

GA, Jul 4, 1778.

Epigram. Satire on the heartless and unwise ministry.

78-107. Dialogue.

"My Lord, your Departure must please you, I'm sure." (54)

PA, Feb 5, 1778.

Dialogue in quatrains. Going home, Cornwallis wishes to bring the war to an end, it being hopeless; but the Scotch William Erskine wishes to continue. Captain Richard Fitzpatrick objects to Scotch ferocity in the war. (From a Boston Gazette.)

78-108. A Dialogue at Court.

"Says [George] to Lord N[orth], this is a sad hobble." (24)

GA, Apr 4, 1778.

Quatrains in couplets. The King and Lord North discuss the progress of the war, the King expressing concern, Lord North reassuring him. The point is that the Americans are much better fighters than anticipated.

78-109. A Dialogue Concerning the Posse Comitatus.

"A Country clown, who heard the news." (100)

M Chron, Jun 27, 1778.

Five-line stanzas. A humorous reaction to the call-up of the militia for the defense of the nation against French invasion.

78-110. A Dialogue on the Times between a Whig and a Tory.

"Whig. These are hard Times." (30)

PA, Mar 13, 1778.

HC. Whig and Tory agree that North should go, and that Hancock should punish him.

78-111. The Difference between Animal and Human Optics. An Epigram.

"Pray tell me, bright Phoebus." (6)

L Eve Post, Mar 14, 1778.

Sixain. Satire on the King for blindness. The response, L Eve Post, Apr 4, 1778, insists the King is blind because stubborn: 78-A [Leave prating].

78-112. Dissipation.

"Is there a word of magic sound." (180)

L Eve Post, Apr 11, 1778.

Quatrains. Satire on the social effects of dissipation, with some remarks on the times including American resistance to tyranny and the ministers who, because of their dissipation, cannot conquer America.

78-113. Donnel and Flora.

"When merry hearts were gay." (40)

Calliope, Or The Musical Miscellany (London: Elliott & Kay, 1788), pp. 96-7 (Song #51). With words and music.

Ballad. Flora grieves for her lover, Donnel, who has died fighting with Burgoyne against the rebels. Ironically, despite victory after victory, Donnel died in Burgoyne's campaign. Allan brings Donnell's sword to Flora.

78-114. The Double Encampment. Extempore.

"The French encamp on Gallic Ground." (12)

PA, Jul 28, 1778.

Quatrains. The French and the English are not yet fighting with each other -- all is show. Another version of this poem appeared in PA, Oct 13, 1778 -- "Extempore," beginning "Monsieur encamps on Gallic Coast."

78-115. A Dream.

"As the other night I lay compos'd in sleep." (10)

GA, Feb 13, 1778; L Eve Post, Feb 10, 1778.

Irregular meter in couplets. The ghost of the Duke of Cumberland, who had defeated the Scotch rebels in the '45, weeps that the Scotch again are responsible for blood -- so that he must drive them back home once more.

78-116. The Duke de Chartres to his Officers, on discerning Mr. Keppel's Squadron.

"Tho' superior our Fleet, and courageous each Man." (8)

PA, Jul 30, 1778.

Extempore. Quatrains. Satire on the French. The Duke de Chartres fears to engage Keppel.

78-117. Edward and Ellen.

"Loud howls the wind! the surges beat the shore!" (104)

MP, Jan 7, 1778.

Ballad. Narrates the tragic history of Edward and Ellen -- Edward cruelly killed by a press gang officer for resisting impressment. (Dramatizes the abuse of impressing sailors into the navy.)

78-118. Efficient Cabinet.

"Efficient Cabinet! why call'd so? Tell." (6)

GA, Mar 4, 1778.

HC. A satire on the cabinet (the ministry), efficient only in destruction and implementing its tyranny.

78-119. Ejaculation proper for the Times.

"Wise men suffer, good men grieve." (4)

W Eve Post, Mar 19, 1778.

Epigram. We are being undone by fools and knaves. (Applicable to the current political situation.) "Knaves invent, and fools believe."

Elegiac Lines, inscribed to the Memory of Lieutenant James Gordon. . . . See "Lines Elegiac. Inscribed to the Memory of Lieutenant James Gordon," 78-271.

78-120. An Elegy on the Death of the late Earl of Chatham, Who was the Glory of the British Nation, and a singular Ornament to his Country.

"When Britain's fame surpriz'd the nations round." (18)

G, May 19, 1778.

HC. History will long remember Chatham.

78-121. Elegy on the Death of William Pitt, Earl of Chatham.

"The bell, big-swollen with disastrous woe." (68)

GA, May 18, 1778.

Elegiac quatrains. With Pitt's death, the empire falls. Review of the peace of 1763, for which the Scots are blamed.

78-122. An Elegy on the Death of William Pitt, Earl of Chatham.

"Mourn, mourn, Britannia, for great Chatham's dead!" (c. 150)

T&C 10 (Jun 1778), 326-7.

HC. Lines express sorrow at the death of a great statesman, Chatham, and review in panegyrical terms his leadership. His last speech in Parliament, when he collapsed, is described.

78-123. Elegy on the Earl of Chatham.

"Fate gives the word; all mortal aid is vain." (48)

GA, May 14, 1778; L Chron 43 (May 14, 1778), 468; SM 40 (Jun 1778), 311; UM 62 (May 1778), 260; WM 40 (Jun 3, 1778), 230.

Elegiac quatrains. Mourns Chatham's death, mentions his great days and his days in eclipse because of poor health.

78-124. An Elegy on the much lamented Death of William, late Earl of Chatham.

"Thou muse to whom the monumental wreath." (160)

HM 8 (Jul 1778), 415-16; T&C 10 (May 1778), 269-71.

Elegiac quatrains. Commemorative stanzas in praise of Chatham -- with respect to the empire, France, his oratory, and his family: a great patriot.

78-125. The Encampment.

"As straggling o'er the tented mead." (28)

G, Aug 22, 1778; G Eve Post, Aug 20, 1778; HM 8 (Oct 1778), 584; PA, Aug 21, 1778; West M 6 (Aug 1778), 438.

Quatrains. Patriotic poem. The poet, visiting a military camp, envisions Britannia's genius asserting itself against all enemies.

78-126. [Endow'd with innate virtuous heav'nly light.]

"Endow'd with innate virtuous heav'nly light." (9)

G, Apr 20, 1778.

HC. Panegyric on Charles Lennox, the third Duke of Richmond, who is inspired by Pitt.

78-127. England's Evil Genius.

"Why rages still this savage, horrid strife." (8)

Freeman's J, Jan 29, 1778; L Eve Post, Jan 13, 1778.

Quatrains. A negative on the fruitless war with America, war caused by the

Scotch -- Mansfield and Bute.

78-128. The Englishman's Litany.

"From Parliaments venal, who barter our laws." (28)

L Eve Post, Feb 10, 1778.

Triplets. A satiric poem on the fast. A prayer by a Whig patriot against Tories, corrupt politicians, Scotchmen, and fasts which prolong the war, and for peace.

78-129. An Englishman's Prayer for the Present Day.

"O Lord, stretch forth thy mighty hand." (8)

GA, Feb 27, 1778.

Irregular verse. A prayer that the American war end and that the despotic ministry cease invading English liberty.

78-130. Epigram.

"The common soldier, who has broke." (14)

LP, Aug 26, 1778.

OC. A common soldier receives 500 lashes for desertion and survives to desert again, but Britain is dying from thirteen stripes (the thirteen rebelling American provinces).

78-131. An Epigram.

"Farewell the glory of a mighty state." (16)

GA, Apr 9, 1778.

HC. Bute and Mansfield still appear to threaten the constitution by misleading the King.

78-132. An Epigram.

"The Gallic Lennox, and the Stuart Grafton." (6)

MP, Dec 15, 1778.

Irregular meter, couplets. Satire on the Duke of Richmond (Lennox) and Grafton for supporting the rebels -- and Keppel, too, of the Patriots -- "Rebellion's friends, Old England's foes."

78-133. An Epigram.

"A Gen'rous Minister, who takes, should give." (4)

PA, Feb 28, 1778; W Eve Post, Feb 26, 1778.

HC. North borrows from the Patriots, but does not reward them. (Referring to North's Conciliatory Proposals to the Colonies.)

78-134. An Epigram.

"'Tis said that the soldiers so lazy are grown." (8)

GA, Apr 4, 1778.

Quatrains. Satire on the English soldier for laziness. The English soldier is spending too much on parties (balls) and powder (hair powder).

78-135. An Epigram.

"'Twas candid, after the last Fray." (8)

PA, Aug 27, 1778.

Quatrains. Satire on Keppel. Should Keppel meet Chartres again, he must really win.

78-136. An Epigram.

"Van Keppel was, the other Year." (10)

PA, Sep 14, 1778.

OC. A negative reaction to the thwarted engagement with the French fleet. A defense of Keppel appears on the next day in PA, Sep 15, 1778: "Answer to Something called An Epigram in Yesterday's Paper."

78-137. Epigram.

"Varus, my legions quickly back restore." (18)

MP, Dec 19, 1778.

HC. Burgoyne really has no defense for his defeat by the Americans. (A negative comment on Burgoyne's defense of his conduct in Parliament, and the fact that the King refused to admit him to court and personally hear him.)

78-138. Epigram.

"What news, says Quidnunc, from America, I pray." (2)

L Eve Post, Jan 24, 1778.

Hexameter couplet. Satire on the absurd lies in the government's paper, the Gazette, about the American War.

78-139. An Epigram.

"When Samson wish'd Philistia's realms to burn." (4)

W Eve Post, Mar 31, 1778.

HC. Satire on Charles James Fox, responsible for inflaming the country against Government.

78-140. An Epigram.

"Whilst anxious cares each British brow o'ercast." (4)

LP, Oct 12, 1778; PA, Oct 13, 1778.

HC. Epigram. Satire on Sandwich. All Britain is gloomy, dreading future evils, but Sandwich is happy with his mistress, Miss Ray.

78-141. [Epigram.]

"Ye patriots who so oft complain." (8)

GA, Oct 23, 1778.

OC. Satire on Sandwich who must resign to save the nation, just as the British sacrificed a ship called "Lord Sandwich" to save Rhode Island from the French.

78-142. Epigram, Addressed to the Genius of Scotland.

"Weep Scotia, weep, and thy hard fate deplore."  (6)

New Foundling Hospital for Wit (1786), II, 127.

HC. Ironic satire on the Scotch, who are made to mourn because "stubborn Yankies" rebel, and are thus displacing the Scotch as the only rebels to their King.

78-143. Epigram. [Another.]

"One Fabius, by his wise delays."  (4)

"Quoth Dick to Will, t'appease these clam'rous men."  (4)

MP, Nov 16, 1778; W Eve Post, Nov 14, 1778.

Two satiric epigrams. The lethargic Howe brothers, General William and Admiral Richard, have brought Great Britain to shame. Now they will begin to write their defensive commentaries.

78-144. Epigram. [Another.]

"Says Bute to Chatham, Wilt thou join."  (4)

"'Tis said by Chathamites that Bute."  (4)

Cal Merc, Nov 14, 1778; St J's C, Nov 19, 1778.

Two epigrams. Chatham and his followers refuse an offer from Bute to join a coalition "To save this ruined nation." This firm rejection of the alleged proposal is described in lines printed in Cal Merc, Nov 23, 1778: "Retired from scenes of busy life." See 78-434.

78-145. Epigram. Fratres Fraterrim!

"Mark well those Thunderbolts of War, the H-wes."  (4)

PA, Nov 17, 1778.

Quatrain. Satire on the Howe brothers for corruption.

78-146. Epigram. On the Declared Pregnancy of a Great Lady.

"Peace -- peace -- ye croakers -- here comes sudden help." (2)

GA, Apr 6, 1778; L Eve Post, Apr 2, 1778.

HC. Satire on the Royal Family. Queen Charlotte will give the nation another child (her 13th!), but England has lost an empire.

78-147. Epigram. To a certain Turgid Orator, on Occasion of his two Jesuitical Letters to his Constituents at Bristol.

"Dear Teague, a True with Irish Matters." (4)

PA, Jun 13, 1778.

Quatrain. Vulgar abuse of Burke for his Letter to the Sheriffs of Bristol.

78-148. Epigrammical Memento after the Fast [+ On Reading the Above].

"The God of Love would have us fast, no doubt." (4 + 12)

L Eve Post, Mar 5, 1778.

Related epigrams. The ministers fast, but are unrepentant. North is cited.

78-149. Epigram[s].

"Monsieur declares the English fled." (8)

"Von Keppel says that Chartres fled." (4)

PA, Aug 14, 1778.

Two epigrams. Quatrains. Neither Keppel nor Chartres has won. (The battle off Ushant was aborted.)

78-150. [Epigram(s)] On the Fast.

"What a wretched mistake." (6)

"When Kings at one time." (6)

"Fasting and abstinence mean the same thing." (4)

"If abstinence and fasting mean the same." (2)

"Fasting and pray'r has pow'r (thro' Christ) no doubt." (4)

GA, Feb 6, 1778; L Eve Post, Feb 3, 1778.

A series of epigrams satirizing the proclamation for a fast, the war, hypocrisy, and the ministry.

78-151. Epistle to the Dean of Gloucester, on his State of the Nation.

"My good Mr. Dean." (96)

GA, Mar 20, 1778; PA, Mar 19, 1778.

Two- and three-stress couplets. Ironic remarks on the optimistic review of the state of the nation made by Josiah Tucker: on emigration (including the loss of troops), manufacturing, ship-building, enclosures, fisheries, taxation, debt, and the need for peace. That the country is prosperous is ridiculed.

78-152. An Epitaph.

"Blest with a heart, on life's exalted plan." (14)

G, May 26, 1778.

HC. Praise of Pitt, "an honest man."

78-153. Epitaph.

"The Commons of Great Britain."

GA, Jun 11, 1778.

Epitaphial inscription on the monument honoring Chatham: a summary of his meaning to Britain, irrespective of politics. Introduced with negative comments on the funeral.

78-154. Epitaph.

"Here lies William, Earl of Chatham." (2)

GA, Jun 16, 1778.

Couplet. Would the ministers were dead, instead of Chatham.

78-155. An Epitaph.

"Here sleeps great PITT, who went to rest." (10)

GA, Aug 31, 1778.

An imitation of William Collins' "Ode Written in the Year 1746" is applied to the death of Chatham.

78-156. An Epitaph.

"On / The Master's Side." (c. 20)

GA, Aug 19, 1778;  L Eve Post, Aug 15, 1778.

Sympathetic inscription on the "death," i.e., imprisonment of a patriotic Son of Liberty, the anti-ministerial political writer, "Hystaspes," for debt. "Hystaspes" wrote political poems and letters.

78-157. An Epitaph.

"Wide extended over half the western world." (c. 70)

PL, Dec 5, 1778.

An elaborately long inscription on the loss of the British empire, the result of "the ignorance or treachery of a nefarious (Scotch Jacobite) Junto," through bribery and corruption. It is the loss of America that is meant; and the Minority Opposition, despite its protests, had no effect.

78-158. Epitaph on Lord Chatham.

"Should some good Briton in a future age." (12)

T&C 10 (Jun 1778), 327.

HC. Chatham, "that Atlas of the British state," is no more. Now that the patriot is dead, "Let Bourbon triumph!"

78-159. Epitaph. On Mungo Campbell, Esq; Lieutenant Colonel of his Majesty's 52d Regt of Foot. . . .

"To check Rebellion in her mad career." (14)

MP, May 9, 1778.

HC. Panegyric on Col. Campbell, who died in the storming of Fort Montgomery on the Hudson, Oct. 6, 1777. The British cause is justified.

78-160. Epitaph on the British Navy, Laid up at Spithead.

"Here continue, ingloriously to rot." (c. 15)

G, May 20, 1778; GA, May 21, 1778.

Inscription. Satire on the government. Despite his naval review, Sandwich is responsible for the decay of the British navy.

78-161. Epitaph on the Earl of Chatham.

"Embalmed / In the grateful memory / of his country." (c. 10)

G, Jun 9, 1778; West J, Jun 13, 1778.

Inscription. A severe attack on the Tory government, "A profligate Administration" that wished "to enslave their Country."

78-162. Epitaph on the Earl of Chatham.

"Here lies the Body / of / William Pitt." (c. 10)

GA, May 21, 1778; MP, May 30, 1778; PA, May 20, 1778.

Inscription. Ironic epitaph commemorating great Chatham, whom the King never employed and Parliament treated with contempt. And now they wish to erect a monument to perpetuate the memory of his ability! (GA lacks the prose.)

78-163. Epitaph on the Earl of Chatham.

"Here rests, (And here only could rest)." (19)

G, Jun 9, 1778; PA, Jun 10, 1778.

Inscription. "The great Commoner" Pitt died, his spirit unable to survive "The Loss of Empire,/ The Dignity, the Power,/ And the Constitution of England."

78-164. Epitaph on the Earl of Chatham.

"In distant climes wherever George's arms." (12)

M Chron, Jun 10, 1778;  MP, Jun 16, 1778;  T&C 10 (Jun 1778), 327.

HC.  The achievements of "Pitt's counsels" will be remembered throughout the world.

78-165.  Epitaph on the Late Earl of Chatham.

"The Parliament of Great Britain."  (c. 20)

GA, Jul 4, 1778.

Inscription.  A criticism of the venality of the members of Parliament, contrasted with praise of the integrity of Chatham.

78-166.  Epitaph.  On the much-lamented Earl of Chatham.

"When ev'ry Gift which can our Nature grace."  (10)

PA, May 15, 1778;  W Eve Post, May 14, 1778.

HC.  Panegyric.  Pitt was a great patriot, orator, and statesman.

78-167.  An Epitaph.  On the Right Hon. William Pitt, Earl of Chatham, &c. &c.

"O generous reader."  (c. 45)

M Chron, May 13, 1778.

Panegyric on Chatham, who died May 11, 1778.  He had created the empire, now unhappily divided.

78-168.  [Epitaph on William Pitt, Earl of Chatham.]

"Here lies / William Pitt, / Earl of Chatham / Who inspired by the eloquence of Demosthenes."  (c. 20)

GA, May 13, 1778;  L Eve Post, May 12, 1778.

Inscription.  A political attack on those Tories who opposed Chatham's policies and brought disaster to the nation -- in a review of the highlights of Chatham's career from the 1760's to his death on May 11, 1778.

78-169.  [An Epitaph / Sacred to the memory of.]

"An Epitaph / Sacred to the memory of." (c. 21)

M Chron, Jun 10, 1778.

Inscription in praise of Chatham's virtues for a monument erected by the citizens of London.

78-170. The Etiquette.

"What though America doth pour." (52)

GA, Jun 13, 1778; LM 47 (Jun 1778), 282; LP, Jun 10, 1778; PA, Jun 11, 1778.

Quatrains, each last line having "etiquette" as rhyme. A satiric review of the American troubles from the time of Grenville's tax policy, through the Tea Party, Boston Port Act, Bunker Hill, Howe's failure, Germain's quarrel with Clinton, and Burgoyne's defeat, concluding with the King's unwillingness to hear Burgoyne's defense of his conduct.

78-171. An Excellent new Ballad, written by Patrick Costello, Servant to a Captain in his Majesty's Army now in Winter Quarters in Boston, intended to be sung between the Acts at General Bur[goyne]'s Theatre on his M[ajest]y's Birth-Day.

"To my song, my dear neighbours, pray lend me an ear." (73)

Freeman's J, Jan 8, 1778.

Ballad narrates the failures of the British in their campaigns against the cowardly Americans. Cited are Burgoyne, Yankee Rebels, Boston, Washington, Bunker Hill, Germain, Rigby, and North.

78-172. Extempore.

"Are Frenchman's Hopes or blest or crost." (8)

PA, Aug 8, 1778.

Quatrains. Frenchmen pray; Englishmen fight.

78-173. Extempore.

"If England could gain by American Wars." (8)

PA, Feb 6, 1778.

Quatrains. Fighting the colonies is fruitless. We should fight "our natural Foes," France and Spain, and get something for it.

78-174. Extempore.

"In Insolence Frenchmen have long put their Trust." (8)

PA, Aug 8, 1778.

Quatrains. The English will teach the insolent French a lesson.

78-175. Extempore.

"Monsieur declares he loves us well." (12)

Lloyd's 42 (Mar 25, 1778), 292; W Eve Post, Mar 24, 1778.

Quatrains. Epigram. The people have spoken -- they support the war against France. The voice of the people is the voice of God.

Extempore. "Monsieur encamps on Gallic Coast." (12) PA, Oct 13, 1778. Another version of "The Double Encampment": 78-114.

78-176. Extempore.

"Shall Keppel fight the Duke de Chartres." (8)

G Eve Post, Jul 23, 1778; PA, Jul 25, 1778.

Quatrains. The British are impatient to see Admiral Keppel engage the French Admiral de Chartres off Brest.

78-177. Extempore.

"Some People, doubting England's Fame." (8)

PA, Oct 21, 1778.

Quatrains. The English privateers will protect English shipping from French attack.

78-178. An Extempore.

"Spite of perfidious Gaul's united pow'rs." (6)

MP, Nov 21, 1778.

Couplets (mixed meter). Ironic satire on Government. If we knew how, we would have crushed the colonial rebellion despite France and Chartres (that is, despite French entry into the war and Admiral Chartres' engagement with Keppel).

78-179. Extempore.

"When first th'unnatural War begun." (12)

PA, Jan 2, 1778.

Quatrains. We were told that the Americans "would run"; but many of our young men have been killed and the war is not ended. We must have peace.

78-180. [Extempore.] Another.

"A Truce with your nonsense of Tod and of Fox." (8)

Lloyd's 42 (Mar 25, 1778), 292.

Quatrains. Epigram. Satire on sly Fox who is only interested in a "snug" place for himself in Government.

78-181. Extempore Epigram on Yesterday's Extraordinary Gazette.

"An Extra Gazette! Mud Island taken." (6)

L Eve Post, Jan 10, 1778.

Irregular lines. Satire on Howe who has just taken Mud Island in his Philadelphia campaign. These lines are developed further in "Extempore Lines": 78-182.

78-182. Extempore Lines. On Friday's (Truly Extraordinary) Gazette.

"Huzza! brave Boys, Mud Island's taken." (15)

Freeman's J, Jan 22, 1778; LP, Jan 12, 1778; PA, Jan 12, 1778.

OC. Howe has taken Mud Island, and his ships can now, if he chooses, "run away."

78-183. Extempore. On a Late Event.

"When France the League perfidious made." (24)

G Eve Post, Nov 19, 1778; LP, Nov 18, 1778; PA, Nov 20, 1778.

Quatrains. France's alliance with America only provokes Britain's anger -- France should beware.

78-184. Extempore. On hearing that a certain Great Minister is to put a still Greater General on the Staff. To the Premier.

"Your Deeds were wont to make us laugh." (4)

PA, Jul 15, 1778.

North is threatened with hanging if he appoints Howe to the general staff.

78-185. Extempore on Lord Chatham's Death.

"Here lies the man whom all admir'd." (8)

LM 47 (May 1778), 235; LP, May 22, 1778; PA, May 23, 1778; WM 40 (Jun 10, 1778), 255.

Quatrains. While he lived, political leaders ignored Chatham and rejected his advice; but now that he is dead, they are rendered foolish.

78-186. Extempore. On our late Captures.

"Let Monsieur sail from East or West." (8)

LP, Jan 16, 1778; PA, Nov 18, 1778.

Quatrains. On a recent English defeat of the French fleet -- time and place unspecified.

78-187. Extempore. On Reading the Debates in the Lower House last Week.

"True! B[ur]ke and B[ar]re have no land." (12 + 18)

MP, Mar 11, 1778; St J's C, Apr 14, 1778.

Epigram. Satire on Fox, Burke, and Barre, who have no property in England; hence they hate Old England but love the New. A parody, entitled "Occasioned by reading the above in the Shrewsbury Chronicle of Saturday, March 7," satirizes Barrington, who supports North and taxes on America: St J's C, Apr 14, 1778.

78-188. Extempore. On Seeing Lord Chatham lay in State, June 8, 1778.

"When Boreas with a blast severe." (12)

LP, Jun 17, 1778.

Sixains. The humble working people are secure in peace or war, while the great are insecure when in place -- witness Chatham's history.

78-189. Extempore. On Sir W[illia]m H[ow]e having expressed his Disapppro-bation of the Vigorous and Necessary Measures hereafter to be persued in America and declaring them to be very different from Those which he had observed in carrying on the War.

"What brave Sir W[illia]m says is very true." (4)

PA, Dec 23, 1778.

Quatrain. General Howe did not really fight the Americans. (Negative comment on Howe's defense of his conduct in Parliament.)

78-190. An Extempore. On the Late Long Obscurity of the Sun, and its resuming its Lustre on a Determination for War, Wednesday, March 17, 1778.

"While long dup'd Britain doubted what to do." (6)

Lloyd's 42 (Mar 20, 1778), 275; MP, Mar 21, 1778; St J's C, Mar 31, 1778.

HC. Heaven smiles on Britons, who are "rous'd to War" and determined to support their "cause."

78-191. Extempore. On the News of the Defeat of the French Fleet, by Admiral Keppel.

"The British Lion, now awaken'd, roars." (10)

M Chron, Aug 5, 1778.

HC. Keppel has awakened the British lion in defeating the French fleet. Britain should "Unite as heretofore, and rule the main."

78-192. Extempore. To Mr. T. Townshend, on his resolving to oppose the Address to his Majesty, until the Causes of the public Misfortunes were inquired into.

"If, Master Townshend, you must know." (10)

PA, Dec 10, 1778;  W Eve Post, Dec 8, 1778.

OC. The causes of the trouble Britain is in may be found in the Patriot Opposition, a faction who oppose the public good, and in the generals who will not fight.

78-193. Extempore. Written on Saint Andrew's Day.

"When first St. Andrew travelled South." (4)

PA, Dec 1, 1778.

Epigram. Quatrain. Satire on the Scotch and Lord North.

78-194. A Fable, addressed to the Americans, upon their treaty with France.

"Rejoice, Americans, rejoice." (52)

G Eve Post, Aug 11, 1778; MP, Aug 11, 1778; SM 40 (Aug 1778), 439; WM 41 (Aug 26, 1778), 207-8.

OC. An animal fable with the moral that the Americans should beware their ally, France, who may swallow them up. Frank Moore writes that David Matthews, Mayor of New York City during the Revolution, may be the author of this song. (Songs and Ballads of the American Revolution [1855], pp. 237-40.)

78-195. A Fable. Written in Virginia in the Year 1776, during the Rebellion there.

"It was the custom in all ages." (76)

WM 39 (Jan 21, 1778), 87.

OC. A moral fable about a paper kite which, wishing to be free, crashes into the ground. The moral emphasizes the need for a stronger cord to govern its flight.

78-196. The Fall of the Leaf. An Elegy.

"With what unerring peace the rapid year." (84)

GA, Oct 6, 1778.

Elegiac quatrains (the last five being relevant). Seasons change in nature, man, and states. Britain has passed through several stages from the times of George I to those of George III, the last bringing decline and separation from the colonies.

78-197. The False Prophet.

"When Jemmy Twitcher said and swore." (20)

PA, Mar 13, 1778.

Quatrains. Earl Sandwich believed the war could be won against cowards; but after Burgoyne's defeat, people became sceptical of this false prophet.

78-198. [Farewell the scythe, the sickle and the plough.]

"Farewell the scythe, the sickle and the plough." (16)

GA, Jul 3, 1778; G Eve Post, Jul 2, 1778; SM 40 (Jul 1778), 380; West J, Jul 11, 1778.

HC. An expression of patriotism in the face of the Bourbon threat. The militia and the navy will fight off France.
Another title for this song is "Soldiers and Sailors United."

78-199. A Farewell to Camps.

"Adieu to Coxheath, and to Warley adieu." (32)

G Eve Post, Nov 7, 1778; PA, Nov 9, 1778.

Quatrains. Sadly, Coxheath and Warley, militia camps, are closed down as winter approaches.

78-200. Father Felim O'Flagherty, of the Society of Jesuits, to his honourable Brother Vice Admiral Sir H--- P-------.

"Te Deum was sung for D'Orvillier's retreat." (15)

GA, Dec 24, 1778.

Triplets. Satire on Palliser, being smeared with the Papist brush. A Jesuit thanks Palliser for his lying charges against Keppel and urges him to pursue Admiral Richard Howe.

78-201.  The Fifth of November.

"In ancient Times this Day was deem'd."  (20)

G Eve Post, Nov 3, 1778;  PA, Nov 5, 1778.

Quatrains.  Guy Fawkes Day, but commemorated with bribery, North doing his part.  "We blow the Senate up with Gold, / And blind the Sovereign's Eyes."


78-202.  The Final Opinion of a Party of Ladies upon the Abilities of our several great Speakers.  An Extempore Epigrammatic Versification.  By one of the Party.

"Amazing Speeches, in one day."  (4)

MP, Dec 5, 1778.

Epigram.  Our politicians make excellent speeches, but cannot do much. (Evidence of frustration, no doubt.)


78-203.  Firmness No Proof of Wisdom.

"The friends of pow'r, quick to me bring."  (6)

Freeman's J, Feb 26, 1778;  L Eve Post, Jan 24, 1778.

Extempore.  Advice to the King to change his policy -- to peace.


78-204.  The Fly Catchers.  An Epigram written on Seeing Britain compared to a drowning Fly, in a vase of water.

"Yes, merciful Fly-catcher, Britain indeed."  (6)

GA, Dec 15, 1778;  L Eve Post, Dec 10, 1778.

Satire on the petty-minded King, too busy making buttons to save the nation. A reaction to "On Taking a Fly Out of a Bason of Water," 78-358.


78-205.  The following Airs, &c. set to music by the late Mr. Purcell . . . [Druid Songs.]

"Hear us, great Rugwith, hear."  (32)

W Eve Post, Mar 28, 1778.

The Druids prepare to resist the Roman invasion. These songs relate to the Gallic threat.

78-206. The following Lines were written by a Youth who came from America to England, for Education; and now detained on Account of the present Disturbances.

"Long have I labour'd big with anxious Care." (21)

Cumb Pacq, Nov 10, 1778.

HC. A young American, in England for education, complains of his exile because of the beastly war, and asks for peace.

78-207. The following Song affords a pretty just Picture of former and present Times.

"When good pious George, our King, came to the throne." (64)

GA, Nov 3, 1778.

A song contrasting past and present -- the past when Britain in George II's reign had trounced France, and waxed prosperous and imperial; the present in George III's reign when the Scotch and corruption brought to an end the good and glorious times. But freedom, banished from Britain, blooms in the New World.

78-208. The following Song was composed extempore on receiving the treaties from France.

"God save America." (28)

Freeman's J, Jul 30, 1778; GA, Jul 27, 1778; L Eve Post, Jul 23, 1778.

Seven-line stanzas. Upon the news of the Franco-American treaties, this (American) song blessing America, King Louis, Washington, and Montgomery was composed.

78-209. For the Consideration of the People of England and America.

"The gain of Civil Wars will not allow." (8)

Lloyd's 42 (Feb 2, 1778), 115.

Octave stanza in couplets.  No one can win in a civil war.

78-210.  Freeth, John.
American Contest.  Song.  Tune -- Push about the brisk bowl.

"When luxury reign'd, and court panders obtain'd."  (48)

GA, Sep 25, 1778;  L Chron 44 (Sep 24, 1778), 300;  L Eve Post, Sep 22, 1778.
Freeth, Modern Songs on Various Subjects (1782), pp. 16-17.

In Freeth's collection, this song is entitled "The Contest," and has 40 lines.
The father (Britain) cannot control his son (America), even when helped by German mercenaries and Indians.  Freeth asks for peace because the war, being useless, is fought in vain, only the French gaining from it.  See Freeth, 82-10.


78-211.  Freeth, John.
Britannia's Call to her Sons.  On Expectation of a French War.  Tune, Come then all ye social powers.

"Come ye lads who wish to shine."  (31)

Cumb Pacq, May 5, 1778;  GA, Apr 30, 1778;  Lloyd's 42 (Apr 27, 1778), 404;
L Chron 43 (Apr 30, 1778), 423 & 45 (Jun 24, 1779), 605;  LP, Apr 29, 1778;
SM 40 (Apr 1778), 206;  UM 64 (Supp 1779), 375;  WM 40 (May 13, 1778), 160;
W Misc 12 (Jun 28, 1778), 311-12.  Also in The Vocal Mag (1778), Song 590,
p. 155;  John Freeth, Modern Songs on Various Subjects (1782), pp. 1-2, &
The Political Songster (1790), p. 35;  Poems Serious and Sarcastical, Songs
Loyal and Humourous. . . . By a Briton in New-York (New York: n. p., 1779),
pp. 71-2.  Also G Eve Post, Apr 28, 1778.

Signed "A Warwickshire Lad" in the serials, Freeth's nom de plume.
Various titles are given this anti-Gallican patriotic song:  "Recruiting Song, on the Commencement of Hostilities with the French," "Britain's Glory,"
"A Martial Song."
Britons will now unite to defy France and her ally, Spain.
The American loyalist version adds a few more stanzas.  Cited are Clinton, Cornwallis, Arbuthnot, and James Wallace in this loyalist version.
The music and words of "Come, Now, All ye Social Pow'rs" can be seen in Calliope, or the Musical Miscellany (1788), p. 278.  See Freeth, 82-10.


78-212.  Freeth, John.
The Sailor's Rouze.  Or the Glorious Success of the English Privateers.
Tune, "Hearts of Oak."

"Ye bold British Tars who are strangers to fear."  (31)

Lloyd's 43 (Oct 28, 1778), 420.

Song. The English privateers are praised for taking many rich French prizes.

78-213. [Freeth, John.]
Scale of Talent. A Political Cantata.

"'Twas in the year seventy-seven." (24)

"Were ever British forces in." (12)

"Full of vigour this vaunting commander set out." (20)

Freeman's J, Mar 10, 1778; LP, Jan 14, 1778; L Eve Post, Jan 31, 1778. J. Freeth, The Political Songster (Birmingham: Pearson, 1790), pp. 28-30.

Freeth's title is "Burgoyne's Defeat on the Plains of Saratoga." Three songs narrate the British defeat at Saratoga. See Freeth, 83-15.

78-214. Freeth, John.
The State Beggars.

"Of all the jolly Beggars." (45)

Freeman's J, Jun 11, 1778; GA, Apr 1, 1778; L Eve Post, Mar 28, 1778; LP, May 29, 1778. Freeth, Modern Songs on Various Subjects (1782), pp. 20-1; Freeth, The Political Songster (1790), pp. 38-9.

The serial version has two stanzas not to be seen in the book version. Song. Satire on North, the King, and politicians who beg for an increase in taxes for the war or for pay and pension. See Freeth, 82-10.

78-215. Freeth, John.
Taxation: or, the Courtier's Creed.

"I am the Premier's Scholar bred." (40)

John Freeth, Modern Songs on Various Subjects (1782), pp. 25-7.

Song. A corrupt courtier, follower of North, objects to any attempt to reduce taxation and the King's influence. See Freeth, 82-10.

78-216. [Frenchmen have sure a right to boast.]

"Frenchmen have sure a right to boast." (4)

Freeman's J, Aug 29, 1778; L Eve Post, Aug 15, 1778.

OC. Epigram. Ironic comment on the French escape off Ushant (July 27) from the British fleet under Keppel. The French claimed the escape as a victory!

78-217. [Friend Harry (Tommy), didst thou never pop.]

"Friend Harry [Tommy], didst thou never pop." (49)

LP, Sep 23, 1778; PA, Sep 25, 1778; W Eve Post, Sep 24, 1778.

OC. Satire on Administration because of its failures. The ministry behave like Prior's caged squirrel: they appear to be very active in the war against America, but they succeed only in keeping their places. Cited are tea, army to suppress the rebellion, commissioners for peace, navy, France, and Spain. They are successful neither in war nor in peace.

78-218. From one of the Druids of Salisbury Plain, to the Author of -- An Ode to the Warlike Genius of Great Britain.

"What Sounds awake me from my Bed of Clay." (27)

St J's C, Oct 10, 1778.

HC. Begs that Britain will heed William Tasker's prayer, and that the spirits of Chatham and Garrick will also be stirred, as well as all English poets, to fight France. See Tasker, 78-40.

78-219. A Game for Children Six Feet High.

"A Is for Abingdon, with thoughts half divine." (26)

L Eve Post, Feb 5, 1778.

An alphabet poem praising the minority and some others -- Gates, Abingdon, Barre, Burke, Effingham, et al.

78-220. Garth, Samuel.
The Dispensary. (Extract.)

"Have I, Britannia's safety to insure." (6)

Lloyd's 42 (Feb 20, 1778), 180.

A quotation from Garth (d. 1719); a satire on the Opposition for sowing discord in order to seize power. A commentary on "The Tradesman's Song," 78-513.

78-221. Genealogy of the American War.

"Luxury begot Arbitrary Power." (7)

Freeman's J, Jan 8, 1778; L Eve Post, Jan 1, 1778.

Prose poem. Luxury, Arbitrary Power, and Oppression now lead to Revenge.

78-222. The General Fast.

"Deep in the Dust let Britons hide." (16)

Lloyd's 42 (Feb 25, 1778), 199; PA, Feb 27, 1778.

Quatrains. Britons must be repentant for crimes, forgive the faults of neighbors, and have peace between friends.

78-223. Georgicon or The First Georgic of Virgil, Imitated. Humbly addressed to the Best of Kings.

"How best to till, or sow the fertile field." (173)

PL, Dec 4, 1778.

HC. Imitation of Virgil. Urges the King to show leadership and unify the nation against France. The topics discussed are as follows: the Scottish infiltration of England, bringing exploitation and corruption; the naval show at Spithead; the Bishop of York, Markham; the King's Divine Right; Sandwich, who boasts that his fleet will humble France and America; Germain; and the militia. Urges the King to pursue the war vigorously, unify the country, make the Scotch Jacobites loyal, give freedom to America (but not independence), and control faction.

78-224. Glasgow Loyalty. Tune, Highland March.

"Let old Scotia rejoice, let her rocks all rebound." (48)

WM 39 (Feb 11, 1778), 160.

Song. Glaswegians will conquer Americans or die. They will avenge Burgoyne and Frazer.

78-225. [Go, False, hot Johnstone, cold.]

"Go, False, hot Johnstone, cold." (16)

W Eve Post, May 14, 1778.

Quatrains. George Johnstone is berated for (probably) accepting a place on the Carlisle peace commission. It was "a bribe."

78-226. Great Britain's Triumph; Or, America Conquered: A Ballad. Tune, -- Derry down.

"Of Great Britain's achievements, now crowned with laurels." (44)

Freeman's J, Jan 6, 1778.

Ballad. Satire on Tory failures in America, their policies and the military action. Narrates the cause of the war, the tax on tea, then proceeds to Gage at Boston, Percy at Lexington, Bunker's Hill, Trenton, Sullivan's Island, Howe in Boston, all British defeats.

78-227. [Great Jove, on a day of ambrosial feast.]

"Great Jove, on a day of ambrosial feast." (20)

LP, May 1, 1782.

Quatrains. Satire on North for making peace with the Americans, France, Spain, the Pope, Pretender, and the Devil. (Opposition to North's Conciliatory Proposals.)

78-228. [Had Howe with Burgoyne changed place.]

"Had Howe with Burgoyne changed place." (26)

GA, Jun 18, 1778.

OC. A criticism of Gen. Howe for amorous dalliance, implied as the cause for his inefficient leadership. Burgoyne, on the other hand, was "too hardy." (On May 25, 1778, Howe handed over his command to Clinton.)

78-229. Hall, Thomas.
To the Memory of Lord Chatham.

"Attend, ye nymphs, and from the roseate bower." (112)

M Chron, Aug 31, 1778; PA, Sep 2, 1778.

Blank verse. Panegyric on Chatham. Americans will continue to honor him, an incorruptible patriot. In this critical time, no one like him can lead the nation.

78-230. [---- has Brains, and them to ease.]

"---- has Brains, and them to ease." (18)

St J's C, Aug 29, 1778.

Sixains. Parody, satire on a patriot poet (unknown) who supports the Americans and nauseates the English.

78-231. Hastings, Thomas.
Cox-Heath Camp. A New Song. Tune -- Hearts of Oak.

"Come, brave Britons, advance let us face the proud foe." (31)

M Chron, Aug 15, 1778.

A patriotic anti-Gallican song. The English will fight off any French invasion. Inspired by the victories of the past -- Cressy (Edward, the Black Prince), Agincourt (Henry), and those of great Marlborough -- they will defeat "the sons of false France."

78-232. Hastings, Thomas.
A New Song. To the tune of Thompson's "Rule Britannia."

"When first the tow'ring mountains rose." (37)

M Chron, Sep 26, 1778.

A patriotic song. It is hoped that Britain will succeed in bringing peace to America, and that America will be reasonable and submit to British sovereignty. (Thomson's name is misspelled in the title.)

78-233. The Hasty Message: A Poem. Humbly inscribed to Dick the Pye-Man.

"Britannia's sick, my Richard, haste away." (32)

PA, Oct 6, 1778.

HC. Britain is sick, and the ministry cannot help her.

78-234. Hibernian Impudence to Malagrida.

"Where, Malagrida, art thou gone." (28)

PA, Sep 18, 1778.

Quatrains. Satire on Irish William Petty, Second Earl of Shelburne, patron of Priestley and Price, and colleague of Burke and Barre and Jervoise Clark.

78-235. Homer and Chatham.

"Homer, as ancient Stories say." (8)

L Eve Post, May 14, 1778; LP, May 11, 1778; PA, May 15, 1778; W Eve Post, May 14, 1778.

Quatrains. Epigram. Homer and Chatham have in common the fact that upon their deaths all contending groups honor them.

78-236. [Hopkinson, Francis.]
An American Song. British Valour Display'd; Or, The Battle of the Kegs.

"Gallants attend, and hear a friend." (88)

MP, Jul 17, 1778.

Ballad stanzas narrating an incident of the war near Philadelphia. The kegs were American mines -- one exploded, killing two men and wounding seven others. This ballad was to be sung to the tune of "Yankee Doodle." (Originally published in the Pennsylvania Packet, Mar 4, 1778.)

78-237. [Horace.]
Lines taken from Horace applicable to the Present Times.

The Houses of Parliament, The People of England, The Language of the Minister, Britannia, The King, The War with America, Lord Bute, Lord Chatham.

GA, Apr 11, 1778.

Also lines from Virgil, Book 2 of the Aeneid, GA, Apr 17, 1778.

78-238. [If America's sever'd from this injur'd nation.]

"If America's sever'd from this injur'd nation." (2)

GA, Aug 22, 1778.

Hexameter couplet. The ministry should suffer if America is lost.

78-239. [If sacred Liberty is doom'd to swing.]

"If sacred Liberty is doom'd to swing." (2)

L Eve Post, Feb 17, 1778.

Epigram. Satire on the King, pious but not a lover of liberty.

78-240. [If we have lost America.]

"If we have lost America." (4)

GA, Apr 16, 1778.

Quatrain. Satire on the ministry, who, responsible for the loss of America, must now suffer the consequences -- punishment in Hell.

78-241. [Impeachments were formerly excellent Things.]

"Impeachments were formerly excellent Things." (4)

PA, Nov 26, 1778.

Anapest tetrameter couplets. Extempore. Every corrupt state officer should fear impeachment. Advocates execution of corrupt political leaders to terrify them. (The presumption is that one of the "Fav'rites" is Bute.)

78-242. An Impromptu.

"The Court, to please old talking Will." (12)

M Chron, May 21, 1778.

Quatrains. The court elevated Pitt to the peerage to silence him. Now he is dead and cannot speak at all. No matter -- our politics is meaningless and blundering.

78-243. An Impromptu.

"The Premier snores in Anglia's Land." (4)

PA, Jan 9, 1778.

Three-stress couplets. North and Howe sleep, bringing ruin to the nation.

78-244. Impromptu on the New Year. (Applied to our American Affairs.)

"We've fought some Years to gain Taxation." (4)

LP, Dec 31, 1777-Jan 2, 1778; PA, Jan 3, 1778.

HC. Epigram on the absurdity of fighting over the principle of taxation.

78-245. [In England's various wars with France.]

"In England's various wars with France." (8)

GA, Aug 21, 1778.

Quatrains. The ministry is responsible for the navy's difficulties with its old enemy France. Keppel is the victim of "a wretched Ministry."

78-246. An Inscription.

"Be it remembered, tho' with difficulty." (9)

Freeman's J, Feb 26, 1778; L Eve Post, Jan 24, 1778.

Ironic observation that the term "patriot" is one of reproach in the reign of George III, and that Tories, Jacobites, and Papists are the King's Friends.

78-247. [Inscription for John Bradshaw.]

"Stranger, / 'Ere thou pass, contemplate this cannon." (c. 10)

GA, Feb 2, 1778.

Inscription on Jamaica, honoring the memory of Bradshaw, one of the republican regicides in the Puritan Revolution: a Whig hero who said, "That rebellion to tyrants is obedience to God."

78-248. Inscription for the Monument of William Pitt, Earl of Chatham.

"The [King] and Senate consecrate this stone." (4)

GA, Jun 12, 1778;  L Eve Post, Jun 9, 1778.

Epigram.  Satire on the King and Parliament who commemorate their folly with a monument to Chatham.

78-249.  [Inscription in memory of the Earl of Chatham.]

"Sacred to the Memory / Of that great and able Statesman."  (c. 10)

GA, Oct 1, 1778.

Panegyric on Chatham.  He brought glory to Britain;  but when he was removed from power, Britain declined.

78-250.  Inscription in Memory of William Pitt, Earl of Chatham, who died on the 11th of May, 1778.

"Friend of thy country, and of England's fame."  (26)

GA, Jun 13, 1778;  L Chron 43 (Jun 11, 1778), 568;  WM 41 (Jul 1, 1778), 16.

Blank verse, in honor of Pitt's leadership and eloquence and wisdom.  He died "Ere yet his falling country fell."

78-251.  Inscription on an Obelisk in the front of Lord Amherst's Seat at Riverhead near Sevenoaks in Kent.

G Eve Post, Sep 3, 1778;  SM 40 (Sep 1778), 508.

General Amherst commemorates his victories in America over the French, 1758-62: Louisburgh, Fort Du Quesne, Niagara, Ticonderoga, Crown Point, Quebec, Montreal, and Newfoundland.

78-252.  An Inscription, taken from the Monument erected in Bushley Church, Worcestershire, is said to be written by Mr. Burke.

"To the Memory of / William Dowdeswell."  (c. 25)

GA, Apr 15, 1778;  L Eve Post, Apr 14, 1778;  LP, Apr 10, 1778;  PA, Apr 15, 1778;  St J's C, Apr 11, 1778.

Dowdeswell, died Feb. 4, 1775, is praised by Burke in this epitaph -- for his civic virtues and service to his country, and for his opposition to the American War.  Reprinted 80-168.

78-253. Instructions to a Certain Admiral.

"You are, Sir, sent to make a gallant show." (4)

L Eve Post, Oct 3, 1778.

HC. Instructions to Keppel to return home, should he have to. The publication of these instructions was meant to embarrass the Government because of the exposure of its poor preparations for a French war. Keppel did receive such instructions in May-June 1778.

78-254. Intelligence Extraordinary.

"I, John of Burgoyne, essay'd to alarm." (12)

Freeman's J, Jan 8, 1778; L Eve Post, Jan 1, 1778.

HC. Satire on Burgoyne, alluding to his proclamation allowing Indians to collect scalps and to his defeat by Gates.

78-255. Invocation to Peace.

"Come, lovely peace! celestial maid, descend!" (30)

L Chron 43 (Jan 13, 1778), 52; SM 40 (Mar 1778), 157.

HC. The poet prays that peace will "stop the slaughter of her warring sons."

78-256. Iö Triumphe!

"He comes! he comes! the Monarch comes!" (6)

G, May 20, 1778; GA, May 21, 1778.

OC. Ironic satire on peasants who try to see the King on his way to Spithead, and on Government and the King for joining in the excitement over the naval review off Spithead.

78-257. Irregular Verses on the Reception of the British Commissioners by the Americans.

"We three shall never meet again." (55)

PA, Aug 26, 1778.

Irregular verses. The persona of George Johnstone speaks about the other two commissioners of peace, Earl of Carlisle and William Eden, and the problem he has had in communicating with Congress and with Henry Laurens, its president.

78-258. Jack Ketch, to B[ute] and M[ansfield].

"Your hour approaches: vengeance both must share." (3)

GA, Jun 20, 1778.

A triplet. The common hangman warns Bute and Mansfield that they are doomed.

78-259. Jephson, Robert.
[Applications to the present Times from the Tragedy of Braganza.]

"The Americans. I think we cannot fail -- our Friends are firm." (40)

PA, Apr 7, 1778.

Lines from Jephson's Braganza are applied to the Americans, Washington, Chatham, the French King, Sir George Savile, Burke, Gates, the King, and the Ministry (North).

78-260. John Bull to Lewis Baboon Greeting.

"Baffled so lately, Lewis, why so fond." (13)

Cumb Pacq, Aug 4, 1778.

HC. John Bull, England, takes on King Louis of France, who has been itching to fight ever since the Americans began their war.

78-261. [Kind heaven, that lets presumptuous sinners know.]

"Kind heaven, that lets presumptuous sinners know." (14)

LP, Apr 3, 1778.

HC (rough). Written in 1761, "on hearing that the finest diamond in his majesty's crown had dropped from it, at his coronation," and applied to the present. Restore Pitt, and King and country will be safe again.

78-262. A King his own Minister. A Caution.

"No Minister for me! I am my own." (8)

L Eve Post, Aug 8, 1778.

HC. The King should have a minister and rule under law. (On the fears of George assuming unconstitutional powers.)

78-263. Labour in Vain; Or, the Inefficacy of Truth. Occasioned by reading the following words in the K[in]g's answer to the London Petition, viz. "I can never be persuaded."

"True Britons give o'er." (24)

GA, Mar 30, 1778; L Eve Post, Mar 26, 1778.

Sixains. Satire on the King for rejecting a London petition: behaving like a tyrant, he endangers his crown.

78-264. The Landing of King William.

"As on this Day, to Britain dear." (20)

G Eve Post, Nov 3-5, 1778; PA, Nov 4, 1778.

Quatrains on the Glorious Revolution. Many years ago on this day, William of Orange came to England, seized the helm from Stuart James, and forced tyranny and superstition to fly the land. Let England continue to fight for freedom.

78-265. [Last Night, to our House, came a Man, full of Scars.]

"Last Night, to our House, came a Man, full of Scars." (6)

PA, Jan 16, 1778.

Epigram on the American War. The civil war is the result of an insistence upon prerogative.

78-266. The Last Prayer of the Whigs.

"Great Jove, look down on us poor Whigs." (24)

LP, Jan 5, 1778.

Quatrains. Satire on Whigs, who pray to be restored to power against the "wicked Tories."

78-267. A Late Bon Mot between Two Noble Lords in Office Versified.

"Says Twitch' to North, my Lord, our Fleet." (4)

PA, Jul 28, 1778.

Epigram. Twitcher (Sandwich) declares to North that the fleet will soon engage the French under Chartres, but North is sceptical.

78-268. A Leadenhall-Street Conversation on the Late Report from Madras.

"'Tis Pity he should ever die." (14)

PA, Jan 22, 1778.

OC. Wheat imported from India is endangered by American privateers. Evidence of a trade problem as a result of American privateering. (The lines in the footnote allude to the privateers of the "Yankies.")

78-269. Liberty Lamenting her Injuries in America.

"Shall horrid war the guiltless maid attend." (26)

GA, Jan 22, 1778.

HC. Liberty complains of the destructive American war -- its toll on lives -- and blames it on the Jacobite Scotch Tories, "those who fought a Stuart's cause."

78-270. Life or Death of Old England.

"To save six rascals, 'tis the common creed." (4)

GA, Mar 2, 1778; L Eve Post, Feb 26, 1778.

HC. Satire on the ministry. The ministry ("six rascals") will be punished. (North, Mansfield, Germain, Sandwich, Bute, and Rigby.)

78-271. Lines Elegiac. Inscribed to the Memory of Lieutenant James Gordon, of the 26th Regiment of Foot, who Died at New York, Oct 31, 1777, of the Wounds he Received on his Return from the Attack on Fort Montgomery.

"When life is yielded to command of Fate." (32)

SM 40 (Jan 1778), 38; WM 39 (Mar 4, 1778), 255.

HC. The death of a "Brave Youth" is mourned.


78-272. Lines occasioned by a Late Naval Engagement.

"The sun of Britain is for ever gone." (16)

M Chron, Aug 13, 1778.

Quatrains. Praise of Keppel for his victory over the French fleet and for raising British morale. (The poem is a reaction to the sea battle off Ushant, here claimed as a British victory.)


78-273. Lines Occasioned by the Death of William Earl of Chatham.

"The distant Woe is scarcely heard." (54)

PA, May 15, 1778.

Regular ode in sixains. Chatham had brought honor to the country before; now he may teach by example.


78-274. Lines on seeing the Lord Chancellor pass by St. Martin's Church, in his way to the House of Peers.

"Pass'd now yon spire, the man whose zeal." (8)

M Chron, Dec 19, 1778.

OC. Praise of Thurlow, Lord Chancellor, disinterested, honest, and humble protector of the laws.


78-275. Lines on the Late American War. Written in the Year 1778.

"Upon a trestle Pig was laid." (22)

Salmagundi: A Miscellaneous Combination of Original Poetry. . . The Third Edition, with Corrections (London: Hodson, 1793), pp. 123-4.

OC. An aborted slaughtering of a pig resembles Britain's attempt to destroy America. See "The Butcher and Hog," 71-16, and "On the American dispute," 80-272.

78-276. Lines Sent to Silas Deane, by a Person of Distinction in Paris, on the News of Burgoyne's Capitulation.

"Ton pays a vaincu ses cruels oppresseurs." (4)

MP, Jan 26, 1778.

Quatrain. In French. Praise of the virtuous and invincible Americans for their victory over Burgoyne.

78-277. Lines. To the Hon. Charles James Tod.

"Alas! poor Charles, -- is this thy Merit's Meed." (6)

PA, Apr 15, 1778.

HC. Satiric lines denigrating Fox and his "dark Deeds."

78-278. Lines written by a Lady in the year 1766, on Mr. Pitt's accepting a Peerage.

"When heav'n to save a sinking land." (14)

LP, Jun 1, 1778.

HC. Panegyric on Chatham. Chatham is a patriot, was and will continue one, despite his elevation to the peerage.

78-279. Lines Written in the late Engagement between the Brest Fleet and Admiral Keppel's Squadron.

"Fiercely engag'd, both sides unite." (24)

L Chron 44 (Aug 18, 1778), 173; MP, Aug 17, 1778.

Sixains. Another version (fanciful) of the inconclusive battle between the two fleets, Keppel's and Chartres'.

78-280. Lines Wrote Extempore upon Lord Warwick's advertising a Meeting of the County of Warwick for a Subscription to raise a Regiment.

"My very good Lord." (6)

GA, Feb 5, 1778.

Sixain. An objection to Lord Warwick's wish to raise a regiment.

78-281. [The London Gazette.]

"The London Gazette." (42)

MP, Aug 29, 1778; W Eve Post, Aug 29, 1778.

Song in sixains and chorus. Satire on Keppel for declining to fight the French fleet off Brest.

78-282. The Longest-Day: A Politico-Moral Thought.

"The Sun in bright Meridian Power." (24)

Cumb Pacq, Jun 30, 1778; PA, Jun 20, 1778; W Eve Post, Jun 18, 1778.

Quatrains. The premier may have the royal favor now, but he will inevitably fall.

78-283. A Loyal Song.

"Rouse! rouse, ye brave Britons, no longer delay." (24)

Cumb Pacq, Sep 29, 1778.

A patriotic song. Britain is roused to fight France and Spain.

78-284. Loyal Song, Sung on the 4th of June, 1776, in America. Tune, Cotillon.

"O'er Britannia's happy land." (52)

MP, Jun 2, 1778.

Quatrains and chorus. A song in honor of the King's birthday celebrated by British prisoners of war on an island in the Delaware River. Some of the prisoners are loyalists.

78-285. The Manchester Volunteers. Written and sung by Mr. Craneson, comedian, at the Theatre-royal in that town, on Friday Jan 9. Tune, In story we're told, &c.

"Ye lads of true spirit." (24)

SM 40 (Mar 1778), 157;  WM 39 (Jan 21, 1778), 88.

A loyal recruiting song against the rebellion.

78-286.  The Manchester Wags:  A Song.

"Ye Manchester lads and ye lasses."  (35)

LP, Jan 9, 1778.

Satire on the loyal Manchester volunteers for wishing to rebel (as the Jacobites and Scotch did in the reign of George II), and relying on Bute and North.

78-287.  A Meditation.

"Renown'd Britannia! lov'd parental land."  (14)

W Misc 12 (Jun 28, 1778), 312.

Sonnet (modified Italian).  Britain will be ruined not by France and Spain but from within -- by loss of freedom, mistreatment of the poor, and corruption.

78-288.  The Meeting of Parliament.

"This Day, so George and Fate ordain."  (28)

PA, Nov 26, 1778.

Quatrains.  Ironic lines on the dull and meaningless work engaging the attention of Parliament.

78-289.  Merry Lord Sandwich;  or, the L[yin]g Politician.

"The merry Sandwich ne'er in earnest speaks."  (12)

GA, Feb 6, 1778;  L Eve Post, Feb 3, 1778.

HC.  Satire on Sandwich, whose jests about the American war are absurd lies.  He says that he is America's best friend!  But he wishes to pacify America by means of violent war!

78-290.  Ministerial Repentance.

"Bute, Mansfield, Sandwich, Suffolk." (7)

Freeman's J, Mar 10, 1778; GA, Mar 6, 1778; L Eve Post, Mar 3, 1778.

The ministers -- Bute, Mansfield, Sandwich, Suffolk, North, and Gower -- are not sincerely repentant. They are sorry that Freedom lives and Slavery must die.

78-291. A Modern Character from Shakespeare, parodied. Jemmy Twitcher, Solus.

"Let me see -- ." (7)

L Eve Post, Apr 30, 1778.

Blank verse. Parody of Shakespeare's *Richard III*. Sandwich soliloquizes and ironically betrays himself -- his fear of being criticized for not building a strong navy.
Part of the satiric campaign against Sandwich for inefficiency in administering the navy.

78-292. A New Ballad. To the Tune of "The White Cliffs of Albion."

"Retir'd from the Crowd, in a calm, silent Spot." (24)

PA, Jul 10, 1778; St J's C, Jul 9, 1778.

Song. Quatrains in couplets. The goddesses Pallas (Wisdom), Freedom, and Astraea (Justice) explain why they have left Britain -- for its failure to heed Pitt and Camden, its rejection of Wilkes, and for cherishing North and Bute.

78-293. A New Occasional Prologue, spoken by the Author, April 6, 1778, on the Edinburgh Theatre, at the representation of a petit piece of one act, intitled The Volunteers; the Piece and the Prologue both written by Mr. Woods.

"Just like the tim'rous young recruit I come." (56)

SM 40 (Apr 1778), 206.

HC. The author patriotically adopts the persona of a volunteer in the war against France. Britain will be "united" against the enemy.

78-294. A New Song. Addressed to the Loyal Recruits now raising at Manchester.

"Let Britannia's genius smile." (36)

G, Jan 16, 1778.

A recruiting song -- against "the rebel troops."

78-295.  A New Song for the Times:  In Imitation of Chevy Chace.

"God prosper long Old England's state."  (136)

GA, Nov 5, 1778.

Ballad narrates the resistance of America to oppression -- to Percy at Lexington, to Howe at Bunker Hill, to Carleton at Quebec, to Burgoyne at Saratoga. Cited are Warren, Montgomery, Arnold, Gates, King George.  Concludes with a warning that the King, unable to suppress the "Yankies," will try to "tame" the English, and with a wish for the end of "bloody wars / 'Mongst breth'ren."

78-296.  A New Song to an Old Tune;  or the Downfall of Lord Bute, and his Junto.  Air, "Push about the brisk Bowl."

"Old England to bless."  (28)

PA, Sep 26, 1778.

Against the American war and those responsible for it -- Tories and Scots, Mansfield, Bute, North, Germain, Suffolk, Sandwich, Stormont, and Jenkinson -- who should all be cashiered.

78-297.  A New Song.  To be Sung this Evening by Mr. Vernon, at Vauxhall.

"Rouse, Britain's warlike throng."  (14)

GA, Jul 14, 1778;  Lloyd's 43 (Jul 13, 1778), 52;  L Eve Post, Jul 14, 1778; LP, Jul 10, 1778;  M Chron, Jul 11, 1778;  Vocal Mag (1778), Song 599, p. 158; West J, Jul 18, 1778.  Also G Eve Post, Jul 9, 1778;  Reading Mercury, Jul 20, 1778.

Quatrains.  A patriotic martial song reflecting the new situation, war with France.

78-298.  A New Song.  To the Tune of "There was a Magpye, &c. &c."

"Good people attend, I'll sing you a song."  (96)

GA, Nov. 12, 1778.

Ballad narrates the career of the Earl of Bute as tutor to young Prince

George and as favorite when the young man becomes king, as minister of the peace, and influential adviser at court, etc. All the defeats are blamed on Bute and his oppressive policies: "Sixty thousand brave soldiers" could not stand against the Americans, and thirteen provinces were lost. The West Indies are next.

78-299. A New Song. Tune, Derry Down, &c.

"Immortal brave Britons attend to my lays." (55)

LP, Jun 12, 1778.

Quatrains in couplets with Derry down chorus. An attack on the Opposition for treason -- especially Richmond and Fox; but others are more discreet -- Burke, Shelburne, Saville, and Rockingham.

78-300. A New Version of the Challenge sent by the never-to-be-enough renowned Marquis de la Fayette to the Earl of Carlisle; together with the noble Earl's Answer.

"I never conceited, my very dear Lord." (44 + 18)

L Chron 44 (Dec 12, 1778), 572; MP, Dec 15, 1778; SM 40 (Dec 10, 1778), 680-1.

Satire on the French De la Fayette who is insulted by Carlisle's letter to Congress in which the commissioner has made disparaging remarks on France; he calls Carlisle a liar and challenges him to a duel. The persona of Carlisle rejects the challenge. (The incident is dated from New York, Oct. 11, 1778.)

78-301. A Nocturnal Reverie. Occasioned by Reading some Late Parliamentary Speeches.

"The clock strikes twelve! -- too much engag'd." (50)

M Chron, Dec 26, 1778.

Mixed verse. The "speeches" refer to the debate on Burgoyne's defense. The writer credits North with good leadership, but he questions the effectiveness of Germaine -- his "timid measures / which hourly sink Britannia's treasures"-- because Germaine (in his opinion) was responsible for Burgoyne's defeat. He envisions Frazer's ghost complaining of Germaine's delay in sending help to Burgoyne. He is sympathetic with Burgoyne. "The mere scape-goat of others' crimes."

78-302. Non Chalance; or, The Philosophic Prince: An Epigram.

"'The news, dear Boreas! what's the news to-day.'" (2)

L Eve Post, Apr 7, 1778.

HC. Epigram, satire on the King, who is not perturbed by the loss of an empire.

78-303. The Northern Route; or "Three Children Sliding on the Ice." Paraphrased.

"Through Canada -- some Englishmen." (8)

LP, Jan 14, 1778; PL, Jan 15, 1778.

Quatrains. Satire on Burgoyne's inglorious expedition for an unjust cause: "Britons subverted sacred laws."

78-304. [Now crimson'd discord strews the plain.]

"Now crimson'd discord strews the plain." (20)

Freeman's J, Mar 31, 1778.

Quatrains. Now that France and Spain enter the war, the King asks Ireland to help Britain: "Invites Hibernia to the war, / To share the glories of his reign."

78-305. [Now trembling on the brink of fate.]

"Now trembling on the brink of fate." (56)

AWCour, Feb 17, 1778; G Eve Post, Jan 3, 1778.

Quatrains. Britain is facing a crisis. The Patriots must stop supporting the rebels, or else the country (empire) will be torn apart. Peace is the only resource for the saving of the state, and only Pitt can help.

78-306. [O may the happy aera soon arrive.]

"O may the happy aera soon arrive." (16)

GA, Feb 11, 1778.

"Pacificus" objects in a prose essay to the ministry's "bad policy" and concludes it with a blank verse peroration expressing hope for peace and lasting union with America.

78-307. An Ode.

"Hark! the sound of war's alarms." (73)

GA, Jun 26, 1778; MP, Jun 25, 1778.

Mostly regular ode bewails the Franco-American alliance and urges that the struggle against France be fought vigorously behind Keppel.

78-308. An Ode adapted to the present Times. To the Ministry of Great Britain, and its Subjects.

"Ye ministers! by no example aw'd." (55)

HM 8 (May 1778), 304.

Irregular Pindaric ode. The increase of vice is responsible for Britain's perilous state, as well as oppressive taxation.

78-309. An Ode, addressed to the -----. On the report that Mr. W-dd--b--ne was to be made a Peer.

"Of policy approv'd, and worth." (32)

GA, Apr 9, 1778.

Regular ode in quatrains. An objection to treacherous Scots power. The "race . . . sculk behind the Throne."

78-310. [Ode for the Americans.]

"Yes, Goddess, yes! 'twas thus of old." (29)

G, Jun 13, 1778.

Reverses the meaning of Whitehead's "Birthday Ode" and has it reprinted as if it supported the Americans. See 78-543.

78-311. Ode for the General Fast, Feb. 27.

"Ah me! what means this Morn."  (52)

St J's C, Feb 24, 1778.

Irregular Pindaric.  An objection to a bloody fast.  Freedom has fled to victorious America; Britain should "proffer Bonds of peace" and learn humanity from General Gates.

78-312.  Ode for the New Year.

"Tho' Time in his continu'd race."  (50)

L Eve Post, Jan 13, 1778.

Regular (Horatian) ode in octaves except for a dixain stanza.  The war against America is unjust.  The Americans bravely resist despotism, and the war is unhappily being pursued.  May this civil war cease and the Tories no more surround the throne.

78-313.  Ode in praise and recommendation of Shaftesbury Punch, Esq; humbly offered as a hint to ----- -----, at this critical time.

"Punchinello."  (36)

GA, Mar 30, 1778; L Eve Post, Mar 26, 1778.

Two- and three-stress lines in sixains.  A hint and a hope (expressed ironically) that the Americans will be persuaded to accept Britain's offer of conciliation.  Punch is apparently Lord North.

78-314.  An Ode performed at a Friend's House on New Year's Day: Not wrote by William Whitehead, Esq; nor set to Music by Dr. Boyce.

"When Rival Nations, great in Arts."  (35)

PA, Jan 2, 1778.

A serious parody of Whitehead's ode, urging reconciliation by rescinding all hostile acts.  See 78-544.

78-315.  Ode to Admiral Van Keppel, on his late Glorious Victory.

"Some Hundreds kill'd, some Hundreds wounded."  (20)

PA, Sep 1, 1778.

An ironic ode on the thwarted engagement between the French and English fleets off the coast of France.

78-316. Ode to Charity.

"Daughter of Heav'n, whose feeling eye." (74)

MP, Jan 17, 1778.

Pindaric ode. Ironic satire on the subscription taken for the American prisoners in London. It encourages rebellion -- such is the theme. Cited are Rockingham, Abingdon, North, Germain, Wilkes, Manchester, Birmingham, and treason.

78-317. Ode to Charity, Occasioned by the Subscription for the American Prisoners.

"Thrice hallow'd grace! that keep'st thy pow'r." (38)

GM 47 (Jun 1778), 278; WM 41 (Jul 15, 1778), 63.

Irregular Pindaric ode. Begs the British to show charity for the American prisoners of war in England. Shelburne is praised for his work in their behalf.

78-318. Ode to L[ord] G[eorge] G[ermain].

"In this advent'rous point of time." (24)

MP, Oct 10, 1778.

Regular (Horatian) ode in octaves. Praise of Germain, who will protect the land against the enemy, "tho' successless." (This ode is undoubtedly ironical.)

78-319. Ode to Peace.

"Descend from thy aetherial Car." (40)

St J's C, Feb 7, 1778.

OC. The war must come to an end -- there has been enough bloodshed.

78-320. Ode to Peace.

"Fair Peace! descend and bless our isle." (42)

L Chron 44 (Jul 28, 1778), 104; St J's C, Jul 25, 1778; WM 41 (Sep 23, 1778), 302.

Regular (Horatian) ode in sixains. Let us have peace with our friends and brothers in America; let us hope that the Commissioners sent to America will be successful so that "civil broils no longer rage."

78-321. Ode to Peace. Written by an English Officer at Philadelphia.

"For here are Hills (though lost to Fame)." (29)

St J's C, Jul 28, 1778.

Irregular ode. An English officer says that America is lovely, needs peace, and the Muse of poetry should celebrate the land. The Delaware is cited.

78-322. Ode to Pity.

"Pity! meek-ey'd heav'nly maid." (36)

Cumb Pacq, Aug 25, 1778.

Regular (Horatian) ode in sixains. Pity is invoked to assuage various kinds of suffering, even that in America in the throes of war.

78-323. Ode to the Earl of Chatham, on hearing that he had an Offer of being appointed Secretary for the American Department.

"Come Clio! come, thou best ador'd." (16)

PA, Feb 9, 1778.

Regular ode in quatrains. Chatham may save the country, while Howe sleeps and Burgoyne suffers defeat.

78-324. Ode To The [King].

"Awake, my Muse, awake and speak." (60)

New Foundling Hospital for Wit (1786), IV, 229-31.

Regular ode in sixains. Satiric parody on Whitehead's Birthday Odes, especially their professions of loyalty. Cited are the King, Howe, Carleton,

Samuel Johnson, Hume, Sandwich, Pinchbeck, and Tories.


78-325. An Ode, Written about the Beginning of the Year 1778, when the Intelligence of General Burgoyne's Being Taken With his Army at Saratoga arrived.

"Now from the Pole's inclement shores." (72)

WM 48 (May 9, 1780), 143.

Regular (Horatian) ode in octaves. Burgoyne fought bravely and should not be ashamed of his defeat. Cited are Germain, King George, Wolfe, and North.


78-326. An Ode. Written on the Arrival of the illustrious Duke of Richmond, at Exeter, to take the Command of the Sussex Regiment of Militia . . . of which his Grace is Head-Colonel.

"Let fierce Bellona shout for war." (56)

WM 13 (Oct 18, 1778), 65-6.

Irregular ode. A panegyric on the Duke of Richmond and a defense of his position as a leading member of the Minority Opposition.


78-327. [O'er the green margin of a spacious pool]

"O'er the green margin of a spacious pool." (68)

L Eve Post, Oct 10, 1778.

HC. A dream-vision of the fall of Athens because of tyranny and corruption and civil strife -- a lesson for England.


78-328. [Of Bristol's great city, so loyal the Mayor is.]

"Of Bristol's great city so loyal the Mayor is." (54)

GA, Feb 7, 1778.

Fourteeners, couplets. Satire on the loyalist Mayor of Bristol, who wishes to be knighted.


78-329. [Oh! had the voice of Charity been heard.]

"Oh! had the voice of Charity been heard." (32)

L Eve Post, Sep 29, 1778.

Elegiac quatrains. The British uncharitably attacked the Americans and now sue for peace! But the Commissioners are spurned, and France prepares to attack. We need peace and charity.

78-330. [Oh thou, great God, who art all wise.]

"Oh thou, great God, who art all wise." (24)

L Eve Post, Feb 24, 1778.

Regular (Horatian) ode in sixains. A prayer that the King may see his error and end the criminal and bloody war against America.

78-331. An Old Briton's Complaint.

"Poor England! how hard is thy lot." (32)

Vocal Magazine; or British Songster's Miscellany (1778), p. 202 (Song #766).

Song. France, Spain, and Holland are threatening England -- and her decline is caused by tea. America is cited. We must change from tea to ale, before it is too late.

78-332. [Old England's mock Pilot.]

"Old England's mock Pilot." (8)

W Eve Post, Apr 28, 1778.

Three-stress quatrains. Remarks on the King and the premier who are not steering the ship of state well. Is it time to change pilots?

78-333. The Old Woman of Syracuse. A Scrap of Ancient History.

"By all, but Courtiers vile, abhor'd." (32)

PA, Jul 28, 1778.

Ballad. The old woman prays that the tyrant Dionysius live, for fear that a worse ruler will succeed him.

78-334. On a Certain Trial.

"Whene'er Corruption's hand shall hold the scale." (4)

L Eve Post, Dec 29, 1778.

HC. The court-martial of Keppel will begin soon. Keppel, who is guiltless, will be charged with crimes, because corruption dominates the country.

78-335. On a Debate not a Hundred Years Since.

"When Lords were sat in grave debate." (8)

W Eve Post, Feb 21, 1778.

OC. Satire on Sandwich and the Government's view of the state of the nation. Richmond and Sandwich debate.

78-336. On a Late Capitulation.

"Great, gen'rous heroes! he who firm to meet." (48)

GM 48 (Mar 1778), 134-5; LP, Feb 2, 1778.

HC. A reaction to Burgoyne's surrender to Gates at Saratoga; a protest at the civil war in which both sides lose. But because America burns "With freedom's fever," it is up to the parent "to sooth that frantic rage" and allow candor, reason, and justice to prevail and to bring peace.

78-337. On a late Defeat.

"Caesar of old was not content to fight." (4)

GA, Feb 3, 1778.

Epigram. Satire on Burgoyne for his menacing proclamation, but yet he was defeated.

78-338. On an Approved Patriot.

"If melting monodies could sooth his soul." (16)

WM 12 (May 31, 1778), 216.

Quatrains. Satire on an allegedly destructive journalist, Atticus. Advice to Atticus, an "approved patriot," at a time when Britain needs assistance.

78-339. On General Burgoyne's Avidity for the Canada Expedition.

"Give me ten thousand men -- and I." (8)

LP, Jan 14, 1778; PL, Jan 15, 1778.

Epigram. Burgoyne boasted he would defeat the rebels, but Gates stopped him.

78-340. On Hearing that the King and his Ministers were still bent upon Blood and Slaughter, Fire and Sword.

"God bless the King, but since he has gone further." (8)

L Eve Post, Dec 19, 1778.

Should the King truly repent, he will not rule oppressively and break the law of God (by trying to subdue America).

78-341. On Hypocrisy.

"Hypocrites in religion form a plan." (4)

Freeman's J, Mar 10, 1778; L Eve Post, Mar 3, 1778.

HC. The context is the General Fast calling for success in the war against America. The clergy is hypocritical regarding its ordaining the fast.

78-342. On Lord Chatham's Death.

"And is th'important Moment come." (16)

G Eve Post, May 12, 1778; PA, May 13, 1778; W Eve Post, May 12, 1778.

Quatrains. Praise of Chatham -- for persuasion and conviction, wisdom and worth. Chatham died May 11, 1778.

78-343. On Lord Chatham's Death.

"O Thou, to whose great shade thy country pays." (10)

W Eve Post, Jun 4, 1778.

HC. Praise of Chatham, whose eloquent attempt to save the nation caused his death.

78-344. On Lord North's Appointment to the Wardenship, Together with his Right to the Wrecks on the Coast.

"Now thou hast sav'd thy country, North." (4)

L Eve Post, Jun 20, 1778.

Quatrain. Satire. Ironic remarks on North's new sinecure post, Warden of the Cinque Ports. America is cited.

78-345. On Lord North's Conciliatory Bill.

"When peace might be gain'd." (72)

GA, Feb 27, 1778; L Eve Post, Feb 4, 1778.

Regular (Horatian) ode in sixains, and a long note in prose rejecting the fast. Satire on the ministry for its conciliatory gestures, all hypocritical. Cited are Bute, North, Mansfield, Court, Junto, King, and Bishops -- all responsible for the war.

78-346. On Lord North's Recantation.

"When North first began." (48)

GA, Mar 9, 1778; L Eve Post, Mar 5, 1778.

Regular ode in sixains. North and his Scotch allies are forced to come to terms with America upon Burgoyne's defeat. But America is lost, because the attempt at conciliation is too late. General Howe is cited in these lines on North's Conciliatory Proposals.
Also in Israel Pottinger, The Political Duenna (Philadelphia: R. Bell, 1778), pp. 47-8. The verses are placed at the end of the pamphlet; they are not a part of this farce.

78-347. On Lord North's Recanting Too Late.

"'Tis well that the tyrants begin to confess." (6)

GA, Mar 9, 1778; L Eve Post, Mar 5, 1778.

Alternating rhymes. Of what use is the confession of error by tyrants when it is made too late. The nation is ruined!

78-348. On Lord Shelburne.

"The patriot burns to see his country lost." (14)

M Chron, Dec 3, 1778.

Blank verse. Panegyric on Shelburne of the Patriot Opposition, for his criticism of corrupt government, especially Henry Howard, Earl of Suffolk (Sec. of State for the Northern Department), and Sandwich.

78-349. On Mr. Pitt's Resignation in 1761.

"Ne'er yet in Vain did Heav'n its Omens send." (4)

St J's C, Apr 4, 1778.

When Pitt resigned in 1761, it was an ill omen, prophetic of the loss of America. Ref. to the "largest Jewel falling out of the King's Crown at his Coronation." See 61-26 and 61-33.

78-350. On Mrs. Macaulay's Birth Day.

"Bright was the day, and splendid was the morn." (94)

L Eve Post, Apr 25, 1778.

HC. Panegyric on Catharine Graham Macaulay for integrity in her writing of British history -- William III, bribery and corruption, tyranny.

78-351. On Modern Conquests.

"'Wonders will never cease,' the proverb says." (12)

Freeman's J, Nov 14, 1778; GA, Nov 9, 1778; L Eve Post, Nov 5, 1778; LP, Nov 9, 1778; PA, Nov 10, 1778.

HC. Epigram. Satire on Gage and Howe who sought conquest across the ocean but returned in failure, accomplishing nothing.

78-352. On Reading an Account in the Papers of Lord G. Germain's being to be made a Peer.

"At Minden George a guiltless victim fell." (6)

L Eve Post, May 14, 1778.

HC. Ironic opinion expressed on Germain's elevation -- <u>not</u> for services rendered to the nation. The King is praised for rewarding the guilty!

78-353. On Reading the Celebrated Poem, entitled the Saints, just published. Addressed to the Author.

"Thanks to thy honest zeal and virtuous rage." (6)

G Eve Post, Jan 10, 1778.

Quatrain and couplet. Congratulates Combe for his satire on the "hoary hypocrite," Wesley. See 78-10.

78-354. On Reading the Following Words, spoken by the King at the Review of one of his Camps, viz. "Oh, Amherst! what a heav'nly sight!"

"Make much of thy Heav'n, great G-----, while below." (4)

GA, Dec 15, 1778.

Quatrain. Satire on the King, who may not go to Heaven upon his death.

78-355. On Seeing a small Mezzotinto Print of Dr. Benjamin Franklin in a Watch-Case. A Parody.

"Had but our Nation mov'd, like this great Man." (8)

St J's C, Aug 27, 1778.

HC. Praise of Franklin. Had the British acted wisely and prudently, "like this great Man," they would have had a strong government and a lasting friendship with America. This poem is followed by another, "On seeing the Author of the above in a thoughtful Mood," in which the author is admonished to cheer up because Liberty is transplanted to America, where France may obtain its shoots for transplanting at home.

78-356. On Seeing Strawberry-Hill, the Seat of Horace Walpole, Esq.

"When Walpole's genius watch'd Britannia's fate." (36)

GM 48 (Apr 1778), 183; WM 40 (May 13, 1778), 160.

HC.  Sir Robert Walpole gave England peace.  His leadership made the nation prosperous and stabilized the English monarchy.  But after he was removed, the '45 rebellion broke out.  (This poem is partly political and indirectly reflects on the failure of leadership during the American War.)

78-357.  On seeing the [King] Laughing and Very Merry, in the midst of a group, who, in the year 1745, made his Gr[andfather] look Very Grave.

"View tyranny, midst gay disport."  (32)

GA, Apr 23, 1778.

Quatrains.  A criticism of the King for favoring treacherous Scotch Jacobites and for undermining English liberty.

78-358.  On Taking a Fly out of a Bason of Water.

"In yonder vase behold that drowning fly."  (30)

GA, Sep 23, 1778;  G Eve Post, Sep 22, 1778;  LP, Sep 21, 1778.

HC.  I can save a drowning fly;  and the great politicians must save our sinking country.  See the comment in "The Fly Catchers," L Eve Post, Dec 10, 1778:  78-204.

78-359.  On the Appointment of a First Commissioner.

"Say, whence this glaring folly, and it's blame."  (5)

MP, Jul 9, 1778.

Epigram.  Satire on the Earl of Carlisle, appointed Commissioner to deal with the Americans.  He is a "nothing."

78-360.  On the City's late Request to have Lord Chatham interred in St. Paul's Cathedral.

"Shall Chatham's Bones in Paul's grand Dome."  (12)

L Chron 43 (Jun 18, 1778), 591;  PA, Jun 20, 1778;  West J, Jun 27, 1778.

Quatrains.  The spirit of Chatham is in every Briton's heart;  it makes no difference where he is interred.

78-361. On the Comparison between the Ancient and Modern Manners of the Age. The Subject given for the Vase at Bath-Easton.

"Blest Halcyon days, and early hours." (45)

GA, Jun 16, 1778; W Eve Post, Aug 1, 1778.

Regular ode in five-line stanzas. Luxury, corruption, and the decay of liberty characterize the present. England must be inspired by past greatness and "ristine Honour" in order to face France.

78-362. On the Conduct of the Ministry in the two Extremes of Peace and War.

"Our Ministry are doom'd by Fate." (18)

PA, Jul 31, 1778; W Eve Post, Jul 30, 1778.

Sixains. Howe could not give us success in war, nor Johnstone (one of the commissioners) in peace. The ineptitude of the ministry is demonstrated in their choices.

78-363. On the Death of General Frazer.

"While Britain mourns the death of thousands slain." (34)

WM 39 (Jan 14, 1778), 63.

HC. Frazer and others died bravely (in the Burgoyne campaign).

78-364. On the Death of Lord Chatham.

"As o'er yon sacred mount I bent my way." (36)

Cumb Pacq, Jul 7, 1778.

Elegiac quatrains. Britannia mourns the death of Chatham, asks for unity and the end of destructive faction and fraud.

78-365. On the Death of Lord Chatham.

"Where wast thou, Virtue, in the awful hour." (36)

M Chron, Sep 3, 1778; PA, Sep 4, 1778.

Elegiac stanzas grieve over Chatham's death, ask that his spirit inspire

Britain, and thank the nation for his monument.

78-366. On the Death of that Great Patriot, and able Statesman, William Pitt, Earl of Chatham.

"Britannia's sons your parent's loss deplore." (28)

GA, May 16, 1778; L Chron 43 (May 16, 1778), 477; SM 40 (May 1778), 261.

Quatrains. Let us all mourn the death of Chatham, "For sure there's cause for more than common woe."

78-367. On the Deaths of Lord Chatham and M. de Voltaire.

"Voltaire was the Pride and the Boast of the Age." (8)

G Eve Post, Jun 18, 1778; PA, Jun 19, 1778.

Quatrains. Praise of Chatham for his wisdom and virtue, which are comparable to Voltaire's learning, genius, and wit in influencing the world. (Voltaire died May 30, 1778.)

78-368. On the Departure of the Portsmouth Fleet, Under Admiral Keppel.

"In thee, great Keppel, Britain rests her hope." (14)

M Chron, Jun 22, 1778.

HC. England has confidence in Admiral Keppel who will teach the faithless French, that is, her naval leaders D'Estaing and Chartres, a terrible lesson.

78-369. [On the Departure of the Portsmouth Fleet Under Admiral Keppel: An Imitation.]

"On thee, bold Keppel, Britannia rests her anchor." (15)

M Chron, Jun 25, 1778.

Hexameter couplets. An earthy imitation of the preceding poem, with notes.

78-370. On the Dispute relative to the Place intended for the Interment of the late Earl of Chatham.

"Blush! hypocrites, blush! nor pretend to respect." (16)

L Eve Post, May 30, 1778.

Hexameter couplets. Satire on the hypocrites in Parliament who dispute with the City over the place for Chatham's interment.

78-371. On the Earl of Chatham's being prevented from Replying to his G[race] the D[uk]e of R[i]ch[mon]d, on the Subject of American Independence, by his sudden Indisposition in the House of Lords, on Tuesday the 7th of April, 1778.

"R[i]ch[mon]d forbear, -- restrain thy patriot rage." (20)

T&C 10 (Apr 1778), 216.

Quatrains. Chatham collapsed, when objecting to Richmond's acquiescence to America's independence, which he thought would be the ruin of his country.

78-372. On the Ensuing Fast Day.

"Can God propitiate a day." (c. 120)

L Eve Post, Feb 17, 1778.

Hudibrastic couplets. An objection to the nation's fast for success in an unjust war that is shamefully supported by bishops and other clergy.

78-373. [On the Ensuing Fast Day.] By the Same.

"The Colonies against us pray." (8)

L Eve Post, Feb 17, 1778.

Ironic satire on the fast and the name-calling of the bishops.

78-374. On the Fast.

"A King's commandment is a sacred thing." (20)

GA, Feb 27, 1778.

Quatrains. Objects to the fast and the war against America.

78-375. On the Fast.

"To fast and pray." (24)

L Eve Post, Feb 24, 1778.

Regular ode in sixains. Satire on the fast, proclaimed for February 27, 1778. The Tories pray for bloody success against the Yankees, but I pray for those who fight for freedom.

78-376. On the Fast Appointed to be Kept the 27th of February, 1778.

"Ye Britons, hark! the thunders roar." (60)

GA, Feb 26, 1778.

Quatrains. An objection to the fast and all who are responsible for it.

78-377. On the Following Words in a Proclamation for a Fast, viz. "By the King's command."

"'By command of the King,' if I am not mista'en." (4)

L Eve Post, Feb 5, 1778.

Epigram. Satire. An objection to the hypocrisy of the King's call for a fast at a time of an unjust American War. The fast does not end the slaughter.

78-378. On the Important News relative to Egg-Bay, communicated by the last Gazette.

"A Gazette! a Gazette! O ye powers divine." (13)

M Chron, Dec 4, 1778.

Irregular lines. Playful satire on North for exaggerating the importance of a minor victory over the colonists at the cost of a whole empire.

78-379. On the King's Message to Parliament for the Maintenance of his Children.

"Beggars may now beg with a grace." (12)

The Craftsman, or London Intelligencer, Apr 25, 1778; GA, Apr 20, 1778; L Eve Post, Apr 16, 1778.

Quatrains. These are "disgraceful times -- an empire lost," and the King has to beg for money.

78-380. On the King's sending the E. of D--b--gh to Lord Ch----m.

"To send D[enbeigh] to Ch[atha]m was certainly wise." (2)

GA, Apr 3, 1778; L Eve Post, Mar 31, 1778.

HC. Chatham is called to assist the ministry, but to send him Earl Denbeigh was unwise, for Chatham detests him. (From another point of view, this embassy was wise, for the idea was to keep Chatham out!)

78-381. On the Late Action between the English and French Fleets.

"See Chartres gains the wish'd for coast." (12)

L Eve Post, Aug 6, 1778.

OC. Chartres escapes Keppel's attack. (This action had terrible consequences. The poem comments on the inconclusive action off Ushant on July 27, 1778, that led to the court-martial of Keppel and Palliser.) See 78-383.

78-382. On the Late Fast Day.

"Lord, hear a suppliant Nation's cry." (24)

W Eve Post, Mar 3, 1778.

Quatrains. Hymn. A prayer that the rebellion end "In Albion's distant lands."

78-383. On the Late Sea-Fight.

"The Evening approaching, the Fleets in Array." (8)

PA, Aug 8, 1778.

Quatrain. The naval battle between Keppel and the Duke de Chartres was aborted. (The poem is about the celebrated battle off Ushant which resulted in the famous court-martial of Keppel and Palliser.) See 78-381.

78-384. On the Naval Review.

"On Twitcher's hobby, Solomon." (38)

G, May 7, 1778.

OC. Satire on Sandwich, Secretary of the Admiralty, and his difficulties preparing a seaworthy fleet and meeting the criticism of the Opposition. See the corrected version, Gazetteer, Jun 10, 1778, of 42 lines.

78-385. On the Naval Reviews.

"Shall S[andwich] of Britannia's navy boast." (8)

L Eve Post. May 14, 1778; WM 40 (May 20, 1778), 208.

HC. Extempore. Satire on Sandwich, who provides a naval show but fails to protect the coast from privateers.

78-386. On the Present Scotch Junto.

"With these the historian our annals will stain." (8)

M Chron, Aug 18, 1778.

Anapest tetrameter couplets. Satire on the present Scottish leadership responsible for draining England of its wealth.

78-387. On the Present State of Great Britain.

"Now trembling on the brink of fate." (56)

WM 39 (Jan 28, 1778), 111.

Quatrains. Only Pitt can now bring peace and save the empire. The "patriots" only "for int'rest bawl."

78-388. On the Queen's Pregnancy with her Thirteenth Child.

"Let croakers croak, for croak they will." (16)

GA, Apr 17, 1778; L Eve Post, Apr 14, 1778.

Quatrains. Satire on the Royal Family. For each revolted American province lost, the King has presented the nation with a child.

78-389. On the Recovery of his Grace the Duke of Richmond.

"When first Britannia heard it said." (20)

L Eve Post, Dec 22, 1778.

Quatrains. Panegyric on Charles Lennox, Duke of Richmond (of the Minority), for his integrity and concern for freedom and the public good.

78-390. On the Reduction of Mud-Island.

"Our commanders and statesmen, a comical herd."  (4)

LP, Jan 14, 1778;  PL, Jan 15, 1778.

Epigram. Satire. The commanders besiege an island of mud, but the politicians leading Government plan dirtier work.

78-391. On the Reflection of Lord North (now lord warden of the Cinque Ports) being Re-Elected for the illustrious Borough of Banbury, in Oxfordshire.

"What, chose again!  He is in troth."  (8)

LP, Jun 26, 1778.

Quatrains. Satire on North and the corrupt electors of Banbury who have chosen him again, despite conscience, honor, and oath.

78-392. On the Report of Lord B[u]te being converted to the Roman Catholic faith, when he was last at Rome.

"Blest aera of returning pow'r."  (52)

GA, Oct 17, 1778.

Quatrains. Fears of Popery in Great Britain. Indignation at concessions made to Roman Catholics in Canada and Ireland -- and an invocation to King William to return to protect English liberty.

78-393. On the Report of Lord Chatham's becoming Prime Minister.

"The World in Terror and Amaze."  (23)

St J's C, Apr 4, 1778.

OC. The thought that Chatham might again lead the nation is inspiring to Britain, and France will not be pleased.

78-394. On the Right Hon. Earl Bathurst's Resignation of the Office of Lord High Chancellor, 3 June 1778.

"Long time have Party Scribblers, through the Press."  (41)

G, Jun 9, 1778.

HC, panegyric on incorruptible Henry, Earl Bathurst, retiring from the office of Lord High Chancellor (a position he held since 1771).  (He had broken with North on June 2, 1778, ostensibly over American policy.)

78-395. On the Royal Trip to Portsmouth.

"How gloriously our navy rides."  (26)

L Eve Post, May 9, 1778.

OC.  A criticism of Sandwich for maladministration of naval affairs.  Satire on the review of the navy.  The point is that such a review does not mean a fighting active navy.

78-396. On the Several Generals to whose Conduct the American Warfare has been intrusted.

"First General Gage commenc'd the War in vain."  (4)

GA, Mar 3, 1778;  PA, Mar 4, 1778.

Epigram.  Generals Gage, Howe, and Burgoyne have led the campaigns in America; Britain's last hope is the General Fast.  (In Horace Walpole, Journal of the Reign of George the Third, ed. Doran [London: Bentley, 1869], II, 214.)

On the Talk of a Dutch War.  Probably written late 1778 and printed early 1779:  see 79-360.

78-397. On the Word Howe.

"How Britain seems still with Atlantic Trips Sea-sick."  (24)

PA, Jul 14, 1778.

Anapest tetrameter couplets.  A satiric review of Britain's American troubles, which are blamed upon Gen. Howe and Lord Germain.

78-398. On the Year 1777.

"To thee, foul year, replete with woes, adieu." (32)

G Eve Post, Jan 3, 1778.

HC. The year 1777 was an abomination because of the civil war; but one good thing happened -- the Subscription for American prisoners.

78-399. [Once more our Rulers call a Fast.]

"Once more our Rulers call a Fast." (12)

L Eve Post, Feb 10, 1778.

Quatrains. An objection that the fast is supported by hypocritical and bloody bishops.

78-400. Cancelled.

78-401. The Only Fast.

"Did thy blest Spirit, Lord, inspire one B[isho]p's heart." (4)

GA, Feb 11, 1778; L Eve Post, Feb 7, 1778.

Hexameter couplets. Satire on the fast and the bishops for their pride and their cruelty in condoning the war. "Self-denial is the only fast."

78-402. A Panegyric On Lord North.

"Hail! Minister, by paradoxes great!" (23)

L Eve Post, Jan 13, 1778; LP, Jan 5, 1778; New Foundling Hospital for Wit (1786), IV, 218; Jeffery Dunstan, Fugitive Pieces (1789), pp. 54-5.

HC. A panegyric (somewhat ironic) on North, whose character and policies, and effect on others are paradoxical; for example, his failures in the war, his "tame campaigns."

78-403. Parody.

"When tuneful bards in lofty verse." (30)

LM 47 (Jan 1778), 42;  PA, Jan 7, 1778;  WM 39 (Feb 25, 1778), 208.

Parody of Whitehead's New Year's Ode, 1778 (78-544).  A satire on the laureat for grafting politics on New Year's day and for roaming across the seas with his prostituted verse.  The parodist begs Whitehead to "Quit politics" and ask forgiveness of Dullness.

78-404.  A Parody.  From the King's soliloquy in Hamlet.

"Oh! my offence is rank;  it smells to Heav'n."  (31)

GA, Mar 2, 1778;  L Eve Post, Feb 26, 1778.

Satire on Germain and his qualms of conscience.  Only a few words are altered to make Claudius's soliloquy applicable to the American War and the fast.

78-405.  A Parody on the Bath Advertisement for a Meeting, to the Tune of King John and the Abbot of Canterbury.

"Ye gay sons of Bladud, high-flyers and all."  (35)

GA, Feb 13, 1778.

Song.  Satire on the Tories who believe it reasonable to suppress the American rebellion.

78-406.  Parody.  The Lads at Water Still.

"The Lads at Water Still."  (32)

PA, Apr 18, 1778;  W Eve Post, Apr 21, 1778.

Song.  A parody of a Scotch song, "The Lass of Peaties Mill."  Burgoyne sings about his defeat to the conquering Americans, for whom he has great respect.

78-407.  [Penn came from America humbly to crave.]

"Penn came from America humbly to crave."  (10)

GA, Oct 15, 1778.

Extempore.  Charles II rejected Penn's petition;  likewise, Congress rejects the petition of the Carlisle Commission.

78-408. A Play for Children Six Feet High.

"A Is one Arnold -- who our heroes outshine." (26)

L Cour, Feb 28, 1778.

An abecedarian poem that favors the Americans. Cited are Arnold, Burgoyne, Carleton, Dunmore, Franklin, Washington, et al.

78-409. Poetical Epistle to a Friend. (Wrote in August.)

"Dear L----, Whence this din of arms." (68)

T&C 10 (Dec 1778), 661-2.

OC. The writer complains of the war that disturbs the pastoral peace. He remarks on the French war and points to America where "Britain's disobedient sons" war "against their rightful sovereign," while their French ally "Applauds the direful parricide." But Britain will assert its power and law over the rebel traitors.

78-410. A Poetical Paraphrase of the Supplement to the Gazette of France.

"The weather, which kept us in harbour past doubt." (48)

SM 40 (Sep 1778), 507-8.

Anapest tetrameter couplets. A versification of the French report on the aborted battle off Ushant between Keppel and the French D'Orvilliers.

78-411. Political Aphorisms.

[Who kills a giant, should his armour take.] (4)

[Angels might weep when England's glory dies.] (4)

On the Decline of ancient Empires. (8)

GA, Aug 26, 1778; L Eve Post, Aug 22, 1778.

Three epigrams. Richmond should succeed Chatham; the King's Friends rejoice at England's fall; Sandwich's lust contributes to the decline of England.

78-412. A Political Elegy.

"Sorrowing upon Hibernia's sea-girt strand." (68)

LP, Jul 1, 1778.

Elegiac stanzas. Britain complains of the American War, styled "The King's War." Cited are Lexington, Bunker's Hill, the need for peace, and the King.

78-413. Political Epigrams.

The Oxford Definition of Rebellion. [And "See non-resistance prov'd as axioms clear."]

"To crush all Nature, heav'n's own will oppose." (6)

GA, Jul 31, 1778.

Two epigrams, HC. Oxford's Tory political and religious principles are attacked: their support of tyranny and old Stuart views.

78-414. Political Epigrams.

Roman and British Senates Compared. [And] Wolfe and Arnold Compared.

"Thy Senators, like Rome's, are most august." (6)

"Wolfe fought for empire, Arnold's nobler end." (6)

GA, Jul 31, 1778; L Eve Post, Jul 28, 1778.

Two epigrams in HC. Bute controls the puppets in Parliament. Wolfe fought for empire, but Arnold fights for freedom, a "nobler end."

78-415. Political Epigrams.

[Tho' Bute o'er earth and seas, or Kings had pow'r.] (12)

[Two parties slay whole hecatombs to Jove.] (10)

[What makes the Yankies such enthusiasts hot.] (6)

[The Howes would root up ev'ry Freedom's fence.] (6)

GA, Aug 5, 1778; L Eve Post, Aug 1, 1778; W Eve Post, Aug 13, 1778.

The last epigram is not in W Eve Post, Aug 13, 1778.
An attack on Bute for suppressing freedom. An objection to "Bute's cabals"

for splitting the nation. The Yankees fight well because they believe in
natural freedom. A few, like Wilkes, defend Boston and freedom from the
assault of the Howes.

78-416. The Poor Ghost of Old England. A Ballad.

"When Chatham the glorious directed the state." (62)

LP, Jul 20, 1778.

Song. Triplets with tail as chorus. England is a poor ghost of its former
triumphant self because of the destructive machinations of the Scotch and the
inept ministry. The American War should be stopped so that the nation can
unite against France and Spain. Cited are Mansfield, Bute, Sandwich, Germain.

78-417. Cancelled.

The Pope's Address to his good Friends in England. A Song. Tune, -- As I was
a driving my waggon one day. "In Rome's rigid clime, when it came to be known."
(40) GA, Jul 20, 1778; L Eve Post, Jul 16, 1778. A song by John Free(th) writ-
ten in 1774 in reaction to the Quebec Act. See 74-90. The Pope praises King
George for helping the Catholics. The American War affords an opportunity for
the Stuarts and Papists to have their way. Reprinted in reaction to the passage
of bills relaxing the anti-Catholic penal laws. See 78-392.

78-418. The Portrait Painter. Duke of Richmond.

"Take him as a soldier, patriot, or man." (8)

GA, Apr 23, 1778; West M 6 (Dec 1778), 672.

HC. Praise of Richmond, a man of incomparable virtue, envied for his merit.

78-419. The Portrait-Painter. Lord Mansfield.

"An Owl, long at Athens, adored for her skill." (22)

GA, Apr 4, 1778; West M 6 (Nov 1778), 600-1.

Anapest tetrameter couplets. Satire on Mansfield for lack of genuine wis-
dom. His bloody advice on America is alluded to.

78-420. The Portrait Painter. Lord North.

"A Farmer had long kept a servant in pay." (36)

GA, Apr 20, 1778.

Anapest tetrameter couplets. A fable that illustrates the mistake the King made in cashiering Pitt and accepting North as prime minister.

78-421. The Portrait Painter. L[or]d Sand[wic]h.

"While at the helm he quaffs and drinks." (4)

GA, Apr 4, 1778; West M 6 (Dec 1778), 672.

Quatrains in OC. Satiric portrait of Sandwich, a licentious character unconcerned over the crisis faced by the nation.

78-422. Portsmouth-Fair, or the Raree-Shew, at Spithead. A Song.

"Let ev'ry thoughtless Englishman." (25)

GA, May 1, 1778; L Eve Post, Apr 28, 1778.

Song. Satire on the King and his ministers and the unprepared fleet. At the Portsmouth naval review there will be a fine show -- including the ministers who have lost the colonies.

78-423. The Praises of Manchester. An Ode. Calculated to be set to Music.

"When first Rebellion rear'd his crest." (48)

Lloyd's 42 (Mar 20, 1778), 275.

Regular (Horatian) ode in sixains. On Manchester, the first town to offer a loyal address at the outbreak of the American Rebellion, and the town which, despite Burgoyne's defeat, still is loyal and supportive of Government by now offering the first regiment. See Whitaker, 77-28.

The Present Age. "No More, my friends, of vain applause." (72) W Misc 9 (Mar 16, 1778), 575-6. See 67-38, 75-219.

Privateering. A New Ballad. See "The British Tars," 78-77.

78-424. The Profits of the American War.

"To gain a paltry tax, what work we've made." (8)

GA, Feb 11, 1778; L Eve Post, Feb 7, 1778.

HC. Satire on the Scotch. The English have lost men, money, and trade for a paltry tax, and the Scotch are to blame. Only the Scotch can gain from our success in the war.


78-425. Prologue. At the opening of the Theatre Royal in New-York, Jan. 6, 1778.

"Now that hoar winter o'er the frozen plain." (40)

Lloyd's 42 (Mar 27, 1778), 300; LP, Feb 18, 1778; M Chron, Mar 28, 1778; W Eve Post, Mar 28, 1778.

Originally printed by James Rivington in his Royal (American) Gazette (New York), January 10, 1778.
HC. Now that the year's campaign is over upon the coming of winter, the theater season opens in New York. This performance is dedicated to the slain soldiers of the American War and to their widows and orphaned children. Despite the aspersions of "scowling faction's interested band," we honor these dead "champions of the country's laws."
Rivington declares the verses were "written by a distinguished character, who, in the midst of superior avocations, does not appear unmindful of the Muse by whom he is so much favour'd."


78-426. Prologue. Spoken by a Gentleman of the Army, at the opening of the Theatre in Southwark, Philadelphia. . . .

"Once more, ambitious of theatric glory." (42)

G Eve Post, Apr 21, 1778; Lloyd's 42 (Apr 24, 1778), 388; L Chron 43 (Apr 23, 1778), 396; LP, Apr 20, 1778.

HC. "Howe's strolling company" perform for charity to help widows and orphans of soldiers killed in the service.


78-427. Prologue to the Invasion.

"The Muse in change and fashion still delighting." (47)

L Chron 44 (Nov 7, 1778), 453; GA, Nov 10, 1778; LP, Nov 6, 1778.

HC. Patriotic lines on the contemporary scene, particularly the war against France, "Perfidious Gaul." (By Frederick Pilon.)

78-428. A Question, with the Answer Thereunto.

"Good now sit down, and tell me, he that knows." (50)

L Eve Post, Nov 14, 1778.

HC and Hudibrastics. The question is asked about the reason for such vast war preparations. The answer is the court's policy regarding America, given in a distorted history of the American Revolution to date.

78-429. Reasons for Concealing the Treaty between France and the Colonies.

"To raise six millions, who'd not tell a lie." (4)

L Eve Post, Mar 26, 1778.

The ministry (Gower and North) will conceal the treaty between France and America so that they can more easily raise the revenue.

78-430. The Rebel Maker and Rebel Keeper.

"For making Rebels Mansfield is the man." (2)

GA, Feb 26, 1778; L Eve Post, Feb 26, 1778.

Epigram. Satire. King George and Lord Mansfield are (largely) responsible for the rebellion.

78-431. The Recess.

"And now our senators are gone." (36)

GA, Jun 13, 1778; LM 47 (Jun 1778), 282; PA, Jun 12, 1778; WM 41 (Jul 22, 1778), 87-8; W Eve Post, Jul 25, 1778.

Quatrains. Satire on the recessed Parliament for its inability to subdue the rebels and for its overall confusion concerning the American War. Parliament went in recess June 3, 1778, despite the objections of Opposition.

78-432. A Reflection on the Fast, composed while meditating on the following words of King David: "I will wash my hands in innocency; so will I approach thine altar."

"With cruel hearts and bloody hands." (8)

Freeman's J, Mar 10, 1778; GA, Mar 6, 1778; L Eve Post, Mar 3, 1778.

Quatrains. The Ministry are not sincere about repenting their criminal war against America. See also the verses "On Reading the Above" for a comment on this poem (same sources): North recants, and denies his crime. He, like the others, is a hypocrite. (In Horace Walpole, Journal of the Reign of George the Third, ed. Doran [London: Bentley, 1869], II, 214.)

78-433. The Restoration. A Reflection on Seeing a Man Loaded With Two Sacks, and an Oaken Bough in his Hat. . . .

"Still must thy neck support the load." (16)

L Chron 43 (May 28, 1778), 520.

Quatrains. The working class continues to toil like slaves; but the great continue to share the spoil. Liberty is merely a word.

78-434. [Retir'd from scenes of busy life.]

"Retir'd from scenes of busy life." (24)

Cal Merc, Nov 23, 1778.

OC. An account of Chatham's rejection of Bute's proposal to form a coalition. See "Epigram. [Another]," 78-144.

78-435. A Retort.

"When modern mock-patriots exult that the fates." (4)

MP, Jan 26, 1778.

Hexameter couplets. An answer to the patriots who were pleased at Gates's victory over Burgoyne in the form of Howes' victory at Mud Island (on the Delaware, near Philadelphia).

78-436. The Royal Contrivance; or, Britannia's Relief: An Epigram. [And] On Reading the Above.

"In disgrace and in blood." (12 + 8)

L Eve Post, Mar 28, 1778.

Sixains and quatrains. Satire on the King. Britain is suffering, and the

King can only make things worse for the country.  The commenting stanza says that not even the doctors can restore spirit to the nation.

78-437.  Royal Curiosity.

"The King, distrustful of his ships."  (128)

L Eve Post, May 14, 1778.

Quatrains.  Satire on the Portsmouth naval review and the times, King George, and Sandwich.  A review is not cause for celebration; it is not a victory over the French who threaten England and America.  The country is being ruined; but the ministry, guilty of ruining the empire, still thrives.

78-438.  A Royal Dream.

"'Twas night -- and sleep weigh'd down the monarch's eyes."  (30)

LP, Jan 14, 1778;  PL, Jan 15, 1778.

HC.  Britannia appears in a dream before King George and begs for peace.

78-439.  The Royal Masquerade.  An Epigram on the same answer [by the King].

"The King, by giving his assent."  (8)

GA, Mar 30, 1778;  L Eve Post, Mar 26, 1778.

Quatrains.  The King is really still tyrannical in his behavior, for he did reject the London petition.  See "Labour in Vain," which precedes this epigram in the two papers:  78-263.

78-440.  St. Paul's Advice to the Citizens.

"Says old Father Paul, with a blush on his nose."  (16)

W Eve Post, Jun 9, 1778.

Anapest tetrameter couplets.  Chatham will be interred at St. Paul's, and a monument erected to his memory in Westminster Abbey.

78-441.  Scamper and Slyboots:  or General Burgoyne's Detachment.

"Says Scamper to Slyboots, pray what is the reason."  (12)

L Eve Post, Mar 28, 1778.

Anapest tetrameter couplets. Satire on Burgoyne, now a prisoner of the Americans.

78-442. Scene between Zamolxis, a Scythian prince, and Publius Cassius, legate from Caesar.

"Explain thy business, Roman, and be brief." (c. 325)

LP, Nov 13 & 18, 1778.

Blank verse. A morality playlet in two installments on the theme of liberty. Rome, proud, tyrannical, and imperial, demands submission from barbaric Scythia, and encounters resistance. Rome is portrayed as a venal state riddled with corruption; it is remote from the primitive virtue of nature. The application to the contest between America and Britain is obvious.

78-443. Scotch Loyalty, Always the Same. An Epigram.

"Scotchmen are virtual rebels their own way." (4)

New Foundling Hospital for Wit (1786), II, 127.

HC. Scotchmen are treacherous.

78-444. Scotch Pride and Meanness.

"Scotch pride and meanness nearly are ally'd." (2)

Freeman's J, Feb 26, 1778; L Eve Post, Jan 24, 1778.

Epigram. Couplet. Vulgar satire on the Scotch.

78-445. [The Scripture bids us love our foes.]

"The Scripture bids us love our foes." (4)

GA, Jul 17, 1778.

Quatrain. A criticism of the King for loving his country's enemies -- the Scots -- and hating his friends, the English (and the Americans?).

78-446. A Select Albion's Song.

"Ye tuneful nine my song inspire." (36)

Vocal Magazine; or British Songster's Miscellany (1778), p. 80 (Song #298).

A drinking and patriotic song directed at France and Spain.


Shakespeare, William. [Characters from Shakespeare.] See 78-82, 78-83, 78-404.

78-447. [Shakespeare, William.]
[John of Gaunt to Richard II.]

"Who dost thou thus give thy anointed body." (27)

GA, Jan 31, 1778.

Blank verse (excerpt). The speech of John Gaunt to Richard II illuminates the mistake George III is making by accepting the advice of evil counsellors who are ruining the country.

78-448. Shakespeare, William.
On England. On the French. On America.

"Behold the wounds, the most unnatural wounds." (8 + 1 + 6)

M Chron, Nov 24, 1778.

Three quotations from Henry VI, Part 1, adapted to the present situation resulting from the Franco-American alliance: the difficulty England faces because of the perfidious treachery of France in entering the war; and a hope that America will return to England because France is unreliable and selfish. (There are many quotations from Shakespeare's plays in the papers at this time. Only a sampling is given here.)

78-449. [Shakespeare, William]
The Times.

"No treachery but want of men and money." (5)

GA, Apr 21, 1778.

Blank verse. A quotation from Shakespeare's Henry VI is used to admonish the English nobility to fight France before America is lost.


78-450. A Short View of the Present State of Great Britain, in regard to her

Home and Foreign Support.

"Ireland -- trembling." (12)

GA, Mar 23, 1778.

Dimeter couplets. America is triumphant while England is alone -- and Ireland trembles, Scotland dissembles, and all Europe jeers.


78-451. Shylock and Sir Archy. An Impromptu. On his Majesty's bespeaking "The Merchant of Venice" without "Love a-la-mode."

"Whether in foul or fair, or doubtful weather." (6)

L Eve Post, Jan 29, 1778.

Hexameter couplets. The King cannot accept satire on the Scots.


78-452. *Sine Corde sine Cerebro*: A Fragment.

"A King should have a heart or head, nay both." (4)

L Eve Post, Feb 5, 1778.

The King has neither heart nor head -- witness the war and his politics.


78-453. Sketch of an Ode, intended for the Celebration of Earl Mansfield's Birth-Day, March 22, 1778.

"Shall future ages boast a name." (36)

M Chron, Apr 6, 1778.

Regular ode in sixains. Praise of Judge Mansfield, who never was the enemy of legal liberty.


Soldiers and Sailors United. See [Farewell the scythe, the sickle and the plough], 78-198.


78-454. A Solemn Truth.

"While Placemen, and Bishops, and Scots, are in play." (2)

859

GA, Feb 6, 1778;  L Eve Post, Feb 3, 1778.

Epigram.  Satire on the alliance of placemen, bishops, and Scots -- the cause of English disaster.

78-455.  Something Like an Epigram.  [And Another.]

"North by finance and learn'd debates."  (10)

"Germaine, for forfeiting his fame."  (16)

GA, Oct 14, 1778;  L Eve Post, Oct 10, 1778.

OC.  Satiric epigrams.  Satire on the King, North, and Germaine.  North loses the American provinces, but gains the Cinque Ports!  Germaine, having lost his reputation in battle, is given the office of Secretary of State for the American Colonies -- and plans the war!  (Modern spelling is Germain.)

78-456.  Song.

"'To arms!  To arms!' Britannia calls."  (26)

W Eve Post, Jun 25, 1778.

A recruiting song.  England's enemies "insult her coast";  England must now fight France and Spain.

78-457.  A Song.

"When young Absalom drove his old father abroad."  (32)

GA, Mar 11, 1778.

Double quatrains.  Would that the modern Achitophel (Bute) end his life, it would please all Englishmen.  Another disaster will make the English angry, and Gen. Howe's writings have this effect.

78-458.  Song for 1778.

"John Bull we know."  (24)

LP, Jun 19, 1778;  PA, Jun 20, 1778.

Sixains.  England now fears the French fleet.  The administration is responsible for the danger the nation is now in.

78-459. Song. On Hearing the News of the French Fleet having been driven into Brest.

"Since Gallia's sons to invade British land." (25)

M Chron, Sep 1, 1778.

Patriotic anti-gallican song. The French fleet was forced to retreat to Brest, and so the English must still be brave, contrary to some criticism.

78-460. Song. Tune, -- Heart of Oak.

"Ye Lancashire lads! whom no dangers affright." (32)

G Eve Post, Feb 12, 1778.

Song. A recruiting song. Lancashire, especially Manchester, loyally supports the war against America.

78-461. Sonnet.

"To Chatham let Affection's tribute proud." (14)

L Eve Post, Jun 16, 1778.

Italian sonnet. A criticism of the hypocrites who now honor Chatham, after opposing him when he was alive.

78-462. Sonnet, addressed to the Rev. Mr. **** [Price]. By an American Prisoner.

"Pardon O [Price] the muse whose accents rude." (14)

L Eve Post, Mar 3, 1778.

Italian sonnet. Thanks rendered to Price by an American prisoner for help rendered to "The United States of America."

78-463. A Speech, Supposed to be Spoken by Lord C[arlis]le, addressing the Congress.

"Behold me, good Sirs, I am the Earl of C-----le." (18)

G, May 20, 1778; GA, May 21, 1778; LM 47 (May 1778), 235; WM 40 (Jun 10, 1778), 255.

Anapest tetrameter couplets. Satire on the British Commissioners for Peace, who bring North's supposedly generous conciliatory proposals to Congress.

78-464. The Spithead Slumber. A Lilliputian Ode. Written previous to the sailing of Admiral Keppel's Fleet.

"Across the Sea, with hostile Force." (36)

St J's C, Aug 8, 1778.

Regular ode in triplets with a tail. Satire on the lack of preparedness of Sandwich's navy. While Keppel's fleet lies idle at Spithead, Admiral D'Estaing is free to sail anywhere, Admiral Howe's ships are destroyed or captured, Philadelphia is blockaded, Spain defies Britain, Paul Jones raids Whitehaven and plunders Scotland. North is asked to follow the example of Chatham and become active.

78-465. Stanza on the General Fast.

"If killing and slaying, and fasting and praying." (4)

L Eve Post, Feb 5, 1778.

Quatrain. An objection to the hypocrisy of the fast.

78-466. Stanzas occasioned by reading the King's Proclamation for a General Fast. . . .

"Here, by the King, a proclamation." (18)

L Eve Post, Feb 5, 1778.

Sixains. An objection to the hypocrisy of the fast.

78-467. Stanzas on Modern Patriotism.

"In times, such as these, of confusion and riot." (20)

MP, Oct 14, 1778.

Quatrains. Satire on the Patriots -- really lying and hypocritical parricides who are zealous for America's welfare, not Britain's.

78-468. State of Slavery in the British West India Islands.

"There Afric's swarthy sons their toils repeat." (38)

GA, May 12, 1778.

HC. Objections to the inhumanity of English slavery in the West Indies. English craving for luxury results in the loss of the rights of man.


78-469. [Strange were the times, should kings refuse their ear.]

"Strange were the times, should kings refuse their ear." (14)

LP, Oct 21, 1778.

HC. A protest against the war and a criticism of the King for choosing foolish and corrupt ministers and for killing their subjects in a civil war.


Supposed to be spoken by Lord C[arlis]le addressing the Congress. "Behold me, good Sirs, I am the Earl of C-----le." (18) GA, May 21, 1778; WM 40 (Jun 10, 1778), 255. See 78-463.


78-470. Cancelled.


78-471. A Temporary Extempore Anacreontic.

"Some their unceasing Thoughts bestow." (12)

PA, Jan 12, 1778.

OC. Some are concerned about the American War, but I am concerned for my love of Delia.


78-472. A Temporary Parody on certain Verses of Dryden.

"Two mighty Generals, in one Country born." (8)

PA, Jul 23, 1778.

Parody on Dryden's verses on Milton. A protest against the generalship of Howe and Burgoyne, and a demand that the King hang them and get a third general. Burgoyne lost an army, but Howe lost an empire.


78-473. Temporary Verses.

"While France is arming at Toulon and Brest." (8)

PA, May 5, 1778.

Epigram. HC. Satire. North is sleeping, planning nothing to protect the country.

78-474. Things As They Are. Things As They Should Be.

"A king out of office." (14)

LP, Feb 23, 1778.

Prose-poem (?). Satire on the King, his favorites, the ministers, and Parliament. Another work with the same title (as the first part) appeared in London Evening Post, July 28, 1778. See 78-A.

78-475. The Thirtieth of January.

"In the First Charles' inglorious Days." (24)

PA, Jan 30, 1778.

Quatrains, commemorating the day Charles I was executed. Attempting tyranny, Charles was executed for defying Parliament, and so provided a lesson to future British kings. (Implied, perhaps, is support for the present constitutional monarch.)

78-476. [Tho' some ill-natur'd Wits may say.]

"Tho' some ill-natured Wits may say." (8)

PA, Aug 15, 1778.

Quatrains. Extempore. Satire on Keppel. If Hawke had been in command instead of Keppel, Chartres would not have escaped.

78-477. The Three Brunswicks.

"In German modes our two Brunswicks school'd." (8)

GA, Mar 26, 1778; L Eve Post, Mar 21, 1778.

HC. Extempore. The country prospered under the first two Georges; but George the Third, influenced by Scotchmen and Jacobites, has cost England freedom, commerce, and America.

78-478. Tickell, Richard.
Prologue to The Camp: An Interlude.

"The stage is still the mirror of the day." (48)

G, Oct 24, 1778; GA, Oct 24, 1778; G Eve Post, Oct 22, 1778; GM 48 (Oct 1778), 487; Lady's M 9 (Oct 1778), 549; L Chron 44 (Oct 22, 1778), 397; L Eve Post, Oct 22, 1778; LP, Oct 21, 1778; M Chron, Oct 23, 1778; MP, Oct 23, 1778; PA, Oct 23, 1778; SM 40 (Oct 1778), 557; West M 6 (Oct 1778), 553; W Eve Post, Oct 22, 1778. Also LM 47 (Nov 1778), 520-1.

HC. The French war affects a variety of people in different ways.

78-479. The Timber Review.

"Our gracious King to Portsmouth went." (100)

GA, May 25, 1778; L Eve Post, May 30, 1778.

Ballad. Satire on the King and the Portsmouth naval review. Narrates the absurd inspection of the fleet by royalty, concluding with a remark that the American War will end by hanging Bute, Suffolk, North, and Mansfield.

78-480. The Times.

"Adieu to dull Lectures in Gravity's School." (32)

PA, Oct 16, 1778.

Elegiac stanzas on the failure of the navy and army to accomplish anything, the farcical militia, and the poor English spirit that once caused Spain and France to tremble.

78-481. The Times: Or, Things As They Are.

"Prophets may see what is to come." (98)

LM 47 (Sep 1778), 422-3; PA, Sep 18, 1778; W Eve Post, Sep 12, 1778.

Hudibrastic couplets. Light satire that reviews the situation at home and the several fighting fronts in America and on the high seas. Cited are the Government leaders, the Opposition, the peace commissioners, the generals -- and the last event on the high seas, the failure of Keppel to defeat D'Orvilliers and the French fleet decisively.  The satirist is not pleased with the way the war is fought or with the political leaders.

78-482.  "'Tis a bad Wind that blows nobody Good."

  "Ill-fated Isle!  Where's all thy ancient Worth."  (8)

  PA, Feb 25, 1778.

  HC.  The Scotch and North are driving the country to ruin.

78-483.  ['Tis fear'd by many, as we hear.]

  "'Tis fear'd by many, as we hear."  (10)

  PA, Oct 8, 1778;  W Eve Post, Oct 6, 1778.

  OC.  Epigram.  Satire on Keppel for running from the French.

78-484.  To a Gentleman who blam'd Keppel's Conduct in a very large and consequential manner, because he did not pursue the French fleet. . . .

  "All you have said amounts to nought."  (12)

  M Chron, Aug 19, 1778.

  A defense of Keppel's conduct.

78-485.  To Admiral Keppel.

  "Brave Man! -- stand firm -- your hour of trial see."  (8)

  GA, Dec 30, 1778;  L Eve Post, Dec 26, 1778;  W Eve Post, Dec 29, 1778.

  HC.  An expression of support for Keppel against his "designing foes." (His court-martial will soon begin.)

78-486.  To Four Great Personages.

  "Greatly wanted two hundred pounds."  (60)

  M Chron, Nov 17, 1778.

  Regular ode in quatrains.  Satire.  The poet addresses the King, North,

Sandwich, and Germain, declaring he will praise them and take their sides for ₤200. America, France, and Spain are cited.

78-487. To General Burgoyne.

"Ill-starr'd Burgoyne! tho' friends, nay en'mies say." (24)

GA, Jul 22, 1778.

HC. Burgoyne fought bravely, but his cause was unjust. Burgoyne is urged to speak out honestly about the war. Cited are Germain and King George.

78-488. To Him Whom it Most Concerns, an Honest and Warm Expostulation.

"To what, Sir, does your obstinacy tend." (13)

L Eve Post, Jul 14, 1778.

HC. Satire on the King for stubbornly accepting the counsel of Stuarts -- Bute and Mansfield -- and for being the Junto's tool, who have lost America and the control of the seas.

78-489. To his Grace the Duke of Richmond.

"How vast his talents! born to rule." (10)

GA, Sep 17, 1778.

OC. Praise of the Duke of Richmond for integrity and all the virtues, and hope that he will form a new administration.

78-490. To his Protesting ----- of -----.

"When Draco's sanguinary laws." (108)

L Eve Post, Jun 23, 1778.

Regular ode in sixains. A harsh satire on Archbishop of York, Markham. An objection to the American War, the Quebec Bill, and North.

78-491. To Mr. James Twitcher on his Naval Exhibition at Portsmouth.

"Dear Twitcher, cease to be so vain." (4)

PA, May 5, 1778.

Epigram. Satire. Sandwich should first have the navy attack in the Caribbean and then have his naval review.

78-492. To Sir Hugh Palliser.

"'Envy will merit as its shade pursue.'" (22)

M Chron, Nov 12, 1778.

HC. Advice to Palliser to be careful for the truth about the recent naval action off Brest. (Now the politics surrounding this naval episode surfaces.)

78-493. To Sir Hugh Palliser.

"Keppel fought as a brave." (6)

L Eve Post, Dec 29, 1778.

Triplets. On the court-martial regarding the Ushant action, July 27.
Why did Palliser not obey Keppel's order? (The order was to obey a signal to rejoin the main body of the fleet with his squadron, so that Keppel could re-attack the French fleet the same day, July 27.)

78-494. To Sir Hugh Palliser.

"My good master Hugh." (28)

GA, Dec 22, 1778.

Quatrains. Satire on Palliser for his "damnable lies" (regarding Keppel and the escape of the French fleet).

78-495. To the Author of Anticipation.

"I've read your Pamphlet, and admire your Wit." (4)

PA, Nov 28, 1778.

HC. An objection to the propriety of Richard Tickell's <u>Anticipation</u>, a humorous satire, at a time of serious crisis.

78-496. To the Author of Warley. A Poem.

"Ah! George, to satire do not give thy mind." (4)

M Chron, Nov 30, 1778.

HC. Extempore. George Huddesford wrote <u>Warley: A Satire</u> in 1778, a few lines of which allude to the American War. The above poem simply says that Huddesford should not write satire, but should write sublime and dignified poetry, like the paintings of Reynolds. For Huddesford, see 78-20.

78-497. To the British Seamen, on the Late Action.

"Or is it Peace, or is it War." (4)

GA, Sep 1, 1778.

Extempore. Quatrain. A criticism of the navy for failing to defeat the French fleet decisively.

78-498. To the Earl of Abingdon, on reading his Thoughts on the Letter of Edmund Burke to the Sheriffs of Bristol.

"When venal senators for dirty pay." (59)

GA, Mar 28, 1778.

HC. Praise of Abingdon for his anti-Tory sentiments, his opposition to absolute monarchy, and his opposition to the American War. The Scots are blamed for all the ruinous court policies. The Tories cited are the writers Samuel Johnson, John Shebbeare, and John Wesley; and the politicians Bute and Mansfield.

78-499. To the Earl of Chatham.

"Once in a Storm, thou dids't our Vessel save." (4)

PA, Feb 20, 1778.

HC. Epigram. Only Chatham can save the country, now in distress.

78-500. To the King.

"Look round, great George, survey your group of friends." (12)

GA, Apr 16, 1778; L Eve Post, Apr 14, 1778.

HC.  Advice to the King to purge his court of untrustworthy ministers --
Mansfield, Sandwich, North, and Suffolk.

78-501.  To the K[ing], on the Present Men and Measures.

"Thy sceptre turn into an iron rod."  (6)

GA, Jan 26, 1778;  L Eve Post, Jan 24, 1778.

HC.  Advice to the King to be firm, to cashier the ministry (North and Bute) because Britain is suffering from the American War.  He should favor the Whigs, too.  (Such is the aftermath of the news of Burgoyne's surrender.)

78-502.  To the King's Real Friends.

"Use ev'ry means to prop our falling state."  (14)

GA, Apr 11, 1778.

HC.  Admonishes Britons to save the ship of state and provide direction for it under a new ministry with Chatham as PM and Richmond solidifying it.

78-503.  To the Memory of Lord Chatham.

"France, proudly bent on universal sway."  (106)

L Eve Post, May 19, 1778.

HC.  A panegyrical review of Chatham's achievement in defeating France, defending the constitution, and bringing glory to England.  See the supplement -- "The Contrast," 78-96.

78-504.  [To the memory of / The Earl of C(hatham).]

"To the memory of / The Earl of C[hatham], / A Man of superior abilities."
(c. 40)

G Eve Post, Jun 13, 1778.

Inscription.  A critical epitaph blaming Chatham for the loss of the American colonies.  In "the aera of 1763" he sowed "the seeds of rebellion amongst the revolting Colonists," brought on the repeal of the Stamp Act, etc., and contributed to "the total loss of North-America."

78-505. [To the Memory / of / William Pitt, Earl of Chatham.]

"To the Memory / of / William Pitt, Earl of Chatham."  (3)

GA, Jun 23, 1778.

A brief inscription.  A compliment to Chatham, a statesman in the reign of George III, for dying "A Poor Man."  (That is, he was incorruptible.)

78-506. To the Minister.

"Had Aesop been living, what mortal so able."  (30)

G, Dec 26, 1778;  M Chron, Dec 11, 1778.

Mixed verse.  Another version of Aesop's moral fable of the goose that laid golden eggs applied to English greed regarding America.

78-507. To the [Ministry].

"Canst thou think by Carnage dire."  (27)

PA, Dec 26, 1778.

Trochaic tetrameter couplets.  The war with our American brothers should end;  the war should be directed against France.

78-508. To the Minority in both Houses.

"The labour that you take, is all in vain."  (4)

L Eve Post, Dec 19, 1778.

HC.  The Minority Opposition is advised to secede.

78-509. To the Minority of Both Houses.

"Whilst in pack'd houses you shall still remain."  (5)

L Eve Post, Dec 10, 1778.

HC.  Advice to the Minority to secede from the corrupt Parliament.

78-510. To the Poetical Correspondents.

"Is't not just, my dear brothers, that now ev'ry muse." (40)

WM 42 (Oct 14, 1778), 62-3.

Anapest tetrameter couplets. Satire, advises poets to sing of the failures of the ministry and the generals unable to defeat "the obstinate Yankees." Cited are tea, Saratoga, Howe, the Minority, North, Chatham. But the next theme is the war with France.

78-511. To the Sons of Liberty who commemorate the Glorious Revolution. Song for the 4th of November, 1778. To the Tune of, Fame let thy Trumpet sound.

"Once more the rolling Year." (42)

PA, Nov 11, 1778.

Song in praise of King William, the deliverer, who saved the country from Stuart slavery; and the Duke of Cumberland. (Cumberland defeated Prince Charles at Culloden.) See "The Landing of King William," 78-264.

78-512. A Touch at the Times.

"How topsy-turvy Things are grown." (26)

LM 47 (Appendix 1778), 603; PA, Dec 17, 1778.

OC. A satire on the top figures in these terrible times -- on George and North for poor leadership, on the Opposition (Burke and Barre) who support the rebels, and on generals and admirals who fail (Howe, Keppel, and Palliser).

78-513. Tradesmen's Song. For her Majesty's Birth Day, 1778. Tune, When all the Attic Fire was fled.

"Again the annual Morn returns." (30)

Lloyd's 42 (Jan 19, 1778), 71.

Regular ode in sixains. Praise of Queen Charlotte by the loyal tradesmen who oppose the American Rebellion and the Minority who encourage it. See Garth, 78-220.

78-514. The Trip to Portsmouth; Or, The Wonders of the Naval Review. A Descriptive Poem. Addressed to a Great Personage.

"'Twas at the Royal shew off Portsmouth town." (66)

GA, May 9, 1778.

Sixains. Satire on the King's inspection tour of the navy at Portsmouth. One stanza has him express the hope of the defeat of America. Cited are the Archbishop of York and Whitehead.

78-515. A True Catch, as it was lately sung at a Great House near Westminster Hall. By James Twitcher, Esq; and Many Voices.

"First Voice. You said you'd make our en'mies rue." (7)

GA, Jun 2, 1778.

Song. Sandwich defends himself from the accusation of lying when he said Britain could fight off its enemies, France and Spain, as well as take care of America.

78-516. [Turk, French, Spaniard, or a Dutchman.]

"Turk, French, Spaniard, or a Dutchman." (2)

L Eve Post, Feb 5, 1778.

Epigram. Even the Americans abhor the Scotch, preferring as allies Turks, French, Spaniards, and Dutch.

78-517. ['Twas Av'rice, Pride, and wild Delusion.]

"'Twas Av'rice, Pride, and wild Delusion." (20)

PA, Jan 31, 1778.

OC. The writer calls this poem an "Extemporary in Doggerels." Satire on the American rebels who revolt without reason. Praise of Jacob Duche, loyalist, for his Letter Addressed to his Excellency General Washington (1777).

78-518. ['Twas on the evening of that solemn day.]

"'Twas on the evening of that solemn day." (64)

L Eve Post, Mar 31, 1778.

HC. A complaint at the misfortunes suffered by Britain as a result of the

American war. Cited are taxation, mercenary troops, Indians; and the need for peace with America, now that there is danger from France.

78-519. [Two Wights there are, without Dispute.]

"Two Wights there are, without Dispute." (4)

PA, Oct 22, 1778.

Quatrain. Epigram. Satire on Bute and North.

78-520. Upon the American War, and the Raising Scotch Regiments to Support the English Constitution.

"Erst from Arabia's barren coast." (32)

GA, Feb 4, 1778.

Quatrains. The Scotch have crossed to England as the Jews came to the Promised Land, and brought on the war. Cited are Arnold, Burgoyne, Mansfield, and Howe.

78-521. Upon the Largest Jewel's Dropping out of his Majesty's Crown on his Coronation.

"Well I remember on that crouded day." (8)

GA, Mar 13, 1778.

HC. When the largest jewel fell from the crown upon the King's coronation, it was an ill omen signifying the loss of America. See 61-26 and 61-33.

78-522. Upon the several Alfreds of Thomson, Mallet, and Home.

"Vainly three frigid Caledonians strive." (12)

Freeman's J, Feb 26, 1778; L Eve Post, Jan 24, 1778.

HC. Scotchmen cannot appreciate the contributions to liberty made by Alfred -- juries and respect for the law by magistrates.

78-523. Upon the Thane's Vindication of Himself.

"Falsehood and fraud spring up in ev'ry place." (6)

GA, Nov 13, 1778.

HC. Extempore. Satire on Bute and the Scotch for their "Falsehood and fraud."

78-524. [Vainly on India's Wealth our Hopes we rest.]

"Vainly on India's Wealth our Hopes we rest." (4)

PA, Oct 22, 1778.

Quatrain. Epigram. Britain will not compensate the loss of America with wealth from India.

78-525. Verses made by the Carpenter of the [Warship] Monarch.

"See above the Hero's head." (32)

MP, Oct 10, 1778.

Quatrains. Patriotic stanzas on British preparations for an attack on the French fleet under Chartres. The British sailors are ready, led by "Brave Keppel."

78-526. Verses on the Times.

"Amidst th' warm, the inflam'd address." (16)

C, Apr 17, 1778.

Quatrains in OC. The times reflect a split in politics that endangers the constitution. Burke wishes to strengthen Parliament's rights; Mansfield the royal prerogative. Either view brings tyranny. But Abingdon will save the country by striking a balance.

78-527. Verses Written by Mr. [Thomas] Burke, a Delegate from North Carolina, and Miss ---, of Philadelphia, June 1777.

"You ask me, fair Chloe, to strike the gay lyre." (180)

GM 48 (Apr 1778), 184, & (May 1778), 231.

Quatrains. An American rebel protests the "tyrant Ambition" that has destroyed the pastoral peace of America, started a civil war, and called him away from his beloved.

78-528. [Villains in France to Death condemn'd.]

"Villains in France to Death condemn'd." (14)

PA, Feb 27, 1778.

OC. North is a traitor and ought to be condemned for his misdeeds. Like a criminal, he should honestly confess his crimes -- buying votes for the continuation of the war and calling liberty by the name of sedition.

78-529. The Volunteer.

"Hark! the loud and rattling drum." (36)

Cal Merc, Mar 2, 1778.

Quatrains. Generalized praise of the volunteer soldier.

78-530. The Volunteers.

"Noble is the Soldier's Calling." (32)

Cal Merc, Oct 5, 1778; LP, Oct 9, 1778; M Chron, Oct 13, 1778; SM 40 (Sep 1778), 508.

Song. A trio that "concludes the Entertainment of the Volunteers, written by Mr. Woods." A patriotic song climaxed with a call for unity of "Young and Old . . . Rich and Poor" against France.

78-531. Warley Camp; or, The Review.

"In Pomp and Circumstance of war." (28)

L Chron 44 (Oct 20, 1778), 391; LP, Oct 21, 1778; PA, Oct 22, 1778; West M 6 (Oct 1778), 553.

Quatrains. A description of the review at Warley Camp by the King and Amherst. See Huddesford, 78-20.

78-532. A War-Song, sung by Mrs. Wrighten, at Vauxhall.

"Sound the fife, -- beat the drum, -- to my standard repair." (24)

SM 40 (Aug 1778), 440.

The women urge their men to be courageous and to fight for King and country.

78-533. What is Man?

"Now strictly to say what a Man, I presume, is." (4)

W Eve Post, Mar 19, 1778.

Epigram. Satire on Man, who simply requires tarring and feathering.

78-534. [What nation, but is rash and vain.]

"What nation, but is rash and vain." (8)

GA, Sep 5, 1778.

OC. The French fleet escaped from Keppel and returned (shamefully) to Brest for safety.

78-535. [What -- though the Witlings of last Year.]

"What -- though the Witlings of last Year." (6)

PA, Jan 7, 1778.

Epigram. Sixain. Lord Effingham had resigned his commission and was accused of cowardice, but now he has become martial.

78-536. [What's to be done, prays North, to save the Nation.]

"What's to be done, prays North, to save the Nation." (4)

PA, May 26, 1778.

Quatrain. Extempore. Satire on North who, in a quandary, wishes to know how to save the nation; Fox advises him to resign.

78-537. [When senates vote their country's rights away.]

"When senates vote their country's rights away." (16)

LP, Apr 17, 1778.

Quatrains. Verses on an inn window at Chester. The country needs to reassert its spirit, its love of freedom.

78-538.  [When Taylor North some Patch-work has in View.]

"When Taylor North some Patch-work has in View."  (8)

PA, Mar 3, 1778;  W Eve Post, Mar 3, 1778.

HC.  Epigram.  North had used the Patriots to pass his Conciliation Bill, but he did not reward them.

78-539.  [When Twitcher, Scandal of a venal Court.]

"When Twitcher, Scandal of a venal Court."  (4)

PA, May 6, 1778.

Epigram.  Satire.  Sandwich does not care to use the fleet;  instead, he puts on a show.

78-540.  [When Varro, by his Rashness lost.]

"When Varro, by his Rashness lost."  (24)

PA, Jul 17, 1778.

Quatrains.  Satire.  An attack on Howe, for losing the war and the empire.  Instead of being cashiered, he is still favored!

78-541.  [When wicked Ministers aloud proclaim.]

"When wicked Ministers aloud proclaim."  (14)

GA, Feb 27, 1778.

HC.  Humanity objects to the hypocrisy of the fast which, instead of peace, is used to encourage war!

78-542.  [While rebel sons with ruffian hand.]  Tune, Rule Britannia, &c.

"While rebel sons with ruffian hand."  (39)

WM 39 (Feb 18, 1778), 183-4.

Song. Imprisoned American loyalists celebrate the King's birthday in song despite rebel protests. (Reprinted from the Pennsylvania Evening Post, Dec. 11, 1777.)

78-543. Whitehead, William.
Ode for his Majesty's Birth-Day, written by William Whitehead, Esq; Poet Laureat, and set to Music by Dr. Boyce, Master of his Majesty's Band of Musicians, performed before the Royal Family, on Thursday, June 4.

"Arm'd with her native force, behold." (40)

AR, 1778, p. 193; Cumb Pacq, Jun 16, 1778; G, Jun 4, 1778; GA, Jun 5, 1778; G Eve Post, Jun 4, 1778; GM 47 (Jun 1778), 278; HM 8 (Jul 1778), 415; Lady's M 9 (Jun 1778), 325; Lloyd's 42 (Jun 5, 1778), 540; L Eve Post, Jun 4, 1778; LP, Jun 5, 1778; M Chron, Jun 6, 1778; MP, Jun 8, 1778; PA, Jun 6, 1778; St J's C, Jun 4, 1778; T&C 10 (Jun 1778), 327-8; West J, Jun 13, 1778; W Eve Post, Jun 4, 1778. Also L Chron 43 (Jun 4, 1778), 538; LM 47 (Jun 1778), 281.

Irregular Pindaric ode. The nation, stronger now than in feudal days, will again fight France. Freedom now gives "new force to glory's charms." A correspondent to the Gazetteer, Jun 13, 1778, reprints the Birthday Ode with the comment that the laureat had been writing for the Americans! See [Ode for the Americans], 78-310.

78-544. Whitehead, William.
Ode for the New Year, Jan. 1, 1778. Written by W. Whitehead, Esq; and set to Music by Dr. Boyce, Master of the King's Band of Musicians.

"When rival nations great in arms." (30)

AR, 1778, p. 192; Cumb Pacq, Jan 6, 1778; DJ, Jan 6, 1778; Freeman's J, Jan 6, 1778; G, Jan 1, 1778; G Eve Post, Dec 30, 1777-Jan 1, 1778; GM 48 (Jan 1778), 39; Lady's M 8 (Supp 1777), 711; Lloyd's 42 (Dec 31, 1777-Jan 2, 1778), 1; LM 47 (Jan 1778), 42; LP, Dec 31, 1777-Jan 2, 1778; MP, Jan 1, 1778; PA, Jan 1, 1778; St J's C, Dec 30, 1777-Jan 1, 1778; T&C 10 (Jan 1778), 45; West J, Jan 4, 1778; W Eve Post, Dec 30, 1777-Jan 1, 1778. Also L Chron 43 (Dec 30, 1777-Jan 1, 1778), 8.

Irregular Pindaric ode. The laureat mourns the enmity between former "friends" -- America and Britain. He prays that they be forgiving, reconcile their differences, and "reunite." But he also appeals to God to settle the quarrel and "reunite / The foes who once were friends."

78-545. [Why all this rout, why all this pother.]

"Why all this rout, why all this pother." (8)

L Eve Post, Jan 1, 1778.

Irregular stanza. A defense of the Howe brothers, who cannot work miracles -- i.e., subdue America.

78-546. Winter. A Moral Sentiment.

"Tho' Sol withdraws his genial ray." (8)

UM 63 (Dec 1778), 316.

Quatrains. The coming of spring is not warmed with the friendship of America.

78-547. A Wish.

"The worst of all curses may Scotchmen obtain." (2)

L Eve Post, Feb 10, 1778.

Epigram. Satire on the Scotch. The worst that can happen to Scotchmen is to return to their own country.

78-548. A Word to the Addressers, who have offered their Lives and Fortunes, and two Words to the Manchester Rebels.

"Ye loyal Addressers who've offer'd your lives." (22)

L Eve Post, Jan 8, 1778.

Fourteener couplets. Satire on the Manchester loyalists, Jacobites and Tories, for their loyal address to the King regarding the American War. Cited are the Americans and George II.

78-549. Wynne, J. H.
Ode for the New Year.

"On Time's fleet pinions, passing swift away." (38)

G, Jan 1, 1778; W Eve Post, Dec 30, 1777-Jan 1, 1778.

Irregular Pindaric. Wynne asserts the justice of Britain's cause and asks that peace permit a reconciliation with America.

78-550. [Ye Manchester shavers.] Tune -- "Of Jacobites our Town is full, &c."

"Ye Manchester shavers." (42)

L Eve Post, Feb 14, 1778.

Song. Ironic satire on the Manchester Volunteers for being Jacobites. Cited are Bute, Yankees, Howe, Clinton, Burgoyne, and Irish Papists.

78-551. [Ye poor simple people.] Tune -- A Cobler there was, &c.

"Ye poor simple people, who foolishly think." (40)

L Eve Post, Mar 17, 1778.

Song with Derry down chorus. Satire on Germain and North, especially the former for cowardice and poor leadership.

78-552. [Ye true honest Britons, who love your land.] Sung at Ranelagh.

"Ye true honest Britons, who love your land." (18)

Vocal Magazine; or, British Songster's Miscellany (1778), p. 200 (Song #763).

A patriotic song against the French and threats of invasion.

Prints

78-553. Admiral Keppel Triumphant or Monsieurs in the Suds.

"Each Briton join chorus with me." (26)

Engr. broadside with quatrains and chorus.  C. 1778.

BL C.116.i.7 (260).

Song, defends Admiral Keppel's courage and seamanship in forcing the French fleet to retreat to its base at Brest and, unfortunately, to safety. This song may be one of the earliest reactions in verse to the naval encounter off Brest, the Battle of Ushant, July 27, 1778, which resulted in the court-martial trial of Admiral Keppel upon charges brought by Sir Hugh Palliser -- a scandalous party issue.

78-554. The City in an Uproar--or the Re-Taking of Umbrage--By Sir Tony Candlestick Knt.

"While grim Sr Tony, that sagacious Blade." (8)

Engr. with HC.  September 29, 1778.

George 5488 (V, 296-7).

Satire on the Irish Volunteers of Dublin, another aspect of the recruitment campaign.

78-555. The Englishman in Paris.

"An American Goose Came Hot from the Spit." (8)

Engr. with couplets.  C. 1777-8.

George 5477 (V, 291).

An Englishman proceeds to devour an American goose, but is interrupted by a Frenchman who also wishes to eat it.

78-556. Folly on both sides, or a Veiw of the Political State of the Nation.

"Come de first ting as you see in dis collection of Vile Beasts (who're met." (100)

Engr. with satiric couplets in rough heptameter lines.  May 11 (?), 1778.

R. T. A. Halsey presented a photocopy to the BM Department of Prints, 1940.

A Frenchman exhibits the follies of the government and the opposition: North, Sandwich, Germaine, et al., and Barre, Fox, Wilkes, Richmond, Camden, et al. In this survey, the minority is accused of selling out the nation, and the government of lying, ineptitude, and corruption.

78-557.  The State of the Nation.

"In a certain Great House that there is in this Land."  (4)

Engr. with tetrameter couplets.  1778 (?)

George 5480 (V, 292).

Scatological satire of government and its supporters, including Johnson, as well as some members of the opposition: Wilkes, Richmond, Barre. The scene in a necessary house represents Parliament in a mess.

78-558.  A Tete A Tete Between the Premier and J^no Hancock Esqr.

"Hancock and N--th, Suppos'd to Meet."  (8)

Engr. with OC.  C. 1778.    .

George 5476 (V, 290).  Wynn Jones, p. 111.

Hancock refuses North's overtures for peace (the Conciliatory Propositions). The Franco-American treaty was signed February 6, 1778.

1779  Books & Pamphlets

79-1. The Anti-Palliseriad: Or, Britain's Triumphs over France. Dedicated to the Honorable Augustus Keppel, Admiral of the British Fleet.
   London: Bew, 1779. iv + 5-23p.

"Hear the loud voice of Honor: martial sons." (c. 360)

Notices: CR 47 (Feb 1779), 154; MR 60 (Mar 1779), 230; LR 9 (Mar 1779), 201-2.

Copies: NUC CtY.

Blank verse. Dedication is dated February 3, 1779. Anti-Gallican poem. After a historical review of Anglo-French relations, the author praises Keppel, recently acquitted by a court-martial. Although the present civil war in America originated in English injustice, the poet concludes that when France, England's old tyrannical enemy, pretended to help America to liberty, American patriotic principles were corrupted, and anarchy and demagoguery set in. Thus continuing the war against America is justified. Cited are the Seven Years' War, Pitt, Hawke, Saunders, Pococke, Wolfe and Quebec, and the inadequate peace; Congress, and the "Palliserian fraud." Berates Palliser for the wrong done Keppel and the country. Praise of Gen. Clinton, commander of the British troops in America.


79-2. The Auspices of War; An Ode. Inscribed to the Honourable Admiral Boscawen. To Which Is Added, The Prophecy of the Union; A Narrative Poem.
   London: Dodsley, 1779. 5-8-15p.

"Yes--'tis the omen of successful war--." (64)

Notices: MR 60 (Jun 1779), 476.

Sabin 2393.

Copies: BL 11630.e.1 (8); NUC DFo.

Regular Pindaric ode, but lacking a third part. A sublime patriotic poem. Britons will remember Wolfe, now that the French are at war with them, and will conquer France as well as Spain, as in the past. The second poem is not relevant. (Edward Boscawen was one of the naval leaders in the Seven Years' War, and participated with Amherst as naval commander of the expedition that captured Louisbourg.)


79-3. The Bostonian Prophet. An Heroi-Comico-Serious-Parodical-Pindaric Ode, In

Imitation Of The Bard. With Notes Critical, Satirical, and Explanatory By The Editor.
   London: Etherington, 1779. [4]-5-12-[xiii]-xivp.

   "'Ruin comes, thou luckless Land." (144)

   Notices: MR 60 (Jun 1779), 479; LR 10 (Oct 1779), 257-8.

   Sabin 6511.

   Copies: BL 164.n.52, 11630.e.16 (16); NUC DLC, MB, MH.

   Regular Pindaric ode, imitation of Gray's Bard. Ironic satire. The prophet foretells defeat and disgrace for the English. Although the Americans are now dying, they will triumph in the future. He damns Fox; mourns the death of Chatham, "the Senate's thunderer," noting that no one can take his place; points to North who is asleep; and is critical of Howe who also slumbers in peace or "In mischianza cloud he flies!" Cited are Germaine, the Tea Act, Montgomery, Warren, Mercer, corruption and faction, and Sandwich.


79-4. [Cartwright, Edmund]
   The Prince of Peace; And Other Poems.
   London: Murray, 1779. 44 + [2]p.

   The Prince of Peace, An Ode. "O Thou! that on the sapphire throne." (190) pp. 7-16.

   Notices: CR 47 (Apr 1779), 301-3; MR 60 (May 1779), 372-4.

   Copies: BL 643.k.23, 11630.d.7 (2); Bod 2799.f.95; NUC CtY, IU, MH, MiU-C, NN.

   Regular Horatian ode in dixains. Invokes the spirit of peace to bring an end to the "Revengeful War" of "thoughtless Albion" against fraternal Americans, "From cold Canadia's hills to Georgia's distant plains." Savage Indian warfare horrifies the poet-- murder of innocent children, old men, and women--and it is shameful and infamous that Britain should sanction it. That Britain be humane may be a vain hope, but he prays for peace. In the "Advertisement," he disavows "Party of every kind." He insists that he writes not "to serve the interested purposes of narrow-minded men," but to serve only "Humanity and Religion." Cited is the late Marquis of Granby. Incidentally, the engraved title vignette portrays the attack on Jane McCrea, the object of Indian atrocity in Burgoyne's campaign. See 86-1.


79-5. Causidicus, A Poetic Lash: In Three Parts. Containing: A real Picture of the Times; The Study at the Temple; With a Visit to a certain Judge; and A most Extraordinary Trial. The Second Edition.
   London: Bowen, Wilkie, Faulder, 1779. 50p.

   "When ****** was King, and it is said." (c. 330)

   Notices: CR 47 (May 1779), 392; MR 61 (Jul 1779), 74; LR 10 (Appendix 1779), 454.

Copies: BL 163.1.17 (1st ed); NUC CtY, ICN, RPJCB (2nd ed).

Hudibrastics. Satire on the times in a narrative of a learned Templar's adventures up to his engagement in the trial concerning the sex of the Chevalier D'Eon. Only the first part is relevant, a satire on British treatment of the American colonies, including North's responsibility for the American troubles, his plan for reconciliation, and the quarrel between Howe and Germain. Cited are Chatham and Bute, King George and Coxheath Camp, and Wesley.

79-6. Cole, John.
The American War, An Ode. Being An impartial Description of the most material, Military and Naval Transactions there; From the Commencement of Hostilities, to the end of the second Campaign. Interspersed Occasionally With humourous satyrical Animadversions on the conduct of both Parties, with Explanatory Notes through the Whole. . . . To Which Is Added, An Appendix. Wherein the Author has traced the origin of that Peoples revolt, to a cause which he never saw yet adverted to; With The many concurring Circumstances which have thus far accelerated the execution of their Plan. By John Cole, Late of Plymouth, but now of Beverley, in Yorkshire.
 [Yorkshire, 1779.] 123p.

"When ancient Greece and famous Troy." (c. 1250)

Sabin 14289.

Copies: BL 11688.c.25; NUC DLC, ICU, RPJCB.

Preface dated September 20, 1779, from Beverley. A narrative poem in quatrains, not a characteristic ode (in the mid-section, pp. 9-66, the rest being prose). Cole's theme is "most melancholy," "our lost domain." He does not favor the Americans, thinking them "contumacious," "arrogant and vain" in their "Rebellious War" against "their parent state." Their leaders are "demagogues," ambitious, intending independence, and theirs is "a bad cause." It is difficult for him to praise heroic Americans--e.g., Warren. Gen. Lee is a "renegade," and the American soldiers are often called "poltroons."
  Cole's motive in writing this narrative is to inspire British youth to arms now, "when our former friends have entered into an unnatural alliance with our rival enemies." A prelude to the revolt was, he believes, the breaking out of party spirit soon after the Peace of 1763; this factionalism may be the origin of the rebellion. Then he reviews the commotions in Boston, the search for arms in the Bay Colony, the actions at Lexington (Smith and Percy) and Bunker's Hill, Howe's evacuation of Boston, the rebel attack on Canada (Arnold and Montgomery), Carleton's invading New York, the Charles Town campaign, South Carolina (Parker and Clinton), Howe's campaign in Long Island and the New York area, and the "unhappy affair" at Trenton (Colonel Rall), which concludes the second campaign and the narrative. Cole is severe with Howe, blaming him for failure to crush the rebellion when he had the opportunity in his Long Island successes.
  The notes to the poem form a connected history of the events described: "The History

of the American War." Here he defends the Peace of 1763 and provides his own military plan for suppressing the rebellion. In the second appendix, he supports the Declaratory Act binding subjects to Parliament law in all cases whatsoever, but he thought it inexpedient to assert that right when it was attempted. Finally, he argues that the failure to provide a suitable governmental structure for the colonies that was clearly subordinated to Parliament was the cause of the troubles. (Also in his A Miscellany: or Collection of Poems, Odes, and Songs [Hull, 1791].)

79-7. [Colvill, Robert]
The Caledonians: A Poem.
Edinburgh: n. p., 1779. 5-10p.

"Heard you dread Mars his brazen clarion sound." (144)

Notices: WM 45 (Jul 25, 1779), 110-11.

Copies: BL 11602.gg.25 (17), 11602.h.13 (3*), C.108.F.5; NUC CtY.

Heroic quatrains. Dated May 1779. A patriot poem calling the Scots peerage to arms against the "faithless Bourbon" whose purpose is to arouse the American colonies, "th'infernal brood," to "Parricide against the Parent Isle," to civil war. (The made-up volume includes The Caledonians (pp. 5-10), 77-4 Atalanta and To the Memory of the Hon. W[illiam] L[eslie], 75-6 Sacred to the Memory of Col. Abercrombie . . . Bunker's Hill, July 17, 1775, and 59-1 Verses for General Wolfe's Monument. See also 89-1 : his Poetical Works.)

79-8. [Combe, William ?]
Fanatical Conversion; or, Methodism Displayed. A Satire.
London: Bew, 1779. 55p.

"Of visionary Gifts and fancy'd Grace." (c. 620)

Notices: CR 47 (Feb 1779), 155; MR 60 (Jun 1779), 478; LR 9 (Mar 1779), 210.

Copies: BL 643.k.10 (6), 840.1.33 (2); NUC IU.

HC. Satire on Wesley and the Methodists, basically not relevant. But a brief comment in a prefatory note to Wesley's inflammatory Calm Addresses is pertinent. The author complains of the hypocrisy of one objecting to profit made from satires against Methodists but who at the same time, "(pretending to preach the Gospel of Peace) can from the Pulpit calmly blow up the Flames of Civil War between his own Countrymen, for the sake of selling a few hundreds of Twopenny Sermons . . . to a fanatic Mob" (Preface, p. x, note).

79-9. [Combe, William]
An Heroic Epistle to Sir James Wright.
London: Bew, 1779. 22p.

"Knight, Broker, Patriot! by whatever name." (c. 200)

Notices:  CR 47 (Jan 1779), 75;  MR 60 (Jan 1779), 65.

Copies:  840.1.17 (14), 11630.d.7 (12), 11630.e.4 (11);  NUC  MH.

HC.  Defense of the character of William Pitt, Earl of Chatham.  The prose preface defends his reputation against Wright's calumnies, a tool of Bute.  It illustrates Pitt's effect upon some Englishmen who believed that, had he lived, his political leadership could have saved the empire.  The poem is anti-Scotch in sentiment, a satire on Wright for slandering Chatham.  Wright was Captain General and Governor of Georgia at the time of the American War.  He had successfully fought off the attacks of the French under D'Estaing and the Americans under Gen. Lincoln upon Savannah in October 1779.  But in this poem he does not figure in his capacity as an American loyalist or British officer in the American administration.

79-10.  [-----]
The World As It Goes, A Poem.  By the Author of The Diaboliad.  Dedicated to One of the Best Men in His Majesty's Dominions, &c.
London:  Bew, 1779.  37p.

"There was a Time, a boyish blushing Time." (c. 650)

Notices:  CR 47 (Jun 1779), 473;  MR 61 (Aug 1779), 109-10;  LR 10 (Jul 1779), 22.

Copies:  BL 163.m.27 (1st ed), 11602.gg.1 (16) (2nd ed);  NUC  CtY, CSmH, ICN, ICU, MH, & NN (1st ed), MH (2nd ed).

HC.  Satire on society.  The Satiric Muse presents a visionary representation of the current world--of mercenary countries, ladies of easy virtue, oppression, misery, hypocrites, and other vicious types.  The satire on the vicious includes "base and crafty Senators" who "betray/ Their King and Country's dearest rights for pay."  But praises the Duke of Portland who, unlike others, is not motivated by sordid self-interest. Among the others are Sandwich, Palliser, Mansfield.  At the end, the satirist asserts the Patriot themes:  merit oppressed, freedom undermined (even by the King), the corruption of the church by the court, the corruption of the MP's, a king foolish enough to betray "the sacred rights" of his people and to impose tyranny.  The poet courageously will not "spare a Vice,--tho' seated on a throne."

79-11.  Delineation, A Poem.
London:  Kearsly, 1779.  5-30p.

"From those dull regions where the sacred light." (450)

Notices:  CR 47 (Apr 1779), 315;  MR 60 (Apr 1779), 317;  LR 9 (Appendix 1779), 465.

Copies: BL T.669 (4); NUC NN.

HC. The poet begs the muses to aid him in lashing vice and folly and praising virtue--the model for the latter being Lord North, who controls the opposition (Barré, Fox, Burke), has the broad view of empire, attends to the war yet is eager for peace, and is protected by truth (pp. 10-11). Then he proceeds to a series of characters, including Thomas Lyttelton, whom he criticizes (pp. 12-13); Fox, with whom he is severe; the Duke of Richmond, with whom he is especially angry as exceptionally factious--"basely urg'd by treachery and pride,/ Leagues with his [the King's] foreign and domestic foes," and "basely seeks . . . To tear the brightest jewel [America] from his crown" (p. 17). He praises the court martial that acquitted Keppel, and Barrington, too (pp. 17-20); condemns Camden as "The factious leader of a factious crew," who engage to sacrifice their country's rights (pp. 20-21); but cannot praise Germain, although he acknowledges the rebel Congress can (p. 22)! He also praises Shelburne for trying to stop the war and yet being loyal (p. 22). His severe strictures on Gen. Howe are noteworthy, accusing him of delay for the sake of money, unwillingness to crush the rebellion (e.g., the forces under Washington at Long Island), and the loss of Burgoyne's northern army (pp. 22-4).

79-12. England's Defiance. An Irregular Ode.
   London: Payne, 1779. 14p.

"Her hostile purpose Spain at length declares." (c. 250)

Notices: CR 48 (Jul 1779), 74; MR 61 (Oct 1779), 313; LR 10 (Aug 1779), 124-5; MP Sep 18, 1779.

Copies: NUC MiD-B.

Irregular Pindaric ode. Attacks France and Spain, the Bourbon allies, for aiding "our rebel Colonies," fostering "foul rebellions," but vows that Britain will fight against the foe and rule the seas; asks a "hapless, fallen America" to repent and reject her alliance with France and to recognize Britain as her real friend, "just, beneficent, and mild"; accuses Franklin of being "the chief incendiary" of the rebellion and cause of the French alliance; yet expresses hope that even if America should be victorious and maintain her independence, Britain and she will form a firm alliance based on a mutual love of liberty. Cited also are "Brave Palliser" versus D'Orvilliers, and the need for domestic unity.

79-13. An Epistle From A Young Lady To An Ensign In The Guards, Upon His Being Ordered to America.
   London: Sewell, Whieldon & Waller, Faulder, 1779. [5]-17p.

"Alas! what dreadful sounds awake my fear." (c. 220)

Notices: CR 48 (Aug 1779), 157; MR 60 (Jul 1779), 76; LR 10 (Oct 1779), 275.

Sabin 22690.

Copies: BL 1486.1.17 (3), 11630.d.11 (13); NUC DLC.

HC. A satire on a courtesan who tries to seduce a soldier from performing his duty. The woman of pleasure protests when she learns her young lover (of the moment) must leave her embraces and the gaiety of London society for the horrid war in America. The satire may extend to the officer who is attracted to the erotic demimonde.

79-14. An Epistle from Edward, An American Prisoner in England, To Harriett, In America.
London: Fielding & Walker, et al., 1779. i + 9p.

"From the vile confines of a prison's gloom." (c. 110)

Notices: CR 47 (Mar 1779), 230; MR 60 (Mar 1779), 231-2; LR 9 (Mar 1779), 211-12.

Copies: BL T.12 (7); NUC CtY, DLC, ICN, MiU-C, RPJCB.

HC. Edward writes to Harriet, informing her of his capture at sea and his being sent to Britain, and declares that all nations perish under "puny statesmen" and tyrants who banish freedom. He believes that England, once the pride of Europe, is now scorned and ridiculed in her hard fortune. America is the future home of "Freedom and Empire." Americans may be called rebels, but they revive the spirit of England's great "Rebel-Chiefs"--Hampden, Sydney, and Russell, who fought "Oppressive pow'r [under the Stuarts], and seal'd their cause with blood." (The profits from this publication, the editor assures the readers, will be applied to the relief of Americans suffering imprisonment in England.)

79-15. [Greene, Edward Burnaby]
The Satires of Persius Paraphrastically Imitated, and Adapted to the Times. With a Preface.
London: Dodsley, Spilsbury, 1779. xxxviii + 71p.

Monumental Inscription. "Tears from a Nation's eye to Merit flow." (26) pp. vii-viii.

Sonnet, Addressed to the Honourable Augustus Keppel. "I will not tell Thee,--Thou may'st little deem." (14) p. 71.

Notices: CR 47 (Jun 1779), 474; MR 60 (Jun 1779), 479-80; LR 10 (Oct 1779), 223-6.

Copies: BL 161.k.32; Bod Godwyn Pamph 1280 (7); NUC RPJCB.

"Monumental Inscription"--HC. Signed with the author's name and dated May 12, 1778. Greene mourns the death of Chatham. "Sonnet, Addressed to the Honourable Augustus Keppel"--praises Keppel for forgiving malicious faction. An English sonnet.

In the "Argument on the American Contest" (pp. ix-xiii), a prose essay, Greene asserts Britain's war with America to be illegal sophistry. The colonies are free except for certain revenues and properties retained by the King. Parliament has no authority in such contracts between King and colonies. The colonies are bound to observe the Act of Navigation and bound to the Mother Country for external security. But, though free to rebel, they cannot justify the arrogation of independence.

The verse satires do not contain relevant commentary, and appear to be unrelated to the initial prose "Argument." The sonnet to Keppel at the very end appears to be an afterthought, Greene's comment on Keppel's acquittal.

79-16. The Guardians, A Poem. By A Young Lady of Portsmouth.
London: Robinson, 1779.

Notices: CR 48 (Oct 1779), 318; MR 61 (Sep 1779), 234; LR 10 (Oct 1779), 259.

Copies: none located.

The argument: "Britannia, reclining on a rock, laments her hero Keppel, being brought to trial. Her guardian genius comes to comfort her, by assuring her, that the hero will be safe. Truth and Justice join them, and promise to bring him off with honour. On this they repair to the court, and gain the love and admiration of all the members, who honourably acquit the much-injured admiral." (From the Critical Review.)

79-17. [Hayley, William]
Epistle to Admiral Keppel.
London: Fielding & Walker, 1779. 20p.

"Swiftly, ye Spirits of the sea and air." (c. 250)

Notices: CR 47 (Feb 1779), 154-5; MR 60 (Feb 1779), 163; LR 9 (Feb 1779), 140.

Copies: BL 164.n.56; NUC ICN, NcD, TxU.

HC. Party satire. Virulent attack on the ministry; nor is Palliser spared. Hails Keppel's acquittal from Palliser's charges, and the defeat of "insidious Craft" and "slander." The spirits of "departed Naval Chiefs" from Drake to Anson come to share this triumph. "Envy's wild rage" has been "reduc'd to silent shame," and "the dark stab of ministerial art," although distressing, evaded. The indignant poet has contempt for those responsible for this "False accusation"--to him, the "Pernicious child of a corrupted state." Palliser, however, must have had a disordered mind, motivated by "wild passion; pride and spleen combin'd" to make these false charges. Hayley speculates that England became corrupted when the evil Scotch came to power. Still, he concludes in a patriotic expression of hope, we must not despair of the state, not even when led by weak statesmen or when Germain "plans the dire campaign,/ The curse of Minden's Field, or Saratoga's plain" (p. 18). The navy, if not undermined by dissension, can protect Britain from the common foe.


79-18. An Heroic Congratulation, Addressed To The Honourable Augustus Keppel, Admiral of the Blue; On His being Unanimously, Honourably, and Fully acquitted of the Five Malicious and Ill-founded Charges exhibited against Him by Sir Hugh Palliser, Vice Admiral of the Blue. To which is annexed, An Address to the Public, Containing the Five Charges, interspersed with Metaphors, Animadversions, and Allusions, suitable to the Subject, to display their Absurdity, and vindicate the untarnished Honour of the British Navy.
London: Dodsley, Almon, et al., [1779]. 32p.

"Illustrious Keppel! who canst well abide." (c. 570)

Notices: CR 47 (Mar 1779), 228; MR 60 (Mar 1779), 230; LR 9 (Apr 1779), 284-5.

Copies: BL 11630.e.1 (3); NUC NN.

HC. Celebrates Keppel's acquittal of Palliser's charges resulting from the episode with the French fleet off Ushant, near Brest, in 1778, when "perfidious" France "Had in our civil Quarrel interfer'd,/ And had the Flag of bold Defiance rear'd." Recounts the Ushant "battle" when the French fleet scurried back to Brest rather than engage, the basis of Palliser's charges that Keppel "was tardy" and "seem'd tim'rously to shun the Fleet of Gaul." What the poet sees in the charges is an attempt by Keppel's enemies to destroy his life and reputation, and make the attempt "The hateful Ground-work of a Civil Strife," especially when unanimity against France was needed. In the Address he describes the naval actions in which Keppel participated, evidence of bravery and attention to duty, and then reviews the charges of negligence and remissness in the performance of duty.


79-19. Keppel For Ever!
[London, 1779]

"Smile, smile, Britannia smile." (49)

Copies: BL Rox III.660.

Broadside. A song in seven-line stanzas praising and congratulating Keppel, who has been acquitted of the malicious charges of Sandwich and "his dupe," Palliser.

79-20. The Keppeliad; Or, Injur'd Virtue Triumphant. A Poem.
  London: Harrison & Co., 1779. 19p.

"The Sun broke forth, the Morning was serene." (c. 420)

Notices: CR 47 (Mar 1779), 228; MR 60 (Mar 1779), 231.

Copies: BL 11602.gg.29 (13).

HC. Dedicated to Marquis of Rockingham. A fanciful rendition of the Ushant episode in July 1778 and the court-martial trial of Keppel, favoring him. Palliser, it is speculated, was moved by "Some private Pique, some Views sinister" or "Resentment" and anger at a sense of insult to disobey or neglect to obey Keppel's orders to renew the attack upon the French, thereby allowing their fleet to escape combat by returning to Brest and safety. Keppel's bravery in the past is reviewed, and his right to command the fleet confirmed. Unlike Palliser, he is not guided by "private Pique" or revenge.-- Palliser charges Keppel with misconduct on that July day. Impeached, Keppel is supported by witnesses who testify that he did his best to perform his duty, and so the court-martial awards him an honorable acquittal.

79-21. Lucas, Henry.
  Poems to her Majesty [Queen Charlotte]. . . .
  London: Davis et al., 1779. 24p.

The Oblation, A Lyric Poem, On her Majesty's Happy Delivery of a Daughter, the Now Amiable Princess Sophia, November 3, 1777. "Empress of Britain's love! whose gentle sway." (c. 160) pp. 13-24.

Copies: BL 11630.e.8 (2); NUC CtY, ICN, InU, MH, NIC.

Irregular Pindaric ode. Another loyal panegyric by Lucas. On the taking of Philadelphia by Gen. Howe, which Lucas believes an omen of the war's end. He proposes to rename the newborn princess "Americana" in honor of the event and the happy conclusion of the rebellion. He concludes with praise of Clinton's successes, probably the taking of Savannah late in 1778, presaging--he hopes--the end of the war.

79-22. Mason, William.
  Ode to the Naval Officers of Great-Britain. Written Immediately after the Trial of Admiral Keppel, February 11, 1779. By W. Mason, M.A.
  London: Cadell, 1779. 8p.

"Hence to thy Hell! thou Fiend accursed." (184)

Notices: CR 47 (Apr 1779), 310-11; MR 60 (Apr 1779), 316; GM 49 (Apr 1779), 199-200; LR 9 (May 1779), 351; PA Mar 25, 1779; W Eve Post Apr 3, 1779.

Copies:  BL 161.m.4, 840.1.4 (11), 11630.d.7 (7);  NUC   CSmH, CtY, IEN, MB, MH, TxU.

Regular Pindaric ode, concluding with ten dixains.  Written as an antidote to the virulent attacks by Keppel's enemies on his character and his cause.  Mason challenges the detractors and praises the fleet officers who resisted the temptations of the court.  (These are the British commanders who presided at Keppel's court-martial or gave their evidence in his favor.)  He invokes Neptune to save Britain from herself, and the "Spirit of the Deep" demands to know why Britain crosses the Atlantic "To stain thy hands with parricide," and condemns "thy cause unbless'd."  Then he demands that Britain "Turn from this ill-omen's war" to fight France, her foe and Freedom's.  With France subdued by Keppel, "fraternal strife shall cease,/ And firm, on Freedom's base, be fix'd an empire's peace."  (In "A Critical Ode, Addressed to Mr. Mason," *Morning Chronicle*, May 20, 1779, note a criticism of Mason's ambiguity in II: 3, line 3--"the truly brave.")

79-23.  Maurice, Thomas.
   Poems and Miscellaneous Pieces, With a Free Translation of the *Oedipus Tyrannus* of Sophocles.  By the Rev. Thomas Maurice, A.B. of University College, Oxford.
   London:  Dodsley, 1779.

Verses Written in the Year 1774.  "'What shouts were those;  what fierce and martial train."  (112)  pp. 38-43.

Notices:  MR 62 (May 1780), 391-7.

Copies:  BL 11630.e.8 (1);  Bod Vet A5d.260;  NUC   CSmH, CtY, NjP, NN.

HC.  Imagines the Genius of Britain standing above Boston harbor, surveying a scene of battle ("scene of guilt").  The spirit remarks that these lands, once settled by Englishmen, are now the home of a "race unworthy those immortal sires," including Wolfe and Braddock who lost their lives for America, because they have taken up arms to shed "brothers' blood."  The spirit urges the colonists to accept peace with Britain and join the fight against France and Spain.  (These verses clearly were revised <u>after</u> 1774.)  The poem was retitled "Verses Written during the American War" for a later edition: *Poems, Epistolary, Lyric, and Elegiacal* (London:  Bulwer,  Wright, 1800), pp. 48-51.


79-24.  Meritorious Disobedience:  An Epistle to a Ministerial Marine Favourite upon his Late Unexpected Escape from the Hands of Justice.
   London:  Bew, 1779.

Notices:  CR 47 (Jun 1779), 472;  MR 60 (Jun 1779), 477.

Copies:  none located.

Satire on Palliser and the administration.  Some lines of satire on Samuel Johnson as a pensioned writer.  *Monthly Review*:  Palliser "now takes his turn for a scalping."

79-25. The Milesian; Or, The Injuries of Ireland. A Poem. In Four Books. With Notes Illustrative and Explanatory.
London: Almon, Dilly, & Dodsley, 1779. 50 + [1]p.

"Fitzgerald! first of Ireland's noble sons." (c. 1550)

Notices: L Eve Post Aug 7, 12, 17, 1779.

Copies: NUC PPL.

HC. A state poem. In the prose preface and the verse, "The Milesian Bard" relates the experience of Ireland with British oppression to the American War. Criticizes the corrupt British government for subjecting Ireland to cruel and unjust controls on trade and industry, especially trade with America. Thus, he argues, Ireland, oppressed and impoverished, may go the way of America—rebel, seek independence and freedom. Often criticizes the vice and corruption in England that are the ultimate causes of the immoral insistence that power makes right, thereby undermining the British Constitution and the principle of consent. Had England subjugated the American colonies, the precedent would have encouraged it to force Ireland to surrender all her rights and to transform Great Britain into "an arbitrary monarchy." Cited are emigration (denied to the Irish), Johnson and Gibbon ("the hireling defenders of a corrupt, blundering Administration"), and Richmond, Camden, and Burke—all praised. Also objects to Ireland's forced participation in the war against America. James Fitzgerald was the Duke of Leinster. (The London Evening Post excerpted three portions, for a total of 160 lines, that ask Ireland to be raised from her torpor and that England relax her restrictions and monopolies on Irish trade in order to bring prosperity to the land.)

79-26. Momus; Or, The Fall of Britain. A Poem.
London: Cadell, 1779. 20p.

"Now vengeful War, with all her Gorgon train." (316)

Notices: CR 47 (Mar 1779), 228; MR 60 (May 1779), 396; LR 9 (Appendix 1779), 466.

Copies: BL 164.n.51; NUC InU, MB.

HC. Britain in peace and prosperity arouses the Arch-Fiend's rage and envy, who thereupon asks his hellish council how to destroy her. Mammon replies that Britain is destroying herself by means of Corruption, gold from India, bringing in its train Dissipation. But Momus, the God of mockery, protests that this method is too slow; he advocates union with the Fury Alecto whose mischief includes fraternal war and parricide: wherever she is found there is "Discord's deadly rage" and "War's iron scourges desolate the land" (pp. 15-16). This venomous Fury will extinguish concord; senates will be destroyed as "Passion, Pride, or Party lead the way," politics will be unstable, "Patriots shall rave in black Sedition's cause" and negate everything, thereby inciting rebellion and civil war and transforming "Columbian [American] mice" to powerful men--Franklin, Adams, Hancock, Arnold--"The spawn of Faction, and the tools of France." He also includes Dr. Witherspoon (pp. 17-18). Momus's argument pleases the Stygian powers, but Satan feels that, combined with Mammon, Alecto will effectively enable Britain to ruin herself.

79-27. Neptune. A Poem. Inscribed to the Hon. Augustus Keppel.
London: Kearsly, 1779.

Notices: CR 47 (Feb 1779), 154; MR 60 (Mar 1779), 231; LR 9 (Feb 1779), 137-8.

Copies: none located.

Praise of Keppel.

79-28. Nereus's Prophecy: A Sea-Piece, Sketched off Ushant on the Memorable Morning of the 28th of July, 1778.
London: Bew, 1779. 25p.

"When Gallia's Doves, by British Eagles press'd." (c. 250)

Notices: CR 47 (Apr 1779), 310; MR 60 (Apr 1779), 317; LR 9 (Appendix 1779), 465.

Copies: BL 1346.k.19.

HC and mixed or irregular forms. An Opposition poem. Nereus is an American (p. 16), and the poem was written after Keppel's acquittal by the court-martial and is dedicated to him. Blames Palliser for Keppel's failure to engage the French fleet in battle off Ushant, and Bute and his faction for the attempt to impeach Keppel. Negative remarks on the fast for 1779, Germain, Quebec Act and the repeal of the penal acts against Papists, John Wesley, and Sandwich. Prophesies a powerful, united, and wealthy America, to which English emigrants will swarm.
  Written by the same person, perhaps, responsible for The Watch, Royal Perseverance, Tyranny the Worst Taxation, Captain Parolles, An Epistle to Lord Mansfield, the Most Unpopular Man in the Kingdom, and The Favourite, all favorable to the minority. (Nereus is introduced originally by Horace as a prophet, denouncing to Paris, when he conveyed Helena to Troy, the fatal catastrophe of that city.)

79-29. Ode To The Privateer-Commanders Of Great Britain: Being A Parody On Mr. Mason's Ode To The Naval Officers Of Great Britain. Written, Immediately After Reading His Ode, April The Sixteenth, 1779. By --- --- ---, B.A.
Oxford: J. & J. Fletcher; London: Rivington, Payne, 1779. 8p.

"Hence down to Hell! ye hulks accurst." (84)

Notices: CR 47 (May 1779), 390; MR 61 (Jul 1779), 76; LR 10 (Appendix 1779), 455.

Copies: BL 840.1.4 (12); NUC CtY, DLC.

Abbreviated regular Pindaric ode, parody of 79-22: Mason's <u>Ode to the Naval Officers</u>. Instead of naval commanders, hireling courtiers, venal peers, and a gigantic deity communicating his advice to Britannia, the poet has substituted privateer commanders, hireling colliers, venal tars, and an enormous shark, the private monarch of the ocean, giving his instructions to Liverpool, haven of many of the privateers. The poet contends that these commanders deserve praise, although the sailors in the navy belittle them, and although their sole motive is "Interest"--profit. The shark advises them to aim at rich French ships from the East Indies, for such captures will eventually impoverish France.

79-30. On the Preference of Virtue to Genius. A Poetical Epistle.
London: Cadell, 1779. 20p.

"**, the wonder of a venal age." (c. 390)

Notices: CR 47 (May 1779), 391-2; MR 60 (Jun 1779), 474-6.

Copies: NUC NN, OCU.

HC. A moral poem on the high abstract level of virtue, that descends in the conclusion (p. 20) with a specific reference to the American war. The poet urges that political leaders be guided by wisdom, virtue, that they give up corruption, "Recall our armies o'er the Atlantic flood," end the war, and restore commerce.

79-31. Party-Satire Satirized. A Poem.
London: Bladon, 1779. 27p.

"Patience assist me! must my Ears still ring." (c. 320)

Notices: CR 47 (Jan 1779), 75; MR 60 (Mar 1779), 229; LR 9 (Appendix 1779), 466.

Sabin 58971.

Copies: BL 643.k.22, 11630.e.16 (12).

HC. A loyal Tory satire. The poet asserts in the prose Preface that "<u>political Satire</u> . . . has its just Limits. It should not exceed the Bounds of Loyalty or Decency." Thus he doubts "true patriotism and sound policy" characterize the satiric effusions of the so-called "patriot" poets. He questions all attacks on North, Bute, Mansfield, Germaine, and the King--to him, evidence of treason, libels, and lies. The poets are being "enlisted now/ Into the Corps of <u>Washington</u>, or <u>Howe</u>" (at this time

Howe, returned from America, was severely criticized by the Establishment for his failures). They are schooled by Price, led by Barré, Fox, and Burke. They rejoice to see America rise by England's fall--and become rebels themselves. Near the conclusion, he accuses them of being anti-monarchist republicans and demands that they be transported to America or, better still, ignored like tiny insects.

79-32. A Pastoral. By An Officer, Belonging to the Canadian Army.
London: Becket, 1779. ii + 20p.

"Colin. What dreadful news is this, the Shepherds tell." (c. 380)

Notices: CR 47 (Apr 1779), 311; MR 60 (Mar 1779), 232; L Mag 48 (Jan 1779), 39; LR 9 (Appendix 1779), 463.

Copies: NUC MiU-C.

HC. A narrative poem framed in the classical pastoral mode, with a digression on Burgoyne's campaign. Begins with a rapid review of the history of Britain's colonies until France is swept from the new world. Then peace is transformed into a rebellion led by "designing men" who impose their own form of tyranny. Describes Burgoyne's campaign, "the late Expedition across the Lakes," and mourns his defeat at Saratoga. Burgoyne is honored, despite his surrender. His troops were outnumbered six to one; his misfortune should generate pity. No one can say he acted wrong. Then the poet completes the narrative of a friend who, almost fatally wounded in the fight "for king, his country, and its laws," has made a miraculously rapid recovery.

79-33. Patriotic Perfidy, A Satire.
London: Bell, 1779. 29p.

"--I'll hear no more--in Mischief's reign." (c. 440)

Notices: CR 47 (Jun 1779), 472; MR 60 (Jun 1779), 477-8; LR 9 (Appendix 1779), 464.

Sabin 59096.

Copies: Bod Godwyn Pamph 1700 (18).

HC. Satire on the minority lords. The poet's point is made in the prefatory "Apology": "the public, though it does not feel the galling yoke of monarchy, groans under the load of ARISTOCRATIC INSOLENCE" (this dated June 9, 1779). In the poem, the author indignantly attacks "Faction's minions," the so-called patriots who pursue treason and are guided by self-interest. They are real rebels for they deliberately create disorder to push North and Sandwich from office. They are the real causes of the American rebellion; they contribute at present to the French triumph. They "keep rebellious perfidy alive" by increasing discord. Among these are Richmond, Weymouth, Camden, B[urlingto]n. All undermine the ministry by means of malicious defamation--Mansfield, Germaine, North, and Sandwich. Concludes with an attack on all internal dissenters who seek to elevate themselves at the expense of their country's ruin: "Britain's vipers [who] in her bosom lie."

79-34. Paul Jones: Or The Fife Coast Garland. A Heroi-Comical Poem. In Four Parts. In Which Is Contained The Oyster Wives of Newhaven's Letter To Lord Sandwich. Edinburgh: n. p., 1779. 37p.

"Pray, tell us, good neighbours, whence all this affray." (c. 1150)

Sabin 36566.

Copies: BL 11602.h.14 (2); NUC RPJCB.

Anapestic tetrameter couplets, doggerel. The letter, Part 4, is dated Newhaven, October 30, 1779. Part 1: "The pirate, traitor [Jones] comes," and the inhabitants of the Scottish Fife coast scurry away to safety or prepare to defend themselves against Jones's raiding forces. The narrative dramatizes the chaotic state of civil defense in the region. Parts 2 and 3 humorously narrate some "queer episodes" about Jones--some genuine raids and some mock or show raids by thieves and robbers assuming his name.

Part 4: A complaint at Jones's disturbing Scots "fisheries." The people, defenceless because their men are lost to the war service, are prey to Jones's raiders. The complaint extends to the patriots in the political opposition, who wish to topple the ministry and "murder the state" (p. 29). Besides, they are inexperienced and unable to lead the country in crisis. Fraudulent patriots, unlike (George?) Johnstone and Capt. Farmer, they oppose "the rights of their country [and] brand her with crimes." Thus they strengthen the enemy, as they are "pleas'd with our disgraces." The women wish Sandwich to order warships north to protect the Scottish coast. Jones is called a "knave, / A Traytor, a pirate, a congressional knave" and a "d----d Scots French American pirate" (pp. 19, 25).

79-35. Ruin seize thee, ruthless King! A Pindaric Ode, Not Written by Mr. Gray. London: Almon, 1779. 3-11p.

"'Ruin seize thee, ruthless King." (144)

Notices: CR 48 (Dec 1779), 471-2; MR 62 (Feb 1780), 171; LR 11 (Appendix 1780), 447; PA, Dec 14, 1779.

Copies: NUC CtY, DLC, MH, MiU-C, NjP.

Regular Pindaric ode, imitation of Gray's Bard. Abusive satire on the king and his ministry. George is portrayed as a "pious Nero" and his ministers as oppressive tyrants. The poet objects to the American War and demands that it cease. He stands by the Thames and berates the times as the king, in his barge, is rowed to Woolwich. Cited are Ireland, Sandwich, Tory, North, Germain, Ushant (Keppel and Palliser), Washington, and Samuel Johnson. Possibly by William Mason. The author is indicated in an advertisement appearing in The Dean and the Squire (1782).

79-36. Satire For The King's Birth-Day. By No Poet-Laureate.
London: Wilkie, 1779. 3-16p.

"Friend. What! you a Poet? and not sing." (c. 180)

Notices: CR 47 (Jun 1779), 472; MR 60 (Jun 1779), 478; L Eve Post Jun 1, 1779; LR 9 (Appendix 1779), 465.

Copies: NUC CSmH, CtY.

Octosyllabic couplets. Satire, imitation of Horace, through a dialogue between a poet and his friend. The friend advises him to compete with laureate Whitehead and offer his eulogy to the king. But the poet, being satiric by nature, is unable to comply. Instead, he writes an ironic satire that is really praise of the king--who loves his people, would extend the toleration even to Catholics (certainly he is not arbitrary), is a good husband and father, keeps his (political) servants in place, is charitable, sober, and moral. The queen is equally virtuous, a dutiful mother, humble, and sincerely devout. The friend concludes that "A SATIRE in this mode/ Is equal to-- a birth-day ODE."

79-37. The Se'er, Or The American Prophecy. A Poem. Being the Second Sight of that celebrated Ohio Man, or Indian Seer, Oomianouskipittiwantipaw, In the Year One Thousand Five Hundred and Eighty Eight.
London: Harrison & Co., 1779. 35p.

"Where the wide waste Columbus first explor'd." (642)

Notices: CR 47 (Apr 1779), 310; MR 60 (Apr 1779), 318; LR 9 (Appendix 1779), 464.

Sabin 78870.

Copies: Bod Godwyn Pamph 1692 (16).

HC. Satire on King George and the Scots. An Indian seer, upon the English arrival to the new world, foretells the nature of George III's reign under Scots influence. He prophesies the loss of the lands by the despot because he was misled by corrupt and fawning courtiers, like Bute and Mansfield, who tell him "Monarchs can do nothing wrong." After severe characters of North, Sandwich, Germaine, and others, he sees England fall in flames and the New World arise like a phoenix.

79-38. Spirit And Unanimity, A Poem, Inscribed To His Grace the Duke of Rich---d.
London: Piguenit, Bew, Ridley, & Tayler, 1779. 40p.

"Rouse, Britons! from inglorious prospects rouse." (c. 600)

Notices: CR 47 (May 1779), 390; MR 60 (Jun 1779), 478.

Copies: BL 1600/1517.

HC. Patriotic verses meant to awaken Britons to their danger and to inspire them with love of their country. At war with powerful enemies and its American colonies now allied with France, Britain is obstructed by treachery at home. So that Howe, Keppel, Clinton, and Percy can fight with spirit and effectiveness, there must be no undermining "discord, hate, faction," or "party." Regarding his objections to party, the poet takes issue with Burke, Richmond, Fox, Barré, Luttrell, Shelburne, who should lead the country to proper action instead of trying to prove the court and ministers wrong. They should move the "inactive" armies and "ling'ring fleets." The poet is angry at those shameless and remorseless politicians who "foment rebellion's flame" and "treach'rously rebellion's cause espouse." Unanimity, reconciliation, must be the "first great aim," and all else will follow--the disappearance of rancor, suspicion, doubt, distrust. Concludes with praise of Savile, Thurlow, Dunning, Camden, and Northumberland (Percy's father).

79-39. [Tasker, William]
A Congratulatory Ode To Admiral Keppel . . . . By the Author of the Ode To The Warlike Genius of Great Britain.
London: Dodsley, Bew, Becket, et al., 1779. [15p.]

"O Muse! the noblest of the Nine." (226)

Notices: CR 47 (Feb 1779), 154-5; MR 60 (Mar 1779), 231; G Eve Post, Apr 3, 1779; L Eve Post, Apr 1, 1779; LR 9 (Feb 1779), 136-7; St J's Chron, Mar 30, 1779.

Copies: BL 1346.k.25 (1st ed); Bod Godwyn Pamph 1698 (2nd ed); NUC CtY, ICU (2nd ed).

Irregular Pindaric ode. Written the day news of Keppel's acquittal reached London. Panegyric on Keppel: "Malice and Envy" were responsible for the attacks on his reputation. But Neptune lent aid to "Keppel's injur'd cause," and his truth and honor withstood party rage and calumny. Even Britain helped, insisting that truth and justice shall prevail, his cause being righteous, his virtue heroic. The judges will acquit this patriot. Keppel's heroic exploits are reviewed, starting with his role in Anson's circumnavigation of the earth and including his capturing the Island of Goree, Senegal, in 1759 and his bravery in the siege of Havannah in 1762. Concludes with a prayer to Concord for unity in a vigorous struggle against France and Spain, and for peace with America: he bids "British Sires again embrace/ Their Children of Columbean race," bringing triumph to the British and the King. The criticism of Palliser is evidence of party zeal.
Parts of the ode, especially stanza 17, were set to music and performed at the Haymarket--see London Evening Post and General Evening Post, above. 2 eds in 1779.

79-40. The Tears of Britannia: A Solemn Appeal To All Her Sons At This Tremendous Juncture: A Poem Addressed To The First Lord of the Admiralty, The Commissioners of

the Militia, And The Great Trading Body of this Kingdom.
   London: Rivington; Oxford: Prince, 1779. iv + 57p.

"As on the wave-beat Beach with pensive Mien."  (c. 1250)

   Notices:  CR 47 (Feb 1779), 155;  MR 60 (Mar 1779), 229-30;  LR 9 (Appendix 1779), 465.

Sabin 94567.

   Copies:  BL 164.n.55, 11630.e.4 (9);  NUC  CtY.

HC.  A loyal poem, occasioned by the problematical sea-fight off Ushant between Keppel and the French, July 27, 1778. Britannia laments the degeneration of her sons, corrupted by luxury, with the example of Rome's ruin; urges unanimity in the present crisis, Keppel's failure to defeat the French fleet. In fact, destroying this fleet is more significant than losing America. Refers to the union of America and France—America characterized as "Rebellion with ferocious hand," "America's false alien Heart"; also to the subversive Opposition ("With freedom's Name baptiz'd a rebel Cause"), Fox and Burke, who have joined with the enemy and exalted his cause, and who praise Washington and Lee but blame Clinton. This is a dishonest Opposition. The Howes are criticized for having performed nothing.


79-41.  [Tickell, Richard]
   Epistle From The Honourable Charles Fox, Partridge-Shooting, To The Honourable John Townshend, Cruising.
   London: Faulder, 1779. 5-14p.

"While you, dear Townshend, o'er the billows ride."  (133)

   Notices:  CR 48 (Dec 1779), 473-4;  MR 62 (Feb 1780), 170-1;  GM 50 (Jan 1780), 35-6; L Eve Post Jan 22, 1780;  MP Dec 17, 1779;  PA Jan 24, 1780;  WM 47 (Jan 17, 1780), 206-7;  W Eve Post Jan 20, 1780.

Sabin 95795.

   Copies:  BL 164.n.57, 11630.e.9 (8) (1st ed), 11659.cc.19 (rev ed), 11602.g.31 (4) (3rd ed, 1780);  Bod Godwyn Pamph 1695;  NUC CtY, DLC, ICN, IU, MH, PU, RPJCB (1st ed).

HC.  Light satire on Fox, one of the chief speakers in the Opposition, imagined in the country, addressing his friend Townshend at sea. Fox, using shots wadded with Gazettes (government publications) and "Almon's bold sheets" (Almon published pamphlets and the like against the ministry), cannot wholly forget the cares of state. He describes the hunt in terms like parliamentary procedure, explaining his technique of teasing and delaying Administration, then invites Townshend to the pleasures of St. James's and to the fun at Brooks' Club of Whig wits and politicians. There they wish Fox "better sport to gain" and Townshend "more glory, from the next campaign," alluding to Fox's opposition to Administration. The pointer dogs have "patriot names": Washington, Paul Jones, Franklin, Silas Deane--"No servile ministerial runners they!" (But the satire, as Horace Walpole noted, really lacks political point.) (Also in The New Foundling Hospital for Wit [1786], I, 318-23. See Namier & Brooke's House of Commons 1754-1790 (1964), volumes 2-3 for entries on Fox and Townshend.) The poem appeared in at least 3 eds 1779-80.

79-42. [Tickell, Richard ?]
Opposition Mornings: With Betty's Remarks.
Dublin: Byrn & Son, 1779. 72p.

"Blest seeds of discord! sown by Heaven's own hand." (4)

Notices: CR 47 (Jun 1779), 471; MR 60 (Jun 1779), 473; L Chron 45 (Jun 1, 1779), 521; LR 9 (Jun 1779), 430; PA, Jun 22, 1779.

Sabin 95797.

Copies: NUC CSmH, CtY, DLC, ICN, MH, MiU-C.

HC. Fictional minutes of Opposition meetings from November 1778 to March 1779, satirizing the members by exposing their absurd strategy on how to proceed in Parliament to obstruct Administration. This is prose but for two couplets of ironic verse on the last page, emphasizing the discord sown by these alleged patriots: "'tis these patriots' fate,/ By discord only to preserve the state."
The preface is signed "Elizabeth O'Neill." The Critical Review identifies Mrs. Betty O'Neill as the "fruiterer in St. James's Street." See 80-61.

79-43. Verses in Memory of Colonel Ackland, With Some Letters to a Noble Lord. Particularly on the Advantages arising from the Newfoundland Fishery, to Great-Britain and Ireland.
London: Brown, 1779.

Notices: CR 47 (Jan 1779), 76; MR 60 (Jan 1779), 71; LR 9 (Mar 1779), 213.

Sabin 99299.

Copies: none located.

79-44. The Vision: A Poem, On The Death of Lord Lyttelton. Inscribed To The Right Hon. the Earl of Abingdon.
London: Millidge, 1779. iv + 13p.

"When darkness reign'd with universal sway." (c. 240)

Notices: CR 49 (Jan 1780), 73; MR 62 (Jan 1780), 87-8; GA Dec 25, 1779; LR 11 (Feb 1780), 143-4.

Copies: NUC CtY.

The Advertisement insinuates that Lyttelton (1744-79) was poisoned to remove him from the political scene before he could expose the ministry's machinations.
HC. At a time when England's state of affairs is rotten from the minority's point of view--Fox, Richmond, Manchester, Rockingham, Camden, Shelburne, Abingdon, Effingham, and Keppel are all praised--a vision awakens the sleeping Lyttelton, foretelling his death in three days and urging him to restore his "drooping fame." He bemoans this "bleeding Country" oppressed by "savage Laws" and "secret Foes"--Bute, Sandwich, Germaine, North, Mansfield, and Wedderburne. The vision replies that heaven knows his secret worth, that he must accept his fate, but that in time Britain's "guilty Sons," "titled Traitors," will be revealed.

79-45. [Wharton, Charles Henry]
A Poetical Epistle To His Excellency George Washington, Esq. Commander In Chief Of The Armies Of The United States Of America, From An Inhabitant of the State of Maryland. To Which Is Annexed, A Short Sketch Of General Washington's Life and Character.
Annapolis, 1779; repr. London: Dilly, Almon, et al., 1780. iv + [5]-13 + 14-24p.

"While many a servile Muse her succour lends." (c. 200)

Notices: CR 49 (Jun 1780), 472-4; MR 62 (May 1780), 389-91; WM 49 (Aug 1780), 190-1.

Evans 16677, 17435-6, 17801; Sabin 103093.

Copies: BL 11630.b.1 (12), 11630.c.13 (14); NUC CtY, DLC, ICN, MH, MiU-C, NN, RPJCB. (Listed are only copies of the London reprint of the first edition in America, 1779.)

This pamphlet was sold to raise money to relieve the distress of American prisoners in English jails.
HC. This poem is offered as a trophy to praise Washington, the "Great Chief," and welcomes Liberty to the banks of the Potomac. Reviews Washington's role in the battle for freedom. Britain will curse the day she thought to force America to submit. America will be "The great asylum of oppress'd mankind," "free without faction," a republic "Aw'd by no titles," the home of true religion, the world center of commerce, a land of justice, "And never curs'd with Mansfields, Norths, or Butes." The great patriot Washington will be the model for America's sons, the future subject of poetry and praise. Cited are Whitehead's laureate odes, German mercenaries. (The prose sketch of Washington's life and character appears at the end, pp. 14-24.)

Serials

79-46. The Accession.

"When George the Great had wing'd his way." (28)

G Eve Post, Oct 23, 1779.

Quatrains. For the anniversary of George III's accession, October 25. The spirit of George II (called George the Great) assures Britain that George the Good (known as George III) is a ruler to be trusted.

79-47. Account of the Camp at Warley. By a Somerset Grasier, in an Epistle to his Wife.

"I zaid, my dear Jenny, as how I would write." (42)

G Eve Post, Oct 16, 1779; WM 46 (Oct 27, 1779), 112.

Sixains. Dialect poem. An account of the good time had during the review at Warley.

79-48. An Address to Great Britain.

"Britons arise! nor longer drooping stand." (7)

MP, Sep 23, 1779.

HC. Britain should unite to fight France. "Engage unanimous, and on [the French] fall."

79-49. An Address to John Wilkes, Esq.

"To thee, O Wilkes! I dedicate my lays." (144)

LP, Nov 29 & Dec 1, 1779.

HC. Panegyric on Wilkes and a summary of his political significance. The clergy are attacked for profaning true religion, and Wilkes is asked to purify the higher clergy! Cited are the King, North, Germain, Camden, corruption, General Warrants, and Natural Rights.

79-50.  An Address to the British Army and Navy, and the Militia of this Kingdom.

"To Arms, to Arms, ye injur'd Men."  (16)

PA, Aug 11, 1779;  W Eve Post, Aug 10, 1779.

Quatrains.  Let us fight France, our natural enemy.  (Signed P. S. E. M. in W Eve Post.)

79-51.  Addressed to the Court-Martial, Now Sitting upon an Honourable Admiral.

"Smile on, smile on, Britannia bids thee smile."  (26)

GA, Feb 10, 1779.

HC.  Praise of Keppel for his honesty.

79-52.  Admiral Lee Shore's Soliloquy.

"Let Hardy seamen rule the main."  (12)

MP, Apr 16, 1779.

Quatrains.  Satire on Keppel, who is supported by Whig party faction.  Indirectly praises Sir Charles Hardy.

79-53.  Advice to Both Parties on the Present State of Affairs.

"Dumb now be Faction;  Party cease to roar."  (10)

G Eve Post, Jul 6, 1779;  WM 45 (Jul 28, 1779), 111.

HC.  Let Britain be united against the Bourbons, France, and Spain.

79-54.  [Ah! happy Townshend! envy'd youth.]

"Ah! happy Townshend! envy'd youth."  (16)

L Cour, Dec 10, 1779.

Quatrains.  The poet advises young John Townshend, Fox's friend, not to risk his life on the seas when England's navy is poorly managed (by venal Sandwich).  See Tickell, 79-41.

79-55. [Ah! 'tis a dismal circumstance.]

"Ah! 'tis a dismal circumstance." (36)

Freeman's J, Feb 11, 1779.

Sixains. Administration is bringing ruin to the nation despite all of Pitt's efforts. Now Keppel is being attacked by "False Palliser." But justice will clear "valiant Keppel" from malicious charges.

79-56. The Alarm.

"Invasion! Invasion! -- Where to be seen?" (16)

G, Sep 27, 1779.

Quatrains. The cry of invasion is only a state trick, Dean Tucker declares in his Thoughts on the present Posture of Affairs. But this poet does not believe him.

79-57. Alderman Crosby's Address to Admiral Keppel, on Presenting his Freedom, &c.

"Illustrious Keppel, Mars' son." (64)

Lloyd's 45 (Dec 29, 1779), 626.

Quatrains. London, through Alderman Crosby, honors Admiral Keppel by presenting his "Freedom of the City" for his victory over D'Orvilliers (and his acquittal by the court-martial). The politics of this episode is emphasized when Crosby asks that Keppel help unseat "fat Boreas" (North).

79-58. The Alehouse Politicians.

"A Pint of Purl -- a Glass of Gin." (28)

Cumb Pacq, Nov 2, 1779; LP, Oct 13, 1779; PA, Oct 15, 1779.

Quatrains. Pub politicians converse about the war that is not going so well for Britain. Admirals Hardy and D'Estaing are cited -- Hardy at Spithead while D'Estaing is in the West Indies threatening British possessions.

79-59. An Alphabetical Account of Opposition.

"A Stands for Abing[don], who late had a call." (20)

MP, Dec 8. 1779.

Anapest tetrameter couplets, on some of the leading figures in politics mostly -- Abingdon, Burke, Effingham, Fox, Howe, Keppel, Richmond, Shelburne, Townshend, and Wilkes. With notes.

79-60. America. An Elegy.

"Where, where alas, are fled the blissful hours." (52)

Lloyd's 44 (Mar 19, 1779), 276; MP, Mar 20, 1779.

Elegiac quatrains. In the past, Britain had a good relationship with America. Like Cromwell's rebellion, the American rebellion is doomed. America will thereupon return like a prodigal to its parent.

79-61. America's Address to England.

"England, remember th'opprobrious lot." (10)

L Eve Post, Sep 21, 1779.

HC. America admonishes England to beware the Scotch and carry the torch of liberty.

79-62. [And so, my friend Miller, the secret is out.]

"And so, my friend Miller, the secret is out." (38)

L Eve Post, Feb 18, 1779.

Anapest tetrameter couplets. A humorous reaction to the verdict clearing Keppel. Comment on the rioting resulting from the announcement of the acquittal. John Miller, the editor of the London Evening Post, asked for an enquiry into the cause of the riots, which this poem attempts to answer with a good deal of cant diction.

Andre, John. See "Verses intended to have been spoken at the Mischianza," 79-504; also "Address intended to have been spoken at the Mischianza," 78-51.

79-63. Application to the American War, from Macbeth.

"Says the King to the Queen, pretty Charlotte, my dear." (20)

L Cour, Dec 28, 1779.

Song. Satire on the King, overconfident in his belief that he can stop the French, should they invade. At the time of the threat, the King had ordered a new set of horse furniture!

79-64. Are the Common Council of London Culpable in Refusing to assist Government in the Present Situation of Affairs?

"Is't right or wrong to save a sinking state?" (20)

Cal Merc, Sep 6, 1779.

HC. Those who do not help their country in need are traitors. Thus those "by faction led" should be banished. When France and Popery threaten, all Protestants must fight for their lives and religion. So "London merits endless blame."

79-65. [Aristides of old.]

"Aristides of old." (36)

GA, Mar 17, 1779.

Sixains. Satire on Palliser. Palliser wishes to punish Keppel only because Keppel is honest and brave.

79-66. [As list'ning to the wild waves solemn roar.]

"As list'ning to the wild waves solemn roar." (39)

L Eve Post, Feb 16, 1779.

HC. England's genius praises Keppel, who has been vindicated by the Portsmouth court-martial, January 12-February 11, 1779.

79-67. Ballad, Humbly Inscribed to Admiral Keppel.

"From his shining bed of coral." (48)

GA, Feb 4, 1779.

Ballad. Keppel is praised (from the grave) for his bravery and patriotism by all the old heroic naval chiefs -- Russel, Saunders, Blake, and Boscawen.

79-68. The Battle of Minden: A parody of "the joy-inspiring Horn," humbly dedicated to Lord G. Germaine.

"Hark! heroes, hark! the martial horn." (24)

Freeman's J, Jun 17, 1779.

Sixains. Satire on Germain for his cowardice at Minden. The English defeat the French badly at Minden, but Germain (Sackville) behaves cowardly and joins the battle when it is over.

79-69. Beelzebub Outwitted.

"Sly Beelzebub, with Wealth and Pride." (16)

PA, Apr 7, 1779; St J's C, Apr 10, 1779.

Ironic quatrains on the loss of commerce, the cause of luxury, thereby improving souls at the expense of prosperity and the devil. (The Patriot Opposition is right to criticize Government.)

79-70. Behold! the Brave Keppel.

"Quite steady, serene and calm." (14)

L Eve Post, Jan 30, 1779.

Quatrains and sixain. Defense of Keppel. Keppel is brave, Sandwich is fearful. The King is advised by Sandwich to support Palliser.

79-71. [The bells of ***** ding dong, dong ding.]

"The bells of ***** ding dong, dong ding." (32)

L Eve Post, Oct 2, 1779.

OC. Satire on the failure of the war with America. Bellmen are not earning any money because the bells are not ringing to celebrate victories, which do not occur. The King has lost an empire, and they their bread.

79-72. Both to Blame. An Epigram.

"Two witlings late discours'd, 'tis said by fame." (18)

GM 49 (Jun 1779), 318; WM 45 (Jul 7, 1779), 39.

HC. Two "witlings" complain of Keppel and Palliser, saying both are to blame; but "a reverend sage" decides the dispute by saying that in a matter of politics "ministers of state" should be allowed to "debate."

79-73. Britain's Address to her Sons on the Prorogation, 1779.

"'Tis done! The Senate's awful train." (40)

G, Jul 15, 1779.

Quatrains. Unanimity in the face of Britain's enemies is the requirement of the present hour.

79-74. Britannia and the Moth.

"The Moth around the Candle flies." (8)

PA, Sep 4, 1779; W Eve Post, Sep 2, 1779.

A simile. Quatrains. Britain, with respect to America, is like the moth and the candle flame. Both are destroyed.

79-75. Britannia Reviving.

"Her Lance inverted, Head reclin'd." (16)

West J, Aug 21, 1779.

Quatrains. Admirals Richard Howe, Keppel, and Robert Harland have restored Britannia's spirit, for now she has sovereignty over the seas again. (Written by "A Lover of Whig Admirals"!) Robert Harland was second-in-command under Keppel off Ushant, 1778-79.

79-76. Britannia. To her Militia at Coxheath Camp and Warley Common.

"When men like these defend their country's cause." (92)

G Eve Post, Jul 22, 1779; MP, Aug 3, 1779.

HC. Patriotic praise of the British soldier's life placed in the tradition of courageous action against France.

79-77. Britannia's Acknowledgement to Sir Charles Hardy, for his prudential Conduct.

"Rome in her Caesar, nurs'd a dauntless Chief." (4)

G Eve Post, Sep 18, 1779; MP, Sep 20, 1779.

HC. Admiral Sir Charles Hardy deserves praise for combining Caesar's fire with Fabius's judgment. By Causidicus of Cirencester. See "Verses, . . ." 78-A.

79-78. Britannia's Address to the People of England. To the Tune of "Hear me, gallant Sailor, hear me."

"Hear me, valiant Britons, hear me." (32)

L Chron 46 (Sep 16, 1779), 268; PA, Sep 17, 1779; St J's C, Sep 14, 1779.

A patriotic war song directed against France.

79-79. Britannia's Appeal to her Navy. Courage, Mes Amis!

"Did not high Heav'n of old the law ordain." (65)

G, Aug 17, 1779; G Eve Post, Aug 14, 1779; West J, Aug 21, 1779.

HC. Britannia urges her sons to fight courageously as of old, against the Bourbons.

79-80. The British Flag Triumphant. To the Tune of, To Britons I attune the Lyre.

"God of the Waves, great Neptune, smile." (36)

Lloyd's 44 (May 12, 1779), 461.

Song. Britain is badly defeating the French on the seas -- her India and Domingo fleets are captured, St. Lucia in the Caribbean is captured. Britain must not allow discord to interfere with the war.

79-81. The British Maiden's Remonstrance and Petition to Lord S[andwic]h.

"Sure never, my Lord, was a Time more distressing." (8)

PA, Jul 14, 1779.

Quatrains. A humorous objection to the practice of pressing (impressment) to man the fleets.

79-82. The British Oak. Tune, Hearts of Oak.

"Behold from afar, still for glory renown'd." (46)

Lloyd's 44 (Apr 77, 1779), 342; PA, Apr 7, 1779.

An anti-gallican naval song. Cited: "threats of invasion."

79-83. [Britons, awake! unsheath the blade.]

"Britons, awake! unsheath the blade." (20)

G, Sep 1, 1779; G Eve Post, Aug 31, 1779.

Quatrains. Another patriotic lyric directed against France and Spain.

79-84. By a Friend of the Late Captain Farmer's, just returned to England.

"Weep, Britons, weep, the irrevocable Doom." (10)

St J's C, Nov 9, 1779.

HC. Brave Capt. Farmer died bravely and will be remembered.

79-85. Catch, for the Times.

"The French are come, and Spaniards too." (12)

G Eve Post, Aug 24, 1779; Lloyd's 45 (Aug 25, 1779), 198; L Chron 46 (Aug 25, 1779), 195; SM 41 (Sep 1779), 502; WM 45 (Sep 8, 1779), 258.

Song. Quatrains. On the threatened French and Spanish invasion: should they try, they will rue it. But they have gone.

79-86. Catch for three Voices, to be performed before the Board of Admiralty, by the First Lord, &c. &c. The Tune, "'Twas you that kiss'd the pretty Girl, &c."

"'Twas you, Sir, 'twas you, Sir." (28)

GA, Feb 3, 1779; LM 48 (Feb 1779), 90; PA, Feb 4, 1779.

Satire on Palliser, who is blamed for poor sailing and improper behavior. Keppel is exonerated.

79-87. Catch, in a New Style. Composed for Jemmy Twitcher.

"Alack a day! what do I see." (12)

GA, Jan 14, 1779.

Song. Satire on Sandwich. Sandwich's "plot" against Keppel is now "unrav'ling." The allusion is to the court-martial.

79-88. Catch. The Stock Jobbers.

"New Loan! I sell! at sixty-one." (6)

G, Aug 14, 1779; G Eve Post, Aug 21, 1779; Lloyd's 45 (Aug 23, 1779), 188; L Chron 46 (Aug 21, 1779), 179; MP, Aug 24, 1779; St J's C, Aug 21, 1779; WM 45 (Sep 15, 1779), 279; West J, Aug 28, 1779.

Song. The Bulls and Bears have their way despite the war.

79-89. The Chace.

"Father. Tho' Monsieur shou'd invade, hand in hand with the don." (16)

L Cour, Dec 25, 1779.

Parody. Cantata. Satire on the King and his family enjoying a hunt while the empire is collapsing -- the Caribbean islands "going" and the American colonies "gone," and the Bourbons threatening invasion.

79-90. Characteristic Odes, Adapted to the Times. Ode 1. The British Soldier.

"Sluggards from my soul I scorn." (40)

W Eve Post, Oct 26, 1779.

Regular ode in quatrains, honoring the conquering British soldier, at a time when provoked by France to fight.

79-91. Characteristic Odes, Adapted to the Times. Ode III. The Satirist.

"In these bold, loose, licentious times." (70)

W Eve Post, Oct 30, 1779.

OC. The function of satire is to expose vice and folly, knaves and fools, particularly Nabobs from the East, corrupt ministers, and pampered peers.

79-92. Characteristic Odes, Adapted to the Times. Ode IV. The British Sailor.

"I'm sure that, like Boteler, I am not afraid." (24)

W Eve Post, Nov 2, 1779.

Regular ode in quatrains, honoring the British sailor for bravery in action against France. Cited are Boteler of the Ardent and Farmer of the Quebec.

79-93. Characteristic Odes, Adapted to the Times. Ode VII. The British Heroine.

"Can a Woman of Spirit, inactive, behold." (32)

W Eve Post, Nov 23, 1779.

Regular ode in quatrains. A feminist poem. In times of great danger, women can also fight bravely for the country.

79-94. [Chearful Peace is fled afar.]

"Chearful Peace is fled afar." (60)

GA, Feb 11, 1779.

OC. The country needs leaders like Keppel at this critical time, not like Palliser.

79-95. Chubby Chubb: An Ode.

"Chubb, Father of the Sceptic Band." (24)

PA, Jul 24, 1779.

Regular ode in sixains. Satire on Gibbon, recently appointed Commissioner of Trade and Plantations. Chubb was a deist. Gibbon is satirized for leaving the Whigs and accepting a place.

79-96. Col. M'Carmick's Invitation to his Country-men; Or, A Challenge to France and Spain. (To the Tune of, Social Powers.)

"Come, my Lads, and serve the King." (20)

MP, Oct 5, 1779.

A patriotic recruiting song. The nation needs soldiers in the war against France and Spain.

79-97. The Comparison; Or, What's the Difference?

"As Tom Bowline was prowling the streets with his gang." (18)

GM 49 (Oct 1779), 509; PA, Sep 25, 1779; W Eve Post, Sep 23, 1779.

Anapest tetrameter couplets. There is no difference between the French Lettre de Cachet and the English Press Warrant; both simply deprive men of their liberty.

79-98. The Complaint [and] The Consolation.

"Branded, like Cain, ah! whither can I turn." (4 + 4)

L Eve Post, Feb 20, 1779; LP, Feb 22, 1779; PA, Feb 20, 1779.

Extempore. Satire on Palliser. Palliser complains of loss of reputation and the burning of his house and effigy; but he should be consoled with the friendship of Sandwich and Germain, Henry Bate (editor of the Morning Post) and John Strutt (the only MP to oppose the February 18 Commons vote of thanks to Keppel for his services).

79-99. Comte D'Estaing's Address to General Prevost: In Imitation of Punch's Address to Minos.

"You soon will know by my Slang, Sir." (33)

MP, Dec 27, 1779; PA, Dec 28, 1779.

Satire on D'Estaing whose persona threatens General Prevost, in Savannah, with extermination unless he surrenders. (It must be remembered, of course, that Prevost blunted the Franco-American attack.)

79-100. Congratulatory Ode, addressed to William Wyndham, Esq; of Felbrigg, Norfolk.

"To Wyndham tune no venal Lyre." (90)

PA, Jan 22, 1779; UM 64 (Jan 1779), 41-2; New Foundling Hospital for Wit (1786), II, 124-6; Jeffery Dunstan, Fugitive Pieces (1789), pp. 104-8.

Regular (Horatian) ode in sixains. Praise of Windham of the Patriot Opposition, with Burke, Cavendish, Savile, and Townshend. Reviews the Keppel-Palliser episode from the Patriot position; attacks the bishops who support the war.

79-101. The Contrast.

"America (tho' wrong) yet merits Fame." (6)

PA, Dec 22, 1779.

Extempore. Sixain. America's behavior, contrasted with Ireland's, is noble.

79-102. A Conversation between the One and the Other.

"Jemmy! I sent for you to tell you we must part." (48)

PA, May 15, 1779.

Blank verse. On the Earl of Sandwich who defends himself from accusations of vice, and expresses remorse over his betrayal of Wilkes. Allusion to Wilkes, Sir Frances Dashwood, and the so-called Medmenham Monks and their orgies.

79-103. A Critical Ode, Addressed to Mr. Mason.

"Well, Sir, in Milton let us look." (120)

M Chron, May 20, 1779.

Regular (Horatian) ode in sixains. A criticism of Mason's Ode to the Naval Officers of Great-Britain (1779), in Stanza 15, ll. 85-90: see 79-22.

The Defeat of D'Estaing at Savannah. See Freeth, "British Arms Triumphant," 79-193.

79-104. The Desponding Frenchman. A New Song.

"What a pother is here about leaving of Brest!" (32)

G, Jul 20, 1779; G Eve Post, Jul 27, 1779; L Chron 46 (Jul 20, 1779), 69.

Satire on the French. The French tars are made to complain of English effectiveness in naval battle and of Spanish ineffectiveness. Ushant is cited.

79-105. A Dialogue between Dean Tucker and the Devil; occasioned by a late Publication, entitled "Thoughts on the Present Posture of Affairs."

"The Dean and Devil, in free conversation." (26)

L Eve Post, Aug 12, 1779; LP, Aug 27, 1779.

Anapest tetrameter couplets. The Rev. Josiah Tucker believes that the French will not invade. Cited are Congress, Saratoga, Independence, Bunker's Hill, and Richard Price. (Tucker argued for colonial independence in previous pamphlets.) See "On Dean Tucker's Address," 79-327.

79-106. A Dialogue between Lord N[orth] and a Great Person.

"N----. Believe me, great Sir, what I say is most true." (12)

L Eve Post, Sep 2, 1779.

Hexameter couplets. North advises the King to take Dean Tucker's advice -- get Mansfield to indict and try the Whigs as rebels, "Republicans vile."

79-107. A Dialogue between the K[ing], Ministers of Great Britain, and Echo.

"S[andwic]h. Behold my pride, my boasted fleet, in safety ride in port." (22)

GA, Sep 11, 1779.

Fourteeners. Scepticism about the optimistic plans of the ministry -- e.g., North's hope of subduing America, Germain's assertion of bravery and willingness to lead the troops against America, and Sandwich's boast that the fleet is invincible.

79-108. Difference of Swallow. Scotch Thistle Broth.

"An Ass will mumble thistles, though not bite." (2 + 2)

L Eve Post, Aug 19, 1779.

Two extempores. Satire on the Scotch, whom King George favors. Bute is cited.

79-109. Dirge for the Peaching Admiral. Chevy Chace.

"The night was black! the tempest roar'd." (20)

L Eve Post, Feb 18, 1779.

Parody on the Chevy Chace ballad. Satire on Palliser for his attempt to ruin Keppel: Palliser is made to commit suicide.

Dodd, J. S. See "Prologue to the new Comedy of Gaelic Gratitude, or the Frenchmen in India," 79-382.

79-110. Dull Verses on a late preaching, teaching, retching, pining, whining, DECLINING, Justifying MEMORIAL.

"When Gibbon blots th' Historic Page." (6)

PA, Nov 11, 1779.

Sixain. Satire on Gibbon's *Memoire Justificatif* -- a sceptic in religion and a Methodist in politics.

79-111. Dunce's Den.

"Alas, O Britons! of what now can you boast!" (28)

WM 46 (Sep 29, 1779), 16.

HC. Britons must resolve to respond to the Bourbon insult of sending their combined fleet to sail by Plymouth.

79-112. The Durham Militia Ballad. Written on the additional Battalion to be forthwith raised by Subscription, &c.

"Our Country now calls, my brave Boys, let us arm." (44 + chorus)

St J's C, Aug 28, 1779.

A patriotic song with "Derry down" chorus, meant to inspire the Durham militia against a French invasion.

79-113. [Each Heart to incite.]

"Each Heart to incite." (30)

PA, Sep 29, 1779.

Regular ode in sixains. A patriotic lyric on Britain's just war.

79-114. The Election.

"In our Forefathers Days." (18)

PA, Oct 20, 1779.

Sixains. North learned from Sir Robert Walpole that "every Man [has] his Price."

79-115. Elizabeth's Reply to her People.

"Thanks, loving subjects! in whose loyal hearts." (18)

G Eve Post, Aug 12, 1779; West J, Aug 21, 1779; W Eve Post, Aug 12, 1779.

Song from a "Musical Piece" entitled "The Prophecy." A patriotic lyric that recalls the British defeat of the French at Cressy and Agincourt, and of the Spanish Armada.

79-116. The Encampments.

"Now the British Boys with Spirit." (24)

G Eve Post, Jul 3, 1779; PA, Jul 5, 1779; W Eve Post, Jul 3, 1779.

Quatrains. In praise of the militia gone to camps to prepare for the war with France and Spain.

79-117. England's Wish, for 1779.

"May firmest union in our councils sit." (9)

G, Jul 8, 1779; G Eve Post, Jul 6, 1779.

HC. The poet hopes for unanimity in the struggle against the country's enemies, as in 1759 when guided by Pitt.

79-118. Epigram.

"Great George, whose Virtues well are known." (6)

PA, Jun 9, 1779; W Eve Post, Jun 9, 1779.

Sixain. The nation has a greater claim to virtue than the King.

79-119. Epigram.

"Hawke in a Tempest, dared the Gallic Shore." (6)

PA, Feb 24, 1779.

HC. Praise of Palliser, despite his defeat off Ushant, July 27, 1778. (After the acquittal of Keppel of the charges brought against him by Palliser, this epigram is probably most ironical.)

79-120. Epigram.

"The King, who is Minister, Senate, and all." (2)

L Cour, Dec 10, 1779.

Couplet. Satire on the King for dominating the cabinet and Parliament.

79-121. Epigram.

"Louis, Most Christian King, declares." (12)

G, Jul 24, 1779; Lloyd's 45 (Jul 23, 1779), 84.

Sixains. A warning to the French King and to his allies, the Spaniards, to beware defeat by England.

79-122. Epigram.

"The Patriot N[orth], twelve years in place." (12)

G, Jul 17, 1779; PA, Jul 16, 1779.

Quatrains. Praise of Lord North, a model of honesty and integrity for "courtiers."

79-123. An Epigram.

"Poor Palliser has play'd a losing Game." (6)

PA, May 5, 1779.

HC. Palliser should die, or his honor and places restored.

79-124. Epigram.

"A Rocket, the true court machine." (8)

MP, Sep 14, 1779.

Quatrains. Satire on Keppel. Keppel's integrity and reputation will quickly disappear, like a rocket.

79-125. Epigram.

"Say, when will England be from Faction freed." (4)

GA, Apr 8, 1779.

Quatrain. England will be freed from "Faction" and "Domestic Quarrels" only when Bute dies.

79-126. An Epigram.

"Says Infidelity to Chubby." (12)

PA, Jul 29, 1779.

Sixains. Criticism of Gibbon for giving up principle by accepting the place of Lord Commissioner of Trade.

79-127. An Epigram.

"Ungrateful Keppel, whither drives thy Speed." (4)

PA, May 5, 1779.

HC. Lines against Keppel for being severe with Palliser.

79-128. An Epigram.

"When *Chubby Chubb*, more proud than wise." (12)

PA, Oct 30, 1779.

Sixains. Scatological satire on Gibbon for attempting to imitate Johnson's literary style in his Memoire Justificatif.

79-129. An Epigram.

"When Gibbon late, in his Decline." (12)

PA, Oct 23, 1779.

Sixains. Gibbon is damned for accepting a place on the Board of Trade.

79-130. An Epigram.

"When red-heel'd Carlisle and the Scottish Laird." (6)

PA, Feb 1, 1779.

HC. The Peace Commissioners, Carlisle and Eden, were told they "might go all to H-LL" by the Americans.

79-131. [Epigram. Imitation of Martial, VI, 19.]

"The Question as all Europe sees." (12)

PA, Mar 16, 1779.

OC. The problem is how to regain the colonies, as Whigs (Luttrell) and Tories (Rigby) disagree.

79-132. Epigram. Occasioned by the Question at the Court Martial, "Did Admiral Keppel tarnish the Lustre of the Navy?"

"To give Lustre, and cause all our Navy to shine." (4)

St J's C, Feb 18, 1779.

Epigram. After Keppel's trial and acquittal. Satire on Keppel for his failure to fight the French.

79-133. Epigram on a late Speech.

"Joe scann'd it o'er, and seem'd provok'd." (12)

LP, Dec 13, 1779.

OC. An expression of shock that the King in his address to the new Parliament failed to show concern for America -- evidence of British weakness and inability to save the empire.

79-134. An Epigram on Sir Hugh Palliser.

"From Keppel's defence, it doth plainly appear." (11)

GA, Mar 17, 1779.

Anapest tetrameter couplets. Satire on Palliser for being blind and deaf, failing to see the signal and to hear the order.

79-135. Epigram. On the death of Captain Farmer, of the Quebec, who was blown up with his ship in an engagement with a French frigate, Oct. 6, 1779.

"Thus saints and heroes, sacred and profane." (4)

"Thy name, Quebec, these grateful isles revere." (4)

GM 49 (Oct 1779), 512; LP, Nov 1, 1779; PA, Nov 3, 1779; St J's C, Oct 30, 1779.

Two epigrams (or epitaphs) mourn the death of unlucky Farmer whose victory was snatched by death. (He was killed when his ship suddenly blew up. See 79-144.)

79-136. An Epigram. On the Late Rejoicings.

"Ye courtly Heroes, who so boldly vote." (8)

PA, Feb 20, 1779.

HC. Rejoices at Keppel's acquittal and then attacks the Carlisle Commission (Johnstone, Eden, and Carlisle) threatening to dismember America.

79-137. An Epigram. On the Proclamation for a Fast.

"When British Arms, in Anna's Reign." (8)

PA, Dec 18, 1779.

Quatrains. This third fast should bring results -- thanksgiving upon the defeat of France.

79-138. An Epigram. On the Vote passed by the City for presenting to Admiral Keppel an Oak Box with their Freedom.

"As Selwin and Gibbon were talking with Fox." (8)

MP, Dec 13, 1779; PA, Dec 14, 1779.

Anapest tetrameter couplets. Satire on those (Fox) who would have London offer the Freedom of the City to Keppel. George Selwin does not wish to do so.

79-139. An Epigram. To Vice Admiral Sir Hugh Palliser on his Conduct in the Action with the French Fleet on the 27th July last [1778].

"Ne'er shall a thousand windows blaze." (6)

MP, May 8, 1779.

Sixain. A reflection on Palliser's court-martial trial, April 12-May 5, 1779. Keppel was prudent, but Palliser was brave. (This difference in behavior may explain the basis of the quarrel between Palliser and Keppel.)

Epigram. Upon Edw. Gibbon, Esq; . . . being made a Lord of Trade. See "Upon Edward Gibbon, Esq;" 79-501.

79-140. Epigrams. On the King. On Lord G. G. On Lord Sandwich.

"Of thirteen provinces, poor G----- bereft." (2 + 2 + 2)

GA, May 21, 1779.

Three epigrams on King George, Germain, and Sandwich. The King does not have thirteen children to compensate for the loss of the thirteen provinces.

79-141. Epigrams on the Late Trial of Admiral Keppel.

"Keppel Loquitur." Etc. (7 in all) (34)

West M 7 (Feb 1779), 110.

Seven epigrams, some having been recorded already. All honor Keppel but attack Palliser for cowardice. See 79-217, 79-219.

79-142. An Epistle to Sir H[ugh] P[alliser]. From a Foremastman in the Fleet.

"Gentle Sir Hugh, now tell me why." (28)

GA, Feb 8, 1779.

Quatrains. Palliser's behavior in an apparent conspiracy formed to ruin Keppel is questioned.

79-143. An Epitaph for a certain Admiral. Addressed to the Hon. Augustus K[eppe]l.

"Pass over the reliques deposited here." (40)

MP, Dec 30, 1779.

Anapest tetrameter couplets. A satire on Keppel, reviewing the whole business of the Ushant engagement, his association with Opposition, his use by Opposition to subvert Government, and his Whig Republican allies.

79-144. Epitaph for Captain Farmer.

"Too oft has Pride an unmourn'd Tablet rais'd." (4)

St J's C, Nov 13, 1779.

HC. Capt. Farmer's lost remains survive in British hearts. (Capt. Farmer, the Quebec, engaged Monsieur de Couedic, Commander of the Surveillante, off Ushant, October 6, 1779.) See 79-135.

79-145. Epitaph [for George Augustus, Viscount Keppel].

"Here is entomb'd the dust of / Augustus Van Keppel." (c. 25)

M Chron, Aug 31, 1779.

Inscription. A severe indictment of Keppel for taking up with "a desperate faction" and betraying his country. (A prose response appeared in M Chron, Sept. 1, 1779.) This inscription is supposed to match the attack on Howe, "Inscription on a monument," 79-228.

79-146. [Epitaph.] In Eternal Memory of G[eorge] A[ugustus] K[eppel].

"Know indignant Reader." (c. 25)

MP, Sep 6, 1779.

Inscription. Another epitaph on Keppel like the preceding. An attack on Keppel for protecting America, for being a part of a faction dignifying rebellion and debasing the nation, etc. See "Epitaph [George Augustus, Viscount Keppel]," 79-145.

79-147. Epitaph in Memory of [England's] once flourishing Existence.

"Behold! Here lyeth a Nation." (c. 6)

PA, Jan 26, 1779.

Inscription. After providing reasons that the American War cannot be won and declaring that even if the Americans were defeated it would mean loss of liberties at home, the writer concludes with an epitaph predicting collapse of the nation because of corruption and maladministration.

79-148. Epitaph. On the Honourable Colonel Maitland.

"When Gallic perfidy, and Rebel pride." (8)

DJ, Jan 15, 1780; G Eve Post, Jan 8, 1780; SM 41 (Dec 1779), 684; WM 47 (Jan 7, 1780), 53; W Eve Post, Jan 6, 1780.

Quatrains. Maitland dashed with his troops from Beaufort, N. C., to Savannah, Ga., only to die repelling the combined Franco-American attack. He had saved Savannah for the British.
This epitaph differs from Colvill's "To the Immortal Memory of the Hon. Colonel John Maitland," 80-74, 89-1. See Stud. in Scot. Lit. 17 (1982), 87-8.

79-149. Epitaph: On the Writer of the Epitaph on G. A. V. K.

"Here lies, / Consign'd to infamy." (c. 10)

M Chron, Sep 9, 1779.

An answer in defense of George Augustus Van Keppel's character to the political attacks on Keppel in the M Chron Aug. 31, 1779, and MP Oct. 6, 1779. See these, 79-145 and 79-146.

79-150. Extempore.

"Chactaws, Chicksaws, and Catabaws." (12)

PA, Jul 27, 1779.

Quatrains. Britain will persevere against all her enemies, including Indians.

79-151. Extempore.

"'D[amn] these Frenchmen,' cries a Briton." (4)

PA, Sep 4, 1779.

Quatrain. A complaint by those impatient to get on with the war against France. This is answered by a wish to "Call back the Ghost of Chatham."

79-152. Extempore.

"Gallant Britons, join your Arms." (12)

G Eve Post, Aug 24, 1779; PA, Aug 25, 1779.

Quatrains. In the past Britons "maul'd" the French and will do so again.

79-153. Extempore.

"In George the Second's gallant days." (12)

L Eve Post, Jul 20, 1779; PA, Jul 22, 1779.

Quatrains. North has lost what George II had won. North is only capable of naval and military reviews. We should really begin to <u>fight</u> the French.

79-154. An Extempore.

"In spight of haughty Bourbon's union." (4)

MP, Jun 23, 1779.

Couplets. Despite the alliance of Roman Catholic France and Spain, England will be well protected by its admirals Byron, Howe, and Hardy.

79-155. Extempore.

"John Bull, a Squire of Eminence and Worth." (8)

PA, May 26, 1779.

HC. Satire on the Scotch, the abettors of the American War. The cure for

Britain's problems with the colonies -- war -- is worse than the disease.

79-156. An Extempore.

"Our men at the helm deserve laurels of flax." (2)

GA, Jun 4, 1779.

HC. An objection to increased taxes.

79-157. An Extempore.

"Our Men at the Helm, not an Inch will relax." (2)

PA, Mar 20, 1779.

Couplet -- anapest tetrameter. The administration relentlessly imposes taxes on the nation. No relief is in sight.

79-158. An Extempore.

"Quebec! a lov'd and yet a fatal sound." (4)

G Eve Post, Nov 16, 1779; MP, Nov 17, 1779.

HC. Quebec, Captain Farmer's ship, recalls Wolfe's death, and now is "Again ennobled by brave Farmer's name."

79-159. Extempore.

"Since Tyranny's become a Trade." (8)

PA, Aug 7, 1779; W Eve Post, Aug 5, 1779.

Epigram. Quatrains. Women wish to fight, too, and do not fear impressment. See "[Well, since I've thus succeeded in my plan]," 79-512, to which this poem, with its sexual pun, may be an answer.

79-160. Extempore.

"Tell me not of idle Dreaming." (20)

PA, Sep 4, 1779.

Quatrains. The British seamen will defeat France and Spain.

79-161. Extempore.

"'Tis a whimsical war we are waging with France." (12)

L Chron 46 (Aug 26, 1779), 195; W Eve Post, Sep 2, 1779.

Quatrains. The naval war between Britain and France is taking a long time to begin.

79-162. Extempore.

"To gratify a restless Nation." (4)

PA, Sep 11, 1779.

Quatrain. Satire on Sandwich, who has failed to build up the English navy.

79-163. Extempore.

"To invade Old England, France and Spain." (8)

G Eve Post, Sep 7, 1779; MP, Sep 9, 1779.

OC. The combined fleets of France and Spain sailed across the Channel and back again, lacking courage to fight Hardy's forces.

79-164. Extempore.

"Unhappy Kep. severe tho' just thy lot." (6)

MP, Sep 16, 1779.

HC. Satire on Keppel, who is neglected and forgotten -- a severe though just fate.

79-165. Extempore.

"When Britain first, by Heaven's Command." (12)

PA, Jun 9, 1779; W Eve Post, Jun 9, 1779.

Quatrains. Satire on Lord North's resort to bribery, and his responsibility for the nation's loss of "public Credit."

79-166. Extempore.

"When William reign'd Religion shone." (8)

PA, Jun 10, 1779; W Eve Post, Jun 8. 1779.

Quatrains. Epigram. The reign of George III is noted for increased taxes, but neither peace nor war.

79-167. Extempore.

"Whilst Britain's wrangling Sons debate." (8)

PA, May 26, 1779.

Quatrains. Britain's leadership is confused; the nation is in hell.

79-168. [Extempore.] Another.

"His Grace of Richmond, and his Coals." (8)

PA, Jun 9, 1779.

Quatrains. Richmond's source of wealth, his coal mines, has enabled him to buy hack writers, "many a partial Pen." Only Truth suffers from their abuse.

79-169. Extempore Lines on Hearing the Report of Count D'Estaing's being lost in a Storm, on the Coast of America.

"Escap'd from the Gibbet for Breach of Parole." (6)

PA, Dec 21, 1779.

Anapest tetrameter couplets. Epigram. D'Estaing will never be drowned, because he is born to be hanged.

79-170. An Extempore. On a Late Memorable Engagement between Admiral Keppel and Count D'Orvilliers, wherein each party obtained a negative victory.

"Two Naval Commanders their banners display." (4)

MP, Feb 18, 1779.

Satire on Keppel and his acquittal. Ironic comment on the indecisive engagement between Keppel's naval forces and Count D'Orvillier's fleet. Neither merits praise.

79-171. Extempore. On a Noble L[or]d's falling asleep in a Great As[sembl]y. By a Member of Opposition who was present.

"To rouze that sleeping L--d no Effort make." (2)

PA, Mar 20, 1779.

HC. On Lord North's habit of sleeping during Parliamentary speeches. The Opposition MP wishes North would never wake.

79-172. An Extempore. On Admiral Keppel.

"Full forty years a British tar." (4)

MP, Apr 8, 1779.

Quatrain. Keppel deserves no illuminations (celebration).

79-173. An Extempore. On Mr. Fox's Motions.

"A Fox was th'animal that Sampson chose." (8)

MP, Mar 15, 1779.

Hexameter couplets. The Whig Fox's attempts to criticize Government are as ineffective as the abortive attempts to destroy the nation by John the Painter.

79-174. An Extempore. On Reading in the Gazette the different conduct of the British and Spanish Commanders in the late Affair of Fort Omoa.

"When Nugent's sword was given in the field." (4)

MP, Dec 21, 1779.

Quatrain. The Britons treat their prisoners humanely; the Spanish cruelly.

79-175. Extempore. On Reading in the Morning Post of the 7th Instant of an expected Invasion.

"Why this foolish false alarm." (12)

MP, Oct 13, 1779.

OC. The alarm because of a threatened invasion is foolish: Britons will never retreat before the French and Spaniards, because there is nothing to fear from them.

79-176. Extempore. On Reading the Names of the Minority Lords who subscribed the PROTEST, as published in the 4th Page of this Paper of Monday the 21st of May 1779.

"Here Richmond heads protesting Peers." (4)

PA, Jun 25, 1779.

Quatrain. Epigram. Richmond and the protesting lords of the Minority are foolish.

79-177. An Extempore. On the ever memorable Action between the British and Gallic Fleets, on the 27th of July, 1778.

"Great D'Orvilliers, great Kep. did beat." (8)

MP, Jul 29, 1779.

Octave, alternating rhymes. Ironic comment on the indecisive Ushant engagement between D'Orvilliers and Keppel on July 27, 1778 (which resulted in the courts-martial of Keppel and Palliser).

79-178. An Extempore. On the Late Illuminations.

"Keppel, is this your patriot zeal." (6)

MP, Feb 19, 1779.

OC. Satire on Keppel for his failure to beat the French. Ironic comment on the indecisive engagement between the forces of Keppel and Count D'Orvilliers. Keppel does not deserve praise.

79-179. An Extempore. On the late Illuminations.

"Our Mob huzza! -- with candles we must treat 'em." (4)

MP, Feb 15, 1779.

Satire on Keppel and his acquittal. An ironic reaction to the indecisive engagement between the English fleet under Keppel and the French fleet under Count D'Orvilliers.

79-180. An Extempore. Supposed to be spoken by Liberty.

"Great pity that Cities, renown'd for their Wit." (4)

MP, May 26, 1779.

Anapest tetrameter couplets. Satire on those cities rewarding Keppel with the Gold Box of Freedom, especially when Keppel sold out liberty. (London was one of these cities.)

79-181. An Extempore. To Lord North. On Reading the Paper this Evening.

"From stinking bogs, perfumes new strength acquire." (8)

MP, Nov 10, 1779.

HC. North looks good in contrast with his opponents. (Although precisely why, it is not clear!)

79-182. An Extempore. To the Fools Who lately Illuminated.

"Why all those candles, all that blaze." (4)

MP, Mar 30, 1779.

Quatrain. Keppel deserves no praise, no celebration, for he was not victorious over France like Admirals Barrington and Vernon.

79-183. An Extempore. Upon his G[rac]e of R[ichmon]d's Indisposition.

"A Disease of the mind, as the learned agree." (4)

MP, Feb 26, 1779.

Vulgar satire on the Duke of Richmond (of the Opposition) for being ill at the news of British victories in Georgia and St. Lucie.

79-184. The Fair American.

"From those unhappy shores where British blood." (20)

T&C 11 (Nov 1779), 607.

Elegiac quatrains. Praise of a beautiful young female American loyalist who has come to England for safety because of the rebellion.

79-185. The Fall of Opposition. A Tragedy.

"Lelaps. The dawn of Liberty is overcast." (96 + 126)

MP, Jul 31 & Aug 31, 1779.

Blank verse mini-tragedy in two installments ("Never concluded"). About Roman politicians but really about the English political scene of the time. The Opposition is maligned as republican and unprincipled malcontents.

79-186. A Favourite New Ballad which they sing at Portsmouth.

"Come listen every honest tar." (40)

M Chron, Jan 29, 1779.

Ballad narrates the source of the conflict between "Whig and Tory," Keppel and Palliser, and Sandwich: the inconclusive battle and the aftermath, the trial of Keppel.

79-187. A Favourite New Song. Sung in Plymouth.

"Ye Devonshire lads, and ye lasses." (32)

G, Aug 31, 1779; G Eve Post, Aug 26, 1779; L Eve Post, Aug 28, 1779; WM 45 (Sep 8, 1779), 258.

Humorous song. With their challenge, Plymouth women frighten the combined fleets of France and Spain so that they do not invade, but instead they return to their home ports.

79-188. The following lines were written by a young Lady on the night of the general illuminations and rejoicing for the honourable acquittal of Admiral Keppel.

"May every false ungrateful heart." (6)

GA, Mar 11, 1779.

OC.  Palliser deserves punishment, Keppel praise and fame.

The following Song was Introduced in the new Entertainment called The Liverpool Prize.  "Behold upon the swelling wave."  (23)  See "The Hyaena," 79-211.

79-189.  The following verses on the appearance of the combined fleets off Plymouth were written by a young man lately elected from our first publick school to the university. . . .

"Constitit Anglorum Genius turbatus ad oram."  (24)

GM 49 (Sep 1779), 463.

A Latin poem.  Translated as "Verses on the Appearance of the Combined Fleets being seen off Plymouth."  See 79-507.

79-190.  The following Verses were written by a young school-boy . . . [and] express the sentiments of the better sort of people in the metropolis.

"Had British Hawke been sent to fight."  (8)

MP, Mar 5, 1779.

Quatrains critical of Keppel's indecisive engagement with the French fleet.

79-191.  For the King's Birth-Day.

"Hail to George's natal Day."  (24)

W Eve Post, Jun 3, 1779.

Quatrains.  Relates the birthday celebrations with the Revolution when William of Nassau helped establish the Brunswick line.

79-192.  [France and Spain unite together.]

"France and Spain unite together."  (14)

M Chron, Nov 3, 1779.

Quatrains.  The Bourbon allies can be defeated by British courage.

79-193.  Freeth, John.

British Arms Triumphant. Or D'Estaing's Defeat at Savannah. A New Song, by an Old Soldier. Tune, Over the Hills, and far away.

"Hark! from o'er the Western Main." (31)

Lloyd's 46 (Jan 26, 1780), 92; WM 47 (Jan 17, 1780), 207. Freeth, Modern Songs on Various Subjects (1782), pp. 3-4, & The Political Songster (1790), p. 36.

In Freeth's collections, this song is entitled "The Defeat of D'Estaing at Savannah."
The song celebrates the repulse by the forces under British General Prevost of the combined French and American attack on Savannah, October 9, 1779, led by D'Estaing and Lincoln. The song treats the episode as a French defeat and mentions only D'Estaing.

79-194. [Freeth, John.]
The British Lion: A Song.

"The Lion of England, a score years ago." (32)

L Eve Post, Nov 23, 1779.

Song. In the past, France feared England; but now, a few years later, the situation is reversed. The Scotch are to blame, and Germain and Sandwich of the ministry.

79-195. Freeth, John.
Col. Keating's Birmingham Volunteers. Song. Tune, Jolly Mortals fill your Glasses.

"Jolly Sons of mirth and spirit." (24)

Lloyd's 45 (Sep 20, 1779), 284; PA, Sep 23, 1779.

Birmingham loyally supports the war against France and Spain with a volunteer regiment.

79-196. Freeth, John.
Jemmy Twitcher and Jolly Dick: A Song.

"Two statesmen, who were seldom known." (52)

L Eve Post, Feb 13, 1779; John Freeth, Modern Songs, On Various Subjects (1782), pp. 18-20.

Signed "F." -- John Freeth. Ballad satirizes Richard Rigby and Sandwich on their way of spending the Fast Day, with comments on hypocrisy.

79-197. Freeth, John.
Paul Jones: A Song. Tune, -- "Stick a pin there."

"Of heroes and statesmen I'll just mention four." (20)

L Eve Post, Oct 12, 1779; Freeth, Modern Songs on Various Subjects (1782), pp. 10-11; Freeth, The Political Songster (1784), pp. 19-20.

Song in quatrains of couplets. Merchants suffer as a result of Jones's privateering. However, contractors are pirates, too; and Germain, North, and Sandwich match him in infamy. See Freeth, 82-10.

[Freeth, John.] Song sung at Vauxhall, by Mr. Vernon, and set to Music by Mr. Heron. "Come, ye lads who wish to shine." (28) L Chron 45 (Jun 24, 1779), 605; UM 64 (Supp 1779), 375. Also G Eve Post, Jun 22, 1779. See Freeth, "Britannia's Call to her Sons," 78-211.

79-198. [Freeth, John.]
A Song, To the Tune of The Jolly Young Waterman. By the Author of Come ye Lads who wish to shine, &c.

"In spite of a treacherous base combination." (24)

G Eve Post, Jul 13, 1779; Lloyd's 45 (Jul 9, 1779), 36.

A song on the threatened French invasion. Britain is united as "Party, Contention, and Discord are dying."

79-199. A French Invasion -- a mere Goose-Chace Enterprise.

"Were Broglio's mighty Host to land." (12)

PA, Sep 4, 1779.

Epigram in sixains. Satire. Geese will help guard the land from French invasion.

79-200. Fugitive Verses. To Administration: To those who rule and do not rule the roast.

"God bless you, now you all are met." (94)

LM 48 (Apr 1779), 186; PA, Jan 28, 1779; SM 41 (Jan 1779), 46; WM 43 (Feb 17, 1779), 183.

OC. Satire on the placemen obedient to Lord North; and on the Opposition interested only in plunder. Cited are Jenkinson, Rigby, Welbore Ellis, and Grey Cooper; and Burke, Barre, and Keppel.

79-201. A Gasconade. Translated from the French.

"Lewis, with sixty-sail, sought Britain's shore." (6)

St J's C, Aug 24, 1779.

HC. Two satires on the threatened French invasion of England, which failed to materialize.

79-202. A General Toast, in Imitation of the Song in the School for Scandal.

"Here's to great North, at the helm so serene." (24)

L Eve Post, Oct 26, 1779; LM 48 (Nov 1779), 520; LP, Nov 1, 1779; WM 46 (Dec 15, 1779), 280.

Song. Satiric toast to ministers and courtiers -- North, Mansfield, Germain, Fletcher Norton, Rigby, and others, as well as John Wesley -- and the hope that they will be "swinging together."

79-203. A Glee. In Honour of the renowned Admiral Keppel.

"Ned Boscawen, 'tis true." (12)

PA, Mar 3, 1779.

Song. Perhaps ironic on Keppel's defeat of Palliser, because of the protest against Keppel's friends who broke the windows of the house belonging to the wife of the late Admiral Boscawen.

79-204. Governor Johnstone [and] Keppel.

"'Tis too apparent, in this age of vice." (8)

MP, Apr 23, 1779.

Two epigrams. On Johnstone, who has been bribed, and on Keppel, a Patriot who has lost his good reputation.

79-205. The Halcyon Days of Old England; or the Wisdom of Administration demonstrated. A Ballad.

"Come list to my song, I'll not tell you a story." (48 + chorus)

L Cour, Dec 31, 1779; L Eve Post, Dec 30, 1779; LP, Dec 31, 1779.

Song. Satire on the ministry for failing to conduct the American War wisely and effectively. Also reviews the American controversy leading to the war -- tea, taxes, the attrition, the Indians, the failures of the campaigns. Additions to the 1777 version include remarks on the failure of the navy to engage the Bourbon fleets, the resignations of Howe and Burgoyne, the stupidity of the King. See the earlier form in L Eve Post, Dec 25, 1777: 77-144.

79-206. Hark! Britannia sounds the Trump of War.

"Exert your Pow'rs, ye Sons of Might." (12)

PA, Jun 25, 1779.

Quatrains. The politicians must unite "In Britain's rightful Cause" and unanimously pursue the war, "For Honour and for Peace."

79-207. Hastings, Thomas.
An Ode for the Birth-Day of his Royal Highness the Prince of Wales.

"'Twas when the guardian tribes round Albion's shore." (52)

M Chron, Aug 12, 1779.

Pindaric ode, oratorio, honoring those who are in the military camps protecting Britain from France and Spain.

79-208. The Honest Tar's Double Wish.

"Come, here's to the Vice of the Blue." (12)

MP, Sep 15, 1779.

Sixains. Praise of Palliser; criticism of Keppel for his failure at Ushant.

79-209. Hor. Ode XII. Lib 1. Adapted to the Present Times, -- and addressed to that Elegant and Courtly Historian and Poet E[DWAR]D G[I]BB[O]N, Esq;

"What Minister or clerk in Place." (78)

PA, Nov 25, 1779.

Imitation of Horace. Ode in sixains. Satire encompassing the times and figures such as Gen. Howe, Gen. Burgoyne, and Admiral Keppel. Their failures are rewarded, the poet exclaims in disgust, and he concludes with a prayer for divine guidance in the crisis.

79-210. [How blest are we seamen! how jovial, how gay!]

"How blest are we seamen! how jovial, how gay!" (21)

G, Sep 6, 1779.

Patriotic naval song. The brave, jolly British tars will fight to the death for their country.

79-211. The Hyaena. Inscribed to the Girls of Gainsborough. By Captain E. Thompson.

"Behold upon the swelling wave." (24 + chorus)

GA, Mar 3, 1779; Lloyd's 44 (Mar 3, 1779), 220; L Chron 45 (Mar 2, 1779), 212; M Chron, Mar 1, 1779; MP, Mar 3 & Oct 8, 1779; St J's C, Oct 5, 1779.

A popular song about privateering, which was also the concluding pendant of F. Pilon's farce or entertainment, The Liverpool Prize (London: Evans, 1779), pp. 40-1, with the added stanza on Keppel. This stanza pictures Keppel again assuming the direction of the navy (after his trial and acquittal). The last stanza declares war against France and the world, but asks for peace with America. The Hyaena was the name of the frigate commanded by Thompson.

79-212. [I think, when in a former reign.]

"I think, when in a former reign." (8)

Cumb Pacq, Jan 19, 1779.

Quatrains. The coming third fast will not be followed by a thanksgiving for success, like the fasts during the war with France in the reign of George II.

79-213. An Idyllion on Content. Inscribed to a Lady at Philadelphia.

"Oh, when will content find this bosom again." (28)

MP, Dec 9, 1779.

Hexameter couplets (in quatrains). A young man in England complains of his separation from his beloved lady in Philadelphia.

79-214. [Imperial Brunswick's Line.]

"Imperial Brunswick's Line." (18)

PA, Dec 31, 1779.

Ode in sixains. Prince Henry will crush France and Spain and save British honor. (On the war against the Bourbons.)

79-215. Impromptu.

"Regardless of a Factious Roar." (4)

MP, Apr 27, 1779.

Quatrain. A defense of Sandwich, who stands firm against factious criticism.

79-216. An Impromptu.

"Sir Hugh insists -- let no denial." (4)

GA, Mar 12, 1779.

Quatrain. Epigram. Palliser, the devil, should have his due -- a trial that he wants.

79-217. Impromptu.

"To exculpate himself from renewing the Fight." (4)

St J's C, Feb 16, 1779; West M 7 (Feb 1779), 110.

Anapest tetrameter couplets. Satire on Palliser. See also 79-141.

79-218. Impromptu. On Observing Centinels guarding the Exchequer.

"From sun-set to day-break, whilst folks are asleep." (6)

L Eve Post, Sep 30, 1779; W Eve Post, Oct 5, 1779.

Anapest tetrameter couplets. Satire on the Court and its corruption. The Exchequer is guarded carefully at night; but during the day thieves may seize the treasure!

79-219. An Impromptu on Reading the Sentence of the Court Martial on Admiral Keppel's Trial.

"The more to bless this happy Land." (4)

PA, Feb 19, 1779; St J's C, Feb 16, 1779; West M 7 (Feb 1779), 110.

Quatrain. Satire. Ironic verses on Keppel's acquittal: now we should have Sackville (Germain) lead the armies and Palliser the navy. Also entitled "Martial on Admiral Keppel's Tryal." See also 79-141.

79-220. Impromptu: On the Threatened Invasion.

"The French enrag'd, their trade so lost." (8)

G Eve Post, May 6, 1779; PA, May 7, 1779; WM 44 (May 26, 1779), 228.

Quatrains. Satire on the French for their threatened invasion of England. Nothing will come of it.

79-221. Impromptu on Union.

"Whilst angry discord, round thy sea-girt isle." (19)

Cumb Pacq, Feb 23, 1779.

Blank verse. A complaint at disunion or faction at a time when the country is at war and in danger.

79-222. [In English hearts extremes will force their way.]

"In English hearts extremes will force their way." (11)

Cumb Pacq, Mar 9, 1779; G Eve Post, Feb 27, 1779.

HC. The English go to extremes, i.e., are extremely emotional people: e.g. -- Wilkes, Garrick, Keppel, sedition or rebellion at home. They will be "undone" "by riot and excess."


[In the -- -- Year of Nabonnassar, &c. &c.] See [Inscription on a monument lately found amongst the ruins of Nineveh], 79-228.

79-223. [In the Year 1763, Britain triumphed.]

"In the Year 1763, Britain triumphed." (c. 7)

Cal Merc, Sep 20, 1779.

Inscription. On Britain's decline from the year 1763 when triumphant over her enemies and flourishing. (Who is responsible? The present ministry?)

79-224. [In vain the Cits attempt to coax.]

"In vain the Cits attempt to coax." (6)

PA, Mar 5, 1779.

OC. The City should not give Keppel an award. It is absurd to believe him a victor: he had turned away from the French!

79-225. The Incitement.

"When mighty Nations rise in Arms." (24)

PA, Sep 8, 1779.

Quatrains. Britons must unite to defeat their enemies.

79-226. The Inconsistent Patriot.

"While Sol yet lay dissolved in sleep." (70)

PA, Aug 2, 1779.

HC. Satire on the "patriot" who asserts principles of freedom but who, at the same time, is a slave to his wife.

79-227. Inscribed to the Defender of his Country's Rights, the Right Honourable Lord Viscount Bulkeley.

"When Britain, by a direful war." (40)

LP, Dec 27, 1779.

Regular (Horatian) ode in octaves, but only occasionally do rhymes appear. Bulkeley is praised for preventing the Court's venal slaves in Parliament from imposing enclosures on Wales. The Welsh affair is linked with the American War and a call for an end of it is made.

79-228. [Inscription on a monument lately found amongst the ruins of Nineveh.]

"In the -- -- Year of Nabonassar, &c. &c." (c. 25)

Cal Merc, Aug 23, 1779; Cumb Pacq, Aug 14, 1779; L Chron 46 (Aug 14, 1779), 159.

Inscription. General Howe is maligned as the treacherous cause of British defeat in America. He deliberately wished to prolong the war for private gain. The attack is disguised as an ancient Assyrian inscription. See 79-145.

79-229. The Invasion. A Ballad.

"Should Monsieur come." (42)

WM 43 (Feb 10, 1779), 160.

A patriotic song. Should the French come, the British will unite and reconcile their parties to fight and trounce them. Taken from "A Ballad," 78-65.

79-230. The Invasion; A Love Song about Murder. (Or, The Soldier's and Sailor's Defiance.) To be sung by all the Hearts of Oak in Old England.

"Ay, ay, let 'em come and be damn'd." (28)

Lloyd's 45 (Aug 1, 1779), 219; MP, Aug 30, 1779; PA, Jul 24, 1779.

Song. The French and Spanish will not succeed in their invasion anywhere in Great Britain -- England, Scotland, Ireland.

79-231. The Invasion: A Satire.

"Why dread Invasion from the Foreign Foe." (116)

PA, Aug 25, Sep 2 & 8, 1779.

HC. A defence of Chatham and his leadership, and an attack on incompetent North for the calamities destroying the nation. He is asked to resign. As in Chatham's time, we need unanimity. Cited are corruption and "lost" America.

79-232. The Invasion; or French Gasconade.

"What heroes croud the beach? What warriors stand." (103)

MP, Aug 27, 1779

HC. Causidicus patriotically urges the British to repel the French, as in the past. He cites the great models -- Beaufort, Percy, Amherst, Townshend, who led and are leading the nation -- and urges unity of Whig and Tory in this crisis.

79-233. The Invocation: A Song.

"Dear Boreas, I wish, you more briskly would blow." (25)

PA, Mar 2, 1779.

Song with "Derry down" chorus. North should wake up and lead the nation in battle; his rhetoric is as tame as Burke's.

79-234. The Irish Debate.

"Hibernia's Sons, in high Debate." (8)

LP, Oct 25, 1779; PA, Oct 27, 1779.

OC (with variations). The Irish should be granted free trade. Generous concessions will earn their gratitude.

79-235. The Irishman's Ditty to Sir Hugh Palliser.

"Arrah, my dear Hugh." (30)

L Eve Post, Feb 11, 1779.

Trimeter triplets. Ballad satire on Palliser. Cited are Keppel and Hood.

79-236. John Bull's Advice to all Parties.

"Says my Lord to the Senate, -- 'This base Opposition.'" (22)

L Chron 46 (Jul 20, 1779), 72; SM 41 (Aug 1779), 441.

Hexameter couplets. Britain advises the Opposition and the Majority to cease their squabbles and focus on the war with the Bourbons, "the Family Compact." "Turn all your rage on the French and the Spaniards."

79-237. The Jolly Soldiers. A New Song.

"Club your firelocks, my lads! Let us march to the coast." (30)

L Chron 46 (Jul 8, 1779), 31; UM 65 (Jul 1779), 39; WM 45 (Aug 11, 1779), 159; Calliope, or The Musical Miscellany (London: Elliott & Kay, 1788), Song 35, pp. 64-65. Words and music.

A patriotic song directed against the French and Spanish.

79-238. The Jolly Tars of Old England. A New Song. Tune, Hearts of Oak.

"Come cheer up, my Lads, let us haste to the main." (29)

L Chron 45 (Jun 26, 1779), 611; PA, Jul 3, 1779; SM 41 (Jun 1779), 337; WM 45 (Jul 14, 1779), 63.

The British sailors are happy to fight the Spaniards, especially for their "dollars."

79-239. Justice Triumphant. A Song. Tune, -- Of the famous Ninety two.

"Swell'd with foaming rage, and fir'd with spleen." (44)

L Eve Post, Feb 27, 1779.

Song. A narrative of the Keppel-Palliser affair to the conclusion -- the vindication of Keppel's honor.

79-240. [Keppel, who long sustain'd the fight.]

"Keppel, who long sustain'd the fight." (48)

Freeman's J, Jan 14, 1779.

Anti-Palliser verses. A ballad narrates the story of the conflict between brave Keppel and "base, degen'rate Palliser." The point is also made that the cowardly (Germain) must not guide the war.

79-241. Keppel's Triumph. Tune, "Oh the days when I was young!"

"Oh! the days when I did run." (12)

MP, Mar 25, 1779.

Song. Satire on Keppel and the lee-shore episode in the abortive naval engagement off Ushant.

79-242. King George and Old England for ever!  A New Song and Chorus, as sung at Vauxhall by Mr. Vernon and others.

"The French fleet is sail'd, if loud Rumour speaks right."  (28)

Lloyd's 44 (Jun 25, 1779), 62;  L Chron 45 (Jun 24, 1779), 605;  L Eve Post, Jun 24, 1779;  M Chron, Jun 25, 1779;  MP, Jun 25, 1779;  PA, Jun 26, 1779;  St J's C, Jun 24, 1779;  UM 64 (Supp 1779), 375;  WM 45 (Jul 7, 1779), 38-9;  West J, Jul 17, 1779.  Also G Eve Post, Jun 24, 1779.

The British tars are prepared to fight the French and the Spanish squadrons.  Their cause is "fair Freedom."

79-243. The King Laughs -- The People Suffer. -- A Merry King, and a Sad People.

"To our Monarch, we are told, when danger is near."  (6 + 4)

L Eve Post, Aug 26, 1779.

Hexameter couplets.  Satire on the cruel, unfeeling King, who enjoys himself with North, while the war is in progress.

79-244. The Ladies Privateer.

"Shall we call it the Sue, or the Nancy."  (28)

PA, Sep 15, 1779;  W Eve Post, Sep 16, 1779.

Quatrains.  Women are joining the navy to fight the French.

79-245. Last Dying Speech and Confession of the Notorious Malefactor, who was hang'd and burn'd at Whitehall, Tyburn, and sundry other Places of Public Execution, on Thursday, February the 11th, 1779.

"All you, my Dying Speech that hear."  (44)

GA, Feb 17, 1779.

Ballad.  Satire on Palliser who is made to utter his dying speech before being burned in effigy (after Keppel's acquittal by the court-martial on February 11, 1779).  Palliser blames his accomplices in crime -- Sandwich and Constantine John Phipps, the latter having testified for him.

79-246. Law-Maxims Reconciled.

"Princes can ne'er do wrong, -- the Courtier cries." (4)

L Cour, Dec 13, 1779.

HC. Epigram. Neither the King nor the people err (so a Tory and a Whig claim); but the King cannot be punished, even though "Heads fall."

79-247. [Let France and Spain triumphant boast.]

"Let France and Spain triumphant boast." (20)

PA, Dec 2, 1779.

Song on the war against France, Spain, and America. The British tars enjoy the struggle despite anything France and Spain, Paul Jones, D'Estaing, or the American Congress may do.

79-248. Liberty, An Ode. By a Young Lady.

"How fair yon landscape rises to the eye." (44)

HM 9 (Nov 1779), 648; UM 65 (Oct 1779), 206; WM 46 (Nov 10, 1779), 158-9.

Quatrains. Liberty makes Britain attractive; but oppression, civil discord, and war destroy it. We must avoid these destructive evils. (Very generalized, these ideas probably have significance for the present times.)

79-249. Lines. From Col. Donnop to Sir W[illiam] H[owe].

"From Myrtle shades, and Amaranthine bow'rs." (38)

MP, Sep 28, 1779.

HC. The persona of Donnop (the Hessian officer who was killed at Trenton) berates General Howe and asks for vengeance. He refers to "an unnat'ral war," which Howe prolonged by his excessive caution and improper behavior.

79-250. Lines. On the Gentlemen of the Military Association in the Artillery Ground.

"Hail! gen'rous Youths, brave London Volunteers." (28)

MP, Sep 8, 1779.

HC. Praise of the brave London volunteers, who will repel France and Spain combin'd "in this dang'rous hour."

79-251. Lines on the Impending War.

"What! the Dons up in arms, with huge whiskers to fright us." (20)

MP, Jun 24, 1779.

Fourteener couplets. Britain will resist the formidable, threatening alliance of France and Spain.


79-252. Lines On the Late Rejoicings for Admiral Keppel's Acquittal. By a Seaman.

"While Peers and Commons head the riot." (26)

MP, May 14, 1779.

OC. An attack on Keppel, who little deserves praise. He is compared with Admiral Byng, and the English with the French fleet in the Ushant engagement (July 27, 1778).


79-253. Lines. On the Loss of the Serapis and Quebec Frigates.

"When Britain's Navy shunn'd th'unequal fight." (8)

MP, Oct 25, 1779.

HC. In praise of the bravery of Capt. Pearson of the Serapis (defeated in a fight with Paul Jones) and Capt. Farmer of the Quebec (blown up by the French). Their heroism is contrasted with Keppel's behavior (alluded to indirectly).


79-254. Lines. To a Friend Who was Thrown by an American Horse.

"Hogarth, believe me, never drew." (16)

MP, Jan 1, 1779.

OC. If the Americans had been treated kindly, instead of with coercion, they would never have rebelled. N.B. There is a print that illustrates this poem -- "The Horse America, throwing his Master," George, Catalogue of Political and Personal Satires, #5549 (V, 332).


79-255. Lord North's Ejaculation.

"Was ever Minister in such a Plight." (8)

St J's C, Jul 8, 1779.

HC. The persona of North complains that he is criticized for anything that he might do.

79-256. Lord N[orth]'s Soliloquy.

"Curse on this coward conscience -- how it stings." (29)

G, Sep 15, 1779; PA, Sep 15, 1779.

Blank verse parody of King Claudius's soliloquy in Hamlet. Now that the war is enlarged with the entry of the Bourbon powers, North's persona develops a guilty conscience, for (he admits) his ambition is the cause of "these broils and slaughters."

79-257. A Loyal Ballad.

"Of Modern Patriotic cause." (16)

MP, Sep 30, 1779.

Ballad. Satire on the Opposition, Keppel and Howe. The nation will win without them.

79-258. Loyal Stanzas.

"Ye gen'rous sons of Albion's pile." (24)

MP, Sep 9, 1779.

Regular ode in sixains, praising Palliser (who has been cleared by a court-martial), despite Keppel and the Opposition. Britons must now unite against the French.

79-259. A Loyal Wish for the Year 1779.

"Before the rising year." (32)

Freeman's J, Jan 9, 1779; LP, Jan 1, 1779.

Quatrains. A prayer for peace between America and Britain so that France and Spain will not benefit from the conflict.

79-260. The Ludlow Rope.

"In Ludlow once a year, the throng." (20)

L Eve Post, Mar 13, 1779.

Quatrains. Satire on the ministry. Those who rend and tear the vitals of a nation deserve execution.

79-261. A Lyric Ode, written at the Conclusion of the Year 1779.

"Down the rapid stream of time." (96)

WM 48 (Apr 6, 1780), 14-15.

Regular Pindaric ode. The year 1779 was shameful and inglorious. The navy ran from the French; the factious Opposition treacherously reported this fiasco to America, thereby strengthening its resolve; England, the "wretched isle," became "to filial foes a prey" (an allusion to Paul Jones); and factious chiefs betrayed the country. Concludes with a hope for the end of dissension and the development of aggressive fighting forces that will "retrieve" Britain's "former name."

79-262. Lyttelton, Thomas.
[Elegy on Lord Chatham.]

"See, where in yonder Abbey's hallow'd walls." (16)

G, Dec 9, 1779; LP, Dec 6, 1779.

Elegiac stanzas, part of a longer poem. Praise of the incorruptible patriot Chatham, coupled with criticism of a corrupt senate and a fallen, slavish country, led by "garter'd knaves." England's pride and glory disappeared with the passing of Chatham. (I have been unable to locate the complete poem.)

79-263. A Medley for the Light Infantry. By a Soldier. Written at New-York.

"Soldier, whilst the flowing bowl." (64)

MP, Sep 13, 1779.

Five songs about English troops on active service. Song (1) -- About shelter and warmth from rain. (2) -- Arising in the morning and forming ranks. (3) -- In action trying "to set sad America free," they pursue the fleeing "fanatic crowd." (4) -- Mercy is shown to a captured Rebel Officer, who is urged to fight for Britain and be truly free. (5) -- If the rebels persist, we will push harder in the next campaign.

79-264. Merlyne his Prophecie. The Sexte Fitte.

"Aurthur hee satte att his tabel rounde." (32)

MP, Aug 28, 1779.

Quatrains. Medieval imitation. Merlin prophesies that Britain shall be overthrown but shall rise again -- by means of her navy -- and be "The Conquerours of the Worlde."

79-265. [The moderate Man exclaims, "Here, Waiter, here."]

"The moderate Man exclaims, 'Here, Waiter, here.'" (6)

PA, Mar 20, 1779.

Epigram. HC. Five newspapers satisfy the coffee-politicians of varying hues -- the moderate call for the Public Advertiser or Gazetteer; "red-hot patriots" call for the Public Ledger or the General Evening Post; and the courtier calls for the Morning Post.

79-266. [The most Catholic King declares that his Right.]

"The most Catholic King declares that his Right." (8)

PA, Jul 29, 1779.

Quatrains. Epigram. It is odd that monarchs all believe that God is on their side; thus the devil must be responsible for their actions.

The Moth and the Candle. PA, Sep 4, 1779; W Eve Post, Sep 2, 1779. See "Britannia and the Moth," 79-74.

79-267. A Naval Ballad.

"I sing of the perils there is in a battle." (36)

MP, Apr 3, 1779.

Ballad. Satire on Keppel for his apparent blunder in the engagement with D'Orvilliers. Cited is Sir Hugh Palliser.

79-268. Neptune and Britannia.

"Thus late Britannia, sunk in Grief." (28)

PA, Sep 17, 1779.

Ballad complaint about the poor state of the navy and the poor leadership among the "Statesmen and Commanders."

79-269. Neptune to Keppel.

"Says Neptune to Keppel, 'Attend my brave Son.'" (16 + 12)

PA, Mar 4, 1779.

Quatrains. Praise of Keppel. A brief sarcastic response belittling Keppel appeared soon after: "A Landsman's Answer to the Naval Poet in Yesterday's Paper," PA, March 20, 1779.

79-270. A New Ballad.

"Rouse Britons! at length." (36)

G Eve Post, Jul 8, 1779; MP, Jul 9, 1779; WM 45 (Aug 4, 1779), 134.

A patriotic song. "Old England's a match, / And more -- for Old Scratch, / A Frenchman, -- a Spaniard, -- and Yankee!"

79-271. A New Ballad on the Times.

"Good People of England, attend to my Song." (60)

West M 7 (Dec 1779), 650-1.

Ballad reviews the current state of affairs -- Britain without allies, America allied with treacherous France, France allied with Spain, Holland turning away from Britain, Ireland demanding free trade at England's expense, and the Scotch feathering their nest in England. The nation must be careful not to defeat itself.

79-272. A New Ballad to be Sung in both H[ouse]s of P[arliamen]t, at their next merry Meeting.

"Good Neighbours, attend." (60)

G Eve Post, Sep 4, 1779.

Ballad in sixains, questions the strange alliance of New England fanatic Saints of the Good Old Cause and the Bourbon Papists. The Americans are encouraged by the so-called Patriots of both Houses of Parliament. But Congress will end enslaved to the Bourbons.

79-273. A New Ballad. To the tune of -- "A Jolly Parson, that lived at Norton-Falgate, &c."

"I'll sing you a song of a Parson." (80)

LP, Oct 11, 1779.

Ballad narrative of the history of a refugee parson in Delwyn, Herts., with a few stanzas on his experience in the state of Maryland and his forced return to England.

79-274. A New Court Song. Tune, -- Black Joke.

"When Conscience, with its piercing dart." (11)

GA, Mar 29, 1779.

A song about the corrupting power of a bribe (at court). (Is the background the Keppel-Palliser trials?) In general, the country suffers.

79-275. A New Dance, called The Cabinet. Tune, -- "Scotch Reel."

"King. My Lord North, first fidler, do pray begin." (20)

LP, Nov 3, 1779.

Satire on the court by means of the metaphor of a court dance. The King, North, Hillsborough, Stormont, Mansfield, Gower, Weymouth, Talbot, Amherst, Germain, Carlisle, all figure in the changing of places.

79-276. A New Loyal Song.

"I sing of George's golden days." (56)

L Eve Post, Sep 23, 1779; also GA, Jan 15, 1782.

The GA version has slight verbal changes with the title "Who's the Noodle. A New Song."
Satire on the King for his failures in America and Europe. The American

War is damned; the Americans are praised; but the Scots are ridiculed. "Yankee doodle" chorus.

79-277. A New Song.

"Hark! the drum beats to arms, let's obey the brisk call." (20 + chorus)

L Chron 46 (Jul 10, 1779), 35; SM 41 (Jul 1779), 378.

Anti-gallican song with "Derry down" chorus. Britons are a match for anything France and Spain will do.

79-278. A New Song, call'd Great Palliser!!!

"Who does not extol our Vice Admiral." (32)

M Chron, Feb 11, 1779.

Song. Satire on Palliser for failure in courage and for improper conduct in battle.

79-279. A New Song called The Court Martial. Tune, -- Deserves to be reckon'd an Ass.

"Brave Keppel last war, as well known to each Tar." (40)

GA, Jan 19, 1779.

Ballad narrative of the Keppel-Palliser scandal gives details of Keppel's court-martial, attacks the ministry for its politics that engendered rebellion and war.

79-280. A New Song for the Times.

"Ye Monsieurs of France, and ye Dons of proud Spain." (36)

WM 45 (Sep 1, 1779), 232.

A patriotic lyric directed at France and Spain.

79-281. A New Song. To an old tune (the Vicar of Bray).

"In good King George's golden days." (48)

Freeman's J, Sep 23, 1779.

A satire on Josiah Tucker, Dean of Gloucester, for maligning the Opposition by calling them "all republicans." The reference is to Tucker's address, Thoughts on the Present Posture of Affairs (1779). See "A Dialogue between Dean Tucker and the Devil," 79-105, and "On Dean Tucker's Address," 79-327.

79-282. A New Song. To the Tune of "Britannia, rule the Waves."

"Let Bourbons join their host and fleet." (29)

L Chron 46 (Jul 6, 1779), 19.

Another naval war song against "False Frenchmen [in] league with haughty Spain."

79-283. A New Song. Tune, -- Roast Beef, &c.

"When dastards are plac'd in the list of promotions." (24)

G, Jan 29, 1779.

A criticism of the nation's leadership. All the men at the helm are inept traitors, especially Sandwich and Germain. Keppel is needed "to guide."

79-284. A New-Year's Gift; or, The Poor Cobler's Advice to his Unfortunate Countrymen, who are now out of Employ; a New Song, proper for the Year 1779.

"When the men of Messina, to feed a few leeches." (40)

GA, Feb 11, 1779.

Ballad narrating how "The Cobler of Cripplegate" would reduce taxes and end the ministry responsible for the American war. Cited are Rigby, North, Sandwich, Germain, Weymouth, King George, and Parliament. He urges that the people speak directly with MP's and the King, because petitions are ignored.

79-285. News from the Clouds.

"The Gods conven'd one day of late." (88)

GA, Feb 16, 1779.

Quatrains in OC. Mercury reports bad news to the assembled gods, including the menace of France, Spain, and America, and concludes with complaints of internal dissension that have weakened the nation and with praise of Keppel, who has been allegedly maligned basely.

79-286. The News of the Day.

"The News of the Day." (36)

PA, Sep 17, 1779.

Sixains. The news of the day is uncertain -- that is, it is not certain if the English will fight the French or if they will win.

79-287. Now or Never.

"Now or Never is the time, Boys." (16)

W Eve Post, Aug 10, 1779.

Quatrains. The "meddling" of the French and Spanish (in the American War) is dishonorable, and their decisive defeat is deserved.

79-288. Number 45 Reviv'd.

"It gives me great pleasure to revive." (6)

G, Nov 30, 1779; PA, Nov 30, 1779.

Mixed verse. Praise of Wilkes, now Chamberlain of the City of London (the lucrative office that he filled until his death in 1797).

79-289. Observation on the Log Book in Lat. 50. 40.

"Say, why, with wonder struck so dumb, so pale." (22)

L Eve Post, Feb 11, 1779.

HC. An expression of indignation at the enemies of Keppel for tampering with the evidence -- the log book.

79-290. An Occasional Address to the Gentlemen Volunteers of Plymouth and Plymouth Dock, written by Mr. Perry and spoken by Mrs. Thornton, at the Theatre in Plymouth.

"Weak were the task, in high-flown gasconade." (72)

G, Sep 23, 1779; PA, Sep 24, 1779.

HC. On the threat of the French invasion and Plymouth's contribution to the defence.

79-291. An Ode.

"Gibbon, for Shame! another Change." (36)

L Eve Post, Jul 15, 1779; PA, Jul 17, 1779.

Regular ode in sixains. Satire on Gibbon for shifting his religious (and political) principles; now he belongs to Government, as he shifts from Whig to Tory principles because of selfish interest.

79-292. An Ode.

"The K[ing] (God bless him) rules the realm." (42)

L Cour, Nov 27, 1779.

Regular (Horatian) ode in sixains. A criticism of the ministry, North, Rigby, and Thurlow, for weakening the nation before the Bourbon powers. The Opposition, proscribed and helpless because of denial of Habeas Corpus, should rise again and dare to be free.

79-293. Ode. Ad Populum.

"Grind the axe, the scaffold rear." (40)

L Eve Post, Jul 6, 1779.

Regular ode in quatrains. Advice to the people to unseat the ministers responsible for the danger the country now is in from France and Spain; and to the Americans to continue the fight. Cited are North, Keppel, Harland. (Robert Harland was second-in-command under Keppel off Ushant, 1778-79.)

79-294. An Ode. Addressed to a certain Admiral.

"Mynheer Van Keppel! 'tis in vain." (49)

MP, Apr 13, 1779.

Regular (Horatian) ode in septains against Keppel, who is undeserving of any fame and who is wrong to persecute Palliser.

79-295. An Ode for his Majesty's Birth-Day. (Not the Laureat's.)

"George this day is forty-one." (13)

GA, Jun 4, 1779.

OC. Negative comment on Whitehead's laureate odes. This is no time to rejoice, for America is lost, Ireland up in arms, Scotland disturbed, and England in depression -- all in contrast with the glorious days of George II.

79-296. An Ode for New-Year's Day; in Imitation of the late Colley Cibber, Esq;

"Chearful flow the Rymes along." (30)

PA, Jan 1, 1779.

A serious imitation of Cibber's manner in praise of Whitehead's politically oriented laureate odes that give "the State of present Times, / In honest Verse, and pleasing Rhymes."

79-297. Ode for Quarter-Day, June 24, 1779.

"While lofty Bards, with Fortune's favours blest." (36)

Lloyd's 44 (Jun 23, 1779), 606.

Quatrains in praise of the farmer who will be productive because he has peace. But in America because of war there will be no plenty. The landlords must not tyrannize their tenants on this day, when rents are due.

79-298. Ode for the New Year. As it will be performed before the Congress.

"To arms, to arms, ye sons of might." (53)

GA, Jan 2, 1779.

Irregular Pindaric ode, parody of Whitehead's Establishment ode (1779), taking the American point of view and that of "the People's Majesty." A Whig poem directed at ministerial oppression.

79-299. An Ode in Praise of Military Bravery.

"Let British youth be taught t'endure." (30)

G, Sep 13, 1779.

Regular ode in sixains. A patriotic poem asserting the bravery of the English against the combined Bourbon forces.

79-300. Ode, in the Manner of Anacreon.

"With wine I'll chace those cares away." (24)

GM 49 (May 1779), 262; LM 48 (Aug 1779), 377.

Sixains. Let us drink, love, and be merry in the face of the war. North should worry!

70-301. Ode, Occasioned by a late glorious Decision. Humbly inscrib'd to the Honourable Augustus Keppel.

"O! for his Heaven descended fire." (72)

L Eve Post, Mar 6, 1779.

Panegyrical ode in sixains honoring Keppel, now vindicated by the court-martial.

79-302. An Ode of Gray. Characters revers'd and adapted to the Nature of the Times.

"Tyburn seize thee ruthless Peer." (68)

L Eve Post, Feb 4, 1779.

Irregular Pindaric. Parody on Gray's Bard. Satire on Sandwich for trying to ruin Keppel. Cited are John the Painter, North, Thurlow, Richmond, Rockingham, and Chatham.

79-303. Ode on a late Treasury Warrant. Addressed to the Gentlemen of Wales.

"To Arms, to Arms, ye Sons of Whores." (25)

LP, Jan 1, 1779; PA, Jan 4, 1779.

Irregular Pindaric ode. Parody. Satire on Whitehead's New Year's Ode for 1779 and on those who plunder the Treasury.

79-304. An Ode on the Gallant Behaviour of Capt. Pearson, and Capt. Piercy, who engaged Paul Jones.

"Far on the azure concave of the main." (70)

West M 7 (Nov 1779), 596-7.

Regular ode in dixains. A sublime poem that describes the heroic battle between Jones's squadron and the Bon Homme Richard with Captain Pearson's Serapis, September 23, 1779.

79-305. Ode on the threatened French Invasion.

"On envious Gallia's hostile coast." (44)

G, Aug 5, 1779;  G Eve Post, Aug 3, 1779.

Regular ode in quatrains. Let us rouse our forces against the combined might of France and Spain, attracted by "British spoil."

79-306. Ode on the Tory Fast. Ad Furores, (anglice) Tories.

"Audiet justus Deus obsecrantes." (20)

LP, Dec 29, 1779.

Regular (Horatian) ode. A Latin poem from Manchester satirizing the Tory clergy for supporting the American war.

79-307. Ode on the Trial of Admiral Keppel.

"Tho' well-try'd courage steel the hardy soul." (50)

GA, Feb 23, 1779.

Regular ode in dixains. Praise of courageous and noble Keppel after his acquittal. Now the nation can focus its attention on the enemy, France. The government is criticized for allowing "Faction" and "private views" to cause maladministration so that Keppel, as well as Clinton and Burgoyne, cannot operate effectively against the enemy.

79-308. Ode on the 25th of October, being the Day of his Majesty's Accession to the Crown.

"Revolving years their destin'd course maintain." (42)

Regular ode in sixains. Nineteen years after his accession, which began auspiciously with victory in war and increase in trade, George now deserves support at a time of "foul Rebellion" and attack by "foreign foes." Britain's sons will assert their country's rights.

79-309. Ode on the Victory at Savannah, in Georgia, on hearing the Guns fired for it.

"Hark! hark! the Park and Tower's guns." (58)

PA, Dec 29, 1779.

A formal ode, in the manner of an oratorio, celebrating the victory at Savannah (October 9, 1779) over the rebels -- a costly victory which should encourage the Americans to return to duty under Britain.

79-310. Ode to Boreas.

"Rise, Boreas, with thy Blasts, arise." (48)

PA, Apr 6, 1779.

Regular ode in sixains. Satire on North. Lord North should wake up and assert himself energetically with the help of the character of several people -- Germain, Mansfield, Suffolk, Sandwich, Gower, Rigby, Wedderburne, Jenkinson, Cowper, Weymouth, Carlisle, and Thurloe.

79-311. Ode to Britannia.

"Awake, great Albion's Queen, awake." (57)

MP, Aug 7, 1779.

Regular ode in twelve-line stanzas (two of which are slightly irregular). Admiral Charles Hardy protects Britain from the combined fleets of France and Spain.

79-312. Ode to Calumny.

"Avaunt, thou worst of fiends, avaunt." (24)

L Eve Post, Aug 10, 1779.

Regular ode in sixains. Calumny is the work of Palliser, tool of Sandwich or North, against Keppel. (This is a satire on Henry Bate of the *Morning Post* for defending Palliser and attacking Keppel.)

79-313. Ode to Liberty.

"For sceptered Pride the Laurel Wreath." (12)

St J's C, Oct 5, 1779.

Regular ode in sixains. "Led by the Genius of old Rome," the poet dedicates himself to the cause of liberty (i.e., republican liberty).

79-314. Ode to Lord North.

"My good Lord North, what Patriot now." (108)

L Cour, Dec 3, 1779.

Regular (Horatian) ode in sixains. Ironic satire on North, advising him to be politic and optimistic in the threatening times so that the Ministry can maintain its majority. Cited are America, Ireland, Jamaica, D'Estaing, Paul Jones, the budget, and Sandwich. (Bod copy is torn; BL copy is perfect.)

79-315. Ode to Peace. Written by a British Officer while the Army was in Philadelphia, in the year 1777.

"Oh, bounteous Peace! with lavish hand." (29)

MP, Dec 29, 1779.

A slightly irregular ode, largely in quatrains. American scenery is as beautiful as the nature of ancient Greece, and the Muse can enjoy it in peace, particularly the Delaware River, Pennsylvania.

79-316. Ode. To the Memory of the Officers and Crew of his Majesty's late ship the Quebec, commanded by Captain Farmer . . . Written in 1779.

"Hail ye! who for your country bled." (18)

MH, Jan 10, 1782.

Ode in sixains, recalling and honoring Capt. Farmer and his crew who died when their battleship, the <u>Quebec</u>, blew up. (The ship exploded Oct. 6, 1779.)

79-317. Ode II. Book I, of Horace adapted to the present Times, and addressed to that "illustrious Band," the Lords and Gentlemen in Opposition.

"Enough hath Jove, with red Right Hand." (90)

PA, Dec 2, 1779.

Imitation of Horace. Ode in sixains. Satire on the Opposition -- Richmond, Rockingham, Dunning, Barre, Pratt (Camden), Keppel, Fox -- eager to take the helm of the ship of state. But they will perform the job poorly.


79-318. [Odell, Jonathan.]
The Congratulation.

"Joy to great Congress, Joy an hundred fold." (180)

PA, Dec 30, 1779.

HC. Reprinted from Rivington's Royal Gazette (N.Y.), Nov. 6, 1779. Satire on the Congress by an American loyalist for its alliance with France; it will not help the rebels escape disaster. Odell exults in the British success over the French at Savannah. Repr. W. Sargent, The Loyal Verses of Joseph Stansbury and Doctor Jonathan Odell (Albany: Munsell, 1860), pp. 45-50 + Notes.


79-319. Of Nobility.

"What are the Badges of heroic Blood." (8)

PA, Aug 11, 1779; W Eve Post, Aug 10, 1779.

Octave. "Honours" do not make a good man: "Outward Greatness" is meaningless "without inward Good." See "The True Honor of the Truly Honorable," 79-493.


Old Mother Dover's Farewell Speech; Or, The Spanish Manifesto. "The World can bear witness that nothing cou'd ruffle." (48) MP, Jun 30, 1779. Another title of "The Spanish Manifesto," 79-425.


An Old Woman's Remonstrance, To one of the best of Sublunary Beings; being as true, and perhaps more important than any, or all, presented by the Loyal Citizens of London. "His faithful subject, Martha Bird." (50) GA, Aug 31, 1779. OC. A complaint at the rise in prices by a common subject, especially the prices of food, beer, coals, and clothing, which will result in emigration to France, Spain, and America. A reprint of a poem that was first published in July-August 1771: see 71-70. A couplet on Wilkes is omitted.


79-320. Cancelled.

79-321. On a Certain Admiral Bred at St. Omer's

"Tell me, ye sailors, generous free and brave." (18)

GA, Jan 18, 1779.

HC. Satire on Palliser, now accused of being a treacherous Papist. The Keppel court-martial is the reference.

79-322. On a Certain Assembly not far from Westminster.

"Pitt found them Puppets, and he made 'em Men." (2)

PA, May 12, 1779.

Epigram. Pitt made Parliament independent and strong; Bute made it servile.

79-323. On a Late Event.

"When Temple sought the blissful Fields." (8)

PA, Jun 21, 1779.

Irregular stanza. Earl Temple died and joined Chatham, leaving corrupt Britain for a place of "endless Peace, and endless Virtue."

79-324. On a late Tryal.

"No longer doubt distracts the anxious Mind." (6)

St J's C, Feb 16, 1779; West M 7 (Feb 1779), 110.

HC. Keppel's trial. Now that Keppel is exonerated, Palliser is exposed as an evil "Fiend."

79-325. On Admiral d'Estaing and the French Fleet.

"When Monsieur D'Estaing." (12)

PA, May 27, 1779.

Sixains. Admiral D'Estaing cannot frighten British sailors. Reference to the Jersey incident, a skirmish in which the French were repelled.

79-326. On Admiral K[eppe]l.

"With all this Route of K[eppel]'s Name." (4)

PA, Feb 13, 1779.

Extempore. Quatrain. Keppel escaped blame, but does not merit praise.

79-327. On Dean Tucker's Address.

"The King proclaims invasion in a pother." (10)

L Eve Post, Aug 21, 1779; PA, Aug 25, 1779.

HC. Satire on Dean Tucker for underestimating the threat from France, and for contributing to the loss of America. (This poem may be alluding to Josiah Tucker's Thoughts on the Present Posture of Affairs [1779]; see "A Dialogue between Dean Tucker and the Devil," 79-105.)

79-328. On Hearing Lord North smiled at the Spanish Manifesto; addressed to a Lady Extempore.

"Pray, why is Lord North like a bold British tar?" (4)

M Chron, Jul 21, 1779.

Hexameter couplets. Epigram. North is happy to fight Spain because victory should be easy and wealth will be gained.

79-329. On Lord North's Continuing Minister.

"So refin'd is his policy, though it seem strange." (2)

L Eve Post, Apr 29, 1779.

Epigram. Satire on North and his questionable policies.

79-330. On Mansfield's Leaving the Efficient Cabinet.

"Mansfield has left the Cabinet, 'tis said." (2 + 2)

L Eve Post, Sep 7, 1779.

Two epigrams in couplets. Mansfield has quit the cabinet, fearing for his head, like all the Scotch.

79-331. On Prosecuting the American War.

"The King, whose great wisdom makes enemies friends." (2)

L Eve Post, Apr 29, 1779.

Epigram. Ironic satire on the King. The King, responsible for the (miraculous) alliance between France and Spain, will somehow succeed (in the war).

79-332. On Resignation.

"Says the Premier, I feel the raps and the knocks." (8)

G, Jul 8, 1779.

Anapest tetrameter couplets. Lord North will not resign until another one like him is found to take his place. (It will not be Fox!)

79-333. On Sir Hugh Palliser.

"Let Envy, Malice, Falsehood join." (4)

MP, Apr 27, 1779.

Quatrain. A defense of Palliser against unjust criticism.

79-334. On Sir Hugh P[alliser].

"P ull from the ship of war the recreant flag." (8)

L Eve Post, Feb 18, 1779.

Acrostic. After Keppel's trial and acquittal. Satire on Palliser -- he should be punished for his crimes.

79-335. On the Appearance of Edward Gibbon, Esq. in the Court Calendar.

"It must be so, thou reason'st well." (4)

St J's C, Jul 22, 1779.

Epigram. Quatrain. Satire on Gibbon whose elevation is a sign that Britain is declining. He was appointed to the Board of Trade and Plantations in June of 1779.

79-336. On the Changing of Generals and Admirals, instead of Ministers.

"What chopping and changing of men in command." (10)

L Eve Post, Oct 26, 1779.

Hexameter couplets. Satire on the administration. It would be a real improvement if the ministry were changed instead of the generals and admirals. (Written by the author of "Scotch Comfort and Accentuation," 79-406.)

79-337. On the City's Box for Admiral Keppel.

"Last year when Keppel ran away." (16)

MP, Sep 14, 1779.

OC. Satire on Keppel, who was awarded the Freedom of the City by London. But he does not merit this honor.

79-338. On the Committee and Burgoyne.

"The enquiring Committee, with mighty Parade a." (8)

PA, May 25, 1779.

Anapest tetrameter couplets. The committee enquiring into Burgoyne's defeat should know that Gates defeated the English because they were starving.

79-339. On the Cutting Down Mount Edgecombe Woods.

"I hear the thund'ring peel that rends the shore." (32)

MP, Sep 13, 1779.

Elegiac quatrains. The woods are being cut down for the British navy, donated to the nation by patriotic Constantine John Phipps, Baron Mulgrave.

79-340. On the Death of Captain Farmer.

"When Heroes seek the Realms above." (12)

PA, Oct 21, 1779; W Eve Post, Oct 19, 1779.

Quatrains. Brave Capt. Farmer, "asserting" his "country's right," was killed when his ship blew up in an engagement with a French frigate.

79-341. On the Death of Lord Temple.

"At Grenville's death, Truth seiz'd her silver pen." (4)

G Eve Post, Sep 14, 1779; L Eve Post, Sep 14, 1779; PA, Sep 15, 1779.

HC. Flattering lines on the death of Richard Grenville, 2nd Earl Temple (1711-1779). (He was notorious for his patronage of Wilkes. Temple also succeeded in exposing John the Painter.)

79-342. On the Defence of Sir Hugh.

"Impartial Justice says, Sir Hugh is cast." (2 + 3)

L Eve Post, May 8, 1779.

Two epigrams. Satire on Palliser and his testimony at his court-martial. (The "mast" evidence.) Palliser's trial was over May 5, 1779.

79-343. On the Fast.

"Bow down, says G[eorge], be humbled to the dust." (8)

GA, Feb 10, 1779.

HC. Satire on the King for ordering the fast, fruitless because of blundering ministers and stubborn Americans. The fast was proclaimed for February 10, 1779.

79-344. On the Firing the Tower Guns last Monday Evening.

"Our Ministers wise." (6)

PA, Dec 24, 1779.

Sixain. Satire on the ministry. Not the victory at Savannah but ignorance and foolishness at court are being celebrated. (News of Prevost's success at withstanding the attack of D'Estaing and Lincoln on Savannah has just reached London.)

79-345. On the French coming.

"Let the French come here." (12)

G, Aug 27, 1779.

Sixains. United, the English will resist the French invasion.

79-346. On the Honourable Acquittal of Admiral Keppel.

"See! Albion crown'd with Keppel's praise." (10)

GA, Feb 13, 1779.

Rough HC. Justice triumphs over vice; Keppel has been acquitted! (Keppel's court-martial trial began January 12 and ended February 11, 1779.)

79-347. On the Idea of a French Invasion.

"Gallia's pale Genius stands aghast." (6)

WM 43 (Jan 27, 1779), 113.

Sixain. The British lion roars and terrifies France.

79-348. On the Impending Force against this Country.

"What! shall our treach'rous foes now dare to say." (66)

M Chron, Aug 25, 1779; PA, Aug 26, 1779.

HC (irregular). Let the world know that Britain will sustain the united force of France and Spain, while still "oppress'd by offsprings of her care, / Taught Independance by false France to rear."

79-349. On the Impending War.

"Hark! the drum beats up to arms." (42)

MP, Jul 5, 1779.

Trochaic tetrameter couplets. The classical goddess Pallas Athena predicts victory over France in the impending war.

79-350. On the Late Knighthood of Capt. H[oo]d, for Bringing Home the Commissioners from America.

"Jemmy Twitcher, fie for shame." (13)

GA, Jan 23, 1779.

OC. Satire on Sandwich for offering a knighthood to Capt. Hood, who accepted.

79-351. On the Late Public Illuminations.

"As Palliser is hunted down." (4)

W Eve Post, Apr 1, 1779.

Quatrain. Epigram on the Keppel-Palliser affair. Satire on Keppel, tool of the Opposition, used to hunt down Palliser and demolish North.

79-352. On the Loss of the Ardent Man of War.

"Boteler, I hail thee well! 'twas bravely done." (24)

W Eve Post, Sep 2, 1779.

Quatrains. Mourns the loss of Captain Boteler and his *Ardent*, man-of-war, defeated by a large French force, and criticizes the unpatriotic "Patriots" for their destructive factionalism.

79-353. On the Pompous Account given in the Morning Post of the 15th instant, of the Manner in which the King spends the day. An Epigram.

"The K--g, God bless him, is the first of men." (2)

GA, May 17, 1779.

HC. Satire on the *Morning Post* and on the simplicity of the King's life.

79-354. On the Present Wretched Condition of Great Britain.

"Unhappy Britain, doom'd to endless chains." (112)

L Eve Post, Jul 8, 1779.

HC. Pessimistic satire on Parliament, corrupt and tyrannical, that keeps the war against America going and that fails to protect the nation from France. The Duke of Richmond cannot move the MP's. The "people" must "interpose" to save the state, for "Bute guides the King" and "Freedom's extinct." North deserves execution.

79-355. On the pretended Invasion.

"With haughty Spirit, and a grand Parade." (6)

St J's C, Jul 27, 1779.

HC. For some reason, the French have called off their invasion of England.

79-356. On the Promotion of E. Gibbon, Esq;

"Of Jacobites Hundreds have Pensions and Places." (8)

PA, Jul 14, 1779; St J's C, Jul 13, 1779.

Hexameter couplets. Satire on Gibbon, "heretic," favored by the King, along with Jacobites and Papists, and other favorites like "wicked" Sandwich. North appointed Gibbon to the Board of Trade and Plantations on June 20, 1779.

79-357. On the Prospect of an Invasion.

"Britons! glory calls once more." (20)

L Chron 46 (Sep 25, 1779), 300; SM 41 (Sep 1779), 502.

Quatrains. All Britons should come to the defence of their country.

79-358. On the Reported Invasion of the British Islands by the French and Spaniards.

"Loud rumour speaks, 'The French and Spaniards steer.'" (60)

L Eve Post, Sep 7, 1779.

HC. The corrupt Parliament and ministry are responsible for the dangerous situation the country is facing -- threats of invasion by the French and Spaniards. Britons and the Irish should cooperate; Britons and Americans should be reconciled.

79-359. On the Sending Out a Fleet in Pursuit of Paul Jones.

"Our Ministers vex'd." (24)

PA, Oct 1, 1779.

Sixains. John Paul Jones eludes the British and keeps his privateering fleet intact.

79-360. On the Talk of a Dutch War.

"That the French far exceed us in ev'ry mean art." (18)

Vocal Magazine; or British Songster's Miscellany (1778), p. 281 (Song #1028).

Patriotic song (probably early 1779). The French are getting the Dutch to join them, but England "shall conquer them all."

79-361. On the Trial of Admiral Keppel by a Court Martial.

"Tories and thieves brave Keppel dare t'arraign." (28)

GA, Jan 8, 1779; L Eve Post, Jan 5, 1779.

HC. Tory traitor Sandwich is responsible for the persecution of Keppel, who will be vindicated.

79-362. On Titles and Distinctions.

"A Title's a Trifle, most Men will allow." (4)

LM 49 (Sep 1779), 424; PA, Jul 14, 1779.

Quatrain. Epigram. A freeholder is as good as a peer.

79-363. The One Thing Needful.

"To save the State, in this dark Hour." (12)

PA, Jun 25, 1779; W Eve Post, Jul 3, 1779.

Quatrain. A poll-tax, that is, a head-tax or execution, is recommended for those responsible for the terrible state of the country.

79-364. Original Lines from a Seaman now at Portsmouth, to his Comrade, containing a rough opinion upon the present Trial, &c.

"Well, Tom! -- If so be, as the Vice of the Blue." (28)

MP, Apr 24, 1779.

Anapest tetrameter couplets. On Palliser's court-martial trial, April 12-May 5, 1779. The persona of a sailor defends Palliser against Keppel's unjust criticism; declares Keppel is a tool of the politically minded Duke of Richmond.

79-365. An Outline of the Earl of [Mansfield]. A Fragment.

"Stuarts he lov'd, but robb'd of that pretence." (19)

L Eve Post, Jul 17, 1779.

HC. Satire on "high Tory" or Jacobite Mansfield (in part) for the American rebellion, by his counsels for "a weak Prince." He advised proclaiming the Americans as rebels, here considered "A fatal transaction."

79-366. The Ox and the Frogs. A Fable for the Times.

"Before I'll be humm'd by the Frogs, (cries the Ox)." (12)

PA, Sep 1, 1779; W Eve Post, Aug 31, 1779.

Quatrains. Animal fable. The British will simply trample all over the treacherous French.

79-367. [A Papist! no; I hope not, for then I.]

"A Papist! no; I hope not, for then I." (54)

Freeman's J, Feb 23, 1779.

Quatrains and OC. Satire on Palliser and Germain, North and Sandwich, who are beloved by the Devil.

79-368. The Parliament Man.

"Demure and profound." (42)

LM 49 (Jan 1780), 39-40; PA, Dec 31, 1779.

Sixains. Satire on a typically corrupt politician without principle.

79-369. Parody, by a Hittite. Serjeant North Recruiting the Gibbonite. A Duetto. To the Tune of a Favourite Air in the Camp.

"Thou little Historian, come list with me." (18)

PA, Aug 12, 1779.

HC. A satire on Gibbon's appointment by North to the Board of Trade regardless of serious principle.

79-370. Parody on Part of the Old Song of Chevy-Chace.

"God prosper long our Noble King." (32)

Lloyd's 45 (Sep 15, 1779), 267; PA, Sep 16, 1779.

Ironic satire on Sandwich and the navy. Ballad on the failure of Admiral Hardy, after receiving negative orders from Sandwich to engage the French fleet off Plymouth.

79-371. Pasquinade. Addressed to ----- -----, Esquire.

"Bred at Newmarket, Almack's, White's." (39)

L Eve Post, Jul 3, 1779.

OC. Satire on an MP patronized by the ministerial majority, concluding with cutting remarks on Germain.

79-372. A Patriotic, Sentimental Toast in Verse.

"B. M. S. N. G. may the halter dispatch 'em." (4)

LP, Dec 13, 1779.

Hexameter couplets. Bute, Mansfield, Sandwich, North, Germain, and Parson Bate, publisher of the Morning Post, should be hanged. "So infernal a crew!"

79-373. Patriotic Stanzas.

"For ages Britain's sons have fought." (28)

MP, Jul 1, 1779.

Quatrains. Luxury, bribery, and faction weakened Britain, but now Britain's genius is rising again in the figure of John Strutt, MP from Essex. (The Morning Post, having become a Government subsidized newspaper edited by Parson Henry Bate, now praises Strutt, the only member of the House of Commons to oppose openly a vote of thanks to Keppel for his services in 1779. An independent country gentleman with Tory ideas, he was of course a steady supporter of North's ministry.)

79-374. Patriotic Tergiversation. An Epigram.

"Some Men may wonder that, 'midst all this Work." (6)

PA, Feb 11, 1779.

HC. Scatological and nasty satire on Burke's oratory, "only Wind."

79-375. A Patriotick Wish.

"Long may brave Hardy British Hearts inspire." (4)

St J's C, Jul 3, 1779.

HC. Captain Charles Hardy (of the navy) deserves praise for his courage.

79-376. Political Duck-Hunting.

"Once on a Time some idle Folks." (36)

PA, Jun 21, 1779.

Sixains. Animal fable about the war between France and Britain, in which Russia, Prussia, and Holland declare their neutrality.

79-377. The Poor Man's Soliloquy to his Tobacco Pipe.

"Farewell, my Pipe, my social Pipe adieu." (31)

LP, Apr 9, 1779.

HC. A smoker bewails the loss of tobacco, the trade with America having been ruined, and blames the Scotch.

A Portrait of the Sublime and Beautiful, from the Apology for the Times. "Then many a B[----], in flow'r-enamell'd tale." (24) MP, Oct 1, 1779. HC. Satire on Burke for his florid oratory and support of the Rebellion. From Daniel Chandler, An Apology for the Times (1778): see 78-7.

79-378. The Portrait-Painter. No. III. Admiral Keppel.

"O for a Muse! -- to waft my flight." (12)

WM 44 (Jun 2, 1779), 250;  West M 7 (Mar 1779), 158.

Irregular stanzas.  Keppel is apotheosized in these lines.

79-379.  A Prayer.  Said to be Written at Philadelphia soon after the Last Proclamation of the Commissioners threatening the Extremes of War and Desolation.

"O Thou! by whose almighty nod, the scale." (29)

L Eve Post, Feb 13, 1779.

Blank verse.  An American prayer to save American liberty from tyranny, and an invitation to those oppressed in Europe to live in America and to share her freedom.

79-380.  The Premier's Orison to Dulness:  A Dreaming Rhapsody.

"In seven-fold fog conceal'd from couch of lead." (66)

L Eve Post, Jun 22, 1779.

HC.  The persona of North, bored, confesses to the power of dullness.  He is haunted by the vision of rebels and patriots, fears impeachment and execution for the loss of empire, confesses that he is a tool and that his councils "echo to a Bute" and the Tory maxims of Mansfield.

79-381.  Private Thoughts of a Modern Patriot.

"Let Shame o'ertake th'apostate slave." (12)

MP, Apr 12, 1779.

Quatrains.  Ironic remarks on the politics of interest, which motivate both ins and outs, Opposition and Government.

79-382.  Prologue to the new Comedy of Gaelic Gratitude, or The Frenchman in India.  Spoken by Mrs. Jackson, in the Character of Britannia.  Written by J. S. Dodd.

"France, from my first existence, well I know." (42)

WM 45 (Jul 7, 1779), 38.

HC. Britain complains of treacherous and ungrateful France, her mortal foe, who has interfered in the American War and hopes to gain some spoil.

79-383. [A Prophecy by the Devil's Oracle.]

"If British armies reach th'American shore." (4)

L Eve Post, Jan 2, 1779.

HC. John the Painter is made to prophesy the end of the British empire, if America is attacked.

79-384. A Prophecy, Found among the Manuscripts of a Gentleman, lately deceased. Written in the Year 1690.

"Tho' William's arm hath quell'd the Foe." (36)

GA, Apr 1, 1779.

OC. A prophecy that within a century, the Revolution Constitution established in King William's reign will be overthrown (by Tories) by Scotsmen, who succeed the Whigs and who are responsible for excessive taxation, General Warrants, wars, emigration, and corruption. Cited are North, Mansfield, and Wedderburne. A useful summary of the popular grievances that disturbed the reign of George III (in this period).

79-385. The Prorogation.

"The Session, methinks, grows tedious and late." (8)

G Eve Post, Jun 24, 1779; PA, Jun 26, 1779.

Hexameter couplets. On the frustrations of politics in Parliament: nothing can get done! Burke and the Spanish Manifesto are cited. Burke wished to conclude "this American Work."

79-386. A Protest Against What have been Offered as the Terms of the Loan for 1779. . . . Addressed to the Right Honourable Frederick Lord North.

"When all was wrapt in dark midnight." (36)

L Eve Post, Jan 23, 1779.

Ballad. Parody of "Margaret's Ghost." An objection to "the extravagance" of North's plan for the subscription to the state loan for 1779.

79-387. Punchinello to the K[ing], on the Late Glorious Success of his M[ajesty]'s Arms in America.

"When first your Cannon so clear-o." (41)

PA, Dec 24, 1779.

Mixed verse. Satire on the British military leadership. The British at Savannah repelled the attack by the forces under Admiral D'Estaing and General Lincoln; but British General Prevost is still blocked there, despite the victory. The point is that the British are unable to manage a clear-cut victory over the rebel forces.

79-388. Question and Answer.

"Q. Was there a viler Ministry e'er known." (4)

LP, Dec 13, 1779.

HC. Epigram. The ministry is vile, and the Scotch dominate it, and the King is pleased with it.

79-389. Reason Why Keppel Smiled at Palliser's Questions.

"With malice curs'd, and full of subtle wiles." (6)

GA, Jan 29, 1779.

HC. Defense of Keppel against Palliser's wiles. An incident at Keppel's court-martial.

79-390. Receipt to make a Modern Minister.

"To form a minister, th'ingredients." (16)

LM 48 (Appendix 1779), 599.

OC. A minister must play many roles; he must be an opportunist. North is the model, "a mixture / Of broker, sycophant, and trickster."

79-391. The Recess of Parliament.

"Retiring from the winter's fight." (28)

G Eve Post, Jul 6, 1779; Lloyd's 45 (Jul 7, 1779), 28; LM 48 (Aug 1779),

377; PA, Jul 8, 1779; WM 45 (Jul 21, 1779), 86-7; W Eve Post, Jul 6, 1779.

Quatrains. Urges Parliament to cease wrangling, because the need is for unanimity, now that Spain has declared war on Britain. (Yet Parliament went into recess!)

79-392. The Reign of Indolence.

"Voluptuous goddess! in whose fairy bow'rs." (171)

L Cour, Dec 18, 1779.

HC. Satire on lethargic Administration. Important is the section demanding action on the need to relieve Ireland by giving it free trade. Criticized is the poor state of the navy, as are the tyrant King, Sandwich, Germain, Dundass, the "bloody" bishops, and North. Cited also are Fox, Paul Jones, and Burgoyne.

79-393. The Restoration.

"When Charles from Foreign Climes return'd." (24)

PA, May 29, 1779; W Eve Post, May 27, 1779.

Quatrains. Ironic praise (?) of the Opposition: Richmond, Grafton, "The sons of England's deadliest foes / Are now her warmest friends."

79-394. Rome and Britain.

"Rome in her greatest brightest Hour." (12)

PA, Apr 8, 1779.

Quatrains. Unlike Rome, Britain is fighting a senseless war against half the world.

79-395. A Rondeau.

"Tell me when, inconstant Rover." (14)

PA, Jul 29, 1779.

A song. The sailor's sweetheart hopes her lover will return.

79-396. [Rouze, Briton, rouse! awake your genuine flame.]

"Rouze, Briton, rouse! awake your genuine flame." (24)

M Chron, Aug 23, 1779.

Patriotic song against the Bourbon enemy. "Let party discord cease, and all unite / T'oppose our foe, defend our country's right."

79-397. [Rowe's *Fair Penitent*.]

"Lord G[eorge] G[ermaine] I knew him well; he was sagacious, cunning." (14)

G, Mar 15, 1779.

Extracts from Nicholas Rowe's play are applied to the current scene. Criticisms of Lord Germain, Sir Hugh Palliser, and Parliament; and praise of Admiral Keppel. Parliament is "weak, divided, irresolute."

79-398. Royal Pity.

"When o'er a new Express G. throws his eyes." (6)

GA, Jan 12, 1779.

Satire on King George and Premier North for being cruel and bloodthirsty regarding Americans: burning "villages and churches," and scalping men, women, and children.

79-399. Royal Resolutions.

"When our Master, God bless him, ascended the Throne." (64)

L Eve Post, Mar 4, 1779; PA, Mar 3, 1779; Jeffery Dunstan, Fugitive Pieces (1789), pp. 99-102.

Hexameter triplets. An imitation of Andrew Marvell's ballad, "Royal Resolutions," written in the reign of Charles II. Satire on George III, his obstinacy and manner of ruling the nation. George stubbornly resolves to be corrupt, to restore the Tories, to choose North, Germain, and Sandwich as his ministers, to coerce the Americans, to use German mercenaries, etc., to ruin the country and to be responsible for the decline of Britain.

79-400. The Sailor's Farewell.

"Farewell, ye buxom Lasses all." (16)

PA, Jul 31, 1779.

Quatrains. The sailor boasts that he will return rich with Spanish plunder.

79-401. The Sailor's Song.

"Come listen my lads, to my song lend an ear." (48)

Freeman's J, Mar 11, 1779; GA, Mar 2, 1779.

Ballad. On brave Keppel.

79-402. [A Sailor's voice, untun'd can raise.]

"A Sailor's voice, untun'd can raise." (32)

GA, Feb 10, 1779.

Quatrains. In defense of Keppel.

79-403. Satire on the King's Birth-Day.

"Come Truth, and help me, whilst I sing." (94)

PA, Jun 30, 1779.

OC. Ironic satire that is meant to be sincere praise of King George, including his generous attitude towards the Catholics. The Queen, too, is praised for her virtue.

79-404. Saunders's Ghost. A Song, to the Tune of "Welcome, welcome, brother Debtor," enrolled this Morning in divers Streets at the West End of the Town. . . .

"Haste, thee! Saunders, England calls thee." (48)

Freeman's J, Jan 14, 1779; G, Jan 28, 1779; L Eve Post, Jan 7, 1779.

Song, in defense of Keppel, disciple of Admiral Saunders, under whom he had served in the Seven Years' War. Saunders' ghost defends Keppel from the malice of Palliser. The music for "Welcome, welcome, brother debtor" may be seen in Calliope, or The Musical Miscellany (1788), p. 30. To the Tune of "Cease, rude Boreas."

79-405. [Say, Muse, with whom shall I begin.]

"Say, Muse, with whom shall I begin." (20)

PA, Nov 26, 1779.

OC. A satire that introduces a prose essay on the seditious Opposition -- Burke, Richmond, and others -- regarding Ireland. Signed "Alfred."

79-406. Scotch Comfort and Accentuation.

"Tho' we from prize American." (8)

L Eve Post, Oct 26, 1779.

Alternate rhymes. Satire on the Scotch at Court. The Scotch are not afraid, even though America is lost, for "the King is his own Minister." (That is, the King will protect them.) See 79-336.

79-407. The Sentence of a Late Court-Martial, Doggrelized.

"In the action of the day, you fought." (6 + 2)

L Eve Post, May 29, 1779.

Two extempores. The reference is to the trial and acquittal of Palliser, April 12-May 5, 1779. The court found his conduct exemplary but questioned why he did not inform Keppel of the disabled state of his ship. Hence the allusion to the "rotten mast" and the fact that the sentence was both censorious and acquitting, a little less than a totally honorable acquittal.

79-408. September. To the Sportsmen.

"Now, now, while France and Spain combine." (24)

G Eve Post, Aug 31, 1779; Lloyd's 45 (Aug 1, 1779), 219; L Chron 46 (Aug 31, 1779), 215; M Chron, Sep 2, 1779; MP, Sep 2, 1779; PA, Sep 1, 1779; W Eve Post, Aug 31, 1779. Also repr. GA, Sep 5, 1782; L Cour, Sep 6, 1782.

Quatrains. On the war with France and Spain. The season now opens to hunt down the enemy, France and Spain.

79-409. A Shew Man's Song at Bartle-My-Fair.

"First you see the Court so fine-a." (32 + chorus)

L Eve Post, Sep 7, 1779.

Song, with "Doodle, doo" chorus. Several scenes are represented ironically -- the King and Queen at Court, the corrupt ministers, the fleet, Westminster volunteers, the Irish who want a share in trade, the Americans defeating Burgoyne, and the Temple-bar.

79-410. A Sketch.

"Alas! how chang'd from him whose patriot ire." (11)

MP, Mar 27, 1779.

Irregular couplets (mostly trochaic). Satire on Keppel, who -- like Wilkes -- has lost his reputation because he became involved in party politics: "A dupe to Faction," his name "Sunk in Sedition's jakes."

79-411. The Soldier's Soliloquy.

"To fight or not to fight? that is the question." (19)

W Misc 13 (Dec 27, 1779), 312.

Parody on Hamlet's soliloquy adapted to the war with the French: Should we have war or peace, that is the question.

79-412. The Solemn Appeal of Britannia to her Sons.

"Old England's genius sparkling in his eyes." (50)

G Eve Post, May 20, 1779; SM 41 (May 1779), 267; WM 44 (Jun 2, 1779), 250.

HC. A patriotic poem. Chatham's spirit rises, the genius of Britain "sparkling in his eyes," invokes the past, including Wolfe, to conquer France. A question is asked: "Shall now Rebellion with ferocious hand, / Combin'd with Bourbon, crush this once-fam'd land?" Another question relates to internal dissension.

79-413. [The son of Adam slew his brother.]

"The son of Adam slew his brother." (20)

L Cour, Dec 4, 1779.

OC. Almon's paper says there was a conspiracy to kill Charles James Fox.

William Adam challenged Fox to a duel (late November, 1779) as a result of Fox's ridicule when Adam announced he would vote against the motion for the removal of the ministry. Fox was slightly wounded. See <u>Paradise Regain'd:</u> <u>Or, The Battle of Adam And The Fox</u> (1780), 80-24.

79-414. A Song.

"Sir Hugh, with courage stout and bold." (64)

GA, Mar 24, 1779.

Ballad. Satire on Palliser. He was unable to injure Keppel in his court testimony. This lyric presents some of the details of the Ushant episode and the Keppel court-martial, and stresses Palliser's allegedly dishonorable behavior.

79-415. Song. Captain Briton, placing his men on each side of him, sings,

"Come, my lads, with souls befitting." (32)

L Chron 45 (Mar 27, 1779), 300; M Chron, Mar 29, 1779; SM 41 (Jun 1779), 336.

A patriotic war song. Britain will depend on her navy to "avenge" her wrongs and to "support her injur'd trade."

79-416. A Song for the Sailors. Tune, The Gods of the Greeks.

"Once Old England's brave Tars." (18)

PA, Sep 11, 1779.

A war song against the French and the Spanish, who will be defeated once the navy is permitted to engage.

79-417. Song from the Royal Nursery.

"Georgy was crying, if story says true." (30)

L Cour, Dec 15, 1779; PM 2 (May 1780), 160.

Satire on the King. He prefers to play at military affairs; but he is simply angered by the loss of America.

Song in The Liverpool Prize. See "The Hyaena," 79-211.

79-418.  Song.  To be sung at the Court of Comus, in Smithfield.

"Fill our Bowls, good Mistress G."  (45)

St J's C, Mar 25, 1779.

A drinking song honoring the navy, which will again (it is hoped) "beat both France and Spain."

79-419.  Song.  To the Tune of, "On The white Cliffs of Albion," &c.

"Behold, on yon cliff, how Britannia appears."  (48)

M Chron, Feb 15, 1779;  PA, Feb 16, 1779.

Lyric in quatrains, attacks Palliser and his supporters, but defends Keppel and his supporters.

79-420.  Song.  To the Tune of, "Over the Hills and Far Away!"

"Britons, while th'invading foe."  (12)

MP, Sep 30, 1779.

Patriotic lyric:  Admiral Hardy will protect the coasts from French invasion.

79-421.  Song.  To the Tune of -- "To all you Ladies now at Land."  Written by an Officer on board Sir Charles Hardy's Fleet.

"To all our Countrymen at Land."  (42)

PA, Sep 3, 1779.

If the British navy is defeated by the combined French and Spanish fleet, then the fault is Sandwich's.

79-422.  Song.  Written by a Gentleman of Philadelphia.

"Late a council of Gods by the mandate of Jove."  (32)

MP, Jun 7, 1779.

Satire on Howe and Burgoyne -- Howe for his ineffectiveness and Burgoyne for his poor leadership and surrender.

79-423. Songs sung by Mr. Vernon, on Saturday Night at Drury-lane Theatre, in a new Piece called Britons Strike Home, or, The Sailors Rehearsal. Song. Tune, Then why should we quarrel for riches.

"Come, the mates of my fortune, be cheary." (20 + chorus)

L Chron 45 (Mar 27, 1779), 300.

The second song is entitled "Song. Captain Briton. . . ." Patriotic anti-gallican song. See 79-415.

79-424. The Spanish Manifest. Painted in its true Colours. By a Travestie thereof in the Style of Hudibras.

"The World undoubtedly can see." (c. 120)

MP, Jun 26, 1779.

Imitation of Hudibras. Doggerel, tetrameter couplets. Speaking in persona, a Spanish minister reveals Spain's true intentions regarding England and the American rebellion. Cited are the French, Yankees, and Indians. (Spain enters the war on the side of France, June 21, 1779.)

79-425. The Spanish Manifesto.

"The World can bear Witness that nothing cou'd ruffle." (48)

MP, Jun 30, 1779; PA, Jul 8, 1779.

Hexameter couplets. A humorous presentation of the reasons Spain decided to give for declaring war on Britain. (The title is "Old-Mother-Dover's Farewell Speech; Or, The Spanish Manifesto," in MP.) Cited are Indians, France, and English encroachments on Spanish possessions in the Caribbean. (Spain enters the war on the side of France, June 21, 1779.)

79-426. Spanish War.

"Now Sandwich and North are deep in the Dumps." (4)

PA, Jun 30, 1779.

Quatrain. Extempore. North and Sandwich are in unenviable difficulty, now that France and Spain are in the war.

79-427. The Spanish War. Addressed to the Tars of Old England.

"Now, my jolly Boys, attack 'em." (28)

Lloyd's 44 (Jun 28, 1779), 619; PA, Jun 29, 1779; W Eve Post, Jul 3, 1779.

Quatrains. A patriotic lyric on the war against Spain. British sailors are happy to have the "dollars" of "the haughty Dons."

79-428. A Speech. By a Great Little Man. Delivered July 3d, 1779.

"I thank you for services many and great." (24)

HM 9 (Nov 1779), 648; LM 48 (Oct 1779), 473; PA, Jul 8, 1779.

Anapest tetrameter couplets. Just before the recess, the King's persona thanks Parliament for its services, especially for its "most noble supplies" to carry on the war in view of the "outrageous attack" on the English crown.

79-429. A Speech On B---E's Motion to Rid the Soldiery from Slavery.

"Mr. Speaker, Who 'lists for life, B---e pitys much." (24)

MP, Feb 29, 1779.

Quatrains, in defense of the practice to keep officers in rank for life against Barre's motion.

79-430. A Speedy way to get rid of Liberty.

"To quick destruction would you Freedom bring." (2)

LP, Dec 13, 1779.

HC. Epigram. King George, "some Saintlike King," is an effective instrument for the destruction of freedom.

79-431. Stag Hunting. A New Ballad.

"Sing Hudibras, the charming sight." (80)

LP, Nov 22, 1779.

Ballad narrative of the American contest. King George hunts the stag and loses the colonies in the war of the rebellion. The rhyme tag is "stag" throughout the ballad.

79-432. Stanzas Addressed to the Right Honourable Lord Amherst, on reading the Warlike Ode to the Genius of Great Britain, dedicated to his Lordship.

"When Patriot Bards attune the lyre." (20)

MP, Feb 10, 1779.

Quatrains, in praise of Amherst, to whom Tasker's inspiring ode was dedicated. (Amherst had declined to lead a command against the Americans, and was inactive until early 1778 when, after France entered the war, he accepted a full generalship and command of British land forces in Britain, with membership in the cabinet.) For Tasker's ode, see 78-40, 78-41, and 78-42.

79-433. Stanzas, By Way of Exhortation to our British Youth.

"Britons be bold! nor let thy god-like fame." (20)

M Chron, Aug 26, 1779; PA, Aug 27, 1779.

HC. British youth are exhorted to be patriotic and to support Keppel in the fight against France and Spain.

79-434. Stanzas occasioned by a late Naval Speech at Portsmouth.

"Whilst poor Sir Hugh is swoln with Spite." (18)

PA, Feb 5, 1779.

Sixains. A reaction to the court-martial proceedings against Keppel. The poet blames not Palliser or Keppel for the failure to defeat the French fleet, but the King and his cowardly policy. These stanzas occasioned a defense of the King. See "To the Anonymous Author," PA, Feb 11, 1779: 79-478.

79-435. Stanzas on the British Navy.

"How oft we've seen in ev'ry form." (20)

G Eve Post, Jun 26, 1779; MP, Jun 28, 1779; WM 45 (Jul 7, 1779), 39.

Quatrains. Britain should not fear the Bourbon alliance, the unity of "haughty Dons" and "French chicane."

79-436. Stanzas. On the Fate of the Late Brave Captain Farmer.

"Why are the Muses mute so long." (30)

MP, Oct 22, 1779.

Regular ode in sixains, in praise of Capt. Farmer who went down with his ship, blown up by the French (Oct. 6, 1779).

79-437. Stanzas on the present War.

"See France and Spain to battle dare." (18)

G Eve Post, Aug 17, 1779; MP, Aug 19, 1779.

Regular ode in sixains. Patriotic stanzas inspiring Britons to arm against the alliance of France and Spain -- invoking past glory: Cressy and Agincourt. See Frank Moore, Diary of the American Revolution (1860), II, 251.

79-438. Stanzas to Britons.

"Insidious Foes may hope in vain." (20)

MP, Jul 23, 1779.

Regular ode in cinquains. Patriotic stanzas written in the face of the combined threat from France and Spain. Britons will unite and, as before, will conquer their foes.

79-439. Stanzas. To Sir Charles Hardy.

"Go, unappall'd, brave Hardy, to the fight." (16)

MP, Sep 23, 1779.

Quatrains. Praises brave Hardy and urges him to sustain British sovereignty over the seas.

79-440. Stanzas to the Grand Fleet, on their Late Sailing from Portsmouth.

"Once more, ye gallant youths, the Bard who sung." (56)

MP, Jul 14, 1779.

Heroic quatrains exhorting naval officers heading the fleet that will soon attack the French -- Barrington, Wallace, Hardy, Ross, Lockhart, Digby, and Darby.

79-441. Stanzas To the Members of the late Court-Martial.

"What radiant forms salute my sight." (28)

MP, May 22, 1779.

Quatrains. The reference is Palliser's trial, April 12-May 5, 1779. Impartial praise of the court-martial members for rendering justice. Apparently anti-Keppel in sentiment because "Faction" is criticized.

79-442. The State of the Nation.

"Down Ruin's track, a headlong steep!" (76)

LM 48 (Jul 1779), 326-7.

Quatrains. A protest at the fruitless war run by politicians who protect themselves from effective criticism by means of corruption.

79-443. The State Quacks.

"Britannia was sick, for a Doctor they sent." (20)

UM 64 (Jan 1779), 43-4; WM 43 (Mar 3, 1779), 232.

Quatrains. The doctors cannot help Britain, who is dying. A reprint of 77-290.

79-444. [A Strong Gale from the West.]

"A Strong Gale from the West." (9 + 8)

PA, Sep 15, 1779.

Two epigrams on Admiral Hardy's recent skirmish with the French fleet.

79-445. [Struck with the chilling northern blast.]

"Struck with the chilling northern blast." (8)

L Cour, Dec 31, 1779.

Quatrains. Pessimistic view of the state of the nation: Britain is being ruined, and no one wishes to save her.

79-446. A Tale for the Times. Inscribed to Sir Philip Jennings Clerke, Bart.

"I once a pack of foxhounds knew." (66)

GM 49 (Jul 1779), 368.

OC. An allegorical tale about poor leadership that causes disorder and rebellion and emigration.

79-447. The Tar's Invitation. Tune, A cruising we will go. A Parody on the Song called the Hyena.

"Behold upon the swelling wave." (24)

MP, Oct 15, 1779.

A serious imitation of Thompson's "Hyaena" -- in which it is asserted that the sailors will "curb the pride / Of Rebels, Spain and France"; and Britons are also admonished to "unite" against all its foes! See "The Hyaena," 79-211.

79-448. Tempora Mutantur! --

"In ancient Story, we are told." (16)

PA, Feb 20, 1779.

Sixains. There is little cause to rejoice at Keppel's disgrace.

79-449. Tempora Mutantur. Verses for the 27th of April, (N. S.) being the Anniversary of the Battle of Culloden, fought April 16, 1746, (O. S.). . . .

"On this bright Day, with Vict'ry red." (12)

PA, May 5, 1779.

Quatrains. In George II's day, the Scotch were considered rebels; but now the Scotch are prime loyalists and the English seditious.

79-450. [That D'Orvilliers and Hardy.]

"That D'Orvilliers and Hardy." (24)

PA, Aug 28, 1779.

Sixains. Admiral Hardy is tardy in engaging the fleet under D'Orvilliers, but the French will soon be defeated once the British begin their attack.

Thompson, Edward. See "The Hyaena. Inscribed to the Girls of Gainsborough," 79-211.

79-451. [Thou! whose arms, so oft victorious.]

"Thou! whose arms, so oft victorious." (32)

GA, Feb 12, 1779.

Quatrains. Praise of Keppel by a lady in Portsmouth.

79-452. The Times.

"America -- contending." (11)

DJ, Apr 13, 1779;   L Eve Post, Apr 8, 1779.

Prose-poem (?). A catalogue of observations on the nations at this time of the American War.

79-453. The Times.

"Attend my good Folks to the Song that I sing." (32)

PA, Oct 23, 1779.

A song. Satire on the times. The country is declining, but lawyers flourish. The soldiers deserve more pay; the sailors, we hope, will provide "a true Touch on the Times." Cited, too, are taxes and the premier.

79-454. The Times.

"The ministers bad." (36)

LM 48 (Appendix 1779), 598-9;   LP, Oct 13, 1779;   PA, Oct 14, 1779.

Sixains. Divided Britain is surrounded by enemies -- even the Dutch. Perhaps Britain may receive assistance from Prussia and Russia. Joseph Yorke, Ambassador to Holland, is cited.

79-455. The Times, at Sea.

"I sing of the War ere it closes." (24)

PA, Aug 14, 1779; W Eve Post, Aug 12, 1779.

Quatrains. Satire on Sandwich and his ineffectual navy.

79-456. Those Times, and These Times.

"In Fifty nine, illustrious Hawke." (32)

PA, Nov 25, 1779.

Double quatrains. At the time of George II, France was at bay; but today in George III's reign, France is threatening Britain. Those responsible for this change must be punished.

79-457. To a Beggar on Horseback.

"You I hate for prancing so." (46)

PA, Feb 24, 1779.

OC. A review of a variety of distasteful experiences, concluding with a reference to the Court and the King's Friends (Bute).

79-458. To Admiral Keppel.

"True son of Albion, in thyself compleat." (28)

L Eve Post, Jan 30, 1779.

HC. Praise of Keppel who, with Hawke, will continue to crush France.

79-459. To Admiral Keppel on his Trial.

"Thine enemies are cover'd with disgrace." (4)

L Eve Post, Feb 6, 1779.

Extempore. HC. Keppel's honor is cleared; Palliser is shamed. The trial is nearing its end.

79-460. To Admiral Lord Hawke [et al.].

"My Lords, and Gentlemen." (c. 8)

GA, Jan 7, 1779.

An inscription praising the members of the court martial for Keppel for their (it is hoped) defense of Keppel.

79-461. [To arms! when Whitehead cry'd the other day.]

"To arms! when Whitehead cry'd the other day." (30)

Freeman's J, Jan 26, 1779; L Eve Post, Jan 9, 1779.

HC. Satire on the inefficiency of the administration and the war effort. Cited are Whitehead, the King, North, and the fast.

79-462. To Britannia's Sons.

"Rise, Britons! rise -- your utmost pow'rs unite." (12)

Cumb Pacq, Apr 27, 1779.

HC. Britons are urged to banish vice, be virtuous, and unite in order to defeat France.

79-463. To Captain Collingwood.

"Ye heav'nly nymphs! your poet's breast inspire." (32)

West M 13 (May 1785), 269.

HC. An address to a captain of a naval vessel by a sailor who prays for his discharge and return to England. He has had enough of war.

79-464. To Charles Fox, Esq. An Impromptu.

"Ah, Charles! would some blest power divide." (6)

MP, Apr 1, 1779.

Sixain. Fox speaks eloquently and admirably; but his mind, poor and detestable, deserves scorn.

79-465. To David Hartley, Esq; on his Motion to Reconcile America and Great

Britain.

"David, thy sense is bright, thy judgment sound." (14)

L Eve Post, Jun 24, 1779.

HC. Hartley is praised for his attempt to reconcile America and Great Britain, but his plan will fail because of Tory and tyrannical policies, "Scotchmen and prerogative."

79-466. To Gallia.

"Weep! Gallia, weep! thy crested flow'rs." (20)

G, Sep 2, 1779; W Eve Post, Jul 24, 1779.

Quatrains. Treacherous France has reason to fear Britain, now strengthened by the spirit of unanimity.

79-467. To Lord M[ansfiel]d.

"Think not, base Scot, when all the mischief's done." (4)

L Eve Post, Sep 7, 1779.

HC. Satire on Mansfield. Mansfield, "base Scot," will pay the penalty for his crimes -- he cannot escape the wrath of the people.

79-468. To Peace.

"Come lovely, gentle peace of mind." (28)

W Misc 13 (Dec 27, 1779), 312.

Quatrains blessing peace of mind away from "the crowded court," in the country.

79-469. To Sir Charles Bunbury, on his Oration Recommending a Coalition of Parties, and Complimenting Both Sides. . . .

"And so, Sir Charles, you'll save the State." (18)

GA, Feb 2, 1779.

Ode in sixains. Ironic satire on Bunbury for his diplomatic oration advocating a union of parties -- of North and Thurlow with Burke, Fox, and Dunning. The unanimity theme begins.

79-470. To Sir Hugh Palliser.

"Accept, much injur'd man! this humble verse." (16)

MP, May 4, 1779.

HC. Brave Palliser is undeserving of the criticism inspired by malicious Shelburne and Richmond.

79-471. To Sir Hugh Palliser.

"Aloof from Envy's grasp is he." (72)

GA, Jan 22, 1779.

Quatrains. Satire on Palliser for his dishonorable behavior. Some questions are raised about his testimony at Keppel's trial.

79-472. To Sir Hugh P[alliser].

"Fie upon you, Sir Hugh, who your honour survive." (6)

L Eve Post, Apr 1, 1779.

Three epigrams. Satire on Sandwich and Palliser for their dishonorable role in the Keppel trial.

79-473. To Sir Hugh Palliser.

"For once, Sir Hugh, your cards you've manag'd ill." (4)

GA, Jan 9, 1779.

Quatrain. Criticism of Palliser. Attempting to destroy Keppel's reputation, he only destroyed his own.

79-474. To Sir H[ugh] P[alliser].

"My good friend, Sir H[ugh]." (48)

GA, Mar 9, 1779.

Sixains. Satire on Palliser. The Devil Satan and Judas the Traitor send greetings from Hell to Palliser; Sandwich and Palliser deserve to be in Hell, Satan declares, for there traitors and treason are enjoyed. Bate of the Morning Post is also welcomed.

79-475. To Sir [Hugh Palliser].

"Well then -- the Jury pack'd -- the Verdict got." (10)

St J's C, Dec 31, 1779.

HC. Sir Hugh Palliser and Lord Sandwich seek Keppel's life in vain, for the sailors are behind him.

79-476. To Sir H[ugh] P[alliser], in the Act of Splicing and Knotting, on the 27th of July, 1778, instead of obeying Mr. Keppel's Long Displayed Signal for Battle.

"On that sad day, ah! day of woful name." (12)

GA, Jan 7, 1779.

Quatrains. Anger at Palliser for allowing himself to be used by Sandwich.

79-477. To Sir John Lockhart Ross.

"My good Sir John Ross." (24)

PA, Sep 29, 1779.

Sixains. Capt. Ross, assigned the job of finding American marauder John Paul Jones, is warned not to announce his plans in the seditious patriot press.

79-478. To the Anonymous Author of the Infamous Lines reflecting on the King's Conduct in the Affair of Keppel and Palliser, in the Public Advertiser of Friday Feb. 5.

"Seditious Wretch! whoe'er thou art." (48)

PA, Feb 11, 1779.

Sixains. "Stanzas occasioned by a late Naval Speech" (79-434) were written by a seditious anti-monarchist. The King maintains the cause against France and Spain, contrary to what the defamatory subversive thinks.

79-479. To the Honourable Admiral Keppel.

"Hold fast, brave Keppel, never fear." (56)

GA, Jan 21, 1779.

Quatrains. Defense of Keppel against the infamous attacks by the ministers and their tools.

79-480. To the Honourable Members of the Committee for Ways and Means.

"Since ways and means you can devise." (28)

G, Jul 24, 1779; L Eve Post, Jul 13, 1779.

Quatrains. Find ways and means to save the country, cure corruption, heal Britain's "bleeding wound," and bring peace and save America and the empire.

79-481. To the [King].

"Canst thou think by carnage dire." (29)

GA, Jan 28, 1779.

OC. The poet believes the King to be foolish for trying to suppress America and liberty, and urges him and the ministry to direct their energies at the rightful enemy, France.

To the Lady of the Right Honourable Lord George Sackville. "Grieve no more, if Ills depress." (30) PA, Mar 17, 1779. Praise and defense of Sackville (Germain) against all traducers. A reprint of a poem originally published in September 1759. See 59-36.

79-482. To the Ministers, On the Return of Generals, Admirals, and Commissioners.

"Alike whate'er ye undertake, succeeds." (4)

PA, Jan 2, 1779; W. Eve Post, Dec 31, 1778-Jan 2, 1779.

Epigram. Satire. All failures, the peace commissioners, the generals, and the admirals, are interested only in "Gold."

79-483.  To the Nation.

"Now, ye Britons, join to damn 'em."  (28)

PA, Sep 11, 1779; W. Eve Post, Sep 11, 1779.

Quatrains.  A patriotic war poem.


79-484.  To the People.

"God save the King! and grant him eyes."  (23)

L Eve Post, Sep 11, 1779.

OC.  Grant that the King recognize "his real enemies":  Germain, North, Sandwich, Mansfield, and Bute -- the ministry.  Then America and Britain will be reconciled, and Britain will fight its real enemy, France.


79-485.  To the People.  On Sir Hugh Palliser.

"Judge not in haste, but wait and see."  (4)

MP, Apr 20, 1779.

Quatrain.  Admonishes the people to judge Palliser impartially and fairly. Palliser should not be pre-judged guilty until all the facts are in.


79-486.  To the Right Hon. Earl Sandwich.  Written by C. W., an impressed Youth on board the Hulk at Plymouth Dock.

"Sandwich to thee the captive Stripling pray'd."  (10)

PA, Jul 31, 1779.

HC.  A youth thanks Sandwich for freeing him from impressment.


79-487.  To the Right Honourable Lord Amherst, Commander in Chief of his Majesty's Forces; the Petition of Francis Palmer, a Lieutenant on half-pay.

"A Soldier's woes, a Poet's pray'r."  (18)

MP, Aug 10, 1779.

OC.  A veteran of Britain's wars petitions Amherst to increase his annuity.

79-488.  To the Tars of Old England.

"Attack them, Hearts of English Oak."  (24)

L Chron 46 (Aug 26, 1779), 199;  MP, Aug 28, 1779;  PA, Aug 27, 1779;  SM 41 (Sep 1779), 501;  WM 45 (Sep 15, 1779), 278-9;  West J, Sep 4, 1779;  W Eve Post, Sep 4, 1779.

Song.  Quatrains.  Patriotic lyric inspiring British sailors to attack the "insidious" French and "imperious" Don with courage.

79-489.  To the tune of, "A Cobler there was."

"Ye poor foolish people who think of to-morrow."  (40)

GA, Feb 9, 1779.

Ballad narrates the Palliser-Keppel dispute, favoring Keppel, the Whig, against all his enemies, Sandwich, Parson Bate (of the Morning Post), and others.

79-490.  To the Tune of Chevy-Chase.

"Hugh Palliser, a trusty knight."  (8)

GA, Mar 9, 1779.

Ballad fragment.  Satire on Palliser, belittles him for his mean treatment of Keppel;  but Palliser has failed to injure Keppel.

79-491.  A Touch at the Times.

"How topsy-turvy things are grown."  (26)

WM 43 (Feb 10, 1779), 160.

OC.  Satire on the times.  All things are awry: King George is cowardly, North is beautiful, the Irish are our friends, generals insult the nation, admirals do not fight, etc.

79-492.  [A Triumph in Honor of Sir Hugh Palliser.]

"Those who are but friends to me."  (16)

L Eve Post, May 8, 1779.

Satire on Sandwich and Palliser. An ironic comment on the request for a "triumph" honoring Palliser upon his acquittal by the court-martial, May 5 -- which was seriously proposed in the Morning Post. The difference in the politics of the London Evening Post and the Morning Post is manifest.

79-493. The True Honor of the Truly Honorable.

"Neither the Birth drawn through in long Descent." (8)

PA, Aug 11, 1779; W Eve Post, Aug 10, 1779.

Octave. True nobility is found in virtue and the noble mind. See "Of Nobility," 79-319.

79-494. The True Sailor's Garland, Or, Admiral Keppel's Triumph. A New Song. To the Tune of A Free and an Accepted Mason.

"Brother tars, now arise." (97)

Jeffery Dunstan, Fugitive Pieces (1789), pp. 109-12.

Praise of Keppel, now vindicated by the court-martial acquittal against the claims of Sandwich and Palliser. See 89-2 for Dunstan's miscellany.

79-495. Twelfth-Day.

"Now the jovial Girls and Boys." (16)

W Eve Post, Jan 5, 1779.

Quatrains. Cynical view of all people engaged in politics as selfish children "struggling for the Cake."

79-496. Twitcher and Palliser.

"To Palliser Twitcher said, Prythee, Sir Hugh." (3)

GA, Jan 20, 1779.

Triplet. Ironic satire. Sandwich's persona is made to confess guilt and to deserve execution -- with Palliser.

79-497. [Two Commissioners were sent to th'American shore.]

"Two Commissioners were sent to th'American shore."  (10)

G, Mar 4, 1779.

Hexameter couplets. An ironic comparison of the Howe Commission (1776) and the Carlisle Commission (1778).

79-498. The Ultima Ratio Regum. (To the Tune of Whitehead's Song -- "King George and Old England For Ever!")

"Pray hear a New Song."  (24)

PA, Aug 28, 1779.

Song. On the war against France and Spain, whom we shall teach a lesson.

79-499. Unanimity.

"We're all undone, say B-rke and modest B-rre."  (10)

G, Jul 31, 1779; PA, Aug 2, 1779.

HC. The Patriot Opposition, Burke and Barre, should cease its endless and fruitless criticism of Government and unite with it to beat the French.

79-500. The Unnatural Alliance.

"America begs the assistance of France."  (12)

G Eve Post, Jun 29, 1779; PA, Jun 30, 1779; WM 45 (Jul 14, 1779), 63.

Quatrains. Being "unnatural," the alliance between Dissenters and Catholics, Americans and French, cannot last. Only the Devil could have coupled "True Freedom and Slav'ry."

79-501. Upon Edward Gibbon, Esq; Author of the Decline of the Roman Empire, being made a Lord of Trade.

"King George in a fright."  (18)

PA, Jul 7, 1779; WM 45 (Jul 21, 1779), 87; New Foundling Hospital for Wit (1786), I, 35. Also repr. W Eve Post, Oct 11, 1781.

Sixains. Epigram. Satire on Gibbon for accepting a place in North's Government. Gibbon's "degen'racy" confirms his own work on Rome. The King's bribery of Gibbon is also an example of the degeneracy in Britain which will cause its decline. The author, according to W Eve Post, Oct 11, 1781, is Charles Fox.

79-502. Upon Lord S[helburn]e.

"An Atheist Priest on either side." (4)

MP, Apr 17, 1779.

Quatrain. Epigram. Satire on Shelburne, hypocritical atheist, who -- should he become premier -- will undermine religion. "An Atheist Priest on either side" is an allusion to Price and Priestley.

79-503. Verses addressed to Britannia.

"Shall Britain see insulting Gaul." (28)

WM 46 (Sep 29, 1779), 16.

Quatrains. Urges Britain to fight bravely against France.

79-504. Verses intended to have been spoken at the Mischianza, a superb entertainment given to Gen. Howe at Philadelphia, on his leaving the army; but which his Excellency would not permit to be spoken.

"Down from the starry threshold of Jove's court." (42)

GM 49 (Sep 1779), 461; M Chron, Sep 14, 1779; PA, Sep 15, 1779; SM 41 (Sep 1779), 501; WM 46 (Oct 13, 1779), 63-4; New Foundling Hospital for Wit (1786), II, 138-9.

HC. The "vet'rans" of Howe's army honor their general, who is returning to England, and vow to be "true" to his successor, Clinton. These verses may have been written by John Andre, Howe's adjutant in Philadelphia. See 78-51.

79-505. Verses, occasioned by the Recess of Parliament.

"When Freedom rear'd her throne in Britain's isle." (36)

G, Jun 14, 1779.

Quatrains. Parliament, when renewed, will continue to accept effective leadership of the country, especially union against the threat of France and Spain. See "The Recess of Parliament," another call for union: 79-391.

Verses on Mr. G[ibbon]'s Accepting a Place under Government in the Year 1779. New Foundling Hospital for Wit (1786), I, 35. See 79-501.


79-506. Cancelled.


79-507. Verses on the Appearance of the Combined Fleets being seen off Plymouth.

"Where Devon's borders check the rising flood." (24)

GM 49 (Oct 1779), 510; St J's C, Sep 18, 25, & 28, 1779; UM 65 (Oct 1779), 206.

HC. An English translation of a Latin poem on the combined French and Spanish fleets off Plymouth. The Latin poem appears in GM 49 (Sep 1779), 463, and two other translations appear in GM 49 (Oct 1779), 509-10. The Latin verses and two translations appear in St J's C. See also 79-189.
The poem complains that the English do not attack the Bourbon fleets.


79-508. Verses on the present French and Spanish War.

"Where is the Patron of the present Age." (40)

St J's C, Jul 20, 1779.

Quatrains, patriotically asserting the justice of Britain's cause against France and Spain, and the American "Rebels." Britons must be determined to win.


79-509. Verses to Chubby Chub, Esq; on his late dull, Bombastical, and Inflated Performance called the <u>Memoire Justificatif</u>.

"When chubby Gibbon strips to buff." (18)

PA, Oct 21, 1779.

Sixains. Coarse satire on Gibbon for accepting a position on the Board of Trade.


79-510. A Very Ancient Prediction of Merlin, the British Wizard. Supposed to be Delivered as Long Ago as the Year 779.

"Whan the Third Husbande-Manne shall rayne." (44)

MP, Jun 10, 1779.

Medieval imitation. Quatrains. Satire on the Patriot Opposition for being traitors to the country: Keppel, Fox, Richmond, Savile. The nation must be unified to win the war.

[Warton, Thomas.] [Poem addressed to Lord Chatham.] "Nor thine the Pomp of indolent Debate." (10) St J's C, Dec 25, 1779. A reprinting of Warton's panegyric on Chatham, which describes the character of a complete, incorruptible minister, a model for the current leadership. See Wharton, "To Mr. Secretary Pitt," 61-49.

79-511. Ways and Means; or the Minister's Reflection.

"I want more Cash, the Premier says." (4)

PA, Jun 17, 1779.

Quatrain. Epigram. Lord North will do anything to have more money for the war.

79-512. [Well, since I've thus succeeded in my plan.]

"Well, since I've thus succeeded in my plan." (34)

M Chron, Jul 16, 1779; PA, Jul 17, 1779.

HC. Should women raise an army, they will quickly bring the "tedious" American War to an end. See 79-159.

79-513. [Wesley, Charles.]
For the Fast-Day, Feb. 10, 1779.

"Tremendous God, Thy work we see." (48)

AM 3 (Oct 1780), 566-8.

Hymn in sixains. The war against America and the discord at home are the central themes of this hymn. Wesley complains of "our guilty brethren" against whom the war continues, and of the partisan fury of those who protest against the war and "thee [God] and thy vicegerent [the King] scorn."

79-514. [Wesley, John.]
2 Sam. xviii. 5. _Deal_ _gently_ _for_ _my_ _sake_ _with_ _the_ _young_ _man,_ _even_ _with_ _Absalom._

"Full of unutterable grace." (12)

AM 2 (Nov 1779), 607-8.

A short hymn. Wesley asks that the rebel son be dealt with gently.

79-515. [When Fox abjures the Name of Tod.]

"When Fox abjures the Name of Tod." (6)

PA, Oct 30, 1779.

Sixain. Epigram. Fox was given the nickname Tod, a sign of his bestiality.

79-516. [When M(ansfiel)d's Artifice a Civil War provok'd.]

"When M[ansfiel]d's Artifice a Civil War provok'd." (8)

PA, Jun 25, 1779.

Hexameter couplets. Mansfield's belligerent attitude towards the American colonies was responsible for the American War.

79-517. [When Roman virtue fell beneath the stroke.]

"When Roman virtue fell beneath the stroke." (18)

L Cour, Dec 17, 1779.

HC. England has no Cato to resist tyranny. This poem is a criticism of the King's "insidious plan" to control Government and Parliament and "to triumph o'er the rights of man."

79-518. [When treach'rous measures don't succeed.]

"When treach'rous measures don't succeed." (40)

Freeman's J, Jan 9, 1779.

Quatrains. Favors Keppel in the controversy with Palliser -- and detects a Tory plot in the affair.

79-519. [While Fame expands her hero's praise around.]

"While Fame expands her hero's praise around." (24)

GA, May 13, 1779.

HC. Generalized panegyric on Keppel.


79-520. A Whimsical War. Extempore.

"'Tis a whimsical war we are waging with France." (12)

L Chron 46 (Aug 26, 1779), 195; PA, Aug 27, 1779; SM 41 (Sep 1779), 502; W Eve Post, Sep 2, 1779.

Quatrains. The fleets of Britain and France appear to be avoiding engagement.


79-521. Whitehead, William.
Ode for his Majesty's birth-day, June 4, 1779. By William Whitehead, Esq; Poet Laureat. And set to Music by Mr. Stanley.

"Let Gallia mourn! th'insulting foe." (44)

AR, 1779, pp. 170-1; Cumb Pacq, Jun 15, 1779; DJ, Jun 10, 1779; G, Jun 4, 1779; GM 49 (Jun 1779), 317; Lady's M 10 (Jun 1779), 325; Lloyd's 44 (Jun 2, 1779), 535; L Eve Post, Jun 3, 1779; MP, Jun 5, 1779; PA, Jun 5, 1779; St J's C, Jun 3, 1779; SM 41 (Jun 1779), 336; W Misc 12 (Jun 21, 1779), 287; West J, Jun 5, 1779; W Eve Post, Jun 3, 1779. Also G Eve Post, Jun 3-5, 1779; L Chron 45 (Jun 1-3, 1779), 532; LM 48 (Jun 1779), 278-9.

Irregular Pindaric ode. France is making a dreadful mistake when treacherously deciding on war with Britain who, she thought, was "lost . . . in deep dismay, / Forlorn, distress'd." Britain will respond with force from the East (India) to the West Indies (St. Lucia).


79-522. Whitehead, William.
Ode for the New-Year. Written by Wm. Whitehead, Esq; And set to Music by Dr. Boyce.

"To arms, to arms, ye sons of might." (34)

AR, 1779, p. 169; Cumb Pacq, Jan 12, 1779; DJ, Jan 7, 1779; G, Jan 1, 1779; G Eve Post, Jan 1, 1779; GM 49 (Jan 1779), 37; Lady's M 10 (Jan 1779), 45-6; Lloyd's 44 (Dec 30, 1778-Jan 1, 1779), 7; L Eve Post, Dec 31, 1778-Jan 2, 1779; LP, Dec 31, 1778-Jan 2, 1779; MP, Jan 1 & 2, 1779; PA, Jan 1, 1779; W Misc 11 (Jan 11, 1779), 360; West J, Jan 2, 1779; W Eve Post, Dec 31, 1778-Jan 2, 1779. Also G Eve Post, Dec 31, 1778-Jan 2, 1779; L Chron 45 (Dec 31, 1778-Jan 2, 1779), 5; LM 48 (Jan 1779), 40.

Irregular Pindaric ode. Whitehead calls Britons to arms for the new French war: "New cause for just offence has Albion found." Furthermore, the French people want freedom; their government is despotic and tyrannical. But the English are happier with their "well-mixed state / Which blends the Monarch's with the Subject's fate." The English are unified in their war against France.

79-523. Who'll Suffer Most.

"A King to his People -- but not in this Age." (12)

St J's C, Aug 31, 1779.

Anapest tetrameter couplets. Satire on the King, who is threatened with loss of America to her ally, France.

79-524. Who's Afraid?

"With sixty-sail of fighting ships." (8)

G, Sep 2, 1779.

Quatrains. Extempore. Although outnumbered two to one, brave Admiral Hardy will fight off the powerful French fleet.

79-525. Written on Board the Victory.

"So long as we." (84)

GA, Feb 13, 1779.

Ode in sixains. Praise of Keppel; criticism of Palliser.

79-526. Wynne, J. H.
  Ode for the New Year, 1779.

"Still in the Western climes afar." (48)

G, Jan 1, 1779.

Three sixteen-line stanzas. Britain will still persist in the war, asserting her claim to sovereignty over the colonies, despite the objections of "Her old, insidious, nat'ral foes."

79-527. Yankee Doodle's Expedition to Rhode Island, written at Philadelphia, 1778.

"From Lewis, Monsieur Gerard came." (50)

M Chron, Jul 13, 1779; PA, Jul 14, 1779.

Ballad. Satire on the failure of the American troops under General Sullivan to dislodge the British under General Pigot in Rhode Island. Admiral D'Estaing's French fleet could not assist the Americans. With Yankee Doodle chorus. Originally published in Rivington's Royal Gazette (New York), Oct. 3, 1778.


[Ye Devonshire lads, and ye lasses.] Song. See "A Favourite New Song," 79-187.


79-528. [You Lords of the waves, amidst Europe's gay slaves.]

"You Lords of the waves, amidst Europe's gay slaves." (44)

GA, Jul 9, 1779.

Ballad. A complaint at Britain's isolation in the struggle -- at the failure of her former friends to aid her: Russia, Holland, and Prussia. But Britain can stand alone if unified and helped by Ireland. Closes with hope that England will atone for its harsh treatment of Ireland in the past.

Prints

79-529. The Birth-Day Ode: The Distresses of the Nation.

"Now Caesar sits on Throne sublime." (79)

Engr. on a printed broadside, regular Pindaric ode in two parts. June 1779.

George 5540 (V, 324-6).

A parody of Whitehead's laureate odes, possibly by John Wolcot although not included in his works. Satire on the King, Mansfield, Sandwich, Germaine, Lowth (Bishop of London), and Samuel Plumbe, the Lord Mayor of London.

79-530. A Dance by the Virtue of British Oak.

"Let others barter Servile Faith for Gold." (4)

Engr. with HC. September 1779.

George 5554 (V, 335).

At this time the allied French and Spanish fleets were in the Channel and England was in danger of invasion. A patriotic poem directed against France and Spain, "French Perfidy and Spanish Arrogance."

79-531. [Freedom, Peace, Plenty, all in vain advance.]

"Freedom, Peace, Plenty, all in vain advance." (8)

Engr. with HC. C. 1779.

John Carter Brown Library. Copy in Lewis-Walpole Library.

America, dupe to France, is a subversive scourger of the land, hypocritical, tyrannical, and Popish. (A reaction to the Franco-American treaty of alliance.)

79-532. A Meeting of City Politicians.

"With staring Eye, and Open Ear." (6)

Engr. with octosyllabic triplets. July 30, 1779.

George 5613 (V, 361).

Satire on tradesmen and artisans who neglect business for political news in the local pub.

79-533. Mr. Trade and Family or the State of the Nation.

"Oh Wash'gton is there not some Chosen Curse." (4)

Engr. with blank verse. December 1779.

George 5574 (V, 346).

Lines addressed to Washington (adapted from Addison's Cato) by a ruined merchant who asks that those politicians responsible for the country's ruin be punished.

79-534. The Political See-Saw, or Minhir Nic Frog Turn'd Balance Master.

"For Now the Field is not far off." (26)

Engr. with Hudibrastic verse. November 6, 1779.

George 5568 (V, 340-1).

Quotations from Hudibras plus an original poem (26 ll.), all emphasizing Britain's critical predicament, especially with the Dutch. The British must prepare to fight an enlarged war.

79-535. Saunders's Ghost.

"Haste thee! Saunders, England calls thee." (48)

Engr. with song in double quatrains. 1779 (?).

George 5538 (V, 323).

A song about Keppel and Palliser, favoring the former. Saunders was the naval officer who helped Wolfe win Canada from the French. See "Saunders's Ghost. A Song," 79-404.

79-536. The Terror of France, or the Westminster Volunteers, 1779.

"Can we invasions dread, when Volunteers." (4)

Engr. with HC. August 26, 1779.

George 5552 (V, 334). Repr. 1776: The British Story of the American Revolution. Catalogue (1976), p. 91.

Comical satire on the London militia, organized to defend the country against a French invasion. At this time, the French fleet was in the Channel.

1780  Books & Pamphlets

80-1. Alves, Robert.
  Ode to Britannia. (For the Year 1780.)  Occasioned By Our late Successes.  By Robert Alves, A. M.
  Edinburgh:  Creech, 1780.  12p.

  "At last Britannia wakes to war."  (102)

  Notices:  MR 62 (Mar 1780), 246;  SM 42 (Jan 1780), 41.

  Sabin 985.

  Copies:  BL 11630.b.8 (16);  NUC  RPJCB.

  Irregular Pindaric ode.  In this sublime poem, Alves celebrates the British victory over the rebel Americans and their French allies at Savannah, where Col. Maitland, a Scots officer, had died.  Maitland is praised for saving the Southern army before his death.  Alves also honors Ireland, which (restrictions on her commerce now relaxed) can now join England's struggle against the Bourbons.  England, strong again, will now control the seas and defeat the rebels.  (Repr. minus the note praising Maitland in his Poems [Edinburgh:  Creech; London: Cadell, 1782], pp. 43-8, with the title changed to "Ode for the Year 1780.  Occasioned by our Successes in the War.")  See 82-2.

80-2. André, John.
  The Cow Chace: An Heroic Poem, in Three Cantos.  Written at New York, 1780.  By the late Major André, With Explanatory Notes, by the Editor.
  London:  Fielding, 1781.  32p.

  "To drive the Kine, one summer's morn."  (284)

  Notices:  CR 52 (Sep 1781), 236;  MR 66 (Jan 1782), 72.

  Evans 16697;  Sabin 1450.

  Copies:  BL 643.k.15 (5) [11687.cc.11 (1780 Amer. ed)];  Bod Godwyn Pamph 1708;  NUC  CtY, DLC, MB, PHi, RPJCB.

  First appeared in Rivington's New York Royal Gazette--August 16, 1780 (Canto 1), August 30, 1780 (Canto 2), September 23, 1780 (Canto 3)--then separately as Cow-Chace, in three Cantos.  Published on Occasion of the Rebel General Wayne's Attack of the Refugees Block-House On Hudson's River on Friday the 21st of July, 1780 (New York:

Rivington, 1780).

Ballad, imitation of Chevy Chace. Narrates the attempt by Wayne's forces to drive a herd of loyalist cattle within the American lines near Fort Lee, on the Hudson River. They attacked a loyalist stockaded blockhouse, Bull's Ferry, New Jersey, on July 20-21, 1780 (4 miles north of Hoboken), but failed in their mission. The third canto of this mock epic ballad was published the day André was captured with documents exposing Arnold's plan to surrender West Point to the British. Generally humorous, the poem has some serious verses describing the tragic effect of the rebellion upon the loyalists (II, pp. 18-19), described as "The loyal Heroes" (II, p. 20).

80-3. Anstey, Christopher.
Speculation; Or, A Defence of Mankind: A Poem.
London: Dodsley, 1780. 52p.

"Ah me! what Spleen, Revenge, and Hate." (c. 900)

Notices: MR 62 (Jun 1780), 474-9; W Misc 14 (Sep 4, 1780), 551-2; W Eve Post Jul 20, 1780.

Copies: BL 643.k.10 (11), 11630.c.11 (1), 11658.h.1 (3); NUC CtY, DLC, IU, MH, MiU, TxU.

Octosyllabic couplets. Social satire; basically, the poem is about investing wealth, losing or making money. Embedded in the satire are two sections that are significant. In an early episode, a Bear (in the stock market) deliberately tries to depress the stocks by forging bad news--"Paul Jones, a Shipwreck, or a plague" (p. 18), and pessimistically emphasizes the dire straits in which the nation finds itself, without allies and commerce (pp. 15-6) but with quarrels at home (p. 16) and with Ireland "discontented" (p. 17)--thereby affecting "Speculation" (p. 18). In another section, Anstey ironically describes the behavior of Parliament, where debates expose all state secrets, thereby injuring the nation (pp. 30-3). He also refers ironically to the alleged success of the armed forces, without any allies--meaning their failure, of course.

80-4. The Britoniad, A Poem.
London: Kearsly, 1780. 23p.

"Resistless truths all-powerful cause I sing." (c. 340)

Notices: CR 49 (Mar 1780), 236; MR 63 (Jul 1780), 72.

Copies: BL 163.m.30; Bod Godwyn Pamph 1498 (5).

HC. Satire on the patriot minority, the Americans, and the government for its "wavering councils" demoralizing the armed forces (p. 15). Chastises America for wreaking vengeance on Britain who "Rais'd and nurtur'd thee"--but also criticizes those in England who advised the King to reject or refuse to hear American grievances. The poet grants America all British rights, but strenuously objects to its independence from Britain and its alliance with France (pp. 8-9). He also objects to the lack of common sense of "modern Whigs" who comfort the Bourbon enemy and undermine the security of the nation by propagating discord, and whom he thinks republicans (p. 12). They do not inspire confidence; they do not deserve to lead (p. 14). But Shelburne, disciple of Chatham, who observes the constitutional balance of the estates, is deserving of the leadership (pp. 16-17). Finally, the poet objects to party divisions, Tory and Whig, his interest being to "Unite contending parties, crush the foe" (p. 23).

80-5. Colvill, Robert.
Savannah A Poem In Two Cantos To The Memory Of The Honourable Colonel John Maitland. . . . Second Edition.
London: Cadell, 1780. [3-4] + 5-20p.

"Wasted by war's annoyance rude." (354)

Notices: L Chron 47 (Mar 18, 1780), 276-7.

Sabin 14902.

Copies: NUC NN (1st ed), CtY, DLC, MiU-C, & RPJCB (2nd ed), MiU-C & PHi (3rd ed).

Dedicated to Col. John Maitland, MP, who led the Caledonian forces, "Frazers Highlanders," at Savannah, having died (like Wolfe, at the moment of victory) after repelling the combined American and French forces, October 9, 1779. Dedication and poem both dated January 27, 1780.
Ballad in octaves. Narrative of the successful British defence of besieged Savannah against the French under Count D'Estaing and the Americans under Rutledge and Lincoln--"Rebellion's ruthless train,/ Worst fiends of discord, war, and death" (p. 6)--through the bravery and leadership of Maitland. Colvill execrates the French for one of the "blackest crimes:/ Rebellion's impious steel to guide,/ The sons to pierce the parents breast" (p. 16). (Repr. in London Chronicle, 47 [March 18, 1780], 276-7, and in 89-1: his Poetical Works, pp. 145-60.) See R. C. Cole, Stud. in Scot. Lit. 17 (1982), 81-98.

80-6. -----.
To The Memory Of Allan Malcolm, Esq; Of Lochore; Heir and Representative of the ancient Knights Baronets of Lochore, Captain in the 33d Regiment of Foot, who was mortally wounded at the head of the Advanced Guard, in the moment of victory, over the Provincial Army, and expired with many brave Gentlemen on the field of battle, before the walls of Charlestown.

"Hark! the wailing voice of sorrow." (176)

In 89-1: his Poetical Works, pp. 183-90.

Elegiac verses in octaves. Mourns the death of Capt. Malcolm, about May 11, 1780, when the rebel Gen. Lincoln surrendered Charleston, S. C., to the British under Gen. Clinton and Gen. Leslie, after a siege of seven weeks. The poem is notable for its style, that of a genuinely bardic or Caledonian poem mourning the death of a heroic warrior, scarcely hinting at the nature of the American contest except in the long explanatory title.

80-7. [Combe, William ?]
The Castle of Infamy. A Poetical Vision. In Two Parts.
London: Bew, 1780. 80p.

"How droop'd the Muse when [Darby]'s casting Voice." (1500)

Notices: CR 50 (Sep 1780), 235-6; MR 62 (Jun 1780), 495; LR 11 (Appendix 1780), 448.

Copies: BL 11632.f.10; Bod Godwyn Pamph 1703 (9), 1709 (8) (annotated in contemporary hand); NUC ICN, MH.

Attributed to William Combe. HC. Satire on the ministry, corrupt traitors, placemen and pensioners, and the politics of the time in which America figures, the author citing evidence from history of Administration's infamy and its "vile War" with America (p. 53). Shocked by the court-martial's acquittal of Palliser, the poet lapses into sleep and is possessed by a nightmare in which he envisions a host of nasty people, one of whom is severely castigated for urging war against America--William Henry Lyttelton, Baron Westcote (p. 12). He ridicules Gov. Johnstone of the Carlisle Peace Commission for trying to "bribe a Congress" (pp. 28, 43); believes taxation or wealth "made America rebel" (p. 33); belittles Germaine for his cowardice at Minden and for his attempts to destroy America from the safety of his cabinet (p. 37); blasts the "ruinous" American War because it is fought on the principle of power, not right, citing the government's use of Samuel Johnson (p. 39); and is horrified by the fighting at Lexington, Concord, Bunker's Hill, and Saratoga, and by Prevost's burning of Fairfield and Norwalk (pp. 41-2). Other significant citations include King George, Bute, North, Sandwich, Mansfield, Keppel and Palliser, William Markham (Archbishop of York), the Scots, Quebec Act, Corruption, and Fast Days.

80-8. [Combe, William]
The Fast-Day: A Lambeth Eclogue. By The Author Of The Auction.
London: Bew, 1780. xiii + 15-32p.

"'Twas on the ev'ning of that sullen day." (c. 250)

Notices: CR 49 (Apr 1780), 312-13; MR 62 (May 1780), 408-9; LR 11 (May 1780), 351.

Copies: BL 11630.e.9 (9); NUC CSmH, CtY, ICU, MH, NcD.

Dedicated to the Hon. Mrs. C[ornwalli]s, the wife of the Archbishop of Canterbury,

Frederick Cornwallis.

HC. Satire on the way Piscopella, a bishop's wife, observes and criticizes the Fast-Day: "this slow-pac'd, canting day," "When holy dulness, by supreme command,/ Scatters Hypocrisy through half the land" (p. 17). The woman would rather play cards. But her maid Comb-brush objects to her scandalous thoughts and insists that she show discipline: "it is but one short day,/ Whose pray'rs will conquer all America" (p. 28). Piscopella answers, "What, what are all those Colonies to me,/ That I should yield an hour of liberty?" As a matter of fact, she views the colonies with a friendly eye, for "They hate a Bishop's yoke, and so do I." She has nothing to do with taxes or coercion; those "who urg'd the horrid mischief [should] pray." She prefers cards and company to prayers over the war. Her maid insists, and Piscopella--to avoid scandal-- agrees to be devout for once and to go to prayers. (An ironic note on corruption appears on p. 18.)


80-9. The Crisis. Now or Never. Addressed To The People Of England. Concluding With A Poetical Invocation To The Genius of England: With A Word of Advice to the C---- M---------. By a Gloucestershire Freeholder.
   London: Rivington, 1780. 34 + 35-42p.

"Genius of England, who, in gloomy Hour." (c. 240)

Notices: CR 50 (Oct 1780), 316; MR 62 (Jun 1780), 489.

Copies: BL 102.g.49; NUC CtY.

The prose essay complains of the calamitous state of the country, and declares that the blame must be placed squarely on the inept leadership of the present administration, "weak, insufficient, and injudiciously appointed," whose judgment is poor and management of resources ineffective. They are certainly responsible for aiding France by causing the colonies to separate from the parent state. On the other hand, the minority must be praised for its opposition to this incompetent government's destructive measures, especially its opposition to the American War. The author also severely criticizes the king, but blames the "Tools of Power" for transforming him into "a Party Man." He believes that "Tory Administrations have been ever fatal to the Welfare of this Country."
   HC. The poem expresses similar ideas: complaining of "Court Influence," high taxation, and calling for reform to eliminate corruption and force the present blundering ministry out, because it is responsible for "The crumbling Empire," "the mangled Colonies dismember'd." There are better men entitled to lead the nation. These new leaders must be found out. Admiral Rodney provides a good example of courageous leadership in crushing the French, the immediate task. Britons must unite, but "New Men must wield the Thunder of the Realm."


80-10. [Croft, Herbert]
   The Abbey of Kilkhampton; Or Monumental Records For The Year 1980. Faithfully Transcribed From the Original Inscriptions, which are still perfect, and appear to be drawn up in a Stile devoid of fulsome Panegyric, or unmerited Detraction; And Compiled with a View to ascertain, with Precision, the Manners which prevailed in Great

Britain during the last Fifty Years of the Eighteenth Century. The Fifth Edition.
London: Kearsly, 1780. 141p.

Notices: CR 50 (Oct & Nov 1780), 253-6, 445-9; MR 63 (Nov 1780), 392-3; M Chron Sep 7, Oct 11, Nov 27, Nov 28, 1780; SM 42 (Oct 1780), 542; WM 49 (Oct 5, 1780), 406-7, 50 (Oct 26, 1780), 86-7, 50 (Dec 21, 1780), 331-2, 50 (Dec 28, 1780), 362-3; L Mag 49 (Sep 1780), 429-30.

Copies: BL T.661 (1) & 11630.e.6 (12) (1st ed), 643.k.10 (10) (5th ed); NUC TxU (1st ed), CtY, ICN, IU, MiU-C, NN, & MH (3rd ed), DLC, MB, MiU-C, & TxU (5th ed), ICN, NcD, & TxU (6th ed). [This is not exhaustive.]

8 eds in 1780, 9 eds to 1788; Part 2 added in 5th ed. 1st ed--75p.; 2nd ed "with considerable additions"--78p.; 3rd & 4th eds--78p.; 5th ed--Part I 82p., Part II pp. 83-141, with index.
Epitaphs or "characters" largely of the nobility and gentry, in the form of inscriptions presented to the nation supposedly two hundred years after the year 1780, mildly satiric in some instances, or simply descriptive. Those that are relevant are of Burke, Camden, Henry Clinton, Cornwallis, Fox, Germain, Richard & William Howe, Keppel, Mansfield, North, Palliser, Richmond, Saville, Shelburne, Thurlow, and Wilkes. It is remarkable that Chatham, Rockingham, and Richard Price are not included; Samuel Johnson is the only literary figure included. (However, Chatham had died in 1778, and all the "epitaphs" are on those alive in 1780.) See Abbey of Kilkhampton, 1780 serials.

80-11. The Deserted City. A Poem.
London: n. p., 1780. v-vii + 20p.

"Thou LONDON! whose extended fame was known." (c. 350)

Notices: CR 49 (Jun 1780), 474-5; MR 63 (Jul 1780), 74; G Jun 28, 1780; LR 11 (Apr 1780), 280-2.

Copies: BL 11602.g.3 (3).

HC. London became prosperous and great through industry and commerce, but as a result of the disastrous war with the American colonies it has been ruined, and its inhabitants and Liberty have emigrated to America. Those responsible for this destructive war, those "Who lost our Colonies by tyrant force," deserve damnation. (The Advertisement distinguishes this poem from Thomas Lyttelton's The State of England, 80-19 below.)


80-12. Egerton, Charles.
A New History of England in Verse; Or the Entertaining British Memorialist. Containing the Annals of Great Britain, From The Roman Invasion to the Present Time. Designed More particularly for the Use of Youth; But Serving at the same Time to Refresh the Memories of Persons in Riper Years. With An Introduction Concerning The Nature And Study Of History.
London: Cooke, [1780 ?]. vi + 240p.

"Albion, a sea girt isle, long known to Fame."  (c. 6000)

Notices:  CR 49 (Feb 1780), 158;  MR 63 (Nov 1780), 387.

Copies:  NUC  CtY, NjP.

HC. Two portions are relevant. The introduction describes Great Britain, "a sea girt isle," including its origin, general character, chief product, and source of wealth in trade; the constitution (a limited monarchy) is the basis of its liberty. The historical review proceeds from the reign of the first monarch, Ecgbert the Great, in 801, to the first part of the reign of George III, 1760-74:  the last years of the Seven Years War, the resignation of Pitt, the war against Spain (Havana, Manilla), the defence of Portugal, the end of the war, the Duke of Cumberland's death, the East India Co.; and remarks on the American contest (pp. 236-40):  the beginning with the Stamp Act and its repeal, the tea duty and the Boston Tea Party, and the commencement of hostilities at Concord, Bunker's Hill, and Charles Town.  Egerton asserts the need for peace and friendship instead of a ruinous civil war, which he describes in general "poetical imagery."  He concludes with a hope for peace and reconciliation:  "May Britain, and her Colonies, unite,/ And be each other's comfort and delight."

80-13.  Elegiac Epistles On The Calamities of Love and War.  Including a genuine Description of the Tragical Engagement between his Majesty's Ships the Serapis and Countess of Scarborough, and the Enemy's Squadron under the Command of Paul Jones, on the Twenty-third of September, 1779.
London: Pridden, 1780.  70p.

"From scenes where Fancy droops her languid wing."  (485)

Notices:  CR 49 (Apr 1780), 311;  MR 62 (Jun 1780), 493-4;  L Mag 49 (Apr 1780), 180.

Sabin 22110.

Copies:  NUC  DLC, MiU-C.

HC. Epistle third only. Letters in verse supposed to have passed between a sailor and his wife.  She writes first, lamenting his cruel absence. He responds with four epistles, the third (in two parts) describing the famous bloody encounter with Jones. Jones' squadron intercepted the English Baltic merchant fleet under convoy of the "Serapis," commanded by Richard Pearson, and the "Countess of Scarborough."  This naval battle cost the lives of many men; although Jones won, his ship "Bonhomme Richard" was sunk.  The British become prisoners and are brought to the Dutch island of Texel. Their escape attempt fails.  The Americans and Jones are condemned for joining with "the common enemy," France, and for taking up arms against their country, for "unlawful war."

80-14. Farrer, John.
America A Poem. By John Farrer, of Queen's College, Oxford.
London: Evans; Oxford: Fletcher; Cambridge: T. & J. Merrill, 1780. 24p.

"'What angry Demon lull'd to fatal sleep.'" (470)

Notices: CR 50 (Dec 1780), 470-1; MR 64 (Jan 1781), 152; G Eve Post Dec 21, 1780; PA Dec 23, 1780.

Sabin 23882.

Copies: Bod Vet A 4.d.11 (3); NUC NN, RPJCB.

Ode in dixains. Britannia and America engage in dialogue. Britain berates America for turning from an indulgent parent who had shielded her from "Insidious France," losing heroic Wolfe in the process: "By his heroic fall I saw a Nation freed." But now America repays this kindness with rebellion and asserts its power and intends to "rise a Western Rome," led by Washington (Fabius) and Congress (senates). However, America turns repentant suppliant, begging for pardon, which Britannia graciously grants. Thereupon, Britannia prophesies greatness for America, "a State by British counsels blest,/ With British laws, with peace and plenty crown'd." In this state, the wild natives will accept British leadership and "two kindred Realms" will unite under the Brunswick monarchy.

80-15. The Genius of Britain, A Poem. Addressed to the Gentlemen of the British Navy.
Edinburgh: Creech, 1780. 19p.

"On yonder rugged rock, with hoary front." (c. 360)

Copies: ICN.

Blank verse. Patriotic poem. Britannia waxes indignant over the Bourbon threat to its shores, its navy, and its merchant fleet, and recalls the past when the fleets of France and Spain were swept from the seas and British trade and industry flourished. A section near the end alludes to America, her fall from "her envied height" through "disobedience and rebellion proud." But now repentant, America returns submissive and enjoys the blessings of a British reign. Before this peace, the hypocrisy of some Americans had lured simple people to rebellion's standard "beneath the borrow'd garb/ Of Liberty, the simulated guise," and there was bloody violence on the banks of the Ohio and Delaware. Now there will be peace and prosperity when the two, Britannia and her sons, form a "sacred bond of union" (pp. 15-18).

80-16. The Gladiators: An Heroic Epistle, Addressed To The Bravoes of Administration.
London: Richardson, 1780. 15p.

"The gloom of sorrow clouds Britannia's brow." (c. 210)

Notices: CR 51 (Jan 1781), 73-4; MR 64 (Feb 1781), 153; L Eve Post Dec 2, 1780;

L Mag 49 (Dec 1780), 573.

   Copies: BL 643.m.16 (27).

HC. Britannia mourns the wretched state of the nation--her treasure plundered by Scotsmen, the disgrace suffered by her armed forces, "patriot generals driven from their place," the decline in trade and the arts. The patriotic bard will speak the truth about Mansfield, Germaine, Sandwich, Loughborough (A. Wedderburn), and Palliser, and about the present reign--its corruption (beginning with Bute), tyranny, revolted colonies, confederated enemies menacing the land, venal Scots and MPs. But Fox deserves praise for his integrity as he exposes the terrible state of affairs brought on by the ministry--in particular Germaine and Sandwich, for they, the poet declares, planned Fox's assassination. The allusion is to the duel with a Scotsman, Adam, which failed of its purpose, the elimination of Fox. The poet protests this immoral method of attacking honest patriots: "Shall England tamely see her favorite meet/ Each <u>Gladiator</u> that infests the street?" (p. 15)


80-17. Green[e], Edward Burnaby.
   Ode, inscribed to Leonard Smelt, Esq. By Edward Burnaby Green.
   London: Faulder, 1780.

   Notices: CR 49 (May 1780), 396; MR 63 (Aug 1780), 149; LR 12 (Jul 1780), 59-60.

   Copies: none located.


80-18. Heroic Epistle From Hamet The Moor, Slipper-Maker In London, To The Emperor Of Morocco. With an Apology for Publication, Addressed To The Lutheran And Calvinistical Ambassadors.
   London: Cadell, 1780. 27p.

   "Prostrate, and faithful slave, may Hamet dare." (c. 230)

   Notices: CR 49 (Feb 1780), 157; MR 63 (Jul 1780), 71.

   Copies: BL 163.m.17 (imperfect), 11626.h.14 (3); NUC CtY, MH.

HC. The author is identified in the Yale copy as "Fielding, son of Henry." Apparently an ironic satire on the Opposition and Administration. The United States are mentioned in a reference to the American flag--"Rebellion's <u>stripes</u> . . . a motley rag," in connection with the desperate situation in which England, alone, faces its many enemies. But it does so ineffectively. The point of the poem may be that England, now in desperate straits, will seek help of the Emperor of Morocco to form a "barb'rous league." The Opposition members are mentioned--Fox, Saville, (John or Simon?) Luttrell, Dunning, Barré, Burke--as lending their support, among others including Samuel Johnson.

80-19. [Lyttelton, Thomas]
The State of England, In the Year 2199.

"And now thro' broken paths and rugged ways." (c. 280)

In his Poems, By A Young Nobleman, Of Distinguished Abilities, lately deceased; Particularly, The State Of England, And The once flourishing City of London. In a Letter from an American Traveller, Dated from the Ruinous Portico of St. Paul's, in the Year 2199, To A Friend settled in Boston, the Metropolis of the Western Empire. Also, Sundry Fugitive Pieces, principally wrote whilst upon his Travels on the Continent (London: Kearsly, 1780), pp. 1-16.

Notices: CR 49 (Feb 1780), 123-7; MR 62 (Feb 1780), 128-31; GM 50 (Feb 1780), 89; LR 11 (Feb 1780), 126-8.

Sabin 42894 (2nd ed).

Copies: BL 643.k.10 (12) (1st ed); Bod Godwyn Pamph 1734 (1st ed), Godwyn Pamph 1494 (4) & 1738 (11) (2nd ed); NUC CSmH, CtY, DLC, ICN, MH, & MiU-C (1st ed); CSmH, CtY, InU, NN, & RPJCB (2nd ed).

Five eds in 1780. Only this poem is relevant. Blank verse. Dated March 21, 1771, it prophetically describes the decline and downfall of Britain, especially the ruins of London, once a center of wealth, trade, and liberty. The nation had destroyed itself by legislative corruption, which brought on civil strife, a division exploited by France and Spain. But America had become all powerful, and France and Spain will fight over her. Still, according to a prediction in the conclusion, Britain and America "combin'd may conquer worlds yet unknown." (See 80-11.)

80-20. Macaulay, J[ohn].
Unanimity. A Poem.
[London]: Cadell, et al., [1780]. 18p.

"When dire Misfortune o'er a sinking land." (244)

Notices: CR 49 (Mar 1780), 235; MR 62 (May 1780), 409-10; L Chron 30 (Mar 30, 1780), 313; LR 11 (Mar 1780), 206-8.

Copies: BL 162.m.55 (1st ed), 11630.d.7 (6) (2nd ed).

Dedication "To his Grace Hugh Duke of Northumberland, Earl Percy, &c.," dated March 13, 1780. HC. Patriotic poem, written when England was menaced by the Bourbon powers; so the theme of political unity became urgent. In an allegorical dialogue, France engages in debate with Britain, criticizes her enemy for corruption, and notes her decline as oppressed Americans rebel and receive aid from France and Spain (ll. 91-110). Britain insists that France has no claim to virtue and freedom, its government despotic and its people slavish. In a brief review of history from Alfred and the Danes to the present, Macaulay illustrates how in the past Britain's desire for liberty prevailed in difficult times and will continue to prevail against France and Spain; America, he predicts, will rejoin her parent (ll. 223-5).

80-21. Nisbet, W.
  Poems, Chiefly Composed from Recent Events.
  Edinburgh: n. p., 1780. 129p.

  The Times: An Ode. Written during the Late Riots. "Sweet Peace, fair daughter of the sky." (56) pp. 3-5.

  Ode. On the Late Action at Savannah. "How blest who in life's youthful bloom" (12) p. 10.

  Ode. On the Last New Levies in Scotland. To the Right Hon. Lord M'Donald. "O Thou! who sway'st the wide domain." (48) pp. 11-13.

  Ode. To the Trident Man of War, in which the Commissioners sailed for America. "Thou long the pride of Windsor grove." (32) pp. 24-5.

  Elegy VII. The Captive. "Now, o'er the sky dim twilight throws her veil." (84) pp. 76-80.

  The Exile. "Where fair Virginia's fertile plains extend." (214) pp. 95-106.

  Notices: CR 51 (Apr 1781), 314; MR 64 (Jun 1781), 467.

  Copies: BL 1162.k.10; NUC CtY, ICN, IU, NN.

  Dedication to George Inglis signed "W. Nisbet." The author, a young man, published his poems with the assistance of many subscribers. He writes in the classical mode: odes, elegies, anacreontics, eclogues, and epistles. The listed poems refer to America; "The Exile" is the complaint of a Virginia loyalist planter.

80-22. [Odell, Jonathan ?]
  The American Times: A Satire. In Three Parts. In Which Are Delineated The Characters of the Leaders of the American Rebellion. Amongst the Principal Are, Franklin, Laurens, Adams, Hancock, Jay, Duer, Duane, Wilson, Pulaski, Witherspoon, Reed, M'Kean, Washington, Roberdeau, Morris, Chase, &c. By Camillo Querno, Poet-Laureat To the Congress.
  London: Richardson, 1780. i + 40p.

  "When Faction, pois'nous as the scorpion's sting." (c. 1000)

Notices: CR 49 (Apr 1780), 307-11; MR 62 (Jun 1780), 495-6.

Sabin 56713.

Copies: BL 11687.cc.11 (1780 New York ed, with André's Cow-Chace); NUC CSmH, DLC, ICN, MB, MH, NN, PHi.

HC. Satire by a loyalist American on rebels--members of Congress, army officers, foreign officers, governors, preachers, lawyers, writers--and on American state affairs--anarchy, mob action, tyranny and confusion, worthless paper currency, heartlessness and dishonor. But he is not quite so certain about British policy on taxation, his point being that it was madness to impose taxes on America, but that it was equally mad to rebel against them. Incidentally, Jefferson also is targeted, but briefly. (The question about Odell's authorship has not been settled.)

80-23. Panegyric: An Essay On Some Of The Worthiest Characters In The Kingdom. London: Fielding & Walker, 1780. 33p.

"'With ills opprest, and worn with care.'" (c. 570)

Notices: CR 49 (Apr 1780), 309; MR 63 (Sep 1780), 229.

Copies: BL T.13 (5).

Octosyllabic couplets. The poet complains that poetry is not profitable. Truth, agreeing that "Wit and Fact were not design'd/ To be in social couplets join'd," advises the writing of fiction--e.g., Whitehead's birth-day odes (pp. 8-10)--and of panegyrics as the way to success, wealth, and power. The youthful poet thereupon engages in praise (ironically, of course) of "wise Germaine" who leads the forces against the allied enemy powers: France, Spain, Holland, and America. At this point, Congress is also satirized (pp. 19-22). Others praised and defended ironically are Sandwich and North (pp. 22-4), Gen. Howe (pp. 25-7), Fox (pp. 27-8), and Burgoyne (p. 29), the last two perhaps more obviously ridiculed.

80-24. Paradise Regain'd: Or, The Battle of Adam And The Fox. An Heroick Poem. London: Bew, 1780. 39p.

"Sing, heav'nly muse, that on the sacred top." (c. 790)

Notices: CR 49 (Mar 1780), 237; MR 62 (Apr 1780), 323; LR 11 (May 1780), 352.

Copies: BL 163.m.21; NUC CtY, ICN, IU, MH, MiU-C, TxU.

Dedication (ironic) to Lord North, signed A. B. Blank verse. A mock epic in the Miltonic style that ridicules William Adam, described as unhappy in Scotland out of

Paradise--i.e., the grace of the English ministry. Adam is put on his guard against the seductive eloquence of Richmond, Rockingham, Shelburne, Saville, and Burke, the minority patriots (pp. 19-23), and encouraged to remove the Fox (Charles James Fox). Thereupon the duel with Fox follows, in which Fox is wounded (pp. 35-6). Adam is restored to Paradise.

Fox was a leading critic of the North ministry and all its measures, especially its policies and actions towards America. Adam was a firm believer in the need to suppress the rebellion, and was unsympathetic with North's peace gestures of 1777-8. Believing that incompetent commanders more than the ministry were to blame for the ill success of the war, he decided (in November 1779) to support the ministry rather than the minority who, in his opinion, made abject concessions to the Americans. Fox ridiculed Adam, who then challenged Fox to a duel, as described in this poem.

80-25. The Patriotic Mice; Or, Modern H***e of C*****s: A Poem. By A Gentleman [Mr. J. Y.].
London: Wade, 1780.

Notices: CR 51 (Jan 1781), 71-2; MR 63 (Dec 1780), 551; MH Dec 23, 1780.

Copies: none located.

80-26. Paul Jones, A New Song.
[Broadside, 1780 ?]

"Of heroes and statesmen I'll just mention four." (24)

Copies: BL Rox. III. 613.

Song. Satire on the ministry and its war. Merchants and contractors complain of trade at a stand-still because of Paul Jones's raids. But England has worse enemies than Jones. If the ministerial leaders--Germain, Sandwich, and North--can be purged and Jones "converted," then England will be "free."

80-27. [Piercy, John William]
An Epistle to the Right Honourable John Earl of Sandwich &c. Or, The British Hero Displayed. A Poem.
London: Rivington, Payne; Cambridge: Deighton, 1780. 23p.

"While merry bards in strains harmonious sing." (c. 320)

Notices: CR 50 (Jul 1780), 69; MR 63 (Jul 1780), 72.

Copies: BL 11630.e.16 (13); NUC MH.

HC. A patriotic poem. Britain's heroic warriors surpass those of antiquity in prowess and other qualities--Wolfe, Marlborough, Capt. Farmer of the Quebec, Rodney. Sandwich deserves praise for choosing naval heroes to help Britain "re-assume the trident of the main."

80-28. A Poem Occasioned By The Late Calamities Of England; In Particular, Those on the Sixth and Seventh of June, 1780.
London: Becket, 1780. 27p.

"What nobly-plaintive sad Sicilian Muse." (419)

Notices: CR 50 (Nov 1780), 391-3; MR 64 (Feb 1781), 150.

Copies: Bod Godwyn Pamph 1704 (4); NUC MiU-C.

HC. Blames England's calamities, including the American rebellion and the Gordon Riots, upon "the fatal calamities of the Stuart line and their consequences to this kingdom." (p. 10) Bewails Burgoyne's defeat at Saratoga (p. 22), but alludes with pleasure to the repeal of oppressive laws injurious to Ireland's trade. England, the poet concludes, has no friend, and the loss of Mansfield's great library in the riots is a calamity, indeed. The poet imitates the diction of Chatterton's Rowley with pleasure, and that of Milton, Shakespeare, Dante, Gray, and the Bible.

80-29. Poems Fit For A Bishop; Which Two Bishops will read. An American Prayer. Address to Religion. Saul at Endor, an Ode. Inscription in Memory of the Earl of Chatham.
London: Almon, 1780. 13p.

An American Prayer, For the Year 1777. "O Universal Love divine." (60) pp. 1-4.

Address to Religion. "Come, sovereign source of heavenly love." (34) pp. 5-6.

Saul at Endor. "On Gilboa's hight, in terror stands." (c. 85) pp. 7-11.

Inscription In Memory Of William Pitt, Earl of Chatham, Who Died on The 11th of May, 1778. "Friend of thy Country, and of England's fame." (25) pp. 12-13.

Notices: CR 49 (Feb 1780), 155-6; MR 62 (Mar 1780), 246.

Sabin 63615.

Copies: BL 11632.g.7; Bod Godwyn Pamph 1302 (11); NUC CtY, MH, MiU-C, RPJCB.

"An American Prayer," which was "written about three years ago on the day appointed for imploring the divine blessing on the British arms in the American civil war," asks for mercy from the Lord, declaring that the aim of the war is not "Dominion's rod [to] extend."
"Address to Religion," meant for a Fast Day (Feb. 4), asks, in a prayer to the God of Justice and Mercy, for an end to the civil war--"Allay the thirst of kindred life." Chatham appears in the other two poems--in the last as a great man who died "Ere yet his falling country fell."
These poems do not express the views of the Establishment regarding the American War.

80-30. Poems On The Several Successes In America. Edinburgh: n. p., 1780. 29p.

[1] Ode On the Taking of Charlestown, by his Excellency Sir Henry Clinton. "As o'er America's hostile plain." (42) pp. 7-10.

[2] Ode on the Action at Savannah. "How blest, who in life's youthful bloom." (12) p. 11.

[3] The Death of General Fraser, An Ode. "Ah! where is British honour fled." (32) pp. 12-13.

[4] The Capitulation, A Poem, To His Excellency Sir Henry Clinton, on the Surrender of Charleston. "While you, the support of Britannia's cause." (128) pp. 14-21.

[5] Camden. A Poem, To the Right Hon. Charles Earl Cornwallis. "While sad despondence marks each downcast brow." (148) pp. 22-9.

Copies: NUC RPJCB.

Four odes on the southern campaign in South Carolina and Georgia, a great success for Gen. Clinton. Dedicated to Lord North "Who, by a Steadiness of Conduct,/ Has endeavoured to maintain the Interests of his Country;/ And though Opposed by the United Powers/ Of a Formidable Faction, To Persevere in the Plan most likely/ To accomplish the Reduction of her/ Rebellious States." The Preface admits that the victories gained have few advantages. But the poet must pay "a tribute of gratitude to the endeavours of friends."
[1] Regular Horatian ode in sixains. Britain should no longer despair after the defeat at Saratoga. The triumph at Charleston, S. C., should help restore peace to America. [2] Regular Horatian ode in quatrains. Imitation of Collins' "Ode, Written in the Year 1746." The patriots who fought honorably and died for freedom (at Savannah) are mourned and blessed. [3] Regular Horatian ode in quatrains. Fraser, a Scots officer who died at Saratoga, did not tamely surrender, insisting to the end that the British cause was just. [4] HC. Written immediately after Charleston capitulated, upon the premise that the American Rebellion would soon end. The campaign is described from the beginning at York, the loyalists in the British army are mentioned, Clinton is praised for his humanity. He had given the Americans two chances to surrender peacefully, but they gladly accepted the second. The conquering troops show pity and compassion "at their friends distress." Yet conquest "o'er Britons gain'd . . . loses half its charms." [5] HC. Mourns the death of Maitland at Savannah, where the British defeated French and American forces; cites Clinton's victory at Charleston. The poet damns those Americans responsible for the war: "curse the men, who on their Country's shame,/ Were proud to raise Distinction's splendid name." That Cornwallis's stunning victory (over Gates at Camden, S. C.) would bring peace and that "Returning love each rebel breast possess" would give him great pleasure.

Poems on Various Subjects.
   Edinburgh: Gordon & Murray; London: Richardson & Urquhart, 1780.

   Copies: BL 1467.c.24.

   A miscellany. See pp. 110-21. Includes The Tears of Britannia--see 76-36.


80-31. The Poetical Review, A Poem. Being a Satirical Display of the Literal Characters of Mr. G*rr*ck, Mr. C*lm*n, Mr. Sh*r**n, Genl. B**rg***e, Mr. M*ckl*n, Dr. K*nr**k. The Second Edition, with Additions.
   London: n. p., [1780?]. 28p.

   "Returning Summer's sweet refreshing Morn." (c. 440)

   Copies: BL 644.k.18 (2); NUC ICN (2nd ed), MB (3rd ed).

   HC. Mostly on writers for the theater. But twelve lines (p. 4) comment on General Burgoyne as a "comic Bard" who, risking "e'en Capitulation," came "to a tragic End!"


80-32. Private Thoughts On Public Affairs: With Some Apology for the Conduct of our late Commanders in Chief: A Poetical Essay. By a Stander-By.
   London: Payne, 1780.

   Notices: CR 49 (May 1780), 395-6; MR 62 (Jun 1780), 496; LR 11 (Appendix 1780), 449.

   Sabin 65727.

   Copies: none located.

   The poet has no respect for either party, the ins or the outs. He writes about Howe and Burgoyne, especially their literary campaigns in defense of their reputations, and also about Howe's failure to suppress the rebellion. (From the excerpts in the Critical Review.)


80-33. The Prophecy: A Poem. Addressed to Mr. Burke, On His Plan for the Oeconomical Reformation Of The Civil And Other Establishments.
   London: Becket, 1780. 11p.

   "Though many a Duke, who snores away." (c. 175)

   Notices: CR 49 (Apr 1780), 308-9; MR 62 (Jun 1780), 497; LR 11 (Appendix 1780), 449.

   Copies: NUC CtY.

Tetrameter couplets. Praise of Burke for his incorruptible integrity, his simple establishment at Beaconsfield unencumbered with a large piece of property, and his merit as an MP, especially his intellect and oratory. But the poet predicts defeat for his attempt at parliamentary reform; it will "Be strangled by the hand of Pow'r." Fox, Barré, Shelburne, Richmond, and Rockingham will grieve at its defeat. But the In-group of corrupt politicians will be merry at the prospect of its defeat--all the "pension'd Commoners and Peers . . . smiling Placemen, and Vote-Sellers"--Germain, Rigby, as well as Gibbon, Soame Jenyns, among others, commissioners of the Board of Trade which Burke marked for abolishment.

Querno, Camillo, Poet-Laureat To The Congress. See 80-22.

80-34. Rebellion And Opposition: Or, The American War. A Poem.
London: Bladon, 1780. 48p.

"When Britain reign'd sole mistress of the Main." (c. 800)

Notices: CR 49 (Mar 1780), 236; MR 62 (Apr 1780), 319-20; LR 11 (Appendix 1780), 447.

Sabin 68324.

Copies: NUC DLC, NN.

HC. An elaborate Tory apology for the North ministry, in a historical review of major policies and events from the peace of Paris in 1763 to the present time.
Dedicated to the King in June 1780. The writer's motive is to expose "the ambitious Views of the Rebels" and the treasonable behavior of the Opposition for abetting the rebellion and the Opposition's ill-founded pretensions to patriotism. Book I defends the Peace of Paris and Bute against the attacks of Wilkes and his partisans. The colonies are criticized for aspiring to independent sovereignty early, despite all the aid received from Britain. Britain certainly had the right to tax the colonies, a right denied by "a factious band . . . The spawn of mad Republicans" in Cromwell's day, sedition led by S. Adams, Hancock, and Franklin. But these are less to blame than the hypocritical subversives who masquerade as patriots, who deliberately create chaos by thwarting "the measures of the best of kings." They have nursed the rebellion; they encouraged persecuting American loyalists. The two Howes and Keppel, "intimately connected with Opposition," have brought disgrace to the nation. Germaine and North do not deserve vilification; at least they try to reunite the colonies with the parent state, not to grant them independence.
Book II. The Opposition leaders want the ability to lead the nation. Rockingham, with Burke and Richmond, was responsible for the Declaratory Act. Grafton and Shelburne were responsible for the Townshend Act. (Incidentally, the poet defends the Stamp Act.) North's tax policy made sense, the repeal of all taxes except that on tea, which provoked

the Boston Tea Party. In the war to suppress the rebellion that ensued, the Howe brothers neglected their duty. The poet is very severe on Gen. William Howe, believing that he was guilty of the loss of Burgoyne's army, and of failure to cooperate with Burgoyne. When France entered the war, the Opposition gave comfort to Britain's natural enemy, criminally weakening the government before its foreign enemies. He prays, however, that Britain will be unified under the present Administration, which will thereupon succeed in bringing peace and defeating faction and rebellion.

80-35. A Satire On The Present Times.
London: Stockdale, 1780. 5-15p.

"In days of yore, (if Rumour tell no lies,)." (c. 160)

Notices: CR 50 (Dec 1780), 470; MR 64 (Feb 1781), 153.

Copies: NUC MiU-C.

HC. Satire on Parson Bate and "Perdita" Robinson. The first part satirizes Henry Bate, editor of the Morning Herald, a new Government subsidized newspaper. The poet protests the hack paid by the ministry to become its tool. Bate fears no persecution or lawyers for slanderous abuse in his paper. He conceals the truth about the American War, "Turns our disasters to ridicule," i.e., insists that they are insignificant when contrasted to those suffered by our enemies. If we lose, it is nothing; if we succeed, it is "a mighty feat." The poet complains of the disappearance of the boasted spirit of Britons. Once it was deemed virtue to rebel (p. 10). Cited are Lord North (as Boreas, who has bribed Bate) and the American General Lincoln. The second part alludes to the adultery of Mary "Perdita" Robinson with the Prince of Wales (later George IV), apparently with the blessing or connivance of clergy, in particular the Bishop of Osnaburgh. Thus the poem focuses on two types of corruption.

80-36. Seduction: The Spirit of the Times, or Petitions Unmasked. A Poem. Wherein is considered the dangerous Tendency of Associations, and Committees of Correspondence, for the Redress of Grievances. By a Real Patriot.
London: Beecroft, 1780.

Notices: CR 49 (Apr 1780), 308; MR 62 (Apr 1780), 323; LR 12 (Jul 1780), 58-9.

Copies: none located.

80-37. A Sketch of the Times. A Satire.
London: Bew, 1780. 3-40p.

"Poet. Yes; still unaw'd, my independent muse." (c. 650)

Notices:  CR 49 (May 1780), 394-5;  MR 62 (Jun 1780), 497;  LR 11 (Appendix 1780), 449.

Copies:  BL 11630.d.11 (14);  NUC  MH, TxU.

HC.  Imitation of Horace.  Party satire.  The poet and his editor debate the limits of satire in these times, citing all sorts of possible targets.  The poet prides himself on his courage, for his rough "independent Muse" does not serve "Courts without shame," unlike the laureate Whitehead (pp. 3-4).  The editor advises him to use "playful irony" and other techniques upon "living Vice" because of the safety factor.  The poet insists upon honesty;  but he will not, because of the danger to his life from assassins hired by the Scotch junto, attack the ministry and the Scots (pp. 14-15).  The editor responds that not all Scots are to blame for "Colonial broils" or "intestine war" at home.  Besides, there is fair game for satire in placemen, pensioners, and government contractors, now the objects of Burke's reform of the economy.  Gibbon is cited (p. 16).  The poet objects to aristocratic privilege assuming the mantle of immunity;  but he will expose Wesley's deceit and the corruption of the Archbishops of York (Markham) and Canterbury (Cornwallis) (pp. 30-2).  At the same time, he praises other religious leaders: Price, Bishop Hinchcliff of Peterborough, and the Bishops of St. Asaph and Carlisle. Finally, the editor advises ironically that the poet make new friends by praising court favorites like Palliser (pp. 36-7).

80-38.  The State Mountebank, or Duke or no Duke.  A Tale.
   London:  Fielding & Walker, 1780.

Notices:  CR 50 (Jul 1780), 68;  MR 63 (Nov 1780), 387.

Copies:  none located.

80-39.  [Steele, Anne]
   Miscellaneous Pieces, in Verse and Prose.
   Bristol and London:  Cadell, Mills, Evans, et al., 1780.  3 vols, xxiii + 224p.

On a day of prayer for success in War.  "Lord, how shall wretched sinners dare." (32)  III, 123-4.

Notices:  MR 66 (May 1782), 337-9;  W Misc 18 (Aug 19, 1782), 504.

Copies:  BL 11632.e.59;  NUC  CtY, MB, MH.

In this Fast Day hymn, Theodosia (Anne Steele's adopted pseudonym) prays that God guide British councils and grant success to British arms.  This religious poem is too general to be applied to any current event.  Also Lady's Poetical Magazine (London: Harrison, 1781-2), IV, 456-7.

80-40.  Unanimity.  A Poem.  Most respectfully inscribed to that truly patriotic Nobleman, The Duke of Leinster.
   London:  Bew, 1780.  36p.

"While costive Bards fatigue th'obstetric Nine." (c. 700)

Notices: CR 49 (Mar 1780), 235-6; MR 62 (Apr 1780), 319-20.

Copies: NUC ICN (London ed), MiU-C (Dublin ed).

HC. Satire on the Tory ministry and Jacobite Tory ideas (the royal prerogative), Scots and the political writers who vent despotic principles--Samuel Johnson, John Lind, James Macpherson, John Shebbeare. The poet believes the shibboleth <u>unanimity</u> will be abused by Tories and Scots to further their own corrupt ends, and so he objects to bribed "sycophantic Minions" in the House of Lords, and bribed MP's in the Commons-- all unanimous in their wish to restore bankrupt Stuart principles, impose a tyranny upon America ("Enforcing Pow'r without Pretence of Right," meaning the Declaratory Act), and shed much American or "filial" blood. Thus in Britain (England and Scotland) factions are inclined to unity, but upon despicable motives. Yet the poet is pleased with the unity of a "Patriot Spirit" in North America and Ireland. Such "independent Unanimity," operating effectively in America, will now occur in Ireland, where one might hope to "Behold another <u>Patriot Congress</u> form." Thus tyranny will be purged from court and country, and freedom and the natural rights of man restored to British subjects. Cited are Bute, Sandwich, Germaine, Palliser, North, Wilkes and Luttrell, Mansfield, corruption, and Henry Laurens.

80-41. Unity and Public Spirit, Recommended in An Address to the Inhabitants of London and Westminster. To which are added Two Odes: Viz. The Miseries of Dissension and Civil War, and The True Patriot, inscribed to Earl Cornwallis, and Sir George Brydges Rodney, Bart.
London: Davis, Walter, Richardson, & Urquhart, [1780]. 60p.

"O For a Muse that might inspire." (c. 175)

"Far! far! be Faction's partial train." (c. 120)

Notices: CR 50 (Nov 1780), 337-41; MR 64 (Feb 1781), 147-8; MP Nov 7, 1780.

Sabin 97996.

Copies: NUC CtY, MiU-C, RPJCB.

Dedication to Jonas Hanway, dated October 1780, recommends "a spirit of <u>Concord</u>, <u>Patriotism</u>, and <u>Religion</u>." The prose address reflects on the present critical state of affairs, the danger to the nation beset by numerous enemies, and argues "for more union and vigour" against the advice of the patriots, the minority opposition. Although an Opposition is necessary in a free government, the present one goes too far in condemning every measure of government. It certainly has contributed to the "birth and increase" of the American Rebellion by its "zealous approbation of the Congress," and by its encouraging Congress to reject "our proposals of conciliation." Now that America has declared its independence, it is difficult to vindicate the Opposition's support of the American cause. They are sowing the seeds of dissension with the reform associations, plans for economy, and schemes for a more equal representation and for restoring annual or triennial parliaments. He fears these associations will subvert the order of the state, as did the Protestant Association in the June riots. The inflammatory speeches of Fox, Day, and Hartley subvert Parliament's authority by using the American experience with Congress as a model. "The Leaders of Rebellion in America" contemplate with pleasure the movements of Opposition and the progress of the associations. The present time, it is clear, demands unanimity and public spirit.

Both poems are irregular Pindaric odes. The first, "Miseries of Dissension," objects to the American Rebellion, a civil war, masked in Liberty and supported by Hypocrisy, Envy, and Hate. Loyalty expires; the madness of Rebellion generates terrible crimes as it "bears Law, Order, Pity, Peace away!" The poet demands revenge upon factious traitors who are destroying Britain, "Friendless and unsustain'd," beset by "war and civil rage."

The second, "The True Patriot," damns the factious wretch who "spurns . . . His Country's sacred rights," and celebrates the hero who steadily pursues "his country's good." The models are Amherst, Wolfe, Boscawen, Hawke, Rodney, and General Cornwallis--alluding to the defeat of "The Rebel Chiefs on Camden's plain."

80-42. [Wesley, Charles]
Hymns Written in the Time Of The Tumults, June 1780.
Bristol: n. p., 1780. 19p.

I. "The floods, O Lord, lift up their voice." (24)

II. "Thou most compassionate High-priest." (36)

III. "Saviour, Thou dost their threatenings see." (32)

IV. "God omnipotent, arise." (32)

V. "Omniscient God, to whom alone." (48)

VII. Upon Notice Sent One That His House Was <u>Marked</u>. "In vain doth the assassin dark." (12)

VIII. "Thou God who hears't the prayer." (32)

IX. "Arm of the Lord, awake, awake." (56)

X. "Most righteous God of boundless power." (64)

XII. For The Magistrates. "Thou, Lord of lords, and King of kings." (36)

XIII. Thanksgiving. "All glory to God! Pluck'd out of the flame." (24)

Copies: BL 3437.e.30, 3441.r.13 (5).

Thirteen hymns on the Gordon Riots, June 1780; two are not relevant here.
I. Wesley notes the violence, discord, destruction, danger, "blaspheming multitudes," and "this tyranny" of the mob. II. He condemns the leaders, "cruel, persecuting men," "Christian wolves, reform'd in name," responsible for misguiding the ignorant, and asks for help "to the distress'd," to those who honor the king, God's mild vicegerent, "Our king by right divine." III. He protests the destructive fury of the mob, the arson, the subversive conspiracy responsible: "Gallia exults and London burns!" IV. Wesley damns the rebels, "the tools of anarchy," who oppose God. V. God should expose "Britain's subtlest enemies,/ The dark conspirators," who planned the destruction of London and the nation, the villainous "assassin band," "who patient majesty blaspheme," and "doom Britannia to the fire."
VII. He trusts in God to protect his house marked for destruction, and laughs at "the leagues of hell." VIII. He defends the king against those traitors who blacken his character as a papist, "the friend/ Of anti-Christian Rome," and likens the king to God. IX. He thanks God for saving London, destroying "the hostile powers," suppressing "the dire conspiracy," dispersing "th'assassinating band," "Rebels and traitors in disguise," whose design was "To slander thine anointed" (the king). X. He blames the destructive riots upon Americans (stanza 5), "her felons . . . / Her savages," and "Assassins," "Britains most apostate sons."
XII. Wesley praises the king, "vicegerent" of God and his subordinate magistrates to whom the people submit joyfully; he asks that they be empowered to deal firmly with "our desperate, sworn, intestine foes." XIII. In the last hymn, he offers thanks to God's aid in quenching fires and restoring peace. (Hymns II and IV appeared in Arminian Magazine 4 [Dec 1781], 674-5, and [Aug 1781], 455, respectively.)

Serials

The Abbey of Kilkhampton. L Chron 48 (Sep 5 & 12, Oct 3, 1780), 231, 255, 327; M Chron Sep 7, Oct 11, Nov 27 & 28, 1780; SM 42 (Oct 1780), 542; WM 49 (Oct 5, 1780), 406-7; 50 (Oct 26, Dec 21 & 28, 1780), 86-7, 331-2, 362-3. Epitaphs on Frederick North, Lord North; Edmund Burke; Edward, Lord Thurlow; Sir William Howe; Hugh Percy, Duke of Northumberland; Viscount Gage; William Murray, Earl of Mansfield; Fitzroy, Duke of Grafton; Lord George Germain; Frederick Howard, Earl of Carlisle; Charles James Fox; John Wilkes; Samuel Johnson, et al. See Croft, 80-10.

80-43. Ad Inclytum Keppel.

"Keppel O, vivas celebrande semper." (24)

LP, Mar 13, 1780.

Horatian ode in Latin, praising Keppel. (An example of the occasional Latin political poems in the papers.)

80-44. An Additional Verse to the Litany for 1781.

"From the false list'ning Spy, th 'informing Knave." (10)

W Eve Post, Nov 21, 1780.

HC. Heaven protect us from reviewers, duns, Wilkes, Gordon, the false spy and informing knave, and a variety of other people.

Address to the City. "Ye Citizens of London, why." (80) PA, Jun 23, 1780. By Charles Wesley, 80-345, 81-17.

80-45. An Address to the city of Bristol, occasioned by reading a paragraph in one of the papers, giving an account of their hanging and burning the Effigies of our valiant Commanders, at the time of their receiving the news of the battle at Camden.

"Already Bristol, blasted in thy fame." (48)

LP, Oct 23, 1780.

HC. Bristol is castigated for being Tory and not electing Burke as MP. The poem does not mention the Battle of Camden, or the British officers.

80-46. Admiral Rodney's Reply to the Vote of Thanks from both Houses of Parliament.

"The thanks of the Senate, my dear Jemmy Twitcher."  (10)

L Cour, Mar 4, 1780; St J's C, Mar 14, 1780.

Hexameter couplets.  Rodney complains that he's still poor and that Sandwich of the ministry is not providing his fleet with enough ships, men, and stores to beat the enemy again.

80-47.  Advice to a Great Personage.  A Tale.

"In Rome, when Lucius bore the sway."  (108)

L Cour, Feb 18, 1780.

OC.  A moral tale that applies to the American contest.  The King wishes to be informed on his reputation among the people: his steward flatters him with a lie; his Chamberlain advises him to be <u>great</u> <u>and</u> <u>good</u> and blames his council; but his fool advises him to seek counsel in his own mind, which the King does with wisdom.  George is thus advised!

80-48.  Airs in the New Comick Opera of <u>Fire</u> and <u>Water</u>.

"When we sound and we thump it."  (16)
"The hardy Sons of Britain's Isle."  (12)
"If ever they venture to land on our Coast."  (13)

M Chron, Jul 10, 1780; St J's C, Jul 8, 1780.

Three patriotic lyrics from <u>Fire</u> <u>and</u> <u>Water</u>, a comic opera.

80-49.  All Fool's Day.  A Dialogue.

"England.  Who says that England's Sons are Fools."  (23)

PA, Apr 1, 1780; W Eve Post, Mar 30, 1780.

Quatrains.  France, Spain and America call England a fool.  But all are fools in their way, although England is prince of them all.

80-50.  American Colours.

"Of winnings great let Yanky crack."  (4)

Cal Merc, Nov 25, 1780.

Quatrain.  Epigram.  The American flag reflects the beating cowardly Americans are getting, despite their alliance with France -- thirteen red, bleeding stripes.

80-51. The Ancient State of America.

"When to this land of peace Columbus came." (24)

W Misc 14 (Aug 21, 1780), 504.

Blank verse sentimental impression of the primitive and pastoral state of America around the time the white Europeans came and brought war.

Andre to Washington. (Taken from the gallant Major Andre's letter to Washington, written the day before his execution.) "The man unconscious of a base design." (24) T&C 16 (Oct 1784), 550. See J. Marjoribanks, <u>Trifles in Verse</u> (1784), 84-9. Andre was captured with incriminating papers September 23, 1780, and hanged October 2, 1780.

80-52. Another Birth-Day Ode, 1780.

"Still folly does o'er Britain reign." (39)

L Cour, Jun 6, 1780, PM 2 (May 1780), 160.

Irregular Pindaric ode, parody of Whitehead's "Birth-Day Ode, 1780." A foolish King reigns in Britain; France and Spain control the seas. The unjust civil war will destroy the once prosperous land. Only the patriotic associations can restore Britain by rooting out domestic foes.

80-53. Another Translation from the Latin, on the Horrid Commotions in London, Set on Foot (as is reported) by the Insidious Arts of France.

"False, cruel, baffled, stung with mad Despair." (8)

PA, Jun 30, 1780.

Quatrains. France thinks to wage a more successful war against Britain by hired thugs and arsonists. The Latin poem appeared in PA, Jun 23, 1780; 80-A. See 80-383.

80-54. Another Translation of Mons. de la Fayette's proclamation.

"Thy love by our Monarch to Canada shewn." (18)

SM 42 (Oct 1780), 542.

Hexameter couplets. Ironic satire on De La Fayette whose persona reveals the true intentions of the French to encourage their countrymen in Canada to start a murderous religious war and get the Indian savages to assist in murder. See SM 42 (Oct 1780), 534-5, for the prose.

80-55. The Anti-Gallican Ode. Sun at Drapers-Hall Thirty Years Ago.

"Where Arthur in th' Elysian plain." (60)

G, Apr 24, 1780.

A patriotic song that recalls past glory: Edward the Black Prince, Henry, Elizabeth, William in victories against France and Spain.

80-56. [Apostrophe on Dr. Benjamin Franklin.]

"Alas! / That great natural talents." (c. 20)

MP, Aug 22, 1780.

Inscription. Prose poem, like the "Apostrophe on George Washington," 80-57, below. Franklin has prostituted his talents to the crime of rebellion. But he may be restored to the righteous if, repentant, he brings peace and concord again.

80-57. [Apostrophe on George Washington.]

"The American FABIUS / (So called)." (c. 6)

MP, Aug 15, 1780.

Inscription. Prose poem. The infamous rebel, Washington, had he been loyal, "Might have been esteem'd / An honest and good Man!"

80-58. Apostrophe to Peace.

"Daughter of him, at whose command." (32)

British Chronicle, or Pugh's Hereford Journal, Aug 24, 1780; St J's C, Jul 18, 1780; WM 49 (Aug 10, 1780), 146.

Quatrains. Prays for the blessings of peace, for the end of "foreign tumult and intestine rage."

80-59. Barre and Dundass; or, A Proper Reply.

"Talk not of independency." (6)

L Cour, Mar 31, 1780.

Irregular verse. Barre asserts his freedom and independency (from place) against Dundass's charge of self-interest.

80-60. [Behold in pensive, awful state Britannia mourns.]

"Behold in pensive, awful state Britannia mourns." (6)

MP, Oct 7, 1780.

Sixain. The Queen's delivery of another child compensates Britain for the filial ingratitude of the American rebels, "Her degenerate sons."

80-61. Betty of St. James's Street. To the Hon. Charles James Tod. A Sapphic Ode.

"Awake, my Charles, my Nut-brown James." (66)

PA, Feb 19, 1780.

Ode in sixains. Satire on Fox who is asked ironically to give up his seditious behaviour, his treason. Cited are North, Keppel, Burke, Barre, Wilkes, Franklin, Shelburne. See Tickell, 79-42.

80-62. The Birth-Day Ode, Anticipated.

"On Monday Whitehead's Verse will shine." (26)

PA, Jun 3, 1780.

OC. Satire on Whitehead who neglects the truth about "blind" King George, and Germaine, Sandwich, Rigby, North, Bute. Mentioned is the inability to conquer America since "Hill of Bunker."

The Birth of the Taxes. W Eve Post, Jul 20, 1780; W Misc 14 (Sep 4, 1780), 551-2. A substantial excerpt (130 ll.) from Christopher Anstey's Speculation: 80-3.

80-63. The Breaking-Up of the Camps.

"The Soldiers now are gone to sleep." (12)

PA, Oct 28, 1780.

Quatrains. Now that winter has set in, the military camps have broken up and the women have gone away.

80-64. Britain's Elect.

"Pitt found 'em Puppets, and he made 'em Men." (11)

LP, Mar 15, 1780.

HC. Burke and Savile are asked to make men of the English, now puppets made by Bute and North, and restore them to the state in which Pitt had left them.

80-65. [Britannia still maintains her ground.]

"Britannia still maintains her ground."  (8)

W Eve Post, Dec 28, 1780.

OC.  In great danger fighting allied forces alone, Britain may be defeated.  Then she will "mourn the fatal error past!"  Presumably, the error is the American War.

The British Arms Triumphant, or D'Estaing's Defeat at Savannah.  A New Song, by an Old Soldier.  Lloyd's 46 (Jan 26, 1780), 92; WM 47 (Jan 17, 1780), 207.  See John Freeth, 79-193.

Britons, Strike Home!  "Chearly my hearts, of courage true."  (30)  G Eve Post, Jan 11, 1780; M Chron, Jan 13, 1780.  See Sheridan, [Songs in Harlequin Fortunatus,] 80-326.

80-66.  Burke, a Favourite at Court.

"Hutton and Smelt, and all the courtier fry."  (9)

L Eve Post, Oct 5, 1780.

Burke appears to be favored by Tories such as Smelt and Hutton, as he was rejected by Bristol for MP.  (Hutton, according to a note, was "a constant attendant on his Majesty.")

80-67.  [Busy in BLOOD, and eager to destroy.]

"Busy in BLOOD, and eager to destroy."  (4)

The Scourge 2 (Feb 5, 1780), 7.

HC.  Epigraph of an essay addressed "To the King."  These lines are critical of a bloody tyrant.

80-68.  [Can ye, O Britons, UNCONCERNED, behold.]

"Can ye, O Britons, UNCONCERNED, behold."  (8)

The Scourge 3 (Feb 12, 1780), 13.

HC.  Epigraph of an essay addressed "To the People," warning them of the threats to their rights and freedom.

80-69.  The Change of the Ministry:  Addressed to the King.

"In Eastern pomp though Smelt would hide the King." (28)

L Eve Post, Sep 7, 1780.

HC. The poet advises the Opposition assume the Ministry and guide the King, despite Smelt's Toryism. He wants Richmond, Shelburne, Burke, Fox, Dunning, Howe, Camden, Rockingham to displace Hillsborough, Germaine, North, Sandwich, Mansfield, Stormont, Bute.

80-70. Characteristic Odes, Adapted to the Times. The Croaker.

"Insulted now by France and Spain." (32)

W Eve Post, Jul 20, 1780.

Quatrains. Criticism of the British navy for its inadequacy in the face of French strength.

80-71. Charles-Town.

"The Howes averr'd that none cou'd do." (4)

PA, Jun 19, 1780; W Eve Post, Jun 17, 1780.

Epigram. Gen. Clinton and Adm. Arbuthnot, in seizing Charles-Town, May 12, 1780, have shown the Howes how to act.

80-72. A Christmas Epistle. Parson Sheridan to the Fair Clarinda.

"Dear Clara, should the humour please." (c. 150)

WM 47 (Jan 7, 1780), 52-3.

OC. Incidental remarks on Col. Maitland against the rebels, North against seditious mock patriots, Irish fencibles, Paul Jones.

80-73. The Christmas Tale, for 1780. Addressed to Mr. Burke, &c. &c. &c.

"In ages past, when men did prize." (98)

MP, Jan 27, 1780.

Hudibrastics. Satire on the disunited Opposition -- Richmond, Fox, Luttrell. North is defended.

80-74. Colvill, Robert.

[Epitaph.] To the Immortal Memory of the Hon. Colonel / John Maitland . . . (c. 10)

Colvill, The Poetical Works (1789), pp. 143-4.

Inscription. Dated Jan 27, 1780. Colvill praises his brave and loyal countryman who gave his life to help defeat the allied Franco-American attack on Savannah, in October 1779. See 79-148, 89-1.

80-75. [Come on my brave tars.]

"Come on my brave tars." (43)

Calliope, or the Musical Miscellany (London: Elliott and Kay, 1788), Song 74, pp. 142-3, 224-5. Words and music.

A patriotic naval war song directed against France and Spain. Let us hope that "eighty" will be like "fam'd fifty-nine."

80-76. Congratulatory Verses to the Morning Post, on Introducing a New Occasional Paper, called, The Examiner.

"While each day we see swarms of itinerant Papers." (28)

MP, Nov 18, 1780.

Hexameter couplets. A defense of Government against misleading faction, its "lies and detraction."

80-77. The Contrast. Charles II Compared with his present Majesty.

"When base fanatic cant, and bigot zeal." (48)

M Chron, Feb 10, 1780.

HC. "An American Refugee," a loyalist, defends the righteous British cause against the rebel Congress now united with France and Spain, as he praises George III.

80-78. The Contrast; or the Blessings of Monarchy, and the Plagues of Republicanism.

"Be mine to love and still obey." (12)

MP, Sep 29, 1780.

Quatrains. A loyal defense of the King and monarchy against the republican American Congress which brings "Tyranny and Chains."

80-79. The Contrast; or, the Wisdom of N****** County, opposed, on same late occasions, to the Folly of N******* Town.

"If, when fell Discord with her ruthless band." (24)

G Eve Post, Aug 1, 1780.

HC. The contrast is between those who sow sedition and disunity and those who support the King, law and order. The reformers and Opposition are satirized.

80-80. The Coronation Day.

"This day, Britannia's annual boast." (8)

Lloyd's 47 (Sep 20, 1780), 288; W Eve Post, Sep 20, 1780.

Quatrains. A Tory poem. On this festal day, the Coronation Day, we should loyally toast the Brunswick line. Note the references to "right divine" and "Delegate of Heav'n."

80-81. Count D'Estaing.

"So Count d'Estaing is sick, they say." (6)

G, Aug 18, 1780.

OC. Extempore. Count d'Estaing is ill and demoralized, because his fleet is blocked by British Admiral Geary (and cannot leave for America). Geary was stationed at Plymouth at this time.

80-82. The Daily Prayer of Modern Patriots.

"Heav'n! Congress bless! -- and send this nation." (14)

MP, Dec 8, 1780.

Generally OC. Satire on the Opposition and the reformers, especially "the Westminster Congress" or association led by Fox. The prose essay below the poem is Examiner, No. 10, an ironic satire on "the Westminster Congress," indicted because its strategy and the structure of its forces are indebted "to our brethren in America." The point in the essay and the poem is that the Opposition or Patriots are traitors, "Saints" or Dissenters, rioters, "drunkards, madmen, low and great."

80-83. [Death of Colonel Maitland. Written by a Lady now in America.] The Spirit of Colonel Maitland to Mrs. D[e Lance]y.

"O'er Maitland's corse, as vict'ry reclin'd." (20)
"From these blest realms where joys eternal reign." (22)

GA, Jun 19, 1780.

HC.  Two poems on the death of Col. Maitland.  Maitland died at Savannah October 1779; he is praised for his patriotism, and his spirit thanks the woman for her generous and sympathetic lines.  See R. Cole, Georgia Hist. Qtrly 65 (1981), 201.

80-84.  A Dissertation on Wigs, Alias Old Whigs.  Addressed to a Worthy Old Peer.

"Dissertations on Heads now so common are grown."  (36)

G Eve Post, Aug 1, 1780.

Hexameter couplets.  A defense of Old Whigs against "base Jacobites, Tories, and Scotch."  The time has now come for Whigs to "stand forth, or most certain's our ruin."

80-85.  The Doctors.

"Poor BRITAIN, torn with rank Disease."  (12)

Cal Merc, Jun 14, 1780.

Quatrains.  Britain, being destroyed by the Patriots, may be assisted by "Scourers"; but the Patriots will do nothing because they hope to plunder her after she dies.

80-86.  An Elegiac Epistle.  To a Right Hon. Commissioner, from his afflicted Brother, W. E. Esq; on the Sudden and Violent Decease of the Board of Trade.

"This Quill, that whilom with Success apply'd."  (78)

PA, Apr 4, 1780; St J's C, Mar 30, 1780; GM 52 (Mar 1782), 133-4.

HC.  Ironic satire through the persona of William Eden, one the Commissioners of the Board of Trade and Plantations.  Eden complains to Lord Carlisle, President of the Board, and to Gibbon, Jenyns, and Richard Cumberland, other members, of the abolishment of the Board of Trade and its rich sinecures as a result of Burke's reform of the government's economy.

80-87.  Elegiac Ode for the 1st of January, 1780.

"When smiling peace each happy prospect crown'd."  (40)

HM 10 (Feb 1780), 110.

Regular ode in cinquains.  The war has ruined commerce and brought an economic depression to the country.  The people are suffering.

80-88. [Elegy on the Death of Captain Farmer.]

"What distant sorrows o'er the stormy beach." (40)

L Cour, Jan 22, 1780.

Elegiac stanzas. Let us mourn the death of intrepid Captain Farmer.

80-89. An Elegy. Written by a Lieutenant in the Light Infantry, now at Charles Town, and enclosed in a Letter to a Young Lady.

"Yes! Aura, yes, o'er foreign plains I stray." (36)

G, Jul 19, 1780; UM 67 (Jul 1780), 39-40.

Elegiac quatrains. The soldier remembers his beloved at home while seeking glory in combat abroad.

80-90. England's Lamentation, or Scotland's Triumph! A New Ballad, To the Tune of Welcome, Welcome, Brother Debtor.

"England, England, where's thy glory." (36)

L Cour, Jan 15, 1780; LP, Jan 19, 1780.

Song, ballad. A criticism of the Tory Scots for corrupting the government, strengthening the power of the crown, and ruining the country. Cited are Bute, Mansfield, North, Jenkinson, Sandwich, taxes, and William Allen.

80-91. Epigram.

"Britain, at length deliver'd from restraint." (6)

W Eve Post, Dec 5, 1780.

HC. Bute no longer will represent Scotland in Parliament. The King will now be free.

80-92. Epigram.

"Grant Louis and proud Spain agree." (12)

G, Jul 19, 1780; Say's, Jul 22, 1780.

Quatrains. Spain will pay for the war, whether England or France wins.

80-93. Epigram.

"I swore (said Louis, t'other day)." (8)

G, Aug 23, 1780.

Quatrains. Neptune supports Britain's command over the seas, despite France's claim.

80-94. Epigram.

"The Opposition is a drowned Cause." (4)

PA, Jun 7, 1780.

The Opposition is dead.

80-95. Epigram.

"Thou Hercules of eloquence." (8)

L Cour, Mar 4, 1780; LP, Mar 10, 1780.

Quatrains. Praise of Burke for his reform bill meant to end corruption.

80-96. Epigram.

"Three hours fine talk from Jesuit Burke." (6)

PA, Jun 24, 1780.

OC. North sleeps through the thunderous speeches of Fox and Burke.

80-97. An Epigram.

"'Tis said that Satan often tries." (8)

MP, Apr 6, 1780.

Quatrains. The reformers, rebels, are led by Satan in the form of Christopher Wyvill, a leader of the Reform Movement and organizer of the Yorkshire Association.

80-98. An Epigram.

"United now by kindred care." (4)

MP, Feb 11, 1780.

Satire. Grafton and Richmond, of the Opposition, now have a motive to support the war: Grafton for his heirs, Richmond for his coal mines.

80-99. An Epigram.

"Why rage the Patriots, thus, for public Thrift." (4)

PA, Jan 21, 1780.

HC. Satire on the Patriot Opposition regarding their bankrupt policy, their self-interest in the reform of the budget.

80-100. Epigram.

"Your Wisdom, London's Council, far." (8)

St J's C, Mar 16, 1780.

The London City Council is praised for its gift to Rodney and Keppel -- gold to poor Rodney, but a wooden box to Keppel.

80-101. Epigram. Occasioned by the strong Aurora Borealis that appeared on Tuesday night.

"When Keppel triumph'd, alias ran away." (6)

MP, Mar 2, 1780.

HC. If not the people, the heavens illuminate and celebrate Rodney's victory (over the Spanish fleet). Keppel is criticized.

80-102. Epigram. On Paul Jones's Refusing the Challenge of Lieutenant Sullivan.

"Great Jones, now free from future reprobation." (8)

British Mercury and Evening Advertiser, Dec 9, 1780; W Eve Post, Dec 5, 1780.

Mixed verse. Satire on Jones, concerned more for money than honor. Paul Jones refuses to fight Sullivan; but his conscience is clear because he has secured a good deal of booty.

80-103. Epigram. On the Citizens of London presenting one Admiral with a Box of Gold, another with Heart of Oak.

"Each Admiral's defective Part." (4)

L Chron 47 (Mar 16, 1780), 271; St J's C, Mar 16, 1780; WM 47 (Mar 29, 1780), 367.

Quatrain. London is commended for its irony in presenting suitable gifts to Keppel and Rodney: the former, lacking courage, receives wood; the latter, poor, receives gold.

80-104.  Epigram on the Resurrection of the Hon. C. J. Fox.

"When Rumour's voice proclaim'd Charles Fox was dead."  (8)

GA, Oct 13, 1780.

HC.  In praise of Fox, the people's friend who was not killed in a duel, as "Rumour" proclaimed it.

80-105.  Epigram.  On the Taxes for the Current Year.

"What!  Porter, Salt, Wine, Spirits, Tea, and Coal."  (4)

St J's C, Mar 16, 1780; Say's, Apr 1, 1780; WM 47 (Mar 29, 1780), 367.

HC.  A complaint directed at North's numerous taxes.

80-106.  Epigram.  On the Unjust Charge of Prodigality Made so Often by the Minority upon our Present Ministers.

"O!  Cease, ye factious Patriots, to complain."  (6)

G, Sep 12, 1780.

HC.  Evidence suggests the ministry will be able to economize effectively.

80-107.  Epigram.  On the Wisdom and Oeconomy of John Bull.

"Kitty P-L-M, in Kent, was Greenwich-Park Keeper."  (6)

PA, Mar 1, 1780.

Satire on wasteful spending by the government, and the need for economy.

80-108.  Epigram.  Subject appointed by the University of Cambridge for Sir William Browne's Prize Epigram, 1780.

"If true the theme for Cambridge prize."  (4)

MP, Feb 3, 1780.

Quatrain.  Epigram.  The Opposition orators are belittled for their treason.

80-109.  [Epigrams.  On Admiral Rodney.]

"What Noise, and what Popping, Rejoicing and Lighting."  (4)
"Let those who wou'd set Rodney's Vict'ry at nought."  (6)

Cal Merc, Jun 10 & Jun 14, 1780.

The first asks ironically if we are celebrating Clinton's victory or Rodney's defeat. The second responds in defense of Rodney's modest victory over the French off Martinique, April 17, 1780 (really an inconclusive engagement).

80-110. Epistle to Mr. Hayley, Addressed to Mr. Urban, on completing the Lth Volume of The Gentleman's Magazine.

"Thy yearly task once more complete, again." (80)

GM 50 (1780), ii.

Dated Dec. 30, 1780. Mourns the prostitution of poetry to "Power" and "Interest," the exception, however, being Hayley. About 25 lines are relevant.

80-111. Epistle II. From a Resident at Bath to his Friend in the Country.

"In my last I reported Bath's royal success." (86)

L Chron 47 (Mar 11, 1780), 253.

Anapest tetrameter couplets. A complaint at the waste and expense of the war, at bribery and corruption, and at the future decline of Britain, included in remarks on the resort in Bath.

80-112. An Epitaph.

"Here lieth, / In ever-during stench and corruption." (c. 90)

L Cour, Sep 16, 1780.

Inscription. Prose poem. Satire on the Third Parliament of George III's reign, dissolved September 1, 1780, for its corruption, for being under the King's influence, and for losing America.

80-113. An Epitaph.

"Mingling / With the mass of common matter." (c. 30)

MP, Nov 16, 1780.

Inscription. Satire on Fox for his opposition to Government: "He disgraced his passions in the slavery of a faction." He was "An American in his conduct."

80-114. [Epitaph from Kilkhampton Abbey.]

"If to prostitute superior Talents in the service." (c. 15)

MP, Dec 13, 1780.

Inscription. "A faithful transcript of one of the epitaphs from Kilkhampton Abbey." Really an addition to Croft's epitaphs from Kilkhampton Abbey -- a strong satire on Fox, undoubtedly. See Croft, Abbey of Kilkhampton (1780), 80-10.

80-115. Epitaph of Bradshaw, President of the High Court of Justice, who passed Sentence of Death on Charles the First.

"Stranger, / Ere thou pass, contemplate this Cannon:" (c. 15)

PA, Jun 1, 1780; W Misc 18 (Jul 8, 1782), 343-4.

An inscription that should explain why the war against the Americans is fought so bitterly. It is an anti-Whig war! "And never, never forget, / That Rebellion to Tyrants / Is Obedience to God."

80-116. An Epitaph on A[dmira]l K[eppe]l.

"Beneath this marble rests free from all storms." (c. 12)

MP, Oct 9, 1780.

Inscription. An attack on Keppel as a partisan of seditious faction.

80-117. Epitaph on Major Andre.

"Is there no bright reversion in the sky." (16)

HM 11 (Jan 1781), 45; LM 49 (Dec 1780), 578; MH, Dec 5, 1780; SM 43 (Jun 1781), 41; UM 67 (Supplement 1780), 375; WM 51 (Jan 18, 1781), 53-4.

HC. An optimistic answer to the question if Andre will be rewarded in Heaven; moreover he will be avenged. (Andre was executed October 2, 1780.)

80-118. An Epitaph on Sir H[ugh] P[alliser].

"Whose earthly part is now consigned to the cold embrace." (c. 10)

MP, Oct 13, 1780.

Inscription. Prose poem. A defense of Palliser, a true patriot, for his bravery and honorable conduct, against the supporters of Keppel. Perhaps an imitation of the epitaphs in Herbert Croft's Abbey of Kilkhampton (1780): see 80-10.

80-119. Epitaph on the Death of Major Andre. By an Officer in the British Army.

"Ye who in sadness tread these lonely aisles." (22)

MH, Nov 22, 1780.

HC. An imaginative rendering of the circumstances of Andre's capture. Washington will be haunted by guilt because of his responsibility for Andre's death.

Epitaph on the Honourable Colonel Maitland. "When Gallic perfidy, and Rebel pride." See 79-148.

80-120. Epitaph on the Late Parliament.

"On the first day of September." (c. 25)

C Chron, Sep 15, 1780; L Cour, Sep 4, 1780.

Inscription. Prose poem. A diatribe against the corrupt Third Parliament of King George III for its vicious war against America.

80-121. Epitaph upon King Charles the Second.

"Here lies the Mutton-eating King." (8)

PA, Feb 26, 1780.

Quatrains. The epitaph on Charles is parodied and applied to King George, "the Button-making King," who will lose an empire.

80-122. Epitaph upon the late General Wolfe. Written in 1772, but never printed.

"Here lies the body." (c. 12)

GM 50 (Mar 1780), 143.

Inscription. A satire on the destructive military mind, using Wolfe as the vehicle!

80-123. An Eulogium on the K[ing], and the Present Administration. Loyally composed and humbly presented.

"Could I thy virtues, G---, rehearse." (96)

L Cour, Nov 29, 1780.

Regular (Horatian) ode in sixains. A tremendously ironic satire on the King and his ministry -- Bute, Thurlow, Sandwich, North, Hillsborough, Germaine, Stormont, Archbishop Markham of York, Gower, Rigby.

80-124. The Exploits of the Unfortunate Count. A New Song. To the tune of, -- "Derry Down."

"Come now, my brave boys, and I'll sing you a song." (75)

MP, Oct 10, 1780.

Ballad narrates Count D'Estaing's history up to his abortive attack on the British in Savannah, which was defended by Gen. Prevost.

80-125. Extempore.

"Britain's Prince comes back triumphant." (8)

PA, Mar 11, 1780.

Quatrains. Prince William, serving under Rodney, contributed to the naval victory against the Spaniards off Cape Vincent.

80-126. Extempore.

"When Laurens was taken, the Minister, blest." (13)

PA, Oct 11, 1780.

Quatrains. Henry Laurens was taken prisoner and sent to the Tower; North was pleased but had nothing much to say. (Laurens, President of the American Congress, was captured on a vessel bound for Holland, and committed to the Tower, October 6, 1780.) See Frank Moore, Diary of the American Revolution (1860), II, 353-5n.

80-127. An Extempore Hint, to the Sleepy Premier.

"N[orth] thinks, as Ireland he can keep." (6)

PA, Jan 22, 1780.

Sixain. Now that Britain "can keep" Ireland (having satisfied her with a free trade), North thinks he can sleep. But should England "still be losing," he will be awakened "with Vengeance."

80-128. Extempore Lines.

"Hail to the glorious deeds of this fair year." (14)

MP, Feb 21, 1780.

HC. At last the British are fighting bravely as in the past against France and Spain. Rodney is the exemplar; but Keppel is justly execrated.

80-129. Extempore Lines, Written on reading the Gazette that contained the brilliant Success of Sir G. B. Rodney over the Spaniards.

"With sounds of triumph strike the lyre." (46)

West M 8 (Mar 1780), 161.

A celebration of Rodney's defeat of the Spanish fleet off St. Vincent's in January 1780.

80-130. Extempore. [On a late Altercation in the H(ous)e of C(ommo)ns.]

"Sir Bullface Double-Fee, who, firm for years." (6)

L Chron 47 (Mar 18, 1780), 271; MP, Mar 17, 1780; SM 42 (Jun 1780), 320.

HC. Fletcher Norton, Speaker of the House (known as Sir Bullface Double-Fee, a corrupt politician) now joins the Opposition, but he has been motivated by self-interest, like all the patriots.

80-131. Extempore. Sum Solus.

"If e'er consistence gave a right to fame." (4)

LP, Nov 20, 1780; MH, Nov 22, 1780.

Benedict Arnold is certainly consistent in his behavior. Known as "one Arnold," he escaped (deserted) by himself. (Is there a suggestion here that because he escaped while Andre was captured, his behavior was not quite admirable?) MH has exclamation point at end of the title.

80-132. Extempore. To the K[in]g.

"Oh, Royal Sir, if a plebeian heart." (9)

Lloyd's 47 (Dec 27, 1780), 624.

HC. Advice to the King to continue pressure on the Dutch by attacking their trade.

80-133. Fable. Captain John Bull in a Storm. By Timothy Tickle.

"On board the Dreadnought stout and trim." (52)

Cal Merc, Nov 6, 1780; MP, Oct 30, 1780; SM 42 (Oct 1780), 543; W Eve Post, Oct 28, 1780.

OC. A moral fable about Captain John Bull's ship, whose crew mutinies, thereby causing the ship (of state) to founder. The moral is meant to promote unanimity, and is directed against factionalism, Burke and Fox.

80-134. The Fall of Faction. A Tragic Interlude. (Parodied from Macbeth.)

"Protervus. Hail, mighty Stasia! Goddess we adore." (c. 125)

MP, Dec 18, 1780.

A playlet in HC. A loyal defence of Government by means of satire on the factious Opposition that matches The Fall of Opposition, in MP Jul 31 & Aug 31, 1779. The Opposition is damned as republican and eager to foment party strife. Fox and Wilkes can be identified; the others are to be guessed. The point is made at the end that despite the American rebellion, Spain, France, and the combination of "northern pow'rs," Britain will persevere, guided by North and Sandwich. See 79-185.

80-135. A Farewel [sic] to Liberty. Occasioned by the Dissolution of the Last Parliament.

"Farewel, sweet Liberty, farewel!" (74)

An Asylum for Fugitive Pieces, in Prose & Verse (1785), I, 16-8.

OC. The King dissolved the Third Parliament on September 1, 1780. The poet complains that this Parliament yielded the natural rights of men, "Britannia's boast," and so liberty has deserted Britain.

80-136. Farewell 1779.

"Ere yet the Laureat trims his lay." (30)

G, Jan 4, 1780.

OC. A hope that Shelburne, should he take the helm, will be an improvement over North. The poem is signed "One Arnold," and Arnold's reputation was not tarnished until the Andre episode at the end of the year.

80-137. [A Fast-Day! what can be absurder.]

"A Fast-Day! what can be absurder." (76)

Freeman's J, Nov 23, 1780.

OC. A Protestant clergyman answers a Roman Catholic objection to the General Fast -- as carried on in Ireland.


Fire and Water. Airs. See Airs in the New Comick Opera of Fire and Water: 80-48.

80-138. The following Epitaph, on Major Andre, was originally intended to have been addressed to the Gentlemen of the London Association.

"Major John Andre, a British Officer." (c. 30)

M Chron, Dec 23, 1780; PA, Dec 25, 1780.

Inscription. As expression of indignation at the death and manner of death of Andre.

80-139. The following Verses were written on a late exchange of prisoners at New York.

"A Refugee Captain lost two of his men." (8)

MP, Nov 17, 1780.

Hexameter couplets. Humorous lines on a prisoner exchange -- two Americans for six British!

80-140. The Fox and Geese. A Fable. By Timothy Tickle, Esq.

"What human prudence can oppose." (c. 100)

MP, Oct 21, 1780.

OC. Animal fable. A satire on Fox and the Opposition for simply wishing to get "in."

80-141. A Fragment, which Some may Suppose to have been written in the Reign of King Charles the Second.

"Where'er great Caesar turns his kingly eyes." (30)

L Cour, Feb 2, 1780.

HC. Satire on the tyrant King, his knavish ministers and flatterers (like the laureat, Whitehead).

80-142. Freeth, John.
Birmingham Recruits. Tune, -- Jolly Mortals.

"Jolly sons of mirth and spirit." (20)

Modern Songs on Various Subjects (1782), pp. 49-50; The Political Songster (1790), p. 38.

Song. Not a town sends more volunteers to the army than Birmingham.

Freeth, John. The British Arms Triumphant, or D'Estaing's Defeat at Savannah. A New Song, by an Old Soldier. "Hark! from o'er the western main." (31) Lloyd's 46 (Jan 26, 1780), 92; WM 47 (Jan 17, 1780), 207. See 79-193.

80-143. Freeth, John.
The British Flag Triumphant. A Song, on the Defeat of the Spanish Fleet. [Langara's Defeat: or, The British Flag Triumphant. Tune, -- The Vicar and Moses.]

"With party away." (48)

Lloyd's 46 (Mar 10, 1780), 244. Also in John Freeth, Modern Songs on Various Subjects (1782), pp. 4-6; The Political Songster (1784), pp. 17-9 and (1790), pp. 33-4. (Only 42 ll. in these collections.)

Song in praise of Admiral Rodney for his defeat of Langara and the Spanish fleet off Cape St. Vincent's, Portugal, January 16, 1780, thereby relieving the threat to Gilbraltar. The same title for a different song appears in 79-80.

80-144. Freeth, John.
Charles Town Bar: or the Cabinet Council's Lamentation. A Song. Tune -- The Sun was in the Firmament.

"When vile mishaps had judg'd it fit." (48)

John Freeth, The Political Songster (1790), pp. 75-6.

Song. General Clinton's men attacked Charlestown, S.C., March 29, 1780, besieged it, and the Americans surrendered May 11, 1780. Freeth recounts an episode at the beginning of the campaign when the British had difficulty moving their troops into position.

80-145. Freeth, John.
The Cottager's Complaint. On the Intended Bill for Enclosing Sutton-Coldfield. Tune, -- Oh the Broom, the bonny bonny Broom.

"How sweetly did the moments glide." (42)

John Freeth, Modern Songs on Various Subjects (1782), pp. 37-9.

Song. A old cottager mourns the enclosure of his cot and grounds and the loss of his content because he has nowhere to go. No longer young, he cannot fly to a market-town, nor can he emigrate (it is assumed).

80-146. Freeth, John.
The Diaboliad.

"When Pluto, as told." (60)

John Freeth, Modern Songs on Various Subjects (1782), pp. 11-4; The Political Songster (1790), pp. 31-3.

Song. The occasion is Sandwich's appointment of Palliser, in early 1780, to the position of Governor of Greenwich Hospital. Thus Freeth satirizes those who support this promotion -- Germaine, Mansfield, Sandwich, and the Rev. Henry Bate (Dudley), proprietor of the <u>Morning Post</u>.

80-147. Freeth, John.
Lord G. Gordon's Procession. Tune, -- The Black Joke.

"Old England, alas! What is come to thy sons." (32)

John Freeth, Modern Songs on Various Subjects (1782), pp. 24-5; The Political Songster (1790), pp. 64-5.

Song. Freeth deplores the London riots and criticizes Lord George Gordon and the fanatics for creating divisions at home while the country is at war abroad. (Gordon was committed to the Tower June 9, 1780.)

80-148. Freeth, John.
The Stream of Corruption; A modern Song. By a State Pensioner. Tune, -- Cassini.

"My song is of Corruption's stream." (40-48)

L Eve Post, Jul 25, 1780; W Eve Post, Aug 8, 1780; John Freeth, Modern Songs on Various Subjects (1782), pp. 31-3; The Political Songster (1790), pp. 65-6.

The text varies. An ironic satire on politicians who enjoy the benefits of corruption and who object to reforms proposed by Opposition. Sandwich is cited.

80-149. Freeth, John.
The Trading War; Or, A Dip in the Loan. A Song. Tune, -- Liberty Hall.

"To get a snug penny since fighting began." (40)

G, Aug 14, 1780. John Freeth, Modern Songs on Various Subjects (1782), pp. 58-60; The Political Songster (1790), pp. 46-7.

Satire on corruption, on all those who benefit from a prolongation of the American War -- financiers, contractors, the generals and admirals, especially the Howes and Benedict Arnold (who prefers English coin). Self-interest motivates Government and Opposition.

80-150. [From all, and more than I have written here.]

"From all, and more than I have written here." (24)

G Eve Post, Dec 21, 1780.

HC. Christmas wishes presumably from the Commonwealth period are adapted to the present times -- wishes to be protected from civil war, hypocritical and fanatic Saints, "new reformers," "bold rebellion," faction, mob government, admirals who do not fight.

80-151. A General Toast.

"While British Heroes bleed in hostile Fields." (12)

Cal Merc, Oct 14, 1780.

HC. A toast to the brave British heroes who have fought to suppress "fierce Rebellion."

80-152. The Genius of England. An Ode. Occasioned by the News from America.

"Ye Muses strike the sounding wire." (54)

T&C 12 (Jul 1780), 380.

Regular (Horatian) ode in sixains. A celebration of Clinton's success (at Charleston, S.C.), which should bring peace to America and return the prodigal to "its parent's arms."

80-153. Good from Evil, and Evil from Good.

"'Tis said this Ferment in the Nation." (10)

PA, Jun 24, 1780.

HC. The disturbances have caused a reconciliation of the King and his brothers, Wilkes and the ministry, but has caused a break between Wilkes and Bull.

80-154. [The Greeks the Letter H discard.]

"The Greeks the Letter H discard." (4)

PA, May 5, 1780.

Quatrain. Extempore. Rebels (Hampden, Hancock) are supported by patriots in Parliament (Hartley) and equated with hell.

80-155. Green, Henry.
The Wooden Walls of Britain. An Ode. Written by Henry Green, and set to music by Dr. Arne. Sung on Tuesday the 25th ult. at Covent Garden Theatre.

"When Britain, on her sea-girt shore." (40)

Lloyd's 46 (Apr 12, 1780), 356; LM 49 (Apr 1780), 184; PA, Apr 13, 1780; WM 48 (May 9, 1780), 144.

A patriotic naval war song. "Britain's best bulwarks are her wooden Walls," her battleships. Reprint of 73-37.

80-156. Griffith, Amyas.
A New Song on the Associations of Ireland, written by Amyas Griffith, Esq; an Officer in the Carbery independent Company of the County of Corke, and Kingdom of Ireland. Air; Rule Britannia, &c.

"Now Ireland has by Heav'n's decree." (52)

G, Aug 3, 1780.

Free Ireland offers volunteers to engage in freedom's cause. The occasion of this song is a grand review of the Irish volunteers at Belfast.

80-157. Heroic Epistle from Serjeant Bradshaw, in the Shades, to John Dunning, Esq;

"Pride of the wond'ring bar! whose potent art." (c. 200)

SM 42 (Jun 1780), 319-20; WM 48 (May 25, 1780), 209-10.

Forty lines appear in MP, May 6, 1780, under a different title: "Serjeant Bradshaw in the Shades. To John Dunning." -- HC. A Tory satire, a defence of George III and monarchy. The persona of John Bradshaw (president of the High Court of Justice that tried Charles I) greets Dunning, "Prince of Chicane," saying Democracy calls for his demagogic aid. His "tools" are Fox, satirized for his gambling and "Poverty" (want of property); Wyvill, for his factious associations; and Fletcher Norton, for his greed and betrayal of North. The point is made that the present monarchy is unlike that of Charles I; and George III does not wish to increase his prerogative, regardless of what Dunning, Burke, and other republican demagogues believe.

80-158. The Hertfordshire Protest. A New Song.

"Impell'd by our fears." (48)

L Cour, Feb 5, 1780.

Song. Satire on a group of peers who protest the economic reform that would deprive them of their places, pensions, and sinecures -- Cranbourne, Essex, Duke of Marlborough, Marchmont, Sir Charles Cocks, Earl of Sandwich.

Hesitation. See "[Of late one sympathetic Word]," 80-251.

80-159. [Hibernian Burke, with holy Zeal.]

"Hibernian Burke, with holy Zeal." (6)

PA, Mar 1, 1780.

Epigram. Sixain. Satire on Burke as a Catholic. His call for reform is specious.

80-160. A Hint to Englishmen.

"Sweden's sworn monarch glory'd in the name." (8)

L Cour, Oct 20, 1780.

HC. Britain should learn a lesson from the tyranny of Sweden's king.

80-161. A Hint to Ministers, Members of Parliament, and others.

"If all the grants -- for money wants --." (16)

G Eve Post, Jan 20, 1780.

Quatrains. On the reform of the economy. If revenues were budgeted properly and needless pensions laid aside, there would be peace at home and no unnecessary and absurd taxes.

80-162. An Honest Man's Wish.

"Keppel return'd; it joys me much." (12)

L Cour, Oct 4, 1780.

Sixains. An expression of pleasure that Keppel was elected MP for Surrey.

80-163. Hor. Ode VI. Lib. I. imitated, and addressed to Sir W[illiam] H[o]we, K. B.

"Your Fame, O H[o]we, in Battle fierce." (30)

PA, Jan 14, 1780.

Imitation of Horace; regular ode in sixains. Satire on Gen. Howe, Keppel, and Burgoyne for leading the struggle so ineffectually. By the same poet who wrote "Ode X. Lib. I. Hor.," Richard Fitzpatrick (?), friend of Charles Fox, (or by one who pretends to be Fitzpatrick).

80-164. Cancelled.

80-165. Idea of Mr. Burke's Eloquence. With a Hint at Its Present State.

"A Stream so various, and so copious too." (11)

L Cour, Feb 25, 1780.

HC. Praise of Burke's oratory despite the malice of North's ministry for ten years.

80-166. Impromptu.

"Bristol! thou Seat of Dulness and of Gain." (8)

PA, Sep 27, 1780.

Quatrains. In the election for the coming Parliament, Bristol cast off Burke; but Burke really is too good for Bristol.

80-167. The Inconsistent Whig.

"'Trust not in man,' the Holy Scripture says." (4)

MP, Jul 21, 1780.

Extempore. Wilkes has changed his politics and become penitent (probably as a result of the Gordon riots).

80-168. [Inscription for William Dowdeswell].

"To the Memory of / William Dowdeswell." (c. 25)

GA, Jan 12, 1780.

A panegyrical inscription on William Dowdeswell, said to be by Edmund Burke: Dowdeswell was an honest member of the Opposition which objected to coercive measures against America. He died in 1775. Reprint of 78-252.

80-169. [Inscription on a Column for Keppel].

"To the immortal honour of / The British Admiral." (c. 10)

MP, Oct 25, 1780.

Inscription. Satire on Keppel, including a prose introduction that waxes ironic on the Howes and Burgoyne. Rockingham, it is made clear, gains from the Keppel episode.

80-170. Inscription to the Memory of the Authors of the Kilkhampton Abbey Epitaphs.

"Consigned to undisturbed oblivion." (c. 25)

M Chron, Dec 1, 1780.

Inscription. A satire on the author of the Kilkhampton epitaphs for compiling a very confusing and self-contradictory work.

80-171. An Inscription Written by a Friend on the brave Major John Andre, who was taken in disguise and put to Death by the Rebels in America.

"When France and Spain by treach'rous league combin'd." (14)

M Chron, Dec 5, 1780.

HC. Andre "died a Hero in his country's cause," despite an infamous and shameful death.

80-172. Instructions for County Meetings, 1780.

"And so think I -- How vain the expectation." (20)

L Eve Post, Mar 28, 1780.

Hexameter couplets. A criticism of Burke for failing to support the Reform Movement, because of his aristocratic bias. Burke here is seen as giving up his Oeconomical Reform Bill and unwilling to remove the North ministry.

80-173. The Invitation.

"The Don, and Mounsieur." (24)

LP, Mar 1, 1780.

Sixains. Satire. The combined fleets of France and Spain are invited to Plymouth again, and "their old friend" Palliser will greet them.

80-174. Irish Manufacture. A New Ballad.

"Ye Noblemen, in place or out." (36)

Freeman's J, Sep 12, 1780.

Ballad with "Irish Manufacture" as refrain. The Irish should wear Irish-made clothing and save their weavers from starvation. Thus the Irish will retaliate against English trade restrictions.

80-175. Irregular Ode to Fortune. Inscribed to the Right Hon. Lord George Germaine, &c. &c.

"Goddess! whose pow'r the nations own." (50)

MP, Feb 29, 1780.

Irregular Pindaric ode. Fortune is invoked to assist Britain, led by Lord Germain, in the struggle against France and Spain.

80-176. John Bull's Reply to Paddy's Address. Another New Ballad. Tune <u>Larry Grogan</u>.

"By Saint George, Paddy Whack." (60)

PA, Feb 12, 1780.

Song. Ballad stanzas responding to "Paddy's Address" (PA, Feb 10, 1780), defending England from criticism of its exploitation of Ireland and asking for continued friendship in the war against America and the Bourbons. See 80-293.

80-177. Johnson, [Samuel.]
An Apology for our present Situation. By Dr. Johnson.

"Zealous for truth and careless of applause." (18)

WM 48 (Apr 22, 1780), 79.

HC. Possibly by Samuel Johnson. A moral comment on the times. Nothing works for Britain, because all pursue their private interest; all wish to satisfy their avarice and pride.

80-178. The K[ing] and Keppel. Question and Answer.

"Q. Why is proud Keppel hated by the K[ing]." (3)

L Eve Post, Sep 14, 1780.

Triplet. The King hates Keppel because he is popular.

80-179. The King's Dear Friends.

"What numbers of dear friends the King has got." (4)

L Eve Post, Oct 14, 1780.

HC. Epigram. The King's friends, "so dearly bought, they are a nation's curse," are really bought by the people's purse, not the King's.

80-180. A Knotty Question.

"If Gazettes lye not, then 'tis plain." (12)

PA, May 18, 1780.

Quatrains. That Washington, although often defeated, still has armies in the field and refuses to submit to King George is a riddle to Sandwich and Germaine.

80-181. A Late Electioneering Advertisement Versified.

"To the free and independent Electors of Glocester." (22)

L Cour, Apr 25, 1780.

Anapest tetrameter couplets. Ironic satire on a Tory who, up for election to the House of Commons, defends the monarchy and its prerogatives, as well as the rights of placemen, against reformers. He is George Augustus Selwyn, a placeman.

80-182. A Late Epistle Versified.

"You'll receive, Sir, with this humble Scrawl of my own." (28)

PA, Mar 9, 1780.

Anapest tetrameter couplets. A report of an English seizure of a valuable French prize, two ships, a victory by Admiral Richard Howe near Gibraltar.

80-183. Lie down, Laugh, and Tickle. A new Song to an old Tune.

"Ye patriots so bluff." (72)

L Cour, Nov 17, 1780.

Song. Inspired by Tickell, the country (including the Patriots) should be amused. Satire on the courtiers and the Scotch.

80-184. Lines delivered extempore by a Lady, on reading his Majesty's Proclamation against the Dutch.

"Oh, glorious George! Great-Britain's native King." (9)

Lloyd's 47 (Dec 22, 1780), 603.

HC. In praise of George for his declaration of war against Holland for breaking its treaties. Britain declared war on Holland, December 21, 1780.

80-185. Lines on Hearing the Guns fir'd last Monday Morning.

"What means that thunder in the sky serene." (28)

MP, Mar 1, 1780.

HC. The "Mock Patriots" (Richmond, Rockingham, Shelburne, Priestley, Keppel) are not pleased by Rodney's victory over Langara and the Spanish fleet (January 16, 1780).

80-186. Lines on the Arrival of Prince William with the joyful News of another Valuable capture.

"Once more ye _Patriots_, tremble and turn pale." (32)

MP, Mar 7, 1780.

HC. Another attack on the factious Patriot Opposition for their failure to support the war.

80-187. Lines on the Death of Sir Charles Hardy.

"Why is each face o'erclouded with despair." (c. 65)

MP, May 24, 1780.

HC. The French navy assumed sovereignty over the seas until Captain Hardy began to fight. The common complaint is again made that France and Spain threaten Britain, weakened by the American rebellion abroad and faction at home.

80-188. Lines on the Riots.

"Whilst wild Sedition stalks around." (16)

MP, Jun 12, 1780.

Quatrains. The (Gordon) riots are properly suppressed, and law and order restored.

80-189. Lines Selected from an Eulogy on the English Nation; written by a Dutchman, Mr. Van Haren.

"O Generous Nation! faithful to your Friends." (24)

PA, Oct 21, 1780.

Regular ode in sixains. Praise of Britain for maintaining the balance of power in Europe, and criticism of France for basely violating treaty obligations.

80-190. Lines written extempore by a Lady, on reading the account of Major Andre's Execution and the Promotion of Arnold to the Rank of Brigadier General.

"To what a pass are matters driven." (6)

British Mercury, Nov 16, 1780.

OC. A reaction of disgust that Andre, a loyal subject, should die while Arnold, a traitor, should be promoted to the rank of Brigadier General.

80-191. A List of Candidates, for a Dodekarchy.

"Here's a List of twelve Speakers, great Speakers and small." (38)

PA, Mar 7, 1780.

Anapest tetrameter couplets. Satire on Opposition -- Burke, Fox, Barre, Dunning, and others -- when they were debating Burke's bill for economical reform, which would weaken the King's power.

80-192. A Look Backward and Forward.

"St. Stephen's House was full of Grace." (18)

GA, Mar 22, 1780.

Sixains. Britons must rid Parliament of corruption, which has benefited Scotland.

80-193. Lord Mayor's Dilemma.

"The Riot quite confus'd the Mayor." (4)

W Eve Post, Jun 17, 1780.

Quatrain. Epigram. Mayor Kennet of London could not cope with the Gordon Riots.

80-194. Lord N[or]th's Epitaph, by Anticipation.

"Here lies a man, to all well known." (8)

L Cour, Jul 11, 1780.

OC. Satire on North, responsible for reducing the empire by one third and making "a part more than the whole."

A Lyric Ode, written at the Conclusion of the Year 1779. "Down the rapid stream of time." (96) WM 48 (Apr 6, 1780), 14-5. See 79-261.

80-195. The Magnanimity of Sandwich.

"A Nation's hatred Sandwich nobly bears." (4)

L Eve Post, Sep 9, 1780.

HC. Epigram. It is difficult to understand how the King can love Sandwich, a man who is hated by the nation.

80-196. Martha Mark'em to Kitty Curious.

"I hope you will kindly excuse." (26)

PA, Oct 19, 1780.

Hexameter couplets. Martha Mark'em continues her review of the news: a visit to a Debating Society, the coming election, the victories of Cornwallis, and the capture of Laurens.

80-197. Martha Mark'em to Kitty Curious. A Second Weeks News, August 26, 1780.

"Well, the Lion and Bear have not come to blows." (38)

PA, Aug 30, 1780.

Hexameter couplets. The English have come to terms with the Russians (who are allowed to trade with France); and news from the West is not forthcoming. But a big naval disaster has struck -- more than forty vessels in a fleet have been lost to France and Spain. Sandwich is not entirely responsible. See "Week's News," PA, Aug 19, 1780: 80-394.

80-198. The Marvellous Adventures of a Rough-Rider, alias Colonel H-LR-D, a new Song, sung at Coventry with great eclat. Tune, -- And a cruising we will go.

"A Stout and valiant Sussex wight." (50)

L Cour, Oct 14, 1780.

A ballad narrating the history of a corrupt politician from Coventry.

80-199. Mary Cay. Or, Miss in Her Teens. An old Canterbury Tale, from Chaucer.

"Good Neighbours, if you'll give me Leave." (148)

PA, May 17, 1780.

Ballad narrative with "Yanky Doodle" chorus, by a N. Y. Tory, about the American rebellion in allegory -- a story of a daughter's resistance to her mother. Cited are Sammy (Sam Adams), Dick and Will (the Howe brothers), Jack (John Burgoyne), Harry (Clinton), France, and War with Spain and France, and (hopefully) a break between America and France.

80-200. Merlin's Prophecy. Addressed to the Poet Laureate on his incomparable Birth-Day Ode, in 1776.

"'Can Britain Fail?' Will Whitehead cries." (12)

L Cour, Dec 30, 1780.

Sixain and OC. Satire on the King for losing America, and on Whitehead for faulty prophetic strains. Merlin prophesies the fall of North and King George.

80-201. A Merry Song, About Murder.

"There was and a very great Fool." (45)

L Cour, Jan 25, 1780; LP, Jan 26, 1780.

Song. About a King, George III, who enjoyed slaughtering his subjects. (May be an allegory about the American War.)

80-202. Milton's Doctrine of Government, abridged and versified.

"The Government's ungirt when Justice dies." (18)

W Eve Post, May 27, 1780.

HC. Justice and laws are basic to government, and Kings must also obey these laws. Should they break them, then "power reverts to its original," the people. (This is a Whig declaration.)

The Miseries of Dissension and Civil War, an Ode. MP, Nov 7, 1780. An extract from Unity and Public Spirit (1780); see 80-41. Stresses three themes: the treachery of Opposition in supporting America, the Gordon Riots, and Britain alone against the hostile world.

80-203. Mr. Fox's Congratulation to Admiral Keppel, on the Success of the Surrey Election.

"Says Fox to Keppel, 'Honest Tar'." (24)

MP, Oct 2, 1780.

Quatrains. Ironic use of Fox's persona betrays Fox as a hypocrite and Keppel as a coward. The Fourth Parliament of George III's reign begins October 31, 1780.

80-204. A Modern Well Known Character.

"To all that's proud, add all that's proudly mean." (10)

L Eve Post, Sep 21, 1780.

HC. A personal satire on Sandwich.

80-205. [Monsieur Sartine, what do you mean.] To the tune of, "What cheer, my honest Messmates?"

"Monsieur Sartine, what do you mean." (64)

G Eve Post, Jan 1, 1780.

Patriotic song by a British sailor, a prisoner in France, about French harassment of English prisoners in order to encourage them to desert. He urges "unanimity" in defence of King and country and "British laws."

80-206. A Monumental Inscription.

"Beneath this load of Marble." (c. 25)

MH, Dec 21, 1780.

Epitaph. Satire, invective directed at Sir Herbert Croft, author of The Abbey of Kilkhampton, for maliciously attacking "Characters the most respectable."

80-207. Motto. For the New Branch of the Legislature.

"To this Belief you may may devoutly keep." (2)

PA, Nov 22, 1780.

HC. Aphorism. The new Parliament will be just like the old.

80-208. Murphy. A. C.
On the Queen's Birth-Day. Ode for Musick.

"Perfidious Bourbon lifts her hostile lance." (64)

W Eve Post, Jan 15, 1780.

Irregular Pindaric ode. Patriotic ode for music directed against the Bourbon powers, France and Spain, and America: "Dismay'd, beneath Columbian skies,/Lo! fierce Rebellion prostrate lies!"

80-209. [Must LITTLE Villains then submit to Fate.]

"Must LITTLE Villains then submit to Fate." (2)

The Scourge 7 (Mar 11, 1780), 37.

HC. Epigraph of an essay addressed "To the notorious Plunderer of the People, Corrupter of Parliaments, State Criminal, and public Traitor LORD NORTH." "Little villains" suffer so that the "Great ones" can enjoy freedom.

80-210. [A nation that we pity and admire.]

"A nation that we pity and admire." (11)

L Cour, May 22, 1780.

HC. The English nobility, having rejected the Contractor's bill, should beware becoming like the French nobility: "born to cringe and to command," etc.

80-211. Nevill, Valentine.
On Admiral Rodney's Account of the Action with the French Fleet, the 17th of April, 1780.

"Kind Nature smiling, -- some are born to write." (52)

West M 8 (Jun 1780), 332.

Rodney is praised for his success off Martinique.

80-212. Nevill, Valentine.
On the British Fleet Rendezvousing at Spithead, for Channel Service.

"Now vernal gales refresh the cheerful sky." (40)

Lloyd's 46 (May 19, 1780), 486; M Chron, May 20, 1780.

HC, in praise of Admiral Rodney and Captain Hardy who have defeated D'Estaing at Grenada and elsewhere.

80-213. Nevill, Valentine.
On the late gallant Defeat of the Spanish Squadron, by Admiral Rodney.

"Let Faction, now, its idle clamours cease." (14)

T&C 12 (Apr 1780), 216.

HC. Rodney has reasserted Britain's "empire o'er the main" by fighting. Dated Feb 29, 1780, this poem refers to Langara's defeat.

80-214. Nevill, Valentine.
On the Much Lamented Death of Admiral Sir Charles Hardy.

"By constant prudence o'er life's waves insur'd." (16)

M Chron, May 27, 1780; Lloyd's 46 (May 22, 1780), 494.

HC. All parties join in praise of Admiral Hardy, who has just died.

80-215. A New Ballad. Entitled and called, The Petitioner's Delight; Or, the Westminster Committee. To the Tune of, "That's a Jubilee."

"Come you who sign Petitions, Sir." (42)

MP, Jun 1, 1780.

Song. Satire on the Reform Movement in Westminster for concocting treason.

80-216. A New Ballad. On Mr. Burke's Bill. To the tune of, <u>Oh my kitten, my kitten</u>!

"Oh, my baby! my baby!" (72)

MP, Apr 14, 1780.

Song. Burke's Bill for Oeconomical Reform is demeaned as seditious, disloyal, and republican. It encourages rebellion. The Reform Movement is traduced, including its supporters in the Opposition: Richmond, Price, Wyvill, Burke.

80-217. A New Ballad on the Times.

"Good people of England, attend to my song." (60)

LP, Jan 19, 1780.

Ballad narrative of the situation in early 1780: Prussia, Russia, and Holland are indifferent to Britain's problem with France and America; Britain has lost America to France; Ireland insists on Free Trade; Scotland is selfish; internal dissension will destroy Britain.

80-218. New England's Glory; Or, the English Independant.

"Ye gentle, generous Whigs give ear." (49)

MP, Dec 19, 1780.

Song, tune not given. A satire on the New England Whig rebels and Dissenters who are identified with the Puritan roundheads and republicans, "Sovereign-killing" and "Prelate-kicking English Independant[s]." (sic)

80-219. A New Lecture on Heads. [Part I.]

"See the Head of his Worship in brass." (52)

LP, Aug 21, 1780.

Quatrains. Satire on the King and Court -- Wedderburne, Sandwich, Germaine, Mansfield, to be followed by another lecture on Opposition figures in Part II.

80-220. A New Lecture on Heads. Part II.

"Ye gentlemen all, and ye ladies." (44)

LP, Aug 23, 1780.

A continuation of "A New Lecture on Heads. [Part I.], 80-219. This part considers favorably the Opposition -- the Dukes of Richmond, Portland, Devonshire, Manchester, and Savile, Barre, Burke, Wilkes, Fox.

80-221. The New Naval Ode for 1780. Sung at Vauxhall by Mr. Vernon, Mrs. Weichsell, Mrs. Wrighten, Miss Thornton, and others. Composed by Mr. Hook.

"Since Discord still rages, we'll plough the salt main." (32)

G Eve Post, May 18, 1780; HM 10 (Jul 1780), 399; Lloyd's 46 (May 19, 1780), 484; L Chron 47 (May 18, 1780), 484; L Eve Post, May 18, 1780; PA, May 20, 1780; St J's C, May 18, 1780; SM 42 (May 1780), 268; WM 48 (Jun 2, 1780), 242; West J, May 27, 1780; W Eve Post, May 23, 1780.

A patriotic war song. British sailors will wage "bloody war" against France and Spain "Till Britain's acknowledg'd the Queen of the main."

80-222. A New Old Epigram.

"When Samson, full of Wrath, devis'd." (8)

PA, Mar 2, 1780.

Quatrains. Fox, says North, is a dangerous and fearful incendiary.

80-223. A New Song, intitled and called The Voter. To the old Tune -- "A Begging we will go."

"Of all the Entertainments." (45)

Cal Merc, Sep 11, 1780.

Satire on elections. Candidates for election ply the voters with food and wine in order to secure their support.

80-224. A New Song. Sung (at the late Masquerade) at the Pantheon, and distributed by Mr. Merlin from his Sailing-Boat.

"Ye Hearts of Oak, who wish to try." (24)

G Eve Post, Apr 6, 1780; L Chron 47 (Apr 4, 1780), 332; MP, Apr 5, 1780; St J's C, Apr 6, 1780; WM 48 (Apr 22, 1780), 79.

Patriotic naval song against the French and Spanish.

80-225. A New Song. Sung at Vauxhall, by Mrs. Wrighten. Set to Music by Mr. Heron. Words by Mr. Dobey.

"To hear the jar of noisy war." (24)

G Eve Post, Jul 11, 1780; L Chron, 48 (Jul 15, 1780), 45; LP, Jul 19, 1780; M Chron, Jul 14, 1780; W Eve Post, Jul 25, 1780.

A frivolous woman's point of view regarding the war. A woman of fashion is more worried about hats and feathers than principles.

80-226. A New Song to an Old Tune.

"The State Botchers humbled." (36)

W Eve Post, Dec 14, 1780.

Sixains. If the various members of Administration were cashiered, there would be peace: Sandwich, Rigby, North, Mansfield, Germaine, the Scotch, Palliser, *et al.*

80-227. A New Song. To the Tune of, -- "A Cobler there was."

"Good people, attend to my song, I beseech." (44)

L Cour, Jan 19, 1780; LP, Feb 16, 1780.

Song. Ballad, narrates the effect of Leonard Smelt's Tory speech upon the Yorkshire reform assembly.

80-228. A New Song. Tune, Highland March.

"Ye brave Caledons! from your mountains come down." (18)

WM 47 (Jan 24, 1780), 112.

An enlistment song. The Scots are asked to join the army in order to "cross the Atlantic, the Yankies subdue," for the English are unable to do it.

80-229. A New Song. Tune, -- "O the Roast Beef of Old England."

"Ye Sons of True Britons, assist me to sing." (21)

Bodleian. Warwick b. 1 (481).

Broadside election song countering two loyal Tory songs, "A Song. To the Tune of Derry Down," and "Truth and Loyalty," 80-336 & 80-387. A Whig retort, and like the Tory songs, it dredges up the past and uses old party labels, as it favors Rockingham, Richmond, Craven, Shelburne, Burke, Fox, and Barre. (These three broadside songs illustrate the emotion generated by a hotly contested election during the American War.)

80-230. N-rth-mpt-n Address.

"To his Majesty Royal." (30)

St J's C, Jul 6, 1780.

Regular ode in sixains. An ironic petition to the King (a button maker) begging him to make shoes! A satire on the "loyal" electors or freemen of Northampton and the King.

80-231. Now or Never. A Song. Addressed to all worthy Electors. Tune, -- Come, ye Lads who wish to shine, &c.

"Britons, now's your time to rouze." (23)

L Chron 48 (Sep 14, 1780), 261; L Eve Post, Sep 12, 1780; PA, Sep 15, 1780.

A song for free elections, against corruption (especially the sale of votes) and those candidates favoring "persecution."

80-232. Ode.

"Spirit of great Eliza, rise!" (43)

Lloyd's 46 (Apr 7, 1780), 337.

Irregular Pindaric ode. Patriotically recollects the past when in Queen Elizabeth's day Spain was trounced; and now soon Spain again will be defeated.

80-233. An Ode.

"While anxious cares my people wait." (72)

L Cour, Feb 1, 1780.

Regular (Horatian) ode in sixains. Satire on the King as a Tory tyrant, a source of corruption. The King's persona ironically betrays himself as stubbornly adhering to the lessons of Bute and Mansfield, to a "System" that has influenced people to change sides, among them Gibbon, Johnstone, and Smelt.

80-234. Ode.

"Ye dastard Gauls, and haughty Dons." (24)

MP, Jul 19, 1780.

Regular (Horatian) ode in sixains. Britain will overlook America's rebellion against her "lawful rights" because she is all-powerful in the world.

80-235. Ode, address'd to Captain Smelt.

"How could you, in the face of day." (102)

L Cour, Feb 22, 1780.

Regular (Horatian) ode in sixains. Ironic satire on Leonard Smelt, a Tory defender of the King's prerogative and opponent of the Yorkshire reformers. Cited are corruption or bribery, Gibbon, Johnstone, North, Fox, Chatham, Richmond, Gower, the Loyalist Yankees, and others. This ode could have been written by John Almon; it is not by Edward Burnaby Greene (80-17).

80-236. Ode for the 4th of June, 1780.

"Hail to the happy, joyful Day." (40)

PA, Jun 5, 1780.

Irregular Pindaric ode. Apparent panegyric on George III, for his achievements, including the war with America. Unanimity will restore profitable trade. This ode is probably ironic -- especially when the following boast is made: "His Deeds in Arms, his conquests won, / The Race of Glory nobly run, / To win the Rebel Mind." The prose essay that precedes this poem confirms the intended irony.

80-237. Ode for the Last Day in the Old Year. By W. Wronghead, Esq.

"And dares the sneaking Dutch pretend." (40)

L Eve Post, Jan 15, 1780; LP, Jan 19, 1980.

Pindaric ode. Parody on Whitehead's New-Year's Ode, 1780. Satire on those responsible for Britain's misery and disgraceful losses: the secret Tory junto, North, Germaine, Palliser, Sandwich, Mansfield, Bute.

80-238. Ode for the New Year, 1780.

"What! tho' confusion rages wide." (87)

PA, Jan 1, 1780.

Regular ode in double quatrains with chorus. An ironic parody on Whitehead's New Year's Odes, an elaborate satire on the King for his obstinacy and the nation for its pride. Cited are Captain Farmer, Pinchbeck, Gibraltar.

80-239. Ode for Thursday the 6th of April, 1780.

"What shall the British People give." (75)

St. J's C, Apr 4-6, 1780.

Irregular Pindaric ode, honoring "this thrice solemn Day," on which Dunning's motion was passed. The Patriots, supported by the spirit of Liberty, will purify the nation of corruption.

80-240. An Ode. In Honour of his Majesty's Birth-Day. Written by the Rev. Mr. Jacobs, one of his Majesty's Chaplains in Ordinary, and recited at Carlisle-house, on Sunday the 4th of June.

"Rodney, proceed! in GEORGE's cause proceed." (76)

MP, Jun 23, 1780.

Regular Pindaric ode. Prays that Rodney will be victorious and restore "fall'n America."

80-241. Ode in the Manner, but not in Imitation of Fenton's Ode to Lord Gower, on our late signal Successes by Sea and Land.

"The summer suns have sear'd the plain." (101)

G, Aug 19, 1780; G Eve Post, Aug 19, 1780.

Regular Pindaric ode. A loyal "Prize poem." Asserts Britain's rights over America, lauds Rodney and the navy, and Clinton for his victory at Savannah, and hopes that Britain's power over America will be restored. Alternate title is "Ode on our late signal Successes by Sea and Land," G Eve Post.

Ode on our late signal Successes by Sea and Land. "The summer suns have sear'd the plain." (101) G Eve Post, Aug 19-22, 1780. A reprint of the "Ode in the Manner, but not in Imitation of Fenton's Ode to Gower," 80-241.

80-242. Ode on the approaching General Election. In the Manner of Gay.

"The senate now dissolv'd -- again." (60)

G, Sep 8, 1780; G Eve Post, Sep 7, 1780; W Eve Post, Sep 7, 1780.

Regular (Horatian) ode in dixains. A cynical lyric about "Free Elections," stressing the need for honesty.

80-243. Ode. On the last New Levies in Scotland. To the Right Hon. L--D M--D---LD.

"O Thou! who sway'st the wide domain." (48)

WM 49 (Jul 27, 1780), 81.

Regular ode in twelve-line stanzas. An anti-Opposition poem, directed against patriot faction, the demagoguery of those partisans who cry of "injur'd rights" and cause discord.

80-244. Ode . . . Performed at the Castle in Dublin, on his Majesty's Birthday.

"Far hence, thou fiend accurs'd, to deepest hell." (7)

DJ, Jun 6, 1780; GA, Jun 11, 1780.

Excerpt. The poet in this Establishment poem invites Faction to Hell and begs for an end to the Civil War and the return of lasting prosperity in which Ireland may share. Refers to Irish Free Trade, now made law.

80-245. Ode X, Lib. 1. Hor. imitated, and addressed to the Hon. Charles James Tod. [Fox.]

"Glib Grandson of old Stephen Tod." (30)

PA, Jan 5, 1780.

Imitation of Horace; regular ode in sixains. Satire on Fox for gambling and encouraging sedition. Cited are his friends Thomas Townshend and Richard Fitzpatrick; and his enemies, North and De Grey.

80-246. An Ode to Fortitude.

"Hail, high-born virgin, mountain maid." (40)

HM 10 (Oct 1780), 567-8.

Regular (Horatian) ode in octaves. An invocation to "Fortitude" to support Britain "At this alarming crisis," attacked by many powerful enemies who threaten the loss of its liberties.

80-247. Ode to Janus. Written February, 1780.

"Janus, bifronted Deity." (112)

St J's C, Feb 17, 1780.

Regular ode in octaves, except concluding stanza. Advises the ministry to end the war against America, an unjust war that cannot succeed. How times have changed when in the past Britain was great and victorious, and the American colonies sought our aid!

80-248. Ode to the Muse. Occasioned by the present Tumults.

"While noise and fire-eye'd tumult reigns." (60)

T&C 12 (Jun 1780), 327.

Sixains. Begs the Gordon rioters, "factious bands," to cease their "internal strife" and turn their vengeance on France and Spain who "aid rebellion's bad designs, / Still to prolong the natal fight."

80-249. Ode to Unanimity.

"Britannia's tow'ring Isle now singly stands." (40)

Adams Weekly Courant, Oct 31, 1780.

Regular (Horatian) ode in dixains. Because Britain must fight the whole world, including Congress, unity is a necessity. Cited are the "arm'd Neutrality," Spain, France, Rodney, Clinton.

An Ode, Written about the Beginning of the Year 1778, when the Intelligence of General Burgoyne's Being Taken With his Army at Saratoga arrived. WM 48 (May 9, 1780), 143. See 78-325.

[Odell, Jonathan.] An Epigram. Wrote on Doctor Franklin, by a Gentleman, on seeing a stove of the Doctor's Invention, in which the flame descended through a flew. MP, Nov 16, 1780. A reprint of Odell's "Inscription on a Curious Chamber Stove," 77-187.

80-250. Oeconomy Commended and Reprobated.

"When our Third George began his happy reign." (12)

L Cour, Nov 29, 1780.

HC. At the beginning of the present reign, George and Bute urged "strict oeconomy." But now they oppose it, branding it with "High Treason"!

80-251. [Of late one sympathetic Word.]

"Of late one sympathetic Word." (32)

PA, Aug 17, 1780; W Eve Post, Aug 12, 1780.

Quatrains. The North ministry is timid and hesitant, incapable of firm and forthright action. Witness its cowardice during the Gordon Riots, the timidity of its treatment of Lord George Gordon. See "Reply to T. V. Author of Hesitation," 80-316.

80-252. [Oh! for a spark of heav'nly fire.]

"Oh! for a spark of heav'nly fire." (36)

LP, Mar 27, 1780.

Regular (Horatian) ode in sixains, honoring Rodney who, like Fabricius, fought bravely for his country and could not be corrupted.

80-253. On a Certain Gentleman who refused to accept a Place in the Ministry in case it should be offered him.

"F[ox] having fix'd, by Insolence and Vice." (6)

PA, Mar 23, 1780.

HC. Satire on Fox who wishes to get a literally juicy place in Government, the Treasury.

80-254. On a Gentleman's Asserting that "Honor was not to be found in a Dutch Dictionary," at the King's Arms Society.

"'Twas lately declared, that honor's a sound." (20)

M Chron, Oct 11, 1780.

Hexameter couplets. The Dutch are accused of being so motivated by avarice that they have lost all their honor.

On a late Altercation. See "Extempore. [On a late Altercation in the H(ous)e of C(ommo)ns,]" 80-130.

80-255. On a Late County Meeting.

"You have heard, I suppose, of our great County Meeting." (22)

G Eve Post, Jan 8, 1780.

Hexameter couplets, doggerel. Satire on the Yorkshire Reform Association for their republicanism and for wishing the defeat of the British forces. Cited are Congress (ironically); Gens. Dalrymple, Prevost, Howe.

80-256. On a Late Division. Addressed to the Mob.

"Rejoice, O Mob! -- for now 'tis plain." (67)

Cal Merc, Apr 24, 1780.

OC. The Patriot Opposition are selfish botchers; untrustworthy, they should not be allowed to rule the country. Cited are Fox, North, Burgoyne, Keppel.

80-257. On Admiral Rodney's insisting on the Release of the British Seamen confin'd in Prisons, before he wou'd agree to the Spanish Admiral's Request of Freedom on Parole.

"Let others paint the Pomp of War." (40)

Cal Merc, Mar 8, 1780.

Quatrains. British sailors face great dangers as they patriotically fight for their country; Rodney is to be praised for freeing them from Spanish prisons. The reference is the defeat of the Spanish Langara off Cape St. Vincent, and the relief of Gibraltar, January 16, 1780.

80-258. On Colonel Tarleton's Victory over General Sumpter.

"'I came, I saw, I conquer'd;" Caesar said." (4)

MP, Nov 21, 1780.

Quatrain. Epigram. Praise of Tarleton for his quick victory over General Sumpter (at Camden, S.C., August 18, 1780).

80-259. On Irish and American Liberty.

"When clouds and darkness hover'd round." (40)

WM 47 (Mar 4, 1780), 269.

OC. England has given Ireland a free trade. Would that the same be given America! All faction and discord should then cease. Humane treatment will generate humane attitudes.

80-260. On Mr. Twitcher declaring at Huntingdon, that, "if he could find another Lord Chatham, he would take him by the hand."

"No, Jemmy, should great Chatham now revive." (6)

L Cour, Jan 28, 1780.

HC. Were he alive, Chatham would reject with indignation any offer from corrupt Sandwich.

80-261. On Mr. Wilkes's preserving the Bank of England, in the Late Riots.

"I heard it mention'd t'other day." (18)

L Eve Post, Jul 18, 1780.

OC. Wilkes courageously helped restore law and order during the riots, and saved the public credit by protecting the Bank of England.

80-262. On Reading a Gasconading Article, dated Paris, in which is predicted the complete Conquest of the British West India Islands, and the Channel Fleet under Admiral Geary.

"Presumptuous France! cannot experience teach." (14)

G, Aug 16, 1780.

HC. Boastful France will be defeated. D'Estaing will be beaten by Rodney.

80-263. On reading an Account of the Character of the accomplished and unfortunate Major Andree, and of his Behaviour at his Death.

"As once in Greece the injur'd Phocion met." (10)

Cal Merc, Nov 22, 1780; SM 42 (Nov 1780), 608; MP, Oct 28, 1780.

HC. Andre, like Phocion, a general of ancient Greece, met his unjust death with great fortitude. Although no one present at his execution mourned, yet he turned it into a triumph and has become as famous as Phocion.

80-264. On Reading some Late Debates.

"This Patriot calls aloud for instant Peace." (4)

Cal Merc, Nov 13, 1780.

HC. Extempore. Two patriots of Opposition, Fox and Abingdon, would make it impossible to carry on the war.

80-265. On reading the Archdeacon of Rochester's late charge to the Clergy in favour of Popery.

"Hark! how proud Rome for joy Te Deum sings." (8)

LP, Mar 29, 1780.

HC. An illustration of Anti-Romanist attitudes. The Archdeacon of Rochester is castigated for his Papist leanings.

80-266. On St. Stephen's Chapel.

"To Stephen sacred was this House of yore." (4)

PA, Feb 10, 1780.

HC. Epigram. Satire on the Opposition who throw dirt on North; but he only falls asleep.

80-267. On Seeing the Earl of Mansfield's House burnt by the Rabble.

"With Truth, O Mansfield, has thy Fame." (8)

M Chron, Jul 22, 1780; MP, Jun 22, 1780; PA, Jun 21, 1780; St J's C, Jun 20, 1780; WM 48 (Jul 5, 1780), 374.

Epigram. Quatrains. Mansfield and Cicero have much in common -- eloquence and legal knowledge, and a house burned by the rabble.

80-268. On Septennial Parliaments. A Fragment.

"If Patriotism be a Trade." (55)

PA, Jun 24, 1780.

OC. Satire on the House of Commons, for its self-interest and corruption and its failure to represent the people. (There is a suggestion of the need for the reform of Parliamentary representation in this poem.)

80-269. On the Action of the 10th of May, 1780, between his Majesty's ship Milford, Captain Sir William Burnaby, and The Duke de Coigny, French Privateer of 28 Guns. -- Tune, "How little do the landsmen know."

"'Twas up the wind, three leagues or more." (36)

M Chron, Jun 28, 1780; PA, Jun 29, 1780; W Eve Post, Aug 29, 1780.

Ballad narrative of a minor British naval victory over the French.

80-270. On the Adjournment of Parliament.

"Christmas gives rest to various ranks." (16)

GA, Jan 21, 1780.

OC. The adjournment of Parliament is welcome, permitting time and rest to think, for Richmond, Sandwich, Burke, North, Rigby, Fox, et al.

80-271. On the amazing Resolutions lately published by some of the Mechanics of Dublin, "That the present Irish Parliament should be dissolved; to address his Majesty for that Purpose; and to enter into a Non-importation Agreement of any Goods from Great-Britain."

"How bless'd are we in this bright Age." (24)

PA, Sep 27, 1780.

Regular ode in sixains. An ironic satire on the mechanics and artisans for presuming to dictate to the Irish Commons. They will be punished for their presumption, for their refusal to help Britain.

80-272. On the American Dispute.

"Upon a trestle Pig was laid." (21)

L Cour, Sep 20, 1780; St J's C, Sep 19, 1780; WM 49 (Oct 5, 1780), 410. Also AR 1789, p. 160.

OC. Animal fable. A pig rebels against slaughter and escapes. No one helps capture him. This allegory illuminates the fundamental nature of the American War. Alternate title in the AR is "On the Late American War." See 78-275, 71-16.

80-273. On the Brave Cornwallis.

"Ye Generals whose sham campaigns." (24)

MP, Nov 9, 1780.

Regular (Horatian) ode in sixains, praising Cornwallis who, unlike Howe and Burgoyne, has won a victory (Camden) that will help restore his country's rights. (Cornwallis defeated Baron DeKalb and General Gates at Camden, S.C., August 16, 1780.)

80-274. On the Commitment of President Laurens to the Tower.

"Says Dick, 'Why this joy in each face that I meet?'" (4)

SM 42 (Oct 1780), 542.

Extempore. Anapest tetrameter couplets. An expression of pleasure that Laurens, captured on the high seas, has been imprisoned in the Tower, October 6, 1780. See "Extempore. [When Laurens was taken,]" 80-126.

80-275. On the Conduct of the Powers of Europe, in the Present War.

"Like some rash Youth whom Wine inflames. (28)

Cal Merc, Apr 24, 1780.

Quatrains. Bitter satire on the European powers -- France, Spain, Holland, Russia -- for interfering in the American War and checking Britain's strength.

80-276. On the death of Captain Philip Browne, late of his Majesty's ship Rose, so honourably mentioned in the public letters of General Prevost and Commodore Henry, for his spirited behaviour in the defence of Savannah; and who died in Georgia, a few days after Colonel Maitland, and of a like fever, contracted by the severe duties he went through during the siege.

"True to thy king, and to thy country true." (40)

L Cour, Dec 18, 1780.

HC. Praise of a good man and soldier, Captain Philip Browne.

80-277. On the Destruction of the Rebel Fleet at Penobscott, and the Reduction of Charles-Town.

"Whigs of all denominations." (72)

PA, Aug 21, 1780.

Octaves. Whigs of all denominations are damned, now that the rebels have been badly defeated at Penobscot Bay, New England, August 15, 1779, and at Charleston, S.C., May 12, 1780. Cited are the French alliance, Hancock, Adams, Franklin, Congress, Dissenters, Washington, Lee, Sullivan, Arnold, Cornwallis, Clinton.

80-278. On the Dissolution of Parliament.

"Let Britons gratefully remember."  (4)
"Slaves to corruption from their earliest youth."  (4)
"Britons! be gay (now only are ye free)."  (4)

L Cour, Sep 7, 1780; W Eve Post, Sep 5, 1780.

Quatrains. Three epigrams on the dissolution of the Third Parliament in George III's reign (September 1, 1780), criticizing its corruption and rapacity and praising Dunning's motion.

80-279. On the Dissolution of Parliament. [And] On a late joyful Dissolution.

"If ev'ry venal Wretch in Place."  (6)
"On Friday last, dissolv'd apace."  (4)

PA, Sep 5, 1780; W Eve Post, Sep 2, 1780.

Two epigrams; sixain and quatrain. If the corrupt politicians were to dissolve like this vile and arbitrary Third Parliament, it would be wonderful.

80-280. On the Glorious Conquest of Charlestown, By Sir Henry Clinton, K.B.

"See Britain's Genius now arise."  (32)

MP, Jun 20, 1780.

Song. (The melody is not given.) Clinton is to be praised for defeating the traitors and rebels supported by faction and France, restoring honor to Britain. Charlestown was captured May 12, 1780.

80-281. On the King's Accession to the Throne.

"When George the Brave resign'd his breath."  (24)

Lloyd's 47 (Oct 23, 1780), 400.

Quatrains. Briton's prospects are clouded; but through the naval victories of Rodney and Walsingham, Britain feels more confident now.

80-282. On the Late Battle in the West Indies.

"On her Snow white Clifts reclining."  (16)

St J's C, May 27, 1780.

Quatrains. Britain, mourning Hardy, is gladdened by Rodney's victory over the

French in the West Indies (Martinique, April 17, 1780). It was really an inconclusive engagement.

80-283. On the Late Public Fast.

"To fast for our sins; why 'tis decent enough." (4)

MP, Feb 11, 1780; also in New Foundling Hospital for Wit (1786), V, 188.

Epigram. Satire on Keppel. The National Fast on February 4, 1780, must give our forces "a stomach to fight." This courage was wanting in Keppel. -- Alternate title: "Epigram. On a Fast During the War."

80-284. On the Late R[IO]TS.

"For his religion, it is fit." (32)

MP, Sep 8, 1780.

OC, doggerel (Hudibrastics). An excerpt from Samuel Butler's Hudibras, I, 189-235, damning Presbyterians. (A few of the original lines are omitted.)

80-285. On the Late Successes.

"On the rude rocks which guard the Cambrian shore." (124)

L Chron 48 (Jul 18, 1780), 61; PA, Jul 22, 1780.

Heroic quatrains. (PA, 100 11.) An expression of pleasure, after the defeat at Saratoga and off Ushant, in Rodney's victory off Gibraltar and Clinton's at Charles-Town. Cited are the Bourbon countries, the Armed Neutrality, Holland, Farmer. Refers to the American rebels as "blind, mistaken men!"

80-286. On the Late Tumults.

"When wanton Riot stalk'd at large." (12)

PA, Jul 21, 1780.

Quatrains. We should in this tumultuous time (Gordon Riots) help our neighbor, thereby helping ourselves: "Self-Love and Social are the same."

80-287. On the National Loss, in the Consumption of Lord Mansfield's Manuscripts.

"Ah! how will Ages yet unborn, when told." (16)

M Chron, Jun 30, 1780; PA, Jun 30, 1780.

Quatrains. The loss of Mansfield's library of rare manuscripts in the Gordon Riots should be compensated by long life to Mansfield; and his eloquence shall endure longer than faction.

80-288. On the Present Political Times.

"Why does my friend such apprehensions raise." (26)

L Cour, Jul 14, 1780; LP, Jul 14, 1780.

HC. These times require the leadership of another Chatham; but all the politicians are scheming self-seekers, both in Government and in Opposition.

80-289. On the Report of Mr. Fox being killed in a Duel.

"Is all this true -- that's bruited through the town." (2)

L Eve Post, Sep 30, 1780.

Epigram. Fox is safe -- not killed in his duel with Adam.

80-290. On the Taking of Charlestown and that Scoundrel Lincoln.

"Hail! worthy Clinton, valiant chief." (24)

M Chron, Jul 7, 1780.

Regular ode in octaves. Praise of the officers who defeated the rebels May 12, 1780, at Charlestown, S. C. -- Clinton, Arbuthnot, Moncrieffe -- and criticism of factious Richmond, Fox, and Shelburne of the Opposition.

80-291. The Orator. Epigrams. By the Author of the Song on Mr. Burke's Bill. On Mr. Burke's Bill. [&c.]

"In Burke's new model of each antient tax." (12)

MP, May 5, 1780.

Six satiric epigrams -- on Burke, Barre, Bishop of Peterborough (John Hinchcliffe), Lord George Gordon, and Fox.

80-292. The Outs and Ins. Tune, The Children in the Wood, or the three Estates together by the Ears.

"Whilst Maj. and Min. thro' thick and thin." (16)

PA, Jun 16, 1780; St J's C, Jun 13, 1780.

Quatrains.  Satire on the majority and minority -- the former wanting only money, the latter wanting power.

80-293.  Paddy's Address to John Bull.  A New Ballad.  Tune, <u>Larry Grogan</u>.

"By your Leave, Gossip John."  (60)

PA, Feb 10, 1780.

Song.  An Irish complaint in which John Bull is asked for a free trade in this time of war.  See "John Bull's Reply to Paddy's Address," 80-176.

80-294.  Paine, Thomas.
[The rain pours down -- the city looks forlorn.]

"The rain pours down -- the city looks forlorn."  (62)

L Cour, Jan 6, 1780; LP, Jan 5, 1780.

HC.  A meditative poem in which Paine tries to find a spiritual meaning in the war and its cruel and destructive violence, but can only damn to death the British responsible:  King George, seen as Cain the murderer, and General Howe, seen as a second Cain, "man of blood."  He cries for revenge.  The British texts are not so explicit as that in <u>The Life and Writings of Thomas Paine</u>, ed. Daniel Edwin Wheeler (New York:  Parke, 1908), X, 338-41, where it is entitled, "An Address to Lord Howe."

80-295.  The Parliament Man.  A New Ballad.  To the Tune of "The Warwickshire Lad."

"Ye Quidnuncs and politic asses."  (56)

Freeman's J, May 16, 1780.  (Adds 7 more stanzas, 49 lines.)  L Cour, May 3, 1780; LP, May 3, 1780.

Seven line stanzas.  On Dunning's motion to diminish the influence of the crown upon Parliament by bribery.  Satire on those who sell their votes, on the Scotch. Cited are Lord North and members of the Opposition -- Fox, Burke, Barre, Savile, and Dunning.  (Seven more stanzas in Irish version on Irish politics.)

80-296.  Parliamenteering.

"For vacant seats in Parliament."  (36)

G, Sep 6, 1780; Say's, Sep 9, 1780.

Quatrains.  A cynical satire on the election process which, to this poet, is corrupted by avarice and self-interest.

80-297. A Parody of the well-known Epigram written at the time when King George the First sent a Regiment to Oxford, and a Library of Books to Cambridge.

"Keppel and Rodney, with discerning eyes." (6)

MP, Mar 11, 1780.

HC. Rodney has more merit than Keppel.

80-298. Past, Present, and Future.

"There was a time, when Britain's daring sons." (20)

G, Aug 22, 1780; Lloyd's 47 (Aug 21, 1780), 179; LP, Aug 23, 1780; PA, Aug 22, 1780; W Eve Post, Aug 17, 1780; also G Eve Post, Aug 19, 1780.

HC. At present, the rebels oppose Britain's "just and lenient sway," and "insult the Sovereign of the main." But soon Britain will assert itself with determination.

80-299. A patriotic Song on Sir Charles Bampfylde's being returned one of the Representatives in Parliament for the City of Exeter.

"Ye sons of fair Freedom, unite and rejoice." (26)

T&C 12 (Oct 1780), 551.

A patriotic song honoring Bampfylde's election as MP. (Bampfylde had voted for Dunning's resolution, April 6, 1780, and voted with Opposition.) See Lewis Namier and John Brooke, The House of Commons 1754-1790 (1964), II, 45.

80-300. The Patriot's Petition.

"Good people in power, ye see me inclin'd." (24)

MP, Dec 20, 1780; WM 50 (Dec 28, 1780), 375.

Quatrains. Satire on Opposition Patriots for their hypocrisy and self-interest.

80-301. The Patriots. Written about the Year 1700.

"Ye Patriots, go on." (15)

W Eve Post, May 16, 1780.

Cinquains. Satire on the Patriots, who simply are selfish. A Tory poem.

80-302. Peace. An Ode.

"O Peace! the offspring of the skies." (48)

W Misc 15 (Nov 27, 1780), 211-2.

Regular (Horatian) ode in twelve-line stanzas. A generalized paean on the blessings of peace, liberty, and "The natural rights of men."

80-303. The Petitioners.

"No, no, says bold Richmond, the laws shall not find." (14)

MP, Feb 22, 1780.

Hexameter couplets. Attack on Richmond and the Opposition for using America to topple the ministry. Ireland, France, Spain are cited, and the Reform Associations.

80-304. A Piece of Natural History unknown to Fox-Hunters.

"Sly Reynard, whose cunning had brought him renown." (12)

MP, Mar 21, 1780.

Anapest tetrameter couplets. A nasty satire on Fox for corruption.

80-305. The Political Footpads; An Ode for rough Music.

"Roar'd the Outs to the Ins -- 'Surrender your places! --'" (c. 74)

MH, Dec 23, 1780.

Burlesque oratorio. Satire on the Outs (the Opposition against war policies) for their ritual attacks on the ministry, for treacherously betraying the nation to America, for being republican and seditious: Barre, Fox, Keppel, Mawbey, Hartley, Price, et al. (The Morning Herald, founded Nov. 1, 1780, was a Tory paper sponsored by Government.)

80-306. Political Truths.

"That the present Ministry hath committed Faults and Errors." (c. 70)

DJ, May 23, 1780.

Prose poem, a political litany in defense of North's ministry. Others were to blame for the American troubles -- Rockingham, Grafton, Shelburne. Unanimity is important now, not reform. Cited: Stamp Act, Tea Duty, Townshend Act of 1767.

80-307. [The Premier, determin'd to raise the Supplies.]

"The Premier, determin'd to raise the Supplies." (4)

PA, May 6, 1780.

Quatrain. Extempore. Lord North, determined to increase the supplies, must levy additional taxes.

The Present Times. "Why does my friend such apprehensions raise." (26) L Cour, Jul 14, 1780. Same as "On the Present Political Times," 80-288.

80-308. Prologue, The Humours of an Election.

"Before we poll, the town I wish to sound." (29)

G Eve Post, Oct 21, 1780; L Chron 48 (Oct 21, 1780), 388.

HC. Frederick Pilon, the dramatist, hopes that peace will come upon the expected successes of Cornwallis and Tarleton, "when vengeance shall foul treachery repay."

80-309. Prologue to Deaf Indeed.

"What, more forc'd humour, and unmeaning mirth." (42)

G Eve Post, Dec 5, 1780; L Cour, Dec 7, 1780.

HC. General remarks on hypocritical politics, "prudent deafness," involving bribery and sinecures, secession, and independence.

80-310. The Question Answered.

"What are 'True Patriots?' -- Growlers base." (4)

MP, Nov 13, 1780.

OC. The Tory *Morning Post* again satirizes so-called "True Patriots," as interested only in pensions and places.

80-311. A Question Resolved.

"Q. Must Kings be treated, Sir, like common men." (6)

L Eve Post, Oct 14, 1780.

HC. Epigram. Kings are treated just like common men, despised if foolish, hated if cruel, honored if wise, loved if kind.

80-312. [Quoth George Tuffy to North, "I'll have nothing to do."]

"Quoth George Tuffy to North, "I'll have nothing to do." (22)

G, Feb 15, 1780.

Hexameter couplets. King George complains of the Middlesex voters because he cannot bribe them.

80-313. The Raree Show; or, Camp in St. James's Park.

"Here you see my rare show--ee." (25)

L Eve Post, Jul 15, 1780.

Song. Satire on the King and the soldiers upon review in St. James's Park. The war appears to be all false show.

80-314. A Reflection on Seeing the Execution Yesterday.

"The little knave submits to angry fate." (16)

L Cour, Jul 14, 1780.

HC. Little thieves pay with their lives for robbery; but great men who plunder the state escape punishment and gain awards. Cited are North, Jonathan Wilde, Stuart. By Causidicus Cirencester.

80-315. The Religious Savages.

"Alas! how hath fanatic Rage." (8)

PA, Jun 22, 1780.

OC. Criticism of Gordon for sparking the riots that destroyed Mansfield's library.

80-316. Reply to T. V. Author of Hesitation.

"In the Public Advertiser." (36)

PA, Aug 19, 1780.

Quatrains. Defense of the ministry and King. The ministry's alleged hesitation is not timidity or cowardice, but prudence. Besides, the criticism emanates from the Patriot Opposition -- Richmond, Savile, Dunning, Burke, Barre, -- who wish to displace North. See "Of late one sympathetic word," PA, Aug 17, 1780: 80-251.

80-317. Richmond and Grafton, Rockingham and Shelburne, Fox, Barre, Burke, and Hartley.

"It hurts one's pride to name these eight." (4)

MP, Feb 2, 1780.

OC. Epigram. The Opposition is made up of factious, vicious, foolish, subversive men.

80-318. Rigby's Generosity.

"Oeconomy, Dick Rigby cannot bear." (4)

PA, Dec 12, 1780.

HC. Satire on Richard Rigby, Paymaster General, who does not believe in economy reforms because he spends the nation's money lavishly.

80-319. Rigby's Perplexity.

"Why war American does Rigby hate." (7)

L Cour, Nov 29, 1780.

HC. Only fresh taxes imposed by Lord North will make Richard Rigby (who is Paymaster of the Forces) support the American War. (Rigby is often caricatured as "Jolly Dick.")

80-320. R[oya]l Oeconomy.

"In merry Old England it once was a rule." (4)

L Cour, Jan 13, 1780.

Quatrain. Epigram. Satire on George for being a fool and a king, thereby saving money.

80-321. Royal Reflexions. In Imitation of Royal Resolutions.

"A certain great Person whose Name you may guess." (55)

PA, Apr 27, 1780.

Hexameter triplets (after a seven-line introductory stanza). Ironic satire on the King through his persona: for sacking Pitt and engaging Bute and friends, for his wish to assume absolute power, and for his obstinacy. Cited are Ireland (free trade) and America (through rebellion lost to the Crown). He is called "King Wilful the Third." See 79-399, another version of Andrew Marvell's poem.

80-322. The Sailor's Adieu to his Mistress. A Ballad.

"Distress me with these tears no more." (24)

MH, Nov 8, 1780.

Ballad. The sailor bids farewell to his weeping sweetheart; and concludes with a reference to the war and the popular cause -- England fighting against allied forces to avenge the wrong done to her.

80-323. St. George and the Dragon. Sung at the Anniversary Meeting of the Sons of St. George. Tune, -- Black Sloven.

"Ye Sons of St. George, here assembled to-day." (28)

LP, Nov 29, 1780; MP, Nov 30, 1780.

A loyalist song. The English today will fight as they did in the past at Cressy, Poitiers, and Agincourt. Witness Minden and Quebec.

80-324. [Says Barre to Burke, "Odd's blood! did you hear."]

"Says Barre to Burke, 'Odd's blood! did you hear.'" (21)

M Chron, Dec 8, 1780; MP, Dec 11, 1780.

Hexameter couplets. The persona of Barre speaks, thereby ironically satirizing himself and Opposition leaders, Burke and Fox, for their determined attack on the reputation of Sir Hugh Palliser. Sir Hugh was returned to Parliament in October 1780, taking a seat representing Huntingdon, on Sandwich's interest. See Lewis Namier and John Brooke, The House of Commons, 1754-1790 (1962), p. 247. Alternate title in M Chron: "Says Isaac to Edmund -- 'Ads blood did you hear.'"

Serjeant Bradshaw in the Shades. To John Dunning. "Why tho' my sentence deem'd my King to bleed." (40) MP, May 6, 1780. See "Heroic Epistle from Serjeant Bradshaw, in the Shades, to John Dunning, Esq;" 80-157.

80-325. Seventeen Hundred and Eighty; or What D'ye Stare At?

"'Tis a year of great Wonders I sing of." (24)

PA, Aug 17, 1780.

Ballad. 1780 is an unusual year: English protestants fight with each other (Church and Dissent); Spain and France agree to help America; the Irish are fearless; the Scotch prosperous; the Russians and Dutch artful; the Danes and Swedes cautious; Rodney defeated the French fleet; and, finally, Lord George Gordon is imprisoned in the Tower.

80-326. [Sheridan, Richard Brinsley(?)]
The following Songs are sung in Harlequin Fortunatus, and said to be written by R. B. Sheridan, Esq.

"When 'tis night, and the mid-watch is come." (20)
"Cheerly my hearts, of courage true." (30)

Lady's M 10 (Supplement 1779), 715-6; L Cour, Jan 13, 1780; LP, Jan 10, 1780 (second song); PA, Jan 14, 1780; West J, Jan 15, 1780 (second song); W Eve Post, Jan 11, 1780; also G Eve Post, Jan 11, 1780; LM 49 (Feb 1780), 87-8.

Two patriotic sailor songs against the French and Spanish foe. See "Britons Strike Home!" another title for the second song with the chorus, "Britain, strike home! revenge your country's wrong!"

A Short Essay on Charles Churchill. Written in 1764. With Notes and Alterations in 1774. To a Friend. GM 50 (Sep 1780), 433-4 & (Oct 1780), 485-6. See 64-86.

80-327. [Shou'd we take from Lord North.]

"Shou'd we take from Lord North." (6)

GA, Jan 1, 1780.

Sixain. North should be expelled from the House of Commons for interfering with the Middlesex election.

80-328. Sir Hugh Palliser and Admiral Keppel.

"Sir Hugh and Keppel share a different fate." (14)

L Cour, Dec 12, 1780.

HC. A satire on the King for favoring hated Palliser but rejecting popular Keppel.

80-329. A Sketch of Modern Patriotism.

"Nero, of Old, -- Rome once on Fire." (8)

PA, Oct 3, 1780.

Quatrains. Satire on Opposition. Nero rejoiced while Rome burned; modern Patriots also enjoy "Ruin."

80-330. The Sleeping Coachman.

"Let ever-waking Faction bawl." (12)

Cal Merc, Nov 13, 1780; MH, Nov 16, 1780.

Quatrains. Lord North sleeps through the Parliamentary debates engineered by Fox and the Patriot Opposition. He knows what he is doing!

80-331. The Soliloquy of a Little Man, on the 21st of December, 1779.

"While loud huzzas and shouts proclaim." (66)

L Cour, Jan 7, 1780.

Sixains. Ironic satire on a Tory supporter of the ministry. The persona of Jervoise Clarke Jervoise complains of poor treatment by his electorate and reveals his true self. Cited are Chatham, North, Sandwich. "A little man" means a follower, in contrast to "a great man," a leader, a premier. (Jervoise urged punishment for Boston rebels and allied with Markham, Bishop of York.)

80-332. Song.

"Now Fox and Rodney, hand in hand." (16)

L Cour, Sep 27, 1780.

Quatrains. An election song for Fox, candidate for MP in Westminster: for freedom, against corruption.

80-333. [Song: from Love in a Village, a Comic Opera.]

"When a man of fashion sets." (12)

L Cour, May 26, 1780.

An air describes an officer, a young "man of fashion," as going to America rather than paying his debts. Hopefully, there he will fight and not run away.

80-334. Song on the Fast. Tune, That the World is a Lottery, &c.

"Give attention, ye patriots! awhile to my song." (57)

L Cour, Jan 6, 1780.

Song. Ironic satire directed at those politicians and clergymen who advocate a fast as a solution to the American troubles -- Germain, Sandwich, Dartmouth, North, and Bishop Cornwallis, all hypocrites.

80-335. Song. The Lords of the Main. Tune, -- Nottingham Ale.

"When Faction, in league with the treach'rous Gaul." (48)

MP, Dec 5, 1780.

Loyal naval song directed at Britain's enemies: Spain, France, and "Congo" (the American Congress) who are being helped by the factious and treacherous Opposition. Keppel is alluded to as a coward.

80-336. A Song. To the Tune of Derry down.

"Come all you brave Freemen and sons of True Blue." (30)

Bodleian. Warwick b. 1 (407).

Broadside election song with "Derry down" chorus for John Baker-Holroyd and Edward Roe Yeo in the riotous and expensive contest for Coventry, the general election of 1780. In this song, Holroyd is presented as "a Friend to the King" but "No Friend. to the fanatic dissembling brood." Also "No American Treason e'er sullied his Fame," and no County Reform Associations saw his name. He is presented as a staunch Tory supporter of Government (from which he had received a good deal of money for his electioneering expenses). See Lewis Namier and John Brooke, The House of Commons 1754-1790 (1962), II, 43; III, 673. See a related song, "Truth and Loyalty," 80-387.

80-337. Sonnet. To the Right Hon. Lord Mansfield.

"O Noble Mansfield! scorn the intemperate zeal." (14)

M Chron, Jun 13, 1780.

Italian sonnet. Defense and praise of Mansfield as judge.


The Spirit of Colonel Maitland to Mrs. D--y. See "[Death of Colonel Maitland. Written by a Lady now in America,]" 80-83.

80-338. Spoken Extempore in the Gallery of the House on Wednesday, the 8th of March, 1780.

"Reform, Reform!" -- That Word is odd." (8)

PA, Mar 23, 1780.

OC. Satire on Burke and Fox who preach reform; but because Burke is a jesuit and Fox a spendthrift, they have no credibility.

80-339. [Stansbury, Joseph.]
Pasquinades on a certain General, and on a certain Admiral. Copy of a Pasquinade

stuck up in the City of New York, August 12, 1780. Copy of a second Pasquinade, stuck up at New York, August 12, 1780. Copy of a third Pasquinade, stuck up on the 25th of August, 1780.

"You know there goes a tale." (40)
"From Arb[o]th[no]t, my friend, pray, tell me the news." (12)
"Has the Marquis la Fayette." (30)

M Chron, May 18, 1781 (3); PM 2 (May 1781), 291 (3); Cal Merc, May 28, 1781 (1); PA, May 21, 1781 (1).

Two of the sources publish only the third pasquinade; two publish all three. Satire by an American loyalist of the British General Clinton and Admiral Arbuthnot for their inactivity.-- The first is reprinted in Winthrop Sargent, The Loyalist Poetry of The Revolution (Philadelphia, 1857), pp. 134-6; and the other two in his Loyal Verses of Joseph Stansbury . . . (Albany: Munsell, 1860), pp. 66-8.


80-340. Stanzas on the Late Dreadful Insurrections in the Cities of London and Westminster, and the Irreparable National Loss in the Consumption of Lord Mansfield's Manuscripts.

"Oppress'd and struggling with a weight of woe." (64)

M Chron, Jun 30, 1780; PA, Jun 30, 1780.

Elegiac stanzas. The loss of Mansfield's library of treasured MSS is mourned. Faction is blamed for the loss.


80-341. Surrey.

"Come, gallant Keppel, come and prove." (16)

L Eve Post, Sep 26, 1780.

Octaves. An election poem praising Keppel who will "ward Corruption's blow" -- Keppel, candidate for Surrey. (He was elected.)


80-342. The Times.

"Attend to my Song." (36)

PA, Jul 29, 1780.

Song. Praise of Wilkes for actively stemming the riots; but the other city officers, Mayor Kennet, Aldermen Hart and Wooldridge, did very little or nothing.


80-343. The Times.

"Come, Genius of Nonsense, attend to my Song." (32)

L Cour, Oct 6, 1780; LP, Oct 4, 1780; PA, Oct 4, 1780.

Song with "Derry down" chorus. Satire on the ministry for persisting optimistically in its attempts to conquer the American rebels, despite its failures: North, Sandwich, Germain, Rigby, Dundas, Jenkinson.

80-344. The Times.

"I sing not of Burleigh, of Pelham, of Pitt." (95)

L Cour, Mar 25, 1780.

Song. Satiric attack on North's ministry for its undiminished imposition of taxes, inefficient administration of the war, corrupting influence; also on the tyranny of the King, the corrupt and acquiescent Parliament. Favors the Reform Movement and its beneficial effects and goals -- annual Parliaments and reduction of pensions and sinecures.

80-345. The Times as They Are. *It is a merry World, my Masters*!

"The French are playing Scurvy Tricks." (c. 30)

L Chron 48 (Sep 28, 1780), 311; PA, Sep 30, 1780.

A review of the situation in September 1780 -- France, Holland, Russia, Ireland, the naval war, the Colonies, Bute, North, the ministry, Parliament. Britain is alone as the Colonies rebel, etc.

80-346. ['Tis plain to every Man of Sense.]

"'Tis plain to every Man of Sense." (6)

St J's C, Apr 8, 1780.

OC. Although North has only a minority, he wins the divisions in the House because of the "Crown's Influence."

80-347. To a Certain Speaker. Extempore.

"Fie for shame, old Sir *Bullface*! to make such a pother." (8)

MP, Mar 20, 1780.

Anapest tetrameter couplets. Praise of North and criticism of Speaker Norton for selfishness and malice because his greed was not satisfied.

80-348. To a Great Person.

"The hearts of all thy real friends are gone." (9)

LP, Mar 6, 1780.

Triplets. Advice to the King, now unpopular, to choose better counsellors and friends, and not "rely / On force or fraud."

80-349. To a Great Person.

"If thou'rt a King by compact and by law." (4)

L Eve Post, Sep 14, 1780.

HC. Extempore criticism of the King.

80-350. To Admiral Rodney.

"Rodney, go on -- fresh victories explore." (8)

T&C 12 (Apr 1780), 216.

HC. A great man of action, Rodney is praised for his successes.

80-351. To all Gentlemen, Freeholders, and Others, who Signed and are now signing Petitions, Associations, &c. An Epigram.

"When malignant Sots, Gamesters, and such worthless elves." (8)

MP, Apr 4, 1780.

Hexameter couplets. Satire on the Reform Movement. The reformers are republicans and would introduce a tyranny of the many.

80-352. To Britannia.

"Rouse, Britain! rouse! nor let corroding care." (42)

MP, Jul 3, 1780.

Irregular Pindaric ode. Clinton's victory in the west has restored honor, along with Rodney's successes, to Britain in her glorious cause: "now Treason 'fore thee [Britannia] flies" and "rank Rebellion falls obedient to her laws!" The reference is the taking of Charleston, S. C., May 12, 1780.

80-353. To J[ohn] W[ilkes].

"'Tis sixteen years ago, and turn'd." (22)

L Eve Post, Jan 11, 1780; LP, Jan 12, 1780.

OC. How Wilkes has changed since he opposed the King sixteen years ago! He is a hypocrite!

80-354. To John Wilkes, Esq; On his late Spirited Defence of Popery.

"Thine active Zeal let other Pens commend." (21)

PA, Jul 5, 1780.

HC. A criticism of Wilkes for appearing to help the Papists, no longer supporting freedom. Wilkes has sold out. See PA, Jun 29, 1780, "To John Wilkes; On . . . Riots," of which it is a parody: 80-355.

80-355. To John Wilkes, Esq; On his Spirited Behaviour, During the late Riots.

"Thy active Zeal let Scoundrels discommend." (24)

PA, Jun 29, 1780.

HC. Praise of Wilkes for helping quiet the disorders. Wilkes does not deserve the satire of the Morning Post. See "To John Wilkes, On his late Spirited Defence of Popery," 80-354.

80-356. To Leonard Smelt, Esq; the King's Friend.

"If you'd hang ev'ry man who rails at the K[ing]." (4)

L Eve Post, Sep 30, 1780.

Epigram. Couplets. Satire on Smelt for his extreme Toryism regarding monarchy. Really, the whole nation despises the King.

80-357. To Lord North.

"A[bingdo]n, of quarterage possessed." (24)

M Chron, Aug 19, 1780.

Sixains. An elusive satire on Abingdon.

80-358. To Lord North.

"No more the Ministers of France." (26)

L Cour, Mar 25, 1780.

OC. Satire on North for his financial chicanery.

80-359. To Lord North.

"Stand boldly forth, illustrious North."  (6)

PA, Jan 22, 1780.

OC. Praise of North for "native Worth" and honesty.

80-360. To Lord N[ort]h.

"To act as Minister, and yet be lov'd."  (56)

St J's C, Jan 8, 1780.

Decasyllabic, alternate rhymes. A defence of Lord North and an attack on Opposition for factionalism, avarice and vanity; and an assertion of the need for unanimity. Burke and Fox are cited. A prose postscript enriches the verse.

80-361. To Lord North. Extempore.

"Would you, my Lord, retain Sir Fletcher."  (6)

MP, Mar 21, 1780.

OC. Another satire on Sir Fletcher Norton for self-interest against all principle, because he broke with North.

80-362. To Mr. Ad[a]m.

"By wounding Fox, to all mankind 'tis clear."  (4)

L Eve Post, Sep 30, 1780.

HC. Satire on William Adam, a Scot, who (it is alleged) received a reward for wounding Fox in a duel.

80-363. To Mr. Burke.

"Think not, O Burke! in dull inglorious Rest."  (12)

PA, Oct 9, 1780.

Quatrains. Praise of Burke, who, in retreat, is begged to return to Parliament, for his country needs him.

80-364. [To perpetuate / The Memory and Actions.]

"To perpetuate / The Memory and Actions." (c. 20)

PA, Jul 20, 1780.

Inscription. An attack, probably by an American Loyalist, on Opposition for its seditious encouragement of the American rebels, just defeated at ruined Charlestown, S. C.

80-365. To Sir Ralph Milbank, on Seeing his North York Regiment of Militia Reviewed.

"Let *Gallia's* faithless sons in crowds come o'er." (13)

MP, May 29, 1780.

HC. Milbank's genuine patriotism will prevent the French invasion and give the lie to Fox's demagoguery.

80-366. To the American Planter.

"Yet, Planter, let humanity prevail." (28)

W Misc 13 (Feb 7, 1780), 455-6.

Blank verse. An anti-slavery poem. Slavery should be abolished. Men should not be enslaved because of color.

80-367. To the Electors of W[es]t[minste]r.

"'Tis the son of old Reynard solicits your voice." (20)

MP, Sep 19, 1780.

An ironic election song, with Derry down chorus, against Fox.

80-368. To the Freemen of the Town of Lancaster. A Parody on an Advertisement that has appeared in the Morning Post.

"Sir George having giv'n up ev'ry pretension." (18)

GA, Mar 11, 1780.

Anapest tetrameter couplets. A parody of a political advertisement begging for support, but ironically betraying a corrupt person (John Fenton) running for a seat in the Commons.

80-369. To the Genius of Britain.

"Genius of Britain, spread thy guardian wing." (18)

T&C 12 (Dec 1780), 669.

HC. The poet prays that "the Genius of Britain" will protect the nation in the war against the Bourbon powers.

80-370. To the Honourable Ch[arle]s F[o]x.

"Dear Charley, if you'd hear the truth." (24)

MP, May 3, 1780.

Quatrains (with some irregularity). Fox should mend his manners, stop abusing the ministers at court, and so improve his fortune.

80-371. To the Hon. Temple Luttrell.

"Fraught with true Patriot fires to save the state." (47)

LP, Mar 27, 1780.

HC. Panegyric on Temple Luttrell (Opposition MP for Milborne Port) for his honesty and integrity and for his part in Parliamentary reform.

80-372. To the Hon. W. Pitt, Second Son of the Late Lord Chatham.

"As skilful gard'ners, of a rising tree." (12)

L Cour, Mar 31, 1780; LP, Mar 31, 1780.

HC. It is hoped that the younger Pitt, here praised, will follow his father's politics, "no slave to party, unallured by gold."

80-373. To the Inhabitants of Westminster.

"All ye who think freedom the root of all evil." (24)

L Cour, Sep 23, 1780.

Quatrains. In the coming election, Fox should be supported by the Westminster freemen.

80-374. To [the King].

"Your Americans, -- rebels to you and the state." (6)

MP, Feb 23, 1780.

Anapest tetrameter couplets. The King should subdue America like Scotland, "make them [his] friends." He should also "master" Parliament, both the "ins" and the "outs."

80-375. To the New Parliament.

"Since solemn ye're met, at this crisis so dread." (12)

G Eve Post, Nov 9, 1780; PA, Nov 10, 1780; W Misc 15 (Nov 27, 1780), 216.

Quatrains. In this time of crisis, when England is beset by many enemies, the new Parliament should be just, and united.

80-376. To the Patriots.

"Ye Patriots, wont to rail and roar." (24)

W Eve Post, Jun 24, 1780; MP, Jul 5, 1780.

Regular (Horatian) ode in quatrains. Satire on Opposition for their ineffectual stumbling blocks placed before Administration (Gordon Riots); Clinton has achieved a victory in the seizure of Charleston which should make them "sick and sore."

80-377. To the Promoters and Protracters of the American War, on both Sides of the Atlantic.

"Whither, ah! whither adverse rush." (28)

GM 50 (Aug 1780), 385.

Regular ode, in quatrains. Imitation of Horace. An objection to the irrational and unnatural civil war in America, from which only France and Spain can gain.

80-378. To the Reverend Clergyman of St. Giles's, who declar'd in publick company, that Charles Fox would not be suffered to live in a well regulated Society.

"Since Fox, adorn'd with ev'ry powerful art." (34)

L Eve Post, Oct 10, 1780.

HC. A defense of Fox's honor and integrity against venal statesmen of the court -- Sandwich, North, Hillsborough, Germaine, Mansfield, Bute, Bishop Southcote (of London).

80-379. To the Tars of Old England.

"Now, my Jolly Boys, the Time is." (12)

PA, Dec 12, 1780.

Quatrains. The sailors should strike hard at the French.

80-380. To the Well Meaning News-Paper Adventurers in Epigrams, Paragraphs, and Essays. A Word of Advice.

"'Gainst Court and Ministers why still inveigh." (10)

LP, Nov 20, 1780.

HC. Satire on Government, "Dead to all sense of honour or of shame." It is vain to try to influence the "Court and Ministers." Same as 80-412.

80-381. To the Wise Men of Gotham.

"Ambassador Laurens, by chance in your pow'r." (6)

W Eve Post, Oct 24, 1780.

Hexameter couplets. Satire on the City Patriots who, because they are not true to their country, deserve imprisonment far more than Henry Laurens.

80-382. [To Town came I a staring Lad.]

"To Town came I a staring Lad." (48)

PA, Jan 20, 1780.

Octaves in OC. Ironic stanzas about Mr. Woodfall's role as purveyor of truthful journalism in his Public Advertiser. Cited are Sheridan, the King and Queen, Smelt, Association, the Peace Commissioners.

80-383. A Translation from the Latin. Wrote on the late Horrid Tumults supposed to have been hatched by French Corruption.

"France is grown diffident in Arms at length." (12)

PA, Jun 28, 1780.

HC. France cunningly fomented the late riots in London. The Latin poem appeared in PA, Jun 23, 1780, and is by William Cowper. See 80-A and 80-53.

80-384. Transmigration.

"Britons, at length, like Indian Bramins, own." (18)

L Cour, Oct 23, 1780.

HC. The soul of Sejanus is in Lord North, of Jeffries in Mansfield or Wedderburn, the old Stuarts in the present monarchy.

80-385. Tray in Disgrace; or, The Danger of Prosperity: A Shandean Fable. Inscribed to Sir William Howe. By Timothy Tickle, Esq.

"To guard the flocks from devastation." (46)

Cal Merc, Nov 6, 1780; MP, Oct 28, 1780; SM 42 (Nov 1780), 608.

Animal fable. OC. Satire on Gen. Sir William Howe for corruption and failing to suppress the American rebellion.

80-386. A Truism.

"Thy Reign, O George! began all fair and bright." (4)

PA, Feb 21, 1780.

Epigram. HC. Bute is responsible for the decline of King George's reign.

80-387. Truth and Loyalty: A New Song. Tune, -- "O the Roast Beef of England."

"The Slaves of a Faction, who Rebels approve." (21)

Bodleian. Warwick b. 1. (409).

Broadside election song for loyal Tories against disloyal Whigs who side with the American rebels, hate the King, applauded the "horrid Murder" of Charles I, particularly Fox, Burke, Rockingham, and Camden (?). This song is for Holroyd and Yeo of Coventry. See "A Song. To the Tune of Derry down," 80-336.

80-388. The Tyranno-Phoby; or, Epidemical Madness.

"The Wretch, who 'midst the Summer's sultry heats." (12)

MP, Mar 9, 1780.

Extempore. Satire on the Opposition for their "barking," protesting.

80-389. Unanimity.

"When ancient Romans spread their martial Fame." (14)

St J's C, Oct 17, 1780.

HC.  Britain must not be divided; or, like ancient Rome, it will fall.


80-390.  Verses addressed to Sir H[ugh] P[alliser].

"I pray thee, Sir Hugh."  (30)

L Eve Post, Dec 16, 1780.

Sixains.  Satire on Palliser for being protected by the court, and praise of Keppel.


80-391.  Verses on the Death of Major Andre.

"When common men return to dust."  (48)

MP, Dec 1, 1780; G Eve Post, Dec 21, 1780.

Regular (Horatian) ode in sixains.  A British officer demands revenge and retaliation for the rebel murder of Andre, "The British Hero."


80-392.  The Victory off St. Vincent's, Obtained over the Spanish Squadron under Admiral Don Langara, Jan 16, 1780.

"'Twas Noon of Day -- the Storm was high."  (90)

St J's C, Mar 2, 1780.

Ballad narrative in sixains of Rodney's celebrated defeat of Langara off St. Vincent's, "the southern promontory of Portugal."


80-393.  The Weathercock:  A Character.

"Reading the News -- those mighty Themes."  (44)

Cal Merc, Oct 21, 1780.

OC.  Satire on the avid but confused newspaper reader unable to unravel the often contradictory and unreliable reports in the papers, but turns with them like a weathercock -- e.g., news about America, Ireland, North, Sandwich, Rodney, Fox, Burke, Cornwallis.


80-394.  The Week's News, Aug 19, 1780.  Martha Mark'em to Kitty Curious.

"Well, we now are relieved from a Part of our Pain."  (42)

PA, Aug 25, 1780.

Hexameter couplets. A gossipy letter expressing anxiety for news from Rodney and Clinton; and news of an agreement (Armed Neutrality) among Russia and other powers is disturbing and confusing, perhaps, a serious threat.

80-395. Wesley, Charles.
Address to the City.

"Ye Citizens of London, why." (80)

PA, Jun 23, 1780.

Dated London, June 22, 1780. OC. On the Gordon Riots, June 2-9, 1780. Only the King's troops were able to maintain order; yet they are not thanked by the City! Reprinted with Charles Wesley's The Protestant Association (1781): see 81-17.

80-396. Wesley, Charles.
Party Loyalty. Written in the year 1780. ["No longer Pipe, no longer Dance."]

"The First and Second George were wise." (22)

AM 4 (Jun 1781), 340. Also in the Poetical Works of John and Charles Wesley, ed. G. Osborn (1868-72), VIII, 447-8.

OC. The author is Charles Wesley. (See Frank Baker, Representative Verse of Charles Wesley [1962], pp. 338-9.) The occasion is John Dunning's resolution, passed April 6, 1780, "That the influence of the Crown has increased, is increasing, and ought to be diminished." Wesley takes exception to the attacks on George III by those who support the rebels. He believes that the King is subject to attack only because he is impartial and above party: "All Seats and Parties reconciles, / Alike on Whig and Tory smiles."

80-397. [Wesley, Charles.]
A Prayer for King George.

"Why do the Christened Heathens rage." (48)

AM 3 (Dec 1780), 677-8.

Sixains. Wesley asks why the English fearlessly "rage" against George III, against God's "dread Vicegerent here." He believes they are plotting against the throne and hopes God will protect George. Also in The Poetical Works of John and Charles Wesley, ed. G. Osborn (1870), VIII, 484-5.

Wesley, Charles. A Prayer, written at the time of the Insurrection, June 1780. "God omnipotent, arise." (32) AM 4 (Aug 1781), 455. Also in Charles Wesley's Hymns in the Time of the Tumults, June 1780 (1780), Hymn 4: see 80-42.

Wesley, Charles. A Prayer Written at the time of the Insurrection, June 1780. "Thou most compassionate High-Priest." (36) AM 4 (Dec 1781), 674-5, Also in Charles Wesley's Hymns in the Time of the Tumults, June 1780 (1780), Hymn 2: see 80-42.

80-398. [Wesley, Charles?]
Short Hymns: Prince of universal peace.

"Prince of universal peace." (32)

AM 3 (Nov 1780), 620-1.

A hymn for the end of enmity and discord, for peace.

80-399. Wesley, Charles.
Written After Passing By Whitehall.

"Unhappy Charles, mistaken and misled." (29)

Poetical Works of John and Charles Wesley, ed. G. Osborn (1870), VIII, 445.

HC. Frank Baker, Representative Verse of Charles Wesley (1962), pp. 328-9, dates the composition of this MS poem "at some time in the 1770's." Charles Wesley, writing in "these furious times," defends Charles I from his detractors who "blacken [his] memory with fictitious crimes."

80-400. Westminster Committee of Association.

"Whereas from the dust lately rais'd in the City." (47)

MP, Nov 15, 1780.

Anapest tetrameter couplets. Ironic satire on the Westminster Association for its contributions to "Reform" and to the end of the war with America. Cited are Saville, Sawbridge, the Patriots, Burke, Fox.

80-401. [What a clattering noise and strange botheration.]

"What a clattering noise and strange botheration." (18)

M Chron, Dec 13, 1780.

Hexameter couplets. The poet begs for unity against France and Spain, an end to the fracas and the bickering between "Majors and Minors," after the Keppel-Palliser episode.

[What distant sorrows o'er the stormy beach.] See [Elegy on the Death of Captain Farmer]: 80-88.

80-402. [When first on North George cast his gracious eye.]

"When first on North George cast his gracious eye." (6)

W Eve Post, Nov 7, 1780.

Epigram. HC. King George favors North and Sandwich, and so dominates the devil and the flesh.

80-403. [When France is join'd with haughty Spain.]

"When France is join'd with haughty Spain." (6)

GA, Jun 28, 1780.

Epigram. Satire on Britain, especially the court, powerless in the face of foes. Thus Britain is no longer Great but Little.

80-404. [When great George the Second rul'd us.] Tune, -- Hosier's Ghost.

"When great George the Second rul'd us." (32)

L Cour, Jun 14, 1780.

Song. Satire on the Tory ministry. In the reign of George II, Britain conquered France and Spain. But in the reign of George III, France and Spain rejoice because the King is under the influence of Bute and the Scots; the ministry is controlled by Tories -- North, Sandwich, Mansfield, Germaine; and [the Whigs] Keppel, Howe, and Burgoyne are banished.

80-405. [Where is Germain the great and victorious.]

"Where is Germain the great and victorious." (6)

L Cour, Jan 15, 1780.

Irregular meter, couplets. Satire on the ministry and King. In these dreadful days, the lethargic and incompetent leaders -- Germain, Bute, North, Sandwich, King George -- are doing nothing useful.

80-406. [Whilst with success a British Premier crown'd.]

"Whilst with success a British Premier crown'd." (10)

Freeman's J, Nov 7, 1780.

A mix of prose and verse. The resistance of America should prove to be a lesson to Britain regarding her policy for Ireland. Britain must give freedom to Ireland.

80-407. Whitehead, William.
Ode for his Majesty's Birth-Day, June 4, 1780. Written by William Whitehead, Esq; Poet-Laureat.

"Still o'er the deep does Britain reign." (36)

AR 1780, p. 194; G, Jun 6, 1780; G Eve Post, Jun 3, 1780; GM 50 (Jun 1780), 291; Lady's M 11 (Jun 1780), 325; Lloyd's 46 (Jun 2, 1780), 534; L Chron 47 (Jun 3, 1780), 541; L Cour, Jun 5, 1780; L Eve Post, Jun 3, 1780; M Chron, Jun 5, 1780; NAR 1780, II, 190-1; PM 2 (May 1780), 159-60; PA, Jun 6, 1780; St J's C, Jun 3, 1780; W Misc 14 (Jun 19, 1780), 280-1; West J, Jun 8, 1780; LM 49 (Jun 1780), 278.

Irregular Pindaric ode. Anti-Bourbon poem. "Still o'er the deep shall Britain reign." Britain's foes will beg for "that peace which their injustice broke."

80-408. Whitehead, William.
Ode for the New-Year 1780.

"And dares insulting France pretend." (40)

AR 1780, pp. 193-4; Cal Merc, Jan 10, 1780; DJ, Jan 6, 1780; GA, Jan 3, 1780; Lady's M 10 (Supplement 1779), 718; Lloyd's 46 (Dec 31/79-Jan 3, 1780), 4; L Cour, Dec 30/79-Jan 1, 1780; L Eve Post, Dec 30/79-Jan 1, 1780; M Chron, Jan 1, 1780; NAR, 1780, II, 178-9); PA, Jan 1, 1780; St J's C, Dec 30/79-Jan 2, 1780; WM 47 (Jan 7, 1780), 53; W Misc 13 (Jan 17, 1780), 384; West J, Jan 8, 1780; W Eve Post, Dec 30/79-Jan 1, 1780. Also G Eve Post, Dec 30, 1779-Jan 1, 1780; L Chron 47 (Dec 30/79-Jan 1, 1780), 7; LM 49 (Jan 1780), 37-8.

Irregular Pindaric ode. Whitehead and Britain defy "United Bourbon's giant pride." God has delegated his power to Britain, who has justice on her side, and decreed that she "should reign sole empress of the sea."

80-409. [Why shou'd just Heaven pursue the *junior* Crime.]

"Why shou'd just Heaven pursue the *junior* Crime." (4)

The Scourge 11 (Apr 8, 1780), 61.

HC. Epigraph of an essay addressed "To the King." Lines critical of ambitious Kings, "exalted Criminals" who, because of their lust for power, would "devour" the world.

80-410. The Wish. An Imitation of Horace.

"Propitious Fortune! only grant." (30)

PA, Aug 8, 1780.

Imitation of Horace. Ode in sixains. Let those who wish it have power like North, Sandwich, Germaine, Rigby; and let Fox debate the war; let the fight go on. But I will be contented with a guinea a day.

80-411. [With Periods round, whilst frothy B(ur)ke.]

"With Periods round, whilst frothy B[ur]ke." (12)

PA, Feb 12, 1780.

Epigram. Satire on Burke and Rockingham. Burke's rhetoric simply means he wants a place, and he is making Rockingham his tool!

80-412. A Word of Advice. To the Well-Meaning News-Paper Adventurers in Epigrams, Paragraphs, and Essays.

"'Gainst Court and Ministers why still inveigh." (10)

PA, Nov 22, 1780.

HC. Criticism or praise of the ministry is useless; it is dead. Same as 80-380.

80-413. Written on Mr. Burke's Plan for Promoting Public Oeconomy.

"What! so much to give up." (6)

M Chron, Feb 22, 1780; LP, Mar 1, 1780.

Sixain. Extempore. The Establishment, fearing loss of their "gains," object to Burke's plan and the petitions for reform.

80-414. Wrote upon the Election of Mr. Burke for the Borough of Malton, the 7th of December.

"Sons of Freedom, haste away." (28)

British Mercury and Evening Advertiser, Dec 15, 1780; L Eve Post, Dec 12, 1780.

Tetrameter couplets. Burke had failed being re-elected from Bristol. He is praised for being "elected" by the Borough of Malton (Rockingham's pocket borough!). He can now resume his work in the Commons, rejoin the Patriots and withstand "a venal crew" who seek "their country's ruin."

80-415. Wynne, J. H.
Ode for the New Year, 1780.

"Lo! like the phoenix rising to the view." (32)

G, Jan 1, 1780.

Irregular Pindaric ode. The war still rages in America, "hapless land! where civil discord reigns," and has enlarged with the entry of France and Spain. Yet in England, stable and fixed, peace, plenty, and freedom will continue.

80-416.  [You know, worthy Mat, that our wise Corporation.]

"You know, worthy Mat, that our wise Corporation."  (40)

MP, Sep 21, 1780.

Anapest tetrameter couplets.  Satire on the opponents of Government in Bristol -- republicans like Cruger who do not protect Bristol traders from "French pirates."

Prints

80-417. Britannia and Her Daughter.

"Miss America North, so News-paper records." (32)

Engr. with song. March 8. 1780.

George 5647 (V, 385-6).

A song about the quarrel between mother (Britain) and daughter (America). America insists upon playing a dangerous game with her allies, or lovers. The end refers to Rodney's triumphs over Spanish naval squadrons.

80-418. The Bull Broke Loose.

"Here, as in a glass you see." (28)

Engr. with OC. March 1, 1780.

George 5645 (V, 383-4).

The bull, England, protests at the abuses of government; that is, the reform movement makes some headway in Parliament. America appears in the print as an Indian with a scalping knife.

80-419. The Bull Over-Drove: or the Drivers in Danger.

"The State Drovers to madness had drove the poor Bull." (8)

Engr. with couplets in quatrains. February 21, 1780.

George 5640 (V, 379). Dolmetsch, pp. 124-5. Wynn Jones, p. 141.

The bull, England, kicks at the political leaders responsible for England's near destruction: North, Sandwich, and Germain. This activity is viewed with alarm by England's enemies: France, America, and Spain.

80-420. The Bull Roasted: Or the Political Cooks Serving their Customers.

"Behold the Bull! once Britannia's chief boast." (8)

Engr. with hexameter couplets in quatrains. February 12, 1780.

George 5636 (V, 376). Dolmetsch, pp. 122-3. Wynn Jones, p. 141.

The bull, England, is being roasted by those responsible for its demise: George, Bute, Sandwich, North. The enemies are served beef: the French, Americans, Spaniards, and Dutch.

80-421. Dutch Gratitude Display'd.

"See Holland oppress'd by his old Spanish Foe." (8)

Engr. with couplets in quatrains. May 4, 1780.

George 5663 (V, 396-7).

A satire. Holland had been helped by Britain before, but now when Britain is beset by France, Spain, and America, Holland insists upon being neutral.

80-422. The Engagement between D'Orvilliers & K--P-L.

"Don't you think my good Friends this a comical Farce is." (6)

Engr. with couplets. By T. Low. January 12, 1780.

George 5626 (V, 369-70).

Keppel's court martial took place January 1780. These anti-Keppel lines refer to an indecisive engagement between the French and English fleets on July 27, 1778.

80-423. An Englishman's Delight or News of all Sorts.

"All Englishmen delight in News." (16)

Engr. with OC. December 30, 1780.

George 5792 (V, 479-80).

Londoners are supplied with morning, afternoon, evening, and Sunday newspapers to satisfy their curiosity, especially their interest in the American war.

80-424. An Herioglyphical Epistle from Britannia to Admiral Rodney.

"To you my darling Child I deign to write." (20)

Engr. with rebus in HC. April 4, 1780.

George 5658 (V, 393-4). M. D. George, English Political Caricatures to 1792 (1959), p. 132.

On Rodney's naval victories, which will turn America from Spain and France back to Britain in peace and prosperity.

80-425. John Bull Triumphant.

"The Bull see enrag'd, has the Spaniard engag'd." (8)

Engr. with quatrains. January 4, 1780.

George 5624 (V, 368-9). Dolmetsch, pp. 120-1.

A pro-government satire, celebrates the victory in October 1779 of the English over the Spanish at Omoa in the Bay of Honduras. England, a charging bull, throws Spain in the air, causing dollar coins to fall from his pocket. The bull prepares to attack a Frenchman, behind whom hides an American.

80-426. Lewis Baboon about to Teach Nic Frog the Louvre.

"Ornamented with Butter Fish Cheese does appear." (8)

Engr. with hexameter couplets. 1780.

George 5664 (V, 397-8).

Satire on Holland, which is being invited by France and Spain to join them in the war against Britain.

80-427. Ministerial Purgations, or State Gripings.

"The People I've Tax'd 'till with rage now they burn." (20)

Engr. with hexameter couplets. February 9, 1780.

George 5632 (V, 373-4).

Another scatological broadside on the leaders of government (the King, Mansfield, Sandwich, and Germaine) in association with the devil, who are all having trouble on their stools in private closets.

80-428. Rodneys Triumph.

"My Name is Sr G. Rodney." (8)

Engr. with rough quatrains. March 10, 1780.

George 5648 (V, 386-7).

On Rodney's triumphs over the Spaniards in January and February, 1780.

80-429.  The State Dunces.

"Tis my Maxim still I say."  (10)

Engr. with couplets.  December 2, 1780.

George 5707 (V, 423-4).

Satire on the government for mismanaging the war.  Fox flogs North.  Sandwich and Germain are worried.

80-430.  The State Tinkers.

"The National Kettle, which once was a good one."  (8)

Engr. with couplets in quatrains.  By James Gillray.  February 10, 1780.

George 5635 (V, 375).  Repr. Wynn Jones, Cartoon Hist. of Britain (1971), p. 66.

Satire on North, Sandwich, and Germain (as well as Bute!) for mismanaging the government, and on King George for being despotic.

1781  Books & Pamphlets

81-1. Alves, Robert.
Ode For The Year 1781.  Being an Invocation to the Public Virtues.

"O Ye whose star-like lustre bright."  (131)

In 82-1:  his Poems, pp. 49-56.

Notices:  SM 43 (Nov 1781), 599-600.

Irregular Pindaric ode.  Alves begs the Public Virtues to visit England, who keeps the balance of power in Europe and dominates the main, and to inspire each British soul: Charity, Benevolence, Candour, Justice, Patriotism, Freedom--the last supported by a powerful navy and a large merchant marine "to awe Americ's rebel-bands" and to control France and Spain.  Thus, under the leadership of Mansfield and North, happiness, peace, and glory will come to the land.
A note in Scots Magazine 43 (November 1781), 600, remarks that because of "our late calamity in Virginia" (Cornwallis's defeat at Yorktown), parts of the poem "may seem a little unseasonable."  But Alves hopes that Britain will continue the struggle despite "the loss of 7000 men."


81-2. Burton, William.
Superstition, Fanaticism, and Faction.  A Poem.
London:  Flexney, 1781.

Notices:  CR 51 (Jun 1781), 472;  MR 65 (Sep 1781), 236.

Copies:  none located.

A Tory poem against the Opposition.


81-3. [Cockings, George]
The American War, A Poem;  In Six Books.  In Which The Names Of The Officers Who Have Distinguished Themselves, During The War, Are Introduced.
London:  Richardson, Hooper, & Broke, 1781.  ii + 181p.

"Of arms I sing, and trans-Atlantic war."  (c. 4700)

Notices:  CR 52 (Aug 1781), 146-7;  MR 65 (Dec 1781), 469.

Sabin 14108.

Copies: BL 992.k.26 (1); NUC CtY, DLC, ICN, MH, NjP, NN, RPJCB.

HC. Six books record the transactions of the contest between the American colonies and England, and describe the battles of the war through 1779. Politics are "studiously avoided." The narrative includes comments on the Stamp Act, Boston Tea Party, Congress, Battle of Lexington, siege of Boston, Bunker's Hill, Howe, Burgoyne, Clinton; the Canada expedition of Montgomery and Arnold, Carleton's defense of Quebec, Dunmore's defeat in Virginia; Washington's assumption of command, Howe's evacuation of Boston, Clinton and Sir Peter Parker's unsuccessful attack on Fort Sullivan; Howe's New York and Long Island campaign, Washington at Trenton; Burgoyne's campaign and its disastrous end at Saratoga, defeated by Gates; the battles at Brandywine, German Town, Mud Island; D'Estaing at Rhode Island, Wayne at Stoney Point, D'Estaing, Lincoln, and Pulaski's assault on Savannah and its failure.

81-4. Colvill, Robert.
Sacred to the Memory of Major Andre.

"If dying Patriots claim a nation's tear." (32)

In 89-1: his Poetical Works, pp. 265-6.

HC. A severe criticism of the Americans, "Goths" and "ruthless Traitors," responsible for the barbaric "felon's death" of André, "Britain's Hero." News of his death reached Britain in December 1780. His monument was installed in Westminster Abbey November-December 1782.

81-5. Conflagration: A Satire.
London: Richardson, 1781. 29p.

"Should you bedeck a clumsy, country swain." (c. 440)

Notices: CR 51 (Jan 1781), 70-1; MR 64 (Apr 1781), 312.

Copies: NUC CtY.

HC. Ironic satire on the leading members of Administration--North (Boreas) and Germain (Germanicus), portrayed as ill-qualified for office. North calls a meeting of the council while the mob is rioting, informs the members of his method of corrupting and controlling parliament, but confesses his failure with Opposition. He presents his plan for ending the riots of the Protestant Association, and accuses Amherst, General of the Army, of failing to quell the rioters. Amherst declares the army, blocked by civil authority, was powerless to suppress the lawlessness. Germain, after ironically betraying his cowardly character, recommends that North propose additional taxes to provide funds for compensating the victims of the disorder and call out the army. North admits he has been responsible for "the revolted provinces," the anti-

British alliance of France and Spain and the Armed Neutrality, poor finance ("taxes grievous," etc.), self-interest, poor state of the navy, increase of the public debt.

81-6. Ditis Chorus: Or, Hell Broke Loose. A Poem. Translated from the Satyricon of Petronius Arbiter, and faithfully adapted to the Times.
London: Kirby, 1781.

Notices: CR 53 (Jan 1782), 67-8; MR 66 (Feb 1782), 147.

Copies: none located.

81-7. A Familiar Epistle from A Cat at the Qu--n's P-l-ce, To Edmund Burke, Esq; On his Motion for the better Regulation of his Majesty's Civil Establishment, &c.
London: Kearsly, 1781. 26p.

"I doubt not, Mr. Burke, but you'll much wonder at." (402)

Notices: CR 52 (Aug 1781), 148; MR 65 (Aug 1781), 155.

Copies: Bod Godwyn Pamph 1739 (15); NUC CtY, NN.

Anapestic tetrameter couplets. The cat and a friend review the politics of the preceding period in the 1760's and blame the bad peace of 1763 on Bute's interference, insinuating that he had been bribed by the French who received from it all that they wanted. This peace led to "unhappy divisions" and, eventually, to civil war, war against America and difficult times and disunity in the nation, "to the great joy of our natural rivals" (pp. 14-16). The cat blames the loss of empire to the "perverseness and mismanagement" of the king's servants, especially Bute and Mansfield, "the Rubicon Lord." They keep their master misinformed and are responsible for Britain's standing alone before numerous enemies. After these remarks, the patriot puss concludes with a discussion of "that rebel Burke" and his plan to reform the civil establishment. The court junto, Mansfield and Jenkinson, are opposed to reform because it would destroy their system of parliamentary corruption.

The cat is a staunch Whig and reports with distaste the hostility of the court for Keppel and their support of Palliser. He also has Bute take credit for "the Popish Quebec Bill." Also cited are Wolfe, the year 1759 when England was at the peak of her glory, just before George II died and "the Butean system," "The source of our ills," was introduced, and all the Whigs displaced by Tories.

81-8. Penrose, Thomas.
Poems by the Rev. Thomas Penrose.
London: Walter, 1781. viii + 120p.

Notices: CR 53 (Jan 1782), 72-3; MR 66 (May 1782), 334-7; GM 52 (Jan 1782), 33-4, (Feb 1782), 86-7; SM 44 (Feb 1782), 100; WM 56 (Jul 4, 1782), 400-1; Eur M 1 (Mar 1782), 201-2; L Mag 51 (Jan 1782), 40; UM 70 (Jan 1782), 28-9.

Copies: BL 81.a.34; NUV InU & MH, DLC & PPL (1782 Dublin ed).

Includes "Flights of Fancy" (pp. 23-37), "Address to the Genius of Great Britain" (pp. 38-47), "Donnington Castle" (pp. 93-6). See 75-14, 75-15, & 75-16. (Another ed: <u>Poems by The Rev. Thomas Penrose, Late Rector of Beckington and Standerwick, Somersetshire</u> [Dublin: W. & H. Whitestone & T. Walker, 1782].)

81-9. A Pindaric Ode, Inscribed to the Right Honourable Lord North.
London: Rivington, 1781.

Notices: CR 51 (Jun 1781), 471; MR 65 (Sep 1781), 235.

Copies: none located.

Panegyric on Lord North.

81-10. Pinkerton, John.
Rimes.
London: Dilly, 1781. 136p.

Melody V. On the Military Preparations MDCCLXXIX. "The kingly oaks whose lofty crest." (91) pp. 22-5.

Notices: CR 51 (Mar 1781), 216-19; MR 65 (Jul 1781), 13-17.

Copies: BL 11643.b.40 (1st ed), 11632.b.42 (2nd ed, 1782); NUC CtY (1st ed), CtY, DLC, ICN (2nd ed).

Experimental Pindaric ode, which Pinkerton styles "Melody." He recalls past history, the glorious victories over the French at Cressy, Poictiers, and Agincourt, and over the Spanish Armada, and over the French again by Cromwell, Marlborough, and Wolfe, to inspire English youth to patriotic fervor. (There are some revisions of the text in the 2nd ed.)

81-11. A Poetical Epistle To The Reverend Dr. Robertson, Occasioned By His History of America.
London: Richardson & Urquhart, 1781. [5]-19p.

"Soft as the gentle dews of even." (c. 190)

Notices: CR 51 (Jun 1781), 473; MR 65 (Aug 1781), 234.

Sabin 63644.

Copies: Bod Godwyn Pamph 1704 (6), 1731 (3); NUC CtY, DLC, MiU-C, NjP.

Octosyllabic couplets. Praises Robertson for his exposure in his history of Spain's cruel and criminal exploitation of Spanish America. Now the poet asks Robertson to write the history of British North America, including "the mutual rage / Of brethren that fierce conflict wage." He objects to this civil war, "Fierce Civil Rage," and British use of the savage Indians, an "indelible disgrace." He wishes Britain to bind and reclaim the colonies "gently" and with their consent, "bind / In cords of love the willing mind." The colonial Americans also believe in freedom, like the English: "Why should they even to Britain bend?" They are not slaves. In the future, America will be a land where freedom and justice flourish.

William Robertson promised additional volumes to his History of America (1777), but the American War prevented his completing a history of the North American colonies. (The poem also appeared in An Asylum for Fugitive Pieces, in Prose and Verse [London: Debrett, 1785], I, 141-50.)


81-12. [Polwhele, Richard, ed.]
Poems, Chiefly by Gentlemen of Devonshire and Cornwall.
Bath: Cruttwell, 1792. 2 vols.

Four Odes, Written at Different Periods on Public Occasions. Ode II. "High heaven decreed--the Muse no more." (90) II, 39-43.

Copies: BL 992.d.32, 11660.ee.24; NUC CtY, DLC, ICN, IU, MH, NN, TxU.

Regular Horatian ode in dixains. A prophetic lyric emphasizing the future growth and greatness of America, the land of liberty. The Muse no more sings of the great nation that was Britain, now in ruin; but, following liberty, she is now inspired by Washington, honest, modest, just, and by Gen. Nathanael Greene, who was embarrassed by the American triumph at Saratoga. The Muse is happy to see Britain rise again in the prosperity, order, arts, and adventurous, expansive spirit of America, which should reach across the continent to California and south to include the regions now possessed by tyrannical Spain. The Muse should leave "this little, this polluted shore," Britain, in Europe, for "Ohio's banks" and "America's broad lakes" and "wide-stretch'd limits."

The poem is signed "V," who prefers to remain anonymous. It was probably written about 1781.


81-13. Satirical Ballads, &c. On the Times. Printed for the Benefit of the Unhappy Sufferers in the West Indies.
London: Asperne, 1781.

Notices: CR 51 (May 1781), 392; MR 64 (Jun 1781), 467.

Sabin 77137.

Copies: none located.

81-14. Seward, Anna.
Monody on Major André. By Miss Seward. (Author Of The Elegy On Capt. Cook.) To Which Are Added Letters Addressed To Her By Major André, In The Year 1769.
Lichfield: Jackson; London: Robinson, Cadell & Evans; Oxford: Prince; Cambridge: Merrill; Bath: Pratt & Clinch, 1781. iv + 47p.

"Loud howls the storm! the vex'd Atlantic roars." (c. 500)

Notices: CR 51 (Mar 1781), 230-2; MR 64 (May 1781), 371-6; GM 51 (Apr 1781), 178-9; NAR 1781 (III, 201-3); PM 2 (1st Supplement 1781), 173.

Evans 17368, 17719; Sabin 79477, 79478 (2nd ed).

Copies: BL 11630.d.8 (14), 11630.d.11 (17) (2nd ed); NUC CSmH, ICN, MH, NN, PHi, RPJCB, & TxU (1st ed), CtY, InU, MH, MiU-C, NN, & RPJCB (2nd ed).

HC. The 2nd ed includes William Hayley's poem "To Miss Seward. Impromptu."
Dedicated to Gen. Sir Henry Clinton, André's senior officer. Seward notes that André's Cow-Chace, "a satiric poem . . . upon the Americans . . . was suppos'd to have stimulated their barbarity towards him."
Disappointed in love, André joined the army to fight the rebels, who he thought were in the wrong, and to seek glory. He became a member of Clinton's general staff, and volunteered to perform the "fatal embassy" to Benedict Arnold, who wished to rejoin the British because of America's "unnatural compact" with France. Although Seward felt that the war was misguided, that it was unwise for Britain to try to conquer America, she was aroused to patriotic indignation at Congress's rejecting English peace overtures and accepting a French alliance: "throw Your country's Freedom to our mutual Foe!--Infatuate Land!" This act polluted the American cause. Justice, liberty, truth, mercy were no longer with the Americans; and so André, trapped by this circumstance, is treated mercilessly. Seward blames Washington for being unnecessarily cruel and barbaric, remorseless and unjust, for treating André as a base felon ruffian, denying him a brave soldier's honorable death. She predicts the same fate for him when his armies are defeated. (André was executed October 2, 1780.)

81-15. The Traitor. A Poetical Rhapsody.
London: Bew, Faulder, & Bowen, 1781. xi + 34p.

"Nature, for ever faithful to her plan." (c. 650)

Notices: CR 51 (Feb 1781), 155; MR 64 (Apr 1781), 312.

Copies: NUC PU.

The prose "Introduction," dated from Oxford, Dec. 8, 1780, belittles Franklin as unfit to be recognized as the ambassador from the American colonies to France, and portrays the French court as unable to treat him with respect and shows the French people as unhappy with their participation in the war. It also asserts that the Americans depend most on the disunion of the British for their success in the war--as demonstrated in the provincial reform associations, the Irish discontents, the London tumults, inflammatory speeches, and anti-ministerial publications.

HC. The verse is a bitter satire that presents Franklin at the French court, motivated by disappointed ambition to become a cunning fraud, bloody rebel parricide, and destructive traitor responsible for the American war, American independence, and the Franco-American alliance. The poet scourges faithless and perfidious Bourbon France, a tyranny, as a most unnatural ally of America, drawing "her gallant Sword in Freedom's Cause"! He predicts that French deception will end with Franklin in the Bastille and doomed to infamy. Then Franklin will no longer be commended by patriots sympathetic to the rebels, by John Almon the publisher, by Richard Price. He closes with an appeal for union in councils and on the battlefields, for the end of faction and discord, and for trust in the British cause; and he hopes that "Rebel Breth'ren, by false arts betray'd," will return to the bosom of the parent country.


81-16. Wells, Christopher.
Address To The Genius of America. A Poem. By the Rev. Ch. Wells, One of his Majesty's Chaplains in the Royal Navy, And Chaplain to the Right Hon. Earl Harcourt.
Canterbury: Simmons & Kirkby; Margate: Hall & Silver, 1781. v-viii + 27p.

"Come genial spirit at the earnest call." (300)

Sabin 102585.

Copies: BL 11632.g.58; NUC ICN, MB, NNC.

Dedication dated September 1781 to Rear-Admiral Francis Samuel Drake.
Blank verse. America, once prosperous, productive, and busily engaged in commerce, was contented. Envious France intervened, building forts on the banks of the Ohio. But Britain protected America, giving generously of her blood (Wolfe). How all is reversed as horrid rebellion stalks the land! Now the abettors of this sedition, this "rebellious war," are joining with France, once America's enemy! "Science" is driven out, by "rebel hands polluted and destroyed"; and peace and plenty are gone-- all caused by "ambition, thirst of lawless rule" and "mad revolt." Who can reunite Britain and America, and restore peace and prosperity? Cornwallis! He will wipe the tear from "Britain's parent eye,/ Who weeps while she corrects."
See 76-41 for 1st ed, only 110 lines.


81-17. [Wesley, Charles]
The Protestant Association, Written In The Midst Of The Tumults, June 1780.
London: Paramore, 1781. 34p.

"Arms, and the good old Cause I sing." (c. 540)

Notices: MR 65 (Nov 1781), 386-7; PA Jun 23, 1780 ("Address to the City").

Copies: BL 11631.aaa.33; NUC NNUT.

Octosyllabic couplets. Includes two "Addresses to the City" and "Advice to the City." Wesley blames the Gordon riots upon the Republicans and Dissenters in the old Puritan tradition, those who please "France, America, and hell" with their subversive activity. These traitors, including those like "John the Painter," Scots, patriots, "And all the friends of Congress," march in the ranks of hell. Wesley then proceeds to narrate the various acts of destruction committed by the rioters: the destruction of mass houses and chapels, the burning of jails and freeing of prisoners, the attacks on the Bank and on Mansfield and the burning and looting of his home (he praises Mansfield), and the indiscriminate plundering of property in the City. In the conclusion, Wesley speculates on the cause of the riots. He believes there must have been a plot, citing several traitors (in his opinion)--Franklyn, Burke, Fox. He cannot believe that the Opposition, along with the rebellious Americans, was not responsible for plotting the riot. It was not an accident, as the patriots say: "Were none of the Associators / American or English traitors?" ("Second Address to the City. Written in June 1780.")

See Frank Baker, _Representative Verse of Charles Wesley_ (London: Epworth Press, 1962), pp. 339-40.

Serials

81-18. The Accession.

"William secur'd great Brunswick's line." (16)

Lloyd's 49 (Oct 24, 1781), 402; St J's C, Oct 23, 1781; W Eve Post, Oct 24, 1781.

Quatrains. The patriot calls for peace and freedom, which William had secured for the Brunswick line. The crown needs peace now.

81-19. An Address to the Lovers of Freedom.

"Return, Britannia's Sons, no longer stray." (37)

Cumb Pacq, Oct 2, 1781.

HC. A woman asks Englishmen not to ape the French but to fight them and other insidious foes.

81-20. Addressed to no Minister nor Great Man.

"With all thy titles, all thy large estate." (52)

L Cour, Aug 27, 1781.

Quatrains. Satire on a frivolous courtier -- no really great man. He did not have the foresight to save the American colonies from France.

81-21. Admiral Rodney. A New Song to an old Tune.

"Saint George, he is our patron, boys, and Royal George our King." (29)

Lady's M 12 (May 1781), insert after p. 272. (With music); M Chron, May 3, 1781.

A patriotic song honoring the King and Rodney for victories over Langara, De Grasse, and the Dutch of St. Eustatius.

81-22. Afflictus melius considere rebus.

"Hence from the breast be ev'ry fear expell'd." (71)

M Chron, Mar 24, 1781.

Blank verse. Britain should not fear her confederated foes, nor the Opposition who, apostate, enjoy the discord that weakens the nation. Britain has her heroes who will fight the allied enemies and America -- especially Rodney.

81-23. Answer to the Last Enigma.

"By my faith now I think, that I'm sure I've found out." (38)

Cumb Pacq, Jul 3, 1781.

Anapest tetrameter couplets. The real answer to the "aenigma" printed August 7, 1781, was "a Hole in my Stocking." Here the writer suggests "a Bank Bill," and he alludes to "Congress-Notes sinking . . . below par."

81-24. Cancelled.

81-25. Ballad for the Day.

"Mynheer Gra'af lay asleep, on Banks of the Deep." (16)

PA, Mar 19, 1781.

Ballad quatrains on the circumstances of Rodney's defeat of Dutch Governor de Graafe at St. Eustatia, February 3, 1781.

81-26. A Blunt but Just Reflection.

"Since the King turn'd his tail on Pitt." (2)

L Cour, Dec 6, 1781.

Epigram. Satiric, vulgar observation that since the time the King removed William Pitt, his councils have been worthless.

81-27. A Bon Mot, at the Hazard Table.

"Says Selwyn to Fox, prithee Charles, let me hear." (4)

MH, Aug 15, 1781.

Hexameter couplets. Fox puns, declaring that English credit in the war with France and Spain, like his, "must depend on the Main!"

81-28. Britain's Genius deploring her Heroes fallen in the present War.

"Thro' sacred fanes deplore my heroes slain." (38)

G, Aug 20, 1781.

HC. A pessimistic poem mourning the dead and the defeat of Britain.

81-29. Britannia.

"As on a shelving cliff, above the sea." (c. 120)

T&C 13 (Sep 1781), 494-5.

HC. Britain mourns the war in which, without allies, she is "the scorn of each insulting foe," and she fears defeat and loss of control of the seas. Neptune urges her to activate her navy and attack the enemy everywhere. Britain, her martial spirit restored, calls for vengeance. But Prudence intervenes and urges peace and reconciliation between Washington and Cornwallis, which will enable Britain to restore her former glory.

81-30. The British Heroes. A New Ballad.

"Prythee tell me no more." (36)

MH, May 14, 1781.

Song in sixains. The British have great heroes the equal of those in the past: Cornwallis, Clinton, and Rodney.

81-31. British Spirit Revived. An Ode.

"Lo! along the sea-girt shores." (50, 60)

GM 51 (May 1781), 235; L Chron 49 (Feb 27, 1781), 204; LM 2 (Jun 1784), 458-9; SM 43 (Mar 1781), 159.

Regular (Horatian) ode in dixains. (LM has another stanza. The title varies: "The Revival of British Spirit, An Ode.") A patriotic poem. An united Britain will withstand the combined efforts of France, Spain, and Holland.

81-32. A Calm Address to a Celebrated Irish Orator, on the Important Question, "Why should Ireland be Dependent on Great-Britain."

"Methinks I hear the voice of Faction roar." (16)

G Eve Post, Dec 25, 1781.

HC. An attack on the demagoguery of Henry Flood, who is subverting the Anglo-Irish relationship by calling for independence and separation from Britain.

81-33. The Captain. A New Song. To the Tune of, Hey, my Kitten, &c.

"O my Captain, my Captain." (87)

L Cour, Dec 25, 1781.

Song. Satire on the King and his ministers for getting into a "mess" (after the defeat of the army at Yorktown). Cited are Sandwich, North, Germain, Yankees, Scotch.

81-34. Case.

"Sir, says the brave Parker, our fleet met the Dutch. (10)

Cal Merc, Sep 8, 1781.

Hexameter couplets. Admiral Parker boasts that he defeated the stronger Dutch fleet under Zoutman; but the Dutch assert theirs was a victory with fewer vessels. See "Counter Case," 81-46.

81-35. Cat - O - Nine Tails to Kikero.

"O! Galloway, Galloway, hold thy silly tongue." (8)

L Cour, Jan 11, 16, 1781.

Quatrain and HC. Two satires on Joseph Galloway (for his attacks on Gen. Howe).

81-36. [Cease Hibernians, cease to mourn.] Wrote Extempore by a Lady.

"Cease Hibernians, cease to mourn." (32)

Freeman's J, Mar 31, 1781.

Quatrains. Ironic observation that although Ireland was denied a Free Trade, she was given Eden. (William Eden, Lord Auckland, came to negotiate with the Irish.)

81-37. Character of a True Englishman. Addressed to the Pope, by the late Cardinal Howard.

"The freeborn English, gen'rous and wise." (c. 30)

L Cour, Dec 12, 1781.

HC. The Englishman hates oppression and illegal abuse of power, and this antagonism to the usurpation of laws extends to tyranny, to kings. (This poem is meant to be a commentary on the unconstitutional politics of corruption engaged in by King George.)

81-38. Character of Lord Sandwich, from the Saucepan.

"True to his trust, he sought the State's relief." (10)

MH, Jun 19, 1781.

HC. A favorable character of John Montagu, Lord Sandwich.

81-39. The Cobler of Messina. A Political Song.

"A Cobler there was, -- at Messina long since." (20)

L Cour, Dec 15, 1781.

Song, with "Derry down" chorus. Satire on the ministry. A cobbler devised a sure method of eliminating poor ministers and removing grievances. Cited are Mansfield, Bute, North, Stormont, Germain, Sandwich, Hillsborough, and Loughborough.

81-40. A Colloquial Epigram. Between a Patriot and a Courtier.

"P. What! thirty Millions at one Grant." (8)

PA, Nov 3, 1781.

Quatrains. A dialogue between a Patriot (in Opposition) and a Courtier (in Government) about taxation, the former complaining that the poor in the workhouses and the bankrupt in debtor's prison are evidence that the nation cannot afford new taxes.

81-41. The Complaint of Commerce.

"In Thought absorb'd, and swell'd with Anguish." (8)

PA, Sep 1, 1781.

Quatrains. Commerce is languishing and complains that only peace will nourish her.

81-42. A Condolatory Ode to Opposition.

"Great Menders of the State! What Game." (36)

PA, Aug 30, 1781.

Regular (Horatian) ode in sixains. Satire on the bankrupt platform of the Opposition, the members having nothing to help them but misfortune. Cited are "the Massachusetts War," Keppel, Saratoga and Burgoyne, York Petition on Reform, Wilkes, Fox, Thomas Townshend.

81-43. A Constitutional Song, on the British Militia. *Pro aris et socis*.

"Let honour's pure principles bind every heart." (36)

Cumb Pacq, Jul 31, 1781.

Song. The English militia will defend the nation against French incursions.

81-44. The Contrast; -- or *C'est une autre chose*.

"If hostile standards wave on Brabant's coast." (8)

MH, Jan 24, 1781.

Quatrains in HC. Britain has helped Holland in the past; but now Holland now refuses to reciprocate and to honor its treaties.

81-45. [Could the bold sculpture animate the bust.]

"Could the bold sculpture animate the bust." (6)

L Cour, Sep 19, 1781.

Extempore. HC. Satire on Sandwich, who is accused of having "Nero's soul" and a sexual relationship with "his Niece."

81-46. Counter Case.

"Tho' Zoutman declares, how a fleet of eleven." (6)

Cal Merc, Sep 10, 1781.

Hexameter couplets. Admiral Parker has defeated the Dutch fleet under Zoutman. See "Case," 81-34.

81-47. Court Odour.

"At Court, so delicate is ev'ry nose." (2)

L Cour, Jan 16, 1781.

Epigram. HC. Vulgar satire on the favored Scotch at court.

81-48. A Crazy Tale.

"Last night in bed, to my surprise." (47)

MP, Feb 8, 1781.

Mixed verse. Satire on General Howe and on Admiral Keppel for their failures in the war, and for their support of the Opposition, which helps the enemy; and on Fox as well.

81-49. Cursory Thoughts in Verse. English News-Papers.

"To those who freedom's rights revere." (72)

T&C 13 (Jan 1781), 48.

OC. In praise of English newspapers, which have far more freedom than foreign papers. Suppression of newspapers would seal "the death of Liberty" and silence coffee-house politicians.

81-50. The Devil and the Ministry.

"That Old Satan's in Hell we know is his curse." (18)

L Cour, Nov 30, 1781.

Hexameter couplets. Satire on North and Parliament who are identified with the Devil and Hell.

81-51. A Dialogue.

"A. Stript of her friends, and freed from all aliance." (5)

L Cour, Jan 1, 1781.

Epigram. Satire on the Scotch, the only allies of the English -- but interested only in England's wealth.

81-52. A Discarded Minister.

"In Heaven old Satan held high place." (18)

HM 11 (Feb 1781), 102.

Sixains. The discarded minister's prototype is Satan, the arch-rebel. (No living political figure is specified.)

81-53. The Election.

"Let Faction hold her tongue to-day." (20)

W Eve Post, Sep 25, 1781.

Quatrains. Humorous remarks on the poll among the London livery for their representative in Parliament (Alderman Richard Clark vs. Sir Watkin Lewes).

81-54. England and North.

"England lies sick; North vows he'll give her ease." (6)

L Cour, Mar 20, 1781.

HC. Satire on North -- England is sick of him, and wishes to be rid of him, "the quack."

81-55. England's Four Ministers.

"Walpole's good nature gain'd him many friends." (4)

L Cour, Dec 14, 1781.

HC. Satire on North. Compared with Robert Walpole, Pelham (Duke of Newcastle), and Chatham, North is a terrible minister.

81-56. [English, Robert.]
A Tribute to the Memory of Admiral Lord Hawke. By the Author of The Naval Review, A Poem.

"Illustrious Hawke is fall'n! who towr'd so high." (22)

G Eve Post, Nov 8, 1781; Lloyd's 49 (Nov 14, 1781), 478; M Chron, Nov 16, 1781; MH, Nov 26, 1781; PA, Nov 16, 1781; St J's C, Nov 10, 1781.

HC. Panegyric on Edward Hawke, died October 17, 1781. He had triumphed over French and Spanish forces. See Robert English, The Naval Review: 73-5.

81-57. Epigram.

"What vain Ambition Louis fills thy Pate." (6)

PA, Dec 12, 1781; St J's C, Dec 8, 1781.

HC. Ironic comment on the French victory at Yorktown. King Louis may have America and Ireland, etc., but George will still be King of France!

81-58. Epigram.

"Why so much Rout about this Year." (8)

PA, Sep 13, 1781.

Quatrains. Admiral Hyde Parker, willing to fight, is far more meritorious than Keppel.

81-59. Epigram. On a certain Person shedding Tears on the Departure of a B[isho]p.

"Nero o'er burning Rome exulting play'd." (4)

W Eve Post, Jan 2, 1781.

HC. Satire on the King, whose values have gone awry. He laughs at the loss of America, but mourns the death of a child.

81-60. Epigram. On Lord North's Conflict in the House of Commons.

"With mighty Breath when Boreas blows." (8)

PA, Jun 19, 1781.

Quatrains. The "dread Blast" of Boreas, Lord North, silences Burke, Barre, and Fox in the House of Commons' debates.

81-61. Epigram. On the Unjust Charge of Prodigality made so often by the Minority upon our present Ministers.

"O! Cease, ye factious Patriots, to complain." (6)

St J's C, Sep 8, 1781.

HC. Ironic satire on the inability of the ministry to control spending in the war.

81-62. An Epitaph on Lord Mansfield, humbly offered to the Gentleman who proposes giving £20 for the best that can be produced.

"Here lies, alas! now mould'ring in the dust." (8)

L Cour, Mar 15, 1781.

HC. Satire on Mansfield who is here ironically eulogized.

81-63. Epitaph on the gallant Major Pierson, who was killed in repulsing the French Invaders at Jersey.

"What need of sculptur'd Marble to impart." (6)

Cal Merc, Jan 24, 1781.

HC. Brave Pierson was killed in the French attack on Jersey, January 6, 1781.

81-64. Extempore.

"Some few Years back <u>one</u> Arnold's Name." (8)

PA, Jun 30, 1781.

Epigram. Quatrains. Arnold's reputation is tainted by his treachery. Should Washington capture him, it would make no difference what the Court might think of him.

81-65. Extempore.

"When gen'rous <u>Andre</u> yields his Breath." (12)

PA, Jul 18, 1781; W Eve Post, Jul 17, 1781.

Quatrains. Andre and La Motte, both equally patriotic, suffered execution; and others will suffer and die so "Long as Ambition must prevail." See "On Mr. La Motte," 81-155.

81-66. Extempore.

"When Rodney's Fleet approach'd the Coast." (12)

PA, Mar 15, 1781.

Quatrains. Epigram. Rodney defeated the Dutch under Admiral DeWitt.

81-67. Extempore. On Hearing that Mr. Fox said lately in the House of Commons, that he earnestly wished for a Peace. . . .

"Fox, tir'd of War and its Alarms." (5)

PA, Mar 14, 1781.

Epigram. OC. Fox is satirized for saying he wished North could be blamed for a bad peace.

81-68. Extempore. On Reading Something in this Paper, relative to a Bull Feast given by a Certain Orator.

"To make Oeconomy his Theme and Rule." (6)

PA, Mar 23, 1781.

Epigram. HC. Burke's drive for economic reforms ("Oeconomy") is a delusion, for there is nothing to save.

81-69. Extempore. On the Abuse of Mr. Burke, in the Newspapers.

"While little Malice vents its Rage." (6)

PA, Jan 26, 1781.

Sixain. Burke, the patriotic and dignified sage, ignores petty party malice.

81-70. Extempore Verses on Viewing the R[oyal] Countenance at the Theatre.

"No traces of a nation's sad disgrace." (6)

L Cour, Feb 7, 1781.

Satire on the King, whose smiling face does not betray the anxiety of the nation.

81-71. An Extraordinary Gazette.

"Captain S[mith] t'other day with dispatches was sent." (12)

W Eve Post, Jun 26, 1781.

Hexameter couplets. A report of an inconclusive naval action against the French. See another report on the same episode, "The Late Gazette Extraordinary," 81-107.

81-72. A Familiar Epistle to Sir P. J. Clerke, on his Saying in the House, that many of the American Refugees deserved a Halter better than a Pension. By a Refugee.

"My father fled abroad, a rope to shun." (30)

L Cour, Mar 2, 1781.

HC. Ironic satire on a mercenary American rascally refugee, whose persona here betrays him. (The epistle is addressed to Philip Jennings-Clerke, MP for Totnes, 1768-88. On May 28, 1781, he moved for an account of the money spent on the American loyalists.)

81-73. The Fatties.

"We like a *fat* coachman, our horses to steady." (4)

L Cour, Jan 16, 1781.

Epigram. Satire on the King and Lord North.

81-74. The First Ode of Horace Imitated, and Addressed to Lord George Germain. Written in the Attic Story of a Country Seat, 1781.

"O Germain! sprung from War's great Kings." (48)

L Cour, Aug 10, 1781.

OC. Satire on Germain, who "guide[s] in War the martial strife," for his reputation as a coward.

81-75. The following are Specimens of the Songs in the Dramatic Pieces exhibited at the Casino.

"Nothing's heard there but dismal noise and sorrow." (56)

W Eve Post, Jan 9, 1781.

Four songs. Light satire on the times, including the politics, concluding with patriotic sentiments on the need for all to prepare to fight and defend England's right.

81-76. The following Lines were written some short time before the Restoration, and seem equally to suit the present Times.

"From all, and more than I have written here." (24)

Cumb Pacq, Jan 2, 1781.

HC. A prayer against civil war, "Saints" and sectaries, reformers, traitors, faction, and the rabble.

Fox, Charles James. Verses on Mr. Gibbon accepting a Place under Government in the Year 1779. By Mr. C. Fox. W Eve Post, Oct 11, 1781. See "Upon Edward Gibbon, Esq; . . ." 79-501.

81-77. Freeth, John.
Admiral Parker's Engagement with the Dutch Fleet. Tune, -- "Welcome, welcome, brother Debtor."

"On a summer's Sunday morning." (40)

G Eve Post, Sep 11, 1781; also Freeth, Modern Songs on Various Subjects (1782), pp. 51-3, & The Political Songster (1790), pp. 44-5.

Ballad narrates the bloody defeat of a Dutch squadron by the British commanded by Admiral Hyde Parker, August 5, 1781.

81-78. Freeth, John.
The Contrast. Tune, -- Hearts of Oak.

"Ye steady supporters of honour and worth." (26)

John Freeth, Modern Songs on Various Subjects (1782), pp. 53-4.

Song. In the last war, Britain, led by Pitt, controlled the seas; but now she is demeaned and, because of poor leadership (especially by Sandwich), must slink across the seas! See Freeth, 82-10.

81-79. Freeth, John.
The Jersey Expedition.

"Christmas gambols to make, being valiant and stout." (16)

"To St. Maloes was sent an express." (24)

John Freeth, Modern Songs on Various Subjects (1782), pp. 7-9; and The Political Songster (1790), pp. 37-8.

Two songs, on the French attack on the island of Jersey, repelled January 6, 1781; but Major Pierson lost his life opposing the attempted invasion. See Freeth, 82-10.

81-80. [The French paid a Visit of late to Tobago.]

"The French paid a Visit of late to Tobago." (4)

PA, Jul 27, 1781.

Epigram. Hexameter couplets. France has been defeated at Tobago, and Spain at Gibraltar.

81-81. Galloway and Minden; or Heads and Tails.

"Their heads old Galloway and Minden join." (4)

L Cour, Feb 2, 1781.

Epigram. Satire on Galloway and Germain for their poor, ineffectual writing against General Howe.

81-82. The Garden of Eden. A New Song. By the Writer of the Constitutional Watchman.

"Ye men of Hibernia, for centuries vext." (48)

Freeman's J, Feb 20 & 22, 1781.

Song. Two printings. Ironic satire on William Eden, Secretary to Lord Carlisle, who will bring paradise (presumably) to Ireland, the cost being the loss of freedom.

81-83. Gazette Extraordinary. Jersey Invaded.

"The French embark'd on Jersey's shore." (4)

L Cour, Jan 12, 1781.

Extempore. Humorous quatrain on the defeat of the French trying to invade Jersey.

81-84. G[eorge] the Third, surnamed the Pious.

"You who attentive read th'historic page." (14)

"Whoe'er thou art, that dost with pleasure trace." (30)

L Cour, Jan 23 & 26, 1781.

HC. Two translations of a Latin satire on Neronic King George, who has done a good deal of evil and lost an empire.

81-85. The Gratitude of Europe -- with a Word to Ourselves.

"Not one Ally on faithless Europe's ground." (4)

MH, Jan 29, 1781.

Quatrain in HC. Britain, "united," can and must stand alone in the war.

81-86. Guy Fox, or the 5th of November.

"Each single man's internal frame." (20)

MH, Nov 6, 1781.

Quatrains. Satire on Fox as a subversive and destructive factious Guy Fawkes (of the celebrated Gunpowder Plot to blow up Parliament).

81-87. Hatchway, John.
On the Times.

"The French and the Spaniards -- the Dutchman and Dane." (21)

Cal Merc, Jan 6, 1781.

Septains. John Bull, Sawney the Scot, and Paddy will together fight off all Europe on the seas and on land.

81-88. Hayley, William.
To Miss Seward. Impromptu, by Mr. Hayley.

"As Britain mourn'd, with all a Mother's pain." (26)

GM 51 (Jun 1781), 284; WM 53 (Sep 27, 1781), 370; W Eve Post, Jun 14, 1781.

HC. Encomium on Seward for the evocative power of her monody on Andre. Included in the second edition of the monody: 81-14. Repr. W Eve Post, Sept 13, 1783.

81-89. The Herald Game-Cock to the Post-Dunghills, on their total Silence of Rodney's Late Success. An Extempore Mattinet.

"Sleep still ye Dunghills on a row." (4)

MH, Apr 24, 1781.

Extempore. Quatrain. The Morning Herald is glad to crow the great news of Rodney's defeat of the Dutch at St. Eustatius, unlike most other papers.

81-90. A Hint to the Financier.

"When N[or]th has drain'd the realm by bribe and vote." (2)

L Cour, Jan 30, 1781.

Epigram. HC. Satire on North for draining the Treasury with bribes.

81-91. Horace; Book V. Epode vii. Imitated. To my Countrymen, on the present Civil War with America.

"What demon, jealous of Britannia's weal." (32)

L Cour, Dec 27, 1781.

Quatrains. Satire on the King and his ministry. The Civil War with America is absurd, unjust, and irrational. The only explanation for it is a "Fatal Influence," despite the wisdom of the Minority Opposition, the influence of the "rebel Scots," who have taught King George the ways of a "Tyrant Stuart."

81-92. Horace. Ode IV. Book II. Imitated.

"Why, Charles, pray, why so much afraid." (24)

PA, Jan 23, 1781.

Regular ode in sixains. An imitation of Horace. Light satire on Charles Fox's infatuation for a low-class wench. Presumably written by Richard Fitzpatrick who cites Keppel, Burgoyne, and Grafton as precedents.

81-93. [How strange, how perverse, is Britannia's Fate.]

"How strange, how perverse, is Britannia's Fate." (12)

PA, Dec 13, 1781.

HC. Satire on Government leadership during the American War. In all their business, they are too late. (A reaction of disgust to the news of Cornwallis's capitulation at Yorktown, which reached London November 23-25, 1781.)

81-94. An Hudibrastic Epistle to Colonel Tarleton.

"Whoever taught you first to fight." (48)

L Chron 49 (Mar 8, 1781), 236; PA, Mar 8, 1781; SM 43 (Apr 1781), 215.

OC. Ironic verses praising Tarleton for his victories, for which he received little glory, because in the past Howe and Keppel were praised for retreat and defeat and hurting the nation.

81-95. An Impromptu.

"France, Spain and America, leagued with the Dutch." (10)

MH, Mar 22, 1781.

Anapest tetrameter couplets. Britain can manage in its war with France, Spain, America, and now Holland.

81-96. [Inscription near Kilkhampton Abbey.]

"Slanderer! or Robber! or Assassin." (c. 30)

St J's C, Jan 11, 1781.

Parody and satire on Herbert Croft, author of the Kilhampton Abbey epitaphs, for character assassination.

81-97. [Inscription on a Memorial Urn for Chatham.]

"Sacred to pure Affection / This simple Urn." (c. 14)

L Chron 50 (Oct 2, 1781), 327; LM 50 (Appendix 1781), 626; West J, Oct 6, 1781; W Eve Post, Oct 2, 1781; also G Eve Post, Sep 29, 1781.

The inscription will be used for a statue of Chatham to be placed in Westminster Abbey. The memorial was prepared by Lady Chatham.

81-98. Inscription on the Coffin [of Major Pierson].

"The remains / Of Major Francis Pierson, who by his / Courage." (c. 6)

G Eve Post, Jan 20, 1781; L Cour, Jan 26, 1781.

Epitaphial inscription for young Major Pierson, killed defending Jersey against French attack, January 6, 1781.

Inscriptions on an Obelisk at Lord Amherst's Seat, Riverhead, Kent. W Misc 17 (Dec 31, 1781), 326-7. All the major victories over the French in Canada, 1758-62. See 60-18.

81-99. [Inscriptions . . . upon the Pedestal of the Statue of King William.]

"The Volunteers of Ireland." (c. 8)

W Eve Post, Nov 13, 1781.

The Irish demand "A Real Free Trade," "A Declaration of Rights," and a repeal of the Mutiny Bill — or else "A Glorious Revolution."

81-100. The Intolerable Affront.

"With loaded shoulders in the crouded street." (19)

GM 51 (Jan 1781), 37.

HC. There is no greater insult than to be called "a parliament man."

81-101. The Issue of a Debate.

"In the long struggle of a warm debate." (6)

L Cour, Feb 2, 1781.

HC. North wins every debate by bribery.

81-102. [J. Cicero! to Second Cataline!!!]

"J. Cicero! to Second Cataline." (87)

L Cour, Feb 15, 1781.

OC. Satire on Joseph (Cicero) Galloway for urging an efficient suppression of the American rebellion. Cited are taxation, Saratoga, Congress, the Armed Neutrality, Opposition, Lexington, Lord Percy, Miss M'Crea, Laurens, and refugees.

Johnson, S. To Miss Seward, on her Monody on Major Andre. GM 51 (May 1781), 235-6; G Eve Post, Apr 10, 1781; MH, Apr 13, 1781. See "To Miss Seward, on her Monody on Major Andre," 81-227.

81-103. Justice.

"Is this the justice of that creature, man." (64)

W Eve Post, Apr 19, 1781.

HC. A general satire on the equivocal behavior of blind justice that includes an allusion to the (in)justice of Congress and Washington regarding Andre's execution.

81-104. Kilkhampton Abbey.

"America Restor'd." (c. 32)

M Chron, Jan 3, 1781.

Inscription, prose poem. A parody of Croft's Kilkhampton epitaphs, adapted to the American War. This inscription is supposedly an expression of American gratitude that the British have saved the colonies from France. (The Morning Chronicle, like the Morning Herald, was a government-sponsored newspaper at this time.) See Croft, 80-10.

[Kilkhampton Abbey.] "Slanderer! or Robber! or Assassin." St J's C, Jan 11, 1781. See [Inscription near Kilkhampton Abbey], 81-96.

81-105. King Bute for ever!

"That the Thane rules, no man will sure dispute." (2)

L Cour, Feb 8, 1781.

Epigram. HC. Satire on Bute, whose presence is suggested in all state measures.

81-106. A King's Mirth no Cure for his Subjects' Affliction.

"When public woes melt millions into tears." (2)

L Cour, Jan 18, 1781.

HC. Epigram. Satire on the King for laughing while the nation is in tears.

81-107. The Late Gazette Extraordinary Versified.

"From the Admiralty Office. Came home just this hour." (35)

PA, Jul 12, 1781.

Hexameter couplets. On the indecisive skirmishing between the French fleet and the English fleet under Rodney and Hood in the Caribbean. St. Kitt is cited. The same episode appears in "An Extraordinary Gazette," 81-71.

81-108. Liberty. A Poem. Inscribed to the People of England.

"As on my pillow, musing on the fate." (115)

PA, Aug 29, 1781.

Blank verse. Liberty admonishes Britain to keep up the tradition, lest she fly to America. Now the country will unite, joining unanimously in a just cause which will bring peace. Signed T. H. (Thomas Hastings?)

81-109. Lines Inscribed to Lord George Gordon on his Honourable Acquittal.

"Hail Sacred Justice -- whose impartial scale." (42)

The Aurora, and Universal Advertiser, Feb 17, 1781.

HC. Honors Lord George Gordon on his acquittal of charges of treason as a result of the great riots. Praise of Thomas Erskine, counsel to Gordon.

81-110. Lines inscribed to the Hon. Charles Feilding, on his Eclogue to his Brother, William, Lord Viscount Feilding.

"Thou generous youth! whose soul, to nature true." (26)

GM 51 (Aug 1781), 382-3.

HC. Panegyric on the young Charles Feilding, in which are included remarks on the brother, Captain William Feilding, who was serving with Cornwallis in America. Cornwallis's victories are mentioned, and a hope is expressed that William will have a triumphal return from the war.

81-111. Lines occasioned by a Perusal of Dr. Johnson's Lives of the Poets, Wherein the Characters of Contemporary Statesmen are occasionally handled.

"When Johnson keen, didactic and morose." (10)

L Cour, Oct 2, 1781. (Corrected Oct 3, 1781.)

Quatrains and couplet. Johnson effectively blames the Patriots ("Patriot Fame") and praises the Court ("the Tools of State").

81-112. Lines on a Certain Gentleman who lately complained in Parliament of an Assertion in one of Cicero's Letters. . . .

"When Old Catiline's crew were accus'd in debate." (8)

MP, Feb 10, 1781.

Hexameter couplets. Part of the debate involving Cicero, a pen-name of a Government supporter who had attacked a member of the Opposition, Catiline, a traitor. See "To Cicero, On his Fifth Letter to Catiline," 81-220. ("Cicero" is Galloway.)

81-113. Lines on the Late Events in America.

"What Muse, O Britain! longs not to relate." (30)

MH, Jan 4, 1781.

HC. Cornwallis is the conquering hero; but Andre, too, is heroic in his death. The British army must revenge Andre's cruel death. Andre's fate should inspire the British to fight harder.

81-114. Lines to the Memory of Captain Drummond, a very amiable and promising English Officer, who died in the late convulsions of Nature in the Western World.

"Drummond! for thee the generous drop shall flow."  (26)

MH, Mar 31, 1781.

HC.  Non-political eulogy of an English officer killed in America.

81-115.  Lines To the Memory of Lieutenant John Money, Aid-de-Camp to Lord Cornwallis, . . . killed . . . at Black Stocks in South Carolina, on the attack and defeat of Mr. Sumpter, an American General, Nov. 9, 1780.

"Fresh bloom the laurel by thy sword acquir'd."  (14)

L Cour, Mar 12, 1781;  MH, Mar 12, 1781.

HC.  Eulogy of the young and heroic Lt. John Money, killed at the age of twenty-four in a battle against the Americans.  Cited are Cornwallis, Tarleton, and Sumpter.

81-116.  Lines to the Memory of Major Pierson.

"When patriots and friends of human race."  (32)

G, Jan 1, 1782;  MH, Dec 31, 1781.

Quatrains, honoring young Pierson, killed defending the Isle of Jersey against French invasion.

81-117.  Lines written upon Ensign Colvile.  A very young Officer in the West Norfolk Militia.

"Accept, brave Youth, the Tribute due."  (21)

Lady's M 12 (Sep 1781), 495;  St J's C, Aug 21, 1781.

OC.  Panegyric on a young officer, Colvile, for foiling French privateer invaders of the English coast.

81-118.  L[or]d N[or]th and his Bravoes.

"When N--th call'd forth his bravoes of defence."  (10)

L Cour, Mar 1, 1781.

HC.  North relies on "bold buffoonery" to have his way in Parliament, and the "hackney'd ribaldry" of John Courtenay.  But the bullies should beware of Sheridan, "for he's a wit."

81-119. Martha Mark'em to Kitty Curious.

"By these Presents, dear Kate, you may understand." (32)

PA, May 30, 1781.

Hexameter couplets. A humorous reaction to the threat of a Dutch attack on England after Rodney's capture of St. Eustatia, and to the seizure of Rodney's St. Eustatia prize by the French fleet.

81-120. Martha Mark'em to Kitty Curious.

"In the letter before me, you say." (32)

PA, Sep 4, 1781.

Hexameter couplets. On the naval war. Martha awaits with suspense some significant news, for all the prints are simply full of surmises. But Britain is being menaced, the siege of Gibraltar is still going on, Washington is besieging New York, and the homeward-bound fleets are endangered.

81-121. Martha Mark'em to Kitty Curious.

"Last Week when I wrote, the close of the Chapter." (31)

PA, Jun 11, 1781.

Hexameter couplets. Newsy reports on the French capture of the prize from St. Eustatia, the costly victory of the forces of Cornwallis over those of "one Green" (Guilford Courthouse, North Carolina), the piratical forays of "Fall," and the oratorical initiation of the younger Pitt, "of the blood and spirit of Chatham."

81-122. Martha Mark'em to Kitty Curious.

"Since my last, which I think was instant the second." (41)

PA, Jun 30, 1781.

Hexameter couplets. Comment on the news: Cornwallis's victory over Green (Guilford Courthouse, N. C.), the King's birthday ball, the behavior of the Prince of Wales, peace this year contrasted with the violent Gordon Riots last year, and Patriot objections to the American War (by "Charles Fox and Co."), which favor France.

81-123. A Military Invocation.

"Say, shall my Britons, whose exalted name." (42)

MH, Jul 31, 1781.

HC. Patriotic lines meant to fire up British spirit in the war with France. Cressy and Marlborough are invoked, and a call for unity concludes the poem.

81-124. Ministerial Squabbles.

"'Twixt Twitcher and Minden the quarrel's a shamm'd one." (2)

L Cour, Jan 16, 1781.

Epigram. Satire on the ministry -- Sandwich, Germain, Thurlow, and North. (Edward Thurlow was openly critical of North at this time.)

81-125. A National Song. Addressed to Sir Joseph Yorke, K.B. By T. N----- of ----- School. Tune, -- English Brown Bear.

"In Britain's cause I dare to sing." (30)

MP, Jan 9, 1781.

Patriotic lyric that stresses the need for union against France and Spain, the neutral states (or "armed neutrality"), and Holland.

81-126. Naval Ballad.

"'Twas on the sixteenth of last January." (45)

MH, Jan 16, 1781.

Ballad narrates the victory, a year before, of Rodney over Langara, off St. Vincent's, January 16, 1780. See Freeth, "The British Flag Triumphant," not the same song: 80-143.

81-127. Naval Ballad. Ghost of Admiral Byng to Admiral Keppel, Who was One of Byng's Court-Martial. Tune, -- Hosier's Ghost.

"As near Bagshot, I was walking." (48)

MH, Jan 8, 1781.

Ballad. The ghost of Admiral John Byng, executed in 1757 for dereliction of duty, berates Keppel and exclaims that politics saved him from a like fate.

81-128. Necessary Qualifications for Making a True Patriot.

"A Real Patriot is a sacred Name." (14)

PA, Oct 5, 1781.

HC. A genuine patriot is independent, uninfluenced by party or king, and incorruptible. He loves his country.

81-129. A New Discovery in 1781.

"The Grand Fleet safe and useless at Torbay." (11)

PA, Nov 24, 1781.

HC. Satire on the fleet, useless at Torbay, permitting the combined French-Spanish fleet to sail along the British coast without challenge.

81-130. A New Occasional Song on the Glorious Success of Sir George Brydges Rodney, Bart. and Gen. Vaughan: Sung at the Theatre-Royal, at Bath, by Mr. Brett.

"To brave Rodney, still watching the motions of Gaul." (24)

MH, Apr 3, 1781.

Song, celebrating the successful attack by Rodney and Gen. Vaughan on the Dutch at St. Eustatia, the island the Dutch were using as a supply base for America.

81-131. A New Occasional Song. To the tune of, -- "In Stories we're told, &c."

"Ye Britons so free." (42)

M Chron, Jan 3, 1781.

A patriotic song against the French, Spanish, Dutch, and the confederates in the "armed neutrality."

81-132. A New Song, called Britons Still your Rights maintain. To the tune of, -- Rule Britannia.

"Britons, to arms, defend your cause." (36)

L Chron 50 (Sep 18, 1781), 274; M Chron, Sep 18, 1781; PA, Sep 20, 1781; WM 53 (Sep 27, 1781), 370-1.

A patriotic song urging unanimity in the defense of the British cause against "The malice of confed'rate foes."

81-133. A New Song, called The Spanish Grenadiers, or, The Galley Slaves Garland.

"In kingdoms of old." (48)

W Eve Post, Aug 28, 1781.

A patriotic song defying Spain and its threats to Gibraltar.

81-134. A New Song. Tune, 'Twas when the Seas were roaring.

"'Twas when the Seas were roaring." (20)

PA, Mar 17, 1781.

Song. Rodney humiliated Dutch Governor de Graafe (at St. Eustatia).

81-135. New Year's Day, 1781. Tune, -- Get you gone, Raw-head and Bloody-bones.

"Oh! Old England, old England." (82)

L Cour, Feb 2, 1781.

Song. Also in Frank Moore, Songs and Ballads of the American Revolution (1855), pp. 342-6.
A complaint at the lack of progress Britain is making in the American War. The satire is directed at Sandwich and the navy, the failure of the armies to defeat America, Lord North and the ineffectual King, the bishops for encouraging papists, and the Scotch, Mansfield and Wedderburne.

81-136. Nil Desperandum.

"Lo! selfish Holland gives up gain." (48)

M Chron, Jul 25, 1781.

Regular ode in sixains. Patriotic lines assert that Britain will be victorious over France and Spain, and now Holland, and will "Preserve Dominion o'er the main."

81-137. O! The Devil! A New Song. To the Old Tune of, -- O! my Kitten, my Kitten.

"O The Devil, the Devil, and O! the Devil. the D----." (31)

L Cour, Dec 1, 1781; reprinted Dec 10, 1781.

Song. Satire on the King and Court for the defeat of Cornwallis at Yorktown, news of which had reached London November 25, 1781. This lyric may be the first significant evidence in English verse of the effects of the Yorktown capitulation. Cited are Arnold, Sandwich, North, Washington, and Burgoyne.

81-138. Ode for the 30th of January.

"The rolling year once more makes known." (42)

L Cour, Feb 2, 1781.

Ode in alternating quatrains and sixains. A republican poem on the anniversary of the death of Charles I. It celebrates the way in which tyranny was terminated by executing a lawless prince; and also urges the present clergy to cease calling Charles a martyr, because he was really a tyrant.

81-139. Ode intended for Christmas-Day.

"Angels of Light transmit from Heaven." (24)

St J's C, Dec 27, 1781.

Regular (Horatian) ode in sixains. A prayer for the successful suppression of the American Rebellion and the triumph "o'er confederate Foes."

81-140. An Ode, neither Written nor set for, nor performed at, St. James's, on New Year's Day, 1781.

"Ask round the world, from Age to Age." (50)

W Eve Post, Dec 31, 1780-Jan 2, 1781.

Irregular Pindaric ode. Parody of Whitehead's New Year's Ode for 1781. England is alone against all Europe; but, if she had the support of her American Colonies, she could succeed.

81-141. An Ode, set to the music of "God save the King," performed before the Committee of Protestant Association at the London Tavern, on Wednesday the 14th instant.

"Britons rejoice and sing." (49)

Freeman's J, Mar 29, 1781.

Song in honor of Lord George Gordon, of the Protestant Association, imprisoned for the riot.

81-142. Ode. The Court-Heroe.

"What if the Heroe of these Strains." (90)

PA, Oct 20, 1781.

Regular (Horatian) ode in sixains. Satire on Germain. A narrative of his career: his behavior at Minden and the court-martial; the duel with George Johnstone; his arrival at court and appointment as Secretary at War to reduce the Rebellion. But he is misplaced; he is unfit for this post, being a coward.

81-143. Ode to E[dmun]d B[urk]e, Esq;

"'Tis Edmund, but a sorry Sight." (42)

PA, Jan 24, 1781.

Regular (Horatian) ode in sixains. A satire on Burke's pretensions to impartiality and virtue regarding the debate on India. (East India problems continue concurrently with West Indian and American problems.) Burke is accused of accepting a bribe from the Rajah.

81-144. An Ode to Hope. Addressed to the People of England.

"Thou blessing sent us from above." (42)

L Cour, Aug 15, 1781.

Regular (Horatian) ode in sixains. Everyone is blessed with hope -- the friendless wretch, the widowed wife, the orphan, etc., including the Patriot who wishes "to prop a falling State," and Britain in its war with France, especially when Rockingham will be the next premier.

81-145. Ode to the Right Hon. Lord George Germain.

"'Tis where, triumphant Isle! thy navy rides." (24)

MH, Mar 23, 1781.

Regular (Horatian) ode in sixains. Germain deserves praise for planning the seizure of Holland's East Indian trade.

81-146. On a Late Motion in the House of Commons.

"When Caesar, who commanded half the Globe." (12)

MH, Dec 12, 1781; PA, Dec 13, 1781.

Quatrains. Satire on Burke as a traitor, perhaps for his motion in the House of Commons, November 29, 1781, for an inquiry into the conduct of Admiral Rodney and General Vaughan at St. Eustatia, which they had plundered for their own gain.

81-147. On a Print of the Hon. Charles Fox, Member for Westminster.

"Behold the picture of a favourite youth." (12)

L Cour, Jan 18, 1781.

HC. A panegyrical character of Fox, compared with "Patriots of the Roman name."

81-148. On Admiral Graves.

"While Gallic foes across the Atlantic waves." (2)

MP, Jan 31, 1781.

Epigram. HC. May the French across the Atlantic meet with our Admiral Graves. (Later in the year, Graves failed to come to the rescue of Cornwallis, trapped at Yorktown.)

81-149. On Admiral Rodney's allowing the Governor of St. Eustatia only One Hour to Consider of a Surrender.

"How vast the gallant Rodney's pow'r." (4)

G Eve Post, Mar 29, 1781; PA, Mar 31, 1781.

Quatrain. Extempore. Rodney gave Governor de Graaffe of St. Eustatia in the Caribbean one hour to surrender and won a great spoil in a brief time.

81-150. On Captain Rodney's Marriage with Miss Harley.

"A Pair so nicely match'd exceeds all story." (2)

L Cour, Apr 13, 1781.

Epigram. HC. Satire on Rodney's match with an heiress: he wanted her money, she his glory.

On Hayley's Observations of Anna Seward, in his *Essay on Epic Poetry*. T&C 17 (Aug 1785), 437-8. Twenty-four lines emphasize the thrilling patriotic inspiration that Seward's monody on Andre provides "a dwindling state" and "a lethargic land." See Seward, 81-14, also 85-40.

81-151. On Hearing Lord North was Taken Ill with a Fever.

"Daughter of Jove! Hygeia fair." (10)

MH, Aug 8, 1781; PA, Aug 10, 1781; St J's C, Aug 7, 1781.

OC. Prayer that Lord North recover from his illness because only he can save the country. Cornwallis's "late Victory" at "Guildford" (Courthouse, N. C.) is cited.

81-152. On Lord North's Sleepiness.

"Rouse, my Lord North, the active Courtier saith." (2)

"Who North would wake, in sleep who's only blest." (2)

L Cour, Jan 23, 1781.

HC. Two translations of a Latin satire on North: "Ad Northium. . . ." L Cour, Jan 20, 1781. The Patriots wish North would suffer the sleep of death.

81-153. On Lord Sandwich requesting to be made a Knight of the Garter.

"Since Sandwich directed the British marine." (8)

L Cour, Dec 27, 1781.

Hexameter couplets. Satire on Sandwich, who deserves a halter more than the garter for his mismanagement of the navy.

81-154. On Mr. G[ibbo]n taking a Place.

"When learned Writers, whose instructive page." (18)

L Cour, Jul 20, 1781.

HC. Satire (ironic) on Gibbon for being corrupt because he accepted a place in Government.

81-155. On Mr. La Motte.

"Let pity weep, -- deplore the wretched fate." (22)

L Cour, Jul 17, 1781.

HC. De la Motte, a French spy (captured in England) has been sentenced to hang. He deserves our pity and admiration, a brave and patriotic man. For the trial and execution of M. Francis Henry De la Motte, see GM 51 (Jul 1781), 341-2, & (Aug 1781), 356-8.

In his Journal of the Reign of King George the Third, From the Year 1771 to 1783, ed. Doran (1859), II, 466, Horace Walpole notes for July 14 the "Trial of Monsieur La Mothe, a spy, after four months of close imprisonment, convicted on the evidence of his accomplice, a Hessian, and most infamous wretch." And for July 27 he notes the execution of "De la Mothe . . . at Tyburn, for being a spy."

See "Extempore [When gen'rous Andre]," 81-65.

81-156. On Reading a Paragraph, Signifying that the Farmers are about to Petition Parliament for some Encouragement of the Corn Trade.

"What pity it is our Condition is such." (15)

Cumb Pacq, Nov 13, 1781.

Anapest tetrameter couplets. Parliament should help the farmers' corn trade.

81-157. On Reading in the Gazette Extraordinary the Account of the Reduction of St. Eustatius, by Admiral Rodney, in one Hour.

"As late at Jove's imperial Throne." (52)

Cumb Pacq, Mar 21, 1781.

Quatrains. Britain mourns divisive faction and discord, and the fact that European nations are pleased at America's struggle for independence, but she is gladdened by Rodney's seizure of St. Eustatius (from the Dutch).

81-158. On Reading Mr. Courtney's Speech on Mr. Burke's Bill.

"Shall that in Courtney be esteem'd as wit." (8)

L Cour, Mar 12, 1781.

HC. Satire on John Courtenay (MP from Tamworth), whose buffoonery at Burke's attempt at reform is asinine. (Courtenay supported the American War, defended the ministry and the prerogatives of the crown.) See "Lord North and his Bravoes," 81-118.

81-159. On Reading the Last Gazette Extraordinary. To the King.

"As some vast ship, Old Albion's pride." (14)

MP, Apr 26, 1781.

OC. The King and the ship of state, guided by North and Germain, will ride out the storm caused by France, Spain, and Holland, as well as the treason of the hostile

Opposition.

81-160. On the Abuse of the Duke of Richmond, by the Morning Post.

"Whilst venal pens revile the Man." (8)

L Cour, Nov 6, 1781.

Quatrains. Richmond is praised for defending himself against the libels of Bate of the Morning Post. (Richmond brought suit for libel and forced the newspaper out of business for a while.)

81-161. On the Beheading of Charles the First.

"To bribe his Parliament, Charles never try'd." (2)

L Cour, Dec 7, 1781.

Epigram. HC. Satire on the King, who (unlike Charles I) succeeds in avoiding the scaffold by bribing Parliament.

81-162. On the Capture of our East and West India Fleets.

"How different is our doom from Spain and France." (2)

MP, Jan 31, 1781.

Epigram. HC. France and Spain beat us by chance; but we win by valor.

81-163. On the Conduct of the Dutch.

"Oh ye perfidious Monsters! will ye dare." (16)

PA, Jan 1, 1781.

HC. The Dutch treacherously betray the English, their friends; instead of helping the English, they join the enemy.

81-164. On the Death of Major Patrick Ferguson, who was killed early in the Action at King's Mountain, South Carolina.

"If an ardent Thirst for Military Fame." (c. 8)

Cal Merc, May 2, 1781.

Epitaphial inscription, "from the New York Gazette of February 14." The brave Major Ferguson died fighting "against Discord." (The Battle of King's Mountain, South Carolina, occurred Oct. 7, 1780. Ferguson commanded a Provincial Brigade from New York.)

81-165. On the Death of Major Pierson.

"Tell me, says Cato, where you found." (24)

GM 51 (Feb 1781), 87.

Quatrains. At the cost of his own life, brave Pierson saved the Channel Island of Jersey from the French.

81-166. On the Disgrace of the French Navy. Addressed to Lord Sandwich.

"No more proud Gallia, make thy boast." (30)

L Cour, Aug 10, 1781.

Regular ode in sixains. The French fleets have been defeated; Britain has nothing to fear from them. (These lines must be wholly ironic!)

81-167. On the Dutch.

"Dutchmen are all alike -- the point is clear." (16)

L Cour, Nov 3, 1781.

HC. Satiric invective against the "artful, knavish, plunder-loving" Dutch.

81-168. On the Dutch War.

"Provok'd by num'rous insults past." (24)

T&C 13 (Apr 1781), 216.

OC. Britain is roused to war against Holland, now allied with France in support of "arm'd Americans."

81-169. On the General Fast.

"Ye nations bow before the Lord." (20)

Lloyd's 48 (Feb 19, 1781), 184.

Quatrains. We must be genuinely penitent before we can receive God's grace. Cited is the war in Canada, Carolina, and China (India?).

81-170. On the Heir Apparent.

"What gloomy prospects strike th'apparent heir." (2)

L Cour, Jan 24, 1781.

Epigram. HC. The heir to the throne faces the gloomy prospect of the loss of an empire.

81-171. On the H[ouse] of C[ommon]s.

"Though Hercules once cleans'd the Augean stable." (2)

L Cour, Jan 12, 1781.

Epigram, couplet. Not even Hercules, who cleansed the Augean stable, can cleanse Parliament.

81-172. On the List of the Officers of the Guards going to America.

"High born, high match'd! Oh, save your precious lives." (2)

L Cour, Jan 16, 1781.

Epigram. HC. Satire on the high-born (or aristocratic) officers going to America.

81-173. On the Ministry adopting a New System in Carrying on the War.

"Our Ministers sage." (6)

PA, Dec 15, 1781.

Sixain. Extempore. The ministry must have a new system to carry on the war, for the old one has not worked.

81-174. On the Present Petitions and Remonstrances.

"Why harass your King thus? -- whose liberal mind." (8)

PA, Dec 13, 1781.

Quatrains. The King does not need criticism. Were he to have our support, America might again be ours. (A reaction to the disaster at Yorktown.) These petitions and remonstrances, like that of the Livery of London, December 4, 1781, urged a discontinuation of the American War.

81-175. On the Right Hon. Lord Thurlow, Lord High Chancellor of Great Britain.

"Whoe'er by visionary hopes misled." (40)

MH, Jan 11, 1781.

Quatrains. Simple, straightforward panegyric on Edward Thurlow for his eloquent and reasonable oratory.

81-176. On the Riots in June, 1780, from Hudibras.

"These feuds by Patriots invented." (170)

M Chron, Jun 8, 1781; PA, Jun 11, 1781.

Hudibrastic couplets; imitation of Samuel Butler's Hudibras. Satire on the Protestant Association for its responsibility in causing the Gordon Riots of June 1780. In this poem, the riots are blamed on the violent elements of the Protestant Association and the Opposition forces outside Parliament. Although Lord George Gordon was acquitted by law of the charge of sedition, he is really guilty.

On the Times. See Hatchway, 81-87.

81-177. On Transmigration.

"Britons, at length, like Indian Bramins, own." (18)

L Cour, Mar 7, 1781.

HC. Satire. Transmigration has occurred in the following -- Sejanus to North, Nero to Charles I to George III, Page and Jeffries to Mansfield.

81-178. [Once -- Ministry were true, in Days of Yore.]

"Once -- Ministry were true, in Days of Yore." (12)

PA, Dec 11, 1781.

Quatrains. In the past, Britain was powerful and triumphant, and her armies fought to win, her aggressive admirals never retreated. But now cowards are protected by interested parties. (This poem is one of the earliest complaints in reaction to the news of the Yorktown disaster.)

81-179. Opposition.

"'Twould make ev'n Heraclitus smile." (8)

T&C 13 (May 1781), 272.

OC. Epigram. A Tory defense of a strong and enduring monarchy and of its prerogatives against the Opposition.

81-180. The Persian and Englishman.

"Xerxes in tears, saw Death's unweary'd pace." (6 + 6 + 8)

L Cour, Feb 10, 1781; also Feb 14, 1781.

Epigram; three versions, presumably translations from the Latin. Satire on the King for enjoying himself while the people suffer and his armies are slaughtered.

81-181. The Priest's Tale.

"'Twas on the day Cumberland gave birth." (38)

L Cour, Apr 23, 1781.

HC. (Extracts.) A long, rambling narrative poem satirizing Archbishop Markham of York, a Tory. Part defines Whig and Tory, the latter identified with Jacobites in whom the King confides. The point is made that, although the Americans were forced to seek the assistance of the French, they are not Tories. Benedict Arnold is execrated as an untrustworthy traitor.

81-182. Questions and Answers.

"Say, can that monarch be or wise or good." (4)

L Cour, Jun 14, 1781.

Epigram. HC. Satire on the ministry (North, Germain, and Sandwich) and on the King for increasing the oppressive burden of taxes.

81-183. The Raffle.

"Rodney went out to play a Bout." (16)

PA, Mar 23, 1781.

Ballad quatrains narrate capture of Dutch St. Eustatius by Rodney and Vaughan.

81-184. [A real Patriot is a sacred name.]

"A real Patriot is a sacred name." (14)

M Chron, Oct 5, 1781.

HC. A real patriot is incorruptible and disinterested. Can one be found in England?

81-185. Reason why Tories are greater Favourites than Whigs.

"Why does ------ hate the Whigs and love the Tories." (6)

L Cour, Feb 15, 1781.

Irregular HC. The Whigs are not in favor at Court because they love liberty; but the Tories are in favor because they are slaves to the King.

81-186. The Recess.

"Now legal Lore, all Pomp and State gone by." (36)

PA, Jul 20, 1781.

HC. Parliament is now in recess, and all the members leave for the country: Rigby, Richmond, Burke, and possibly others such as Thurlow, George Savile, and Wyvill.

81-187. A Recipe to make a Patriot.

"Take a man who is ruin'd, a Gamester, a Sot." (8)

MP, Feb 3, 1781.

Quatrains. A personal and political satire on Fox. He "writes treason with ease."

81-188. The Reduc'd Farmer.

"Pity the Sorrows of a poor old Man." (44)

L Cour, Oct 11, 1781; St J's C, Oct 11, 1781.

Elegiac quatrains. A poor farmer mourns his ruin and the ruin of his family, and asks for pity and relief.

81-189. Reformation. A Poem. Addressed to the Gentlemen of the C[ommo]n C[ounci]l, on their late wise resolves to alter their past conduct.

"Appoint, my Friends, an early day." (40)

Cumb Pacq, Apr 10, 1781; MP, Mar 26, 1781.

Quatrains. London had supported Keppel and the Americans; now it should reform and support Rodney and Cornwallis and Palliser. Signed "A Loyalist."

81-190. The Refugees.

"The Congress hang'd two Refugees for spies." (4)

L Cour, Feb 26, 1781.

HC. Satire on the American refugees -- they should be hanged.

81-191. The Republican. A New Song. Supposed to be Written by that very excellent Poet, and firm Loyalist Mr. A----N S----E.

"When Satan felt his spleen arise." (20)

MP, Mar 20, 1781.

Song. Satire on republicans (like those in the Opposition), who trace their ancestry to Satan and his rebellion against God.

81-192. The Royal and Ministerial Hunt.

"The King and North pursue a diff'rent game." (6)

L Cour, Dec 6, 1781.

Epigram. Satire on the King and North, who both like hunting: the King hunts the stag, the Premier hunts the nation -- to the death.

81-193. Rushton, Edward.
An Irregular Ode.

"As when the rugged blast spreads uproar wide." (83)

Lloyd's 48 (Mar 19, 1781), 276.

Irregular ode.  Rushton wishes Britain and America to settle their differences and to accept a compromise.  Britain should admit that it was oppressive, and the Colonies that they were disloyal, unwise, and imprudent.  Americans must also know that the French alliance will not help, because it will simply unite all Britons against them.

81-194. [Sempronius Johnson, hear Truth's just decree.]

"Sempronius Johnson, hear Truth's just decree." (4)

L Cour, Feb 7, 1781.

Epigram.  HC.  Satire on Gov. Johnstone, whose praise or blame is pointless.  See "To Sempronius Johnstone," 81-230.

81-195. The Sermon Substantiated.

"Fight on, fight, my merry men all." (2)

L Cour, Feb 26, 1781.

HC.  Satire on Government for its policy of attempting to slaughter rebels.

81-196. Sketch of a Lie.

"The Father of Lies is the Devil." (24)

PA, Apr 9, 1781.

Quatrains.  On the history of a lie, originating with the Devil, and associated with the rebel host, the Opposition, and with Lord George Gordon, "a Fanatic Leader." See "Sketch of the Truth," 81-197.

81-197. Sketch of the Truth. [In Answer to the Sketch of a Lie in Monday's Paper.]

"The Father of Truth is above." (24)

PA, Apr 11, 1781.

Quatrains.  A defence of the Opposition and Lord George Gordon and Thomas Erskine, his counsel;  and an attack on the lying sycophants at court.  See "Sketch of a Lie," 81-196.

81-198. Song, by a Retired Officer, lately returned from America.

"Hence, noisy Strife and turgid War." (20)

PA, Sep 4, 1781.

Quatrains. A soldier, returning from America, sings of the blessings of nature's peace and the love of his "Bright Nymph," Sylvia.

81-199. Song. [From] The New Pantomime of Robinson Crusoe.

"Come, come, my jolly lads, our ship's afloat." (26)

MH, Feb 2, 1781; W Eve Post, Feb 1, 1781.

A patriotic naval song directed against Spain.

Song on the late Sea-Fight. Tune, -- "Welcome! welcome! Brother Debtor." G Eve Post, Sep 11, 1781. Another title for Freeth's song on "Admiral Parker's Engagement with the Dutch Fleet": 81-77.

81-200. Song. Tune, -- "Rule Britannia."

"Hail Britain! hail thou glory's pride." (25)

MH, May 12, 1781.

A patriotic lyric honoring Rodney for his victory over the Dutch at St. Eustatia.

Sonnet, To the Duke of Richmond. On His Motion for Annual Parliaments and Equal Representation. L Cour, Jan 16, 1781. Also Lloyd's 55 (Sep 24, 1784), 303; NAR 1783 (III, 204-5); West M 10 (Nov 1782), 605. See Edmund Cartwright, 83-5.

81-201. Speculation. Subject given for the Vase at Batheaston.

"Methinks, in ev'ry walk of life." (56 + 56)

L Cour, Mar 13 & Dec 5, 1781.

Quatrains. Additional stanzas deepen the satire of this relatively inoffensive poetry about the effect of the war on the cost of marketable products, like sugar from Jamaica, or on business in general. The added stanzas speculate on the effect a reign that favors the Scots and adopts Stuart maxims has on Government and the Church. The thought is also expressed that "this Transatlantic War" is "A DANG'ROUS, DANG'ROUS SPECULATION," and the King is accused of being ambitious to extend his

power.
This poem is not the same as William Tasker's "Ode to Speculation," or Christopher Anstey's Speculation: 80-3.

81-202. Spoken Extempore in the Park, on Hearing the Cannon Fired; Tuesday 13th March.

"Hark! through the Land our thund'ring Guns proclaim." (4)

PA, Mar 17, 1781.

Quatrain. Rodney is victorious again, shaming Howe and Keppel.

81-203. [Stanzas.]

"The fate of that destructive war." (84)

W Eve Post, Jan 6, 1781.

Unrhymed quatrains. An objection to the wasteful civil war between America ("Columbia") and Britain, especially now that France aids America and that Spain has joined the fray. America should reconsider the peace proposals. Cited are Andre, Washington, Arnold, and Clinton. Nathan Hale is alluded to.

81-204. Stanzas on the creating Sir J. Hamilton Captain of the Hector Man of War, a a Baronet, for his services at the Siege of Quebec, by the Americans. . . .

"Immortal as the British name." (24)

MH, May 9, 1781.

Quatrains, honoring (humorously) the naval officer J. Hamilton, who helped save Quebec from the besieging Americans in mid 1776. Cited are Wolfe and Montcalm.

81-205. [Starvation seize that skin-flint Judge.]

"Starvation seize that skin-flint Judge." (12)

L Cour, Jul 10, 1781.

Quatrains. Satire on Alexander Wedderburn, Lord Loughborough, for lack of compassion towards American prisoners, regarding their food allowance.

81-206. The State of Mynheer. An Extempore.

"Holland, by dealings lost the game." (4)

MH, Jan 10, 1781.

Quatrain. Holland's navy has no commander. Holland cannot win without Van Trump.

81-207. The State-Pastry-Cook. An Epigram on the Loan for 1781.

"The First Lord of the Treasury made a Plumb-Cake." (12)

PA, Apr 7, 1781.

Anapest tetrameter couplets. Satire on North, who declares he will continue to bribe if he receives support in Parliament.

81-208. [Staunch to the cause, old Nugent stands.]

"Staunch to the cause, old Nugent stands." (60)

L Cour, Apr 13, 1781.

OC. Satire on Tories. Robert, Earl Nugent, "A Tory of the rankest breed," supports the crown against those petitioners who would reduce its prerogatives; also, Henry "Starvation" Dundass refuses to hear the people. The reference is Lord George Gordon as a demagogue threatening the power and privileges of the King.

81-209. A Stroke at Mynheer.

"Now, my gallant sons of thunder." (24)

Lloyd's 48 (Jan 3, 1781), 24.

Quatrains. Patriotic lines against the Dutch, French, and Spaniards. What ancient valor had performed can now be performed against Britain's enemies.

81-210. ["Such once was Britain!" shall our grandsons say.]

"'Such once was Britain!' shall our grandsons say." (32)

West M 9 (Oct 1781), 603.

Quatrains. British forces on sea and land must be roused to fight aggressively as in the past. They need the leadership of Admirals Howe and Parker, General Cornwallis, and Colonel Tarleton. Admiral Graves is criticized.

81-211. The Tempest. An Extempore.

"From South and West, the tempest blew." (4)

MH, Feb 21, 1781.

OC. Lord North has shocked the nation with his new budget.

81-212. [There is a period in the walk of time.]

"There is a period in the walk of time." (90)

M Chron, Aug 23, 1781; PA, Aug 24, 1781.

HC. Didactic satire by Causidicus, the Cirencester poet, in reaction to Holland's entrance into the war. The Dutch, because of their behavior at Amboyna, are not to be trusted. In this crisis, the country must end domestic factious strife (here the poet denounces Fox and Burke) and must unite against its enemies, who would destroy the nation.

81-213. Thoughts occasioned by the War.

"All hail! ye far-fled distant thrice-blest days." (73)

L Cour, Aug 17, 1781.

HC. Rambling thoughts on the unpatriotic, aristocratic youth who gamble and play at this critical time; a picture of a savage Indian raid on the Ohio; and a declaration of will to wage war.

81-214. The Three Enemies of Britain, or Tria Juncta in Uno.

"Three Bullies in three different Countries born." (6)

PA, Jan 20, 1781; W Eve Post, Jan 18, 1781.

Epigram. HC. Satire on Spain, France, and Holland -- the last assimilating the character of the first two, haughtiness and perfidy. (An imitation of Dryden's epitaph on Milton.)

81-215. A Title for the Peerage Said to Await Admiral Rodney.

"The gallant Rodney, whom our Foes so fear." (12)

PA, Jun 13, 1781.

HC. Rodney deserves praise for his victories, but he made a mistake in sacking an open town, St. Eustatia. Such disgraceful behavior is more suitable to cowardly Germain.

81-216. To a Certain Great Person.

"Long have you loudly laugh'd! when will you cry." (4)

L Cour, Dec 10, 1781.

HC. Satire on the King, stubborn and unshaken in the face of calamities. Only "Contradiction to [his] Royal Will" can "shake" him.

81-217. To Admiral Rodney.

"Rodney, thy fame is great, thy worth still greater." (4)

L Cour, Mar 20, 1781.

HC. Twitcher Sandwich's future is bleak, but Rodney's is glorious.

81-218. To Admirals Rodney, Digby, Ross, &c. &c.

"Who's this on winter seas so bold." (60)

L Chron 49 (Mar 22, 1781), 285; SM 43 (Mar 1781), 159; WM 51 (Apr 5, 1781), 402.

Regular ode in sixains, in praise of the bold naval leaders of Rodney's fleet -- Digby, Ross, et al.

81-219. To Both Houses of Parliament. Alter'd from Prior.

"What though among yourselves, with too much heat." (6)

MH, Nov 26, 1781.

HC. Parliament should cease debate and now zealously get on with the war against Holland, Spain, and France.

81-220. To Cicero, on his Fifth Letter to Catiline, and the Preceding.

"Go on, great Caesar, in thy country's cause." (10)

MP, Jan 17, 1781.

HC. The King should stamp out treason (Fox and Savile?), so urges "Cicero," a pen-name for a ministry supporter who has attacked "Catiline the Second" and the Opposition, including the two Howes and Keppel, in a series of essays. "Cicero" is Joseph Galloway.

81-221. To D----S D----Y, Esq.

"Good Mr. D----s have you sold." (24)

Freeman's J, Dec 13, 1781.

Sixains. Satire on an Irish politician who was bribed to give his vote to Administration and to selling out Grattan and the movement for greater independence from Britain. (The name of the politician has not been identified.)

81-222. To Jemmy Twitcher.

"Hadst thou, Oh, Twitcher! seen the book of fate." (4)

L Cour, Mar 20, 1781.

HC. Satire on Sandwich, who, with Palliser, would have continued to blunder, had not Rodney succeeded in battle.

81-223. To Lord N[or]th.

"Like a big wife, the Budget makes thee swell." (6)

L Cour, Mar 12, 1781.

HC. Satire on North and his new budget.

81-224. To Lord N[or]th and another.

"Of thy corruptions N[orth], so strong the smell." (6)

L Cour, Jan 30, 1781.

Three similar satiric epigrams on Lord North, declaring him unfit for the House of Commons or Lords.

81-225. To Lord Sandwich. On his Late Trip to the Nore.

"When Fortune frowns on thee, as now." (36)

L Cour, Aug 25, 1781.

Sixains. Ironic satire on Sandwich, who is urged to persist despite present misfortune. (He had lost his mistress.)

81-226. To Minden.

"The friends of virtue let me ever join." (8)

L Cour, Feb 14, 1781.

HC and triplets. Satire on Germain for his hostility towards the Howe brothers and Burgoyne, here defended.

81-227. To Miss Seward, on her Monody on Major Andre."

"Above the frigid etiquette of form." (38)

G Eve Post, Apr 10, 1781; GM 51 (May 1781), 235-6; MH, Apr 13, 1781.

Also entitled "Verses addressed to Miss Seward upon her Monody on Major Andre." HC. Praise of Anna Seward's sympathetic poem on Andre. Like Seward, this poet criticizes Washington for his cruelty, his "heart of Nero's colour." Signed S. Johnson of Shrewsbury, who is <u>not</u> the lexicographer, Boswell's Johnson.

81-228. To Mr. Burke, on the Loss of his Saving Bill.

"With wit like lightning, eloquence like thunder." (2)

L Cour, Mar 5, 1781.

Anapest tetrameter couplet. Despite his wit and eloquence, Burke cannot persuade the corrupt politicians to resign their plunder.

81-229. To Mr. Urban, on completing his LIst Volume.

"From scenes of blood and lowering skies." (50)

GM 51 (1781), ii.

OC. Dated Dec. 31, 1781, a review of a variety of publications by Chatterton, Mason, James Harris, Gibbon, and others shows that war and tragic scenes dominate literature and the times. Wars will cease only upon the end of the world.

81-230. To Sempronius Johnstone.

"You went to bite the Congress, and was bit." (6)

L Cour, Jan 24, 1781.

HC. Satire on Gov. Johnstone for his attitude towards Congress. He is compared to Sempronius, a hypocritical patriot: "a deceiver and a traitor."

81-231. To Sir William Howe.

"In hopes to blast a Howe's beloved name." (6)

L Cour, Feb 10, 1781.

HC. In defense of Gen. Howe from the attacks of Scots, refugees (Galloway), and Germain.

81-232. To the Gentlemen of the Edinburgh Defensive Band. Ode on the Anniversary of his Majesty's Accession to the Throne.

"When rude Barbarians from the northern climes." (40)

Cal Merc, Oct 29, 1781.

Regular ode in dixains. A loyal poem. The present Scottish "Defensive Band" emulates the old Scots who drove the invading Danes away; it will guard British liberty at present against the enemy.

81-233. To the K[ing].

"Trust to your Ministers, great Sir, be sure." (2)

L Cour, Jan 20, 1781.

HC. The King has nothing left but to endure and trust his ministers.

81-234. To the Parliamentary Combatants of both Houses.

"The Serpent's teeth of old, whom Cadmus slew." (16)

MP, Feb 7, 1781.

HC. Satire on Britain's internal foes, on Fox, especially.

81-235. To the People of England.

"No generous purpose can enlarge the mind." (39)

L Cour, Jun 25, 1781; W Eve Post, Jun 9, 1781.

HC. Satire on the nation for its luxury and the ministry for corruption and selfishness. The nation is sinking. We need Camden to protect freedom and Chatham to provide leadership in the war crisis.

81-236. To the Right Hon. the Countess of H[untingdo]n.

"As Rats forsake, a falling house." (36)

PA, Aug 8, 1781.

Quatrains. Someone (P--y?) returns to "wrong'd Britannia," after giving up on the American rebels. Soon the rebellion will end and there will be a reconciliation. (P--y is probably a Methodist minister who had briefly sided with the Americans.)

81-237. To the T--y B--h at B---le's C----e-H---e.

"Indeed, my Friends, you're much to blame." (69)

MP, Mar 19, 1781.

OC and mixed verse. An ironic satire on the Opposition, "subtle, sly republicans," who engage in treason and wish for the success of England's enemies: France and America, Holland and Spain.

81-238. To the Vigorous Protesters against the Dutch War.

"In vain, mighty Statesmen, with rage you're possest." (6)

MP, Feb 1, 1781.

Hexameter couplets. Satire on the Opposition for protesting the Dutch war and the war against America.

81-239. To the Volunteers of Ireland. By a young Lady.

"Britannia, sunk in deep distress." (64)

Freeman's J, Jun 16, 1781.

OC. A political moral framed in classical myth. Ireland will provide volunteers to aid Britain in the struggle against France and Spain, should Britain treat her "with true affection."

81-240. Translation. [In Northium Vestris Saltationi attidentem.]

"When cap'ring Vestris, at the opera springs." (14)

"When Vestris' feet, with active leap." (12)

L Cour, Mar 1, 1781.

HC, quatrains. Two translations of a comparison between the celebrated Vestris, a dancer, and Burke, an orator: Vestris lightens the spirit; Burke enlightens the mind. North laughs at Vestris, sleeps at Burke.

81-241. The Treasury. An Ode. Inscribed to Old Barnsley.

"What Minister or Clerk in place." (30)

MP, Mar 28, 1781.

Regular (Horatian) ode in sixains. The point of this incomplete poem is not clear. North and Germain are cited favorably, Fox and Burke unfavorably. The remainder was to be printed March 30, 1781, which was missing from the Burney file.

81-242. The Triumph of Beauty.

"I will persist -- of every Hope bereft." (8)

St J's C, Dec 18, 1781.

HC. Britain shall still be victorious and enslave France, Spain, and America -- through its beautiful women!

81-243. Twitcher's Courage.

"What! France, America, and Spain combin'd." (4)

L Cour, Jan 20, 1781.

HC. Satire on Sandwich, who boasts that Britain can fight the whole world, including America.

81-244. The Two Cabinets. Question and Answer.

"Q. Th'Official Cabinet, whom, Sir, do you call." (4)

L Cour, Dec 14, 1781.

HC. Satire on the King's double cabinet system -- the official cabinet that does nothing, and the "efficient" cabinet or the secret "bloody Council of the Kingdom's Foes."

81-245. The Uniform Emancipation of the Bees. A Fable.

"Such long ago was Nature's state." (118)

Freeman's J, Apr 24, 1781.

OC. Animal fable. A satire on the Church in Ireland for the purpose of securing relief from tithing for landowners and tenants. (Emancipation from the Established Church is desired just as emancipation of the state body politic from English domination.)

81-246. The Union.

"Oh, that damn'd Union! cries the restless Scot." (3)

L Cour, Jan 15, 1781.

Epigram. Triplet. The union of Scot and Englishman is cursed by both.

81-247. The Vain Contest.

"Still, by some fraudful lure led on." (94)

LM 50 (Dec 1781), 596-7.

OC. A plea to end the American War, which is fruitless, especially after the French have become the allies of the Americans. England is now in decline. How changed "since Chatham's days!" Now it is fallen, insulted, alone; once it was powerful and respected. Under these conditions, to prolong the war is "prepost'rous" -- it is wasteful of men and money. (Cornwallis surrendered at Yorktown on October 19; news reached England about November 25.)

Verses addressed to Miss Seward upon her Monody on Major Andre. See "To Miss Seward, on her Monody on Major Andre": 81-227.

81-248. Verses written on hearing the Rev. Dr. R------N's Sermon on the General Fast of February 1781.

"When those we love in peace and safety rest." (60)

Cal Merc, Feb 26, 1781.

A sermon in HC. Britain will suffer decline as a result of "pride, and luxury, and rapine rage," faction tearing the nation apart and exposing her to her fierce, despotic enemies.

81-249. Verses Written on the Great Rejoicings and Illuminations at the Acquittal of Adm. Keppel. By a very gallant seaman.

"While Peers and Commons head the riot." (26)

SM 43 (Mar 1781), 159-60.

OC. Satire on Keppel, who was only acquitted because of politics -- he was a member of the Opposition.

81-250. The Vow.

"No, never, while Britain, the Queen of all Isles." (24)

PA, Apr 6, 1781.

Anapest tetrameter couplets. The English vow to fight for freedom, despite the Dutch ("Van Trowser"), French, and Spaniards. "In justice' fair Cause they'll assert their whole Might."

Wesley, Charles. No longer Pipe, no longer Dance. AM 4 (Jun 1781), 340. Another title for Charles Wesley's Party Loyalty, 80-396.

81-251. [When E(dmun)d his long Bill brings in.]

"When E[dmun]d his long Bill brings in." (24)

PA, Mar 1, 1781.

Regular (Horatian) ode in sixains. Satire on Burke for his long orations (on the India Bill), his self-interest, and his Irish lineage. The Marquis of Rockingham is criticized for being Burke's patron and for securing him a seat in the House of Commons.

81-252. Whitehead, William.
Ode for his Majesty's Birth-Day, June 4, 1781. By W. Whitehead, Esq. Poet Laureat.

"Still does the rage of war prevail." (42)

AR, 1781, pp. 168-9. Cal Merc, Jun 9, 1781; G, Jun 4, 1781; G Eve Post, Jun 2, 1781; GM 51 (Jun 1781), 283; Lloyd's 48 (Jun 1-4, 1781), 536; L Cour, Jun 5, 1781;

MH, Jun 4, 1781; NAR, 1781 (III, 193-4); PA, Jun 4, 1781; St J's C, Jun 2, 1781; W Misc 16 (Jun 18, 1781), 288; West J, Jun 9, 1781; W Eve Post, Jun 2, 1781; L Chron 49 (Jun 2-5, 1781), 533; LM 50 (Jun 1781), 288.

Irregular Pindaric ode. The laureat complains that the war still continues, man being motivated by "Revenge, and pride, and deadly hate, / And avarice," but disguising these evil passions, "hideous band," in the attractive colors of "glory." Nature's "social plan" encourages peace and fraternity; but man blindly wages war.

81-253. Whitehead, William.
Ode for the New Year, 1781. Written by William Whitehead, Esq; Poet Laureat.

"Ask round the world, from age to age." (42)

AR 1781, pp. 167-8; Cal Merc, Jan 8, 1781; Cumb Pacq, Jan 9, 1781; G Eve Post, Dec 31, 1780-Jan 2, 1781; GM 51 (Jan 1781), 36; Lady's M 11 (Supp 1780), 718; Lloyd's 48 (Dec 29, 1780-Jan 1, 1781), 8; L Cour, Jan 2, 1781; M Chron, Jan 1, 1781; MH, Jan 1, 1781; MP, Jan 1, 1781; NAR 1781 (III, 188-9); PA, Jan 1, 1781; St J's C, Dec 30, 1780-Jan 2, 1781; W Misc 15 (Jan 15, 1781), 375-6; West J, Jan 6, 1781; W Eve Post, Dec 30, 1780-Jan 2, 1781; L Chron 49 (Dec 30, 1780-Jan 2, 1781), 5; LM 50 (Jan 1781), 41.

Irregular Pindaric ode. Britain had kept the balance of power in Europe. But now Europe is indifferent to Britain's danger. Without a friend, Britain must depend on herself and "look down with scorn / On an opposing world, and all its wily ways."

81-254. The Wish.

"O may the Sword of War be sheath'd." (12)

PA, Mar 6, 1781.

Quatrains. Let us have trade with the colonies, and let peace prevail.

81-255. The Wrangling Orators. An Ode.

"When Edmund of Hibernian Race." (30)

PA, Jun 26, 1781.

Regular (Horatian) ode in sixains. Satiric characters of Edmund Burke and Henry Dundas, both devilish in their differing ways -- their oratorical style and politics.

81-256. The Wreath and Motto.

"All Heaven was sat in solemn state." (48)

Cumb Pacq, May 15, 1781; G Eve Post, Mar 20, 1781; PA, Mar 21, 1781.

OC. A victory poem for Rodney, who is honored by the gods for his naval triumphs over the Dutch.

81-257. Written by a young Man in a French Prison.

"Thou loathsome Dungeon, in whose dreary womb." (39)

Cumb Pacq, Jan 23, 1781.

HC. A complaint by a British soldier against the terrible condition of a French prison in the Caribbean. Those who have fought against France, Spain, and America deserve better!

81-258. Written by Miss ----- to an American Officer. [And an] Answer.

"With thee thro' dreary wilds I'll go." (16 + 16)

West M 9 (Mar 1781), 156.

Quatrains. The lady insists upon heeding the call of love, despite the fact that her lover is a rebel. Her beloved agrees to be her subject; no longer a rebel, he has been "Subdu'd by Love."

81-259. Yank-Hunting.

"It fell on a time, when plumb-pudding and peace." (50)

L Cour, Dec 26, 1781; Noon Gazette, Dec 26, 1781.

Song with "Derry down" chorus. Both newspapers were owned by John Almon. Satire on the Scotch and the Tories, who are pursuing the war against the Americans. Cited are Bute, North, Rigby, Sandwich, Mansfield, Germain, Amherst, Bunker's Hill, Yanky, George, Burgoyne, Gates, Gen. Howe, Mud Island, Rawdon, Gen. Greene, Cornwallis, and De Grasse.

Prints

81-260. Administration and Opposition as Exhibited April 3, 1780 at the Pantheon Masquerade.

"Let hungry Patriots lick their lips at our rich-season'd dainties." (44)

Engr. with song. January 1781.

George 5829 (V, 497-8).

A satire on the opposition which desires political power but has no real program.

81-261. Antigallican Spirit; humbly Inscrib'd to Capt: Forster & the Managers of the Antigallican Private Ship of War.

"Would Statesmen but this Picture View." (4)

Engr. with quatrain. 1781 (?).

George 5861 (V, 517).

Praise of Capt. Forster for capturing three French ships. If the ministry were so successful as Forster, France and Spain would be easily defeated.

81-262. The Ballance of Power.

"America, dup'd by a trecherous train." (10)

Engr. with anapest tetrameter couplets. January 17, 1781.

George 5827 (V, 495-6). Dolmetsch, pp. 160-1.

Britain asserts that she maintains the balance of power against her enemies -- America, France, Holland, and Spain, and hopes to reunite with America.

81-263. The Dutch in the Dumps.

"Perfidious Dutchmen now beware." (4)

Engr. with quatrain. January 4, 1781.

George 5825 (V, 494).

Britain drubs Holland, now in the war since December 20, 1780, with the others -- Spain, France, and America. A satire on Holland.

81-264. The Dutchman in the Dumps.

"I shall Die, I'm undone!" (10)

Engr. with dimeter couplets. April 9, 1781.

George 5837 (V, 504).

Illustrates the reaction to the loss of St. Eustatia. Another satire on Holland.

81-265. The Junto, in a Bowl Dish.

"Behold the Ministerial foul Fish." (12)

Engr. with OC. February 11, 1781.

George 5831 (V, 499).

Mismanaged, England is assailed by her enemies: America, France, Spain, and Holland.

81-266. State Cooks, or the Downfall of the Fish Kettle.

"O Boreas, the Loss of those Fish will ruin us for ever." (2)

Engr. with couplet. December 10, 1781.

George 5855 (V, 514-15).

At this late date, North with the help of Germain is still hopeful of a victory in America, despite the King's pessimism.

81-267. Tria Juncta in Uno. Or the Three Enemies of Brittain.

"Three Bullys in three distant Countries born." (6)

Engr. with verses. January 17, 1781.

George 5826 (V, 495).

Satire on the three allies-- Holland, France, and Spain -- all at war with Britain. Parody of Dryden's epitaph on Milton.

1782  Books & Pamphlets

82-1. Admiral Rodney's Triumph, Or The French Fleet Defeated.
N. P., n. d. Broadside.

"True Britons all of each degree." (48)

Copies: BL C.121.g.9 (216).

Ballad praising Rodney for his victory of April 12, 1782, over De Grasse in the West Indies. Although the English fleet was outnumbered, they took five French ships of the line and Admiral De Grasse himself. Decorated with a crude woodcut.

82-2. Alves, Robert.
Poems, by Robert Alves, A. M.
Edinburgh: Creech; London: Cadell, 1782. viii + 243p.

Copies: BL 11632.e.3; NUC CtY, DFo, ICN, IU.

Includes "The Miseries of War: An Elegy. Written anno 1769," "Ode for the Year 1780. Occasioned by our Successes in the War," and "Ode for the Year 1781. Being an Invocation to the Public Virtues." See 69-1, 80-1, 81-1. "The Miseries of War" takes on added significance when printed in 1782.

82-3. [Badini, Carl Francis]
The Flames Of Newgate; Or, The New Ministry.
London: Southern, 1782. 66p.

"When Chatham mounted to the bright abodes." (1387)

Notices: CR 54 (Aug 1782), 151; MR 67 (Sep 1782), 237; ERL 3 (Jan 1783), 41-4; GA Jun 1, 1782; L Chron 51 (Jun 1, 1782), 531; L Cour Jun 7 & 20, 1782.

Copies: BL 11630.e.14 (12); Bod Godwyn Pamph 1737 (12); NUC CSmH, CtY, DFo, NN, PU.

HC. Satire on the old ministry of Lord North and panegyric on the new ministry of Lord Rockingham. The poet imagines Chatham being installed a god in the ethereal regions, where he "makes a lamentable description of our surrounding calamities" (Argument). St. Paul appears to give the king advice upon the choice of the new ministry. But first he must be instructed in the times before he can perform his duty. At this point Johnson is satirized: "The slavish tool, by tyrants better fed,/ Reviles that liberty which gave him bread." Parliament in debate is described--Conway favorably, as he makes his motion for peace. Fox is praised for his eloquence. North is made responsible for the loss of America, as well as Germain and Sandwich, both criticized for misleading the king, who complains of the defeat of Cornwallis and the loss of America. At the conclusion, Rockingham, Shelburne, Burke, Fox, Richmond, and Keppel restore wisdom and virtue, honesty and truth, to the ministry.

82-4. The Beauties Of Administration, A Poem. With An Heroic Race To The Palace, Between L--d Sh-lb--ne and the Hon. C. J. F-x.
London: Hooper, [1782]. ii + 71p.

"Adieu, ye bards! whom harmless fancy leads." (c. 1400)

Notices: CR 54 (Nov 1782), 397; MR 68 (Feb 1783), 185; W Eve Post Oct 17 & 27, 1782.

Copies: BL 644.k.21 (17); NUC CtY, DFo, MBAt, MH.

HC. Frontispiece engraving of King George and his Tory council is dated Oct. 1, 1782. Satire on the politics of the time, particularly the Scotch influence and the Tory administration of Lord North. The poet believes that the coming of Scotsmen to the court, led by Bute, brought Corruption (allegorically drawn) and ruin, a destructive civil war that resulted in "One empire ruin'd, and another lost," Burgoyne and Cornwallis defeated, the state's credit gone, and the treasury emptied. The King complains that North, his friend, will now be torn from his council, but Sandwich and Germaine reassure him that the rebellion can still be suppressed. Britannia admonishes the King for the destructive civil war that has desolated the land while bribery dominates a venal Parliament. Impartial characters appear of Bute, Richmond, Mansfield, Thurlow, Fox, Burke, Sandwich, Camden, Effingham, Carlisle, Germaine, Wilkes, and others. At the end, Corruption disappears with the new ministry, but when Rockingham dies, "The Heroic Race" of Shelburne and Fox (who runs for Portland) begins, a race for the premier's office won by Shelburne. (Rockingham had died July 1, 1782.)

82-5. The Blockheads; Or, Fortunate Contractor. An Opera, in Two Acts, As It Was Performed at New York. The Music Entirely New, Composed by several of the most eminent Masters in Europe.
New York; repr. London: Kearsley, 1782. iii-[vi] + 43p.

"Gallic slav'ry hence no more." (12)

"Dear Albion come, my love to prove." (12)

Notices: CR 55 (May 1783), 416; MR 68 (Mar 1783), 271.

Sabin 5944.

Copies: NUC CtY, InU, NN.

An allegorical operatic farce attempts to reconcile Britain and America and to keep France at a distance. Act I: As Liberty becomes violent, all Friendship disappears. France, portrayed as Deception, a quack physician, leads a blind Dutchman, Peace, in a dance. Act II: America decides to help Liberty prepare for war. Contractors become prosperous. But some members of Congress suspect French intentions, call for an expulsion of the French, and declare for Britain. America, duped by French promises, rues the tyranny of French fetters. Deciding to return to Britain, America asks her to "destroy this Gallic chain." The last two airs (pp. 38-40) make the theme explicit.

82-6. Cave, Jane (afterwards Winscom).
On the General Fast, February 8, 1782.

"Omnipotent eternal all." (40)

In 83-6: in her Poems on Various Subjects, pp. 135-7.

Hymn. A prayer to God to work a miracle: to protect "our sinking land," to "direct our king and senators," to preserve "our fleets," to bless "our armies," and to give success to the nation against "our foes." See 75-4.

82-7. Colvill, Robert.
The Downfall Of The Roman Confederacy; Or, The Ever Memorable 12th of April 1782. A Heroic Poem, In Three Cantos. By the Rev. Mr. Colvill of Dysart, V. D. M.
Edinburgh: Darling, 1788.

"Descend dread goddess of the fearless eye." (151)

Copies: BL 11602.h.13 (3) (imperfect, wanting all after Canto 1, p. 12).

HC. Colvill celebrates Rodney's stunning victory April 12, 1782, over Admiral De Grasse and his fleet, which turned the scales on the British side, thereby saving the British empire in the West Indies from extinction.

82-8. -----.
On the Memorable Siege of Gibraltar, Where the Gallant General Elliot with his brave Garrison, for many months baffled all the power of Spain, and in her final defeat, by the distruction [sic] of the Floating Batteries, won immortal laurels.

"Triumphant Victors! o'er the pride of Spain." (46)

Sacred to the Memory of Colonel James Webster.

"Onward to the field where Slaughter." (64)

In 89-1: in his Poetical Works, pp. 261-3, 169-71.

"On the . . . Siege of Gibraltar": HC. Dated St. Salvator's College, St. Andrew's, 1782. A celebration of Gen. Elliot's successful defence of Gibraltar, which lifted the siege October 1782.

"Sacred to the Memory of Col. James Webster": Octosyllabic couplets. Dated St. Salvator's College, St. Andrews, 1782. Colvill mourns the death of Webster, who fought under Cornwallis and was mortally wounded at Guilford, N.C., March 15, 1781.

82-9. [Dorset, Michael]
Condolence: An Elegiac Epistle From Lieut. Gen. B-rg-yne, Captured at Saratoga, Oct 17, 1777, To Lieut. Gen. Earl C-rnw-ll-s, Captured at York-Town, Oct. 17, 1781. With Notes By The Editor.
London: Evans, 1782. 5-32p.

"Tell my, my Lord! can no soft strain." (426)

Notices: CR 53 (Jan 1782), 68-9; MR 66 (Feb 1782), 147; EM 1 (Jan 1782), 28-9; G Eve Post Dec 25, 1781; SM 44 (Feb 1782), 100.

Sabin 9249.

Copies: BL 643.k.2 (6) (1st ed), 11630.e.14 (7) (2nd ed); NUC CSmH, CtY, DLC, ICN, MB, MH, MiU-C, & RPJCB (1st ed), DLC, MiU-C, & RPJCB (2nd ed).

European Magazine 1 (January 1782), 28-9, identifies the author as Captain (Michael) Dorset. Stanzas in sixains. Ironical satire on the war against America. Burgoyne's persona expresses sympathy for Cornwallis, who was also disgraced by defeat in America. Burgoyne is made to admit that British "troops were Freedom's foes"; that he used savage Indians in his army, causing the murder and scalping of Miss Macrae; that Cornwallis opposed the Declaratory Act and supported "the rights of man" but later betrayed his principles. The persona then imagines the effect of Cornwallis's defeat upon the ministry--Mansfield, North, Germain, Rigby, Thurlow, Sandwich. He feels that they, like many others who fought in America, should be rewarded in defeat--for lies will help.

He blames the Tories for the American troubles, which he describes from the Boston Tea Party to the fighting and the "Unvaried vict'ries" which all contribute to Britain's ruin. He confesses that successful coercion of America "was impossible at starting." He prays for peace, which even George Washington craves, and heaps praise on Washington and Franklin. He concludes wishing both to do penance for their crimes.

Cited are Palliser, Clinton, Howe, Henry Bate of the Morning Herald, Gibbon, S. Johnson, Tarleton, and others.

82-10. Free[th], John.
Modern Songs, On Various Subjects: Adapted To Common Tunes. Written On The Immediate Arrival Of The Accounts Of The Different Events. By John Free.
Birmingham: Pearson & Rollason, 1782. viii + 60 + 2p.

The Preface. "By diff'rent views are authors led." (89)

Copies: 11623.aaa.14; NUC DLC.

The 32 songs in this collection were written between 1777 and 1782. More than half, about politics or the war, were published in the newspapers. These songs are included in the section on poetry appearing in serials--for example, "Britain's Glory" (1778), "The Defeat of D'Estaing at Savannah" (1779), "Langara's Defeat" (1780), "Jersey Expedition" (1781), "The English Lion" (1779), "Paul Jones" (1779), "Prescott's Breeches" (1777), "Jolly Dick and Jemmy Twitcher" (Rigby and Sandwich; 1779), "Admiral Parker's Engagement with the Dutch Fleet" (1781), "The Georges. On Lord Sackville's Promotion" (1782), and "The Trading War" (1780).

In the verse Preface (pp. iii-viii), in octosyllabic couplets, Freeth comments on history and the changing times, contrasts the glorious results of the Seven Years War with the poor results of the American War (as in "The Contrast," too), points to the blunders of ministers and generals, to the failures of the American War, to the division and discord in the country. He finds it remarkable that the North ministry remained in power despite all its failures. See 76-13, 83-15.


82-11. [Greene, Edward Burnaby]
The Prophecy Of Andree. An Ode. Written in the Year 1780.
London: Kearsly, Faulder, 1782. 20p.

"Stern on the gently rising plain." (276)

Sabin 28593.

Copies: NUC CSmH, N, RPJCB.

A "Sonnet Devoted to His Majesty," signed by Greene and dated from Kensington on Aug. 5, 1782, follows the English or Shakespearean rhyme scheme. Greene waxes patriotic in the face of the Bourbon confederacy, hopes that discord will soon cease, and that American rebels will be reconciled to Britain and give up independence: "Dismember'd Regions? 'tis the Coward's plan."
The Prophecy is a regular Pindaric ode in six parts, each with three subsections. The expression of this poem is so extremely unusual that the meaning can scarcely be understood. Britannia briefly reviews the history of the new world, its discovery and settlement, including New England and its potentially rebel dissenters; she remarks on the defeat of France (Wolfe and Quebec), thereby protecting the colonies. But "Proud Congress" breaks the relationship with the parent country, and is supported in the parricide by a patriot (Fox?) in Parliament. What is now needed is "Union."
In the conclusion, Andree speaks through Britannia, declaring that Britain must strike the enemy "thro' a Subject's side," that her cause is just, and that freedom is given only to "accordant Subjects."

82-12. [Mason, William]
An Archaeological Epistle, To The Reverend And Worshipful Jeremiah Milles, D. D. Dean of Exeter, President of the Society of Antiquaries, and Editor of a Superb Edition of the Poems of Thomas Rowley, Priest. To Which Is Annexed, A Glossary, Extracted From That Of The Learned Dean.
London: Nichols et al., 1782. 18p.

"As whanne a gronfer with ardurous glowe." (126)

Notices: CR 54 (Jul 1782), 19-22; MR 66 (Apr 1782), 294-8; PA Mar 29 & 30, 1782.

Copies: BL 840.1.17 (16), 11630.d.2 (6), & 11630.d.7 (11) (1st ed), 11630.e.11 (10) (2nd ed, corr); NUC CtY, ICN, IU, MH, TxU.

Attributed to William Mason. The prose preface is dated from Mile-End, March 15, 1782.
Sixain stanzas. An ironic imitation of Chatterton's medieval Rowley forgeries. The preface takes S. Johnson to task for the "venal dereliction" of his political tenets; that is, the surrender of his views on "the constitutional liberty of his fellow subjects." The poem is an ironical Rowleian address to the various writers engaged in the controversy over the authenticity of Chatterton's medieval poems ascribed to Thomas Rowley. But when in the poem the "Gothic terms" degenerate into modern English, Mason comments on the American War (stanzas 15-21).
Indignantly, Mason asks Dr. Milles to spread his "murky antiquarian cloud" over the truth and judgment concerning Chatterton's obvious forgeries and to extend it over Britain's past to obscure her greatness and glory when she had crushed France. He asks Milles also to tell Britain that France's navy is not strong and that only Sandwich and Germaine can save her; that only borrowing money can fill her empty coffers; that bribed lords welcome Germaine to the peerage, for he has been elevated as Viscount Sackville as a reward for his plans to quell the American rebels; and finally that, although two British armies have been subdued, "the free Americans will yield" as the bloody civil war continues. The last stanza ridicules the Archbishop of York, Markham, ambitious to become Archbishop of Canterbury. (Reprinted in The Repository: A Select Collection of Fugitive Pieces of Wit and Humour, in Prose and Verse [London: Dilly, 1783], IV, 277-300, and in The School for Satire [London: Jacques & Co., 1802], pp. 103-23.)


82-13. [-----]
The Dean And The 'Squire: A Political Eclogue. Humbly Dedicated to Soame Jenyns, Esq. By the Author of the Heroic Epistle to Sir William Chambers, &c.
London: Debrett, 1782. iv + 15 + [2]p.

"In Coffee-house of good account." (274)

Notices: CR 53 (May 1782), 392; MR 67 (Oct 1782), 309-11; EM 2 (Sep 1782), 210-12; GM 52 (Jul 1782), 339-40; WM 57 (Aug 14, 1783), 219-21.

Copies:  BL 840.1.17 (17) (1st ed), 11630.e.9 (5) (2nd ed), 11630.e.24 (3rd ed); NUC  CSmH, DLC, & ICN (1st ed); CtY, IU, InU, MH, & MiU-C (2nd ed); CtY, MH, & MiU-C (3rd ed).

Malcolm MacGreggor (the pseudonym of William Mason) dates his dedication from Knightsbridge, May 1st, 1782.

Octosyllabic couplets. Satire on Soame Jenyns and Josiah Tucker, Dean of Gloucester, both Tories, who have a fictional debate on political principles. As Mason informs us, he imitates Jenyns' "Eclogue of the 'Squire and the Parson, written on Occasion of Lord Bute's glorious Peace" and burlesques "the two first Heads of Jenyns' Seventh Disquisition," on Government and Civil Liberty, in <u>Disquisitions on Several Subjects</u> (1782), and Tucker's <u>Treatise Concerning Civil Government</u> (1781). Jenyns tried to controvert basic Lockean Whig principles, particularly the first two: that all men are born equal, that all men are born free, that all government is derived from the people, that all government is a compact between the governors and the governed, that government is useful only so long as it continues to be of equal advantage to the governed and to the governors. He damns (in the poem) the factious Opposition as "the old round-head leaven," the Puritan levellers and republicans. Although the American troubles are not specifically mentioned, this poem is relevant because of its implications concerning the meaning that rebel America held for those who justified their behavior according to the controversial and Whiggish preamble to the Declaration of Independence.

82-14. -----.
  Ode To The Honourable William Pitt. By William Mason, M. A.
  London: Dodsley, 1782. 5-11p.

"'Tis May's meridian reign; yet Eurus cold." (84)

Notices:  CR 54 (Jul 1782), 70;  MR 67 (Oct 1782), 308-9;  GM 52 (Jul 1782), 340-1; W Eve Post Jul 20, 1782.

Copies:  BL 840.1.4 (13), 11630.e.9 (2);  Bod Godwyn Pamph 1726 (10);  NUC  CSmH, CtY, ICN, IU, MH, MiU-C, NN, TxU.

Dated at end from Aston, May 11th, 1782. Regular Horatian ode. Mason hopes that the younger Pitt will be guided by his father's example: "knit the union firm, and bid an Empire live," "Give life, give strength" to freedom, protect "The native Rights of Man from Corruption's baleful power," become "The People's Friend." Cited are Chatham, Keppel, Mason's "Ode to the Naval Officers of Great Britain" (1779). Thus Mason, at the end of the war, heralds a new day in this patriot poem, as the son of Chatham enters the political arena. (Mason later changed the last few lines significantly; e. g., "To claim thy sovereign's love, be thou thy country's friend.")

82-15. Maurice, Thomas.
  Ierne Rediviva: An Ode. Inscribed To The Volunteers Of Ireland. By the Rev. Thomas Maurice, A. B. Chaplain Of His Majesty's Ninety Seventh Regiment.
  [London]: Dodsley & Dilly, 1782. 13p.

"Shall Freedom, on yon favour'd Isle." (192)

Notices: CR 54 (Dec 1782), 478; MR 68 (Mar 1783), 272-3.

Copies: NUC MH.

Quatrains. Maurice honors the Irish who have joined the Volunteers to defend freedom. He condemns Britain's "ungenerous" and unwise tyranny over Ireland. He would break "the kindred ties" and fly to freedom, should "Britain basely act th'oppressor's part." He means "tyrants at the helm," for the "genuine voice of Britain is Liberty." Apparently, Maurice would accept the model of America, which has succeeded in its struggle to break oppression's chain and "share those rights to man by heav'n assign'd." Brutus and republican Rome also provide a model for freedom.

Ireland has its noble and virtuous heroes--Henry Grattan and Charlemont. (James Caulfeild, 1st Earl of Charlemont, joined Grattan in 1780 in the assertion of Irish independence, and was chosen commander-in-chief of the volunteer force.) Maurice takes pleasure in the hope of peace with America and the defeat of treacherous and slavish France, Britain's ancient enemy, now allied with Holland and Spain. Britain had erred (in the war against America), but now her cause is just: "when insulted, [let it be known that Britain] braved a WORLD in fight."

82-16. [Mickle, William Julius]
The Prophecy of Queen Emma; An Ancient Ballad lately discovered. Written by Johannes Turgotus, Prior of Durham, in the Reign of William Rufus. To which is added, by the Editor, An Account of the Discovery, and Hints towards a Vindication of the Authenticity of the Poems of Ossian and Rowley.
London: Bew, 1782. 40p.

"O'er the hills of Cheviot beaming." (128)

Notices: CR 53 (Jun 1782), 419-20; MR 67 (Sep 1782), 237; St J's Chron May 21, 1782; W Eve Post Aug 19, 1783.

Copies: BL 1162.k.6 (3); NUC ICN, MB, MH, NN.

Ballad, imitation of "Chevy Chase." Mickle imagines that the poem was written by Turgotus, the same Saxon monk of the tenth century whom Chatterton claimed as the author of the medieval Latin poems presumably translated by Thomas Rowley.

The ballad narrates the story of the bloody conflict between Queen Emma's sons, Edwin and Edgar. Emma dashes between the two armies to prevent the fratricidal struggle. She upbraids Edgar for his "base alliance" with the Danes, a hateful measure that provoked Edwin's antagonism. The brothers fight, ignoring their mother's plea for a peaceful settlement. Emma, mortally wounded, predicts doom for both. But she believes Edgar's loss and that of his descendants will be greater as she curses the Danish alliance, a radical act contrary to faith, honor, and freedom.

Thus Mickle, in a political allegory, criticizes treacherous American diplomacy, which produced the Franco-American alliance, and foretells the ruin of the colonies. Mickle's note in the prose postscript (p. 28) confirms this interpretation.

Also included in Mickle's Poetical Works (London: Barfield, 1806), pp. 109-13.

82-17. Ode On The Surrender At York-Town. To The Honourable William Pitt.
London: Bowen, 1782. 8p.

"Whence this alarm? this cloud of care." (80)

Notices: CR 54 (Sep 1782), 233; MR 66 (Jun 1782), 473; GA, Mar 1, 1782; T&C 14 (Nov 1782), 603.

Sabin 56704.

Copies: The Paul Mellon Collection, Upperville, Virginia.

Regular Horatian ode in octaves. The poet imagines Cornwallis's surrender of his 7000-man army because, despite their valor, they were "unsupplied" and "promised aid" did not come. He invokes the guardian spirit of Chatham to help Britain, then begs Chatham's son to persuade the ministry to stop the "War, horrid war, their cruel rage / Across th'Atlantic still would wage," arguing from Britain's loss of sea dominion, half the western empire, commerce and credit, and thousands dead.

82-18. [Polwhele, Richard, ed.]
Poems, Chiefly by Gentlemen of Devonshire and Cornwall.
Bath: Cruttwell, 1792. 2 vols.

Four Odes, Written at Different Periods On Public Occasions. Ode I. "How dim, how faded is the ray." (90) II, 35-9.

Copies: BL 992.d.32, 11660.ee.24; NUC CtY, IU, MB, MH, MiU, NN.

Regular Horatian ode in dixains. Britain, fallen from the height of glory where Pitt the elder put her, is now forced to fight France and Spain, "In treacherous league combin'd," while Russia and Europe remain aloof. Indian wealth and its debasing corruption cause England's troubles. Had America not defied the parent state, had the country been blest with concord, England might have stood off Europe--as shown by the brave chiefs, Hood, Parker, Rodney, and Elliot. But England has been "Self-vanquisht."

82-19. Puddicombe, John Newell.
Albion Triumphant: Or, Admiral Rodney's Victory Over The French Fleet. A Poem. By J. N. Puddicombe, M. A.
London: Robson, Debret, Sewell, Johnson, et al., 1782. 19p.

"Awhile my lips the warbling reed forego." (272)

Notices: CR 54 (Aug 1782), 147; MR 67 (Sep 1782), 237; ERL 1 (Apr 1783), 343; MP, Jul 23, 1782.

Sabin 66539.

Copies: BL 11633.g.29.

HC. Puddicombe celebrates "Rodney's glorious deeds," his "dauntless valour" united with "mercy's milder light," his noble patriotic fervor, all exceeding Pompey's or Caesar's. Rodney had "Curb'd with one blow insidious Gallia's pride." Puddicombe describes in general poetic terms the Battle of the Saints, citing the names of the heroic British officers who had achieved this marvellous victory over De Grasse's fleet. But the war continues, and he asks when it will cease, when (alluding to America) "ill-fated strife . . . whom nature's voice, whom interest, bids combine" will end. He also asks the leaders to pursue their policy so that there will be an honorable peace: "Then all who triumph'd at her adverse fate," those who opposed the war, "Shall rue that triumph."

82-20. [-----]
The British Hero In Captivity. A Poem. Dedicated To His Royal Highness The Prince Of Wales.
London: Robson, Walter, & Sewell, 1782. 23p.

"While others ask the tuneful virgin train." (378)

Notices: CR 53 (Mar 1782), 229; MR 66 (Jun 1782), 473; GM 52 (May 1782), 246; MP Mar 28 & Apr 22, 1782.

Sabin 8108.

Copies: BL 11633.g.8; NUC ICN, RPJCB.

Blank verse. Praise of Cornwallis (cf. Eulogium of Lord Cornwallis, Morning Post March 28, 1782), André, Arnold; harsh criticism of America (cf. Lines Addressed to America, Morning Post April 22, 1782). Puddicombe pays tribute to Cornwallis, who should be admired for his courage, resolution, nobility, and humanity in defeat, and pitied for being overwhelmed by immensely superior numbers of French and American troops. He finds the French victory particularly galling.
"Faithless America" is responsible for this sanguinary civil war, for destruction and ruin, because of its "rebellious strife," its "revengeful hate."
Then the shade of André appears to call "vengeance down" on America for its black and pitiless injustice. Puddicombe mourns the death of this heroic patriot, and exalts Arnold for his bravery, noting that Arnold had offered his own life for André's. In conclusion, he believes another hero is crossing the Atlantic to humble "Ruthless America." But he begs "hapless, alienated" America to return to its king and parent: recognize its conduct is "mark'd with dire barbarity and guilt," and "Unite with Albion to confound her foes."

82-21. Robinson, Mary Darby.
Ode to Valour. Inscribed to Colonel Banastre Tarleton.

"Transcendent Valour!--godlike Pow'r." (100)

In <u>Poems by Mrs. M. Robinson</u> (London: Bell, 1791), I, 57-60.

Copies: BL 11642.e.37; NUC CSmH, CtY, DLC.

Irregular ode praising valorous warriors--Tarleton ("the zealous Patriot"), the British on Gibraltar, Wolfe. (Mrs. Robinson does not mention specifically Tarleton's reputation for valor and ferocity in America.) The poem was probably written in 1782 and refers to Tarleton's reputation formed in the American War. See Wolcot, 82-31, on Reynolds' portrait of Tarleton.


82-22. [Rushton, Edward]
The Dismember'd Empire. A Poem.
Liverpool: Gore, Nevett, & Johnson, [1782]. [5]-27p.

"Seven times the globe has made its annual round." (c. 320)

Notices: CR 56 (Aug 1783), 237; MR 68 (Aug 1783), 167; L Cour Feb 4, 1783; PA Feb 6, 1783.

Copies: NUC CtY, MH.

The preface is dated from Liverpool, November 1782.
HC. The war to enslave America has lasted seven years. But America united to resist, "dar'd to vindicate the rights of man," and its "rabble" succeeded in withstanding "all the skill of veteran hosts." The Americans have continued in the tradition of the English struggle for liberty and limited monarchy--against King John for Magna Charta, and against Charles I, which William (of Orange) confirmed in the Glorious Revolution. But America has shamelessly rejected Britain's offer of peace, and ambitiously seeks independence allied with France. Then Spain and Holland joined the conflict against Britain, while the Armed Neutrality enjoyed "th'unequal strife." At the same time that it is faced with foreign foes, Britain is weakened by domestic faction, which insists that Britain should "foul rebellion own." Rushton advises that Britain "never! never! yield to such disgrace," never allow proud rebellion to gain independence, never yield its "just maternal right." (Chatham's view.) For to do so would destroy its empire, all its trade--the West Indies and India, and Britain itself will suffer economic depression and depopulation as its commerce ceases.

All Britains should now unite ("O Unanimity! assume thy reign") to expel faction and discord, and support Shelburne. Britain's navy should resolutely carry on the fight against the Bourbon powers. After "justly punish'd craft would point at Peace," America should be reconciled to its parent, firm and unshaken, "The envy, dread, and wonder of each land."

82-23. Scott, John.
The Poetical Works of John Scott Esq.
London: Buckland, 1782. 341p.

Ode XIII. [On Hearing The Drum.] "I hate that drum's discordant sound." (16) p. 201.

Ode XVII. Privateering. "How Custom steels the human breast." (40) pp. 211-13.

Notices: CR 54 (Jul 1782), 47-50; MR 67 (Sep 1782), 190; BM & R 1 (Dec 1782), 459; L Chron 51 (Jun 13, 1782), 569-70; MH, Jan 1, 1784; NAR 1782 (III, 199).

Copies: BL 79.i.25, 1346.d.28; NUC CSmH, CtY, DLC, InU, NN, & TxU (1st ed), DLC, ICU, PPL, & TxU (2nd ed, 1786).

Regular Horatian odes, anti-war poems by a Quaker. The first expresses Scott's objection to the recruiting of soldiers to fight and die for empire "in foreign lands." To him, war is an atrocity, bringing misery, painful death, destruction. The second objects to barbaric practices of plundering merchant vessels and murdering the passengers. The merchant who suffers the loss goes bankrupt and is imprisoned; but the robber prospers and is honored. This collection of poems also includes "Sonnet V. To Britain. 1766" and "Stanzas on Reading Mrs. Macaulay's History of England. 1766." See 66-16. Scott, in Remarks on the Patriot (1775), had written against Samuel Johnson and the Administration on the policy of coercing the Americans. (The ode "On Hearing The Drum" was reprinted in BM & R, MH, and NAR, the notices above.)

82-24. Stevenson, John Hall.
The Works of John Hall-Stevenson . . . Corrected and Enlarged. With Several Original Poems, Now First Printed, and Explanatory Notes.
London: Debrett, 1795. 3 vols.

Epitaph Upon A General. "Here lies, for so the envious Fates decree." (70) II, 188-95.

Copies: BL 1081.h.6-8, 1081.h.9-11; NUC CSmH, CtY, DLC, InU, MH, PU.

A Latin epitaph on General Charles Lee, died at age 51, October 2, 1782, which Stevenson has translated into English heroic verse. From a section titled "Monkish Epitaphs," published from the author's MS. Lee's character is described, his adoption by the Iroquois Indians and his service with the Americans are mentioned-- "A hardy tribune of the Yanky crew."

82-25. Stevenson, William.
An Ode To Peace. By William Stevenson, M. D. Second Edition Corrected.
Newark: Tomlinson; London: Fielding, 1782. xx + 23p.

"Hail Peace! thou daughter of the skies." (c. 690)

Copies: NUC NjR.

A revision of the edition entered as 78-39. This 1782 edition adds a prose "Preface To The Second Edition" (pp. xi-xx) and a verse "Supplement" (88 ll., pp. 20-3). Slight revisions are also made in the earlier text. In the additional prose, Stevenson notes that now there is no choice but peace for the new administration based upon the independence of America; for only peace can save the nation and the only way towards peace is acknowledging American independence. The same policy applies to Ireland and Irish independence, contrary to the wishes of Lord Abingdon. These views are the result of the nation's suffering "four additional years, mostly of calamity" since 1778.

In the additional verse, Stevenson honors the new leaders Lennox, Wentworth, Fitzmaurice, and Pratt (Richmond, Rockingham, Shelburne, and Camden) who will "save a sinking land." (He also notes the recent untimely death of Rockingham.) He denies power to the bishops and concludes with mention of the miraculous victory of Rodney and the rise of America.

82-26. [Stratford, Thomas]
The First Book of Fontenoy. A Poem, In Nine Books.
London: Dodsley, Becket, et al., 1782. iii + [5]-105p.

Notices: MR 71 (Aug 1784), 95-8.

Copies: BL 161.m.42, 11630.b.1 (6); NUC CtY, MH.

A blank verse epic influenced by Milton, and written in response to Voltaire's poem on the Battle of Fontenoy to vindicate the honor of his heroic countrymen. In the prose essay (pp. 5-21), Stratford calls for "union," the end of faction, so Britain, now standing alone, can face its numerous enemies effectively. He thinks of the Americans as "vipers, the parricides of their country" (p. 17). The poem is not relevant.

82-27. The Triumph Of Liberty, And Peace With America: A Poem. Inscribed To General Conway.
London: Walker, 1782. i + 26p.

"Again Britannia's Genius rears her head." (400)

Notices: CR 53 (May 1782), 391; MR 68 (Feb 1783), 185.

Sabin 59410, 97008.

Copies: Bod Godwyn Pamph 1737 (13); NUC CtY, InU, MiU-C, NHi, RPJCB.

Quatrains, alternating rhymes. Praise of the prospective Rockingham ministry which should effect peace and union with America and bring prosperity and plenty to Britain through trade. The Minority, "Britain's faithful sons," had tried for long to bring peace to the "divided land," and now at last as Conway pleads for an end to the impious American War, even the king should be convinced of the need to end it. Britain was responsible for the Franco-American alliance, but now she must have a genuine reconciliation with "the infant state" to weaken its bonds with France. Britain should stop the war, restore domestic peace, be repentant of her crime, and America should pardon her. After all, Britain must be reconciled to America--"A brave, a guiltless, an industrious race/ Who sought like her with freedom to be blest." Venal influence and corruption will no longer prevail; Britain will regain her power, as America will resume trade. Keppel and Conway will spurn coward Sackville, who cared nothing for freedom. America will "unite with England to chastise its foes." The poet concludes with praise of Henry Seymour Conway (whose motion to stop offensive warfare against the colonies and to concentrate on Britain's European enemies was carried February 27, 1782--and adopted as the theme of the poem).

Incidentally, the poet objects to the use of German mercenary troops.

82-28. A Versification Of Sir Jeffery Dunstan's Most Gracious And Sentimental Speech To The Lords and Commons Of Garrat-Green, On Thursday the 5th of December, 1782.
London: Debrett, 1782. 17p.

"My Knights and Gentlemen,/ Since the close of last Session I've bustled like mad." (c. 120)

Notices: CR 56 (Dec 1782), 478; MR 67 (Dec 1782), 471.

Copies: BL 8133.g.17; NUC DFo.

Anapest tetrameter. Ironic satire of the King's speech to Parliament. Sir Jeffery is a mask for King George. A few topics are briefly discussed ironically, indicating action taken by the King (upon counsel from his ministers): peace with America, economic measures, compensation for the loyalists, the public debt, the high price of bread, Irish free trade. The King is made to declare that his empire will remain intact, but then he admits that "this dear Separation" from America should please everyone because "I consulted your Wishes. . . . For, good Heav'ns! if otherwise, what a Disgrace!" (p. 8) (Sir Jeffery is a historical person, but a mock knight. See Critical Review 56 [April 1784], 314, and the DNB for further details.)

82-29. [Wesley, Charles]
Hymns For The Nation, In 1782.
London: Paramore, 1781. 24p.

I. After The Defeat At The Chesapeak. "The Lord, th'almighty Lord of hosts." (36)

II. For The Loyal Americans. "Father of everlasting love." (48)

III.  "By whom, O God, shall Britain rise."  (48)

VII.  For Concord.  "Divided 'gainst itself so long."  (40)

VIII.  A Prayer For The Congress.  "True is the Oracle Divine."  (32)

IX.  Thy Kingdom Come!  "Jesus supreme in majesty."  (32)

XII.  For The Conversion Of The French.  "Supreme, immortal Potentate."  (48)

Sabin 102677-8-9.

Copies:  NUC  MB, MH, PHi, PPL.

Seventeen hymns, at least seven of which relate to the American Revolution.  These are hymns written for the crisis when Britain, alone, faced hostile nations.  Wesley declaims against "factious demagogues," "fawning sycophants," "rebellious sects," "parricides."  As the war draws to an end, he prays that God will miraculously transform the evil of "perjured parricides," the Americans, into good (Hymn XII).
   I.  Wesley reacts bitterly to Cornwallis's defeat at Yorktown.  The Lord was pleased to bless rebellion's cause, "And crown the wicked with success."
   II.  He prays for the deserted American loyalists whom the English have betrayed.  They may be murdered by the Americans, "remorseless fiends."  He detests the American alliance with the French, "those murderers of fanatic Rome."
   III.  He prays that Britain rise again when a political chief will unselfishly serve "his king's and God's designs,/ America and Britain joins,/ And blends them in his breast."
   VII.  The Americans "blindly serve the treacherous ends/ Of tyranny and Rome," the French.  He prays for the end of fratricidal war and for close friendship between America and Britain.
   VIII.  He damns the Satanic Americans and hopes God will punish them for their terrible sins, the spilling of "rivers . . . of guiltless blood."
   IX.  Eventually, he knows, God will mysteriously transform the American rebellion into good.  The American "rage for power, their fury blind/ Hastens the coming of our Lord."
   XII.  He urges his countrymen to arm against "the common foe," the treacherous French--liars, hypocrites, false corrupters, lustful slaves, papists.
   A 2nd ed includes this and the following work under the title of Hymns For The Nation, In 1782, In Two Parts (London:  Paramore, 1782).


82-30.  [-----]
Hymns For The National Fast, Feb. 8, 1782.
London:  Paramore, [1782].  24p.

II.  "God of tremendous power."  (56)

III.  "Thou awful God of righteousness."  (60)

IV. Habakkuk I. "How long to Thee, O God, shall I." (60)

X. "Can the disciples of our Lord." (40)

XI. "Lord of Hosts, and God most high." (80)

XIII. "Jesus Thy flaming eyes." (48)

XIV. For Peace. "Come thou choicest gift of heaven." (32)

Copies: BL 3437.e.39; NUC MH, NN, PHi, PPL.

Fifteen hymns, seven of which are relevant to the theme of this bibliography. Wesley here asks Britons in their misery to atone for their sins and seek guidance out of the morass into which they were led by their rulers.
  II. A complaint at the factions tearing apart the country, factious traitors who are "Rebellion's sworn allies." These calumniating parricides fire up "th'unthinking people," who are "mad with rage of liberty/ To do whate'er they will."
  III. A complaint at the defeats abroad by the enemy, "the dismember'd empire," the rebel and French "yoke" on America, the torment of the loyalists ("our friends in pieces torn"), the discord dividing the nation, the factious traitors (the Minority) who are "Rebellion's friends," bringing "Wild, independent anarchy" that presages "a nation's fall."
  IV. A complaint at the Franco-American alliance, especially at the French who "like hungry wolves" will "rend and tear America oppress'd."
  X. A complaint at the subversive parricides who are destroying the country, the factious Minority, "friends of Gaul" who "triumph in their Country's fall." Wesley would have the present ministry treat these internal enemies firmly. "Nor suffer Rebels to despise/ Their mild, irresolute lenity!"
  XI. He alludes to the military conduct of General Sir William Howe (whom he identifies in two footnotes) who, because he betrayed his trust, led to "a sad reverse," the failure of Cornwallis at Yorktown, "this last tremendous blow." His idea in this hymn is that God is responsible for these terrible reverses. Britons are mistaken in trusting entirely to themselves and neglecting God. Even though they had such huge forces in America, they failed, because in their pride they were godless.
  XIII. He complains of the Franco-American alliance, satanic Congress, rebel traitors, and their victory. He asks God for revenge and then he asks for an eternal union of "loyal Britons," "In strictest bonds fraternal join'd," "America and Britain, One."
  XIV. Wesley prays that God bring peace, "End this dire intestine war," reconcile "all the British race," restore "Concord" to Americans, and "Melt our hatred into love."

82-31. [Wolcot, John]
Lyric Odes, To The Royal Academicians, For MDCCLXXXII. By Peter Pindar, Esq. A Distant Relation To The Poet Of Thebes.
London: Egerton et al., 1782. 12p.

Ode 1. "My cousin Pindar in his Odes." (42)

Notices: CR 54 (Jul 1782), 71-2; MR 67 (Oct 1782), 308-9.

Copies: BL 11630.c.11 (10), 11632.g.83 (1st ed); NUC CtY, MH, & TxU (1st ed), CtY, TxU (2nd ed).

2nd ed 1784; 8 eds by 1787. Regular Horatian ode in sixains. Wolcot singles out for comment Sir Joshua Reynolds' portrait of Tarleton--"Lo! Tarleton dragging on his boot so tight!/ His horses feel a godlike rage,/ And long with Yankies to engage--/ I think I hear them snorting for the fight!" These remarks suggest a connection with Mrs. Robinson's praise of Tarleton's valor: see 82-21. (8 odes in this collection.)

Serials

82-32. An Acrostic. [General Conway.]

"G ive him who merits praise his just reward." (13)

GA, Mar 19, 1782.

HC. Praise for Conway on his motion to end the American War (February 27, 1782).

82-33. An Acrostic. [Lord Viscount Howe.]

"L ament ye Spaniards, grieve ye abject Gauls." (16)

PA, Nov 29, 1782.

HC. Sir Richard Howe, with his little fleet, repelled the Spaniards. (Admiral Howe relieved Gibraltar, October 11-19, 1782.)

82-34. An Acrostic. [Rodney.]

"R eign long, great Rodney! conqu'ror of the main." (6)

MH, May 23, 1782.

HC. Acrostic on Rodney, who is praised for triumphing over France and Spain.

82-35. An Address of Congratulation, humbly attempted on the Arrival of Lord Rawdon and Lord Cornwallis, from America.

"From scenes of enterprize, mid wars alarms." (48)

M Chron, Feb 5, 1782.

HC. Praise of Francis Rawdon, who served bravely under Clinton and Cornwallis. The poet applauds both officers, despite the defeat at Yorktown.

82-36. An Address to the Real Sons of Britain. On the Present Prospect of National Affairs.

"Europe, O Britons! trembles for your fate." (32)

G Eve Post, Sep 26, 1782.

Quatrains. France is responsible for Britain's problems -- especially with the Americans -- and united Britain should make her bleed.

82-37. Addressed to Lord S[helbur]ne.

"The Cloud is burst, behold a clearer Sky." (70)

PA, Mar 30, 1782.

HC. Causidicus again urges unity and praises Shelburne, who will restore British glory as it once was under Pitt.

82-38. [All hail the Day, the sacred Day.] The following Song was sung . . . at . . . the Anniversary Meeting of the Revolution Society.

"All hail the Day, the sacred Day." (26)

GA, Nov 7, 1782.

Song commemorates King "William's natal day" and honors "The Great Nassau" for banishing James II, a "tyrannic" prince, to France, thereby saving English liberty.

82-39. Allegory on the American War.

"Each morning the fire Betsy lights." (12)

GA, Nov 5, 1782.

OC. The American War "is all about a dish of Tea."

82-40. The Alliance; or, The Praises of Harwich Camp. A Soldier's Song. To the Tune of "The Men of Kent."

"When Harwich Camp was form'd, and Kent and York did meet." (54)

G Eve Post, Aug 13, 1782.

A song about the new Harwich Camp in Kent for Kentish and Yorkshire men -- for the defence of the country against a possible invasion by France. A bland and almost meaningless lyric: e.g., "We love our Majors, Captains, Lieutenants, Ensigns too -- / Nor wou'd forget our Chaplains."

82-41. America to Britannia. Britannia to America.

"Parent of distant Climes to thee we send." (48)

PA, Oct 26, 1782.

HC. Two inter-related poems. America begs for mercy; and Britain, after attempting to crush horrid and disloyal rebellion, now sheds a tear for America and accepts peace, so that Britain and America can be "In Concord joined."

82-42. Another Votum Turpissimum. [Another Most Scandalous Wish.]

"Let Britain make an abject peace." (10)

MP, Dec 4, 1782.

OC. Satire on Fox and his forces who, despite the crisis facing the nation, will do anything to achieve power -- i.e., "storm the throne, / And force [their] party into places."

82-43. An Argument for Prosecuting the American War.

"Twice has the Monarch been let blood." (6)

St J's C, Jan 22, 1782; West M 10 (Jan 1782), 47.

OC. Epigram. Ironic satire on North, who is "bleeding" the nation with terrific losses like those at Saratoga and Yorktown.

82-44. [As late the muse in silent sorrow sat.]

"As late the muse in silent sorrow sat." (51)

Freeman's J, Aug 22, 1782.

HC. Praise of Henry Flood, but criticism of Henry Grattan -- Ireland's freedom being the issue.

82-45. Ballad intended to be sung in the Burlesque Interlude, called, The Relief of Gibraltar.

"Ye friends of old England, attend to my song." (36)

W Eve Post, Nov 12, 1782.

Ballad. On the successful defence of Gibraltar by Gen. Elliot and Admiral Howe against the Spanish forces.

82-46. A Ballad. (Occasioned by an account in the Brussels Gazette that the British arms had been entirely defeated in the West Indies.) Tune, -- Derry down, &c.

"As over the water King Lewis Baboon." (50)

Cumb Pacq, Jun 25, 1782; W Eve Post, Jun 8, 1782.

Satiric ballad narrates the effect on the French King of the false news that De Grasse had defeated Rodney in the West Indies -- but the truth will out.

82-47. Bobadil No Boaster: Or, Nothing's Impossible to British Courage.

"No more the Plan of Bobadil." (12)

PA, Oct 5, 1782.

Quatrains. With his little band of men, Elliott is defying the powers of France and Spain on besieged Gibraltar.

82-48. Britannia Rules the Waves.

"Plac'd in this wave fenc'd Spot by Heaven's great Law." (58)

PA, Jun 22, 1782.

HC. Causidicus declares that Rodney has redeemed Britain's honor. Britain is again Europe's balance and the mistress of the seas. Shelburne is following Pitt's standard, just as Rodney and Howe follow Hawke and Boscawen.

82-49. Britannia to General Elliott, Governor of Gibraltar.

"Hail, my brave Elliott! -- from her sea-girt isles." (14)

G, Oct 24, 1782.

HC. Praise of brave General Elliott, whose forces have withstood a massive attack by the French and Spanish forces (September 13, 1782).

82-50. Britannia Triumphant. Tune, -- "British Grenadiers."

"Ye gallant bold Hibernians come listen to my lay." (48)

HM 12 (Jul 1782), 384.

Song. A ballad that narrates the details of Rodney's great victory over the French, April 12, 1782. Concludes with remarks on the Irish who, having accomplished their reforms, will assist the English in the struggle: "Britannia's cause is ours."

82-51. The British Soldier's Song of Defiance.

"In the cause of religion and liberty arm'd." (42)

T&C 14 (Sep 1782), 479-80.

An anti-Gallican war song.

82-52. British Valour; An Epigram.

"Our ancient Britons, who disdain'd to fly." (4)

GA, Feb 2, 1782.

HC. Unlike ancient Britons who died rather than surrender, contemporary Britons timidly surrender. (This epigram alludes to the last great defeat at Yorktown.)

82-53. [Britons lament, since Rockingham's no more.]

"Britons lament, since Rockingham's no more." (14)

GA, Jul 4, 1782.

HC. Let us mourn for Rockingham, who has just died, July 1, 1782: he labored to stop the American War; he was a noble person.

82-54. [Britons rejoice -- for, lo! th'important Hour.]

"Britons rejoice -- for, lo! th'important Hour." (22)

PA, Mar 29, 1782.

HC. An expression of hope for the political future. The patriots will unite "To realize again the glorious Fifty-nine."

82-55. Burgoyne, John.
Prologue to the Tragedy of Zara. (By General Burgoyne.) Spoken by Lord Rawdon, at Boston. (Never yet published.)

"In Britain once, (it stains th'historic page)." (30)

GA, Sep 2, 1782; G Eve Post, Aug 31, 1782; Lloyd's 51 (Sep 2, 1782), 228; M Chron, Sep 2, 1782; MH, Sep 3, 1782; PA, Sep 2, 1782; St J's C, Aug 31, 1782; W Eve Post, Aug 31, 1782; also L Chron 52 (Aug 31, 1782), 223.

HC. An earlier text of this prologue, published in April 1776, has six more lines than this 1782 version, as well as other variations. But the relevant remarks on the ruinous effect of Cromwell and Puritanism ("the bigots' roar") upon the theatre remain the same. See Burgoyne, 76-77.
There must be some connection between the publication of these lines now and Burgoyne's appointment as commander-in-chief in Ireland by the Rockingham administration.

82-56. Bushy Park: Or Lord North's Soliloquy.

"From Seas of variegated Strife." (24)

MH, Apr 6, 1782; PA, Apr 5, 1780.

Regular (Horatian) ode in sixains. North soliloquizes on the non-political natural pleasures of retirement at his country home, Bushey Park (near Twickenham, London).

82-57. Candid Advice to a Certain Great Man.

"Appease with Sacrifice old Ocean's God."  (32)

PA, Apr 16, 1782.

HC. Causidicus advises "some great Knave" to sacrifice himself for the good of the country, and to "Redeem whole Years of Shame."  (Is it Sandwich? Causidicus is not clear.)

[Cartwright, Edmund.] Sonnet to Richmond; An Ode to the Earl of Effingham, On his Going a Volunteer to the Relief of Gibraltar.  West M 10 (Nov 1782), 605, & (Dec 1782), 662-3.  See Cartwright, 83-5.

82-58. Caution to M[iniste]rs.

"'Tis said that Walpole, bound like hair in Locket."  (12)

PA, Mar 1, 1782.

HC. Epigram. North, like all ministers, should control his temper if slandered.

82-59. Character of a Minister's Myrmidon, from Mr. [Denis?] O'Bryen's Imitation of Juvenal.

"There is a lesser thing, as sadly known."  (40)

MP, Mar 29, 1782.

HC. Imitation of Juvenal. Satire on a loyal but corrupt supporter of the North ministry, who comes to Parliament only to vote. Cited are Grey Cooper, Fox, Burke, Mansfield (Murray), and Pitt.

82-60. The Choice: To the Minden Hero.

"When opposition against power prevail'd."  (6)

GA, Mar 30, 1782.

HC. Satire on Germain. Despite his elevation to the peerage, Germain (now Viscount Sackville) deserves to die by the axe, if not by the gibbet.

82-61. The Christmas Recess.

"The Doors are clos'd; heard ye the Sound."  (32)

PA, Dec 28, 1782; W Eve Post, Dec 26, 1782.

Quatrains. Parliament goes into recess for the Christmas season, and each politician goes home to feast -- North, Fox, and Burke -- secure in the knowledge that no transatlantic enemies can rob him of his beef. "Hostilities at last shall cease."

82-62. [Come, come Britons, rouse.]

"Come, come Britons, rouse." (16)

M Chron, Aug 22, 1782.

Quatrains. A generalized, patriotic lyric. Britain should defy all her foes.

82-63. [Come, generous Britons, let's rejoice.]

"Come, generous Britons, let's rejoice." (42)

M Chron, Dec 28, 1782.

A song (tune not given) in praise of Rodney for his great victory over De Grasse in the West Indies, April 12, 1782.

82-64. [Come rouse up, bold Britons.]

"Come rouse up, bold Britons." (16)

M Chron, Sep 27, 1782; MP, Sep 23, 1782.

Quatrains. Patriotic verses. The British under Elliot defy the Spanish at Gibraltar.

82-65. The Contrast. Addressed to the First Lord of the Treasury.

"North had Honour and Wit -- lov'd, respected, he fell." (4)

MH, Jul 20, 1782; St J's C, Jul 23, 1782.

Epigram. Hexameter couplets. Satire on Shelburne, who is said to be inferior to North as premier.

82-66. The Court Dance.

"They first lead up, then turn about." (6)

GA, Sep 3, 1782; MH, May 27, 1784.

Epigram. Sixain. There is always someone behind the curtain, pulling the strings, no matter who is in or out. See 66-35.

82-67. A Courtly Answer to a Common Request.

"As near to my Heart, as the Church to the Steeple." (6)

L Cour, Mar 4, 1782.

Hexameter couplets. Satire on the King for obstinately maintaining his policy of waging "permanent War" against America in order to achieve "permanent Peace."

82-68. Cowper, William.
On the Loss of the Royal George. Written when the News Arrived.

"Toll for the brave." (36)

Three twelve-line stanzas. The warship sank August 28, 1782. A Latin version, "In Submersionem Navigii Cui Georgius Regale Nomen Inditum," was published in PA, Aug 23, 1783. Both poems were included in a letter to Unwin, July 1783. See Cowper Poetical Works, eds. H. S. Milford & Norma Russell (London: Oxford University Press, 1971), pp. 344-5, 668.

Craven, Elizabeth. Ode, Addressed to General Arnold. See 82-212.

82-69. [Cumberland, Richard.]
Epilogue to the Walloons. By the Author.

"Now men are scarce, and these wide wasting wars." (38)

AR 1782, pp. 201-2; Lady's M 13 (Apr 1782), 215; Lloyd's 50 (Apr 24, 1782), 396; L Cour, Apr 25, 1782; M Chron, Apr 26, 1782; MH, Apr 25, 1782; MP, Apr 25, 1782; PA, Apr 24, 1782; St J's C, Apr 23, 1782; W Eve Post, Apr 23, 1782; also L Chron 51 (May 2, 1782), 431.

HC. The patriot women, "female volunteers," join the navy because the war has depleted the men, and express conventional sentiments on the French, Spaniards, Dutch, and Americans. The last are asked to break with France and return, "and prove / A mother's pardon, and a sister's love."

82-70. The Day after the Fast.

"Reflection! for a Moment come." (24)

PA, Feb 9, 1782; W Eve Post, Feb 7, 1782.

Quatrains. The poet reflects on Fast-Day prayers and questions the motives behind them. He asks if the cause is justice in the American War.

82-71. Deborah Sweep-House lately brushed out of a dark closet a small scroll of Latin which she humbly offers to the public; with a free Translation. . . .

"Descriptio status Britanniae." (6) "Traveller stop -- pray -- why so fast!" (44)

L Eve Post, Feb 9, 1782.

OC. A reaction to the Yorktown defeat and a satire on the times. The ministers still keep their places, despite the coming of the end; the senate is corrupt; the county associations are noisy debating societies; the nobility and clergy are mean and worthless; the generals ineptly carry on the fighting; the times are wretched.

82-72. The Deer and Fawn.

"What Abel Hassen did long since." (12)

G, Mar 12, 1782; PA, Mar 12, 1782.

Quatrains. Britain, the deer, and America, the fawn, in peace will restore commerce and prosperity.

82-73. Description of a Modern Orator.

"'Tis a talking, prating Sir." (20)

MP, Nov 15, 1782.

Hudibrastics. Satire on Fox as a selfish opportunistic politician, completely cold, cunning, and treacherous.

82-74. Description of a Monument erected in Westminster Abbey, for Major John Andre, designed by Robert Adam, Esq. . . . This Monument is composed of a Sarcophagus, elevated on a pedestal, upon the pannel of which is engraved the following inscription:

"Sacred to the Memory / of Major John Andre." (c. 10)

B&BM I:23 (1782), 358-9; GA, Nov 12, 1782; GM 52 (Nov 1782), 514; MP, Nov 12, 1782; UM 71 (Dec 1782), 329; W Misc 19 (Dec 2, 1782), 209; LM 51 (Appendix 1782), 609; L Chron 52 (Nov 9, 1782), 463.

Inscription on the untimely death of Major Andre, October 2, 1780, aged 29. Illustration of the monument in UM 71 (Dec 1782), facing p. 329.

82-75. Description of the State of Britain.

"Stay, Traveller, a little while." (24)

GM 52 (May 1782), 253.

OC. A severe review of the state of affairs in Britain: corruption, a mad senate, "base statesmen" who plunder the country, hireling and useless bishops, the war leaders and generals unfit and corrupt, and cowardly soldiers.

82-76. A Dialogue between K[in]g Pepin and Boreas, on Saturday, March 16, 1782.

"Good morning, friend Boreas, you seem full of thought." (20)

GA, Mar 20, 1782.

Hexameter couplets. The King and Lord North converse, North communicating his fears should he be voted out of his office. He fears execution.

82-77. Dramatic Intelligence Extraordinary. Edmund, Volpone, and Roderigo.

"Volpone. Welcome, good Roderigo; we wanted much." (50)

MP, Nov 12, 1782.

Blank verse mini-play. A satire on Fox and Burke for their scheming politics now that they are out of office. They appear to be making use of the Duke of Portland as a dupe, after the death of Rockingham, their old leader. Shelburne opposes them.

82-78. The Drunken Crew. Verses addressed to all Parties.

"The Ship's at Sea, tremendous lours the Storm." (14)

PA, Feb 23, 1782.

HC. Causidicus satirizes the North ministry in this time of crisis, for quarrelling among themselves.

82-79. Dulce et decorum est pro patria mori.

"Though Gallia's proud, insulting Sons afar." (30)

St J's C, Nov 9, 1782.

HC. Patriotic lines assert Britain's superiority over France and Spain.

82-80. Dulce et Decorum est Pro Patria Mori.

"'Tis done: -- Lo! haughty France hath felt the Blow." (60)

PA, Jun 1, 1782.

HC. Causidicus glows with pride for Admiral Rodney because of his inspiring victory over the French fleet in the Battle of the Saints, April 12, 1782. He calls for unity (again) in the struggle alone and unallied against France, Spain, and Holland.

82-81. Dutch Sincerity.

"Let base Amboyna be forgot." (24)

PA, Feb 23, 1782.

Quatrains. Let us not, after the Amboyna massacre (of English merchants, 1623), overlook Dutch insulting perfidy. Holland must be crushed.


82-82. Ecce, Britannia cadit!

"When Chatham held the ruling Rein." (12)

PA, Feb 23, 1782.

Sixains. When Chatham ruled and Ferdinand and Hawke defeated the enemy, the country gloried in victory; but now, should North and Sandwich still rule, the country faces disaster.


82-83. Cancelled.

An Elegiac Epistle to a Right Honourable Commissioner, from his afflicted Brother, W. E. Esquire, on the very perilous Situation of the Board of Trade, March 14, 1780. "This quill, that whilom with success apply'd." (78) GM 52 (Mar 1782), 133-4. HC. Satire on William Eden and the Board of Trade. Eden's persona complains that the board has been reformed out of existence by "Edmund's myrmidons," so that now he and the other members are deprived of a sinecure. Cited are Burke, Carlisle, Jenyns, Gibbon, and Richard Cumberland (the last being the secretary). A reprint of 80-86.


82-84. An Elegiac Lamentation on the Great National Loss of the Royal George, and her Brave Officers and Seamen.

"Too true, alas! too true the public woe." (36)

GA, Sep 4, 1782.

Elegiac quatrains.


82-85. An Elegy.

"'Twas night -- Britannia melancholy lay." (114)

GA, May 29, 1782; GM 55 (Sep 1785), 733-4.

Sixains in elegiac meter. The reform movement is here associated with the freedom of the separate and independent American colonies and with self-rule for Ireland. Britain must not mourn the loss of America, but give it respect and love for its freedom. Richmond (Lenox), Fox, Sawbridge, John Jebb, John Cartwright, and William Pitt (prematurely) are listed as the reformers. (GM has two additional stanzas.)

82-86. Elegy on Major Andre.

"Such worth, as thine, alas! ill-fated youth." (40)

MP, Aug 9, 1782; T&C 14 (Jul 1782), 382.

Elegiac quatrains. The Americans will be made to pay with horrible war for their cruel murder of Andre. "'Twas lust for vengeance" that made the American rebels commit the "Atrocious deed."

82-87. An Elegy on the Death of Admiral Kempenfelt.

"Now shall the Muse in doleful accents tell." (48)

Cumb Pacq, Oct 8, 1782; L Chron 52 (Sep 28, 1782), 319; L Cour, Sep 28, 1782.

Elegiac stanzas on the tragic sinking of the Royal George, a warship.

82-88. Elegy on the Death of the Marquis of Rockingham.

"To tune the Golden Lyre to softest Strains." (24)

PA, Jul 23, 1782.

Elegiac quatrains. Britain mourns the death of Rockingham, the patriot guardian of the peoples' rights and of the nation against corruption.

82-89. An Elegy. On the much-lamented Death of the most noble and Puissant Prince, Charles Wentworth, Marquis of Rockingham. By Mr. Conway.

"Hail! sacred views!" (30)

GA, Jul 4, 1782.

Pindaric ode. A non-political poem mourning the death of the Patriot, Rockingham. The rhetoric is flat and stale.

82-90. Elliot Triumphant.

"'Which of my sons,' proclaim'd War's God." (30)

G Eve Post, Oct 15, 1782; MP, Oct 12, 1782.

Sixains. Gen. Elliot and his "slender force" fight off the Spanish enemy under Crillon and hold besieged Gibraltar for the English.

82-91. [English, Robert.]
The Invocation. A Poem. By the Author of the Naval Review.

"On balmy plumes, blest harmony! Advance." (26)

GA, May 1, 1782; L Cour, Apr 29, 1782.

HC. The poet invokes Harmony (unanimity) to bring an end to civil war, the fratricidal war, and faction, so that a united Britain can face its enemies. Keppel will be in the tradition of Boscawen, Anson, Saunders, and Hawke.


82-92. Epigram.

"Britannia's dead, her glory now is o'er." (4)

PA, Feb 21, 1782.

HC. Satire on North, responsible for the death of Britain.


82-93. Epigram.

"How could you, friend B[urk]e, when our hearts are all aking." (6)

M Chron, Dec 9, 1782.

Hexameter couplets. A criticism of Burke for committing the impropriety of ridiculing the King's speech. See "Ridicule No Test of Truth," 82-314.


Epigram. "I'm out, cries Old Twitcher; but when in took such care." (4) W Eve Post, Apr 18, 1782. See "Twitcher's Comfort," 82-377.


82-94. Epigram.

"Ned damns the King's Speech with rank Patriot Hate." (10)

PA, Dec 17, 1782.

HC. Causidicus damns the malcontents, Edmund Burke and others, whom neither God nor King can please.


82-95. Epigram.

"Nobility by Birth's a vain Cockade." (16)

PA, Feb 22, 1782.

HC. Causidicus comments on Germain's elevation to the peerage. He believes that merit makes the man.

82-96. Epigram.

"N[or]th thought a Peace would do no Harm." (8)

PA, Sep 2, 1782.

OC. The peace negotiations progress very slowly, although North, Fox, and Shelburne all agree to the need for peace.

82-97. Epigram.

"Such a liar as _Edmund_ I never came nigh." (2)

MP, Oct 3, 1782.

Hexameter couplet. Satire on Burke as a habitual liar.

82-98. Epigram.

"'Twixt Keppel and Rodney 'tis easy discerning." (4)

MH, Jun 5, 1782.

Quatrain. Rodney, contrasted with Keppel, is a better and braver naval officer.

82-99. Epigram.

"When Charley Todd." (16)

PA, Jan 31, 1782.

Sixains and quatrain. Satire on Fox, who does not attack North because he wants his job as Lord of the Treasury.

82-100. Epigram.

"When G--s--e says, 'The Nation is secure.'" (2)

GA, Jan 26, 1782.

HC. Satire on Bamber Gascoigne (?), a loyal Tory supporter of Government.

82-101. Epigram.

"Whence all this clamour, noise and rout." (12)

GA, May 6, 1782; L Cour, May 2, 1782.

Quatrains. Let us hope that the Opposition, formerly out and now in, will never again be out.

82-102. An Epigram. Addressed to R. B. Sheridan, Esq. On being Appointed Under Secretary of State.

"New Ministers have all resign'd." (6)

GA, Mar 30, 1782.

OC. Sheridan joins the new Rockingham ministry and leaves the theater.

82-103. Epigram. Another.

"Who vainly craves for Peace, when Brunswick's Star." (4)

"Now Britain, boast thy ruling Star." (6)

GA, Jul 6, 1782.

HC. Sixain. Two epigrams on the turn in English fortunes, now that Keppel is Secretary of the Navy and Admirals Rodney and Howe are triumphant. England need not sue for peace with France.

82-104. Epigram. Applicable to the Present Times.

"Of Outs and Ins, the common sins." (8)

MP, Jul 19, 1782.

Quatrains. Comment on the situation after the death of Rockingham. Both outs and ins have one object -- maladministration and robbing the nation. The best plan for good government is to choose a few from each sort to rule.

82-105. Epigram. From the Edinburgh Gazette, 1757.

"When Samson full of wrath devis'd." (8)

L Eve Post, Jul 11, 1782.

Quatrains. Charles James Fox outdoes his father and Samson in destroying a nation, complains Lord North.

82-106. Epigram On Admiral Rodney's Not Fighting the French Fleet off Tobago.

"When great Sir George was poor, why then." (8)

Cumb Pacq, Mar 26, 1782.

Octave. Satire on Rodney. Now that Rodney is rich with the spoils of successful war, he does not fight the French. (From "The Jamaica Gazette of the 19th of January.")

82-107. Epigram on General Elliott's burning the Spanish Floating-Batteries that attacked the Fortress of Gibraltar.

"When floating batt'ries ceas'd to float." (8)

GA, Oct 21, 1782; W Misc 19 (Oct 28, 1782), 96.

Quatrains in OC. Gen. Elliott humanely orders that drowning Spaniards, who failed in their grand attack on Gibraltar, be saved (September 13, 1782).

82-108. Epigram on the British Lion.

"Our Lion once did roar, and look'd so grim." (4)

GA, Jan 21, 1782.

HC. As long as Sandwich and Germain continue in office, Britain will be timid and weak.

Epigram on the Burning of the Gun Boats. See "Epigram on General Elliott's burning the Spanish Floating-Batteries," 82-107.

82-109. Epigram. On the Present Administration.

"When Ministers devis'd the State to save." (4)

MH, May 31, 1782.

HC. The present ministry undermines the state by ordering the recall of Rodney, "the Conqu'ring Hero." (Rodney's seizure of St. Eustatia was considered questionable.)

82-110. Epigram on the Recapture of St. Eustatius. Addressed to the gallant and respectable Commanders who had the Honour of taking it. . . .

"Murder awakes God's wrath -- and who can wonder." (2)

L Cour, Jan 16, 1782.

HC. Rodney and Vaughan captured and plundered Dutch St. Eustatius. The French recaptured it, November 27, 1781.

82-111. Epigram. On the Report of Lord Howe Having Retreated from the Combined Fleet.

"The Frenchman cries, 'Ve beat de English now.'" (2)

Cal Merc, Jul 31, 1782.

HC. The British cannot believe that Admiral Richard Howe was defeated by the French.


82-112. Epigram. The Two Buckets in the Well.

"F[ox] calls the M[iniste]r a specious Cheat." (12)

PA, Feb 27, 1782.

HC. Ironic satire on Fox and North. They abuse each other, and both may be right.


82-113. Epigrams. On the Productiveness of Lord North's Taxes. On the Lord Advocate's Recommending a Coalition of Parties. On Lord Surrey's Intended Motion: To Prevent which Lord North Resigned.

"Who says that your Taxes bring nothing about." (2)

"For Coalition, great Advocate, wisely you plead." (2)

"Adjourn, says North, to save Disgrace." (4)

PA, Jul 4, 1782.

Three epigrams comment on taxes and the excitement generated by Lord North's resignation. (North resigned March 20, 1782. The Lord Advocate is Henry Dundas.)


82-114. Epigrams. To Lord North on his Majority of Nine against Dismission. On Lord North's Not Resigning from a Motive of Honour. On Lord North's Not Resigning out of Gratitude.

"What, Corruption's Majority dwindled to nine." (4)

"Quoth the Premier, 'My Honour forbids to resign.'" (4)

"Great Minister, you're wond'rous good." (6)

PA, Jul 2, 1782.

Three satiric epigrams on North, in effect urging the premier's resignation.


Epilogue to the Walloons. By the Author. See Richard Cumberland, 82-69.


Epitaph. "Here lies the body of / BEN FRANKLIN, / Printer." GA, Oct 14, 1782. Franklin compares himself to an old book -- after death, he will be published in a new edition. See "Epitaph on a Printer of Boston," 71-30, an earlier printing.

82-115. An Epitaph.

"Peace to his shade! Here Rockingham! Oh woe." (22)

GA, Jul 8, 1782.

HC. Grenville (Earl Temple) and Rockingham have died this year. No more will incorruptible, freedom-loving Whigs be led by Rockingham. (Temple died in 1779!)

[Epitaph of John Bradshaw.] W Misc 18 (Jul 8, 1782), 343-4. See 80-115.

82-116. Epitaph intended for Lord Barebones.

"Beneath this dirty spot, where thistles shoot." (16)

GA, Apr 20, 1782.

HC. Satire on John, Earl of Bute, whose counsels have caused much trouble for Britain. He is now dead and (presumably) will go to hell. (Bute actually died in 1792.)

82-117. An Epitaph on the Late Ministry.

"Laid Sprites! / -- Fates only mourn. / -- Dark Rites!" (c. 20)

GA, Apr 17, 1782.

Inscription. An expression of hope for a reconciliation with America, while Keppel "shall awe proud France and Spain."

82-118. Esto Perpetua. [May She Endure Forever.]

"Patriots of old, bold, resolute, and free." (4)

MH, Dec 20, 1782.

HC. Satire on the present "patriots" who, unlike genuine patriots of the past, betray the "dearest rights" of the British empire. A protest at the peace negotiations.

82-119. Extempore.

"When Princes and Peers, in a frolicksome Rout." (8)

PA, Feb 7, 1782.

Quatrains. France would gain, should Britain destroy America.

82-120. An Extempore.

"Who ever heard of Fox and Geese." (16)

MH, Apr 16, 1782.

Extempore quatrains. Satire on Charles James Fox, compared with Guy Faux, the incendiary.

82-121. Extempore. On a Scandalously Stupid Contest.

"Britain! take heed! Steer clear, 'tween two black rocks." (2)

MH, Jul 30, 1782.

HC. Satire on the competition for priority in the government between Shelburne and Fox, who are both equally dangerous.

82-122. Extempore, on seeing his Majesty going from the Queen's Palace to St. James's, amidst the Acclamations of his Subjects.

"Who dares insult, when loyal Britons raise." (8)

Lloyd's 51 (Jun 28, 1782), 4.

HC. So long as Britain is united under the respected King, she will triumph over her foes.

82-123. Extempore. On Sir George Rodney's Recall.

"To sap the edifice of state." (4)

MH, May 30, 1782.

Quatrain. The "Patriots," now the Government, are blamed for weakening the state by recalling Rodney. (Rodney's conduct regarding the seizure of St. Eustatius was subject to criticism.)

82-124. Extempore. On the Siege of Gibraltar.

"Ten Grecian Chiefs did 'fore Old Troy advance." (8)

GA, Aug 27, 1782.

HC. Britain has defended Gibraltar successfully and will continue to guard the Straits.

82-125. An Extraordinary Letter, in a Late Extraordinary Gazette, Versified.

"Believe me, Dear Stephen's, I'll tell you the Whole." (60)

PA, Nov 15, 1782.

Ballad narrative of the siege of Gibraltar by the Spaniards and the successful resistance of the British under Elliott, in a letter to the secretary of the Admiralty.

82-126. The Fall of Albion.

"Traitors we have -- too well all Europe knows." (22)

MP, Mar 15, 1782.

Irregular meter, couplets. England dies, but none of the Patriots wish to die with her, all of them really traitors -- Burgoyne, Camden, Shelburne. No one can be crowned with renown by Gibbon. Such is the fall of England -- a tragedy without a noble tragic hero!

82-127. A Familiar Epistle, paraphrased from Horace, and Addressed to my Friend, Joe D-----.

"Good friend, be ca'm. Why shouldst thou fret." (150)

PA, Oct 7, 1782; An Asylum for Fugitive Pieces, in Prose and Verse (London: Debrett, 1785), I, 160-8.

Regular (Horatian) ode in sixains. Imitation of Horace on the theme of Carpe Diem. The first few stanzas allude lightly to the political and military situation of (perhaps) 1779-80, North and taxes, the naval war, and the war in America and Arnold.

82-128. The Fast.

"When modern Wars all Transatlantic." (20)

L Cour, Feb 8, 1782; MH, Feb 8, 1782; PA, Feb 7, 1782; W Eve Post, Feb 5, 1782.

Quatrains. A Fast Day poem, February 8, 1782; and a satire on the situation. The American War is a crime, and it now requires sincere repentance.

82-129. The Fast. [And Answer.]

"In the midst of our shame." (6 + 12)

GA, Feb 7 & 9, 1782; LP, Feb 4 & 7, 1782.

Sixains. A Londoner refuses the order to fast on February 8 (the day proclaimed for the National Fast), finding it shameful (possibly alluding to Cornwallis's defeat). But another rejects his reasoning and damns him to hell.

82-130. Fatality!

"Oh! may the Court accept this special Plea." (10)

PA, Feb 13, 1782.

HC. The "King's Friends" or "Cabinet" could never have caused the crisis facing the country. A doomed nation is simply ruined by fate.

82-131. A few Extempore Lines.

"Elliot's name that s'd be dear." (24)

M Chron, Nov 11, 1782.

Quatrains, in praise of Gen. Elliot, as well as Howe, for saving Gibraltar.

82-132. The First Ode of the First Book of Horace, Applied to the Right Hon. C. J. F.

"O! F[ox] descended from a noble Race." (24)

PA, Apr 22, 1782.

HC. Imitation of Horace. In praise of Fox, "Prince of Orators," for saving England.

82-133. The Following Address spoken by Miss Kirby . . . previous to her leaving the Theatre Royal, Edinburgh.

"If verse be fiction, it ill suits the heart." (43)

Cal Merc, May 8, 1782; PA, Aug 2, 1782.

HC. Praise of two Scottish heroes of the American War -- Simon Frazer and John Maitland -- and a hope for peace to end the civil discord.

82-134. The following Lines are the production of a Young Genius, and his first Essay.

"Ingratitude thy baneful influence own." (48)

M Chron, Sep 18, 1782; PA, Sep 20, 1782.

HC. Satire on Burke and Fox of the new administration -- for their hypocrisy.

82-135. The following Lines were occasioned by the Author's reading in the London Courant that General -------, and the Troops under his Command . . . rendered essential Services to the distressed Inhabitants of B------. . . .

"****** did his duty well perform." (24)

L Cour, Jan 7, 1782.

Sixains. Tarleton (?) behaved humanely after a hurricane in the West Indies, but cruelly in America. Germain is cited.

82-136. The following Lines were written by a young Lady at Table after Dinner, and sung to the Tune of Nancy Dawson, with great Applause.

"Of all the Lords in London town." (24)

Cumb Pacq, Mar 26, 1782; L Cour, Mar 15, 1782.

Song. Ironic satire on Germain and James Cockburn, both honored for cowardice: at Minden and at St. Eustatia. (Cockburn was governor of St. Eustatia in 1781 when it was captured by the French. He was accused of mismanagement, court-martialed, and cashiered in 1783.)

The following Lines were wrote with charcoal, on the walls of the new gaol in Philadelphia. . . . See 76-162.

82-137. For the Political Tomb-Stone of a Dissolving M[inistr]y.

"Here lies contemn'd." (6)

PA, Mar 16, 1782.

Epitaph. Sixain. Let us celebrate the death of "A vile Administration"!

82-138. The Fox. A Song.

"When hope seem'd lost in despair." (16)

M Chron, Apr 17, 1782.

"A song" without music! Animal allegory. Quatrains on Fox's miraculous assumption of political leadership.

82-139. Freeth, John.
Britannia. A Song. In Honour of the gallant Rodney. Tune, -- "All shall yield to the Mulberry Tree."

"Behold from afar what glad tidings are brought." (28)

PA, Jun 29, 1782; West M 10 (Jul 1782), 384; also John Freeth, The Political Songster (1790), pp. 45-6.

PA identifies the author as "a Warwickshire Bard." On the stunning victory over De Grasse, April 12, 1782. In Freeth's collection, the title is "Britannia Triumphant! on the Glorious Victory of April 12, 1782."

82-140. [Freeth, John.]
  Britannia's Relief: A Song. On the Change of the Ministry.

  "Long had the vessel of the state." (60)

  L Cour, Apr 18, 1782.

  Song in dixains. Freeth commends the change from North to Rockingham and praises the new administration of Fox, Burke, Shelburne, Barre, Camden, Cavendish, Conway, and Richmond, all former members of Opposition.
    This song was altered in 1783 to adapt to another change: see "The New Administration, in 1783," 83-107.

82-141. Freeth, John.
  The British Salamanders. A Ballad on the Siege of Gibraltar.

  "Old Gib is safe, with care away." (64)

  G Eve Post, Nov 28, 1782; Freeth, The Political Songster (1790), pp. 42-3.

  Ballad celebrates Elliott's successful defense of Gibraltar on September 13, 1782, against the combined Franco-Spanish attack. Captain Curtis's humanity in saving many enemy lives is cited.

82-142. Freeth, John.
  Corruption Defeated: or the Premier Routed. Tune -- "Give round the Word, dismount, dismount."

  "Give round the word, resign, resign." (32)

  Freeth, The Political Songster (1790), pp. 54-5.

  Song. The English should be pleased at North's resignation (March 20, 1782). Now the reform movement can stem corruption, and there can be "A speedy peace, or glorious war," inspired by Chatham and Temple (Richard Temple Grenville), as the Patriots assume power.

82-143. Freeth, John.
  The Georges: or, Lord Sackville's Promotion. Tune, -- Push about the Jorum.

  "Of great and glorious Names to speak." (48)

  L Cour, Mar 12, 1782; Freeth, Modern Songs on Various Subjects (1782), pp. 56-8, The Political Songster (1784), pp. 1-3, and The Political Songster (1790), pp. 52-3.

Song. Satire on Lord George Germain, elevated to the peerage as Viscount Sackville, February 9, 1782. Germain, the Minden hero, has undeservedly been created a peer by King George. Rodney and Vaughan are worthy of elevation, and so (ironically) are Paul Jones and Benedict Arnold!

82-144. Freeth, John.
Song for the British Tars, on the Sailing of Lord Howe's Fleet.

"The Fort to save, the Fleet is gone." (28)

Freeth, The Political Songster (1790), p. 41.

Admiral Howe's fleet has gone to relieve Gibraltar. The patriotism of Lowther, who himself provided a ship of war, fully outfitted, to the nation, should be an inspiration to all Britons, especially the people of Birmingham.

82-145. Freeth, John.
The State Jockeys; or, the Ins and Outs. Tune, -- Caesar and Pompey were both of them horned.

"What a Noise has there been, what a strange Exclamation." (30, 48)

Cumb Pacq, Sep 3, 1782; West M 10 (Aug 1782), 439; Freeth, The Politican Songster (1790), pp. 47-9.

Song. Freeth reviews the political situation after North resigned and Rockingham died, the confusion that broke out as Fox and Shelburne competed for leadership. He deplores the hunger for power and urges that all parties pull together and work towards "Reformation." See 65-59 for the earliest version. But this lyric was printed in many versions, even the one in West M differing from that in the Cumb Pacq.

82-146. [Friday in the morn, April the Twelfth.]

"Friday in the morn, April the Twelfth." (36)

Lloyd's 50 (May 24, 1782), 498; M Chron, May 25, 1782; MP, Nov 26, 1782; PA, May 27, 1782; W Eve Post, May 23, 1782.

An ode or song in nine-line stanzas, one of the earliest to celebrate the great victory of Rodney and Hood over De Grasse in the Battle of the Saints, April 12, 1782. The title in Public Advertiser is "A Parody."

82-147. G[enera]l C[onwa]y's Motion.

"When Conway speaks, what Energy divine." (20)

L Cour, Mar 5, 1782; PA, Mar 2, 1782.

HC. Causidicus praises Henry Seymour Conway's motion to bring the American War to an end.  Now "America and Britain shall unite."  (Conway's motion to end the American War was rejected February 22, 1782;  his second motion was carried February 27, 1782.)

82-148.  [General Greene's Letter to Congress.]

"A Letter which was lately seen."  (78)

M Chron, Jan 11, 1782.

OC, doggerel.  The persona of Gen. Nathaniel Greene describes the Battle of Eutaw Springs, S. C., in which he forced the British back to Charleston (September 8, 1781).

82-149.  The Genius of England.

"Her equal Gifts great Nature kindly sheds."  (4)

PA, Nov 29, 1782.

HC.  Epigram.  Britons are "brawny" but Frenchmen are crafty.  Thus Britain blunders with peace treaties, while France gains.

82-150.  Gentlemen of the House of Commons.

"My People's prosperity, welfare, and ease."  (11)

L Cour, Mar 5, 1782.

Anapest tetrameter couplets.  Ironic satire on the King, whose persona <u>demands</u> that the war against America continue and that taxes be paid to support it.

82-151.  The Ghosts of the French.  To Lord Sandwich.

"Sandwich! deep-whelm'd beneath the wave."  (28)

MH, May 29, 1782.

Quatrains.  Ironic satire on the new administration.  The drowned French complain to Sandwich of Rodney, who is unlike Keppel and who is unaffected by factious patriots.  France has allies in the Patriots, who have forced Sandwich to resign and have recalled Rodney.

82-152.  Gibbons, Thomas.
An Hymn for the Fast, Feb. 8, 1782.

"Almighty God, whose Sway extends."  (64)

PA, Feb 8, 1782.

Quatrains. A penitent prayer for forgiveness for crimes committed -- and for suppression of the "Rebellion."

82-153. Gibraltar Relieved: A Song. Tune "Hark! the loud Drum," &c.

"In days of yore." (39)

G Eve Post, Nov 26, 1782.

Gibraltar, unlike Troy, will never fall to Spain or France -- as Elliot and Howe demonstrate.

82-154. Give us our Rights.

"When Alfred was founding our Glory by Sea." (51)

GA, May 3, 1782.

Song about the need to reform Parliamentary elections and representation: for annual Parliaments and for an extension of the suffrage on the basis of men, not property. The song title is from Major John Cartwright's pamphlet, <u>Give us our Rights! or a Letter to the present electors of Middlesex and the Metropolis, shewing what those rights are: and that . . . Middlesex and the Metropolis are intitled to have fifty members in the Commons House of Parliament</u> (London: Dilly, et al., [1782]).
The fifth stanza alludes to America and to the need for honest representation.

82-155. Good Terms; Addressed to four Great Personages.

"In these days of damn'd party rage." (152)

M Chron, Jan 2, 1782; PA, Jan 4, 1782.

Quatrains. Satire on venality in government, as the poet imagines himself ironically defending some politicians for money. The "four Great Personages" are the King, North, Sandwich, and Germain. Cited are Cornwallis, Burgoyne, "Yankey war," and fasts.

82-156. Hastings, Thomas.
Ode For the Birth-Day of his Royal Highness the Prince of Wales, August 12, 1782.

"Who dares -- tho' ev'n of Patriot name." (32)

GA, Aug 13, 1782; M Chron, Aug 12, 1782; PA, Aug 12, 1782; West M 10 (Aug 1782), 439.

Regular ode in sixteen-line stanzas. Hastings does not wish to give up the American colonies. To do so means "to alienate a George's Royal Right!" Reprinted in W. Sargent, <u>The Loyalist Poetry of the American Revolution</u> (Philadelphia, 1857), pp. 140-41, who derives it from <u>Rivington's</u> (New York) <u>Royal Gazette</u>, November 2, 1782.

82-157. He Don't Fight Fair: An Impromptu on General Elliott's firing red-hot Balls at the Spanish Floating-Batteries, when they attacked the Fortress of Gibraltar.

"When Hawke, the British Neptune, reign'd." (12)

DJ, Oct 24, 1782; G Eve Post, Oct 15, 1782; W Misc 19 (Oct 28, 1782), 96; W Eve Post, Oct 10, 1782.

Quatrains. Gen. Eliott defeated the Spaniards who attacked Gibraltar (September 13, 1782) and is accused by them of fighting unfairly!

Howard, G. E. Wrote Extempore over a Bottle on a Discourse of Ireland's Late Restor'd Rights. See 82-407.

82-158. Imitation of the 2d Epistle of the 1st Book of Horace, modernized.

"The matchless Bard, who sings the War of Troy." (30)

GM 52 (Oct 1782), 494-5; M Chron, Oct 16, 1782; PA, Oct 17, 1782; St J's C, Oct 26, 1782.

HC. This imitation of Horace introduces contemporary politicians -- Conway, Shelburne, and North -- and damns party faction that encourages anarchy.

82-159. Imitation of the Second Ode of the First Book of Horace. Addressed to the Right Hon. Lord Sh[elburn]e.

"Enough of Hail and Snow dire Jove has spent." (42)

PA, May 9, 1782.

HC. Imitation of Horace. Shelburne will call to justice those traitors who had almost ruined the country, "and sneak'd off again."

82-160. Imitation of the Sixth Ode, of the First Book of Horace. Addressed to the Right Hon. Earl Cornwallis.

"In British Verse shall Whitehead sing your Name." (26)

PA, May 30, 1782.

HC. Imitation of Horace. Praise of Cornwallis's martial exploits, which merit Whitehead's laureate verse.

82-161. Impromptu.

"Sages of old allow'd for truth." (12)

L Eve Post, Jan 22, 1782.

Sixains. Despite petitions to the contrary, King George and Lord North stubbornly persevere in the tenets of Bute, thereby ruining the nation.

82-162. Impromptu. Ins and Outs.

"'Mongst Outs and Ins what routs and dins." (4)

MH, Mar 25, 1782.

Quatrain. Damn the competing parties!

82-163. Impromptu. Logic and Morals. Addressed to Lord Shelburne.

"By promises Shelburne can ne'er come to shame." (6)

MH, Jul 24, 1782; W Eve Post, Jul 27, 1782; New Foundling Hospital for Wit (1786), IV, 259.

Hexameter couplets. Shelburne opposes reform and, as a supporter of the King, is more Tory than Tories!

82-164. Impromptu. On Lord Shelburne's acknowledging in his last Speech, the great Talents, and Integrity of Mr. Fox, and Lord John Cavendish.

"Parts, and Virtue to Ca'ndish, and Fox you ascrib'd." (4)

MH, Jul 30, 1782; W Eve Post, Jul 27, 1782.

Quatrain. Satire on Shelburne. Will Barre and Dunning admit your great talents and integrity?

82-165. Impromptu. On Lord Shelburne's appealing to Heaven for the sincerity of his concern, on the death of the Marquis of Rockingham.

"Fitz-Maurice to Heaven appeals for his grief." (4)

MH, Jul 29, 1782; W Eve Post, Jul 27, 1782.

Impromptu. Only in Heaven -- never on earth -- will Shelburne's sincerity concerning his grief over Rockingham's death be believed.

82-166. Impromptu. On Reading Wednesday's Debates in the House of Commons.

"'Tis done! th'unnat'ral Conflict is o'er." (12)

PA, Mar 1, 1782.

Quatrains. The Commons has voted to stop the American War; now France and Span should have no great hopes.

82-167. Impromptu. On Seeing General Arnold again at Court.

"In Wentworth's spendour, Arnold kept his den." (2)

MH, Jul 24, 1782; W Eve Post, Jul 27, 1782; New Foundling Hospital for Wit (1786), IV, 259.

HC. When Rockingham was premier, Arnold kept hidden; but when Shelburne becomes premier, he comes out of his den.

82-168. Impromptu. Physical Necessity. An Apology for Lord Shelburne's having asserted three falsehoods in his last Speech. By Dr. P----.

"Three fibs in one speech! -- Priestley makes the cause plain." (6)

MH, Jul 24, 1782; W Eve Post, Jul 27, 1782.

Hexameter couplets. Satire on Shelburne, through the persona of Priestley, whose patron was Shelburne.

82-169. [In the rich Ruins of a falling State.]

"In the rich Ruins of a falling State." (118)

PA, Mar 26, 1782.

HC. Causidicus calls for the end of "Party's Madness" and for unity under the ministry of Shelburne.

82-170. Innuendo to Both Parties. Jeu D'Esprit.

"The bow-string round her neck, with dying eyes." (6)

MP, Mar 2, 1782; PA, Mar 6, 1782.

Extempore. HC. An objection to destructive party conflict. The two rival parties are choking Britain to death, thereby serving the enemy. By Causidicus of Cirencester.

Inscription for a Column at Runnymeade. PA, Feb 9, 1782. See Capel Lofft, "Runnymede," 82-185.

Inscription [on a Monument for John Andre erected in Westminster Abbey]. B&BM I:23 (1782), 358-9; MP, Nov 12, 1782. See "Description of a Monument . . . " 82-74.

82-171. Io Triumphe! Io Paean!

"Let Britain sing her Song of Joy."  (20)

PA, Mar 2, 1782.

Quatrains.  Let Britain celebrate the peace -- the American War has come to an end! "No more our faithful Brethren we / Shall tread beneath our Feet."

82-172. Jeu D'Esprit.

"The Toast of each Briton in War's dread alarms."  (4)

MH, Nov 16, 1782.

Hexameter couplets.  The British soldiers are brave and fight to win; but the French are cowardly and run away.

82-173. Johnson, Samuel.
Marmor Norfolciense: An Ancient Prophetical Inscription . . . To Posterity.

"Whene'er this Stone now hid beneath the lake."  (26)

L Cour, Jan 4, 1782;  L Eve Post, Jan 8, 1782.

Johnson's poem critical of Sir Robert Walpole is reprinted without comment.

82-174. The Late P[remie]r was very Fond of Declaring in the H[ouse], "That he took the Helm of Affairs in a Turbulent, Tempestuous Time. . . ." -- But how hath he left it?

"North in the Senate said, vain-glorious Plea."  (64)

PA, Apr 19, 1782.

HC.  Causidicus praises the unanimity of the new leaders in bringing the American War to a successful conclusion, which North could not do.  He mentions Shelburne first among these leaders, then Rockingham and others, but he does not mention Fox!  (Clearly, Causidicus favors Shelburne.)
"See! pleas'd America, her Heart expand, / And cordial clasp the peaceful Olive Wand."

82-175. The Levellers.  A Catch.

"Why John, Ralph, Sal! -- Why don't you come?"  (6)

G Eve Post, Jun 15, 1782;  M Chron, Jun 18, 1782;  PA, Jun 17, 1782.

The servants demand equality of status; but the master insists that they must work and he must rule, "lest all should starve."

82-176. Lines addressed to the Honourable William Pitt.

"Success is your's, and gratitude inclines." (18)

L Cour, Jan 15, 1782.

HC. Panegyric on the younger Pitt, who, it is hoped, will surpass his father in fame.

82-177. Lines Inscribed to the Right Hon. Lord North. By a Lady.

"Retir'd from storms by party's clamour rais'd." (28)

M Chron, Apr 3, 1782; PA, Apr 8, 1782.

HC. Praise of North, now retired, for his service to the nation "'gainst Opposition's Tide," despite his failures.

82-178. Lines on the Death of Lord Rockingham.

"Is Wentworth then no more? That peerless Peer." (18)

St J's C, Jul 4, 1782.

HC. An eulogy of the Marquis of Rockingham, lately deceased.

82-179. Lines on the late Melancholy Catastrophe at Spithead.

"With weeping Eyes, that spoke the Grief she bore." (28)

St J's C, Oct 1, 1782.

HC. Neptune consoles Britannia for the tragic loss of the Royal George (which sank August 29, 1782, a large piece of her bottom having suddenly fallen out).

82-180. Lines on the Return of Admiral Rodney from the West-Indies.

"When ancient Rome, the Empress of the World." (36)

M Chron, Sep 26, 1782.

HC. Because of his great success, Rodney must be given a Roman triumph upon his return to England. Rodney saved "Our wretched Empire."

82-181. Lines to Sir James Lowther's Offering a Seventy-Four Gun Ship to his Majesty. Inscribed to the Right Hon. William Pitt.

"The name of Lowther sweet shall be." (16)

GA, Sep 25, 1782.

OC. Panegyric on Lowther, a wealthy landowner in northern England, who has patriotically presented to Britain a naval war ship in return for what the country has done for him.

82-182. Lines to the Lords Rodney and Hood.

"Illustrious pair! to whom 'twas given." (12)

MH, Jun 12, 1782.

Quatrains. Rodney and Hood have restored supremacy on the seas to Britain. Nothing can detract from their achievement.

82-183. Lines to the Memory of Major Pierson.

"When patriots, and friends of human race." (32)

G, Jan 1, 1782.

Quatrains commemorating Pierson, who lost his life repelling the French attack on Jersey, in early January 1781. (The text was too blurred for copying.)

82-184. Lofft, Capel.
A Monody. In Imitation of Aristotle's Ode to Virtue.

"Virtue, whose heaven-beaming eye." (62)

Eur M 2 (Aug 1782), 152.

Unrhymed "free numbers." In praise of public virtue; in effect an attack on corruption and self-interest. Lofft invokes virtue, associating this spirit with freedom and those who sacrificed their lives in the struggle against tyranny: Brutus and the great Whig martyrs, Algernon Sydney and Lord William Russell. Virtue is the "Guardian of Liberty and equal Law."

82-185. Lofft, Capel.
Runnymede.

"Whoe'er thou art, if love of human kind." (39)

Eur M 2 (Dec 1782), 472; PA, Feb 9, 1782.

Blank verse. A tribute to the place associated with Magna Charta and English freedom, where "the Commons, to their right restor'd, / Became indeed a people" and "the equal rule / Of free consent" was certified. A thoroughly Whig poem in its assertion of "the Rights of Men." Lofft also stresses the need for "annual Parliaments."

82-186. [Marjoribanks, J.]
  To the Memory of Major Marjoribanks, late of his Majesty's 19th Regiment of Foot.

  "Unskill'd in verse, I boast no poet's art."  (50)

  L Chron 51 (May 2, 1782), 431;  PA, May 1, 1782;  WM 56 (May 16, 1782), 175.

  HC.  A soldier son pays tribute to his father, killed in the American War, Eutaw Springs, S. C., September 9, 1781.  See 84-9.

82-187.  A Melancholy Case.  Addressed to the Gentlemen of the Faculty.

  "An Irish orator, with words full fraught."  (32)

  MP, Dec 16, 1782.

  Quatrains.  Satire on Burke who, having resigned his post in Administration, now engages in Opposition.

82-188.  Merlin's Prophecy.

  "When Boreas guides the helm of state."  (4)

  GA, Jan 18, 1782.

  Quatrain.  North and Sandwich are unreliable and untrustworthy leaders of the nation. As long as they are in office, the nation is in danger.

82-189.  Ministerial Alliance.

  "Says Sandwich to North, when I fall you can't stand."  (8)

  GA, Jan 29, 1782.

  Hexameter couplets.  Epigram.  North assures Sandwich that he will bag "the Fox."

82-190.  The Minister's Budget.

  "As Pandora threw open her Box."  (8)

  PA, Feb 27, 1782;  W Eve Post, Feb 28, 1782.

  Quatrains.  Because of the heavy taxes called for in the budget, we should end this "sad war."

82-191.  The Moderator;  or Advice to Mechanical Patriots.

  "Of F[o]x or S[hel]b[urn]e, why this rage."  (16)

G, Aug 9, 1782.

Quatrains. It makes no difference which great politician has power, Fox or Shelburne. The humble must still pay taxes.

82-192. Modern Characters. American War.

"Is all our travel turn'd to this effect." (8)

MP, Mar 14, 1782.

Shakespeare's Henry VI is quoted to reflect an objection to any attempt to "conclude effeminate peace."

82-193. Musical Mottos.

"Lord Camden. By virtue illumin'd his actions appear." (30)

GA, Jan 16 & Jan 17, 1782.

Selected quotations from songs that are used to provide characters of Lord Camden, Earl of Effingham, Lord Amherst, Gibbon, Savile, and the younger Pitt -- all favoring the politics of the Opposition. Gibbon is satirized for corruption; Savile, Camden, and Effingham are praised. Keppel, Palliser, North, Rigby, Abingdon appear in the second group.

82-194. A Naval Ode On Sir George Rodney's complete Victory over the French Fleet in the West Indies. Performed in Vauxhall Gardens. Set by Mr. Barthelemon.

"Hark! triumphant shouts proclaim." (38)

G Eve Post, May 25, 1782; Lloyd's 50 (May 27, 1782), 508; L Chron 51 (May 28, 1782), 515; M Chron, May 28, 1782; PA, May 27, 1782; St J's C, May 28, 1782; WM 56 (Jun 6, 1782), 274.

A lyrical extravaganza, with chorus and airs, celebrating Rodney's great victory over De Grasse and the French fleet in the Battle of the Saints, April 12, 1782.

82-195. Neptune and Britannia. Occasioned by our late Successes in the West-Indies.

"With hair dishevelled, with tear-dew'd cheeks." (24)

PA, Jun 7, 1782; UM 70 (Jun 1782), 321.

HC. Rodney's great victory has restored Britain's sovereignty over the seas.

82-196. Neptune's Second Resignation. A Song. On the Late Successes in the West Indies.

"Deep in the Bosom of the Main." (54)

PA, Jun 13, 1782.

Neptune is impressed by the latest British naval victory over the French, and so yields to Britain the rule of the sea, thanks to Rodney and Hood.

82-197. Nevill, Valentine.
On the Late Animated Exertion of the Noble Efficients and great Instruments of the New Administration.

"Blest Friends of Britain! turn your longing eyes." (62)

West M 10 (Apr 1782), 210-11.

HC. Panegyric on members of the Rockingham ministry: Camden, Thurlow, Conway, John Cavendish, Surrey (Charles Howard), and Fox.

82-198. Nevill, Valentine.
To the Right Honourable William Pitt, Chancellor of the Exchequer.

"While poor Britannia, like a wretched maid." (12)

M Chron, Dec 31, 1782.

HC. Praise of the younger Pitt who as Chancellor of the Exchequer is still the disinterested and incorruptible patriot. (He accepted the office in Shelburne's administration from July 1782 to April 1783.)

82-199. A New Martial Song. By an Officer in the Kingston [Jamaica] Militia.

"Hark; from each quarter dire alarms." (36)

M Chron, May 17, 1782.

A song directed at the French and Spanish, who covet Jamaica; but the Kingston militia will resist.

82-200. A New Song. Intituled and Called, EO: Or, the Man of Abilities. To the Tune of, -- "I went to Abingdon."

"Have you abilities? -- heigh, Sir! ho, Sir." (36)

W Eve Post, Jul 18, 1782.

Satire on Fox, gambler, who wishes to be in place as a minister; but his abilities are questioned, as well as his integrity.

82-201. A New Song. "O Ponder well, ye Parents dear."

"O! ponder well, my Charly dear." (40)

MP, Oct 22, 1782.

Song. Satire on Fox, recently "in," but now "out." (Shelburne assumes the leadership on July 13, 1782.)

82-202. A New Song, on the Naval Volunteers of Ireland.

"Brave sons of Hibernia, your freedom's declar'd." (16)

HM 12 (Sep 1782), 496.

Quatrains with "Derry down" chorus. Now that Ireland has her freedom and all her "former injuries [are] fully repair'd," she provides "twenty-thousand brave seamen to fight, / In defence of their king, and their country's right," against France, Spain, and Holland.

82-203. A New Song. Suitable to the present Time. Tune -- the Dublin Volunteer Quick-step.

"Since liberty at last is come." (48)

Freeman's J, Mar 21, 1782.

Song in octaves. The Irish volunteers will loyally support the King against his enemies, so long as Ireland is free.

82-204. A New Song. To the Tune of Roast Beef.

"Once more we have hopes, that Old England will stand." (15)

GA, Mar 23, 1782.

North's ministry must resign -- and the war against the French, Dutch, and Spaniards must be carried on -- as Fox "should rule this land." (The Rockingham Administration was announced in the General Advertiser, March 26, 1782.)

82-205. A New Song. Tune, -- "In Stories we're told, / How our Monarchs of old / In France had their royal domain," &c.

"The man at the helm." (72)

MP, Jul 20, 1782; W Eve Post, Jul 18, 1782.

Song in sixains. Satire on Burke and Fox, who were briefly in place and now are out. The difficulty of bringing the American War to an end is alluded to.

82-206. Nichols, T.
An Ode, Occasioned by the Loss of the Royal George, August 27, 1782, wherein One Thousand Lives were lost in the Space of a few Minutes.

"God of the wave saline." (c. 65)

GA, Sep 7, 1782.

Irregular ode.

82-207. O Tempora! O Mores! Verses Addressed to All Parties.

"Lo! mad Disunion claps her Raven Wings." (77)

PA, Mar 7, 1782.

HC. Causidicus traces the history of the English Constitution and damns those fomenters of faction who would undermine it, the perfect English system of government. Fox appears to be the target of these critical remarks.

82-208. An Odd Resemblance. On Stag Hunting. On a Great Personage.

"Lord N--th's like the K--g as one egg's like another." (6)

L Cour, Mar 20, 1782.

Three satiric epigrams. The King resembles Lord North; the King will never catch Washington; and the King loves stag-hunting.

82-209. Ode.

"Beyond the vast Atlantic wave." (72)

MP, Dec 13, 1782.

Regular (Horatian) ode in sixains. A bitter poem in defence of the Loyalists. Britain owes something to the American Loyalists -- she will not desert them. Carleton will never "plighted faith forego." The genuine traitors, the Catilines in Britain, deserve execution.

82-210. Ode.

"Sacred to Truth's and Virtue's cause." (48)

MH, Mar 30, 1782.

Regular (Horatian) ode in sixains. Praise of the virtues of Sandwich, whom venal faction defames, especially Fox. (The Morning Herald was subsidized by the crown.)

82-211. Ode.

"When Rome for Arts and Arms Renown'd." (28)

GA, Jul 15, 1782.

Irregular ode. Complains that Rockingham, who has just died, is now neglected, and that he has not been given public honors.

82-212. Ode, Addressed to General Arnold. By Lady [Elizabeth] Craven.

"Welcome one Arnold to our Shore." (72)

Eur M 1 (May 1782), 385-6; L Chron 51 (Feb 19, 1782), 182; GA, Feb 18, 1782; L Cour, Feb 21, 1782; LP, Feb 13, 1782; PA, Feb 14, 1782; W Misc 17 (Mar 4, 1782), 551-2; W Eve Post, Feb 16, 1782. Also repr. New Foundling Hospital for Wit (1786), IV, 259-62.

Regular (Horatian) ode in sixains. Satire, from the side of the Patriots, on Arnold and the ministry who welcome him to England, especially Germain, and on the inability of the government's forces to conquer America. Cited are Washington, Galloway, Palliser, Sandwich, Carleton, Amherst, Loyalist refugees, Abingdon, Burgoyne, Mansfield, Clinton, Paul Jones, and Wedderburne. Also repr. in Winthrop Sargent, Life and Career of Major Andre, ed. W. Abbatt (1902), pp. 511-12.

82-213. An Ode. Composed for his Majesty's Birth-Day. By an Officer of Marines on Board the Prince George, one of Lord Rodney's Fleet, then Lying at Jamaica.

"Hark! hear Apollo strikes his lyre." (92)

Cal Merc, Aug 19, 1782; MP, Aug 31, 1782.

Irregular Pindaric ode. The British cause against "ingrate sons" was just. Now Britain wants peace, and her loyal supporters dutifully agree. Cited are France, Spain, Rodney, King George, and Jamaica.

82-214. Ode for the New Year, January 1, 1782.

"O Wond'rous Power of golden worth." (36)

L Cour, Jan 25, 1782.

A serious parody of Whitehead's New Year's Ode for 1782 (82-397). Irregular Pindaric. Corruption still menaces freedom. But (after Yorktown) freedom "calls" to end "th'unnatural War" with America.

82-215. Ode in Honour of British Bravery: In Imitation of Horace. By Mr. G----.

"Let British Youth be taught t'endure." (30)

PA, Jul 24, 1782.

Ode in sixains. Imitation of Horace. Let British youth train to fight for their country, especially against France. "How sweet, how glorious 'tis to die / In Arms for England's Public Weal."

82-216. Ode on Ireland.

"As through the sable gloom of night." (42)

M Chron, Sep 11, 1782; PA, Sep 12, 1782.

Regular ode in Quatrains. A celebration of the freedom bloodlessly gained by Ireland, and an expression of confidence in the leadership of Henry Flood and Charles Coote, Earl of Bellamont. Grattan is rejected.

82-217. Ode on the King's Birth-Day.

"Ye minstrells join the tuneful choir." (70)

M Chron, Jun 14, 1782.

Irregular Pindaric ode. A loyal ode honoring the King because the nation has again, as a result of Rodney's victory over the French fleet, achieved sovereignty on the seas.

82-218. Ode on the Progress of Party, Written in Imitation of Mr. Gray's celebrated Ode on the Progress of Poesy.

"Awake Athenian Lyre, awake." (112)

Eur M 2 (Oct 1782), 310-11.

Parody of part of Thomas Gray's regular Pindaric Ode on the Progress of Poetry. An objection to destructive party spirit which originates in hell, inspires civil war as in Scotland, and the murder of monarchs. In England, the exemplars of the "wild madness" of faction are Cromwell, the First Earl of Shaftesbury, and the Duke of Marlborough. No contemporary figure is cited; but implications for the times are clear in this anti-Whig poem.

82-219. An Ode on the Times. Addressed to the Members of the House of Commons . . . by a Freeholder of the Three Counties [of Gloucester, Monmouth, and Glamorgan].

"Long have we fought, but fought in vain." (246)

GA, Jan 7. 1782.

Regular (Horatian) ode in sixains. (Fills two columns.) Reflections on the American War, doubts about its propriety and success. Advises Parliament to control the budget and thereby control the war, which is the immediate goal of the Reform Movement, here related to the American War and national politics. References to the surrender of Burgoyne and Cornwallis, North, corruption, England against the world and in decline, and virtuous America.

82-220. Ode to Peace.

"O sweet Peace! thou heaven-born maid." (18)

Cal Merc, Jul 17, 1782; G, Jul 25, 1782; GA, Jul 25, 1782.

Regular ode in sixains. The poet yearns for the end of the prolonged civil war: "Too long [have] brothers been by brother slain."

82-221. Ode to the Genius of Great Britain, Occasioned by the Late Success in the West Indies.

"Long had thy generous Spirit borne." (36)

Cumb Pacq, Jun 18, 1782.

Regular ode in quatrains. Britain has been fighting Spain, Holland, France, and America; and now, at last, Rodney carries the flag and ends the bloody war.

Ode. To the Memory of the Officers and Crew of his Majesty's ship the Quebec, commanded by Capt. Farmer . . . Written in 1779. MH, Jan 10, 1782. See 79-316.

82-222. An Ode, written on hearing the News of the Defeat of the French Fleet, by Admiral Rodney.

"Too long hath fair Britannia been oppress'd." (30)

WM 56 (Jul 11, 1782), 432; West M 10 (Jun 1782), 327-8.

Regular ode in sixains. A celebration of Rodney's great victory over the French, Battle of the Saints, April 12, 1782.

82-223. Old Reynard's Prediction. An Ode.

"When by an armed Force of Squibs." (54)

PA, Nov 12, 1782.

Regular ode in sixains, "from the 15th Ode of the 1st Book of Horace, and applied to some political Period of this Country." A satire on Fox, who had been in government, taking North's place. But after Rockingham's death, he has been politically isolated, having the opposition of Barre, Dunning, and Shelburne, although the support of Burke, John Cavendish, and Thomas Townshend. The poet hopes Fox will be hanged.

82-224. On a Certain Gentleman's Attributing all our National Misfortunes to Providence.

"Who shall dispute what E---- says." (12)

PA, Mar 14, 1782.

Quatrain. Sandwich, Sackville (Germain), and North deserve to be hanged.

82-225. On a Certain Nobleman's Affecting to Appear Since his Dismission from Employment, at public places.

"Why strut my Lord, with an unmeaning face." (8)

L Cour, Apr 12, 1782.

HC. A Scotch politician, a Murray, now out, is advised to keep at home: "The M[u]rr[a]ys ever were detested T[raito]rs."

82-226. On a certain Variable Peer.

"Ireland's sole ***e; her l-st of Peers, the prime." (26)

Freeman's J, Nov 30, 1782.

HC. A satire on an Irish peer of protean politics. He is thoroughly unstable and unreliable. (His identity is not given.)

82-227. On a Change of Ministry. Addressed to the Right Hon. L[or]d N[ort]h.

"When the Aeternal first from Chaos hurl'd." (32)

MP, Apr 4, 1782.

HC. All things decay, and so North need not repine at losing power. May the new rulers save the country from ruin.

82-228. On a Late Change.

"In firmest phalanx, see the patriot band." (6)

GA, Apr 8, 1782.

HC. The new ministry will bring peace to "Columbia" (America) without the recourse to bribery.

82-229. On a Late Singular Transaction.

"Some Men are hang'd, and others rise to Fame." (16)

PA, May 4, 1782.

HC. Causidicus remarks on Sackville (Germain), responsible for Britain's undoing, yet is elevated to the peerage and is rewarded with a pension for his pains.

82-230. On a Recent Event. On Lord North's Tax upon Soap.

"Should the Ministry Now." (6)

"If I had Lord North in my Power." (8)

PA, Mar 22, 1782.

Two epigrams. Sixain and quatrains. The new ministry cannot be worse than the old ones and their tax policies. North's tax on soap is objectionable.

82-231. On Admiral Rodney.

"On thee, brave Rodney, may each Blessing flow." (8)

PA, Jun 22, 1782.

HC. Rodney deserves immortal fame for his great victory.

82-232. On Admiral Rodney's taking the Ville De Paris.

"France, the lost gem of England's regal Crown." (2)

W Eve Post, May 28, 1782.

Epigram. On Rodney's defeat of De Grasse and capture of the French flagship in the Battle of the Saints, April 12, 1782.

82-233. On B. B.'s approved Motion for granting an enormous SUM to Harry Clapper-Clack for his uncertain Services to his country.

"Search Europe, trace the globe's extended round." (60)

Freeman's J, Dec 19, 1782.

HC. Satire on Henry Grattan for the enormous grant of £50,000 awarded by the Irish

Parliament. Grattan is an orgiast who has deserted the cause of his country. (Grattan initiated a motion to petition the crown for full independence of the Irish legislature; and, when partial consent was gained [but not implemented] from the British government, the grateful Irish Parliament granted him this sum of money.)

82-234. On Colonel Barre.

"Britannia boasts the gallant Barre's name." (4)

GA, Feb 1, 1782.

HC. Barre should be admired for his patriot virtue.

82-235. On General Burgoyne's Appointment to the Chief Command in Ireland. Epigrammatic.

"An Empire's lost on Saratoga's plains." (6)

MH, Apr 27, 1782.

HC. Satire on Burgoyne, who had failed at Saratoga and will fail again in Ireland.

82-236. On General Eliott and Captain Curtis.

"Descend, fair Calliope and sing." (77)

M Chron, Dec 27, 1782; PA, Dec 28, 1782.

Regular (Horatian) ode in eleven-line stanzas. An account of the defeat of the Spanish forces attacking Gibraltar by the British under Gen. Eliott and Capt. Curtis. (The PA version has only 33 lines.)

82-237. On Harry G--t--n's late conduct in Parliament.

"G[ratta]n, the idol of a bounteous nation." (10)

Freeman's J, Jul 27, 1782.

HC (irregular). Grattan was voted £50,000 for his efforts to achieve Irish freedom; and now he wishes to curb the freedom of the press. He is a hypocrite, and the nation is deceived in him!

82-238. On Hearing that General Eliott was expected before Christmas.

"See the conquering Hero comes." (39)

M Chron. Dec 10, 1782.

Song (no tune given) in honor of Gen. Eliott, conqueror of the French and Spaniards.

82-239. On his Excellency the L[or]d L[ieu]T[enan]T's arrival. A Doubt.

"T****E's arriv'd, but what he'll be." (50)

Freeman's J, Sep 24, 1782.

OC. The Irish are doubtful about the new Lord Lieutenant Temple's views on Irish rights and freedom. They do not trust him. Grattan is belittled.

82-240. On Lord Shelburne's Boasting on a late Occasion, in the House of Lords, of his Candour and Veracity.

"Fitzmaurice talks loud of his Candour and Truth." (4)

MH, Jul 20, 1782; St J's C, Jul 23, 1782.

Epigram. Anapest tetrameter couplets. Satire on Shelburne (William Fitzmaurice Petty, nicknamed Malagrida).

82-241. On Mr. Hollis's Print of the Reverend Dr. Mayhew, of Boston in America.

"Ere civil Strife, on Boston's menac'd shore." (26)

GM 52 (Mar 1782), 133.

HC. Praise of Jonathan Mayhew (pastor of the West Church in Boston, from 1747 to his death in 1766), who prevented the introduction of corrupt bishops to America. He did not live to see the violence of the rebellion. He was an example of "one firm Priest" committed to religious liberty and integrity, "whose unpolluted soul / No lust of gain could warp."

82-242. On News-Papers.

"In ev'ry Newspaper -- that copious sheet." (22)

GA, Oct 18, 1782.

HC. The newspaper displays the times, but it is impossible to say which reports are true and which false.

82-243. On our late Successes in the West-Indies.

"Praying that o'er my drowsy Head." (8)

St J's C, May 28, 1782.

OC. Rodney has awakened Britain with his naval victories.

82-244. On our Late Victory.

"A backward season damps these northern parts." (8)

GA, Jul 1, 1782; W Eve Post, May 28, 1782.

HC. Epigram. On Rodney's victory over De Grasse, described in an agricultural metaphor.

82-245. On Representation.

"To represent, is but to personate." (6)

GA, Aug 29, 1782.

HC. Honest representation means no bribery or corruption (no sale of seats).

82-246. On Sir George Brydges Rodney's Victory with the British fleet over the fleet of France, commanded by the Comte de Grasse, on the 12th of April, 1782. Written by a common Sailor. . . .

"From Heav'n behold a clearing ray." (76)

M Chron, Jul 19, 1782; PA, Jul 20, 1782.

Ballad narrating Rodney's great victory in the Battle of the Saints in the West Indies.

82-247. On Sir James Lowther's Present to his Majesty.

"Victory claims a nation's thankful voice." (21)

M Chron, Sep 26, 1782.

HC. Panegyric on Lowther for "his loyal gift," a "full mann'd ship o' line," a war ship. He is disinterested, thoroughly incorruptible!

82-248. On the British Merchants Seeking Protection from Neutral Flags.

"Time was when Britain's Sons, with Sails outspread." (32)

PA, Sep 25, 1782.

Elegiac quatrains. Those responsible for diminishing the power of British commercial shipping deserve censure -- "Whether of English, Scotch, or Irish Birth."

82-249. On the Death of a late Noble Marquis.

"Alas! Britannia, mourn and weep." (16)

L Eve Post, Jul 6, 1782; M Chron, Jul 8, 1782; PA, Jul 9, 1782.

Quatrains. Let us mourn the death of noble Rockingham, a great loss to the nation that he has tried to save. Rockingham died July 1, 1782.

82-250. On the Death of the Marquis of Rockingham.

"Great men must die; it is the will of fate." (14)

G, Jul 11, 1782; PA, Jul 9, 1782.

HC. Causidicus mourns the death of the patriot Rockingham, and is consoled because "great Shelburne . . . lives to guide the helm." This poem was reprinted in the Weekly Entertainer 1 (May 12, 1783), 456, with the name of Fox substituted for Shelburne!

82-251. On the Death of the Marquis of Rockingham.

"Rise, conscious Gratitude! thy Tribute pay." (25)

GA, Jul 26, 1782.

Blank verse. A conventional tribute.

82-252. On the Death of the Marquis of Rockingham.

"The Sun of Britain's set, at Heaven's Command." (2)

MH, Jul 20, 1782; St J's C, Jul 23, 1782.

Epigram. HC. Upon the death of Rockingham, Shelburne usurped command of the government.

82-253. On the Death of the Marquis of Rockingham.

"'Twas in the synod of the blest." (78)

Eur M 2 (Nov 1782), 389-90.

Sixains. Chatham welcomes Rockingham to Elysium, deplores faction, and assures Britain that Shelburne was left behind "Virtue's cause [to] defend," to humble France, and to make peace.

82-254. On the Death of the Marquis of Rockingham.

"Whene'er the great, the virtuous and the just." (19)

GA, Jul 9, 1782.

HC. Praise of "the truly Noble Man / Who in his Country's cause uprightly stood, / And stem'd Corruption's overwhelming flood." (Otherwise conventional and cliche-ridden.)

82-255. On the Defeat of the French Fleet in the West-Indies on the 12th of April Last.

"Ye sons of great Albion -- fam'd Rodney's the toast." (20)

M Chron, Aug 30, 1782.

Anapest tetrameter couplets in quatrains. A toast to "bold Rodney" and the navy for saving "our islands."

82-256. On the Famous Sir George Brydges Rodney, Admiral of the White.

"Ye friends of Old England! say was there a Tar." (16)

GA, May 25, 1782.

Hexameter couplets in quatrains. Generalized praise of Rodney, conqueror of the French and Spanish fleets.

82-257. On the French Fleet being driven back to Brest.

"England's best friends still hover in the skies." (2)

GA, Jan 29, 1782.

Epigram. HC. Fortunately, England was saved by the storms that drove the French fleet back to Brest.

On the late Animated Exertion of the Noble Efficients and great Instruments of the New Administration. See Nevill, 82-197.

82-258. On the Late Death of Mr. Pendrell, a Descendant of Pendrell, who attended King Charles II. when Searched in the Royal Oak.

"The Tories long, long Time, have had their Day." (10)

PA, Apr 1, 1782.

HC. May there be "Patriot Pendrells" to keep England's monarchy alive, now that Whigs have displaced the Tories.

82-259. On the late Expedition to Gibraltar. A Comic Poem.

"In Gibraltar straits, roll'd with disdain." (54)

B&BM I:21 (1782), 333.

OC. Narrative poem on the success of Admiral Richard Howe in eluding the combined French and Spanish fleets and in supplying Gibraltar, where General Elliott had fought off the Spanish siege.

82-260. On the Late Happy Revolution.

"Some folks look sad, whilst all around rejoice." (4)

L Cour, Apr 25, 1782.

Epigram. HC. Those who are not pleased with the new administration (the Rockingham ministry that displaced North's ministry) deserve execution.

82-261. On the Late Ministry.

"Our late good Men to serve the State." (4)

PA, Apr 25, 1782.

Quatrain. Epigram. Satire on the North ministry, which was guided solely by self-interest.

82-262. On the Late Repulse of the French and Spaniards in their attempt to storm Gibraltar by Sea and Land.

"Firm as the rock itself the English stand." (14)

GA, Oct 14, 1782; MH, Oct 24, 1782.

HC. Unlike Troy, Gibraltar has successfully withstood the siege by France and Spain (September 13, 1782).

82-263. On the Memorable 12th of April 1782. Extempore, by a Young Lady.

"Whilst you rejoice for Rodney's great success." (6)

Cal Merc, Jun 5, 1782.

HC. Although we rejoice in Rodney's success, we must not forget those brave officers who were killed -- Blair, Bayne, and Manners.

82-264. On the Minority becoming the Majority.

"'Twixt Major and Minor, and Minor and Major." (8)

PA, Mar 2, 1782.

Quatrains. Extempore. The Minority or Opposition has now control of Government and has become the Majority.


82-265. On the Political Death of the Late Pay-Master.

"Here lies in your corner." (30)

MP, Sep 6, 1782.

Doggerel, three-stress with rough rhymes. Satire on Burke, for his Irish background. Burke was at this time Pay-Master of the Forces.


82-266. On the Proposed Tax on Theatrical Amusements.

"To dismember a State." (6)

PA, Mar 16, 1782.

Sixain. Extempore. North dismembered a state; now, through taxes, he wishes to attack the stage.


82-267. On the Release of Mr. Laurens, followed by the Arrival of General Arnold.

"With captive Armies proud, and British Spoils." (8)

L Cour, Jan 31, 1782.

Quatrains. Britain, after Yorktown, is forced to give up Henry Laurens for Gen. Arnold. An allusion to the captured army of Cornwallis (but Gen. Cornwallis is not cited).


82-268. On the Report of Mr. Ogle's accepting a Colonel's Commission in the Fencibles.

"Does Ogle stoop t'accept a Menial's hire." (46)

Freeman's J, Sep 3, 1782.

HC. A protest at Ogle, who is here accused of deserting Ireland's cause, and a call for Irish unity in the struggle for their rights against Britain, which "is seldom merciful and just."


82-269. On the Report of the Duchess of Kingston Having unnaturally celebrated the Capture of Lord Cornwallis, and Banished from her all Attachments to this Country.

"Though Kingston we've lost." (6)

PA, Jan 4, 1782.

Sixain. Satire on the notorious alleged bigamist, the Duchess of Kingston, for demonstrating her pleasure at the capture of Cornwallis.

82-270. On the Revolution in Irish Affairs. By a Lady.

"Long had Hibernia borne oppression's rod." (48)

Freeman's J, Aug 24, 1782.

HC. Ireland must be restored to her native right, and must not be exploited and oppressed by England.

82-271. On the Siege of Gibraltar. [Written by a young Gentleman of Merchant Taylors School in school hours. . . .]

"'Tho' Hector his victorious Legions led." (20)

GA, Oct 10, 1782.

Quatrains. The achievement of Elliott in repelling the siege of Gibraltar by the French and Spaniards surpasses that of Hector and Troy.

82-272. On the State of the Nation.

"Oh! what a State is ours." (10)

PA, Jul 31, 1782.

Doggerel, with play on a single rhyme. A pessimistic view of the state of the nation as chaotic. Even the peace makers are "stumbling."

82-273. On the Success of Gen. Conway's Motion, to discontinue Offensive War with America.

"In a long-wish'd for and auspicious hour." (6)

L Cour, Mar 7, 1782.

HC. Parliament at last asserts its power by passing Henry Seymour Conway's motion (Feb. 27, 1782) to end the war against America.

82-274. On the Triumphant Arrival of Lord Rodney. By Mr. Conway.

"He comes like Caesar! Rodney comes." (44)

GA, Sep 28, 1782.

Quatrains. Praise of heroic Rodney for his defeat of Langara, and now De Grasse, thereby restoring British sovereignty over the main. (A conventional tribute.)

82-275. On the Victory gained by Admiral Rodney over Count de Grasse.

"Much have we heard of coups of late." (4)

Cal Merc, May 29, 1782.

Epigram. Admiral Rodney captured Count de Grasse. May Britain's foes share his fate -- "the coup de Grasse"!

82-276. On the Vote of Thanks to Admiral Rodney, On Account of his Late Victory.

"Two votes of thanks have pass'd the house." (4)

MH, May 31, 1782.

Epigram. Quatrain. Satire on Keppel, who is contrasted unfavorably with Rodney. Keppel deserves no thanks. Rodney's victory over De Grasse is the reference.

82-277. On Two Seceding Ministers. (Parodied from Dryden's Young Statesman.)

"North had wit and sober sense!" (21)

MP, Oct 5, 1782; W Eve Post, Oct 3, 1782.

Quatrains. Satire on Burke and Fox, "seceding ministers" from Shelburne's administration. (Actually, Fox and Burke resigned upon the death of Rockingham.)

82-278. [Once more, my messmates, brave and bold.]

"Once more, my messmates, brave and bold." (21)

M Chron, Oct 19, 1782.

A naval war song affirming British supremacy over the seas, "which gallant Rodney did regain."

82-279. Opposition's Reasons for Urging the Necessity of Dismissing the First L[or]d of the A[dmiralt]y at this Perilous Juncture, Versified.

"S[andwic]h must fall, it is the Will of Fate." (30)

PA, Feb 20, 1782.

1250

HC. The patriot Causidicus calls for the dismissal of Sandwich because he is too old, inefficient, and unpopular.

82-280. [Panegyric upon Mr. Burke, extracted from one of Mr. O'Brien's Poems.]

"When this wide mass of blockheads shall subside." (32)

MP, Mar 23, 1782.

HC. Praise of Burke for his integrity and incorruptible vision, by Denis (?) O'Bryen.

82-281. The Pantomime Orator.

"Let B[urke], with Vanity, not Glory smit." (47)

PA, Dec 20, 1782.

HC. A critical reaction to Burke's rhetoric: it has color but lacks persuasion.

82-282. A Paraphrase of Patriotism; or, the Freeholder's Rattle.

"A Patriot's scull, bereft of brains." (42)

GA, Jul 24, 1782.

Sixains. A satire on Fox, whom one former but now disillusioned follower refuses to acknowledge any more as leader. (A reflection of the split among the Whigs.)

82-283. A Paraphrase on Horace. Lib. IV, Ode 13.

"Thank God! we have obtain'd our pray'r." (52)

MP, Jul 30, 1782.

Quatrains. Satire on Fox, gloating that he has lost his position in the government. Burke and Pitt are cited.

82-284. A Paraphrase on Peace.

"Behold yon field! how dreadful is the sight." (14)

GA, Apr 11, 1782.

HC. A new administration has come in, and so the movement for peace with America gains momentum. A picture of the dreadful carnage of civil war is presented.

82-285. Parliamentary Exhibition of Pictures for the Year 1781-2.

Earl Cornwallis. No. 20. "It is success that colours all in life." (4 + 29)

G, Jan 1, 1782.

Brief quotations from Shakespeare's plays that provide characters of Cornwallis, Clinton, Effingham, William Eden, Charles Jenkinson, George Savile, Hugh Palliser, and others.

82-286. Parody from Othello. Being a real Soliloquy, as it was lately most pathetically spoken at the back of the Pay-Office, (by a celebrated Actor of St. Stephen's).

"I had been happy, whoe'er the Treasury did preside." (19)

G, Sep 19, 1782.

Blank verse. Satire on Burke, who complains of his loss of place as Pay-Master of the forces. The contention among the leading politicians -- Shelburne, Portland, and Fox -- is of no account so long as this gentleman retains his place and its perquisites. (Burke lost this position upon the death of Rockingham in July 1782.)

82-287. Parody on the First Part of Gray's Pindar.

"Ruin seize thee! shameless thing." (14)

MP, Mar 8, 1782.

Parody of Thomas Gray's Bard. Satire on Fox and Burke for supporting France. Shelburne is cited.

82-288. Parody on the Song of Moderation.

"Of an old Song wrote by an old English pate." (52)

L Cour, Mar 25, 1782.

Song. A satire on George III. Pitt made George II and his court great with his victories; and the times of George II were great indeed. But when George III reigned, times changed for the worse, including the treatment of America.

82-289. The Patriot: A New Song. To the tune of, "As I went to Abingdon, &c."

"What is a Patriot? heigh! Sir! oh! Sir." (66)

W Eve Post, Dec 19, 1782.

Song. Satire on the so-called "patriots" of the day -- harshly critical when out and selfish when in, interested in reform, yet basically selfish. How can they be silenced? By kicks or a pension? Cited is Shelburne.

82-290. A Patriotic Address to Mr. Fox, On his Spirited Resignation. By Mr. Conway.

"Let Patriots hail the ruling star." (42)

GA, Jul 18, 1782.

Sixains. A complaint at the split in the Whig party after Rockingham's death. Fox, disagreeing with Shelburne, resigns in order to end the war, and the poet approves. Bute and Burke are cited.

82-291. Patriotic Wishes. Most Respectfully addressed to the virtuous Champions of Patriotism.

"Heav'n guard thy Hero! swell his sails." (24)

GA, Aug 2, 1782.

Quatrains. Admiral Richard Howe relieved besieged Gibraltar, and peace with the USA is on its way. "Our kindred States . . . Sign Bonds of Peace," and Britain will be "re-ally'd" with them "By Ties of Trade, and Liberty."

82-292. The Patriotism of the King's Speech.

"Come, honest Truth, and pour thy grateful strain." (58)

PA, Dec 19, 1782.

HC. Causidicus praises King George as an exemplary constitutional monarch for his virtue and patriotism; and he welcomes the peace to come, "on liberal plan, by Justice known," for which Shelburne is striving.

82-293. The Patriot's Wish.

"Oh! might a simple Youth presume." (12)

GA, Feb 22, 1782.

Sixains. The Patriot wishes sincerely for the nation's wounds to heal, the ministers brought to justice, and the end of the war.

82-294. The Pear-Tree.

"High on a lofty tree there grew." (10)

MP, Aug 22, 1782.

OC. Simile. Shelburne, like a beautiful pear, "reigns supreme"; but the Foxites, like fallen, rotten pears, lie below.

82-295. Pinchbeck, Christopher.
An Ode in Honour of her Majesty's Birth-Day.

"Though Dutch and French and all combine." (36) (Extract 6)

M Chron, Jan 19, 1782.

Ode in sixains. Pinchbeck, the King's toyman, optimistically asserts that Britain will conquer the Dutch, French, "and all" who combine with "rebellious subjects."

82-296. A Poem. Written by a Descendant of the Illustrious Mr. Sternhold, the Poet, and Executed in his Best Manner.

"God prosper long the Morning Post." (32)

L Cour, May 1, 1782.

Quatrains. The several London newspapers are briefly characterized -- Morning Post, Morning Herald, Morning Chronicle, Public Advertiser, General Advertiser, London Courant, Daily Advertiser, Gazetteer, and Public Ledger.

82-297. The Poetical Inspector. Number VI.

"O For the martial Muse who thee inspir'd." (42)

T&C 14 (Sep 1782), 479.

HC. Patriotic lines directed against France. The poet provides generalized war aims for which the British are fighting: "British freedom, British laws," and "our naval lustre to regain," that is, British sovereignty over the seas.

Poetical-Political Squibs, Pro and Con. Impromptu. Logic and Morals. Addressed to Lord Shelburne [Etc.]. MH, Jul 24, 29, 30, 1782; W Eve Post, Jul 27, 1782. Five Epigrams satirizing Shelburne. See Impromptu(s): 82-163-5, 82-168.

82-298. The Poet's Corner -- a What d'ye call it?

"Too long, by G-----, I've stood the dupe." (28)

GA, Oct 26, 1782.

Quatrains. Light satire on the people's poetry. "The Poet's Corner," or column, speaks, forbidding amateur and untalented poetasters to contribute, and damning them should they "force" the muses to sing "Against their inclination." (This poem suggests the origins of much of the poetry appearing in the newspapers.)

82-299. A Political Fable, Addressed to the P[remie]r.

"A Man, a travelling with his Ass the Road." (20)

PA, Feb 19, 1782.

HC. An animal fable by Causidicus, "The Discontented Patriot," satirizes the ministry (of North), which does not serve the country well.

82-300. The Political Fast.

"In th' midst of our Shame." (6)

PA, Jan 12, 1782.

Sixain. Sandwich will enjoy the national Fast with a feast of trout and wine, as his persona confesses.

82-301. The Politicians: A Fragment.

"Precisely at the Hour of Six." (50)

PA, Apr 17, 1782; W Eve Post, Apr 16, 1782.

OC. Unanimity should be the theme guiding the new ministry, for it will make the nation strong.

82-302. Pro Deo, et Rege; pro Patria, ejusque Libertate!

"No rude, no despicable song I sing." (14)

G, Mar 20, 1782.

HC, favoring the establishment of an asylum for orphans of those soldiers fallen in defence of their country, "since the commencement of the present war."

82-303. Prologue to [the Late New Farce of] Retaliation.

"Trite seems our Authour's Task, when all Creation." (44)

G Eve Post, May 11, 1782; L Chron 51 (May 9, 1782), 450; MH, May 11, 1782; St J's C, May 11, 1782.

HC. Britain will now retaliate upon France, Holland, and Spain; Britain, united, is confident against the world in arms.

82-304. A Prophecy.

"Through Boreas, Twitcher, and Minden." (4)

L Cour, Jan 28, 1782.

Epigram. North, Sandwich, and Germain will ruin Britain with their poor leadership, and North will tax us "to starve in the streets."

82-305. Puddicombe, John Newell.
The Tears of Britain; Or, An Elegy on the Loss of the Royal George. By J. N. Puddicombe, M.A.

"Midnight had spread her sable wings around." (144)

Eur M 2 (Sep 1782), 233-4.

Elegiac stanzas. An expression of grief over the disastrous sinking, without warning, of Admiral Richard Kempenfelt's 100-gun battleship, with the loss of 400 seamen and officers, including Kempenfelt and 200 women, August 28, 1782.

82-306. Query to Common Sense. Common Sense's Answer.

"Thou best and truest Pilot of the Heart." (14)

PA, Nov 16, 1782.

HC. What is a Whig? The Whig is dead since 1688; and at present what passes as a Whig is a swindler (Fox) leagued with a Jesuit (Burke).

82-307. [Quoth Clodio to a Brother Patriot Peer.]

"Quoth Clodio to a Brother Patriot Peer." (6)

PA, Feb 20, 1782.

Epigram. HC. Causidicus believes that one worthless peer who objects to Germain's elevation to the peerage is hypocritical.

82-308. A Recipe to Make a Modern Minister.

"When Jove, to scourge a self-rebelling nation." (18)

MP, Oct 16, 1782.

HC. Satire on Fox, his appearance, oratory, and character.

82-309. Reformation, -- A Tale.

"Where Britain's sea-girt Isle arose." (26)

Cumb Pacq, Mar 19, 1782.

OC. The loss of America and the Atlantic trade will mean the end of luxury. Thus good comes from evil, Britain's fall.

82-310. The Refugees.

"How long, ye guardian powers that rule the world." (106)

HM 12 (Jul 1782), 383-4; T&C 14 (Jun 1782), 325-6.

HC. The Poet (R. D. J.) asks the Americans to end their parricidal rebellion and to restore peace with the parent's blessing. He describes the anguish of those wretched American loyalists "forc'd for safety from their native land," Virginia. Lonely, he is discontented in London. He prays that "each wanderer" be restored to his own country and hopes that the Government will bring peace and reunion -- "join the parent to the child again."

82-311. Retaliation. An Original Prologue.

"To curb the Passions, and to mend the Heart." (56)

L Eve Post, Sep 24, 1782; PA, Oct 4, 1782.

HC. Naval retaliation is proper; likewise, Wolfe's retaliation against the French in Canada, and British retaliation upon Holland for joining with Spain, the mutual enemy. This prologue to <u>Retaliation</u> differs from the one published May 11, 1782. See "Prologue to the Late New Farce of Retaliation," 82-303.

82-312. The Revenge of France: A Parody on Dr. Warton's Ode, entitled, The Revenge of America.

"As late Britannia's bulwarks rode." (30)

MH, Jun 8, 1782.

OC. France complains of British victories, of Rodney; and again Keppel is blamed for failing to fight the French off Ushant on July 27, 1778.

82-313. The Revival of British Spirit; An Ode. Written soon after Rodney's Victory in the West Indies.

"Lo! along the sea-girt shores." (60)

An Asylum for Fugitive Pieces in Prose and Verse (1785), I, 19-21.

Regular (Horatian) ode in dixains. A patriotic poem. Rodney's spectacular victory over De Grasse and the French fleet, April 12, 1782, has restored British dominion over the ocean. "Th'ungrateful league" of powers opposing Britain will not withstand her vengeance.

82-314. Ridicule No Test of Truth.

"What will not Party dare, her Point to gain." (16)

PA, Dec 24, 1782.

HC. Causidicus objects to Burke's ridicule of the King's speech, which he believes one of the King's best. (See "The Patriotism of the King's Speech," 82-292.) Causidicus is glad to learn that the younger Pitt deplored the ridicule and reproved Burke. For the comments made by Burke and Pitt, see The Parliamentary History of England (London: Hansard, 1814), XXIII, 266-72, 272-5 (Dec. 6, 1782).

82-315. [Robertson, Thomas.]
To the Right Honourable Lord Shelburne. The humble Petition of the worshipful Company of Poets and News-writers.

"That your honour's petitioners (dealers in rhymes)." (36)

M Chron, Aug 30, 1782.

Anapest tetrameter couplets. Ironic satire on Shelburne and his administration for failing to provide targets for railing criticism, for not giving captious critics anything to say.

82-316. Rodney for Ever, A Favourite Song, sung by Mrs. Kennedy at Vauxhall, and set by Mr. Hook.

"Again Britannia smile." (18)

G Eve Post, Jun 22, 1782; Lloyd's 50 (Jun 24, 1782), 604; L Chron 51 (Jun 27, 1782), 622; M Chron, Jun 24, 1782; MH, Jun 25, 1782; PA, Jun 25, 1782.

A song that celebrates Rodney's victory over the French in the West Indies, April 12, 1782, and the re-establishment of "British empire o'er the main."

82-317. Rodney's Victory: A New Song. Tune, -- "The Wat'ry God." Chorus, to the Tune of -- "Rule Britannia."

"As bending o'er the azure tide." (58)

MP, Dec 2, 1782.

Song in sixains and chorus. On Rodney's celebrated defeat of the French fleet in the West Indies. Britain still rules the seas, despite the combined efforts of all her foes.

82-318. The R[oya]l Philosopher. Addressed to a Great Person.

"Though Fortune's foot-ball, none could ever trace." (4)

L Cour, Feb 8, 1782.

Epigram. HC. Satire on the King for failure to express sorrow for the great loss at Yorktown.

82-319. Rubicon's Solemn Protestation.

"That Bute he has not seen these fourteen years." (4)

GA, Jan 29, 1782.

HC. A Tory, Mansfield, confesses to conversation with Bute (not seen for fourteen years), "by the K[ing']s command."

82-320. Rushton, Edward.
To the People of England.

"When bellowing warfare lords it round." (80)

MP, Oct 11, 1782.

Regular ode in dixains. A patriotic poem. Britain stands alone against France, Spain, Holland, and America. In this crisis, including "foul rebellion," Britons must rouse, unite, and be strong. There are a few exemplary patriots left, the Suffolk family (Henry Howard, Thomas Howard), Sir James Lowther. Some comments on the difficulties of reaching a peace with America appear.

82-321. Sailor's Song. In Mr. Keefe's New Farce of the Positive Man.

"Sweet Poll of Plymouth was my dear." (24)

MP, Mar 18, 1782.

Ballad. Sweet Poll of Plymouth dies of grief because the press gang has taken her sweetheart away.

82-322. [Say whence this noise -- this needless rout.]

"Say whence this noise -- this needless rout." (6)

M Chron, Jul 11, 1782.

Sixain. Epigram. Cynical satire on party divisions as meaningless and futile. The Outs and Ins should all be hanged.

82-323. Second Song.

"After four years expence, the Grand Monarch of Spain." (28)

M Chron, Dec 28, 1782.

Ballad narrates the great victory of Gen. Eliott over the attacking Spaniards and French at Gibraltar, September 13, 1782.

82-324. The Senate of Pluto. (In Addition the Senate of the Gods.)

"Pluto, on high imperial Seat." (20)

PA, Jan 12, 1782.

Quatrains in OC. France, Spain, and Holland all must go to hell.

82-325. The Senator. An Extempore.

"Where nervous sense with polish'd phrase unite." (10)

MH, Dec 21, 1782.

HC. Praise of "Honest North," for the candor, "nervous sense," and straightforward eloquence that reflect steadiness, seriousness, and constancy of purpose, in contrast with devious insincerity and "rage of words" of Patriot oratory.

82-326. Seventeen Hundred and Eighty-Two; Or, A Sketch of the Times: An Ode. Addressed to Sir James Lowther, Baronet.

"For Lowther weave the wreath of fame." (120)

PA, Nov 28, 1782; W Eve Post, Nov 26, 1782; New Foundling Hospital for Wit (1786), IV, 232-8.

Regular (Horatian) ode in sixains. Light satire on the times. Following the example of Lowther, who supplied the money to build a naval warship, several people contribute saleable objects to raise money to build more ships. A sketch of the politics of the time in which Shelburne plays the leading role. Shelburne's unwillingness to grant independence to America is dealt with in one stanza. Cited also are Henry Flood and the threat of Irish revolution.

82-327. Seward, Anna.
The Celebrated Old Ballad of the Battle of La Hogue, Altered and applied to the late Naval Victory in the West-Indies. By Miss Seward.

"When April wak'd the dawn with lucky gales." (40)

G Eve Post, Jul 20, 1782; GM 52 (Sep 1782), 447; HM 12 (Aug 1782), 439; LP, Jul 22, 1782; M Chron, Jul 23, 1782; MH, Jul 24, 1782; St J's C, Jul 20, 1782; West M 10 (Aug 1782), 440; W Eve Post, Jul 23, 1782.

Song. Seward offers an impressionistic piece on Rodney's defeat of the French fleet, and capture of De Grasse and his flagship, the *Ville de Paris*, April 12, 1782.

82-328. Seward, Anna.
Verses by Miss Seward, inviting Stella to Tea on the Public Fast-Day, February 1782, written the preceding Evening.

"Dear Stella, 'midst the pious sorrow." (52)

M Chron, May 6, 1782; West M 10 (May 1782), 267-8.

OC. An invitation to tea with remarks on the hypocrisy of the National Fast Days and on tea as the cause of the American War.

82-329. Shelburne.

"Three months -- no more? -- to ride his Ass." (4)

St J's C, Oct 15, 1782.

Extempore. Quatrain. Satire on Shelburne. To date, Shelburne has been in power three months (since July 13, 1782). He cannot be premier much longer. (His ministry resigned February 24, 1783.)

82-330. The Siege of Gibraltar. A Martial Review.

"The Dons around, in close array." (60)

GA, Sep 11, 1782.

Regular ode in sixains. A dramatic review of the fighting in defence of George Augustus Eliott's besieged Gibraltar, the last significant engagement of the American War. (On September 13, 1782, a large Franco-Spanish force was repelled.)

82-331. The Silence of the Patriotic Alderman.

"While Englishmen for Freedom loudly speak." (6)

St J's C, Mar 16, 1782.

Epigram. HC. Wilkes, Chamberlain of London, has been very quiet. Should he be made a tax-collector, he will change his political creed and side with the Court. (Wilkes is no longer among the patriots!)

82-332. [Since Whigs now rule Old England's glorious State.]

"Since Whigs now rule Old England's glorious State." (8)

PA, Apr 12, 1782.

HC. Now that the Whigs rule the nation, Britain may again resume her former triumphant place among the nations of the world.

82-333. Sketches of the Characters of the Right Honorable Charles James Fox, and the Right Honorable Edmund Burke, Delineated in Verse.

"Curst be the man, who in these dubious times." (165)

An Asylum for Fugitive Pieces, in Prose and Verse (London: Debrett, 1786), II, 216-23.

HC. The poet affects impartiality, candor, and freedom in an estimate of Fox and Burke. Regarding Fox, his eloquence is admired, but his addiction to gaming, his dissipation is deplored. Regarding Burke, his oratory is admired for being informative and rhetorically striking, as in the Speeches on American Taxation and Reform; their qualities will pass the test of time.

82-334. Soliloquy. Overheard in Park-street, Westminster, spoken by a Gentleman upon his return on Tuesday from the House of Commons.

"Farewell; a long farewell to all my Greatness." (13)

GA, Jun 28, 1782.

Blank verse. An important but here unknown politician bemoans his fall from grace.

82-335. A Song.

"See, ye Patriots; see, ye Placemen." (36)

M Chron, Sep 30, 1782.

An election ode in sixains for Henry Thornton, standing for Southwark in September 1782. (He did not bribe the electors!)

82-336. A Song. In Commemoration of the Sea-Fight, between Admiral Rodney, and the Count de Grasse, On the 12th of April, 1782. To the tune of "Hearts of Oak."

"Whilst Russel's bold deeds are with glory renown'd." (36)

B&BM I:19 (Nov 1782), 301-2.

Song in praise of Rodney's defeat of the French fleet and capture of many ships including the flagship, the Ville de Paris, and its commander Admiral de Grasse.

82-337. Song in the Second Act of the Walloons. Set by Mr. Arne.

"'Twas up the Wind, three Leagues and more." (37)

L Chron 51 (May 7, 1782), 445; M Chron, May 10, 1782; MH, May 9, 1782; MP, May 8, 1782; PA, May 9, 1782.

A generalized naval war ballad that narrates the defeat of Dutch and French ships by British sailors who intend "to rule the waves." Richard Cumberland wrote the play.

82-338. Song. Introduc'd last night at Mr. Astley's Riding-School.

"Come my lads with souls befitting." (16)

MH, May 23, 1782.

Song in quatrains. A patriotic lyric in praise of Rodney, who will defeat the French, and Howe, the Dutch.

82-339. Song. To the Tune of "Hearts of Oak."

"Too long has resounded the murmurs of woe." (16)

G Eve Post, Jun 8, 1782.

Song honoring Rodney for his great victory over Dr Grasse in the West Indies, April 12, 1782. Britain has waited long for such a victory.

82-340. Stanzas ad Hominem.

"Say! why does black suspicion lurk." (32)

MH, Jun 3, 1782.

Quatrains. A criticism of Burke and Fox for their misleading and delusive eloquence.

82-341. Stanzas. Ode to the British Commanders in the Sea Fight, between the English and the French on the 27th of July, 1778.

"Ye bards of Great Britain." (38)

MH, Jul 27, 1782.

Irregular ode, trimeter. Satire on Keppel, malicious and vulgar, written for a "day of National Disgrace," when Keppel had failed to engage the French channel fleet. The *Morning Herald* thus tries to embarrass the ministry, of which Keppel was a member, by referring to "this day's direful calamities" in a black-bordered notice commemorating July 27, 1778.

82-342. Stanzas on a Glorious View of the Grand Fleet setting Sail under the Command of Lord Howe. By Mr. Conway.

"Hail, Brunswic, hail the glorious day."  (28)

GA, Sep 17, 1782.

Quatrains.  The British navy, led by Admirals Richard Howe and Samuel Barrington, sets out to engage the French in order to relieve Elliott, who is besieged in Gibraltar.

82-343.  Stanzas.  On our Late Glorious Successes.  Addressed to the Right Hon. Lord Rodney, Commander in Chief of His Majesty's Forces at the Leeward Islands.

"Rich in herself, yet fond to bless Mankind."  (36)

PA, Jul 11, 1782;  St J's C, Jul 6, 1782.

Regular (Horatian) ode in sixains.  A tribute to Rodney for his victory over the French fleet, Battle of the Saints, April 12, 1782.

82-344.  Stanzas on the Victory of the 12th of April 1782.  Addressed to the Commanders of the British Navy, who had the honor to serve with the Gallant Rodney on that glorious day.

"From Heav'n behold a chearing ray."  (76)

MH, Jul 18, 1782.

Quatrains.

82-345.  Stanzas on the Year 1782.

"Britain, thy fame, in eighty-two."  (50)

English Chronicle, or Universal Evening Post, Dec 3, 1782.

Regular ode in dixains.  A patriotic poem.  The fame of Britain in 1782 surpasses that of 1759 because now Britain, alone and without allies, has defeated her enemies France and Spain on the seas and at Gibraltar.

82-346.  Stanzas to the Gallant Elliot, on the Siege of Gibraltar.

"No more attun'd to just disdain."  (26)

W Eve Post, Oct 17, 1782.

Irregular stanzas.

82-347.  Stanzas written in Westminster Abbey.  Inscribed to L[aurence] Cox, Esq; M.P.

"Ah! whence those sounds, that thus in sorrows strain." (36)

MH, Aug 31, 1782.

Elegiac quatrains. Britannia mourns her troubles -- the colonies have broken away aided by France and Spain, and now Ireland wishes to do the same; and faction tears the nation apart. Unanimity is wanted in Parliament and the fighting forces. (Laurence Cox, a London merchant, was a war contractor, and generally a supporter of North's Administration. See Lewis Namier and John Brooke, The House of Commons 1754-1790 [1964], II, 266.)
These stanzas are not ironic.

82-348. [The Star which marks the Noble Breast.]

"The Star which marks the Noble Breast." (12)

L Cour, Feb 16, 1782; PA, Feb 13, 1782; W Eve Post, Feb 14, 1782.

Quatrains. General satire on spurious nobility; but the specific occasion for reprinting these favorite verses at this time is the objection to the elevation of George Germain to the peerage. The point is made that only virtue or merit distinguishes the nobility of a peer, endowing him with worth and dignity. As these lines emphasize "true worth," "true greatness," irrespective of hereditary birth, they appear to favor republican or levelling ideals. For the "Lord's Protest" to Germain's elevation, see L Chron 51 (Feb 19, 1782), 182. For versions of this favorite poem, see 64-85 (with many other references), and 66-127.

82-349. The State Doctors: A Poem. Addressed to Doctors J[eb]b and B[rockleb]y.

"Too poor old England, sick, and like to die." (158)

MH, Aug 27, 1782.

HC. Satire on the former Patriot Opposition, now the members of the ruling ministry, for sedition, republican principles, and treachery, that is, helping the Americans win the war: especially Gen. Sir William Howe, Burgoyne, Fox, Burke, and Barre. Also included are remarks on Ireland (related to America).

Steele, Ann. On a Day of Prayer for Success in War. "Lord, how shall wretched sinners dare." (32) W Misc 18 (Aug 19, 1782), 504. See 80-39.

82-350. [Tasker, William.]
The following Verses are said to be an extemporaneous "jeu d'esprit" of the Reverend Mr. Tasker.

"Daughter of Poesy divine." (70)

M Chron, Jun 17, 1782; W Eve Post, Jun 15, 1782.

OC. A reaction to Seward's invitation to Stella, 82-328, with some light remarks on politics and the end of the American War.

82-351. Taxation: A New Song.

"Would he Tax but the rich folks, I should not much care." (32)

GA, Mar 22, 1782.

A Scotch complaint that North is not taxing the people fairly in order to pay for the American War.

82-352. [Than Marlborough Rodney more glorious by far is.]

"Than Marlborough Rodney more glorious by far is." (2)

W Eve Post, May 28, 1782.

Epigram. On Rodney's defeat of De Grasse, April 12, 1782. General Marlborough threatened Paris; but Rodney captured it. (He captured De Grasse's flagship, the Ville de Paris.)

82-353. [Thinking the storm was o'er, and the winds at peace.]

"Thinking the storm was o'er, and the winds at peace." (c. 90)

GA, Jul 30, 1782.

HC. The pleasures of politics in reading the newspapers when Parliament is in session; concludes with praise of Rockingham, "the boast of English pride."

82-354. [This house may England represent, 'tis plain.]

"This house may England represent, 'tis plain." (2)

L Cour, Mar 5, 1782.

Epigram. HC. Taken "from the Wall of a Water Closet." Vulgar satire on Germain's poor and ineffectual leadership during the American War.

82-355. Thomas, E. (Astronomer.)
An Ode. Most Respectfully Dedicated to the President, Gentlemen, &c., Promoters of the Briddyn Column, in Honour of Lord Rodney.

"Brave men with bravery will their leaders fire." (c. 60)

GA, Aug 15, 1782.

Song. A Welshman honors Rodney.

82-356. To a Young Lady on the return of her Lover from America.

"Harriet, prepare! thy captain's come." (24)

LM 51 (Mar 1782), 140.

Quatrains. Generalized advice to the young woman to love the veteran returning from the American War.

82-357. To Colonel T*****.

"Far as the distant north, the voice of Fame." (36)

MH, Sep 10, 1782.

HC. A criticism of Colonel Tarleton, brave in battle but cruel to a woman whose reputation he had ruined. Relevant because of the lines on Tarleton's military reputation. (He was charged with brutality by the colonists.)

82-358. To L[ord] N[orth].

"Behold th'indignant Muse depress'd with chains." (21)

L Cour, Apr 15, 1782.

HC. Satire on North, who is asked to leave the stage and seek obscurity. (North resigned March 20, 1782.)

82-359. To Lord North, on Hearing of his intended Tax upon Dogs.

"A Tax upon dogs, my good Lord, you propose." (14)

MP, Mar 14, 1782.

Hexameter couplets. Satire on North. A poor dog objects to Lord North's desperate measure to raise revenue by a tax upon dogs.

82-360. To Mr. Fox, on his late excellent Speech upon the Irish Bill.

"To speak at once thy own and People's sense." (8)

St J's C, Oct 1, 1782.

HC. Praise of Fox's oratorical style. (By this time, Fox had broken with Shelburne and left the ministry.)

To Peace. GA, Jul 25, 1782. See "Ode to Peace," 82-220.

82-361. To the Americans.

"Cervus equum pugna melior communibus herbis." (5)

"Once upon a time (I think 'tis Aesop's brood)." (8)

MH, Apr 5, 1782.

HC. Animal fable. Latin and English. Once curbed (by the French), the Americans will not be free.

82-362. To the Glorious Defenders of Liberty.

"While fawning sycophants to the Nine implore." (36)

GA, Jul 20, 1782.

HC. Praise of those in the former minority who had consistently opposed the (Tory) ministers and their war policy. These patriots (now in power) are the guardians of Britain's laws and liberties.

82-363. To the Honorable C. J. Fox.

"Is there no Daemon unexplor'd." (48)

MH, Sep 9, 1782.

Quatrains. Satire on Fox. And Burke, motivated by ambition, associates with Fox.

82-364. To the K[ing]. Answer to the Above.

"To create Lord Sackville was wisely advised." (4)

L Cour, Feb 26, 1782; PA, Feb 26, 1782.

Epigram. Satire on Germain and the King, who has the power to create a peer of anyone he wishes.

82-365. To the King's Most Excellent Majesty.

"Illustrious George! remember now." (6)

M Chron, Mar 30, 1782.

OC. Extempore. "Modern Whigs," General Sir William Howe and Admiral Augustus Keppel, are responsible for the King's loss of an empire.

82-366. To the Memory of General Lee, who died in America, having served more Nations than Britain.

"Warriour, farewell! excentrically brave." (18)

St J's C, Nov 26, 1782.

HC. A character of Gen. Lee -- mercenary, republican, proud, fearless, solitary, etc. (The character is generally unsympathetic yet respectful.) Charles Lee died at Philadelphia, October 2, 1782.

82-367. To the Memory of John Hugh Griffith, Esq; First Lieutenant of Marines, who was killed by an explosion of a cartridge on board the Prudente, in the late action between Hood and De Grasse: being the fragment of a letter to his Mother, written after he was wounded.

"Amidst these bleeding wounds and social tears." (76)

M Chron, Apr 5, 1782.

Blank verse. After seven years' service in America, since 1775, Griffith was mortally wounded in an explosion on board his ship. He describes the action before he dies, and a friend completes the letter and asks for peace with America.

To the Memory of Major Marjoribanks, late of his Majesty's 19th Regiment of Foot. "Unskill'd in verse, I boast no poet's art." (50) L Chron 51 (May 2, 1782), 431; PA, May 1, 1782. See John Marjoribanks, 82-186, 84-9.

82-368. To the Memory of the Late Marquis of Rockingham.

"He's gone, alas! great Rockingham is gone." (20)

M Chron, Jul 4, 1782.

HC. Eulogy on Rockingham, who has died, July 1, 1782. The country now needs leaders desperately, or farewell liberty! But Richmond gives hope.

82-369. To the "Old Whig."

"Hail! learned Sir! thou wisest of the Times." (34)

PA, Jul 2, 1782.

Blank verse. Praise of an "old Whig," not identified, for indicting North, Germain, and Sandwich for Britain's failures and for being unwilling to allow them to make the peace. But now that Britain has defeated the French fleet, she must whip France and force her to submit to a proper peace.

82-370. To the Paym[aste]r-General on the Late Changes.

"A Word or two, good Edm--d B--ke." (84)

PA, May 17, 1782; W Eve Post, May 21, 1782.

Regular (Horatian) ode in seven-line stanzas. The poet admonishes Burke and the new ministry to reward all those honest politicians who were overlooked in the last appointments, all friends who were unrewarded -- like Temple Luttrell or even Henry Cruger. Some appointments are questioned: Burgoyne, David Hartley. See 83-173.

82-371. To the People. -- An Ode.

"When [Fox] with insolent command." (42)

MH, Jun 21, 1782.

OC. Satire on Fox, who is not fit for political leadership.

To the Right Honourable William Pitt, Chancellor of the Exchequer. See Valentine Nevill, "To the Right Honourable William Pitt . . ." 82-198.

82-372. To the Thane.

"Quarrel not St[uar]t with thy sentence mild." (8)

L Cour, Apr 24, 1782.

HC. Bute is still reviled for his hatred of liberty; he is a Stuart like his great relations, Charles I and James II -- the one executed, the other banished.

82-373. [Too long has resounded the murmurs of woe.]

"Too long has resounded the murmurs of woe." (16)

G Eve Post, Jun 8, 1782.

Song in praise of Admiral Rodney for conquering De Grasse in the West Indies.

82-374. The Triple Cord. King, Lords, and Commons.

"King. Lords, and Commons, strenuous in one Plan." (102)

PA, Mar 13, 1782.

HC. Causidicus objects to national disunity and, invoking the spirit of Chatham, demands that Britain (a triple cord) unite against France.

82-375. The Triumph of Rodney.

"With trembling Hand the God of Day." (84)

Cumb Pacq, Jun 11, 1782.

Ballad in sixains narrates the naval battle in the West Indies, in which Rodney defeated De Grasse and captured the Ville de Paris and Hector.

82-376. Twitcher in Retirement.

"Into the free and open Air." (24)

PA, Apr 11, 1782.

Regular (Horatian) ode in sixains. A satire on Sandwich going into retirement with "His Bottle and his W[hore]." He will no longer be concerned with fighting "The Vet'ran Washington," or with naval reviews.

82-377. Twitcher's Comfort.

"I'm out, cries old Twitcher, but when IN took such care." (4)

St J's C, Apr 9, 1782; WM 56 (Apr 18, 1782), 50; W Eve Post, Apr 18, 1782.

Epigram. Satire on Sandwich, whose persona boasts that he has damaged the ship of state beyond repair.

82-378. Unanimity. A Song on the change of the ministry in 1782. By G. Rollos, Author of the Royal Quatorze, printed in the Lond. Mag. for October 1780. Vol. XLIX. Tune. Rural Felicity.

"Ye true honest Britons and friends to the nation." (60)

LM 51 (Apr 1782), 186.

Song in dixains. Unanimity is the theme. Rollos, a pseudonym, welcomes the new ministry and expresses a hope for the end of "party-commotions."

82-379. Unanimity: Or, The Downfall of Faction.

"Greatness distress'd will ev'n dissolve." (16)

PA, Apr 2, 1782; W Eve Post, Mar 30, 1782.

Quatrains. Unanimity will enable Britain to maintain her freedom, greatness, and prosperity against her "num'rous Hosts of Foes."

82-380.  Upon Arnold's standing near the King, when the Commons presented their Address.

"If by his company a man is known."  (10)

L Cour, Mar 7, 1782.

HC.  Arnold boasts the he will fight for the King and beat the Rebels;  but he should fear hanging by Congress.  He may get a ribbon from the King, but a rope from Congress!

82-381.  Upon the Late Dismission of his Majesty's Ministers.

"The King, in a pet, his affairs all derang'd."  (4)

W Eve Post, May 9, 1782.

Anapest tetrameter couplets.  Satiric epigram.  The King should have ordered that the North ministry be hanged.

82-382.  Verses Addressed to All Parties.

"Heaven sometimes to chastise flagitious Times."  (61)

PA, Feb 13, 1782.

HC.  Satire by Causidicus denouncing faction and division, and calling for unity against the Bourbon enemy.  Cited are Rockingham and Stormont, Fox and North, and Richmond and Thurlow.

82-383.  Verses Applicable to the Present Crisis.

"Says France's Monarch to the King of Spain."  (8)

GA, Dec 11, 1782.

HC.  The King of France indicates to the King of Spain that, although the English cannot be beaten in the field, they will lose the peace.  (Alludes to the Peace of 1763.)  They "Make War like lions, but make Peace like fools."

82-384.  Verses on the Duke of Portland's being appointed Lord-Lieutenant of Ireland.

"Such welcome Tidings to Hibernia's Shore."  (15)

GA, Apr 19, 1782;  St J's C, Apr 16, 1782.

HC.  Praise of William Henry Cavendish-Bentinck, Third Duke of Portland, who will be an honorable and uncorrupt Viceroy of Ireland.

82-385. Cancelled.

82-386. Verses, to the Memory of Mr. Richard Stevens, a young Officer who was killed at Gibraltar, in October, 1781.

"In hostile wars, where dying cries." (24)

Lady's M 13 (Dec 1782), 663-4.

Quatrains. Generalized lines on the death of a heroic soldier who "nobly fell" at Gibraltar.

82-387. Verses written by an American after his Arrival in London.

"Distant, far distant from his native soil." (40)

T&C 14 (Jan 1782), 47-8.

Elegiac quatrains. A young loyalist flees to England, leaving his sweetheart and parents behind; he vows to shun dissipation and be good.

82-388. The Vicar of Bray. Tune, In Charles the Second's Merry Days.

"In good King Charles's golden days." (52)

W Misc 18 (Jun 24, 1782), 305-7. The Convivial Songster (London: Highley, n.d. [c. 1788]), pp. 238-9.

The old Restoration song of the Vicar of Bray who shifted allegiance to save his skin is brought up to date when the Tory Government was displaced by the Whig Opposition in 1782. (The Vocal Magazine [1778], Song 843, p. 226, prints the six-stanza version which reaches to the reign of George II.)

82-389. Warton, Thomas.
Imitation of Horace, Book II. Ode VIII. By the Rev. Thomas Warton, B. D. Ulla si juris, &c. To the Prime Minister.

"If ever Justice with her iron hand." (40)

L Cour, Jan 3, 1782.

HC in irregular stanzas. North (resigned as premier March 20, 1782) should beware corruption.

82-390. [Wesley, Charles.]
A Motion of the Minority.

"Agreed! let it be as the Patriots hope." (10)

AM 5 (Mar 1782), 167; repr. The Poetical Works of John and Charles Wesley, ed. G. Osborn (1870), VIII, 480.

Anapestic tetrameter couplets. Frank Baker, <u>Representative Verse of Charles Wesley</u> (London: Epworth Press, 1962), p. 347, assigns this poem to Charles Wesley and declares that "it may relate to the vote of February 22, 1782, [on Conway's motion to end the war,] which almost forced the seeking of peace terms with the American colonists." Baker also relates the poem (pp. 346-7) to another poem by Charles Wesley, still in MS, "Written on a Late Vote Febr. 22, 1782."

82-391. [Wesley, Charles.]
Non Tali Auxilio, Nec Defensoribus Istis Tempus Eget. -- Virgil. [Wreckers of the Realm.]

"What hope of safety for our Realm." (60)

The Poetical Works of John and Charles Wesley, ed. G. Osborn (1870), VIII, 480-2 (wanting last two stanzas); Representative Verse of Charles Wesley, ed. Frank Baker (1962), pp. 349-50.

Regular ode in sixains. Not published in serials. Baker assigns this MS poem to Charles Wesley, and dates it "shortly after the overthrow of North's ministry early in 1782." (North resigned March 20, 1782.) The poet expresses distaste for the Opposition, especially Wilkes and Fox, for wrecking the realm, committing treason, and feeding rebellion's fire, raising civil discord "higher." Insincere, they are motivated by self-interest, "avarice and ambition." They are the heirs of Cromwell.

82-392. [Wesley, Charles. (?)]
On General Wolfe.

"In various climes immortal honours won." (22)

AM 5 (Aug 1782), 447.

HC. In praise of Wolfe, England's national hero, a great leader.

82-393. [Wesley, Charles.]
Written on a Late Declaration of Lord C[ornwallis] that the Conquest of America by Fire and Sword is not to be accomplished.

"True is the Patriotic word." (48)

AM 5 (Sep 1782), 500-2; M Chron, Oct 2, 1782; PA, Oct 3, 1782.

Sixains in OC. Frank Baker, <u>Representative Verse of Charles Wesley</u> (London: Epworth Press, 1962), pp. 344-7, assigns this poem to Charles Wesley. In the poem, Wesley hopes that Carleton will continue the war against America and criticizes Howe and Cornwallis for their failure. Also repr. in <u>The Poetical Works of John and Charles Wesley</u>, ed. G. Osborn (1870), VIII, 482-4.

82-394. The Westminster Harangue.

"Like Wilkes or old Poplicola, with art." (4)

MH, May 15, 1782.

HC. Satire on Fox. The rabble, who are like geese, should beware Fox's seductive oratory. (Fox is a demagogue like Wilkes.)

82-395. [When Rome its ancient glory lost.]

"When Rome its ancient glory lost." (31)

M Chron, Aug 30, 1782.

Irregular verse. Who can save declining England?

82-396. Whitehead, William.
Ode for the King's Birth-Day, June 4, 1782. Written by W. Whitehead, Esq. Poet Laureat. Set to Music by Mr. Stanley, Master of the King's Band of Musicians.

"Still does reluctant Peace refuse." (54)

AR 1782, pp. 187-8; Cal Merc, Jun 8, 1782; Cumb Pacq, Jun 11, 1782; DJ, Jun 8, 1782; G Eve Post, Jun 1-4, 1782; GM 52 (Jun 1782), 302; Lady's M 13 (Jun 1782), 325; Lloyd's 50 (Jun 3, 1782), 532; M Chron, Jun 4, 1782; MH, Jun 4, 1782; NAR 1782 (III, 182-3); PA, Jun 4, 1782; St J's C, Jun 1-4, 1782; T&C 14 (Jun 1782), 326; WM 56 (Jun 13, 1782), 303; W Misc 18 (Jun 17, 1782), 282-3; W Eve Post, Jun 1-4, 1782; also L Chron 51 (Jun 1-4, 1782), 535.

Irregular Pindaric ode. Whitehead reviews the situation in 1782. Peace still does not come. But Holland has had enough of war "And [should] know her ancient friends again." It is hoped that America and Britain, after a bloody and destructive civil war, will be reconciled and reunited. The French have suffered defeat in the West Indies, and "the Gallic star" sinks below the horizon.

82-397. Whitehead, William.
Ode for the New Year, Jan. 1, 1782. Written by W. Whitehead, Esq. Poet Laureat.

"O Wondrous power of inborn worth." (36)

AR 1782, p. 186; Cal Merc, Jan 5, 1782; Cumb Pacq, Jan 8, 1782; DJ, Jan 5, 1782; G, Jan 1, 1782; G Eve Post, Dec 29, 1781-Jan 1, 1782; GM 52 (Jan 1782), 36; Lady's

M 12 (Supplement 1781), 718; Lloyd's 50 (Dec 31, 1781-Jan 2, 1782), 4; MH, Jan 1, 1782; NAR 1782 (III, 180-1); PA, Jan 1, 1782; RWM 7: 3 (Jan 9, 1782), 22; St J's C, Dec 29, 1781-Jan 1, 1782; W Misc 17 (Jan 14, 1782), 383; W Eve Post, Dec 29, 1781-Jan 1, 1782; also L Chron 51 (Dec 29, 1781-Jan 1, 1782), 7.

Regular ode in twelve-line stanzas. Although Britain stands alone in her struggle against many nations, "She cannot fall," for God "Does still her arduous cause maintain."

Who's the Noodle. A New Song. GA, Jan 15, 1782. See "A New Loyal Song," 79-276.

82-398. A Wish for the New Year.

"The fleeting year, late call'd our own." (30)

Lady's M 13 (Feb 1782), 103-4.

Sixains. May Britain defeat the French and Spanish, and may peace come again.

82-399. [With Englishmen 'tis still the same.]

"With Englishmen 'tis still the same." (50)

Cumb Pacq, Jun 4, 1782.

OC. Rodney is defended from hasty, ill-conceived criticism of being mercenary. The blame for contradictory measures is placed upon the new ministry, which wished to blame someone for their weakness.

82-400. [With floods of praise Ierne's sons.]

"With floods of praise Ierne's sons." (44)

GA, Sep 18, 1782; M Chron, Sep 16, 1782.

Regular ode in quatrains. A tribute to those Irish political leaders who succeeded in achieving freedom for Ireland.

82-401. The Wits, a Satire.

"Ill-Fated poetry by fashion made." (c. 180)

LM 51 (Oct 1782), 485-6.

HC. A complaint that satire is not serving its function in this age. Critical judgments are made on George Colman (the Elder, the dramatist), James Scot (the client of Sandwich), Samuel Johnson, William Mason, and Junius. The writer wishes for the return of Junius.

82-402. [Wo(e) to this land whereon we tread.]

"Wo[e] to this land whereon we tread." (54)

GA, Mar 18, 1782.

Regular ode in sixains. The end of England's glory is mourned, and those who try to do her good are libelled as rebels. The old North ministry is still in power.

82-403. The Wooden Walls of England. A favourite Song, sung by Mr. Cubitt, at Vauxhall Gardens. Set to Music by Mr. Barthelemon.

"When Britain on her sea-girt shore." (40)

G Eve Post, Jun 18, 1782; MH, Jun 20, 1782; St J's C, Jun 18, 1782; UM 70 (Jun 1782), 321-2; W Misc 18 (Jul 1, 1782), 332-3; W Eve Post, Jun 20, 1782.

"Britain's best bulwarks are her Wooden Walls," her warships. By Henry Green, reprinted for the occasion of the recent naval victories: see 73-37 and 80-155.

82-404. Written Extempore by a Person Unknown, May 10, 1782.

"Britannia looks -- and loves the Man." (18)

GA, May 16, 1782.

Mixed verse. The virtuous Patriot, Fox, will save the sinking state: "Freedom -- and a Fox [are] the same."

82-405. Written in 1782, Upon the Bust of the Earl of Chatham.

"Her trophies faded, and revers'd her spear." (10)

An Asylum for Fugitive Pieces. A New Edition (London: Debrett, 1785), I, 51.

HC. England became great under Chatham and suffered a disastrous decline upon his death.

82-406. Written on the Change of Ministry.

"Says the Whig to the Tory, If you govern much longer." (22)

GA, May 7, 1782.

Fourteener couplets. The new ministry of Whigs, led by Fox, will begin a total reform as it sweeps out the old, corrupt Tory government.

82-407. Wrote Extempore over a Bottle on a Discourse of Ireland's Late Restor'd

Rights.  By G. E. Howard.

"Whilst Nations who have been distress'd."  (12)

DJ, May 30, 1782.

Extempore in sixains.  Ireland, unlike America, remained loyal, did not rebel and begin a civil war in order to have its rights restored.

82-408.  [Ye Britons! boast not that your Kings of yore.]

"Ye Britons! boast not that your Kings of yore."  (12)

GA, Feb 20, 1782.

HC.  Ironic satire on the King for making a button and for elevating Germain to the peerage as Lord Sackville -- two *great* achievements!

Prints

82-409. The American Rattle Snake.

"Two British Armies I have thus Burgoyn'd." (6)

Engr. with couplet and quatrain. By James Gillray. April 12, 1782.

George 5973 (V, 569). Dolmetsch, pp. 170-1.

The American rattlesnake has surrounded the armies of Burgoyne and Cornwallis, and is prepared to surround a third.

82-410. The American Rattlesnake Presenting Monsieur His Ally a Dish of Frogs.

"Monsieur be pleas'd to accept the frogs." (10)

Engr. with couplets and sixain. November 8, 1782.

George 6039 (V, 616-17). Repr. The British Look at America During the Age of Samuel Johnson (1971), #92.

Britons are advised to separate the Rattlesnake (the colonies) from the French; otherwise, the colonies will be lost to France.

82-411. The British Lion Engaging Four Powers.

"Behold the Dutch and Spanish Currs." (6)

Engr. with OC. June 14, 1782.

George 6004 (V, 593). Dolmetsch, pp. 180-1.

The several powers engage in peace negotiations and assert their claims -- and Britain appears to resist, supported by Fox. America is a rattlesnake and asserts her independence.

82-412. The Chase. To the Tune of the Dusky Night.

"From Nimrod to these happier days." (51)

Engr. with song. February 16, 1782.

George 5961 (V, 560-1).

The satiric song is directed at the King and his government. He simply prefers to go hunting despite the disasters on land and sea in the war against the Allies. Cited also are Fox, Burke, and Barré.

82-413. Date obolum Belisario.

"Rome's Veteran fought her rebel Foes." (8)

Engr. with quatrains. August 24, 1782.

George 6028 (V, 610).

Lord Shelburne rewards Col. Barre with a pension of £3,000 per annum.

82-414. The Five Travellers.

"A Robber from America first View." (12)

Engr. with couplets. 1782 (?).

Copy in Lewis-Walpole Library.

Two of the evil travellers are an American (possibly John Jay) who wishes to plunder Ireland and Charles James Fox, who is crafty and treacherous. Cited are Orde, Mason, Ireland, Hillsborough. (Written from the point of view of protecting the English interest over Ireland.)

82-415. The Grumbling Princes Or the Dev-l take the Monsieurs.

"I swore (said Lewis) t'other day." (8)

Engr. with two quatrains. June 12, 1782.

George 6000 (V, 590-1).

King Louis of France boasts that his navy will make the English submit; but Rodney's victory gave him the lie. (Rodney says "Da-n the Peace," as he has DeGrasse prisoner along with six warships.)

82-416. Labour in Vain or Let them Tug and Be Da-nd.

"Four Foes to old England have Wickedly Join'd." (8)

Engr. with quatrains. November 27, 1782.

George 6040 (V, 617).

Britain resists the four allies, her enemies: America, Spain, France, and Holland. America is portrayed as an Indian woman with a feather headdress and sandals, holding a tomahawk.

82-417. Lord North in the Suds.

"For Taxing of Salt Tobacco and Soap." (4)

Engr. with doggerel verse in couplets. March 27, 1782.

George 5968 (V, 565).

New taxes are sought by the North government, and North is here belittled.

82-418. The Minister In. The Minister Out.

"When the Ministers In, how subservient his Friends." (8)

Engr. with two quatrains. By Gillray. April 22, 1782.

George 5978 (V, 572).

When the ministers are in power, they are treated with great deference; but when out of power, they are treated disgracefully. Fox and North are mentioned.

82-419. The Reconciliation between Britania and her daughter America.

"A curse upon all Artifice." (8)

Engr. with quatrains. March 1782.

George 5989 (V, 582-3). Dolmetsch, pp. 178-9.

America is being reconciled with Britain while France and Spain protest and Holland appears neutral. The ministers are to be cashiered.

82-420. Reynards Mirror.

"In this slight Sketch behold the Man portray'd." (33)

Engr. with verses. March 4, 1782.

Copy at Lewis-Walpole Library.

Satire in heroic couplets, on Fox for betraying the nation to the enemy, the French and the Americans. Britons should beware of this traitor.

82-421. The State Cooks Making Peace--Porridge.

"The State Cooks a making Peace-Porridge are found." (8)

Engr. with couplets in quatrains. July 6, 1782.

George 6009 (V, 597-8). Wynn Jones, p. 175.

On the difficulties of making peace. Fox is cited.

1783  Books & Pamphlets

83-1. An Address from the Members of the Constitutional Body to their Sovereign on the Change of the Ministry. By an American Loyalist.
London: Bladon, 1783.

Notices: CR 56 (Jul 1783), 74; MR 68 (Jun 1783), 540.

Copies: none located.


83-2. Arx Herculea Servata, quum ab Hispanis simul ac Gallis obsideretur; Anno MDCCLXXXII. Or, Gibraltar Delivered, A Poem, In Latin And English. Inscribed to the Right Honourable Admiral Lord Viscount Howe, and the Right Honourable General George Aug. Elliot, K. B.
London: Davis, 1783.

Notices: CR 56 (Aug 1783), 151; MR 69 (Nov 1783), 436; ERL 2 (Jul 1783), 70.

Copies: none located.

In Latin, with English translation. Celebrates the praises of Gen. Elliott and his brave garrison, victorious in Gibraltar over the besieging Bourbon powers.


83-3. Brice, Thomas.
The State Coach in the Mire, A Modern Tale; In Four Parts. By Thomas Brice.
London: Scatcherd & Whitaker; Exeter: Woolmer & The Author, 1783. 32p.

"The old State-Coach, which long had borne." (c. 750)

Notices: CR 56 (Sep 1783), 235-7; ERL 3 (Aug 1783), 147.

Copies: BL 11601.ff.1 (6); NUC MH (imperfect).

Hudibrastic doggerel verse. Political allegory. Traces the major outlines of politics from 1760 to c. 1782-3. I. Pitt had left the state coach in excellent condition until Bute mired it. Bute resigned buy "by proxy" continued to hold the reins and drive crazily through North's ministry. Sandwich would blame the people for getting stuck in the quagmire, not the ministry. The ghost of Pitt (Chatham) warns the King that this leadership will destroy the kingdom and advises that more skillful and wise drivers succeed them.
II. Conway declares that the North ministry lost the American trade, started a civil war ("Two armies of kindred brood,/ Who deluge all the scene with blood"), undermined the prosperity of the West Indies, aroused Ireland to rebel, dethroned Britain

as monarch of the seas. Germaine resigned (Feb. 11, 1782); and after some delay Sandwich and North gave up the reins (Mar. 20, 1782), to be replaced by Conway and his friends.

III. Rockingham, now the chief minister, effects a few reforms (excludes contractors and excise men from parliament). Meanwhile, Rodney thrashes De Grasse. When Rockingham dies, Fox and Shelburne compete for the driver's seat, which the latter wins after a scuffle. Guided purely by politics, Fox thereupon forms a coalition with North, despite his contempt for the former premier. North describes it as "A very nat'ral coalition"! Its purpose was to prevent Shelburne from having his peace, thus forcing his resignation. Portland succeeds in the driver's seat, with Fox and North as assistants. However, the younger Pitt, urged by his father's ghost, intervenes.

IV. The younger Pitt begins a reformation. But encountering resistance, he compromises with North, which produces a debate led by Thomas Powys. At the close, Brice urges all to unite to "work the rightful reformation," so that the state coach will move again.


83-4. Brown, T.
The Times: A Satire. To the King; and Dedicated to the Emperor of Germany.
By T. Brown.
London: Edgerton, 1783.

"In solitary dales, unknown of pain."

Notices: CR 55 (May 1783), 408-9; MR 68 (Jun 1783), 540; ERL 1 (May 1783), 424.

Copies: none located.


83-5. [Cartwright, Edmund]
Sonnets To Eminent Men. And An Ode To The Earl of Effingham.
London: Murray, Becket, 1783. 15p.

VI. To The Duke Of Richmond. On His Motion For Annual Parliaments, And Equal Representation, 1780. "The stream that, wandering from its parent source." (14) p. 8.

Ode To The Earl of Effingham, On His Going A Volunteer To The Relief of Gibraltar. "Severely shall the heart repine." (60) pp. 11-15.

Notices: CR 54 (Dec 1782), 478; MR 68 (Jan 1783), 46; ERL 1 (Jan 1783), 58-9. The sonnet to Richmond also appeared in Lloyd's Eve Post 55 (Sep 24, 1784), 303; L Cour, Jan 16, 1781; NAR 1783 (III, 204-5); West Mag 10 (Nov 1782), 605; and W Eve Post, Sep 23, 1784. The ode appeared in West Mag 10 (Dec 1782), 662-3.

Copies: BL 1601/311; NUC CtY, MBAt, MH.

Six Italian sonnets, one clearly relevant here--To Richmond. Cartwright praises Richmond (an important leader of the Minority during North's ministry) for his motion to prevent corruption by reforming the laws about parliamentary elections and representation. He has become "Freedom's Champion, and THE PEOPLE'S FRIEND." See 86-A.

"Ode to Effingham"--regular Horatian ode in sixains. Cartwright also praises Thomas Howard, 3rd Earl of Effingham, for resigning his commission rather than fight the American colonists. He had refused "to quench in kindred gore/ . . . Freedom's holy rays," and had joined "the chosen few, the patriot band," or Minority. Now that the war grew to include France and Spain, Effingham can maintain his principles, become active again, and exhibit his patriotism and courage with Gen. Elliott on Gibraltar. See 86-1.

83-6. Cave, Jane (afterwards Winscom).
Poems on Various Subjects, Entertaining, Elegiac, and Religious.
Winchester: Sadler, 1783. iv + 150 + 26p.

Copies: BL 11632.aaa.10; 993.c.43 (1) (1786 ed); NUC CtY, ICN, IU, MB, MH, PU.

Two poems: see 75-4, 82-6.

83-7. The Coalition Ballad. As sung at the Shakespeare.
[London, 1783.] Broadside.

"Come listen awhile, and I'll give you a song." (40)

Copies: BL C.121.g.9 (217).

Ballad with Derry down chorus. Narrates the formation of the Fox-North coalition. North was angrily opposed by Fox and Burke only to join them soon after the fall of his ministry, and form (to the indignation of the balladist) a "Damn'd Coalition." But the younger Pitt inspires confidence. At the end, the poet asks the electors (of Westminster) to vote for Sir Cecil Wray and Admiral Samuel Hood, rather than for Fox. Decorated with engraving of heads of Fox, Burke, and North.

83-8. Coombe, Thomas.
The Peasant of Auburn; Or, The Emigrant. A Poem. Inscribed To The Earl of Carlisle. By T. Coombe, D. D.
London: Elmsly, Robson, 1783. 5-18p.

"Dark was the sky, and fatal was the morn." (232)

Notices: CR 55 (Aug 1783), 149-50; MR 69 (Sep 1783), 258-9; ERL 2 (Sep 1783), 224-5; GM 53 (Oct 1783), 862-3; Lloyd's Eve Post 53 (Sep 17, 1783), 276; L Chron 54 (Sep 13, 1783), 265; NAR 1783 (III, 211-12).

Sabin 16390-1.

Copies: BL T.3 (6), 11630.b.6 (3); NUC CtY, DLC, ICN, MH, NN, PHi, RPJCB.

HC. A sentimental poem against emigration. Inspired by Goldsmith's <u>Deserted Village</u>, which is imitated in theme, thought, and expression. Coombe contrasts through an emigrant Edwin the present miseries of life beside the "wild Ohio," "the scene of Braddock's defeat," and the past pleasures of the simple life in the village of Auburn.

Edwin, driven off the land by the usurpation of a "tyrant lord," emigrates to America. But the three-month wintry voyage across the Atlantic killed his wife Emma and his two little sons. In America, his only surviving child Lucy is carried off by savage Indian "fiends." Civil war, sickness, and famine also take their toll of the emigrants. Alone, with "no pitying friend, no meek-ey'd stranger near," Edwin despairs. Emigration, it is clear, is a terrible mistake. The dreams of freedom and prosperity for the poor who leave for America are "baseless" fantasies. (Also repr. in <u>An Asylum for Fugitive Pieces in Prose and Verse</u> [London: Debrett, 1786], II, 233-43.)

83-9. Crawford, Charles.
Liberty: A Pindaric Ode. By Charles Crawford, Esq.
Tunbridge-Wells: Sprange; Canterbury: Simmons & Kirkby; Maidstone: Blake; London: Rivington, [1783]. iii + 12p.

"Take, O Muse! the breathing Lyre." (174)

Evans 17894 (Philadelphia, 1783), 30297 (The Progress of Liberty [Philadelphia, 1796]); Sabin 17434 (note on Philadelphia ed, 1796).

Copies: BL 1465.d.1 (3) (dated 1789 by BLC); Bod Godwyn Pamph 1737 (19); NUC DLC, MH, PPL, & RPB (Philadelphia, 1783, ed only).

Regular Pindaric ode. Written in Antigua; dated 1783 on internal evidence: Crawford states the North ministry, "a late Ministry," should be brought to trial for engaging the nation in the criminal American War (p. 8).

The Preface argues fro freedom in the Whig tradition of Algernon Sidney, Milton, Locke, and Price, and asserts that the Roman Catholic religion encourages tyranny.

The poem declares that the people's consent ("free and general Choice") delegates authority to a monarch (First Strophe), thereby setting the basis of constitutional monarchy. Love of freedom is traced back to the Greek struggle against the Persians, and to the Roman republic until, corrupted by luxury, it submitted "to th'imperial yoke." Crawford celebrates William of Nassau for rescuing Britain from "a Bigot Tyrant" (James II) and raising "The hallow'd Banner of just Liberty." Britons are motivated by Liberty as demonstrated by Magna Charta and the leadership of Hampden; Crawford asks her "To practice Justice on that venal Band," the last ministry, for its war on the American colonies—"the mad Aim her distant Children to enslave." He also objects to British slavery in the West Indies and American slavery in the southern colonies, and praises Washington for his declaration against slavery. When America shall abolish slavery, it will follow in the tradition of liberty and "Thrive and exult" as "The kind and common Refuge of th'oppresst." (Also repr. in full in G, July 31, 1783.)

83-10. [Cunningham, Peter]
Chatsworth Or The Genius Of England's Prophecy. A Poem. By The Author Of The Naval Triumph.
Chesterfield: Bradley; London: Parker, 1783. 18p.

"Ye Dells, and woodland Wilds, in song unknown." (220)

Notices: CR 57 (Apr 1784), 314-15; MR 71 (Sep 1784), 228.

Copies: BL 1600/83; NUC CtY, DFo, TxU.

Heroic quatrains. An elegant descriptive poem of the Cavendish manorial estate, home of the Duke of Devonshire. Cunningham alludes to the "civil Furies" that disturb the realm, "an envious World [that] in Arms prevail'd," Britain's "matchless Empire's rapid Fall," and America "spurn'd" by Britain and turning to France. But (now that peace is being negotiated) he warns of French treachery. Rodney in his naval victories, the poet Mason in his Ode to . . . William Pitt, and the patriot Thomas Day in his Reflections upon the Present State of England and the Independence of America, "recently republished with additions," will contribute to the revival of Britain's "pristine spirit." And William Cavendish (the Duke of Devonshire, who had been in consistent opposition to North's ministry) will save the country and bring peace with America ("No more on bleeding Brothers waste your Ire"), and with Ireland, who will prosper through free trade. Although Britain's glory has set in the West, it will rise again in the East.


83-11. [-----]
The Naval Triumph. A Poem.
London: Kearsley, 1783. 16p.

"From western climes, where the fierce Lord of Day." (270)

Notices: CR 54 (Dec 1782), 478; MR 68 (Apr 1783), 356-8; ERL 1 (Jan 1783), 62-3.

Sabin 52088.

Copies: NUC CtY, OCU, RPJCB.

Regular Horatian ode in sixains. Panegyric on Admiral Rodney, celebrating his great victory over De Grasse in the Battle of the Saints, in the West Indies on April 12, 1782, which Miss Seward neglected to do. Rodney, who earlier defeated Langara of Spain and seized St. Eustatia from the Dutch, chastises Burke for maligning him (p. 6). Cunningham mourns the death of young Manners, praises some other officers, and, at the conclusion, welcomes peace. (André is cited.)

83-12. [Davies, Jeremiah]
An Epilogue To The Late Peace, Addressed to the Right Honourable The Earl N----. London: Baldwin, 1783. 31p.

"You'll give me credit, good my Lord, I trust." (c. 680)

Notices: CR 55 (Jun 1783), 488; MR 70 (Jan 1784), 77; ERL 3 (May 1784), 389.

Sabin 22685.

Copies: NUC NN, RPJCB.

HC. A bitter protest at British injustice perpetrated against the loyalists. Davies had supported North, but because North lacked "vigour . . . or at least success," Davies agreed that Rockingham was preferable. But when Rockingham died, he is forced to acknowledge Shelburne as chief. Davies has no confidence in Shelburne because of his deceitful nature and his unacceptable peace. Shelburne is careless with the American loyalists, especially in Carolina and Georgia, who, fearing "rebel madness and fanatic zeal/ . . . From tyrant saints and tyrant patriots' hate,/ Flee to the deserts" for safety. Shelburne has no sympathy for the loyalists, and so Davies asks Britons not to forget "those heroes" who fought for them, for they are now exposed "To all the rancour of malignant foes," e. g., "savage Washington" whose "stern decrees" were responsible for Asgill's torment. Shelburne has given Washington and the rebels a free hand with the loyalists. Davies also invokes the spirit of André to tarnish Washington's fame. After all that Britain had done in the past for America, rebel Americans are now behaving meanly, especially in seeking French aid, an unforgivable crime! Davies predicts anarchy in America as its inhabitants are dominated by ambition, "lust of pow'r." He concludes with a denunciation of France, "foremost savage on the roll of shame," for "breach of faith, and deeds of blood"; and a protest at the terrible injustice of British exploitation of India.

83-13. Day, Thomas.
[Epitaph Upon the Death of Colonel Laurens.]

"Here the last prey of that destructive rage." (20)

[Additional Verses on the Death of John Laurens.]

"On by the Delawar's resounding shores." (50)

Notices: EM 19 (Jun 1791), 473; James Keir, <u>An Account of the Life and Writings of Thomas Day, Esq.</u> (London: Stockdale, 1791), pp. 114-17. Also in <u>Select Miscellaneous Productions of Mrs. Day, and Thomas Day, Esq. in Verse and Prose</u> (London: Jones & Cadell, 1805), pp. 10-13.

Day mourns the early death of his friend Colonel John Laurens, killed August 27, 1782, in an obscure skirmish of the irregular warfare that persisted in South Carolina: thus he "seal'd a nation's liberties in death." (Young Laurens, son to Henry Laurens of South Carolina, President of the Congress, was admitted to the Middle Temple, London, September 16, 1772, for the study of law.)

In the second poem, Day pictures the destruction caused by the war in the regions of the Delaware, Bronx, and Saratoga, mourns the numerous dead, but does not think there was "a nobler victim slain/ To glut the bloody rites of freedom's fane" than when Laurens died.

83-14. [Edwards, Bryan]
Poems, On Subjects Arising In England, And The West Indies. . . . By A Native Of The West Indies.
London: Faulder, 1783. vii + i + 108p.

The Antigua Planter; Or War And Famine. "Of that small isle, where oft the planter stands." (219) pp. 23-44.

Ode On Admiral Rodney's Victory, On The Twelfth Of April. "Gallia once more in fair array." (66) pp. 66-9.

Ode To General Elliott, On His Brave Defence Of Gibraltar. "Ye lofty muses, deign a while." (72) pp. 70-4.

Notices: CR 57 (Feb 1784), 110-12; MR 72 (Jun 1785), 467; ERL 2 (Dec 1783), 433-6.

Copies: BL 11630.e.15 (8).

Twenty poems, many on Negro slavery emphasizing the tragedy of slavery in the West Indies.
"The Antigua Planter": HC. Written in 1779 when the French fleets dominated the seas and Antigua suffered drouth and famine. But Edwards focuses far more sharply on the suffering of the slaves than on their white masters.
"Ode on Rodney's Victory": regular Horatian ode in sixains. Describes the naval victory over De Grasse, in general terms.
"Ode to General Elliott": regular Horatian ode in sixains. Praise of Elliott for breaking the siege of Gibraltar.

83-15. Free[th], John.
A Touch On The Times: Or, The Modern Songster, On Various Subjects: Adapted To Common Tunes. By John Free.
Birmingham: Pearson & Rollason, 1783. viii + 76p. (Pp. *57-*60 after p. 60.)

Copies: BL 11621.e.15; NUC MH.

The Political Songster; Or, A Touch on the Times. Third edition.
Birmingham: Pearson & Rollason, 1784. viii + 60p.

Notices: CR 58 (Jul 1784), 73; MR 71 (Nov 1784), 386.

Copies: NUC   CtY, NN.

The Political Songster: Or, A Touch On The Times, On Various Subjects, Adapted To Common Tunes. The 4th ed. By John Freeth.
  Birmingham: Pearson & Rollason, 1786.

Copies: NUC   DFo.

The Political Songster. . . . The 6th ed., with additions.
  Birmingham: Pearson, 1790. xvi + 220 + 11p.

Copies: NUC   CtY, DLC, ICU, OCl.

   These editions of Freeth's songs should be collated with the preceding collections listed in 76-13 and 82-10. Many songs, as before, appeared in journals or newspapers, and are listed in the serial section of this bibliography.
   Songs for 1782 include "Britannia Triumphant! On the Glorious Victory of April 12, 1782," "The Ins and Outs; or, The State Jockies," "The Georges; or Lord Sackville's Promotion," "Corruption Defeated; or the Premier Routed," and "Britannia's Relief."
   Songs for 1783 include "The Budget," "The New Administration, in 1783," "The Old King's Ghost," "On the Prospect for Peace," "The State Pensioners," "The Wonderful Coalition," and "Written on the Day of Thanksgiving for a General Peace" (four songs).

83-16. [Hayley, William ?]
  Ode To A Friend, On Our Leaving, Together, South-Carolina. Written in June 1780.
  London: Dodsley, 1783. 15p.

"Friend of my inmost heart, oh! say." (144)

Notices: CR 55 (Feb 1783), 146-7; MR 69 (Aug 1783), 165-6; ERL 1 (Jun 1783), 515-16; GM 53 (Feb 1783), 155.

Sabin 56707.

Copies: NUC   CSmH, DLC, MH, MiU-C, NN, PHi.

   Regular Horatian ode in adapted Spenserian nine-line stanzas. The poet feels that the pleasures of friendship should alleviate the fury of the war, perhaps bring better days and peace. Unfortunately, however, the slaves cannot share in these domestic pleasures, doomed as they are to eternal oppression. The poet is pained "To see the hand of Freedom wave,/ Aloft, the scorpion lash that rules the slave," and to be unable to do anything about it. He consoles himself with the thought that some in Carolina, like Laura, are color blind and capable of expressing sympathy for the slaves.
   Not by Jayley, but by an anonymous poet who adopted (as he writes in the Advertisement) "the Stanza of Hayley's charming Ode to Mr. Howard," a nine-line stanza.

83-17. -----.
Ode to Mr. Wright of Derby. 1783.

"Away! ye sweet but trivial Forms." (108)

In his <u>Poems and Plays, by William Hayley, Esq. in Six Volumes</u>. A New Edition (London: Cadell, 1788), I, 141-7. (1st ed, 1785.)

Notices: MR 74 (Jan 1786), 69; W Eve Post, Mar 5, 1785.

Copies: BL 11607.c.14 (1785), 239.h.10 (1788); NUC CtY, DLC, MH, & TxU (1785), DLC, InU, & NN (1788).

Regular Horatian ode in adapted Spenserian nine-line stanzas. The poet addresses Joseph Wright, the painter (called Wright of Derby), who is celebrating on a large canvas the successful British repulse under Elliott and Curtis of the Spanish besieging Gibraltar. The defeat occurred September 13, 1782. (Also repr. in <u>An Asylum for Fugitive Pieces in Prose and Verse</u>. A New Edition [London: Debrett, 1785], pp. 68-71.) First edition of the poem--Chichester: Dennett Jaques, 1783. (5-11p.)


83-18. An Heroic Epistle To The Right Honourable Lord Viscount Sackville.
London: Kearsley, 1783. 21p.

"Son of Quirinus! or to greet thine ear." (288)

Notices: CR 55 (Feb 1783), 146; MR 68 (Apr 1783), 355; ERL 1 (Feb 1783), 159-61; GA, Feb 3, 1783.

Copies: BL 11632.h.1 (11); Bod Godwyn Pamph 1709 (10); NUC CSmH, CtY.

Dated from Oxford December 5, 1782. HC. Satire on George Germain, created Viscount Sackville February 11, 1782. But patriot peers will feel only contempt for him who betrayed his cowardice at Minden and dishonored his name. It was certainly mad to appoint this coward Secretary of State for the American Department (from which he resigned in February 1782) and entrust to such a timid, fearful, meek person the execution of the military plans, "'midst flames of civil war," and "'gainst sons of liberty," heroes "flaming with the zeal/ Of patriot glory." America and freedom are ascendant in the western world; but Britain's empire is falling, her honors fading, glories dying. England is being destroyed from within by luxury.
Includes incidental ironic and satiric remarks on King George, who penetrated the aspersions of Germain's character to his "real" merit.


83-19. Independence: A Poem, In Hudibrastic Verse. Addressed to <u>Richard Brinsley Sheridan</u>, Esq.
[London:] Flexney, 1783. 52p.

"When dire disputes, and thirst of power." (c. 1750)

Notices: CR 56 (Jul 1783), 71-2;  MR 69 (Oct 1783), 343;  ERL 2 (Jul 1783), 71.

Copies: NUC  CtY, NcD.

Hudibrastic verse. Imitation of Samuel Butler's Hudibras, satire on politics. The chief characters in this farcical burlesque are Germain, North (or the North ministry taken ensemble), the selfish Scotch, King George (enamored of the Scotch), King Louis of France, and Gen. Washington. The war to suppress the rebellion of the American colonies is presented in a political allegory--the court against thirteen towns. This war is blamed on the Scotch (p. 11). Germain and his squire are tarred and feathered (Canto II), then attacked by Amazons led by one representing Washington (Canto III). The King is presented as a stubborn imbecile obviously in the wrong: "Tho' an estate he shou'd lose by't" (p. 42). He is also considered oppressive and uncharitable. The poet reviews past history from the time Pitt was removed from office at the end of the last war with France and the choice of Bute in his stead, a political act that bred discord. This review takes in the American rebellion, the Declaration of Independence, the Franco-American alliance, including the peace that gave freedom to America. For England, however, it turns out to be a poor peace, like the one negotiated at the end of the last war (Canto IV).

83-20. Neitherside, Nicholas, pseud.
The Political Squabble; Or, A Scramble for the Loaves and Fishes. A Poetical Essay: (Partly In Hudibrastic Verse,) Adapted to the Public Characters of our Statesmen in general, From the Demise of his late Majesty to the present Date. Addressed To All Parties, And Dedicated To The Right Hon. the Marquis of Carmarthen. By Nicholas Neitherside, Gent.
London: Barker, Fielding, 1783. 30p.

"In Britain's Realm, where Freedom reigns." (c. 550)

Notices: CR 55 (Mar 1783), 232;  MR 68 (Mar 1783), 273;  ERL 1 (Mar 1783), 255-6.

Copies: BL 1489.f.35;  NUC  NN.

The date on title page is incorrectly printed MDCCLXXIII. The dedication to the Marquess of Carmarthen is dated January 28, 1783. Carmarthen is praised for integrity. In 1780 he had decided to support the Opposition; as a result, he was quickly removed from his court position.

Hudibrastic verse. A cynical rejection of the politics of 1782, after Rockingham's death. Material self-interest and corruption dominate British life and politics. Yet only virtue marks the man, and "Greatness centers/ . . . In true Nobility of soul," like Hampden, Chatham, Camden. Selfishness, pride, and avarice produce faction and sedition, which undermine the stability of government.

There was union under Pitt near the end of the last war when Britain was gloriously victorious over France. But this happy state of affairs lasted only until Bute and the Scots introduced faction to court. Bute accepted French bribes to make a peace favorable to France. Scots also attempted despotically to banish liberty by filling all the positions of state, monopolizing the power, controlling the state.  This revolution brought protest and civil disturbances along with bribery and corruption ("The dearest Rights are bought and sold/ At common Mart," etc.), subverting the electoral process and eventually causing the American War (pp. 23-4).  The war continued tediously year after year ("ineffective each Campaign") until France formed an alliance with the colonies and brought in Spain and Holland.  Despite this awful combination, the corrupt ministry, instead of resigning, continued as usual to serve up "Loaves and Fishes," "their only View and Aim," until forced to resign and leave to Opposition (Wentworth-Rockingham) the difficulty of negotiating peace and repairing "The Ravage of a tedious War."  When unselfish Rockingham died, Shelburne succeeded to the honors and profits of the premiership; Fox, enraged, resigned from the government.  Thus self-interest and faction persist, impeding administration, confusing negotiations for peace, defeating the country's basic interests.


83-21. Newman, Henry Charles Christian.
   The Love of our Country, A Poem, Dedicated by Permission To His Grace The Duke of Devonshire.  By the Reverend Henry Charles Christian Newman, A. B.  Of Trinity College, Cambridge, and Vicar of Stotfold, in the County of Bedford.
   London: Faulder, Debrett, Egerton, Mattews, Kearsley, & Bladon, 1783.  viii + 21p.

   "Ye chosen Band! whose well exerted zeal." (c. 420)

   Notices:  CR 56 (Jul 1783), 62-3;  MR 70 (Jan 1784), 78;  ERL 3 (May 1784), 388-9.

   Copies:  BL 11630.e.17 (2).

   HC.  A panegyric of the Rockingham ministry begins the poem.  Praise of the "chosen Band," the "happy Few," with whom William Cavendish, the 5th Duke of Devonshire, has joined--Portland, Burke, Fox, Townshend, Conway--"Blest race! who caus'd Britannia's tears to cease."  The poet uses America as the model for freedom and independence, the basis for genuine and disinterested patriotism, "untainted by corruption" and the influence of monarchy (p. 6).  Then Newman describes at great length but in general terms the need for a disinterested love of the country.
   At the end, he appears to refer to a reconciliation between America and Britain.  He hopes the child (America), which Britain will "to maturity and vigor rear," should some day return the favor and help her in her need.


83-22. Noyes, Robert.
   Distress, A Poem.  By Robert Noyes, Cranbrook, Kent.
   Canterbury: Smith; London: Law, Wilkie, Richardson & Urquhart, 1783.  34p.

   "Is there a Muse will her assistance lend." (c. 700)

   Notices:  CR 55 (Feb 1783), 147;  MR 69 (Sep 1783), 260;  ERL 1 (Feb 1783), 165-7;  GM 53 (Jan 1783), 61.

Copies: BL 1465.d.1 (4), 1465.k.12, & 12269.c.8 (1st ed), 11643.aa.45 (1805 ed, with sketch of author's life); NUC ICN & IU (1st ed), InU (1805 ed), IU (1808 ed, with corrected life of author and some account of the poem's composition).

HC. Amidst the private and public scenes of distress described, two are drawn from North America and another from Spithead. The scenes of anguish in America include the catastrophic battle at Bunker's Hill and savage Indian warfare. Noyes narrates the tragic end of an innocent Pennsylvanian family cruelly destroyed by Indians who take the young mother into captivity after murdering her aged father, her husband, and infant son. She dies trying to escape. Near the end, Noyes describes the calamity at Spithead where Admiral Kempenfelt's flagship The Royal George sank at anchor August 29, 1782, with 796 persons on board, 495 of whom were drowned, including the admiral.

83-23. Ode on the Late Change in Administration. Inscribed to the Right Hon. Charles J. Fox.
Bath: Cruttwell, 1783.

Notices: CR 55 (Mar 1783), 230-1; MR 68 (Apr 1783), 355; ERL 1 (Mar 1783), 256.

Copies: none located.

The poet, triumphant on the overthrow of Lord North's ministry, invokes the Genius of Albion and prophesies that "A firm, united patriot band/ Shall save the ruins of thy sinking land," and steer the ship of state clear from quicksands. The poet exhorts them not to surrender "their hard earn'd conquests again." A Compliment to the Americans and the Rockingham administration closes the poem. (Bases on the notices above.))

83-24. An Ode To Mr. Lewis Hendrie, &c. &c. &c. Principal Bear-Killer In the Metropolis of England, And Comb-Maker in Ordinary to His Majesty.
[London:] Bladon, 1783. 18p.

"Not to the notes of Epic lyres." (c. 150)

Notices: CR 55 (May 1783), 406-7; MR 68 (Jun 1783), 539-40; ERL 2 (Jul 1783), 70-1.

Copies: BL 11630.e.14 (13); Bod Godwyn Pamph 1723 (22); NUC CtY, ICN.

Preface dated from Lincoln's Inn, March 18, 1783.
Irregular Pindaric ode. Burlesque satire on the coalition ministry. The poet develops a new theme, Lewis Hendrie, who markets bear-grease "for strengthening and thickening the hair." But he soon turns to politics, asking Hendrie to regenerate the land with "An Ointment of Politic Life." This ointment, he conjectures, will be produced from the members of Parliament--Fox ("strength of lung, / Bred on democratic dung"), Dundass (lubrication), North (a glue which can "In monstrous coalition bind/ Tories

before and Whigs behind"), Burke ("froth and fume"). This "Senatorial broth," when applied, should have "a potent influence" on Britain; that is, "Britain's force [will] be felt in armed pride." Concludes with personal but non-political satire on Samuel Johnson, another bear.

83-25. Parkin, Miles.
  Columba, A Poetical Epistle, Heroic And Satirical; To The Right Honourable Charles, Earl Cornwallis. By The Rev. Miles Parkin, A. B. of Queen's College, Oxford.
  [London:] Debrett, 1783. 36p.

"Silent for ever shall the Muse deplore." (516)

  Notices: CR 56 (Oct 1783), 311-12; MR 69 (Nov 1783), 437; Cumb Pacq, Dec 30, 1783; ERL 3 (Mar 1784), 230-1.

  Sabin 58782.

  Copies: NUC MiU-C, RPJCB.

  Dedication to Cornwallis dated from Kingston, near Tetsworth, Oxfordshire, January 1, 1783.
  HC. Patriotic poem, the word "Columba" is used for America which Parkin finds "too trite and feeble to be admitted into a chaste English couplet." Parkin takes it upon himself to present "Britain's cause," to rouse the country to unite at a time when Britain is threatened by France, Spain, and Holland. He writes encomiums on Cornwallis, Elliott, and other officers, and eulogies on those who perished in defence of Britain: Fraser and others. He pleads for a reconciliation of America to the mother country.
  The major details appear in the following order: He laments Burgoyne's defeat, the death of Fraser, Monckton, and Webster. He is angered at America's shameful alliance with France--"Columba's Hero [Washington] forges Britain's chain!" But Rodney's victory over De Grasse pleases him, despite the tragic death of young Manners. The loss of Minorca by Gen. Murray, and his court-martial, cause dismay. Admiral Richard Howe's relief of besieged Gibraltar and Gen. Elliott's brilliant defense of the fortress deserve celebration. Tarlton is praised for his courage, and so are those who seized India from the French--Laurence, Clive, Coote, Caillaud. Cornwallis also deserves praise, "Caress'd by all, and yet no Tool of State."
  Next Parkin addresses Columba, mourning the broken tie with Britain. He pictures Britain at once begging America to "Return . . . to thy Parent's Arms," and threatening her with revenge (pp. 25-26). He hopes Columba will join Britain "'gainst perfidious Gaul," so that the two can dominate the world. He concludes with a panegyric on Cornwallis, who is now in England (after his defeat at Yorktown), and insists that Cornwallis merits honor.
  Also briefly cited are Arnold, Ackland, Asgill, André, Kempenfelt.

83-26. -----.
Rodney Triumphant. A New Song.

"A Health to bold Rodney, triumphant and brave." (36)

In 83-25: his Columba, pp. 34-6.

Dated May 30, 1782, and, according to a note on p. 16, taken from the Oxford Journal, June 22, 1782. This "tributary song" praises Rodney for his victories over Langara of Spain, the Dutch, and De Grasse and Bougainville of France.

83-27. Pugh, David.
A Poem on the Approaching Peace. By David Pugh.
London: Fielding, 1783.

Notices: CR 55 (Feb 1783), 149; MR 68 (Mar 1783), 273; EM 3 (Feb 1783), 136.

Sabin 66606.

Copies: none located.

HC. Pugh describes the horrors of war as it affects individuals, families, and the nation, hails the return of peace, and pays tribute to the memory of those heroes who distinguished themselves in the late war. He praises the ministry responsible for the peace, and concludes with a compliment to the king and queen. (European Magazine.)

83-28. Pye, Henry James.
The Progress of Refinement. A Poem. In Three Parts.
Oxford: Clarendon, 1783. 104p.

"As when the stream by casual fountains fed." (I: 679; II: 782; III: 601)

Notices: CR 55 (Jun 1783), 427-31; MR 69 (Oct 1783), 282-5; GM 53 (Jun 1783), 513; L Chron 54 (Sep 4, 1783), 233.

Copies: BL 11633.g.30; NUC CtY, DFo, ICN, MH, TxU.

HC. Two sections are relevant in Part II. In the first, Pye laments the little encouragement given to poetry in the present time, despite the achievements of a trio of celebrated contemporary poets--William Mason, William Hayley, and Anna Seward. He also adds Thomas Warton and Thomas Chatterton. In approving Seward, he notes the effect her poem on André had on the British conscience (ll. 569-72).
In the second, in the conclusion of a review of civilization, "Refinement," Pye refers to the American War just ended, and optimistically hopes that America will carry the torch of English freedom and "Extend o'er half the globe Britannia's laws" (ll. 761-70).

83-29. The Rescue. Inscribed To The Right Honourable Charles James Fox.
London: Debrett, 1783. 28p.

"Oh thou! by all the patriot virtues fir'd." (260)

Notices: CR 55 (Jul 1783), 72-3; MR 69 (Aug 1783), 167; ERL 3 (Mar 1784), 228-9.

Copies: NUC InU, MiD.

HC. Panegyric on the new Portland (William Henry Cavendish-Bentinck, 3rd Duke of Portland) administration including Fox, Burke, Keppel, Carlisle, Savile, Burgoyne, and others. Fox rescued Britain from Thurlow's power and "with gen'rous zeal his Country's chains unbound," permitting "Freedom" to rear her head. Others for various reasons were found wanting, therefore incapable; e.g., Shelburne, who is deceitful and given to pride; Pitt, who is overly ambitious; young Onslow, who is more interested in cultivating taste than politics; Johnstone, who is too furious (he had gone to America as one of the Commissioners for Peace, certainly not the proper person to conciliate America, the poet makes clear); Grafton, who is treacherous; etc.

83-30. Rice, Woodford.
The Rutland Volunteer Influenza'd: Or, A Receipt To Make A Patriot, a Soldier, or a Poet. By Woodford Rice, Esquire.
London: Kearsley, 1783. 51p.

"Take noble Dorset's smile, and bend." (c. 675)

Notices: CR 55 (May 1783), 407-8.

Copies: BL 011586.t.18, 643.k.2 (7), 643.k.15 (10); NUC DLC, NjP, RPJCB.

Four stress couplets. An obscure, intensely personal and highly allusive poem in which Rice, a soldier, appears to be begging for favors, as he cites everyone he knows, or has read about, a vast body of acquaintances, and mentions his achievements as a warrior in the Peninsula Campaign of the Seven Years War and in the following American War when France joined in.
Incidentally, twice he refers to America. The first reference is to Shelburne's peace strategy, which is working: "America is at your feet,/ Proclaim it loud in every street./ Direct your force 'gainst France and Spain,/ And Peace--oh, Peace, you'll get again."
He also alludes to the peace with America in connection with Barré, Sir George (?), and Robert (?) Pigot, who meet with Franklyn and Washington: "For universal peace they'll treat." But King "George shall bid proud France defiance,/ And laugh at paltry Dutch alliance" (pp. 29-30, 46).
See M. Dorothy George, Catalogue of Political and Personal Satires, vol. 5, p. 761, #6316.

83-31. Rushton, Edward.
American Independency.

"Ye men of Columbia! oh! hail the great day." (40)

In his Poems and Other Writings (London: Wilson, 1824), pp. 38-40.

Copies: BL 993.1.36; Bod 24.695; NUC DLC, InU.

This poem was probably written between 1783 and 1785. Regular Horatian ode in double quatrains. Rushton hails the American Declaration of Independence and those who gave their lives for the cause of freedom--Warren and Montgomery, and Washington's leadership. He asks that America's "spoilers" be detested, by whom he means the slave-owners who deny Negroes their freedom and the rights of mankind for which America fought. (Rushton also wrote a severe Expostulatory Letter to George Washington of Mount Vernon, in Virginia, on his continuing to be a Proprietor of Slaves [1797].)


83-32. Tasker, William.
Annus Mirabilis; Or, The Eventful Year Eighty-Two. An Historical Poem. By the Rev. W. Tasker. A. B. Author of the Ode to the Warlike Genius of Great-Britain, &c.
Exeter: Thorn & Son; London: Baldwin & Dodsley, [1783]. ii + [5]-44p.

The Second Edition. Exeter: Thorn & Son; London: Baldwin & Dodsley, [1783]. ii + [5]-45p.

"Historic Muse! fair daughter of the skies." (832)

Notices: 1st ed: CR 55 (Mar 1783), 229-30; MR 68 (Feb 1783), 120-3; B Mag 2 (Mar 1783), 216; ERL 1 (Apr 1783), 341-2; EM 3 (Mar 1783), 202-3; GM 53 (Feb 1783), 156; L Mag 52 (Jan 1783), 39, 43; St J's Chron, Feb 1, 1783. 2nd ed: CR 55 (Aug 1783), 237; GM 53 (Aug 1783), 691-2; L Mag (NS) 1 (Sep 1783), 241-2; M Chron, Aug 7, 1783, & Apr 9, 1784; MP, Aug 20, 1783; PA, Aug 15, 1783; St J's Chron, Aug 5, 1783; W Ent 2 (Aug 25, 1783), 190.

Copies: BL 643.k.15 (8) (1st ed); Bod Godwyn Pamph 2799.d.146 (2nd ed); NUC CSmH & MH (1st ed).

HC. Inspired by John Dryden's Annus Mirabilis for 1666. Preface to the 1st ed is dated from Devon, Jan. 1, 1783. Appendix to the Preface in the 2nd ed is dated from Exeter, July 16, 1783; this edition is revised and corrected. The principal addition to the poem is the section on the "Georgian Star," Herschel's discovery; also the political situation had changed upon Rockingham's death in June 1782, to which Tasker responded with appropriate alterations in his text.
In the Preface, Tasker declares his political impartiality and explains the patriotic motive underlying the poem about the chief events of 1782: "a desire of inspiring Military and political Virtue, and of rendering the Nation sensible of her own unconquerable Powers, against combined, numerous, and mighty Enemies."
In the poem, he laments the calamitous national situation--the "unnatural war" with America, the disgraceful dependence on German mercenaries, the surrender of the armies led by Burgoyne and Cornwallis, the loss to Spain of Minorca under Gen. Murray, the

rise of the national debt, the increase of taxes, the loss of trade, the corruption of the court. But 1782 brings "The Patriot Band," the "New Pilots" who will save the "sinking Land." Tasker praises Conway, Fox, Burke, Barré, Dunning, Shelburne, Sheridan, the younger Pitt, Sir George Yonge, and Rockingham (who dies Jul 1, 1782); he describes Burke's plan for royal "Oeconomy" at court, and the beginning of the peace negotiations and the difficulties of treating with France, Spain, and Holland; and he asks for a reconciliation of the independent Americans with their "British Sires."

Among domestic achievements, Tasker also points to the repeal of Poinings Act, which granted a virtual free trade to Ireland. He celebrates at great length the great victory of Rodney over De Grasse in the Battle of the Saints, and narrates the successful defence by Elliott and Curtis of Gibraltar against the combined forces of France and Spain, and its relief by Admiral Richard Howe. Near the end he also describes "the fatal dissention of the Patriots, the resignation of Fox and Burke," and the sinking of the Royal George.

83-33. [Williams, Helen Maria]
An Ode On The Peace. By The Author Of Edwin And Eltruda.
London: Cadell, 1783. 20p.

"As wand'ring late on Albion's shore." (272)

Notices: CR 55 (Mar 1783), 232; MR 69 (Aug 1783), 167; ERL 1 (Apr 1783), 340-1; GM 53 (Mar 1783), 245; NAR 1783 (III, 205-7).

Sabin 104227.

Copies: BL 11641.h.4 (3); Bod Godwyn Pamph 1723 (23); NUC CtY, DLC, MH, PU, RPJCB.

Regular Horatian ode in octaves. Williams imagines the terrible effects of war and presents two stanzas on Major André, mourning his early death and praising Anna Seward's monody on him. Three stanzas describe the frantic effects of Captain Charles Asgill's mother to save his life (he was selected by lot for execution in retaliation for a loyalist hanging of a rebel officer). Welcomes peace and its attendant virtues, and the re-establishment of commerce. Pictures the reconciliation of America with Britain, "the Parent-Isle," who together in "firm united Band" will face France. (Also repr. with revisions in her Poems [London: Cadell, 1786], pp. 35-57.)

83-34. Wolcot, John (Peter Pindar, pseud.).
More Lyric Odes, To The Royal Academicians, By Peter Pindar, Esquire. By A Distant Relation To The Poet of Themes, And Laureate to the Academy.
London: Egerton, 1783. 23p.

Ode II. "Now for my criticism on paints." (62) pp. 7-9.

Notices: CR 55 (Jul 1783), 73; MR 70 (Jan 1784), 75-7.

Copies: BL 11630.c.11 (12); NUC CtY, MH, TxU.

Irregular ode. Satire on "the British Raphael," Benjamin West. In the conclusion, Wolcot alludes meanly to America, where "ev'ry Scoundrel convict is a _king_," after giving ironic advice to "our Yankey painter," West. Wolcot makes "that artist a handsome Offer of an American Immortality," should West take the advice for the improvement of his paintings. Five editions to 1789.

Serials

83-35. An Acrostic. [James Lowther.]

"Join'd in an hostile league, but join'd in vain." (12)

HM 13 (Jan 1783), 48.

Lowther and other Patriots will help England fight off the "quadruple" alliance of the American Congress, Holland, France, and Spain.

83-36. An Address to the Independent Electors of Westminster, Versified.

"My accepting an office this letter denotes." (16)

MP, Apr 5, 1783.

Anapest tetrameter couplets. Satire on Fox, who is up for election in Westminster. Here, ironically, he is made, in his persona, to rationalize his behavior, his alliance with the Tory North.

83-37. American Eclogues. Eclogue 1. Morning; or the Complaint. (By a Gentleman of Liverpool.)

"Far from the savage banditt's fierce alarms." (c. 170)

GM 53 (Dec 1783), 1043-4; GM 54 (Jan 1784), 46 (errata).

HC. An anti-slavery poem. The scene is Pennsylvania. A tortured Negro slave begs for freedom. The name of the poet is the Rev. Mr. Gregory. See 84-22. This and the second eclogue (in GM 54 [Jan 1784], 45-6) provide a harsh indictment of American inhumanity.

83-38. American Independence.

"When pregnant Nature strove relief to gain." (6)

G, Jul 25, 1783; W Eve Post, Jul 31, 1783.

HC. Epigram. The birth of American independence was brought about by Washington and Paine; and America has rapidly developed into manhood, assisted by France, Britain, Congress, and God.

83-39. Andrews, Miles Peter.
The (Royal) British Tar. A New Song. Sung by Mr. Arrowsmith at Vauxhall. Written by Miles Peter Andrews, Esq; Set to Music by Dr. Arnold.

"Sons of Ocean, fam'd in story." (30)

E Chron, Jul 12, 1783; Lloyd's 53 (Jul 14, 1783), 53; M Chron, Jul 15, 1783; MP, Jul 15, 1783; WM 57 (Jul 31, 1783), 147; W Eve Post, Jul 12, 1783; L Chron 54 (Jul 12, 1783), 55.

A popular song in praise of the British sailor, bland and generalized. The lyric really is in praise of Prince William, the "Royal Tar."

83-40. Annus Mirabilis; Or, The Downfall of the Church and its Champion, within a Year of each other.

"Once Mother Church, with Terrors arm'd." (12)

PA, Mar 5, 1783.

Sixains. A complaint that the King no longer can defend the church in America because of the nature of the agreed peace. He can no longer be called "Defender of the Faith" because of "the Enfranchisement of America."

83-41. Antient Rome to Great Britain.

"I who the conquer'd world so long had swayed." (18)

GA, Mar 21, 1783.

HC. Britain will be a ruin and a memory like ancient Rome, should the Opposition (at this time the Tories) come to power. (Or does the poem allude to the opposition to Shelburne's peace by the Foxites and North?)

83-42. Aut Caesar aut nullus.

"Now, now, or never, cry'd th'ambitious F[o]x." (16)

PA, Mar 29, 1783.

HC. Causidicus satirizes Fox, comparing him to Satan, who desires to rule even though in Hell.

83-43. The Beef-Steakes of Old England. A New Song.

"While others swell high in full numbers divine." (38)

M Chron, Jan 4, 1783.

Song. Celebrates the heroic and triumphant officers -- Rodney, Hood, Curtis, Hughes, Howe, Parker, Pigot, and Eliott -- "all British true blues."

83-44. Billa Vera. An Epigram.

"Quoth Fox to Burke, 'We've made a Rout.'" (8)

PA, Mar 6, 1783.

Quatrains. Dialogue. Satire on Fox and Burke, who complain that their maneuvers (against Shelburne) did not succeed, for they received nothing.

83-45. The Blessings of War.

"First Jew Cred. Speak, Brother, is the deed yet done." (23)

MP, Feb 25, 1783.

Satire on Fox in the form of a rough parody of the witches in Macbeth. Sham patriots and Jewish creditors ironically cast shame upon Charles James Fox, who is here portrayed as a corrupt war monger and spendthrift. That is, he objected to Shelburne's peace, thereby protracting the war.

83-46. [Boreas through Fear of losing his Head.]

"Boreas through Fear of losing his Head." (4)

PA, Mar 11, 1783.

HC. North and Fox will both suffer, despite their coalition.

83-47. [Bright primal Stars thirteen.]

"Bright primal Stars thirteen." (14)

"Six thousand times thro' Glass enlarg'd." (6)

PA, Mar 17, 1783; St J's C, Mar 13, 1783.

Couplets, mixed and OC. Two epigrams on the loss of the thirteen United States and, in compensation, the gain of the Georgian Star, discovered by the astronomer William Herschel.

83-48. Britannia's Tale.

"Stabb'd by her Sons, oppress'd by Foreign Power." (9)

MH, Apr 21, 1783; St J's C, Apr 17, 1783.

HC. Satire on politicians. Britain is betrayed by America, threatened by foreign powers, but the politicians are greedy for places!

83-49. The Broad-Bottomed Administration. Or Mr. F's Genuine Thanks to his Westminster Electors.

"Quoth N[orth] to F[ox], 'You've got your Ends.'" (8)

PA, Apr 9, 1783.

Quatrains. Vulgar satire on Fox, who in his coalition with North is leading his friends by the nose.

Burnby, John. See "A Thought in 1781," 83-249.

83-50. A Call in Vain.

"France, Spain, the Dutch, have with the Rebels join'd." (14)

PA, Sep 30, 1783.

HC. An objection to the peace. Britain is sleeping and must be awakened; for the peace is "treach'rous."

83-51. Calumniari Fortiter, ut aliquid adhertat.

"Calumniate boldly, something will adhere." (22)

PA, Jan 14, 1783.

HC. Causidicus defends Shelburne from Burke's offensive calumnies.

83-52. Character of the late Marquis of Rockingham.

"In lovely virtue first, and first in fame." (14)

GA, Mar 20, 1783.

HC. Panegyric on Rockingham for his integrity. He died (July 1, 1782) at an "inauspicious hour."

83-53. The Coalition.

"From morn to night, my head I strain." (60)

MH, Apr 14, 1783.

Regular ode in sixains, with "coalition" as an important rhyimg word. Satire on the Fox-North coalition for wishing to plunder the state "by partition," to weaken the King, and to exploit the people.

83-54. Coalition.

"Nor human maxims, nor divine." (8)

G, Jul 17, 1783.

OC. An answer to "A Desirable Coalition" (83-65) insists that corruption, bribery, and unfair and heavy taxes are the real issues, and that they must cease.

83-55. The Coalition.

"Quoth Sir John to his chaplain, a sound politician." (6)

SM 45 (Apr 1783), 207.

Epigram. Sixain. Some good may come of the Fox-North coalition, a blend of opposites, spirit with weakness, acid with sweet.

83-56. Coalition of Parties.

"When juggling Knaves get places by Partition." (2)

St J's C, Feb 27, 1783.

Epigram. HC. Satire on the Fox-North coalition -- the politicians are simply conniving for places. (The Tories and Rockingham Whigs combine to censure the Shelburne ministry for making too many concessions in the peace. This is the early sign of the Fox-North coalition, to result, on April 2-5, 1783, in the new Portland ministry.)

83-57. The Coalition. On the Same.

"To-Day the People's Friend and Foe unite." (2)

"Faction be dumb; Lord North and Fox are one." (2)

PA, Apr 8, 1783; St J's C, Apr 3, 1783.

HC. Two epigrams. Fox and North unite today; but tomorrow they will fall out. Should Fox and North be divided, England will be undone. (The second is undoubtedly ironic.)

83-58. The Coalition. Or, The Man of the People.

"Old Sarah said unto her recreant son." (8)

PA, May 15, 1783.

HC in quatrains. Causidicus satirizes Fox and the coalition again.

83-59. Colvill, Robert.
On the Late Great Naval and Military Preparations; Humbly Inscribed to the Most Noble James Marquis of Graham, Colonel of the Caledonian Band of Heroes.

"Heard you dread Mars his brazen clarion sound." (180)

SM 45 (Apr 1783), 207-8 (extract ll. 25-64). Colvill, The Poetical Works (London: Dodsley et al., 1789), pp. 75-84.

Heroic quatrains. Scotland too joins in the war against France and Spain -- tyrants who have aided the American rebels (ll. 13-16). Rodney has won a tremendous victory in the Battle of the Saints, April 12, 1782, saving the British empire from total destruction. The Scottish nobility has joined the struggle -- Gordon, Campbell, Atholl, as well as the citizens of Edinburgh, et al. Colvill cites Maitland, who died at Savannah, and other Scottish heroes. See Colvill, 89-1.


83-60. Compositive Epigrammatical Epitaph on the Death of the Subtle, Ingenious, metallic Mr. Pinchbeck, inventor of that metal.

"Here lies a burnish'd bastard got on gold." (4)

WM 57 (Jul 31, 1783), 147.

Epitaph on Christopher Pinchbeck, the celebrated toyman and clockmaker, and the personal favorite of the King.


83-61. The Contrast; Or, This Year and the Last.

"Reyn. So great for my country's repose is my zeal." (64)

W Eve Post, Sep 11, 1783.

Anapest tetrameter couplets. Ironic satire on Fox and North, whose personae are made to explain their coalition. Fox's objections to Shelburne's peace with America, his "changing principles" now that the American War is over, and North's profession of sincerity and assertion that he was not responsible for the disastrous American War are in the argument.


83-62. [Corruption has her baneful Pinion spread.]

"Corruption has her baneful Pinion spread." (8)

PA, Mar 24, 1783.

HC. An expression of hope that wisdom and truth will return and disperse the cloud of corruption hovering over the land.


83-63. [The Country and the Town.]

"The Country and the Town." (24)

PA, Jun 27, 1783; W Eve Post, Jun 24, 1783.

Song, no tune given. A satire on the coalition ministry because of its difficulties in making a satisfactory peace with Holland and America. Cited are David Hartley (a negotiator) and Fox.

The Country Politicians. "'Had I my Wish,' says honest Ned.'" (36) Cumb Pacq, May 20, 1783. First published in 1774: see 74-49.

83-64. The Court Dance.

"They first lead up, then turn about." (6)

W Ent 1 (Jun 2, 1783), 528.

Epigram. Sixain. The politics at court is like a dance, but someone behind the curtain is calling the tune. An adaptation of 66-35.

Cowper, William. In Submersionem Navigii Cui Georgius Regale Nomen Inditum. "Plangimus fortes -- periere fortes." (32) PA, Aug 23, 1783. Cowper's Latin version of his poem "On the Loss of the Royal George," both written 1782-83. See 82-68.

83-65. A Desirable Coalition.

"Tell me what Maxims, human or divine." (4)

G, Jul 15, 1783; PA, Jul 11, 1783; St J's C, Jul 8, 1783.

HC. The Coalition is good and useful -- "old Enemies" can join to "preserve the State." Answered in "Coalition," 83-54, and "Extempore on Reading, . . ." 83-95.

83-66. The Desperate Alternative.

"Ill fated Britain! What must thou endure." (12)

PA, Nov 28, 1783.

HC. A criticism of the "ignominious" peace and of Shelburne, who still exerts influence through Pitt and Temple (George Nugent-Temple Grenville).

83-67. The Devil and Arnold. A Dialogue.

"<u>Dev</u>. Where art thou, Arnold?" (2)

L Cour, Feb 7, 1783.

The Devil invites Arnold to come to Hell, now that America is free.

83-68. The Disappointed Placeman. Another Canterbury Tale.

"A Man, no matter who -- unnam'd." (60)

PA, Aug 4, 1783.

Sixains. Satire on corruption. A man from the west country returns home frustrated and unhappy because his noble patron has not secured him a place in London.

83-69. A Drama. Enter Two Devils. -- Scene a Barren Prospect. [Two Parts.]

"Both. Double, double, toil and trouble." (42)

MP, Mar 4 & 7, 1783.

Parody of the witches' scene in Shakespeare's Macbeth. Satire on the Fox-North coalition ("monstrous friendship") including Keppel, Johnstone, Hartley, and others, who wish to unseat Shelburne and who use others (Sackville, Grattan, and Arnold) for their nefarious purposes.

83-70. Eliott's Wreath; or, Gibraltar Preserved. A Cantata. Written by Dr. Houlton, and Set to Music by Signor Giordani.

"Peaceful silence cease to reign." (82)

Freeman's J, Sep 23, 1783.

This cantata (airs and recitatives) celebrates the successful resistance of General Eliott's forces to the onslaught of the Spaniards at fortress Gibraltar. Eliott fought humanely; his was "polish'd warfare."

83-71. The Emigrant's Farewell.

"Swift on the wings of never-resting Time." (56)

WM 58 (Oct 23, 1783), 113.

Elegiac quatrains. A prospective emigrant to "Columbia," where the "Fair Ohio floats upon her oozy bed," mourns as he bids farewell to his "Dear native plains." But he is consoled with the hope of securing the benefits of productive industry and liberty.

83-72. England's Happiness; or, The Blessings of the Coalition.

"While, under North's broad Shield, Fox greatly fights." (10)

PA, May 23, 1783; St J's C, May 20, 1783.

HC. The Fox-North coalition is good for England because it prevents bribery and corruption in Parliament by "base Contractors" and other "Miscreants."

83-73. The English and Irish Patriot.

"The Patriot English prattles, bullies, swaggers." (4)

St J's C, Nov 11, 1783.

Satire on the Irish leaders. The English patriot is quieted by a bribe or pension; but the Irish patriot cannot be satisfied, his greed being bottomless. (The reference is the enormous award of £50,000 granted to Grattan.)

83-74. Epigram.

"Caligula, as Hist'ry doth relate." (12)

PA, Aug 19, 1783.

HC. Ironic satire on corrupt ministers. Caligula made his horse a minister of state, and he was honest and absolutely incorruptible. Indeed, "His parts were equal to our Statesmen's now!"

83-75. Epigram.

"God of his Mercy grant, that we may yet." (2)

PA, Apr 2, 1783; St J's C, Mar 29, 1783.

HC. The present faction of Fox and North governing the country should be destroyed, and "a[nother] Pitt" should be restored to leadership.

83-76. Epigram.

"Having tir'd and drain'd the Jews of the East." (4)

MP, Mar 27, 1783.

Quatrain. Satire on the profligate Fox, who is moving from the money lenders of the East to North.

83-77. Epigram.

"If Stormont, or Mansfield, or Bute, 'tis all one." (4)

St J's C, Mar 20 & 22, 1783.

HC. Two versions of an epigram. Satire on Tory leaders (Stormont, Mansfield, and Bute) and on Whig leaders (Burke and Fox). The country will be undone if either group captures the ministry. (David Murray, Viscount Stormont, was the nephew of William Murray, Earl Mansfield.)

83-78. Epigram.

"Ill-fated Britannia, how lost in thy Wishes." (4)

St J's C, May 10, 1783.

Anapest tetrameter couplets. Satire on the Coalition. The greed of the politicians is the ruin of the country.

83-79. An Epigram.

"Premier! says Fox, I'll have a tax." (4)

W Eve Post, Jun 17, 1783.

Quatrain. Satire on Fox, for his penury: he will not have enough money to purchase anything, and so the new Receipt Tax will not affect him.

83-80. Epigram.

"What mean these Tears, Britannia, tell us why." (4)

St J's C, Jul 1, 1783.

HC. Satire on the Fox-North coalition -- the greed of the two. North lost half the empire, Fox threatens the other half.

83-81. Epigram.

"When from the North the silent Gaul." (12)

G, Jul 29, 1783.

Sixains. Fox will bring ruin to the nation.

83-82. Epigram.

"The Wisdom of the Nation, Patriots say." (16)

PA, Mar 19, 1783; St J's C, Mar 15, 1783.

HC. North's ministry of nine years accomplished nothing but the loss of America; perhaps the future will improve. (An allusion, no doubt, to the Fox-North coalition.)

83-83. An Epigram. Impromptu.

"Our blessed Lord, to save mankind." (4)

MP, May 26, 1783.

Quatrain. Satire on Fox and North and their followers, because they crucified Shelburne for saving the country.

83-84. Epigram. On a Late Great Party.

"In Nature 'tis common as well as in Party." (4)

PA, Apr 2, 1783.

Hexameter couplets. Praise of the Rockingham party led by Fox and Burke: Fox has the "Brains," Burke the "Tongue and Face."

83-85. Epigram. On Certain Specious Explanations.

"Freddy, and Freddy's Schemes lay hid in Night." (2)

PA, Mar 29, 1783.

HC. Fox (somehow) will illuminate the mystery of his union with North.

83-86. Epigram on Mr. Fox.

"To have Britannia's strength restor'd." (6)

MP, Mar 19, 1783.

Sixain. Satire on Fox as hypocrite. He wanted a peace before; but, now that Shelburne has given the nation peace, he opposes it, his object being a place.

83-87. Epigram. On the People of Ireland appointing the Earl of Bristol their Delegate to Dungannon.

"Where Ireland's Sons prepar'd to frame." (5)

Cal Merc, Sep 1, 1783.

Sixain. The Irish trusted Frederick Augustus Hervey, 4th Earl of Bristol, to get them "An equal Legislation," not the English Parliament. (He was Bishop of Cloyne, 1767-68, and Bishop of Derry, 1768-1803.)

83-88. An Epigram on the Times.

"To what End are Contentions? To what Use is Tongue War?" (2)

PA, Jun 19, 1783.

Anapest tetrameter couplet. Contentious debates are useless, doing nothing for the country until it is ruined.

83-89. Epigram, Said to be Written by the Late General Lee, on Himself.

"Seduc'd by error, to misfortune born." (4)

MH, Feb 7, 1783.

HC. The persona of Gen. Lee complains of his mistakes. He is hopeless, deceived by Congress, rejected by England, and wanting friends.

83-90. Epigram. To Mr. Chancellor Pitt.

"The Time of War, in any Nation." (10)

PA, Jan 8, 1783; W Eve Post, Jan 7, 1783.

OC. Political advice to young Pitt, chancellor, at a difficult time of transition from war to peace.

83-91. An Epitaph.

"A few days since were quietly interred." (c. 20)

L Cour, Jan 14, 1783.

Epitaph. Satiric inscription. A mock epitaph on the failures of General Sir William Howe in America, taken from an American (loyalist) newspaper, the Philadelphia Independent Gazetteer, Nov. 26, 1782.

83-92. The Epitaphs on the New Monuments intended for the Speedy Decoration of Henry the Seventh's Chapel, Westminster Abbey.

"This artless record of my death receive." (2)

Cal Merc, Aug 25, 1783.

HC. An epitaph (selected) on the King who is made to complain of Burke's economic reforms that have cost him money -- and the end of his reign.

83-93. Cancelled.

An Extempore. "A Bear very lately was order'd by Fate." See 83-95.

83-94. An Extempore!

"Shelburne is gone, and has bequeathed us peace." (6)

MH, Apr 7, 1783.

HC. Fox and North, a "monstrous" combination, joined to force out Shelburne, who gave the country peace. (Shelburne resigned March 29, 1783; he was succeeded by the Fox-North coalition, April 2, 1783.)

83-95. Extempore on Reading a Few Lines in the Public Advertiser of Friday, July 11, entitled "A Desirable Coalition."

"A Bear very lately was order'd by Fate." (8)

MH, Jul 21, 1783; PA, Jul 18, 1783.

Anapest tetrameter couplets. Animal fable. Satire on Fox, who cleverly joins with North and deceives fools into thinking he is wise. Entitled "An Extempore" in MH. See "A Desirable Coalition," 83-65.

83-96. Extempore on Reading Mr. Pitt's Speech in Opposition to Mr. F[ox].

"Now, Master Charles, will all your art." (12)

MP, May 23, 1783.

Quatrains. A warning to Fox, that he will be disarmed by Pitt, despite his coalition with North.

83-97. An Extempore. On the Two Famous Champions in the Irish Parliament, Mr. G[ratta]n and Mr. F[loo]d.

"Both kingdoms boast of F[loo]d and G[ratta]n." (4)

MP, Nov 26, 1783.

OC. Flood and Grattan are not a credit to Ireland or England.

83-98. Extempore. On Viewing Hayes-Place, Kent, the Seat of the Hon. W. Pitt.

"Here Chatham, Saviour of his Country." (16)

GA, Feb 7, 1783; PA, Feb 13, 1783; St J's C, Feb 22, 1783.

HC. Alludes to Chatham's stroke while debating the American War, and uses him as a model of patriotic statesmanship.


83-99. Extempore. To the Premier. On reading the Speech of a New Orator in the House of Commons, on Monday last, when the Articles of Peace were held in Discussion.

"Shelburne! 'tis Time thy Premiership to drop." (4)

PA, Feb 21, 1783.

HC. Shelburne should resign for concluding "so damn'd a Peace." (A majority of the Commons voted for censuring the terms of the peace, February 21, 1783, forcing Shelburne to resign, March 29, 1783.)


83-100. The following lines are inscribed to those noted Literary Impostors, and Lurking Blockheads called the Monthly Reviewers.

"Though critics in their skulls have all the nine." (8)

MP, Sep 22, 1783.

HC (largely). An objection to the mean language of the monthly reviews -- and criticism of the uncreative, destructive, and corrupt critics in these reviews.


83-101. Fox, Charles James.
Invocation to Poverty. By the Hon. C. Fox.

"Oh Poverty! of pale, consumptive hue." (26)

SM 45 (Jul 1783), 379.

HC. Ironic satire on Fox. The persona of Fox prays that poverty keep him honest and capable of sympathy, free, wise, and healthy, as well as from the temptations of ambition and avarice. (Fox was often satirized as being poor, hence dependent and motivated by greed and self-interest. This poem must be part of the satiric campaign against his integrity.)


83-102. Fox and Bear.

"When a Fox gives his hand to an awkward fat Bear." (6)

G, Jul 25, 1783; PA, Jul 23, 1783; St J's C, Jul 19, 1783.

Anapest tetrameter couplets. Epigram. Satire on the preposterous Coalition. But Fox and North, although allied, have not changed -- North is still vicious, and Fox hypocritical.


83-103. The Fox and Hounds.

"A Wily Fox who long had been." (42)

PA, Feb 6, 1783.

OC. Animal fable. The hounds that allowed the fox to escape deserve hanging. This fable may apply to the British armed forces in America.

83-104. The Fox and the Badger.

"Mark Anthony and Caesar both unite." (16)

PA, Mar 18, 1783.

HC. Causidicus attacks the North-Fox coalition and defends Shelburne again, for he had saved the country. But making the peace was the occasion of the political death of Shelburne.

83-105. [France in her Richlieu saw a dauntless Chief.]

"France in her Richlieu saw a dauntless Chief." (28)

PA, Mar 13, 1783.

HC. Causidicus again defends Shelburne. Despite the fact that honest Shelburne brought peace and satisfied the public, he was forced to resign. "Factions damn the Man . . . who dar'd his Country save."

83-106. Freeth, John.
The Budget. Tune, -- Shawnbree.

"The Budget's disclos'd -- fresh Taxes impos'd." (24)

Freeth, The Political Songster (1790), pp. 74-5.

Song. A protest against new taxes imposed even though the war is over (May-June 1783). Taxes encourage emigration! The new Receipt Tax is cited.

83-107. Freeth, John.
The New Administration, in 1783. Tune, -- Hark, hark away, away to the Downs!

"Long had the vessel of the state." (50)

Freeth, The Political Songster (1790), pp. 55-6.

This song, in its original form, was entitled "Britannia's Relief. On the Change of the Ministry," 82-140, about the welcomed change to the Rockingham ministry. The revision reflects the change to Shelburne's ministry, without the forces of Fox and Burke. Shelburne was premier from July 13, 1782, to March 29, 1783, and was succeeded by the Fox-North administration on April 2, 1783.

83-108. Freeth, John.
　The Old King's Ghost.  Tune, -- Teague's Ramble to London.

　"The clock had struck twelve, old Morpheus's hour."  (48)

　Freeth, The Political Songster (1790), pp. 50-51.

　Song in hexameter couplets in octaves. The ghost of George II complains that his grandson George III has destroyed the empire by bringing in Bute and Germain and by forcing Chatham out: "Your Empire dismember'd -- America lost!"

83-109. Freeth, John.
　On the Prospect of Peace.  Tune, -- Now's the Time for Mirth and Glee.

　"Now away with pining care."  (24)

　Freeth, The Political Songster (1790), pp. 53-4.

　Song on the coming peace. The Peace Preliminaries between Great Britain and France and Spain were signed January 20, 1783. Peace is welcomed by "Merchants, tradesmen, farmers, factors, -- / All but greedy State Contractors." Birmingham will profit from the peace.

83-110. Freeth, John.
　The Wonderful Coalition.  Tune, -- As I was a driving my Waggon one Day.

　"At a period when all public virtue is lost."  (44)

　MP, Apr 7, 1783; Freeth, The Political Songster (1790), pp. 86-8.

　Song. Satire on the confusing and strange coalition of Fox and North, which was meant to undermine Shelburne and his peace. Fox is portrayed as selfishly concerned with his personal welfare: "'Tis not for our int'rest that faction yet cease, / I the War always d[am]n'd, and I'll now d[am]n the Peace." Likewise, North is interested in securing his pension and providing for his son. MP says this was "Written by a very ingenious and honest Publican at Birmingham."

83-111. Freeth, John.
　Written on the Day of Thanksgiving for a General Peace.  Tune -- Two Welchmen partners in a Cow, &c.

　"Thanksgiving days so rarely come."  (12)

　Tune -- Ye Warwickshire Lads and ye Lasses.
　"The people were seiz'd with a phrenzy."  (28)

　Tune -- Drink and set your hearts at rest.
　"Sons of trade for mirth prepare."  (15)

　Tune -- Come ye party jangling Swains.

"Now no more to distant lands." (12)

Freeth, The Political Songster (1790), pp. 120-2.

Four songs on the Definitive Treaty of Peace between Great Britain and France, Spain, and America, signed September 3, 1783. Peace was proclaimed October 6, 1783. The second song is especially pertinent, a satire on the ill-managed war and on Fox's objections to Shelburne's peace: as soon as Shelburne secured peace, "A legion of parties united attend / To run down what none had the power to mend."

83-112. Grattan and Flood. Dialogue Between A. and B.

"A. Flood aims at Grattan -- Grattan strikes at Flood." (4)

St J's C, Nov 11, 1783.

Dialogue. Satire on the Irish leaders Flood and Grattan, in dispute over the large reward to Grattan. But both are knaves.

83-113. Grattan and Flood. Question and Answer.

"Q. Pray, what has giv'n to Flood a mortal wound." (4)

G Eve Post, Nov 8, 1783; St J's C, Nov 6, 1783.

Dialogue. Satire on the Irish political leaders. Grattan, the Irish statesman, received a £50,000 reward for services in Parliament; but Flood is envious. Another version appeared in Cumb Pacq, Nov 25, 1783: "Questions and Answers," 83-A.

Gregory, (?) See "American Eclogues, Eclogue 1," 83-37.

83-114. A Hasty Defence of a Late Coalition.

"Says F[ox], 'If I ever my Honour should place.'" (16)

PA, Mar 15, 1783; St J's C, Mar 11, 1783.

Quatrains in anapest tetrameter couplets. Satire on the Coalition. Neither Fox nor North can be trusted; they deserve each other.

83-115. [Heaven sometimes to chastise flagitious Times.]

"Heaven sometimes to chastise flagitious Times." (24)

PA, May 21, 1783.

HC. Causidicus satirizes North (called Squab) and blames him for England's problems. "Undone by Squab, see bleeding Albion stands / . . . / Plung'd in the Miseries of War and Debt, / Her Empire crush'd, her Sun of Glory set." See also 84-78.

83-116. The Historical Column.

"Liberty, / (who dares deny it)." (c. 50)

PA, Mar 21 & 22, 1783.

Inscription, in Latin and an English translation. An American loyalist in England objects to American treason and independence, the alliance with France, and loss of liberty, because a treacherous and "villainous Rabble" has taken over the colonies.

83-117. The Honesty of Fox, and the Wisdom of North.

"To save the State Fox clos'd with North, 'tis said." (4)

St J's C, Aug 19, 1783.

HC. Satire on the Fox-North Coalition: Fox "to save the State" and North "to save his Head." A wretched coalition!

83-118. Humanity's Petition.

"Peace to the direful din of arms." (40)

HM 13 (Jan 1783), 47-8.

Quatrains. An expression of pleasure that the destructive war is over.

83-119. Imitation. From Gibbon's Decline and Fall, &c.

"North doz'd, 'tis true, some precious Hours away." (4)

PA, Mar 15, 1783; St J's C, Mar 11, 1783.

Epigram. HC. If North slept less, and Shelburne more, Britain would be the gainer.

83-120. An Impromptu.

"Men who so well together suit." (4)

MP, Mar 15, 1783.

Quatrain. Satire on the Fox-North alliance, an odd suit.

83-121. Impromptu. From the Philadelphia Gazette.

"We have got independence the world must allow." (2)

G, May 20, 1783; MP, May 19, 1783.

Satire on William Howe. America has its independence as a result of General Howe's blunders. There are two more epigrams in the Morning Post (following the first), one of them also being anti-Howe: see same title, 83-A.

83-122. Impromptu. Occasioned by the Squabbles for Peace amongst the Great.

"Civilians make a mighty Stir." (12)

PA, Mar 10, 1783.

Sixains. The debate on the peace dismays this poet; he concludes that the King should rule alone because, if he cannot err, he needs no base counsellors or courtiers.

Impromptu on the Present P[eac]e. L Cour, Feb 25, 1783. See "On the Present P[eac]e. Impromptu," 83-201.

83-123. Impromptu. To Garter King at Arms.

"Where are the Trophies brought from far." (4)

W Eve Post, Sep 16, 1783.

OC. A rejection of the peace to end a shameful war: there are no trophies! (The Definitive Treaty of Peace between Great Britain and France, Spain, and America was signed on September 3, 1783.)

83-124. Impromptu. To General Washington, On hearing that the Loyalists were to be Recommended to Congress.

"If thou canst prove there's aught amiss in those." (8)

W Eve Post, Feb 20, 1783.

HC. An expression of fear that the loyalists in America would be abandoned. The loyalists should not be mistreated because they tried to help Britain. Revenge and retaliation must be the work of God -- not men. (Articles 5 and 6 of the Provisional Articles of Peace accepted by Britain and the United States of America were concerned with the loyalists. Their implementation depended only on the good will of the Americans. Hence the anxiety expressed in these lines.)

83-125. Impromptus on the Receipt-Tax.

"A Receipt-tax must do for the people at large." (8)

MH, Jun 21, 1783; PA, Jun 20, 1783; W Ent 2 (Jul 7, 1783), 24.

Two epigrams on taxes (the invariable state problem) -- this time, a new receipt tax which will benefit the gentry and the aristocracy at the expense of the middle-class merchants.

83-126. In Answer to some Lines signed MERLIN, which appeared in last Friday's Paper.

"Shall disaffected spirits dare." (16)

M Chron, Jan 13, 1783.

Quatrains defend the King against the insulting satire "On the King's Commanding" (Mrs. Siddons) in M Chron, Jan 10, 1783: 83-195.

Inscription on a Chamber-Stove in the Form of an Urn, invented by Dr. Franklin, and so contrived that the Flame, instead of ascending, descended. GA, Jul 1, 1783; St J's C, Jun 26, 1783; West M 11 (Dec 1783), 663-4. Jonathan Odell's poem: see 77-187.

83-127. The Interview between Fox and North.

"Charles. Come to my arms, my dear much valu'd friend." (42)

GM 53 (Mar 1783), 247; MP, Feb 26, 1783; SM 45 (Feb 1783), 101; WM 57 (Jul 17, 1783), 82.

HC. Dialogue between Fox and North, that ironically satirizes their coalition of forces which, after their mutual recriminations during the course of the American War, suggests insincerity and hypocrisy as well as self-interest. Entitled "The Interview" in MP.

83-128. Invocation to Peace.

"Too long the earth has mourn'd her children's blood." (34)

GA, Jan 29, 1783.

HC. A general invocation to peace, and all its virtues.

83-129. [The Irish Emancipation.]

"Arm'd capapee forth from the martial band." (42)

Freeman's J, Jul 8, 1783.

HC. Extracts from a poem protesting the mistreatment of Ireland by Britain. America provides a lesson for Ireland, which needs to be free. Immediately preceding this poem is a report on the resolve of the organized working silk weavers to emigrate to America for favorable economic conditions. (From an unpublished poem.)

83-130. Jeu D'Esprit.

"As a certain great Lord was discussing the Peace." (6)

MH, Feb 24, 1783; W Eve Post, Feb 23, 1783.

Hexameter couplets. Praise of North, who -- because of his imperturbable control in debate -- may yet protect the nation.

83-131. John Bull's Clock. A Companion to King Stephen's Watch.

"Whene'er in town you're ask'd to dine." (116)

GA, Feb 6, 1783.

OC. A fable of the clock that needed repair, to illustrate the need for reform of the government machinery, which Lord North opposes but which the younger Pitt proposes.

83-132. Cancelled.

Liberty. A Pindaric Ode. "Take, O Muse! the breathing lyre." (160) G, Jul 31, 1783. Regular Pindaric ode in four parts, each with strophe, anti-strophe, and epode. The poem is preceded with a heading, "American Poetry." The ode in praise of freedom focuses upon slavery in the Caribbean, urges that Britain legally abolish the slave trade and that America abolish its slavery, and refers to Thomas Day's "Dying Negro," 73-2. A reprint of the poem by Charles Crawford, 83-9.

83-133. [Liberty is, after God. An Inscription for a Monument.]

"Liberty is, after God." (c. 20)

Cumb Pacq, Mar 25, 1783.

An American inscription in Latin, and translated into English, honors the King of France because his country helped America achieve liberty.

83-134. Lines Humbly Inscribed to the Right Honourable Charles James Fox, one of his Majesty's Principal Secretaries of State.

"When from her course by adverse billows borne." (38)

M Chron, Dec 22, 1783; PA, Dec 24, 1783.

HC. Fox will guide the ship of state safely to port; there, she will become strong again.

83-135. Lines on New Year's Day, 1783.

"Britannia, seated 'midst her hostile foes." (13)

MH, Jan 2, 1783.

Irregular stanza. Britannia will not be defeated if unanimity prevails -- America, Holland, France, and Spain will all lose from British unanimity: America will "Be sicken'd of her new gain'd liberty."

83-136. Lines on the Life of the Late Lord Chatham.

"'Tis long since Britain's guardian angel fled." (40)

MH, Feb 14, 1783.

HC. Praise of Chatham's persuasive oratory. But Chatham is not dead; he lives in his son, the younger Pitt.

83-137. Lines Said to be Written by Richard Hill, Esq. . . On the Coalition between Lord North and Mr. Fox.

"In an old-fashion'd book we read an old story." (14)

MH, Mar 24, 1783.

Hexameter couplets. Fox and North, a strange combination of Whig and Tory, is explained by their opposition to Shelburne.

83-138. Lines to the Memory of Mr. Christopher Pinchbeck. By A. Bicknell.

"Let not alone the great, the brave, the gay." (22)

MP, Mar 26, 1783.

HC. A eulogy on Pinchbeck, the target of William Mason's satire.

83-139. Lines Written by a Common Soldier, soon after the Floating Batteries were destroyed by the brave General Eliott, at Gibraltar.

"On Calp's mount, where numerous batteries rise." (55)

GA, Jan 16, 1783.

HC. A common soldier narrates a patriotic version of the celebrated Franco-Spanish attack on Gibraltar that was repelled by Eliott and his forces.

83-140. Lines written by a Lady, on the Ratification of the Peace.

"Now the noise of war no more." (18)

W Ent 1 (Feb 24, 1783), 184.

Regular ode in sixains. Generalized observations of the end of the war.

83-141. Maurice, Thomas.
An Address to Ireland.

"Ierne hail! in whom renew'd." (20)

W Ent 1 (Jun 16, 1783), 575-6.

Quatrains honoring Irish oratory, especially that of Grattan aimed at corruption.

83-142. Mavor, W. F.
Ode for the New Year.

"Long has Bellona's thund'ring car." (48)

SM 45 (Jan 1783), 40.

Quatrains. Let peace come to India, Europe, Gibraltar, and America ("Beyond th'Atlantic's liquid plain").

83-143. The Meaning of Mr. Fox's Speech on Monday last. Versified Hudibrastically.

"Sir, You see me rise as usual." (76)

MP, Mar 30, 1783.

OC. Satire on Fox through his persona for simply using politics to gratify his self-interest, his private welfare. Cited are Lord North and the King, especially North, with whom Fox is now friendly. (The Morning Post consistently attacked Fox and North for their coalition, which it believed should be "the ruin of the nation.")

83-144. Merlin to Mrs. Siddons.

"Think not, because you lead and charm the town." (90)

M Chron, Feb 4 & Mar 24, 1783.

HC. Two installments. A satire with angry words on generals who lost the war, on Shelburne, who lost the peace, on Franklin ("that hoary traitor"), and on the terrible peace.

83-145. Cancelled.

83-146. MERLIN to T. S. in reply to his Stanzas in favour of Mrs. Siddons.

"The soul of sympathy, the eye of woe." (28)

M Chron, Jan 17, 1783.

HC. Merlin responds to criticism of his satire on effeminate England, defeated in the war, by additional harsh satire on the moral causes of English decline. See "On the King's Commanding," 83-195, and "In Answer," 83-126.

83-147. Mr. Fox's Address of Thanks to the Westminster Electors.

"Gentlemen, Altho' on the Hustings I cou'd get no hearing." (26)

MP, Apr 14, 1783.

Anapest tetrameter couplets. Satire on Fox, whose persona is made to exhibit his hypocrisy when standing for election in a Westminster that holds him in contempt.

83-148. Mr. H[il]l's Observation Versified.

"Their Country ruin'd, F[ox] and N[orth] unite." (8)

PA, Mar 7, 1783.

HC. Causidicus, believing Shelburne is being crucified for his peace, attacks the Fox-North friendship as the alliance of Herod and Pontius Pilate. Richard Hill's speech, Feb 21, 1783, is reported in Lewis Namier and John Brooke, History of Parliament: The House of Commons (1964), II, 624.

83-149. A Monody, On the Death of Captain Asgill, As Related in the Philadelphia Gazette of the First of June 1782. By the Rev. Mr. Thomas.

"In some lone wood's impenetrable shade." (96)

BM&R 2 (Feb 1783), 135-6.

Elegiac quatrains. On the disasters suffered by Britannia -- divided empire, surrounded by enemies, Cornwallis captured, Andre hanged, and now Captain Charles Asgill cruelly executed. But the poet's report on the death of young Asgill proved to be premature. He died in 1823. Asgill, a prisoner of the Americans, was to be executed in retaliation for the murder of American Captain Huddy by "Refugees" or loyalists. Eventually, after the intervention of his mother with Ambassador Vergennes, who took the case to the French court, he was released by Act of Congress, November 7, 1782. See AR 1783, pp. 241-4, for the documents supporting this interesting story.

83-150. [Mother England was sick, and just ready to die.]

"Mother England was sick, and just ready to die." (12)

G, Jun 16, 1783; St J's C, Jun 12, 1783.

Hexameter couplets. England is sick, her constitution ruined, and will die because she lacks "virtue," or power. England's decline is owing to internal discord (which may also suggest the American Rebellion).

83-151. A New Alphabet. For the Abecedarians in Politics. 1783.

"A was an Ashburton, sunk to a Lord." (25)

PA, Apr 30, 1783.

Alphabet poem. The leading politicians are characterized -- Ashburton (John Dunning), Bute, Conway, Dundass, Benjamin Franklin, Jenkinson, the King, Laurens, North, Pitt the younger, Shelburne, Richmond, and Thurlow.

83-152. A New Catch for the Coalition.

"Bring every flow'r that can be got." (8)

MP, Apr 19, 1783.

Song in quatrains. Satire on the Coalition of Fox and North, "rogues."

83-153. The New Ministry.

"In twelve short months, three Ministries are pass'd." (10)

PA, Apr 11, 1783; St J's C, Apr 8, 1783; W Eve Post, Apr 10, 1783.

HC. The new coalition ministry will last as long as Bute agrees with it. A cynical view of what has happened to government in the last year, including the attempts at a peace. Bute is to blame for the turmoil. (The ministries are North, Rockingham, Shelburne, and now Fox-North.)

83-154. New Occasional Prologue, On the Prospect of Peace with America, Written by Mr. W. Cowdroy, of Chester, and Spoken by Mr. Austin. At the Opening of the Theatre-Royal, Manchester, on Wednesday the First of January, 1783.

"When hydra-headed War with all her Train." (48)

G Eve Post, Jan 11, 1783.

HC. The "Sons of Manchester" are honored for fighting in Freedom's cause, as well as Rodney, Elliott, and Curtis, upon the restoration of peace.

83-155. A New Song.

"Huzza for Gibraltar, the place of renown." (37)

GA, Mar 27, 1783.

No tune is given. A loyal, patriotic song that insists that Gibraltar will long remain British.

83-156. A New State Flash Song.

"From Seventy-three to the Year Eighty-one." (56)

PA, Dec 19, 1783.

A satiric song expressing indignation that North should be accepted as minister after being stigmatized by the Opposition for ten years. Cited are Fox, Burke, Cavendish, and Shelburne. In effect, this is a satire on the so-called "Patriots" for their self-interest. But Pitt is favored.

83-157. The New Year's Address of the Men who Distribute the Whitehall Evening-Post to their Worthy Masters and Mistresses, on the Entrance of the year 1783.

"Masters, I'm told, (and most folks know it)." (82)

W Eve Post, Jan 4, 1783.

OC. A newspaper distributor reviews last year's news, including Rodney's naval successes; but he is also happy to welcome the blessings of peace that will end the horrors of war. The poor common man is unaffected by politics.

83-158. [Nor Civil Broils, nor proud tyrannic Sway.]

"Nor Civil Broils, nor proud tyrannic Sway." (60)

PA, Aug 26, 1783.

HC, signed "A Youngster," in honor of British battle heroes in the war -- Hawke, Parker, Macartney, Rodney, Eliott, Curtis, Cornwallis, Tarleton, and Rawdon.

83-159. [Nothing can soften Malice; her fell Rage.]

"Nothing can soften Malice; her fell Rage." (74)

PA, Jan 23, 1783.

HC. Again Causidicus defends Shelburne and his peace policy from the attacks of Fox and Burke and from "Faction's rude licentious Tongue."

83-160. [O Liberty, thou Goddess bright.]

"O Liberty, thou Goddess bright." (90)

GA, Jul 3, 1783; PA, May 6, 1783.

OC. Argues for the prevention of waste and corruption, for Parliamentary election reforms, "Of equal Rights and equal Laws / In equal choosing Parliament / By ev'ry Briton's free Consent."

83-161. Ode.

"What Wonder Things are as they are." (28)

PA, Nov 11, 1783.

Regular (Horatian) ode in quatrains. An indictment of the selfish, sensual, and materialistic English after "a damn'd War" and "a mock Peace." They are content with infamy and dishonor.

83-162. Ode, On signing the Preliminary Articles of Peace. Addressed to Henry Fletcher, Bart. Chairman to the East India Direction.

"Now shall the Muse, all tranquil ride." (24)

M Chron, Feb 1, 1783.

Quatrains. On the pleasures of peace. The Preliminary Articles of Peace between England and France, Spain, and America were signed at Versailles, January 20, 1783. (See Parliamentary History of England [1814; repr. 1966], XXIII, 345-58.)

83-163. Ode on the Approach of Peace.

"Hark! aloft methinks I hear." (48)

T&C 15 (Feb 1783), 101.

Regular (Horatian) ode in octaves. Peace comes, and Britannia ceases its mourning as its commerce revives.

83-164. Ode on the Proclamation of Peace.

"War's dire Alarms no more are heard." (44)

PA, Oct 9, 1783.

Irregular ode, but largely sixains. After a devastating war, peace and its blessings are welcomed. (A conventional poem with generalized imagery.) Peace was proclaimed October 6, 1783.

83-165. Ode sur la Paix.

"Descends de la voute eternelle." (50)

Eur M 3 (Apr 1783), 312.

Regular (Horatian) ode in dixains. A French poem. England's persona confesses the mistake of "striking America with a vengeful sword," instead of sparing her, and complains of Eliott's costly victory at Gibraltar.

83-166. Ode to a Terrier. Who interrupted the Debate in the House of Commons.

"Dear Snap, of that true terrier breed." (28)

MP, Mar 14, 1783.

Quatrains. Satire on North in large measure, and then a little on "That tattling turnspit Burke," for their attack on (Shelburne's) peace.

83-167. Ode to Peace.

"Cease the dreadful din of arms." (16)

G, Feb 19, 1783.

Quatrains. Peace will restore commerce, friendship, and love.

83-168. An Ode to Peace.

"Fell war, avaunt, thou bane of every good." (36)

L Chron 53 (Feb 1, 1783), 116; PA, Feb 6, 1783; W Ent 1 (Feb 24, 1783), 190-1.

Regular ode in twelve-line stanzas. Peace and plenty can come, now that the war is over.

83-169. Ode to Peace.

"Long now the God of Arms." (36)

GA, Feb 19, 1783.

Quatrains. General invocation to peace, which should displace war and its horrors.

83-170. Ode to Peace.

"O Thou who bad'st thy turtles bear." (24)

L Cour, Apr 10, 1783; MH, Mar 20, 1783; St J's C, Apr 22, 1783; UM 72 (Mar 1783), 160; WM 57 (Jul 31, 1783), 147.

Regular (Horatian) ode in sixains. Britain welcomes the return of peace.

83-171. An Ode To the Memory of the late Dr. William Hunter, Physician Extraordinary to the Queen, Teacher of Anatomy, &c. &c.

"And why should fear delay." (68)

M Chron, Apr 10, 1783.

Irregular Pindaric ode. The poet imagines that the fame of Dr. Hunter (the distinguished physician, anatomist, and medical teacher) reaches America in the future, where science carries on, and that, although America may have dominion over Britain in the future, Hunter will still be remembered.

83-172. An Ode to the Premier.

"Great Lord, who rul'st the Loaves and Fishes." (42)

PA, Jan 2, 1783.

Regular (Horatian) ode in sixains. A satire on Shelburne, the premier, declaring that he owes his position to Bute.

83-173. Ode II. To a Late Paymaster General.

"Pasquin, who promis'd ere 'twas long." (91)

PA, Jan 3, 1783; W Eve Post, Jan 2, 1783.

Regular (Horatian) ode in septains. A satire on Burke and the domestic politics involving self-interest. This satire is the sequel written last May by the same author, Pasquin: PA, May 17, 1782, "To the Paymaster-General on the Late Changes," 82-370. Cited are Fox, Shelburne (Malagrida), et al.

83-174. [Oh! Squab, the F(o)x and B(urk)e combine to praise.]

"Oh! Squab, the F[o]x and B[urk]e combine to praise." (6)

PA, Apr 8, 1783.

HC. Satire by Causidicus on the coalition. Fox and Burke try to raise the character of North, but he is still evil.

83-175. The Olive Branch.

"Oft has the rose its fragrance shed." (8)

G, Jan 29, 1783.

Quatrains. Peace now comes, bringing love.

83-176. On a Late Coalition.

"Charles Fox and Lord North, both Patriots sound." (6)

PA, Apr 5, 1783; St J's C, Apr 1, 1783.

Hexameter couplets. Satire on the Fox-North coalition. Because Fox and North are ill-coupled, their ministry will go down.

83-177. On a Late Detested Political Association.

"Quoth Volpone to Boreas, we two are the Thing." (7)

MP, Mar 12, 1783; PA, Mar 13, 1783.

Hexameter couplets. Satire on the association of Fox and North. The devil is behind it.

83-178. On a Late Resignation! O my Country!

"Savile resign'd -- O cursed Coalition." (4)

PA, Dec 18, 1783.

Quatrain. Now that Savile has retired, the nation has lost hope. (Savile was in poor health. He died January 10, 1784, shortly after leaving Parliament.)

83-179. On a Politician.

"Here lies a man who read Newspapers." (2)

Lloyd's 53 (Aug 6, 1783), 132.

Ironic satire on newspapers. Epigram on a reader who killed himself because the newspapers made him ill.

83-180. On an Interruption which is related in the General Advertiser to have taken place while Lord North was speaking in the Debate on the Address of Thanks on the Preliminaries of Peace.

"When North, great Statesman, who has given." (29)

GA, Feb 26, 1783.

OC. A protest at North's objections to the Peace Preliminaries, especially his support of the Loyalists.

83-181. On Ins and Outs. A Dialogue.

"Prithee, dear Tom! what means this rout." (12)

W Eve Post, Apr 3, 1783.

OC in quatrains. Ins and Outs -- is there any difference? Both are equally selfish.

83-182. On Lord Temple's Administration.

"Friend to his country and mankind." (66)

Freeman's J, Mar 8, 1783; GA, Mar 19, 1783.

OC. The new Lord Lieutenant of Ireland, (Viceroy) Lord Temple (George Nugent-Temple Grenville), is praised. He will give Ireland "equal freedom," a Bill of Rights.

83-183. On Peace.

"Hail, placid Peace! return'd once more." (48)

G, Mar 10, 1783.

Quatrains. The long war having come to an end, trade is resumed and prosperity is restored.

83-184. On Peace.

"Rejoice, O Isles! and be your praises heard." (46)

Lloyd's 53 (Oct 10, 1783), 356.

Blank verse. Peace has been officially signed on September 3 and proclaimed October 6, 1783. Rejoices over the new peace and conventionally admonishes people in high and low station to take advantage of the blessings of peace. Social improvements should now be the concern of the rulers.

83-185. On Peace.

"With solemn song and unrestrained lay." (16)

M Chron, Feb 5, 1783.

Irregular lines, OC and HC, welcoming the peace.


83-186. On Reading the New Year's Ode.

"The <u>nations</u> doubtless will attend." (40)

GM 53 (Jan 1783), 64.

Irregular ode. A satiric criticism of "Goody Whitehead's" New Year's Ode, 1783. The poet objects to the lack of spirit in Whitehead's poem and to the message that all will turn out well if Britain has faith in God -- including the return of America.


83-187. On Seeing a small Mezzotinto Print of Doctor Franklin in the Case of a Watch, 1778. By an Englishman.

"Had but our nation mov'd like this great man." (20)

L Chron 53 (May 8, 1783), 444; W Ent 1 (May 26, 1783), 484-5.

HC. Prophetic lines at the end of an essay, "Some Account of Benjamin Franklin, L.L.D. and F.R.S." Britain should have taken the advice of sage Franklin; had it done so, it would have remained friendly with the colonies. But there is the consolation that, while liberty has disappeared in England, it is flourishing in America.


83-188. On Seeing the Shattered Remains of the Forty-fifth Regiment of Foot pass through Town from America.

"Welcome! thrice welcome, Heaven-born Peace." (32)

M Chron, Oct 22, 1783.

Quatrains. "Shatter'd Battalions here return / With Peace their only prize." But the dead "lie, on yon curs'd shore [America] expos'd, / Chain'd down with martial sleep."


83-189. On the British Empire in America. Written by an English Officer, some years ago, at Boston in New England.

"A crafty American walking one day." (20)

LM 52 (Mar 1783), 142.

Quatrains. The British Empire in America at the time the British were under siege in Boston (1775) does not extend westward beyond Canada, but is confined to Boston only.


83-190. On the Cessation of Hostilities.

"Hail smiling Peace, I greet thy milder reign."  (34)

MP, Mar 5, 1783.

HC.  Peace brings trade and prosperity;  and may unanimity guide our senate, and may the King stand firm "in Virtue's cause."

83-191.  On the Death of Mr. Pinchbeck.

"Long had Pinchey by letters."  (6)

PA, Mar 22, 1783;  W Eve Post, Mar 20, 1783.

Sixain.  Christopher Pinchbeck, the inventor of candle snuffers (whom William Mason had satirized), is dead.  See 76-19.

83-192.  On the Death of Mr. R. S., a Young Officer killed at Gibraltar.

"In hostile war, where dying cries."  (24)

GA, Apr 7, 1783.

Conventional memorial to a brave young officer killed at Gibraltar.

83-193.  On the Death of the Marquis of Rockingham.  Written by a Lady.

"Great men must die, it is the will of fate."  (14)

W Ent 1 (May 12, 1783), 456.

HC.  Although Britain has suffered a great loss in the death of patriot Rockingham, Fox is still living to provide leadership.  A poem by Causidicus is here corrupted by changing politics -- Fox's name substituted for Shelburne's!  See 82-250.

83-194.  On the Frequent Ministerial Changes and Arrangements.

"Such Shifting and Changing."  (6)

PA, Mar 1, 1783;  W Eve Post, Feb 27, 1783.

Sixain.  On Shelburne's removal;  there is so much changing of ministerial personnel that it should end in execution of these politicians.

83-195.  On the King's Commanding the Tragedy of the Grecian Daughter, on Thursday the 2d Instant.  Epigrammatic.

"Siddons, to see King, Lords, and Commons run."  (18)

M Chron, Jan 10, 1783.

HC. The country is neglected and going to the dogs, since all the leaders are interested in the acting of Mrs. Siddons: Shelburne, Fox, Thurlow, Townsend. See "In Answer," 83-126.

83-196. On the Miseries of War.

"Thou dire destroyer War! whose dreadful way." (60)

B&BM 2: 4 (1783), 62-3.

HC. A description of the destructive effects of war -- including British soldiers killed at Bunker's Hill -- until, after a period of mourning, peace and prosperity return and knowledge can be pursued once again.

83-197. On the Peace.

"Long has Europe, war's dire carnage mourn'd." (10)

B&BM 2: 14 (1783), 212.

HC. In praise of peace in Europe after a long war: "Now peace returns, see commerce lifts her head." The imagery is generalized and conventional.

83-198. On the Peace.

"War is over, Peace is come." (10)

GA, Feb 3, 1783.

OC. The soldier who returns home from "a sev'n years war" has nothing but scars to show for it; nevertheless, he is glad for the peace.

83-199. On the Present Alarming Crisis.

"Ill-fated Nation, torn by Faction's Pow'r." (4)

PA, Mar 27, 1783.

HC. In this crisis, the Fox-North coalition, with Bute behind it, will ruin the country. Who can save the nation?

83-200. On the Present Ministerial Confusion, and on the Late Promotion of Baronets.

"Cheat by clean hearts is seldom understood." (8)

MP, Dec 23, 1783.

HC. Kings who are misled by ministers are dangerous. (Fox and North were dismissed from office, as a result of the failure of Fox's India Bill, Dec. 18, 1783; and on the following day Pitt accepted the Premiership!)

83-201. On the Present P[eac]e. Impromptu.

"The Moment's come when Britain shall no more." (14)

GA, Mar 5, 1783; L Cour, Feb 25, 1783; PA, Feb 17, 1783.

HC. A complaint against the "shameful Peace" that has "sealed the Ruin" of England. If North were premier, Britain would not suffer this terrible peace.

83-202. On the Present Times.

"In twenty Months, or thereabouts." (4)

PA, Dec 27, 1783; W Eve Post, Dec 25, 1783.

Quatrain. A grim satire on postwar instability and confusion. The nation has had five ministerial changes since March 1781: North, Rockingham, Shelburne, Portland (the nominal head of the Fox-North Coalition), and now Pitt. All will be damned for "crimes" when out of power. (Pitt became Prime Minister on December 19, 1783, after the failure of Fox's India Bill.)

83-203. On the Proclamation of Peace.

"Alas! Poor Britain! falsely styled Great." (6)

PA, Oct 7, 1783.

HC. Britain is reduced to littleness by the Treaty of Paris -- its glory has set. The trouble started with the Stamp Tax. (The Peace Treaty was signed in Paris, September 3, and proclaimed October 6, 1783.)

83-204. On the Repulse of the French and Spaniards by General Elliot and Captain Curtis, on their Attempt to Storm Gibraltar by Sea and Land.

"Firm as the rock itself the English stand." (14)

W Ent 1 (May 12, 1783), 456.

HC. The British are as firm as the rock of Gibraltar in their defense of the fortress against the French and Spaniards -- a modern siege of Troy with one difference: the British did not surrender.

83-205. Paraphrase of an Order said to have been sent from St. James's, after the Meeting of Parliament, Nov. 1783, to my Lords the Bishops, to omit the Prayer against

America.

"Our Royal Will now publish'd to the nation." (7)

New Foundling Hospital for Wit (1786), I, 260.

HC. A satire on the King regarding the end of the American War, after the Americans achieved independence in the peace.

83-206. P[arliamentar]y Justice.

"What Justice can a Government bestow." (4)

St J's C, May 27, 1783.

Epigram. Satire on the government for corruption. A corrupt government cannot administer justice. Witness the (probable) acquittal of Thomas Rumbold (of the East India Company, charged with mismanagement and corruption, but acquitted in June 1783 by a Parliamentary inquiry).

83-207. Parody from the Third Act of Macbeth. Scene the First.

"Enter Britannia with an Old Man." (33)

MP, Mar 3, 1783.

Blank verse. Parody of Macbeth. Satire on the forces under Fox and Burke and North, who formed a strange union to oppose Shelburne's peace measures. They are accused of weakening the throne.

83-208. A Parody on a Favourite Duet, (in the Burlesque of Tom Thumb) between Mr. Noodle and Mr. Doodle.

"Sure such a Year, so renown'd, so astonishing." (12)

PA, Apr 14, 1783.

Fourteener couplets. The coalition of Fox and North, once enemies, is evidence of their knavery.

83-209. A Parody on the Favourite Duet in Rosina. The Maid of the Mill for me.

"N[orth]. I find that to quarrel will ne'er get a place." (26)

MP, Apr 4, 1783.

Song. Satire on Fox and North, both selfishly interested -- North in a sinecure post, Fox in enrichment at the Treasury.

83-210. The Patriotic Resolution.

"Quoth F[ox] to Lord N[orth], let us kiss and be friends." (4)

L Chron 53 (Jun 24, 1783), 608; MH, Jun 26, 1783; PA, Jun 25, 1783; St J's C, Jun 21, 1783; W Ent 2 (Jul 21, 1783), 72.

Epigram. Hexameter couplets. Satire on the Coalition, the motives of lust for power and greed underlying it. Fox proposes to North their union so that both will have money and power.

83-211. The Patriot's Plan.

"The Constitution is the Patriot's Sign." (2)

St J's C, Aug 19, 1783.

HC. Satire on Fox (undoubtedly). The "Patriots" cry "Constitution" deceptively in order to rob the treasury.

83-212. Pax Bello Potior.

"In the vast World of Waters, Ocean's Queen." (56)

PA, Jan 25, 1783.

HC. Causidicus portrays England standing courageously and triumphant among her enemies, with Shelburne now as her leader; and Shelburne wishes for peace and prosperity, and for friendship with America. When Britain becomes strong again, "America shall seek her Friend once more."

83-213. Peace.

"Returning Peace once more begins to smile." (96)

M Chron, Sep 19, 1783; PA, Sep 22, 1783.

HC. Peace comes with all its pleasures. Now "husbandry and commerce both increase." (The Definitive Treaty of Peace between Great Britain and France, Spain, and America was signed September 3, 1783.)

83-214. The Peace. A Vision.

"Rapt with poetic ardour, as I stray'd." (36)

B&BM 2: 12 (1783), 178.

Quatrains. The poet has a nightmare of Britain at war and wakes up as a result of thunder to find the vision has disappeared and himself in bed.

83-215. Cancelled.

83-216. A Poetical Preface to be Prefixed to the Pamphlet called "The Defence of the Earl of Shelburne;" necessary to be read by all those who wish not to be the Dupes of meretricious Eloquence and Party Prejudice.

"Reader, whoe'er thou art, thou here wilt find." (30)

PA, Feb 21, 1783.

HC. Causidicus continues to defend Shelburne from his malicious and factious detractors, who favor Fox instead.

83-217. Political Bathos; or, The Art of Sinking. A New Song. Sung by Lord N[orth] in his New Farce. To the Tune of, -- Here we go up, up, up, &c.

"Come let us sing, merry men all." (54)

MP, Mar 25, 1783.

Satire on Lord North for becoming friendly with Fox and for being self-interested: "A fig for the loss of my morals."

83-218. The Political Death of L[ord] N[orth], which happened on the memorable Night when Antipathies ceased between the Fox and the Badger, to the Astonishment of all sedulous Investigators of Nature.

"If Heaven is pleas'd when Sinners sin no more." (4)

PA, Mar 19, 1783.

HC. Satire on North, who will die politically when joining with Fox. By Causidicus?

83-219. The Politicians; a Simile. Imitated from Prior.

"'Thomas, didst thou never pop.'" (26)

GA, Apr 12, 1783.

OC. Satire on the lower middle classes who love to talk politics and never get their work done. (The point is that politics is for the upper classes.) Mentioned is the failure of the country, meaning the failure of the peace.

83-220. Portentous Transformation!

"Strange Tameness! See! on France, Nails pared, Teeth drawn." (2)

PA, Nov 18, 1783.

HC. An objection to the peace. Britain has been tamed by France -- a strange sight!

83-221. [P(ortlan)d of Mongrel Breed, 'twixt Whig and Tory.]

"P[ortlan]d of Mongrel Breed, 'twixt Whig and Tory." (8)

PA, Apr 10, 1783.

Epigram. Quatrains. William Henry Cavendish-Bentinck, 3rd Duke of Portland, neither Whig nor Tory, is suitable for the Fox-North Coalition, of which he is the nominal head. (On April 5, 1783, he assumed the office of Lord High Treasurer, or Prime Minister.)

83-222. Prerogative and Privilege.

"How more than blest must every Briton be." (10)

MP, Mar 8, 1783; PA, Mar 7, 1783; St J's C, Mar 4, 1783.

HC. Ironic satire on the coalition of Whig and Tory, Fox and North.

83-223. The Preservation of English Liberty.

"In Britain's days when papal zealots reign'd." (28)

GA, Mar 26, 1783; GM 53 (Feb 1783), 160-1.

HC. King William ("Nassau") forced the bigot papists from England and enabled religious freedom to flourish.

83-224. The Principal Argument in Favour of the Coalition between the cold-blooded Octavius and the rapacious Anthony.

"Of two great Ills 'tis wise to chuse the least." (8)

PA, Apr 3, 1783.

HC. Causidicus satirizes Burke for joining Fox and North.

83-225. Problem.

"There are, it seems, who think a black mask'd War."  (4)

PA, Nov 15, 1783.

HC. An obscure criticism of Shelburne, "the Godfather of Franklin's peace."

83-226. [The Proclamation of Peace.]

"O Yes O Yes, and a third Time O Yes."  (52)

PA, Oct 9, 1783.

OC. Intended as an ironical paraphrase of the peace proclamation, this verse is really a criticism of a poor peace and the man most responsible for it, Shelburne (Malagrida). Peace was proclaimed Oct. 6, 1783.

83-227. The Prospect of Peace.

"When Wisdom's Beam its Light denies."  (66)

Cumb Pacq, Feb 25, 1783.

Regular (Horatian) ode in sixains. Peace and commerce are welcomed. America has tranquillity and Britain supplies cloth to India. But freedom and prosperity are marred by the inhumane slave trade.

83-228. Quassata Republica.

"Alas! Britannia, thy fate."  (28)

MP, Apr 28, 1783.

Quatrains. Satire on the "unnatural" Fox-North coalition, including Burke, for undoing the church and state. North's corruption continues apace. Liberty, denied "relief" in England, must seek a place in America.

83-229. A Question Answered.

"What gives the Subjects safety, Princes awe."  (2)

L Cour, Feb 7, 1783.

HC. Epigram. The people are safe only when the King's powers are limited by law.

[Quoth F(o)x to Lord N(orth), let us kiss and be Friends.] St J's C, Jun 21, 1783. See The Patriotic Resolution, 83-210.

83-230. [Reader, / With solemn thought. Inscription on the Royal George.]

"Reader, / With solemn thought / Survey this grave." (c. 22)

Cumb Pacq, Apr 29, 1783; GA, Apr 19, 1783; G Eve Post, Apr 19, 1783; L Chron 53 (Apr 19, 1783), 381; L Cour, Apr 21, 1783; LP, Apr 18, 1783; W Eve Post, Apr 19, 1783.

A monument commemorating the tragic foundering of the Royal George with the loss of Admiral Kempenfelt and over 400 men, August 29, 1782.

83-231. Recollection. An Extempore.

"In former Wars, we Heav'n besought." (16)

PA, Apr 24, 1783; W Eve Post, Apr 22, 1783.

Quatrains. "In former Wars," Britain achieved glory; today, "our civil Jars" bring "Disgrace and endless Shame." We need another Pitt!

83-232. Red Hot Balls. A New Song. Addressed to General Elliott, alias Salamander. Tune, "Roast Beef of Old England."

"When Elliot commanded the fam'd Gibraltar." (30)

Ram M 1 (Jan 1783), 35.

Another song celebrating the defeat of the combined Franco-Spanish attack on Gibraltar, September 13, 1782.

83-233. The Return of Peace. A New Ode. Performed in Vauxhall Gardens, and set to Music by Mr. Hook.

"Hark! Hark! it is Peace who revisits the Plain." (27)

GA, May 16, 1783; G Eve Post, May 13, 1783; MH, May 15, 1783; PA, May 14, 1783; St J's C, May 13, 1783; W Eve Post, May 17, 1783.

Airs and chorus in celebration of the peace. "The Wars are all over," and Britain is at peace.

83-234. The Rival Statesmen of Two Generations.

"Two Rival Statesmen of Britannia's realm." (26)

L Chron 53 (Jun 24, 1783), 608; PA, Jun 27, 1783.

HC. William Pitt and Stephen Fox are contrasted; likewise, their sons, Charles James Fox and the younger Pitt. The sons are the opposite of their fathers, as they are of each other. This poem was improved and enlarged in L Chron 55 (May 27, 1784), 516. See 84-165.

83-235. Rivington's Reflections.

"The more I Reflect, the more plain it appears." (96)

Cumb Pacq, Mar 4, 1783.

Anapest tetrameter couplets. Ironic and pathetic poem by James Rivington, the New York printer, about his dilemma (and that of all American loyalists) at the time of the peace -- what to do and where to go. Cited are Nova Scotia, Carleton, Clinton, Cornwallis, New York, Charleston, and Asgill. This poem appeared in Rivington's (New York) Gazette, Dec 14, 1782. See Contrast and Connection: Bicentennial Essays in Anglo-American History, eds. H.C. Allen and Roger Thompson (London: Bell, 1976), pp. 141-3.

The Royal British Tar. See Miles Peter Andrews, 83-39.

83-236. The Royal Review; or a Trip to the Camp.

"'Tis in vain, my dear girl, yet to think of repose." (36)

Lady's M 14 (Feb 1783), 104.

Hexameter couplets. Female Londoners have an exciting visit to Cox-heath camp when the King is there for the review.

83-237. St. Stephen's Chapel and Westminster-Hall.

"In Stephen's dark chapel though Honour can't thrive." (6)

St J's C, Jul 22, 1783.

Anapest tetrameter couplets. Honor cannot prosper in Parliament; but justice will be given at Westminster-Hall: "Court Thieves and State Plunderers" will be punished.

83-238. Saturday the 12th of April, being the Anniversary of Lord Rodney's Victory in the West-Indies, the Day was celebrated by a number of his Lordship's Friends and Admirers, at the Bush Tavern in Bristol, by whom the following extempore Production was sung on the occasion. Tune, The Anacreontic Song.

"The Gods were assembled in weighty debate." (63)

GA, Apr 23, 1783; L Cour, May 9, 1783.

Song. Rodney's great victory over the French in the Battle of the Saints, April 12, 1782, is here celebrated, for it recalls Britain's past glory, in contrast with its present sunken fame.
"An Anacreontic Song," by Ralph Tomlinson, provided the tune for the American national anthem, "The Star-Spangled Banner." See Tomlinson, 78-A & 80-A.

83-239. [Shelburne is gone, and has bequeath'd us Peace.]

"Shelburne is gone, and has bequeath'd us Peace." (6)

MH, Apr 7, 1783; PA, Mar 1, 1783.

HC. Shelburne has resigned, and the "monstrous" and hypocritical coalition of Fox and North, "Opposites," has displaced him. (Apparently, these changes were not quite official yet.)

83-240. The Siege of Gibraltar. Written by a Young Gentleman of the Grammar School in the Close of Salisbury.

"Long had the foes insulting fix'd their eyes." (50)

W Ent 2 (Sep 29, 1783), 310-11.

HC, commemorates the great victory of the besieged forces under General Eliott and Captain Curtis over the French and Spaniards at Gibraltar (in the last year, September-October 1782).

83-241. Song for the New Year.

"Thank God at last, the old year is past." (24)

Ram M 1 (Jan 1783), 35-6.

Quatrains. No tune is given. The theme is that peace and plenty will come again through the revival of trade, "tho' America's lost."

83-242. Song. On the Prospect of Peace with America. To the Tune of -- Heart of Oak.

"Hark! the Lion is rous'd, and the Cannons they roar." (23)

GA, Jan 11, 1783; PA, Jan 16, 1783; St J's C, Jan 9, 1783; W Eve Post, Jan 7, 1783.

France and Spain will be taught a lesson; but we shall have peace with America. The song has Britain say to America, "let us be Friends, and the World we defy."

83-243. A Song on the Wise Coalition, compleated the first of April, 1783. To the Tune of, -- Nancy Dawson.

"Of all the Leaders in the State." (32)

MP, Apr 21, 1783.

Song. A satire on Fox, North, and Burke, "that artful Jesuit" -- the leaders of the new ministry.

83-244. Sonnet. To Miss Seward.

"Poetic daughter, whose sweet lyre conveys." (14)

GM 53 (Oct 1783), 870.

Modified Italian sonnet. A tribute to Seward's sympathetic evocation of pity for "Andre's strangled corse." Her powerful poetry should melt even the pitiless breast of Congress, frozen by oppression, so that Congress too would love Andre.

83-245. Splendide Mendax. Hor.

"Some Men are born to dazzle and surprise." (18)

PA, Jan 11, 1783.

HC. Satire by Causidicus on Fox as a hypocrite in a position of political power.

83-246. Stanzas, Addressed to his Excellency Earl Temple.

"In ocean's wat'ry bosom laid." (108)

Freeman's J, Apr 19, 1783.

Sixains. Panegyric on Earl Temple, Lord Lieutenant of Ireland, who regretfully has resigned his post and is leaving for England, after having done much for Ireland's national health. (George Nugent-Temple Grenville was extremely bitter towards North when recalled by the Coalition.)

83-247. The State of Party Two Years Ago in this Little Restless Island. The State of Party at Present. Epigram.

"Ned blasted Tom, and call'd him a State Fool." (14)

MP, Mar 8, 1783; PA, Mar 7, 1783.

Two epigrams. HC. Causidicus satirizes Fox and North, and again defends Shelburne from factions who, dissatisfied with his peace, have unseated him, although he saved King and country with his peace measures.

83-248. [This day / will depart. . . . Inscription Honoring George Grenville-Nugent, Earl Temple.]

"This day / will depart from the Government of this kingdom." (c. 65)

Freeman's J, Jun 3, 1783.

An inscription honoring the Viceroy of Ireland, Earl Temple, leaving for England, after a brief period of nine months as Lord Lieutenant, for his positive attitude towards Ireland.

83-249. A Thought in 1781. By Mr. John Burnby.

"Our present Constitution's like." (4)

PA, Sep 3, 1783.

OC. A simile. The constitution is like a muddy ditch. It is being corrupted by the political leaders, by "every venal Wretch in Power."

83-250. A Thought upon Statesmen and Patriots.

"In Heaven Old Satan held high place." (18)

W Eve Post, Apr 3, 1783.

Sixains. Selfish politicians are compared to Satan.

83-251. Thoughts on Peace.

"Monarchs, 'tis true, shou'd calm the storms of war." (12)

M Chron, Feb 26, 1783.

HC. Doubts about the quality of the preliminary peace treaties just concluded: "A peace in haste concluded cannot last."

83-252. The Times. -- An Epigram.

"Whilst some with their Souls may for ever in Hell burn." (10)

W Eve Post, May 20, 1783.

Hexameter couplets. Opinion is divided between Shelburne and Fox, but this writer refuses to accept either. Cited are "the [peace] Measures of Shelburne."

83-253. The Times. Sung at the Pantheon 1st of May.

"For my country's good I care not a souse." (24)

G Eve Post, May 1, 1783.

A light-hearted and cynical song about the times -- the politics of peace, corruption, and Fox.

83-254. To a Chosen Seven. An Extempore.

"If ye are all good Men and true." (8)

PA, Apr 26, 1783.

Satire on the "hotch-potch" Fox-North ministry. See "To the New Cabinet Ministry," 83-265.

83-255. To a Friend, on the past and present measures of G[overnmen]t.

"As a friend to my country, without any guile." (36)

LM 52 (Mar 1783), 144.

Anapest tetrameter couplets. Apparently, an objection to the "American measures" of the Shelburne ministry.

83-256. To Captain -----, on his return from America to his paternal estate.

"Milo's from home, and Milo being gone." (4)

GA, Mar 31, 1783.

HC. A British officer returned from America to find that his wife had borne a son.

83-257. To Lord G[eorge] G[ordon].

"If Shelburne would his Wisdom shew." (12)

PA, Jan 23, 1783.

Quatrains. A defense of Shelburne from the criticism of Lord George Gordon, who plans "Again to light Sedition's Fire."

To Miss Seward. Impromptu by Mr. Hayley. "As Britain mourn'd, with all a mother's pain." (26) W Eve Post, Sep 13, 1783. A reprint of 81-88.

83-258. To Peace.

"Approach! asupicious Peace with placid Smile."  (28)

PA, May 20, 1783.

HC.  An invocation to peace, which now has come, with plenty and commerce in its train.

83-259.  To Peace.  An Invocation.

"Come, Peace! pure Virgin of the sky."  (20)

G Eve Post, Jan 2, 1783.

Quatrains.  Peace is welcomed, and commerce may revive.  (The Provisional Articles of Peace between England and America were signed in Paris on November 30, 1782.  See Parliamentary History of England [1814; repr. 1966], XXIII, 279, 354 ff.)

83-260.  To Sir George Savile.

"Farewell! great Guardian of our charter'd Rights."  (24)

PA, Dec 5, 1783;  St J's C, Nov 29, 1783.

Blank verse. A tribute to the incorruptible patriot and guardian of civil rights, Savile, upon his retirement.  Cited also are Richmond, Pitt, James Martin -- all deeply concerned to support their "Country's Welfare."  Savile died shortly after leaving Parliament, January 10, 1784.

83-261.  To the Censurers of Two Certain Ministers.

"To decry F[o]x and N[ort]h."  (6)

PA, Apr 10, 1783.

Sixain.  Satire on Fox and North, each "a d[amna]ble K[na]ve."

83-262.  To the Chancellor of the Exchequer.

"Repeal the Duty on Receipts."  (8)

PA, Oct 3, 1783.

Quatrains.  Advises the Chancellor of the Exchequer to repeal the tax on receipts and to impose, instead, a small stamp tax on paper.  (This poem carries overtones of irony, for it echoes reactions to the celebrated Stamp Tax of 1765.)

83-263.  To the Chiefs of the Coalition.

"Go on, ye Chiefs, through policy refin'd." (24)

MP, Apr 18, 1783.

HC. Satire on the Fox-North Coalition, just come to power: North to stem the opposition in the Lords, Fox in the Commons.

83-264. To the Electors of Westminster, who dined with the Man of the People.

"When the son of old Isaac, disgracing his cloth." (6)

MP, Apr 10, 1783.

Anapest tetrameter couplets. Attack on Fox for selling his birth-right for pottage.

83-265. To the New Cabinet Ministry, or the Illustrious Seven.

"Britain's Hope, illustrious Seven." (8)

G Eve Post, Apr 17, 1783.

Quatrains. Praise of the new Portland ministry, which took office April 8, 1783: Stormont, Earl of Carlisle, Fox and North, Duke of Portland, Cavendish, and C. Townshend. See "To a Chosen Seven," 83-254.

83-266. To the Right Hon. William Pitt.

"Whilst impious Statesmen struggling for command." (42)

MP, Mar 11, 1783.

HC. The factious Fox-North coalition (that unseated Shelburne) is ruining the country. Perhaps Pitt the Younger can save the country, with the assistance of William Petty, Viscount Fitzmaurice (i.e., Shelburne).

83-267. To the Rising Warlike Genius of Britain. Being the First Poetical Effort of a Disbanded Officer. Tune, -- "Rule Britannia."

"Britannia, by her foes oppress'd." (31)

MP, Jul 19, 1783.

Patriotic song honoring young Prince William, "our great George's son," for leading the battle against the fleets of Spain, France, and Holland. The young man served in the navy during the latter part of the war.

83-268. A Translation of the Hodge Podge in the Gazetteer of Yesterday.

"Is this a time, my friend, to smile." (12)

G, Jul 11, 1783.

OC. A commentary on the news, deploring "the base and mean" and foolish coalition of Fox and North, which will only prolong the practice of corruption.

83-269. Truth.

"How are Great-Britons from themselves estranged." (24)

PA, Oct 16, 1783.

Elegiac quatrains. Wretched Britain is ruined: the peace is disgraceful and dishonorable. Who is to blame? Faction! (Shelburne or Fox is the target of this pessimistic reaction to the peace treaty.)

83-270. The Two Chiefs.

"N[orth] plung'd us in a cruel War." (16)

PA, May 28, 1783.

Quatrains. It is disgraceful that North, who is responsible for so much evil, is rewarded, while Shelburne, who brought peace, "From Honour is discarded."

83-271. The Two Secretaries.

"Says F[ox] to N[orth], 'What a great rout.'" (4)

PA, Apr 26, 1783.

OC. Satire on the coalition of Fox and North -- "knaves"! Fox and North were the principal Secretaries of State.

83-272. The Two Secretaries. Fiat Justitia!

"Joy to you! many a one will cry." (46)

PA, May 9, 1783.

OC. Ironic satire on the coalition of Fox and North: "who can deny / Your Virtue and Integrity? / Rank you with those who made the Peace?"

83-273. The Union of the Fox and the Badger. Addressed to the Country Gentlemen.

"Let Order die, and let Confusion stand." (48)

PA, Mar 15, 1783.

HC. Causidicus, using an animal metaphor, satirizes the peculiar union of Fox and North. Certainly, this alliance should wake up the Country Gentlemen in the House of Commons.

83-274. Verses addressed to Miss Seward, on the publication of her Monody on Major Andre.

"Enchanting harmonist! whose Muse complains." (26)

GM 53 (Jun 1783), 519-20; MP, Jul 11, 1783; W Eve Post, Jul 8, 1783.

HC. Seward's monody on Andre's death was published in 1781 (81-14). Hayley's response to the monody (81-88) differs from this poem. A friend pays tribute to the power of sympathy in Seward's monody.

83-275. Verses on the Peace.

"Satiate of blood, with battles tir'd." (32)

W Ent 1 (Feb 10, 1783), 144.

Quatrains. France and Spain wish the war to come to an end, and Britain agrees: "In peaceful councils, none more fam'd [than British 'chiefs'] / For mercy, equity, and right."

83-276. [When Britain surfeited with wealth and ease.]

"When Britain surfeited with wealth and ease." (45)

Freeman's J, Jun 19, 1783.

HC. Ireland must emulate America ("Boston's sons") and seek freedom and equality with Britain, thereby bringing prosperity, the arts, and toleration to the country. But Ireland does not seek independence.

83-277. Whitehead, William.
Ode for his Majesty's Birth-Day, June 4, 1783. By William Whitehead, Esq. Poet-Laureat.

"At length the troubled waters rest." (40)

AR 1783, pp. 180-1; Cal Merc, Jun 9, 1783; Cumb Pacq, Jun 10, 1783; DJ, Jun 10, 1783; G, Jun 4, 1783; G Eve Post, Jun 3, 1783; GM 53 (Jun 1783), 519; Lady's M 14 (Jun 1783), 325; Lloyd's 52 (Jun 2-4, 1783), 536; MH, Jun 4, 1783; MP, Jun 5, 1783; NAR, 1783 (III, 209-10); PA, Jun 4, 1783; RWM 8: 25 (Jun 11, 1783), 197; St J's C, Jun 3, 1783; W Ent 9 (Jun 16, 1783), 574-5; L Chron 53 (Jun 3-5, 1783), 529.

Irregular Pindaric ode. Peace has come, commerce revives. The world enjoys the blessings of peace. The man of peace, who has the capacity for sympathy (presumably King George), is the friend of man.

83-278. Whitehead, William.
Ode for the New Year, 1783. By William Whitehead, Esq; Poet-Laureat.

"Ye Nations, hear th'important tale." (44)

AR, 1783, pp. 179-80; Cal Merc, Jan 4, 1783; Cumb Pacq, Jan 7, 1783; DJ, Jan 7, 1783; GA, Jan 1, 1783; GM 53 (Jan 1783), 62; Lady's M 14 (Jan 1783), 45; Lloyd's 52 (Dec 30, 1782-Jan 1, 1783), 8; MH, Jan 1, 1783; NAR, 1783 (III, 196-7); PA, Jan 1, 1783; RWM, Jan 8, 1783; St J's C, Dec 31, 1782-Jan 2, 1783; SM 45 (Jan 1783), 40; W Ent 1 (Jan 13, 1783), 46-7; W Eve Post, Dec 30, 1782-Jan 2, 1783. Also L Chron 53 (Dec 31, 1782-Jan 1, 1783), 1; LM 52 (Jan 1783), 40-1.

Irregular Pindaric Ode. Britain is still firmly planted on Gibraltar (Calpe), despite the efforts of the united Bourbons to dislodge her. Britain's strength has not deserted her. Britain is still sovereign over the seas; her "glory [shall] gild the wreath of peace."

83-279. [The Wise in Government behold the Disease.]

"The Wise in Government behold the Disease." (4)

PA, Mar 27, 1783.

Epigram. Blank verse. "Written at the Settlement of the present Peace." In the future, the errors of the present peace will have to be corrected.

83-280. A Wish.

"Long may this Administration last." (2)

G, Jul 11, 1783; St J's C, Jul 5, 1783.

HC. A hope that the Fox-North coalition will "cure the fatal blunders of the past."

83-281. The Wonders. A New Song.

"Ye Friends to Old England, untainted by Gold." (28)

L Chron 53 (Mar 11, 1783), 235; PA, Mar 6, 1783.

Song with "Derry down" chorus. It is absurdly fantastic that Fox and North should form a coalition. Cited are Burke, Pitt, Shelburne, Sandwich, and Wilkes.

83-282. Written for the Twelfth of April.

"High on a craggy Cliff, whose bending Head." (30)

PA, Apr 14, 1783.

HC. Rodney should not be forgotten. This poem commemorates Rodney's celebrated victory over De Grasse in the West Indies last year, April 12, 1782.

83-283. Written on a Blank Leaf of Mr. Day's Admirable Reflexions on the Present State of England.

"Britains Horizon Night spread o'er." (4)

St J's C, Mar 6, 1783.

Quatrain. Epigram. Praise of Thomas Day's essay, Reflexions Upon the Present State of England, And the Independence of America (1782). See MR 67 (Nov 1782), 321-8.

83-284. Written on reading one of the supposed Preliminary Articles to a General Peace, said to be proposed by the French Ministry; that "France should no longer acknowledge the Sovereignty of the British Flag."

"What then! -- Shall haughty Bourbon's Giant Pride." (28)

Cumb Pacq, Jan 21, 1783.

Quatrains. Britain shall never surrender sovereignty over the seas to the Bourbon powers. Did not Rodney defeat them?

83-285. Written on the Following Question, Lately Agitated in the British Council; -- "In Case of a War between Russia and the Porte, Shall Great Britain espouse the Cause of Russia?"

"Plain is the Answer; Britain shall not wage." (28)

Cumb Pacq, Oct 7, 1783.

Heroic quatrains. The Armed Neutrality policy is cited against Queen Catherine of Russia; and, besides, she is a foe to freedom. Britain will not help such a monarch in her war against Turkey.

83-286. Written on the Twenty-third of April, 1783; -- The Anniversary of Paul Jones's Attempt to Burn the Town and Shipping of Whitehaven.

"The purple Currents tinge no more the Main." (53)

Cumb Pacq, Apr 29, 1783.

HC. John Paul Jones is criticized for his evil attempt to destroy Whitehaven, where he had many friends. (Jones raided Whitehaven April 23, 1778.)

Prints

83-287.  An Air Balloon Engagement for the Empire of the Sky.

"Some think we shall soon."  (18)

Engr. with verses.  December 1783.

Copy in Lewis-Walpole Library.

Soon we shall be fighting for the empire of the sky as we are now fighting for the ocean.

83-288.  The [Ass]-Headed and [Cow-Heart]-ed Ministry Making the British [Lion] Give Up the Pull.

"My honour'd Sirs, who me pretend to lead."  (22)

Engr. with HC.  May 8, 1783.

George 6229 (V, 709-10).  Dolmetsch, pp. 202-3.

Part rebus.  Critical of the patriots who have checked the power of Britain, enabling her enemies to take advantage of her weakness and America to achieve independence.

83-289.  Boreas helping the patriotic Weather-cock to snap a Goose.

"Mars doth his Iron Chariot stop."  (8)

Engr. with quatrains.  April 4, 1783.

Dolmetsch, pp. 196-7.

Fox and North join forces against Shelburne, the Prime Minister, during the peace negotiations.  North is seen blowing the geese, Fox's political enemies, toward Fox's open mouth.

83-290.  The British Tar's Triumph.

"The English Tar Triumphant Rides Mynheer."  (8)

Engr. with HC in quatrains.  October 22, 1783.

George 6268 (V, 734).

Britain gained some spectacular naval victories at the end of the war, thereby strengthening its position at the peace table.

83-291. The Coalition.

"Thou you are a Fox by name and nature." (16)

Engr. with two couplets and OC. [February, 1783.]

George 6179 (V, 678-9). HM 13 (Apr 1783), facing p. 189.

Fox and North discuss the possibility of a coalition to displace Shelburne, and cynically mention the peace.

83-292. The General P--s, or Peace.

"Come all who love friendship, and wonder and see." (16)

Engr. with quatrains. January 16, 1783.

Lewis-Walpole Library.

A satire on the peace that Britain has made with America and her allies, a peace that has given America independence through the connivance of the patriots.

83-293. Lord Shelburne Begging Monsieur to Make Piss or Peace.

"He's no heart of Oak." (12)

Engr. with sixains. January 21, 1783.

George 6168 (V, 671).

On the difficulties Shelburne is having with the peace. He became unpopular as a result of his peace negotiations.

83-294. The Monster. 1783.

"This many-headed Monster of the Land." (10)

Engr. with HC. April 2, 1783.

George 6203 (V, 690-1).

Fox is satirized as a politician simply motivated by self-interest.

83-295. Peace Porridge All Hot / The Best To Be Got. [Tune, Roast Beef.]

"The Frenchman & Spaniard are both Cock-a-hoop." (18)

Engr. with song. February 11, 1783.

George 6172 (V, 674). Repr. The British Look at America during the Age of Samuel Johnson (1971), #94.

England must make the best of a bad peace (with France, Spain, Holland, and the United States), but now peace will bring prosperity.

83-296. Proclamation of Peace.

"Peace! Peace! crys Monsieur, before Hood again calls." (6)

Engr. with couplets. October 21, 1783.

George 6267 (V, 733). Jones, p. 181.

Peace (formally proclaimed October 3, although signed September 2-3) blows a trumpet and waves an olive branch as it flies over the five belligerents. America boasts of its liberty; but Britain says America will be the worse for it.

83-297. The Savages Let Loose, or the Cruel Fate of the Loyalists.

"Is this a Peace, when Loyalists must bleed." (2)

Engr. with couplet. March 1783.

George 6182 (V, 679-80).

A protest against the savage treatment of the American loyalists.

83-298. Wonders Wonders Wonders & Wonders.

"Come, Come, shake hands, & lets be Friends." (4)

Engr. with couplets. 1783.

George 6162 (V, 668).

America is happy to conclude a peace, now that her ends have been gained. Sandwich forgives Burke and Fox. Cited are Shelburne and Lord Denbigh, Wilkes and the King now reconciled.

Epilogue 1784-1800

1784  Books & Pamphlets

84-1. The Christmas Tale, A Poetical Address And Remonstrance To The Young Ministry.
London: Faulder, 1784. 27p.

"Most potent, grave, and reverend Juniors, lend." (c. 390)

Notices: CR 57 (Jan 1784), 77; MR 70 (Feb 1784), 155; M Chron, Jan 27, 1784.

Copies: BL 1600/1300; NUC CtY, DLC, MH, NN.

HC. A condescending satire on the ministry of the younger Pitt because of their youth. But they have succeeded in displacing the veterans. The poet believes that they receive the reluctant assistance of the older statesmen, and that they should return to school and learn to follow before they lead. Satiric remarks on Shelburne's terrible peace are significant (pp. 18-19).

84-2. The Coalitionist. A Satire.
London: Murray, Johnson, Sewel, Blamire, & Faulder, [1784]. iv + 28p.

"Poet.--For shame! for shame!" (c. 550)

Notices: CR 58 (Dec 1784), 476; ERL 4 (Nov 1784), 398.

Copies: BL 1490.de.15.

In the prose dedication "To the Public," the poet expresses indignation at the shameful and "unnatural combination" of Fox and North, and "dread for the consequences," because it may signify that the principles for which these men stood are "totally altered, or totally banished."
HC. Imitation of Horace, satire on Fox and North. The poem shows that "Liberty can only stand on a tottering foundation, if such advocates as these Coalitionists are to be depended on for its support," for they are guided by private interest. The people, he concludes, must protect and maintain their rights. As it is said by the poet: "What makes the difference if the bustling game/ 'Twixt Whig and Tory should be just the same?/ Plunder's the Patriot, now" (p. 8). He laments the instability, the constantly varying ministries, the transformation of principles into "a standing joke." A substantial part of the poem is given to the definition of Whig and Tory, and it is clear that he dislikes the Tory's ideology: "His creed in one small word consists-- OBEY" (p. 20). Even servility towards tyrants is the Tory practice. But the poet insists upon freedom and Magna Charta: the Whig "stands . . . the people's friend,/ Of all his actions, liberty the end" (p. 21). But not to the point of Democracy, which introduces lawlessness and equality, and subverts "all distinction." The Whig

understands liberty under law, which "Limits alike the subject and the crown." A genuine Whig actively protects his rights.

The poet calls the coalition "the foul design," "black cabal," formed by "selfish meanness." He reviews Fox's methods of standing up for "the people's right" against North's ministry: Fox had called for their execution and did "The western cause intrepidly espouse" (p. 25). Now sceptical of Fox's sincerity, he concludes that Fox's motive must have been simply plunder.


84-3. Edwards, John.
The Patriot Soldier; A Poem. By John Edwards, Esq. Major of Light Dragoons in the Volunteer Army of Ireland.
Nottingham: Tupman; London: Longman, T. & W. Lowndes, 1784. vii + 35p.

"To fire the soul with thirst of martial deeds." (c. 600)

Notices: MR 73 (Oct 1785), 305; ERL 4 (Dec 1784), 463, & 5 (Apr 1785), 412.

Copies: BL 643.k.15 (11); NUC IU (Dublin, 1784).

A patriotic poem in praise of the Irish Volunteer Army, a civilian army. Dedication to the Earl of Charlemont, dated from Old Court, July the First, 1784.
HC. In the poem, Edwards writes that the troops stationed in Ireland for its defence were transported to America, "to stem the western main,/ In foreign climes to forge the galling chain" (p. 4), leaving the country "an easy conquest" for a foreign power. And so the patriot Volunteer Army was born.
During the war, Ireland was "unassail'd"; and when Britain needed reinforcements upon the surrender of Burgoyne's army, Ireland "spar'd to thee [Britain] the nation's standing force./ Which by one generous act at once repair'd/ The sad disgrace thy captive army shar'd"--5000 soldiers (p. 10). Ireland also helped strengthen Britain's navy. Then Edwards criticizes Britain for her unwise and oppressive policy which keeps Ireland poor and weak. He objects to British exploitation of Ireland's resources and bluntly declares, "No more, Ierne will thy chains endure" (p. 11).


84-4. An Epitaph On The Late Illustrious Earl of Chatham.
London: Davies & Sewel, 1784. 16p.

"Here continue,/ Insensibly to mingle with their original dust." (c. 245)

Notices: CR 57 (Jun 1784), 480; MR 70 (Jun 1784), 479; ERL 3 (May 1784), 388.

Copies: BL 992.h.20 (1).

Dedication to William Pitt, dated March 31, 1784. This epitaph, by the author's admission, was written many years ago and printed now so that the son will have in view the example of his most illustrious and "incomparable Father" and be guided

accordingly in his "ministerial Course."
   In the form of a long panegyrical inscription, the epitaph reviews the political career of the Earl of Chatham from the time of his leadership in the Seven Years War to his death after his last participation in the debate on the American War.


84-5. The Fourth Satire Of Persius Imitated, And Much Enlarged On. In Application To The Right Honourable William Pitt.
   London: Bladon, 1784. [5]-24p.

   "Dost thou, Pitt, govern? (think, young man, you hear." (c. 210)

   Notices: CR 57 (Feb 1784), 152-3; MR 70 (Jan 1784), 311.

   Copies: BL 11630.e.1 (12).

   HC. Imitation of Persius. Satire on the younger Pitt for being too young and inexperienced for the government of a great country. The poet insinuates that Pitt is guided by "Secret Influence," because all that he can use in Parliament is fluent speech. But Pitt's words are not particularly persuasive, lacking "facts and arguments." Pitt condemns the Fox-North Coalition--Fox for joining North "who carried on that war, that cursed war." But the poet declares Pitt is equally to blame as he forms alliances "with different persons, just the same"--Thurlow, Gower, Jenkinson, and Dundas (p. 21)! Pitt, according to the satirist, is self-deceived; he should resign from the position he cannot justly claim.


84-6. Hayley, William.
   Sonnet To Mrs. Hayley, On her Voyage to America. 1784.

   "Thou vext Atlantic, who hast lately seen." (14)

   In his <u>Poems and Plays, by William Hayley, Esq. in Six Volumes. A New Edition</u> (London: Cadell, 1788), I, 167. (1st ed, 1785.)

   Modified sonnet. Hayley asks the Atlantic Ocean, lately the scene of British anger at America, to be gentle while his wife sails to America. Hayley refers to "the blind parent, in her frantic spleen,/ Pouring weak vengeance on a filial world!"


84-7. Hurn, William.
   The Blessings Of Peace, And The Guilt Of War, A Lyric Poem. By The Reverend William Hurn.
   London: Johnson, 1784. 5-28p.

   "Discord, baneful power, away." (c. 410)

   Notices: CR 57 (Aug 1784), 152; MR 73 (Sep 1785), 229; ERL 4 (Sep 1784), 224.

Copies: NUC CtY, MH.

Octosyllabic couplets (largely). Hurn is glad that the cruel war has ended and that sweet peace has returned, and with it "Imperial Commerce." He complains of the vicious slavery in America, now "free," and pleads for the mitigation of the torments of the Negroes (pp. 15-19). He cites "an American farmer" as witness of the terrible crimes performed against the slaves.

84-8.  Knights-Hill Farm The Statemen's Retreat, A Poem, Descriptive and Political.
London: Bew, 1784. 46p.

"Imperial Thames! thou Britain's Joy and Pride." (c. 800)

Notices: CR 58 (Nov 1784), 395; ERL 4 (Dec 1784), 426-7.

Copies: BL 1493.h.12.

HC. A topographical, political poem about "sweetly rural Dulwich" and key post-war political figures, focusing on the conflict between the younger Pitt, allied with Thurlow, and the Fox-North coalition. Favors Pitt and the King, who used his prerogative to sustain Pitt despite his minority in the Commons. Praises Shelburne for the peace that "broke Rebellion's Pow'r." Castigates North for the ruinous war; imagines Cromwell's ghost advising Fox on how to weaken the King, beginning with breaking the King's power in America. Accuses Gen. Howe of losing at Long Island a chance to end rebellion.

84-9.  [Marjoribanks, J.]
  Trifles in Verse. By a Young Soldier.
  Kelso: Palmer; London: Macklew; Edinburgh: Bell, 1784. 2 vols.

André To Washington. "The man unconscious of a base design." (24) I, 41-2.

The Sweets Of Sleep. [Extract] "Sleep . . . what mighty wonders in thy realms we find." (34) I, 6-7.

Thoughts On Leaving Britain. "Oh! must I leave my native British shore." (12) II, 30.

To Mr. -----. Watchmaker And Politician. "By what strange means the secrets did you gain." (22) I, 42-3.

To The Memory of Major Marjoribanks, Late of the 19th Regiment of Foot. "Unskill'd in verse, I boast no Poet's art." (50) I, 103-6.

Notices: CR 58 (Oct 1784), 294-7; MR 72 (Feb 1785), 151; ERL 4 (Nov 1784), 344-6; L Chron 56 (Nov 2, 1784), 433; Town & Country Mag 16 (Oct 1784), 550 (repr. "André To Washington").

Copies: BL 1163.a.26-27 (1st ed), 11632.aa.34 (2nd ed, 1785); NUC ICN, MiU-C.

"André To Washington": HC. André begs Washington to be allowed to die nobly. (André's letter to Washington, written the day before his execution, versified.)

"The Sweets Of Sleep": Extract. HC. The poet dreams of the successful end of the American War, the Congress in captivity, and André's ghost damning "The Rebel Chief."

"Thoughts On Leaving Britain": HC. The soldier, leaving for America, has difficulty parting from friends and family.

"To Mr. -----. Watchmaker And Politician": HC. Satire on one who appears to be privy to all military and naval secrets. Cited are D'Estaing, Rodney, Parker, Washington, Clinton, North, and others.

"To The Memory Of Major Marjoribanks": HC. A soldier son pays tribute to his father, who died in the American War (Battle of Eutaw Springs, South Carolina, September 9, 1781).

84-10. Maurice, Thomas.
Westminster Abbey: An Elegiac Poem. By The Revd. Thomas Maurice, A.B. Of University-College, Oxford.
London: Dodsley, Kearsley; Oxford: Fletcher & Prince; Cambridge: Merrill, 1784. viii + 22p.

"Majestic monument of pious toil." (164)

Notices: CR 58 (Jul 1784), 70-1; MR 72 (Jun 1785), 463-5.

Copies: BL 11630.e.25 (1st ed), 78.g.31 (1813 ed); Bod Vct A 5 d.135 (3); NUC CtY, DFo, ICN, IU, MH, NN, & PHi (1st ed); DLC, ICN, InU, MH, & NN (1813ed).

Elegiac quatrains. Inspired by Gray's Elegy. Maurice pays tribute to the dead important in British history and refers to the present in his broad elegiac survey that relates history, politics, and poetry (p. vii). Coming to the warriors commemorated in Westminster Abbey, he mourns the heroic soldiers like Townshend, Wolfe, Howe, all killed in the campaigns against France in America; for example, (George Augustus) Howe, killed at Ticonderoga, "Whose triumphs made the western world our own." But to no avail, because what he had fought for is now lost. And André lost his life because of "curst civil rage" (p. 9).

A later version, published 1800, has revisions, one of which is significant. Here, Maurice advises Howe, who had given his life for victory against the French in North America, to "Tear not the laurels from thy veteran brow,/ In lost Columbia all the parent glows." Some of Maurice's bitterness has disappeared; he accepts American independence. (Thomas Maurice, Poems, Epistolary, Lyric, and Elegiacal [London: Bulmer & Wright, 1800], p. 213.) But the stanza on Howe is omitted in the enlarged 1813 edition! (Probably owing to changed circumstances again, the War of 1812.)

84-11. The Political Remembrancer. A Poem. In Hudibrastic Verse.
London: Macklew, 1784.

Notices: CR 57 (Feb 1784), 153; ERL 3 (Jan 1784), 64.

Copies: none located.

84-12. The Progress of Politics; Or A Key to Prior's Alma. First Canto.
London: Cadell, 1784.

Notices: CR 57 (Jun 1784), 470-1; MR 70 (Jan 1784), 311-12; ERL 3 (May 1784), 386.

Copies: none located.

The extract in the Critical Review alludes to Burgoyne and Gates.


84-13. Puddicombe, John Newell.
An Irregular Ode; Addressed To The Hon. William Pitt.
London: Robson, 1784.

Notices: MR 70 (Mar 1784), 235 (1st ed), 70 (Apr 1784), 383 (2nd ed); ERL 3 (May 1784), 387; PA, Mar 20, 1784.

Copies: none located. But see Puddicombe, 84-A, a version printed in PA.


84-14. Regular Ode Addressed To The Honourable William Pitt.
[London:] Robson, 1784. 11p.

"Immerst in more than midnight gloom." (136)

Notices: CR 57 (Mar 1784), 232.

Copies: BL 11633.g.28.

Regular Horatian ode in octaves. Panegyric on the younger Pitt. Britain is portrayed as oppressed and ruined by faction, with France triumphing over her. But Pitt has restored her vitality and liberty, and has suppressed faction: "in Thee/ With reverence and with joy we see/ Thy much-lov'd Sire revive," his eloquence, judgment, and "manly sense." The young man, incorruptible, is affected by "No selfish mercenary aim." He should glory in his youth.


84-15. A Rhodomontade Of Politics; Or, A Series Of Fables, With Notes Variorum; to be continued occasionally.
London: Appleyard, 1784.

Notices: CR 59 (Jun 1785), 474; MR 72 (Apr 1785), 389; ERL 4 (Dec 1784), 427-8.

Copies: none located.

On North, Sheridan, Burke, and others. (English Review of Literature)

84-16. The Sick Queen And Physicians, A Poetical Tale. In Five Cantos.
London: Stockdale, 1784. 58p.

"Where'er our roving thoughts can range." (1096)

Notices: CR 57 (Jun 1784), 473; MR 71 (Sep 1784), 227.

Copies: NUC CtY, CaBVaU.

Hudibrastic couplets. An allegorical review of the political state of Britain from the accession of George III to the last change of administration. I: The queen is Britannia, who is prosperous and healthy at the beginning, and "from fell taxation free." But when pride and ambition attack her, she is advised to collect taxes from North America; and so start the great troubles: the tarring and feathering of English excise officers, the rebel resistance, the use of force, the disastrous campaigns, concluding with General Gage's advice to engage in peaceful measures.
II: Boreas (North), who had learned his science from Bute, is appointed Britannia's physician. He prescribes a medicine that causes a nightmare, the loss of "the brightest gem" of her crown. But Britannia is advised to be firm and to subdue the rebels with force, under Howe's generalship. There is bloody violence, Burgoyne and all his troops are captured, and all the campaigns of Howe and Clinton are frustrated, for the Americans have formed an alliance with the French. Then Cornwallis, trapped by Washington, returns to report the sinking of British glory.
III: A new quack, Fox, displaces North, and promises a cure with the assistance of "The artful Jesuit" Burke and the advice of Rockingham. Britannia gives up America, Rockingham dies, Shelburne replaces Fox and brings peace.
IV: The coalition of former foes, Fox and North, is formed. Fox musters his friends, Burke, Hartley, and Sheridan, to help. But Britannia protests this hateful combination, which is solely guided by self-interest and plunder; and so the Portland ministry, with the assistance of Cavendish, is formed.
V: Britain's condition fails to improve, despite Fox's India Bill. Fox is portrayed as a complete hypocrite, lacking any conscience whatsoever. In anger, the King turns out the coalition, enabling Doctors Thurlow and Pitt to come in, "Great men, without a sordid view" (p. 57).

84-17. Speech To The Sun Of The Political Hemisphere, By A Fallen Angel. Embellished With A Beautiful Frontispiece.
London: Stockdale, 1784. 5-10p.

"O! Thou that with the Royal Favour crown'd." (66)

Notices: CR 57 (Feb 1784), 151-2; MR 70 (Feb 1784), 155.

Copies: NUC CtY, NN.

Blank verse. Parody on Milton's Paradise Lost IV, 32-113. A satire on Fox. The fallen angel Satan is Fox, who is made to admonish the sun, the new minister Pitt, against "overstretched Ambition" and treachery to the king--all that had unseated and ruined him. As a result, Fox's persona must complain that, out of office, he cannot repay his debts. Unable to placate the king, unable to submit to the king, the persona is made to say that he will make the House of Commons his king and that he will rule England through his domination of the Commons.

The Yale pamphlet wants the frontispiece.


84-18. Vanity Of Fame: A Poem Illustrated By Some Characters Of The Present Age. Written In Imitation Of Pope's Didactic Essays. Addressed To Sir Carnaby Haggerston, Bart.
London: Murray, 1784. 49p.

"The thirst of Fame, how wide it spreads, how small." (812)

Notices: CR 58 (Oct 1784), 309; MR 72 (Feb 1785), 151.

Copies: NUC CtY.

HC. Homiletic satire on those mortals who seek enduring fame. But their search is vain because fame is characteristically ephemeral. Certain characters involved in the American war and used to illustrate this theme are here relevant--Keppel (p. 7), Cornwallis, whose defeat is mentioned (pp. 7-8), Capt. Farmer (p. 15), Robert Manners (pp. 16-17), Gen. Eliott on Gibraltar (pp. 19-20), Chatham (pp. 24-7), Sandwich (pp. 41-2), and Rodney (pp. 44-5). "Virtue alone is never-ending fame!"

America is presented as a base parricide allied with France (p. 43, ll. 697-714). The decline of Britain (pp. 34-5, ll. 549-68) is also described.


84-19. The Voluntary Exile, A Political Essay.
London: Scott, 1784. vii + 7-31p.

"Theron. O yet awhile thy rash resolves suspend." (c. 230)

Notices: CR 57 (Feb 1784), 152-3; MR 70 (Jan 1784), 310-11.

Copies: BL 11630.c.11 (2); NUC MH.

HC. Based on Juvenal's Third Satire. Dedication in verse to Fox complains that, although the war has ended, England is now suffering from "domestic woes" under a "lawless" leadership that betrays the public trust. The poet asks Fox, the uncorrupt patriot, to accept his poem, for Fox will never betray his country's freedom. The satire is meant to illustrate the disgust felt by the poet as a result of "foul corruption" which no patriot can dispel, now that Fox (through exertion of the king's power) has been removed from the political helm and displaced by Pitt and his ministers: Thurlow, Jenkinson, Dundass, Gower. Had Chatham, Pitt's father, been alive to see the members of Pitt's ministry, he would have been saddened and angered. The poet is very severe on Pitt for strengthening the king's prerogative against "the people's rights." He believes that Jenkinson and the others are secretly influencing and deluding the young chancellor with their Tory views. And so the poet's persona decides to leave England "And woo fair Freedom on some distant shore." The place of exile is not specified--it could be America.

Included in the satire is irony directed at the king: "The fatal plans of whose inglorious reign/ One half had sever'd from his rich domain." The king, it is clear, is not an exemplary model for the corrupt times. But Fox still can be "the guardian of this falling state," still can save "the shatter'd remnants" of the people's rights.

Cited is Bute ("the thane").

## Serials

84-20. Advice to Electors.

"Elections mingled Chaos now behold." (14)

Lloyd's 54 (Apr 10, 1784), 371; St J's C, Apr 13, 1784.

HC. Advice to electors to avoid corrupt candidates, to test a man by his actions, and to "choose none but Friends to Freedom and the Laws."

84-21. Advice to Mr. Fox.

"If you'd save yourself C[har]les from many hard Rubs." (4)

PA, Feb 9, 1784; St J's C, Feb 5, 1784.

Anapest tetrameter couplets. Satire on North and the House of Lords. Fox should drop Lord North and send him to the House of Lords; the peers should be sent to the devil!

84-22. American Eclogues. Eclogue II. Evening; or The Fugitive. By the Rev. Mr. Gregory.

"Say whither, wanderer, points thy chearless way." (c. 150)

GM 54 (Jan 1784), 45-6, & (Feb 1784), 123 (errata).

HC. An anti-slavery poem. A Negro slave, a fugitive, mourns his hard lot and the loss of his freedom and happy family life in his native Angola. 83-37, Eclogue I.

Andre to Washington. (Taken from the gallant Major Andre's letter to Washington, written the day before his execution.) "The man unconscious of a base design." (24) T&C 16 (Oct 1784), 550. See Marjoribanks, 84-9.

84-23. The Apparition; or, Chatham's Ghost.

"When all was wrapt in dark midnight." (64)

MH, Mar 17, 1784.

Ballad. Chatham's ghost appears to his son and admonishes him for aligning with cunning Jenkinson (of Secret Influence fame), a friend of Bute, and at the same time gives his view of the history of the reign of George III. He urges his son to resign his place, in order to maintain the Commons' rights. (The King was maintaining Pitt in power despite the fact that he was in the minority.)

84-24. [As the wise Cato understood.]

"As the wise Cato understood." (26)

St J's C, Oct 5, 1784.

OC. King George, like wise Cato, is a good ruler, above mean and paltry politics, "Secure in Virtue, and in Love."

84-25. Cancelled.

84-26. The Baby and Nurse. A Song. Written soon after the Dissolution of Parliament, 1784. . . .

"List, all ye young Masters! to you a bard sings." (48)

Lloyd's 55 (Aug 4, 1784), 127; MH, Jul 26, 1784.

Ballad with "Derry down" chorus. In defense of Fox against Pitt, who is here presented as a minion and tool of the court.

84-27. The Belly and the Members. A Fable. Addressed to Old England in the year 1784.

"Neglected by the hands and feet." (36)

M Chron, Feb 10, 1784.

OC. Moral fable. Infant peace is endangered by the jangling debates in Parliament between Fox and Pitt.

84-28. Billy to Jack the Ratcatcher.

"Dear Jacky, your servant, my good Satan, adieu." (8)

GA, May 8, 1784.

Hexameter couplets. Satire on Pitt and Wilkes, now allied. The poet has Pitt advise Wilkes to sow seeds of dissension and discord in order to confuse the people.

84-29. [Blest is the man, whose happier fate.]

"Blest is the man, whose happier fate." (64)

M Chron, Mar 1, 1784.

Regular (Horatian) ode in quatrains. A retirement poem that exhibits disillusionment with politics, yet praises Shelburne and Grafton as "wise State Pilots" who should steer the ship of state soon, incorruptible patriots.

84-30. The Boar and the Monkey. A Fable.

"Dissolv'd in peace, fearing no ill." (32)

PA, Aug 2, 1784.

Animal fable, quatrains, with the moral of the need for naval preparedness. Britain should not let down its guard but must continue to build up its navy, should it wish to maintain its claim as mistress of the seas.

84-31. [Britannia, when th'ungen'rous foe.]

"Britannia, when th'ungen'rous foe." (20)

West M 12 (Apr 1784), 214-15.

Quatrains. Hood and Rodney had saved Britain before; now that faction is tearing the country apart, after the loss "of half [her] realms," Pitt can save Britain.

84-32. The British Toast.

"Replenish your glasses, and crown them to Pitt." (16)

GA, Sep 30, 1784.

Quatrains. Pitt will be a successful leader, like his father, Chatham.

84-33. B[ur]ke's Glasgow Promotion.

"Unqualified in Senates to declaim." (8)

St J's C, Apr 22, 1784.

Quatrains. Satire on Burke, just elected Lord Rector of the University of Glasgow. Burke is more qualified to declaim over boys than to orate in Parliament. (Burke was elected rector November 15, 1783; he visited the University of Glasgow in April 1784, when he was installed in office. See The Correspondence of Edmund Burke [Cambridge: University Press, 1965], V, 117-18.)

84-34. C[harle]s F[ox]'s Lamentation at the Treasury Gate; a Parody on the Lamentation of Mary Queen of Scots.

"I sigh and lament me in vain." (24)

PA, Feb 11, 1784.

Double quatrains. Satire on Fox, whose persona weeps over the loss of his treasury position when displaced by Pitt.

84-35. The Chimera Realized.

"Though Horace flouted long ago." (36)

St J's C, Nov 9, 1784.

Regular (Horatian) ode in sixains. Satire on the monstrous coalition of opposition figures -- Fox, North, Burke, Sheridan, and John Courtenay. (The last was surveyor general of ordnance in the coalition of 1783.)

84-36. A Coalition.

"What, more Removes! Already change the Dishes." (16)

PA, Jan 30, 1784.

HC. The Fox-North ministry is out, and now there is another ministry! "All honest Men" should unite to form a genuine coalition in order to save the nation.

84-37. Come Haste to the Hustings. A New Song. To the Tune of "Rural Felicity."

"Come haste to the hustings all honest Electors." (40)

M Chron, Apr 1, 1784.

Song. Parliament was dissolved March 25, 1784. Thereupon, the election for the next Parliament began. "Honest electors" will not desert Fox for Sir Cecil Wray (his opponent in Westminster). Wray favors the maid tax and will not help the veteran soldiers. True Whigs will vote against this Tory.

84-38. A Conversation.

"Says a Man in the Lobby, 'What's doing within.'" (26)

PA, Feb 18, 1784.

Hexameter couplets. Satire on Fox and North. The King is obeying the constitution; but all the excitement is caused by Fox and North, because they wish to unseat him!

84-39. Counter Song to that Published in the Chronicle of the 5th March, 1784. Intitled the State Juggler, or a Plain Guide to Secret Influence, by way of back stairs.

"A Juggler there is, and he has from his youth." (84)

M Chron, Mar 11, 1784.

A ballad narrates the history of the period of the American Revolution, from 1763 to the present in 1784, from Bute to the Younger Pitt. Cited are Parliament, the Peace (1763 and 1783), Chatham, Fox, Secret Influence, Grenville, the Stamp Act, and

Rockingham. Fox is presented as an honest defender of freedom. The loss of the American colonies is blamed on the Peace of 1763, but the Peace of 1783 is considered equally disastrous. See 84-109.

84-40. Detur Digniori.

"Gods! what a pother in the realm of late." (8)

W Eve Post, Apr 15, 1784.

HC. A satire on Fox and North. "Pitt and Thurlow, men of clean renown," deserve to be in; Fox and North deserve to be forced out.

84-41. A Dialogue between Malagrida and Master Billy, on some of the New Taxes.

"Thanks to my stars! I've train'd the boy." (42)

M Chron, Aug 14, 1784.

Sixains. Satire on Pitt and Shelburne and their vexing tax policy. Pitt vows to raise money through a variety of new taxes, and Shelburne applauds. Thus Pitt will be a Tory and Fox "the People's man."

84-42. The Dinner Bell.

"Burke once harangu'd on ev'ry subject long." (4)

W Eve Post, Mar 2, 1784.

HC. Satire on Burke for his long, tiresome speeches. Burke has become a signal for "the Dinner-Bell." Slightly improves the first line of 84-43.

84-43. The Dinner-Bell.

"M----n B[ur]ke harangu'd on every Subject long." (4)

St J's C, Feb 24, 1784.

Epigram. HC. Burke's oratory is ineffective -- it simply announces the dinner-bell.

84-44. The Dissolution Dialogue between Jack and Will.

"J. What makes the Town and Country, Will, so sad." (10)

St J's C, Mar 27, 1784.

HC. The King is to be blessed for dissolving Parliament, ending the coalition ministry of Fox and North and a variety of abuses. Jack is Wilkes, and Will is Pitt.

84-45. An Elegy, written in St. Stephen's. A Parody.

"Gazettes now toll the melancholy knell." (64)

M Chron, Jan 2, 1784; PA, Jan 5, 1784.

Elegiac quatrains. Parody of Gray's Elegy. Satire on Parliament and its venal members. Fox is a target.

84-46. An Epigram.

"A Daniel (cries Shylock) in Raptures distort." (4)

PA, Feb 16, 1784; St J's C, Feb 12, 1784.

Anapest couplets. The father can be seen in the younger Pitt.

84-47. Epigram.

"The land was doubly tax'd, we thought." (8 or 12)

G, Aug 18, 1784; GA, Aug 19, 1784; MH, Aug 18, 1784; PA, Aug 18, 1784; St J's C, Aug 14, 1784; W Eve Post, Aug 17, 1784.

Quatrains. On the vexing problem of raising money through taxation. The war at an end, the peace must still be paid for in high taxes; and, regardless, the people must pay whether "the Great make war or peace." (Only the G version has two quatrains.)

84-48. Epigram.

"Too long has Fox's tongue prevail'd." (12)

M Chron, Mar 18, 1784.

Quatrains. Too long has Fox prevailed; we are happy that Pitt has assumed the leadership. Pitt respects the King; Fox does not.

84-49. Epigram. Georgium Sidus, the New-Discovered Planet.

"Britain, in spite of ev'ry Blow." (4)

M Chron, Mar 18, 1784; PA, Mar 19, 1784; LM (NS) 3 (Oct 1784), 297.

Quatrain. Herschel gave George a new kingdom in the sky to compensate for the loss of America.

84-50. Epigram. On Mr. Fox's Credit.

"Of the Credit of Fox what Jew can despond." (2)

Lloyd's 54 (May 26, 1784), 508; W Eve Post, May 25, 1784.

Anapest tetrameter couplet. Satire on Fox because, without credit, he is not credible.

84-51. Epigram. On Seeing a Herse and Mourning Coaches fall in with Mr. Pitt's Procession to the City. . . .

"As by his zealots Pitt was led." (6)

M Chron, Mar 1, 1784.

Sixain. Pitt's procession to the City falls in with a funeral, symbolizing the burial of the Constitution.

84-52. Epigram on the Objection to the Age of the Right Hon. Will Pitt, Esq.

"As G[eor]ge is sagacious, determined, and cool." (4)

MH, May 21, 1784.

HC. King George is wise to choose young Pitt as his minister, because he now has a willing tool. George long had wished to have his own wish.

84-53. Epigrammatic Soliloquy. [And] Ditto.

"The Devil's in the Dice -- I'm ruin'd past a doubt." (2 + 4)

PA, May 31, 1784.

Two epigrams satirize Fox, who complains that he is ruined.

84-54. Epistle. From Miss Mark'em, in London, to Lady Barbara Courtley, at Castle Lizard in the County of Cornwall. Written in Feb. 1784.

"Sweet Lady Bab, According to Promise I got my dear Aunt." (58 + 52 + 56 + 56 + 70)

PA, May 6, 10, 12, 14, & Jun 18, 1784.

Five installments of a chatty verse letter. Hexameter couplets. 1. Miss Mark'em visits the House of Commons to see the followers of Fox contesting those of Pitt. Wilkes is praised: "he assists the Prerogative Scale," that is, Pitt and the King.
2. Fox and North are satirized. 3. Pitt assails Fox in the debate over the India Bill. 4. Burke's oratory is the target of Miss Mark'em's satire. 5. Remarks on party factionalism.

84-55. Epistle to C[harles] F[ox], From an Intimate Acquaintance.

"Dear Charles, whose Eloquence I prize." (76)

St J's C, Oct 19, 1784.

Quatrains. Satire on Fox and his supporters North, Sheridan, and Burke. He is urged to take up Methodism, thereby securing disciples.


84-56. An Epitaph.

"Beneath the accumulated weight." (c. 20)

W Eve Post, Feb 17, 1784.

An inscription. Satire on the Fox-North coalition -- its demise. But both Fox and the opposition and North and his ministry were both responsible for prolonging the unnatural American War and losing the colonies.


84-57. An Epitaph, Designed for an Old Patriot.

"Here lies a wretch, who made a noise." (48)

G, Mar 19, 1784.

OC. Satire on Wilkes as selfish and unprincipled turncoat in a survey of his political career. This epitaph marks his political death as a true patriot.


84-58. Epitaph, Extempore. On George Alexander Stevens, the famous Lecturer on Heads. By Capt. [Edward] Thompson.

"A Second Alexander here lies dead." (2)

MH, Oct 7, 1784; St J's C, Oct 2, 1784.

HC. On the death of George A. Stevens, the celebrated lecturer on heads and the song writer. See "The Heads," 76-175.


84-59. Epitaph. On a Defunct Coalition.

"Underneath this stone doth lye." (4)

W Eve Post, Mar 2, 1784.

Satire on the Fox-North coalition and its demise. (After the failure of Fox's India Bill, the coalition collapsed and the younger Pitt became Premier, December 27, 1783.)

[Epitaph on General Wolfe . . . in the Parish Church of Westerham.] GM 54 (Oct 1784), 731. See 60-13.

84-60. Epitaph. On Sir George Savile.

"Oh Liberty! -- thy once lov'd Savile view." (14)

MH, Jan 20, 1784.

HC. A sincere patriot, an independent and honorable man of great integrity, has just died (January 10, 1784) -- Sir George Savile.

84-61. Epitaph on the Late House of Commons.

"This House was the best, that e'er Motion was made in." (4)

PA, Mar 26, 1784.

Hexameter couplets. Satire on the House of Commons for factionalism and chaos, and for disregard of the people's rights and the royal prerogative.

84-62. An Excellent New Song. To the tune of "The Children in the Wood."

"Ye Britons all, come, mourn with me." (28)

MH, Mar 3, 1784.

Ballad. Young Pitt does not follow in his father's footsteps. A Tory, he supports prerogative, but opposes constitutional liberty, a strong Commons, and Fox.

84-63. Extempore.

"A Dutchman seldom looks for bays." (4)

MP, Nov 10, 1784.

Quatrain. Satire on the Dutch because they are simply mercenary.

84-64. Extempore. On Doctor Samuel Johnson.

"O Johnson! thou wer't honest, learned, rough." (10)

MH, Dec 29, 1784.

HC. Panegyric on Johnson (in a sense), dead and freed from errors, party rage, and pension. An allusion to Taxation No Tyranny. Johnson died December 13, 1784.

84-65. Factious Oratory.

"How Athens rose, historians tell." (28)

G, Aug 26, 1784.

Quatrains. The Athenian empire, including the colonies, was destroyed by seditious demagogues; the British empire, likewise, has been destroyed by the Burkes and Foxes of the time, since they have "render'd freedom's effort vain."

84-66. A Familiar Epistle, paraphrased from Horace, and addressed to Joe D----, by his old friend Will G----.

"The Muse, who lov'd him, gave her Will." (162)

SM 46 (Aug 1784), 428-9.

Quatrains in introduction (12 lines), then sixains. This poem was written after Arnold's apostasy but before the end of the war. Only the first part is relevant, because it touches on the American War from late 1780 to early 1781. Allusions to Yankee privateering raids, the failure of the generals and admirals.

84-67. [Far from those scenes of horror and distress.]

"Far from those scenes of horror and distress." (24)

Lloyd's 55 (Nov 22, 1784), 503.

Quatrains. Verses by a retired "Half-Pay Officer" who reminisces about the war -- he feels pity for those hurt by the war, but pleasure in having served his country.

84-68. A favourite Cantata as performed at the Shakespear Tavern, Covent-Garden. Composed by G. J. Esq. Set to Music by L--- S---h.

"Roar, all ye winds! ye distant Mountains roar." (128)

M Chron, Feb 26, 1784.

A series of airs tied together with recitative. A satire on Fox and North. Fox complains of Pitt's appointment to the premiership. He will have his revenge. North confesses to self-interest, regardless of party, Whig or Tory.

84-69. Favourite Songs out of different Operas, sung by people of the first rank on the late change of ministry.

"The K[in]g. Though they think me such a ninny." (c. 60)

M Chron, Jan 10, 1784.

Quotations from several popular operas -- Maid of the Mill, Cymon, Beggar's Opera, et al. -- are applied to the King, Bute and Jenkinson, Pitt, Savile, and others.

84-70. The Female Canvasser. A Song. On the Westminster Election. Tune, -- Push about the Jorum.

"When Charles in contest hard was run." (56)

W Eve Post, May 20, 1784.

Song. Satire on Fox and his canvasser, the Duchess of Devonshire, in his difficult competition for MP with Sir Cecil Wray, the government-supported candidate.

84-71. A Finance Dialogue in the Cabinet.

"Th[urlo]w. Rotten Taxes by G[o]d." (5)

MH, Jul 7, 1784.

Hexameter couplets. Satire on Thurlow and Pitt for their demeaning tax policy.

84-72. The Following is a Copy of What Was Sent on Thursday to the Officer of a Great Assembly.

"Oh, heedless Commons, where's your Spirit gone." (34)

PA, Feb 2, 1784.

HC. Satire on North, Fox, and Pitt, who, lacking principle, all basely pursue their selfish ends. What the nation needs is effective leadership, and the King can give it, if allowed.

84-73. The Following was the Last Speech of a Criminal, Lately Executed in Palace Yard.

"Good Christians all who here attend." (28)

Lloyd's 54 (Mar 22, 1784), 284; PA, Mar 20, 1784.

OC. Satire on Fox for betraying his country, etc., thereby losing his place to Pitt. He begs North to avenge his political death.

84-74. For Great-Britain. A Funeral Dirge.

"O Nation! numbered with the dead." (8)

PA, Oct 26, 1784; W Eve Post, Oct 23, 1784.

Epitaph in quatrains. Britain's "vital principle," honor, is wanting, and so the nation is spiritually dead.

84-75. The Fox Outwitted. A Dialogue.

"Fox. Where are these mighty loaves and fishes." (6)

WM 59 (Mar 4, 1784), 289.

Sixain. Satire on Fox for his greed. North leaves him India to plunder.


84-76. Franklin, Benjamin.
Epitaph on Miss Shipley's Squirrel, killed by her Dog. By Dr. Benjamin Franklin.

"Alas! poor Mungo." (23)

G Eve Post, Sep 18, 1784; W Eve Post, Sep 25, 1784.

Inscription, printed on the first page of the General Evening Post. The moral, perhaps applicable to America, is that an excess of liberty leads to destruction and death: "apparent restraint / Is real liberty."


84-77. The Frenchman. The Republican. The Honest Englishman.

"True to Religion, and the Gospel Text." (68)

PA, Aug 4, 1784.

HC. Causidicus satirizes the shallow French and the irreligious Republican; in contrast, he praises the honest, moderate Englishman and defines proper church-state relations. The poem includes a panegyric on the King and Pitt.


Gregory, (?). See American Eclogues. Eclogue II, 84-22.


84-78. [Heaven often, to chastise flagitious Times.]

"Heaven often, to chastise flagitious Times." (54)

PA, Feb 18, 1784.

HC. Satire on Fox. Causidicus attacks Fox for faction and sedition, and Burke for supporting him. An improvement of Causidicus's poem in 83-115.


84-79. His Majesty's most gracious Answer to the Mover of the late humble, loyal, dutiful, respectful Address.

"With all humility I own." (33)

Cal Merc, Mar 15, 1784; M Chron, Mar 10, 1784; W Eve Post, Mar 6, 1784; LM (NS) 2 (Apr 1784), 329.

OC. A satire on Fox, spoken ironically in the persona of the King, for attempting to reduce the King's prerogative, which the King was using to keep Pitt in power, despite the fact that he was in the minority.

84-80. "Honi soit qui mal y pense."

"When Britain acts by British laws." (12)

PA, Dec 10, 1784.

Sixains. Britain shall teach her enemies the meaning of her motto -- evil to him who evil thinks.

84-81. [If to degrade thy country, blast her fame.]

"If to degrade thy country, blast her fame." (46)

PA, Jun 23, 1784; W Eve Post, Jun 22, 1784.

HC. Causidicus targets for satire the Fox-North coalition, thrust out by the Pitt-Thurlow alliance. A severe indictment of Fox.

84-82. The Importance of the Coalition to the Public Safety. An Ode.

"'Tis strange! yet still the kingdom stands." (30)

G, Sep 2, 1784.

Regular ode in sixains. The Coalitionists, or Pittites, must be doing the right thing, for they are not destroying the country, whose prosperity appears to depend on measures, not men.

84-83. Impromptu.

"Who calls Charles Fox a selfish man." (4)

W Eve Post, Jul 13, 1784.

Quatrain. Satire on Fox, who will do anything to be Prime Minister.

84-84. Impromptu. On the Distinction of Whig and Tory.

"O what is a Whig, Sir -- O what is a Whig." (8)

G, Jun 26, 1784; PA, Jun 25, 1784.

Quatrains. Satire on corruption in politics. Whig and Tory are alike in that they can be bribed for preferment.

84-85. Impromptu, To the Compiler of a List of the late House of Commons, in which the Friends of Mr. Pitt are distinguished by Stars, and those of Mr. Fox by Daggers.

"With Prices shewn by Figures wrote." (8)

PA, May 14, 1784.

Quatrains. Pitt will save the nation; Fox, a traitor, will destroy it.

84-86. [Indignant see! the God of War.]

"Indignant see! the God of War." (24)

M Chron, Oct 27, 1784.

Quatrains. Critical comments on Holland threatened by war and unable to secure help, not even from America. Holland wanted American money, not its liberty.

84-87. The Ins and Outs.

"Friend Tummus, didst thou never ken." (18)

WM 59 (Jan 29, 1784), 144; W Eve Post, Jan 15, 1784.

Nine-line stanzas. The Outs simply wish to return to office.

84-88. The Ins and Outs.

"If the In[n]s and the Outs should struggle much longer." (4)

PA, Feb 9, 1784; St J's C, Feb 5, 1784; WM 59 (Mar 4, 1784), 289.

Anapest tetrameter couplets. The prolonged struggle for power between ins and outs creates chaos, which will ruin the country.

84-89. The Ins and Outs.

"Of Ins and Outs, no more let Quidnuncs prate." (4)

G Eve Post, Jan 17, 1784.

HC. Statesmen (politicians) must be measured by the quality of their service to their country, not by party or faction.

84-90. Inscription. On the Pedestal of a Plaister-of-Paris Image of Peace.

"What, Britons, by out-numbering foes distressed." (4)

PA, Oct 9, 1784.

Quatrain. A rejection of the "false peace."

84-91. An Irregular Ode for the Year 1784.

"Thy gates, oh Janus, now are clos'd." (72)

MH, Jan 21, 1784.

Irregular ode. Peace has come and the soldiers are returning home from the war. Could there be political unity, we would all rejoice. By C. Meadows.

84-92. The Judgment of Minerva on the Author of the American War.

"In days of old -- in virtuous days." (40)

Almon's General Advertiser, Dec 13, 1784.

Quatrains. North, the author of the American War, is judged not to exile but to scorn.

The King's Answer to the Motion for a certain Representation, being part of Sir Richard Hill's Speech last night versified. W Eve Post, Mar 6, 1784. See "His Majesty's most gracious Answer," 84-79.

84-93. The Lamentation of a fallen Statesman recounting his Losses in a Soliloquy.

"By Pride and Obstinacy toss'd." (12)

PA, Jan 30, 1784; W Eve Post, Feb 5, 1784.

OC. An ironic satire on Lord North, who complains of all that he has lost -- America, place, power, and honor.

84-94. The Lamentation of Lord N[orth].

"Ah me! what dire misfortunes flow." (14)

Ram M 2 (Jan 1784), 37.

OC. Ironic satire on Lord North, who confesses in a soliloquy his weakness and ignorance, resulting in the loss of America, of immense sums of money, and of his reputation and place. A plagiary of 84-93.

84-95. Liberty Jack.

"When Liberty Jack was in mighty Renown." (12)

St J's C, Aug 31, 1784.

Anapest tetrameter couplets. Satire on Wilkes for breaking his faith, deserting his friends, and seeking the King's approval.

84-96. Lines on Certain Pitiable Honors.

"Time was, when Sovereign sense, and British spirit." (6)

MH, Nov 26, 1784.

HC. Shelburne asks for honors before meriting them. (He was created Marquess of Lansdowne in 1784.)

84-97. Lines on Mr. Pitt.

"Against Pitt, tho' you vent all your spleen." (4)

MP, Oct 26, 1784.

Quatrain. The youth of Prime Minister Pitt cannot be held against him, for he becomes older every day!

84-98. Lines on Mr. Pitt.

"When Chatham died, Britannia bow'd." (4)

PA, Jul 30, 1784.

Quatrain. The Earl of Chatham's spirit reappears in his son.

84-99. Lines on the Fifth of November.

"This day the City Muse, in annual rhymes." (34)

PA, Nov 6, 1784.

HC. Guy Fawkes Day is reinterpreted in the light of the alleged plot of Fox (Faux, "the old way spelling Fox") and North to undermine the nation -- to rule and ruin it. But Pitt is the country's savior! (How Fox and North have fallen in British esteem!)

84-100. Lines to Lord Mahon.

"A Tax upon Dogs, my good Lord, you propose." (12)

MH, Aug 31, 1784.

Hexameter couplets. Satire upon taxes, especially those on dogs, proposed by Charles Stanhope, Lord Mahon.

84-101. Lines. To the Right Hon. the Earl of -----.

"Some men there are, whom, spite of wealth, and name." (27)

MH, Feb 9, 1784.

HC. A satire on an unidentified Tory peer -- ambitious, proud, timid, and vain.

84-102. Lines written by Mr. Gray, upon Mr. Fox's Father's Retiring to his Seat at Kingsland, in Kent. [And Parody.]

"Old and abandon'd by his venal friends." (48)

M Chron, Jan 22, 1784; PA, Jan 23, 1784; W Eve Post, Jan 20, 1784.

Elegiac quatrains, by Thomas Gray. Ironic verses on Henry Fox, Lord Holland, returning to his country estate to build fake ruins and complaining that if Bute and others of his political friends had their way they could have ruined London. The verses are parodied in lines that are applied to the son, Charles James Fox, here harshly satirized for wishing to destroy the constitution.

84-103. Lines Written on a Pedestal which supported the Statue of Minerva (in a Gentleman's Garden at Parsons Green,) by a Lady who had decorated it with flowers on the day appointed for returning God thanks for the Peace made by Lord S[helburn]e.

"While venal senates, sacred rites prophane." (22)

MH, Aug 2, 1784.

HC. Praise of Fox's patriot virtue.

84-104. Maurice, Thomas.
An Epistle to the Right Hon. Charles James Fox, on his Bill "for vesting the Affairs of the East India Company in the Hands of Certain Commissioners," &c.

"Thou guardian Genius of a sinking state." (c. 180)

Eur M 6 (Oct 1784), 322-4.

HC. A severe indictment of British avarice, which has almost destroyed India; and praise of Fox, "Undaunted Champion of the rights of man," for pleading her cause. Dated January 1784.

84-105. The Modern Alcides.

"O'erwhelm'd by foreign and domestic blows." (48)

W Eve Post, May 8, 1784.

Sixains. Praise of the younger Pitt, who has subdued "the Hydra Faction" and will restore the nation to its former glory, her empire over land and sea.

The Modern Clodio . . . A Memento to my Countrymen. Lloyd's 54 (May 5, 1784), 434-5; W Eve Post, May 4, 1784. See "To the Worthy Freeholders of England," 84-198.

84-106. Modern Gratitude Exemplified.

"N[orth] hath his Country ruin'd, King betray'd." (48)

PA, Feb 11, 1784.

HC. Causidicus abuses Lord North for all that is terrible and wrong with the nation; North is seditious and factious despite gaining enormous wealth from the nation.

84-107. Modern Zimri, or the Political Weathercock.

"Drag Zimri forth, expose the wretch to view." (48)

W Eve Post, Mar 13, 1784.

HC. Causidicus pens a satire on a political trimmer, identity not known. (He could be North.) The trimmer sometimes supports Fox; at other times, he supports the King.

84-108. [Mourn! Britons, mourn! for Freedom's gone.]

"Mourn! Britons mourn! for Freedom's gone." (12)

GA, Jun 23, 1784.

Quatrains. Freedom has gone from England, for the young Pitt is responsible for discord. Only unanimity can restore England's fame.

84-109. A New Ballad. To the Tune of, "There was an Old Woman, and what do you think."

"There was an old F-x, and what do you think." (55)

M Chron, Mar 5, 1784.

A satire on Fox for shifting his "principles" or views; the peace and North are dealt with. This song inspired the "Counter Song," 84-39.

84-110. New Coalitions.

"When Foes like Oil and Vinegar unite."  (10)

St J's C, May 15, 1784;  An Asylum for Fugitive Pieces . . . A New Edition (London: Debrett, 1785), I, 264 (first ed., p. 223).

HC.  It is strange that Wilkes and the King should now love each other.


84-111.  A New Song, entitled, Master Billy's Budget, or a Touch on the Taxes.  To the Tune of "A Cobler there was, &c."

"Ye boobies of Britain, who lately thought fit."  (70)

Lloyd's 55 (Aug 11, 1784), 150-1 (65 ll.);  MH, Jul 21, 1784;  PA, Jul 21, 1784; W Eve Post, Aug 12, 1784.

Ballad with "Derry down" chorus.  A satire on the younger Pitt's budget, the new proposals for taxes on hats, dresses, candles, bricks, cotton and linen, horses, paper -- all of which disappoint and disillusion the author.


84-112.  A New Song.  Entitled The Grocer's Delight;  or A Sugar Plumb [sic] for Master Billy.  To the Tune of "The Roast Beef of Old England."

"When good George the Second did sit on the Throne."  (37)

M Chron, Mar 2, 1784.

Song.  Satire on Pitt, a Tory who "stands up for Prerogative strong."  Young Pitt has deserted "the Old Whigs" that his father favored for the lords of "the Back Stairs," Jenkinson, Dundas, and Thurlow.


84-113.  A New Song, entituled, The Budget;  or, A Word to the Wise.  To the Tune of, "A Cobler there was."

"Ye People of Britain, your hopes reassume."  (60)

GA, Sep 9, 1784.

Ballad with "Derry down" chorus.  Praise of Pitt's tax policy because it imposes equal taxes on the people.


84-114.  New Song.  To the Tune of Langolee.

"Good People, I'll tell ye a pitiful story."  (40)

M Chron, Feb 17, 1784;  PM 6 (Feb 1784), 86.

Song in double quatrains.  The M Chron version is addressed to Woodfall, the printer of the paper:  "Mr. Woodfall, I'll tell ye a pitiful story."  A satire on Fox because of his difficulties in speaking from the hustings to the electors of Westminster.

84-115. A New Song. To the Tune of "O my Kitten, my Kitten."

"All you who are willing to know." (64)

M Chron, Jan 24, 1784; PA, Jan 26, 1784.

A Whig song. A satire on the monarchy, its prerogatives, and its Tory supporters. The theme states the need for the people to maintain their rights against the crown. The Tories are now favored by the King.

84-116. A New Song, upon the New Times.

"To Kings who aspire to an absolute reign." (24)

G, Jan 19, 1784.

Quatrains. No tune is given. The "back-stairs" is the way to achieve credit with the King and to evade the requirements of a parliamentary monarchy. Pitt is the example. Camden and Shelburne, George Grenville (Earl Temple), and others are mentioned in various roles.

84-117. A New State Song.

"A Statesman there is, and his name I can tell." (52)

M Chron, Feb 7, 1784.

A ballad with "Derry down" chorus. Satire on Fox, who demagogically and hypocritically prostituted Liberty's name to feed "the American flame," then formed a union with "an absolute Tory"; but the Lords will not accept his India Bill.

84-118. A New Year's Ode for the First of January; Alias a New Song called, A Touch on the Times: Or the Downfall of the Coalition.

"Come all honest Britons attend to my Song." (64)

PA, Jan 22, 1784.

Ballad with "Derry down" chorus narrates the downfall of the cursed coalition of North and Fox and expresses hope for the new ministry of Pitt.

84-119. The Newspaper: An Ode.

"Hail, spreader of amusive news." (68)

M Chron, Apr 27, 1784.

Regular (Horatian) ode in quatrains. The newspaper has many uses for its diverse readers -- including the information about "public contests" or politics and the publishing of "th'inferior poet[s]."

84-120. [N(ort)h, while the Star still beams upon his Breast.]

"N[ort]h, while the Star still beams upon his Breast." (6)

Lloyd's 54 (Mar 10, 1784), 248; PA, Jan 24, 1784; St J's C, Mar 9, 1784.

HC. North is shameless in his alliance with Fox, because he is greedy for a handsome annuity.

84-121. N[or]th's Opinion of Parliamentary Reformation.

"Senates reform'd (N[orth] crys) he ever hated." (6)

St J's C, Jun 8, 1784.

HC. Satire on North, who here is made to accept corruption in government as standard, and reformation as foolish.

84-122. Ode, Addressed to the Hon. Charles James Fox, Esq.

"As when the tempest low'rs around." (42)

MH, Apr 7, 1784.

Regular (Horatian) ode in sixains. Let us support Fox in the present election. Fox is in the tradition of Hampden and liberty.

84-123. Ode for the Anniversary Dinner of the Quintuple Alliance, June 17, 1784. To Freedom.

"Of every higher Joy the Queen." (30)

PA, Jul 7, 1784.

Ode largely in sixains. Wilkes presided over a meeting dedicated to the continuation of political reform for "Equal Laws." Capel Lofft and Major Cartwright spoke at this affair.

84-124. Ode, Humbly Inscribed to the Right Honourable George Earl Temple.

"Stunn'd by a venal factious Crew." (48)

PA, Apr 10, 1784.

Regular (Horatian) ode in sixains. Panegyric on George Nugent-Temple (2nd Earl Temple). He will cleanse Britain of the venal and factious (meaning the followers of Fox and North), and, like Washington, he will be above party.

84-125. Ode occasioned by a late Address, and the Answer to that Address.

"Why sleeps the Muse, while Faction bold." (36)

M Chron, Mar 8, 1784.

Pindaric ode. A defense of Pitt's ministry. Let us honor the new ministry of the younger Pitt, supported by Thurlow. It will make landed wealth pay an equal tax, instead of shifting the burden upon the laboring class and the merchants. See the Parliamentary History of England (1815), XXIV, 668-9, 677-8, 699, & 717-18.

84-126. Ode to Mr. Pitt.

"O thou, a fainting Nation's stay!" (52)

Lloyd's 55 (Nov 3, 1784), 434; M Chron, Nov 4, 1784; PA, Nov 5, 1784.

Quatrains. The poet counsels the younger Pitt to be careful in politics and to remain pure, uncorrupted, and independent.

84-127. Ode to Mr. Pitt, on the late Entertainment at Grocers Hall.

"'Twas at the Grocers feast, for power won." (c. 130)

M Chron, Mar 8, 1784; MH, Mar 5, 1784; SM 46 (Apr 1784), 211-12.

Irregular Pindaric ode; parody on Dryden's Alexander's Feast. A satire on the young Pitt, now premier, indicating his difficulties in maintaining this office in the face of Fox's strong opposition. Also Asylum for Fugitive Pieces (1785), pp. 78-82.

84-128. Ode to the New Year.

"With brighter fates another year." (44)

M Chron, Jan 16, 1784.

Irregular Pindaric ode. Praise of Shelburne for his peace, and thanks for the peace and the prosperity that it brings. Britain is still great and victorious.

84-129. An Ode Written on New Year's Day.

"Once more bifronted Janus knows." (24)

PA, Feb 13, 1784.

Regular (Horatian) ode in sixains. Satire. Britain is at peace but is menaced by

Fox and North, who should be sent to the devil.  Portland can be left alone, and Conway kicked a little;  Keppel should suffer guilt, and all those who in Parliament are self-interested should be imprisoned.

84-130.  [Of three competitors to rule the State.]

"Of three competitors to rule the State."  (12)

PA, Nov 22, 1784.

Two impromptus in HC.  Pitt can handle Indian affairs better than Fox can, although he has less experience (like that of the American crisis) than North has -- and he will restore England's glory.

84-131.  Omnium Gatherum; or, the Political Hodge-Podge.  To the Tune of "Mrs. Arne, Mrs. Arne, it gives me concern."

"Kit Wyvill, Kit Wyvill."  (85)

G, Apr 8, 1784.

Song.  Satire on the leaders of the reform movement:  Christopher Wyvill, Thomas Howard (Earl of Effingham), Charles Stanhope (Lord Mahon), William Mason, and others.

84-132.  On a Certain Great Oratour's Being Cough'd Down.

"B[ur]ke on again!  How shall we get him off."  (2)

St J's C, Jun 22, 1784.

HC.  Satire on Burke as orator.  One way to prevent Burke from speaking is to "cough" him down.

84-133.  On Seeing a Hedger with a bundle of Sticks upon his Shoulder, and an Electioneering Bill in his Hand.

"Poor fellow! what hast thou to do."  (20)

G, Feb 7, 1784;  GA, May 17, 1784;  PA, May 15, 1784;  St J's C, May 11 & 13, 1784; W Eve Post, Jan 29, 1784.

Quatrains.  Satire on the anti-democratic times.  Those in the laboring class, despite changes in government, must still work.  To them politics is irrelevant and liberty "but a name."  Also entitled "Stanzas by the late Alexander Thistlethwayte." Adapted to the Fox-Pitt strife in the May version.

84-134.  On Seeing the Earl of Chatham's Monument in Westminster-Abbey.

"When this high, stately Monument, attentively I view."  (26)

M Chron, Dec 29, 1784.

Hexameter couplets. Panegyric of Pitt, Earl of Chatham: he made Britain great, in the East and in the West.

84-135. On Seeing the Exultations, at the Close of the Poll in Westminster.

"Princes of old the envy'd laurel gain'd." (5)

Lloyd's, Jun 11, 1784; W Eve Post, Jun 10, 1784.

HC. Satire on Fox, at the end of the election poll, for having gambling friends, including the Prince of Wales (later George IV), and for being factious.

84-136. On the Commutation Tax.

"Wow! what's this Pitt? Some unco spark." (72)

Cal Merc, Nov 8, 1784.

Six-line, bob-tail stanza associated with Burns; in Scots dialect. Satire on the younger Pitt's commutation (window-light) tax. Pitt had withdrawn the tea tax, but this act does not compensate for the other additional tax. See <u>Parliamentary History of England</u> (1815), XXIV, 1332 ff. On August 10, 1784, the bill for repealing the several duties on tea, and for granting other duties in lieu thereof and several additional duties on houses, windows, or lights, etc., was introduced and debated, and passed by the Commons.

84-137. On the Death of the Celebrated G. Alexander Stevens.

"Poor Stevens, alas! thy HEAD is laid low." (4)

W Eve Post, Sep 11, 1784.

Quatrains. A notice in verse on the death of George Alexander Stevens, who wrote songs, delivered lectures on heads, and may have written the celebrated song on "The Heads," 76-175.

84-138. On the Horse Tax.

"Tho' the tax upon horses much treasure amasses." (2)

W Eve Post, Oct 30, 1784.

Anapest tetrameter couplet. Satire upon taxes. A tax upon asses would be more productive than that on horses.

84-139. On the India Bill. A Constitutional Song. To the Tune of, -- The Vicar of Bray.

"The Grecian Bards may sing about." (68)

Lloyd's 54 (Feb 6, 1784), 135;  PA, Feb 13, 1784.

A ballad narrates some political history, including Septennial Parliaments, Scotch politics, Wilkes and Luttrell, Fox and North, Reforms, and the Coalition, up to the India Bill.  The theme emphasizes self-interest:  "That men in power, let who will reign, / By interest will be guided."

84-140.  On the Late Dissolution of the Last Parliament.

"The Coalition Parliament." (4)

PA, May 31, 1784;  W Eve Post, May 29, 1784.

OC.  Impromptu.  The Coalition Parliament has been dissolved (March 25, 1784).

84-141.  On the Late Fall of Virtue into a Pitt.

"Virtue, dear girl! full oft essay'd." (12)

G, Mar 23, 1784.

Quatrains.  Pitt may not be an honest statesman.  Virtue has fallen into a Pitt and may be raised with "a Plumb," an attractive office in government.

84-142.  On the new-created Marqueses.

"Our Sister Isles, in diff'rent factions rav'd." (20)

PA, Dec 16, 1784.

HC in quatrains.  Praise of Temple and Shelburne elevated to Marquis.  George Grenville, Earl Temple, was created Marquess of Buckingham;  William Fitzmaurice Petty, Earl of Shelburne, was created Marquess of Lansdowne.  Temple soothed Ireland;  Shelburne brought the American War to an end.

84-143.  On the Political Death of Sir Boreas Broadbottom, who departed the Ministerial Life some Time in December last.

"If Heaven is pleas'd when Sinners sin no more." (4)

PA, May 11, 1784.

HC.  Causidicus is pleased to bury North in a political grave.  (The Fox-North Coalition fell from power December 19-23, 1783, after the defeat of Fox's India Bill.)

84-144. On the Treatment Mr. F[o]x lately met with at Westminster from the Mob, who compelled him to take refuge at the King's-Arms Tavern, Palace-Yard.

"The <u>Man of the People</u>, at Westminster Justled."  (8)

W Eve Post, Feb 24, 1784.

Quatrains.  Satire on Fox, so-called "Man of the People," who is rejected by them.

84-145. On Two of the Minister's New Taxes. An Epigrammatic.

"Folks call Pitt clever! -- so they may."  (4)

MH, Jul 3, 1784; W Eve Post, Jul 13, 1784.

Quatrain.  Satire on Pitt for imposing a Candle Tax and a Window Tax.

84-146. The Oratour and the Ass.

"How wise, when silent E----d B--ke appears."  (4)

St J's C, Jul 3, 1784.

HC.  Satire on Burke for his absurd and asinine oratory.  The campaign against Burke continues.

84-147. Par Nobile Fratrum.

"How oft hath F[ox], in fury of debate."  (34)

W Eve Post, Jan 27, 1784.

HC.  A satire by Causidicus on "A Pair of Noble Brethren," Fox and North, now in coalition.  Fox and North reprobated each other often in debate, and their accusations were just.

84-148. A Paraphrase.

"Inform'd you before, that I knew full as well."  (28)

PA, Mar 19, 1784.

Anapest tetrameter couplets.  A paraphrase of the King's thoughts about the possibility of a broad-bottom administration, which he appears to believe has little or no foundation and which he rejects.  (Thus he refuses to ask the Pitt ministry to resign.)

84-149. The Patriot.

"In good Sir Robert's golden Days." (57)

PA, Jun 4, 1784; St J's C, Jun 1, 1784.

A song, tune not given but easily recognizable as the old "Vicar of Bray." A review of the ministries from Bute to Pitt. A satire on a venal MP who simply sides with those in power, despite principles. Cited are Sir Robert Walpole, Bute, North, Rockingham, Shelburne, the Fox-North Coalition, and the Pitt-Thurlow-Gower Coalition.

84-150. Plan of Ministerial Power. To L[or]d N[orth].

"Thou witty, laughing, gay, unfeeling Man." (12)

PA, Mar 5, 1784.

HC. North, responsible for much evil including the loss of America, is saved from punishment by his coalition with his former opponent Fox.

84-151. The Political Boxers; or Labour in Vain.

"Puff'd up with raging Party Zeal." (16)

PA, May 31, 1784.

Quatrains. The Butcher and Cobbler dispute the merits of Fox and Pitt; but to what end? They cannot benefit from the advance of either.

84-152. Political Consistency.

"What! Liberty Wilkes, of oppression the hater." (8)

MH, May 3, 1784; An Asylum for Fugitives, in Prose and Verse (1785), p. 170.

Hexameter couplets. Satire on Wilkes, who has consistently been guided by self-interest. He is not a turncoat!

84-153. The Political Death of Carlo Khan, who departed the Ministerial Life some Time in December last, to the great Joy of most honest Men in the Kingdom, to the Regret of only hungry Dependance and disappointed Faction.

"O Carlo Khan, how great thy fall." (24)

PA, Aug 13, 1784.

Regular (Horatian) ode in sixains. A satire on Fox, the cheat who is in eclipse. (After the rejection of Fox's India Bill, his ministry was forced to resign, December 19, 1783.)

84-154. Political Matrimony. A Dialogue.

"Had not I seen thy fair bewitching Face." (11)

PA, Mar 19, 1784; St J's C, Mar 16, 1784.

HC. Satire on the Fox-North coalition, which did not turn out so well for Fox. He wants to be rid of North, but North refuses to part.

84-155. Political Principle.

"'An union on principle,' cries Fox, 'I require!'" (10)

WM 60 (Apr 29, 1784), 136.

Hexameter couplets. Satire. Fox and others are without principle.

84-156. The Political Roscius, An Ode.

"Skill'd in the labyrinths of mind." (54)

M Chron, Sep 22, 1784.

Regular ode in sixains. A satire on Fox, who will do anything to destroy the present Pitt ministry.

84-157. Political Rumours. A Poem.

"What ills from civil discord rise!" (44)

M Chron, Oct 21, 1784.

Quatrains. Satire on politics. All sorts of rumors contaminate the political scene, all causing needless fears and generated by faction: about Europe, Ireland, emigration, government funds, prerogative and the constitution, smuggling tea, taxes, trade.

84-158. Political Squibs thrown at Carlo Khan and his Powder Bag Committee.

"When Dust is thrown in Charley's Eyes." (40)

PA, Feb 28, 1784.

Eight epigrams satirizing Fox.

84-159. A Pregnant Query.

"A Nation with her own perdition pleased." (4)

PA, Oct 26, 1784;  W Eve Post, Oct 23, 1784.

HC.  Is there any hope for Britain, dismembered, degenerate, insane, and "with her own perdition pleased"?

84-160.  Prerogative and Privilege.  Question and Answer.

"Q.  To what good Purpose, or what glorious End."  (6)

PA, Feb 9, 1784;  St J's C, Feb 5, 1784.

HC.  The King and the nobility contend for power at the expense of the nation.

84-161.  The Private Reflections of a Patriot.  To the Tune of "The Roast Beef of Old England."

"A Certain great Patriot, whose Name you may guess."  (145)

M Chron, Feb 2, 1784;  PA, Feb 16, 1784.

Ballad.  Satire on Fox, self-interested throughout -- narrating his history from the time he opposed North, supported America and Keppel, etc.  Cited are Sandwich, Conway, Burke, Rockingham, Shelburne, the Loyalists, the Coalition, Pitt, and Thurlow.

84-162.  Psalm.  Te Laudamus.

"We praise thee, O George;  we acknowledge thee to be the King."  (46 vv)

GA, Jun 24, 1784.

A parody of Biblical prose-poetry.  Satire on the King and Pitt, and advice to the King to dismiss the young and inexperienced Pitt in order to restore liberty to England.  The King's views on America are presented in a few verses.

84-163.  Remarkable Occurrences in the Year 1783.

"When ---- by War had ruin'd all."  (40)

PA, Jan 1, 1784.

Quatrains critical of the coalition of Fox and North, but praise of the new ministry of the younger Pitt.  Shelburne and the peace are alluded to.

84-164.  A Requiem.  In the Manner of Charles Churchill.

"Peace to his ashes! may his virtues live."  (14)

MH, Dec 27, 1784.

HC. On Samuel Johnson's Tory ideology. Johnson lacked one virtue -- that of withstanding despotic power; and Britons now appear to be surrendering liberty. (Johnson died December 13, 1784.)

The Revival of British Spirit, An Ode. LM 2 (Jun 1784), 458-9. See "British Spirit Revived. An Ode," 81-31.

84-165. The Rival Statesmen of Two Generations.

"Two Rival Statesmen of Britannia's realm." (58)

L Chron 55 (May 27, 1784), 516; also 53 (Jun 24, 1783), 608, in 26 lines.

See 83-234. This poem takes the careers of Fox and Pitt up to the new Parliament, when Pitt received the support of the electorate, spring 1784. It is a neat summary of the political situation in 1783 and 1784.

84-166. The Sale of Opposition's House-Hold Stuff. A New Song.

"Opposition has broken up house." (88)

PA, Aug 16, 1784.

Ballad. Satire on the present opposition (to Pitt's ministry), including Conway, Surrey, Fox, North, Burke, Cavendish, Adam, Sheridan, and others, no longer in power.

84-167. The Scavengers.

"Street and State, Scavengers are much at one." (2)

St J's C, Apr 1, 1784.

Epigram. Satire on corruption. Business will only be done with bribes -- on state or street level.

84-168. Scheme For paying off the National Debt.

"While patriots are stunning the ears of the nation." (21)

PA, Aug 13, 1784; W Eve Post, Aug 10, 1784.

Anapest tetrameter couplets. The satirist suggests a tax on hypocrites and on the taxes themselves.

84-169. The Search; or, Virtue found in a Pitt.

"An Hermit, who long had sequester'd from men." (90)

G, Mar 8, 1784.

Anapest tetrameter couplets in sixains. A hermit searches everywhere for virtue -- East and West, House of Lords and of Commons -- and eventually finds it in the young Pitt, the son of old Chatham, who, unlike the fraudulent North and Fox, will reduce taxes and bring peace to the nation.

84-170. Secret Influence.

"While wordy Charles at Secret Influence rails." (4)

PA, Feb 16, 1784.

HC. Fox is secretly influenced by the devil.

84-171. Some Events of the Reign of Charles the First, compared with the present Times.

"When Britain to avenge her wrongs of old." (36)

M Chron, Sep 11, 1784.

Quatrains. What happened in the reign of Charles I -- tyranny and civil war -- was repeated in the reign of George III, who strengthened his prerogative to wage a destructive war on America. Cited are the Stamp Act, Bute, and North.

84-172. A Song.

"It was more than once said." (54)

Lloyd's, Mar 3, 1784; M Chron, Mar 4, 1784.

Song in sixains (without a tune). A satire on Fox, who has been deprived of his ministry by Pitt. It is hoped that Fox "will ne'er have a place."

84-173. A Song.

"Ye sons of fair freedom who sense have to save." (45)

MH, Feb 25, 1784.

A ballad, without tune but with a "Derry down" chorus. An attack on Pitt and Thurlow, Tories who would weaken the House of Commons and the constitution by strengthening the crown's prerogative. (In effect, a pro-Fox poem.)

84-174. Song. A Stroke at the Budget. By a Madeley-Wood Collier. Tune -- "Jolly Mortals fill your Glasses."

"'Twas in sultry summer weather." (48)

PA, Aug 28, 1784.

Quatrains. A satire on taxes. The government is thinking of taxing coal mined at the pit ("Pit Coal"), but the colliers will resist. Manchester and Coventry gained from the (American) War; they should be taxed double!

84-175. A Song. On the Restoration of the Forfeited Estates of Scotland. Tune -- Lochiel's Reel: Or, The Haughs of Cromdale.

"As o'er the Highland hills I hied." (40)

Cal Merc, Nov 10, 1784.

An ode in octaves honoring the Scottish clans whose forfeited estates have now been restored, because they are now loyal to the King and nation: the Camerons, Lochiels, McLeods, McDonalds, MacPhersons, Frasers, and McLeans. The debates in Parliament on the Forfeited Estates Bill took place on August 2 and 16, 1784. See the Parliamentary History of England (1815), XXIV, 1316 ff., 1363 ff.

84-176. Song. The Trimmer.

"Fear-Shaken fools, by conscience aw'd." (24)

Lloyd's 55 (Sep 22, 1784), 294; MH, Sep 24, 1784.

Quatrains. No tune is given. Satire on the trimmer who always moves to the strongest side, regardless of serious principles. But the trimmer endures because he is compliant.

84-177. Song. To Mr. Pitt.

"Indeed, Mr. Pitt." (24)

Lloyd's 54 (Apr 12, 1784), 354.

No tune is given. Sixains in praise of Pitt for opposing Fox and for being friendly to the King.

84-178. Song. To the Tune of Ballynamona Oro.

"To Th[ur]l[o]w and G[o]w[e]r, many praises belong." (54)

MH, Mar 18, 1784.

Song. A satire on the younger Pitt for his threats to freedom and his equivocation. Apparently, he desires only power, and he will not resign despite being in the minority.

84-179. The Source of the Evil: Or, The Saddle Laid on the Right Horse. A New Song. To the Tune of "A Cobler there was," &c.

"I'm an Englishman true, and all taxes I hate." (80)

PA, Sep 11, 1784; St J's C, Sep 7, 1784.

Ballad with "Derry down" chorus. The source of the evil, the need for revenue, is in North's American War, exacerbated by the waste of the Fox-North coalition. Pitt must be praised for bringing order to the government with his tax policy.

Stanzas by the late Alexander Thistlethwayte, Esq; occasioned by his meeting a man loaded with sacks. . . . See "On Seeing a Hedger with a bundle of Sticks upon his Shoulder, and an Electioneering Bill in his Hand," 84-133.

84-180. Stanzas on the Late Budget.

"Uprising from the Treasury rows." (24)

Lloyd's 55 (Jul 30, 1784), 111; MH, Jul 22, 1784; PA, Aug 4, 1784; W Eve Post, Aug 3, 1784.

Quatrains. A complaint against Pitt's excessive taxes -- on candles, clothing (hats), soap, bricks, and even noses!

84-181. Stanzas on the New Year.

"How swift return renewing years." (24)

Lloyd's 54 (Dec 31, 1783-Jan 2, 1784), 7; MH, Jan 2, 1784.

Sixains. Remarks on the end of the bloody rebellion and the coming of peace. The veteran remembers the death of Lord Robert Manners (who, badly wounded in the Battle of the Saints, died after tetanus set in, April 23, 1782); he also remembers the defeat of Cornwallis, who had "lost th'inglorious war."

84-182. The State Jehu Haranguing the Mob.

"Now, now, or never, cries the ambitious F[o]x." (69)

PA, Feb 2, 1784.

HC. Causidicus abuses Fox as a demagogue who wishes to rule at the price of good sense and honesty.

84-183. State Wonders; or, The World Turned Upside Down.

"When Whigs and Jacobites shake hands in peace." (12)

SM 46 (Apr 1784), 212; WM 59 (Mar 11, 1784), 311.

HC. In Pitt's ministry, opposites join in an alliance -- Scotsmen are friends of William Pitt, and they were enemies of his father!

84-184. Substance of Mr. Fox's Declamation against Mr. Pitt.

"I am out, and you are in." (4)

Lloyd's 55 (Sep 1, 1784), 218; W Eve Post, Aug 31, 1784.

OC. Satire on Fox for being factious and selfish. He simply wishes to be "in," to be in power. (Perhaps the debates on India inspired these lines.)

84-185. Tally-Ho!

"Ye Statesmen, draw near, who with riot and noise." (24)

W Eve Post, Feb 24, 1784.

No tune is given for the song. The heading: "A Fox-hunter distributed the following laughable Song at the last Masquerade." The "Opposition" have difficulty hunting down Fox.

84-186. The Taxes. A Tale. By Mr. R. Tattam.

"Great Jove, tho' seated far on high." (74)

W Eve Post, Dec 14, 1784.

OC. Jove learns of taxes through a farmer's complaints about the window and horse taxes, etc. Thereupon, he produces walls instead of windows, the horses die of fright, the farmer's wife miscarries. In pity, Jove restores the farmer's condition to its former state. Moral: there are worse evils than taxes.

84-187. [Thalia, my friend.]

"Thalia, my friend." (49)

PA, Feb 6, 1784.

Song. No tune is given. Satire on this "whimsical Age." There is a good deal of conflict between the outs and the ins and between politicians once friends, like North and Dundas. We need leaders like Pitt or Shelburne to prevent party dissension.

84-188. To a Certain Minister of State.

"May you have all you wish, 'scape all you fear." (16)

St J's C, Mar 4, 1784.

HC. A satire on Pitt, the new chief minister, by a pseudo-hack flatterer who slavishly (but really ironically) begs the premier's favors.

84-189. To E[DMUN]D B[UR]KE.

"To thee, O B[ur]ke! since Speeching's of no Use." (2)

St J's C, Feb 24, 1784.

Epigram. HC. Burke is urged to try silence, because his oratory has been useless.

84-190. To His Majesty.

"Oh had I power, with what supreme delight." (20)

Lloyd's 54 (Mar 5, 1784), 232.

HC. The poet sings the praises of the King supported by "the generous Pitt"; he damns Fox and, to some extent, North.

84-191. To John Sawbridge, Esq. on his Re-election as Representative in Parliament for the City of London.

"When sinking Britain needs the Patriot's aid." (16)

GA, May 20, 1784; M Chron, May 15, 1784.

HC. Sawbridge deserves his reelection to Parliament as a sincere patriot who will guard the rights of the people of London.

84-192. To Mr. B[u]rk[e].

"In this long Interval of Time." (48)

St J's C, Dec 28, 1784.

Quatrains. A satire on Burke for misusing his oratorical powers to undermine Pitt's ministry -- by supporting Fox's India policy and North, who was responsible for the civil war and the loss of the American colonies. Burke inconsistently censures Hastings but not North.

84-193. To Mr. Pitt.

"O Pitt! to thee, and to thy Father's Name." (20)

St J's C, Feb 24, 1784.

HC. Pitt is asked, as heir to his father's name, to suppress faction (the union of Fox and North, which weakens the monarchy) and to steer the ship of state.

84-194. To the Memory of Sir George Saville.

"When Brutus fell, the pillar of the state." (18)

WM 59 (Jan 29, 1784), 144.

HC. Savile died because faction undermined freedom.

84-195. To the Right Honourable Earl Percy on his late promotion.

"While from the earliest bloom of youth." (24)

M Chron, Nov 24, 1784; MP, Nov 24, 1784; PA, Dec 2, 1784.

Quatrains. Upon his appointment as Colonel of 2 Troop Horse Grenadier Guards, Percy is here praised for his humanitarian feeling for his soldiers at Bunker's Hill and elsewhere.

84-196. To the Right Hon. The Earl -----.

"Some men there are, whom, spite of wealth, and name." (27)

MH, Feb 9, 1784.

HC. Satire on an unidentified peer, Earl -----, for presuming to advise the King. He is careless about the people's rights and is a genuine Tory.

84-197. To the Right Hon. William Pitt.

"When factious Rage embroil'd the British State." (38)

PA, May 27, 1784.

HC. Panegyric on young Pitt, who follows his great father. Chosen by the King to assume the helm of the state, he restores order and saves the country.

84-198. To the Worthy Freeholders of England.

"Think Tygers gentle and polite the Bear." (72)

Lloyd's 54 (May 5, 1784), 434-5; PA, Apr 20, 1784; W Eve Post, May 4, 1784.

HC. A satiric character by Causidicus, who again blasts Fox. Fox is not to be trusted because he is a gambler and spendthrift, and basically insincere. (Fox, for some strange reason, is identified as "Ned," Burke's nickname.) Also entitled "The

Modern Clodio . . . A Memento to my Countrymen."

84-199. The True Patriotick Spirit of Whigs and Tories.

"With Loaves and Fishes ever in the Eye." (4)

St J's C, Apr 3, 1784.

HC. Cynical satire on Whigs and Tories, equally corrupt.

84-200. Tune. -- Sweet Willy O!

"The first of all Statesmen is sweet Charley O!" (20)

G, Apr 7, 1784.

An election song in praise of Charles James Fox, patriot and "man of the people," up for MP from Westminster.

84-201. Two Characters. The Contrast. Earnestly recommended to the Two H[ouses] of P[arliament], and the People at large, at this critical Juncture.

"Is there a man to honour strictly just." (32 + 40)

W Eve Post, Feb 24, 1784.

HC. A satire and panegyric by Causidicus. Pitt (the Younger) is the good leader; but North is the evil leader.

84-202. Unanimity.

"How long shall Britain feel the force." (60)

GA, Oct 2, 1784.

Regular (Horatian) ode in sixains. Mean, self-interested, and corrupt politicians, the "aristocratic few," should not tear our country apart. We need unanimity and stability, and less party strife. (The criticism is aimed at Fox's supporters.)

84-203. Union of Parties. An Expedient recommended to the Congress at the St. Alban's Tavern.

"What's N[or]th, and what's F[o]x." (12)

PA, Feb 16, 1784; St J's C, Feb 12, 1784.

Sixains. Were the state plunderers Fox and North hanged, there would be no debate, all parties would unite, and things would go well.

84-204. Verses Addressed to Henry Cruger, Esq. Member for Bristol. On his safe Arrival in that City, from America.

"Hail! Cruger, hail! whose gen'rous soul." (20)

Lady's M 15 (Oct 1784), 550.

OC in quatrains. "The friend of virtue and the poor" and the assertor "Of commerce, liberty, and laws," Cruger, returning from America, is welcomed home. (Cruger, a New York merchant, was elected MP for Bristol in the 1784 Parliament, although he was in America at the time. He was a follower of Pitt.)

84-205. Verses addressed to the Hon. Mr. Grosvenor, Chairman of the Committee for the Redemption of the Nation from the Slavery and Tyranny of Faction.

"Genius of England, who in dreary Hour." (92)

PA, Feb 4 & 6, 1784.

HC. Causidicus complains of faction and discord in this time of crisis, damns North and the Coalition, calls on the Country Gentlemen to perform against party, and concludes with an expression of hope for salvation.

84-206. Verses Addressed to the King.

"Come, Panegyric, pour thy smoothest strain." (40)

W Eve Post, Mar 16, 1784.

HC. Causidicus writes a panegyric on George III, for showing concern for the people, for obedience to the nation's laws, and for observing the Constitution.

84-207. Verses on Mr. Pitt.

"O'er Albion's cliffs I pensive stray'd." (68)

L Chron 55 (Apr 8, 1784), 350; UM 74 (Mar 1784), 154.

Quatrains. The poet mourns the "cruel war" which ended in an "inglorious peace," an "empire torn," and the faction and discord which now shake the state. But Pitt will save the nation and restore its glory.

84-208. Verses to be Fix'd on the House of Commons.

"Gold rules within, and reigns without the doors." (8)

GA, Sep 24, 1784.

HC. Satire on Parliamentary corruption. The MP is like a whore who prostitutes herself -- both sell themselves for gain.

84-209. Verses. To R. H-v-de, Esq.; With a Purse formed of the Thirteen American Stripes, and Presented on his Birth-Day. By a Lady.

"This day, which still with joy I sing." (46)

MH, Dec 9, 1784.

OC. A gift of a purse symbolizes the new United States of America, a land characterized by simplicity, integrity, and valor.

84-210. Verses to the Memory of Lieutenant James Abernethie, of the Ninety-Second Regiment, who was unfortunately lost on board the Glorieux, September 17, 1782.

"Each weeping Muse assist my mournful pen." (40)

Lady's M 15 (Supplement 1784), 717-18.

HC. The death of a young man, another casualty in the war, is mourned.

84-211. A Vindication and Reply.

"A. You've abus'd my friend F[o]x; but I pray do him right." (12)

W Eve Post, Feb 14, 1784.

Anapest tetrameter couplets. Satire on Fox. Fox is clever; but, like the devil, he belongs in hell.

84-212. Voila la Difference.

"Some men are hang'd, and others rise to fame." (37)

W Eve Post, Apr 15, 1784.

HC. Satire on North by Causidicus. North is damned, despite the eloquent support of Burke.

84-213. [The *Ways and Means* again deferr'd.]

"The *Ways and Means* again deferr'd." (12)

W Eve Post, Feb 17, 1784.

OC. Satire on Fox for his gambling. He is not quite the man to be in charge of the Treasury, and so he is forced to resign.

84-214. [We your Majesty's Subjects, Potwallopers all.]

"We your Majesty's Subjects, Potwallopers all." (16)

PA, Feb 10, 1784.

Anapest tetrameter couplets. Ironical criticism of Pitt (meant as praise) and praise of Fox (meant as criticism) by seditious subversives like Catiline, Jack Cade, Wat Tyler, and John Straw.


84-215. The Westminster Meeting; Or, The Back Stairs. An Excellent New Song, To the Tune of "Mrs. Arne, Mrs. Arne, It gives me consarne." [And] Another Excellent Song. Being a Second Part of the same Tune.

"Sir Cecil, Sir Cecil." (108)

"Mr. Fox, Mr. Fox." (94)

M Chron, Feb 18, 1784; MH, Feb 17, 1784; PM 6 (Feb 1784), 86-88.

Songs on the politics of the Westminster election for Parliament: Sir Cecil Wray vs. Charles Fox. (The Morning Herald prints only the first part.)


84-216. [When dauntless Abingdon, with ardent Zeal.]

"When dauntless Abingdon, with ardent Zeal." (12)

St J's C, Mar 4, 1784.

HC. Abingdon (apparently) joins Pitt against Fox and other gamblers who have entered politics in order to ruin the state by their factionalism.


84-217. Whitehead, William.
Ode for His Majesty's Birth-Day. June 4, 1784. Written by W. Whitehead, Esq. Poet-Laureat.

"Hail to the day, whose beams again." (44)

AR 1784-85, II, 132-3; Cal Merc, Jun 9, 1784; DJ, Jun 8, 1784; G, Jun 4, 1784; GA, Jun 4, 1784; G Eve Post, Jun 3, 1784; GM 54 (Jun 1784), 453; Johnson's British Gazette & Sunday Monitor, Jun 6, 1784; Lloyd's 54 (Jun 2, 1784), 536; M Chron, Jun 4, 1784; MH, Jun 4, 1784; NAR 1784, III, 199-200; PA, Jun 4, 1784; St J's C, Jun 3, 1784; W Ent 3 (Jun 21, 1784), 598-9; LM (NS) 2 Jun 1784), 456.

Irregular Pindaric ode. A celebration of the English constitution, "That wond'rous plan . . . Which curbs licentiousness and pride, / Yet leaves true liberty." This is what King William of Nassau achieved and the Georges of Brunswick "perfected."


84-218. Whitehead, William.

Ode for the New Year. Written by W. Whitehead, Esq. Poet Laureat. And set to Music by Mr. Stanley.

"Enough of arms. To happier ends."  (44)

AR 1784-85, II, 131-2;  Cal Merc, Jan 7, 1784;  G, Jan 1, 1784;  DJ, Jan 6, 1784; G Eve Post, Dec 30, 1783-Jan 1, 1784;  GM 54 (Jan 1784), 45;  Lady's M 15 (Jan 1784), 45;  Lloyd's 54 (Dec 31, 1783-Jan 2, 1784), 2;  MH, Jan 1, 1784;  NAR 1784 (III, 197-8);  PA, Jan 1, 1784;  W Ent 3 (Jan 12, 1784), 46-7;  LM (NS) 2 (Jan 1784), 17.

Irregular Pindaric ode. A didactic poem. The war is over, and now Britain resumes the arts of peace. Only "frugal industry" can make the nation "truly great." Adults should be models of patriotism to youth and should teach them "to bleed, to die, in Britain's cause," and to guard their birthright, liberty, "from faction nobly free."

84-219.  [With Noise for Argument, Abuse for Wit.]

"With Noise for Argument, Abuse for Wit."  (22)

PA, Jan 3, 1784.

HC.  Satiric abuse of a Scots politician, probably Wedderburn.

Prints

84-220. Harlequin Junior; or the Magic Cestus.

"As Fancy does his heart incline." (48)

Engr. series of 8 frames and quatrains. November 17, 1784 (?).

Lewis-Walpole Library.

London Stage Index gives a date of 1784 for this pantomime. Harlequin deserts his Columbine for a series of adventures, including investing in American bonds and helping Elliot defend Gibraltar.

1785  Books & Pamphlets

85-1. The Bees, The Lion, The Asses, And Other Beasts, A Fable.
London: Debrett, 1785.

Notices: CR 60 (Oct 1785), 314; MR 73 (Sep 1785), 230; ERL 6 (Jul 1785), 72.

Copies: none located.

"The American war, the k--g, and lord N---h, form the subject of this rhapsody" (Critical Review). "The rise and progress of the American war, and abuse of the K--g, and Lord N---h make up the contents of this publication" (English Review of Literature).

85-2. Cowper, William.
The Task, A Poem, In Six Books. By William Cowper, Of The Inner Temple, Esq.
London: Johnson, 1785. 359p. (283p. for The Task)

"I sing the Sofa. I who lately sang." (c. 5500)

Notices: CR 60 (Oct 1785), 251-6; MR 74 (Jun 1785), 416-25.

Copies: BL C.116.bb.30, C.71.c.22, Ashley 2995; NUC MH.

Blank verse. Many editions. Probably begun June-July 1783; completed September 1784. Didactic poem, partly satiric, partly meditative. Selections comment on the current scene--Book 2, pp. 56-60 (c. 80 ll.): Writing as a patriot, Cowper praises Chatham's inspiring eloquence and Wolfe's military genius. He blames the effeminate English nobility for losing an empire to France; the men were more interested in horse racing than in building a strong navy to withstand France. (Note the allusion to the jewel falling out of the king's crown.)
  Book 4, pp. 137-41 (c. 80 ll.): Cowper describes the pleasures of reading a newspaper, comments ironically on British troops sleeping in America and on political debates.
  Book 5, pp. 204-8 (c. 90 ll.): he expresses his love of his country for its civil and political liberty, despite the loss of its empire and its inferiority to France in politeness. However, he predicts its doom because of the corruption of its political idealism.

85-3. Day, Thomas.
[Stanzas Written On The Failure Of The Application For An Equal Representation In Parliament.]

"When faithless senates venally betray." (16)

In James Keir, An Account of the Life and Writings of Thomas Day, Esq. (London: Stockdale, 1791), p. 60. Rpt. in European Magazine, 19 (June 1791), 473.

Quatrains. Written c. April 1785. The attempt at a reform of parliamentary representation by the younger Pitt having failed, Day angrily deplores the corruption of "faithless senates" and a slavish "degenerate" aristocracy. He accuses these "parasites" of the king of betraying the nation and its liberty. Indignant, he retires from politics.


85-4. Fletcher, John William, and Joshua Gilpin.
An Essay Upon The Peace of 1783. Dedicated To The Archbishop of Paris. Translated From The French Of The Rev. J. Fletcher, Late Vicar Of Madeley, Salop. By The Rev. J. Gilpin, Vicar Of Wrockardine, Salop.
London: Hindmarsh, Longman, et al., 1785. 79p.

"Th'Eternal Father from his radiant Throne." (c. 1300)

Notices: CR 59 (Feb 1785), 154, 60 (Nov 1785), 335-6, & 60 (Dec 1785), 465; MR 72 (Jan 1785), 68, & 74 (Feb 1786), 147-8.

Copies: BL 643.k.15 (13); NUC CtY, CU-S, DLC, MH.

Dedication to Mrs. Fletcher by the translator Joshua Gilpin is dated from Madeley, August 28, 1785. Fletcher's dedication to the Archbishop of Paris is dated from Madeley, January 28, 1784. The French version appeared first in 1784; then, additions were made. In this later form, as explained in "The Advertisement," "it is introduced as an Episode into a larger poem, lately published, under the title of La Grace et la Nature."
HC, with an epic flavor. Fletcher seconds the French Archbishop's call for peace and reconciliation in his own essay of four cantos. I: The French king "invites his Britannic Majesty to put a Period to the Calamities of War" in the West Indies (where Rodney and De Grasse fought), in America ("where civil Discord reigns,/ And falling Britons strew the tented plains"), before Gibraltar, and in India.
II: The British king welcomes peace with France and relinquishes his claim to America. He hopes that Congress will not be despotic and Americans "Themselves enslav'd." He bewails the expense, destruction, waste, and the dead as a result of war. He alludes to the loss of armies at Saratoga (Burgoyne), Virginia (Cornwallis), and Savannah; the loss of Kempenfelt and the Royal George--all "the dire Events of War." He concludes with the decree "That a new World, with Independence crown'd,/ Should rise the Glory of the Nations round."
III: The blessings of peace are heaped on "the United States of America," and "Another England rises into Fame." "The English are consoled for the Sacrifices They have made on her Account"; and "the French ('on Mississippi's far extended coast') are

invited to maintain the Peace they have promoted." Incidentally, he refers to the Opposition "in foul Conspiracy" encouraging the rebel Americans. He praises Shelburne and Vergennes as advocates of peace, and especially thanks Vergennes for Asgill's release from captivity.

IV: Fletcher concludes with a vision of "Christ's peaceable Kingdom."


85-5. Hayley, William.
Poems and Plays, by William Hayley. Esq. In Six Volumes.
London: Cadell, 1785. 6 vols.

Notices: MR 74 (Jan 1786), 69.

Copies: BL 11607.c.14 (1st ed), 239.h.10 ("A New Edition," 1788); NUC CtY, DLC, MH, & TxU (1st ed), DLC, InU, & NN (1788 ed).

See 83-17: "Ode to Mr. Wright of Derby" and 84-6: "Sonnet to Mrs. Hayley, on her Voyage to America."


85-6. Humphries, David.
A Poem Addressed To The Armies Of The Unites States Of America. By David Humphries, Esq; Colonel in the Service of the United States, and Aid-De-Camp to His Excellency, the Commander in Chief.
New Haven: T. & S. Green, 1784; rpt. Paris, 1785, & London: Kearsly, 1785. 28p.

"Ye martial bands! Columbia's fairest pride." (c. 460)

Notices: CR 59 (Jun 1785), 472-3; MR 72 (May 1785), 388-9; ERL 5 (Apr 1785), 312-14; GM 55 (Apr 1785), 302.

Evans 16801 (1780 ed); Sabin 33811.

Copies: BL 11630.b.1 (4), 11686.h.11; Bod Godwyn Pamph 1737 (14) (Paris ed); NUC CtY.

HC. First published in New Haven, 1780. This version may have been written c. 1780-81, "when the army was in the field," the sixth year of independence (pp. 5, 20). Humphries inspires Americans with a patriotic review of the glorious war for independence, concluding with the defeat of Britain, and with a prophetic vision of the new nation's future as it turns westward. The review includes remarks on British despotism as the cause of the war, the Battle of Concord, Bunker Hill and the fall of Warren, the coming of Washington from Virginia, the death of Humphries' friends in battle, the death of young John Laurens, the use of barbaric German mercenaries. He dramatizes Washington's crossing the Delaware and defeating the Germans at Trenton; alludes to Mercer, Gates and Saratoga, Wayne, Greene and the war in the South, and finally the defeat at Yorktown with French aid (pp. 19-20), and the end as France, Spain, and

Holland close in on "Th'exhausted foe" (p. 22), making possible the golden years of American freedom, peace, and prosperity.

Humphries is bitter at the British because they were fighting a dirty war, including such barbarities as the attempted assassination of Washington and the starvation of prisoners.


85-7. Ireland, John.
   The Emigrant. A Poem. By J. Ireland.
   London: Richardson & Urquhart, & Stockdale; Whitehaven: Ware & Son, 1785. 23 + i (Errata) p.

"Near Duddon's silver stream, where oft I've trac'd." (c. 300)

Notices: CR 59 (Mar 1785), 236; MR 73 (Aug 1785), 152; ERL 5 (Mar 1785), 232; GM 55 (Apr 1785), 303.

Copies: NUC MiU.

HC. A moral tale illustrating the folly of emigration from England to America. A Lancashire farmer makes the mistake of emigrating with his family from a land where he is secure, comfortable, and prosperous.
   After his wife dies at the end of the crossing to Carolina, he begins to farm; but, unfortunately, the American War "In Carolina rears its ghastly head/ . . . And fell Rebellion's flag victorious flies." The ruffian rebels seize his property; in anger, he, a loyalist, "joins th'intrepid band/ Of bold Cornwallis." He is captured; but before he dies of his wounds, he confesses to the folly of emigrating to America, complains of his orphaned children left behind in poverty, probably to be sold as slaves, and moralizes that such may be the fate of others who emigrate.


85-8. Lovibond, Edward.
   Poems On Several Occasions, By The Late Edward Lovibond.
   London: Dodsley, 1785. 200p.

Notices: CR 60 (Sep 1785), 230; MR 73 (Dec 1785), 432-5.

Copies: BL 11643.aa.54 (1); NUC CtY, MH, TxU.

Includes "To Laura. On Politics." See 65-6.


85-9. The Muse Of Britain: A Dramatic Ode To The Right Honourable William Pitt.
   London: Becket, 1785.

Notices: CR 60 (Oct 1785), 316; MR 73 (Dec 1785), 469.

Copies: none located.

Calls on Pitt to save the sinking nation. (Based on the notices.)

85-10. The Prospect; Or, Re-Union Of Britain and America: A Poem. Addressed To The Right Honourable William Pitt.
London: Bew, 1785. 23p.

"Night now o'er all had spread a solemn shade." (c. 290)

Notices: CR 59 (Apr 1785), 314; MR 73 (Aug 1785), 152; ERL 5 (May 1785), 389-90; GM 55 (Apr 1785), 303.

Sabin 66072.

Copies: NUC  MBAt, RPJCB.

HC. Dedication to the younger Pitt is signed "An American Officer." The "Advertisement" declares the poem "was written by an American Officer at Pittsburgh on the Ohio, last year." The poet hopes that the younger Pitt will emulate his father, for whom Pittsburgh was named, try to bring the two countries together again, and unite against France and Spain. (This poem was probably intended to counteract the effect of the poem by "An American Officer," David Humphries.) The poet is critical of France, who has succeeded in tearing the parent from its offspring. He is also critical of those who were responsible for the loss of "the brightest gem in the British diadem" through their corruption of the principle of freedom--North, Germaine, Fox. Yet although he hopes for a permanent union, he praises the freedom and independence of America where "A just equality o'er all presides."


85-11. Thomas, Ann (of Milbrook, Cornwall).
Poems on Various Subjects, By Ann Thomas.
Plymouth and London: Law, 1785.

Notices: CR 61 (Jan 1786), 72; MR 73 (Nov 1785), 389.

Copies: none located.

A widow of an officer of the Royal Navy celebrates memorable events of the last war. (Based on the notices above.)


85-12. Twisting, Timothy (pseud.).
The Pittiad; Or Poetico-Political History Of William The Second. In Five Cantos. By Timothy Twisting, Esq. Historiographer To The Pitt Administration. Dedicated To The Rev. George Prettyman, D.D.
London: Jarvis, Debrett, Becket, French, 1785. iii-iv + 50p.

"Say Muse, who oft has deign'd to sing." (c. 750)

Notices: CR 60 (Sep 1785), 230; MR 73 (Sep 1785), 231; EM 8 (Jul 1785), 45.

Copies: NUC  IU.

Stanzas in sixains. Ironic satire on the younger Pitt, tracing his early career in politics to the time he became premier and entrenched in office, 1784. I: Pitt's major theme at the very beginning was to reject cooperation with anyone involved in the "cursed YANKEE wars"--"except a chosen few." Fox is rejected because of his coalition with North. II: Pitt is soon rid of Shelburne, through the coalition of Fox-North. Fox begins the arduous task of India reform to prevent nabob corruption of English politics. III: But Pitt sees to the rejection of Fox's India-Bill through manipulation of the peers, forces the coalition to resign, and himself seizes the reins of power. He still refuses to join with North, "Him who AMERICA had lost,/ With millions which the war had cost." Yet he accepts others, "As deep were in the mire," perhaps the "King's Friends" (Jenkinson et al.). IV: Pitt chooses as his "COADJUTORS" Thurlow, Camden, Gower, Dundas; he harasses Fox with the prolonged "Westminster Scrutiny," thereby preventing Fox from taking his seat, despite defeating Sir Cecil Wray in the election. V: Pitt institutes his budget and new tax policies, to raise supplies and impoverish the nation, and subtly suppresses, "With truly Machiavellian art," the movement towards parliamentary reform.


85-13. Urim and Thummin. A Poem. Inscribed To Her Grace The Duchess Of Devonshire.
London: Macklew, [1785]. 31p.

"The rage of slaves, the Tyrants wasteful ire." (c. 600)

Notices: CR 60 (Oct 1785), 315; MR 73 (Sep 1785), 229.

Copies: NUC CtY, DFo, InU.

HC. A narrative in semi-allegorical style of a battle between Foxites armed with Truth and Pittites armed with Prerogative, in which the former are praised and the latter abused. The Hebrew title derives from Ex. xxviii.30 and Lev. viii.8, and, regarding the poem, refers to a favorable divine judgment on the integrity of Fox and his party in their quarrel with slavish and treacherous hypocrites, Pitt and his friends. Objects to the peace that Shelburne negotiated because it "serv'd the mean ambitious ends/ Of our rebellious foes, and damn'd our [Loyalist] friends," and weakened the nation; defends the Fox-North coalition and eulogizes North; finds Pitt inconsistent in rejecting North but not "the partners of his guilt," Charles Jenkinson, John Robinson, Henry Dundas. Pitt is mocked for uniting even with Wilkes, despite his many declamations against "the abettors of the American war and the Coalition."


85-14. The Veteran: A Poem.
London: Debrett, 1785.

Notices: CR 59 (Apr 1785), 315; MR 73 (Oct 1785), 304.

Copies: none located.

An old soldier relates his history during a period of forty years.

Serials

85-15. Addressed to the Minister, with an Appeal to the People of England.

"When Britain's Genius, on Perdition's brink." (86)

Lloyd's 56 (May 13, 1785), 463; W Eve Post, May 10, 1785.

HC. Eulogy of Pitt. Causidicus blesses the day Pitt rose to power against the coalition forces of "proud Democracy," which threatened the state, that is, the monarchy. Soon England shall give Ireland free trade, and commerce will flourish.

Ancell, Samuel. "In Commemoration of the Red-Hot Balls at Gibraltar, 13 September 1782." See 85-32.

Ashby, S. "Receipt for an Epigram." See 85-46.

85-16. The Birth-Day Ode. (The Second Edition.) With Alterations and Amendments.

"Amid the thunders of the lyre." (56)

PA, Jun 8, 1785.

Irregular Pindaric ode, a parody of a parody: Ode No. XXII of the _Probationary Odes for the Laureatship. By Sir John Hawkins, Knt._ (London: Ridgway, 1787), pp. 112-14. This second parody is a satire on the rhetorical conventions of the King's Birth-Day Odes and Whitehead, the dull master of their nonsense. But now Thomas Warton has been chosen to fill the office and improve the kind, "To foster Inspiration's flame."

85-17. A Coalition Parody.

"Three great r[ogue]s in one age born." (6)

PA, Aug 24, 1785.

Parody on Dryden's epitaph on Milton. Satire on Fox, Burke, and North, who formed a coalition in opposition to the ministry of Pitt in order "To attempt their country's ruin."

85-18. Comfort to the Maid-Servents.

"Household Maidens, do not scandal-." (12)

Cal Merc, Jun 11, 1785.

Mixed verse. Light satire on an object of unending concern -- taxes. The tax on maidservants by the younger Pitt will encourage marriage.

85-19. The Dog-Skinner and the Minister, A Modern Tale or Song, to an old Tune.

"As a Skinner was flaying a dead dog one day." (45)

M Chron, Jul 5, 1785.

Ballad with "Derry down" chorus. Satire on Pitt, who wishes to tax just about everything and everyone for revenue "To support our vast burthens laid on since the peace."

85-20. The Downfall of Old England.

"Ah England! ah! once happy isle." (48)

West M 13 (Oct 1785), 551-2.

Sixains. A patriotic call to arms. Britain, now no longer feared by the Bourbon powers, was disgracefully "forc'd to implore" their mercy in the last peace. Now, because they threaten Britain's possessions on the Mosquito shore in the Caribbean, Britons must rouse to arms and avenge their country's right!

An Elegy, Written in 1782. "'Twas night -- Britannia melancholy lay." (126) GM 55 (Sep 1785), 733-4. Signed C. L. See 82-85.

85-21. Epigram.

"Quoth John to my Lady, when talking of taxes." (5)

W Eve Post, Jun 21, 1785.

Anapest tetrameter couplets. Light satire on Pitt's new taxes. In this house, the owner says, we need not fear the tax on maids -- for there is not one maid (i.e. virgin) that we have.

85-22. Epigram. By Mr. T. Tattam.

"Taxes, our wise taxators say." (4)

W Eve Post, May 3, 1785.

OC. Tattam protests taxes on useless things.

85-23. Epigram. On Mr. Eden's Accepting an Appointment under the Present Ministry.

"When Fox, concern'd that Patriots prove untrue." (4)

Lloyd's 57 (Dec 12, 1785), 570; W Eve Post, Dec 10, 1785.

Quatrain. Satire on William Eden (soon to be Baron Auckland), who has shifted his allegiance from the Whigs and Fox to the Tories for selfish ends.

85-24. Epigram[s]. On the Many Unmeaning and Ineffectual Speeches made in the British Senate upon the Subject of Parliamentary Reform.

"As cur dogs worry -- so our Members talk." (2)

"Reform the Senate! -- At the end commence." (6)

G Eve Post, Apr 21, 1785.

(1) The MP's are not sincere about reforming Parliament.
(2) First banish corruption, then try reform. (A corrupt senate is unable to reform itself.)

85-25. An Epistle to William Hayley, Esq.

"On high Parnassus' highest summit plac'd." (c. 250)

Eur M 8 (Nov 1785), 385-7.

HC. Praise of Hayley as a poet provides the occasion for this review celebrating the chief merits of late eighteenth-century English poets, including Churchill, Goldsmith, William Whitehead, Anstey, and Seward. The remarks on Whitehead are especially relevant.

85-26. Epitaph. On a Politician. By Mr. Tattam.

"Free from all broils of opposition." (10)

W Eve Post, Mar 17, 1785.

OC. A generalized epitaph on a politician. Upon his death, even the worms become politicized.

85-27. An Epitaph on W. W[hi]te[hea]d, Esq; intended for his Monument in Westminster Abbey.

"Beneath this stone a Poet Laureat lies." (8)

PA, Apr 27, 1785. An Asylum for Fugitive Pieces . . . A New Edition (London: Debrett, 1785), I, 264 (first ed., pp. 214-5).

HC. Somewhat ironic praise of King George for giving Whitehead, a middling poet, a pension and the laureatship for his flattering odes. Whitehead died April 14, 1785.

85-28. Freeth, John.
Budget-Day. A Song. Tune, -- The Dusky Morn.

"Old Scores to pay, we've seen so much." (40)

Lloyd's 57 (Aug 1, 1785), 118-19; Freeth, The Political Songster (1790), pp. 38-9*.

Freeth's ballad records the objections to the numerous taxes imposed on the people by the Pitt ministry: on trade, female servants, polls, and shops.

85-29. [Freeth, John.]
The Budget Worn Out.

"Britons now your murm'ring cease." (32)

Lloyd's 57 (Nov 23, 1785), 506; W Eve Post, Nov 22, 1785.

Song; no tune is given. Humorous comment on the budget (including provisions for the new taxes) urged by Pitt's ministry. The Shop Tax may be repealed, because all the trading centers objected to it. Also in his Political Songster (1790), pp. 78-9.

85-30. [Freeth, John.]
Song. Nothing at all -- an Hibernian Harangue on the Propositions.

"Well met, brother Peter! Now do not deceive me." (48)

W Eve Post, Oct 8, 1785; Freeth, The Political Songster (1790), pp. 99-100.

Song. A satire on the English for giving Ireland really nothing, when deciding on a free trade. The English petitioned against it, refusing to accept Irish competition in the manufacturing of cloth. Flood is cited.

85-31. Hastings, Thomas.
An Ode on the Birth-Day of his Royal Highness the Prince of Wales, August 12, 1785.

"Hark! from sublime aetherial plains." (59)

M Chron, Aug 12, 1785.

Irregular Pindaric ode. The volunteer laureat poet urges his countrymen (in the fourth and last stanza) to foster the peaceful arts and develop native resources in order to make a paradise of Britain.

85-32. In Commemoration of the Red-Hot Balls at Gibraltar, 13th September 1782.

"Let not this day, of memorable date." (36)

Cal Merc, Sep 17, 1785.

HC, honoring the successful defense of Gibraltar by the forces under General George Augustus Eliott and Captain Roger Curtis against those of France and Spain. Also, on this day in 1759 Wolfe had captured Quebec. (The Scottish regiment quartered in Edinburgh Castle was in both actions.) Signed Samuel Ancell from Edinburgh Castle.

85-33. [Morris, Charles.]
The Banner of Freedom, A New Song. Written by Captain M-----.

"While the rights of mankind and fair Liberty's cause." (56)

M Chron, Feb 15, 1785.

Song. Morris celebrates Fox and the English constitution or limited monarchy that respects "the rights of mankind and fair Liberty's cause"; but he fears the aristocracy who wish to extend the King's prerogative -- Bute, Tories, and Pitt, all the people's oppressors.

85-34. An Ode for the Anniversary of the Revolution; Addressed to the Revolution Society at Leicester, 1785.

"O! for that Lyre which Pindar strung." (60)

G Eve Post, Nov 17, 1785.

Regular (Horatian) ode in sixains. An anti-Stuart commemoration of "the Year, the Day, the Hour" when King William restored freedom to English subjects and taught the King "Respect to Laws." (We should recall that King George III appeared to favor the Stuart cause, to override British rights at the time of the American Revolution.) Hampden and Sydney are cited.

85-35. Ode for the New-Year.

"High let the Laureat take his Flight." (60)

St J's C, Jan 1, 1785.

Regular (Horatian) ode in sixains. This is printed immediately beneath Whitehead's ode, which the poet rejects as conventional and unreal. He will sing on themes Whitehead avoids -- politics, the debts for which North is responsible, the absurd coalition of Fox and North, venal and treacherous orators (such as Burke?) and gamesters (Fox), and young Pitt and his Commutation Bill, both praised.

85-36. Ode to his Majesty, on the Death of W. Whitehead, Esq. Poet Laureat. By a Poor Poet.

"Will. Whitehead, Sir, hath wish'd the world _good night_." (40)

An Asylum for Fugitive Pieces, in Prose and Verse. A New Edition (London: Debrett, 1785), I, 262-3 (first ed., pp. 214-15).

Ode in quatrains and sixains. An ironic satire on Whitehead's laureat poetry by a confessedly "red hot Tory" who hates Charles Fox and the people and damns liberty that diminishes the King's prerogative. Whitehead died April 14, 1785.

85-37. Ode to the Right Honourable W. Pitt.

"Accept, O Pitt! this tribute to thy praise." (48)

M Chron, Mar 21, 1785.

Regular (Horatian) ode in octaves. A panegyric on Pitt, "the Saviour of the State."

85-38. Ode to the Right Hon. William Pitt, Esq.

"Our prayers unbrib'd, unpension'd, rise." (60)

PA, Dec 23, 1785; West M 13 (Dec 1785), 664.

Regular (Horatian) ode in sixains. An ode originally written for the father, the Earl of Chatham, is adapted to the son, William Pitt, whose leadership is here fulsomely praised for bringing prosperity and security to the land.

85-39. On a late spirited but well-timed Flagellation, when the "Man of the People," with great humiliation of his pride, and evident perturbation to his conscious feelings, was most degradingly laid in the lap of pity, and become an object, not of admiration, but general lamentation.

"When Pitt harangu'd, how look'd the people's man." (76)

PA, Jun 7, 1785.

HC. Causidicus again satirizes Fox, Tartuffe and Satan combined, once great but now fallen. Causidicus cannot forgive him the coalition with North, formerly "the nation's curse, Britannia's scourge."

85-40. On Hayley's Observation of Anna Seward, in his *Essay on Epic Poetry*.

"Warm'd by the harmony of Hayley's muse." (104)

T&C 17 (Aug 1785), 437-9.

HC. The poet responds to Hayley's praise of Seward in his *Essay on Epic Poetry* (1782) with an encomium of his own on her monodies evoked by the deaths of Cook and Andre. He devotes twenty-four lines to the patriotic inspiration that Seward's monody on Andre provides "a dwindling state" and "a lethargic land." See Seward, 81-14.

85-41. On Mr. Eden's accepting the Office of Commercial Negociator with the Court of France.

"For a Treaty with France, who than Eden more fit." (8)

Lloyd's 57 (Dec 12, 1785), 570; W Eve Post, Dec 10, 1785.

Quatrains. Epigram. Satire on William Eden's deserting the Whigs for the Tories in order to get a government post.

85-42. On Seeing Lord Mansfield at Guildhall.

"Hail! venerable Sage! in whom appears." (8)

G Eve Post, Aug 6, 1785.

HC. Praise of William Murray, Baron Mansfield ("Astraea's favourite and Apollo's friend"), in his declining years. Mansfield died in 1793.

85-43. On the King of Spain making General Washington a Present of a Jack-Ass.

"The Monarch of Spain." (6)

PA, Dec 6, 1785.

Sixain. Ironic comment on the appropriateness of a gift of an ass by the King of Spain to Washington.

85-44. On the Triumphal Procession of Carlo Khan to Westminster.

"Rejoice not too much, Carlo, at thy fate." (10)

Lloyd's 56 (Mar 18, 1785), 266.

HC. Causidicus belittles Fox's victory in the Westminster election, claiming the victory was won by the Duchess of Devonshire. (Georgiana Spencer Cavendish, wife of William Cavendish, 5th Duke of Devonshire, vigorously canvassed for Fox in the difficult 1784 Westminster election.)

85-45. Political Creed, Proper to be repeated by every True Patriot every Morning and Evening.

"I believe that a kingdom divided against itself cannot stand." (c. 25)

G, Oct 1, 1785.

A bitter political and moral litany including a severe rejection of party conflict, self-interest, faction, and the degradation of the aristocracy, concluding with a belief "in the humiliation of America."

85-46. Receipt for an Epigram. By Mr. S. Ashby.

"Take a portion of wit." (6)

W Eve Post, May 12, 1785.

Epigram in a sixain. The ingredients of an epigram -- pointed wit directed with satire at vice and folly. (Generalized, but useful as a norm.)

85-47. Ridiculous Verses. On a Ridiculous Opposition.

"Pitt-fall'n Coalition." (27)

PA, May 28, 1785.

Doggerel, trimeter couplets. Satire on the ridiculously quibbling opposition of Fox, North, and Burke, who wish to topple the ministry of the younger Pitt.

85-48. Rondeaus. Humbly Inscribed To the Right Honourable William Eden, Envoy Extraordinary and Minister Plenipotentiary of Commercial Affairs at the Court of Versailles.

"Of Eden lost, in ancient days." (15)

"A mere affair of trade t'embrace." (15)

Lloyd's 57 (Dec 14, 1785), 578; W Eve Post, Dec 13, 1785.

Two rondeaus. Satiric remarks on Eden's shift of allegiance to the Tories, upon Pitt's offer of a place in the government. North points to Eden's self-interest.

85-49. The Servant Maids all in an Uproar, About the curious Tax on Female Servants. A New Song.

"Says Hannah the House Maid, to Nelly the Nurse." (35)

M Chron, Sep 22, 1785.

A ballad with "Derry down" chorus in protest at Pitt's tax on maid servants.

85-50. The Shop Tax, A New Song. Tune -- "The Old Sorrowful Ditty of, The Babes in the Wood."

"Now ponder well, O spare our shops." (40)

M Chron, Jun 16, 1785; PA, Jun 18, 1785.

Ballad. A protest against the new and oppressive taxes by Pitt's ministry on the retail trade and on servant maids.

85-51. Smoaking.

"Sedent and by myself I sit." (66)

M Chron, May 16, 1785.

OC. Cynical lines on the major political figures and the issues of the time: Fox, Pitt, India Bills, Irish trade, reform, finances (taxation). No matter what happens, the people will pay. Oppressive taxes will drive people to emigrate.


Tattam, T. See "Epigram," 85-22; and "Epitaph. On a Politician," 85-26.


85-52. To L[or]d G[ermai]n.

"To your Lordship a question I humbly hold out." (8)

PA, May 6, 1785.

Anapest tetrameter couplets. Abusive satire on Germain, who deserves hanging -- an ignominious execution.


85-53. To Miss Farren.

"From where Ohio rolls his rapid tide." (86)

M Chron, Jan 1, 1785.

HC. A romantic and sentimental vision of the American Indian scene. The poet returns from America, enamored of the natural attractiveness of the Indian way of life, only to be disgusted with the deceits of English civilization. However, he is happy to find Elizabeth Farren's acting equal to the integrity of Indian nature. He compares Miss Farren to Immoinda, "a Shawnese Indian": see another poem by the same author, identified as "Virginius," for the comparison -- M Chron, Jan 6, 1785.


85-54. To Mr. Warton on his Birth-Day Ode.

"O Blest in Genius, blest in Fame." (30)

St J's C, Jun 30, 1785.

Irregular Pindaric ode. Praise of the King for choosing Thomas Warton to be the poet laureat upon Whitehead's death: "Dulness yields its wide extended Reign, / And gives to Merit sovereign Power again."


85-55. To the Earl of Mansfield.

"Shall merit find no shelter but the grave." (90)

M Chron, Nov 21, 1785;  PA, Nov 19, 1785.

HC. The poet notes how Rodney was mistreated by "Injurious faction" which "strip'd him of command" after his great victories, the exemplum confirming the truism that living genius is unrecognized in its time. (The allusion is the recall of Rodney by Fox's ministry.) An exception to the truism is Lord Mansfield, who is credited with saving an empire!

85-56. Warton, Thomas.
Ode for His Majesty's Birthday, June 4, 1785. Written by the Rev. T. Warton, Poet Laureat. And set to Musick by Mr. Stanley, Master of the King's Band.

"True Glory scorns the pride of war." (56)

AR 1784-5, pp. 134-6;  DJ, Jun 9, 1785;  GM 55 (Jun 1785), 473;  LM (NS) 4 (Jun 1785), 431-2;  PA, Jun 4, 1785;  W Eve Post, Jun 2-4, 1785.

Irregular Pindaric ode. Warton pays "a blameless homage" to King George as he urges him to pursue the arts of peace and to set a virtuous example for taste, fashion, and knowledge: "Mankind to polish and to teach, / Be this the Monarch's aim." Thus Warton's muse honors George but does not prostitute "the tribute of her lays."

85-57. Whitehead, William.
Ode for the New Year [1785], As performed before their Majesties. Written by William Whitehead, Esq. Poet-Laureat. And set to Musick by Mr. Stanley.

"Delusive is the Poet's dream." (48)

AR 1784-5, II, 133-4;  Cal Merc, Jan 3, 1785;  DJ, Jan 6, 1785;  G Eve Post, Dec 30, 1784-Jan 1, 1785;  GM 55 (Jan 1785), 53;  HM 15 (Feb 1785), 103;  Johnson's British Gazette & Sunday Monitor, Jan 2, 1785;  Lloyd's 56 (Dec 31, 1784-Jan 3, 1785), 1;  M Chron, Jan 1, 1785;  St J's C, Dec 30, 1784-Jan 1, 1785;  W Eve Post, Dec 30, 1784-Jan 1, 1785;  LM (NS) 4 (Jan 1785), 45.

Irregular Pindaric ode. In his last court ode written before his death (April 14, 1785), Whitehead's muse prophecies reconciliation and union between America and Britain, a lasting Anglo-American union of "Two Britains."

85-58. Written immediately after being at Bermondsey Spa, and seeing that excellent Deception the Water-Fall of Niagara in America.

"Fancy, through various climes is known to roam." (32)

West M 13 (Aug 1785), 440.

HC. An appreciation of the magnificence and splendor of America's scenery -- especially Niagara Falls -- inspired by a "wondrous imitation."

Prints

85-59.  The Anti-Patriot:  A Satyrical Poem.

"Hail! mighty Pitt, great Politician hail."  (c. 175)

Engr. with HC.  August 10, 1785.

George 6808 (VI, 240).

A satire on Pitt for his tax policy.  Pitt has taxed almost everything.  And so the problem of taxation persists!

85-60.  The Fall of Achilles.

"Thus do I strive with heart and hand."  (8)

Engr. with couplets.  January 7, 1785.

George 6770 (VI, 219).

Pitt the Younger drives sedition, in the form of North, Fox, and Burke, from the land.  Thus the coalition collapses.

85-61.  The Loss of Eden!--And Eden, Lost!

"Two patriots in the self-same Age was Born."  (9)

Engr. with couplets.  December 21, 1785.

George 6815 (VI, 244-45).  Dolmetsch, pp. 212-13.

William Eden and Benedict Arnold are compared as traitors.  Eden helped solve Irish economic problems and then left the government to go in opposition; but soon he joined the government of Pitt to help negotiate a commercial treaty with France. One renegade is compared with another, both men having been bought off for a price.

1786  Books & Pamphlets

86-1. Cartwright, Edmund.
Poems By Edmund Cartwright, Master Of Arts, And Prebendary Of Lincoln; A New Edition.
N.p., 1786. 97p.

The Prince of Peace. An Ode. (pp. 37-46) See 79-4.

Ode to the Earl of Effingham. (pp. 59-63) See 83-5.

To the Duke of Richmond. On His Motion For Annual Parliaments, And Equal Representation, MDCCLXXX. (p. 92) See 83-5.

Copies: BL 991.k.13 (2); NUC  ICN, IU, MH.


86-2. Morris, Charles.
A Collection of Songs, By The Inimitable Captain Morris. Part The First.
London: Ridgway, 1786. 33p.

Notices: CR 62 (Oct 1786), 313.

Sabin 50803.

Copies: BL T.105 (6) (imperfect); NUC  CSmH, MiU-C.

See 86-3.


86-3. -----.
A Complete Collection of Songs, By Captain Morris. The Twelfth Edition, Revised, Corrected and Enlarged.
London: Ridgway, 1790. 38 + 22p.

Billy's Too Young To Drive Us. "If life's a rough journey, as moralists tell." (84)  pp. 12-16.

Billy Pitt And The Farmer. "Sit down neighbours all." (170)  pp. 17-25.

The Westminster Triumph. "While Vict'ry smiles on patriot worth." (84)  pp. 34-8.

Sabin 50804.

Copies: BL 11622.e.5 (13th ed, 1793); NUC  CtY (12th ed), DFo (13th ed).

Many editions. I have seen the 12th (1790) and the 13th (1793), similarly paginated.
"Billy's Too Young To Drive Us"--written 1783-4. Satire on Pitt, who is accused of being a tool of Bute, Jenkinson, and "a high-flying Jacobite gang." Morris defends the Fox-North coalition.

"Billy Pitt And The Farmer"--written 1784. Satire on Pitt; bred a Whig, he gives up the people and seeks the support of the Nabobs and the help of such Tories as Jenkinson and Henry ("Starvation") Dundas (who argued for the passage of the Boston Port Bill just before the American War).

"The Westminster Triumph"--written 1784. Praise of Fox and the Whigs for winning the hotly contested Westminster election against Sir Cecil Wray, a Tory supported by the king. King George is criticized for abusing his prerogative; i.e., interfering in the election.


86-4. Williams, Helen Maria.
An American Tale.

"'Ah! pity all the pangs I feel.'" (124)

In *Poems, By Helen Maria Williams* (London: Rivington & Marshall, 1786), pp. 3-13.

Notices: CR 62 (Jul 1786), 62-3.

Sabin 104230.

Copies: BL 239.h.3 (1st ed), 994.g.44 (2nd ed, 1791); NUC CtY, ICN, IU, MH, NjP, & NN (1st ed), CtY, MH, & OU (2nd ed).

Ballad. Romantic and sentimental narrative in dialogue on the aftermath of the American War. Placed first in her collection of poems, it dramatizes the important possibility of reconciliation between Britain and America motivated by common personal, charitable, and humane ties, if not by political ones.

Edward, born in America, meets and falls in love with Amelia while at Oxford, but his father opposes the match. During the war, Edward fights against Britain, although with an "erring sword," and has the opportunity to save the life of Amelia's father, a British officer, imprisoned and ill. The daughter comes to America, finds her father, meets Edward, who thereupon informs her that his father no longer opposes their union.

1787   Books & Pamphlets

87-1.   Mickle, William Julius.
  To the Memory of Com. Geo. Johnstone.

  "Though Life's tempestuous sea to thee was given."   (41)

  Poems, And A Tragedy. By William Julius Mickle, Translator of the Lusiad (London: A. Paris, J. Egerton, et al., 1794), pp. 206-8 (p. 208 mispaginated as 212);   The Poetical Works . . . Including Several Original Pieces, With a New Life of the Author (London:   Barfield, 1806), pp. 87-90.

  Copies:   BL 643.k.11 (2) [Poems, 1794],   991.a.16 [Poetical Works, 1806].

  Johnstone died May 24, 1787.
  HC.  The third paragraph of these commemorative lines alludes to Commodore Johnstone's participation in the unsuccessful Carlisle peace commission of 1778 to end "filial strife."  But Mickle notes that, by providing information to the British navy, Johnstone was able to help Rodney's seizure of French and Dutch prizes.
See Mickle, 82-16.

1788  Books & Pamphlets

88-1. Croft, Herbert.
The Wreck Of Westminster Abbey, Alias The Year Two Thousand, Alias The Ordeal Of Sepulchral Candour; Being A Selection From The Monumental Records Of The Most Conspicuous Personages, Who Flourished Towards The Latter End Of The Eighteenth Century . . . By The Author Of Kilkhampton Abbey.
London: Stalker, 2001 [i.e. 1788 ?]. 36p.

On a small Urn in the middle of the Chancel.  "Blessed are the Peace Makers!" (c. 15)  5th ed, p. 21.

Copies:  BL 12298.k.18 (1st ed), 12315.i.46 (5th ed "With considerable Additions"), 840.i.30 (2) (6th ed), 1601/64 (8th ed), 12352.bb.42 (1) (Dublin ed); NUC ViU ("A New Edition"), CtY, DLC, ICN, MH, PU, & TxU (5th ed), TxU (Dublin ed).

Many editions in the same year, perhaps nine, which BLC and NUC indicate as 1788 (?). I have seen the 5th London edition and the Dublin edition, also dated doubtfully as 1788 (?).
These are epitaphs written in the style and manner of Croft's Abbey of Kilkhampton (see 80-10).  Some are satirical, some panegyrical.  The harshly satirical epitaph on the Earl of Shelburne is particularly relevant because it is concerned with Shelburne's "ignominious Peace" that brought the American War to an end.  It could have been written many years earlier, perhaps in 1783-84.

1789  Books & Pamphlets

89-1.  Colvill, Robert.
The Poetical Works Of The Revd. Mr. Colvill V.D.M.  Vol. I & II.
London:  Dodsley, Donaldson, Creech, & Elliot, 1789.  276p.

Copies:  BL 11643.i.3;  NUC NB.

Includes many poems previously published, and discussed individually elsewhere: 71-1 "The Cyrnean Hero"; 83-59 "On the Late Great Naval and Military Preparations"; 59-1 "Verses for the Monument of General Wolfe" (see also 79-7); 75-6 "To the Memory of Major Pitcairn" (see also 79-7); 77-4 "To the Memory of the Honourable William Leslie" (see also 79-7); 80-5 "To the Immortal Memory of the Hon. Colonel John Maitland" (see also 79-148 for another epitaph on Col. Maitland); 80-5 "Savannah"; 82-8 "Sacred to the Memory of Colonel James Webster"; 80-6 "To the Memory of Allan Malcolm"; 82-8 "On the Memorable Siege of Gibraltar"; and 81-4 "Sacred to the Memory of Major Andre."


89-2.  Dunstan, Jeffery.
Fugitive Pieces, Written By <u>Sir Jeffery Dunstan</u>, Member of Parliament, And Mayor For Garrat; Now collected together for the First Time: Among Which Are Inserted A Few Pieces Written By The First Wits Of The Nation, Who have condescended to honour Sir Jeffery with their Correspondence.
London:  Printed For Sir Jeffery, And Sold By The Booksellers, 1789.  vi + 126p.

Copies:  NUC  ICN, NN.

A miscellany of poems humorous, satiric, and serious.  The following have particular relevance:

Ode, Written by Sir Jeffery, in the Year 1777.  (pp. 6-11)  Also entitled "Ode. On the Success of his Majesty's Arms."  See 77-183.

A Supplemental Ode, or a Hint to Lord North, on the State of the Nation.  (pp. 12-19)  See 77-292.

Heads of the Year 1777.  (pp. 31-3)  See 76-175.

Paulus.  A Monody.  "Upon a sea-girt rock the mourner stood."  (70)  pp. 34-7. Irregular stanzas.  The poet mourns the death of James Rogers, an American studying law in London, who was drowned at sea when returning home in Maryland to join his countrymen in the revolt against tyranny.  But the German mercenaries and the Scotch arrived safely on the American shore!  See 75-212.

[Hugh Brackenridge]  The Rising Glory of America.  (pp. 37-46)  See 72-14.

Blooming Dale:  An American Soliloquy.  (pp. 46-7)  See 76-68.

1427

A Panegyric. (pp. 54-5)  See 78-402.

The Lunatic. (pp. 55-6)  See 77-167.

Alexander's Feast, Parodied; Or, the Grand Portsmouth Puppet-Shew. (pp. 65-73)  See 78-56.

The Hen and the Golden Eggs. A Fable. Addressed to the Minister. (pp. 78-79)  See 75-128.

Lines Addressed to S[oame] J[enyns]. (pp. 84-6)  See 76-195.

Royal Resolutions. (pp. 99-102)  See 79-399.

Congratulatory Ode, Addressed to William Wyndham, Esq; of Felbrigg, Norfolk. (pp. 104-8)  See 79-100.

The True Sailor's Garland, Or, Admiral Keppel's Triumph. A New Song. To the Tune of a Free and an Accepted Mason. "Brother tars, now arise." (84 + chorus) pp. 109-12. Praise of Keppel, now vindicated by the judgment of the court martial against the claims of Sandwich and Palliser. See 79-494.

Liberty. An Elegy. "From a black cliff, where bold Cornubia's shore." (168) pp. 118-26.
Elegiac quatrains. Liberty bewails oppression in the reign of George III, and praises all her defenders, the minority Opposition--Wilkes, Savile, Camden, Beckford, Chatham, Rockingham, Burke, Shelburne, Effingham, Abingdon, Bishop of Peterborough, et al. Liberty notes how the war against America was begun--her petitions denied and then America was accused of treason.

Poems annotated above have not been found in other publications.


89-3. An Epistle In Verse. Written From Somersetshire, In The Year 1776. To [James Townshend Oswald], Esq. In Scotland.
  London: Murray, Cooper, 1789. 27p.

"*****, withdrawn to calm retreat." (558)

Notices:  CR 68 (Aug 1789), 152-3.

Copies:  BL 11630.e.4 (16);  NUC  MH.

Octosyllabic couplets. Only the conclusion (pp. 26-7, 44 ll.) is relevant. The poet envisions Alfred prophesying the rapid growth of the British empire, and then its decline and disintegration as a result of corruption. (A placeman, Oswald was MP from Dysart Burghs, 1768-74, and Fifeshire, 1776-79. He supported North.)

1790  Books & Pamphlets

90-1. Murphy, Henry.
The Conquest of Quebec. An Epic Poem in Eight Books. By Henry Murphy. Dublin: Porter, 1790. xix + 308p.

Sabin 51459.

Copies: NUC  CtY, DLC, MB, MH, NN.

Dedicated to the Marquis (George) Townshend. HC. The only relevant part is in Book 8, pp. 272-279. God gives the soul of dead Gen. Wolfe an insight into the future. In a prophetic vision he reveals to Wolfe the principal events that relate to the future greatness of Britain--the exploits of Admiral Hawke, General Amherst, the Marquis of Granby, and Admiral Rodney (Amherst's victory over the French in North America; Granby's over the French on the continent of Europe; after the peace, the Americans in rebellion, supported by France, Spain, Holland; the American War developing into a lopsided contest between Britain and the world, until Rodney's tremendous successes). Cited--the officers who participated in the campaign in Canada: Monkton, Lester, Howe, Townshend, and a force of "Royal Americans."

1792   Books & Pamphlets

92-1.  [Edwards, Bryan]
  Poems, Written Chiefly In The West-Indies.
  Kingston, Jamaica: Aikman, 1792. 67p.

  Sabin 21906.

  Copies:  NUC  CtY, ICN, NN, RPJCB.

  The contents include these items, discussed individually:  77-74 "Stanzas, Occasioned by the Death of Alico, an African Slave, condemned for Rebellion, in Jamaica, 1760";  76-9 "Ode, Written in England, during the American War";  76-211 "Epitaph on General Montgomery, 1776."
  This collection is not the same as that in his Poems, On Subjects Arising In England, And The West-Indies (1783)--see 83-14.

92-2.  [Polwhele, Richard, ed.]
  Poems, Chiefly By Gentlemen Of Devonshire And Cornwall.
  Bath: Cruttwell; London: Cadell, 1792. 2 vols.

  Copies:  BL 992.d.32, 11660.ee.24;  NUC  CtY, DLC, ICN, IU, MB, MH, NN, TxU.

  The contents include these items, discussed individually: 75-8 Edward Drewe's "Lines, Addressed to a Friend, On the Author's Leaving Boston in 1775, for the Cure of his Wounds Sustained at Bunker's Hill";  82-18 "Ode I" of "Four Odes, Written at Different Periods on Public Occasions";  and 81-12 "Ode II" of the same "Four Odes."

1793   Books & Pamphlets

93-1. Blake, William.
America a Prophecy.
Lambeth: Blake, 1793. 18p.

"The shadowy daughter of Urthona stood before red Orc." (226)

Sabin 5797.

Copies: BL C.45.i.13 (1); NUC CSmH, CtY, DLC, MH, TxU.

Political allegory. Unrhymed long lines. Employing his characteristically personal myth, Blake symbolically defines the liberating forces expressed in the American Rebellion and places that event in his view of history. Orc, the spirit of revolt and liberation, is the hero; the Guardian Prince of Albion or Guardian Angel is George III, the villain, typifying the forces of repression. Blake sees the thirteen colonies in apocalyptic revolt against the oppression of George and Archbishop Markham of York; he expresses his satisfaction that after twelve or fourteen years the French are following the Americans.

In the action of the poem, the English king angrily threatens to use force to enslave America; but, led by Washington, the Americans rebel and resist, and issue their Declaration of Independence (Plates 5 & 6). Orc envisions the rebellion led by Washington, Paine, Warren, and prophesies its successful conclusion with the "terrible birth" of the United States, the end of British rule, the destruction of the British armies. The rebellion affects England adversely; and Ireland, Scotland, and Wales are inspired by Orc. Finally, the French receive "the Demon's light," the liberating spirit, shaking the oppressive monarchies of Europe and dooming them.

1800  Books & Pamphlets

1800-1.  Pye, Henry James.
  Carmen Seculare For The Year 1800.
  London: Wright, 1800.  viii + [9]-43p.

"Incessant down the stream of time."  (487)

Copies:  BL 1346.i.11;  NUC  MH, PPL, PU.

  Irregular ode.  Pages 25-31 only are relevant.  Pye reviews British martial history, the growth of empire with the conquest of Canada by the heroic Wolfe.  He cites the exploration of the western seas.  Then sedition destroys peace and the empire.  Here Pye gives a Tory view of the American rebellion (Stanzas 21-22):  Sedition, Sophistry, Envy, Hypocrisy poison America and lure the parricide from Britain.  France intervenes--"the Gaul vindictive aids the traitrous blow."  Soon the French Revolution occurs, bringing with it "the progeny of hell"--Oppression, Lust, Murder, Anarchy, Atheism, the contagion spreading over all of Europe.  But Britain stands alone "freed from the pest."  (Pye was appointed Poet Laureate in 1790, succeeding Thomas Warton.)

Supplement: Additions

55-A

On the Death of Gen. Braddock, said to be slain in an Ambuscade, by the French and Indians, on the Banks of the Ohio, July 9, 1755.

"Beneath some Indian shrub, if chance you spy."  (10)

GM 25 (Aug 1755), 383.

HC. A bitter poem, because British soldiers ran away. Mourn for "murder'd Braddock" and in his memory plant an English oak at the place where he fell--if you can find his grave.

56-A

On the present State of America, and General Braddock's Defeat.

"No more I'll paint in soft descriptive strain."  (59)

LM 25 (Apr 1756), 189.

HC.  A participant describes the disastrous defeat suffered by Braddock's forces near "Monongahela's fatal flood," and the loss of numerous British officers at the hands of the French and their savage Indian allies.  But, he concludes, the French will soon be defeated and Braddock avenged.

59-A

[Inscription on a Monument in Westminster-abbey, to Roger Townshend.]

"This monument was erected by a disconsolate Parent." (c. 15)

L Chron 12 (Nov 16, 1762), 486.

Lt. Col. Roger Townshend was killed near Fort Ticonderoga in the Great War for Empire, July 25, 1759. (His monument is next to that of Major Andre.)

60-A

Advertisement from France.

"Since to Heav'n and Pitt." (24)

L Chron 7 (Jan 15, 1760), 63.

Sixains. Satire on the French, who confess to great losses in their war against England under Pitt's leadership. They complain of their inebriate king and his mistress, Madame Pompadour, and their cowardly "paltry commanders" who fly from Hawke, Boscawen, and Saunders.

Epitaph for General Wolfe.

"Wolfe, the virtuous and the brave." (6)

L Chron 7 (Jan 3, 1760), 30.

OC. Britain will forever mourn Wolfe, the heroic conqueror of Quebec.

French Politicks: Or, Chicane and Gold. A Song.

"As Louis sat pensive and cursing his stars." (66)

L Chron 8 (Oct 14, 1760), 371-2.

Occasioned by Gen. Johnson's defeat of the French under Gen. Dieskau near Lake George, September 7, 1755. The French king is advised to use treacherous diplomacy to cheat the English out of their victories in Canada. King Louis is doubtful that the English can be bribed and cheated.

A Morning Scene in Paris.

"Now morn arose, and in the Gallic clime." (78)

L Chron 7 (Jan 17, 1760), 70.

HC. The persona of King Louis of France complains of the nation's bankrupt state and his failures in the war against Britain. He fears that he will be forced to submit and lose all to Britain, including Cape Breton, Louisburgh, Quebec, Guadalupe, DuQuesne, Niagara, Ticonderoga, and Crown Point.

A New Song, entitled and called, Britain's Remembrancer for the Years 1758 and 1759.

"Come listen awhile and I'll tickle your ears." (40)

L Chron 7 (Jan 31, 1760), 120.

Triplets and chorus. The English gloat over their successes, their defeat of the French in Canada and the West Indies: Guadeloupe, Crown Point, Frontenac, Niagara, Duquesne, Quebec, Breton, etc.


Ode on the happy fate of Canada.

"Where near Quebec St. Lawrence flows." (30)

L Chron 8 (Jul 20, 1760), 82.

Regular (Horatian) ode in sixains. The genius of Canada predicts the defeat of French power and the coming of liberty and civilization, the blessings of peace and commerce, to America under Britain's crown.

61-A

An Ode On his Majesty King George the Third.

"O for a Muse of heavenly fire." (168)

L Chron 10 (Aug 4, 1761), 123.

Regular (Horatian) ode in octaves. A political poem on the situation in 1761 including praise of those, especially the Queen Mother, responsible for the youthful king's successful education ("He loves his people's rights no less / Than the prerog'tives of his crown"); an emphasis on the need to preserve liberty; remarks on the glories of "the fifty-nine" in British annals when Pitt led the conquest of the French in Canada, Europe, and Africa, and "each Indian shore." The poet hopes the British will treat the defeated French in Canada humanely. He views the Great War for Empire as the struggle between "Superstition's gloomy sway" (Roman Catholicism) and "Freedom's gladdening day." The cost, he concludes, was great in human life (Wolfe) and wealth (the large Public Debt). This ode nearly fills up one page of the London Chronicle.


The Seer. To the Right Hon. William Pitt, one of his Majesty's Principal Secretaries of State.

"At Hercules, in vain, you rail -- ." (41)

L Chron 10 (Nov 19, 1761), 495.

Varied meter in couplets. A prediction that Pitt, the incorruptible statesman, will be honored with a star (promotion to the peerage). Posterity will admire his acts and his fame will be enduring. "How long! before another Pitt appears!"

62-A

Delamayne, Thomas Hallie.
  The Oliviad.
  London: Scott, 1762. xii + 9-58p.

  "Dropt on her bended knee, and broken spear." (848)

  Notices: MR 28 (Feb 1763), 162; PA, Oct 24, 1772.

  Copies: NUC CSmH, IU (imperfect).

  HC. Two cantos celebrate the Seven Years War, the Peace, and George's virtues. France recounts her losses in Asia, Africa, and America, although she has won back Minorca. She mourns the loss of Quebec and Montreal, etc., and concludes her complaint with a wish for peace, to which England generously assents.
  Delamayne praises Wolfe's brave conduct in the battle that made him famous, and concludes with praise of Pitt for the unity which his leadership inspired.


On General Monckton's writing home, that he could not find words to render justice to our troops at Martinico.

  "If the French e'er attack, how Fame blazons the story." (20)

  L Chron, 12 (Jul 3, 1762), 23.

  Anapest tetrameter couplets. The French are adept with words even in defeat; English generals must learn to express themselves effectively. Meanwhile, our forces should abate their ardor.


On his Majesty's lately taking a View from Cooper's Hill, of Runnimede, where Magna Charta was signed.

  "When late, from Denham's hill, great George survey'd." (6)

  L Chron 12 (Oct 14, 1762), 366.

  HC. The persona of King George vows to maintain Magna Charta.


Song, At the Wheat-Sheaf, Newport, Mar. 25, 1762, on the taking Martinico. To the Tune of God save the King. Aeterno fulgeant Auro.

"Now Martinico's name." (35)

L Chron 11 (Mar 30, 1762), 307.

Song celebrating the seizure of the French possession in the West Indies, Martinique, a victory of the British forces under Rodney and Monckton, February 13, 1762.

[Survey thy crimes, insidious France! and know.]

"Survey thy crimes, insidious France! and know." (8)

L Chron 12 (Jul 15, 1762), 288.

HC. Latin and English. England should fear the treachery of France when the war ends.

63-A

The Address [and] The Great Man's Reply.

"May your lordship it please." (96)

LM 32 (Dec 1763), 668.

Sixains. Pitt agrees to ward off the tax on cider and perry.


The Battle of the Books.

"How long shall Britannia, so famous in story." (38)

L Chron 14 (Dec 13, 1763), 572.

HC. An objection to party factions, Whig and Tory, and a comparison of political writing in Jonathan Swift's day with the present.


Churchill, Charles.
   The Author. A Poem. By C. Churchill.

London: Flexney, Kearsly, et al., 1763. 19p.

"Accurs'd the man, whom fate ordains, in spite." (398)

Notices: CR 16 (Dec 1763), 446-8; MR 30 (Jan 1764), 26-30; GM 33 (Dec 1763), 610; L Chron 14 (Dec 13, 1763), 574; LM 32 (Appendix 1763), 707-9; St J's C, Dec 22, 1763; UM 33 (Supp 1763), 379-80; WA, Dec 31, 1763, pp. 30-1.

Copies: BL 840.k.5(9), 840.k.16(2); NUC CSmH, CtY, DLC, DFo, ICN, InU, MH, et al.; another ed (1764) CSmH, WU.

HC. Churchill berates the corrupt and stupid peerage that requires exposure by satire. He concludes with an attack on the slavish writers for the court, all bought by "a weak, wicked Ministerial train. / The tools of pow'r, the slaves of int'rest": Tobias Smollett, Arthur Murphy, John Shebbeare, William Guthrie, Philip Francis, and John Kidgell.


Churchill, Charles.
   The Conference. A Poem. By C. Churchill.
   London: Kearsly, Coote, et al., 1763. 19p.

"Grace said in form, which Sceptics must agree." (392)

Notices: CR 16 (Dec 1763), 443-6; MR 29 (Nov 1763), 385-9; L Chron 14 (Nov 24, 1763), 507; Lloyd's 13 (Nov 25, 1763), 517-8; L Eve Post, Nov 24, 1763; LM 32 (Nov 1763), 614-5; St J's C, Nov 24, 1763; UM 33 (Dec 1763), 323-5; WA, Dec 24, 1763, pp. 14-15.

Copies: BL T.655(21), 840.k.16(1); NUC CSmH, CtY, DLC, ICN, IU, MB, MH, NN, TxU; 2nd ed (1764) BL 11661.dd.2(1); CtY, TxU.

HC. An imitation of Pope's 1738 (Horace, Book 2, Satire 1). Churchill converses with a friend about his motives for writing satire and is advised to be prudent. But Churchill insists upon being honest and appeals to "A gen'rous Public" for support of his disinterested and incorruptible satire on "bad actions" that check freedom and destroy the country. He insists, too, on keeping Wilkes his friend and defending him against arbitrary power and oppression, Sir Fletcher Norton, the Attorney General, and Judge Mansfield. (Norton was largely responsible for Wilkes' North Briton, No. 45, being voted a seditious libel in the House of Commons, November 15, 1763.) Bute is satirized as "Hirco" (ll. 55-72).

Churchill, Charles.
An Epistle to William Hogarth. By C. Churchill.
London: J. Coote, 1763. 31p.

"Amongst the sons of men how few are known." (654)

Notices: CR 16 (Jul 1763), 63-7; MR 29 (Aug 1763), 134-8; Court&CM, Jul 1763, pp. 350-6; L Chron 14 (Jun 30, 1763), 6-7; L Eve Post, Jul 2, 1763; LM 32 (Jul 1763), 386-7; RM 9 (Jul 1763), 47; SM 25 (Aug 1763), 447-55; St J's C, Jun 30, 1763; UM 32 (Supp 1763), 374-6.

Copies: BL 1346.k.52, 2nd ed 11602.ff.14(1), 3rd ed 840.k.5(6); NUC CLU-C, IU, MH, NN, TxU.

HC. Churchill writes a good deal about himself, on his choice of satire over panegyric, before engaging on his main theme, Hogarth's character and Hogarth's satire on Wilkes. Churchill execrates Hogarth, characterized by meanness, vanity, and senility, for taking "the murd'rous pencil in his palsied hand," and failing to appreciate the great patriotic and libertarian issues at stake in the campaign against Bute and the peace that he effected with France.
An attempt to ridicule this work was made by adding a third line to each couplet-- Churchill's Epistle to William Hogarth, Esq. Re-versified (London: Burd, 1764, 39p.); noticed CR 17 (Jan 1764), 75; copies NUC CtY, MH, PU, PPULC.

Churchill, Charles.
The Prophecy of Famine. A Scots Pastoral. By C. Churchill. Inscribed to John Wilkes, Esq; ....
London: G. Kearsly, 1763. 28p.

"When Cupid first instructs his darts to fly." (562)

Notices: CR 15 (Jan 1763), 60-2; MR 28 (Jan 1763), 56-61; Lloyd's 12 (Jan 17 & 19, 1763); L Chron 13 (Jan 20, 1763), 76; St J's C, Jan 22, 1763; St J's M 1 (Jan 1763), 345-52; SM 25 (Feb 1763), 103-6, & (May 1763), 287-91.

Copies: BL 840.k.8(6), 3rd ed 11659.e.11; NUC CLU-C, CSmH, DLC, IU, MH, PU, TxU.

At least seven eds in 1763; nine eds by 1765. The annotation is for the 3rd ed, enlarged.

HC. Satire on the Scotch, portrayed as nasty, brutish, and poor, as unrepentant rebels and traitors, Jacobites and Tories still, after the defeats of 1715 and 1745. "The refuse of mankind" and envious haters of the English, they are happy to ravage England's "rich plains," to dominate the English by their cunning, to subvert the English nation by fomenting civil discord and civil war. This is the policy sanctioned by Lord Bute, and to achieve these ends Bute had Pitt removed, settled for the poor peace, and branded with calumny Prince William, Duke of Cumberland (because William opposed the peace and the prosecution of Wilkes for libel).

Rodondo (Cantos 1 & 2) was printed in the SM as an answer (SM 25 [Feb 1763], 106-7, [Jun 1763], 340-5, & [Sep 1763], 499-504), as was John Langhorne's Genius and Valor: A Scotch Pastoral, SM 25 (Oct 1763), 553-7.

An imitation of Churchill's poem appeared as The Prophecy of Famine. A Scots Pastoral. Part the Second, CR 15 (Jun 1783), 486.

Churchill, Charles.
Verses written in Windsor Park.

"When Pope to Satire gave its lawful way." (18)

BM 4 (Sep 1763), 495; GM 33 (Aug 1763), 408; L Chron 14 (Aug 11, 1763), 146; LM 32 (Aug 1763), 442; SM 25 (Aug 1763), 456.

HC. Churchill praises Prince William, Duke of Cumberland, "the saviour of his country" and "the image [of William] of Nassau." (The Duke was Keeper and Ranger of Windsor Great Park.) See the answer, "On Mr. Churchill's late poems. Occasioned by his Verses Written in Windsor Park," below.

Epigram.

"Much has been writ, O Wilkes! in vain." (8)

AR 1763, pp. 231-2; G, Nov 28, 1763; L Chron 14 (Nov 26, 1763), 519.

OC. Wilkes' friends wish him dead (wish him to suffer martyrdom); but his foes wish to keep him alive.

Epigram. Natural Account of a Political Weathercock.

"P[u]lt[e]n[e]y, complaining of his side." (20)

LM 32 (Dec 1763), 675.

Quatrains. William Pulteney, Earl of Bath, and Charles Townshend, exhibiting "wavering conduct" and unable to stick with one political "side" or party, are accused of being unsteady in principle. See "An Extempore Answer to the Author of the Political Weathercock," 64-A.

An Excellent New Ballad. To the Old Tune of Chevy Chace.

"God prosper long our noble King." (96)

L Chron 14 (Oct 27, 1763), 415-6.

Ballad. A humorous narrative of the way in which Wilkes deflected Capt. Forbes' challenge to a duel and kept his honor.

An Ode, sacred to the Memory of a late eminently distinguished Placeman, on his retiring from Business.

"Father of politicks, to whose great name." (84)

L Chron 13 (Mar 8, 1763), 235-6.

Regular (Horatian) ode in sixains, with explanatory notes. Satire on Thomas Pelham-Holles, Duke of Newcastle, who resigned the post of first minister in a conflict with Bute and the court, May 25, 1762. He had brought to perfection a system of bribery. The poet criticizes "the unsteadiness" of government's measures injurious to the American colonies.

On Mr. Churchill's late poems. Occasioned by his Verses written in Windsor park.

"Forbear, fond bard, thy prostituted lays." (26)

L Chron 14 (Aug 20, 1763), 182; SM 25 (Aug 1763), 456.

HC. Satire on Churchill, who (it is here affirmed) is incapable of praise. His talent is satire, malice and slander, as in the "Verses Written in Windsor Park," a poem that, written against George III, contributes to "Faction." Duke William (of Cumberland) is also abused for his cruelty at Culloden.

Peace, 1763. A Cantata.

"'Come Gentle peace,' victorious Albion cry'd." (36)

UM 33 (Sep 1763), 153.

Cantata: recitative, air, and chorus. Satire on the financiers and merchant capitalists (Bulls and Bears) who regret the end of the war.

Political Squib. Extempore.

"Immoral W[ilke]s to moral B[ut]e." (4)

L Chron 14 (Dec 1, 1763), 536.

Satire on Churchill and Wilkes, both immoral characters.

The Snarling Pug and Dancing Bear. A Fable. Addressed to Messrs. Hogarth and Churchill.

"Lest, Hogarth, thou shouldst draw again." (c. 200)

AR 1763, pp. 232-6.

Hudibrastics. A warning to aging Hogarth not to antagonize Churchill.

To the Glorious Defenders of Liberty.

"Whilst fawning sycophants the Nine implore." (36)

WA, Dec 24, 1763, p. 16.

HC. Praise of Justice Pratt for espousing the cause of liberty. He "stem'd the ministerial tide."

To the Right Hon. William Pitt, Esq; L Chron 14 (Aug 9, 1763), 142-3. See 63-9: same as "An Address to the Right Hon. Mr. Pitt."

Wilmot, John, Earl of Rochester.
  [Your loyal subjects humbly crave.]

"Your loyal subjects humbly crave." (6)

L Chron 14 (Sep 10, 1763), 253.

Rochester's satire on the Whigs who would reduce Charles II's prerogative is applied to Pitt, here considered as an "Ambitious Minister." Also applied to the Opposition in 1779: see 79-A, Wilmot.

64-A

Answer to an Epigram on the Death of Mr. Churchill.

"If Churchill's Muse from Heaven came." (4)

L Chron 16 (Dec 18, 1764), 586.

Epigram, quatrain. Satire on "factious Whigs" who maintain that Churchill came from Heaven.

Answer to the Epigrams on the New Pavement.

"Cease, factious fry, in shameful rhymes." (16)

L Chron 16 (Nov 20, 1764), 491.

OC. A defense of Scotsmen, and a protest at the slanderous satire on Scotland for providing paving stones to London.

Answer to the Epitaph on Churchill and Lloyd.

"Silence best shews the Anguish of the heart." (10)

L Chron 16 (Dec 25, 1764), 610.

HC. The poet mourns the loss of Charles Churchill and Robert Lloyd: "Satire, manly Sense, with Wit allied, / Expir'd" when they died. A continuation of "Epitaph," below: 64-A.

An Attempt.

"What, Churchill dead! -- and silent ev'ry Bard." (18)

L Chron 16 (Nov 20, 1764), 491.

HC. A defense of Churchill's satire which was "fir'd" by love of liberty. The poet asks Robert Lloyd and William Woty "to chaunt his praise."
"A Counter-Attempt" presents the opposite opinion of Churchill: see below, 64-A.

The British Coffee-House. A Poem.
London: Nicol, Flexney, Ridley, Moran, 1764. 24p.

"Muse speak the Scots, who since Culloden's woe." (c. 480)

Notices: CR 16 (Dec 1763), 479; MR 30 (Feb 1764), 157.

Copies: BL 1487.r.6; NUC CtY, DFo, MH, NN.

HC. Anti-Scots satire. Demeans the Scotch, rude and ignorant and filthy, for their invasion of London and their undeserving rise to place, dignity, and power. Wilkes is mentioned twice, but he is not at the center of this satire. "The Scottish Club" is located in the British Coffee-House. Internal similarities suggest that the same poet wrote The Thistle (1773).

Churchill, Charles.
   The Candidate. A Poem. By C. Churchill.
   London: Flexney, Kearsly, et al., 1764. 38p.

"Enough of Actors -- let them play the play'r." (806)

CR 17 (May 1764), 365-70; MR 30 (May 1764), 415; AR 1764, pp. 237-9; Freeman's J, May 19, 1764; GM 34 (May 1764), 243-4; Lloyd's 14 (May 11, 1764), 461-2; L Chron 15 (May 12, 1764), 463-4; L Eve Post, May 10, 1764; St J's M 4 (May 1764), 248-56; WA, Jun 9, 1764, pp. 399-400.

Copies: BL T.1558(2), 840.k.16(5); NUC CSmH, CtY, DLC, ICN, InU, MH, et al.

HC. Ironic satire on John Montagu, Earl of Sandwich, on the occasion of the election of the High Steward for Cambridge University, March 30, 1764. Churchill ironically announces that he has "quit the losing for the winning side," left Wilkes and the Opposition for Sandwich and the Tory court, in order to write this "Panegyrick," which is really an attempt to blacken Sandwich's character (Sandwich's link with the Medmenham Monks does not escape caustic mention) and to prevent his election to the Cambridge office. In the course of this vituperation of the candidate, Churchill alludes to national politics -- Bute's resignation, the budget of the Grenville administration, and Parliamentary privilege.

Churchill, Charles.
   The Duellist. A Poem. In Three Books. By C. Churchill.
   London: Kearsly, Flexney, et al., 1764. 49p.

"The Clock struck twelve; o'er half the globe." (1016)

Notices: CR 17 (Jan 1764), 39-43; MR 29 (Dec 1763), 531-8; AR 1764, pp. 233-4; BM 5 (Jan 1764), 43-4; GM 34 (Jan 1764), 39-40; L Chron 15 (Jan 19, 1764), 68; L Eve Post, Jan 19, 1764; LM 33 (Jan 1764), 47-8; SM 26 (Apr 1764), 217; WA, Feb 11, 1764, pp. 126-8.

Copies: BL 840.k.5(10), 840.k.16(3), 2nd ed 11630.d.1(7); NUC CSmH, CtY, ICN, IU, InU, MH, NN, et al., 2nd ed MH, TxU.

OC. Churchill comments on the events leading to Wilkes's duel with Samuel Martin, November 16, 1763, which, as he presents the evidence, was a vicious conspiratorial plot by William Warburton (Bishop of Gloucester), Sir Fletcher Norton (the Attorney General), and John Montagu (4th Earl of Sandwich) to have Wilkes assassinated, thereby strengthening Bute's position and undermining freedom. Churchill places Wilkes in the tradition of the struggle for freedom with John Hampden and Algernon Sidney. He deplores the corruption of MP's, notes the ruin of the House of Commons and the destruction of the freedom of the press as a result of the persecution of Wilkes.

Other assassins alluded to include Captain John Forbes, a Scots officer in the French service, who challenged Wilkes to a duel (Paris, August 15, 1763), and Alexander Dunn, a young Scotsman who threatened Wilkes's life, December 8, 1763.

Churchill, Charles.
Gotham. A Poem. Book I. By C. Churchill.
London: Flexney, Kearsly, et al., 1764. 24p. [Book II, 32p. Book III, 31p.]

"Far off (no matter whether East or West)." (500 + 678 + 664)

Notices: CR 17 (Feb 1764), 144-6, (Apr 1764), 288-92, & 18 (Aug 1764), 107-11; MR 30 (Feb 1764), 151-4, (Apr 1764), 291-6, & 31 (Aug 1764), 101-5; AR 1764, pp. 234-6; Court C&CM, Feb 1764, pp. 25-8; Freeman's J, Apr 7 & Aug 25, 1764; GM 34 (Feb & Aug 1764), 90-1 & 391; L Chron 15 (Feb 21, 1764), 180-1, (Mar 24, 1764), 291, & 16 (Aug 9, 1764), 142; L Eve Post, Aug 9, 1764; LM 33 (Aug 1764), 422; St J's C, Feb 21, 1764; St J's M 4 (Mar 1764), 79-84; SM 26 (Apr 1764), 217-8, & (Sep 1764), 507-8; WA, Feb 25 (all in 1764), p. 159, Mar 3, pp. 175-6, Mar 17, pp. 206-8, Apr 21, pp. 287-8, Sep 1, pp. 591-2, & Dec 22, pp. 847-8.

Copies: BL Bk 1 840.k.16(4), Bk 2 1490.ee.48, Bk 3 840.k.16(4**); NUC CSmH, CLU-C, CtY, ICN, IU, InU, MH, PU.

HC. Published Feb 21, Mar 28, & Aug 10, 1764. In the guise of a ruler of Gotham, an Utopia, Churchill passes critical remarks on the four Stuart rulers of England in the seventeenth century and then provides his ideal character of a Patriot King.

In Book II, after presenting norms for criticism and poetry, Churchill takes his stand on freedom against the "Stuart's tyrant race." He would rather see the country in ruin than "live to see a Stuart wear her crown" and enslave the people. Harshly critical of James I, Churchill cannot forgive him the execution of Raleigh and "The bloody Legacy of Right Divine." He believes Charles I was undone by the counsel of Strafford and Laud, "who boldly dar'd avow / The trait'rous doctrines taught by Tories now," by the wish to assume an unlimited "Prerogative." The oppression of his reign inevitably resulted in civil war, and so Charles the Tyrant was martyred. Charles II, he declares, sought only pleasure; but James II proved to be an arbitrary bigot who undermined freedom and the English constitution until the tyrant was driven out. The Revolution and William of Nassau thereupon secured liberty and law for England.

In Book III, Churchill portrays an ideal Patriot King, one who, despite the burdens of the crown, would assume responsibility for good, clean government by his servants and proxies to whom his power is delegated. He will not tolerate abuse of his subjects, nor plead ignorance when his subjects protest or rebel. He will be guided by the public good, ruling with wisdom and understanding. He will reward only those who, possessing merit, are truly deserving; and he will always be accessible to the petitions of his subjects. (So Churchill admonishes the young George III and his ministers.)

Churchill, Charles.
  Independence. A Poem. Addressed to the Minority. By C. Churchill. London: Almon, Coote, et al., 1764. 28p.

  "Happy the Bard (tho' few such Bards we find)." (600)

  Notices: CR 18 (Oct 1764), 265-70; MR 31 (Oct 1764), 271-5; L Chron 16 (Oct 2, 1764), 324-5; LM 33 (Oct 1764), 533-4; SM 26 (Oct 1764), 557-60; WA, Oct 27, 1764, pp. 718-20.

  Copies: BL 11656.r.48, 11661.dd.2(10); NUC CSmH, CLU-C, DLC, ICN, MH, NN, TxU, et al.

  HC. Churchill asserts his independence as a poet beholden not to a rich and powerful aristocratic patron but to the public that appreciates his merit. He satirizes venal lords and takes great pride in being "A poor, but honest Bard, who dares be free / Amidst Corruption." But he does praise one lord, Earl Temple, his ideal of an old "great Noble." Nor does he have any use for "pidling Witlings," Arthur Murphy, William Mason, William Whitehead, and their "measur'd prose, which they call verse"; nor for "the weak Bard, with prostituted stain," who praises "that proud Scot [Bute], whom all good men disdain." Bravely, he declares his independence of the present "Administration," despite its malice and strength as represented by Mansfield and Norton, and despite all the fear, flattery, hypocrisy, bribery, and corruption all around.


A Conference on a late Event.

  "Where's W[ilkes]? you cry -- O! Friend, forgive my laughter." (11)

  L Chron 15 (Jan 3, 1764), 16.

  HC (irregular). Wilkes's sincerity is questioned because he has sent his daughter to France for an education, where "She bigottry [sic] imbibes 'mongst Gallic slaves."


A Counter Attempt.

  "What, Churchill dead! -- and silent ev'ry bard." (18)

  L Chron 16 (Dec 1, 1764), 535.

  A harsh negative view of Churchill, "a mean cringing tool" to Wilkes, self-interested, "to party rage a fool," etc. An answer to "An Attempt," above: 64-A.


Counter-Epitaph to the Memory of the late Mr. Charles Churchill.

  "Scurrility, no more! O Death, 'twas hard." (4)

L Chron 16 (Dec 1, 1764), 535.

An answer to the "Epitaph to the Memory of . . . Churchill" (64-36), expressing pleasure in the death of the "favourite Bard" of "Party."

Epigram.

"Cambridge! would'st thou, in antient Learning's stead." (4)

L Chron 15 (Mar 8, 1764), 240.

Quatrain. Satire on Sandwich's candidacy for High Steward of Cambridge University. Sandwich is not quite the proper candidate; nor is Wilkes, for that matter.

An Epigram. Addressed to the Earl of B[u]te's Coachman.

"In driving Mac, how great your reputation." (2)

L Chron 16 (Aug 7, 1764), 133.

Satiric couplet on Bute: he "drives" (guides) the King.

Epitaph.

"Ah! what avail the verdant bays." (8)

L Chron 16 (Dec 20, 1764), 594.

OC. The poet, overcome with grief at the death of Churchill and Lloyd, is unable to complete the poem. However, he does proceed in his "Answer to the Epitaph on Churchill and Lloyd," for which see above. (Robert Lloyd, Churchill's close friend, died December 15, 1764. Churchill died November 4, 1764.)

An Extempore Answer to the Author of the Political Weathercock.

"On Will and Charles, for shifting sides." (16)

LM 33 (Feb 1764), 104.

Quatrains. A defense of Charles Townshend for "shifting sides." The true test of a patriotic statesman is sincerity and independence, not party; principle and wisdom, not foolish obstinacy. See "Epigram. Natural Account of a Political Weathercock," 63-A.

A Monody. On the Death of Mr. Charles Churchill.

"Ye verdant Laurels, and ye gloomy Pines." (70)

PA, Dec 5, 1764; WA, Dec 29, 1764, p. 864.

Decasyllabics, but irregularly rhymed. Who will defend freedom, now that Churchill has died? "Nor venal Lords, nor Ministers, would [he] spare / To lash the highly Vicious was his care."

Ode to Ambition.

"Away, Ambition, let me rest." (30)

L Chron 15 (Feb 23, 1764), 192.

Regular (Horatian) ode in sixains. Satire on Wilkes. The persona of Wilkes takes comfort (in his exile) that, when Bute denied him the place of Governor of Canada, he drove Bute from power.

On the C[alv]es-H[ea]d-C[lu]b in 1764.

"At last, 'tis plain, some W[hi]gs are as of yore." (6)

L Chron 15 (Feb 2, 1764), 120.

HC. King George is warned against the Whigs because they are king-killing republicans. (The Calves Head Club was established shortly after the execution of Charles I in 1649 and held its meetings on the anniversary of the execution, January 30.)

Patriotism A-La-Mode.

"At Court the great ones jar and quarrel." (14)

WA, May 19, 1764, p. 352.

HC. General satire on corrupt and selfish courtiers who wish "to cheat the nation."

[The sentence pass'd, poor Wilkes undone.]

"The sentence pass'd, poor Wilkes undone." (13)

L Chron 15 (Feb 9, 1764), 139.

OC. Remarks somewhat impartially on Wilkes's duel with Martin and his escape to France. But, the poet insists, England still suffers from the evil of a great public debt and the "favour'd Scot."

Soliloquy, supposed to be spoken by Mr. W[ilkes].

"Return, or not return, that is the question." (29)

L Chron 15 (Jan 28, 1764), 98.

Blank verse, parody on Shakespeare's *Hamlet*. Satire on Wilkes, whose persona weighs the consequences of his flight to safety in France, the loss of English liberty. Reference to Wilkes' ambition to be "Governor of Canada."

The Statesmen: A Satirical Ballad. See Freeth, 64-40.

To E. G.

"In future annals should our children read." (12)

L Chron 15 (May 24, 1764), 504.

HC. A defense of the King's dismissal of Conway from his several places. King George used his prerogative properly in this episode: he "*dar'd be King*." Probably an answer to 64-62. E. G. is another versifier.

To the Author of Verses on Mr. Churchill's dying of a malignant Fever.

"Vain man, forbear; in peace let Churchill rest." (16)

L Chron 16 (Nov 20, 1764), 491.

Quatrains. A defense of Churchill's honest and manly satire: "Whate'er the man, the poet still was great."

65-A

A Bad Omen for the Scot.

"The Scottish pavement having reach'd as far." (4)

L Eve Post, Jul 25, 1765.

HC. The Scottish pavement has now reached Temple-Bar where the heads of the executed Scottish rebels have been spiked -- a bad omen signifying "the end of the Scot's glory."

A Character.

"Urim was civil, and not void of sense." (36)

L Chron 17 (Apr 11, 1765), 359.

HC. Satire on John "Estimate" Brown for the hypocritical insincerity of his social criticism. Entering politics, he now flatters the court, praises "the Fav'rite" Bute instead of Pitt, weakens the cause of liberty by blaming faction for fomenting sedition, but ignoring the "Faction near the throne," and undermining the freedom of the press to criticize ministers. A useful summary of the abuses of government from the popular position.

An Epigram.

"'Greatest of Poets!' Wilkes to Churchill cry'd." (8)

L Chron 17 (Apr 16, 1765), 370.

HC. The rough partisans of Wilkes and Churchill support their admiration of the two with violence. Thus the people speak!

Epigrams.

"The Court is surely most unjust." (4)

"A Grecian horse in days of yore." (4)

"Both hot and cold this nation blows." (4)

"Wilkes says, we lost our liberty." (4)

L Chron 17 (Mar 2, 1765), 221.

A series of satires encompassing John Williams, printer, and the freedom of the press, subversion, secret influence and its effect on politics, and John Wilkes and his flight to France for safety.

Epitaph at Thebes in Boeotia.

"Here lies a Greek, who took universal pains." (10)

L Chron 17 (May 30, 1765), 523.

HC. An objection to tyranny in England, to "the tyrant-scene" -- the undermining of Magna Charta, the rights of parliament, the disappearance of trial by jury, the use of capital and other cruel forms of punishment to control the people.

An Ode. Inscrib'd to the Right Hon. H[enry] S[eymour] C[onwa]y, Esq.

"At length the labours of the senate cease." (40)

L Chron 18 (Jul 20, 1765), 77.

Cinquains. An eulogium of Conway, patriot -- martial in war, zealous champion of liberty in peace.

An Old Experienced Courtier's Advice to his Nephew, whose Bread was to be Earned by Ministerial Attendance. "Those fine-spun notions which so high you rate" (57)
L Chron 18 (Aug 1, 1765), 118. Same as 65-27.

On St. Sepulchre's Bells Ringing [and] On the Death of His Royal Highness William Duke of Cumberland.

"Joy shone in every Traitor's eye." (4)

"True Britons, for their William gone." (8)

L Chron 18 (Nov 2, 1765), 438.

Quatrains. The enemies of England are pleased at Cumberland's death, including Sandwich and James Scott (Anti-Sejanus).

On the Report of a Change of the Ministry.

"They're out to-day -- but will be in to-morrow." (4)

L Eve Post, Jul 2, 1765.

HC. A sceptical reaction to the accession of the Rockingham ministry, which will be unable to keep the members of the preceding government out of office, out of power.

To Benjamin Franklin, Esq; LL.D. F.R.S. Occasioned by hearing him play on the Armonica. Written in Philadelphia, 1763.

"Long had we, lost in grateful wonder, view'd." (48)

L Chron 18 (Aug 31, 1765), 219.

HC. A panegyric on Franklin for his great scientific and cultural achievements -- the lightning rod and now the harmonica.

Verses Extempore, On Reading some Late Political Papers.

"Ye baulers and grumblers, who ever complain." (20)

L Chron 18 (Aug 27, 1765), 203.

Quatrains, but single rhyme throughout. Urges honesty upon the political writers when focusing upon Bute, Pitt, and the King; and continued support of natural rights and freedom of the press.

66-A

The Character of a Good King.

"With pure religion let the monarch glow." (26)

WA, Apr 19, 1766, p. 255.

HC. A generalized portrait. A good king should be pacific, yet prepared for war; generous and concerned for the public good; kind to virtue's friends, but stern to her foes; modest, rational, and cultivated in intellectual pursuits.

[Free(th), John.]
  The Times.

"What a shame to the Land! what a cursed vexation!" (36)

L Chron 19 (Feb 25, 1766), 200.

Song. A complaint at the starvation of the poor, caused by corruption, enclosures, decline of commerce, and oppressive taxation. Reprinted in his Warwickshire Medley (Birmingham: Pearson & Rollason, [1776]), pp. 24-5, with a total of six lines omitted from the fourth and fifth stanzas. See 75-119.

[Mourn, Albion mourn, the wretched change deplore.]

"Mourn, Albion mourn, the wretched change deplore." (40)

L Chron 20 (Aug 7, 1766), 143.

HC. Bute is responsible for corrupting Pitt.

Political Squibs.

"'Tis too apparent, in this age of vice." (4)

"No letters more full or expressive can be." (4)

"Here dead to Fame lies patriot will." (4)

"What pains have been taken, in verse and in prose." (4)

"Cease, Grub-street, cease the vulgar to inflame." (4)

L Chron 20 (Aug 12, 21, & 26, 1766), 159, 192, 207.

Epigrams on Pitt's elevation to the peerage and its effect on his political career.

Pride: A Poem. Inscribed to John Wilkes, Esquire. By An Englishman. London: Almon, 1766. viii + 23p.

"O Happiness! thou transient partial good." (c. 400)

Notices: CR 21 (Feb 1766), 152-3; Lloyd's 22 (May 25, 1768), 508; L Chron 19 (Feb 13 & 20, 1766), 159, 181; UM 38 (Feb 1766), 101; WA, Mar 8, 1766. pp. 159-60.

Copies: BL 1480.bb.2; NUC CtY, IU, OCU, TxU.

HC. In the prose Apology, the poet complains of the enforced exile of Wilkes, Britain's "choicest son." In the verse, he pities the Corsicans, who are fighting for honor and for freedom from the Genoese (pp. 9-13). They, especially Paoli, provide models of genuine patriotism to British legislators. However, he berates British senators for corruption, and objects to Bute's control of the court. He mourns the loss of William, Duke of Cumberland, and the exile of Temple, Pitt, and Wilkes. In the conclusion, he asks that Wilkes return to "Drive cowards, knaves, and blockheads from the th[ro]ne."
Boswell quoted from the Corsican section: see 68-49.

[Shall P(it)t, to sacred Freedom late so dear.]

"Shall P[it]t, to sacred Freedom late so dear." (6)

L Chron 20 (Jul 31, 1766), 120.

HC. Doubts that Pitt will maintain his integrity. He will become like Grenville, Bute, and Bedford, as he joins the court party and deserts the popular patriot cause.

A Song: To the Tune of the Roast Beef of Old England.

"The World is a Bubble and full of Deceit." (30)

L Chron 19 (Apr 10, 1766), 351.

The great ones who run the nation disagree among themselves, the result being chaos in government. Taxation is a problem. Perhaps, as the Cyder Act has been repealed, the tax on ale will also go.

'Tis False! He is Not Fallen From What He Was.

"Tho' snarling critics, void of wit." (6)

L Chron 20 (Aug 7, 1766), 143.

Despite his acceptance of an earldom, Pitt, now Chatham, is still actuated by "Honour and Justice."

Verses to the Memory of his late Royal Highness, William Duke of Cumberland.

"While ripe in honour and in manhood's bloom."  (74)

LM 35 (March 1766), 158-9.

HC.  Eulogy on the Duke of Cumberland, son of George II and uncle of George III. He had fought bravely in Germany against France; he had defeated the Scottish rebels who defended "a Romish vagrant's cause," assisted by his good friend George Keppel.

67-A

On Political Justice.

"'Tis not enough you scorn a private claim." (8)

WA, May 2, 1767, p. 287.

HC. A generalized plea for justice, for using just means to ends by the state and by individuals.

68-A

An Addressicle.

"May it please your Gumpship; for 'tis clever." (58)

L Chron 24 (Jul 24, 1768), 50-1.

Hudibrastic couplets. A satire on Francis Bernard, Governor of Massachusetts, ironically parodying the exchange between the council and the governor on the boundary dispute with New York. From the Boston Gazette, Jun 6, 1768.

Epigram.

"Sure justice now is at an end." (4)

LM 37 (Jun 1768), 323.

Quatrain. An angry reaction to the generous but unjust treatment that "power" has accorded the "Scotchmen" responsible for murder at the St. George's Fields riot. They are freed on bail, while Englishmen are jailed!

Extempore by a Gentleman (who was drinking Yorkshire Ale) on hearing the following Toast, Success to the two Cans (meaning the Americans and Corsicans) given by a Gentleman who was drinking French Brandy Punch.

"There is no doubt they're brave and bold." (8)

L Chron 24 (Sep 24, 1768), 303.

Quatrains. The Yorkshireman favors a can of Yorkshire ale for a toast to the Corsicans and Americans.

Extempore. On Reading that Mr. Serjeant Glynn is to be distinguished by the Title of The Great Commoner.

"For England's credit, be it said." (12)

L Chron 24 (Dec 27, 1768), 623.

Quatrains. Glynn merits the title of the Great Commoner, unlike Pitt, who demeaned it by willing to be "a Little Lord."

Extempore. On the Report that a Certain Clergyman has a View to a Seat in the House of Commons.

"And is it true? and can it be?" (8)

L Chron 24 (Dec 22, 1768), 608.

Quatrains. Praise for "a Patriot Priest," Horne, who may become "a righteous Member."

Impromptu.

"When Stuart Anne by death was call'd." (12)

L Chron 24 (Dec 15, 1768), 580.

Quatrains. The administration is venal and corrupt, "engag'd in dirty Jobbs," with its hired "mobs."

Jaffier Ali Cawn's Ghost to the Free Burgesses of P-----ct in particular; and all British Electors in general, who are in danger from naturalized Nabobs.

"From those unbounded realms which mortal view." (42)

L Chron 24 (Oct 18, 1768), 383.

Blank verse. The ghost of a ruined and dethroned monarch in India (who had been deceived by Clive) warns Britons against the deceit of the nabobs who corrupt the election process in England through the purchase of votes: "Scorn to be sold like abject Eastern slaves, / Assert your rights, and study to be free."

Lines, applicable to the death of W. Allen, jun. from a Versification of Part of the 5th Book of Telemachus.

"Some fierce infernal hand sure struck the blow." (18)

LM 37 (Jun 1768), 323.

HC. Lines from Telemachus, by Francois de Salignac de la Mothe Fenelon, describe the death of a young man who could have been Allen, killed by Scots soldiers in the course of the St. George's Fields riot.

On Occasion of the Election at Brentford.

"O Truth! from whom vast crouds wou'd crib." (4)

L Chron 24 (Dec 10, 1768), 561.

Quatrain. Epigram. Truth is a victim of the election speeches of Glynn and Proctor (Middlesex election).

On the Late Riot at Brentford.

"How fatal to England this dreadful alarm is!" (2)

L Chron 24 (Dec 13, 1768), 576.

Hexameter couplet. Epigram. A protest at violence in elections. Senate seats are gained "Vi & Armis."

On Two Late Advertisements.

"S[erjean]t G[lyn]n, ever fond of good order and quiet." (8)

L Chron 24 (Dec 15, 1768), 584.

Hexameter couplets. William Beauchamp Proctor and Serjeant Glynn accuse each other of improper behavior during the Middlesex election. But Proctor uses violence, "the Bludgeon."

A Pill for the Candidates.

"Friend Hodge, you'll surely vote for Glynn?" (12 + 12 + 12)

L Chron 24 (Dec 6, 10, 13, 1768), 552, 568, 576.

Quatrains, dialogue. Hodge and Parson Horne discuss the candidates Glynn and Proctor, during the Middlesex election.

The State Coach; a Tale; in Imitation of the Manner of Dr. Swift.

"Once on a time a grand lord-may'r." (176)

L Chron 23 (Jan 30, 1768), 109.

OC. Animal moral fable, satire on the nobility. Guided by self-interest, the horses are unable to pull together; but succeeding in securing pensions for themselves and their descendants, they refuse to work. Because the master (King George) is too meek and mild and cannot get them to work, someone like "Stern boisterous Cromwell" must discipline them.

The Thieves and Butcher: A Fable.

"Two men, of base, dissembling heart." (26)

L Chron 24 (Dec 15, 1768), 580.

OC. The ministry is accused of protecting the violent bruisers and thugs responsible for the mob violence at elections.

To the Person, who, disguis'd in a Mask, &c. and known to the Mob by no other Name, than that of the Devil, gave considerable Sums of Money to the Voters at a certain Election.

"'Tis hard, you cannot calumny escape." (14)

L Chron 23 (Apr 2, 1768), 325.

HC. A warning that it is really the Devil who corrupts elections by purchasing votes.

Verses occasioned by the Death of a Middlesex Cook.

"Hail, Middlesex! Behold, your wish complete." (14)

L Chron 23 (Jun 23, 1768), 603.

HC. Impromptu. A "South-Briton" urges support of Serjeant Glynn in the forthcoming Middlesex election: Glynn "the Guardian Saint of Number--FORTY-FIVE."

69-A

The Alphabetical Gimcrack.

"A was an Alderman, factious and proud." (26)

L Chron 26 (Aug 3-5, 1769), 127.

An abecedarian poem that reflects the troubles disturbing London and the court: riotous mobs, sedition, Wilkes, Horne, Bellas. Cited is George Onslow (who had moved [Apr 15, 1769] that Luttrell be declared duly elected for Middlesex, despite the fact that Wilkes secured more votes).

A Conversation between the two Heads upon Temple-Bar.

"Says Townley to Fletcher, What causes this rout." (36)

L Chron 25 (Mar 23, 1769), 287.

Hexameter couplets. Two Scotch rebel traitors, Fletcher and Townley, executed twenty-three years ago, comment on the mob that is roughing up the merchants and Scotchmen who offer their foul-smelling loyal addresses to the King. See "Dialogue between the two Heads . . ." 69-53, also "On the Merchants' Address," 69-A.

A Dialogue, political and polemical, between Brothers, W. and B.

"W. Britannia, Sir, can truly boast." (51)

L Chron 26 (Dec 26, 1769), 617.

OC. This satire demonstrates that every man has his price (as Sir. R. Walpole has said): there would have been no trouble if Wilkes were offered the Viceroyship of Canada, Glynn made a judge or lord high chancellor, and Horne given a bishopric.

The Enchantment.

"Thrice the Horn-Owl shriek'd." (c. 100)

L Chron 25 (Jan 24, 1769), 83.

Parody of the three prophetic witches in Macbeth; satire on Wilkes and his leading supporters, John Horne and Humphrey Coates, who deliberately drive the mob into a frenzy through the issues of Bute's peace (No. 45) and the suppression of liberty. The Essay on Woman is also cited in connection with the King's mother.

An Epigram.

"O! noble Duke, I fear thy fall." (4)

L Chron 25 (Jan 19, 1769), 66.

Quatrain. Grafton will fall from power; his "friend," Conway, will be responsible.

Epigram for the Politicians.

"Go to war! cries a grave Politician, to war." (4)

L Chron 26 (Nov 18, 1769), 496.

An objection to starting a war in order to "end" Wilkes and faction. The response protests that Wilkes must be stopped, else the country will be destroyed: L Chron 26 (Dec 9, 1769), 564.

Epitaph on William Allen. "Sacred to the memory of / William Allen." L Chron 26 (Jul 20, 1769), 75. Same as 69-194.

Extempore. On the Issuing 4000 l. from the Treasury, for the Payment of the Money recovered by John Wilkes, Esq; from Lord Halifax. By a Liberty-Boy.

"Cease, Courtiers, longer to complain." (4)

L Chron 26 (Nov 25, 1769), 519.

Quatrain, epigram. Wilkes won his suit against government, but at the expense of the public.

A Fable.

"A Flock of Cranes newly come over." (35)

L Chron 26 (Nov 7, 1769), 455.

OC (largely), moral animal fable. A man is really known not by his words but by his deeds. When a placeman behaves like the Tories, he is "a time-serving slave." He cannot be a Whig.

[Gray, Thomas.]
Ode performed in the Senate-House at Cambridge, July 1, 1769, at the installation of His Grace Augustus-Henry Fitzroy, Duke of Grafton, Chancellor of the University. Set to Music by Dr. Randal, Professor of Music.

Cambridge: J. Archdeacon, T. & J. Merrill, 1769. 8p.

See 69-135 & 136, and next item below.


[Gray, Thomas.]
 Ode Performed in the Senate-House at Cambridge, July 1, 1769 . . . . [2nd ed]
 Cambridge: J. Archdeacon, 1769. 8p.

"Hence, avaunt, ('tis holy ground)." (94)

Notices: CR 28 (Sep 1769), 233-4; MR 41 (Aug 1769), 159-60.

Copies: BL 1st ed C.59.f.1, 2nd ed 840.k.11 (9), 840.l.4 (4); NUC 2nd ed CtY, DLC, ICN, IU, MH, TxU.

"A grand anthem," as it is described in GM 39 (Jul 1769), 361, in the form of a sublime irregular Pindaric, this Installation Ode honoring the Duke of Grafton has political relevance when it celebrates John Milton as the friend of freedom and, in the concluding Grand Chorus, praises the steadiness of Grafton's conduct during the popular clamor against him. The support of the political establishment -- Grafton, the prime minister, and his friends among the nobility (who attended the festivities at Cambridge) -- is noted with disfavor in the three satiric parodies on the poem (69-136) and on the epitaph in Gray's Elegy (69-66).
 Altogether three parodies appeared: [1] PA, Jul 17, 1769; St J's C, Jul 13, 1769 -- "Hence! avaunt! 'tis sacred ground" (94); [2] LM 38 (Jul 1769), 380-1; St J's C, Jul 8, 1769 -- "Hence! avaunt! 'tis _venal_ ground" (94); and [3] L Chron 26 (Sep 14, 1769), 267 -- Ode to Liberty, intended to be performed in the Matted Gallery Society: "Hence! avaunt! 'tis patriotic ground" (32). See also New Foundling Hospital for Wit (1771), IV, 8-22, for the parodies.


[If Alderman Squint is a ****** in grain.]

"If Alderman Squint is a ****** in grain." (4)

L Chron 25 (May 2, 1769), 423.

Hexameter couplets. Ironic satire on Wilkes; he inspires admiration for profaning God and King and making it profitable!


Impromptu, by a Lady, On the Election of an Alderman.

"That words are arbitrary, is most true." (7)

L Chron 25 (Jan 10, 1769), 40.

HC. Wilkes, not an "honest sober Cit," is unfit to be an alderman.

Oakman, J.
   The Mastiff in Prison. A Fable.

   "Some Fables have been deem'd of old." (72)

   L Chron 25 (May 25, 1769), 503; PA, May 27, 1769; W Eve Post, May 27, 1769.

   OC. Animal fable retells the story of Wilkes who, opposing Bute and the Scotch influence on the King, was banished. But he returns, only to be imprisoned. Though elected to city office, he is kept in prison until, finally, the King relents. Then all is peaceful once more.


Occasioned by the Pardon of MacQuirk and Balfe, the hired Murderers of Mr. George Clarke, at the Middlesex Election, A.D. 1768.

   "Behold what wonders we Court S[teward]s work." (6)

   L Chron 25 (Apr 22, 1769), 387.

   Impromptu protest at the pardon of the murderers who bludgeoned George Clarke to death late in 1768.


On a late repeated Expulsion.

   "What! again! Mr. Printer, our choice they are mocking." (12)

   L Chron 25 (May 23, 1769), 491.

   Hexameter couplets. Ironic satire on the persona of a Wilkes supporter who objects to Wilkes's third expulsion from Parliament which, he believes, has no right to expel him.


On Reading Mrs. Macaulay's History of England.

   "To Albion's bards, the Muse of history spoke." (16)

   LM 38 (Dec 1769), 644.

   Quatrains. Mrs. Macaulay, "freedom's faithful advocate," has written effectively against tyranny, slavery, and oppression.


On the Defection of the Corsicans. An Elegy.

   "Blame not my tears, they must in floods descend." (88)

   L Chron 26 (Nov 7, 1769), 452.

Elegiac quatrains. The poet complains that the Corsicans have been bought off by King Louis, thereby bartering their precious liberty for gold, betraying their chief Paoli and their country. He begs them to renew the struggle, to recall Paoli.

On the Merchants' Address.

"Tho' a vast City mob, with ordure vile." (8)

L Chron 25 (Apr 4, 1769), 327.

HC. Realistic satiric picture of a London riot, the mob pelting with filth the loyal merchants who present an anti-Wilkes address to the King. The public money will be used to clean up the mess! See "A Conversation Between the Two Heads Upon Temple-Bar," 69-A, above.

On the Opinion given by the Master, Wardens, and Surgeons, at their Hall, relating to the Death of Mr. Clarke.

"Alas, poor Clarke? how hard his Case." (6 + 2)

LM 38 (Mar 1769), 164.

OC & HC. Two epigrams. Cynical questions are raised about the murder of George Clarke, who was bludgeoned to death at Brentford, Dec. 14, 1768, possibly by the bully and assassin McQuirk.

The poetical Wish of a Middlesex Freeholder.

"If e'er I the cause of fair Freedom betray." (16)

L Chron 25 (May 20, 1769), 484.

Hexameter couplets. A rioter _hopes_ to stand firm in freedom's cause. An allusion is made to the "dirty" Merchants' Address. (That no irony is intended is demonstrated in 69-8, The Middlesex Freeholder.)

A Political Genealogy.

"Arbitrary power begot oppression." (7)

A Companion for a Leisure Hour (London: Almon, 1769), p. 151.

Prose-poem. A critical observation on the "murder" of William Allen in the St. George's Fields massacre, May 10, 1768. The cause is the oppressive and arbitrary power of government. These lines were also entered in 1773 (73-86); but no doubt they were first written before, probably in 1768-69, as the publication in a miscellany, Almon's Companion, suggests. Other versions appear in 70-164 and 76-285.

The Prophecy of Liberty.

"In the days when Good Sense and True Virtue prevail." (6)

L Chron 25 (Jan 3, 1769), 11.

Hexameter couplets. Now that Wilkes has been elected alderman by Farringdon Without, England will soon recognize his worth.

The Ribband, a sure Omen.

"By a blue ribband's going, we may guess." (6)

L Chron 26 (Sep 26, 1769), 312.

HC. The King is awarding ribbons to the peerage, a sign that "the great" are unaffected by the complaints and petitions of the seditious and factious, and that Grafton will not resign.

Teague's Address to his Countrymen.

"Riot on, my Dear Joys, nor fear what may betide." (11)

L Chron 25 (May 4, 1769), 429.

Hexameter couplets. Knowing that the law protects him, an Irishman enjoys the London riots which, incidentally, he suggests, Scotch bullies have started.

To Governours from Subjects.

"One rule, or its reverse, is ever true." (6)

L Chron 25 (May 23, 1769), 491.

HC. Epigram. A warning to officials of government (and elected representatives) to be guided by the welfare of the public they serve. A comment on Wilkes' third expulsion by Parliament.

To the Celebrated Mrs. Macaulay, the Historian of Liberty.

"Wonder not, fair Historian, to behold." (6)

L Chron 25 (Jun 27, 1769), 611.

HC. Impromptu. Mrs. Macaulay is advised to ignore the criticisms of "Court-slobbers" and reviewers.


To the Farringdon Ward Without, the following Epigram is humbly addressed by a Gentleman in the Country.

"Since Wilkes is your Alderman, pray change your name." (2)

L Chron 25 (Jan 28, 1769), 103.

Couplet. The citizens who elected Wilkes alderman have brought shame to Farringdon. Two answers follow: L Chron 25 (Jan 28 & 31), 103, 105.

[Underwood, Thomas.]
Copy of Mr. Underwood's lines, inscribed on the monument of Mr. Churchill, which was lately erected at Dover, to the memory of that celebrated satyrist, at Mr. Underwood's expence.

"The Rich and Great no sooner gone." (14)

L Chron 26 (Aug 3, 1769), 127.

OC. Indignant that Churchill has died and is forgotten, the poet provides a memorial. See 69-67.


Verses written at the New-England Coffee-House, on seeing Mr. -----, one of the Supporters of the Bill of Rights, tamely submit to be twice pulled by the Nose.

"Degenerate indeed! -- are these the Wights." (10)

L Chron 25 (Apr 4, 1769), 327.

HC. Humorous satiric squib by a loyal citizen directed at a supporter of Wilkes and Horne.

70-A

Address to Britannia.

"Renown'd Britannia! lov'd parental land!" (14)

L Chron 27 (May 31, 1770), 523.

Sonnet. Britain shall decline in power because of internal corruption: the complaints of the starving poor, oppression by the rich, bribery of the senate, and loss of free men's natural rights.

The Blunt Courtier.

"Round Royal George, in triple rows." (8)

L Chron 28 (Sep 27, 1770), 309.

Quatrains. Ironic satire on the corruption at court: the air is so thick with insincere flattery that it causes disgust.

De Brent, John.
To Mrs. Catharine Macaulay: With a Swan-Quill Pen, cut by the Author John De Brent, M.A.

"Go, raw, uneducated thing." (c. 110)

L Chron 28 (Jun 30, 1770), 4.

OC. Panegyric on Mrs. Macaulay for writing against tyranny and popery. Her defense of liberty emancipates the minds of men against the "senseless cackle" of Tories, their prejudice for unlimited monarchy and the divine right of kings.

An Elegy to the Memory of the late Right Hon. W. Beckford, Esq; twice Lord Mayor of London.

"To Fame let flatt'ry her proud column raise." (10)

LM 39 (Sep 1770), 485.

HC. Beckford, no mean hypocritical sycophant, is now facing his maker in heaven; there no sycophants can undermine his petition as they did at George's court.

Epigram.

"Caligula, as hist'ry doth relate." (12)

LM 39 (Sep 1770), 485.

HC. Ironic satire. Caligula made his horse a minister of state, and he had all the virtues. Certainly, "His parts were equal to our statesmen now!"

Epigram on the Times.

"Now patriot and pickpurse for what they can get." (4)

LM 39 (Apr 1770), 217.

Quatrain. Cynical satire on politics. Self-interest guides politicians. The reference is to Wilkes, who uses "liberty" for personal gain.

Ketch, John, pseud.
The Infallible Receipt, For the Cure of Court Corruption, By John Ketch, M.D.

"Let a scaffold be rais'd upon fam'd Tower-hill." (10)

L Chron 27 (Apr 17, 1770), 376.

Hexameter couplets. Ketch's prescription for an end to political corruption is the threat of execution.

An Ode to Palinurus.
London: Wilkie, 1770. 11p.

"When bad bold men, in years of yore." (96)

Notices: CR 29 (Mar 1770), 233; MR 42 (Mar 1770), 250; L Chron 27 (Mar 15, 1770), 257; LM 39 (Apr 1770), 212.

Copies: BL 840.k.11 (11); NUC CtY, IU, MH.

Regular Horatian ode in octaves. A tribute to Charles Pratt, Lord Camden, a political piece on the popular side written in January 1770 when Lord North had just become premier and Camden had resigned his post as Chancellor. The poet urges Camden to return to his post, advises a gracious reception to petitions and a reversal of the Middlesex election business (to permit Wilkes to take his seat), as the best methods of reestablishing political tranquillity. Cited are Sawbridge, Horne, Glynn, Junius, Saville, Luttrell, Burke.

On a Celebrated Female Writer.

"To shame the lukewarm Patriots of the age." (4)

L Chron 27 (May 10, 1772), 452.

Hexameter couplets. Praise of Mrs. Macaulay, the personification of Liberty.

Parody upon Mr. Gray's Elegy on the Death of a Favourite Cat. By an anti-ministerial Grub-Street Poet.

"'Twas on the lofty Treasury's Side." (42)

BLJ, Aug 11, 1770.

Parody on Gray's ode on the death of a cat is applied to Bute attracted by gold. Wilkes is cited.

Spoken Extempore on Three Patriotic Orators.

"Great Chatham, it's true." (12)

L Chron 28 (Dec 4, 1770), 543.

Sixains. Chatham, Burke, and Barré, of the minority opposition, cannot succeed "While England is rul'd by the North," meaning while Bute exerts his influence.

Stanzas on a Late Resignation.

"Hail, Camden, hail! who patriotic zeal." (24)

L Chron 27 (Jan 25, 1770), 96.

Heroic quatrains. Praise of Camden (who had followed Chatham in attacking the Administration in January 1770) for resigning from his position as Lord Chancellor. (Grafton's administration was giving over to that of North.)

The Superiority of England. Never before published.

"While every nation a pretension lays." (44)

LM 39 (Jul 1770), 380.

HC. An eulogium on Britain and George III. Britain is superior to France and Spain in every way. A Briton is guided by justice, honor, liberty, and fame; he scorns hypocrisy, deceit, art. Good King George, "that godlike youth," is "The heir of virtue and the child of truth."

To a Friend in the Country, with a File of News-Papers.

"Since you say we in town the advantage have got." (41)

L Chron 27 (Mar 29, 1770), 312.

Hexameter couplets. Chatham is reported to be well, recovered "from his fit, / A Patriot as staunch as when only Will. Pitt."

To Mrs. Macaulay.

"'Envy will merit, as its shade pursue.'" (19)

L Chron 28 (Nov 20, 1770), 495.

HC. A defense of Mrs. Macaulay, who eventually will achieve fame and triumph over her detractors and "the ribaldry of [their] buffoon lays."

The Vine and the Bramble. A Political Fable.

"Is there a Briton hopes to see." (58)

LM 39 (Apr 1770), 217-8.

OC. Moral fable which emphasizes the advantage of monarchy as the best form of government, especially the monarchy of George III. A tory anti-republican poem. (This poem is printed immediately following "On the Scum of the Earth"!)

## 71-A

Addressed to the Two Patriots, on their late Differences.

"For shame, ye Patriots, spar no more." (12)

L Chron 29 (Jan 24, 1771), 91.

Sixains. Wilkes and Horne are urged to cease disputing with each other and to join their pens "To quell despotick sway," else "Liberty must fall."

Ode to Alderman Oliver in the Tower.

"Hark! heard ye not yon raging cries." (108)

LM 40 (Apr 1771), 228-9.

Same as 71-110, which wants the noun "Ode" in the title; also, this version omits stanzas xv-xviii asking for the assassination of North.

On the Dispute among the Popular Party.

"Patriots, alas! Your cause is laugh'd to scorn." (2)

L Chron 29 (Jan 29, 1771), 72.

The dispute between Wilkes and Horne is hurting their cause.

72-A

Colvill, Robert.
   For General Wolfe's Monument, By the Rev. Mr. Colvill.

   "In sable robes, majestic in her grief." (26)

   L Chron 32 (Oct 3, 1772), 335.

   HC. Britannia mourns the death of her hero. This epitaph by Colvill repeats a few lines from the poem written earlier (59-1), but it is basically another poem.


[Epitaph, To the Memory of the late General Wolfe.]

   "To the admired memory of Major General / JAMES WOLFE." (c. 35)

   L Chron 32 (Aug 11, 1772), 148.

   An elaborate inscription, described as a "sketch for an Epitaph" that tells us how to react to the death of Wolfe with respect to the conquest of Canada.


The Genius of the London Magazine Unmasking the Times.

   "Blest Genius! still be thine the arduous task." (4)

   LM 41 (1772), frontispiece with verse.

   Not in Cat. of Pol. and Pers. Satires.

   This journal sees itself as a moral instrument for the exposure of evil, thereby stemming "the torrent of Iniquity," including corruption, "State Sharping," high food prices, "Prerogative, Pension, Patriotism," and other evils of the times.


A Notable Remark on reading some Epitaphs on General Wolfe. To the Epitaph Writers.

   "Who blunders now, that write, enrag'd Teague cries." (2)

   L Chron 32 (Nov 19, 1772), 492.

   Wolfe is immortal; he requires no epitaph. Another couplet epitaph follows the above with a similar sentiment.

73-A

From the Massachusetts Spy. A Tragic-comic Scene, lately acted at the Theatre Loyal in Liberty Lane.

"Have you to private friends or betters." (44)

L Chron 34 (Sep 18, 1773), 281.

A satiric mini-drama about the conflict between Governor Thomas Hutchinson, his secretary Andrew Oliver, and the Massachusetts Assembly -- after the exposure of their letters by Franklin. The "scene" favors the Assembly, and Boston is urged to break the yoke of tyranny and be free.

On a late Remonstrance.

"To please the cits, out of their wits." (8)

LM 42 (May 1773), 253.

Quatrains. Satire on low townspeople, fickle and witless. Give them a shorter parliament which they crave, they will soon beg for the present septennial again.

Puddicombe, J. N.
  Verses on his Majesty's Birth-Day, June 4, 1773.

"Rise, Albion, rise, proclaim thy joy." (36)

LM 42 (May 1773), 250.

Heroic quatrains. A loyal panegyric on George III from "a suppliant youth" ("Of flatt'ry void, but led by Truth") who, confessing the theme exceeds his slender poetic powers, allows his muse to "yield to Whitehead's softer strain."

The Thistle.
  London: Bladon, 1773. vi + 14p.

"Hail! thriving plant of Highland Scottish birth." (c. 260)

Notices: CR 35 (Jun 1773), 474; MR 49 (Jul 1773), 65; LM 42 (Jun 1773), 302.

Copies: BL 11656.r.12; NUC NN.

Fulsome dedication in prose to John Wilkes, praised for his virtues, "the first and most complete Gentleman of the Age," equal in genius, intrepidity, and sensibility to Brutus and Sidney. Defends him from the malicious envy of the City politicians, Sawbridge, Townsend, and Oliver, as well as Parson Horne.

HC. Anti-Scots satire. Objects to the preference shown the Scots at the English court, and criticizes Macpherson, Dalrymple (for his Tory history that damns Sidney and "Censure[s] Patriots to give Stuarts grace"), Samuel Johnson ("a pensioner to Kings," "The very rankest Tory of his Time"), Goldsmith, and other authors. The Scots are portrayed as venal, Tory hypocrites, characterized by "cringing Cunning" and "Pride and Poverty." But the poet prides himself on his independence and begs for Wilkes's friendship.

The frontispiece is a print illustrating Bute, North, and Mansfield dancing to "The Thistle Reel," the last holding an open scroll identified as the Quebec Bill in his left hand. But the bill is not mentioned in the poem. This poet must have also written The British Coffee-House (64-A).

The engraving reappeared in LM 44 (Feb 1775), 56, when it was adapted to the situation about two years later with an interpretation, "The Thistle Reel, A Vision," including a complaint by "the injured ghost of poor America . . . that her country [Britain] would ruin ours -- and France and Spain would profit by the downfall of both," and concluding with a warning of a coming "civil war." See also Mary D. George, Catalogue of Political and Personal Satires (1935), #5285 (V, 197-8).


To the Memory of William Lord Russell.

"Whilst crouds to thee their general plaudits raise." (42)

LM 42 (Aug 1773), 407.

HC. A patriot defense of Lord William Russell (1639-1683), Whig martyr, executed July 21, 1683, as an accessory in the Rye House Plot to kill Charles II. Russell "dar'd a Stuart's rising pow'r controul"; he was incorruptible in his opposition to Stuart tyranny. Soon his Whig principles were confirmed in the coming of William of Nassau, "our great deliverer," who protected English freedom and established the Brunswick line.

74-A

Goldsmith, Oliver.
   Retaliation: A Poem. By Doctor Goldsmith. Including Epitaphs On The Most Distinguished Wits of this Metropolis.
   London: Kearsly, 1774. iii + 5-16p.

"Of old, when Scarron his companions invited." (146)

Notices: CR 37 (May 1774), 392; MR 50 (Apr 1774), 313-4; GM 44 (Apr 1774), 184; HM 4 (May 1774), 293-5; L Chron 35 (Apr 23, 1774), 396.

Copies: BL 643.k.12 (5), Ashley 3271, 11632.h.7 (3rd ed); Bod II 33 (14) Art, 13 Theta 119 (2nd ed), 13 Theta 9 (4) (3rd ed); NUC CSmH, CtY, ICN, IU, MH.

Seven eds appeared before the end of 1774; and an eighth ed appeared in 1776 or 1777. Corrections of the errata of the first and second eds are incorporated in the third and following eds. Many libraries own the later eds, including the added lines. HM printed the entire poem.
Goldsmith died Apr 4, 1774. This poem, unfinished at his death, was published Apr 19. Hexameter couplets. A series of semi-jocular epitaphs on some of Goldsmith's friends, the poem becomes political in the character of Edmund Burke, the Rockinghamite, treated as a political figure dominated by ambiguity. He is portrayed as a man of principle, not an opportunist, yet also a man of party. But he is not an enthusiastic "patriot." At this time, Burke spoke for the Rockingham opposition and must have been preparing his celebrated speech on American taxation, delivered Apr 19, 1774. Also entered in 74-98.

75-A

On a Ropemaker who had long expressed a great Desire to see the House of Commons, and his Remarks on the Congregation of the Chapel of St. Stephen.

"A plain sober man, who lived far out of town."  (12)

LM 44 (Jun 1775), 318.

Quatrains.  Satire on the House of Commons.  The ropemaker, "a plain sober man," disgusted with most of the members of the Commons, wishes to hang them.

Remarks on the Slavery of the Negroes.  To which is prefixed a short View of a Free Country.

"Calm was the air, serene the sky appear'd."  (127)

LM 44 (May & Jun 1775), 262, 317-8.

HC.  Anti-slavery sentiments.  Slavery in the Barbadoes is relentless -- by cruel and oppressive means, families are torn apart, and the blacks chained, exposed to the burning sun, whipped, and tortured.  It is criminal to disregard the inhumanity of tyrannical slave owners.  The end of the slave trade, in which Christians are engaged, should bring peace and prosperity for the blacks in Africa.

76-A

The Contented Man.

"If Fortune smile, if Fortune frown." (24)

L Chron 39 (Jan 25, 1776), 96.

Sixains, regular ode. The contented man is modest, seeking neither riches nor fame. Pleased with a simple life seasoned with humor, he does not fear the French or Spanish fleet; nor does he care if Hancock or North is victorious. He rejects the fame sought by Lord Percy in battle and the vanity of life at court. See 76-195.

Epigram. On the different Fate of the Great and Little Knaves.

"The Little Knave submits to angry Fate." (12)

MJ, Sep 19, 1776.

HC. Satire on corruption. Causidicus cynically points to the fact that the big thief who robs the public weal escapes punishment, while the little thief who robs the private weal is hanged.

On Real Slavery.

"Anguish in sounds the Slave reveal'd." (46)

MJ, Sep 19, 1776.

OC. Anti-slavery poem. A Negro slave protests his hellish enslavement to "Whites remorseless." He cries for revenge and revolt against "tyrant Whites."

[One Hannibal from Carthage pass'd the Alps.]

"One Hannibal from Carthage pass'd the Alps." (4)

L Chron 39 (Jan 20, 1776), 77.

Epigram, quatrain. The poet admires Benedict Arnold for his astonishing exploit--marching hundreds of miles through the dangerous Indian "wilderness of Scalps" (and in wintry weather) to attack Quebec--successfully, the author mistakenly believes. His feat matches that of Hannibal passing over the Alps with his army to attack Rome.

Parody. The Minister's Song in the new Pantomime called the Budget. As performed at St. Stephen's Chapel, Wednesday, April 15, 1776. Song.

"From Downing-street hither I've drove in a crack." (36)

MJ, Apr 27, 1776.

Parody of "The Coachman's Song," MJ, Apr 23, 1776. A song about corruption of the MP's.


The Real Patriot.

"Happy the man! thrice happy! -- blest is he." (69)

M Chron, Apr 6, 1776.

Blank verse. Praise of a Scottish laird. The genuine patriot will fight for his country's cause, unlike the mock patriots--and Argyle is the exemplar (John Campbell, 5th Duke of Argyll [Scottish]).


[See the dread Harbinger of human Woe.]

"See the dread Harbinger of human Woe." (6)

Engr. with verses. Not in George.

LM 45 (1776), frontispiece.

The print is pessimistic: Mars introduces his sister Bellona to Britannia, kindling a civil war. But the verses express a hope for peace and harmony, although the "Bond" between the colonies and Britain has been "broke."

77-A

Impertinent Curiosity.

"This race of triflers, active as the bee." (44)

L Chron 41 (Mar 13, 1777), 253.

HC. The poet objects to barbershop gossips who talk a good deal and know nothing about politics and the war, especially the good work of the Howes and the capture of Gen. Charles Lee.


Ode to Peace. Written by a British Officer while the Army was in Philadelphia, in the year 1777. "Oh, bounteous Peace! with lavish hand." (29) MP, Dec 29, 1779. See 79-315.


A Spurious Speech which appeared in a morning paper a few days ago, versified.

"In the name of the Commons, I'm come on my knees." (14)

L Eve Post, May 10, 1777.

Anapest tetrameter couplets. Ironic satire on the King, whose persona here begs the House of Commons for money. See 77-161.

78-A

Extempore.

"Monsieur declares the English fled." (8)

G Eve Post, Aug 13, 1778.

Quatrains. Cynical verses on the aborted engagement between Keppel and Chartres off Ushant. Both had run away, according to the poet.

[Here rest the remains / Of William Pitt, Earl of Chatham.]

"Here rest the remains / Of William Pitt, Earl of Chatham." (c. 25)

G Eve Post, Jul 9, 1778.

Epitaphial inscription honors Chatham, his patriotism and integrity, and his great achievement, the enlargement of the empire.

[Leave prating to Phoebus.]

"Leave prating to Phoebus." (6)

L Eve Post, Apr 4, 1778.

Epigram. Sixain. A response to 78-111.

Lines On the Death of Major Sill, who was killed at Fort Clinton. By a young Lady.

"When WOLFE expir'd, e'en VICT'RY dropt a tear." (14)

MP, Feb 16, 1778.

HC. Major Sill died a conquering hero like Wolfe, and Britain suffers. Germain is cited critically. (Sill served under Gen. Henry Clinton and died in the successful attack on Forts Montgomery and Clinton north of Peekskill, on the Hudson River, in early October 1777 -- Clinton's aborted attempt to provide relief to Burgoyne's army under great pressure further north.)

The Noble Cricketers: A Poetical And Familiar Epistle, Address'd To Two Of The Idlest Lords In His Majesty's Three Kingdoms.
  London: J. Bew, 1778. 22p.

"Whilst Britain for her slaughter'd Legions sighs." (c. 340)

Copies: Bod 2799.d.28.

HC. Satire on the youthful Duke of Dorset and Earl of Tankerville because, "negligent of Birth and Fame," they would rather play cricket than attend Parliament and assist their country engaged in war with America. (Charles Bennet, 4th Earl of Tankerville, a noted cricketer, recorded dissents to the ministry's measures towards the American colonists in 1775 and supported Chatham's bill to conciliate the colonies, 1775. But John Frederick Sackville, 3rd Duke of Dorset, supported the North ministry, of which his uncle George Sackville was a member from December 1775.)

[O Pitt! once grac'd with eloquence divine.]

"O Pitt! once grac'd with eloquence divine." (8)

G Eve Post, Jun 9, 1778.

HC. Britain mourns Pitt, now dead.

On Ingratitude.

"Ingratitude! monster uncurb'd!" (44)

G Eve Post, Sep 24, 1778.

Quatrains. The poet blames the venom of the personification "Ingratitude" for the grievous trouble between "mother" Britain and "her lov'd children."

On the Earl of Chatham's Funeral.

"See Britain her departed Patriot mourn!" (10)

G Eve Post, Jun 9, 1778.

HC. Nature mourns Chatham's death. It is raining during the funeral.

A Poetical Paraphrase of the Supplement to the Gazette of France.

"The weather, which kept us in harbour past doubt." (49)

SM 40 (Sep 1778), 507-8.

Anapest tetrameter couplets. The Keppel-Chartres episode off Ushant, July 27, 1778, from the French point of view. See 78-52.

Things as they Are.

"France ---- insulting." (11)

L Eve Post, Jul 28, 1778.

Prose-poem. A catalogue of observations on the European nations at this time of the American War. America is triumphant and France, Spain, England, Holland, et al., are doing a variety of things. Scotland is fattening! See 78-474.

Tomlinson, Ralph.
An Anacreontic Song. By Ralph Tomlinson, late President of the Anacreontic Society.

"To Anacreon, in Heav'n, where he sat in full glee." (48)

The Vocal Magazine, or British Songster's Miscellany, . . . Volume the First. London: J. Harrison, J. Bew, 1778. Song 566, pp. 147-8.

The first appearance of this spirited classical drinking song, the air of which was chosen during the War of 1812 by Francis Scott Key in September 1814 for a patriotic song. Key's lyric became the national anthem of the United States, "The Star Spangled Banner." See Tomlinson, 80-A, for later publication in newspapers and magazines.

Verses addressed to my Countrymen in Camp.

"Rome in her Caesar, nurs'd a dauntless Chief." (70)

G Eve Post, Aug 6, 1778.

HC. Causidicus patriotically urges Britons to fight the French. See 79-77.

79-A

Answer to Paddy's Address to John Bull. To the same tune, Larry Grogan.

"Is it so, Gossip Pat." (60)

GA, Dec 29, 1779.

Song. Satire on the Irish for being so selfishly concerned at a critical time when the state of the nation has gone awry. "Since America's gone, / All things have been wrong."


The Brest Council.

"Says Count D'Orvillier." (12)

G Eve Post, Jul 29, 1779.

Sixains. The persona of the French admiral confesses that he dare not risk battle with the English Channel fleet under Hardy.


Britannia to her Sons.

"Britons, awake! your wonted port assume." (48)

G Eve Post, Aug 28, 1779.

HC. Causidicus recalls the glorious past and urges Britons to be courageous in the struggle against the Bourbons.


Britannia's Admonition to her Sons, at this tremendous juncture, for Unanimity and Mutual Exertion.

"'Tis Freedom's task to watch with jealous eye." (22)

G Eve Post, Sep 25, 1779.

HC. Causidicus damns the Patriot Opposition for maligning England and siding with the rebel enemy. He objects to their praise of Lee and Washington and to their criticism of Clinton. He believes, "This is not honest Opposition." It is divisive. Now the times require unanimity; now, he declares, we must unite!


A Congratulatory Address to Admiral Keppel. On the Issue of his late Tryal.

"Hail, Keppel! to thy country dear!" (50)

LM 48 (Mar 1779), 135-6.

OC. Eulogy of Keppel, whose integrity has been confirmed by the positive conclusion of his court-martial trial. His virtue and innocence have been vindicated against the accusations of Palliser, "a paltry knave." See LM 48 (Jul 1779), 327, for corrections in the Latin epigraph.


Cowper, William.
An Address to the Mob, on Occasion of the Late Riot at the House of Sir Hugh Palliser.

"And is it thus, ye base and blind." (25)

G Eve Post, Feb 18, 1779.

OC. The riot that inspired this poem occurred on the night of Feb 11, 1779. Cowper objects to the "base and blind" rioters celebrating the court martial acquittal of Admiral Keppel by destroying Palliser's house. Although sympathetic with Palliser, Cowper does not appear to believe his testimony.
See The Poems of William Cowper, Vol. I: 1748-1782, ed. John D. Baird and Charles Ryskamp (Oxford: Clarendon Press, 1980), pp. 212-3. But the publication of this poem in the General Evening Post is not indicated in this work.


Cowper, William.
Epinikion.

"Who pities France? her Enterprizes cross'd." (16)

HC. MS poem, repr. in Charles Ryskamp, William Cowper of the Inner Temple, Esq. (Cambridge: University Press, 1959), p. 237. Written 1779 (?). The title means "victory song."
An objection to French participation in the American War. France deserves no pity for her losses in the East and in the West. She has encouraged America, "the thankless Child," to rebel, "To aim a Poignard at the Parent's Breast," and to seek independence, "Helped him to Pick a Gem from England's Crown." The allusions may be to the loss of Pondicherry, Oct 16, 1778, and of St. Lucia, Dec 18-30, 1778.


Cowper, William.
On the Trial of Admiral Keppel.

"Keppel, returning from afar." (16)

Quatrains. MS copy published in Universal Review 7 (Jun 1890), 289. Written in Feb 1779. A defense of Keppel. Cowper cannot believe the charges against Keppel because of his reputation for bravery. (Keppel's court martial ran from Jan 7 to Feb 11, 1779. After his acquittal, the fleet fired congratulatory salutes and London was illuminated in his honor.)

See *The Poems of William Cowper*, Vol. I: *1748-1782*, ed. John D. Baird and Charles Ryskamp (Oxford: Clarendon Press, 1980), pp. 211-2.

Cowper, William.
A Present for the Queen of France.

"The Bruiser e'er he Strikes a Blow." (48)

OC. MS poem, repr. in Charles Ryskamp, *William Cowper of the Inner Temple, Esq.* (Cambridge: University Press, 1959), pp. 238-9. Written November-December 1779. France having gone to war with England, Cowper ironically offers a gift to her queen -- the American Congress in miniature. Ryskamp declares that the poem, like "To Sir Joshua Reynolds," was inspired by the defeat of D'Estaing at St. Lucia in December 1778 and at Savannah in October 1779. See *The Poems of William Cowper, Vol. I: 1748-1782*, ed. John D. Baird and Charles Ryskamp (Oxford: Clarendon Press, 1980), pp. 219-20, 496.

[Exert your pow'rs, ye sons of might.]

"Exert your pow'rs, ye sons of might." (12)

G Eve Post, Jul 10, 1779.

Quatrains. Extempore. A plea for unanimity so that the war can be pursued vigorously.

The following Verses were distributed at the Masquerade last night, by a Gentleman in the character of Merlin. From Merlin's Cave.

"'Midst sacred oaks on Mona's brow." (42)

G Eve Post, Feb 4, 1779.

OC. Merlin is urged by the Druid spirits to "bid fraternal discords cease" so that the war against the combined Bourbon powers can be fought effectively. Keppel is honored.

French Peace.

"The French boldly threaten to make peace in London." (4)

G Eve Post, Jul 24, 1779.

Hexameter couplets. Impromptu. A Londoner defies France.

[The French sail'd to Jersey, a visit to pay.]

"The French sail'd to Jersey, a visit to pay."

G Eve Post, May 25, 1779.

Hexameter couplets. Impromptu. Satire on the French, whose attack on Jersey was repelled.

[Hail to the Son of Fame in yonder sky!]

"Hail to the Son of Fame in yonder sky!" (19)

G Eve Post, Oct 25, 1779.

Blank verse. An eulogy of the brave Captain Farmer.

A Hint to Admiral Keppel.

"Some forty years, (I think you say)." (20)

G Eve Post, Mar 16, 1779.

Quatrains. Keppel is advised to distrust "party zeal," because it is as fickle as that of a mob. The loss of "fame" suffered by Wilkes and Horne provides the lesson. See answer, "['Tis true that Keppel pants for fame]," below.

[Lead on, lead on, brave Britons bold.]

"Lead on, lead on, brave Britons bold." (24)

G Eve Post, Dec 4, 1779.

Quatrains. A patriotic lyric, "made for a select party of the Military Association."

Modern Mobbing; A New Song. To the tune, "Come, let us prepare, &c."

"Now since licence we've got." (36)

M Chron, Mar 11, 1779.

Song. Satire on Fox and the Minority for encouraging rioting. Fox is said to have declared, "That mobs may destroy the whole nation."

The Sequel of Britannia's Address to her Militia.

"Tempests and clouds oft' dreadfully surround." (76)

G Eve Post, Jul 29, 1779.

HC. A patriotic poem. The theme is unity and courage, "In this great anxious moment of distress." The spirit of Chatham dares Englishmen to conquer France or to die.

['Tis true that Keppel pants for fame.]

"'Tis true that Keppel pants for fame." (8)

G Eve Post, Mar 23, 1779.

OC. Extempore answer to "A Hint to Admiral Keppel," above. A defense of Keppel. He does not need mob support. "He loves the people, not the noise."

The Volunteer's Rouse. A new Song.

"Ye free-born souls of Britain's isle." (37)

G Eve Post, Sep 21, 1779.

A song from Birmingham, whose volunteers are urged to stand for their country.

[While Byron and Barrington guard the West-seas.]

"While Byron and Barrington guard the West-seas." (22)

G Eve Post, Jul 15, 1779.

Probably a song, although no tune is given. The British navy has active officers like Samuel Barrington and John Byron, and defies the French; "While Keppel, [Robert] Harland, and [Richard] Howe love their ease."

Wilmot, John, Earl of Rochester.
  [In all humility we crave.]

"In all humility we crave." (14)

G Eve Post, Nov 6, 1779; Manchester Mercury, Nov 16, 1779.

OC. Satire on the Opposition. Rochester's ironic petition to Charles II is reprinted as a criticism of Opposition's self-interest -- its treacherous wish to secure power at the expense of the King's prerogative. Some of these lines were also applied to "a certain great commoner," Pitt, who like all "Ambitious Ministers" spoke the same language before being forced to resign. See Wilmot in 63-A.

Woods, W.
   Lyric Ode to Public Courage. By W. Woods. Set to Music by Mr. Corri. Performed at the Theatre-Royal Edinburgh, before his Grace the Duke of Buccleuch, and Officers of the South Fencibles.

   "Hark! the loud and rattling drum." (44)

   M Chron, Apr 7, 1779.

   A patriotic musical extravaganza honoring the volunteers who answered the call to arms.

80-A

Address to Parliament, on their first Session.

"Hail! glorious Senate, welcome as the day." (32)

L Chron 48 (Dec 23, 1780), 604.

HC. The new Parliament begins its work; and should it be guided by "strict union" and English law, the slavish French, Tories, and papists will be defeated.


A Comparison.

"In ancient times old Father Care." (20)

LM 49 (Mar 1780), 132.

Quatrains. Satire on the ineffective British army. In the past, British soldiers were heroic and had conquered the Bourbon powers; now they are effeminate and "drove or led," so that mercenaries must be hired.


Cowper, William.
In Seditionem Horrendam, Corruptelis Gallicis (Ut Fertur) Londini Nuper Exortam. [The Same in English.]

"Perfida, crudelis, Victa et Lymphata Furore." (8)

"False, cruel, disappointed, Stung to th' Heart." (8)

Written June 1780. First published in William Hayley, The Life and Posthumous Writings of William Cowper, Esq. (1804), III, 41. Cowper berates the French for instigating the Gordon Riots. The Latin poem appeared in PA, Jun 23, 1780. For other contemporary English translations, see 80-53 & 383.


Cowper, William.
On the Victory Gained by Sir George Rodney over the Spanish Fleet off Gibraltar in 1780. For which he has since been Rewarded with the Lieutenant Generalship of the Marines.

"From Shades of Tartarus and Realms of Woe." (6)

HC. MS copy repr. in Ryskamp, William Cowper of the Inner Temple, Esq. (Cambridge: University Press, 1959), p. 237. Written March 1780. Cowper agrees that Rodney deserves to be rewarded for his defeat of a Spanish squadron off Cape St. Vincent, Jan 16, 1780, thereby relieving besieged Gibraltar.

Cowper, William.
   To Sir Joshua Reynolds.

   "Dear President, whose Art sublime." (42)

   OC. Dated c. 1780; in the letters to Unwin. Cowper instructs Reynolds to paint a picture, or a political cartoon, of "British Glory," the defeat of France, America, Spain, and Holland -- particularly the defeat of D'Estaing at St. Lucia in December 1778 and at Savannah in October 1779, the failure or fall of Independence, identified as a kite flown by France and shredded by "Britannia's Lightning" and the wind "into thirteen pieces," which are laid "at George's feet."


An Epitaph.

   "A few days since were quietly interred." (c. 25)

   L Chron 48 (Oct 3, 1780), 327; SM 42 (Oct 1780), 542; WM 50 (Oct 26, 1780), 86-7.

   Inscription-type epitaphial satire from Croft's Kilkhampton Abbey severely criticizing Gen. Sir William Howe for losing the American War and destroying Britain. See 80-10, Herbert Croft, The Abbey of Kilkhampton (5th ed, 1780), pp. 39-40.


Tomlinson, Ralph. An Anacreontic Song. "To Anacreon, in Heav'n, where he sat in full glee." (48) G Eve Post, Mar 23, 1780; GM 50 (May 1780), 224-5; L Chron 47 (Mar 25, 1780), 301; LM 49 (Mar 1780), 134; LP, Mar 22, 1780; PA, Mar 27, 1780; St J's C, Mar 23, 1780; Say's, Apr 1, 1780. Also The Vocal Enchantress (London: J. Fielding [1783]), pp. 336-7, Song 167. The entry Tomlinson, 78-A, lists the first publication of this popular song, the tune of which was adopted for the American national anthem. See Oscar G. T. Sonneck, The Star Spangled Banner (Washington: Government Printing Office, 1914), pp. 32-5, where many sources from 1780 to 1804 are listed; but the newspapers are overlooked. Tom Paine had written two lyrics to the air of this song: The Boston Patriotic Song ("Ye sons of Columbia who bravely have fought." [73]); and Columbia ("To Columbia who, gladly reclined at her ease." [54]) The first was written near the end of the of the struggle; the second, probably a few years after the peace.

81-A

Epilogue to the Royal Suppliants.

"Well! -- these heroic times -- I scarce can speak." (36)

LM 50 (Mar 1781), 146-7.

HC. An example of contemporary "heroic virtue," Captain Farmer is pictured going down with his burning ship, defying the French enemy to the last.

An Epistle to William Hayley, Esq.

"On high Parnassus' highest summit plac'd." (134)

T&C 13 (May 1781), 271-2.

HC. A young poet reviews the characteristics of the chief poets of the eighteenth century -- Pope, Thomson, Akenside, Goldsmith, Gray, Collins, Mason, Shenstone, Lyttelton, Churchill, Beattie, Warton, Glover, concluding with remarks on William Whitehead, Anna Seward, Anna Laetitia (Aikin) Barbauld, Mickle, and Hayley, among others. The remarks on some of these poets at the end have a certain relevance.

[The fate of that destructive war.] W Eve Post, Jan 6, 1781. See [Stanzas], 81-203.

The Parliamentary Duellists. Inscribed to both Majority and Minority.

"As soon as Cadmus had the dragon slain." (20)

LM 50 (Jan 1781), 42.

HC. A bitter denunciation of Parliamentary politics. Administration and Opposition hate each other and dispute in Parliament. Would that they destroy each other and end faction; then Britain could regain its former glory.

Pasquinades on a certain General, and on a certain Admiral. . . M Chron, May 18, 1781; PM 2 (May 1781), 291; Cal Merc, May 28, 1781; PA, May 21, 1781. See Stansbury, 80-339.

82-A

Cowper, William.
  Poems By William Cowper, Of the Inner Temple, Esq.
  London:  J. Johnson, 1782.  vii + 367p.

  Notices:  CR 53 (Apr 1782), 287-90;  MR 67 (Oct 1782), 262-5;  GM 52 (Mar 1782), 130-1;  LM 51 (May 1782), 245 (rev.), 247-8 (two poems);  T&C 14 (May 1782), 269 (name is spelled Cooper).

  Copies:  BL C.116.bb.27, C.116.bb.29, Ashley 2994;  NUC  CSmH, CtY, ICN, IU, MH, TxU.

  Four poems are relevant:  Table Talk, The Modern Patriot, On the Burning of Lord Mansfield's Library (2).  Vol. 2, same title, published 1785, includes The Task (the first edition).  See Cowper, 85-2.

  Table Talk (pp. 1-40).  "A.  You told me, I remember, glory built."  (771)
  HC.  Written Jan-Feb 1781.  A rambling satire on the times, embodying Cowper's favorite topics and briefly alluding to the American War -- specifically to General Howe and Admiral Keppel (ll. 192-8), to the isolation of England like "a devoted deer" (l. 362) hunted by the hostile nations of the world:  the Armed Neutrality, the Bourbon powers, Holland, and America.  Cowper lavishes praise on George III, his moral character, his sincerity, and "his gentle reign" (ll. 65-90); also praises English traditions of constitutional liberty (ll. 200 ff.) and notes English objections to despotism or "proud Prerogative" (l. 230), in contrast to the slavish French.  He takes exception, however, to the excesses of the Gordon Riots (ll. 310-29).  Cowper is also suspicious of the motives of the popular "patriots," believing that they are self-interested (l. 191) and that Chatham (d. 1778) was the last genuine patriot (l. 339);  and his estimate of England's future is pessimistic, believing that the nation is enervated by "effeminacy, folly, lust" (l. 394) and corrupted by venality and bribery (ll. 416-7), which will cause its scourging ruin.  Finally, Cowper includes critical remarks on some eighteenth-century poets, providing a fine appreciation of Charles Churchill as man and poet (ll. 670-89).
  The original verse for ll. 13-28 (in Cowper's MS record book) describes Britain at bay in the American War, standing alone against the united "Western colonies," France, Spain, Holland, and the Armed Neutrality.  Cowper expresses sympathy for Britain's just cause and wishes "large redress" for his country and "Honor and Success" for his king.  The Poems of William Cowper, Vol. I: 1748-1782, ed. John D. Baird and Charles Ryskamp (Oxford:  Clarendon Press, 1980), p. 241n.

  The Modern Patriot (pp. 313-4).  "Rebellion is my theme all day."  (24)
  Quatrains.  Written Feb 1780.  Satire on the "patriots."  Cowper assumes the persona of a patriot in order to exhibit the "modern patriot" as a lawless rebel who delights in "civil broils."  The Americans are portrayed as "roaring boys, who rave and fight / On t'other side th'Atlantic."

On the Burning of Lord Mansfield's Library Together with his MSS. By the Mob, in the Month of June 1780 (p. 318). "So then -- the Vandals of our isle." (12)
   Quatrains. Written June 22, 1780. Mansfield will mourn his personal loss; "But ages yet to come shall mourn" the loss of his treasure.

On the Same [On the Burning of Lord Mansfield's Library . . . June 1780] (p. 319). "When wit and genius meet their doom." (16)
   Quatrains. Written June 1780. Murray was not harmed by the mob; his library has been destroyed, but Murray's eloquence is still remarkable.


Freeth, John.
   The State Pensioners. Tune, -- Strange rumours of War &c.

   "That miracles never will cease." (64)

   Freeth, The Political Songster (1790), pp. 84-6.

   Song in double quatrains. Probably composed in the fall of 1782. A satire on those who received large pensions from the state -- North upon his resignation, and Barre upon becoming a member of Rockingham's government. All the statesmen want pensions!


The Nonconformists' Nosegay, (From A Corrected Copy, 1782.) By Miss * * * * *.

   "Various in colour, odour, shape, and size." (59)

   GM 52 (Nov 1782), 543; LM 51 (Dec 1782), 583-4.

   HC. A clever poem reviews the characteristic traits of several dissenting ministers important at this time in comparison with "Vegetation," such as laurel, sunflower, sweet-briar, myrtle, etc. Richard Price is compared with a bramble -- a rough, prickly shrub: "In Speculation's mazes long run wild, / Price offers up the parent to the child. / For nature's common, law and grace dethrones, / The foremost Bramble Desolation owns." Thus he is judged harshly because of his pro-American views.


Ode On The Emancipation Of Ireland, 1782.
   Dublin: William Porter, 1806. 9p.

   "Was it from Heaven, a voice divine." (74)

   Copies: BL 11641.h.7 (4)

   Regular Pindaric ode in two parts. A celebration of Irish independence under the British crown.
   Dedicated to Henry Grattan, this poem "celebrates an Event, chiefly due to the Exertions of his Eloquence." The "Advertisement" declares that the poem was written to express the moderate position that the "repeal of the 6th of Geo. I. declaring a right to exist in the parliament of Great Britain of binding Ireland"

was a sufficient guarantee of Ireland's freedom and independence within Great Britain, contrary to Flood's view "that an express renunciation of such right was requisite." (Fox's motion, made May 18, 1782, to repeal the "obnoxious" Act for Securing the Dependency of Ireland was adopted by the House of Commons.)

Written subsequent to the repeal, this ode was recited in February 1783 to the audience attending Kemble's benefit at the Theatre-Royal, Dublin. Thus the Irish, as the poet states, did not, "for our birth-right, wade / Through Destruction, Death, and Blood."

An Ode to be performed at the Altar of Discord, on the great anniversary of the most antient and honourable fraternity of Anti-Musicians. Composed by -----, founder and grand president of the order. Ode to Discord.

"Prepare, prepare, the mystic rites prepare." (c. 160)

LM 51 (Aug 1782), 389-91.

Elaborate high or irregular Pindaric ode. A burlesque satire ironically celebrating discord, chaos, anarchy productive of "ceaseless ruin, ceaseless wars." Among all those fired by disharmony is Benjamin Franklin, worshipped by his brethren "In Bostonia's favour'd shore."

Wesley, Charles.
The American War Under The Conduct Of Sir William Howe. By the Rev. Charles Wesley, M.A. Edited, with an Introduction & Notes, by Donald Baker, M.A., M.Phil.
London: Keepsake Press, 1975. 37p.

"The Americans, we all allow." (615)

Copies: BL Cup.510.agb 36.

A manuscript poem in three parts, written in 1782, printed for the first time as a contribution to the celebrations of the Bicentenary of the American Declaration of Independence.

Hudibrastic OC. Wesley adopts Joseph Galloway's opinions on Gen. Howe's alleged treacherous procrastination, on his unwillingness to press home any military advantage and crush Washington's "Undisciplin'd, half-arm'd, half-fed" forces, although his own were "six times stronger," because it was to his personal interest to prolong the war and an advantage to his party. Like Keppel, Howe was motivated by partisan considerations. Furthermore, he deliberately suppressed Loyalist assistance; and he disobeyed orders to join forces with "The brave, unfortunate Burgoyne," a deliberate lapse that cost Britain the loss of Burgoyne's army and a quick end to the war.

83-A

The Ghost of Lord Chatham to his Son, Mr. William Pitt.

"Mark me, -- lend thy serious hearing."  (25 + c. 30)

MP, Nov 27, 1783.

Blank verse (irregular) and prose. Parody on Shakespeare's Hamlet. Incidentally, the speech refers to "the late wretched peace" and warns against Shelburne and Fox. Specifically, the persona of Chatham warns his son against Fox's India Bill, focusing on the evil "set of miscreants," the rulers of the East India Company who have committed murders and who refuse to be bound by justice, law, and humanity. They insist upon their cruel monopoly so that they can continue to plunder India.

Imitation of the Song, O Nancy, &c. Written by the Bishop of Dromore. Addressed to a Lady. By an Officer going to embark for America. [And] Answer.

"O Nancy, wilt thou go with me."  (32 + 32)

GM 53 (Aug 1783), 696.

Double quatrains. Imitation of a ballad by Thomas Percy, author of the celebrated Reliques of Ancient Poetry (1765); a simple but pathetic ballad on the enforced separation of lovers because of the American War. The lady declares that she will be faithful; and should he die "in the virtuous cause / Of glory," she will die of a broken heart. Bishop Percy's original popular song was published in Dodsley's miscellany, A Collection of Poems . . . By Several Hands (London: J. Dodsley, 1775), VI, 233-4.

Impromptu. From the Philadelphia Gazette.

"One H[OW]E is dead, G[o]d rest his soul."  (4)

MP, May 19, 1783.

Quatrain. George Augustus Howe, now dead, did little for America; but his brother, William Howe, because of a love of gambling, helped America win. See 83-121.

A Minister's Reasoning.

"Should I once plead, says N[orth], for Reformation."  (2)

PA, May 23, 1783.

HC. Epigram. Ironic satire on North, whose persona admits that to support Parliamentary reform will be at the cost of his political life. (This poem contradicts "England's Happiness," which is printed immediately beneath it in the newspaper. See 83-72.)

The Order of St. Patrick, an Ode, dedicated to the Right Hon. the Earl of Bellamont.
   London: Debrett, 1783.

   Notices: CR 56 (Sep 1783), 237; MR 69 (Aug 1783), 166.

   Copies: None located.

   MR: "The subject of this Ode . . . is the restoration of the rights of Ireland."

The Quack. "John Bull, a 'squire of eminence and worth." (18) LM 52 (Jun 1783), 297. Repr. of 76-295 (St J's C, Nov 12, 1776), but with ten added lines and some verbal improvements. The Tory Scots are still blamed for the American War; and the poem, now that the war is lost and Britain has officially given the colonies their independence, is even more poignantly applicable.

Questions and Answers.

   "What makes Flood's passion burst all decent bounds?" (4)

   Cumb Pacq, Nov 25, 1783.

   HC. Satire on Flood and Grattan, the Irish political leaders. Flood's objections to the £50,000 awarded to Grattan can only be silenced by the same amount.

Wesley, Charles.
   American Independency.

   "What harm, if Ministers agree." (168)

   MS Poem, printed in Frank Baker, <u>Representative Verse of Charles Wesley</u> (London: Epworth Press, 1962), pp. 357-61.
   OC. Written after the Peace of Paris, Sep 3, 1783. A bitter criticism of those Britons responsible for losing the American War. Wesley blames Gen. William Howe for his unwillingness to defeat "the Yankies" decisively (at Brandywine, Sep 11, 1777, for example), preferring to betray his country "for double pay" as he prolongs the war. Howe also failed to help Burgoyne, likewise betraying "his rival." Wesley charges Admiral Richard Howe for failing to blockade American harbors and starving the rebels into submission. British generals, he declares, did not fight in earnest; nor did they allow the Loyalists to fight. They conspired with the treacherous "Patriots" in Parliament to defeat the effort to subdue the rebellion. Wesley even blames Cornwallis for surrendering at Yorktown and leaving

the Loyalists to the mercy "of those Fiends from hell." In conclusion, Wesley associates the unnecessary loss of the colonies with a betrayal of King George and a weakening of his power to the point of forcing him to abdicate and setting up a republic "following Congress's example."

84-A

Burns, Robert.
A Fragment. Tune -- "Gillicrankie."

"When Guilford good our Pilot stood." (72)

Poems, Chiefly in the Scottish Dialect, By Robert Burns (Edinburgh: Creech, 1787), pp. 311-5; The Works of Robert Burns; With An Account of His Life, and A Criticism on his Writings, ed. J. Currie (London: Cadell & Davies; Edinburgh: Creech, 1801), III, 266-70.

A ballad in double quatrains on the rhyme "aw." Written probably 1784; printed first in the Edinburgh edition, 1787. In a relatively humorous, but neutral or impartial manner, Burns narrates the history of politics from the beginning of the American War with the Boston Tea Party to the several ministries, ending finally with that of the younger Pitt. He refers to the American expedition to Canada that resulted in Montgomery's death; Gage in Boston; Howe in New York and Philadelphia; Burgoyne and Fraser in Saratoga; Cornwallis and Clinton; Germain, Fox, Burke, Rockingham, Shelburne, the Fox-North Coalition, the fall of Fox and the assumption of "Chatham's boy," Pitt. Repr. Frank Moore, _Songs and Ballads of the American Revolution_ (1855), pp. 380-4; and in _The Poems and Songs of Robert Burns_, ed. James Kinsley (Oxford: Clarendon Press, 1968), I, 49-51; II, 1026-9.


Consistency of the Patriotic Alderman. "What! Liberty W[il]kes! of Oppression the Hater!" (8) An Asylum for Fugitives, in Prose and Verse (1785), p. 170. See 84-152.


Dialogue Between a Certain Personage and his Minister: -- Imitated from the 9th Ode of Horace, Book 3.

"K[ing]. When heedless of your birth and name." (36)

An Asylum for Fugitives, in Prose and Verse (London: Debrett, 1785), pp. 75-6.

Sixains. Satire on the King and Pitt, who has accepted the power of the office of prime minister in order to protect the King's prerogative, to "keep [the] _Commons_ down," and to undermine Wyvill and the movement for reform. Pitt is presented as a hypocrite.


On the Candle and Window Tax.

"Jove said, Let there be light -- and, lo!" (10)

MH, Aug 20, 1784; An Asylum for Fugitive Pieces, in Prose and Verse (London: Debrett, 1785), p. 239.

OC. Satire on the new taxes of Pitt's ministry.


Puddicombe, John N.
   Ode To the Right Hon. William Pitt.

   "Again the tuneful powers of verse."  (88)

   PA, Mar 20, 1784.

   Regular (Horatian) ode in octaves, signed "J. N. Puddicombe." A fulsome eulogy of the younger Pitt decorated with a good deal of classical imagery.
   The "Illustrious youth" has raised Britain's "drooping Genius," and the "beams" shed by his "diffusive glories . . . Add lustre to the blaze encircling [his] father's head." Spain and Holland will again fear British naval power. Not the same poem recorded as 84-13, the title of which also differs.


Thompson, Edward. "Epitaph, Extempore. On George Alexander Stevens." See 84-58.


Verses on the King.

   "In private life when splendid virtues shine." (23)

   Lloyd's 55 (Nov 5, 1784), 447.

   HC. An eulogy on the King for his many virtues as a private person.

INDEX
(Additions in the Supplement are identified by year followed by Capital "A".)

Part I

Authors and their Poems, and Titles of
Anonymous Pamphlet Poems


Addison, Joseph (1672-1719). Poet, essayist, journalist, and Whig politician.
    "Address to Liberty," **72**-5 (in Junius's *Compilation*)
*Admiral Rodney's Triumph, Or the French Fleet Defeated* (1782), **82**-1
*The Alderman's Letter to the Lord Mayor. Relative to Wilkes* (1768), **68**-1
Allen, William (1704-80). Colonial jurist, industrialist, and Loyalist.
    *The American Crisis. A Letter . . . to the Earl Gower* (1774), **74**-1
Almon, John (1737-1805). Journalist, printer, and publisher.
    "The Congratulation: Addressed to the Sons of Freedom, On the Change of
        Ministry in 1766," **66**-32
    "Ode, addressed to Captain Smelt," **80**-235
    **About**: **78**-43; **79**-41, **81**-259
        and Fox, **79**-413
        a "patriot" sympathetic with American Rebels, **81**-15
Alves, Robert (1745-94). Scottish schoolmaster and poet.
    *The Miseries of War. An Elegy* (1769), **69**-1, **82**-2
    *Ode for the Year 1781* (1781, 1782), **81**-2, **82**-2
    *Ode to Britannia. (For the Year 1780.)* (1780), **80**-1, **82**-2
    *Poems* (1782), **82**-2
*America Lost. A Poem of Condolence, Addressed to Britannia* (1778), **76**-5, **78**-1
An American.
    "An Epitaph on the Ministry," **74**-78
    "Epitaph on Wolfe," **72**-46
    *Oppression* (1765), **65**-8
    *The Yankees War-Hoop . . . The Victorious Defeat at Boston* (1775), **75**-26
An American Loyalist.
    *An Address from the Members of the Constitutional Body . . . on the Change
        of the Ministry* (1783), **83**-1
American Poems. By Americans. **55**-2, **57**-2, **58**-1, 2, 3, **59**-5, 6, **60**-7, 8,
  **61**-2, **62**-3, 4, 8, 9, **63**-5, **65**-8, **66**-15, 64, 67, **68**-26, 95, **70**-190, 243, **71**-
  30, **72**-14, 46, **73**-11, **74**-1, 78, 216, **75**-26, 51, 148, **76**-86, **77**-9, 14, **78**-
  51, 59, 66, 73, 107, 206, 208, 236, **79**-504, **83**-1, 8, **84**-76, **89**-2
    "Addressicle," **68**-A
    by an "American" in the West Indies, **83**-9
    "From the Massachusetts Spy," **73**-A
    in honor of the King of France, **83**-133
American Poems. By Americans against British coercion and the American War.
  **66**-67, **68**-95, **72**-14, **74**-8, 216, **75**-23, 25, 101, 143, 148, 251, 252, 275,
  288, 289, **76**-9, 97, 166, 169, 211, 275, 276, 282, 290, **77**-14, 178, 188; **78**-
  73, **79**-14, 45, 379, **80**-294, **83**-14, **85**-6, 10, **89**-2, **92**-1

"Impromptu," **83**-A
Montgomery and Canada, **76**-183
Tomlinson & Paine, **80**-A
American Poems. By American Loyalists, **76**-86, **77**-129, 172, 186, 187, 188, 189, 243, **78**-194, 195, 211, 284, 542, **79**-422, **80**-22, 30, 77, 83, 199, 323, 339, 364, **81**-72, **83**-1, 8, 91, 116, 235
Americanus. (pseud.) "A Cabinet Dialogue," **75**-51
André, John (1751-80). "The British Hero." Major in British Army; Gen. Howe's adjutant, 1778; with Gen. Clinton, 1778-80; executed as spy, October 2, 1780. Friend of Miss Seward, the poet.
"Address intended to have been spoken at the Mischianza," **78**-51
*The Cow-Chace: An Heroic Poem in Three Cantos* (1781), **80**-2
"Verses intended for the Mischianza," **79**-504
**About**: **80**-117, 119, 171, 190, 263, 391, **81**-4, 14, 88, 203, **82**-11, 19, **83**-11, 25, 28, 33, 244, 274, **84**-9, 10, 40
American guilt for an atrocity, **82**-86
and French spy La Motte, **81**-65
epitaph, **80**-138
injustice of André's execution, **81**-103
monument in Westminster Abbey, **82**-74
must be avenged, **81**-113
Ancell, Samuel (d. 1802). Military writer; served with the army at the siege of Gibraltar, 1779-83.
"In commemoration of the Red-Hot Balls at Gibraltar," **85**-32
Andrews, Miles Peter (d. 1814). Dramatist, author of *The Election* (1774), a musical interlude, and *Fire and Water* (1780), a ballad opera; friend of Ld Lyttelton.
"The (Royal) British Tar. A New Song," **83**-39
Anstey, Christopher (1724-1805). Poet, author of the popular rhymed letters, *The New Bath Guide* (1766) and *The Election Ball* (1776), clever satires on the times.
"A Parody on the Laureat's Ode for the New Year," **73**-13
*Speculation; or A Defence of Mankind* (1780), **80**-3
**About**: **85**-25
*The Anti-Palliseriad, or, Britain's Triumphs over France* (1779), **79**-1
Arnot, Hugo (1749-86). Scottish historical writer; a Jacobite.
*The XLV. Chapter of the Prophecies of Thomas the Rhymer . . . Dedicated to Doctor Silverspoon. . . .* (1776), **76**-1
*Arx Herculea Servata, . . . or, Gibraltar Delivered* (1783), **83**-2
Ashby, S. Newspaper poet.
"Receipt for an Epigram," **85**-46
*The Asses Ears, A Fable* (1777), **77**-1
*An Asylum for Fugitive Pieces in Prose and Verse* (1785), **66**-32, **80**-135, **81**-11, **82**-127, 313, 333, 405, **83**-8, 17, **84**-110, 127, 152, **85**-27, 36
"Dialogue, . . . " and "On the Candle and Window Tax"), **84**-A
*An Asylum for Fugitives* (1776), **75**-61, 166, 242, **76**-57, 65, 88, 133, 181, 190, 213, 218, 307, 334, 386, 387
Atkinson, Joseph (1743-1818). British captain, 46th Foot Regiment; later a dramatist, his plays produced after 1785.
*Congratulatory Ode, to General Sir William Howe* (1778), **78**-2
*The Auspices of War; An Ode* (1779), **79**-2
Averay, Robert.
*Britannia and the Gods in Council; A Dramatic Poem* (1756), **56**-1

Badini, Carl Francis. Translator, opera librettist, editor of the *Morning Post* as of July 1783.
    *The Flames of Newgate; or, The New Ministry* (1782), **82**-3
*Baratariana. A Select Collection of Fugitive Political Pieces* (1773, 1777), **70**-15, **71**-46, 130
Barbauld, Anna Laetitia (née Aikin) (1743-1825). Poet and miscellaneous writer.
    "Corsica" (1769), in *Poems* (1773), **69**-2
    **About**: **81**-A ("Epistle to Hayley")
Barebones, Ebenezer (pseud.).
    *Venality. A Poem* (1775), **75**-1
*Battle of Bunker Hill. This Song Composed by the British . . .* (1775), **75**-2
*The Battle of the Quills; or, Wilkes Attacked and Defended* (1768), **68**-2, 31, 60, 62, 112, 113
Bayly, Mary (1715-71?). Anti-papist patriotic poet.
    *Old Woman's Loyalty* (1762), **62**-1
*The Beauties of Administration* (1782), **82**-4
*Bedlam, A Ball, and Dr. Price's Observations on the Nature of Civil Liberty* (1776), **76**-2
*The Bees, The Lion, The Asses, and other Beasts, A Fable* (1785), **85**-1
*Bellona; Or, The Genius of Britain; . . . Inscribed to John Dunning* (1778), **78**-3
Bentley, Richard (1708-82). Poet, playwright, and pamphleteer; friend of Horace Walpole and the poet Gray.
    *Patriotism: A Mock Heroic in [Five] Six Cantos* (1763-65), **63**-1, 2
Berkeley, George (1685-1753). Bishop of Cloyne; celebrated philosopher.
    "Verses on the Prospect of Planting Arts and Learning in America," **75**-41
    **About**: **74**-25
Bertie, Willoughby, Fourth Earl of Abingdon. (pseud.)
    *An Adieu to the Turf . . . from the Earl of Abingdon to . . . the Archbishop of York* (1778), **78**-4
Bicknell, Alexander (d. 1796). Author in many genres—biography, novel, history and polemical essays.
    "Lines to the Memory of Mr. Christopher Pinchbeck," **83**-138
Blackburn, Peter. Schoolboy poet, "under fourteen years of age."
    "On the Reduction of the Havannah by the British Arms," **62**-43
Blake, William (1757-1827). Radical poet and artist whose genius was recognized and honored long after his death.
    *America a Prophecy* (1793), **93**-1
*The Blessings of Liberty Displayed; With the Fall of Corsica* (1769), **69**-3
*The Blockheads; or, Fortunate Contractor* (1782), **82**-5
A Bostonian.
    "The Lamentation of a Bostonian Addressed to England," **75**-148
    "The Wise Men of Gotham, and the Goose. A Fable," **74**-216
*The Bostonian Prophet* (1779), **79**-3
Boyce, Samuel (d. 1775). Dramatist and poet.
    "An Ode. Addressed to Sir Joseph Mawbey," **69**-39, **71**-14
Boyce, William (1710-79). Composer, Master of the Royal Band. Composed the music for Garrick's patriotic lyric, "Heart of Oak," and the music for Whitehead's laureat odes.
    "A New Song," Heart of Oak, **60**-16
Brackenridge, Hugh Henry (1748-1816). Philip Freneau (1752-1832). Youthful American authors.

*The Rising Glory of America* (1771), **72**-14, **78**-73, **89**-2
Brewood, J. D. A journal poet from Staffordshire.
    "A Letter of Remonstrance and Condolence, . . ." **74**-106
Brice, Thomas. A provincial printer and publisher of *The Postmaster; or The Loyal Mercury* of Exeter.
    *The State Coach in the Mire, A Modern Tale* (1783), **83**-3
Bridges, Thomas (fl. 1759-75). Dramatist, novelist, and parodist.
    *The Battle of the Bonnets. A Political Poem* (1768?), **65**-2
    *The Battle of the Genii. A Fragment. In Three Canto's* (1765), **65**-1
*Britain, A Poem; in Three Books* (1757), **57**-1
*Britannia's Garland, Containing four excellent New Songs* (1777?).
    "Britannia's Call to her Sons on Expectation of a French War," Song I, **77**-2 (see also **78**-211, Freeth)
    "The Soldiers Farewell," Song III, **77**-2
*Britannia's Intercession for the Deliverance of John Wilkes* (1768), **68**-3
*The British Coffee-House. A Poem* (1764), **64-A**
    **See**: *The Thistle* (1773), **73-A**.
*The Britoniad, A Poem* (1780), **80**-4
Brown, T. Unidentified poet.
    *The Times. A Satire. To the King* (1783), **83**-4
Browne, Moses (1704-87). Clergyman, poet.
    "Verses (written the evening of the royal funeral) on occasion of the late King's death," **60**-10
Bruce, Michael (1746-67). Young Scottish poet.
    *Poems on Several Occasions* (1770), "Ode: To Paoli," **67**-1, **70**-1
Burgoyne, John (1723-92). MP, 1761-92. Dramatist, and general officer in British army.
    [Proclamation at beginning of his New York campaign, "Inversed"], **77**-44, 45, 136, **78**-254
    "A Prologue . . . spoken at Boston in New England, before the Tragedy of Zara," **76**-77, **82**-55
    "A Vaudeville . . . call'd the Boston Blockade," **77**-43
    **See** Part II of Index for entries about Burgoyne.
Burke, Edmund (1729-97). MP, 1765-94, and New York Agent. Author of political tracts and published speeches supporting America against North's ministry.
    "Inscription for William Dowdeswell," **80**-168
    **See** Part II of Index for entries about Burke.
Burke, Thomas (c. 1747-83). Member Continental Congress from North Carolina, 1776-81, and Governor of North Carolina, 1781.
    "Verses Written by Mr. [Thomas] Burke, a Delegate from North Carolina," **78**-527
Burnby, John. A newspaper contributor; objects to the corruption of the "present constitution."
    "A Thought in 1781," **83**-249
Burton, William. A Tory partisan against Opposition.
    *Superstition, Fanaticism, and Faction. A Poem* (1781), **81**-2
Butler, Samuel (1612-80). Satiric anti-Puritan poet of the Interregnum and Restoration, noted for his mock-heroic *Hudibras*, a Tory attack on Republicans and puritan dissenters, the Whigs of a later time.
    *Hudibras* (1663-78), **79**-534, **80**-284 (excerpts)
Burns, Robert (1759-96). Scottish poet, satirist and lyricist.
    "A Fragment," **84-A**
Byrom, John (1692-1763). Mystic and poet.

"Almighty Lord of Hosts, by whose commands," **76-78**
*Caledonia. A Poem* (1778), **78-5**
*The Caledoniad* (1775), **66-7, 72-87, 75-3**
*Calliope; or, The Musical Miscellany* (1788), **75-256, 78-113, 211, 238, 79-404, 80-75.**
*Captain Parolles at Minden . . . Dedicated to Temple Luttrell* (1778), **78-6**
Cartwright, Edmund (1743-1823). Poet and inventor of the power-loom, and other agricultural machines; opposed the American War.
    *Poems* (1786), **86-1**
    *The Prince of Peace; And Other Poems* (1779), **79-4, 86-1**
    Sonnet, to the Duke of Richmond. On His Motion for Annual Parliaments and Equal Representation, 1780," **83-5, 86-1**
    Sonnets to Eminent Men. And an Ode to the Earl of Effingham (1783), **83-5, 86-1**
Cartwright, John (1740-1824). Older brother of Edmund C; known as the "Father of Reform." Opposed American taxation and slave trade.
    *Give us our Rights* (1782), **82-154**
    **About**: America, Ireland, freedom and reform, **82-85**
        Wilkes, Lofft, and reform, **84-123**
Cato Redivivus. (pseud.)
    *Patriotism: A Political Satire* (1767), **67-5**
Causidicus. (pseud.) The Cirencester poet, "The Discontented Patriot," a defender of Shelburne and the younger Pitt. All his poems were published in newspapers, **75-257, 76-47, 69, 79-77, 232, 80-314, 81-212, 82-37, 48, 57, 169, 170, 174, 207, 229, 250** (and **83-193**), **279, 292, 299, 307, 314, 374, 382, 83-42, 51, 58, 104, 105, 115, 148, 159, 174, 212, 216, 218, 224, 245, 247, 273, 84-77, 78** (and **83-115**), **81, 106, 107, 143, 147, 182, 198, 201**
    and Burke, **82-94**
    and Germain, **82-95**
    "Britannia to her Sons," **79-A**
    "Britannia's Admonition," **79-A**
    "Epigram. On . . .," **76-A**
    on Conway's motion to end American War, **82-147**
    on the failing North ministry, **82-78**
    on George III, **84-206**
    praise of Rodney, **82-80**
    praise of younger Pitt, **85-15**
    "Verses," **78-A**
    vs. Fox, **85-39, 44**
    vs. Fox and faction, **84-205**
    vs. North, **84-212**
*Causidicus, A Poetic Lash* (1779), **79-5**
Cautious, Timothy. (pseud.)
    "An Answer to the Quiet Man's Opinion of the Times," **63-11**
    "A Quiet Man's Opinion of the Times," **63-133**
Cave, Jane (afterwards Winscom) (fl. 1750-1800). A religious poet.
    "On the First General Fast after the Commencement of the Late War," in *Poems on Various Subjects* (1783), **75-4, 82-6, 83-6**
    "On the General Fast, February 8, 1782," in *Poems on Various Subjects* (1783), **75-4, 82-6, 83-6**
Champion, Joseph. A Tory poet hopes the King will crush the American rebellion.
    *The Progress of Freedom. A Poem* (1776), **76-3**
Chandler, Daniel. Supposed author, a staunch Tory criticizes the American rebels

and the English Opposition.
*An Apology for the Times . . . Addressed to the King* (1778), **78-7**

Chatterton, Thomas (1752-70). The young creator of the medieval Rowley poems here appears as a political satirist and Wilkesite partisan.
    "The Consuliad. An Heroic Poem" **70-35**
    "Resignation," **70-36**
    **About:** **77-252**, **81-229**, **83-28**
        his medieval style, **71-116**
        Rowley imitated, **80-28**, **82-12**
        Turgotus, Chatterton and Mickle, **82-16**

Children, Poems by, and Young People, **62-43**, **75-139**, 298, **77-204**, 247, **78-21**, **79-190**, 240
    an impressed youth, **79-486**
    young American in England, **78-206**
    young man, **79-189**
    "A Youngster," **83-158**
    a youth, **82-134 & 271**

*The Christmas Tale, A Poetical Address . . . to the Young Ministry* (1784), **84-1**

Churchill, Charles (1731-64). Leading verse satirist of the 1760's, a prolific and powerful ally of Wilkes.
    *The Author* (1763), **63-A**
    *The Candidate* (1764), **64-A**
    *The Conference* (1763), **63-A**
    *The Duellist* (1764), **64-A**, **70-209**
    *An Epistle to William Hogarth* (1763), **63-A**
    *The Ghost* (1763), **61-3**
    *Gotham* (1764), **64-A**
    *Independence* (1764), **64-A**
    [Lines on Wilkes], **68-4**
    *The Prophecy of Famine* (1763), **63-A**
    *The Times* (1764), **64-61**
    "Verses Written in Windsor Park," **63-A**
    **About:** **62-47**, **63-4**, 20, 59, 128, 152, 154, 187, **64-6**, 13, 18, 19, 27, 30, 36, 44, 46, 49, 59, 61, 66, 68, 69, 82, 86, 99, **65-4**, 5, 6, 10, 11, 13, 23, 70, 73, 87, 97, 115, 139, **66-7**, 81, 84, **67-6**, 8, **68-6**, 33, 103, **69-67**, 77, 254, **70-2**, 3, **72-77**, **73-8**, **74-13**, **76-184**, **85-25**
        "Answer" [2], **64-A**
        "Attempt," **64-A**
        "Copy of Mr. Underwood's Lines," **69-A**
        "Counter" [2], **64-A**
        Cowper's "Table Talk," **82-A**
        "An Epigram," **65-A**
        "Epitaph," **64-A**
        in Junius's *Compilation*, **72-5**
        "Monody," **64-A**
        "On Mr. Churchill's Late Poems," **63-A**
        "Political Squib," **63-A**
        "Snarling Pug," **63-A**
        "To The Author," **64-A**

Cibberius Secundus. (pseud.)
    "A New Ode for the New Year, 1773," **73-57**.

*The Ciceroniad. A Poem. Inscribed to William Earl of Mansfield* (1777), **77-3**

*City Patriotism Displayed. A Poem . . . To the Rt. Hon. Frederick Lord North* (1773), **73**-1
*Civil War; A Poem. Written in the Year 1775* (1775), **75**-5
*The Coalitionist. A Satire* (1784), **84**-2
Cockings, George (d. 1802). Writer; had a small place in the British government at Boston, Massachusetts; held post of registrar of the Society of Arts, Manufactures & Commerce in the Adelphi for thirty years to his death.
    *The American War, A Poem; In Six Books* (1781), **81**-3
    *The Conquest of Canada; or The Siege of Quebec. An Historical Tragedy* (1766), **66**-1
    *The Paoliad; or Corsican Memoirs. A Poem* (1769), **69**-4
    *War: An Heroic Poem from the taking of Minorca, by the French; to the Reduction of the Havannah, by the Earl of Albemarle, Sir George Pocock . . .* (1760), **60**-1, 2, 3
Cole, John (fl. 1779-91). Poet historian of the American War up to the British defeat at Trenton, December 1776; believed the rebellion to be unjustified.
    *The American War, An Ode* (1779), **79**-6
Cole, R. A Tory versifier vs. Dissenters and the "saints," and a memorialist of Charles I.
    "Advice to the Presbyterians," **65**-16
    "On The Thirtieth of January," **65**-89
    "Supplement to the Advice to the Presbyterians," **65**-117
    "Thirtieth of January for Ever and Ever," **75**-57
    **About**: **65**-125, 126
Colvill, Robert (d. 1788). A patriotic Scottish clergyman and Tory poet from Dysart.
    *Atalanta* (1777), **75**-6, **76**-83, **77**-4, **79**-7
    *The Caledonians* (1779), **59**-1, **76**-83, **79**-7
    *The Cyrnean Hero* (1771), **71**-1, **89**-1
    *The Downfall of the Roman Confederacy; or, The Ever Memorable 12th of April 1782* (1788), **82**-7
    "For General Wolfe's Monument," **72**-A
    *Occasional Poems* (1771), **71**-1
    "On the Late Great Naval and Military Preparations," **83**-59; **89**-1
    "On the Memorable Siege of Gibraltar," **82**-8, **89**-1
    *Poetical Works* (1789), **59**-1, **71**-1, **75**-6, **76**-83, **77**-58, **80**-6, 74, **81**-4, **83**-59, **89**-1
    "Sacred to the Memory of Col. Abercrombie, of Major Pitcairne, . . ." (1775), **75**-6, **76**-83, **77**-4, **79**-7, **89**-1
    "Sacred to the Memory of James Webster," **82**-8, **89**-1
    "Sacred to the Memory of Major André," **81**-4, **89**-1
    *Savannah, a Poem in Two Cantos* (1780), **80**-5, **89**-1
    "To The Immortal Memory of the Hon. Colonel John Maitland," **80**-5, 74, **89**-1
    "To The Memory of Allan Malcolm," **80**-6, **89**-1
    "To The Memory of the Hon. William Leslie," **77**-4, 58, **79**-7, **89**-1
    "Verses for General Wolfe's Monument," **59**-1, **79**-7, **89**-1
Combe, William (1741-1823). Poet, satirist, friend of Laurence Sterne; later in life noted as a political pamphleteer and the author of *Tours of Dr. Syntax* (1812-21), with Rowlandson plates.
    *The Castle of Infamy* (1780), **80**-7
    *The Crisis, Now or Never* (1780), **80**-9
    *Fanatical Conversion; or Methodism Displayed* (1779), **79**-8

  *The Fast-Day: A Lambeth Eclogue* (1780), **80-8**
  *The Heroic Epistle Answered: By . . . Lord Craven* (1776), **76-4**
  *An Heroic Epistle to an Unfortunate Monarch* (1778), **78-8**
  *A Heroic Epistle to Sir James Wright* (1779), **79-9**
  *An Heroic Epistle to the Right Honourable the Lord Craven* (1775), **75-7**
  *The Justification: A Poem* (1777), **77-5**
  *Perfection. A Poetical Epistle Calmly Addressed to the Greatest Hypocrite in England* (1778), **78-9**
  *The Saints, A Satire* (1778), **78-10**
  *Sketches for Tabernacle-Frames* (1778), **78-11**
  *The World as It Goes, A Poem* (1779), **79-10**
  **About:** **76-176** (about **75-7**); **77-316**; **78-353**
*A Companion for a Leisure Hour* (1769), **68-30, 31, 52, 64, 108**
  "A Political Genealogy," **69-A**
*The Complaint: Or Britannia Lamenting the Loss of Her Children* (1776), **76-5, 78-1**
*Conflagration: A Satire* (1781), **81-5**
*The Conquerors. A Poem. Displaying the Glorious Campaigns of 1775, 1776, 1777* (1778), **78-12**
*The Convivial Songster* (c. 1788), **82-388**
Conway, -----. Poet for *Parker's General Advertiser*.
  "An Elegy. On the Much-lamented Death of . . . Charles Wentworth, Marquis of Rockingham," **82-89**
  "On the Triumphant Arrival of Lord Rodney," **82-274**
  "A Patriotic Address to Mr. Fox, On His Spirited Resignation," **82-290**
  "Stanzas on a View of the Fleet of Lord Howe," **82-342**
Cooke, William (1746-?). Fellow, New College, Oxford.
  *The Conquest of Quebec: A Poem* (1769), **69-5**
Coombe, Thomas (1747-1822). American Loyalist; Anglican clergyman and poet.
  *The Peasant of Auburn; or, The Emigrant* (1783), **83-8**
Cooper, Myles (1737-85). American clergyman, President of King's College, New York (later Columbia University); Loyalist.
  "Stanzas Written on the Evening of the 10th of May, 1776," **76-86**
Costello, Patrick. Poetic Irish servant of an English army captain in Boston at the time of the siege.
  "An Excellent new Ballad . . . intended to be sung . . . on his Majesty's Birth-Day," **78-171**
Couper, Robert (1750-1818). Scottish poet and M. D. Served as tutor in a family of Virginia; but on the outbreak of hostilities in America returned to Scotland, 1776.
  "Epitaph. On the Honourable Colonel Maitland," **79-148**
Cowdroy, William. A loyal poet, editor of the *Chester Chronicle*.
  "New Occasional Prologue. On the Prospect of Peace with America," **83-154**
Cowper, William (1731-1800). Leading poet of latter half of 18th century. Regarding the American Revolution, Cowper shared the opinions of the Tory Establishment: he wished to see the American rebels defeated.
  "An Address to the Mob," **79-A**
  "Another Translation from the Latin, on the Horrid Commotions in London," **80-53**
  "Epinikion," **79-A**
  "In Seditionem Horrendam," **80-A**
  "On the Loss of the Royal George," **82-68**
  "On the Trial of Admiral Keppel," **79-A**

"On the Victory Gained by Rodney off Gibraltar in 1780," **80-A**
*Poems* including:
   "The Modern Patriot," **82-A**
   "On the Burning of Lord Mansfield's Library," **82-A**
   "Table Talk," **82-A**
"A Present for the Queen of France," **79-A**
*The Task, A Poem, in Six Books* (1785), **85-2**
"To Sir Joshua Reynolds," **80-A**
"A Translation from the Latin. Wrote on the late Horrid Tumults," **80-383**

Crabtree, Christopher. An admirer of Churchill's poetry.
  "The Feast of Fancy, A Pastoral Elegy" (1764), **64-18**

Craven, Elizabeth (1750-1828). Author. Wife of Ld William Craven; later, upon his death, became Margravine of Anspach.
  "Ode, Addressed to General Arnold," **82-212**

Crawford, Charles (1752-?). Of Antigua, West Indies. Fellow commoner, Queen's College, Cambridge; wrote on political, social, and religious subjects, including slavery.
  *Liberty: A Pindaric Ode* (1783), **83-9**

*The Crisis*. (91 numbers, January 20, 1775-October 12, 1776). The "flaming" periodical; issue No. 3 was ordered burned by the common hangman, March 6, 1775; but the journal persisted until October 12, 1776. Assumed the Whig republican perspective against government's policy of coercion.
  *An Epistle to William, Earl of Mansfield* (1778), first published in *Crisis*, May 13, 1775, **78-15**
  "Gardner's Ghost, A Prophetic Ballad," **76-165**
  "The Prophecy of Ruin," **75-223**
  "A Rough Sketch for the Royal Academy," **75-239**
  "These mighty crimes will sure ere long provoke," **75-261**
  "To the King," **75-276**
  *Tyranny the Worst Taxation* (1778), first published in *Crisis*, May 20, 1775, **78-44**
  **About**: **75-90, 78-23**

*The Crisis: An Ode to John Wilkes, Esq;* (1763), **63-3**

*The Crisis: Being Three State Poems . . . I. The Northern Dictator . . . II. On the Reduction and Surrender of the Havannah, and Conclusion of the Late Peace. III. Caledonia . . .* (1764), **64-1**

*The Crisis. Now or Never* (1780), **80-9**

Croft, Herbert (1751-1816). Author, friend of Thomas Maurice; wrote an epistolary novel, *Love and Madness* (1780), on Martha Ray, mistress of Ld Sandwich, which includes letters of Chatterton; also wrote on Gordon riots.
  *The Abbey of Kilkhampton; Or Monumental Records for the Year 1980* (1780), (1780), **80-10**
  *The Wreck of Westminster Abbey* (1788), **88-1**
  **About**: **80-114,**
    character assassin, **81-96**
    criticized, **80-170 & 206**
    parody, **81-104**

Cumberland, Richard (1732-1811). Playwright and poet; clerk and secretary to the Board of Trade and Plantations, 1776-81; private agent for Germain, Secretary of State for the Colonies.
  "The Election. [A Song on Liberty,]", **74-60**
  "The Election, Epilogue," **74-51**
  "Epilogue to the Walloons," **82-69**
  "The Patriotic Secession: An Ode," **77-249**

"Song in the Second act of the Walloons," **82**-337
    **About**: **77**-175 (an answer to **77**-249); **80**-86

Cunningham, John (1729-73). Poet, born in Dublin. Strolling actor; wrote occasional prologues.
    "An Elegiac Ode on the Death of [George II]," **60**-12
    "Occasional Stanzas for the Corsicans," **69**-51

Cunningham, Peter (d. 1805). Poet, clergyman; friend of Anna Seward.
    *Chatsworth or the Genius of England's Prophecy* (1783), **83**-10
    *The Naval Triumph. A Poem* (1783), **83**-11

Cunningham, Thomas. Of Queen's College, Oxford; defended John Williams, the pilloried printer, and the freedom of the press.
    "To The Wise Men of Gotham," **65**-132

Dalrymple, Hugh (d. 1774). A Scottish defender of Bute, and critic of Pitt, Wilkes, and Churchill.
    *Rodondo; or, The State Jugglers* (1763-70), **63**-4

Darly, Matthew (d. 1781). Caricaturist, engraver, designer. Published political prints which were collected annually under the title of *Political and Satirical History*.
    *General Sanguinaire Mark-ham*, **77**-33

Darwall, John. Vicar of Walsall, Staffordshire, England; critic of rebellious Americans.
    *Political Lamentations Written in the Years 1775 and 1776* (1777), **77**-6

Davies, Jeremiah. Clergyman, poet; denounced British injustice to American Loyalists.
    *An Epilogue to the Late Peace* (1783), **83**-12

Dawes, Matthew (or Manasseh) (d. 1829). Miscellaneous writer; barrister of the Inner Temple; opposed the American War.
    *The Prospect from Malvern Hill; or, Liberty Bewailing her Injuries in America* (1777), **77**-7
    *The War in America* (1778), **78**-102

Day, Thomas (1748-89). Author of the pedagogical novel, *Sandford and Merton* (1783-89); friend of the Laurens family and American cause; supported reform and anti-slavery movements.
    "Additional verses on the Death of John Laurens, **83**-13
    *America, An Ode* (1776), **76**-6
    *The Desolation of America* (1777), **77**-8
    *The Devoted Legions* (1776), **76**-7, 8
    *The Dying Negro* (1773), **73**-2
    "Epitaph upon the Death of Colonel Laurens," **83**-13
    "Stanzas . . . on the Failure of . . . an equal Representation," **85**-3
    **About**: **73**-98, **80**-41, **83**-9, 10, 283

De Brent, John. Poet, admirer of Mrs. Macaulay.
    "To Mrs. Catharine Macaulay," **70**-A

De Fleury, Maria (fl. 1770-1800). Poet, wrote religious verse and *Poems, occasioned by the confinement and acquittal of Lord George Gordon*, 1781.
    "Elegy on the Death of . . . Beckford," **70**-47

De La Cour, James (1709-85). Poet, Irish clergyman from Cork.
    "Epitaph on General James Wolfe, in the Military Style of Scripture," **72**-40

Delamayne, Thomas Hallie (1718-73). Poet, satirist; educated at Trinity College, Dublin; barrister in London. Supporter of Wilkes, and Whig politicians.
    *The Banished Patriot* (1768), **68**-6
    *The City Patricians* (1773), **73**-3

*An Elegy on the Approaching Dissolution of Parliament* (1774), **74-5**
*The Oliviad* (1762), **62**-A
*The Patricians . . . of the House of Lords* (1773), **73-4**
*The Senators: . . . of St. Stephen's Chapel* (1772), **72-1**
**About: 73-**100

DeLancey, Margaret Allen. Wife of prominent American Loyalist from New York, James Delancey (1732-1800), and daughter of Chief Justice Allen of Pennsylvania.
"Death of Colonel Maitland," **80-83**
"The Spirit of Colonel Maitland to Mrs. DeLancey," **80-83**
**See** Benjamin Moore.

*Delineation, A Poem* (1779), **79-11**
*The Deserted City. A Poem* (1780), **80-11**
*The Dialogue: Addressed to John Wilkes, Esq.* (1770), **70-2**

Dickinson, John (1732-1808). Colonial American statesman and pamphleteer, the "Penman of the Revolution."
"A Song, Now much in vogue in North America" [The Liberty Song], **68-75**
**About: 76-**22

*Ditis Charms; or Hell Broke Loose. A Poem* (1781), **81-6**

Dodd, James Solas (1721-1805). Surgeon, lecturer, actor.
"Prologue to the new Comedy of Gaelic Gratitude, or the Frenchman in India," **79-382**

Dorset, Michael. Captain in the Sussex militia; opponent of the American War, like his friend and patron, the Duke of Richmond.
*Condolence: An Elegiac Epistle from . . . Burgoyne, . . . To Cornwallis . . (1782)*, **82-9**

Draper, William (1721-87). General, helped conquer India, 1757-59; married daughter of Oliver DeLancey, Tory, of New York; active in the futile defense of Minorca, 1781.
"Epitaph on General Wolfe," **72-49**
**About: 69-**106, 200

Drewe, Edward. British officer from Exeter; badly wounded at Bunker Hill, 1775.
"Lines, Addressed to a Friend, On . . . Bunker's Hill," in *Military Sketches* (1784), **75-8**
*Poems, Chiefly by Gentlemen of Devonshire and Cornwall* (1792), **75-8, 81-12**
**About: 75-**277

DuBois, Dorothea (1728-74). Poet, playwright, and miscellaneous author.
"The New Year's Gift," **68-36**

Duché, Jacob (1738-98). Chaplain of Congress, 1776, but soon turned Loyalist and was considered a traitor by the Americans.
"Episode, From the Indian Treaty, A Poem," *Caspipina's Letters* (1774, 1777), **77-9**
**About: 78-**517

Duncombe, John (1729-86). Cambridge scholar, antiquarian, poet, and clergyman.
*The Works of Horace, in English Verse, . . . To Which Are Added Many Imitations* (1767), **55-1, 59-2, 3, 60-5, 61-1, 62-2, 64-2, 65-3, 67-2**

Dunstan, Jeffery (1759?-97). A mock knight and mock Lord Mayor of Garrett-Green, London. Not an MP, as he claims.
*Fugitive Pieces* (1789), **72-14, 75-**128, 212, **76-**68, 175, 195, **77-**167, 183, 292, **78-**56, 402, **79-**100, 399, 494
"Liberty" (cross referenced in 1776), **89-2**
**About: 82-**28

*The Earl of Chatham's Apology. A Poem* (1766), **66-2**

Edwards, Bryan (1743-1800). Poet from Antigua, West Indies; merchant, historian, and English politician (from 1796).
    "Montgomery Falls! Let no fond breast repine," **76-211**, **92-1**
    *Ode for the New Year, 1776* (1776), **76-9**, **92-1**
    "Ode, Written in England, during the American War," **76-9**, **92-1**
    *Poems, On Subjects Arising in England and the West Indies* (1783), **83-14**
    *Poems, Written Chiefly in the West Indies* (1792), **76-9**, **92-1**
    "Stanzas occasioned by the Death of Alico, an African Slave," **77-74**, **92-1**

Edwards, John (1751-1832). Irish poet; Major of the Light Dragoons in the Volunteer Army of Ireland.
    *The Patriot Soldier; A Poem* (1784), **84-3**

Egerton, Charles. Probably a schoolmaster.
    *A New History of England in Verse* (1780?), **80-12**

*An Elegiac Epistle from an Unfortunate Elector of Germany* (1776), **76-10**

*Elegiac Epistles on the Calamities of Love and War* (1780), **80-13**

*An Elegy on the Approaching Dissolution of Parliament* (1774), **74-5**. Attributed to Delamayne, *Critical Review* 38 (June 1774), 472.

*An Elegy on the Late Rt. Hon. William Pitt, Esq.* (1766), **66-3**

*Eleutheria: A Poem. Inscribed to Mrs. Macaulay* (1768), **68-7**

*England's Defiance. An Irregular Ode* (1779), **79-12**

*England's Tears: A Poem* (1774), **74-6**

English, Robert (1722-84). Chaplain to the 12th Regiment of Foot, and to Edward Ld Hawke.
    *An Elegy, On the Death of the Right Hon. Sir Charles Saunders* (1777), **77-10**
    "The Invocation, A Poem," **82-91**
    *The Naval Review. A Poem* (1773), **73-5**
    "A Tribute to the Memory of Admiral Ld Hawke," **81-56**
    **About**: 73-70

*An Epistle from a Young Lady to an Ensign in the Guarda* (1779), **79-13**

*An Epistle from Edward, an American Prisoner* (1779), **79-14**

*An Epistle from the Earl of Chatham to the King* (1778), **78-13**

*An Epistle in Verse. Written from Somersetshire, in the Year 1776* (1789), **89-3**

*An Epistle to the Rt. Hon. Lord George Germaine* (1778), **78-14**

*An Epistle to the Rt. Hon. the Earl of Chatham* (1766), **66-4**

*An Epistle to William, Earl of Mansfield* (1778), **78-15**. (First pub. 1775)

*An Epitaph on the Late Illustrious Earl of Chatham* (1784), **84-4**

*An Essay on Patriotism, in the Style and Manner of Mr. Pope's Essay on Man* (1766), **66-5**

Evans, Nathaniel (1742-67). Colonial poet and Anglican clergyman.
    *An Exercise; containing, A Dialogue & Ode on the Peace* (1763), **63-5**
    *Ode on the late Glorious Successes* (1762), **62-3**
    "Panegyric Ode to Gen. Wolfe," **72-3**
    *Poems on Several Occasions* (1772), **61-2**, **62-4**, **72-3, 4**

*The Exile Triumphant; or Liberty Appeased. A Poem . . . Inscribed to the . . . Liverymen of the City of London*, **68-8**

*The Expostulation; A Poem* (1768), **68-9**

*An Extraordinary Ode to an Extraordinary Man on an Extraordinary Occasion* (1766), **66-6**

Falconer, William (1732-69). Poet and sailor, born in Edinburgh.
    *The Demagogue* (1766), **66-7**
    **About**: **66-119**

*A Familiar Epistle from a Cat . . . to Edmund Burke* (1781), **81-7**
Farrer, John (b. 1759?). Of Queen's College, Oxford.
    *America. A Poem* (1780), **80-14**
Fawkes, Francis (1720-77). Clergyman and poet, translator of classical authors, esp. Duncombe's *Horace*.
    "On the Death of the King [George II]," **60-37**
Female or "Lady" Authors. See "Women as Authors."
Fergusson, Robert (1750-74). Scottish poet.
    "Epigram on the Epitaphs for Gen. Wolfe," **72-26**
    "Epitaph on Gen. Wolfe," **72-44**
    "The King's Birth-Day in Edinburgh," **72-52**
*Fifth Ode of the King of Prussia's Works Paraphrased. On the Present War* (1777), **77-11**
Fitz-James, Oswald. (pseud.)
    *The Wandsworth Epistle* (1762), **62-11**
Fletcher, John William (1729-85). Methodist clergyman; friend of John Wesley.
    A Essay upon the Peace of 1783 (1785), **85-4**
*The Flight of Freedom. A Fragment* (1776), **76-34**. (Probably *not* by John Tait.)
— — — *For Ever! A Poem* (1768), **68-10**
*Four Excellent New Songs, I. The Britons Resolution to Conquer Their Rebels in North America. II. Britannia's Address to her children. . . .* (1776), **76-11**.
Fox, Charles James (1749-1806). MP, 1768-1806; politician, leader of the Opposition at time of the American War. See Part II, Topics and Names, &c.
    "Upon Edward Gibbon, Esq.; . . . being made a Lord of Trade," **79-501**
Franklin, Benjamin (1706-90). American philosopher, scientist, man of letters, and statesman. See Part II, Topics and Names, &c.
    "Epitaph on Miss Shipley's Squirrel," **84-76**
    "Epitaph on a Printer of Boston," **71-30**
*Freedom, Sacred to the Memory of General Richard Montgomery* (1776), **76-12**
Freeman, S. (pseud.)
    *England's Glory, A Poem to the King* (1777), **77-12**
Free(th), John (c. 1740-1805). Birmingham publican and author of lyrics on current events adapted to popular tunes.
    "Admiral Parker's Engagement with the Dutch Fleet," **81-77**
    "American Contest," **74-89**
    "American Contest" [or, "The Contest"], **78-210**
    "The Birmingham Cut," **68-47**
    "Birmingham Recruits," **80-142**
    "Britannia. A Song," **82-139**
    "Britannia's Call to her Sons. On Expectation of a French War," **78-211**
    "Britannia's Relief. A Song," **82-140**
    "British Arms Triumphant" (Defeat of D'Estaing at Savannah), **79-193**
    "The British Flag Triumphant," **80-143**
    "The British Lion: A Song," **79-194**
    "The British Salamanders," **82-141**
    "The Budget," **83-106**
    "The Budget. A Song," **77-131**
    "Budget-Day. A Song," **85-28**
    "The Budget Worn Out," **85-29**
    "Bunker's Hill, or the Soldier's Lamentation," **75-115**
    "Burgoyne's Defeat on the Plains of Saratoga" ("Scale of Talent"), **78-213**
    "Charles Town Bar: or the Cabinet Council's Lamentation," **80-144**
    "Col. Keating's Birmingham Volunteers," **79-195**

"The Contrast," **81**-78, **82**-10
"Corruption Defeated: or the Premier Routed," **82**-142
"The Cottager's Complaint," **80**-145
"The Diaboliad," **80**-146
"A Dialogue," **75**-116
"A Dialogue between a Briton and a North American," **66**-59
"Dudley Rout . . . On the Celebration of the Victory on Long Island," **76**-164
"The George's: or, Lord Sackville's Promotion," **82**-143
"The Ins and Outs," **65**-59, **82**-145
"Jemmy Twitcher and Jolly Dick," **79**-196
"The Jersey Expedition," **81**-79
"Lord George Gordon's Procession," **80**-147
"Lord George Sackville's Promotion," **75**-117
*Modern Songs on Various Subjects* (1782), **77**-132, **78**-210, 211, 214, 215, **79**-193, 196, 197, **80**-142, 143, 145, 146, 147, 148, 149, **81**-77, 78, 79, **82**-10, 143
"The New Administration, in 1783," **83**-107
"A New Song," **63**-59
"The Old King's Ghost," **83**-108
"On the Prospect of Peace," **83**-109
"Paul Jones," **79**-197
*The Political Songster* (1790), **74**-89, **75**-115, **77**-132, **78**-211, 213, 214, **79**-193, 197, **80**-142, 143, 144, 146, 147, 148, 149, **81**-77, 79, **82**-139, 141, 142, 143, 144, 145, **83**-15, 106, 107, 108, 109, 110, 111, **85**-28, 29, 30
"The Pope's Address to his Good Friends in England," **74**-90
"Prescot's Breeches," **77**-132
"Prorogation," **74**-91
"The Sailor's Rouze. On the Glorious Success of the English Privateers," **78**-212
"Scale of Talent. A Political Cantata," **78**-213
"The Soldier's Complaint," **75**-118
"Song for the British Tars, on the Sailing of Lord Howe's Fleet," **82**-144
"Song. *Nothing at all*—A Hibernian Harangue," **85**-30
"A Song, To the Tune of the Jolly Young Waterman," **79**-198
"The State Beggars," **78**-214
"The State Jockeys," **65**-60
"The State Jockeys: or, The Ins and Outs," **82**-145, **65**-59
"The State Pensioners," **82**-A
"The Statesmen," **64**-40
"The Stream of Corruption," **80**-148
"Taxation: or the Courtier's Creed," **78**-215
"The Times," **75**-119, **66**-A
*A Touch on the Times* (1783), **83**-15
"The Trading War," **80**-149
"The Vicar of Brentford," **71**-45
*The Warwickshire Medley*, (1776), **66**-59, **71**-45, **74**-89, 90, 91, **75**-115, 116, 117, 118, 119, **76**-13, 164
"The Wonderful Coalition," **83**-110
"Written on the Day of Thanksgiving for a General Peace," **83**-111
French Poems.
"Monsieur Squinton," **71**-60

"Ode against Oppression," **65-81**
French Poems on the American War.
    "Epitre aux Insurgens" (three translations), **77-106, 107, 312**
    Fletcher's poem on the peace, **85-4**
    "Gasconade," translated, **79-201**
    "Lines Sent to Silas Deane . . . on . . . Burgoyne's Capitulation," **78-276**
    "Ode sur la Paix," **83-165**
Freneau, Philip (1752-1832). American author. See Brackenridge, Part I of Index.
*The Fugitive Miscellany* (1774), **73-47, 61, 62**
*Fugitive Pieces of Irish Politics, During the Administration of Lord Townshend* (1772), **70-15, 73-61**
Garrick, David (1717-79). Actor, playwright, songwriter.
    "A New Song," ["Heart of Oak," sung in *Harlequin's Invasion*], **60-16**
    "Shakespeare's Mulberry Tree," **75-48** (parody on)
    **About**: **71-75, 78-218, 79-222**
Garth, Samuel (1661-1719). English physician and poet in the reign of Queen Anne; wrote little besides *The Dispensary*.
    *The Dispensary* (1699, 1706), **78-220** (excerpt)
*The Genius of Britain. An Ode. In Allusion to the Present Times* (1775), **75-9**
*The Genius of Britain. A Poem* (1780), **80-15**
*The Genius of Britain, To General Howe* (1776), **76-14**
Gentleman, Francis (1728-84). Dramatist, actor, poet, and editor.
    *The General. A Poem* (1764), **64-3**
*A Genuine Collection of the Several Pieces of Political Intelligence* (1766), **66-8, 24, 26, 29, 33, 34, 46-49, 53, 54, 56, 58, 66, 76-79, 86, 93, 97, 98, 101, 102, 107, 117, 123, 127, 132**
Gibbons, Thomas (1720-85). Dissenting minister, writer of poems and hymns, and miscellaneous works; prayed for suppression of the "Rebellion."
    "An Hymn for the Fast, February 8, 1782," **82-152**.
Gillray, James (1757-1815). Caricaturist, his most famous and characteristic work appeared at the time of the French Revolution.
    *The American Rattlesnake*, **82-409**
    *The Minister In. The Minister Out*, **82-418**
    *The State Tinkers*, **80-430**
*The Gladiators: An Heroic Epistle* (1780), **80-16**
Goldsmith, Oliver (1728-74). Man-of-letters: poet, playwright, essayist, and novelist.
    *The Deserted Village. A Poem* (1770), **70-4, 72-5**
    "On the Taking of Quebec," **59-17**
    *Retaliation* (1774), **74-98, 74-A**
    *The Traveller, or A Prospect of Society. A Poem* (1764), **64-4, 72-5**
    **About**: **85-25**
        *The Thistle* **73-A**
        *Deserted Village*, **76-12**
        emigration from Auburn, **76-327**
        influence on Coombe's poem, **83-8**
Gough, James (1712-80). Irish clergyman; poet and religious author.
    *Britannia: A Poem. With Historical Notes* (1767), **67-3**
Gray, Thomas (1716-71). Poet, friend of Horace Walpole.
    "Lines . . . upon Mr. Fox's Father Retiring," **84-102**
    *Ode Performed in the Senate-House at Cambridge, July 1, 1769* (1769), **69-A, 69-135**

"When sly Jemmy Twitcher had smugg'd up his face," 77-325
**About:** 84-10
　imitation, 80-28
　parodies, 69-66, 136, 84-102
**See also:** Imitations of Gray's *Elegy*, and *The Bard*; and Parodies of Gray's *Elegy*, *Installation Ode*, *Ode on Death of a Favourite Cat*, "Lines . . . upon [Henry Fox]" all in Part III of Index.

Green, Henry. Purser of the warship "Ramillies." Author of a popular patriotic naval song.
　"The Wooden Naval Walls of England," 73-37, 80-155, 82-403
　**About:** 73-69

Greene, Edward Burnaby (d. 1788). Poet, satirist, translator, essayist.
　*The Conciliation: A Poem* (1778), 78-17
　*Corsica. An Ode* (1768), 68-11, 12
　*The Laureat. A Poem* (1765), 65-4
　"Liberty" (1769), 69-6
　"Monumental Inscription" [on Pitt] (1779) and "Sonnet, Addressed to . . . Keppel" (1779), 79-15
　*Ode, Inscribed to Leonard Smelt, Esq.* (1780), 80-17
　*Poetical Essays* (1771), 66-9, 69-6, 71-2
　*The Politician. A Poem* (1766), 66-9
　*The Prophecy of Andree. An Ode* (1782), 82-11
　*The Scourge. A Satire* (1765), 65-5
　*The Tower: A Poetical Epistle inscribed to John Wilkes, Esq.;* (1763), 63-6

Gregory, ____. Poet, clergyman from Liverpool who objected to slavery in the United States.
　"American Eclogues. Eclogue 1," 83-37
　"American Eclogues. Eclogue 2," 84-22

Griffith, Amyas. Officer in the Irish Fencibles; song writer.
　"A New Song on the Association of Ireland," 80-156.

Griffith, Richard (d. 1788?). Irish writer (?)
　"Crown'd with Laurels see the Brave," 64-41

*The Guardians, A Poem* (1779), 79-16

Hall, John S. (1739-97). Historical engraver.
　*A Game of Skittles*, 70-244 (a print)

Hall, Thomas. A Newspaper correspondent.
　"To the Memory of Lord Chatham," 78-229

Hastings, Thomas (1740?-1801). Pamphleteer; volunteer laureat of the royal family; itinerant bookseller.
　"The Coronation," 76-170
　"Cox-Heath Camp. A New Song," 78-231
　"Irregular Ode on the Birth-Day of his Majesty," 77-146
　"Liberty. A Poem. Inscribed to the People of England," 80-108
　"A New Song," 78-232
　"Ode for the Birth-Day of the Duke of Gloucester," 76-173
　"Ode for the Birth-Day of George, Prince of Wales," 76-172
　"Ode for the Birth-Day of His Majesty," 76-171
　"Ode for the Birth-Day of the Prince of Wales," 77-147, 79-207, 82-156
　"Ode on the Birthday of the Prince of Wales," 73-40, 85-31
　"On the Birth-Day of her Majesty," 76-174
　"On his Majesty's Coronation Day, September 22, 1775," 75-126
　*The Tears of Britannia On the Death of William Earl of Chatham* (1778),

**78**-18
Hatchway, John. Scottish newspaper poet.
    "On the Times," **81**-87
Havard, William (1710-78). Actor, dramatist, occasional poet.
    "A Coronation Ode," **61**-7
Hayley, William (1745-1820). Popular poet; friend and biographer of Cowper; associated with Blake for a few years.
    *Epistle to Admiral Keppel* (1779), **79**-17
    *Essay on Epic Poetry* (1785), **85**-40
    *Ode to a Friend, On Our Leaving . . . South Carolina . . . June 1780* (1783), **83**-16
    *Ode to Mr. Wright of Derby* (1783), **83**-17, **85**-5
    *Poems and Plays* (1785), **85**-5
    "Sonnet to Mrs. Hayley, On Her Voyage to America," **84**-6, **85**-5
    "To Miss Seward. Impromptu" (1781), **81**-14, 88
    **About:** **80**-110, **83**-28, **85**-25, 40
        "Epistle to . . . Hayley," **81**-A
Hazard, Joseph. A young poet of Lincoln College, Oxford.
    *The Conquest of Quebec. A Poem* (1769), **69**-7
Heart(s) of Oak. A popular patriotic lyric, first sung on the stage in 1759; the music was adapted to a variety of lyrics, English and American. See David Garrick, William Boyce.
    **60**-16, **63**-73, 76, 140, 143, **66**-108, **68**-85, 95, **69**-203, **70**-192, **74**-20, **75**-242, **76**-46, **78**-212, **78**-231, **79**-82, 238, **80**-224
Hedge, Simon. (pseud.)
    *The Poor Man's Prayer. Addressed to the Earl of Chatham* (1766), **66**-12, **72**-5
Henvill, Philip. Opposed the American War and the blundering North ministry.
    *A Poem on the American War* (1778), **78**-19
*An Heroic Congratulation, Addressed to Augustus Keppel* (1779), **79**-18
*Heroic Epistle From Hamet the Moor* (1780), **80**-18
*An Heroic Epistle From Omiah to the Queen of Otaheite* (1775), **75**-10.
    **About Omiah:** **76**-231
*An Heroic Epistle to Lord Viscount Sackville* (1783), **83**-18
Hill, Richard (1733-1808). MP, 1780-1806. Voted against the North ministry, December 1781-March 1782; and for Shelburne's peace terms, February 1783.
    "Lines . . . On the Coalition between Lord North and Mr. Fox," **83**-137
    **About:** **83**-148, **84**-79
Hollway, James. An establishment poet.
    *Merit. A Poem Inscribed to his Grace the Duke of Grafton* (1768), **68**-13
Hopkinson, Francis (1737-91). American poet and pamphleteer; lawyer and member of Continental Congress; signer of Declaration of Independence.
    "The Battle of the Kegs," **78**-236
Hopkinson, Thomas. Young American poet, graduate of the College of Philadelphia (later the University of Pennsylvania).
    "An Exercise, containing a Dialogue, and two Odes," (May 20, 1766), **66**-64
Horace (65-8 B.C). Quintus Horatius Flaccus, ancient Roman poet.
    "Lines taken from Horace applicable to the Present Times," **78**-237
    **See:** Imitations of Horace, Part III of Index.
Howard, Frederick, 5th Earl of Carlisle (1748-1825). House of Lords, 1770-. Friend of C. J. Fox; headed the Peace Commission to America, 1778.
    "Verses, Composed by Lord Carlisle . . . on leaving Eton," **73**-42
    **See:** Index, Part II, for entries about Lord Carlisle.

Howard, Gorges Edmond (1715-86). An Irish miscellaneous writer, solicitor, and occasional versifier.
"Wrote Extempore . . . on . . . Ireland's Late Restor'd Rights," **82-407**
Howard, Middleton. Young poet of Wadham College, Oxford; won the Lichfield prize for the best poem on Wolfe's conquest of Quebec.
*The Conquest of Quebec. A Poem* (1768), **68-14**
Howard, Robert (1626-98). Poet and playwright in reign of Charles II. (The play assigned to him was probably written by his contemporary Nathaniel Lee.)
*Almeyda, or the Rival Queens*, **75-131**
Huddesford, George (1749-1809). Satirical poet; fellow at Oxford; clergyman from the year 1803.
*Warley: A Satire* (1778), **78-20**
**About**: **78-496, 531**
Hughes, Benjamin. Possible author of the verse epistle recommending topics for Junius' satire.
*An Epistle to Junius* (1774), **74-7**
*The Humours of the Times* (1771), **64-73**, **66-2**, 21, 33, 106, 122, **67-4**, **68-37**, 44, 61, 115
Humphreys, David (1752-1818). American poet, miscellaneous writer, soldier and statesman; aide-de-camp to Gen. Washington.
*A Poem Addressed to the Armies of the United States of America* (1785), **85-6**
**About**: **85-10**
Hurd, Richard (1720-1808). Clergyman and author; archdeacon of Gloucester, 1767-74; preceptor to Prince of Wales, 1776, and favorite of George III; bishop of Coventry and Lichfield, 1775-81, and of Worcester, 1781-1808.
*Discord. A Satire* (1773), **73-6**
**About**: **76-384**
Hurn, William (1754-1829). Clergyman and poet.
*The Blessings of Peace, And the Guilt of War. A Lyric Poem* (1784), **84-7**
*Independence: A Poem, In Hudibrastic Verse* (1783), **83-19**
*The Indian Scalp, Or Canadian Tale* (1778), **78-21**
**See**: John Reynolds
Inglis, John (d. 1786). Scottish poet; opposed the Americans and their British friends.
*The Patriots; or, An Evening Prospect on the Atlantic* (1777), **77-13**
Ireland, John (d. 1808). Poet; biographer of Hogarth.
*The Emigrant. A Poem* (1785), **85-7**
Jacobs, _____. One of King George's chaplains.
"An Ode. In Honour of his Majesty's Birth-Day," **80-240**
*Jamaica, A Poem, In Three Parts . . . Written . . . in the Year MDCCLXXVI* (1777), **77-14**
Jenyns, Soame (1704-87). MP, 1742-80; miscellaneous writer and poet.
"America. Addressed to the Rev. Dean Tucker," **76-190**
"On Reading a Poem called Truth in Rhime," **63-99**
**See**: Part II of Index for entries about Jenyns.
Jephson, Robert (1736-1803). Irish poet and dramatist.
*An Heroic Epistle to a Great Orator* (1775), **75-11**
*Braganza* (1775), **78-259**
Jingle, Bob. (pseud.)
*The Association, &c. of the Delegates of the Colonies* (1774), **74-8**
*John and Susan; or, The Intermeddler Rewarded* (1778), **78-22**

Johnson, Samuel (1709-84). Of London and Lichfield; Tory establishment author who defended North's ministry regarding the causes of the American War.
>"An Apology for Our Present Situation," **80**-177
>"*Marmor Norfolciense*: An Ancient Prophetical Inscription," **82**-173
>"Present State of Great Britain," **73**-47
>**About**: **65**-4, **65**-5, 10, **71**-5, 91, **73**-7, 47, 103, **74**-9, **75**-21, 29, 55, 61, 107, 114, 129, 178, 183, 184, 239, 282, **76**-17, 18, 73, 194, 226, 298, 337, **77**-1, 72, 183, **78**-10, 11, 16, 25, 27, 43, 44, 324, 498, 557, **79**-24, 25, 35, **80**-7, 10, 18, 40, 393, **82**-3, 9, 12, 401
>>and J. Wesley, **77**-212
>>and John Scott, **82**-23
>>character, **78**-82
>>death, December 13, 1784, **84**-64
>>*The False Alarm* vs Wilkes, **70**-6, 43
>>Ireland and the lesson of America, **80**-406
>>Johnson's Toryism, **77**-18
>>Johnson's Tory ideology, **84**-164
>>one of Johnson's satires applied to North, **82**-173
>>orthodox Tory, **77**-25
>>personal satire of, **83**-24
>>*Taxation No Tyranny*, **75**-132, 257, **76**-32, 209
>>*The Thistle*, **73**-A
>>Tory bias in *Lives of the Poets*, **81**-111

Johnson, Samuel. Of Shrewsbury, Shropshire.
>"To Miss Seward, on her Monody on Major Andre," **81**-227

Johnson, Walter. A journal poet.
>"On the Peace," **63**-68

*John the Painter's Ghost* (1777), **77**-15.
>**See**: James Aitken, in Part II of Index.

Jones, John. A journal contributor.
>"Whilst some on Pleasure's flow'ry lap reclin'd," **70**-92

Junius (fl. 1769-72). (pseud.) Noted for his prose attacking the Duke of Grafton and his ministry (because of their policies on taxation of the American colonies) and defending the cause of Wilkes.
>"Epitaph for the Monument of General Wolfe," **72**-39
>*Political Poems: A Compilation* (1772), **72**-5
>**See**: Part II of Index for entries about Junius.

*Justice A Poem* (1774), **74**-9

Kenrick, William (1725?-79). Poet, playwright, hack writer; wrote for the *Monthly Review*, 1759-66; edited the *London Review*, 1775-79.
>"An Epistle to Mr. Wilkes, On the Confirmation . . .," **68**-16, **69**-105
>"The Lion in the Toils. A Political Fable," **68**-16, 63
>"The Loaded Ass; or Public Credit. A Political Fable," **68**-15
>"Pitt and Proteus," **67**-26
>*Poems, Ludicrous, Satirical and Moral* (1768, 1770), **66**-66; **67**-26, **68**-15, 63, **69**-105, 106
>"The Political Magnet," **66**-66
>"The Political Scapegoat," **68**-16, **69**-106
>"Verses to a Gentleman, who desired the Author to write Politics," **65**-66

*Keppel For Ever!* (1779), **79**-19

*The Keppeliad; or, Injur'd Virtue Triumphant* (1779), **79**-20

Ketch, John. (pseud.) The real Ketch was the English executioner and public hangman who died in 1686.

"The Infallible Receipt, For the Cure of Court Corruption," **70-A**
Kingsley, _____. A Wilkesite partisan.
    "An Elegy on the Much Lamented Death of Anti-Sejanus," **66-40**
*Knights-Hill Farm. The Statesman's Retreat, A Poem* (1784), **84-8**
*The Lamentation of Britannia for the Two-and-Twenty Months Imprisonment of John Wilkes* (1768), **68-17**
Langhorne, John (1735-79). Clergyman, poet and miscellaneous author; Justice of the Peace, Somerset; also contributed to the *Monthly Review*.
    *The Country Justice* [Part III] (1777), **77-16**
Latin poems and translations from the Latin, **76-29, 77-102, 79-306, 80-43, 81-84, 180, 240, 82-24, 71, 361, 83-2, 116**
    America praises French King Louis, **83-133**
    Cowper, **82-68**
    on Corsica, **73-20**
    "Survey . . .," **62-A**
    translation [of **79-507**], **79-189**
    translation of Cowper's Latin poem [**80-A**], **80-53, 383**
    translation of Latin satire on North, **81-152**
    **See also** in Part III of Index: Imitation of Horace, Juvenal, Martial, Persius, and Virgil.
Latter, Mary (1725-77). Provincial poet from Reading.
    *Liberty and Interest. A Burlesque Poem on the Present Times* (1764), **64-5**
Lewis, _____. "Corrector of the Press," editor of the Dublin *Freeman's Journal*.
    "1770; or, A View of Ireland," **70-186**
    "The Spirit of Popery Displayed," **74-175**
    "The Voice of Ireland," **73-49**
    **About:** **70-210**
Lewis, R. A newspaper correspondent "in the West of England."
    "A New Loyal Song," **63-79**.
*Liberty and Patriotism: A Miscellaneous Ode* (1778), **78-23**
*Liberty: A Poem. To Which is Added the Modern Politician* (1776), **76-15**
*Liberty Deposed, or The Western Election: A Satirical Poem* (1768), **68-18**
Lloyd, Evan (1734-76). Welsh poet, friend of Charles Churchill and Wilkes.
    "On Mr. Churchill's Death," **65-70**
Lockman, John (1698-1771). Poet, miscellaneous writer; secretary to the British Herring Fishery and to Lord George Townshend, Viceroy of Ireland.
    "Albion to Cynthia. An Ode." **67-28**
    "Ode on the Administration of Ireland, under . . . Townshend," **68-67**
    "An Ode: On the Birth-Day of [the] Prince of Wales." **60-20**
    "A Sixth Loyal Song" [on Admiral Hawke's Victory], **60-21**
    "A Song on the taking of Montreal by Gen. Amherst," **60-22**
    "To the Honourable Gen. Townshend," **60-23**
    *To The Honourable General Townshend, on his Arrival from Quebec* (1759), **59-4**
    "Verses: Suggested by the two grand National Subscriptions . . . in 1759," **60-49**
Lofft, Capel (1751-1824). Miscellaneous writer, editor of the *European Magazine*; agitated against American War and slave trade; admirer of Charles Fox and an advocate of reform.
    "A Monody. In Imitation of Aristotle's Ode to Virtue," **82-184**
    "Runnymede," **82-185**
    **About:** **84-123** (Wilkes and Cartwright)

*Lord Chatham's Prophecy. An Ode; Addressed to . . . General Gage* (1776), **76-16**
   (Attributed to William Mason)
Lovibond, Edward (1724-75). Poet and essayist.
   "To Laura. On Politics," in *Poems on Several Occasions* (1785), **65-6, 85-8**
Low, T. A printseller.
   *The Engagement between D'Orvilliers and Keppel*, **80-422** (a print)
Lucas, Henry (fl. 1775-1800). Author of complimentary occasional verse.
   *Poems to her Majesty [Queen Charlotte]* (1779), "The Oblation, A Lyric Poem," **79-21**
   *The Tears of Alnwick; A Pastoral Elegy in Memory of . . . Elizabeth, Dutchess of Northumberland* (1777), **77-17**
   *A Visit from the Shades; or Earl Chatham's Adieu to his Friend Lord Cam[b]den* (1778), **78-24**
Lyttelton, Thomas (1744-79). 6th Baronet; MP, 1768-69; House of Lords, 1773-79; son of George Lyttelton of Hagley.
   "Elegy on Lord Chatham," **79-262**
   "The State of England. In the Year 2199," in *Poems, By a Young Nobleman* (1780), **80-19**
      **About**: **73-104, 75-10, 20, 79-11, 44**
Macaulay, Catharine (1731-91). Whig heroine, libertarian and republican; sister of John Sawbridge, City Whig politician.
   "An Ode," **77-139**
   **See**: Part II of Index for entries about Macaulay.
Macaulay, John (fl. 1780-1801). A patriotic poet.
   *Unanimity. A Poem* (1780), **80-20**
Macgreggor, Malcolm. Pseudonym of William Mason, the poet and satirist.
Mallet, David (1705?-65). Scottish poet, dramatist, and miscellaneous author; secretary to Frederick, Prince of Wales, father of George III.
   *Truth in Rhyme* (1761), **61-3**
   "William and Margaret, Ballad of," **66-14**
      **About**: **63-22, 65-4, 5, 10, 73-7; 77-15**
         answer to *Truth in Rhyme*, **63-99**
         with Thomson and *Masque of Alfred*, **78-522**
Marjoribanks, John. Scottish soldier, poet, son of Major John Marjoribanks, the hero of the Battle of Eutaw Springs, S.C., September 9, 1781.
   "Andre to Washington" (October 1784), **84-9**
   "The Sweets of Sleep," **84-9**
   "Thoughts on Leaving Britain," **84-9**
   "To Mr. _____," **84-9**
   "To the Memory of Major Marjoribanks," **82-186, 84-9**
   *Trifles in Verse. By a Young Soldier* (1784), **84-9**
Mark'em, Martha. (pseud.) Author of a series of newspaper poems, "Martha Mark'em to Kitty Curious." **See**: Women as Authors.
Martin, Alexander (1740-1807). Deputy King's attorney, 1766; judge, 1774-5; and Governor of North Carolina, 1782. Fought against Loyalists in the South during the American War.
   *America: A poem* (1766, 1769), **66-67**
Marvel, Andrew. (pseud.) A newspaper poet who adopted Marvell as his persona.
   "Marvell's Prophecy," **74-109**
   "On the Death of England's Prince of Whigs," **68-82**
   "To John Wilkes, Esq. Upon his Birth-Day," **68-105**
Marvell, Andrew (1621-78). English poet and satirist and politician, MP.
   "Royal Resolutions," **79-399, 80-321**

Mason, William (1725-97). English clergyman, poet and satirist; friend of Gray and Horace Walpole.
- *An Archaeological Epistle to Jeremiah Milles* (1782), **82**-12
- "A Congratulatory Ode, addressed to Lord North," **75**-62 (possibly by Mason)
- *A Congratulatory Poem on the Late Successes of the British Arms* (1776), **76**-17, 18
- *The Dean and the Squire* (1782), **82**-13
- *An Epistle to Dr. Shebbeare: To Which Is Added An Ode to Sir Fletcher Norton* (1777), **77**-18
- *An Heroic Epistle to Sir William Chambers* (1773), **73**-7
- *An Heroic Postscript to the Public* (1774), **74**-11
- *Lord Chatham's Prophecy. An Ode* (1776), **76**-16 (attributed to Mason)
- "Ode, Addressed to the Earl of Dartmouth," **75**-166
- "Ode to Independency," in Junius's *Compilation*, **72**-5
- *Ode to Mr. Pinchbeck, Upon his Newly Invented Patent Candle-Snuffers* (1776), **76**-18, 19
- *Ode to the Honourable William Pitt* (1782), **82**-14
- *Ode to the Naval Officers of Great-Britain* (1779), **79**-22, 103
- *Ruin seize thee, ruthless King! A Pindaric Ode, Not Written by Mr. Gray* (1779), **79**-35 (possibly by Mason)
- **About**: **64**-6, **65**-4, 11, **73**-97, **76**-16, 28, **78**-7, **79**-29, 103, **81**-229, **82**-401, **83**-10, 28, 138
    - and reform, **84**-131
    - Churchill's *Independence*, **64**-A

Massie, Joseph (d. 1784). Writer on trade and finance.
- "Accounts of the Trade between London and Ireland," **74**-110

Mathison, T. A patriotic Scottish clergyman from Brechin.
- "A Sacred Ode. Occasioned by the Late Successes Attending the British Arms," **60**-25

*Matrimonial Overtures, . . . to Lord George Germaine* (1778), **78**-25

Matthews, David. American Loyalist; Mayor of New York City (1776-83); emigrated to Cape Breton, Nova Scotia.
- "A Fable, addressed to the Americans, upon their treaty with France," **78**-194

Maurice, Thomas (1754-1824). Poet and clergyman, chaplain of the 97th Regiment; oriental scholar and historian.
- "An Address to Ireland," **83**-141
- "An Epistle To Charles James Fox," **84**-104
- *Hagley. A Descriptive Poem* (1776), **76**-20
- *Ierne Rediviva. An Ode* (1782), **82**-15
- *A Monody Sacred to the Memory of Elizabeth Dutchess of Northumberland* (1777), **77**-19
- *Poems and Miscellaneous Pieces* (1779), **79**-23
- *Poems, Epistolary, Lyric, and Elegiacal* (1800), **79**-23
- "Verses Written in the Year 1774," **79**-23
- *Westminster Abbey: An Elegiac Poem* (1784), **84**-10

Mavor, William Fordyce (1758-1837). Born in Scotland, later lived in England; poet, educator, and clergyman.
- "Ode for the New Year [1783]," **83**-142

Maxwell, Archibald. A radical Whig supporter of Wilkes.
- *Political Society* (1769), **69**-13 (possible author)

Meadows, C. A newspaper correspondent begs for unity now that peace has come.

"An Irregular Ode for the Year 1784," **84-91**
*Meritorious Disobedience: An Epistle* (1779), **79-24**
Merrick, James (1720-69). An Oxford clergyman, writer of religious poetry.
"On His Majesty's Accession to the Throne," **60-27**
Mickle, William Julius (1735-88). Scottish poet and translator of Camoens' *Lusiads*, 1776; secretary to George Johnstone, 1779.
*The Prophecy of Queen Emma; An Ancient Ballad* (1782), in *Poetical Works* (1806), **82-16**
"To The Memory of Com. George Johnstone," in *Poems, And a Tragedy* (1794), **87-1**
**About**: "Epistle to Hayley," **81-A**
*The Middlesex Freeholder; or, The Triumph of Liberty* (1769), **69-8**; also "The Poetical Wish of a Middlesex Freeholder," **69-A**
*The Middlesex Petition Inversed* (1769), **69-9**
*The Milesian; or, The Injuries of Ireland* (1779), **79-25**
Milton, John (1608-74). Commonwealth poet and republican pamphleteer of the Puritan Revolution; appears in Whig Pantheon.
*Paradise Lost* (1667) and *Paradise Regained* (1671), excerpts, **76-205**
**About**: **68-7, 72-14, 74-4, 78-73, 83-9**
doctrine of government, **80-202**
Gray's *Ode*, **69-A**
*Minister of State. A Satire* (1762), **62-5**
*Momus; or, The Fall of Britain. A Poem* (1779), **79-26**
Moore, Benjamin (1748-1816). American Loyalist; President of Columbia College, New York; after the flight of Myles Cooper.
"The Spirit of Colonel Maitland to Mrs. De Lancey," **80-83**
Moore, Frank (1828-1904). Nineteenth century American author and editor.
*Diary of the American Revolution* (1860), **79-318, 437, 80-126**
*Songs and Ballads of the American Revolution* (1855), **78-194, 81-135, 84-A** (Robert Burns),
Morris, Charles (1745-1838. "Captain Morris," popular songwriter; served in America, c. 1764; a Fox partisan.
"The Banner of Freedom, A New Song," **85-33**
*A Complete Collection of Songs* (1786, 1790), **86-2, 3**
"Billy Pitt and the Farmer"
"Billy's Too Young to Drive Us"
"The Westminster Triumph"
Murphy, A. C. Establishment poet; vs rebel Americans and their allies.
"On the Queen's Birth-Day," **80-208**
Murphy, Henry. Irish poet; glorifies Rodney's role in the American War.
*The Conquest of Quebec. An Epic Poem in Eight Books* (1790), **90-1**
Murray, James (1732-82). Dissenting clergyman from Newcastle; satiric poet who opposed the American War.
*The New Maid of the Oaks: A Tragedy, As Lately Acted Near Saratoga* (1778), **78-26**
Murray, Oliver James. Tory poet critical of Wilkes.
*The Candid Inquisitor, or, Mock Patriotism Displayed* (1771), **71-3**
*The Muse in a Fright; or, Britannia's Lamentation* (1774), **74-12**
*The Muse of Britain: A Dramatic Ode to . . . William Pitt* (1785), **85-9**
*The Muse's Mirror* (1778), ed. Edward Thompson, **65-124, 66-112, 74-113, 114, 75-162, 264, 75-315, 77-74, 269, 327**
*The Muse's Pocket Companion* (1785), **77-74**
*Musical Companion; or Songster's Magazine for the Year 1777* (1777), **77-49**

Neitherside, Nicholas. (pseud.)
> *The Political Squabble; or, A Scramble for the Loaves and Fishes* (1783), **83**-20

*Neptune. A Poem. Inscribed to . . . Keppel* (1779), **79**-27

*Nereus's Prophecy: A Sea Piece, Sketched off Ushant* (1779), **79**-28

Nevill, Valentine. Of Gray's Inn; newspaper correspondent and poet.
> "On Admiral Rodney's Account of the Action with the French Fleet," **80**-211
> "On the British Fleet Rendezvousing at Spithead," **80**-212
> "On the late Animated Exertion of the New Administration," **82**-197
> "On the late gallant Defeat of the Spanish Squadron," **80**-213
> "On the Much Lamented Death of Admiral Sir Charles Hardy," **80**-214
> "To the Right Hon. William Pitt, Chancellor of the Exchequer," **82**-198

*New Foundling Hospital for Wit* (1768), **66**-2, 21, 33, 53, 98, 106, 122, **67**-4, 27, **68**-30
> (1769), **68**-44, 52, 61, 63, 115, **69**-11, 140
> (1771), **70**-112
> (1772), **70**-18
> (1786), **64**-54, **72**-14, **73**-61, 62, 86, **75**-38, 41, 61, 120, 128, 158, 166, 187, 219, 242, **76**-6, 9, 16, 56, 65, 67, 190, 211, 213, 219, 223, 307, 334, **77**-69, 74, 76, 167, 183, 292, **78**-43, 56, 142, 324, 402, 443, **79**-41, 100, 501, **82**-163, 212, 326, **83**-205

Newman, Henry Charles Christian. Vicar of Stotfold, Bedford; poet; admired the Americans.
> *The Love of our Country. A Poem* (1783), **83**-21

Nichols, T. Newspaper correspondent.
> "An Ode, Occasioned by the Loss of the Royal George," **82**-206

Nisbet, W. Young Scottish poet who wrote about the American War.
> *Poems, Chiefly Composed from Recent Events* (1780), **80**-21, 30[2]

*The Noble Cricketers: A Poetical and Familiar Epistle* (1778), **78**-A

Noyes, Robert (d. 1798). Dissenting clergyman and miscellaneous author from Canterbury.
> *Distress, A Poem* (1783), **83**-22

Nugent, Nicholas (1747?-1813?). Bart. Lieutenant, First Regiment of Foot Guards.
> *An Answer to the Tears of the Foot Guards* (1776), **76**-21

Nugent, Robert Craggs (1702-88). Earl Clare and Earl Nugent; MP, 1741-84. Irish supporter of North's ministry.
> *Verses Addressed to the Queen with a New Year's Gift of Irish Manufacture* (1775), **75**-12, 24
> **About:** **72**-1, **77**-18, **81**-208 (a Tory)

Nunnington, ____. Newspaper poet.
> "To the Right Hon. the Lord-Mayor [Crosby]," **71**-122
> **About:** **71**-115

Oakman, J. (pseud.)
> "The Frogs and King. A Fable," **71**-62
> "The Mastiff in Prison. A Fable," **69**-A
> "To the Nobility, Gentry, &c.," **68**-72

O'Bryen, Dennis (1755-1832). Irish, but settled in London; newspaper editor, pamphleteer, and playwright; critic of Shelburne during the peace debates.
> "Character of a Minister's Myrmidon, from Mr. O'Bryen's Imitation of Juvenal," **82**-59
> "Panegyric, upon Mr. Burke, extracted from one of Mr. O'Brien's poems,"

      **82**-280
An Ode, addressed to the Scotch Junto, and their American Commission (1778), **78**-27
Odell, Jonathan (1737-1818). American Loyalist, poet and satirist of the rebel leaders; Episcopal clergyman at Brunswick, New Jersey.
    *The American Times: A Satire* (1780), **80**-22
    "A Birth Day Song," **77**-186
    "The Congratulation," **79**-318
    "The Following Song was composed by a loyal Subject," **77**-129 (possibly by Odell)
    "Inscription on a Curious Chamber Stove," **77**-187
    *Liberty* (1769, 1777), **77**-188
    "Song for St. George's Day," **77**-189
*Ode on the Emancipation of Ireland* (1782), **82**-A
*Ode on the Late Change in Administration . . . to Charles J. Fox* (1783), **83**-23
*Ode on the Surrender at York-Town To . . . William Pitt* (1782), **82**-17
*An Ode to Liberty, Inscribed to the Right Hon. Thomas Harley* (1768), **68**-19
*An Ode to Lord B[ute], On the Peace* (1762), **62**-6
*An Ode to Mars* (1778), **78**-28
*An Ode to Mr. Lewis Hendrie . . . Principal Bear-Killer* (1783), **83**-24
*An Ode to Palinurus* (1770), **70**-A
*Ode to the British Empire* (1775), **75**-13
*Ode to the Earl of Chatham* (1767), **67**-4 (Horace Walpole attributes authorship to Henry Seymour [q.v.].)
*Ode to the Legislator Elect of Russia* (1766), **66**-10
*An Ode to the People of England* (1765), **65**-7
*An Ode to the People of England* (1769), **69**-10
*Ode to the Privateer-Commanders of Great Britain* (1779), **79**-29
*An Ode upon the Present Period of Time* (1769), **69**-11 (Horace Walpole attributes this poem to Henry Seymour [q.v.].)
Ogden, James (1718-1802). A Manchester author; wrote epic narratives about the Seven Years' War and the American War.
    *The British Lion Rous'd* (1762), **62**-7
    *The Contest, A Poem, In Two Parts* (1776), **76**-22
*On the Preference of Virtue to Genius. A Poetical Epistle* (1779), **79**-30
*On the Present War* (1778), **78**-29
*Oppression. A Poem. By an American* (1765), **65**-8
*The Order of St. Patrick, an Ode* (1783), **83**-A
Paine, Thomas (1737-1809). American revolutionary writer.
    "Song on Liberty Tree," **76**-276
    "The rain pours down—the city looks forlorn," **80**-294,
    **About**: 76-315, 80-A (Tomlinson, "Anacreontic Song"), **83**-38, **93**-1
*Panegyric: An Essay On Some Of The Worthiest Characters In The Kingdom* (1780), **80**-23
*Paradise Regain'd; or, The Battle of Adam and the Fox* (1780), **80**-24
*Party-Satire Satirized. A Poem* (1779), **79**-31
Parkin, Miles. "A Cumberland youth" and poet.
    *Columba, A Poetical Epistle, Heroic and Satirical* (1783), **83**-25
    "Rodney Triumphant. A New Song," **83**-26
*A Pastoral. By an Officer, Belonging to the Canadian Army* (1779), **79**-32
Patrick, J. Poet; volunteer on board the warship *Somerset* during the Quebec campaign, 1759.
    *Quebec: A Poetical Essay* (1760), **60**-6

*The Patriot. A Poem. Inscribed to the Supporters of the Bill of Rights* (1773), **73**-8
*The Patriotic Mice* (1780), **80**-25
*The Patriotic Miscellany* (1769), **69**-45, 71, 76, 78, 102, 158, 165, 182, 228
*Patriotic Perfidy, A Satire* (1779), **79**-33
*Patriotism: A Political Satire. By Cato Redivivus* (1767), **67**-5
*The Patriot Minister: A Poem* (1778), **78**-30
*The Patriot Poet, A Satire* (1764), **64**-6
*The Patriots Guide. A Poem* (1771), **71**-4
*The Patriot's Progress, . . . to John Wilkes* (1776), **76**-23
*The Patriot Vision. A Poem* (1778), **78**-31
*Paul Jones, A New Song* (1780?), **80**-26
*Peace, A Poem* (1778), **78**-32
Pearch, George. Miscellany editor and printer.
    *A Collection of Poems* (1770), **66**-16
Peart, Joseph. A solicitor; authorship is doubtful.
    *A Continuation of Hudibras . . . Written in the Time of the Unhappy Contest between Great Britain and America* (1778), **78**-33
Penrose, Thomas (1742-79). Clergyman and poet; served in the marines during the Seven Years' War.
    *Address to the Genius of Britain* (1775), **75**-14, **81**-8
    "Donnington Castle" in *Poems* (1781), **75**-15, **81**-8
    *Flights of Fancy* (1775, 1781), **75**-16, **81**-8
        "The Carousal of Odin"
        "The Helmets, A Fragment"
        "Madness"
Perry, James (1756-1821). Scottish journalist; contributed verses and essays to *General Advertiser* and *London Evening Post*; later, editor of the *Gazetteer*.
    "An Occasional Address to the Gentlemen Volunteers of Plymouth," **79**-290
Piercy, John William. A patriotic establishment poet.
    *An Epistle to . . . John Earl of Sandwich* (1780), **80**-27
Pilon, Frederick (1750-88). Irish playwright and actor.
    *The Liverpool Prize* (1779), includes Edward Thompson's song "The Hyaena," **79**-211
    "Prologue, *The Humours* of an Election," **80**-308
    Prologue to *The Invasion*, **78**-427
Pinchbeck, Christopher (c. 1710-83). Inventor, toyman; "King's Friend."
    "An Ode in Honour of her Majesty's Birth-Day," **82**-295
Pindar, Peter. (pseud.) **See**: John Wolcot.
*A Pindaric Ode, Inscribed to the Right Honourable Lord North* (1781), **81**-9
Pinkerton, John (1758-1826). Scottish antiquary, historian, miscellaneous writer and poet.
    "Melody V. On the Military Preparations 1779," in *Rimes* (1781), **81**-10
*Plain Truth, In Plain English. A Satire* (1768), **68**-20
*The Plaints of Runny-Mead: A Poem* (1775), **75**-17
*A Poem Humbly Inscribed to John Wilkes* (1769), **69**-12
*A Poem Occasioned by the Late Calamities of England* (1780), **80**-28
*Poems, Chiefly by Gentlemen of Devonshire and Cornwall* (1792), **77**-28, **81**-12.
    **See**: Whitaker, **77**-28, **78**-423
*Poems Fit For A Bishop* (1780), **80**-29
*Poems On the Several Successes in America* (1780), **80**-30
*Poems on Various Subjects* (1780), **76**-36 (and p. 1029, a cross reference)
*Poems Serious and Sarcastical, Songs Loyal and Humourous. By A Briton in*

New-York (1779), **78-211**
*A Poetical Address to Almighty God by George III* (1776), **76-24**
*A Poetical Epistle, Addressed to William, Earl of Mansfield* (1778), **78-34**
*A Poetical Epistle To The Reverend Dr. Robertson* (1781), **81-11**
*A Poetical Epistle to the Right Hon. Lord Mansfield* (1768), **68-21**
*Poetical Excursions in the Isle of Wight* (1777), **77-20**
*The Poetical Retrospect; or The Year 1769* (1770), **70-5**
*The Poetical Review, A Poem. Being a Satirical Display* (1780?), **80-31**
*Political Epistles on Various Subjects of the Present Times* (1766), **66-11**
*The Political Looking-Glass* (1775), **75-18**
*The Political Remembrancer. A Poem. In Hudibrastic Verse.* (1784), **84-11**
*The Political Society: A Poetical Essay* (1769), **69-13** (Possible author, Archibald Maxwell)
Polwhele, Richard (1760-1838). Cornish poet and clergyman; historian and miscellaneous writer.
    "Four Odes Written at Different Periods on Public Occasions, Ode II," **81-12**
    "Ode I," **82-18**
    *Poems, Chiefly by Gentlemen of Devonshire and Cornwall* (1792), **81-12, 18, 92-2**
    *The Spirit of Frazer, To General Burgoyne* (1778), **78-35**
*The Poor Man's Prayer. Addressed to the Earl of Chatham* (1766), **66-12**
Pottinger, Israel. Poet and author of farces.
    *The Duenna: A Comic Opera* (1776), **76-25, 26, 78-346**
    *The General Fast; A Lyric Ode* (1776), **76-27**
    *Stanzas Sacred to Liberty* (1769), **69-14**
Preston, William (1753-1807). Irish poet and dramatist.
    *The Age of Loyalty: An Historical Panegyric* (1777), **77-21**
    *The Court Mirrors; or, The Age of Loyalty* (1777), **77-22**
*Pride. A Poem. Inscribed to John Wilkes* (1766), **66-A**
Prime, Benjamin Young (1733-91). Colonial American poet; physician in New York.
    *The Patriot Muse; or Poems on Some of the Principal Events of the Late War* (1764), **64-7** (including the following poems:)
        "An Acrostic [William Pitt]," **59-5**
        "Britain's Glory, or Gallic Pride Humbled on the Taking of Quebec, 1759," **59-6**
        "The Lamentation of Lewis XV . . . 1760," **60-7**
        "Loyal Tears Shed over Royal Dust, on the Death of George II," **60-8**
        "An Ode on the Surrender of Louisbourg, July 27, 1758," **58-1**
        "On General Braddock's Defeat, A.D. 1755," **55-2**
        "On the Peace of Fountainbleau," **62-8**
        "On the Surrender of Fort William-Henry, A.D. 1757," **57-2**
        "On the Surrender of the Havannah, A. D. 1762," **62-9**
        "To General Amherst Passing through Long Island," **58-2**
        "The Unfortunate Hero. An Ode to Viscount George Augustus Howe," **58-3**
*Private Thoughts on Public Affairs* (1780), **80-32**
*The Progress of Politics; or A Key to Prior's Alma* (1784), **84-12**
*The Prophecy: A Poem. Addressed to Mr. Burke* (1780), **80-33**
*Pro-Pinchbeck's Answer to the Ode from the Author* [William Mason], **76-28**
*The Prospect of Liberty* (1767), **67-6**
*The Prospect; or, Re-Union of Britain and America* (1785), **85-10**
*Public Spirit, An Essay* (1777), **77-23**
*Public Spirit: An Ode* (1773), **73-9**

Puddicombe, John Newell. Poet and clergyman.
- *Albion Triumphant; or, Admiral Rodney's Victory over the French Fleet* (1782), **82-19**
- *The British Hero in Captivity. A Poem* (1782), **82-20**
- *An Irregular Ode, Addressed to . . . William Pitt* (1784), **84-13**
- "Ode to the Right Hon. William Pitt," **84-A**
- "The Tears of Britain; or, An Elegy on the Loss of the Royal George," **82-305**
- "Verses on his Majesty's Birth-Day," **73-A**

Pugh, David. (?)
- *A Poem on the Approaching Peace* (1783), **83-27**

Pullein, Samuel (fl. 1758). Irish poet, clergyman, and silkworm specialist.
- "On the Taking of Louisburgh," **58-10**

Pye, Henry James (1745-1813). MP, 1784-90; poet laureat, 1790 to his death.
- *Carmen Seculare for the Year 1800* (1800), **1800-1**
- *The Progress of Refinement* (1783), **83-28**

*Pynsent. A Poem* (1766), **66-13**

*Pynsent's Ghost* (1766), **66-14**

Querno, Camillo. Poet-Laureat to the Congress. See Jonathan Odell, **80-22**

*Rebellion and Opposition; or, The American War* (1780), **80-34**

*Rebellion. A Poem* (1775), **75-19**

*Reflections on Government, With Respect to America* (1776), **76-29**

*Regatta. A Poem. Dedicated to . . . Thomas Lord Lyttelton* (1775), **75-20**

*Regular Ode Addressed to . . . William Pitt* (1784), **84-14**

*The Repository: A Select Collection of Fugitive Pieces* (1783), **82-12**

*The Rescue. Inscribed to . . . Charles James Fox* (1783), **83-29**

*The Resurrection of Liberty; or Advice to the Colonists* (1774), **74-13**

Revere, Paul (1735-1818). American patriot, silversmith, leader of Boston "mechanics," cartoonist, and member of the Boston Tea Party.
- "The Fruits of Arbitrary Power," **70-243** (British print of Boston Massacre)

*A Review of the Poem Intitled "The Patricians"* (1773), **73-10**

*A Review of the Poem Intitled "The Senators," Parts I and II* (1772), **72-6, 72-7**

Reynolds, John (1758-?). Brother of Frederick Reynolds, dramatist; young poet admonishes the British for using savage Indians in the American War.
- *The Indian Scalp; or Canadian Tale* (1778), **78-21**

*A Rhodomontade of Politics* (1784), **84-15**

Rice, Woodford. Soldier, fought in Seven Years' War and American War.
- *The Rutland Volunteer Influenza'd* (1783), **83-30**

Richardson, William (1743-1814). Scottish professor and poet; wrote critical essays on Shakespeare's characters.
- *Corsica: A Poetical Address* (1769), **69-15, 16**
- "Corsica. Written at St. Petersburgh, 1768," (1774), **69-16, 74-14**
- *Poems, Chiefly Rural* (1774, 1781), **74-14**

Rivington, James (1724-1802). Colonial and Loyalist publisher in New York City.
- "Rivington's Reflections," **83-235**
- **About:** **78-425, 79-318, 437, 527, 80-2, 81-164, 82-156**

Robertson, Thomas. Poet and "news-writer" for the *Morning Chronicle*.
- "To the Right Honourable Lord Shelburne," **82-315**

Robinson, Mary M. (1758-1800). Actress, poet and novelist; Della Cruscan; also known as "Perdita," mistress of Prince of Wales and, later, of Col. Tarleton.
- *Elegiac Verses to a Young Lady, On the Death of her Brother . . . at*

*Boston* (1776), **76**-30
"Ode to Valour. Inscribed to Colonal Banastre Tarleton," in *Poems by Mrs. M. Robinson* (1791), **82**-21
   **About**: **80**-35 (mistress of Prince of Wales)
Rogers, Robert (1731-95). Colonial American frontier soldier, commanded Rogers' Rangers during Seven Years' War and Queen's Rangers in American War.
   *Ponteach; or, The Savages of America* (1766), **66**-15
Rowe, Nicholas (1674-1718). Early 18th century poet and dramatist.
   *The Fair Penitent* (1703), **79**-397 (extracts)
Rowling, R. R. A newspaper poet who supported "Wilkes and Liberty."
   "An Address, To the Gentry, Clergy and Freeholders of Kent," **69**-192
   "Nell of Kent," **69**-193
*The Royal Favourite* (1762), **62**-10
*Royal Perseverance. A Poem* (1778), **78**-36
*Ruin seize thee, ruthless King! A Pindaric Ode* (1779), **79**-35
Rushton, Edward (1756-1814). A blind Liverpool bookseller and poet.
   "American Independency," in *Poems and Other Writings* (1824), **83**-31
   *The Dismember'd Empire. A Poem* (1782), **82**-22
   "An Irregular Ode," **81**-193
   *Party Dissected; or, Plain Truth* (1770), **70**-7
   "To the People of England," **82**-320
Ryley, J. C. A newspaper correspondent; Wilkes partisan.
   "An Acrostic [Wilkes.]," **68**-92
*Salmagundi: A Miscellaneous Combination of Original Poetry* (1793), **78**-275
Sargent, Winthrop (1825-70). American editor and historian of the 19th century.
   *The Life and Career of Major André* (1902), **82**-212
   *The Loyal Verses of Joseph Stansbury and Doctor Jonathan Odell* (1860), **77**-186, 187, **80**-339, **82**-156
*Satire for the King's Birth-Day. By No Poet-Laureate* (1779), **79**-36
*A Satire on the Present Times* (1780), **80**-35
*Satires on the Times in Two Parts* (1763), **63**-7
*Satirical Ballads, &c. On the Times* (1781), **81**-13
*The School for Satire* (1802), **82**-12
Scott, John (1730-83). A Quaker poet and essayist from Amwell.
   "On Reading Mrs. Macaulay's History of England" (1766), **66**-16, **82**-23
   *Poetical Works* (1782), **82**-23
      "On Hearing the Drum"
      "Privateering"
   "Sonnet. To Britannia" (1766), **66**-16, **82**-23
Scottish Poets. Robert Alves, Hugo Arnot, Michael Bruce, Robert Burns, Robert Colvill, Robert Couper, Hugh Dalrymple, Robert Fergusson, John Inglis, John Macaulay (?), David Mallet, John Marjoribanks, T. Mathison, William Fordyce Mavor, William Julius Mickle, W. Nisbet, James Perry, John Pinkerton, William Richardson, John Tait, W. Woods.
*Sedition; A Poem* (1770), **70**-8
*The Seducers . . . Dedicated to . . . The Earl of Mansfield* (1778), **78**-38
*Seduction: The Spirit of the Times; or Petitions Unmasked* (1780), **80**-36
*The Se'er; or, The American Prophecy* (1779), **79**-37
Seward, Anna (1747-1809). Poet from Lichfield; friend of John André.
   "The Celebrated Old Ballad of the Battle of La Hogue," **82**-327
   *Monody on Major André* (1781), **81**-14
   "Verses . . . inviting Stella to Tea on the Public Fast-Day, February 1782," **82**-328

>    **About:** **83**-10, 28, 33, 244, 274, **85**-25, 40
>    "Epistle to Hayley," **81**-A
>    Hayley's poem on Seward and André, **81**-14, 88
>    S. Johnson's poem on Seward and André, **81**-227

Seymour, Henry (1729-1807). MP, 1763-80. Country-gentleman, half-brother of John Montagu, Earl of Sandwich.
>    *Ode to the Earl of Chatham* (1767), **67**-4
>    *Ode Upon the Present Period of Time* (1769), **69**-11

Shakespeare, William (1564-1616). Poet, playwright, and actor.
>    Characters and adaptations, **78**-82, 83, 404, 447, 448, 449, **82**-192
>    *Cymbeline* (extract), **76**-313
>    **About:** **80**-28 (imitation). See Part III, Parody on (Shakespeare's plays).

Sharp, William, Jr. (d. 1794). Of the Isle of Wight; a supporter of "Wilkes and Liberty."
>    *The Livery's Remonstrance* (1770), **70**-9
>    "To John Wilkes, Esq.; A Sonnet," **69**-227
>    "To the Right Honourable the Lord Mayor," **71**-99
>    *Verses to the Right Honourable John Wilkes, Lord Mayor* (1775), **75**-21

Shaw, Cuthbert (1738-71). Poet, satirist, hack writer.
>    "Answer to the Verses entitled, Enquiry . . ." (January 4, 1766), **66**-104
>    *Corruption. A Satire. Inscribed to Richard Grenville, Earl Temple* (1768), **68**-22
>    *The Race. By Mercurius Spur, Esq.* (1765), **65**-9, 10

Shebbeare, John (1709-88). "Venal" Tory Jacobite hack writer; political pamphleteer.
>    "That Cuckoo Tone," **77**-276 (adapted from Butler's *Hudibras*)
>    **About:** See Shebbeare in Part II of Index.

Sheridan, Richard Brinsley (1751-1816). MP, 1780-1812. Playwright, lyricist, theatre manager; supporter of Fox and Burke.
>    "Songs," from *Harlequin Fortunatus* ("Chearly my hearts, of courage true," and "When 'tis night, and the mid-watch is come"), **80**-326.
>    **About:** See Sheridan in Part II of Index.

Sherratt, Thomas. Newspaper correspondent who supported the Corsicans.
>    "On Seeing the Picture of Pascal Paoli," **69**-198

*The Sick Queen and Physicians, A Poetical Tale* (1784), **84**-16
*The Siege of Quebec* (1769), **69**-17
*Six Odes, Presented to . . . Mrs. Catharine Macaulay* (1777), **77**-24
*The Sixteenth Ode of the Third Book of Horace Imitated. With a Dedication to Lord North* (1777), **77**-25
*A Sketch of the Times. A Satire* (1780), **80**-37
*A Sketch of the Times, for A.D. 1769* (1771), **69**-18 (possibly by Sir Edward Walpole)
>    **See also:** **69**-199 (a shorter version)

Smith, John Stafford (1750-1836). Supposed composer of music for Ralph Tomlinson's "Anacreon in Heaven."
>    **See:** Ralph Tomlinson, **78**-A, **80**-A, **83**-238 (the melody of the American national anthem)

Smith, William (1727-1803). American Episcopal clergyman and provost of the College of Philadelphia; chaplain of the Continental Congress until he opposed independence and was stigmatized as a Loyalist.
>    "A Dialogue. &c. spoken at the Commencement in . . . Philadelphia," **70**-190
>    **About:** *Sermon on the Present Situation of American Affairs* (1775), **76**-52

Soldier and Sailor Poets and Poetry, 60-6, 66-15, 73-37, 75-8, 76-21, 78-2, 51, 171(?), **79**-32, 263, 296, 315, 447, 504, **80**-2, 89, 119, 322, 391, **81**-12, 198, 249, **82**-9, 186, 213, 246, 367, **83**-139, 189, 267, **84**-3, 9, 67, 181
    enough of war!, **79**-463
    Imitation . . .", **83**-A
    **See also**: John André, John Marjoribanks, and Edward Thompson.
*The South Wiltshire Petitioners, A Mock Heroic Poem* (1776), **76**-31
*Speech to the Sun of the Political Hemisphere* (1784), **84**-17
Spence, Joseph (1699-1768). Clergyman, literary historian, critic, antiquary, and poet.
    "On the Death of King George II. And Inauguration of George III," **60**-43
*Spirit and Unanimity, A Poem* (1779), **79**-38
Stansbury, Joseph (1742-1809). Poet, song writer; Loyalist secret agent involved in the treason of Benedict Arnold.
    "Pasquinades on a certain General, and on a certain Admiral," **80**-339
*The State Mountebank; or, Duke or no Duke* (1780), **80**-38
*State Necessity Not Considered as a Question of Law. A Political Sketch* (1767), **67**-7
Steele, Anne (1717-78). Baptist hymn writer; used the pen-name of Theodosia.
    "On a Day of Prayer for Success in War," in *Miscellaneous Pieces in Verse and Prose* (1780), **80**-39
Stevens, George Alexander (1710-84). Popular songwriter, strolling player, humorist and wit; author of *A Lecture upon Heads* (1764).
    "A Christmas Carroll, Called Liberty-Hall," **70**-196
    "The Heads: Or the Year 1776," **76**-175 (based on Stevens' satiric *Lecture upon Heads* and adapted to the year 1776)
    "Politics," **72**-89
    *Songs, Comic, Satyrical* (1772), **70**-196, **72**-89
    **About**: **84**-58, 137 (death)
Stevenson, John Hall (1718-85). Poet, satirist of Tory politicians; friend of Wilkes and of the novelist Sterne.
    "Epitaph Upon a General," in *The Works* (1795), **82**-24
    *An Essay Upon the King's Friends* (1776), **76**-32
    *Lyric Consolations*, "A Tory Ode" and "Ode" (1769), **69**-19
    *Makarony Fables; Fables for Grown Gentlemen. With the New Fable of the Bees* (1768), **68**-23
    "Queries to the Critical Reviewers," **63**-146
Stevenson, William (1719?-83). Irish M.D.
    *An Ode to Peace; Occasioned by the Present Crisis of the British Empire* (1776), **76**-33, **78**-39, **82**-25
Stewart, Thomas. Dramatist and poet who opposed the American rebels and their cause.
    "Lines on Sedition and American Bravery," **76**-196
Stockdale, Percival (1736-1811). Miscellaneous writer; poet, literary critic, and journalist.
    *Churchill Defended, A Poem: Addressed to the Minority* (1765), **65**-11
    *The Remonstrance. A Poem* (1770), **70**-6
Stratford, Thomas. Irish clergyman; accused the Americans of parricide.
    *The First Book of Fontenoy. A Poem* (1782), **82**-26
Tait, John (1748-1817). Scottish poet, loyal to the Establishment.
    "The Banks of the Dee," **75**-256
    *The Flight of Freedom. A Fragment* (1776), **76**-34 (probably not by Tait)
    *The Land of Liberty. An Allegorical Poem* (1775), **75**-22

"Ode on the Anniversay of his Majesty's Birthday," **71-105**
"Ode to Liberty, On the Anniversary of his Majesty's Accession," **70-198**
*Poetical Legends: Containing the American Captive and The Fall of Faction* (1776), **76-35**
**About**: **76-379**

Tasker, William (1740-1800). Clergyman, poet and antiquary in the Bath-Easton circle.
*Annus Mirabilis; or, The Eventful Year Eighty-Two* (1783), **83-32**
*A Congratulatory Ode to Admiral Keppel* (1779), **79-39**
"The following Verses . . . an extemporaneous 'jeu d'esprit'," **82-350**
*An Ode to the Warlike Genius of Great Britain* (1778), **78-40, 41, 42**
**About**: **78-218, 79-432**

Tattam, R. Poet correspondent of the *Whitehall Evening Post*.
"Epigram," **85-22**
"Epitaph On a Politician," **85-26**
"The Taxes. A Tale," **84-186**

*The Tears of Britannia: A Solemn Appeal to All her Sons* . . . (1779), **79-40**
*The Tears of Britannia. . . . On the present American War* (1780), **76-36**
*The Tears of the Foot Guards, upon their Departure for America* (1776), **76-37, 38**

Temple, Anne Chambers, Countess (c. 1709-77). Wife of Richard Grenville, Earl Temple, patron of Wilkes and Churchill.
"The Jewel in the Tower, A Song," **63-67**

*The Thistle* (1773), **73-A**

Thistlethwaite, James. A Bristol poet and satirist.
*The Prediction of Liberty* (1776), **76-39**

Thomas, _____. Clergyman, poet.
"A Monody, On the Death of Captain Asgill," **83-149**

Thomas, Ann. Of Milbrook, Cornwall; widow of a naval officer.
*Poems on Various Subjects* (1785), **85-11**

Thomas, E. Welshman; astronomer.
"An Ode . . . in Honour of Lord Rodney," **82-355**

Thompson, Edward (1738?-86). Naval officer during American War; lyricist; editor of *The Muse's Mirror*.
"Epitaph, Extempore. On George Alexander Stevens," **84-58**
"The Hyaena. Inscribed to the Girls of Gainsborough," **79-211**
"To the Memory of James Moore, . . ." **75-262**
"To the Memory of Sir Charles Saunders," **76-360**

Thomson, James (1700-45). Scottish poet and playwright. Wrote "Rule Britannia," patriotic lyric for *Alfred* (1740), with Mallet.
estracts from plays, **82-285**

Thorn, Theophilus. See William Falconer.

*Three Excel[l]ent New Songs* (1776), **76-40**
"A New Song on the Battle of America"

Tickell, Richard (1751-93). Poet, satirist, dramatist; pamphleteer vs Opposition.
*Epistle from the Honourable Charles Fox, . . . To John Townshend* (1779), **79-41**
*Opposition Mornings: With Betty's Remarks* (1779), **79-42**
*The Project. A Poem. Dedicated to Dean Tucker* (1778), **78-43**
"Prologue to *The Camp*: An Interlude," **78-478**
**About**: **78-495**

Tickle, Timothy. (pseud.)
    "Fable. Captain John Bull in a Storm," **80-133**
    "The Fox and Geese. A Fable," **80-140**
    "Tray in Disgrace; or, The Danger of Prosperity," **80-385**

*The Times. A Poem* (1769), **69-20**

Tomlinson, Ralph (d. 1779). "Late" president of the Anacreontic Society, founded in 1766; the music for his lyric provided the tune for the national anthem of the United States in the 19th century.
    "An Anacreontic Song," **78-A**, **80-A**
    **About:** 83-238
    **See also:** John Stafford Smith, Part I of Index

Tournay, Thomas. Poet and clergyman.
    *Ambition. An Epistle to Paoli* (1769), **69-21**

*The Traitor. A Poetical Rhapsody* (1781), **81-15**

*The Triumph of Liberty, And Peace with America: A Poem* (1782), **82-27**

*The True-Born Scot: Inscribed to John Earl of Bute* (1764), **64-8**

Trumbull, John (1750-1831). Colonial American poet, one of the Hartford wits.
    *McFingal: A Modern Epic Poem. Or the Town Meeting* (1775), **75-23**

Twisting, Timothy. (pseud.)
    *The Pittiad; or, Poetico-Political History of William the Second* (1785), **85-12**

*Tyranny, The Worst Taxation; . . . to Lord North* (1778), **78-44**

*Unanimity. A Poem . . . to The Duke of Leinster* (1780), **80-40**

Underwood, Thomas (c. 1740-?). Of St. Peter's College, Cambridge; satiric poet; admirer of Churchill.
    "Copy of Mr. Underwood's Lines [on Churchill]," **69-A**
    "Extempore upon the Much-lamented Death of Charles Townshend," **67-9**
    *The Impartialist. A Poem* (1767), **67-8**
    *Liberty, A Poem* (1768), **68-24**
    *Poems* (1768), **67-8**
    *The Snarlers* (1767), **67-8**

*Unity and Public Spirit . . . Two Odes: Viz. the Miseries of Dissension and Civil War, and The True Patriot* (1780), **80-41**

*Vanity of Fame; . . . Some Characters of the Present Age* (1784), **84-18**

*Verses Addressed to John Wilkes . . . At Lynn* (1771), **71-5**

*Verses Addressed to No Minister* (1763), **63-8**

*Verses Addressed to the . . . [Queen]. With Irish Potatoes* (1775), **75-24**

*Verses in Memory of Colonel Ackland* (1779), **79-43**

*A Versification of Sir Jeffery Dunstan's Speech . . . 5th of December, 1782* (1782), **82-28**
    **See:** Jeffery Dunstan

"The Vicar of Bray." Ballad about a clergyman of Bray, a village in Berkshire, England, who held his position by easy conversions of faith according to necessity, from the days of Charles II until the accession of George I; here adapted to an equally venal political opportunist who easily shifts allegiance in the reign of George III.
    **76-308**, **78-20**, **79-281**, **82-388**, **84-149**
    **See also:** Trimmers in Part II of Index.

*The Victim. A Poem. Inscribed to John Wilkes* (1768), **68-25**

Victor, Benjamin (d. 1778). Theatrical manager and writer in Ireland and England; wrote occasional poems for the court at Dublin.
    "An Ode [for] the Birth-Day of George III," **65-82**

Virgil (70-19 B.C.). Publius Vergilius Maro, pre-eminent poet of ancient Rome.
    "Lines from *Aeneid*, Book 2, applicable to the Present Times," **78**-237

*The Vision: A Poem, On the Death of Lord Lyttelton* (1779), **79**-44

*The Vocal Magazine* (1778), **66**-108, **75**-309, **77**-31, 112, **78**-99, 211, 331, 446, 552, **78**-A (Tomlinson), **79**-360, **82**-388

*The Voice of the Minority* (1778), **78**-45

*The Voice of the People. Inscribed to Henry Cruger and Edmund Burke* (1777?), **77**-26

*The Voluntary Exile, A Political Essay* (1784), **84**-19

Walpole, Edward (1706-84). MP, 1730-68; brother of Horace Walpole.
    "A Sketch for A.D. 1769," **69**-199
    *A Sketch of the Times, For A.D. 1769, Corrected and Enlarged: And now reprinted for A.D. 1771* (1771), **69**-18

Warton, Thomas (1728-90). (Also spelled Wharton.) Oxford professor of poetry and ancient history; poet laureat, 1785.
    "Imitation of Horace, Book II, Ode VIII," **82**-389
    "Ode for his Majesty's Birthday, June 4, 1785," **85**-56
    "The Oxford Newsman's Address," **71**-131
    "Revenge of America," **60**-53, **63**-167
    "To Mr. Secretary Pitt," **61**-49
    **About**: **65**-4, **83**-28, **85**-16, 54
        parody on "Revenge of America," **82**-312

Warwick, Thomas. Of University College, Oxford; poet and dramatist; apologist for the British cause against America.
    *The Rights of Sovereignty Asserted. An Ode* (1777), **77**-27

*The Watch, An Ode . . . to . . . Mansfield.* [And] *The Genius of America* (1778), **78**-46, 47

Watkins, T. Journal poet of Bristol; upholds the justice of the British cause against America.
    "On the American Rebellion," **76**-382

Watkins, W. Poet, upholds the justice of the British cause against America.
    "On the American Rebellion," **76**-248 (**76**-389)

Weller, _____. Journal poet.
    "To Fame. An Ode. In Memory of the Late Victory [at Minden]," **59**-33

Wells, Christopher (d. 1800). Clergyman from Cornwall; chaplain in the Royal Navy and to Earl Harcourt.
    *Address to the Genius of America* (1776), **76**-41, **81**-16 (revised)

Wesley, Charles (1707-88). Hymn writer and poet of the religious revival; a "Methodist," like his brother John; a Tory royalist, he detested the American rebels.
    "Address to the City" (1780), **80**-345, **81**-17
    "American Independency," **83**-A
    *The American War under the Conduct of Sir William Howe* (1782), **82**-A
    *Hymns for the Nation, In 1782* (1781), **82**-29
    *Hymns for the National Fast, February 8, 1782* (1782), **82**-30
    *Hymns Written in the Time of the Tumults, June 1780* (1780), **80**-42
    "A Motion of the Minority," **82**-390
    "Non Tali Auxilio, . . ." **82**-391
    "On General Wolfe," **82**-392
    "Party Loyalty. Written in the Year 1780," **80**-396
    "A Prayer for King George," **80**-397
    *The Protestant Association* (1781), with two "Addresses to the City" and

"Advice to the City," **81-**17

"Short Hymns: Prince of universal peace," **80-**398

"Written after Passing by Whitehall," **80-**399

"Written on a Late Declaration of Lord Cornwallis," **82-**393

Wesley, John (1703-91). Evangelical "Methodist"; reversed his opinion of America and in 1776 became a Tory, defending North's policy of coercion.

"For the Fast-Day, February 10, 1779," **79-**513

"On the Troubles in America," **75-**305

"2 Sam. xviii. 5. *Deal gently for my sake with the young man, even with Absalom*," **79-**514

"To a Friend on some Late Infamous Publications," **76-**383

**About:** **75-**97, 181, 282, **76-**25, 354, 397, **78-**10, 44, 47, 353, 498, **79-**5, 8, 28, 202, **80-**37.

*Calm Address to our American Colonies*, **75-**183

*Calm Address to the Inhabitants of England*, **77-**212

Tory, **78-**9

Wharton, Charles Henry (1748-1833). American from Maryland and Roman Catholic priest practicing his religion in Worcester, England, where the poem was written.

*A Poetical Epistle to his Excellency George Washington* (1779), **79-**45

Wheatley, Phillis (c. 1753-84). Freed Negro slave of colonial Boston.

*Poems on Various Subjects* (1773), **73-**11

"To the King's Most Excellent Majesty," **68-**26

"To the Right Honourable William Earl of Dartmouth," **73-**11

**About:** **73-**68

Wheeler, _____. Professor of Poetry at Oxford.

"Ode at the Encoenia, Held at Oxford, July 1773," **73-**62

*The Whig. A Poem* (1776), **76-**42

Whitaker, John (1735-1808). Clergyman; historian of Manchester.

"Manchester, An Ode," in Polwhele's *Poems, Chiefly by Gentlemen of Devonshire and Cornwall* (1792), **77-**28, **78-**423 (also entitled "The Praises of Manchester. An Ode")

White, Dick. (pseud.) Irish weaver.

"Advice from the Liberty, or the Weaver's Garland," **70-**15

Whitehead, Paul (1710-74). Poet and satirist, sometimes confused with William Whitehead, the laureat.

"Song in the Fair," **60-**42

Whitehead, William (1715-85). Poet Laureat, 1757 to death; dramatist and miscellaneous poet.

King's Birthday Odes: **70-**237, **73-**110, **74-**210, **75-**313, **76-**386, **77-**328, **78-**543, **79-**521, **80-**407, **81-**252, **82-**396, **83-**277, **84-**217;

New Year Odes: **60-**50, **61-**50, **62-**66, **63-**170, **65-**140, **67-**50, **71-**135, **72-**107, **73-**109, **74-**211, **76-**387, **77-**329, **78-**544, **79-**522, **80-**408, **81-**253, **82-**397, **83-**278, **84-**218, **85-**56.

**About:** **58-**6, **65-**4, 10, 52, **68-**33, 71, **69-**252, **70-**86, **71-**5, **72-**71, 90, **73-**13, 19, 57, **74-**119, 120, 121, 122, 128, 151, 186, **75-**62, 239, **76-**153 217, 221, 225, 253, 274, 300, 386, **77-**1, 5, 12, 152, 244, **78-**56, 68, 314, 324, 403, 514, **79-**36, 45, 295, 296, 298, 303, 461, **80-**23, 37, 52, 62, 237, 238, **81-**140, **82-**214, **85-**25, 35, 36

and Cornwallis's exploits, **82-**160

Churchill's *Independence*, **64-**A

"Epistle to . . . Hayley," **81-**A

epitaph, **85-**27

    faulty prophetic strains of, **80-200**
    on New Year's Ode for 1777, **77-60**
    on New Year's Ode for 1783, **83-186**
    parody of Birth-Day Odes, **85-16**
    parody of laureat odes, **79-529**
    Puddicombe, **73-A**
    a reversal of meaning of Birth-Day Ode for 1778, **78-310**
    satire on Birth-Day Odes, **78-69**
    support of, **76-65**
    Whitehead as flatterer, **80-141**
Wignell, John (d. 1774). Poet.
    "A Song, on the Taking of the Havanna," **62-53**
*Wilkes and Liberty; or, The Universal Prayer* (1764), **64-9**
Williams, Helen Maria (1762-1827). Poet and miscellaneous author; supported the (coming) French Revolution.
    "An American Tale," in *Poems* (1786), **86-4**
    *An Ode on the Peace* (1783), **83-33**, **86-4**
Wilmot, John (1647-80). 2d Earl of Rochester; poet and satirist; rake at the court of Charles II.
    "Your loyal subjects humbly crave," **63-A**, **79-A** (Wilmot)
Wodhull, Michael (1740-1816). Poet, book collector, translator of Euripides, and an ardent Whig.
    *The Equality of Mankind: A Poem* (1765), **65-12**
Wolcot, John (1738-1819). (Peter Pindar, pseud.) Popular satirist of society and the court.
    "The Birth-Day Ode: The Distresses of the Nation," **79-529**
    *Lyric Odes, To the Royal Academicians, for 1782* (1782), "Ode 1," **82-31**
    *More Lyric Odes, To the Royal Academicians* (1783), **83-34**
Women as Authors, **62-1**, **63-67**, **64-5**, **67-31**, **68-36**, **81**, **69-2**, 238, 254, **70-47**, 72, 210, **71-67**, **72-72**, **73-44**, 65, **74-205**, **75-4**, 256, 298, 299, **76-134**, 135, **78-278**, 527, **79-13**, 16, 42, 188, 248, 425, 451, **80-61**, 83, 184, 190, **81-14**, 19, 36, 239, 258, **82-6**, 136, 211, 212, 260, 263, 270, **83-193**, **84-103**, 209
    and coercion of America, **75-104**
    "Lines on . . . Major Sill," **78-A**
    "Martha Bird," **71-70**
    Martha Mark'em series: **77-168**, **78-89**, **80-196**, 197, 394, **81-119**, 120, 121, 122, **84-54**
    "Nonconformists' Nosegay," **82-A**
    on American War, **76-160**, 228, 269, **77-139**
    on the peace, **83-140**
    praise of American officers, **75-110**
    praise of North, **82-177**
    **See also:** Barbauld, Bayly, Cave, Craven, De Fleury, De Lancey, DuBois, Latter, Macaulay, Robinson, Seward, Steele, Temple, Ann Thomas, Wheatley, Williams.
Woods, W. A Scottish poet.
    "Lyric Ode to Public Courage," **79-A**
The World Turned Upside-Down. A Song. A popular lyric and tune; here the title is used, if not the original words or melody.
    **60-51**, **66-134**, **66-140**, **74-89**(?), **78-210**(?)
Woty, William (1731?-91). Grub Street poet and journalist.
    "Britannia's Genius," **75-50**
    "On the Death of Admiral Boscawen," **61-51**

"Stanzas, Occasioned by the Death of his Late Most Sacred Majesty," **60**-52
**About: 64**-A ("An Attempt")
Wronghead, W. (pseud.)
"Ode for the Last Day in the Old year," **80**-237
Wynne, John Huddleston (1743-88). London journalist, associated with the *Gazetteer*; edited *The Lady's Magazine*.
"Ode for the New Year [1778]," **78**-549
"Ode for the New Year, 1779," **79**-526
"Ode for the New Year, 1780," **80**-415
"Ode on the Birth-Day of George III," **77**-182
*Yankee Doodle*, or (*as now Christened by the Saints of New England*) *The Lexington March* (1777-79?), **75**-25
chorus, **79**-276
tune, **78**-236

INDEX

Part II

Topics: Persons, Places and Events; Themes and Subjects

Abingdon, Earl of. See Willoughby Bertie.
Acadia. French settlement, Nova Scotia, Canada. Population about 10,000 before most were deported by the British in 1755. **56**-1
Acland, John Dyke (1746-78). MP, 1774-78. Major, Brit army; three times wounded, 1776-78, in American War; captured with Burgoyne at Saratoga, 1777; died after a duel, November 23, 1778. Wife accompanied him to America. **78**-14, 40, **79**-43, **83**-25
Adam, William (1751-1839). MP, 1774-94, 1806-12. A Scot; supported the Tory North ministry; wounded Fox in a duel, November 1779; joined Fox-North Coalition 1783.
    duel with Fox, **79**-413, **80**-16, 24, 289, 362, **84**-166
Adams, Samuel (1722-1803). American revolutionary leader in Boston. **75**-2, 29, 48, 92, 150, **76**-11, 22, 97, 298, 390, **77**-134, 292, **78**-7, 66, **79**-26, **80**-22, 34, 199, 277
Africa. **59**-16, 20, 27, **60**-25, **61**-2, 37
    Gorée, **59**-34, **73**-5, **79**-39
    Senegal, **58**-4, **59**-42, **60**-42, **79**-39
Agriculture and the Farmer. **77**-259
    Quarter-Day, June 24, **77**-260
    farmers petition Parliament to help corn trade, **81**-156
    in Britain and America, Quarter-Day, **79**-297
    a ruined farmer begs for relief, **81**-188
    **For more on the economy, see**: Bristol, Debt, Emigration, Finance, and the Poor.
Aitken, James (d. 1777). Called "John the Painter." Scots republican sympathetic with the American cause; arsonist, hanged at Portsmouth. **77**-15, 70, 158, 204, 211, 239, 289, 302, 383, **81**-17
    and Fox, **79**-173
    and Sandwich, **77**-324
Albemarle, 3d Earl of. See George Keppel.
Alexander, William (1726-83). Lord Stirling; served under Massachusetts Gov. Shirley in Seven Years' War. American general captured in Battle of Long Island, August 1776, and exchanged the next month for Gov. Montfort Browne and Cortlandt Skinner. Presided over Lee's court martial and André's board of inquiry. **76**-200, 262
Allen, William, Jr. (d. 1768). Young man martyred in the St. George's Fields massacre, May 10, 1768, at the time Wilkes was to be released from the King's Bench Prison, his outlawry having come to an end. **68**-21, 71, 81, 121, 123, 124, **69**-12, 20, 23, 29, 43, 58, 59, 83, 94, 100, 102, 111, 117, 138, 139,

151, 163, 172, 187, 194, 214, 240, 269, **72**-64, 87, **74**-6, 29, **75**-223, **80**-90
   "Lines," **68**-A
   "A Political Genealogy," **69**-A
America.  Colonies.
   Boston, Massachusetts, **65**-14, 135, **66**-72, **68**-85, 95, 96, **69**-84, 118, **70**-174, **72**-14, **73**-16, **74**-2, 5, 6, 74, 192, 207
      Massachusetts, Ld North, **75**-73
      Massacre, **70**-243
      quartering of troops, **65**-34
   Georgia, **70**-4
   New England and Dissent, **73**-74, **75**-213
   New York, **66**-65
   Philadelphia, **66**-64, **70**-174, 190
   South Carolina, **70**-85, **83**-16
   Virginia, **65**-19, 108, **68**-22, 64, 78
      Stamp Act and Nonimportation, **65**-41
   Wilmington, North Carolina, **66**-67
America.  Colonies.  Before the American War begins.  **65**-7, 8, 29, 34, 77, 102, 116, 140, 147, **66**-4, 10, 13, 19, 43, 61, 64, 70, 72, 74, 90, 113, 134, 137, 138, 139, **67**-3, 4, 5, 7, 35, 37, 50, **68**-6, 7, 9, 12, 23, 42, 47, 78, 85, 98, 108, 117, **69**-1, 3, 13, 19, 21, 54, 95, 123, 149, 179, 268, **70**-15, 28, 77, 101, 190, 216, 242, **73**-17, 40, **74**-13, 42, 53, 68, 78
   and Canada, **69**-5
   Civil war, **68**-20
   Crosby and Oliver, **71**-137
   "Extempore by . . .," **68**-A
   "genius" of America, **69**-92
   Hillsborough, **73**-10
   life in America before the Troubles, **77**-9
   "obstinate and troublesome," **70**-66
   "An Ode," **64**-A
   *The Thistle*, **73**-A
   tranquility in America after repeal of Townshend Acts, **71**-7
   **See also**: America.  Nonimportation and Stamp Act.
America.  Colonies.  Metaphor of children with respect to parent, filial ingratitude, parricide, and the return of the repentant prodigal to the forgiving parent.  **66**-134, 140 (a print), **70**-132, **74**-192, 210, **75**-9, 36, 88, 99, 116, 139, **76**-5, 9, 41, 126, 220, 248, 250, 286, 389, **77**-4, 16, 41, 53, 75, 178, 247, 329, **78**-58, 210, 336, **79**-7, 39, 140, **80**-4, 5, 14, 15, 20, 152, 417 (print), **81**-15, 16, **82**-22, 26, 29, 213, 310, 419, **83**-21, 25, **84**-6, **85**-10
   base parricide allied with France, **84**-18
   Cowper's "Epinikion," **79**-A
   filial ingratitude, **79**-60
   hypocritical parricides, **1800**-1
   "Nonconformist's Nosegay," **82**-A
   "On Ingratitude," **78**-A
   return of the prodigal, **79**-60
   "tyrant mother," **76**-169
America.  Declaration of Independence.  See American War.  Independence.
America.  Icon and Image in Prints.  **82**-409, 410
   as half-naked Indian with feathered head-dress, **65**-147, **66**-138
   as Indian with scalping knife, **80**-418
   as Indian woman with feathered head-dress and sandals and holding a tomahawk, **82**-416

as rattlesnake, **82**-411
America.  Land of Liberty.  **70**-111, **72**-14, 17, **73**-105, **74**-9, 26, 62, 63, 108, 177, 209, **75**-38, **76**-12, 27, 34, 39, 74, 230, 264, 276, 394, **77**-7, 18, 106, 177, 323, **78**-207, 311, 355, 375, 414, 415, **79**-14, 45, **81**-11, **83**-71, 187, 228, **85**-6
    American Patriots, **77**-155
    and English freedom, **83**-28
    liberty defined, **84**-76
    *Not* the Land of Liberty, **75**-22(?), **76**-14, 390, **77**-279, **83**-8, 12, 16, 31, 37, 116, **84**-22
    No. 2, **76**-11
    Roman republican liberty, **77**-107, 312
    Whig freedom, **77**-20
America.  Model of freedom and independence, providing the basis of a disinterested patriotism, untainted by corruption and the influence of monarchy or aristocracy.  **83**-21
    where "A just equality presides o'er all," **85**-10
America.  Model of simplicity, integrity, and valor.  **84**-209
America.  National Flag.
    Cowper's "To Sir Joshua Reynolds," a kite shredded into thirteen pieces, **82**-A
    thirteen red bleeding stripes, **80**-50
    thirteen stars lost, **83**-47
    thirteen stripes, **84**-209
America.  Nonimportation.  **74**-8, 177, **75**-249, 260, **76**-11,
    after Stamp Act, **66**-41
    American Loyalist, **76**-280
    begins again, **74**-20
    effect on British economy
        bankruptcies, **77**-263
        hard times, **76**-46
        tobacco trade ruined, **76**-375
        Tucker's view of prosperity challenged, **78**-151
    end of first nonimportation pact, **70**-190
    **See also**: Agriculture, Bristol, Finance, the Poor.
America.  Portrait.
    Cowper's "Modern Patriot," as lawless rebels and "roaring boys," **82**-A
America.  Postwar Period, 1784-85.
    against slavery in America, **84**-7
    allegorical review of politics of American War, &c, **84**-15
    attractiveness of primitive nature in America, the Indian and external nature, **85**-53, 58
    commemorates events of the war, **85**-11
    discourages emigration to America, **85**-7
    hope for reunion, **85**-10
    investing in American bonds, **84**-220 (a print)
    Maurice rejects America and then revises opinion to accept American independence, **84**-10
    post-war politics and the American War, **84**-8
    rejection of the peace, **85**-13
    review, **85**-1
    vanity of fame and individuals in American War, **84**-18
    a Whig review of American War, Charles I and George III compared, tyranny

and civil war, **84**-171
>    **See also:** Slavery.

America. Rising Glory of.   **72**-14 (same as **78**-13), **74**-25, **75**-41, 221, 222, **76**-9, 294, **78**-35, 47, 63, 73, **79**-14, 28, 37, **81**-12, **82**-25, **83**-18
>    by inversion, **80**-19
>    *Not* the Land of Glory, **83**-8, 34, 171
>    under British sovereignty, **80**-14
>    virtuous America, **82**-219

The American War. Atrocities.
>    American, **75**-93
>    British, **76**-218, **77**-262, **79**-398, **85**-6
>    Civil war as atrocity
>    >    dreadful carnage, **82**-284
>    Indian scalping, **76**-218, **77**-262, **78**-90,
>    >    and Jane McCrea, **79**-4

The American War. Attitudes. British defend American rebellion.
>    1774
>    >    British defend American rebellion [the justice of American resistance to tyranny and of the struggle for freedom], **74**-35, 102, 109, 120, 121, 122, 147, 150, 152, 176, 183, 195
>    1775
>    >    British defend American Rebellion, **75**-5, 15, 16, 21, 29, 31, 34, 42, 44, 59, 62, 64, 67, 80, 81, 82, 83, 84, 86, 99, 105, 120, 131, 136, 149, 150, 151, 159, 169, 186, 202, 253, 259, 261, 265, 279, 293, 297
>    >    >    a mad civil war, **75**-130
>    >    British general support of American rebels, **75**-45, 46, 49, 75, 110, 113, 129, 188, 193, 204, 239, 242, 272, 273, 278, 280, 287, 291
>    >    British protest a landowning peer who supports the war, **75**-295
>    >    British protest profiteering war contractors, **75**-85
>    1776
>    >    British defend American rebellion, **76**-5, 6, 7, 8, 9, 16, 17, 18, 27, 29, 30, 42, 51, 57, 58, 118, 133, 177, 189, 193, 195, 197, 251, 252, 253, 261, 287, 300, 307, 335, 336, 339, 347, 364, 376
>    >    British general support of American rebels, **76**-39, 84, 114, 127, 186, 274, 278, 286, 312, 381
>    >    >    Shakespeare, **76**-313
>    >    British woman protests the war, **76**-160
>    >    British objections to American War as "an unworthy cause," **76**-136, 163, 176, 205, 221, 224, 259, 329
>    >    British objections to war profiteers
>    >    >    contractors, **76**-95
>    1777
>    >    America, at peace in past, at war in present, **77**-69
>    >    British defend American rebellion, **77**-7, 8, 29 (answer to **77**-245), 177, 215, 224, 231, 236
>    >    British general sympathy with America, **77**-11, 18, 20, 22, 23, 173, 236
>    1778
>    >    British general sympathy with America, **78**-14, 26, 27, 32, 275 (and **80**-272), 295, 310, 408
>    >    >    British pity America, **78**-377
>    >    British opposition to American war as unjust, but support of war against France, "the just war," **78**-31, 416, 507
>    >    British opposition to the "foul impious war," **78**-12, 28, 32, 35, 39, 44,

45, 47, 90, 102, 128, 129, 173, 179, 203, 295, 296, 303, 306, 311, 312, 314, 319, 320, 329, 330, 372, 373, 377, 442, 487, 490, 498, 528
    both sides lose, **78-209**, 336
    both sides wrong, **78-57**
    British need peace, **78-438**
    a fruitless war, **78-127**
    the need for peace, **78-412**
    need for peace with America because of French menace, **78-518**
    only the Scotch gain, **78-424**
    a protest against the civil war, **78-469**
    useless war and only France gains, **78-210**
1779
   British general sympathy with America, **79-293**
   British opposition to American War and declare American cause is
      just, **79-5**, 15, 22, 35, 276, 293(?)
      an Irish view, **79-25**
      "an unnat'ral war," **79-249**
   British opposition to American War, but support war against France, **79-4**,
      22, 30, 39, 227, 248, 254, 259, 480, 481
   a senseless war against half the world, **79-394**
1780
   British hope for peace and reconciliation or unity with America, **80-12**,
      14, 15, 20, 30 (No. 5), 199
   British hope for peace, generalized, **80-32**, 399
   British opposition to the unjust American War, **80-12**, 52, 236, 247, 272
      (and **78-275**)
        Fox and Abington, **80-264**
        Ireland and America, **80-259**
        "vile War," ruinous and immoral, **80-7**
   British plea to both sides, American and British, for peace, **80-377**
1781-1784
   an "inglorious war," **84-181**
   British opposition to unjust American War, **81-11**, **82-219**, **83-32**
      and the Fast, **82-70**
      Government's policy, to slaughter rebels, **81-195**
   British sympathy with American cause, **82-9**
   a Whig view of the war, Charles I and George III compared, tyranny and
      civil war, **84-171**
The American War. Attitudes. British defend Government's cause in suppressing
   rebellion, a just war.
   1775, **75-8**, 50, 64, 92, 126, 137, 146, 172, 213, 248, 256, 284, 318
        tradesmen, **75-112**
      British objections to domestic traitors and apostates, patriots of the
        Minority Opposition, for encouraging rebels, **75-19**, 50, 55, 90, 197,
        201, 232, 234
        patriots as parricides, **75-182**
   British opposition to American rebellion, **75-48**, 108, 154, 284
   1776
      British defend Government's just cause, **76-1**, 2, 3, 4, 11, 14, 23, 24, 31,
        35, 41, 63, 64, 65, 142, 196, 248, 257, 261, 289, 317, 330, 356, 382,
        386, 387, 395
        Congress is foolishly obstinate, **76-355**
      British general opposition to American rebellion, **76-94**, 100, 119, 166,
        174, 202, 220, 258, 314, 324

Scottish anti-American poem, **76-279**
British objections to domestic traitors . . . for encouraging rebels, **76-14**, 44, 56, 130, 196
British regret and dislike the war, the coercion, but also dislike the rebellion, **76-41**
British soldiers support the Government in the American War, **76-162**
British woman prays for peace on British terms, **76-228**

1777
British condemn American cause of domestic traitors . . . who encourage the enemy, **77-6**, 13, 27, 75, 218, 247, 279, 289
British defend Government's just cause, **77-2**, 4, 12, 17, 19, 40, 149, 212, 274
British express varied opinions on justice of the war, **77-255**
British general and loyal support of Government's cause, **77-28** (and **78-423**), 29 (answer to **77-245**), 163, 182, 191, 204, 207, 208, 255, 311
    execution of a traitor, James Aitken, **77-158**, 289
    a youthful volunteer, **77-296**
British pray for peace and reconciliation on Government's terms, **77-329**
British regret the war but dislike the rebellion, **77-15**, 185

1778
British condemn American cause and domestic traitors . . . who encourage the enemy, **78-23**, 517
British defend Government's just cause, **78-159**, 190, 308, 409, 508, 549
    especially after France enters, **78-60**
    only against France, **78-175**
British general and loyal support of Government's cause, **78-38**, 78, 423, 460, 513, 520;
British pray for end of American rebellion and for peace and reconciliation on Government's terms, **78-18**, 305, 382, 544
    King's speech, **78-53**
    on basis of North's Conciliatory Propositions, **78-232**

1779
British condemn American cause and its "Patriot" supporters, **79-6**, 7, 12, 23, 513, 514
British defend Government's just cause, **79-308**, 508
British general and loyal support of Government's cause, **79-31**, 32, 113, 263, 526

1780
American Loyalist opposition to American cause: **80-22**, 77, 199
British defend Government's cause, **80-14**, 30 (No. 3), 34, 41, 42, 150, 151, 240, 241, 285, 298
British general and loyal support of Government, **80-39**, 171, 273, 308, 352
    Scotch recruitment song, **80-228**
British hope for peace on Government's terms, **80-58**, 244, 308
foolishness of contending parties, including British and American, **80-410**
miscellaneous, **80-49**, 377,

1781-82
both British and Americans are wrong, **81-193**
British defend Government's cause, **81-1**, 14, 16, 76, 108, 189, **82-11**, 213
    Cowper's "Table Talk," **82-A**
British hope for peace and reconciliation with America, **81-29**, 236,

262 (a print)
        British and Americans must compromise, **81**-193
    British hope for peace, for break between America and France, **81**-15, 18,
        24, 25, 29, **82**-9
        and revival of commerce, **81**-41
        and trade, **81**-254
        hope for honorable peace, **82**-19
        on British terms, **81**-203
American War. Attitudes. British deplore and mourn the war, 1775-76. **75**-47,
    205, 256
    Britain "weeps while she corrects," **76**-41
    laments "the King's War" and loss of America, **76**-5
    a Methodist hymn, **75**-305
    mourns the dead in a war for British "rights," **76**-40
    mourns the war and blames corruption and luxury, **76**-36
The American War. Attitudes. British for peace, compromise, reconciliation.
    1775, **75**-316
    both sides lose, **75**-106
    need for compromise, **75**-309, 321
    no hope; views are irreconcilable, **75**-116
    peace more important than war, **75**-36, 60
    prayer for justice and freedom, **75**-233
    terrible consequences of civil war, **75**-144
    terrible consequences of war, **75**-311
    Whitehead's prayer for peace, union, and concord, **75**-313
    1776, **76**-5, 20, 45, 46, 52, 66, 70, 89, 222, 271, 274, 281, 309, 320, 333,
        363
    after American defeat in Battle of Long Island, **76**-269
    both sides lose, **76**-50
    justice on both sides, for peace and clemency, **76**-53 (same as **76**-380)
    negotiation, not war, **76**-273
    on Government's terms, **76**-35, 228
    peace and punishment of the guilty, **76**-78
    peace guarantees British strength, **76**-358
    pray for peace, not for success in fratricidal war, **76**-235, 236
    1777, **77**-30, 34, 53, 122, 151, 181, 184, 252, 255, 277, 301
    absurd costly war with trifling cause, tax on tea, **77**-48, 117
    both sides mad or mistaken, **77**-62, 167 (and **89**-2)
    common sense requires end of war, **77**-111
    the war must be stopped because of the menace of France, Britain's true
        enemy, **77**-113, 121, 219, 278
    the war must end because America can't be defeated, **77**-115, 139
The American War. Battles and Campaigns. According to Year: A Summary.
    1775
    Bunker Hill
    Invasion of Canada (Quebec and Montreal to 1776)
    Lexington and Concord
    Siege of Boston (to 1776)
    Ticonderoga
    1776
    Carleton's invasion from Canada
    Charleston, South Carolina
    Howe's attack on Long Island and New York
    Siege of Boston

1777
- Admiral Peter Parker and Newport, Rhode Island
- Burgoyne's invasion from Canada to Saratoga
- Clinton and Forts Clinton and Montgomery
- Howe's New Jersey and Pennsylvania campaigns

1778
- American Gen. Sullivan and French Adm. D'Estaing vs. British Gen. Pigot at Rhode Island
- Little Egg Harbor, New Jersey
- Savannah
- Ushant sea battle

1779
- defense of Channel Island of Jersey
- Pigot and Newport
- Savannah

1780
- Camden, South Carolina
- Charleston, South Carolina
- King's Mountain, South Carolina
- Penobscot Bay

1781
- Channel Island of Jersey
- Eutaw Springs, South Carolina
- Guilford Courthouse, North Carolina
- Yorktown

1782
- Lifting the Siege of Gibraltar
- Rodney's Battle of the Saints

**For more sea battles, see**: American War and British Navy, American War and British naval actions, and Gibraltar Besieged

The American War. Battles and Campaigns. Boston Siege, April 1775-March 17, 1776. **75**-135, 143, 166, 185, 198, 210, **76**-17, 18, 22, 77 (and **82**-55), 79, 191, 217, 223, 305, 325, 388, **77**-127, **78**-12, 94, 171, 226, **79**-6, **81**-3, **82**-55, **83**-189. British Gen. William Howe vs. American Gens. Washington, Ward, and Putnam.
- account of British besieged in Boston and their evacuation, **76**-303
- Burgoyne's "Vaudeville," **77**-43
- evacuation of Boston, **76**-150
- memorial inscription on evacuation, **76**-188
- Washington's capture of Boston without bloodshed, **77**-102

The American War. Battles and Campaigns. Bunker Hill, Boston, Massachusetts, June 17, 1775. **75**-2, 6, 8, 25, 26, 115, 157, 162, 277, **76**-5, 16, 22, 30, 37, 38, 40, 83, 165, 202, 217, 218, 223, 298, 340, **77**-71, 313, **78**-8, 12, 94, 170, 171, 226, 295, 412, **79**-6, 105, **80**-7, 12, **81**-3, 259, **83**-22, **85**-6
- death of a devoted lover, **76**-350
- a veteran complains, **75**-118

The American War. Battles and Campaigns. Burgoyne's Invasion from Canada and Defeat at Saratoga, New York, June 13-October 17, 1777. **77**-37, 39, 56, 66, 91, 105, 143, 149, 179, 183, 195, 203, 306, 313, 331, **78**-6, 8, 12, 35, 56, 295, 336, 435, **79**-105, **80**-7, 28, 285, **81**-3, 42, **85**-6
- American victory song, **78**-59
- and the French, **78**-276
- atrocity, **77**-262

Burgoyne's army surrounded by American rattlesnake, **82**-409 (a print)
Burgoyne's defeat caused by Gen. Howe, **79**-11
Burgoyne's proclamation, **77**-44, 45, 214
capture of Ticonderoga, **77**-137, 141
character of Burgoyne's army, **78**-84
death of "Donnel," young lover, **78**-113
death of Gen. Simon Fraser and defeat, **78**-363
defeat, **77**-281, 292, 299, **78**-170, 213, 325, **79**-32
defeat and Burgoyne's proclamation, **78**-254
defeat and Parliament, **77**-318
defeat and Sandwich's remarks on Americans as cowards, **78**-197
failure anticipated, **77**-120
the failure at Saratoga, **78**-510
Germain's responsibility for defeat, **78**-14, 16, 19
North's ministry blamed for defeat, **78**-28
Saratoga, **81**-102
surrender to Gates, **77**-170
surrounded, **77**-199
tragic drama on Burgoyne's defeat, **78**-26
treatment of captured army, **78**-45
**For more on this topic, see**: John Burgoyne and American Gen. Horatio Gates.

The American War. Battles and Campaigns. Camden, South Carolina; American Gen. Gates and Baron De Kalb suffer defeat by British Gen. Cornwallis, August 16-18, 1780. **80**-30[5], 41, 45, 273
Col. Tarleton defeats Gen. Sumter, **80**-258

The American War. Battles and Campaigns. Canadian Invasion and Siege of Quebec, August 1775-October 1776. **76**-5, 12, 16, 27, 37, 38, 223, **78**-12, 295, **79**-6, **81**-3. British Gen. Carleton, Col. Allan McLean and John Hamilton, R.N., vs. American Gens. Montgomery and Arnold.
the Americans who died, **76**-183
and Hamilton, **81**-204
Arnold, **76**-117
Carleton and Wolfe, **76**-296
defeat of American rebels, **76**-43
defeat of the rebels, **76**-321
narrative of the siege, 1775-76, **76**-315

The American War. Battles and Campaigns. Carleton's Offensive against American Forces at Lake Champlain (Valcour Island), June-October 1776, **76**-106, 111, 345, 396, **79**-6. British Gen. Carleton vs. American Gen. Arnold, driving American forces permanently from Canada.
narrative of the campaign, June-October 1776, **77**-202

The American War. Battles and Campaigns. Channel Island of Jersey; British under Major Pierson repel French raid, January 6, 1781. **81**-63, 79, 83
the first attack, **79**-325
"The French sail'd to Jersey," **79**-A

The American War. Battles and Campaigns. Charleston, South Carolina, June 28, 1776. British action against Sullivan's Island, entrance to Charleston Harbor, fails. **76**-105, 123, 218, 277, 374, 377, **77**-313, **78**-12, 226, **79**-6, **81**-3
attack repelled, **76**-208
Charleston bar, **76**-201
Germain plans to take, **76**-206

loss of warships, **76**-214, 239
   **For more on this joint naval and military expedition, see**: Adm.
      Peter Parker and Gen. Henry Clinton
The American War. Battles and Campaigns. Charleston, South Carolina; American
   Gen. Lincoln surrenders his forces to British Gens. Clinton and Leslie after
   a siege of seven weeks, May 12, 1780. **80**-6, 30 [1 & 4], 71, 144, 152, 277,
   280, 285, 290, 364, 376
The American War. Battles and Campaigns. Clinton's Attack on Forts Clinton and
   Montgomery, October 3-22, 1777, to help relieve pressure on Burgoyne's
   forces. **77**-172, **78**-271
      "Lines on . . . Major Sill," **78**-A
The American War. Battles and Campaigns. Eutaw Springs, South Carolina, British
   Col. Alexander Stewart and Capt. John Marjoribanks defeat American Gen.
   Greene, September 8, 1781, the last major engagement in the South before
   Yorktown. **82**-148, 186
The American War. Battles and Campaigns. Guilford Courthouse, North Carolina,
   Cornwallis defeats American Gen. Greene, March 15, 1781. **81**-121, 122, 151
      **For more, see**: Cornwallis and Nathanael Greene
The American War. Battles and Campaigns. Howe's Long Island and New York Cam-
   paign, August 27-November 20, 1776, against Gen. Washington. The first
   pitched battle of the American War was fought on Long Island. **76**-14, 87, 90,
   102. 107, 108, 131, 132, 164, 178, 196, 202, 245, 247, 262, 263, 268, 269,
   306, 307, 332, 365, **77**-133, 150, 313, **78**-12, 94, **79**-6, **81**-3
      the beginning, **76**-66
      capture of three American generals: William Alexander [Lord Stirling],
         John Sullivan and Nathaniel Woodhull, **76**-200
      the first news of American defeat, **76**-319
      Hell Gate, **77**-127
      pleasure in Howe's victory, August 27, 1776, **76**-257
The American War. Battles and Campaigns. Howe's New Jersey and Pennsylvania
   Campaign, to the Capture of Philadelphia, November 1776-September 1777.
   **77**-56, 59, 127, 149, 174, 241, 268, 291, 332
      Battle of Princeton, **77**-58, 76
      capture of Philadelphia, **79**-21
      Red Bank and Mud Island, forts on Delaware River, **77**-91, 292, **78**-62, 94,
         181, 182, 236, 390, 435, **81**-3, 259
      Trenton, **77**-71, 102, 284, 313, **78**-94, 226, **79**-6, **81**-3
      Trenton and Washington, **78**-12, **81**-3, **85**-6
      **For more on Gen. Howe, see**: William Howe
The American War. Battles and Campaigns. King's Mountain, South Carolina,
   defeat of Southern Loyalists under Patrick Ferguson by American patriot
   partisans, October 7, 1780. **80**-164
The American War. Battles and Campaigns. Lexington and Concord, April 19, 1775,
   the first land action of "The Massachusetts War." **75**-25, 87, 141, 155, 162,
   211, **76**-5, 16, 22, 37, 38, 40, 133, 223, **77**-71, 134, **78**-8, 12, 16, 226, 295,
   412, **79**-6, **80**-7, 12, **81**-3, **85**-6
      **For more, see**: Gen. Gage and Gen. Percy
The American War. Battles and Campaigns. Little Egg Harbor, New Jersey, October
   4-5, 1778, a raid led by Capt. Patrick Ferguson.
      a minor British victory, **78**-378
The American War. Battles and Campaigns. Newport, Rhode Island, captured by
   Gen. Henry Clinton and Admiral Sir Peter Parker, in a joint military and
   naval operation, December 8, 1776. **77**-35, 228, **78**-12

The American War. Battles and Campaigns. Newport, Rhode Island; Gen. Robert
    Pigot repels offensive by American Gen. John Sullivan and French Admiral
    D'Estaing, July-August 1778. **79**-527, **81**-3
    **For more, see**: Pigot and D'Estaing
The American War. Battles and Campaigns. Penobscot Bay, New England [Maine];
    British successfully repel American attack, July-August 1779. **80**-277
The American War. Battles and Campaigns. Reviews in Verse.
    by Humphreys of the American War, **85**-6
    of American resistance, 1775-77, **78**-295
    of battles through 1779, **81**-3
    of failures in 1775-76, **78**-226
    of failures up to Burgoyne's defeat, **78**-171
    of the major failures by Howe, Burgoyne, Clinton, and Cornwallis, **84**-16
    of the Savannah defense, **79**-387
    of the second campaign from beginning to end, December 1776, **79**-6
The American War. Battles and Campaigns. Savannah, Georgia, captured by British
    Col. Archibald Campbell, December 29, 1778; and defended by British Gen.
    Prevost against American Gen. Lincoln and French Adm. D'Estaing, October 9,
    1779. **79**-9, 21, 99, 183, 309, 318, 344, 387, **80**-1, 21, 30 [2 and 5], 124,
    241, **81**-3, **85**-4
    death of a soldier, **80**-276
The American War. Battles and Campaigns. Ticonderoga, captured by Americans
    Ethan Allen and Benedict Arnold, May 10, 1775. **75**-46, 109
The American War. Battles and Campaigns. Yorktown, Va., the last important
    American campaign, resulting in the capitulation of the British army under
    Gen. Cornwallis, October 19, 1781, and the end of the American War.
    Alves' poem [**81**-1] republished, **82**-2
    British in a political "mess" after Yorktown defeat, **81**-33
    British surrender suggests British loss of valor, **82**-52
    Charles Wesley reacts bitterly to victory of Satanic Americans and French
        papists, **82**-29
    a complaint at lack of British aggressive spirit and the Yorktown sur-
        render, **81**-178
    Cornwallis' army surrounded by American rattlesnake, **82**-409 (print)
    Cornwallis reports sinking of British glory, **84**-16
    Cornwallis' surrender, demoralizing effect on war policy, **82**-17
    criticism of Cornwallis, ironic estimate of effect of Yorktown defeat on
        North ministry, and praise of Washington and Franklin, **82**-9
    death of Col. Webster, **82**-8
    demoralizing effect of the terrific defeat, **82**-30, 43
    disgust with Government leadership upon news of capitulation at Yorktown,
        **81**-93
    the exchange of Henry Laurens for captured Gen. Arnold, **82**-267
    first significant verse reaction to Yorktown defeat, satire on King and
        court, **81**-137
    Humphreys' poem, remarks on British defeat at Yorktown, the end of the
        American War, **85**-6
    ironic comment on French victory at Yorktown, **81**-57
    ironic couplet on, and criticism of, Adm. Graves, **81**-148, 210
    King George fails to express sorrow at Yorktown loss, **82**-318
    King is pessimistic but North is still hopeful after Yorktown in December
        1781, **81**-266 (print)
    objection to petitions and remonstrances urging end of American War, **81**-174

a plea to end American War, a reaction to the Yorktown defeat, **81**-247
satire on unchanging corruption of wretched times despite Yorktown defeat, **82**-71
victory of French and Americans is galling, and patriotic Puddicombe wishes to continue war against faithless Americans, **82**-20
Yorktown defeat and Alves' poem for year 1781, **81**-1

The American War. Beginning of the crisis and war, 1774-76. **74**-1, 2, 3, 4, 5, 8, 9, 75, 121, 122, 151, 159, 183, 193, 207, **75**-9, 45, 71, 104, 114, 169, 171, 240, **84**-16
    America cannot be suppressed, **75**-122
    Bostonian prays for Chatham's aid against British oppression, **75**-148
    excitement among the people, **75**-217
    generates excitement in Britain, **75**-30
    high spirit of Americans, **75**-247, 289
    "Liberty," denial of American petitions, **89**-2
    oratorical excitement, **75**-283
    prayer for reconciliation, **75**-14
    "See the dread harbinger of Woe"; war breaks out, **76**-A (a print)

The American War. Beginning; preparing for the War against America, **75**-51, 135, 136, 176, 204, 300

The American War. British Navy.
    Before the American War,
        attack on Brest, **59**-29
        Britain all-powerful, **64**-41
        Britain "mistress of the seas," **62**-51
        Britain rules the waves, **60**-45
        Britain's all-powerful navy, **74**-211
        Britain's "empire of the main," **70**-198
        Britain's imperial navy, **73**-37, **80**-155
        Britain's sovereignty over the seas, **73**-81
        ministry weakens navy, **73**-69
        a powerful warship, **59**-11
        review of Britain's power, **73**-5
        summary of year 1759, **59**-42
        the year 1759, **60**-34
    France, Spain and the American War, **79**-163, 238, 242, 370, 418, 427, 435, 520, 524, **81**-7
        and America, **79**-247
        and decay of British navy, **78**-160
        British, French and Spanish sailors, **79**-104
        British still supreme on the main, **75**-203
        confidence in navy personnel, **79**-154, 160, **80**-155
        dissension and weak navy, **79**-17
        fears and surmises, summer 1781, **81**-119, 120
        French defeated in East and West Indies, **79**-80
        loss of confidence in naval leaders, **79**-268
        loss of control over seas, **81**-78
        loss of forty vessels to Bourbons, **80**-197
        loss of sovereignty over seas to France, **78**-488
        menace of Britain's Bourbon enemies, **75**-301
        naval war with France, **79**-161
        preparations, **78**-525
        the sea war, **80**-345

                    unprepared for French war, **78-245**, 253, 395, 464
                    unspecified victory over French, **78-186**
                    "Whig admirals," Howe, Keppel, Harland, restore British sovereignty
                        over the seas, **79-75**
                    the year 1779, **79-261**
            References to, **77-246, 79-409, 80-93**, 407, 408, **82-127**
                    and British sovereignty, **79-439**
                    Britain at end of war controls seas, **83-278**, 284
                    Britain depends on navy, **81-27**
                    Britain dominates seas, **81-1**
                    Britain must maintain its naval power, **84-30**
                    Britain's spectacular triumphs at end of war, **83-290**
                    British valor, **81-162**
                    and effeminate nobility, **85-2**
                    praise of naval officers, **83-43**
                    praise of Rodney's fleet officers, **81-218**
                    praise of "the Royal Tar," Prince William, **83-39**
                    preparation for engaging French fleet, **79-440**, 450
                    vs. French, **81-166**
                    a young sailor begs to be discharged, **79-463**
            Weak state of, **79-392**, 421, 434, 455, 507, **80-70, 81-5**
                    and loss of control over seas, **81-78**
                    unprepared navy, **81-129**
            **See also:** Gibraltar Besieged, the Ushant Episode
    The American War. British Navy, and American Rebels.
            American privateer engages armed British merchantman, **77-77**
            British minimize loss of two warships to American navy, **77-322**
            Capt. Bligh against American privateers, **77-162**
            Charleston, South Carolina, **76-214**, 239
            French support of America on the seas, **77-235**
            possible first British casualty in sea actions against rebels, **75-262**
            resisting French attack on Rhode Island, **78-141**
            **See also:** Admiral Peter Parker and Charleston, South Carolina, John Paul
                Jones, Privateering
    The American War. British Navy, and Holland, 1781-82.
            Adm. De Witt, **81-66**
            British vs. Dutch and French, **82-337**
            minor skirmish, August 5, 1781, **81-77**
            retaliation on Holland justified, **82-311**
            **See also:** Holland and St. Eustatius in American War, West Indies
                Actions
    The American War. British Navy, and Rodney's Engagements and Victories.
            Defeat of Spanish Admiral Langara off St. Vincent's and the relief of
                Gibraltar, January 16, 1780. **80-101**, 143, 257, 283, 392, **81-126**
                    Cowper's "On the Victory,", **80-A**
            Martinique, West Indies, April 17, 1780: **80-109**, 282
            St. Eustatius, West Indies, captured February 3, 1781, **81-21**, 25,
                89, 119
                    Adm. "Van Trowser," eponym for Dutch Governor Johannes de Graef, **81-183**
                    and Dutch Governor, **81-134**, 149
                    and Gov. James Cockburn, **82-136**
            French recapture of Eustatius, November 27, 1781, **82-109**, 110

negative reaction to Rodney's capture, **81-264**
praise of Rodney and Gen. Vaughan for their success, **81-130**
Rodney defended, **82-399**
Rodney loses his prize to the French, **81-121**
Rodney sacks an "open" town, **81-215**
Sea Battle of the Saints, West Indies, April 12, 1782, **82-**1, 7, 19, 46, 63, 139, 194, 195, 196, 217, 221, 222, 243, 244, 263, 275, 313, 316, 317, 327, 336, 343, 344, 345, 415 (print), **83-**14, 32, 59, 157, 238, 282
earliest song celebrating this victory, **82-146**
narrative, **82-246**, 375
narrative details of the battle, **82-50**
**For more on the naval war, see**: Gibraltar Besieged, Privateering, the *Royal George*, Ushant Episode.

The American War. British Navy, and West Indies Actions.
St. Kitt, **81-71**, 101
St. Lucia, **79-183**
Cowper's "Epinikion" and "Present for the Queen," **79-A**
Tobago (off Trinidad), **81-80**, **82-106**
**For more on naval operations in the West Indies, see**: under American War, British Navy, Rodney's Engagements and Victories.

The American War. British Successes over American Forces.
Clinton at Charleston, South Carolina, **80-152**, 280, 290
Cornwallis and Tarleton in the South, **80-308**
Cornwallis at Camden, South Carolina, **80-273**
dreams of success over Americans, **84-9**
general comment, **80-50**
Penobscot Bay, New England, and Charleston, South Carolina, **80-277**
Rodney off Gibraltar and Clinton at Charleston, South Carolina, **80-285**
**For more on this topic, see**: The American War. Battles and British Navy.

The American War. Called "The King's War." **78-412**.
The American War. Cause of, and cause of all related troubles. For more evidence of this topic before 1774-75, see Taxation and Stamp Act.
American ambition, **78-2**
American faithlessness, **82-20**
American hypocrisy, **78-33**
American ingratitude, **76-187**
"On Ingratitude," **80-A**
American lies and propaganda, **76-248**, 389
American "madness," **76-387**
American sin and evil passions, **77-6**
American tyrants, **79-32**
American War cause of French hegemony, **78-92**
bishops, **78-345**
bishops, placemen, and Scotch, **78-454**
Boston "Saints," **75-213**
Britain's desire "for power" or sovereignty, and Bute, **78-27**
Britain's initiation of tax tribute from America, **78-19**
British coercion of Americans, **79-254**
British despotism, **85-6**
British dominion or sovereignty over America, **76-371**, **80-29**
British pride, **76-50**, **84-16**
British provocations, abuse of natural rights, Stamp Act, and Proclamation

of Rebellion, August 23, 1775, **76**-58
Burke, E., **84**-65
Bute, **76**-362, 370, **78**-27, 127, 298, 345, 498, **83**-108
    ambition, **77**-23
    and Tories, **81**-7
    Mansfield, North, **75**-194
    responsible for decline of Britain, **80**-386
    Scotch, and King bring corruption and civil war and ruin, **82**-4
    Scotch, North, King George III, Mansfield, Markham, **75**-30, 33, 34, 55
    Scotch, Tories, **80**-404
Congress, "republican faction" pushing for independence, and "Puritanic rage," **78**-2
corruption, **78**-327, **79**-25, **80**-19
    Cowper's "Table Talk," **80**-A
corruption, luxury, immorality, **76**-36
corruption, maladministration, **79**-147
Cowper's "Table Talk": effeminacy, venality, bribery, **82**-A
cruel Mansfield and a "loathed Ministry," **76**-346
"designing" American tyrants, **79**-32
desire for power and conquest, **78**-95
effeminate English nobility, **85**-2
    Cowper's "Table Talk," **82**-A
faction, **76**-363
faction responsible for dishonorable peace, **83**-269
factious subversion by Fox and Burke destroys British empire, **84**-65
failures caused by Patriot Opposition and generals who do not fight, **78**-192
"faithless America," **82**-20
fate and chief ministers, **82**-224
fate, not the King's Friends, **82**-130
Fox, C. J., **84**-56, 65, **85**-10
France, **82**-36
Franklin, **79**-12, **80**-56, **81**-15
"fraudful Patriots," Minority Opposition, **76**-196
a frivolous courtier who drove America to France, **81**-20
Germain, **83**-108, **85**-10
Germain responsible for Yorktown disaster, **81**-178
the "Great National Cause, Constitutional Subordination," **76**-371
greed, **75**-103, **76**-155, 398, 399
    and golden eggs, **74**-216, **75**-128, **78**-506 (**See also**: American War. Cause of, and Fable of the Goose that laid Golden Eggs.)
    blind fury, **79**-26
"Grenville's wild Revenue Plan," Stamp Tax, then tea tax, **77**-125
Howe, **83**-121
    lost American War in Battle of Long Island, **84**-8
Howe's delays lose America, **78**-91
    C. Wesley, "American Independency," **83**-A
immorality, **76**-71
India, wealth and corruption, faction and disunion, **82**-18
insistence upon prerogative, tyranny, **78**-265
Jacobite Scotch Tories, the "Stuart's cause," **78**-269
King, **75**-276, **76**-22, **78**-68, **79**-399, 434, 478, 484

and Bute, Germain and Pitt's dismissal, **83**-108
               and Mansfield, **78**-430
               North ministry, Bute, bishops, **78**-345
       King's corruption and subversion of Parliament and constitution, **75**-261
       "King's Friends," **77**-108, **78**-102, **81**-91
       King's Friends, who advised the American War, **78**-100, **80**-237
       King's insistence upon "Prerogative," **77**-253
       legislative corruption and civil strife, **80**-19
       luxury, **83**-18
               arbitrary power, oppression, revenge, **78**-221
       lying Americans, **76**-389
       "Mad Faction," **76**-363
       "the madness" of a few Americans, **76**-387
       Mansfield, **76**-346, **78**-16, 127, 430, **79**-365
       Mansfield, North, Bute, **75**-95, 218
       Mansfield's belligerency, **79**-516
       ministry, **75**-27, **76**-346, **78**-418, **80**-11
               inept, **80**-9
               prolongs the war, **80**-226
               tyranny of, **80**-11
       Minority lords, "aristocratic insolence," **79**-33
       Minority Opposition support of rebels, **80**-34
       "Modern Whigs," Howe and Keppel, **82**-265
       moral cause, Britain's pride and ambition; immediate cause, taxation of
           Americans, **84**-16
       North, **77**-94, **78**-39, 482, **80**-194, **81**-5, **83**-115
               and Bute, Mansfield, **75**-33, 34, 55, 95, 194, 218, **76**-346
               and Fox prolong war and lose America, **84**-56
               and Germain and Fox responsible for loss of America, **85**-10
               and Germain and Sandwich mislead King and lose America, **82**-3
               "author of the American War," **84**-92
               ministry, **78**-345, 501, **79**-256, 279, 285, **83**-3
               responsible for civil war and loss of America, **84**-192
       "On Ingratitude," **78**-A
       Opposition, **80**-85
       Opposition, especially Fox and Wilkes, traitors, responsible for loss of
           war and wreck of realm, **82**-391
       Opposition, Rockingham, Grafton, Shelburne, **80**-306
       Opposition support of rebels, **80**-34
       "a paltry tax" on tea, **77**-22
               and Scotch, **78**-424
       party faction as result of Peace of 1763, **79**-6
       party rancor, **75**-30
       the Peace of 1763, **79**-6, **84**-39
       placemen, **78**-454
       poor leadership, **79**-446
       pound of tea, **77**-48, 84
       Presbyterian Puritanism, American hypocrisy, **78**-33
       pride, luxury, faction, and war responsible for Britain's decline, **81**-248
       "The Quack," Tory Scots; also C. Wesley's "American Independency," Gen.
           Howe, **83**-A
       removal of Pitt from power, **78**-249, **83**-108
       repeal of Stamp Act, **78**-7

Scotch, **75**-244, **76**-184, **77**-7, 297, **78**-102, 115, 207, 424, 454, 520, **79**-155, **83**-19, 20
    and Bute and Mansfield, **78**-127
    and the devil, **76**-376
    and ministry, **78**-416
    and North, **78**-482
    and Tories, **78**-296, **79**-384
    corruption, **77**-114
    influence through Bute causes British failure in the war, **76**-225
    Jacobite Junto through bribery and corruption, **78**-157, 269
    policies, **76**-295
secret influence of Scotch, "King's Friends," **81**-91
secret Tory junto responsible for Britain's misery and losses, **80**-237
self-interest of Opposition, **80**-85
Stamp tax, **77**-125
    repeal, **78**-7
"the Stuart line," **80**-28
taxation, **74**-212, **75**-30, **78**-19, **84**-8
    America's wealth, **80**-7
    nonimportation, smuggling, coercion, **75**-249
tea, **75**-228, **77**-48, 84, **78**-331, **82**-39, 328
    tax, principle of taxation, **77**-22, 125, **78**-226, 244
Tories, **78**-75, **80**-28, **82**-9
    and Bute, **78**-498
    Scotch, **78**-296, **79**-384
Tory Jacobite Scotch, **76**-339
Tory Scotch, **80**-90
    "The Quack," **83**-A
tyranny, **75**-31, **76**-230, **78**-221, **80**-11
    and corruption, **78**-327
    and prerogative, **76**-74, **78**-265
vice, corruption, **79**-25
    and taxation, **78**-308
Whig aristocracy, **79**-33
Whigs and Tories, Scotch and King's Friends, **78**-102

The American War. Cause of, and Fable of the Goose that laid Golden Eggs. (Britain's greed for American gold), **74**-216, **75**-103, 128, **76**-155, 398, 399 (a print), **77**-300, **78**-506 (same as **75**-128)
    English and French appetite for American goose, **78**-555 (a print)

The American War. Confidence in Leadership, the Generals and Admirals.
    Carleton, **76**-342
    Clinton, Percy, **76**-332
    Howe brothers, **76**-245, 324
    Wm. Howe, **78**-2

The American War. Conscientious Objectors to "an unnatural civil war."
    James Wilson, MP in Irish Parliament, **76**-343
    the Minority, **77**-298
    **See also**: Thomas Howard, 3d Earl of Effingham, and Augustus Keppel.

The American War. The Difficulty or Impossibility of Subduing "the obstinate Yankees." **74**-121, 151, 218, **75**-5, 10, 129, 162, 165, 166, 237, 269, **76**-25, 27, 79, 200, 201, 203, 225, 226, 316, **77**-46, 50, 109, 115, 126, 139, 144, 148, 155, 230, 241, 251, 258, 284, 292, 313, 314, **78**-45, 47, 64, 97, 107, 108, 112, 178, 179, 405, 431, 510, **79**-58, 107, 133, 205, 387, **80**-62, 343, **82**-9, 12

    after Yorktown, a plea to end the war, **81**-247
    after Yorktown, a plea to ministry to end the war, **82**-17
    American invincibility, **78**-66
    blundering ministers and stubborn Americans, **79**-343
    British cannot win in a civil war, **76**-249
    British frustration in Parliament, **78**-202
    collapse of British campaign against America, **77**-237
    the danger of waging war against America, **81**-201
    failure of English spirit, **78**-480
    failures of the generals, **77**-240
    fruitless, **79**-442
    God on American side, **76**-376
    logistics, **76**-316
    a summary of defeats, **78**-226
    the war continues, war fatigue, **81**-252
    Washington's leadership, **80**-180
The American War. The Ease of Defeating America. See also Soldiers, American. **75**-195, 249
    ironic, Americans not really cowardly, **76**-214
    should have been bribed, **76**-378
The American War. Effect of war on _____.
    American family, **78**-90
    bellmen and king, **79**-71
    Bristol trade, **77**-252
    British, dying from thirteen stripes, **78**-130
    British nation, because of waste and expense of war, **80**-111
    British officer, upon returning home from America, **83**-256
    British people, suffering because of ruin of commerce, **80**-87
    daughter's fears for her father, an army officer at Boston, **75**-298
    emigrants, **76**-327, **83**-8
    England, loss of men, money, and trade, but Scotland gains, **78**-424
    friendship, **77**-5
    "Imitation": separated lovers, **83**-A
    king and family, **79**-89
    love vs. war, **78**-471
    lovers across battle lines, **81**-258
    lower class British family, **76**-272
    loyal tradesmen who oppose American rebellion, **78**-513
    the national budget, **77**-131
    newly married couple, **75**-294
    on young American or British lovers, **76**-68, 349, 350
    on taxes and national debt, **78**-47
    price of tobacco, **76**-375
    profits of contractors and jobbers, **77**-174
    a ruined merchant, **79**-533
    separated lovers, **80**-322
    separated young lovers, **77**-282
    separation of American lovers, **79**-213
    separation of husband and wife, **78**-79
    separation of lovers, **77**-49, 105, **78**-527
    separation of sailor and his sweetheart, **79**-395
    separation of young lovers, **75**-299
    the state of nature in America, **80**-51

    stock jobbers, bulls and bears, **79-88**
    trade in American tobacco, **79-377**
    wife's fears for husband leaving to fight the rebels, **76-351**
    young American in England for education exiled from native home, **78-206**
    young lovers, **78-113**
    young loyalist, separated from sweetheart and parents, **82-387**
    young man separated from native home, **77-64**
    young soldier leaving family for America, **84-9**
The American War. The End.
    Conway's motion to end the American War, **82-32**
    the end of the fighting, and France, Spain, and Holland, **85-6**
    the end of the war, defeat of Cornwallis, and coming peace, **84-191**
    peace and re-alliance with America are on the way, **82-291**
    petitions urging peace after the Yorktown defeat, **81-174**
    remarks on the end of the war, **82-350**
The American war. The End. Britain's Loss of America. **81-59, 82-3**, 4, 28, 30, 309, 347, **83-10**
    and the Georgian Star, **83-47, 84-49**
    and king, **83-108**
    and North ministry, **83-82**
    blamed on Gen. Howe and Adm. Keppel, **82-365**
    to France, **82-410**
The American War. The End. Hope for Reconciliation and Reunion with America. **83-21**, 30, 32, 33, 212, 242
    after the peace, a reconciliation, **83-298**
    America reunites with England "to chastise its foes," **82-27**
    Britain and America reunite against France, **83-25**
    Britain and America will be reallied, **82-291**
    France and Spain protest reconciliation of Britain with America, **82-419**
    Loyalist hopes for reunion, **82-310**
    of Britain and America against France, **82-5**
    peace with America, but war against France, **82-15**, 69
    return of America, **83-186**
    reunion, **82-396, 86-4**
    reunion, Anglo-American union of "Two Britains," **85-10**, 57
The American War. The End. Peace. **82-28**, 29, 32, 61, 72, 117, 119, 133, 142, 166, 171, 174, 213, 214, 293
    and Ireland, **82-202**
    and North's resignation, **82-204**
    debate on the peace in Parliament, **83-122**
    incredible view of the way peace has come, **82-41**
    King resists petitions against war, **82-161**
    the need for peace, **82-220**
    new Rockingham ministry will bring peace to America, **82-228**
    peace is elusive, **82-396**
    peace is welcomed, **83-11**
    Peace Preliminaries, January 20, 1783, **83-109**
    Shelburne and peace, **82-253**
    Shelburne's peace, **82-292**
    a soldier asks for peace with America, **82-367**
    Who is to make the peace?, **82-369**
The American War. The End. Peace Negotiations. (Provisional Articles of Peace between England and America, signed in Paris, November 30, 1782.)

and Franco-American alliance, **83**-12
and the Portland ministry, February 1783-December 1783, **83**-29
the beginning of negotiations in 1782, **83**-32
beware French treachery, **83**-10
Britain blunders at peace treaties, **82**-149
British resist American independence supported by Fox, **82**-411 (a print)
the Coalition and the peace with America and Holland, **83**-63
comments on peace with America, **82**-320
difficulties of making peace, **82**-421 (a print)
difficulty of ending American War, **82**-205
doubts concerning preliminary peace treaties, **83**-251
need to separate colonies from France, **82**-410
negotiators "stumbling," **82**-272
North's support of American Loyalists, **83**-180
Peace of 1763 and Peace of 1783, Britain blunders at treaties with France, **82**-383
a peace that frees America, **83**-19
peace with America will be followed by ties of trade and liberty, **82**-291
progress slowly, **82**-96
protest at, **82**-118
rejection of an "effeminate peace," **82**-192
Shelburne unwilling to grant independence to America, **82**-326
Shelburne's difficulties, **83**-289, 293 (prints)
three ministries and their peace attempts, **83**-153
The American War. The End. Reception of Peace Treaty, 1783. (Peace officially signed September 3, 1783; proclaimed October 6, 1783).
    acceptance of peace treaty, **83**-167, 168, 169, 170, 175, 183, 184, 185, 190, 197, 198, 213, 214, 227, 233, 258, 259, 275, 277, 296 (a print) **84**-91, 128, 218, **85**-4
    accepted but for slavery in America, **84**-7
    accepts the peace, **83**-27
    the common man welcomes peace, **83**-157
    defense of Shelburne's peace, **83**-83, 86
    Definitive Treaty of Peace, September 3, 1783, and Shelburne, **83**-111
    French view of the peace, **83**-165
    infamous, "a damn'd War" and "a mock Peace," **83**-161
    peace and American Loyalists, **83**-124, 180, 297 (a print),
    pleasure in, **83**-118, 128, 142, 163, 164
        after signing Preliminary Articles, **83**-162
    a poor peace, deplored, **83**-19
    rejection of, and ends a shameful war, **83**-123
    rejection of peace treaty, **83**-220, **84**-1, **85**-13
        a bad peace, but England must make the best of it, **83**-292 (a print), 295 (a print)
        base, **83**-269
        errors of must be corrected, **83**-279
        failure, **83**-219
        "false peace," **84**-90
        Great Britain now little, **83**-203
        "inglorious peace," **84**-207
        proclamation ironically paraphrased, **83**-226
        "shameful," ruinous, **83**-201
    Shelburne's peace criticized, **83**-66

terrible peace, **83**-144
"treacherous" peace, **83**-50

The American War. Enlarged. The Armed Neutrality, 1780-1783. **80**-249, 285, 325, 394, **81**-102, 125, 131, **82**-22
    and Russia, **83**-285
    Cowper's "Table Talk," **82**-A
    Russia, Prussia, Holland, **79**-376
    **See**: Russia, and the Armed Neutrality, 1779-80.

The American War. Enlarged and Transformed into a French War, March 17, 1778, because of Franco-American treaty of alliance, February 6, 1778. **77**-11, 27, 305, **78**-18, 22, 172, 173, 174, 175, 423
    alliance condemned, and Arnold and André, **81**-14
    Americans in alliance are not Tories, **81**-181
    anti-Gallican recruiting song and additional recruits leave for America, **77**-2
    anti-Gallican song, **78**-211, 231
        on expected invasion, **78**-65
    beginning of war with France, **78**-40
    Britain surrounded by enemies, including Holland, **79**-454
    condemned as unnatural alliance, **81**-15
    effect of alliance after Yorktown, **81**-247
    fear of France, **79**-194
    Franco-American alliance, **78**-194
        condemned, **80**-13, 14
    French alliance dangerous to America, **80**-417
    French intervention, **78**-33, 81
    Holland as enemy, **79**-534
    Holland prepares to join France against Britain, **79**-360
    hope that Franco-American alliance will be broken and Britain reconciled with America, **82**-5, 11, 22, 27, 29, 30, **83**-19, 25
        alliance condemned, **82**-16, **83**-116
        France will enslave America, **82**-361
    ingratitude of America, **81**-104
    isolated, Britain needs Ireland's help, **79**-528
    loss of America to France, **80**-199, 217
    loyal song upon expectation of a French War, **77**-28
    menace of France, **78**-3
        in Canada and De Lafayette, **80**-54
    the menace of France, Spain, and Holland, **78**-331
    ministry's quandary now that France and Spain are in the war, **79**-426
    need for reconciliation with America because of danger of Bourbon war, **79**-358
    the need to fight France, **78**-218
    objection to alliance, **81**-16
    objection to France and Spain "meddling" in American War, **79**-287, 382
    peace with America, but war with France, **79**-484
    Pitt and a "just" war, **78**-43, 60
    preparations for French War, **78**-114
    recruiting song, **77**-265 (same as **77**-2)
    review of situation 1779, **79**-271
    summary view of effect of Franco-American alliance, **84**-16
    support of and opposition to French War, **78**-280
    unjust war becomes just, even against America, **79**-1

war against France, but peace with America, **79**-211
war against France, Spain and America, **79**-247, 270, 285, 348, 447, 526
war with France, **79**-411
whole world in opposition, **78**-87
will unite Britain against America, **81**-193
**See also:** American War Enlarged and Transformed into a "World War": Britain against Confederated Powers; France (and Britain).

The American War. Enlarged and Transformed into a French War: Patriotic Support of the French War, **78**-175, 177, 178, 198, 283, 293, 307, 361, 416, 427, 446, 448, 449, 478, 510, 518, 543 (see **78**-310), **79**-2, 6, 7, 12, 50, 76, 78, 79, 82, 83, 96, 111, 112, 115, 116, 121, 151, 152, 153, 192, 210, 214, 237, 238, 242, 251, 277, 280, 282, 299, 360, 366, 396, 408, 415, 416, 418, 423, 437, 483, 488, 498, 503, 521, 522, **80**-15, 20, 27, 48, 55, 75, 155, 175, 189, 205, 221, 224, 232, 322, 323, 326, 365, 368, 379, 407, 408, **81**-10, 19, 43, 75, 87, 123, 125, 131, 132, 133, 136, 198, 209, 213, 214, 250, **82**-11, 51, 62, 79, 80, 215, 297, 313, 320, 324, 338, 345, 398
   and Dutch, **81**-21
   and Ireland, **78**-304
   Britain welcomes the French War, **78**-260
   Fast Day verse, **82**-6
   from Jamaica, for peace, **82**-213
   from Jamaica, vs. France and Spain, **82**-199
   Gibraltar remains British, **83**-155
   the London volunteers, **79**-250
   Patriotic verse against Bourbon enemies and America, **79**-A ("Britannia to her Sons," "French Peace," "Lead On," "The Sequel of Britannia's Address," "The Volunteer's Rouse," Woods' "Lyric Ode"), **80**-208, 234 (?), 335, 352, **81**-1, 210, 262, **82**-295
   preparations for a French War, **78**-428
   recruiting song, **78**-456
   Scotch poem, **81**-232

The American War. Enlarged and Transformed into a "World War": Britain against Confederated Powers. **80**-3, 18, 23, 28, 41, 65, 134, 217, 246, 249, 272, 275, 345, 375, 417 (a print), 419 (a print), **81**-7, 22, 29, 31, 85, 87, 157, 168, 242, 247, 250, 253, 262 (a print), 263 (a print), 265 a print), 267 (a print), **82**-18, 29, 219, 303, 313, 411 (a print), 412 (a print), **83**-10, 32, 48
   alone, but Britain cannot fall, **82**-397
   and the peace, **83**-50
   Britain against the world, **90**-1
   Britain requires assistance of America to defeat all Europe, **81**-140
   Britain will manage, **81**-95
   Cowper's "Table Talk," **82**-A
   England eaten up by enemies, **80**-420 (a print)
   the fame of Britain in 1782, **82**-345
   Holland refuses to help Britain, **80**-421 (a print)
   North's Government will win, **81**-159
   Rodney ends this war with a great victory, **82**-221
   unanimity will save Britain, **83**-135
   vs. the "quadruple" alliance, **83**-35

The American War. Failure of Leadership. Generals, **78**-192, 481, 512, **79**-387, **82**-71, 75, **83**-91
   British officers, failure of martial spirit, **77**-232
   British troops sleeping in America, **85**-2

Burgoyne, **76**-325, **77**-134, 144, 240, **78**-396, 472, **79**-422, **80**-32, 163
    defense of, **79**-32
    "too hardy," **78**-228
Carleton, **77**-240
Clinton, **77**-240
Cornwallis, **82**-393, **83**-A (in C. Wesley's "American Independency")
Dunmore, **77**-240
failures of generals and admirals, **84**-66
Gage, **76**-325, **77**-134, 240, **78**-351, 396
generals who lost the war, **83**-144
Howe, **77**-90, 134, 144, 148, 240, **78**-91, 94, 170, 189, 351, 396, 472, **79**-6, 40, 387, **84**-8
    amorous dalliance of, **78**-228
    and brother Richard, **78**-143
    and Burgoyne, **79**-422, **80**-32, 163
    and Cornwallis, **82**-393, **83**-A (C. Wesley's "American Independency")
    and Germain, **77**-148
    and Keppel, **80**-163, **81**-48
    blamed for British defeat, **79**-228, 249
    excessive dilatoriness, **77**-257, 261
    lethargic character and delays, **78**-91, 94, 143, 170, 189, 228, 540, **79**-6, 40, 228, 249
    lost the war and the empire, **78**-540, **83**-144
    poems on, **80**-A ("A Comparison," "An Epitaph")
    **See also**: Howe Brothers
incompetent commanders, **80**-24
self-interested generals, **79**-482
The American War. Failure of Leadership. King and Premier North and Ministry. **82**-219
    Army and Navy, **77**-307, 323, **78**-480, 481, **81**-135
    British forces in America, **82**-212, **83**-103
    British isolated among enemies, **83**-149
    clergy, **82**-75
    confused leadership, ship of state rudderless, **79**-167
    Cornwallis, **83**-149
    cowardly soldiers, **82**-75
    a divided empire, **83**-149
    "execution" of Asgill, **83**-149
    failures, **83**-149
    generals, **82**-75
    Germain, **82**-10, 354, 369
        blamed for Burgoyne's defeat, **78**-6
        "timid measures," **78**-301
    hanging of André, **83**-149
    King, **78**-102, 436, 477, **79**-89, 276, 446, **82**-10
        and ministry, **79**-205, 446
        and North, **78**-332, 512, **81**-135
    Majority in Parliament, **79**-446, **82**-75
    ministry, **78**-96, 100, 106, 217, 356, **79**-205, 446, **80**-9, 18, **81**-93, 173, **82**-75
        and generals, **78**-510
    need for a Pitt, **78**-229, 393
    North, **77**-23, 251, 310, **78**-106, 217, 332, 512, **82**-177, 369

and Germain, **78**-551
and King, **81**-135
premier, **78**-402, 536, **79**-233
Sandwich, **78**-103, 260, 267, 291, **82**-279, 369, 377
  inept administration, **78**-16, 27, 54, 56
self-interested peace commissioners, generals and admirals, **79**-482
"Statesmen and Senators," **77**-327
Tory policy, **78**-226
Wesley's "American Independency": blames failures on generals and Minority Opposition, **83**-A
whole leadership, especially Germain and Sandwich, **79**-283
Yorktown, **81**-93

The American War. Foreign Aid.
Britain warns America to be content with British rule because the alternative, French arbitrary government, is worse, **76**-229
Britain warns America not to seek foreign aid, **76**-269
Britain will soon chastise France for assisting America, **77**-246

The American War. Hypocrisy of Americans. (The British reaction to Franco-American alliance.) **80**-15, 41, 77, **84**-18
Americans as seditious and hypocritical parricides, **1800**-1
America as subversive, hypocritical, and Popish, **79**-531 (print)
American betrayal of Britain, **83**-48
faithless, ruthless, barbarous, and guilt-ridden, **82**-20
hypocritical fanatical saints, **80**-150
"perjur'd parricides," **82**-29
Presbyterian Puritanism and French alliance, **78**-33
treacherous American diplomacy, **82**-16

The American War. Independence. (The Struggle for Independence.) **80**-309, **83**-135
acceptance of, **82**-25
achieved with the connivance of "Patriots," the former Minority Opposition during North's ministry, **83**-288 (print), 292 (print)
America achieves independence and concludes a peace, **83**-298 (print)
America aspired to independence early in the 1760's, **80**-34
American Loyalist objects to, **83**-116
and church, **83**-205
and Dean Tucker, **79**-105
and the effect on the church in America, **83**-40
and France, **79**-348
and Ireland, **83**-276
and Louis XVI, **83**-133
and reform movement, **82**-85
birth of U.S.A., **93**-1
bitterness over, **85**-45
Britain must give freedom [independence] to America, **78**-336
Britain predicts Americans will not benefit from independence, **83**-296 (print)
Britain should solve the American problem by means of amputation, **76**-175
British offer freedom but not independence, **78**-223
celebration of an independent America, **85**-4
colonies provoked to declare independence, **78**-12, 45
Cowper's "To Sir Joshua Reynolds," predicts failure of independence, **80**-A
Declaration of Independence, **83**-19, **93**-1

praise of, **83**-31
versified, **78**-63
defense of, **78**-36
effect on Ireland and France, **93**-1
effect on the church in America, **83**-340
Gen. Howe's blunders and American independence, **83**-121
hope that America will give up independence and return to Britain, **82**-11
"Independency" as motive, March 1, 1776, **76**-243
inept ministry provoked colonies to separate, **80**-9
Jenyns on American independence, **76**-190
"Lawless Independency," **77**-6
Maurice changes mind about American independence, **84**-10
opposed and condemned, **79**-6, 15
opposition to, **80**-4
American independence, **82**-156, 326
preamble to Declaration attacked by Jenyns, **82**-13
prophesied, **78**-63
Richmond and Pitt (Chatham) on American independence, **78**-371
support of America's rights but opposition to its independence, **82**-22
Washington, Paine, France, Britain, Congress and God and the birth of independence, **83**-38
The American War. Minority Opposition. See Minority Opposition during North's ministry, the period of the American War.
The American War. Prisoners.
American, **76**-200, **78**-89, 316, 317, 398, 462, **79**-14, 45, **81**-205
British starvation of, **85**-6
American Loyalist, **76**-162, **78**-284
British, **80**-21
and Spanish, treatment contrasted, **79**-174
in France, **80**-205
in French prisons, West Indies, **81**-257
sailors in Spanish prison, **80**-257
Exchange of American and British, **80**-139
"Hulks" (prison ships on Thames), **76**-320
**See also**: John André, Henry Laurens.
The American War. Prophecy of ruin to come, civil war, loss of America, dismemberment of the empire, defeat, and a variety of hopes. **71**-90, **74**-16, 25, 35, 67, 109, 170, 172, 209, 210, 212, 218, **75**-13, 32, 66, 70, 111, 120, 121, 131, 140, 221, 222, 223, 224, **76**-6, 7, 8, 39, 54, 55, 59, 165, 239, 260, 271, 292, 293, 294, 357, 367, **77**-33,
America lost, **79**-295
to the crown, **80**-321
America, a nation powerful and pure, **78**-47
America will rejoin Britain, **80**-20
America's greatness, union of America and Britain, **80**-19
America's triumph, **79**-3
anarchy in America dominated by "lust of pow'r," **83**-12
by America, a pessimistic view, **76**-289
Britain doomed to perish because of its criminal war, **78**-63
Britain will mourn "the fatal error" of the American War, **80**-65
Britain will soon assert its power, **80**-298
Britain "sick" and declining, **78**-233, 287
Britain's glory has set in West, will rise again in East, **83**-10

Britain's overthrow, but navy will restore her hegemony, 79-264
British isolated and alone in March 1778, 78-450
British victory and end of rebellion, 79-21
collapse of Britain, loss of liberties and America, 79-147
the collapse of the British campaign against America, 77-237
Congress enslaved to Bourbons, 79-272
decline and death of Britain, 77-290 (same as 79-243), 79-443 (same as 77-290)
decline of Britain and separation of colonies, 78-196
the declining nation, 78-358
defeat, 77-173
    of America, 81-14
        at Charleston, South Carolina, May 12, 1780, should end the war, 80-152
    of American rebels, 80-208
    of Burgoyne and loss of America, 77-120
    of D'Estaing and France, 80-262
desire for peace and loss of America, 77-54
destruction of empire, 78-100
dethronement of King, 78-8
division of empire, 78-167
doom of American rebellion, 79-60
end of British empire, 79-383
epitaph on death of British empire, 78-157
execution of North and Bute, 74-225
failure to suppress American rebellion and oppression at home, 78-295
fall of Britain, 79-26
fall of North and King George, 80-200
fall of North ministry and effect on Britain's enemies, 80-419
for year 1776, 76-291
future greatness of America, 81-12
future greatness of Britain after Seven Years' War, and then its decline and fall, 90-1
the future of U.S.A. as it expands westward, 85-6
George III will lose an empire, 80-121
loss of America, 79-37, 431
    and West Indies, 78-298
    to France, 79-523
loss of America and Atlantic trade means end of luxury, 82-309
loss of colonies through revolt presages decline of grandeur, 78-24
loss of empire, 75-79, 78-302
loss of Pitt and empire, 78-349
Minority in place and colonies dominate Britain, a dream, 77-73
nation in ruin, constitution undermined, 78-37
North, Sandwich, Germain will ruin Britain, 82-304
North's ministry will win against Opposition and Confederated Powers, 81-159
of victory of Tories, 77-57
only Pitt can bring peace and save the empire, 78-387, 499
the Patriots in power will restore Britain's glory, 82-54
Pitt's death and fall of empire, 78-121, 163
powerful, united, and wealthy America, 79-28
the rebellion will be crushed, 76-94

reconciliation of Britain and America upon France's entry into war, **78-22**
revival of trade will bring prosperity, although America is lost, **83-241**
Rodney's victories and America's return to Britain, **80-424**
ruin, **78-16**
    of America because of French alliance, **82-16**
    of Britain, **79-445**
    of the nation, **77-327**
a ruinous civil war, **75-68**
suppression and failure of Burke's plan for Parliament's reform, **80-33**
Tory overthrow of Glorious Revolution Constitution, **79-384**
traitors of Opposition and defeat, **79-510**
victory of America, helped by France and Spain, **78-44**
victory over America, France and Spain, **77-292**
victory over France, **79-349**
Washington's victory, **77-143**

The American War. Punishment of Criminals Responsible for the Ruinous War.
damnation in hell for those urging coercion of America, **80-11**
execution of Bute, Suffolk, North, Mansfield, **78-479**
execution of North, Mansfield, Germain, Rigby, John Wesley, **79-202**
execution of those responsible, **79-363**
the genuine traitors, the Catilines, are the Opposition to North's ministry, **82-209**
Germain, **82-60**
    deserves hanging, **82-224**, **85-52**
ironically anticipated defeat and punishment of the leading rebels, **77-183**
King, for his failures, **80-161**
the ministers should be brought to justice, **82-293, 381, 83-9**
North, **82-76, 224**
    is saved from punishment by his coalition with Fox, **84-150**
Sandwich, **82-57**
    for mismanagement, **81-153**
Sandwich, North, Germain deserve hanging, **82-224**
Shelburne will punish the traitors, **82-159**
urges trial of North ministry for its criminal war, **83-9**

The American War. Veterans. See Veteran Soldiers.
Americans in England. See Henry Cruger, Arthur and William Lee, Stephen Sayre, James Rogers.
Amherst, Jeffrey (1717-97). British general, conqueror of Canada in French and Indian war; Governor of Virginia, 1763, and loses this fat sinecure to Ld Botetourt in 1768; declined a command against America, although he supported Government's coercive policies towards the Americans. **58-1, 2, 5, 59-5, 16, 60-5, 18, 22, 29, 41, 42, 48, 62-7, 64-7, 67-25, 68-22, 64, 78, 108, 76-16, 78-14, 354, 531, 79-232, 275, 432, 487, 80-41, 81-259, 82-193, 212, 90-1**
character, **78-84**
Gordon Riots, **81-5**
obelisk commemorating his victories over the French in America, **1758-62**
    [see also **60-18**], **78-251**
André, John (1751-1780). See Part I of Index.
Anson, George (1697-1762). MP, 1745-47; British admiral; circumnavigated the world, 1740-44, young Augustus Keppel being with him; First Lord of the Admiralty, 1751-62, and Keppel, **79-39, 82-91**
Anti-Papist Sentiments. **62-1**

**See also:** Quebec Bill, Gordon Riots.
Arbuthnot, Marriott (1711-94). Blundering British admiral, commanded a
    squadron in American waters, 1779-81. **78**-211, **80**-71
        Charleston, South Carolina, **80**-290
        criticized for inactivity, **80**-339
Armed Neutrality. See American War. Enlarged. The Armed Neutrality; also
    Russia, and the Armed Neutrality.
Army Officers (American) serving in the American War, 1775-83.
        William Alexander (Stirling), Benedict Arnold, Horatio Gates, John
        Laurens, Benjamin Lincoln, Hugh Mercer, Richard Montgomery, Israel Putnam,
        Thomas Sumter, Artemas Ward, George Washington.
Army Officers (American) serving in the French and Indian (or Seven Years') War,
    1755-63.
        William Alexander (Stirling), Benedict Arnold, Horatio Gates, Hugh Mercer,
        Richard Montgomery, Israel Putnam, Artemas Ward, George Washington.
Army Officers (British) serving in the American War, 1775-83.
        John D. Acland, Charles Asgill, John Burgoyne, Mungo Campbell, Guy
        Carleton, Henry Clinton, James Cockburn, Charles Cornwallis, John
        Dalrymple, William Draper, George Augustus Eliott, William Erskine,
        William Feilding, Patrick Ferguson, Richard Fitzpatrick, Simon Fraser,
        Thomas Gage, Francis Geary, Jr., William Howe, John Maitland, John
        Marjoribanks, James Moncrieff, John Money, James Murray, Hugh Percy,
        Francis Pierson, Robert Pigot, Richard Prescott, Augustine Prevost,
        Francis Rawdon, Banastre Tarleton, John Vaughan.
Army Officers (British) serving in the Seven Years' War, 1755-63.
        Jeffrey Amherst, Isaac Barré, Edward Braddock, John Burgoyne, James
        Cockburn, Henry Seymour Conway, Charles Cornwallis, William Draper, George
        Augustus Eliott, William Erskine, Simon Fraser, Thomas Gage, George
        Germain (Sackville), George Augustus Howe, William Howe, William Johnson,
        John Manners (Granby), John Marjoribanks, Robert Monckton, James
        Moncrieff, James Murray, Hugh Percy, Richard Prescott, Augustine Prevost,
        Roger Townshend, John Vaughan, James Wolfe.
Arnold, Benedict (1741-1801). American general and traitor; joined the British
    after André's capture and execution. **76**-27, 243, 315, 321, 342, **77**-47, 66,
    178, 183, 202, 203, 285, 292, **78**-8, 12, 25, 64, 295, 408, 520, **79**-26, **80**-136,
    149, 190, 277, **81**-3, 181, 203, **82**-20, 127, 143, **83**-25, 69, **84**-66
        and André, **80**-131, **81**-14
        and Burgoyne, **77**-199
        and the devil, **83**-67
        and Eden, both traitors, **85**-61
        and Gen. Prescott, **77**-192, 237
        and Wolfe, **78**-414
        at court, **82**-380
        at George's court, **82**-167
        exchanged for Henry Laurens, **82**-267
        Lady Craven's ode, **82**-212
        "one Arnold," **76**-17
        "One Hannibal," **76**-A
        reputation at George's court, **81**-64
Asgill, Charles (c. 1762-1823). Young British captain captured at Yorktown,
    selected by lot for execution in retaliation for a loyalist hanging of a
    rebel American officer, 1782. **83**-25, 33, 149, 235, **85**-4
Atticus. (pseud.) An allegedly destructive journalist, an "approved patriot,"
    i.e., a Tory. **78**-338

Balf, Lawrence. A bruiser hired by the court party and tried with MacQuirk for the murder of George Clark. See Edward MacQuirk.

Ballooning, the War in the Air. **83**-287 (a print)

Bampfylde, Charles W. (1753-1823). MP, 1774-90, 1796-1812. Independent country gentleman who often supported the opposition against North. **80**-299

Barnard, John (c. 1685-1764). MP, 1722-61; Alderman, 1720-58; and Lord Mayor, 1737-38, of London. **72**-7, 12

Barré, Isaac (1726-1802). MP, 1761-90. Served with Wolfe at Quebec, where he lost an eye; protégé of and spokesman for Shelburne; supported Wilkes and America, where he was regarded as a hero; a severe critic of the American War. **66**-64, 75, 129, **70**-101, 107, 113, 178, 195, **72**-1, **74**-5, **75**-78, 177, **76**-44, 82, 92, 202, 290, **77**-13, 119, 149, 270, 271, 292, 299, **78**-23, 34, 38, 43, 66, 187, 219, 234, 512, 556, 557, **79**-11, 31, 38, 200, 317, 429, 499, **80**-18, 33, 59, 61, 191, 220, 229, 291, 295, 305, 316, 317, 324, **81**-60, **82**-164, 234, 349, 412 (a print), 413 (a print), **83**-30, 32

    America and liberty, **74**-17

    Boston Port Bill, **74**-32

    Freeth and pension, **82**-A

    Shelburne awards Barré a pension, **82**-413 (a print)

    "Spoken . . . ," **70**-A

    vs. Fox, **82**-223

Barrington, Samuel (1729-1800). British naval officer; served under Hawke, Byron, and Rodney in Seven Years' War; rear admiral in command in West Indies, captured St. Lucia, 1778; under Richard Howe in the Channel Fleet and at relief of Gibraltar, 1782. **79**-182, 440, **82**-342

    "While Byron and Barrington," **79**-A

Barrington, William Wildman, 2d Viscount Barrington (1717-93). MP, 1740-78. Secretary-at-War, 1755-61, 1765-78. Ordered the military to suppress the Wilkesite riots, especially the one at St. George's Fields, May 10, 1768. Believed America could not be subdued but loyally voted with the North ministry for military coercion. **59**-16, **60**-17, 25, **68**-121, **69**-12, 59, 214, **70**-18, 28, 32, 112, 120, **72**-1, 6, **76**-213, 307, 313, **78**-187, **79**-11

Bate, Henry (1745-1824). The "Fighting Parson." Editor of the *Morning Post*, government supported newspaper; also edited the *Morning Herald*, beginning November 1, 1780, a new government organ. Assumed the additional name of Dudley in 1784. **79**-98, 372, 373, 474, 489, **80**-35, **82**-9

    and libels of Richmond, **81**-160

    and Palliser, **80**-146

    *Morning Post* vs. *London Evening Post,* **79**-492

    satire on, regarding Keppel-Palliser scandal, **79**-312

Bathurst, Henry. 2d Earl Bathurst (1714-94). MP, 1735-54; then House of Lords. Lord High Chancellor in North's ministry, 1771-78. **77**-12, **78**-7

    resigns as Lord High Chancellor, **78**-394

Battles of the American War of Independence. See American War. Battles and Campaigns.

Beauchamp-Proctor, William (1722-73). MP, for Middlesex, 1747-68. Lost to Glynn in the exciting and expensive contest for MP, Brentford, Middlesex, 1768. Whig; voted with opposition on Wilkes issues and general warrants, 1763-64. **68**-37, **69**-81, 112

    "On Occasion," "On Two," and "A Pill," **68**-A

Beaufort, Duke of. See Henry Somerset.

Beaumarchais, de. Assumed name of Pierre Augustin Caron (1732-99). French secret agent who secured needed supplies for America.

    and Franklin, **77**-149

Beckford, William (1709-70). MP, 1747-70; alderman, sheriff, and lord mayor of London. Wealthy Jamaican sugar planter and merchant; a Tory under George II, but a radical under George III, supported the causes of Wilkes and the American colonists. **63**-179, **69**-126, 129, 202, **70**-6, 8, 26, 42, 47, 48, 63, 75, 76, 95, 103, 104, 134, 135, 136, 137, 144, 145, 146, 162, 170, 187, 194, 199, 212, 217, 218, 219, 229, 233, 234, 239, 242, **71**-120, 137, **72**-7, 12, 54, 87, **76**-10, **78**-44
    and Whig liberty, **74**-17
    Beckford's remonstrance, **70**-19, 20
    "An Elegy . . .," **70**-A
    "Liberty," **89**-2
Bedford, 4th Duke of. See John Russell.
Bellamont, Earl of. See Charles Coote.
Bellas, George. Attorney, Wilkesite partisan, London Common Councilman from Castle Baynard; a moving spirit, along with Horne, Sawbridge, and James Townsend, of the Society of Supporters of the Bill of Rights, especially the preparation of the great Middlesex Petition to the King, May 1769. **69**-14, 126, **70**-101, **73**-3
    "Alphabetical," **69**-A
Bennet, Charles, 4th Earl of Tankerville (1743-1822). In House of Lords, he opposed the North Ministry regarding Wilkes and coercion of the colonies. *Noble Cricketers*, **78**-A
Bentinck, William Henry. See William Henry Cavendish-Bentinck.
Berkeley, Norborne (c. 1717-70). MP, 1741-63; then House of Lords. Baron Botetourt, 1764. A Tory with several places in the King's household, supported Bute and Grenville; appointed Royal Governor of Virginia replacing Amherst, 1768; died in Virginia. **68**-78
Bernard, Francis (1712-79). Governor of New Jersey, 1758-60; governor of Massachusetts, 1760-71; recalled to England because his administration was too strict and unpopular, making government impossible. **69**-26, 84, 118, **74**-209
    "An Addressicle," **68**-A
Bernard, Robert (1739?-89). MP, 1765-68, 1770-74. Helped found the Bill of Rights Society, 1769, but voted for its dissolution in 1771 and, breaking with Wilkes, joined the rival Constitutional Society with Horne. Led the reform movement in his county of Huntingdonshire. **67**-6
Bertet de la Clue Sabran (c. 1696-1764). French admiral of the Toulon fleet during the Seven Years' War; defeated in Lagos Bay, August 1759, by Boscawen, when he attempted to join his fleet with the Brest fleet of Admiral Conflans. **60**-14
Bertie, Willoughby Montagu, 4th Earl of Abingdon (1740-99). A frequent speaker in the House of Lords; loyally backed Wilkes in the 1760's and friend of Rockingham, but went beyond the Rockingham Whigs in support of popular rights; steadily opposed the coercive measures of the North ministry; a Yankee sympathizer. **75**-35, 42, **76**-176, **77**-7, 29, 55, 85, 88, 95, 128, 215, 245, 304, **78**-4, 14, 45, 64, 219, 316, 498, 526, **79**-44, 59, **80**-357, **82**-193, 212
    and independence of Ireland, **82**-25
    and Markham, **78**-43
    and the war, **80**-264
    joins Pitt against Fox, **84**-216
Berton de Balbe, Louis de; Duc de Crillon (1718-96). Head of the Bourbon forces making the grand final assault on Gibraltar, September 1782. **82**-90
The Bible. See Part III of Index, Imitations of the Bible.

Board of Trade and Plantations. Established by William III, 1696; abolished by Parliament, March 1780, and dismantled, 1782. A government agency serving as an advisory body to Parliament regarding imperial policies, especially North American colonial development and trade. Lords (or Commissioners) of Trade in the period of the American Revolution: Richard Cumberland, clerk and secretary, 1776-81; Thomas De Grey, 1777-81 (also under-secretary of state for the American dept, 1777-80); George Montagu Dunk, Earl Halifax, President, 1748-61; William Eden, 1776-82; Bamber Gascoigne, 1763-65, 1772-79; Edward Gibbon, June 1779-May 1782; Frederick Howard, Earl of Carlisle, President, 1779-82; Soame Jenyns, 1755-80; William Legge, Earl of Dartmouth, President, 1765-66, 1772-75; Richard Rigby, 1755-60, Hans Sloane-Stanley, 1780-82.
    abolished, **80**-86
    marked for abolishment in Burke's plan for Parliamentary reform, **80**-33
    **For more, see especially**: Edward Gibbon.

Boscawen, Edward (1711-61). Admiral, commanded the expeditions that captured Louisburg, 1758, and Lagos, 1759, in Seven Years' War. **56**-1, **58**-1, 4, 5, **59**-10, 16, 42, **60**-14, 17, 25, 42, 48, **61**-9, 51, **62**-17, **63**-17, **79**-1, 67, 203, **80**-41, **82**-48, 91
    "Advertisement . . . ," **60**-A
    death, **61**-35

Boston, Massachusetts. **65**-14, 135, **66**-25, 75, **70**-243 (print of Massacre), **78**-73 (same as **72**-14)
    celebrated for opposition to tyranny, **72**-14
    "From the Massachusetts Spy," **73**-A
    Loyalists, **74**-21
    "Massacre," **71**-13, **73**-16, 86
    quartering of troops, **65**-34

Boston, Massachusetts. "Rebellious Boston" and its Troubles. **74**-29, 31, 70, 106, 142, 212, 216, 222, **75**-10, 34, 37, 38, 44, 45, 48, 55, 71, 75, 122, 123, 124, 133, 148, 162, 168, 215, 220, 227, 240, 241, 311, 317, **76**-6, 19, 22, 43, 182, **77**-4, **78**-15, 415, **79**-6, **80**-19
    British atrocities in, **76**-70
    Magna Carta and American Rights, **74**-23, 114
    New England Fishery Bill, March 30, 1775, **75**-84
    Port and other Intolerable Acts, **74**-8, 15, 20, 32, 33, 56, 69, 83, 85, 89, 131, 139, 183, 189, **75**-1, 197, 199, 223, 314, **76**-46, **78**-15, 170
    **For more on Boston, see**: Boston Siege and Bunker Hill in American War. Battles and Campaigns; Quebec Bill; Thomas Gage; Tea (Boston Tea Party).

Boswell, James (1740-95). The biographer of Samuel Johnson; his account of Paoli and Corsica, 1768, excited much sympathy for the Corsican struggle for liberty from Genoa and from France. **68**-12, 49, **69**-2, 4, 38, 198, 256, **70**-6, **71**-1

Boteler, Philip (d. 1787?). Captain of the *Ardent*, man-of-war, defeated in a heroic action by a French force. **79**-92, 352

Botetourt, 4th Baron. See Norborne Berkeley.

Braddock, Edward (1695?-1755). British general died in a French and Indian ambush on the way to an attack on Fort Duquesne, July 9-13, 1755. Washington was Braddock's aide-de-camp. **57**-1, 2, **60**-17, 41, **62**-7, **63**-164, **66**-67, **69**-19, **72**-14, **75**-13, **78**-73, **79**-23, **83**-8
    beginning of the Ohio campaign, **55**-1
    defeat and death, **55**-2
    "On the Death of Gen. Braddock,", **55**-A

"On . . . Gen. Braddock's Defeat," **56**-A

Bradshaw, John (1602-59). Puritan regicide and Whig hero; president of the "high court of justice" which tried Charles I. Buried in Westminster Abbey; Bradford's experience teaches "That Rebellion to Tyrants / Is Obedience to God." **76**-189, **78**-247, **80**-115, **80**-157

Bristol, the city of. **65**-93, **70**-35
- and Henry Cruger, and complaint against "French pirates," **80**-416
- Burke, **80**-166, 414
- effect of American War on trade, **77**-252
- loyalist mayor, **78**-328
- Tory, fails to elect Burke, **80**-45

Britain.
- Britain appears to be unaffected by American War, **80**-45
- Britain assisted in birth of American independence, **83**-38
- Britain defies its enemies, **84**-80
- Britain is satirized for pride and King for obstinacy, **80**-238
- Horace and Virgil comment on American War, Britain and several political leaders, **78**-237

Britain. Anglo-American Union and British Power and Leadership. **68**-98, **74**-34, 219, 221, **75**-36, **76**-58, 190

Britain. Decline and Fall of, and an Empire Lost. **74**-109, 172, 209, **75**-20, 32, 79, 221, 222, 223, 224, **76**-292, 294, 367, **77**-33, 54, 73, 87, 112, 114, 120, 290, 443, **78**-68, 88, 95, 249, 378, 379, 488, 546, **79**-26, 37, 147, 223, 295, 383, 431, 443, 445, 523, **80**-11, 16, 19, 20, 29, 111, **81**-12, 28, 59, 84, 170 **82**-219, 309, 402, **83**-41, 115, 119
- "Address to Britannia," **70**-A
- after disastrous American War, **84**-18
- after Yorktown, **81**-247
- and Chatham, **82**-405
- and corruption, **89**-3
- and Seward on André, **85**-40
- Britain declines, America rises in glory, **74**-25, **83**-18
- Britain destroying self in American War, **79**-74
- Bute and Mansfield responsible, **81**-7
- caused by "Patriots," Minority Opposition, **80**-85
- Cowper's "Table Talk," **82**-A
- Cowper's *Task*, **85**-2
- dishonored, spiritually dead, **84**-74
- dismembered, degenerate, **84**-159
- economic depression, hard times, **80**-87
- empire dismembered, **83**-108
- "empire torn," **84**-207
- the factors of decline, **81**-248
- Great Britain reduced by peace to littleness, **83**-203
- impotent after the peace, **85**-20
- loss of trade, **83**-32
- moral factors of Britain's decline, **83**-146
- nation needs leadership, **81**-235
- needs leadership, **82**-395
- no longer land of liberty, **80**-135
- North and loss of America, **84**-93
- "Patriot" traitors of Opposition responsible, **82**-126
- powerless in face of foes, **80**-403

responsibility of King George, Bute, North, Sandwich, **80**-420
rise and fall of Britain, **90**-1
Scottish union accurst, **81**-246
sick and defeated by internal discord and American War, **83**-150
vision of ruin, **71**-90
**For more, see**: American War. Prophecy of ruin.
Britain. Height of Power. **74**-211, **75**-207, **84**-16
in year 1759, **81**-7
Britain. Liberty. **76**-175, **78**-287, 292
loss of liberty, **84**-164
no longer land of liberty, **80**-135
no loss of liberty, despite loss of America, **85**-2
vs. French tyranny, **80**-20
Britain. Prosperity and American Trade. **74**-110, 117
Brocklesby, Richard (1722-97). Prominent physician. **82**-349
Broglie, Victor François, Duc De (1718-1804). French officer, served under Contades at Minden in the Seven Years' War. (Name is misspelled in the original texts.) **59**-43 (a print), **61**-32
Brown, John (1715-66). Clergyman, author of *Estimate of the Manners and Principles of the Times* (1757-58), a popular satire on society. **65**-75
"A character," **65**-A
The Budget. **67**-30, **73**-15
Bulkeley, Thomas James, 7th Visct Bulkeley (1752-1822). MP, 1774-84; until 1779 supported the North ministry, thereafter in opposition. **79**-227
Bull, Frederick (c. 1714-84). MP, 1773-84; sheriff, alderman, and Lord Mayor of London, 1773-4. Tea merchant, dissenter, radical, anti-Papist; opposed North ministry and supported Wilkes and American cause. Treasurer of Society of Supporters of Bill of Rights. **71**-61, 101, 114, **72**-87, **73**-1, 38, 111, **74**-9, 194, 214
Gordon Riots and Wilkes, **80**-153
Bunbury, Thomas Charles (1740-1821). MP, 1761-84, 1790-1821. Recommended (January 26, 1779) a coalition of parties for the sake of union in the war with France. A racing man and owner of property on Grenada in West Indies. **79**-469
Burgoyne, John (1723-92). MP, 1761-92. Dramatist and officer in British army; captain and colonel in Seven Years' War, general in American War; appointed Commander-in-Chief in Ireland by Rockingham, August 1782-84. Was with Howe at Bunker Hill; surrendered to Gates at Saratoga, October 1777. **61**-17, **62**-2, **75**-107, 110, 127, 135, 136, 176, 204, **76**-104, 226, 325, **77**-37, 44, 45, 66, 105, 135, 136, 137, 156, 170, 195, 199, 203, 240, 258, 285, 313, 331, **78**-6, 7, 47, 59, 64, 68, 171, 224, 295, 300, 303, 323, 325, 337, 339, 346, 408, 423, 487, 520, 550, **79**-32, 307, 392, **80**-23, 31, 32, 163, 169, 199, 256, 404, **81**-3, 42, 92, 259, **82**-4, 9, 126, 155, 212, 219, 349, 370, **83**-32, **84**-12, 16
aftermath of surrender, **78**-501
and Cornwallis, **81**-137
and George III, **78**-170
and Germain, **78**-14, 16, 25, **81**-226
and North, **78**-93
and North's Ministry, **78**-28
and Saratoga, **85**-4
anticipation of failure to link up with Howe's forces, **77**-120
before House of Commons, May 23, 1778, **78**-137
Burns, **84**-A

character, **78**-82
Commander-in-Chief, Ireland, **82**-235
criticized, **78**-254
defeat, **77**-126, **78**-406, 472, **79**-409, **83**-25
in Portland administration, **83**-29
Indians and Jane McCrea, **79**-4
leadership criticized, **78**-228
parliamentary inquiry into defeat, **79**-338
prisoner of America, **78**-441
resignation, **79**-205
returns to England after defeat, **78**-97
tragedy of Saratoga, **78**-26
Wesley's *American War*, on Howe and Burgoyne, **82**-A
**See**: Part I of Index for Burgoyne as author.

Burke, Edmund (1729-97). MP, 1765-94. Author of political tracts and published speeches supporting America against North's ministry. **65**-1, **68**-107, **69**-13, 129, 131, 140, 258, **70**-101, 103, 105, 113, 178, 192, 195, 211, **72**-1, 6, **75**-35, 49, 63, 78, 91, 145, 223, 240, **76**-12, 16, 22, 29, 80, 92, 122, 133, 290, 337, 341, **77**-7, 29, 55, 85, 128, 149, 207, 215, 220, 245, 248, 249, 270, 271, 292, 299, **78**-7, 14, 23, 38, 43, 64, 66, 147, 187, 219, 234, 252, 259, 299, 498, 512, 526, **79**-11, 25, 31, 38, 40, 59, 100, 200, 233, 385, 405, 499, **80**-10, 18, 24, 33, 34, 37, 45, 61, 64, 66, 69, 73, 157, 191, 220, 229, 270, 291, 295, 316, 317, 324, 363, 393, 400, **81**-7, 17, 60, 69, 186, 241, **82**-3, 4, 59, 61, 97, 134, 280, 283, 287, 290, 340, 412, **83**-21, 32, 77, 84, 156, 173 (sequel to **82**-370), **84**-15, 16, 35, 55, 78, 166, 212, **85**-35, 47,
America and liberty, **74**-17
and Abingdon, **78**-4
and abolishment of Board of Trade, **80**-86
and Bristol, **80**-166
and Dundas, **81**-255
and George III, **82**-93, 94
and India, **81**-143
and King's speech, **82**-314
and reform, **80**-338, 413, **81**-228
 corruption, **80**-95
and Rodney, **83**-11
and St. Eustatius and Rodney, **81**-146
appointment by Rockingham ministry, **82**-370
 sequel, **83**-173
aristocratic bias and failure to support reform, **80**-172
as Irish Catholic reformer, **80**-159
Boston Port Bill, **74**-32
Burns, **84**-A
chosen by Malton, Rockingham's pocket borough, **80**-414
coughed down, **84**-132
criticized for encouraging America, **77**-125
delusion of reforms, **81**-68
denounced, **81**-212
estimate of, **82**-333
factious, **80**-133
 subverts war effort, **80**-360
Fox, **82**-363, **84**-161
 and North, **83**-174, 207

and Shelburne, **82**-77
Fox-North Coalition, **83**-7, 224, 243, 281
Goldsmith's *Retaliation*, **74**-98, **74**-A
*History of the Late Ministry*, **66**-131
in Opposition to Shelburne, **82**-187, 205
in Portland ministry, **83**-29
India Bill orations, Rockingham, and Irish lineage, **81**-251
Jesuitical Whig, **82**-306
"Liberty," **89**-2
Lord Rector of University of Glasgow, **84**-33
loss of place, **82**-286
    as Paymaster of Forces, **82**-265
*Ode to Palinurus* and "Spoken Extempore on . . .," **70**-A
orator, **80**-96, **81**-240
oratory, **80**-165, **82**-281, **83**-24, **84**-54, 146, 189
    "the Dinner Bell," **84**-42, 43
    misused against Pitt, **84**-192
Reform Bill attacked, **80**-216
reforms and George III, **83**-92
resigns from Administration upon Rockingham's death, **82**-277
satire on Burke's oratory, **79**-374
seditious, **82**-349
self-interested, **77**-79, **80**-411
Shelburne, **83**-44, 51
    peace policy, **83**-159, 166
a "son of liberty," **77**-26
*Thoughts on the Present Discontents*, **70**-46
**See also:** Part I, for Burke as author.
Burlington, 1st Earl of. See George Augustus Henry Cavendish (1754-1834).
Bussy, François de (1699-1780). French minister plenipotentiary at London, 1761-62. **61**-4, 6, 31
Bute, Earl of. See John Stuart, Earl of Bute.
Byng, John (1704-57). British admiral. Court-martialed and shot for naval misjudgment regarding the defense of Minorca, Seven Years' War. **59**-10
Byron, John (1723-86). Naval officer, captained the *Dolphin* under Admiral Anson in a voyage around the world, 1764-66; Governor of Newfoundland, 1769-72; admiral in command of squadron defeated off Grenada by D'Estaing, 1779.
    "While Byron and Barrington," **79**-A
Cabinet. See King's Friends.
Cade, Jack (d. 1450). English seditious rebel.
    and Fox, **84**-214
    and seditious Wilkesite rioters, **70**-96
    and Wilkes, **68**-100, **69**-139
Calvert, John (1726-1804). MP, 1754-1802. Wealthy brewer; voted with Opposition on Wilkes and general warrants, 1763-64, but to expel Wilkes from Parliament, 1769; supported North's measures against America.
    Thrale and Whitbread vs. Wilkes, **69**-80
Camden, 1st Baron and 1st Earl. See Charles Pratt.
Campbell, Mungo (d. 1777). Brave Scots officer; Lieutenant Colonel of the 52d Regiment of Foot, killed in the storming of Fort Montgomery on the Hudson, October 6, 1777. **78**-159
Campbell, John, 5th Duke of Argyll (1723-1806). MP, 1744-61, 1765-66. Scottish laird; commander of the forces in Scotland, 1767-78.
    "The Real Patriot," **76**-A

Campbell, William (c. 1732-78). MP, 1764-66; naval officer. Scots governor of Nova Scotia, 1766-73, and of South Carolina, 1773-76. **76**-244
Camps, Militia. Established under threat of French invasion. **78**-81, 125, 223, 354, **79**-76, 116, 206, **80**-63
    Cox-Heath (Kent, near Maidstone), **78**-40, 80, 98, 99, 231, **79**-5, **83**-235
        and Warley, **78**-199, **81**-43
    Harwich (Kent), **82**-40
    Warley (Essex), **78**-20, 531, **79**-47
Canada. **61**-1, 37, **62**-7, 8, **63**-21, 60, 173, **64**-1, **66**-1, **67**-25, 28
    American War, **76**-43, 183
    Nova Scotia, **83**-235
    "Ode on . . .," **60**-A
    Roman Catholicism, **74**-6, 76
    Wolfe's tomb *is* Canada, **73**-46
    **See also**: Seven Years' War, Louisburg, Quebec, Montreal, and Canadian Invasion under rubric of American War, Battles and Campaigns.
Caribs, St. Vincent's, West Indies.
    war against, **73**-61
Carleton, Guy (1724-1808). British general, Anglo-Irish origin; served in Canada with Amherst and Wolfe in French and Indian War; lieutenant-governor and commanding officer of Canada from 1766; drove Americans permanently from Canada, 1776; commander-in-chief of all British forces in America after defeat of Cornwallis, 1782. **76**-43, 44, 63, 106, 166, 223, 252, 296, 321, 342, 345, **77**-33, 202, 240, **78**-47, 295, 324, 408, **81**-3, 212, **83**-235
    and American Loyalists, **82**-209
    should continue the war against America, **81**-393
Carlton House. Palace of the Queen Dowager, George III's mother, in London. See Queen Dowager.
Carlisle, 5th Earl of. See Frederick Howard, 5th Earl of Carlisle (1748-1825).
Carlisle Peace Commission, 1778. Comprising Frederick Howard, Earl of Carlisle, Howe brothers, William Eden, George Johnstone, and Adam Ferguson, secretary, the commission was sent to negotiate with the American Congress April 16, 1778, on the basis of North's Conciliatory Proposals. **78**-16, 27, 28, 70, 217, 225, 320, 359, 481, **80**-21, 382
    and Congress, **78**-463
    compared with Howe Peace Commission, 1776, **79**-497
    Congress rejects petition, **78**-407
    criticized, **79**-136
    Johnstone, **87**-1
    reception by America, **78**-257
    return to Britain, **79**-350
    told to leave America, **79**-130
Carmarthen, Marquess of. See Francis Godolphin Osborne.
Cartwright, John (1740-1824). See in Part I of Index.
Cato, Marcus Porcius (95-46 B.C.). Roman philosopher and statesman, called *Uticensis*; opposed Julius Caesar in the civil war; represented as a model of virtue and disinterestedness. As a Whig idol, he became a symbol of incorruptible integrity.
    Addison's *Cato,* **79**-533
        and America, **66**-25
        and Pitt, **66**-57
    and Gen. Prescott, **77**-227
    and George III, **84**-24

    and Pitt, **66**-18
    and Whig ideas, **67**-5
    and Wilkes, **68**-104, **69**-71, 73, **70**-11, **75**-102
        and Hampden, **70**-208
    and Wolfe, **73**-32
    Beckford, **70**-217, 242
    character of, **69**-46
    England wants a Cato to resist tyranny, **79**-517
    in republican and Whig pantheon, **70**-95
    parody on Addison's *Cato*, **63**-126

Caulfeild, James, 1st Earl of Charlemont (1728-99). Large landowner in Ireland, but lived most of the time in London; associated with Flood and Grattan to advance the cause of Irish self-government. Commanded Irish Volunteers, 1780-84. **82**-15
    and Irish volunteers and American War, **84**-3

Cavendish, George Augustus Henry, 1st Earl of Burlington (1754-1834). MP, 1775-1831. Styled Lord George Cavendish until 1831 when created Baron Cavendish and Earl of Burlington. Opposed the North ministry like the rest of his family. **79**-33

Cavendish, John (1732-96). MP, 1754-84, 1794-96. Friend of Burke; supported Wilkes and opposed American War and North policies; Ld of Treasury in Rockingham ministry, 1765-66, and chancellor of Exchequer, 1782-83; rejected Shelburne's peace terms. **82**-197, 223, **83**-156, 265, **84**-166
    chancellor of Exchequer and Receipt Tax, **83**-262
    Fox and Shelburne, **82**-164
    in Rockingham ministry, **66**-69

Cavendish, William, 4th Duke of Devonshire (1720-64). 1st Lord of the Treasury, 1756-57; Lord Chamberlain, 1757-62, but dismissed for opposing Bute's policies, 1762; opposed Bute's peace terms, 1762, and cider tax, 1763, and restrictions on parliamentary privilege in the case of Wilkes.
    and Duke of Cumberland, **65**-94
    on death, **66**-50
    resignation, **62**-46

Cavendish, William, 5th Duke of Devonshire (1748-1811). Like his father, a Whig; consistently in opposition to North's ministry and its colonial measures. **80**-220, **83**-21
    of Chatsworth, **83**-10

Cavendish-Bentinck, William Henry, 3d Duke of Portland (1738-1809). A Newcastle-Rockingham Whig, opposed the North Ministry, 1770-82; nominal leader of the Rockingham party, 1782; and of the Portland ministry or Fox-North Coalition, April-December 1783. **76**-42, **77**-23, **79**-10, 100, **80**-220, **82**-286, **83**-3, 21, 29, 56, 265, **84**-16
    and Fox and Burke, **82**-77
    appointed Viceroy of Ireland, **82**-384
    nominal head of Fox-North Coalition, **83**-221

Chads, Henry (d. 1799). British naval officer, captained the *Cerberus*, which brought the three British generals Burgoyne, Clinton, and Howe, to New England to begin the attempt at suppressing the American rebellion.
    brought back to England the bad news of Bunker Hill, 1775, **75**-26

Charlemont, Earl of. See James Caulfeild.

Charles I, Charles II. See the Tory Tradition, The Stuarts.

Charleston, South Carolina.
    and Rivington, **83**-235

**See also:** American War. Battles and Campaigns. Charleston, South
   Carolina.
Charlotte, Queen (1744-1818). Princess Sophie Charlotte of Mecklenburg-Strelitz,
   married George III on September 8, 1761.
   and American War, **76**-222
Chartres, Duc de, Louis Philippe Joseph, afterwards Duc d'Orleans (1747-93).
   The Philippe Égalité of the French Revolution. Commander of the van of the
   French Squadron under D'Orvilliers that quit the engagement with Admiral
   Keppel at Ushant. **78**-116, 149, 176, 178, 368, 381, 383, 476
   **See also:** Ushant Episode.
Chesterfield, 4th Earl. See Philip Dormer Stanhope.
Chubb, Thomas (1679-1747). Deist.
   and Gibbon, **79**-95, 356, 509
Church of England. Bishops.
   and Fox, **80**-378
   criticism for encouraging papists, **81**-135
   criticized for ordaining the fast, 1778, **78**-341, 372, 373, 399
   criticized for support of North's war policy—"bloody Bishops," **75**-105, **76**-
      11, 27, 227, **78**-20, 39, 47, 399, 401, **79**-49, 100, 392, **80**-29
      Bishop Hurd, **76**-384
      except Hinchcliffe, **77**-309
      except Shipley, **75**-186
      hypocritical, **78**-345
      Latin poem, **79**-306
   criticized for supporting Quebec Bill in House of Lords, **74**-71, 113, 115,
      179, 217, **75**-223
      hireling bishops, **82**-75
      hypocritical and mean, **71**-8
      Junius should satirize, **74**-7
      Mayhew's opposition to bishops in America, **82**-241
      support North, **70**-112
      vs. bishops, **82**-25
      with few exceptions support oppression, **73**-4
   **See also:** Frederick Cornwallis, John Hinchcliffe, Richard Hurd, Edmund
      Law, Robert Lowth, William Markham, Jonathan Shipley, William
      Warburton.
Church of England. Clergy. **72**-16, 24, **76**-49
   and Charles I, **81**-138
   the Church and independent America, **83**-40, 205
   Church contributes to the country's ruin, **76**-293
   conflict with Dissent, **80**-325
   corrupted by the court, **79**-10
   criticized for Papist bias, **80**-265
   mean and worthless, **82**-71
   protest against Dissenters, **72**-67, **73**-74
   religious Loyalists in Boston, **74**-21
   threat of Scotch Jacobites and Papists to State Church, **73**-84
   Tory, teach the "exploded doctrines of the Stuart's reign," **77**-23, 238
   **For more on this topic, see:** Fast Days, Gordon Riots and Protestant
      Association, Charles Wesley, and John Wesley.
Cities (Loyal) supporting the American War. See Loyal Cities.
Clare, Earl. See in Part I of Index, Robert Craggs Nugent.
Clark, George (d. 1768). Of Brentford, Middlesex. Young man, like William

Allen, a martyred victim of the violence which Grafton's administration allegedly engineered against Wilkes' supporters. He died December 8, 1768, from a bully's headblow at a riot during Glynn's electioneering in Brentford. His murderers, MacQuirk and Balf, were pardoned. **69**-12, 23, 43, 100, 102, 111, 172, **74**-6

    "Occasion'd . . ." and "On the Opinions," **69**-A

Clark, Richard (1739-1831). Attorney, alderman of London, 1776-98; sheriff, 1777; lord mayor, 1784; chamberlain, 1798-1831. **81**-53

Clarke, Jervoise (1733?-1808). MP, 1768-69, 1774-1808. Voted consistently against North's ministry. **78**-234

    satirized as Tory supporter of the North ministry and ally of Markham, Archbishop of York [totally at variance with information in the reference sources!]. **80**-331

Class Consciousness.
- aristocratic arrogance, **75**-7
- common man's needs and politics, **66**-68
- country farmer vs. landed aristocracy, **71**-89
- "country farmers" and politics, **62**-13
- country farmers on the upper and lower class, **74**-49
- farm laborer vs. lord of the manor, **66**-37
- Goldsmith's *Deserted Village* on peasantry vs. wealthy merchant engrosser, **70**-4
- the great and the scum of the earth, **70**-151
- the high cost of food, **67**-19, 20
- "Impertinent curiosity" of lower class ignoramuses, **77**-A
- John Scott on the working poor and the powerful rich, **66**-16
- lower class artisans and high politics, **66**-38
- lower class illiterates and politics, **75**-217
- lower middle class and politics, **83**-219
- masters, servants, and equality, **82**-175
- "mechanics" and politics, **75**-192
- on the breakdown of "subordination" and class divisions, **71**-81
- the poor and political power, **67**-49
- "rabble" and American rebellion, **83**-116
- tradesmen and artisans and politics, **79**-532
- Wilkes misleads the common people, **70**-7

    **See also:** The Poor.

Clergy. See Church of England.

Clerke, Philip Jennings. See Philip Jennings-Clerke.

Clinton, Henry (1730-95). MP, 1772-84, 1790-94; British general, served in Germany during Seven Years' War, 1760-63, and in America, 1776-82; commander-in-chief in America, 1778-82. Grew up in New York, father being Governor of New York, 1741-51. **75**-107, 110, 127, 135, 136, 176, 204, 226, 332, 374, 377, **77**-132, 149, 172, 240, 313, **78**-20, 211, 550, **79**-1, 38, 40, 307, **80**-10, 30 (1, 4, 5), 71, 144, 152, 199, 241, 249, 277, 352, 394, **81**-3, 203, **82**-9, 212, 285, **83**-235, **84**-9, 16
- and André, **81**-14
- and Charleston, **80**-280, 290
- and Savannah, **79**-21
- British hero, **81**-30
- Burns, **84**-A
- criticized for inactivity, **80**-339
- "Lines on . . . Major Sill," **78**-A

       quarrel with Germain, **78**-170
       Sullivan's Island, Charleston, **76**-208
       victory at Charleston and Opposition, **80**-376
Clinton, Thomas Pelham (1752-95). Tory MP, 1774-94; candidate for Parliament from Westminster, with Hugh Percy, 1774, his election subsidized by the North ministry; aide to cousin Gen. Clinton in America, 1779-81, **74**-42, 118
Clive, Robert (1725-74). MP, 1754-55, 1761-74. The conqueror of India, from which he became fabulously wealthy. His role in East India Company politics affected national politics. **59**-10, **64**-55, **70**-123, 124, **72**-7, **75**-191, **83**-25
Clubs.
    Almack's, **72**-38, 56, 69
      and White's, **79**-371
    Brooks', **79**-41
    George's, White's, Arthur's, Almack's, **64**-52
    Wildman's, **64**-9, 104
The Coalition. See Fox-North Coalition.
Cockburn, James (1723-1809). With Wolfe at Quebec, 1759, and with Gage at Bunker Hill, 1775; Governor of St. Eustatius, 1781, when it was captured by the French. **82**-136
Collingwood, Cuthbert (1750-1810). Captain in British navy in West Indies and American waters, 1776-81. **79**-463
Colman, George (1732-94). The Elder; dramatist and theater manager, Covent Garden and Haymarket. **82**-401
Columbia (name for America). **62**-7, **79**-26, **81**-203, **82**-228, **83**-71, **84**-10
    "Columba," **83**-25
    Tomlinson, "Anacreontic Song," **80**-A
Conflans, Hubert de Brienne, Comte de (d. 1777). French admiral, defeated by Hawke, Battle of Quiberon Bay, November 20-21, 1759, resulting in abandonment of a French invasion of England. **59**-25, 42, **60**-14, 42, **70**-74
Congress (American). **75**-24, 34, 108, 154, 164, **76**-6, 12, 22, 107, 108, 145, 250, 314, 352, 355, 356, 396, **77**-133, 167, 178, 183, 216, 291, **78**-45, 257, 300, **79**-1, 105, 247, 298, **80**-23, 255, 277, **81**-3, 102, **85**-4
    and American independence, **83**-38
    and André, **80**-103
    and Charles Lee, **83**-89
    and Franklin and France, **77**-287
    and French alliance, **79**-318, **80**-77
    and Johnstone, **81**-194, 230
    captured, in fantasy, **84**-9
    flees from Philadelphia, **77**-332
    nonimportation, **74**-8
    Peace Commission, **78**-407
    pitiless, **83**-244
    republican, **80**-78
    seditious Whigs and devils, **76**-366
    separates from Britain, **82**-11
The Constitution (English). **75**-263, **76**-270, 297, **77**-7, 13, 320, 329, **78**-37, 475
    and factious rumors, **84**-157
    and Fox, **84**-102
    and George III, **84**-206
    and limited monarchy, **83**-9
      William III and Georges of Brunswick, **84**-217

and tyranny of George III, **80**-37
and the younger Pitt, **84**-51, 62, 116
corrupted by political leaders, **83**-249
Cowper's "Table Talk," **82**-A
King his own minister, **78**-262
perfect English system of government, **82**-207
prerogative vs. privilege, king vs. nobility, **84**-160
satirized, **80**-22
threatened by secret influence of Bute and Mansfield, **78**-131
"The Triple Cord," King, Lords, Commons, **80**-374
ultimate responsibility for government, monarch or people, **79**-246
vs. Tories and younger Pitt, **85**-33
**See also**: Corruption, King's Friends, Rights.
Contentment vs. politics and war. **70**-109, **72**-9, **76**-85
Contractors and Jobbers (American War). **75**-88, 118, 278, **77**-174, **79**-197, **80**-26, **82**-5, 347
and excisemen excluded from Parliment, **83**-3
corruption and Fox-North Coalition, **83**-72
displeased by peace, **83**-109
objections to contractors as MP's, **76**-95
Wombwell and Sandwich, **77**-315
**See also**: Thomas Harley, George Wombwell, and Laurence Cox.
Conway, Francis Seymour, Earl of Hertford (1718-94). Older brother of Henry S. Conway; supported the North ministry. **72**-81
Conway, Henry Seymour (1719-95). MP, 1741-84. A Rockingham Whig, he opposed the measures of the Grenville and North ministries against the American colonists. Conway moved the repeal of the Stamp Act in 1766, and the end of the American War in February 1782. **64**-25, 29, 62, 63, 90, **65**-8, 62, 74, 76, 124, **66**-64, 69, 74, 75, 120, **68**-78, **70**-18, **72**-1, **72**-7, **76**-22, **82**-25, 158, 197, **83**-3, 21, 32, 151, **84**-129, 166
and Fox, **84**-161
"An Epigram," **69**-A
motions to end American War, **82**-3, 27, 32, 147, 273, 390
"Ode to . . . Conway," **65**-A
"To E.G.," **64**-A
Conway, Thomas (1733-1800?). Irish-Frenchman volunteer in American War; involved in the so-called "Conway Cabal," Winter 1777-78. **77**-285
Cooper, Grey (c. 1726-1801). MP, 1765-84, 1786-90. Loyally served as undersecretary of the treasury with Rockingham, Grafton, and North. **79**-200, 310, **82**-59
Coote, Charles, Earl of Bellamont (1738-1800). Irish Parliament, 1761-66; Irish patriot. **82**-216
Cornwall, Charles Wolfran (1735-89). MP, 1768-72, 1774-89. Supported the views of Jenkinson and North against America. Speaker of the House of Commons, 1780, after Norton. **66**-20, **68**-18, **72**-1, **75**-120
Cornwallis, Charles, 1st Marquis and 2d Earl Cornwallis (1738-1805). MP, 1760-62; then House of Lords. Served in Seven Years' War as aide to Granby and was at Minden. Voted against the Declaratory Act, 1766, and the measures that caused the insurrection; yet accepted a command in American War; general officer. **76**-226, 273, **77**-59, 208, 298, 211, **80**-10, 30 (5), 41, 277, 308, 393, **81**-30, 113, 115, 210, 259, **82**-4, 9, 29, 30, 35, 155, 219, 285, **83**-25, 32, 158, 235, **84**-16, 18, 181
and Capt. William Feilding, **81**-110

and Yorktown, **85**-4
Battle of Camden, **80**-273
Burns, **84**-A
can re-unite Britain and America, **81**-16
character, **78**-83
defeat, **82**-129
    at Yorktown, **81**-137
defeated, but the war continues, **82**-20
Duchess of Kingston and capture of C, **82**-269
effect of Yorktown defeat, **82**-3
Guilford Courthouse, **81**-151
praise of martial exploits, **82**-160
reconciliation with Washington, **81**-29
victories, **80**-196
victory over Greene at Guilford Courthouse, **81**-121, 122
Wesley criticizes Cornwallis, **82**-393
Wesley's "American Independency," **83**-A
wishes to end the war, **78**-107

Cornwallis, Frederick (1713-83). Archbishop of Canterbury, 1768-83; uncle of Gen. Charles Cornwallis.
    corrupt, **80**-37
    hypocrite for ordaining a fast, **80**-334

Corruption (self-interest as motive; bribery subverting the right of election through purchase of votes of freemen, and through purchase of votes in Parliament in exchange for titles, places and pensions offered by King and ministry; patronage and control of elections in rotten boroughs; patronage and party faction; non-political luxury, immorality and licentiousness of the times—such as gambling and horse-racing by the aristocracy). **58**-13, **60**-53, **61**-11, 46, **62**-5, 16, 21, **63**-1, 2, 6, 7, 9, 17, 21, 43, 48, 49, 72, 73, 83, 89, 92, 100, 107, 113, 114, 119, 132, 135, 142, 167, **64**-4, 9, 10, 14, 45, 47, 49, 74, 75, 81, 88, 97, 102, **65**-5, 17, 20, 25, 27, 28, 30, 59, 61, 68, 75, 79, 106, 111, 123, 139, **66**-2, 6, 14, 16, 22, 24, 33, 76-79, 93, 128, 139, **67**-5, 8, 15, 21, 22, 27, 31, 34, 38, 42, 45, **68**-1, 7, 9, 10, 18, 22, 24, 25, 30, 48, 52, 57, 86, 101, 108, 123, 124,, **69**-6, 8, 13, 14, 20, 29, 42, 46, 66, 81, 82, 93, 95, 107, 115, 136, 161, 169, 170, 176, 181, 182, 187, 203, 207, 219, 247, 255, **70**-7, 9, 12, 15, 22, 23, 26, 31, 34, 36, 37, 43, 49, 65, 70, 91, 92, 99, 111, 112, 114, 118, 126, 128, 131, 147, 153, 156, 163, 171, 182, 211, 214, 228, **71**-6, 8, 14, 20, 22, 33, 35, 36, 63, 76, 81, 86, 104, 108, **72**-1, 8, 20, 53, 54, 67, 68, 85, 89, 91, 94, 106, **73**-8, 9, 12, 14, 23, 34, 47, 50, 52, 53, 55, 79, 83, 85, 87, 88, 107, **74**-11, 12, 19, 28, 38, 39, 48, 51, 59, 60, 61, 75, 76, 78, 82, 88, 89, 96, 125, 153, 171, 173, 176, 188, 208, 220, **75**-1, 10, 13, 17, 33, 39, 55, 65, 75, 219, 223, 226, 236, **76**-6, 7, 8, 9, 15, 22, 27, 36, 39, 175, 288, 298, 301, 310, 320, 372, **77**-7, 22, 23, 24, 25, 33, 65, 97, 197, 275, 288, 315, 327,, **78**-11, 12, 19, 20, 39, 44, 50, 75, 128, 145, 157, 201, 214, 215, 308, 327, 334, 350, 361, 442,, **79**-3, 10, 17, 26, 30, 37, 39, 49, 69, 91, 231, 274, 303, 480, **80**-7, 8, 20, 33, 40, 90, 111, 158, 161, 235, 242, 309, **82**-14, 59, 75, 155, 214, 219, **83**-62, 68, **84**-72, 84, 167
    "Address to Britannia," **70**-A
    America, **74**-27
        American policy and corruption, **75**-247
    and American War, **76**-192, **80**-149
    and coercion of America, **75**-98
    and Cowper (the poet), **85**-2

and decline of Britain, **89**-3
and dissipation, **78**-112
and Dunning, **80**-239
  motion, **80**-295
and elections, **80**-231
and English after "a damn'd War" and "a mock Peace," **83**-161
and Fox-North Coalition, **83**-54
and Junius, **69**-233
and nobility, indifferent to reform, **85**-3
and North, **79**-114, **81**-207, **82**-389, **84**-121
  and nation's integrity, **79**-165
  and bribes, **81**-90, 101
  ministry and Parliament, **80**-344
and Parliamentary justice, **83**-206
and reform, **80**-148
and Rockingham, **82**-88, 254
  after his death, **83**-20
  new ministry, **82**-228
and ruin of Britain, **78**-287
and targets of satire, **80**-37
and the nation, **76**-166
and the 3d Parliament, dissolved September 1, 1780, **80**-112
and Younger Pitt, **84**-141
attack on corruption, **82**-184
Banbury and North, **78**-391
Bate and journalism, **80**-35
"Blunt Courtier," **70**-A
bribery and luxury, **76**-34
Britain, **79**-323
Bute and Scotch, **82**-4
buying votes for continuation of war, **78**-528
Churchill's *Duellist, Independence,* "Patriotism-A-la-Mode," **64**-A
a "clean" election, **82**-335
contractors and corruption, **75**-118
contractors and Fox-North Coalition, **83**-72
corrupt ministers, **83**-74
a corrupt politician, **80**-198
the court, **64**-78, **79**-218, **83**-32
  motivated by self-interest, **78**-102
"Dialogue," **69**-A
Dunning's motion, **80**-295
English and Irish, **83**-73
"Epigram. On . . . Great and Little Knaves," **76**-A
"Epigram on the Times," **70**-A
Fox vs. corruption, **80**-332
  self-interested Fox and India Bill, **84**-139
freeholders vs. corruption, **69**-220
George III, **79**-399, **80**-233, **81**-37
  reign of, **80**-16
Gibbon, **79**-95, **81**-154
greedy ministers, **77**-18
impeachments and accountability of corrupt officials, **78**-241
in America, **68**-95

    incorruptible Middlesex freeholders, **80**-312
    Ireland, **83**-141
    Irish, **74**-131
    "Jaffier . . . " and nabobs, **68**-A
    Johnstone, **78**-225
    Ketch and cure of corruption, **70**-A
    King and Parliament, **77**-161
    Keppel vs. corruption, **80**-341
    luxury, **78**-7
        and slavery, **78**-468
    nabobs, **69**-3
    nation and ministry, **81**-235
    Norton, **74**-145
    "oeconomy," **63**-123
    of America, **76**-378
    of poetry, **80**-110
    of politicians, **83**-48
    Parliament, **75**-251 **80**-192, 268, **83**-237, **84**-45, 208, **85**-24
    "Parody. The Minister's Song," **76**-A
    politicians and American War, **79**-442
    reform and end of corruption, **80**-95
    "Representative," (its meaning and bribery) **63**-124
    sale of titles at court, **74**-101
    Scotch, **74**-107, **78**-207
    self-interest, **77**-330
        all self-interested, **80**-177
    self-interested politicians, **76**-368
    solution to the problem, **70**-177
    taxes, placemen and pensions, **76**-143
    Tory Scotch, **79**-384
    true patriot is incorruptible, **81**-128
    virtue of, **78**-38
    Whigs and Tories, **84**-199
    Wilkes incorruptible, **69**-64
    **For more on corruption and related topics, see**: Bute (and his alleged sale of the Peace of 1763 to King Louis of France); faction (and party divisions); Pitt (and his elevation to the peerage); elections and the electoral process; reform and reform movement; Gibbon, Johnson.

Corsica (and Pascal Paoli), Freedom's Cause against Oppression. **67**-1, **68**-5, 12, 24, 49, 80, 117, **69**-1, 2, 3, 4, 16, 38, 50, 51, 62, 99, 157, 198, 249, **71**-1, **73**-20, **76**-16, **77**-188, **78**-3
    "Extempore by . . .," **68**-A
    "On the Defection . . .," **69**-A
    *Pride*, **66**-A
    **See also**: Paoli, and James Boswell.

Cotes, Humphrey (d. 1775). A wine merchant, general factotum to Wilkes, and prominent supporter of the Bill of Rights.
    "Enchantment," **69**-A
    loses election to Tories, Percy and Clinton, **74**-42

Courtenay, John (1738-1816). MP, 1780-1807. One of North's bravoes speaking for the ministry from 1780; urged that more support be given to British forces in America since "every wound given to America was a wound to the House of Bourbon." **81**-118, **84**-35

vs. Burke's attempts at reform, **81-158**
Cox, Laurence (d. 1792). MP, 1774-84; London merchant and war contractor; supporter of the North ministry. **82-347**
Craven, William, Baron (1738-91). Husband of Lady Elizabeth Craven, the poet; in the House of Lords, consistently opposed the North ministry on Wilkes, Falklands Islands, coercion of America, the Quebec Act, and a peerage for Germain. **75**-7, 42, **76**-4, 176, **80**-229
Crillon, Duc de. See Berton de Balbe, Louis de.
Cromwell, Oliver (1599-1658). Puritan leader who led the struggle against the royalist forces supporting Charles I, but in the end he turned against Parliament; and so, with regard to the Whig view of freedom, his reputation is ambiguous.
    and death of tyrant Charles I, **65-126**
    and liberty and the opposition of Wilkes, Glyn, and Rockingham, **68-124**
    inspires American patriots fighting against King's army, **75-29**
    like Cromwell's, the American rebellion is doomed and America will be restored to Britain, **79-60**
    on the ruinous effect of Cromwell and bigoted Puritans on the theatre, **76-77**, **82-55**
    Pitt resembles Cromwell, **66-61**
    "The State Coach," a stern Cromwell is needed to restore order in government, **68-A**
    a Tory view, American rebels are "the spawn of mad republicans" of Cromwell's day, **80-34**
    a Tory view, the Opposition to North's ministry are traitors, heirs of Cromwell, **82-391**
    vs. tyranny, **75-200**
    Wilkes, like Cromwell, is seditious, **69-139**
        and foments civil war, **72-12**
    Wilkes, like Cromwell, produces tyranny, **69-173**
    Wilkes, like Cromwell, to be distrusted, **69**-44, **73**-24
    Wilkes' supporters, the spawn of "Old Nol" and Presbyterian hypocrites, **69-35**
    with Hampden and Sidney, inspires "sons of freedom" against coercion of America, **74-9**
    with Sidney, symbolic of Whig suffering under tyranny, **71-110**
Crosby, Brass (1725-93). MP, 1768-74. Sheriff in 1764-65, alderman from 1765, lord mayor of London, 1770-71. Supported Wilkes, 1769 and thereafter; sent briefly to the Tower for championing John Miller and other London printers, in defiance of the House of Commons, 1771; also opposed press warrants while mayor. **71**-26, 44, 48, 51, 64, 65, 66, 68, 79, 99, 102, 103, 115, 116, 118, 119, 120, 137, **72**-7, 22, 93, **73**-1, 3, 80, **75-255**
    and Keppel, **79-57**
Cruger, Henry (1739-1827). MP for Bristol, 1774-80, 1784-90. Bristol Common Council, 1766-90; sheriff, 1766-67; lord mayor, 1781-82. Son of a New York merchant and educated at King's College (later Columbia). Supported Wilkes and opposed coercive and tax measures directed against America.
    criticism of Opposition in Bristol, **80-416**
    recommended for place in Rockingham administration, **82-370**
    returns from America to attend Parliament, **84-204**
    a "son of liberty," **77-26**
Cumberland, William Augustus, Duke of (1721-65). 3d son of George II and uncle of George III. Led the British forces that suppressed the Scotch Jacobite

rebellion, 1745, an attempt to restore the Stuarts to the British throne; thus a Whig prince. Opposed Bute's peace and the persecution of Wilkes. **64**-9, **65**-44, 50, 76, 94, 95, 99, 108, 116, 143, 144, **66**-50, **70**-27, **76**-9, **78**-511

    Churchill's *Prophecy of Famine* and "Verses . . .," **63**-A
    Culloden, **64**-2
    death, **80**-12
    his ghost damns the Scotch, **78**-115
    "On St. Sepulchre's Bells," **65**-A
    *Pride*, "Verses," **66**-A
    vs. "General Excise" taxes, **63**-187

Curtis, Roger (1746-1816). British naval officer; served three years in Newfoundland, 1762-64; commanded Admiral Richard Howe's flagship in American waters, 1777; captain, with Gen. Eliott, in the final climactic assault on Gibraltar, September 1782. **82**-141, 236, **83**-17, 32, 43, 154, 158, 204, 240, **85**-32

Cushing, Thomas (1725-88). Merchant, politician; speaker of the Massachusetts General Court (Assembly) and member of Congress, although he had reservations about independence. **78**-66

Dalrymple, John, 4th Baronet (1726-1810). Scotch legal historian, solicitor to the Board of Excise and baron of the Scottish exchequer, 1776-1807; maligned the Whig cause and its leaders, Hampden, Sidney, and Russell, in his history of England from the time of Charles II, 1771. **73**-25, 94, **75**-114, **77**-20

    *The Thistle*, **73**-A

Dalrymple, John, Viscount Dalrymple (1749-1821). British army captain, served in Boston, 1768, when the colonists refused to provide quarters for his men; also served in the American War, 1778-81. **80**-255

Dartmouth, 2d Earl of. See William Legge.

Dashwood, Francis (1708-81). MP, 1741-63. Supporter of Bute and Grenville. Member of the disreputable "Hell-Fire Club" and of the Medmenham Club, in which he was a crony (briefly) of Wilkes and Sandwich. **63**-75, **73**-18

    Wilkes and Medmenham Monks, **79**-102

Deane, Silas (1737-89). American congressman, first American diplomat abroad; assisted in the formation of the Franco-American alliance. **78**-4, 276, **79**-41

Debt, National. **74**-68, 75, 86, 96, **78**-47, 151, **81**-5

    rises because of war, **83**-32

Declaratory Act, March 18, 1766. Accompanied the repeal of the Stamp Act; Parliament asserted its authority to make laws binding the American colonies "in all cases whatsoever." Pitt, Earl of Chatham, tried to amend it in February 1775, but failed; Sir William Meredith moved to repeal it, seconded by Cecil Wray, April 6, 1778, and also failed. **78**-66, **79**-6, **80**-40

    and Cornwallis, **82**-9
    Opposition leaders responsible for, **80**-34

DeGrasse, Comte. See François-Joseph-Paul Grasse-Tilly.

DeGrey, Thomas (1748-1818). Son of William DeGrey. MP, 1774-81; undersecretary of state for the colonies, 1778-80, and member of Board of Trade and Plantations, 1777-81. Supported the North ministry consistently.

    enemy of Fox, **80**-245

DeGrey, William (1719-81). MP, 1761-71; solicitor general, 1763-66, and attorney general, 1766-71; conducted the legal measures against Wilkes; involved in the persecution of the press, 1770. **70**-165

DeKalb, Johann (1721-80). Bavarian volunteer in American army; general, known as "Baron de Kalb," died from wounds received in Battle of Camden, August 16, 1780.

death, Camden, South Carolina, **80**-273

De la Clue. See Bertet de la Clue Sabran.

Delaval, Francis Blake (1727-71). MP, 1751-68. Chairman of the Society of Supporters of the Bill of Rights, meeting at the London Tavern, 1769; supported Wilkes and liberty (but not trusted by Wilkes). **69**-154, **70**-178, **74**-45

Denbigh, 6th Earl. See Basil Feilding.

Denis, Peter (1713-78). MP, 1754-68. Naval officer in Seven Years' War under Hawke; member of the court-martial of Admiral Byng, 1756; fought at Quiberon Bay, 1759; became a rear-admiral in 1770; supported the Rockingham administration, 1765-66. **60**-48, **70**-74

D'Éon, Madamoiselle (also Chevalier d'Éon) (1728-1810). A notorious hermaphrodite; used by a poet who assumes her persona to satirize Germain. **78**-25, **79**-5

Dering, Edward (1732-98). MP, 1761-70, 1774-8. Generally Tory and supporter of the North ministry in the period of American troubles but his voting record was erratic for he voted against Sandwich for Keppel. **74**-18, 94, 144, 187, 188, 204, 213

De Velasco, Lewis (d. 1762). Spanish governor of the Morro Castle, Havana, captured by the English after a forty-day siege, July 30, 1762; Havana surrendered August 10, 1762, to Pocock and Albemarle (George Keppel). **62**-31

Devonshire, Duchess of. See Georgiana Spencer.

Devonshire, 4th and 5th Dukes. See William Cavendish (1720-64) and William Cavendish (1748-1811).

Dieskau, Ludwig August, Baron (d. 1767). French general, defeated by Gen. William Johnson, Lake George, New York, September 7, 1755.
    "French Politicks," **60**-A

Dissent, Dissenters (British and American). **75**-227, **76**-1, 390, **80**-277, **82**-11
    blamed for Gordon Riots, **81**-17
    a hypocritical parson as leader of America, **76**-400
    **See also:** Church of England: Clergy; and Presbyterians.

Donop, Carl Emil Kurt von (c. 1740-77). Hessian officer thought to be killed in Washington's attack on Trenton, December 26, 1776. Actually, Col. Rall, having relieved Donop on December 14, was killed; and Donop was mortally wounded in the attack on Ft. Mercer (Red Bank), New Jersey, October 22, 1777, in Howe's Philadelphia campaign. **79**-249

Dowdeswell, William (1721-75). MP, 1747-54, 1761-75. Chancellor of the Exchequer in Rockingham's ministry, 1765-66; directed the Rockingham Opposition to his death; supported Wilkes and opposed coercion of America. **65**-62, **65**-74, 76, **66**-20, 60, **70**-107, 113, **72**-1
    Burke's inscription, **78**-252, **80**-168

Dryden, John (1631-1700). English Restoration poet and dramatist. **64**-46, 59, **65**-11

Dudley, Henry Bate. See Henry Bate, who assumed the additional name of Dudley in compliance with the will of a relation of that name.

Dudley, 2d Viscount. See John Ward (1725-1788).

Dundas, Henry (1742-1811). MP, 1774-1802. Solicitor general for Scotland, 1766-1775, and lord advocate for Scotland, 1775-1783. Tory, of the "Scotch gang" among leaders of the North majority during the American War (Gilbert Elliot, Welbore Ellis, Wedderburne, and Thurlow); stood for no concessions to America until it acknowledged the absolute supremacy of Britain. **75**-120, **77**-13, **79**-392, **80**-59, 343, **81**-208, **82**-113, **83**-151, **84**-112
    and Burke, **81**-255

and Fox-North Coalition, **83**-24
and North, **84**-187
and Pitt, **85**-12, 13, **86**-3
in Pitt's camp, **84**-5, 19

Dunk, George Montagu, 3d Earl of Halifax (1716-1771). North's uncle, president of Board of Trade and Plantations, 1748-1761; secretary of state, northern and southern department, 1762-1763, and northern department, 1771. From the start in the campaign against Wilkes with the issuance of a General Warrant; in Bute's cabinet and Grenville's too. **62**-5, **63**-2, **65**-54, 113, **68**-122, **69**-262, **70**-152, **71**-40, 126, **78**-14

Dunmore, Earl of. See John Murray, 4th Earl of Dunmore.

Dunn, Alexander. Young Scotsman, threatened Wilkes' life, December 8, 1763; arrested, found insane, and confined to a private madhouse, May 1764; allegedly hired by Sandwich to assassinate Wilkes. **63**-44, **68**-27
   Churchill's *Duellist*, **64**-A

Dunning, John (1731-1783). MP, 1768-82. A staunch Whig member of the Minority Opposition to North's coercive American policies. His famous resolution, April 6, 1780—that the influence of the Crown had increased, was increasing, and ought to be diminished—contributed much to North's fall in 1782 and the momentum towards Parliamentary reform. **70**-113, **72**-1, 6, **76**-80, **77**-23, 142, **78**-3, **79**-38, 317, **80**-18, 69, 157, 191, 316, 396, **82**-164, **83**-32, 151
   against Fox, **82**-223
   honoring the day on which Dunning's motion was passed, **80**-239
   motion praised, **80**-278, 295
   North and "Crown's influence" on Parliament, **80**-346

Dyson, Jeremiah (1722-1776). MP, 1762-1776. Tory placeman; secretary to Treasury, 1762-1764; lord of Trade, 1764-1768; lord of Treasury, 1768-1774. Worked in government against Wilkes and supported North's American measures until his death. Called "Mungo," after Isaac Bickerstaff's fictional slave, because of his unflagging capacity for intrigue. **64**-89, **70**-221, **72**-1, 6, **74**-7

East India Company. A trading corporation virtually controlled by the government; because of its lucrative monopoly of commerce with the East Indies, especially India, the company had a profound effect on British imperial policy.
   in a review of history, **80**-12
   North and "that Great Company," the East India Company, **73**-15
   **See also:** Tea; Robert Clive.

Easton, James. American who helped seize Ticonderoga in May 1775. See James Euston.

Eden, William (1744-1814). MP, 1774-1790. Member of Board of Trade, 1776-1782, and of Carlisle Peace Commission, 1778-1779; managed the secret service on continent of North America; Carlisle's secretary, when Carlisle became Viceroy of Ireland, 1780-1782; helped form the Fox-North Coalition; deserts Fox and Whigs to join Tories and Pitt, 1785. **78**-27, 257, **79**-130, **80**-86, **81**-36, 82, **82**-285, **85**-23, 41, 48, 49

Effingham, 3d Earl of. See Thomas Howard (1747-1791).

Egremont, 2d Earl of. See Charles Wyndham.

Elections, Electoral Process.
   and corruption, **70**-228, **84**-20
      bribery, **69**-82, **74**-59
         and "Give me death or liberty," **74**-60
      buying votes, **68**-57
      the City vs. court hirelings, **73**-80

corruption, mob violence, intimidation, **80**-296, **84**-20
    "Thieves and Butcher," **68**-A
    "To the Person," **68**-A
court bribery and corruption, **73**-79
Dering of Kent, **74**-187, 188
election propaganda and party divisions, **74**-213
election song, **73**-93, **74**-204
    and America, **69**-54
    Coventry, **74**-87
    vs. Fox, **80**-367
General election and America, **74**-6
General election and bribery, hypocrisy, **73**-72
General election, March 1768, electioneering, **68**-30
an honest candidate, Henry Thornton, **82**-335
"Jaffier" and nabobs, **68**-A
London mayoralty and Wilkes, **74**-214
need for honest and "free elections," **80**-242
Newcastle and Wilkes, **74**-45
North re-elected for Banbury, and corruption, **78**-391
on buying votes, **75**-72
"On the Late Riot," **68**-A
"On Two Late, . . ." [Brentford election], **68**-A
Percy and Westminster, **68**-88
Percy, Clinton, and America, **74**-42
"The Poetical Wish" on Wilkes' election, **69**-A
riot, Middlesex election, **68**-37
securing votes, **80**-223
song on election of mayor, **72**-80
song vs. bribery, **74**-88
Stephen Fox and corruption, **69**-107
vs. corruption and American War, **80**-231
vs. corruption for honest election, **74**-190
Watkin Lewes at Worcester, **74**-61
Whig vs. Tory, **80**-229, 336, 387
Wilkes and London livery, **68**-68, 112, 113
Wilkes and mayoralty election, **73**-102, 111
Wilkes vs. corruption of buying votes, **73**-83
**For more on this topic, see**: Parliament.

Eliott, George Augustus (1717-1790). Governor and commanding general at Gibraltar, 1777-1790, defending it successfully against besieging French and Spanish forces to the very end of the American War. The climactic grand assault of the combined Bourbon forces was repelled, September 13, 1782. **82**-8, 18, 45, 47, 107, 125, 141, 153, 157, 238, 271, 346, **83**-2, 14, 17, 25, 32, 43, 70, 154, 158, 204, 232, 240, **84**-18, 220
    and Admiral Howe, **82**-131
    and Wolfe, **85**-32
    a French view of Eliott's victory, **82**-165
    **See also**: Gibraltar Besieged.

Elliot, Gilbert (1722-1777). MP, 1753-1777. Scotch, a King's Friend and supporter of North's American policies. Among the leaders of the Majority (Dundas, Wedderburne, Ellis, and Thurlow) at time of American War. **75**-120, **76**-62, 91

Ellis, Welbore (1713-1802). MP, 1741-1794; secretary at war, 1762-1765, and

treasurer of the navy, 1777-1782; in "the Scotch gang" that opposed any concessions to the colonies, even Shelburne's peace.  **74**-7, **75**-120, **77**-67, **79**-200
Emigration (to North America).  **64**-4, **66**-139, **67**-24, **68**-17, **70**-4, 31, **71**-70, **72**-8, 85, **73**-59, **74**-84, 95, 140, 154, 161, **76**-12, **77**-259, 260, **78**-73, **79**-28, 446, **83**-71
    America invites immigrants, **79**-379
    and enclosures, **80**-145
    and loss of troops, **78**-151
    and religious persecution, **72**-14
    and rumors and faction, **84**-157
    and Scotch influence, **75**-17
    and taxes, **83**-106
    causes of, **73**-105, **74**-47, 62, 63
    Goldsmith's Auburn, **76**-327
    Ireland, **74**-191, **79**-25
    of Irish silkweavers to America, **83**-129
    of Liberty, **76**-394, **80**-11, 135
    oppressive taxes and emigration, **85**-51
    Scotland, **76**-99, **78**-5
    Tory Scots responsible for emigration, **79**-384
    vs. emigration to America, **83**-8, **85**-7
    **See also**: Scottish Emigration.
Encaenia.  Dedication festival; annual university ceremony at Oxford of commemoration with recital of poems and essays and conferring of degrees.  **73**-50, 61, 62.
Enclosures (of common lands), "Monopoly."  **70**-4, **72**-8, **80**-145
    Freeth, "The Times," **66**-A
Erskine, Thomas (1750-1823).  MP, 1783-1784, 1790-1806.  Barrister and friend of Sheridan and Fox.  Counsel to Admiral Keppel in his court martial trial, 1779; and to Ld George Gordon on trial for treason as a result of the London riots, 1780; and to Tom Paine on trial for treason, 1793; defense successful in the first two, **81**-109
    attacked and defended, **81**-196, 197
Erskine, William (1728-1795).  Scotch officer, served in Germany, Seven Years' War; as general fought in Battle of Long Island, August 1776; in Monmouth, New Jersey, Campaign, 1778; second in command to Tryon in the Connecticut coast raid, July 1779; commanded eastern district of Long Island, New York, 1778-1779.  Returned to London, summer 1779.
    urges continuation of war, **78**-107
Estaing, Charles Hector Théodat, Count d' (1729-1794).  French admiral, commander of the French fleet in American waters during American War.  **78**-368, 464, **79**-9, 169, 247, 314, 325, 387, 527, **80**-5, 212, **84**-9
    and General Prescott before Savannah, **79**-99
    at Rhode Island and at Savannah, **81**-3
    Cowper's "Present for the Queen of France," **79**-A
    defeated at Savannah, **79**-193
    fleet blocked by Adm. Geary, **80**-81
    his history, **80**-124
    threatens British in West Indies, **79**-58
Euston (Easton), James.  American from Massachusetts, leader of some volunteers who helped seize Ft. Ticonderoga, May 13, 1775, according to American ballad narrative.  **75**-109

Faction (Party Division). **63**-121, **64**-4, 14, 24, 47, 48, 50, 81, **65**-25, 40, 43, 61, 71, 116, 122, **66**-109, **67**-5, 31, **68**-24, 59, **69**-6, 18, 22, 43, 149, 161, 162, 164, 173, **70**-2, 3, 7, 13, 80, 92, 175, 188, 198, 230, **71**-3, 69, 83, 105, 113, **72**-7, 22, **73**-6, 36, 47, **74**-65, **75**-20, 22, **76**-309, **79**-3, **80**-150, 157, **82**-10, **83**-20, **84**-87, 88, 89, **85**-45
    American rebels, **74**-21, **75**-35, **78**-425
        British faction helps, **77**-146
        British factions support, **74**-118
    and discord, Fox vs. Pitt, **84**-207
    and Fox-Pitt contest, **84**-54
    and Rockingham's death, July, 1782, **82**-104
    and the English constitution, **82**-207
    "Battle," Whig and Tory factions, **63**-A
    blamed for loss of Mansfield's library, **80**-340
    Bute responsible, **79**-125
    causes British defeat, **82**-18
    condemns party faction, **82**-158
    condemns "Party Madness," **82**-169, 170
    denounced, **82**-382
    end of, **82**-379
    Fox subdued by Pitt, **84**-105
    Fox-Pitt debates tear nation apart, **84**-27, 31
    generates fears by rumor, **84**-157
    hellish, **80**-244
    Junius, **70**-61
    "lies and detraction" of factious Opposition, **80**-76
    ministry accused of, **79**-307
    objection to, **80**-4
    opposition to, **79**-38, 215, 221
    "Parliamentary Duellists," **81**-A
    "Party commotions" end under Rockingham, **82**-378
    "Patriot" factions: Chathamites, Rockinghamites, Wilkesites, **65**-47
    undermines unity of empire, **82**-347
    weakens nation, **79**-285
    Whig faction denounced, **82**-218
    will destroy Britain, **80**-217
    Younger Pitt suppresses faction, Fox-North Coalition, **84**-14
    **See also**: Minority Opposition during American War, Ins and Outs, Whigs and Tories.

Farmer, George (1732-1779). Captain who went down with his exploding ship, the *Quebec*, October 6, 1779, at the moment of victory over a French frigate. **79**-34, 84, 92, 135, 144, 316, 340, 436, **80**-27, 88, 238, 285, **84**-18
    and Pierson and Keppel, **79**-253
    and Wolfe, **79**-158
    "Epilogue . . . ," **81**-A
    "Hail to the Son," **79**-A

Farren, Elizabeth (c. 1759-1829). A celebrated actress and great beauty.
    and the romantic view of the American Indian. **85**-53

Fast Days. **80**-29 (1777 & ?), 39
    December 13, 1776, **76**-27, 72, 112, 127, 128, 131, 147, 156, 158, 193, 227, 235, 236, 250, 251, 252, 264, 312, 376, 381, **77**-6, **77**-130
        hypocrisy of, **76**-163
    February 27, 1778, **78**-222, 311, 341, 345, 372, 373, 374, 375, 376, 377,

                382, 396, 399, 401, 404, 432, 465, 466, 541
            fast prolongs the war, **78**-128
            hypocrisy, **78**-148, 150
        February 10, 1779, **79**-28, 461
            fruitless, **79**-212, 343
            proclamation, **79**-137
            Rigby and Sandwich, **79**-196
            Tory fast, **79**-306
        February 4, 1780, **80**-7
            hypocrisy, **80**-8, 334
            Ireland, **80**-137
            vs. Keppel, **80**-283
        February (?), 1781, **81**-169, 248
        February 8, 1782, **82**-6, 30, 155
            hypocrisy of, and tea as cause of American War, **82**-328
            moral crime of American War, **82**-128
            prayer for suppressing "Rebellion," **82**-152
            pro & con, **82**-129
            questions motives of prayers, **82**-70
            Sandwich, **82**-300
        Jane Cave, at commencement of American War, **75**-4
Feilding, Basil, 6th Earl of Denbigh (1719-1799). Tory peer; member of the "cabinet," and supporter of North's policies. **73**-4, **75**-51, 254
    and Pitt, **78**-380
    and Richmond, **78**-43
    and Shelburne reconciled after the peace, **83**-298 (a print)
Feilding, William, Viscount (1760-1799). MP, 1780-1796; captain in British army, with Cornwallis in the southern campaigns of 1781, according to the poem, **81**-110
Fell, Isaac. Publisher of the *Middlesex Journal*, founded 1769, **69**-240
Felton, John (c. 1595-1628). Assassin of the minion of Charles I, the 1st Duke of Buckingham, 1628, **69**-52
Female.
    Duchess of Devonshire, canvasser for Fox, **84**-70, **85**-13
    politician, **69**-83
Feminist Poems, or Women and the Times. **79**-93, 159, 187, 512
    Britain's beauties and the war, **81**-242
    conventional patriotic lyric, women urge men to fight the French, **78**-532
    frivolous women of fashion, **80**-225
    a visit to a militia camp, **83**-235
    women and American War, **82**-69
    women and privateering, **79**-244
    women and returning veteran, **82**-356
Fenton, John (1753-1831). MP, 1783-1796, 1812-1831. During an election contest, which he lost, satirized for corruption. **80**-368
Ferdinand of Brunswick, Prince (1721-1792). See Minden.
Ferguson, Adam (1723-1816). Scottish professor, University of Edinburgh, and author. See Carlyle Peace Commission, of which he was secretary.
Ferguson, Patrick (1744-1780). Scottish officer at Brandywine, 1777; Little Egg Harbor, New Jersey, 1778; and King's Mountain, South Carolina, 1780. **78**-378
    death, **81**-164
Fermor, George, 2d Earl of Pomfret (1722-1785). Courtier; lord of the bedchamber, 1763-1781.

satirized by Delamayne for oppressive arrogance, **73**-4
Finance, Financiers. ("Bulls, Bears, and Jews.")  **72**-57, **73**-108
- Bank of England, Wilkes, and Gordon Riots, **80**-261
- bankrupt commerce, paper credit, **78**-8
- budget, **79**-314
- bulls and bears, **83**-195
- "Congress Notes," financing the Americans, **81**-23
- effect of American War on business and commerce, speculation, **81**-201
- financiers, contractors, and American War, **80**-149
- Jewish creditors, **83**-45
- loss of commerce and corruption, **79**-69
- need of money for war, **78**-81
- North and financing the War, **81**-5
- North's need of money to finance the war, **79**-511
- Parliament's economic measures, **82**-28
- "Peace. 1763", **63**-A
- Pitt's budget and taxes, **84**-111
- speculation and the war, bears, **80**-3
- state credit gone, treasury emptied, and American War, **82**-4, 12
- stock jobbers, bulls, bears, and enlargement of American War, **79**-88
- stock market, **74**-176, **76**-66
- subscription to 1779 government loan, **79**-381
- war budget, **77**-131

**See also:** Budget, Taxes for related topics.

Fitzgerald, William Robert, 2d Duke of Leinster (Irish) (1749-1804). MP (Irish), 1767-1773; in English House of Lords from 1774; protested measures of North ministry against America. **79**-25, **80**-40
- Boston Port Bill, **74**-32

Fitzmaurice, Thomas (1742-1793). MP, 1762-1780. Brother of the Earl of Shelburne and a humane Irish landlord. **74**-191

Fitzpatrick, Richard (1748-1813). MP 1770-1813. Close friend of Charles Fox. Captain in the Foot Guards 1772, colonel in 1782; served in America March 1777 to May 1778. In politics sided with Fox and the Opposition. **80**-163, 245, **81**-92
- objects to Scotch ferocity, **78**-107

Fitzroy, Augustus Henry, 3d Duke of Grafton (1735-1811). Called a "disciple of Bute," both of Stuart origin, Grafton being descended from the illegitimate son of Charles II. Prime Minister, July 1766-January 1770, of the Grafton-Chatham ministry, Pitt (about to accept his peerage) proposing to dominate it. **65**-8, 54, 75, 76, **66**-64, 69, 75, 82, **68**-10, 13, 34, 42, **69**-3, 10, 11, 24, 28, 29, 30, 61, 66, 107, 108, 128, 130, 136, 137, 140, 170, 176, 189, 242, 255, 263, 265, 266, **70**-8, 18, 22, 26, 32, 33, 35, 36, 82, 84, **71**-108, **72**-64, 76, 88, **73**-4, 10, 26, **75**-1, 197, **76**-16, **80**-34, 98, 306, **81**-92, **83**-29
- criticized, **80**-317
- "An Epigram," **69**-A
- Gray's *Ode*, **69**-A
- in Opposition and supporting American rebels, **78**-132, 393
- rejoins the Minority Opposition [to North's ministry], **75**-272, 273
- resigns and runs, **70**-81
- "The Ribband," **69**-A
- "wise" and "incorruptible," **84**-29

**See also:** Grafton-Chatham Ministry, 1766-1770.

Flood, Henry (1732-1791). MP, 1783-1784, 1786-1790. Irish political leader,

urged (for a time) the independence of Ireland from Britain until bribed by North. **74**-154, **81**-32, **85**-30
    and Grattan, **82**-44, 216, **83**-97, 112, 113
    and threat of Irish revolution, **82**-326
    "Questions and Answers," **83**-A
Foote, Samuel (1720-1777). Actor, playwright, and owner of the Haymarket Theatre. **66**-105
Forbes, John (d. 1809). Scots officer in French service; challenged Wilkes to a duel, August 15, 1763, but French authorities prevented it; Sandwich was suspected of hiring Forbes to assassinate Wilkes. **63**-32, 65, 152, **68**-127
    Churchill's *Duellist*, **64**-A
    "Excellent new Ballad," **63**-A
Fort Ticonderoga; formerly Fort Carillon under the French. Located on Lake Champlain, between Albany, New York, and Montreal, Canada, it figured in the French and Indian War and in the American War. **58**-3, **59**-28, 42, **60**-3, 18, **62**-7
    **See also**: George Augustus Howe; American War, Battles and Campaigns, Ticonderoga and Burgoyne's Invasion.
Fort William Henry. At the southern tip of Lake George, New York, it figured in the French and Indian War (Montcalm besieged it) and in Burgoyne's offensive in 1777. **57**-2
Fox, Charles James (1749-1806). MP, 1768-1806; ld of Admiralty, 1770-1772; ld of Treasury, 1773-1774; leader of Minority Opposition at time of the American War. "Prince of Orators," "Man of the People," "the mighty patriot and assertor of American liberty," "the People's Friend," "Charles James Tod," "rough monster." See Part I of Index for poem by Fox. **70**-32, 143 (?), **71**-64, 102, 109, 117, **72**-1, **73**-8, 26, 42, 61, **74**-5, 197, **75**-35, **76**-92, 290, **77**-13, 52, 183, 248, 269, 270, 271, 299, **78**-34, 38, 66, 139, 180, 187, 277, 299, 536, 556, **79**-31, 38, 40, 41, 44, 59, 137, 332, 392, 412, 515, **80**-10, 16, 18, 23, 33, 41, 69, 73, 104, 157, 191, 220, 229, 235, 256, 270, 290, 291, 295, 305, 316, 317, 324, 330, 367, 393, 410, **81**-17, 27, 42, 60, 67, 92, 122, 147, 241, **82**-3, 11, 59, 61, 85, 134, 197, 283, 286, 287, 340, 371, **82**-411 (print), 412 (print), 414 (print), 418 (print), 421 (print), **83**-3, 20, 21, 23, 24, 32, 61, 76, 77, 79, 84, 156, 173, 193, **84**-45, 50, 53, 72, 78 (and **83**-115), 79, 83, 109 (and **84**-39), 158, 172, 185, 200, 211, 213, 214, 215, 216, **85**-51
    advice to, **80**-370
    after Rockingham's death, **82**-223, 277
    ambitious, like Satan, **83**-42
    and Adam, **80**-24, 362
        duel with, **80**-289
    and Aitken, "John the Painter," **79**-173
    and Burke, **82**-363
    and Burns, **84**-A
    and devil, **84**-170
    and Duchess of Devonshire, **84**-70
    and English constitution, **84**-102
    and India Bill, **84**-139
        India Bill rejected by House of Lords, **84**-117
    and King, **84**-48
    and Mrs. Siddons, **83**-195
    and North, **80**-222, 429, **82**-99
        advised to send North to House of Lords, **84**-21

        unity with, **82**-382
and Opposition, **79**-317
and Pitt, **83**-96, **84**-127, 165, 177
        antagonist of, **84**-27
        conflict with, **84**-8
        contrasted, **83**-234, **84**-165
        defended against, **84**-26, **85**-13
        "The Ghost," **83**-A
        opposition to, **84**-35, 85, 156
and reform, **80**-338
and Shelburne, **82**-4, 121, 145, 191, 294, **83**-44
        breaks with, **82**-290
        enemy, **83**-216, 252
        peace, **83**-86, 159, **84**-103
and the war, **80**-264
assumes mantle, **82**-204
Britain's enemy, **81**-234
Burke and Portland, **82**-77
character, good and bad, **79**-464
corrupt, **80**-253, 304
criticized, **79**-11, **82**-73, **84**-2, 17, **85**-39, 44
        by disillusioned follower, **82**-282
        character, **82**-200
damned, **79**-3, **84**-190, 198
defended against hypocrites, Pitt and his friends, **85**-13
demagogue, **80**-365, **84**-182
        like Wilkes, **82**-394
denounced, **81**-212
election, **84**-122, 135
        September 1780, **80**-373
election song, **80**-332
eloquence praised, **82**-360
England's savior, **82**-132
estimate of, **82**-333
an exemplary Whig, **84**-19
factious, **80**-133, **82**-209, **84**-184, 205
factious, pro-American, **80**-113
factious, republican, **80**-134
factious, subversive, **81**-86
factious, undermines war effort, **80**-360
favors Fox, **86**-3
first mention in verse, March 1770, **70**-112
Fox's Westminster Association, reform, and end of American War, **80**-400
fraudulent Whig, **82**-306
greedy, **83**-115, 211, **84**-75
hypocrite, **80**-203, **83**-147, 245
incendiary, **82**-120
leader, **82**-138
"Modern Mobbing," **79**-A
the new Portland administration, **83**-29
North's opinion of, **82**-105, 112
"Ode on Emancipation of Ireland," **82**-A
orator, **80**-96

"Out" again, vs. Shelburne, **82**-201, 205
peace negotiations, **82**-96
"the People's Man," **84**-41
persona speaks, **83**-101
political death, **84**-153
praised, defended, **80**-378, **83**-134, **84**-39
    an exemplary Whig, **84**-19
    for India Bill, **84**-104
review of career, 1775-1784, **84**-161
review of role in period of American War, **84**-16, 39, 109
satirized, **80**-114, **81**-187, **82**-308
seditious, **80**-245
seeks power, **82**-42
self-interested, **80**-140, 253, **83**-264, 294 (print)
support of, in coming election against Cecil Wray, **84**-37
threatened by mob, **84**-144
traitor, **79**-510, **80**-61, **81**-48, 220, **82**-420 (print)
    leader of "the Westminster Congress," or Association, **80**-82
undermines English constitution, **82**-207
unprincipled, **84**-155
venal, factious, **82**-209
virtuous patriot, **82**-404
war monger, spendthrift, **83**-45
weeps over loss of treasury place, **84**-34
Westminster election, **84**-114

Fox, Charles James, the Fox-North Coalition. After the fall of Shelburne's ministry, February 24, 1783, the Fox-North Coalition, with Portland as PM, to December 1783; followed by the ministry of the younger Pitt.
    criticized, **83**-3, 7, 24, 46, 49, 53, 54, 56, 57, 58, 61, 69, 75, 76, 78, 80, 81, 83, 85, 94, 95, 102, 104, 107, 110, 114, 117, 120, 127, 137, 143, 148, 152, 177, 208, 209, 210, 222, 239, 247, 254, 261, 263, 266, 271, 272, 273, 281, 289 and 291 (prints), **84**-1, 16
        and Bute, **83**-153, 199
        and peace with America, **83**-63
        answer to **83**-65, **83**-95
        Burke, **83**-224, 225, 243
        Burns, **84**-A
        cannot endure, **83**-174, 176
        dismissed from office, **83**-200
        especially North, **83**-156
        fall of, **84**-36
        foolish and corrupt, **83**-268
        Pitt's attitude, **84**-5
        weakens throne, **83**-207
    defended, **83**-36, 55, 65, 72, 82(?), 265, 280

Fox, Charles James, the Fox-North Opposition to Pitt's Ministry. After December 1783; includes Conway, Burke, Sheridan, John Courtenay, Portland, et al. **84**-21, 35, 38, 55, 59, 68, 73, 81, 117, 120, 129, 147, 149, 161, 163, **85**-17, 35, 47
    and loss of colonies and American War, **84**-56
    as faction which Pitt must suppress, **84**-193
    Coalition Parliament dissolved, March 1784, **84**-140
    criticized, **84**-202, 203

        deserve to be out, **84**-40
        downfall of Coalition, **84**-118
        Fox and followers vs. Pitt, **84**-54
        Fox breaks with North, **84**-154
        Fox driven out by Pitt, **84**-60 (print)
        Pitt, **84**-99, 130
        satirized, **84**-166
Fox, Henry, 1st Baron Holland (1705-1774). MP, 1735-1763. Worked with Bute to secure the Peace of 1763. Father of Charles James Fox. **62**-20, 28, **63**-187, **64**-40, **65**-8, 71, 149, **69**-261, **71**-64, **84**-102
Fox, Stephen, 2d Baron Holland (1745-1774). MP, 1768-1774. Older brother of C. J. Fox; considered "a tool of Bute"; supported Grafton and North ministries. **68**-122, **69**-80, 107, **70**-3, 143(?), **71**-64
France (and Britain), 1755-1763.
        Defeat of France, **59**-34, **60**-19, 38, 39, 44, **60**-A, **61**-15, 16, 17, 31, 32, 35, **62**-1, 8, **67**-25, 28, **69**-5, 7, 17, **78**-207, **82**-11
        The French and Indian War, **55**-1, 2, **55**-A, **56**-1, **56**-A, **57**-1, 2, **58**-1, 2, 3, 4, 5, 12
        French Parliament (evil), **63**-111
        Pro-French Tories, **63**-15
            and Bute, **63**-80
        Return of French prisoners, **63**-47
        **See also**: Seven Years' War.
France (and Britain), 1764-1773.
        Corsica, **68**-87, **69**-1, 2, 3, 4, 15, 16, 21, 50, 51, 62, 99, 151, 157, **71**-1
        Fear of France, **65**-30, 79, 83, 116, **66**-103
        French tyranny, **72**-19, 39.
        **See also**: Corsica (and Pascal Paoli).
France (and Britain), 1774-1783 and after. **74**-15, **75**-121, 130, 203, 209, 215, 300, 301, **76**-9, 14, 16, 20, 85, 166, 197, 229, 273, 324, 356, 363, **77**-27, 33, 112, 113, 116, 121, 131, 133, 158, 164, 188, 219, 224, 235, 246, 278, 284, 305, 332, **78**-18, 19, 22, 33, 47, 60, 75, 173, 217, 355, 429, 437, 473, 486, 516, **79**-1, 2, 13, 18, 22, **80**-199, 249, 403
        after Rodney's great victory, April 12, 1782, **82**-396
        alliance with America, **78**-183, 194, **79**-40, **80**-277
        American poem on French alliance, **78**-208
        and American independence, and on the Mississippi, **85**-4
        and Franklin, **77**-287, **78**-17
        and invasion, **76**-126
        blockades English fleet, **78**-101
        Bourbon alliance and America against Britain, **80**-325
        Bourbon nations, **80**-285
        Britain need not sue for peace with France, **82**-103
        complains of Rodney, **82**-312
        controls the seas, **80**-52
        Cowper's "Epinikion," **79**-A
        "The Family Compact," alliance of France and Spain, **79**-331, 426
        fleet, **82**-257
        Fox and French loans to America, **77**-269
        France and American independence, **83**-38, **85**-10
        France denounced, **83**-12
        France intervenes in American War, French Revolution, **1800**-1
        France, the real enemy, **75**-321

France responsible for Britain's problems, **82**-36
France rules the ocean, **78**-103
French and West Indies, **80**-262
French fleet retreats to Brest, **78**-459
French motivation, greed, **78**-555
French Revolution, **93**-1
peace, **82**-213
Pitt (the Elder), **77**-206
strange Franco-American alliance, **79**-272
tyranny of French government, **80**-20
war against France and Spain, **80**-128, 303
**For more, see**: American War, Enlarged and Transformed into a French War; American War, British Navy; American War, Rodney's Engagements.
**See also in Part I of Index**: French Poems on American War.

France (French). Threat of Invasion of Britain, 1778-1779. **78**-65, 81, 109, 205, 231, 427, 456, 458, 552, **79**-56, 63, 82, 85, 105, 112, 175, 198, 199, 201, 220, 229, 230, 231, 232, 290, 305, 327, 345, 347, 357, 358, 420, 530, 536
and women, **79**-187
"French Peace," **79**-A
July, end of fear of, **79**-355

Francis, Philip (1740-1818). MP, 1784-1807. Court writer for Henry Fox; tutor to Charles James Fox; the most likely author of Junius' letters.
Churchill's *Author*, **63**-A

Franklin, Benjamin (1706-1790). American philosopher, scientist, man of letters, and statesman; postmaster general of the colonies, 1753-1774; agent for Pennsylvania, Georgia, and Massachusetts, 1764, 1768, 1770; secured repeal of Stamp Act; helped draft the Declaration of Independence; secured the French alliance; chief negotiator of the peace. **72**-14, **73**-101, **74**-73, 74, 165, 181, **75**-108, 252, 275, **76**-5, 16, 306, **77**-29, 128, 183, 187, 269, 287, 292, **78**-4, 17, 73, 355, 408, **79**-12, 26, 41, **80**-22, 34, 56, 61, 277, **81**-17, **82**-9, **83**-151, 187
and France, **76**-237
and George III, **77**-86
"From the Massachusetts Spy," **73**-A
"hoary traitor," **83**-144
in France, **77**-149
"Ode to Discord," **82**-A
rumored to be in London, **77**-99
"To Benjamin Franklin," **64**-A
traitor, **81**-15
**See** Part I of Index for Franklin's poems.

Fraser, Simon (d. 1777). General, a Scottish hero of the American War. Was at Louisburg, 1758, and with Wolfe at Quebec, 1759; aide to Viscount Townshend, Viceroy of Ireland, 1767-1772; served with Howe in Boston; mortally wounded in Burgoyne's invasion of New York, Saratoga, October 7, 1777. **77**-137, **78**-14, 224, 301, 363, **80**-30(3), **83**-25
Burgoyne's defeat, **77**-66
Burns, **84**-A
Fraser's regiment retreats from Boston, **76**-305
ghost urges end of American War, **78**-35
mortally wounded, **77**-222

Free, John. London minister; supporter of Wilkes; preached at funeral of William

Allen, martyr of St. George's Fields riot, May 10, 1768, and an anniversary sermon against "political murder" a year later. **69**-97, 254

Freedom of the Press. **See** Rights: Liberty of the Press and Libels.

French and Indian War, 1755-1763. **See** Seven Years' War, 1755-1763.

Gage, Thomas (1721-1787). Captain at Culloden and Colonel under Braddock; commanding general of British forces in the American colonies, 1763-1775; governor of Massachusetts, 1774-1775, and moved the government from Boston to Salem; recalled and replaced by Gen. Howe after Bunker Hill. **74**-6, 159, 207, 209, **75**-23, 26, 30, 37, 62, 87, 100, 101, 123, 162, 169, 188, 195, 227, 264, 296, 315, **76**-11, 12, 16, 40, 79, 88, 223, 252, 298, 325, **77**-134, 240, 314, **78**-8, 226, **84**-16

    Burns, **84**-A

    Gage's proclamation of martial law in verse, **75**-288

    "military government," **74**-27

Galloway, Joseph (c. 1731-1803). Leading Loyalist exile in England; urged aggressive action against the rebels, especially by Gen. Howe, and was with him in Philadelphia. **81**-35, 81, 102, 112, 220, **82**-212

    and Howe, **81**-231

    Charles Wesley's *American War*, **82**-A

Gardner, Thomas (d. 1775). American colonel, Massachusetts, died from wounds suffered at Bunker Hill.

    ghost admonishes George III to cease tyrannizing America, **76**-165

Gascoigne, Bamber (1725-1791). MP, 1761-1786. Member of Board of Trade and Plantations, 1763-1765, 1772-1779; Tory supporter of the coercive policies of the North Administration. **82**-100

Gates, Horatio (1728-1806). American general, born at Maldon, Essex, in England, and named for his godfather Horace Walpole; served under Cornwallis in Nova Scotia, 1750, and under Braddock in 1755; Washington's Adjutant General, 1775; stopped Burgoyne at Saratoga, 1777, but lost to Cornwallis at Camden, South Carolina, 1780. **77**-39, 170, 195, 199, 292, **78**-8, 12, 14, 26, 35, 45, 59, 219, 259, 295, 311, 339; **79**-338, **80**-30(5), **81**-3, 259, **84**-12, **85**-6

    Camden, **80**-273

Geary, Francis (1709-1796). British admiral; at Louisburg and Halifax, 1759; admiral of the blue, 1775, and of the white, 1778. **80**-81

Geary, Francis (d. 1777). Son of Admiral Geary; a cornet, killed in Burgoyne's campaign, March 1777. **77**-223, **77**-306

General Warrants. Legality challenged by Wilkes upon publication of *The North Briton, No. 45*, April 23, 1763; in 1765 declared illegal by Lord Mansfield, and also by Pratt, Lord Camden, except for treason; thus the liberty of person was established against encroachments by the executive. **63**-93, 106, 131, 166, **64**-25, 63, **65**-84, 147, **68**-103, 123, 124, **69**-112, 77, 204, **79**-49, 384

    Star Chamber warrants, **70**-15

    **See also**: Pratt and Wilkes, **63**-passim.

George II (1683-1760). King of England, 1727-1760. **60**-8, 10, 12, 32, 37, 43, 52, **65**-3, **68**-79, **75**-160, **78**-357, 548

    ghost of, complains of George III, **83**-108

    reigns of George II and III contrasted, **78**-207

George III (1738-1820). King of England, 1760-1820; father was Prince Frederick Louis (d. 1751) and grandfather was George II; accession to throne, October 25, 1760. "George the Good"; "Old Freedom's Parent, and her Prop"; "Button-making King." **60**-10, 12, 27, 32, 43, 52, **61**-3, 11, 26, 33, 41, 42, 43, 50, **62**-8, 10, 33, 45, 56, 59, **63**-1, 2, 5, 11, 39, 60, 130, 133, 137, 141, 170, **64**-3, 4, 6, 39, 51, 77, 78, 95, 100, **65**-1, 5, 29, 82, 99, 114, 124, **66**-11, 61,

108, 112, 116, **67**-40, **68**-6, 9, 10, 23, 24, 26, 27, 64, 87, 123, 124, **69**-12, 18, 31, 40, 49, 58, 65, 108, 109, 112, 113, 183, 188, 191, 197, 199, 241, 257, **70**-2, 3, 6, 9, 17, 19, 20, 21, 49, 51, 53, 66, 78, 96, 142, 145, 155, 168, 176, 180, 181, 183, 185, 197, 198, 216, 217, 226, 231, 239, **71**-3, 18, 21, 26, 41, 49, 62, 71, 75, 83, 85, 98, 101, 105, 117, 136, **72**-23, 52, 62, 64, 82, 84, 90, 91, 98, 106, **73**-1, 6, 10, 21, 26, 59, 61, 73, 79, 81, 83, **74**-9, 27, 28, 29, 50, 72, 90, 93, 105, 120, 128, 129, 148, 155, 164, 167, 171, 193, **75**-5, 10, 14, 24, 28, 32, 34, 55, 58, 64, 67, 70, 94, 99, 101, 102, 105, 112, 125, 127, 139, 140, 147, 152, 155, 162, 171, 173, 200, 216, 223, 231, 237, 239, 240, 241, 276, 303, **76**-3, 10, 17, 18, 19, 22, 25, 27, 35, 39, 42, 43, 49, 67, 89, 144, 154, 165, 199, 202, 217, 252, 253, 260, 265, 270, 279, 297, 299, 302, 358, 361, 382, 392, **77**-6, 7, 12, 25, 33, 50, 68, 86, 97, 130, 131, 182, 186, 237, 247, 256, 258, 284, 288, 305, 311, **78**-7, 8, 12, 25, 39, 44, 47, 53, 56, 65, 68, 81, 95, 96, 108, 137, 203, 204, 214, 215, 223, 239, 246, 248, 256, 259, 261, 262, 284, 295, 302, 324, 325, 330, 333, 340, 345, 352, 354, 357, 377, 379, 388, 412, 420, 422, 430, 436, 437, 438, 455, 469, 474, 477, 479, 486, 487, 488, 500, 512, 514, 531, 548, **79**-5, 10, 11, 31, 35, 36, 37, 46, 49, 70, 89, 106, 133, 140, 308, 331, 353, 417, 461, 523, 529, **80**-7, 34, 42, 47, 52, 77, 78, 180, 191, 219, 230, 281, 312, 349, 382, **81**-69, 73, 106, 122, 137, 259, **82**-122, 155, **83**-3, 19, 151, 205, 277, **84**-69, 77, **85**-1, 15, 33, 34

    above self-interest, **84**-72
    advice to George to become a Whig, **77**-294
    advised to pacify Parliament and America by corruption, **80**-374
    ambitious and criminal, **80**-409
    American petitions to, **78**-66
    American rebellion and Ireland, **75**-226
    American Revolution and French Revolution, **93**-1
    and Aitken, "John the Painter," **77**-15
    and Burgoyne, **78**-170
        effect of Burgoyne's surrender, **78**-501
    and Bute, **78**-16
    and Charles I, **76**-98
    and Church in America, **83**-40
    and court, **79**-409
    and debate on peace, **82**-122
    and destruction of freedom, **79**-429
    and dissolution of Parliament, March 25, 1784, **84**-44
    and evil counsellors, **78**-447
    and the Fast, **79**-343
    and Fox-North Coalition, **82**-53, **83**-143
    and Fox's Westminster election, **86**-3
    and French invasion, **79**-63
    and Germain, **82**-364, **83**-18
    and Gordon Riots, **80**-153
    and Keppel, **80**-178
    and King William, **74**-80
    and loss of America, **81**-59
    and ministers, **81**-233
    and ministry, **79**-388
    and Minority, **77**-146
    and nation, **79**-118
    and petitions, **79**-284

and Pitt, **84**-116
    America, **84**-162
and Sandwich, **80**-195
and Scots, **78**-308
    favors, **78**-445, 451
    protects, **79**-406
and Stuarts, **80**-384
and Whitehead, **85**-27
and Wilkes, **84**-110
and Yorktown, **81**-33, **82**-318
as Prince of Wales, **60**-20
as tyrant, **78**-36, **79**-120, 392, 517, **80**-141, 321, 344
    bloody and destructive, **80**-67
    cruel, **80**-201
    like tyrant James II, **74**-66
    obstinate and foolish, **80**-321
    wishes to enlarge power, **81**-201
Battle of Long Island, **76**-131
birthday poem and prayer for peace, **76**-316
birthday song by American Loyalist, **77**-129
"blind," **80**-62
blind, stubborn, **78**-111
briber of Parliament, **77**-161, **81**-161
Burgoyne's defeat, **77**-281, **78**-501
Cain, the murderer, **80**-294
character summary, **70**-182
Charles I, tyranny, and civil war, **84**-171
civil war, France and Spain, **76**-197
compared to Nero, **78**-69
confides in Tory Jacobites, **81**-182
constitutional monarch, **73**-110, **84**-206
continuing the war after Yorktown defeat, **82**-24
coronation, **61**-7
    Coronation Day, **80**-80
corrupt, **80**-348
Cowper's "Table Talk," **82**-A
criticized, **79**-243, **80**-427, **84**-19
crucial influence on Parliament, **80**-346
cruel and bloodthirsty, **79**-398
defended, **80**-316, **83**-126
defense of, after Yorktown, **81**-174
defense of, distinguished from Charles I, **80**-157
defense of King, **76**-24, 28, **77**-13
despised, **80**-356
"Dialogue . . .," **84**-A
enjoys self as people suffer, **81**-180
exemplary constitutional monarch, **82**-292, 314
extension of royal prerogative, **76**-12
favors Palliser over Keppel, **80**-328
favors Scots, **78**-445, 451, **79**-107
favors Tories, **81**-185
General Fast, **76**-193
George II's criticism of, **83**-108

the "great National Cause, . . . Constitutional Subordination," **76**-371
history of reign, 1760-1783, **84**-16
incompetent, **80**-405
influenced by Bute and Scotch, **80**-404
influenced by corrupt politicians, **76**-368
inhumane tyrant, **77**-159
the jewel in the crown, Pitt and America, **78**-349
King and Court as Junto, **75**-308
"Leave prating to Phoebus," **78**-A (answer to **78**-111)
like tyrant James II, **74**-66
losing an empire, **75**-79
loss of America, **79**-431
loss of Prime Minister North, **82**-76
lost America, **80**-200
loyal odes, **82**-213, 217
lusts for American blood, **75**-96
marriage, peace, **61**-10
misled by North, **82**-3
misled by Tory cabinet leaders, **82**-4
mock epitaph, **83**-92
must provide leadership, **78**-102
must punish North ministry, **82**-381
the navy, **79**-434, 478 (answer to **79**-434)
neglects country, **83**-195
Nero and Charles I, **81**-177
Neronic, **81**-84
North and Sandwich, **80**-402
North, hunting, **81**-192
North, Washington, and stag hunting, **82**-208
obstinacy, **74**-172, **76**-54, **79**-399, **80**-238, 321,
    and American War, **82**-67
"Ode on . . . King George the Third," **60**-A
of Brunswick line, **79**-191
opposition to "oeconomy," reform, **80**-250
"a Party Man," **80**-9
persists in war against America, **82**-150
pessimistic over outcome of American War, **81**-266
Pitt his tool, **84**-52
politics of corruption, **81**-37
praised, **79**-403
    with Pitt, **84**-190
prerogative and Pitt's ministry, **84**-8
protects Scots, **79**-406
Puddicombe, **73**-A
reaction to enlargement of war, **79**-428
reconciled with Wilkes, **82**-298 (print)
rejects London petition, **78**-263, 439
satirized, **80**-121, 123, 236, 320, **82**-288, 408, 412
Scotch influence, **77**-295
speech December 5, 1782, on peace with America, **82**-27
"Spurious Speech," **77**-A
statue in New York, **76**-103, 108, 241
sticks to Bute's tenets, **82**-161

Stuart tyrant, dominated by "King's Friends," **81**-91
stubborn, **81**-216
stupid, **79**-205
stupid and foolish, **80**-321
stupid and inhumane, **78**-452
summary of character, **70**-182
supports Pitt's ministry, **84**-148
"The Superiority . . .," **70**-A
"To E. G.," **64**-A
Tory defense of, **80**-396, 397
Tory Jacobite, **75**-52
Tory tyrant, great corruptor, **80**-233
two opposed birthday odes, **76**-220, 221
urges king to peace with America but war with France, **79**-481
uses prerogative to support Pitt's ministry, **84**-8
"Verses Extempore," **65**-A
"Verses on the King," **84**-A
"The Vine and Bramble," **70**-A
virtue and integrity, **63**-99
Warton's first birthday ode, **85**-56
wedding and coronation, **61**-6
Wilmot, **63**-A
Wolfe, **72**-35
worthless, **81**-26
**See also**: Jewel in the Crown.

George III's Secret cabinet. (King George's double cabinet system.) See "The King's Friends."

Germain, George Sackville (1716-85). MP, 1741-1782. Appointed Secretary of State for the American colonies, November 10, 1775, after Dartmouth's resignation; coordinated the campaigns during American War. Created Viscount Sackville, February 11, 1782. **59**-8, 36, **62**-7, **65**-8, **70**-178, 195, **72**-1, 6, **74**-12, **75**-58, 61, 80, 96, 117, 120, 170, 187, 235, **76**-7, 8, 17, 18, 19, 27, 60, 61, 76, 92, 124, 132, 135, 168, 191, 201, 206, 207, 215, 217, 218, 221, 226, 266, 304, 307, 311, 338, 345, 398, **77**-13, 15, 33, 46, 66, 67, 148, 149, 163, 183, 245, 286, 288, 299, **78**-6, 12, 14, 16, 19, 25, 44, 64, 86, 171, 223, 296, 316, 318, 325, 352, 397, 404, 416, 455, 486, 487, 551, 556, **79**-3, 17, 28, 31, 33, 35, 37, 44, 49, 98, 107, 140, 194, 197, 202, 219, 240, 275, 283, 284, 310, 367, 371, 372, 392, 397, 529, **80**-7, 10, 16, 23, 26, 33, 40, 62, 69, 123, 146, 175, 180, 219, 226, 237, 334, 343, 378, 404, 405, 410, 429, 430, **81**-5, 33, 39, 124, 145, 182, 241, 259, 266 (print), **82**-3, 4, 9, 27, 60, 135, 136, 155, 224, 304, 369, **83**-19, 69, **85**-52
and Arnold, **82**-212
and Burns, **84**-A
and Gen. Howe, **81**-81, 231
and George III, **79**-399
coward, **81**-74
criticized, **82**-12
defended, **80**-34
history and character, **83**-18
the Howes and Burgoyne, **81**-226
Minden, **59**-43 (print), **75**-267, **76**-219, **79**-68
and Secretary of State, **75**-160, 163
must resign, **82**-108

narrative of career, **81**-142
peerage, **82**-143, 229, 307, 348, 364
    elevation to peerage, **82**-95
poor leadership, **82**-354
quarrel with Clinton, **78**-170
quarrel with Howe, **79**-5
resigns February 11, 1782, **83**-3
Yorktown disaster, **81**-178
**See also:** Minden.

Gibbon, Edward (1737-94). MP, 1774-1784. Historian, commissioner of Trade and Plantations, June 1779-May 1782; generally supported the North ministry and voted for coercion of America. **79**-25, 110, 126, 128, 129, 138, 209, 291, 335, 369, **80**-33, 37, 86, 233, 235, 229, **82**-9, 193
    and Thomas Chubb, the deist, **79**-95, 509
    bribed and corrupted, **79**-501
    corrupt, **81**-154
    protest at his appointment to Board of Trade, June 20, 1779, **79**-356

Gibbons, Maria, Mrs. A loyalist who spied on Washington in New York, 1776. **77**-321

Gibraltar Besieged, September 12, 1779-February 3, 1783. **80**-182, 238, **81**-80, 120, 133, **82**-8, 21, 157, 345, **83**-2, 32, 70, 232, 240, **85**-4, 32
    Spanish-French assault repelled September 13-14, 1782, the last important engagement of the American War in Europe, **82**-8, 21, 157, 345, **83**-2, 32, 70, 232, 240, **85**-4, 32
        Admiral Howe, **82**-33, 45
            and General Eliott lift siege, **82**-45
            relieves Gibraltar October 11, 1782, **82**-144
        and Effingham, **83**-5
        and siege of Troy, **82**-271
        attack of French and Spaniards repelled, **82**-262
        British still on Gibraltar after the peace, **83**-278
        a common soldier's narrative of, **83**-139
        Eliott and Howe, **83**-25
        Gibraltar saved by Eliott and Howe, **82**-131
        great victory surpassing siege of Troy, **83**-204
        Hayley on Wright of Derby, **85**-5 (same as **83**-17)
        narrative, **82**-237
            of Bourbon attack, September 13, 1782, **82**-141
            of Eliott's victory, **82**-323
            of Howe's success in eluding Bourbon fleets, **82**-259
        painting by Wright of Derby, **83**-17
        review of the fighting, **82**-330
        siege lifted by Eliott and Howe, **82**-153

Glynn, John (1722-79). MP (for Brentford, Middlesex), 1768-1779. Serjeant-at-law, 1763; recorder of London, 1772-d. Member Bill of Rights Society; counsel for printers of *North Briton*, 1764, and for Wilkes, 1768, and for James Townsend, 1772. Supported the American and populist causes. **68**-22, 37, 50, 71, 94, 124, **69**-8, 36, 55, 56, 81, 93, 97, 126, 131, 180, 181, 183, 193, 201, 212, 253, **70**-103, 113, **71**-25, 77, **72**-1, 87, 93, **73**-3, 63, **75**-223, **76**-80, **78**-4
    "Extempore on . . .," **68**-A
    *Ode to Palinurus*, **70**-A
    "On Occasion," **68**-A

"On Two Late . . .," **68-A**
"A Pill," **68-A**
"Verses," **68-A**
Gordon, George (1751-93). MP, 1774-1780. Led the London protest demonstration of the Protestant Association petitioning the House of Commons against Roman-Catholic Relief and sparking no-popery riots that lasted eight days; committed to the Tower, June 9, 1780, for his part, but acquitted of treason, February 1781. **80**-44, 147, 291, **81**-141, 176
    acquitted, **81**-109
    and North ministry, **80**-251
    and Shelburne, **83**-257
    attacked and defended, **81**-196, 197
    defended, **81**-208
    imprisoned in Tower, **80**-325
    sparked the riots, **80**-315
    **See also:** Gordon Riots.
Gordon Riots, London, June 2-9, 1780. Excited by the enormous demonstration against Roman-Catholic relief, mobs burned Catholic chapels, prisons, and homes of people (e.g., Mansfield) until quelled by the army; more than 450 people were killed or injured. **80**-41, 286
    and American rebellion, **80**-28
    and American War, **80**-248
    and London Mayor Kennet, **80**-193
    and North ministry, **80**-251
    blamed on the French; see Cowper's Latin poem, **80**-53, 383
    blamed upon America, "Hymn X," **80**-42
    caused by American and English traitors (Minority), **81**-17
    Cowper's "In Seditionem Horrendam," **80-A**
    Cowper's "On Burning of Mansfield's Library," **82-A**
    Cowper's "Table Talk," **82-A**
    effect on Wilkes, **80**-167
        and King George, **80**-153
    Freeth's song against, **80**-147
    loss of Mansfield's library, **80**-287, 340
    Samuel Butler and Presbyterians, **80**-284
    suppressed, **80**-188
        by army, **80**-395
Gower, 2d Earl. **See:** Granville Leveson-Gower.
Grafton, 3d Duke. **See:** Augustus Henry Fitzroy.
Grafton-Chatham Ministry, July 1766-January 1770. **66**-331, **67**-35, 47, **68**-3, 19, 24, 71, 106, 120, 121, **69**-31, 32, 40, 43, 48, 59, 63, 72, 73, 125, 131, 132, 143, 144, 146, 149, 158, 180, 253, **70**-2, 105, 111, 112, 176, 179, 189, 213, 235, **71**-6, 102
    resigns, **70**-69
    **For more on Grafton, see:** Augustus Henry Fitzroy, 3d Duke of Grafton.
Granby, Marquis of. **See:** John Manners.
Grasse-Tilly, François-Joseph-Paul, Comte de Grasse (1723-1788). French Admiral whose fleet trapped Cornwallis at Yorktown but was destroyed by Rodney, Battle of the Saints, April 1782. **81**-21, 259, **82**-1, 7, 46, 146
Grattan, Henry (1746-1820). Irish political leader; Irish Parliament from 1775; championed legislative independence for Ireland. **81**-221, **82**-15, 239, **83**-69
    against corruption, **83**-141

and Flood, **82**-44, 216, **83**-97, 112, 113
    on the enormous grant of £50,000 by Irish Parliament. **82**-233, 237
    on the grant of money, **83**-73
    "Questions and Answers," **83**-A
Graves, Thomas (1725-1802). British admiral, in command of the British navy on the American station for four months beginning July 4, 1781, and at time of Cornwallis's surrender, October 19, 1781. Graves' failure to extricate Cornwallis trapped in Yorktown virtually brought the American War to an end. **81**-148, 210
"The Great." **See**: Nobility.
Greene, Nathaniel (1742-86). American general; fought Cornwallis at Guilford Courthouse, March 15, 1781; against British at Eutaw Springs, South Carolina, September 8, 1781, and forced them back to Charleston, the last major action in the South, **81**-12, 121, 122, 259
    David Humphreys on, **85**-6
    Eutaw Springs, **82**-148
Grenville, George (1712-70). MP, 1741-1770. PM, 1763-1765; introduced the Stamp Act, 1765; and initiated the proceedings against Wilkes, 1763; but opposed his expulsion from House of Commons, 1769. **63**-2, **64**-100, 106, **65**-8, 39, 61, 76, 105, 113, 147, **66**-60, 84, 91, 96, 110, 119, **67**-4, 7, **68**-10, 23, 107, **69**-11, 81, **70**-8, 77, 107, **75**-1, 239, **76**-22, **77**-125, **78**-170, **84**-39
    epitaph, **70**-62, **71**-31
    "Gentle Shepherd," **66**-33
    on Grenville's Election Act, February 25, 1774, **74**-178
Grenville, George Nugent-Temple, 2d Earl Temple (1753-1813). MP, 1774-1779. 1st son of George Grenville. Leader of the Grenville party in opposition to North, 1774-79, and continued opposition in House of Lords; upset the Coalition. **82**-239, **84**-116, 124
    and peace, **83**-66
    cr. Marquess of Buckingham, **84**-142
    praised from Irish perspective, **82**-246, 248
    Viceroy of Ireland and Irish emancipation, **82**-182
Grenville, James (1715-83). MP, 1742-1770. Brother of George and Richard Temple Grenville; supported Pitt against Bute and against George Grenville. **65**-91.
Grenville, Richard Temple, 1st Earl Temple (1711-79). MP, 1734-1752, and House of Lords. Brother of George, whom he opposed on the Wilkes issue, 1763, and on the Stamp Act, 1765; opposed conciliatory measures towards American colonies. Called "the evil genius of Pitt." **61**-22, **63**-23, 58, 130, 142, 189, **64**-1, 44, 100, **65**-1, 5, 8, 74, 91, 101, 133, **66**-3, 106, 131, **68**-22, 124, **69**- 250, **70**-24, 130, 170, 192, **73**-4, 18, **82**-142
    and Aitken, "John the Painter," **77**-15
    Churchill's *Independence*, **64**-A
    death, **79**-323, 341
Guillouet, Louis, Comte d'Orvilliers (1708-c.92). Admiral of the French Brest fleet in the Ushant engagement, July 22, 1778. **78**-200, 410, 481, **79**-12, 57, 170, 177, 178, 179, 267, 450, **80**-422
    "Brest Council," **79**-A
Guthrie, William (1708-70). Court writer; historian, miscellaneous author.
    Churchill's *Author*, **63**-A
*Habeas Corpus*. Introduced February 6, 1777, the High Treason Bill was meant to suspend *habeas corpus*, i.e., to limit the rights of Englishmen. Naturally, the Opposition took exception to this bill. **77**-59, 142, 314

effect on Opposition, **79**-292
petition against, **77**-160

Hale, Nathan (1755-76). American "Martyr Spy," captured on an intelligence mission within the enemy lines shortly before the battle of Harlem Heights, New York. Executed upon Gen. Howe's orders, September 22, 1776. **81**-203

Halifax, Nova Scotia, Canada, **76**-22

Halifax, 3d Earl. **See**: George Montagu Dunk.

Hallifax, Thomas (1721-1789). MP, 1780-1781, 1784-1789. Banker and London alderman, 1766-d.; sheriff, 1768-1769; and lord mayor, 1776-1777. Opposed press gangs and the High Treason Bill. **77**-160

Hamilton, John (1726-84). British naval officer, saved Quebec from the besieging Americans, mid 1776. **81**-204

Hampden, John (1594-1643). Puritan statesman, sparked the revolt against Stuart tyranny by refusing to pay "ship money" tax. **78**-8 (cited)
denigrated with Hancock and Hartley, **80**-154
Hampden's spirit opposes Stuart tyranny and slavery, **76**-361
**Also see**: Whig Tradition, Invocation of Whig Pantheon, John Hampden.

Hancock, John (1737-93). American revolutionary statesman; president of Congress, 1775-1777, and first signer of Declaration of Independence. **75**-2, 29, 48, 88, 133, 150, **76**-11, 21, 22, 85, 97, 166, 258, 279, 298, 390, **77**-134, **78**-7, 8, 66, 110, 558, **79**-26, **80**-22, 34, 277
and Hampden, **80**-154
compared with Wilkes, **75**-19

Hanway, Jonas (1712-86). Merchant, philanthropist; commissioner of the victualing office, 1762-1783. **80**-41

Harcourt, Simon, Earl (1714-77). Governor to Prince of Wales (later George III), 1751-1752, ambassador to Paris, 1768; Viceroy of Ireland after George Townshend, 1772-1777. **73**-35, 49, 250

Hardy, Charles (1716-80). MP, 1764-1768, 1771-1780. Naval officer and Governor of New York, 1755-1757; with Boscawen at capture of Louisburg, 1758; with Hawke at Brest and Quiberon Bay, 1759; admiral at time of American War, commander of Channel fleet; supported North's ministry. **79**-52, 58, 77, 154, 163, 311, 370, 375, 420, 421, 439, 440, 444, 450, 524, **80**-212, 282
"Brest Council," **79**-A
death, **80**-187
poem on death of, in Nisbet's *Poems*, **80**-21

Harland, Robert (c.1715-84). British admiral, second-in-command, under Keppel, off Ushant, 1778-1779. **79**-75, **79**-293
"While Byron . . .," **79**-A

Harley, Thomas (1730-1804). Brother of 3d Earl of Oxford; MP, 1761-1774, 1776-1802. Wine merchant, banker; alderman, 1761-d., and lord mayor of London, 1767-1768; anti-Wilkes Tory, and King's choice; war contractor and heavy subscriber to Government loans. **68**-1, 19, 71 91, **69**-56, 128, **71**-113, **73**-38
on wisdom of contractor being MP, **76**-95

Harris, James (1709-80). MP, 1761-1780. Classical scholar and philosopher; friend of George Grenville; supporter of North's American policy without reservation.
on wars, **81**-229

Hartley, David (c.1730-1813). MP, 1774-1780, 1782-1784. Patriot, member of Minority Opposition against North's ministry; made eight motions for conciliation with America, but all were defeated; peace negotiator under the Fox-North Coalition, April 1783. **75**-35, **76**-168, **80**-41, 305, 317
and Fox-North Coalition, **83**-69

      and peace with America, **83**-63
      Hampden and Hancock, **80**-154
      in Rockingham administration, **82**-370
      motion to reconcile America and Britain blocked by Tory policies, **79**-465

Hastings, Warren (1732-1818). Of the East India Co.; the first Governor of British India.
      Burke and North, **84**-192

Hawke, Edward (1710-81). MP, 1747-76. British admiral, served in the Seven Years' War and commanded at the victory in Quiberon Bay, 1759; 1st Lord of Admiralty, 1766-1771; supported Grenville ministry and general warrants; member of Keppel's court martial. **59**-3, 25, 29, 42, **60**-14, 17, 21, 25, 42, 48, **66**-1, **70**-29, 74, **73**-5, **78**-476, **79**-1, 190, 456, 458, 460, **80**-41, **82**-48, **83**-158, **90**-1
      "Advertisement from France," **60**-A
      and Keppel, **82**-91
      death, **80**-56

Hayley, George (d. 1781). MP, 1774-1781. Wealthy merchant; alderman of London, 1774, and sheriff, 1775-1776. Brother-in-law of Wilkes. Opposed North Government's American measures.
      berated for betrayal of America and the Opposition, **75**-133

Henry, Patrick (1736-99). American statesman and revolutionary orator. **74**-60

Herschel, William (1738-1822). British astronomer, discoverer on March 13, 1781, of the Georgian Star; proposed the name "Georgium Sidus" (Georgian Planet), but after fifty years the name "Uranus" became generally accepted.
      and loss of America, **84**-49
      and loss of 13 stars, **83**-47

Hervey, Augustus John, 3d Earl of Bristol (1724-79). MP, 1757-1775; then House of Lords. Naval officer, served under Admiral Byng and was at Martinique, St. Lucia, and Havana, 1761-1762; commander of Mediterranean fleet, 1763. Supported Bute and Grenville, Grafton against Wilkes, 1768-1769, and North's measures against America. **59**-29, **68**-34, 75

Hervey, Frederick Augustus, 4th Earl of Bristol (1730-1803). Bishop of Cloyne, 1767-1768; bishop of Derry, 1768-1803. Encouraged the Irish volunteer movement and reform of Parliament.
      and Ireland, **83**-87

Hervey, George William, 2d Earl of Bristol (1721-75). Opposed repeal of the Stamp Act. A corrupt hireling peer, according to William Mason. **74**-11

Hervey, William (1732-1815). MP, 1763-1768. Brother of Augustus, George and Frederick Hervey; gave up the church for a military career; served in America, 1755-1763, and was with Braddock, 1755; was not in America during the American War. **55**-1

Hill, Wills, Earl of Hillsborough (1718-93). MP, 1741-1756; then House of Lords. President, Board of Trade and Plantations, 1763-1765; post-master general, 1766-1768; first secretary of state for colonies, January 20, 1768-August 31, 1772; supported North's ministry and served as secretary of state, southern department, 1779-1782. **68**-108, **70**-28, 32, 71, 82, **73**-4, 10, 26, **74**-127, **79**-275, **80**-69, 123, 378, **81**-39, **82**-414

Hinchcliffe, John (1731-94). Bishop of Peterborough, 1769-1794. Opposed North's anti-American policy.
      opposed the American War, **77**-309
      praised, **78**-12, **80**-37
      satirized, **80**-291

Hogarth, William (1697-1764). Painter and engraver. **63**-53, 75, 100, 152, 157,

181, **64-6, 66**-84
      Churchill's "Epistle to Hogarth," **63**-A
      "The Snarling Pig", **63**-A
Holland (the Dutch). **80**-285, 345, **81**-125, 167, **82**-396
      American ally, **78**-516
      and peace, **83**-63
      breaks with Britain, **81**-44
      Britain at war with, **81**-168
      British ally, **58**-12
      British retaliation on is justified, **82**-311
      character of, **81**-214
      the coming Dutch war, **79**-360, 534
      December 21, 1780, Britain declares war on, **80**-184
      Dutch avarice, **80**-254
      Dutch perfidy, **82**-81
      Holland's entrance into the war, **81**-212
      indifferent to Britain's war with France and America, **80**-217
      insists upon neutrality, **80**-421
      mercenary, **84**-63, 86
      navy attacks Dutch trade, **80**-132
      navy lacks leader, **81**-206
      Rodney seizes St. Eustatius, **81**-25
      satirized, **81**-263 (print)
            Dutch reaction to loss of St. Eustatius, **81**-264
      tempted to war against Britain, **80**-426 (print)
      treacherous, **81**-163
      turning from Britain, **79**-271, 529
      **For more, see under American War:** British Navy, Rodney's Engage-
         ments, St. Eustatius
Hollis, Thomas (1720-74). London libertarian, "Republican" and "true Whig,"
      friend of American Jonathan Mayhew; like his great uncle Thomas Hollis, he
      was a benefactor of Harvard College. **82**-241
Holmes, Charles (1711-61). MP, 1758-1761. Naval officer at the capitulation
      of Quebec, 1759; also served as member of Admiral Byng's court martial, 1757.
      **69**-17
Holroyd, John Baker (1735-1821). MP, 1780, 1781-1784, 1790-1802. Staunch Tory
      opponent of America and Dissent; friend of North (later marrying North's 2d
      daughter), and supporter of the North ministry and Fox-North Coalition.
      Spoke against Conway's motion to end the American War and voted against
      Shelburne's peace preliminaries. Also a very good friend of Gibbon. **80**-
      336, 387
      a corrupt politician, **80**-198
Home, John (1722-1808). Scottish playwright and historian of the '45
      rebellion.
      **65**-11, **78**-522 (and Mallet and James Thomson and Alfred).
Hood, Samuel (1724-1816). MP, 1785-1796. British naval officer; knighted for
      bringing the Carlyle Peace Commission home; rear-admiral with Rodney at St.
      Eustatius and with Graves against the French, September 1781 (Yorktown
      capitulation); also with Rodney in the Battle of the Saints, 1782. **79**-235,
      **81**-107, **82**-18, 146, 182, 196, **83**-43, **84**-31
      and Carlyle Peace Commission, **79**-350
      vs Fox, **83**-7
Hopkins, Esek (1718-1802). First commander-in-chief of the American navy; a

successful sea-captain and privateer in Seven Years' War, but a failure in the American War.  Here reported as having defeated Admiral Howe and Admiral Parker, late 1776.  **77**-124, 228

Horne, John (after 1782, John Horne Tooke) (1736-1812).  Curate at New Brentford, 1760-1763, but gave up clerical life for politics; defended Wilkes and worked for reform, 1765-1771; quarreled with Wilkes and left the Society for Support of Bill of Rights to form the Constitutional Society, 1771; fined and briefly imprisoned for attempting to raise money for American prisoners, 1777-1778. **68**-28, 37, 111, **69**-22, 23, 44, 58, 83, 97, 103, 104, 124, 138, 139, 167, 183, 211, 212, 253, 266, **70**-2, 64, 82, **71**-9, 25, 32, 45, 47, 49, 56, 57, 72, 80, 82, 88, 95, 97, 99, 107, 113, 119, 123, 127, 128, 129, 131, **72**-87, 93, **73**-3, 33, 54, 61, 67, **74**-46, 81, **78**-23

    "Addressed . . .," **71**-A

    "Alphabetical," **69**-A

    denigrated at length, **71**-94

    "Enchantment," **69**-A

    "Extempore on the . . .," **68**-A

    *Ode to Palinurus*, **70**-A

    "On the Dispute . . .," **71**-A

    trial for attempting to aid American rebels, **77**-209

Horse-Racing as Metaphor.  **65**-9, 59, 60, 75, **66**-82, 106, **67**-11, **70**-18, **77**-88, 128, **78**-4

    and effeminate nobility, **85**-2

    anti-Scot satire, **74**-63

Howard, Charles, Earl of Surrey (1746-1815).  MP, 1780-1786.  Succeeded father as 11th Duke of Norfolk, 1786.  Announced on March 20, 1782, a motion in House of Commons to dismiss North ministry, but North anticipated it by declaring that he and his ministry had resigned.  Member of Treasury Board under the Coalition, 1783; a supporter of Fox.  **82**-197

    among the Foxites against Pitt, **84**-166

    and North's resignation, **82**-113

Howard, Frederick, 5th Earl of Carlisle (1748-1825).  House of Lords, 1770-; friend of C. J. Fox; headed the Peace Commission to America, 1778; president Board of Trade and Plantations, 1779-1782; lord lieutenant of Ireland, 1780-1782.  Supported the North ministry to its end and held office in Coalition, 1783.  **78**-25, 27, 257, 300, 359, 463, **79**-275, 310, **80**-86, **82**-4, **83**-29

    dedication to, **83**-8

    in Portland administration, **83**-29, 265

    **See also**: Part I of Index for Lord Carlisle's verse; **see also**: in Part II of Index, Carlisle Peace Commission.

Howard, Henry, 12th Earl of Suffolk (1739-79).  House of Lords; opposed repeal of Stamp Act, 1766, and to Commons' unseating of Wilkes, 1770; headed the Grenville group (after Grenville's death), 1770, and joined North's forces; as Secretary of State Northern Department, opposed any concessions to colonists, 1771-1777.  **73**-4, **75**-197, **77**-67, 318, **78**-27, 290, 296, **78**-348, 479, 500, **79**-310, **82**-320

Howard, Thomas, 3d Earl of Effingham (1747-91).  House of Lords; in the Minority Opposition against policies of North ministry; resigned commission rather than fight America; returned to service against the Bourbons, 1778, and volunteered for action on Gibraltar.  **66**-64, **75**-35, 150, **76**-42, 43, **78**-12, 219, 535, **79**-44, 59, **82**-4, 193, 285, **83**-5, **86**-1

    and reform, **84**-131

    "Liberty," **89**-2

Howe, George Augustus, 3d Viscount Howe (1724-58). MP, 1747-1758. British general, one of the three Howe brothers serving in North America; slain July 6, 1758, on the march to Ticonderoga, New York. A monument to his memory ordered by the province of Massachusetts Bay is in Westminster Abbey. **58**-3, 4, 7, 8, **59**-28, **60**-3, **64**-3, **66**-67, **69**-19, **84**-10, **90**-1.
    "Impromptu," **83**-A

Howe, Richard, 4th Viscount Howe (1726-99). MP, 1757-1802. Admiral, British navy, serving during the Seven Years' War and the American War. He supported Government's punitive measures against the colonies and was commander-in-chief in North American waters; peace commissioner with brother William, 1776. **59**-3, 10, **60**-48, **62**-2, **69**-5, **70**-74, **76**-66, 178, 322, **78**-464, **79**-38, 75, 154, **80**-10, **81**-210, **82**-48, 103, 338, **83**-2, 32, 43
    and French, **82**-111
    failure in America, **79**-40
    Gibraltar, **82**-45, 144, 153, 342
    "Impertinent Curiosity," **77**-A
    naval victory, **80**-182
    relieves Gibraltar, October 1782, **82**-33
    saved Gibraltar with Eliott, **82**-131
    Wesley's "American Independency," **83**-A
    "While Byron . . .," **79**-A

Howe, William (1729-1814). MP, 1758-1780. British general, served with Wolfe at Louisburg and Quebec, and was at Belle Isle, 1761, and Havana, 1762, Seven Years' War; led the British forces in the first three and a half years of the American War, 1775-1778. **58**-7, **75**-2, 107, 110, 127, 135, 136, 162, 176, **76**-77, 166, 191, 226, 258, 307, 388, **77**-12, 38, 90, 109, 132, 156, 167, 171, 173, 202, 208, 240, 247, **78**-2, 7, 20, 32, 64, 184, 295, 324, 346, 520, 540, 550, **79**-59, 205, **80**-10, 23, 69, 163, 255, 404, **81**-3, 94, 259, **82**-9, 30, **84**-16
    and Catiline, a traitor, **81**-112
    and Rodney, **81**-202
    Battle of Long Island and New York Campaign, 1776, **76**-14, 87, 102, 103, 178, 200, 247, 268, 306, 385, **77**-38, 133, 150
        lost American War in, **84**-8
    before Parliament, **78**-189
    blamed for Burgoyne's defeat, **80**-34
    Burns, **84**-A
    character, **78**-82, 243
    contrasted with Tarleton, **80**-164
    corrupt, **77**-174
        and ineffectual, **80**-385
    Cowper's "Table Talk," **82**-A
    Croft's "Epitaph," **80**-A (from **80**-10)
    criticized, **77**-257, 258, 261, 313, 314, **78**-91, 228, **79**-228, **82**-393
    defended, **81**-231
    evacuation of Boston, **76**-150
    failures, **78**-362, 397, 472, 510, **79**-6, 11, 40, **80**-32, **83**-91, 121
    Galloway and Germain, **81**-81
    hopes Howe will defeat the rebels, **77**-189
    Howe and Burgoyne's Campaign, 1777, **77**-105, 120
    Howe's defeat at Boston, **78**-226
    "Impromptu," **83**-A
    in Opposition, **79**-257

inactive, asleep, **79**-3
lost an empire, **82**-365
Mischianza, farewell to his troops, 1778, **78**-51, **79**-504
New Jersey and Philadelphia Campaign, 1776-1777, **77**-56, 58, 59, 92, 200, 231, 241, 256, 268, 291, 332, **78**-62, **79**-21
    Mud Island, **77**-91
not militant, **78**-49
quarrel with Germain, **79**-5
a second Cain, **80**-294
sleeps, **78**-323
supported by Minority Opposition, **79**-31
traitor, **82**-349
Wesley's "American Independency," **83**-A
Wesley's *American War*, **82**-A
writings, **78**-457
**For more on William Howe, see:** Howe's Battles and Campaigns (including Boston Siege and Bunker Hill) in American War, Mischianza, and Reviews in Verse of Battles and Campaigns in American War.

Howe Brothers. **76**-202, 324, 332, 398, **77**-27, 78, 83, 110, 127, 148, 247, 285, **78**-8, 25, 47, 66, 143, 415, **80**-169, 199
    and Battle of Long Island, **76**-245
    and Germain, **81**-226
    attacked by Galloway, **81**-220
    character, **78**-84
    corrupt and self-interested, **80**-149
    corruption, **78**-145
    criticized, **77**-140, 164
    damned as traitors, **80**-34
    defended, **78**-545
    failure, **77**-32
    "Impertinent Curiosity," **77**-A

Howe Brothers' Peace Commission, 1776. **76**-56, 313
    and Carlyle Peace Commission, **79**-497

Hughes, Richard (c.1729-1812). British naval officer; commanded the Halifax station, 1778-1780; served under Howe at Gibraltar, 1782; commanded the Jamaica station, 1784-1786. **83**-43

Hume, David (1711-76). Scottish philosopher and Tory historian. **63**-22, **78**-324

Hunter, William (1718-83). London physician to the Queen; celebrated anatomist and medical teacher, like his brother John (1728-1793).
    and America, **83**-171

Hurd, Richard, Bishop. **See**: Part I of Index.

Hutchinson, Thomas (1711-80). American, Royal Governor of Massachusetts; supported the unpopular Grenville policies, so that his house was pillaged, 1765; after Governor Bernard's withdrawal, he became governor, 1769; upon Franklin's disclosure of his private correspondence, 1773, he was forced to retire to England, 1774. **69**-84, **73**-101, **74**-6, 74, 165, 181, 196, 209
    "From the Massachusetts Spy," **73**-A

Hutton, James (1715-95). English Moravian preacher; "a constant attendant on his Majesty" George III; thought to be Tory like Leonard Smelt, **80**-66

Hystaspes, a patriotic Son of Liberty, anti-ministerial political writer, imprisoned for debt, **78**-156

Ideal character of _____.

alderman, **69**-174
American, **77**-255 (rebel)
beau, **77**-36 ("the beau of 1777")
"Bostonian Saint," **75**-213
Briton, **70-A** ("the Superiority of England")
citizen
    honest independent, **74**-85
    rational political citizen, **70**-80
contented man, **76**-85 (indifferent to American War)
courtier, **70**-167, **75**-156
Englishman
    on the American rebels, **77**-255
    true Englishman, **81**-37
epigram, **85**-46
government, **68**-86 (a "Happy Government")
great man, **72**-105 (vs. a good man)
heroine, **79**-93 (British)
king: **61**-5
    "Character of a Good King," **66-A**
    Churchill's *Gotham*, a patriot king, **64-A**
    King George III, **78**-36
    "The Superiority" of King George, **70-A**
    a Whig king, **70**-160
land of freedom, **75**-22
member of parliament, **64**-60, **73**-89, **79**-368, **84**-208
  **See also:** "politician"
minister
    discarded, **81**-52
    good, **72**-92
    modern, **75**-89, **77**-264, **79**-390, **82**-308
    young, **69**-140
nation
    British, **71**-135
    good, **74**-49
    "The Superiority of England," **70-A**
noble, **64-A** (Churchill's *Independence*, a "great Noble")
patriot, **73**-99, **74**-160, **81**-128, 184
    "complete patriot," **70**-178
    genuine, **70**-156
    "The Real Patriot," Scottish, **76-A**
    true, **70**-163
politician: **64**-60, **67**-42
    corrupt Parliament man, **79**-368
    credentials of a proper candidate for seat in Parliament, **73**-89
    honest and independent-Beckford, **70**-48
    thoroughly rotten and corrupt Parliament, **85**-26
    **See also:** "courtier," "member of Parliament," "modern minister."
sailor, **79**-92 (British)
satirist, **79**-91
Scotsman, **77**-255 (on the American rebel)
soldier, **79**-90 (British)
West Indian, **77**-255 (on the American rebel)
Impressment. **See:** Press Warrants.

Independence. **See**: The American War. Independence.
India (and East Indies). **59**-9, 20, 27, 34, 42, **60**-25, 39, **61**-1, 2, 35, 37, **63**-60, **65**-140, **69**-3, **74**-186, **77**-16, **79**-26, **85**-4
    and America, **74**-67
    and Burke, **81**-251
    Britain supplies cloth to India, **83**-227
    Fox's India Bill, **84**-104, 139
    Fox's India Bill and Pitt, **85**-12
    "The Ghost" and Fox's India Bill, **83**-A
    loss of America, but gain of India, **78**-524
    nabobs, **79**-91
    "Ode on . . . George III," **61**-A
    praise for officers who seized India from the French, **83**-25
    source of wealth and corruption, **82**-17
Indians (of North America). **55**-1, 2, **57**-1, 2, **63**-5, **64**-4, **65**-64, **69**-19, **76**-37, 38, 376, **77**-143, **78**-27, 210, 518, **79**-205, 425, 426
    and immigrants, **83**-8
    as allies of French, **69**-5
    as enemies of Britain, **79**-150
    British use of Indians in American War, **80**-11
    Burgoyne, **82**-9
    "On the Death of General Braddock," **55**-A
    "On the Present State of America," **56**-A
    join the British, **60**-33
    pleased at defeat of America, **76**-257
    Pontiac, **66**-15
    pre-American War, or colonial, episodes illustrating savagery, **77**-9
    raid on Ohio, **80**-213
    romantic view of, **85**-53
    savages, **78**-14, 36, 90
        and atrocious warfare, **79**-4, **83**-22
        and their atrocities, **78**-21
    scalping, **76**-218
        and Burgoyne, **78**-254
        savage practice of, **77**-135
Inn, English. **76**-337 ("real liberty" only at, and America)
Ins and Outs (Government vs Minority Opposition. **63**-104, 110, 115, 121, **65**-31, 39, 41, 65, 90, 103, 105, 123, **67**-14, 32, 49, **68**-45, **70**-52, 55, 107, 166, 215, **71**-52, 83, 131, **72**-10, 20, 66, 89, **74**-213, **76**-15, 318, **78**-266, **79**-381, **80**-292, 305, 401
    both self interested and destructive, **84**-87, 88, 89
    competing parties condemned, **82**-162
    conflict between, **84**-187
    equally self interested, **83**-181
    Fox is out, **84**-184
    minister, in and out, **82**-418
    Minority becomes Majority, **82**-264
    "On the Report," **65**-A
    "Parliamentary Duellists," **81**-A
    party divisions futile, **82**-322
    Patriots, Outs, **72**-79
        always critical, **82**-289
    Pitt and Thurlow deserve to be in, Fox and North deserve to be out, **84**-40

Rockingham's death brings division, **82**-104, 145
**Also see:** Faction; and Minority Opposition during North's Ministry; and Ministries (from 1754 to 1783, to determine "ins".
Ireland (and Irish). **64**-11, **65**-102, **67**-3, 28, **68**-67, **70**-15, 30, 186, 210, 216, **71**-46, 78, 86, **73**-35, **74**-89, 110, 149, 154, **75**-208, 222, 310, **77**-18, **78**-450
    and America and American War, **74**-131, 161, **75**-13, 66, 142, 143, 193, 226, 230, **76**-43, **77**-250, **79**-35, 314, 409, **80**-1, 127, 295, 303, 325, 345, **82**-349, **83**-3
        America and the movement towards Irish freedom, **82**-15
        and American liberty, **80**-259
        and American rebellion, **93**-1
        and Cavendish, 5th Duke of Devonshire, **83**-10
        and Earl of Bristol, "An equal Legislation," **82**-87
        and emancipation, **84**-3
        and faction, **84**-157
        and Fox, **82**-360
        and France, after Yorktown, **81**-57
        and French war, **78**-304
        and Ireland's emancipation, **82**-129
        and the movement towards Irish freedom, **82**-15
        and Palliser, **79**-235
        and seditious Opposition, **79**-405
        and 3d Earl Temple, **84**-142
        and William Eden, **81**-82
        anti-English feeling, **80**-271
        "Answer to Paddy's Address," **79**-A
        Belfast grand review of fencibles, **80**-156
        Britain needs help from Ireland in war, **79**-358, 528
        contrasted with America, **79**-101
        defense of present Anglo-Irish relation and need for cooperation in American War, **80**-176
        discontented, **80**-3
            and source of disunity with England, **81**-15
        Duke of Portland, incorruptible Viceroy of Ireland, **82**-384
        Earl Temple, new Lord Lieutenant, **82**-239
        emancipation from the Established Church of Ireland, **81**-245
        emigration, **73**-105, **74**-12, 95, 191
        English oppression, **82**-270
        English vs Irish patriot, **82**-73
        equality with England, **82**-182
        an Establishment poem, **80**-244
        fencibles or volunteers, **80**-72
        Flood, Grattan, freedom, **82**-44, **83**-97, 112, 113
        free trade, **79**-234, 271, 392, **80**-217, 293, 321, **85**-15, 30, 51
            denied, **81**-36
        freedom, Flood and Coote [Bellamont], but vs Grattan, **82**-216
        Grattan and greater independence from England, **81**-221
        independence for America and Ireland, **82**-25
        Ireland and support of Britain's cause, **82**-50
        Ireland emulates America and seeks freedom and equality, but not independence, **82**-276
        Ireland vs Quebec Bill, **74**-22
        Irish oratory, especially Grattan's, **82**-141

        an Irish politician, **82**-226
        Irish up in arms, **79**-295
        Irish volunteers, **78**-554, **82**-202, 203
            demand freedom, **81**-99
        the lesson of America, **80**-406
        loyal to Britain, yet received its rights, unlike America, **82**-407
        *Ode on the Emancipation of Ireland*, **82**-A
        on protecting the English interest over Ireland against America,
            **82**-414 (print)
        *Order of St. Patrick* and "Questions and Answers," **83**-A
        Papists, **78**-550
        patriot spirit and a "Patriot Congress," **80**-40
        reform, self-rule, and American independence, **82**-85
        repeal of Poinings Act, **82**-32
        repeal of trade restrictions, **80**-28
        should buy native goods and retaliate against English trade restric-
            tions, **80**-174
        threatens to secede from empire, **82**-347
        trade restrictions, **75**-12, 24, **79**-25
        tribute to Irish leaders for achieving liberty, **82**-400
        unity vs Britain, **82**-268
        view of American War to March 1777, **77**-314
        the war and Ireland's desire for freedom, **81**-239
    **For more on Ireland, see**: Henry Flood and Henry Grattan; and Lewis in
        Part I of Index.

Jacobite(s), Scotch rebel(s), the "Forty-five." **See**: Tory Tradition. The
    Stuarts. Tories, Jacobites, and Scotch Rebels.

Jay, John (1745-1829). American statesman, diplomat; took part in the peace
    negotiations, 1782-1783. **80**-22

Jebb, John (1736-86). Prominent dissenter, physician, and scholar; supporter
    of Fox and the reform of Parliament; leader of the Association movement in
    London. **82**-85, 349

Jefferson, Thomas (1743-1826). Founding father, Virginia; statesman, diplomat,
    and author of Declaration of Independence. **80**-22

Jeffreys, George (1648-89). Tory, loyal supporter of James II; presided at
    trial of Algernon Sidney, 1683; "hanging judge," his reputation made by his
    sentences on participants in Monmouth's Rebellion, "bloody assizes," 1685.
    Died in the Tower, April 18, 1689. **64**-65, **70**-240, **75**-268, **81**-177

Jenkinson, Charles (1729-1808). MP, 1761-1786. Loyal public servant under
    Bute and Grenville, Grafton and North, including secretary at war, 1778-
    1782; had great influence on King George as "King's Friend" and probably was
    the real "secret influence" condemned by the Opposition. Member Board of
    Trade, 1784, and president, 1786-1804. **72**-1, **72**-6, **73**-79, **74**-7, 9, **75**-122,
    145, **76**- 62, 217, **77**-67, **78**-27, 296, **79**-200, 310, **80**-90, 343, **82**-285, **83**-
    151, **84**-68, 112
        and Pitt, **85**-12, 13, **86**-3
        in Pitt's camp, **84**-5
        in Pitt's ministry, **84**-19, 23
        opposes reform, **81**-7

Jennings-Clerke, Philip (1722-88). MP, 1768-1788; opponent of North ministry;
    for Wilkes and reform. **79**-446
        on Loyalist refugees, **81**-72

Jenyns, Soame (1704-87). MP, 1742-1780. Miscellaneous author and poet;

member of Board of Trade and Plantations, 1755-1780. **76**-58, 195, 353, **80**-33, 86, **82**-13, **89**-2. **See also:** Part I of Index for Jenyns' poems.
Jervoise, Jervoise Clarke. **See:** Jervoise Clarke.
Jewel in the Crown. Metaphor of loss of France, of Pitt, or of America. **61**-26, 33, **78**-349, 521, **79**-11, **85**-2, 10
    America, "the brightest gem" of Britannia's crown, **84**-16
    Cowper's "Epinikion," **79**-A
    France, "the lost gem of England's regal Crown," **82**-232
    loss of Pitt and of America, **78**-261
Jews.
    and Fox, **83**-76, **84**-50
    creditors, **83**-45
Johnson, Samuel. **See:** Part I of Index for poems by and about Samuel Johnson.
Johnson, William (1715-74). General in the American campaigns of the French and Indian War; large landowner on Mohawk River of upstate New York, **60**-41
    "French Politicks." **60**-A
Johnstone, George (1730-87). MP, 1768-1787. Scotch commodore in navy, Seven Years' War; Governor West Florida, 1763-1767; fought duel with Germain, 1770; member of Carlisle Peace Commission; commanded squadron off Portugal, 1779; director East India Co., 1784-1786. **75**-61, **78**-225, 257, 362, **79**-34, 204, **80**-7, 233, 235, **83**-29
    and American Congress, **81**-194, 230
    and Fox-North Coalition, **83**-69
    death, Carlisle Peace Commission, and Rodney, **87**-1
    duel with Germain, **81**-142
John the Painter. **See:** James Aitken, arsonist.
Jones, John Paul (1747-92). American naval hero, born in Scotland; from the British point of view a marauding pirate. **79**-41, 247, 261, 314, 392, **80**-26, 72, **82**-143, 212
    account of capture of Pearson's *Serapis*, **80**-13
    eludes British fleet, **79**-359
    encounter with Richard Pearson's *Serapis*, September 23, 1779, **79**-253
    infamous privateer, **79**-197
    Jones's attack on Whitehaven, April 23, 1778, **83**-286
    Jones's squadron captures *Serapis*, **79**-304
    mercenary, **80**-102
    raids along Scottish coast, **79**-34
    raids Whitehaven, plunders Scotland, **78**-464
    the search for, **79**-477
Junius (pseud.) (fl. 1769-72). **69**-22, 63, 77, 115, 168, 200, 209, 213, 221, 232, 233, 234, 235, 236, 244, 266, **70**-2, 7, 8, 10, 13, 58, 83, 93, 94, 98, 101, 110, 121, 130, 139, 154, 188, 201, 202, 203, **71**-4, 23, 28, 55, 91, 119, **72**-5, 12, 64, 94, 97, **74**-7, 12, **77**-23, **78**-43, **82**-401
    "Ape of . . . Junius," **75**-114
    Burke as Junius, **71**-27
    "death," **72**-50
    epitaph, **70**-61
    *Ode to Palinurus*, **70**-A
    **See also:** Junius in Part I of Index and Philip Francis in Part II of Index, possible author of Junius' letters.
Junius Americanus. **See:** Arthur Lee.
Kelly, Hugh (1739-77). Irish dramatist and journalist; wrote for the North ministry. **76**-226

Kennet, Brackley (d. 1782). Vintner, alderman of London, 1767; Lord Mayor of London; criticized for ineffectual leadership during the Gordon Riots, June 1780. **80**-342

Keppel, Augustus, Viscount Keppel (1725-86). MP, 1755-1782. Staunch Whig; admiral in British navy; served in Seven Years' War, escorting Braddock and troops to America; victor at Gorée and Senegal in Africa, at Quiberon Bay, 1759, and Havana, 1762. Declared he was ready to do his duty against the French, "but not in the line of America," 1775. Involved in the Ushant episode, 1778. **59**-3, 10, 16, 34, **60**-39, 48, **61**-2, **62**-12, **65**-8, 76, **70**-74, **73**-5, **79**-27, 38, 44, 59, 65, 67, 70, 72, 75, 94, 124, 138, 164, 172, 182, 190, 200, 211, 224, 235, 269, 283, 285, 302, 307, 326, **80**-256, 305, 404, **81**-42, 58, 92, 94, **82**-14, 27, 193, **84**-18, 129
- American War and France, **78**-3, 16, 27, 40, 65, 132, 253, 307, 368, 369, 464, 525, 534, **79**-22
- and American War, **75**-301
- and Byng, **79**-252, **81**-127
- and Fox-North Coalition, **83**-69
- and London, **81**-189
- and Pearson and Farmer, **79**-253
- and politics, **81**-249
- and riots, **79**-222
- and Rodney, **81**-202, **82**-98, 151, 276, 312
- and Ushant Episode, and Palliser, **78**-52, 76, 116, 149, 176, 178, 272, 281, 315, 381, 383, 410, 476, 481, 483, 484, 553, **79**-20, 35, 109, 127, 139, 141, 142, 177, 203, 208, 274, 279, 312, 321, 324, 351, 378, 389, 397, 401, 402, 404, 414, 419, 434, 441, 451, 458, 459, 471, 472, 473, 476, 479, 490, 494, 518, 519, 525, 535, **80**-7, 10, 61, 100, 101, 103, 128, 162, 163, 169, 328, 390, 401, **81**-7
  - and King George, **80**-178
  - and Rodney's victory over Langara, **80**-185
  - and Strutt, **79**-373
  - as focus of patriotic war against Bourbons, **79**-433
  - as seditious partisan, **80**-116
  - as tool of Richmond, **79**-364
  - contrasted with Tarleton, **80**-164
  - criticized as a dupe to seditious faction, **79**-410
  - disgraced, **79**-448
  - "Extempore," and "A Political Paraphrase," **78**-A (the French view)
  - from the "Patriot" Minority perspective, **79**-100
  - "Hint to . . . Keppel," and "'Tis true," **79**-A
  - Latin poem, **80**-43
  - narrative of dispute, **79**-489
  - narrative up to time of Keppel's acquittal, **79**-239, 240
  - Palliser's acquittal, **79**-258
  - traitor, **79**-510
  - victim of "a wretched ministry," **78**-245
  - Whig vs Tory, **79**-186
- anti-Keppel, **80**-422
- attacked by Galloway, **81**-220
- candidate in Surrey, **80**-341
- connection with Whig Opposition, **79**-143
- coward, **80**-203, 283, 335
- Cowper's "Table Talk," **82**-A

criticized, **79**-52, 267, 294
defended, **79**-149
Fox supports, **84**-161
Gold Box of Freedom, **79**-180, 337
in Opposition, **79**-257, 317
in the Portland [Fox-North] administration, **83**-29
in Rockingham's ministry, **82**-3
Keppel's Trial or Court Martial, January 12-February 11, 1779, **78**-334, 485, **79**-1, 11, 16, 17, 18, 19, 20, 28, 39, 51, 55, 57, 86, 87, 132, 136, 170, 219, 289
    acquittal, **79**-62, 66, 178, 179, 301, 346
    "A Congratulatory Address," **79**-A
    Cowper's "Address," **79**-A
    "The following Verses . . .," **79**-A
    "On the Trial of . . . Keppel," **79**-A
    reaction to, **79**-15
less merit than Rodney, **80**-297
libeled, Ushant revived, **82**-341
loss of reputation, **79**-204
lost an empire, **82**-365
naval career, **79**-18
persecuted by Sandwich, **79**-361
role in the new Rockingham ministry, **82**-91
satirized, **79**-241
Secretary of Navy, **82**-103
tool of Opposition, **79**-351
traitor, **79**-145, 146
"While Byron . . .," **79**-A
**See also:** Hugh Palliser; and the Ushant Episode.

Keppel, George, 3d Earl of Albemarle (1724-72). MP, 1746-1754. Older brother of Augustus Keppel. Associate of Duke of Cumberland and Rockingham; member of court martial that found Sackville (Germain) guilty of disobedience at Minden; led the troops to victory at Havana, 1762. **62**-3, 12, 23, 53
    "Verses," **66**-A

Ketch, Jack (d. 1686). Public executioner in reign of Charles II; executed the Whig martyr William, Lord Russell, 1683. **65**-131, **69**-104, 207
    and Bute and Mansfield, **78**-258
    John Ketch, **70**-A

Kidgell, John (1722-90?). Methodist parson. Court writer, early 1760's; exposed the alleged blasphemy of Wilkes' *Essay on Woman*, thereby permitting Government to continue its prosecution and persecution of Wilkes. **63**-30, 41, 42, 52, 70, 90, 139, 149, **64**-22, 34, 71, **65**-5, **69**-121, 268
    Churchill's *Author*, **63**-A

King's Bridge, New York. Important location in Howe's New York Campaign, between northern Manhattan and southern Bronx, on Spuyten Devil Creek, the Harlem River. **76**-247, **77**-150

"The King's Friends." Members of the so-called "secret cabinet," or "double cabinet," who exerted a "secret influence" upon George III; back-door advisors of George III led by Bute and Mansfield and Charles Jenkinson; included Pinchbeck and Eden; also called "the Fatal Influence," "The Scotch Junto." **72**-1, 82, **75**-114, **76**-29, 32, 42, 290, **77**-208, **78**-27, 44, 386, 411, 447, 474, 488, **79**-457, **82**-130, **84**-39
    and American War, **81**-91

"Court Influence," secret influence, **80**-9
"The King's *real* Friends": Pitt, Richmond, *et al.*, **78**-502
"a nation's curse," **80**-179
of Charles II, **77**-267
responsible for policy of oppression and coercion of America, **78**-102
Scotch and Jacobite, **78**-477
the secret "efficient" cabinet, **81**-244
the secret influence, **83**-3
Tories, Jacobites, Papists, **78**-247

Kirkman, John (1741-80). MP, 1780. Alderman of London, 1768-1780; elected MP for the session beginning 1780, but died before he could begin to serve. **73**-3

Knox, William (1732-1810). Placeman in American colonies, agent for Georgia and East Florida; dismissed by Rockingham for supporting Stamp Act; opposed concessions to America as undersecretary of state for the colonies under Germain.
author of *Present State of the Nation*, **68**-107, **69**-258

Ladbroke, Robert (1713?-73). MP for London, 1754-1773; alderman, sheriff, and lord mayor of London in 1740's; voted with the Opposition on the Middlesex election (of Wilkes), 1769-1770, but not a Wilkite; protested the London remonstrance, March 1770.
considered a tool of North, **73**-3

La Fayette, Marie Joseph Paul Yves Roch Gilbert, Marquis de (1757-1834). French aristocrat volunteer in the American Army, 1777-1781. Father was killed at Minden. Challenged Earl of Carlisle to a duel, October 1778. **78**-300, **80**-54, 339

La Motte, Francis Henry De (d. 1781). French spy captured in London; executed July 27, 1781, **81**-65, 155

Langara y Huarte, Juan de (1736-1806). Spanish admiral, defeated by Rodney, January 16, 1780, off Cape St. Vincent (S.W. Portugal), thereby enabling the relief of Gibraltar. **80**-143, 213, 257, 392, **81**-21

Laurens, Henry (1724-92). From South Carolina; after Hancock President of Congress, 1777-1778; captured off Newfoundland on a vessel bound for Holland and committed to the Tower, October 6, 1780. Exchanged for Cornwallis, April 1782. **78**-257, **80**-22, 40, 381, **81**-102, **83**-151
and son John, **83**-13
captured, **80**-126, 196
exchanged for General Arnold [sic], **82**-267
imprisoned, **80**-274

Laurens, John (c.1754-82). Educated in England; aide to General Washington; son of Henry Laurens. Killed in South Carolina, August 27, 1782. Friend of Thomas Day. **85**-6
the death of, **83**-13

Law, Edmund (1703-87). Bishop of Carlisle; supported religious toleration and opposed the North ministry's policy toward the colonies.
praised. **80**-37

Lee, Arthur (1740-92). Junius Americanus; American in London; follower of Wilkes; procured the insertion in Middlesex Petition of a resolution protesting Government's American measures, 1769; London agent for Massachusetts, 1770; helped Beaumarchais during American War; returned to America, 1780. **69**-9, 168, **75**-26(?), 29, **76**-26, **78**-45

Lee, Charles (1731-82). British mercenary soldier of fortune who served as

general in the American army, 1775, subordinate only to Washington and Ward; captured in New Jersey, December 13, 1776; exchanged in April 1778; court martialed and dismissed for insubordination, January 10, 1780; died in Philadelphia October 2, 1782, in poverty. **75**-37, 110, 169, 238, **76**-11, 27, 167, 210, 218, 263, 357, 396, **77**-124, 167, 183, 193, 221, 226, **79**-6, 40, **80**-277, **83**-89
    "Britannia's Admonition," **79**-A
    capture, **77**-59, 63, 77, 92, 218
    death and character (mercenary and republican), **80**-366
    epitaph, **82**-24
    "Impertinent Curiosity," **77**-A

Lee, William (1739-95). American merchant in London; native of Virginia, and older brother of Arthur Lee, and, like him, a follower of Wilkes; "Yankee" sheriff, with Stephen Sayre, of London, 1773; member Society for Support of Bill of Rights; only American to become alderman of London, 1775. His brother Richard Henry Lee proposed the resolution in Congress for separation from the mother country. **73**-51

Legge, Henry Bilson (1708-64). MP, 1740-1764. Son of 1st Earl of Dartmouth; uncle of William Legge, 2d Earl of Dartmouth; friend of Edward Walpole. Dismissed as chancellor of the exchequer, 1754-1761, when he voted against Bute's peace. **64**-58, 76, 83, 94, **65**-49, **66**-50

Legge, William, 2d Earl of Dartmouth (1731-1801). A Rockingham Whig, 1765, and president of Board of Trade and Plantations, 1765-1766; secretary of state for the colonies, 1772-1775, Germain succeeding to this post after "timid Dartmouth" resigned. But he remained in North's cabinet, 1773-1782. **73**-11, **75**-24, 26, 155, 166, 170, 187, **76**-226
    and the Fast, **80**-334

Leinster, 2d Duke of. **See**: William Robert Fitzgerald.

Lennox, Charles, 3d Duke of Richmond (1735-1806). Aide to Prince Ferdinand at Minden, where he distinguished himself; opposed to Bute and Grenville; served under Rockingham, 1765-1766, and opposed North's American policies; supported reform; uncle of Charles James Fox. **66**-120, **73**-4, **74**-70, **75**-10, 35, 49, 150, 170, 240, **76**-16, 42, 81, **77**-23, 207, 220, **78**-14, 66, 132, 299, 326, 335, 389, 411, 418, 489, 502, 556, 557, **79**-25, 38, 44, 59, 183, 302, 317, 354, 393, 405, **80**-10, 24, 33, 34, 69, 73, 98, 220, 229, 235, 270, 290, **81**-186, **82**-3, 4, 25, 85, **83**-151, 260
    and Denbigh, **78**-43
    and his stable of hacks, **79**-168
    and libels by Bate of *Morning Post*, **81**-160
    and Palliser, **79**-470
    and Pitt, **78**-126
    criticized, **79**-11, 33, 176
        for politicizing American War, **80**-303
    factious, **80**-316, 317
    may be leader of Rockingham Whigs, **82**-368
    motion to reform Parliament, **83**-5, **86**-1
    republican traitor, **80**-216
    traitor, **79**-510, **80**-185
    unity with Thurlow, **82**-382

Leveson-Gower, Granville, 2d Earl (1721-1802). MP, 1744-1754, thereafter HL. Leading member of the Bedford clique; friend of Thurlow; supported Bute and opposed repeal of Stamp Act; in North's cabinet to 1779; opposed Shelburne's peace terms. **64**-89, **71**-102, **73**-4, **75**-26, **76**-37, 38, 290, 429, **79**-275, 310, **80**-123, 235

in Pitt's camp, **84**-5, 19, **85**-12
Lewes, Watkin (1740-1821). MP, 1781-1796. Alderman of London, 1772-d; sheriff, 1772-1773; lord mayor, 1780-1781. Leader of Society for Support of Bill of Rights, 1769-1770; and a Wilkesite; voted for reform and against North ministry and against Fox-North Coalition. **73**-93, **74**-61, **75**-255, **77**-160, **81**-53
Lincoln, Benjamin (1733-1810). American general, led the attack on Savannah, October 1779, allied with D'Estaing and assisted by Pulaski; in the Yorktown campaign against Cornwallis. **79**-9, 387, **80**-5, 35, **81**-3
Lind, John (1737-81). Parson; Tory political writer; wrote for Lord Mansfield; friend of Sir Herbert Croft; defended the American War, 1775, and wrote *An Answer to the Declaration of the American Congress*, 1776. **80**-40
Livy (Titus Livius) (59 B.C.-17 A.D.). Ancient Roman historian. **68**-105
Lloyd, Charles (1735-73). George Grenville's private secretary; wrote many political pamphlets in support of Grenville. **69**-258
Lloyd, Robert (1733-64). Poet, journalist, and satirist; Churchill's friend.
    "Answer to the Epitaph," **64**-A
    "Epitaph," **64**-A
Locke, John (1632-1704). English political philosopher; his Whig theories of government were influential in the American Revolution.
    and Magna Carta, Opposition, and America, **77**-23
    and Price, **78**-36
        Pratt and Coke, **78**-45
    and Soame Jenyns, **82**-13
    Milton, Harrington, and Pym, Whig Pantheon, **68**-7
    Whig Pantheon, **72**-95, **77**-294, **83**-9
    **See**: Whig Tradition. Invocation of Heroes and Saints in the Whig Pantheon.
Lockhart Ross, John. **See**: John Lockhart Ross.
London (City Politics). **68**-1, 35, 76, 84, **69**-3, 189, 247, **70**-75, 194, 223, **73**-1, 3, 111, **74**-9
    against King and court, **75**-102
    "Alphabetical . . .," **69**-A
    American rebels and London, **75**-19, 21, 113, 121, 161, 189
    anti-Wilkes, **74**-201
    City Patriots as traitors, **80**-381
    conflict with Parliament over Civil Rights, etc., **70**-9, 19, 20, 21, 199, **71**-4, 58, **73**-10, 77, **74**-194, **75**-285
    Freemen, **71**-33, 39, 44
        "liberty boys," **73**-60
    Livery election, **81**-53
    London common council refuses to help country in the crisis, **79**-64
    petition rejected, **78**-263
    should change its politics and support Rodney, Cornwallis, and Palliser, **81**-189
    Wilkes rejected, **68**-53, 68
    **See**: Brass Crosby, Richard Oliver, John Miller, and John Wilkes.
Louis XV (1710-74). King of France, 1715-1774. **60**-7, 17, **61**-6, **79**-269
    "Advertisement," **60**-A
    "French Politicks," **60**-A
    "A Morning Scene," **60**-A
    "On the Defection . . .," **69**-A
Louis XVI (1754-93). King of France, 1774-1793. **78**-22, 65, 208, 259, **79**-121, **81**-57, **83**-19, 133

and Battle of the Saints, West Indies, **82**-46

Louisburg, Canada. Powerful French fortress on Cape Breton Island at mouth of St. Lawrence River, the gateway into Canada. Captured 1745 by American colonists; returned by treaty to France, 1748; recaptured by British, 1758. **58**-1, 4, 5, 9, 10, **59**-6, 9, 23, **60**-3, 18, 28, 31, 42, **61**-2, 51, **72**-42, **75**-25

    "A Morning Scene in Paris," **60**-A

    "A New Song," **60**-A

Lowth, Robert (1710-1787). Bishop of London. Supported John Wesley; wished to extend influence of the church in the colonies.

    criticized, **79**-529

    praised, **77**-5

Lowther, James, 5th Baronet (1736-1802). MP, 1757-1784. Reckoned the richest commoner in Britain, his enormous fortune based on large estates in the Barbadoes, West Indies, and ownership of collieries at Whitehaven. Celebrated for his patriotic contribution of a fully outfitted 74 gun warship to the nation, 1782. From January 1775 often opposed the North ministry and its American measures. **82**-144, 181, 247, 326, **83**-35

    exemplary patriot, **82**-320

Loyal Cities. Supported Government's American policy with "Loyal Addresses," etc.

    Banbury, **78**-391

    Birmingham, **75**-62, 254, 279, **78**-17, 316, **79**-195, **80**-142

        "The Volunteer's Rouse," **79**-A

    Bristol, **78**-328 (loyalist mayor)

    Coventry, **84**-174 (gained from the American War)

    Durham, **79**-112 (vs French invasion)

    Edinburgh, **78**-293

    Glasgow, **78**-49, 224

    Hampstead, **76**-220.

    Liverpool, **78**-17,

        haven for British privateers, **79**-29

    Manchester, **75**-98, 153, 258, **77**-28, **78**-17, 285, 286, 294, 316, 423, 460, 548, 550, **83**-154, **84**-174

    Northampton, **80**-230 (vs the loyal electors)

    Plymouth, **79**-290 (vs French invasion)

    Warwick, **78**-280

    Worcester, **75**-28

Loyalist(s), or American Tories.

    Allen, William, **74**-1

    American Congress and Britain and refugees, **81**-190

    and Fox, **84**-161

    and Shelburne's peace, **85**-13

    at King's Mountain, South Carolina, October 7, 1780, **81**-164

    compensation for, **82**-28

    Coombe's poem on emigration, **83**-8

    defended, **82**-209, **83**-12

    "fair American" refugee, **79**-184

    Galloway, **81**-35, 102, **82**-212

    in British army, poems by American Loyalist (probably), **80**-30

    in Carolina and Virginia during American War, **85**-7

    in London, **76**-156, 232

    King's birthday poem, **78**-527

a Loyalist engagement in New Jersey, André's *Cow Chace*, **80-2**
Loyalist fears he must support Non-Exportation, **76-280**
Loyalist mayor of New York on Franco-American alliance, **78-194**
Loyalist objects to American treason, independence, and alliance with France, **83-116**
Loyalist Yankees, **80-235**
McFingal and Whigs, **75-23**
Myles Cooper, refugee from New York, **76-86**
North and peace treaty and Loyalists, **83-180**
Odell's *American Times*, **80-22**
Odell's "Congratulation," **79-318**
Odell's poems, **77-129, 186, 187, 188**
parody of "Massachusetts' Song of Liberty," **68-96**
patriotic lyric sung in New York, **80-323**
peace treaty and Loyalists, **83-124**
persecution of Loyalists encouraged by Opposition, **80-34**
protests Franco-American alliance, defends British just cause and George III, **80-77**
refugee parson from Maryland, **79-273**
refugees in London, **75-174, 82-212**
Rivington the printer, **83-235**
satire on American Tory character, **77-217**
satire on mercenary refugee, **81-72**
savagely treated at end of war, **83-297** (print)
song, **78-284**
Stansbury's verses, **80-339**
verses by Margaret DeLancey and Benjamin Moore, **80-83**
Virginian Loyalist hopes for peace and reunion with Britain, **82-310**
Virginian Loyalist planter's complaint, **80-21**
Virginian's poem on rebellion, **78-195**
Wesley's "American Independency," Loyalists and General Howe, **83-A**
Wesley's *American War*, Loyalists and General Howe, **82-A**
Wesley's hymns, **82-29, 30**
young loyalist flees to England, **82-387**
**See also**: American Poems. By American Loyalists, and James Rivington, in Part I of Index; also Joseph Galloway in Part II of Index.

Lucas, Charles (1713-71). Patriotic Irish physician, politician, and pamphleteer stressing Irish grievances against England. **70-200**

Luttrell, Henry Lawes (1737?-1821). MP, 1768-1794, 1817-1821. Army officer, major 1762, colonel 1777, general 1782. Ran against Wilkes in 1769 by-election for Middlesex, polling 296 votes against 1143 for Wilkes, but the House of Commons declared Wilkes ineligible (four times all told) and Luttrell elected, April 15, 1769. Supported the North ministry. **69-12, 30, 55, 129, 130, 131, 216, 222, 225, 259, 263, 70-9, 22, 23, 205, 71-10, 64, 74, 74-6, 76-10**

*Ode to Palinurus*, **70-A**

Luttrell, Temple Simon (1738?-1803). MP, 1775-1780. Brother of Henry Lawes Luttrell, but a vigorous critic of the North ministry; supported Parliamentary reform. **78-6, 79-38, 131, 80-40, 73**

praised, **80-371**

recommended for place in Rockingham ministry, **82-370**

Lyttelton, George, 5th Baronet (1709-73). MP, 1736-1756; then House of Lords. Writer and politician; secretary to Prince of Wales, 1732-1744;

supported Bute against Newcastle, 1762; supported Grenville's ministry and Stamp Act and voted against its repeal, 1766. Father of Thomas Lyttelton. **66**-131, **73**-4, 29, 30

Lyttelton, William Henry, 7th Baronet (1724-1808). MP, 1748-1755, 1774-1790. Governor of South Carolina, 1755-1760, and of Jamaica, 1760-1766. Tory, considered the war against America as a "holy war." Became Baron Westcote, 1776. **80**-7

Macaulay, Catharine (1731-91). Whig heroine, libertarian, republican; sister of John Sawbridge, and with him a supporter of Wilkes and a defender of the Bill of Rights; opposed American War, and in 1784 traveled to America and visited Washington in Mount Vernon for ten days in 1785. See Part I of Index for a poem by her. **66**-16, **68**-7, **70**-6, 8, 10, 46, 207, 236, **72**-12, **74**-177, **75**-62, 184, **76**-28, **77**-24, 154, 190, 210, 319, **78**-23, 35, 44, 350

    DeBrent, **70**-A
    "On a Celebrated Female Writer," **70**-A
    "On Reading . . . ," **69**-A
    "To the Celebrated . . . ," **69**-A
    "To Mrs. Macaulay," **70**-A

Mackreth, Robert (1725?-1819). MP, 1774-1802. "Bob the Waiter" at White's, the gambling club, money lender and dealer in landed estates; sent to Parliament by Lord Orford, Horace Walpole's nephew. Supported the North ministry. **74**-48, 130, 158

Macpherson, James (1736-96). MP, 1780-1796. Scottish Tory author of the Ossian poems, dedicated to Bute, who secured a pension for him; secretary to Governor Johnstone of West Florida, 1764; leading Government writer, 1766-1782, combating Junius and the colonists; in North's opinion wrote the best defence of the American War in *Rights of Great Britain asserted against the claims of America* (1776). **65**-11, **73**-7, 25, **75**-23, **76**-226, **77**-18, **80**-40

    *The Thistle*, **73**-A

MacQuirk, Edward. Irish chairman employed by court party at the Middlesex by-election at Brentford, December 8, 1768. Tried with Lawrence Balf, for murder of George Clark. Both received the royal pardon, March 1769. **69**-43, 218

    "Occasioned by the Pardon of MacQuirk and Balfe," **69**-A
    "On the Opinion . . . relating to the Death of Mr. Clarke," **69**-A
    pardoned, **69**-76

Magna Carta (or Magna Charta). **See**: Rights: Magna Carta.

Maitland, John (1732-79). MP, 1774-1779. Son of the 6th Earl of Lauderdale. Scots colonel on active service in America from 1777. Saved Savannah from capture by forces under Lincoln and D'Estaing, October 1779, only to die like Wolfe at the moment of victory. **79**-148, **80**-1, 5, 30, 72, 74, 83, **82**-133, **83**-59, **89**-1

    death of another soldier at Savannah, like Maitland, **80**-276

Manchester, 7th Earl and 4th Duke of. **See**: George Montagu.

Manners, John, Marquis of Granby (1721-70). General officer in Seven Years' War and at Minden leading cavalry in a crucial charge; commander-in-chief of army, 1766-1770; supported Government over Wilkes and general warrants, and voted against repeal of Stamp-Act, 1766, and against Wilkes, 1769, but supported repeal of tea duty, 1769. **60**-9, 48, **61**-2, **62**-2, **64**-3, **68**-124, **69**-232, **70**-26, 87, **75**-160, 199, **79**-4, **90**-1

    and Whig liberty, **74**-17

Manners, Robert (1758-82). Captain in navy. MP, 1780-1782, but never took his seat. Son of John Manners, Marquis of Granby; served under Keppel at Ushant,

1778, and under Rodney in Battle of the Saints, 1782, when he was mortally wounded. Died of tetanus, April 23, 1782. **82**-263, **83**-11, 25, **84**-18, 181

Mansfield, Earl of. **See**: William Murray, Earl of Mansfield.

Marjoribanks, John (d.1781). Scottish, major in British army, hero of the Battle of Eutaw Springs, South Carolina, September 8, 1781, the last important engagement of American War in the South. Mortally wounded, he died October 23, 1781. **82**-186, **84**-9

    **See**: John Marjoribanks, his son, in Part I of Index.

Markham, William (1719-1807). Archbishop of York from June 1777. Tory, opposed conciliation of America. **75**-34, **77**-12, 25, 29, 128, 212, 245, 292, **78**-4, 223, 490, 514, **80**-7, 37, 123, 331, **81**-181, **82**-12, **93**-1

    and Abingdon, **78**-43

    character, **78**-82

    Tory views, **77**-326

Marlborough, Sarah Jennings, Duchess of (1660-1744).

    and Pitt, Earl of Chatham, **66**-98

Martin, James (1738-1810). MP, 1776-1807. Wealthy banker and independent country gentleman in opposition to the North ministry and American War.

    and Savile. **83**-260

Martin, Samuel (1714-88). MP, 1747-1774. Joint secretary of the Treasury, key office of the civil service. Attacked by Wilkes for supporting Bute, Martin challenged him to a duel and wounded him, November 16, 1763. Martin's half-brother Josiah was Governor of North Carolina, 1771-1775; his father owned an estate on Antigua, West Indies; opposed the Americans. **63**-5, 35, 84, 88, **66**-133, **70**-40

    Churchill's *Duellist*, "the sentence passed . . .," **64**-A

Marvell, Andrew (1621-78). English poet and satirist, associate of John Milton, admirer of Cromwell, and critic of court corruption in reign of Charles II; friend of republicans. **68**-82, 105, 124, **69**-127, **74**-208, 220, **76**-359. **See also**: Andrew Marvel (pseud.) in Part I of Index.

Maubert de Gouvest, Jean-Henri (1721-67). French author; one of the principal political writers of the 18th century. **60**-26

Mawbey, Joseph (1730-98). MP, 1761-1790. Sheriff, Surrey, 1757-1758; alderman, Southwark; wealthy malt distiller and pig dealer; supported Wilkes and helped found Society for Support of Bill of Rights; in Opposition against North during American War, but voted for the North ministry at the end, February-March 1782. **68**-56, **69**-39, 129, **71**-14, **72**-1, 6, **75**-255, **80**-305

Mayhew, Jonathan (1720-66). Pastor of the Unitarian West Church, Boston, 1747-1766; prevented introduction of Anglican bishops to America. Staunch upholder of civil liberty against arbitrary rule. **82**-241

McCrea, Jane (1760?-77). Fiancée of a British solder, a victim of Indian atrocity, a tragic episode of the Burgoyne campaign. **78**-26, **79**-4, **81**-102, **82**-9

Mercenaries (in the American War). **75**-209, 212 (**89**-2), **76**-27, 54, 62, 134, 184, 213, 335, 376, **77**-22, 143, **78**-47, 518, **82**-27, **85**-6, **89**-2

    and George III, **79**-399

    cited for propaganda, **75**-302

    "A Comparison," **80**-A

    German, **78**-40, 71, 210, **79**-45

    Hessians, **77**-292, 313, 314, **79**-249 (Donnop)

Mercer, Hugh (c.1725-77). American general from Pennsylvania and Virginia; wounded at site of Braddock's defeat, 1755; present at Trenton, 1776; killed near Princeton, New Jersey, January 1777. **79**-3, **85**-6

       defeat at Oswego, **59**-1
       mortally wounded, **77**-76
Methodism.  **See**: John and Charles Wesley, John William Fletcher, and satires by William Combe, Part I of Index.
       satires by Combe, **78**-9, 10, 11
Middlesex County (including Brentford) and John Wilkes.
       election of Wilkes, **68**-73, 76, 77, 84, 116, 118, **69**-8, 111, 180, 181, 190, 216, 222, 259, **70**-9, 19, 20, 25
          "On Occasion," **68**-A
       freedom, defense of, **69**-192
       freeholders, **68**-65, 109, **69**-8, 87, 245, **70**-25
          incorruptible, **80**-312
       jury, **64**-57
       petition and America, **69**-9, 183, 257, **70**-23(?)
       1780 election, vs North, **80**-327
       Wilkes, **69**-110, 116, 117
          and Glynn, **69**-93
       **See also**: *The Middlesex Freeholder* and *The Middlesex Petition Inversed* in Part I of Index.
Milbanke, Ralph, 5th Baronet (1722-98).  MP, 1754-68.  From Yorkshire; supported each administration, 1761-68; probably Tory.
       and Fox, **80**-365
The Militia.  **See**: Camps.
Miller, John (d. 1809).  Printer of *London Evening Post*, involved in the struggle for freedom of the press; tried July 1770 for publishing Junius' letter to the king, and was acquitted; arrested with seven other London printers March 1771, for breach of parliamentary privilege (publication of Parliament's debates), which led to the clash between Ld Mayor Crosby and the Commons; in 1773 indicted for libel by Ld Sandwich, who was awarded damages; opposed American War.  **70**-206, **71**-26, **73**-39
       supported Keppel, **79**-62
Milles, Richard (c.1735-1820).  MP, 1761-80.  Country gentleman; elected MP from Canterbury, defeating Dering, 1774; supported Rockingham and voted against Chatham, Grafton, and North.  **74**-144
Milton, John (1608-74).  **See**: Part I of Index.
Minden.  A town on the Weser River, Westphalia, Germany, site of an important battle, August 1, 1759, in the Seven Years' War.  Prince Ferdinand of Brunswick's Anglo-Allied victory over the French under Marshal Contades was marred by Germain's refusal to obey the repeated command of his superior to charge with his cavalry.  This behavior resulted in Germain's court martial, disgrace, and reputation for cowardice.  **59**-8, 23, 24, 27, 33, 34, 42, 43, **60**-25, 39, 42, **61**-44, **75**-117
       and Granby, **64**-3, **70**-87
       and Germain's alleged cowardice, **79**-68
       Germain and Prince Ferdinand, **75**-160
       Germain saved his neck at Minden, **75**-58
       **See also**: George Sackville Germain.
Ministries ("Administration," or "Government").  **64**-40, **65**-40, 54, 59, 60, 76, 77, 91
       changes, in general, **71**-17
       a review, 1755-1767, **70**-77
       **See**: Ministries, from 1754 to 1783, and the individuals as named and listed below:

April 6, 1754: T. H. Pelham, Duke of Newcastle, & Thomas Robinson
November 1755: T. H. Pelham, Duke of Newcastle, and Henry Fox
June 30, 1757: T. H. Pelham, Duke of Newcastle, and William Pitt, the Elder
March 25, 1761: John Stuart, Earl of Bute
May 29, 1762: John Stuart, Earl of Bute, and George Grenville
April 16, 1763: George Grenville
July 13, 1765: Charles Watson-Wentworth, Marquis of Rockingham
August 2, 1766: Augustus Henry Fitzroy, Duke of Grafton, and Charles Townshend to 1767, and Frederick North
February 10, 1770: Frederick North
March 27, 1782: Charles Watson-Wentworth, Marquis of Rockingham
July 13, 1782: William Petty, Earl of Shelburne
April 5, 1783: William Henry Cavendish-Bentinck, Duke of Portland, and Charles James Fox-Frederick North Coalition
December 27, 1783: William Pitt, the Younger

Minority Opposition during North's Ministry, the period of the American War, 1775-81; called "The Patriots," "false Patriots," "subtle sly republicans," "Traitors," etc. **75**-120, 141, 158, 170, 201, 215, **76**-47, 49, **77**-168, 263, **78**-43, 510, **80**-18, 24
    achieving power at last, **81**-144
    advised to give up, **77**-31
    advised to secede, **78**-508, 509
    aid rebels, **77**-73, 146
    America's distrust of, **78**-66
    American Loyalist criticizes Opposition, **80**-364
    and Cruger, **80**-416
    and end of American War, **80**-400
    and Galloway, **81**-102
    and Gordon Riots, **80**-376
    and North, **81**-152, **82**-177
    and the peace, **83**-20
    and Tucker, **79**-281
    attacked for encouraging American rebels, **77**-12, 16, 146, 298
    blamed for Gordon Riots, **81**-17
    Christmas recess, **77**-220
    cowardly, refuse to fight American rebels, **77**-298
    Cowper's "Modern Patriot," a lawless rebel, **82**-A
    Cowper's "Table Talk," self-interested, **82**-A
    criticized, **78**-481, 513, **79**-11, 34, 38, 42, 176, 185, 317, 352, 393, **79**-A ("Britannia's Admonition," "Modern Mobbing," and Wilmot) **80**-4, 73, 191, 243, 265, 290, 303, 388, **81**-179, 191, 196, 212, 260
        blamed for British failures, **78**-192
        by Tory, **78**-23
    dead, **80**-94
    defended, **77**-5, 23, **78**-12, 14, 45, 219, **80**-9, 16, 69, 220, 239, **81**-197
    destroyed the British empire, **84**-65
    destructive, **80**-329
    factious, **80**-133, 134, 317, 360, **82**-22
    Fletcher Norton joins Opposition, **80**-130
    Fox engineers debates in Parliament, **80**-330
    Fox opposes North's policy and supports America, **84**-161
    House of Commons: Adair, Barré, Burke, Conway, Cruger, Dunning, C. J. Fox,

      Glynn, Hartley, Keppel, Savile, Sawbridge, Thomas Townshend, Wilkes
  House of Lords: Abingdon (Bertie), Camden (Pratt), Chatham (Pitt), Craven, Effingham (Howard), Grafton, Manchester, Portland, Richmond, Rockingham, Shelburne; and Bishops, Shipley (St. Asaph), Hinchcliffe (Peterborough)
Howe and Keppel, **81**-48
"in foul conspiracy" to aid American rebels, **85**-4
inconsistent patriot, **79**-226
incorruptible, **76**-328
ineffectual protests, **75**-80, 107, 157, **78**-157
influenced by American rebels, **80**-82
its continual criticism of the ministry, **77**-55
Jenyns critical of, **76**-353
John Wesley's criticism of, **79**-513
"Liberty," written 1776, **89**-2
London City Leaders: Glynn, Sawbridge, James Townsend, Wilkes.
make politics out of American War, **80**-303
Minority must cease its opposition, **79**-236
mock patriots pleased at Burgoyne's defeat, **78**-435
must stop the war, **78**-90
must unite with Government against France, **79**-499
nation will win without the Opposition, **79**-257
need for organization and leadership, **75**-49
North answers Fox and Burke, **77**-248
North borrows from Opposition for Conciliation Bill, **78**-133, 538
objections to the war, **81**-122
other notable MP's, House of Commons, in Opposition: Gen. Wm. Howe and Gen. John Burgoyne (from 1778).
parricides, **78**-467
patriots, "true" or "real"?, **81**-128, 184
Pitt's motion to end the war, May 30, 1777, **77**-206
praised, **79**-69
predict defeat, **77**-285
proscribed, **79**-292
republicans, **81**-179, 191
    and levellers, **82**-13, 349, 391
a review of Opposition opinion, April 1779, **79**-28
a review of Opposition's role in American War, **84**-16
Rockingham ministry, in power officially, March 27, 1782, **82**-27, 54, 101, 264
Sandwich's incompetence, **78**-54, 384
satire on Opposition Lords, **79**-33
secession, **77**-175, 249, **80**-309
    of Rockinghamites, **76**-234
a second-rate patriot poet, **78**-230
self-interested and hypocritical, **80**-34, 99, 130, 140, 149, 300, 301, 310, 316
self-interested outs, **76**-318, 356, **77**-273, **78**-72, 387
self-interested "vile republicans," **79**-106, 185, 200, 381
"sham patriots," **76**-202
should assume ministry and guide King, **80**-69
"simulated Patriots" provoke, inflame quarrel with America, **77**-164
"slain Patriots," **76**-202

support reform, **80**-148, 216, 239
Tory satire on Opposition patriot poets, **78**-31
traitors, **76**-15, 45, 56, 101, **77**-73, 146, **78**-4, 7, 33, 220, 299, 305, 316, 512, 556, **79**-26, 38, 40, 106, 261, 272, 405, 510, **80**-34, 41, 72, 79, 82, 108, 185, 186, 305, 335, 360, 376, 387, **81**-17, 22, 42, 159, 234, 237, 238, **82**-30, 126, 209, 349, 391, 402, **83**-288 (a print)
unable to compete with "King's Friends," **81**-91
uncooperative, **76**-316
unreliable as leaders, **80**-256
wants a program, **81**-260 (a print)

Minority Opposition, or Patriot Press.
seditious, betray information to enemy during American War, **79**-477

Mischianza (Medley). Extravaganza, homage to Gen. Howe and Adm. Howe, in Philadelphia, May 18, 1778, by officers of the British army, upon Gen. Howe's farewell as commander-in-chief of the British armies in America. **78**-51, **79**-504
**See also:** André in Part I of Index.

The Mob ("Mobbing"), Rabble & Rioters. **See also:** Gordon Riots. **63**-78, 145, **66**-6, 112, **67**-24, **68**-27, 34, 110, **69**-12, 18, 83, 177, 184, 199, 205, 241, 248, 250, 253, **70**-96, 98, 113, 119, 129, 149, **71**-24, **74**-132
Boston, **68**-96
Cowper's "Address to the Mob," **79**-A
Cowper's "Modern Mobbing," **79**-A
Cowper's "On the Burning of Mansfield's Library," **82**-A
Fox threatened by mob violence, **84**-144
"Impromptu," **68**-A
"Thieves and Butchers," **68**-A
Wilkes' supporters, **74**-30

Monarchs and Monarchy, and the Monarchy in Britain. **73**-110, **75**-22, **85**-33, 34
accountability, **79**-247
and the American War, **76**-121, 133, **77**-7
and John Milton, **76**-205
and Mrs. Macaulay, **77**-24
Cowper's "Table Talk," constitutional liberty and monarchy, **82**-A
defended against republican American Congress, **80**-78
defended in year 1777, **77**-12
George III as constitutional monarch, **81**-292
George III no longer "Defender of the Faith" in America, **83**-40
God on their side, **79**-266
impartial and above party, reconciles Whig and Tory, **80**-396
Milton's Whig doctrine, **80**-202
oppressive monarchies of Europe and the American Revolution, **93**-1
power must be limited by law, **83**-229
prerogatives defended, **81**-208
present monarchy and Stuarts, **80**-384
rests on trade, **77**-252
Scots strengthened, **80**-90
Tory defense, **81**-179
treated like commoners, **80**-311
tyranny, a lesson from Sweden, **80**-160
vs divine right, unlimited prerogative, **76**-125
**See also:** Tory Tradition and Whig Tradition.

Monckton, Robert (1726-82). MP, 1751-54, 1774, 1778-82. British officer, Seven

Years' War, serving in North America; lt. gov. Nova Scotia, 1755-61; second in command under Wolfe at Quebec, 1759; governor of New York, 1761-65; commander at Martinique, 1762; governor of Portsmouth, 1778-82. Supported administration. **60**-6, 11, 48, **62**-3, 7, 34, 36, 40, 50, **69**-5, 17, **83**-25, **90**-1
    Delamayne's *Oliviad*, **62**-A
    "On Gen. Monckton's . . . ," **62**-A
    "Song," **62**-A

Moncrieff, James (1744-93). Scots army officer, served with distinction at Savannah and Charleston, 1779-80. **80**-290

Money, John (d. 1780). Aide-de-camp to Gen. Cornwallis, killed in action, November 9, 1780, at the age of twenty-four. **81**-115.

Montagu, George, 7th Earl and 4th Duke of Manchester (1737-88). One of the lords of Opposition to North's policy of coercion, 1770-82; sided with Rockinghamites and colonies; ambassador to Paris to make peace, 1783. **77**-23, **78**-12, **79**-44, **80**-220

Montagu, John, 4th Earl of Sandwich (1718-92). Secretary of State, northern department, 1763-65, 1770-71; first ld admiralty, 1771-82; supported all of Government's measures against America; betrayed Wilkes, a friend, 1768, earning name of "Jemmy Twitcher," character in Gay's *Beggar's Opera*. **63**-2, 52, 70, 90, 139, 149, 178, **64**-15, 20, 21, 37, 67, 75, 79, 88, 89, 93, **65**-5, 36, 39, 80, 113, 119, 128, 134, **66**-9, 36, 42, 60, 84, 91, 114, 119, 140, **68**-122, **69**-108, **70**-35, 77, 91, 110, 111, 152, **71**-12, 59, **72**-103, **73**-4, 7, 10, **74**-7, 12, 93, **75**-1, 10, 26, 107, 117, 120, 155, 173, 242, 306, **76**-19, 27, 37, 38, 202, 207, 217, 218, 226, 240, 242, 267, 290, 304, 322, 372, 373, **77**-46, 61, 67, 283, 292, 307, 325, **78**-7, 12, 25, 27, 44, 54, 56, 103, 140, 141, 160, 223, 267, 289, 290, 291, 296, 324, 335, 348, 384, 385, 395, 411, 416, 421, 437, 486, 491, 500, 515, 556, **79**-3, 10, 19, 28, 33, 35, 37, 40, 44, 54, 70, 87, 98, 107, 140, 194, 197, 202, 215, 245, 283, 284, 310, 314, 350, 367, 370, 372, 392, 455, 486, 493, 494, 496, 529, **80**-7, 17, 23, 26, 40, 62, 69, 90, 123, 134, 158, 180, 219, 226, 237, 270, 331, 334, 343, 378, 393, 402, 404, 405, 410, 429, 430; **81**-33, 39, 45, 124, 137, 153, 182, 225, 243, 259, **82**-3, 4, 9, 155, 212, 224, 304, **84**-18
    and cowardly Americans, **78**-197
    and Fox, **84**-161
    and Fox-North Coalition, **83**-281
    and French navy, **81**-166
    and James Aitken, "John the Painter," **77**-15, 324
    and North, **82**-189
    and Pitt, **78**-43, **80**-260
    and Rodney, **80**-46, **81**-222
    and Wombwell, **77**-315
    called Americans cowards, easily coerced, **75**-80
    Churchill's *Candidate, Duellist,* & "Epigram," **64**-A
    criticized, **78**-16, **82**-12
    defense of character against Fox's defamation, **82**-210
    the Fast, **79**-196, **82**-300
    a favorable character, **81**-38
    forgives Burke & Fox at the peace, **83**-298 (print)
    George III, **79**-399
    his future, **81**-217
    incompetent, **78**-539
    Keppel, **79**-302
        enemy of Whig Keppel, **79**-489

    must resign, **82**-108
       and North too, **82**-188
    neglected navy, **79**-162
    "On St. Sepulchre's Bells," **65**-A
    opposes reform, **80**-148
    Opposition urges his dismissal, **82**-279
    "out," cashiered, his failures, **82**-377
    Palliser, **79**-471, 474, 475, 476, **80**-146
    praised, **80**-27
    resigns, March 20, 1782, **83**-3
    retired, **82**-376
    Royal Regatta, **78**-75
    satirized, **80**-204
    Spanish War, **79**-426
    unpopular, **80**-195
    Wilkes and Dashwood, **79**-102

Montcalm, Louis-Joseph de Montcalm-Gozon, Marquis de (1712-59). French general commanding army in Canada during French & Indian War; captured English post at Oswego, 1756, Ft. William Henry, Lake George, 1757; saved Ticonderoga, 1758; but lost Quebec and his life, 1759. **57**-2, **59**-2, 6, 14, 15, 28, 42, **60**-6, **68**-14, **69**-5, 17, **72**-35, **81**-204

Montesquieu, Charles Louis de Secondat, Baron de la Brede et de (1689-1755). French philosophical historian, author of the *Persian Letters*, 1721, and *Spirit of the Laws*, 1748. **78**-43

Montgomery, Richard (1738-75). American general; at siege of Louisburg, Cape Breton, 1758; with Amherst at Ticonderoga, Crown Point, and Montreal, 1760; and at capture of Martinique and Havana, 1762; settled in America, 1773; killed at Quebec, December 31, 1775. **76**-5, 12, 16, 27, 37, 38, 43, 104, 138, 139, 183, 210, 211, 243, 254, 315, 321, 342, 359, **77**-173, **78**-208, 295, **79**-3, **81**-3, **83**-31
    and Wolfe, **76**-255
    Burns, **84**-A

Monthly reviewers (and critics). **65**-88, 98, **66**-99, **67**-8, 36, **68**-24, **70**-7, **74**-137, **80**-44, **83**-100

Montreal, Canada. **60**-18, 22, 26, 28, 29, 41, **78**-251

More, Hannah (1745-1833). Bristol bluestocking author. **77**-252

Morres, Hervey Redmond, 2d Vct Mountmorres (c. 1743-97). Wilkes' candidate for Parliament from Westminster; lost to Earl Percy and Thomas Pelham Clinton, 1774. **74**-42

Morris, John (d. 1776). Captain in British navy; died for an unworthy cause, in the attack on Charleston, South Carolina, June 1776. **76**-136

Morris, Robert (1743-93). Barrister; secretary, Society of Supporters of Magna Carta and the Bill of Rights, 1769, but resigned, 1770; counsel for John Miller, in the Wheble-Thompson freedom of the press case vs. House of Commons. **70**-208

Mountmorres, 2d Viscount. **See**: Hervey Redmond Morres.

Mulgrave, 2d Baron. **See**: Constantine John Phipps.

Murphy, Arthur (1727-1805). Writer for Bute and the court; actor.
    Churchill's *Author*, **63**-A
    Churchill's *Independence*, **64**-A

Murray, David, 7th Viscount Stormont (1727-96). Tory Scot, nephew of William Murray, Earl Mansfield; supporter of North ministry, of which he became a member, 1778-82; supported Fox-North Coalition and then the younger Pitt. **78**-

296, **79**-275, **80**-69, 123, **81**-39, **82**-382, **83**-77, 265
Murray, James (c.1719-94). Scottish general officer; with Wolfe at Louisburg, 1758; on Wolfe's staff at Quebec; Governor of Quebec, 1760-66, Governor of Minorca, 1774-81, and obliged to capitulate to French and Spanish after seven-month siege. **60**-15, **69**-5, 17, **83**-25, 32
Murray, John, 4th Earl of Dunmore (1732-1809). Scottish representative peer, 1761-68, 1776-96; governor of New York, 1769-70, and Virginia, 1772-76; forced to return to England, December 1776; governor Bahamas, 1787-94. **76**-16, 146, 244, 320, **77**-240, **78**-408, **81**-3
    and Negroes, **76**-218
    returns to England, **76**-180
Murray, William, Earl of Mansfield (1705-93). Scottish Tory; lord chief justice of the king's bench, privy councillor and king's serjeant-at-law, 1756-88; speaker of House of Lords, 1760, 1770-71; supported the court on most major issues, Wilkes and libel cases and coercion of American colonies. **61**-3, **63**-2, 95, 118, **64**-8, 65, **65**-5, 8, **66**-109, **68**-21, 22, 38, 115, 119, 122, 123, 124, **69**-10, 12, 19, 29, 30, 41, 81, 126, 263, 269, **70**-8, 17, 28, 32, 34, 51, 54, 89, 95, 100, 111, 112, 113, 120, 159, 165, 206, 240, **71**-6, 64, 77, 112, 125, **72**-50, 57, 64, 95, 96, **73**-4, 7, 10, 61, **74**-9, 24, 29, 36, 78, 152, 174, 185, **75**-34, 43, 54, 55, 66, 80, 81, 134, 184, 194, 218, 239, 268, 270, 314, **76**-12, 16, 19, 27, 39, 43, 49, 62, 69, 88, 184, 217, 287, 346, **77**-3, 12, 33, 66, 67, 130, 209, 215, 237, 245, 313, **78**-7, 12, 15, 25, 27, 34, 38, 44, 47, 127, 131, 258, 290, 296, 345, 416, 419, 430, 453, 479, 498, 500, 520, 526, **79**-10, 31, 33, 37, 44, 45, 106, 275, 310, 330, 372, 384, 516, 529, **80**-7, 10, 16, 40, 69, 90, 146, 219, 226, 233, 237, 378, 404, **81**-7, 17, 39, 62, 135, 259, **82**-4, 9, 59, 212, **83**-77, **85**-42
    and Bute, **81**-319
    and Francis Page, "the hanging judge," **81**-177
    and freedom of speech, **77**-302
    and Judge Jeffreys, **80**-384, **81**-177
    and North, **79**-380
    and Pratt, **78**-43
    the cause of American rebellion, **79**-365
    Churchill's *Conference*, **63**-A
    Churchill's *Independence*, **64**-A
    Cowper's "On the Burning of Mansfield's Library," **82**-A
    decision on slavery in Britain, **77**-14
    house destroyed by Gordon rioters, **80**-267
    loss of library in Gordon Riots, **80**-28, 287
    praised, **76**-331, **80**-337
    saved an empire, **85**-55
    *The Thistle*, **73**-A
    "a true Tory," **77**-18
    unpopular "base Scot," **79**-467
Musgrave, Samuel (1732-80). Physician of Exeter and political polemicist; accused Bute of selling British interests to France in peace of 1763; supported Wilkes and condemned the North ministry. **69**-57, 203, 207
Naval Actions in the American War of Independence. **See**: British Navy under heading of American War.
Naval Officers, American, active in American War, 1775-83. **See**: Esek Hopkins and John Paul Jones.
Naval Officers, American, active in French and Indian War, 1755-63. **See**: Esek Hopkins.

Naval Officers, British, serving in the American War, 1775-83.  **See**: Marriott Arbuthnot, Samuel Barrington, Philip Boteler, John Byron, William Campbell, Henry Chads, Cuthbert Collingwood, Roger Curtis, George Farmer, Francis Geary, Thomas Graves, John Hamilton, Charles Hardy, Robert Harland, Samuel Hood, Richard Howe, George Johnstone, Augustus Keppel, Robert Manners, Hugh Palliser, Hyde Parker, Peter Parker, Richard Pearson, George Brydges Rodney, and John Lockhart Ross.

Naval Officers, British, serving in the Seven Years' War, 1755-63.  **See**: Edward Boscawen, John Byng, William Campbell, Roger Curtis, Peter Denis, Francis Geary, Samuel and Thomas Graves, Charles Hardy, Edward Hawke, Charles Holmes, Samuel Hood, Richard Howe, Richard Hughes, George Johnstone, Augustus Keppel, Hugh Palliser, Hyde Parker, Peter Parker, George Pocock, George Brydges Rodney, John Lockhart Ross, and Charles Saunders.

Naval Review.  "Royal Regatta."
- and Sandwich, **82**-376
- 1773: **73**-5
- 1778: **78**-54, 56, 68, 75, 160, 223, 256, 384, 385, 395, 422, 437, 479, 491, 514

Navy.  **See**: British Navy under heading of American War.

Newcastle, 1st Duke of.  **See**: Pelham-Holles, Thomas.

Newfoundland, Canada.  **62**-1, 19, 24, 26, 60

Newspapers
- American Loyalist, **83**-91
- and North ministry, **80**-380, 412
- Bate's *Morning Herald*, biased news, **80**-35
- confusion and contradictions in news about American War, **80**-393
- lies in Government *Gazette*, **78**-138
- London newspapers characterized: *Morning Post, Morning Herald, Morning Chronicle, Public Advertiser, General Advertiser, London Courant, Daily Advertiser, Gazetteer, Public Ledger*, **82**-296
- a newspaper distributor, the war and politics, **83**-157
- on popular poetry appearing in, **82**-298
- papers and North ministry, **80**-380, 412
- pleasures of, **85**-2
- pleasures of reading about politics in, **82**-353
- praise of English newspapers, **81**-49
- the problem of truth, **82**-242
- satire on, **83**-179
- satire on *Morning Post*, **77**-56
- uncertainty of the news, **79**-286
- uses of, including publication of "th' inferior poets," **84**-119
- variety of London newspapers and American War, **80**-423 (print)
- varying politics of *Public Advertiser, Gazetteer, Public Ledger, General Evening Post,* and *Morning Post*, **79**-265
- Woodfall, Henry S., manager of *Public Advertiser*, **80**-382

New York City.
- besieged by Washington, **81**-120
- Colvill on New York, **77**-4
- in *The Rising Glory of America*, **72**-14, **78**-73
- Rivington, the printer, **83**-235
- **See also**: Howe's Long Island and New York Campaign under heading of American War, Battles and Campaigns.

Nivernoise, Duc de, Louis-Jules-Barbon Mancini-Mazarini (1716-98).  French

diplomat serving at the peace negotiations, 1762. **62**-35.
Nobility (aristocracy).
- and king contend for power, **84**-160
- and Pitt, **66**-127
- and scum of the earth, **70**-151
- and the starving poor, **72**-98
- Churchill's *Author*, on corrupt and stupid peerage, **63**-A
- Combe vs Ld Craven's arrogance, **75**-7
- contemptible, **69**-78
- corrupt, **74**-72
- corrupt peer, **70**-167
- corruption, **74**-72
- Cowper on effeminate nobility, **85**-2
- a criminal peer, **74**-180
- freeholder as good as peer, **79**-362
- Germain and true nobility, **82**-348
- Germain's elevation to peerage, but merit makes the man, **82**-95, 307
- little thieves and "great" thieves, **80**-314
- mean and worthless, **82**-71
- Minority lords accused of "Aristocratic Insolence," **79**-33
- objection to aristocratic privilege, **80**-37
- "The Ribband," the "great" and politics, **69**-A
- satire on English nobility, **80**-210
- satire on frivolous peer who lost America, **81**-20
- self-interested, **76**-297
- "State Coach," lazy and selfish peerage, **68**-A
- "titled slaves" and liberty, **73**-106
- Tory nobility and Pitt wish to extend King's prerogative, **85**-33
- true and false, **64**-85, **79**-319, 493
  - and Pitt, **66**-127
- unpatriotic aristocratic youth, **81**-213
- venal, **70**-38
  - and indifferent to reform, **85**-3

Nonimportation. **See**: America, Nonimportation.

North, Frederick (1732-92). Styled Lord North, 1752; 2d Earl of Guilford, 1790, ld of Treasury, 1759-65; chancellor of Exchequer, October 1767-March 1782; 1st ld of Treasury and PM, January 1770-March 1782; Home sec in Fox-North Coalition, April-December 1783; in Opposition to young Pitt's ministry, 1784-90. Nicknamed "Boreas." **67**-16, **68**-10, **69**-29, **70**-2, 8, 17, 18, 22, 32, 36, 56, 79, 125, 126, 138, 184, 188, 205, **71**-6, 8, 42, 108, 110, 117, 121, **72**-1, 6, 18, 25, 54, 57, 68, 76, 81, 88, **73**-8, 15, 17, 26, 36, 52, 55, 61, 62, 76, 78, 79, 96, **74**-5, 15, 28, 32, 37, 54, 65, 83, 91, 113, 132, 183, 185, 208, 220, 223, **75**-24, 34, 39, 51, 62, 66, 73, 92, 100, 101, 105, 118, 120, 122, 136, 152, 162, 173, 184, 190, 194, 198, 209, 220, 225, 227, 237, 240, 252, 269, 270, 284, 317, **76**-3, 14, 17, 18, 19, 24, 25, 27, 43, 49, 82, 85, 92, 166, 179, 184, 194, 201, 202, 207, 215, 216, 250, 266, 278, 298, 328, 347, 398, **77**-6, 12, 13, 18, 33, 46, 47, 56, 61, 66, 67, 82, 89, 94, 130, 131, 141, 149, 163, 166, 207, 208, 229, 233, 234, 248, 251, 254, 266, 272, 286, 288, 300, 308, 310, **78**-4, 7, 12, 23, 25, 38, 39, 45, 50, 56, 61, 64, 108, 110, 171, 184, 193, 214, 237, 243, 267, 282, 286, 290, 292, 296, 300, 302, 313, 316, 325, 344, 345, 378, 402, 420, 429, 432, 455, 464, 473, 479, 482, 486, 490, 501, 510, 512, 519, 536, 551, 556, **79**-3, 5, 11, 31, 33, 35, 37, 44, 45, 49, 57, 106, 171, 181, 197, 202, 231, 233, 255, 256, 284, 300, 302, 310, 328,

329, 332, 367, 384, 392, 453, **80**-7, 10, 23, 24, 26, 30, 40, 61, 62, 64, 69, 72, 90, 123, 127, 134, 136, 209, 235, 237, 256, 266, 270, 295, 330, 331, 334, 343, 378, 393, 402, 410, 429, 430, **81**-33, 39, 50, 60, 67, 73, 124, 137, 151, 182, 241, 259, **82**-43, 58, 61, 92, 155, 158, 193, 219, 224, 334(?), **83**-115, 119, 151, **84**-9, 15, 16, 72, 107, 120, 149, 166, 171, 190, 212, **85**-1
    abused, **84**-106
    and Abingdon, **80**-357
    and allies, Fox, Burke, Sheridan, satirized, **84**-55
    and Banbury, **78**-391
    and Barré, **77**-119
    and bribery, **81**-101, 207
    and bribes financed by Treasury, **81**-90
    and Burgoyne, **78**-93
    and conciliation, **78**-44
    and "Crown's Influence," **80**-346
    and enemy, **80**-245
    and Fox, **80**-222, **82**-99, 112, **83**-102, **84**-68
        friendly with, **83**-143
    and George III, **79**-399, **82**-208
    and Gibbon, **79**-369
    and Henry Bate, **80**-35
    and Jonathan Wilde, the thief, **80**-314
    and Middlesex election, **80**-327
    and need for money to finance war, **79**-511
    and new budget, **81**-211, 223
    and Norton, **80**-347, 361
    and obedient placemen, **79**-200
    and Opposition, **77**-31
    and peace negotiations, **82**-96
    and Pitt, **75**-290, **77**-280, **85**-12
    and Sandwich must resign, **82**-188
    and Sejanus, **80**-384, **81**-177
    and Shelburne, **82**-65, **83**-270
        peace policy, **83**-166, 207
    and Spanish War, **79**-426
    and tax increase, **80**-307
    and taxes, **80**-105, **82**-266
        new, **82**-417 (print), 418 (print)
        ruinous, **82**-304
    and Yorktown, **82**-9
    as Tory, **77**-25
    beware of America, **76**-348
    broken arm, **76**-148, 233
    castigated for ruinous American War, **84**-8
    character, **78**-82
    coalition with Fox, **83**-24, 36, 46
    compared with other PM's, **81**-55
    Conciliatory Motion, **75**-179
    controls Parliament, **81**-118
    corrupt, **78**-201, **79**-114, 165, **81**-224, **82**-389
        and traitor to cause of liberty, **78**-528
        despite union with Fox, **84**-228
    corruption and reform, **84**-121

     criticized, **79**-153
        severely, **81**-5
     cruel, bloodthirsty, **79**-398
     decline and fall of, **84**-93, 94
     defended, **80**-34, 73
        against factious Opposition, **80**-360
     defends self regarding American War, **83**-61
     deserves execution, **79**-354
     England tired of, **81**-54
     evil leader, **84**-201
     fall from power, **80**-200
     fears impeachment and execution, **79**-380
     fears of losing office, **82**-76
     financial chicanery, **80**-358
     financing the war, **79**-386
     Fox's enemy, **80**-245
     Freeth and pension, **82**-A
     hunts the nation to the death, **81**-192
     in Opposition with Fox and Burke to younger Pitt, **85**-47
     in retirement, **82**-56
     installed as Chancellor of Oxford University, July 1773, **73**-50
     Majority and America, **79**-314
     "A Minister's Reasoning," on reform, **83**-A
     Minority and Conciliation Bill, **78**-538
     model minister, **79**-390
     model of integrity, **79**-122
     political death, **84**-143
        and union with Fox, **83**-218
     praised, **80**-359, **82**-325
        despite failures, **82**-177
        for skillful debate, **83**-130
     reassures Sandwich vs Fox, **82**-189
     refuses to leave Fox, **84**-154
     resignation, March 20, 1782, **82**-113, 114, 142, 204, 358
        and union with Fox, **83**-3
     responsible for American War and loss of empire, **80**-194
     responsible for nation's enormous debts, **85**-35
     Rockingham, North, and end of American War, **82**-174
     satirized, **84**-55
        for self-interested friendship with Fox, **83**-217
        responsible for loss of America, **82**-3
     scorned, **84**-92
     Scotchman's tool, **76**-369
     should be cashiered, **80**-226
     should be sent to House of Lords, **84**-21
     sleeps during debates, **80**-96
     sticks to power and Bute, **82**-161
     still hopes for success in American War, **81**-266 (print)
     vs Fox-North ministry, **83**-156
     will not give up, **77**-292
North Ministry, February 1770-March 1782. Includes Dartmouth, Dyson (to 1776),
     C. J. Fox (to 1774), Germain (from 1775), Gower (to 1779), Grafton (to 1775),
     Hillsborough, Jenkinson, Mansfield, Sandwich, Suffolk, Thurlow, Wedderburne,

Weymouth (to 1779), and Bute as occasional "consultant." **70**-26, 32, 59, 88, 105, 112, 146, 152, **71**-46, 59, 61, 63, 85, 102, 136, **72**-91, **73**-69, **74**-7, 9, 25, 29, 36, 46, 78, 93, 139, 171, **75**-1, 27, 67, 80, 95, 121, 129, 147, 155, 227, 239, 278, **76**-11, 25, 42, 62, 95, 110, 199, 205, 217, 252, 268, 281, 291, 301, 346, 353, 373, 385, **77**-50, 67, 68, 82, 96, 144, 165, 179, 230, 245, 263, 288, 307, **78**-12, 16, 17, 25, 44, 47, 66, 105, 118, 161, 178, 217, 256, 259, 270, 290, 308, 340, 345, 362, 390, 422, 429, 474, 500, **79**-17, 35, 205, 218, 279, 292, **81**-137, **82**-10, 59, 71, 78, **83**-19, 20
    accountable for loss of America, **78**-238, 240
    accused of "faction," **79**-307
    and Arnold, **82**-212
    and Burke, **80**-165
    and failed Stuarts, **76**-304
    and George III, **81**-233
    and Gordon Riots, **80**-251
    and increased taxes, **81**-182
    and Pitt, **78**-380
    and Yorktown, **81**-33, **82**-9
    bankrupt and unable to survive the crisis, **78**-233
    blundering, **78**-96
    Boston and tea, **74**-55
    cannot defeat American rebels, **79**-107
    changing places, **79**-275
    character, **78**-84
    controlled by Tories, **80**-404
    corrupt, **77**-65, **78**-556, **79**-409
       self-interested, **82**-261
    criticized, **80**-7, 26, 40, 344, 380, 427 (print), **81**-5, 39, 124, **82**-299
       for excessive prodigality, **81**-61
       for failures, **78**-101
    defended, **80**-76, 306, 316
       by Tory, **80**-34
    deserve execution, **79**-260
    dissipated, **78**-112
    divided as to how to pursue American War, **76**-311
    economies effected, **80**-106
    epitaph, **82**-117, 137
    falls, **82**-227
    first signs of, **70**-67, 69
    incompetent, **80**-405
       and inept, corrupt and lying, **78**-556
    inefficient, **79**-461
    lacks direction, **78**-242
    lethargic, **79**-392
    may resign, **80**-419
    mismanages the war, **80**-429 (print), **80**-430 (print)
    must be unseated, **79**-293
    must end American War after Yorktown, **82**-17
    must know the rightful enemy is France, **79**-481
    national fast and North's Conciliatory Proposals, **78**-432
    need for change, **79**-336
    negative achievements to date, **74**-157
    on change to Rockingham ministry, **82**-140

real enemy of King, **79**-484
responsible for national crisis, **78**-458
responsible for poor state of navy, **78**-245, 253
satirized, **80**-183, 343, **82**-3, 4
Scotch influence, **74**-146
Scots dominate, **79**-388
should be brought to trial, **83**-9
should be cashiered, **80**-226
should be removed, **80**-69
still in power, **82**-402
swept out, **82**-406
thrives as it ruins nation, **78**-437
to be cashiered, **82**-419 (print)
unable to defeat American rebels, **76**-226
**See also**: John Robinson.

North's Conciliatory Proposals to Congress. Presented to Parliament February 17, 1778, passed March 3, and signed March 11, by King George. **78**-58, 313, 320, 329, **79**-5
America should reconsider, **81**-203
criticized, **78**-55
hypocritical, **78**-345
protest against, **78**-227
rejected by America for French alliance, **81**-14
rejected by Congress, **78**-81
rejected by Hancock, Congress, **78**-558 (print)
Rushton criticizes America for rejecting Britain's peace offer, seeking independence and French alliance, **82**-22
taken from patriot Opposition, **78**-133
too late, **78**-346, 347
**See also**: Carlisle Peace Commission, 1778.

Norton, Fletcher (1716-89). MP, 1756-82. Attorney-general December 1763-July 1765; Speaker House of Commons, 1770-80. Tory, opposed repeal of Stamp Act 1766 and supported Government in its American War to 1777, wavered and went into Opposition 1780. **65**-8, **66**-101, **69**-12, 29, 42, 81, 131, 269, **70**-32, 54, 106, 131, 152, 156, 165, 184, 189, 209, **71**-6, 24, 72, **72**-1, 6, **73**-8, **74**-5, 46, 145, **75**-122, **77**-18, 161, **79**-202, **80**-157
Churchill's *Conference*, **63**-A
Churchill's *Duellist* and *Independence*, **64**-A
criticized for breaking with North, **80**-361
criticized for greed and malice, **80**-347
joins the Opposition, **80**-130
promoted to Privy Councillor, March 22, 1769, **69**-160
"A Spurious Speech," **77**-A

Ogle, _____(?). Irishman in the Fencibles.
need for unity against England, **82**-268

Ohio. Region in western Pennsylvania, location of French Fort Duquesne, now Pittsburgh, where Braddock was defeated and the French and Indian War began. **66**-3
beginning of war, **57**-1
Braddock's defeat, **55**-2, **57**-2
French encroachments on, **62**-17
"A Morning Scene in Paris" and "A New Song" on DuQuesne, **60**-A
"On Death of Gen. Braddock," **55**-A

"On the Present State of America," **56-A**

Scots soldiers in, **61-39**

the war begins on the Ohio, **56-1**

William Hervey with Braddock, **55-1**

Oliver, Richard (1735-84). MP, 1770-80; London alderman, 1770-78, and sheriff, 1772-73. West Indies (Antigua) merchant in London; founding member of Bill of Rights Society 1769-71, but broke with Wilkes and joined Horne to found The Constitutional Society, 1771. Opposed the American War. **70-97**, 104, **71-64**, 66, 67, 71, 102, 110, 116, 137, **72-7**, **73-311**, **74-7**

in Whig pantheon, **70-95**

"Ode to Alderman Oliver," **71-A**

Omiah (or Omai). South Sea islander from Otaheite, visited England, 1774-76. **75-10**

made viceroy of Quebec and Boston, **76-231**

O'Neill, Elizabeth (?). Fruiterer in St. James's Street.

and C. J. Fox, **80-61**

and Minority, **79-42**

Onslow, George, 4th Baron, 1776 (1731-1814). MP, 1754-74; then House of Lords. Voted against Bute's peace preliminaries, December 1762; at first supported Wilkes, 1763, then later in 1768-70 trimmed on Wilkes; supported Rockingham ministry, 1765-66; but supported also the North ministry. **66-69**, **67-5**, **70-18**, **71-64**, **72-1**

"Alphabetical . . .," **69-A**

Onslow, Thomas (1754-1827). MP, 1775-1806. Son of George Onslow; voted with the North administration; and supported North in the Coalition and Fox's India Bill, 1783. **83-29**

Orde, Thomas (1746-1807). MP, 1780-96. Tory supporter of North ministry and its American policy. **82-414** (print)

Orvilliers, Comte d'. **See:** Guillouet, Louis.

Osborne, Francis Godolphin, Marquess of Carmarthen (1751-99). MP, 1774-75, then House of Lords; supported the North ministry and the rights of Britain over America; broke with North, 1780, and joined Opposition, but still believed in the justice of the war against America. **83-20**

Oswald, James Townshend (1748-1814). MP, 1768-74, 1776-79. A Scottish placeman who supported the Grafton and North ministries.

verse epistle to, in 1776, **89-3**

Otis, James (1725-83). American politician, publicist, patriot orator in Massachusetts; according to John Adams, responsible for slogan, "Taxation without representation is tyranny." **75-133**

Oxford.

and Toryism, **78-413**

Encaenia, **73-50**, 61, 62

Palliser, Hugh, 1st Baron (1723-96). British naval officer, with Saunders at Quebec, 1759; governor Newfoundland, 1764-69; comptroller of navy, 1770-75; ld of Admiralty, 1775-79; admiral when charging Keppel with incompetence at Ushant, which led to court martials for both, 1778-79. **78-200**, 493, 494, 553, **79-1**, 10, 12, 17, 18, 19, 20, 24, 28, 35, 39, 65, 70, 72, 86, 94, 98, 109, 119, 123, 134, 139, 141, 142, 208, 216, 217, 219, 235, 267, 278, 294, 321, 333, 334, 342, 364, 367, 397, 404, 470-476, 485, 492, 496, **80-7**, 10, 16, 37, 40, 118, 226, 237, 324, **81-222**, **82-9**, 193, 212, 285

anti-Palliser, **79-240**

appointed by Sandwich as governor of Greenwich Hospital, **80-146**

cleared by court martial, **79-258**

       court martial, **79**-441
       Cowper's "Address," **79**-A
       "False Palliser," **79**-55
       hanged in effigy, **79**-245
       the politics of Ushant surfaces, **78**-492
       satirized, **80**-173
       trial and acquittal, **79**-407
       **See**: Augustus Keppel and the Ushant Episode, July 27, 1778.
Paoli, Pasquale (1725-1807). Corsican patriot. **68**-12, 55, 87, **69**-1, 2, 3, 4,
   13, 21, 31, 50, 90, 151, 198, 242, 243, **71**-1
       and Wilkes, **69**-99
       arrival in England, September 18, 1769, **69**-150
       **See**: James Boswell, and Corsica.
Parker, Hyde, 5th Baronet (1714-83). British admiral; served under Byron in
   American waters, 1778; in action off Grenada, 1779; with Rodney, 1780; fought
   the Dutch, 1781; lost at sea on way to India, 1783. **81**-210, **82**-18, **83**-43,
   158, **84**-9
       ballad narrative of engagement with Dutch Zoutman, **81**-77
       better than Keppel, **81**-58
       engagement with Dutch Admiral Zoutman, **81**-34, 46
Parker, Peter, 1st Baronet (1721-1811). MP, 1784-90. British admiral, led the
   naval squadron in the unsuccessful attack with Clinton on Charleston, S.C.,
   June 1776; supported General Howe's capture of New York, 1776; also led the
   attack on Rhode Island, December 1776-January 1777; commanded the Jamaica
   station, 1777-1783. **76**-123, 214, 218, 277, 374, **77**-35, 228, **81**-3, 34, 46
Parliament. **74**-89, **78**-237, 288, **79**-284
       advice to legislators, **67**-3
       and Henry Fox and Bute, **62**-20, 28
       and horse races, **67**-11
       and King, **66**-11
       and taxation, **80**-25
       Bute's bribes, **65**-79
       Christmas recess and gagging Opposition, **77**-318
       Christmas recess, end of debates, **77**-220
       Corruption, **71**-78, 104, **73**-23, 80, **74**-19, 115, **76**-49, 95, 96, 109, 120,
           133, 161, 261, 264, **76**-293, 310, 367, **77**-18, 97, 161, **78**-165, 201, 370,
           414, 474, 509, 537, **79**-262, **80**-112, 268, 278, 295, 344, **81**-71, **82**-71,
           245, **83**-237
           and America, **74**-157, 251, **76**-34
           and enslaving America, **76**-134
           and incompetent, **77**-557
           and tyrannical, **79**-354
           and Wilkes' arrest, **64**-10
           benefits Scots, **80**-192
           bribery in Parliament, **63**-43
           destroys free Parliament, **65**-106
           election, **63**-92, **68**-30
               and rotten boroughs, **68**-18
           generated American War, **75**-13, 159, 240
           King through bribery is supreme, **75**-263
           new Parliament just like old, **80**-207
           responsible for American War, **80**-120
           responsible for Bourbon threat, **79**-358

        results in excessive power of King George, **76**-270
        Third dissolved, **80**-279
        venal, **82**-4
        votes for more taxation, **77**-51
        yielded the rights of men, **80**-135
    the danger of voting freely, **69**-111
    debates, **78**-43
        reveal state secrets, **80**-3
    election and corruption, **63**-92
        and rotten boroughs, **68**-18
    election song adapted by America, **69**-54
    Elections, 1774-80, **74**-6, **76**-95, 96, **77**-275, **78**-391, **79**-114, **80**-198,
        223, 229, 336, 341, 387
            and America, **74**-42
            and bribery, **74**-96
            Arthur Lee and other leaders of Bill of Rights Society defeated in
                1774 election, **75**-255
    electioneering and corruption, **68**-30
    electoral process in Brentford, **69**-36
    English form of government, **71**-21, **73**-110, **75**-263, 307, **78**-526
    foolish, **78**-248
    free, corruption destroys, **65**-106
    French and English, **63**-111
    frustrations of politics in, **78**-385
    John Williams pilloried by Parliament for printing Wilkes' *North Briton,
        No. 45*, **65**-145, 146
    honest representation means no sale of seats, **82**-245
    MP's and constituents, **63**-124, 147
    mad, **82**-75
    Middlesex election riot, **68**-37
    Middlesex Petition vs arbitrary government, **69**-9
    must control budget and American War, **82**-219
    must unite against European enemies, **81**-219
    on approaching election, **68**-10
    oratory in, **66**-53
    Parliaments in Reign of George III, Second, 1768-74, **74**-75, 76, 77
            dissolution, **74**-5, 91, 208
    Parliaments, Third, 1774-80
            adjourned January 1780, **80**-270
            dissolved September 1, 1780, **80**-112, 278
            a review, **80**-345
    Parliaments, Fourth, 1780-84, **81**-50
            "Address to . . .," **80**-A
            dissolved March 25, 1784, and end of Fox-North Coalition Ministry,
                **84**-37, 44
            epitaph on, and factionalism, **84**-61
            first meeting at a critical time, **80**-375
            must unite against enemies at war, **81**-219
            "a parliament man," **81**-100
            recess, **81**-186, **82**-61
    peace, **82**-61
    persecution of Wilkes by, **64**-43
    Pitt and Peace Treaty of 1763, **63**-9

the power of House of Commons, **69**-142
Power of Parliament, its "rights," arrogance, pride and tyranny, **69**-142, **70**-117, 183, **73**-22, **74**-116, **75**-37, 74, 201, 206, 240, 251, 261, **76**-113
    a challenge to Parliament's privilege, **77**-118
    the King, through corruption of Parliament, becomes supreme tyrant, **75**-263
    the majority and destruction of America, **75**-120
    "On a Ropemaker," **75**-A
    quarrel with London, **71**-65, **74**-194
    "To Governours from Subjects," warning to Parliament, **69**-A
    tyrannical and keeps the war against America going, **79**-354
Quebec Act, **74**-167, 168, 169
recess, June 3, 1778, **78**-431
recess, June 1779, **79**-391, 505
rendered servile and powerless by King's Friends and Bute, **78**-44, **79**-322
Scotch influence, **71**-96
Septennial Parliaments, **63**-92, **70**-23, **73**-77, 87, **84**-139
    criticized, **63**-101
    "On a Late Remonstrance," **73**-A
Southwark and election, **65**-68
threats to free elections, **67**-5
trends in politics, **64**-40
the voting system, **69**-82
"weak, divided, irresolute," **79**-397
yields the rights of men, **80**-135
    **See also**: Corruption, Elections, Faction, Ministries, Minority Opposition, Wilkes, etc.

Pearson, Richard (1731-1806). Naval officer, noted for his command of the *Serapis*, defeated and captured by John Paul Jones' *Bonhomme Richard* and squadron, in a heroic sea battle, September 23, 1779. **79**-253, 304, **80**-13
    **See**: John Paul Jones.

Pelham-Holles, Thomas, 1st Duke of Newcastle (1693-1768). "Prince of Whigs"; first minister in coalition with Pitt during Seven Years' War until their resignation because of conflict with Bute and the court, 1761-62; the greatest political party organizer and dispenser of patronage of his time. **60**-17, **62**-46, **63**-2, 130, 187, **64**-40, **65**-62, **70**-77, **73**-6, 18, **81**-55
    death, **68**-40, 82
    "An Ode," **63**-A

Penn, William (1644-1718). Founder of Pennsylvania, Quaker statesman.
    Penn's petition to Charles II and Carlisle Commission petition to Congress, **78**-407
    with son Thomas (1702-75) assists College of Philadelphia, **65**-29

Percy, Hugh (1742-1817). MP, 1763-76, Tory. Styled Lord Warkworth, 1750-66; later Earl Percy, 1776. British general served at Minden and under Gage at Boston; led the relief column at Concord and retreat to Boston, April 20, 1775; in New York campaign with Howe and returned to England, 1777, **63**-76, **68**-88, **74**-42, 118, 199, **75**-110, 211, **76**-16, 85, 103, 223, 273, 332, **77**-4, 12, 17, 19, 27, 58, 123, 298, **78**-7, 226, 295, **79**-38, 232, **80**-20, **81**-102
    and his soldiers, **84**-195

Peterborough, Bishop of. **See**: John Hinchcliffe.

Petty, William Fitzmaurice, 2d Earl of Shelburne (1737-1805). MP, 1760-61; then House of Lords. Disciple of Pitt, and like him opposed American independence,

but not concessions; PM, 1782-83, after Rockingham's death.  Patron of Joseph Priestley; for his political deviousness, called "Malagrida," after a scheming and unscrupulous Jesuit.  **66**-64, **68**-19, **69**-140, **70**-101, 178, 188, **71**-94, 99, 129, **73**-3, 4, **75**-49, 170, **76**-16, 34, 82, **77**-23, 149, 207, 292, **78**-12, 66, 234, 299, 317, 348, **79**-11, 38, 44, 59, **80**-10, 24, 33, 34, 61, 69, 136, 229, 290, 306, 317, **82**-3, 25, 37, 48, 158, 159, 240, 286, 287, 289, **83**-3, 32, 56, 193
    and Benedict Arnold, **82**-167
    and Bute, **78**-43
    and Fox, **82**-4, 121, 145, 191, 223, 250, 294
        and Burke, **82**-77
        and John Cavendish, **82**-164
        break with Fox, **82**-290
    and ministry, **82**-315, 329
    and North, **82**-65
    and Palliser, **79**-470
    awards Barré a pension, **82**-413
    criticized, **82**-168
    favored by Causidicus, **82**-169, 174
    his peace policy, retention of America in British empire, **82**-22
    peace, **82**-292
    peace negotiations, **82**-96
    praised as future leader, **80**-4
    Rockingham's death, **82**-165
    Shelburne (Petty) as Prime Minister and thereafter, **83**-20, 29, 119, 151, 156, **84**-116
        and Burke, **83**-51, 173
        and Burns, **84**-A
        and Bute, **83**-172
        and Lord Gordon, **83**-257
        and Mrs. Siddons, **83**-195
        and Fox, **84**-161
        and "so damn'd a Peace," **83**-99
        and younger Pitt, **83**-266, **84**-41, **85**-12
        attacked by Fox and North, **83**-289 (print)
        brings peace, **84**-16
            but is "discarded," **83**-270
        created Marquess of Lansdowne, **84**-96, **84**-142
        criticized, **83**-225, 226
        crucified by Fox-North, **83**-83
        crucified for his peace, **83**-148
        defended, **83**-105, 216, 247
        Fox-North Coalition, **83**-110, 281
        Fox's objections to Shelburne's peace, **83**-61, 86, 94
        incorruptible, **84**-29
        lost the peace, **83**-144
        peace, **83**-66, **84**-128
            and Fox, **83**-45
            and his political death, **83**-104
            good, **84**-8
            "ignominious," **88**-1
            objection to, **85**-13
            policy defended from faction, Fox and Burke, **83**-159

strategy, **83**-30
terrible, **84**-1
with America, **83**-298 (print)
platform: peace, prosperity, friendship with America, **83**-212
praised as peace advocate, **85**-4
resignation, **83**-239
vs Fox, **83**-252
Shelburne's Ministry, July 13, 1782-March 29, 1783, **82**-252, 253, 315, 329
and American Loyalists, **82**-209
and Fox-North, **83**-69
and "Vicar of Bray," **84**-149
Freeth's song on, **83**-107
neglect of American Loyalists, **83**-12
objection to its "American measures," **83**-255
peace measures opposed by Fox, Burke, and North, **83**-207
resignation, **83**-194
resignation of Fox and Burke, **83**-32
satirized, **82**-349
takes command to make peace with America and humble France, **82**-253
a Tory criticism of the friend of Price and Priestley, **79**-502
Tory, opposes reform, **82**-163
traitor, **80**-185, **82**-126
unwilling to grant independence to America, **82**-326
usurped command upon Rockingham's death, **82**-252
Philadelphia, Pennsylvania.
blockaded, **78**-464
Brackenridge, *Rising Glory*, **72**-14, **78**-73, **89**-2
College of Philadelphia, **63**-5, **65**-29
Colvill on future greatness of America, **77**-4
peaceful scenery on the Delaware River, **78**-315
**See also:** Howe's New Jersey and Pennsylvania Campaigns in Battles and Campaigns under American War.
Phipps, Constantine John, 2d Baron Mulgrave (1744-92). MP, 1768-90. Naval officer, Admiralty Bd, 1777-82; with Keppel off Ushant, 1778; Bd of Trade, 1784- 86; friend of Sandwich and consistent supporter of North ministry; testified favorably for Palliser at Keppel's court martial, January 12-February 11, 1779; also opposed reform. **76**-372, **79**-245, 339
Piercy, Thomas. British naval captain of the warship *Countess of Scarborough* in Capt. Richard Pearson's convoy attacked by Paul Jones' privateering squadron, September 23, 1779. **79**-304
**See:** John Paul Jones and Richard Pearson.
Pierson, Francis (1756-81). Young major, killed in the successful defense of the Channel Isle of Jersey against French invaders, January 6, 1781. **81**-63, 79, 98, 116, 165, **82**-183
Pigot, Robert (1720-96). MP, 1768-72. Supported Grafton and North ministries. British colonel at Lexington and Bunker Hill, 1775; general of the garrison at Newport, R.I., that successfully fought off a Franco-American attack, July-August, 1778. **79**-527, **83**-30(?), 43
Pinchbeck, Christopher (c.1710-83). George III's personal favorite, allegedly one of the "King's Friends"; toyman and clockmaker who had fabricated an ingenious candle snuffer. **76**-10, 18, 19, 28, 217, 299; **78**-8, 324, **80**-238
death, **83**-191
epitaph, **83**-60
eulogy, **83**-138

Pitt, William, Earl of Chatham (1708-78). MP, 1735-66; then House of Lords. Popular leader of the House of Commons, 1757-61, in the Pitt-Newcastle coalition during the Seven Years' War; objected to the Peace of 1763 negotiated by Bute; supported Wilkes on the issue of Parliamentary privilege, 1763; opposed American policy of Grenville, Stamp Tax, 1765; formed a ministry with Grafton, 1766, but was too ill to lead; too weak also to oppose North's American measures effectively, 1770-78, and to keep America in the empire. **58**-1, 4, **59**-5, 9, 40, **60**-8, 17, 25, 34, 45, **61**-8, 12, 13, 14, 18-32, 34, 36, 40-44, 46-49, **61**-A, **62**-5, 6, 7, 17, 18, 21, 24, 30, 39, 46, 57, 63, 65, 67, **62**-A, **63**-2, 4, 8, 9, 17, 64, 71, 85, 112, 125, 130, 141, 144, 145, 152, 153, 155, 160, 161, 169, 174, 184, 187, **64**-1, 3, 6, 7, 8, 17, 35, 40, 44, 48, 51, 64, 73, 74, 100, 102, 104, **65**-1, 5, 6, 8, 22, 25, 36, 37, 61, 67, 71, 74, 76, 85, 91, 92, 101, 121, 133, 141, **66**-3-6, 8, 18, 21, 22, 24, 26-29, 31-34, 38, 39, 46-49, 51, 53, 54, 56, 57, 61, 66, 71, 76-80, 83-87, 90, 94-99, 102, 103, 107, 111, 117, 119, 122, 123, 125-132, 139, **67**-7, 10, 15, 23, 26, 27, 32, 34, 44, 45-47, **68**-10, 18, 22-24, 51, 52, 59, 124, **69**-10, 17, 29, 68, 90, 214, 237, **70**-2, 6, 24, 50, 101, 104, 123, 130, 170, 172, 207, 227, **71**-137, **72**-13, 27, 57, 64, 93, **73**-4, 10, 18, 26, **74**-5, **75**-10, 11, 223, 274, **76**-81, 167, **78**-97
    "Address," **63**-A
    and America, **66**-7, 8, 30, 43, 53, 62, 64, 67, 72, 74, 75, 101, 113, 120, 121, 137, 138, 140, **67**-4, 25, 37, 61, **69**-140, **70**-77, 85, 111, **71**-4, **72**-60, 74, **74**-12, 35, 41, 53, 89, 93, 113, 152, 177, 189, **75**-13, 35, 49, 105, 148, 150, 198, 227, 240, 266, 273, 317, 319, **76**-3, 12, 14, 16, 22, 29, 320, 347, **77**-5, 7, 13, 16, 23, 111, 173, 206, 251, 288, 318, **78**-12, 14, 15, 18, 23, 35, 40, 47, 75, 86, 96, 102, 292, 323, 349, 387, 419, 502, 510, **79**-1, 3, 9, **82**-3, 17
        American rebellion and French war, **79**-412
        and French intervention, **78**-218
        and George III, **81**-26
        and liberty, **74**-17
        and North, **75**-290, **77**-280
        and Pitt's character, **78**-30
        and Rushton and American independence, **82**-22
        blamed for loss of America, **78**-504
        Boston Port Bill, **74**-32
        Dunstan's "Liberty," and war against America, **89**-2
        honored in America, **78**-229
        only Pitt can save Britain, **78**-305, 499
        Pitt's stroke and America's independence, **78**-371
        refuses Bute's offer to form a coalition, **78**-434
        refuses Bute's offer to save the nation, **78**-144
        restore Pitt, jewel in crown, and America will again be safe, **78**-261
    and Sandwich, **78**-43
    and Seven Years' War, **78**-16
    and starving farmer, **66**-12
    bon mot, **59**-31
    Churchill's *Prophecy of Famine*, **63**-A
    Death, May 11, 1778, and after, **78**-18, 24, 152-155, 158, 185, 188, 235, 237, 242, 248-250, 259, 273, 278, 342, 343, 360, 364-367, 369, 380, 393, 440, 461, **79**-5, 15, 117, 151, 231, 262, 302, 322, **80**-29, 64, 235, 321, 331, **82**-59, 142, 405, **83**-3, 19, 20, **84**-18, 39
        and fall of British empire, **78**-121
        and North, **81**-55

        and Sandwich, **80**-260
        and Scotch and son, **84**-183
        and Shelburne, **82**-48
        and younger Pitt, the son, **84**-14, 46, 98
        Cowper's "Table Talk," **82**-A
        death, **79**-15
        effect on nation, **78**-87, 88
        elder Pitt would reject younger Pitt's "lawless" ministry, **84**-19
        eloquence, **85**-2
        epitaphs on Pitt and his character and achievements as patriot,
            orator, and statesman, **78**-160 to 169
        eulogy, **78**-120, 122
        "The Ghost," **83**-A
        "Here rest," **78**-A
        incorruptible, **78**-505
        memorial in Westminster Abbey, **81**-97
        model for son, **82**-14
        nation, sinking, needs Pitt's leadership, **81**-235
        "O Pitt!", **78**-A
        old Whig Pitt the father vs Tory Pitt the younger, **84**-112
        "On the . . . Funeral," **78**-A
        patriotic statesman, **83**-98
        Pitt's ghost objects to younger Pitt's politics, **84**-23
        poor health and eclipse, **78**-123
        praised, **84**-134
        resignation, 1761, **80**-12
        review of achievements, **78**-503
        review of career for edification of son, **84**-4
        review of his statesmanship, his last speech that brought on the
            mortal stroke, **78**-122
        "The Sequel of Britain's Address," **79**-A
        son and father, **83**-136
        spirit invoked, **82**-374
        summary of achievements regarding empire, oratory, and France, **78**-124
    elevation to peerage as Earl of Chatham, **66**-2
    "Extempore on . . .," **68**-A
    factious, **78**-85
    his leadership in another French war, **78**-3
    in eclipse, **77**-176
    "Mourn," **66**-A
    place among British worthies, and support of "the just war" against France, **78**-31
    "Political Squibs," **66**-A
    resignation from Grafton's ministry, October 1768, **68**-75
    "Shall Pitt," **66**-A
    spirit invoked, **82**-374
    "Spoken . . .," **70**-A
    "'Tis False!," **66**-A
    "To a Friend," **66**-A
    "Verses Extempore," **65**-A
    Wilmot, **63**-A
Pitt, William (the younger) (1759-1806). MP, 1781-1806. 1st ld of Treasury and

chancellor of Exchequer, Prime Minister, December 1783-March 1801, May 1804-d. Second son of William Pitt, Earl of Chatham; opposed North's ministry, joined Shelburne's ministry as privy councillor and chancellor of Exchequer, July 1782; voted for Shelburne's peace; opposed Fox-North Coalition and destroyed it in 1783 to form his own ministry, December 19, 1783. **82**-181, 193, 283, **83**-7, 29, 32, 151, 156, 260, **84**-23, 69, 71, 72, 77, 79, 97-99, 188, **85**-51
- advice to, **83**-90, **84**-126
- ally of Wilkes, **84**-28
- and burial of constitution, **84**-51
- and Burke, **82**-314
- and Burns, **84**-A
- and corruption, **84**-141
- and ending American War after Yorktown, **82**-17
- and father, **82**-176, **84**-46
    - as model, **84**-4
- and Fox, **83**-96, **84**-54
    - contrasted, **83**-234
    - "The Ghost," **83**-A
- and Fox-North Coalition, **83**-281
- and Hastings and North, **84**-192
- and King and Fox, **84**-48
- and Puddicombe, **84**-A
- and re-union with America, **85**-10
- and Shelburne, **83**-266
- and Shelburne's peace, **83**-66
- and taxes, **85**-59 (print)
- and Thurlow, **84**-81
- antagonist of Fox, **84**-27
- assumes office of PM, December 19, 1783; four PM's since March 1781, **83**-200, 202
- brings discord, **84**-108
- can save Britain from disintegrating faction, **84**-31
- conflict with Fox and North, **84**-8
- contrasted with Fox, **84**-165
- criticized, **84**-178
- "Dialogue," **84**-A
- drives sedition and Foxites out, **85**-60 (print)
- father and son, **83**-136
- first sign of interest in politics, March 31, 1780, **80**-372
- Fox and North, **84**-130
- "the generous Pitt," and George III, **84**-190
- guidelines for son of Chatham, **82**-14
- in Shelburne's ministry, **82**-198
- must suppress faction of Fox and North, **84**-193
- nation needs another Pitt, **83**-231
- nation's savior, **84**-207
- new taxes, **84**-145
- objections to, youth, questionable allies, and support of "secret influence," **84**-5
- on American War and his allies, including Wilkes, against Fox, **85**-13
- on American War and suppression of reform movement, **85**-12
- oratorical initiation, **81**-121
- PM after Fox-North Coalition, **83**-3

praised, **84**-32, 40, **84**-169, 177, 197, 201, 214, **85**-35, 37, 38
    for suppressing faction, **84**-14
    for tax policy, **84**-179
reformer, **82**-85
satirized, **84**-127
should assume command, **83**-75
subdued faction, **84**-105
tax policy, **84**-113
tool of Bute, Jacobites and Tories, **86**-3
tool of the court, **84**-26
tool of George III, **84**-52
Tory and unlike his father, **84**-62
Tory Pitt and prerogative, **84**-112
Tory, taxes, and Shelburne, **84**-41
vs Fox, **84**-85
    and "proud Democracy," **85**-15
vs Pitt and Tories, **85**-33
Wilkes, **84**-44
with Thurlow leads the nation, **84**-16

Pitt, William (the younger). Ministry, the Pitt-Thurlow-Gower Coalition, December 27, 1783. **84**-118, 149, 163
    criticized, **84**-173
    Fox, **84**-161
    "lawless" Tory leadership strengthens King's prerogative, **84**-19
    Pitt-Thurlow alliance, **84**-81
    questioned for honesty, **84**-5
    tax policy, **84**-125
    their measures are effective, **84**-82
    their youth, **84**-1

Placemen.
    obedient to North, **79**-200
    **See**: Corruption, passim; George Augustus Selwyn.

Plumbe, Samuel (d. 1784). London alderman, Castle Baynard Ward, 1767-82; Ld Mayor, 1779. Brother-in-law of Henry Thrale, brewer, the friend of Samuel Johnson; supported the North ministry which brought so much distress to the nation, American War, etc.
    satire on the ministry and its supporters, **79**-529 (print)

Pocock, George (1706-92). MP, 1760-68. Admiral, commanded the fleet that captured Havana, for which he received an enormous sum of prize money; supported Bute and Grenville; voted against repeal of Stamp Act, 1766. **62**-23, 53, **79**-1

Poetry and Poets.
    advice to "the Poetical Correspondents," **78**-510
    captious poet satirists, **82**-315
    minor, "City," poets, **74**-44
    popular poetry in newspapers, **82**-296

Politics and Politicians (general).
    effect of four seasons on politicians, **71**-34
    "Epigram" (Caligula's horse), **70**-A
    "Epigram on the Times," **70**-A
    on selfish politicians, **83**-250
    politicians always criticized, **77**-145
    powerful politicians and the constitution, **83**-249

**See also:** Ideal character of (alderman, courtier, member of parliament, minister, modern minister, politician); and Review of Politics, passim.

Pomfret, Earl of. **See:** George Fermor.

The Poor, or Common People (Working poor, mechanics, bankrupts; starvation and hard times).

    "Address to Britain," on complaints of starving poor—oppression by rich, bribery, and loss of natural rights, **70-A**
    British ruin will be caused by mistreatment of poor, **78-287**
    class division between laborer and lord of manor, **66-37**
    colliers object to younger Pitt's tax on coal, **84-174**
    common persons' view of politics, **66-68**
    complaint at monopoly high prices for food, **66-93**
    economic distress drives poor to emigrate to America, **66-139** (print)
    emigration of liberty to America caused by imprisonment for debts, etc., **76-34**
    emigration to America compounds problems of poor, **83-8**
    English commerce helps "the poor," **72-103**
    exploitation of the poor, one corruption of the times, **70-92**
    Freeth again objects to treatment of the poor, starving and oppressed, **75-119**
    Freeth's song on hard times, **66-A**
    future for Britain is dim, dearth and domestic troubles, **74-156**
    hopes for the poor, **68-36**
    ignored by everyone, **73-111**
    in workhouses and bankrupts in debtor's prison and taxes, **81-40**
    the irrelevance of liberty and politics to poor, **84-133, 151, 157**
    John Scott on class division between helpless working poor and powerful rich, **66-16**
    King must help starving poor, else they will emigrate, **73-59**
    ordinary easily deceived, "cullied," people, **69-246**
    petition to King complaining of high prices and taxes that force poor to emigrate, **71-70**
    Pitt's elevation to peerage and loss of leaders of working class, **66-38**
    a poor debtor in prison, **68-97**
    a poor rioter begs to be transported and saved from execution, **67-24**
    poor still suffer, **77-197**
    poor suffer, rich always in power, **67-49**
    protest at abuses in "little" Britain, imprisonment for debt, game laws, and taxation of America, **76-198**
    protest at appointment of contractor to represent poor and others, a veteran of Bunker Hill protests exploitation of poor—a Freeth song, **75-118**
    protest at high price of "corn" (wheat), **66-17**
    protest at oppressive "monopoly" and its effect on food prices, **68-25**
    protest at starvation in Britain, **72-91**
    protests at hard times, **67-38, 39, 40**
    protests at high food prices and taxes, **67-18, 19, 20**
    protests at luxury during hard times, **75-219**
    "Quarter Day," agricultural economy, and growth of "monopoly," **77-259**
    "Quarter Day" and oppression on the farm, **77-260**
    "scum of the earth" as republicans, **70-151**
    social protest by starving poor, **68-72**

starving poor ignored by King and nobility, **72**-98
starving tenant farmer, **66**-12
Wilkes' working class followers, **69**-125
Wilkesites and the high price of food, **72**-87
working class toils like slaves and the great share the spoil, **78**-433
**See also**: Emigration, Enclosures.

Pope, Alexander (1688-1744). Satiric poet.
compared with Churchill, **65**-11
imitations, **60**-24, **66**-5, **70**-186, **84**-18
Churchill's *Conference*, **60**-A
parodies, **66**-60, **73**-82, 83, **75**-220

Portland, 3d Duke, and Portland Ministry, April-December 1783. **See**: William Henry Cavendish-Bentinck.

Powys, Thomas (1743-1800). MP, 1774-97. Independent country gentleman; supported North's ministry regarding America, but became increasingly critical of its failures; voted for Shelburne's peace and denounced Fox-North Coalition.
in administration of younger Pitt, **83**-3

Pratt, Charles, Baron Camden (1714-94). MP, 1757-62; House of Lords, 1765-d. Ld chief justice, common pleas, 1762-66; ld chancellor, 1766-70. Ruled in Wilkes case that gen warrants were illegal and unconstitutional, 1763; and challenged Mansfield's ruling that in libel cases juries could only determine facts of publication. Friend of elder Pitt; opposed colonial taxation and American measures of North ministry. **63**-36, 37, 61, 86, 95, 106, 118, 131, 162, 188, **64**-3, 6, 102, **65**-1, 5, 76, 93, 142, **66**-4, 31, 32, 64, 75, 131, **67**-5, **68**-19, 21, 25, 103, **69**-10, 13, **70**-8, 50, 77, 103, 104, 111, 130, 204, **72**-95, **73**-4, 10, 26, **75**-19, 150, 240, 319, **76**-29, 42, 336, **77**-5, 7, 23, **78**-12, 14, 23, 24, 66, 102, 292, 556, **79**-25, 33, 38, 44, 49, 317, **80**-10, 69, **82**-193, **83**-4, **84**-116
and American liberty, **74**-17
and Mansfield, **78**-43
and Pitt, **85**-17
Boston Port Bill, **74**-32
criticized, **79**-11
dismissed as Ld Chancellor by Grafton, January 1770, **70**-122
in the new Rockingham ministry, **82**-197
in Rockingham's ministry as ld pres, **82**-25
"Liberty," **89**-2
nation needs Pratt to protect freedom of sinking nation, **81**-235
*Ode to Palinurus,* **70**-A
"Stanzas," **70**-A
"To the . . . Defenders of Liberty," **63**-A
traitor, **82**-126

Presbyterians.
attack on Presbyterians as republicans, **65**-16
confusion of Scottish reaction to Wilkes, **68**-89
pro and con, Whig republicanism, regarding Charles I's martyrdom, **65**-126, 127
rejection of Papist criticism of, **65**-117
Whig republican and hypocrite, **65**-56
Wilkes's supporters derive from followers of Cromwell and Presbyterian hypocrites, **69**-35
**See also**: Dissent.

Prescott, Richard (1725-88). British general; served in Germany during Seven Years' War; captured July 10, 1777, in Rhode Island under embarrassing circumstances by Arnold's troops; exchanged for Charles Lee, May 6, 1778. **77-71**, **93**, **132**, **192**, **193**, **201**, **221**, **226**, **227**, **237**

Present, Past, and Future (Comparisons and Contrasts).
    Adm Byng in 1757, Keppel in 1779, **81-127**
    after Yorktown, Britain in Pitt's day and Britain at present, **81-247**
    America before and during the rebellion, **76-14**
    America in future and in present, **74-67**
    America, past and present, in peace and at war, **77-69**
    American colonies sought British aid in past but now at war with Britain, **80-247**
    "Battle of the Books," political writing in Swift's day and the present, **63-A**
    beau of 1777 contrasted with serious matters, **77-36**
    Britain achieved glory in past wars, now Britain suffers shame and disgrace, **83-231**
    Britain once triumphant and powerful; now, after Yorktown disaster, defeated and demoralized, **81-178**
    Britain prosperous fifteen years ago and in shambles now, **76-75**
    Britain under Pitt and under North, **82-82**
    Britain will re-assert itself in American War, **80-298**
    Britain's history up to time of American War, **80-12**
    Britain's navy will chastise France and Spain like the past, **78-246**
    Britain's prosperity, then corruption and oppression, which brings American War, **77-155**
    British brave and fearless in Seven Years' War, but pessimistic and fearful in American War, **76-159**
    British navy under Pitt in past and under Sandwich at present, **81-78**
    "A Comparison," British army in past and present, **80-A**
    contrast between 1782 and 1783, from perspective of North and Fox, **83-61**
    decline and fall of Rome and Britain, **75-20**
    fear of 1777 contrasted with serious matters, **77-36**
    France and Britain in reigns of George II and George III, **78-92**
    Freeth on successes of Seven Years' War and failures of American War, **82-10**
    George I, II, and III, **78-477**
    glorious past and dismal present of civil war, **76-45**
    Howe and Fabius, **78-91**
    Ins and Outs in Walpole's day and the present, **72-66**
    Ireland between 1746-53 and present, **74-95**
    London riotous last year, peaceful this year, **81-122**
    Magna Carta, past and present, **73-85**
    party politics in 1781 and 1783 compared, **83-247**
    reigns of Charles I and George III compared, tyranny and civil war, **84-171**
    reigns of George II and George III, **78-207**, **79-295**, **80-404**, **82-288**
        France in, **79-456**
        the Scotch in, **79-449**
        Whigs and Tories, Britons and Bourbons, **80-404**
    Wolfe and Burgoyne, elder Pitt and North, **78-97**
    year 1782 vs year 1759, **82-345**

Press Warrants (Press Gang). Warrants used to force British subjects into the naval service, sanctioning violence, if necessary. **67-12**, **69-112**, **70-225**,

77-42, 168, **78**-117, **79**-159, 486, **82**-321
    and the French *Lettre de Cachet*, **79**-97
    objection to, **79**-81
Prevost, Augustine (1723-86). British gen officer; served under Wolfe at Quebec, 1759; commanded British southern army, December 1778 and blunted attack on Savannah by D'Estaing and Lincoln, October 9, 1779. **79**-99, 193, 344, 387, **80**-255
    Combe accuses Prevost of burning Fairfield and Norwalk, Connecticut, July 8 and 11, 1779, **80**-7
Price, Richard (1723-91). Dissenter, Presbyterian clergyman; moral philosopher and expert on insurance and finance; supported American and French Revolutions; author of the celebrated *Observations on the Nature of Civil Liberty, the Principles of Government, and the Justice and Policy of the War with America* (1776), for which the City of London awarded him a medal. **76**-2, 12, 16, 28, 34, 69, 238, 284, 314, 315, 337, 341, **77**-29, 160, 276, **78**-7, 23, 36, 39, 45, 234, 462, **79**-105, **80**-37, **81**-15
    and Shelburne, **79**-502
    disloyal republican, **80**-216
    "Nonconformists' Nosegay," **82**-A
    schools the Opposition poets, **79**-31
    traitor, **76**-101, **77**-41
        and republican, **80**-305
Priestley, Joseph (1733-1804). Dissenter, Presbyterian clergyman; patronized by Shelburne; considered "the father of modern chemistry." Opposed the measures of North ministry; supported Shelburne and influenced his brief ministry, 1782-83; emigrated to America, 1794. **78**-234
    and Shelburne, **79**-502, **82**-168
    "Mock Patriot," displeased by Rodney's victory over Langara, **80**-185
The Prime Minister.
    "The Great Man," general comment, **74**-99
Prince of Wales, later George IV (1762-1830). Eldest son of George III. **73**-40, **76**-172, **77**-147, **78**-60, **81**-122
    and the loss of an empire, **81**-170
    friend of Fox, **84**-135
Prince William, later William IV (1765-1837). Third son of George III. The "Royal Tar," served in the British navy during the latter part of the American War. **80**-125, 186, **83**-39, 267
Prior, Matthew (1664-1721). English poet and diplomat. **81**-219, **83**-219, **84**-12
Privateering. **77**-157, 162, 213, 284, **78**-177, 212, 385, **79**-205, 211, 244, 359, **81**-121
    American privateer vs British merchantman, **77**-77
    American privateering and effect on British trade, **78**-268
    and French ships from West Indies, **79**-29
    British merchantmen sail under neutral flags to avoid privateering, **82**-248
    French privateer raiders, **81**-117
    Jones, **78**-464, **79**-197
    objection to, **82**-23
    technique of, **78**-77
    Yankee privateer raids, **84**-66
    **For more on privateering, see:** John Paul Jones.
Prize Poems.
    epitaphs on death of Gen Wolfe, **72**-passim, **73**-passim

       on American War, **76**-223, **80**-241
       on conquest of Quebec, **68**-14, **69**-5, 7
Proctor, **see**: Beauchamp-Proctor.
Protestant Association for the Repeal of the Roman Catholic Relieving Act. The
   act, meant to provide relief to Roman Catholics from certain civil penalties,
   was passed by Parliament in May 1778.  In protest, Protestant Associations
   were formed in Scotland and England, triggering no-popery riots in Edinburgh,
   February 1779, and in London, June 1780.  **80**-28, 41, 42
       **See**:  Gordon Riots and George Gordon.
Prussia, under Frederick the Great (1712-86).  British ally in Seven Years' War.
   **58**-12, **59**-25, **62**-61, **79**-528, **80**-217
Pulaski, Casimir (c. 1748-79).  Polish nobleman, volunteer in American army;
   mortally wounded at Savannah and died October 11, 1779.  **80**-22, **81**-3
Pulteney, William, 1st Earl of Bath (1684-1764).  English politician of preceding
   reigns, his political life ending in 1746; created, with Bolingbroke, the
   concept of a standing opposition to the government.
       and Pitt's apostasy, his elevation to the peerage, **66**-98
       "Epigram.  Natural," criticized for being unsteady in principle, **63**-A
Putnam, Israel (1718-90).  American general; was with Rogers' Rangers and with
   Amherst at Montreal, closing the French and Indian War, 1760; became a Son of
   Liberty, and was at Bunker Hill.  The British recognized his name, often
   repeated in their press.  **59**-28, **75**-26, 27, 29, 110, 150, 162, 188, 238, **76**-
   11, 16, 22, 27, 40, 263, 325, 400, **77**-124, **78**-7
Pynsent, William, 2d Baronet (c. 1679-1765).  MP, 1715-22; wealthy merchant,
   willed his large estate and great fortune to Pitt who, upon his elevation to
   peerage, assumed the title of Earl of Pynsent and Chatham.  **66**-2, 3, 13, 14,
   98, 103

Quartering Act.  **See**: Standing Army.
Quebec Bill, enacted June 22, 1774; called "The Canada Act," or "The Canada
   Bill"; granted French Canadians freedom to practice their Catholic religion;
   also extended Canada's boundaries to the Ohio River; was not received well by
   America and by Britain as evidence of Tory and high church bias.  **74**-6, 8,
   22, 39, 52, 54, 57, 69, 71, 72, 76, 90, 92, 103, 112, 113, 115, 141, 143, 148,
   152, 157, 164, 166-169, 179, 185, 189, 217, **75**-69, 71, 75, 216, **76**-1, 12, 16,
   19, 24, 80, 96, 298, **78**-490, **79**-28, **80**-7
       and corruption, **74**-198
       Irish protest, **75**-230
Quebec, Canada.  **59**-6, 7, 9, 17, 20, 22, 23, 30, 37, **60**-3, 6, 11, 18, 26, 28,
   46, **60**-A (passim), **61**-2, **62**-7, **66**-1, **68**-14, **69**-5, 7, 17, **72**-15, 42, 48, 49,
   **76**-117, **78**-15, **81**-204
       defeat of American rebels, **76**-43
       Delamayne, **62**-A
       Wolfe and Montgomery, **76**-12
       **See also**: Montcalm, Montgomery, and James Wolfe.
Queen Charlotte Sophia, of Mecklenburg-Strelitz (1744-1818).  Married George III,
   September 8, 1761.  **61**-3, 6, 7, 10, **78**-146, 513, **79**-21, 36, 403, **80**-208,
   382, **82**-295
       birth of another child and loss of America, **80**-60
       thirteenth child born, 1778, but England has lost thirteen provinces, an
          empire, **78**-388
Queen Dowager, Augusta of Saxe-Gotha-Altenburg (1719-72).  Married, 1736,
   Frederick, Prince of Wales (1707-51).  George III's mother, alleged mistress
   of Ld Bute.  Her code words are "petticoat rule," implying her influence on

the young king; also "Carlton House," her residence, to which Bute had a backstairs entrance and where he exerted his "secret influence." **68**-23, 35, 91, **69**-119, 188, **70**-23, 37, 41, 54, 182, 197, **71**-6, 85
    "Enchantment," **69**-A
    "An Ode," **61**-A

Rawdon, Francis (1754-1826). British officer, wounded at Bunker Hill; with Clinton at Monmouth, N.J., 1778; raised a provincial Loyalist regiment called "The Volunteers of Ireland," 1778; with Cornwallis in the Carolinas, 1780-81; left for England and captured at sea, 1781, and exchanged after end of American hostilities, 1782. **76**-77, **81**-259, **82**-35, 55, **83**-158

Rebellion, Revolution and Civil War, caused by Oppressive Government.
    another "Political Genealogy" of present civil war, **76**-285
    call to action against tyrants and despots, **73**-56
    "civil war," **72**-9
    objection to anti-American measures of Government which will bring civil war, **74**-147
    oppressive government sparks people's rebellion, **70**-155
    "Pedigree of the Ions," oppression begets revolution, **70**-164
    petition to George III to attend to people's grievances, **71**-117
    a playlet illuminates cause of American War in British tyranny, **78**-442
    "A Political Genealogy," **69**-A
        St. George's Fields and Boston massacres, **73**-86
    prediction of civil war, **70**-195
    Tory criticism of subversive republicans, **72**-12

Reform Movement, Reform Associations, Reformers. Burke's bill on "oeconomy" presents the goals of this movement that relate basically to several types of parliamentary and governmental corruption: "for the better regulation of his Majesty's civil establishments, and of certain public officers; for the limitation of pensions, and the suppression of sundry useless, expensive, and inconvenient places," February 11, 1780. **80**-52, 235, 303, 318, 320, 382, 418 (print)
    and American colonies and Ireland, **82**-85
    and American War, **80**-41
    and corruption, **84**-121
    and George III, **80**-250
    and new ministry of Whigs, **82**-406
    and Parliamentary representation, **80**-268
    and resignation of North, **82**-142
    and system of Parliamentary elections and representation, and America, **82**-154
    and unity of parties, **82**-145
    annual Parliaments and reduction of pensions and sinecures, **80**-344
    associations engage in futile debate, **82**-71
    benefits of, **80**-161
    bribery and representation, **82**-245
    Burke and abolishment of Bd of Trade, **80**-86
    Burke and Fox, **80**-338
    Burke's bill weakens King's prerogative, **80**-191
    Burke's failure to support reform, **80**-172
    Burke's plan, **80**-33, 37, **83**-32
    cause of British disunity, **81**-15
    a corrupt senate cannot reform itself, **85**-24
    corruption, **80**-148

cynicism about, **85**-51
delusive, **81**-68
failure of, **85**-3
failure of Burke's reform, **81**-228
Fox-North Coalition and India Bill, **84**-139
Fox's Westminster Association, **80**-400
leaders satirized, **84**-131
Leonard Smelt, **80**-17
need for economy, **80**-106, 107
need for, opposed by North and proposed by Pitt, **83**-130
objection to Burke's plan by the Establishment, **80**-413
opposed by court junto, **81**-7
Parliament, the budget and American War, **82**-219
Pitt suppresses reform movement, **85**-12
placemen, pensioners, and holders of sinecures, **80**-158
placemen vs reformers, **80**-181
republicans, **80**-351
Rockingham, Pitt and reforms, **83**-3
satire on "new reformers," **80**-150
satirized, **80**-82
    for republicanism and treason, **80**-255
    for treason, **80**-215, 216
seditious reformers vs supporters of King, law and order, **80**-79
to eliminate corruption, **80**-9
unity more important than reform, **80**-306
vs corruption and election laws, **83**-160
Wilkes, Lofft, and Cartwright, **84**-123
Wyvill, **80**-157
Yorkshire petition on reform, February 8, 1780, **81**-42
**See**: Smelt; Wyvill; Yorkshire Association.
Review of Events, or of Politics. (Summary Poems).
additions to Vicar of Bray song to 1782, **82**-388
allegorical review, cause of American War, **76**-230
American colonial development to French entry into war, **78**-19
American contest from Bute's rise to power to British loss of Boston, 1761-76, **76**-22
American contest, Stamp Act to Burgoyne's defeat, **78**-66
American controversy and American War up to its failures, **79**-205
American controversy, 1760-74, **74**-89
American resistance in war, 1775-77, **78**-295
American Revolution in allegory, 1775-80, **80**-200
American troubles, **78**-397
    Grenville's new taxes to 1778, **78**-170
American War and the peace, **85**-4
American War, Lexington to beginning of New York campaign, 1775-June 1776, **76**-223
American War to 1781, **85**-6
  from Whig perspective, **81**-259
American War to 1782, and events and politics of 1782, **83**-32
battles: Lexington, Bunker Hill, Boston Siege and Evacuation, Charleston, S.C., 1775-76, **76**-206
beginning of American War, Concord to Bunker Hill, **75**-162
beginning of war, 1775-76, **77**-134

Britain alone in 1779, state of affairs, **79**-271
British campaigns in America, 1775-77, **78**-12
British liberty, Celtic times to present, **74**-12
British military failures, **78**-171
British Worthies from Alfred to Pitt, **78**-31
Burns on politics and events of American War, Boston Tea Party to accession of younger Pitt, December 1773 to December 1783, **84**-A
Bute's career as tutor to Prince of Wales, future George III, favorite of King George and court advisor during American War, **78**-298
causes of American War, December 1775, **75**-201
causes of and steps leading to present civil war, September 1776, **76**-285
contributing factors leading to American Revolution, 1760 to present, from radical Whig perspective, **75**-223, 276
Delamayne, review of action in Seven Years' War and of events in America, **62**-A
Dunstan on the failure of British army, **77**-183
events leading to horrid rebellion and unnatural Franco-American alliance, **81**-16
failures of British generals, **78**-396
    to November 1777, **77**-240, 258
failures of British to defeat rebel Americans, to March 1777, **77**-314
follies of ministry and Opposition, **78**-556
from 1755 to 1767, "Principal Ministerial Characters," **70**-77
from 1760 to 1769, **69**-108
from 1760 to 1770, **71**-3
from 1763 to 1772, **72**-65
from William III to George III in 1775, radical Whig view, **76**-9, 10
George III's bad traits, 1760-80, stupid, tyrannical, obstinate, **80**-321
Germain's career, Minden to present, 1759-81, **81**-142
goals to achieve, July 1779, **79**-480
history of America through American War, **82**-11
history of American Revolution to 1778, **78**-428
history of Charles Fox, 1775-84, **84**-161
history of English constitution, **82**-207
history, 1755-78, from Whig perspective, **78**-16
Howe's military strategy, 1775-77, **78**-94
James II to George III, 1685-1774, **74**-155
Keppel, Ushant episode and its significance, **79**-143
the merits of 18th century poets, **85**-25
ministries from Bute to younger Pitt, 1760-84, **84**-149
narrative of American contest, **79**-431
negative achievements of politicians, 1774; **74**-157
"A New Song," British successes over the French in 1758 and 1759, **60**-A
news in 1782, **83**-157
"Ode on . . . George III," the situation in 1761 at end of Seven Years' War, **61**-A
of policies and events, 1763-80, from Tory perspective, **80**-34
on British failures, **78**-64 (answer to **77**-258)
Opposition opinion in December 1779, **79**-317
Opposition opinion to April 1779, **79**-28
Parliament's failures, 1768-74, **74**-75, 76
past divisions and internal strife in England, from Tory perspective, **77**-12

Pitt's career, 1760's to death, May 11, 1778, **78-168**
political affairs from accession of George III to ministry of younger Pitt, December 1783, **84-16**
political directions for 1774, **74-156**
political history from Scotch politics to India Bill, 1783, **84-139**
political history, 1760-83, and the peace, **83-3**, 19, 20
political history, 1765-80, and defense of North ministry, **80-306**
politics and American War, May 1776, **76-43**
politics and state of affairs from 1760's to reform movement, 1780-81, **81-7**
post war instability, five ministries from March 1781 to December 1783, **83-202**
present situation, May 1776, **76-212**
principal events, including American War, relating to greatness of Britain, **90-1**
progress of freedom, ancient times to American War, British Tory view, **76-3**
reign of George III from Bute to younger Pitt's ministry, **84-23**, 39
reigns of George I, II, and III, **78-196**
rise and progress of American War, and George III and North, **85-1**
the shameful year 1779, **79-261**
situation after North resigned and Rockingham died, Fox-Shelburne competition, **82-145**
the situation as of January 1776, anti-court view, **76-49**
situation between Britain and America, 1774, **74-16**
situation in Britain, regarding Europe and America, **78-474**
situation in December 1778, **78-81**
situation in early 1780, **80-217**
situation in January 1776, Whig perspective, **76-298**
situation in January 1782, American War, etc., **82-219**
situation in June 1782, as laureat Whitehead explains, and winding down American War, **82-396**
situation in 1777, **77-164**
situation in 1780-82, **82-22**
situation in 1783, Fox and Pitt, **84-165** (**83-234** revised)
state of affairs to December 1777, **77-292** (continuation of **77-183**)
    Government's view, **77-149** (answer to **77-183** and **77-292**)
state of the nation by Tucker challenged, 1778, **78-151**
state of the nation, July 1779, **79-353**, 442
state of the nation, July 1782, **82-272**
"Things As They Are," **78-A**
the 3d Parliament of George III's reign, 1774-80, corrupted, influenced by King George, and has lost America, **80-112**
trends from 1760 to 1777, **77-155**
waste of American War, Fox-North Coalition, and taxes, **84-179**
Wilkes' career, 1757-72, **73-18**
Wilkes' career to 1776, **76-140**
the year 1772, **73-34**
the year 1777, **78-398**
the year 1780, **80-325**
the year 1783, Fox and Pitt, **84-163**
younger Pitt's career from end of American War to his ministry in 1784, **85-12**

**See also:** Rebellion ("Political Genealogies" and "Pedigree of the Ions"), and the Times.

Richmond, 3d Duke of. **See:** Charles Lennox.

Rigaud, Pierre-François de, Marquis de Vaudreuil-Cavagnal (1704-78). Governor of Canada 1755-60; French commander at Montreal, capitulated to General Amherst, September 8, 1760. **60**-29

Rigby, Richard (1722-88). MP, 1745-88. Tory placeman. Friend, secretary, and lieutenant of Duke of Bedford, and member of inner circle of "Bloomsbury gang." Paymaster of the forces, 1768-82, a place that made him very rich. Consistently opposed Wilkes and conciliation to America, such as repeal of Stamp Act, 1766. Supported coercive measures of North against America; and opposed Dunning's resolution and reform movement, 1780. **62**-18, **66**-60, **70**-32, **72**-1, 6, **74**-173, **75**-120, **76**-16, 67, **77**-82, **78**-171, **79**-131, 200, 202, 284, 292, 310, **80**-10, 33, 62, 123, 226, 270, 319, 343, 410, **81**-186, 259, **82**-9, 193

  and the Fast, **79**-196
  opposes reforms, **80**-318

Rights: Civil and Natural Rights of British Subjects. **63**-56, 96, 162, 172, **64**-19, **65**-35, **66**-16, **67**-6, **68**-19, **69**-3, 9, 20, 21, 27, 39, 49, 57, 69, 87, 123, 127, 129, 138, 179, 183, 184, 210, 237, **70**-9, 25, 47, 223, 241, **71**-14, 16, 19, 37, 39, 64, **75**-1, 9, 10, 223, 227, **76**-1, 6, 49, 58, 194, 281, 323, **78**-357, **79**-49, **80**-68

  "Address to Britannia," **70**-A
  and George III, **76**-24
  and Ireland, **80**-40
  and Wilkes, **69**-134
  Bill of Rights Society, **73**-51
  blessings of peace and natural rights of man, **80**-302
  Bute and Stuarts, **75**-229, 245
  Captain Morris defends freedom's cause and natural rights against Pitt and Tory oppressors, **85**-33
  decay of liberty, **78**-361
  defense of freedom, as in America, means "public spirit," **77**-23
  defense of Whig ideology, **84**-2
  "Epitaph at Thebes," **65**-A
  Fox, champion of rights of man, **84**-104
  French praise of English liberty, **65**-81
  George III's tyranny, **79**-517
  Junius, **69**-233
  legal liberty and Mansfield, **78**-453
  Mason advises younger Pitt to protect natural rights from power of corruption, **82**-14
  "On Political Justice," **66**-A
  the people will defend its rights against oppression, **73**-56
  Pratt as defender of civil rights, **72**-95
  Savile, guardian of civil rights, **83**-260
  slavery in America and rights of man, **83**-31
  3d Parliament, 1774-80, yields natural rights of man, **80**-135
  "Verses Extempore," **65**-A
  West Indian slavery and rights of man, **78**-468
  Whig assertion of "the Rights of Men," **82**-185
  Wilkes stands for liberty and rights of people, **73**-102
  **See also:** Charles Pratt (Ld Camden), John Wilkes, and Society of Supporters of Magna Carta and the Bill of Rights.

Rights: Liberty of the Press and Libels. The legality of this issue was resolved and the definition of the freedom of the press was broadened in the early 1770's; thus it became legally possible for the press to publish and debate a variety of opinions about Government's policies and its manner of waging the American War. **63**-53, 105, 122, **64**-65, **65**-16, 20, 32, 132, 137, 148 (print), **70**-28, 51, 73, 89, 102, 153, **71**-26, **72**-61, **73**-10, **74**-12, 46, 149, **75**-90, **77**-205, 302
    Churchill's *Duellist*, **64**-A
    John Miller, printer of *London Evening Post*, **70**-206
    a wish to suppress the speech of "patriot" opponents of American War, **78**-23
    **See**: John Miller, John Williams, and William Murray (Ld Mansfield).

Rights: Magna Carta. Foundation of English liberties, issued at Runnimede June 1215, in reign of King John, against whose tyranny the barons had rebelled. The charter came to be interpreted as a grant to the people of rights that Stuart kings were withholding: trial by jury, principle of *habeas corpus*, right of Parliament to control taxation. **64**-2, **70**-196, **71**-26, 64, **73**-85, **74**-23, 106, 111, 176, **75**-13, 17, 156, **76**-6, **77**-23
    must be preserved, **77**-153
    "On his Majesty's . . . View . . . of Runnimede," **62**-A
    tribute to Runnimede, **82**-185

Riots and Rioters, Civil Discord. **68**-110, **69**-112, 184, 186, 193, **70**-237, **71**-4, 15
    Brentford Election riot, **69**-141. **See also**: George Clark.
    Cowper's
        "Address to the Mob,"**79**-A
        "A Hint to . . . Keppel," **79**-A
        "Modern Mobbing," **79**-A
    "the curst Riot Act," **73**-105
    Edinburgh riot, **80**-21
    English extremism, **79**-222
    London Gordon Riots, **80**-42. **See also**: Gordon Riots.
    martial law and America, **74**-53
    Middlesex Election riots, **68**-37, **69**-8, 197. **See also**: Middlesex County and John Wilkes.
    St. George's Fields' "Massacre," May 10, 1768, **68**-3, 17, 21, 71, 81, 121, **69**-8, 12, 29, 34, 116, 136, 151, 163, 187, 194, 214, **70**-35, 36, 222, **72**-1, **73**-4, 61, 86, **74**-146, 179, **75**-223, **76**-10, **78**-16, 25, 44
        "Alphabetical," **69**-A
        "Conversation," **69**-A
        "Epigram," **68**-A
        "On the Merchants' Address," **69**-A
        "Poetical Wish," **69**-A
        "Political Genealogy," **69**-A
        "Teague's Address," **69**-A
        **See also**: William Allen, Jr.

Rivington, James (1724-1802). **See**: Part I of Index.

Robertson, William (1721-93). Scottish author of *The History of America*, 1777.
    should write a history of the American War, a civil war, **81**-11

Robinson, John (1727-1802). MP, 1764-1802. North's trusted undersecretary, political agent, and confidant, 1770-82. Did not join North in the coalition with Fox, and soon defected to the younger Pitt. **85**-13

Rockingham, 2d Marquess. **See**: Charles Watson-Wentworth.

Rockingham Ministry, July 13, 1765-August 2, 1766 and March 26, 1782-July 1, 1782. **See:** Charles Watson-Wentworth, 2d Marquess of Rockingham, Rockingham Ministry.

Rodney, George Brydges (1718-92). MP, 1751-54, 1759-74, 1780-82. British admiral; governor and commander-in-chief of Newfoundland, 1749-50; served under Boscawen at Louisburg, 1758; stationed in West Indies up to American War; gained spectacular victories over Spanish (Cape Finisterre and Cape St. Vincent, January 8 and 16, 1780), and Dutch (St. Eustatius, February 3, 1781), and French (Battle of the Saints, April 9-12, 1782). **80**-27, 41, 125, 128, 129, 143, 240, 241, 249, 252, 282, 325, 350, 352, 393, 394, 417, **81**-22, 30, 66, 89, 107, **82**-18, 19, 25, 34, 103, 143, 213, 243, 244, 255, 256, 274, 338, 339, 343, 352, 355, 373, 375, **83**-10, 32, 43, 154, 158, 282, **84**-9, 18, 31, **85**-55

    and British navy repel menaces of France and Spain, **75**-301
    and Burke, **81**-130, 146
    and De Grasse, **82**-1, 7, 46
        thrashes, **83**-3
        victory over, **83**-11, 25
    and D'Estaing in West Indies, **80**-212, 262
    and Keppel, **82**-98, 151, 275
    and Langara, **80**-185, 213, 257, **81**-126
    and Rockingham ministry, **82**-399
    and St. Eustatius, **81**-149, 157, 200, **82**-399
        sacking of, **81**-215
    and Sandwich, **80**-46, **81**-217, 222
    and Tobago, **82**-106
    Battle of the Saints, **82**-48, 63, 80, **83**-59
        victory, **82**-139, 194, 195, 196, 231, 232
    capture of St. Eustatius and reaction, **81**-119
    captured Martinique, February 13, 1762, **62**-34, 36
    Cowper's "On the Victory by . . . Rodney," **80**-A
    defeat of Dutch "Van Trowser," Governor Johannes de Graef, of St. Eustatius, **81**-183
    ends war with great success, **82**-221
    financial need, **81**-150
    gift from London City Council, **80**-100, 103
    honored for victories over Dutch, **81**-256
    Howe and Keppel, **81**-202
    many naval victories, **83**-26, **90**-1
    Martinique, **80**-109
    model of courageous leadership, **80**-9
    praise of fleet officers, **81**-218
    praised for victories, **81**-21
    recall by Rockingham ministry, **82**-109, 123
    restored British sovereignty on seas, **82**-182, 217, 278, 316, 317
    saved the empire, **82**-180
    "Song," on Martinique, **62**-A
    superior to Keppel, **80**-297
    triumphs over Spanish navy, **80**-428 (print)
    victories raise British hopes, **80**-281
    victories will restore America to Britain, **80**-424 (print)
    victory over Langara and Spanish fleet, **80**-101, 392
    **See also:** D'Estaing, De Grasse, Langara, Rodney's Engagements and Victories under American War, British Navy.

Rogers, James (d. 1775). Young American law student in England, drowned when returning home to participate in the rebellion.
"Paulus. A Monody," **75**-212, **89**-2
Roman Catholicism (Popery). **64**-102, **65**-79, 117, **66**-93, **69**-6, 268, **72**-67, **73**-84, **74**-38, 52, 72, 76, 90, 141, 147, 148, 164, 166, 167, 168, **75**-216, **76**-12, 199, 308, 376, **77**-197
    America vs, **76**-93
    among King's Friends, **78**-246
    and General Fast in Ireland, **80**-137
    and George III, **79**-403
    anti-papist sentiment, **80**-265
    fears of, in Britain, Canada, and Ireland, **78**-392
    in Ireland, vs bill for Roman Catholic relief, **72**-175
    no popery riots, **80**-21, 42
    opposition to repeal of penal acts against Roman Catholics, **79**-28
    Puritans vs Papists, **77**-314
    toleration of, **79**-36
    **See also**: Gordon Riots, Protestant Association, Quebec Bill.
Ross, John Lockhart (1721-90). MP, 1761-74. Scottish admiral; served at Quiberon Bay, 1758-60, and in the Channel, North Sea, and Mediterranean, 1779-82, including relief of Gibraltar, 1780-81; assigned mission to stop raids of Paul Jones. Voted consistently with the court, Bute, Grenville, Grafton, and North. **79**-440
    and Jones, **79**-477
    and Rodney, **81**-218
The *Royal George*. The 100-gun British warship sank without warning at Spithead, August 29, 1782, with considerable loss of life: over 400 seamen and officers including Admiral Kempenfelt, and 200 women. **82**-68, 84, 179, 206, 305, **83**-22, 25, 32, 230, **85**-4
    and Admiral Kempenfelt, **82**-87
Rumbold, Thomas (1736-91). MP, 1770-75, 1780-90. Clive's aide-de-camp at Plassey, 1757; director of East India Co., indicted for mismanagement and corruption, but acquitted, June 1783; supported North ministry to its end. **83**-206
Russell, John, 4th Duke of Bedford (1710-71). Head of Bedford or Bloomsbury "gang," advocated the strict assertion of British authority over American colonies. Held many court appointments; ambassador to Paris to negotiate (with Bute) peace, 1762-63; influential from 1760, his party allegedly dictating policy, after his death, for North ministry. **62**-5, **63**-14, **65**-113, **66**-60, 96, **68**-10, **69**-11, 108, 109, **70**-111
Russell, William (1639-83). Whig martyr, with Hampden and Sidney. Third son of 1st Duke of Bedford, executed July 1683 for complicity in Rye House Plot to murder Charles II and brother Duke of York, later James II.
    "To the Memory of William Lord Russell," **73**-A
    **See also**: Whig Tradition, Invocation of Heroes and Saints in Whig Pantheon.
Russia, and the Armed Neutrality, 1779-80. The combination of Northern European powers (Russia, Prussia, Denmark, Sweden, Holland) proclaimed by Catherine II, February 29, 1780, to protect neutral trade from British interference. **79**-528, **80**-197, 217, 275, 345, 394, **82**-18
Rutledge, Edward (1749-1800). American politician and officer from South Carolina; served with Lincoln at Savannah, October 9, 1779; captured when Charleston surrendered, May 12, 1780; member of Congress and signer of Declaration of Independence. **80**-5

Sackville, George, Viscount. **See**: George Sackville Germain.
Sackville, John Frederick (1745-99). MP, 1768-69; then House of Lords, where he supported North's ministry; nephew of George Sackville Germain, ambassador to Paris, 1783-89.
    *Noble Cricketers*, **78-A**
St. Clair, Arthur (1737-1818). Scottish officer with Amherst at Louisburg, and with Wolfe at Quebec; general in American army, forced to abandon Ft. Ticonderoga, July 2-5, 1777, by Burgoyne. **77-137, 142**
St. Eustatius (St. Eustacia). Dutch island in West Indies, captured by Rodney and Vaughan, February 3, 1781; a great *entrepôt* of neutral trade with the colonies during the American War, full of booty which Rodney confiscated. **See**: Rodney's Engagements and Victories under American War, British Navy; and George Brydges Rodney.
St. George's Fields' Massacre. **See**: Riots and Rioters, and William Allen, Jr.
St. Stephen. The Patron Saint of Parliament. **See**: Parliament.
Sandwich, 4th Earl. **See**: John Montagu.
Saunders, Charles (1713-75). MP, 1750-75. British admiral, assisted Wolfe and Amherst in the Canada campaigns; friend of Admiral Keppel; a Rockingham Whig; disapproved British neglect of Corsica and voted against unseating Wilkes. **59-9, 16, 60-6, 48, 62-7, 66-1, 69-17, 70-29, 73-5, 77-10**
    "Advertisement from France," **60-A**
    and American War, **75-301, 76-16**
        blames loss of empire on "Stuart pride," **76-9**
        death, and American War that will lose the empire he had won, **76-256**
        death, unhappy at civil discord that will lose an empire, **77-224**
        French intervention justifies continuation of American War, **79-1**
    and Keppel, **82-91**
    panegyric by Edward Thompson, **76-360**
    Saunders' ghost defends Keppel, **79-404, 535**
    Saunders' ghost praises Keppel, **79-67**
Savile, George, 8th Baronet (1726-84). MP, 1759-83. Captain against Jacobites in 1745 uprising; Rockingham Whig, in opposition to Bute, Grenville, Grafton, and North, from 1759; supported Wilkes; urged an immediate end to American War, 1778; presented Wyvill Yorkshire petition for reform to House of Commons, February 8, 1780; detested the Fox-North Coalition. **69-13, 70-2, 101, 103, 114, 156, 195, 71-3, 72-1, 6, 75-35, 76-290, 353, 77-5, 78-14, 17, 259, 299, 79-38, 100, 510, 80-10, 18, 24, 64, 220, 295, 316, 400, 81-186, 82-193, 285, 84-60, 69, 194**
    in Portland ministry, **83-29**
    in retirement, **83-260**
    *Ode to Palinurus*, **70-A**
    resigns Parliament seat, **83-178**
Sawbridge, John (1732-95). MP, 1768-95. Brother of Catharine Macaulay (née Sawbridge); alderman of London from 1769, sheriff, 1770, ld mayor, 1775-76; founding member of Society of Supporters of Bill of Rights, 1769, supported Wilkes and opposed North and the measures against America, and at the end supported Fox against younger Pitt. Considered a radical of the republican type. **69-21, 126, 129, 250, 70-101, 192, 72-1, 63, 93, 73-3, 111, 75-19, 255, 76-28, 77-160, 78-4, 43, 80-400, 82-85**
    *Ode to Palinurus*, **70-A**
    re-elected as representative of London, **84-191**
Sayre, Stephen (1736-1818). Merchant, born on Long Island, N.Y., and opened a

bank in London; "Yankee" sheriff with William Lee, 1773. Arrested October 23, 1775, and committed to the Tower on charge of high treason, for allegedly plotting to seize King George; his plea for *habeas corpus* granted by Ld Mansfield, he was released October 27, 1775, and subsequently discharged for lack of evidence.

    alleged treason, **75**-62, 270
    in Bill of Rights Society, **73**-51

Schuyler, Philip John (1733-1804). American general from old patrician Dutch family of New York; fought in the French and Indian War, Lake George, N.Y., September 1755 and Oswego, 1757; in Albany served as commissary supplying Amherst's forces, 1760; delegate of 2d Continental Congress, 1779-80; Gates took his position when he did not stop Burgoyne, 1777.

    Burgoyne's offensive, **77**-137, 242
    defeat at Oswego, **57**-2

Scot(s), Scotch, Scottish. Targeted for satire from the time when Pitt, a national hero, resigned as PM (1761), and Ld Bute assumed the leadership and then negotiated the Peace of Paris (1763); also satirized when they migrated, with Bute's encouragement and example, in appreciable numbers to London and exerted an influence on government and society. **63**-4, 29, 33, 59, 63, 174 (print), **64**-26, 31-33, 56, 72, **65**-120, 121, **66**-28, 84, **74**-171, **76**-380 (same as **76**-53, with different title), **78**-25, 128, 142, 144, 193, 450, 547, **80**-183, **83**-A (same as **76**-295)

    advised ruinous American War, **77**-237
    Allen, Wilkes and liberty, Bute's bribery, **68**-122 to 124 (prints)
    America abhors, **78**-516
    America, Britain and Scotland are right, and now must compromise, **76**-53
    America distrusts, **79**-61
    and American War, **76**-17, 221, **80**-7
        and corruption, **76**-39
        caused by Scotch, Mansfield and Bute, **78**-127
    and Bute, **64**-8, 10
        favored by King, **68**-9
        introduce factional strife, **64**-50
        vs Wilkes, **64**-105
    and corruption responsible for British decline, **78**-207
    and defeat at Yorktown, **81**-33
    and despotic ministry and America, **75**-129
    and Dunning's motion, **80**-295
    and English resistance to excise tax, **63**-38, 39
    and the General Fast, **76**-147
    and Gen. Howe, **81**-231
    and James Wright, Governor of Georgia, **79**-9
    and London mayor and council, **69**-247
    and loss of America, **78**-68
    and loss of English liberty, **69**-92
    and party spirit, **82**-218
    and Stamp Tax and America, **66**-110
    and Stuart maxims favored at court, **81**-201
    and Tories dominate politics, **64**-40
    and unjust American War, **76**-199
    and venal court and Wilkes, **69**-132
    and Wilkes, **63**-3, 23, 81, **68**-79, 106, **70**-238
        and enemy, **68**-32

>        and liberty, **68**-119
>        and Whig Pantheon, **68**-103
>        dislike Wilkes, but Presbyterians adore him, **68**-89
>        *North Briton*, No. 45, **63**-25, 46, 94
> anniversary of Allen's murder, **69**-163
> "Answer to the Epigrams," **64**-A
> as rebels and traitors, responsible for St. George's Fields' massacre, Scotch like those who voted for Quebec Bill, **74**-179
> as targets for satire, **74**-7
> assassin Alex Dun and Wilkes, **63**-44
> assassin Captain Forbes and Wilkes, **63**-32
> attack on Scotch, **77**-20
> "A Bad Omen," **65**-A
> before Scotch were rebels, now are loyal and the English are seditious, **79**-449
> blamed by Chatterton for English and American troubles, **70**-36
> blamed for decline of Britain and king's abuse of power, **76**-98
> blamed for economic distress and emigration, **66**-139
> blamed for loss of tobacco trade with America, **79**-377
> blamed for poor peace of 1763, **78**-121
> blamed for premature end of Seven Years' War, poor treaty, cider tax, and corruption of Parliament and King, **65**-110
> blamed for reverses, **79**-194
> blamed for ruinous court policies, **78**-498
> bring arbitrary power and oppression, **69**-102
> *British Coffee House*, **64**-A
> Bute and Jacobites and loss of America, **77**-33
> Bute and peace, **62**-6, 11, **64**-1
> Bute and Scotch bring war and ruin, **82**-4
> Bute and Wilkes, **64**-10, 105, **65**-143
> Bute's peace sell-out to France, **63**-168
> cause American War, **76**-55
> cause civil war and destruction of empire, **76**-292
> cause of civil war, **75**-33
> charged with death of the empire, **78**-44
> Churchill's *Prophecy of Famine*, **63**-A
> Churchill's satire, **64**-18
> Colvill praises Paoli, **71**-1
> Colvill, Scotch patriotically support war against France and America, **79**-7
> corrupt, **79**-17, **80**-40, 90, **83**-20
>    Parliament vs Wilkes, **64**-10
>    "Scottish politicians" cause ruin of Britain, **76**-75
> corruption and English liberty, **73**-107
> corruption and Wilkes and liberty, **69**-203
> court dominated by Scots, satirized, **76**-32
> crimes and American War, **76**-112
> criticized for urging war against America, **78**-102
> critics are partial, **67**-36
> "cruel measures" responsible for American War, **77**-297
> death of Allen, **68**-121 (print), **69**-12
> depopulation and emigration to America, **78**-5
> despotic, **65**-131, **77**-22, **80**-40, 90

        and treacherous, **78**-8
        despotic influence, **75**-17
        power banishes English liberty, **71**-133
"dirty Scotch" in government places and church, **73**-41
disliked without distinction as to class, **68**-93
displeased at Wilkes' freedom, **68**-27
do not believe in English traditional freedom, **78**-522
dominate administration, **73**-69
dominate court, **70**-24
dominate England, **65**-83
dominate North ministry, **79**-388
dominate venal and corrupt court, **63**-6
domination results in England's decline, **66**-100
driving the country to ruin, **78**-482
Duke of Cumberland
        death of, **65**-108, 143
        defeated French and Scotch in '45 rebellion, **65**-94
        pleased at his death, **65**-144
eager for American War, **76**-42
        Scottish view of Bunker Hill satirized, **78**-71
effect on nation should Scottish Stuarts rule, **65**-20
endanger English freedom, **69**-20
endanger throne, **69**-14
enemies of England and America, **78**-445
English prejudice against Scottish culture, food, clothing, religion,
    intolerance, and Jacobitism, **63**-16
epistle to James T. Oswald, **89**-3
failure of liberty in Scotland, **69**-181
false and fraudulent, **78**-523
favored at court, **62**-48, **63**-57, 91, **69**-267
fierce Scottish troops at conquest of Quebec, **68**-14
France enjoys Bute, Tories, Scots, Jacobites as allies, **63**-80
France rejoices at Scottish influence on King, **80**-404
friends of younger Pitt, **84**-183
gain by cider and perry tax, **63**-108
gain from American War, **76**-165
gain from Parliament's corruption, **80**-192
government officers forced to leave America, **76**-244
greedy, **65**-115, **75**-286, **81**-51
        and despotic, **73**-162
        and rebellious, **65**-44
        for gold, **63**-126
hackneyed theme, **64**-105
hatred of, **65**-63
have best bar orator in Mansfield and helped conquer Canada, **77**-3
have financial security at English expense, **71**-125
in Burgoyne's army, **77**-143
in the period 1761-66 when Bute exerted his influence on court, **68**-23
influence and enslavement of America and England, **73**-174
influence and Parliament, **71**-96
influence brings ruin to the nation, **74**-24, **79**-37
influence on King and corruption, **73**-55
interest at court, **69**-136

invade England and seek their fortune, **63-186** (print)
Jacobite Scotch cause oppressive civil war against America and tradition
 of freedom, **76-339**
Jacobites and Scots and anti-American policy, **75-161**
Jacobites and Tories, **63-146**
Jacobites create difficulties for America, **69-268**
Jacobites enslave England, **73-82**
join war against Bourbons, especially Scottish nobility, **83-59**
King favors Scots, **75-223**, **76-10**, **78-451**, **79-406**
    treacherous Scottish Jacobites, **78-357**
King poisoned by "Scottish education," i.e., Bute, **77-295**
lead British to ruin and destruction, **78-56**
leadership causes decline of England, **76-367**
leadership responsible for American War, **76-295**
a list of Scots in office, blamed for ruining British empire, **75-244**
London freemen vs Stuarts and rebels, **71-44**
love liberty like Corsicans, English, and Americans, **69-3**
militia, "Defensive Band," **81-232**
murder William Allen, **69-12**
need for British to rebel against venal Scottish government, **75-310**
North and Scottish allies forced to come to terms with America after
 Burgoyne's defeat, **78-346**
objection to Bute's Scotch Toryism, **75-245**
objection to demagoguery of anti-Scottish sentiment, **71-4**
objection to Scottish influence, **74-72**
objection to Scottish Jacobites and court's war policy, **75-67**
objection to "Scottish politics" regarding America, **74-27**
patriotic Scottish song of freedom and independence, **76-185**
peace, **62-22**
peers and new prime minister, North, **70-112**
penetrate English politics through royal family, **63-151**
persecution of Wilkes, **69-263**
places in administration, **65-42**
poet praises Paoli, **67-1**
praise of Mason's satire on Scots, **73-97**
praise of Scottish officers who fought American rebels, **77-58**
prophecy of Bute's execution, **65-109**
prosper at court, **69-53**
prosperous, **80-325**
protest at denigration of Wilkes and liberty, **64-9**
protest at Scottish domination of England, poor peace, and new taxes, **63-185** (print)
proud, **78-444**
rebellious, **65-67**
rebels, **65-1**
regiment responsible for St. George's Fields riot, **70-222**
rejoice at Churchill's death, **65-87**
responsible for American War, **75-247**, **78-520**
restoration of forfeited estates to loyal Scots, **84-175**
ruin government and oppress Whigs, **69-260**
St. George's Fields riot, **68-3**
a satirist fears hired assassins of Scottish Junto, **80-37**
satirized, **63-136 to 141**, **74-7**, **163**, **75-118**, **77-22**, **79-108**, **276**, **81-135**,
 **83-19**

         among those who profit from American War, **77**-174
         as despotic, **77**-22
         as chief grievance, **75**-218
         by Mason, **73**-7
         court favorites, **81**-47
         depopulation and American War, **76**-213
         for gaining at expense of England, **77**-72
         for wishing to suppress freedom of speech, **77**-302
         "Scottish Junto" and secret cabinet, **78**-27
    savagely criticized, **78**-12, 16
    Scotch in administration must be cashiered to bring peace, **80**-226
    Scotch responsible for American policy, **75**-247
    Scottish crimes and American War, **76**-112
    "Scottish Faction" ruthlessly pursue American War, **76**-102
    Scottish influence and American War, **76**-12
    Scottish influence and Bute cause Britain's failure, **76**-225
    Scottish influence causes English decline, **74**-24
    Scottish Jacobites and American War, **76**-9
    Scottish Jacobites cause American rebellion, **76**-59
    Scottish Jacobites will suppress American rebellion, **75**-52
    Scottish Junto at court and American will to resist tyranny, **75**-306
    "Scottish Junto", secret cabinet satirized, **78**-27
    Scottish Murray politician is "out," **82**-225
    Scottish oppression source of all evils in England, **71**-54
    Scottish rebels and American rebels, **75**-76
    Scottish soldier will free his country from "unjust rebellion," **75**-256
    Scottish soldiers vs American rebels, **75**-164
    Scottish Tories and Jacobites attacked by Whigs, **76**-323
    Scottish view of American War, satirized, **76**-212
    self-interested and America, **68**-20
    selfish, **80**-217, **83**-19
         as Britain suffers, **79**-271
         Scotch and American War, **76**-91
    "The sentence pass'd," **64**-A
    should return home, **63**-64, **64**-74
         after peace settlement, **63**-153
    soldiers at Gibraltar and Quebec, **85**-32
    soldiers in North America, **62**-7
    still influential in new North ministry, **70**-152
    subvert English liberty, **63**-172
    *The Thistle*, **73**-A
    Tories and Scotch in power, **78**-26
    Tories drive out Whigs even to America, **69**-19
    Tory, corrupt, despotic, the ruin of Britain, **80**-90
    Tory influence and loss of Corsica, **69**-21
    Tory Scots and Jacobites cause American War, **76**-73
    Tory Scots dominate England and endanger Whig Liberty, **73**-107
    traitors, **73**-146
    treacherous, **78**-443
    Trumbull's *McFingal*, satire on American Tories, **75**-13
    unable to help dying Britain, **77**-290
    undermine English liberty, **69**-195
    union with England accurst, **81**-246

urge militant war against America, **78**-49
venal, **81**-51
assassins, **80**-16
vs America, **75**-13
vs Mansfield and Scotch, **79**-330
vs Scottish infiltration of England, bringing exploitation and corruption, **78**-223
vs Scottish Jacobites, **64**-91
vs Scottish writers and Bute's peace, **63**-22
view of American rebels, **77**-255
"weazel Scotch" satirized, **77**-18
why Scotch fight America, **75**-138
**See also:** John Stuart, Earl of Bute.
Scotch Junto. **See:** King's Friends.
Scott, James (1733-1814). Clergyman, author. Hack polemicist writing under the pen-name of Anti-Sejanus and Old Slyboots in the *Public Advertiser* for Ld Sandwich; wrote against the repeal of the Stamp Act, **65**-5, 75, 134, **66**-9, 40, 55, 63, 91, 92, 114, 118, 119, **70**-220, **73**-7, **82**-401
"On St. Sepulchre's Bells," **65**-A
Scottish Authors: John Dalrymple, John Home, David Hume, James Macpherson, Tobias Smollett. **See:** Part II of Index for these authors; and Scottish Poets in Part I of Index.
Scottish Emigration.
complaint at "extraordinary emigration of the Highlanders," **74**-84
eight hundred oppressed Scotch from Galloway seek freedom and equality in America, **74**-63
epidemic of Scottish emigration to America stopped by American War, **78**-5
oppression and various grievances caused by Tories and Scotch result in emigration, **79**-384
protest at Highland emigration caused by "hard oppression," ruthless monopoly, "barb'rous avarice," change from raising sheep and goats to crop production, **76**-99
Scottish depopulation causes difficulty in raising recruits for American War, **76**-213
Scottish "influence" is oppressive and causes emigration, **75**-17
want and oppression force poor Scotch to emigrate, **74**-47
**See also:** Emigration.
Scottish Soldiers Killed at Bunker Hill. **75**-6, **76**-37, 38, 83 (same as **75**-6)
Secker, Thomas (1693-1768). Bishop of Oxford, 1737-58; dean of St. Paul's, 1750-58; archbishop of Canterbury, 1758-68. Baptised, confirmed, crowned, and married George III to Princess Charlotte; advocated establishing bishoprics in the American colonies. **65**-29
Secret Influence. **See:** King's Friends.
Sejanus, Lucius Aelius (d. 31 A.D.). Favorite and minister of the Roman emperor Tiberius; executed for plotting to seize the throne.
and North, **80**-384, **81**-177
**See also:** James Scott, "Anti-Sejanus."
Selwyn, George Augustus (1719-91). MP, 1747-91. A notorious seeker of sinecures.
opposes awarding Keppel the Freedom of the City, **79**-137
Tory placeman, defends monarchy and opposes reform, **80**-181
Seven Years' War (French and Indian War), 1755-63.
Beginning, **55**-1, 2, **56**-1, **57**-1, 2, **58**-1, 2, 3, **64**-7

End and Peace, **59**-27, **61**-2, 45, 48, **62**-3, 4, 7, 8, 11, 14, 15, 17, 18, 19, 22, 24, 25, 27, 29, 31, 35, 37, 38, 42, 43, 49, 55, 58, 62, 66
    and American colonies, **60**-40
    passim, **60**-A
    "Survey . . .," **62**-A
  The Peace, **63**-1, 2, 5, 9, 17, 22, 27, 34, 38, 55, 63, 68, 79, 80, 82, 98, 117, 129, 132, 147, 153, 172, 174, 177, 184
    Churchill's *Epistle to Hogarth* and *Prophecy of Famine*, **63**-A
  The Peace and "the Shameful Peace," **63**-83, 113, 114, 116, 168, 175, 176, 179, 180, **64**-1, 35, 44, 48, 87, 107, **65**-3, 7, 30, 57, 83, 104, 109, 121, 130, **66**-13, 45, **68**-79, **69**-13, 60, 69, 108, 109, **70**-116, **71**-3, **75**-223, **78**-27, **79**-1, **80**-12, 34
    and Scots, **78**-121
    the fount of all the troubles since, **81**-7
  Pitt's conduct in the War, **66**-5, **66**-7
    "the Seer," **61**-A
  **See also**: William Pitt, Earl of Chatham.
  Victories and Conquests, summaries, **62**-61, **63**-60, **64**-3, 41, **73**-5
    Amherst's successes in America, **78**-251
    Delamayne's *Oliviad*, **62**-A
    "An Ode to George III," **61**-A
  **See also**: France (and Britain), 1755-63; West Indies and Seven Years' War.
Seven Years' War and American War. **77**-27, **79**-1
  contrasted, **82**-10
  "Royal Americans" in Seven Years' War, **90**-1
Seward, Anna. **See**: Part I of Index.
Shebbeare, John (1709-88). "Venal" Tory Jacobite and political pamphleteer, granted a pension of £200 p.a. by Bute; enemy of Wilkes; supported government's coercive policy and wrote against Burke, 1775, and Price, 1776. **70**-221, **73**-7, **75**-62, 63, 78, 114, 184, **76**-17, 18, 73, 194, 226, 298, 337, 341, **77**-18, 100, **78**-43, 498, **80**-40
  Churchill's *Author*, **63**-A
  **See also**: Shebbeare in Index, Part I.
Shelburne, 2d Earl; and Shelburne's Ministry. **See**: William Fitzmaurice Petty.
Sheridan, Richard Brinsley (1751-1816). MP, 1780-1812. Playwright, lyricist, theatre manager; partisan of Fox and Burke. **80**-382, **81**-118, **83**-19, 32, **84**-15, 16, 35, 55, 166
  joins the Rockingham ministry and leaves the theatre, **82**-202
  **See**: Park I of Index.
Shipley, Jonathan (1714-88). Bishop of St. Asaph. Opponent of North's coercive policy.
  praise of, in Minority Opposition, **78**-14
  praised by anti-court satirist, **80**-37
  support of America, **75**-186
  **See also**: Church of England, Bishops.
Siddons, Sarah (1755-1831). Famous English actress. **83**-126
  her fame and political leaders, **83**-195
Sidney, Algernon (1622-83). Whig patron saint; fought in the Civil War; martyred by Charles II. Son of the 2d Earl of Leicester, executed December 1683 for alleged complicity in the Rye House Plot to murder Charles II and his brother the Duke of York, later James II. **76**-326, **78**-44
  **See also**: Whig Tradition, Invocation of Whig Pantheon, Algernon Sidney.

Slavery, Slaves. Political slaves, corruption and bribery of "slaves"; oppression as slavery. **66**-23, 135, **67**-7, **69**-21, 54, 94, 98, **70**-31, **71**-21, 50, **72**-23, 73, **73**-82, 85, 103, **74**-136, 162, 174, **75**-97, **76**-7, 8, 11, 51, 72, 118, 134, 361, **78**-289
    Popery, **74**-22
    Stuart slavery, **78**-511
    "titled slaves," the nobility, **73**-106
    Whigs love liberty, Tories are slaves to the King, **81**-185

Slavery, Slaves and Slave Trade. **58**-13, **63**-54, 56, **66**-115, **69**-3, 21, **72**-75, **73**-2, 11, 68, **76**-376, **77**-74
    American slave owners as "spoilers," **83**-31
    anti-slavery, to "an American planter," probably from Virginia, **80**-366
    Beckford and slaves in Jamaica, **70**-199
    in America, **77**-279
    in South Carolina, **83**-16
    in West Indies, **73**-98, **78**-468
    Jamaica, slave trade, Mansfield's decision, **77**-14
    Negroes as British allies, **76**-218
    objection to slavery in America, **84**-22
    objection to slavery in "free" America, **84**-7
    objection to slavery in West Indies and America, **83**-9
    "On Real Slavery," **76**-A
    peace brings freedom and prosperity, but they are marred by slave trade, **83**-227
    pleased at defeat of America, **76**-257
    "Remarks on . . . Slavery" in West Indies, **75**-A
    tragedy of slavery in West Indies, **83**-14
    vs slavery in Pennsylvania, **83**-37

Smelt, Leonard (c. 1719-1800). Former captain in royal engineers in Canada; sub-governor to Princes George and William, 1771-76; outspoken royalist and Tory opponent of reform. **80**-17, 66, 69, 227, 233, 356, 382
    Almon's ode vs Smelt, **80**-235

Smith, William. American clergyman. **See:** Part I of Index.

Smollett, Tobias George (1721-71). Scottish novelist and editor of *The Critical Review*, 1756-1762, *The Briton*, May 1762-February 1763, and *The British Magazine*, 1760-67. **63**-22, 146, **73**-7
    Churchill's *Author*, **63**-A

Society of Supporters of Magna Carta and the Bill of Rights. Founded 1768-69 by John Wilkes and John Horne. Leading members: Brass Crosby, Frederick Bull, John Glynn, Sir Watkin Lewes, Sir Joseph Mawbey, Richard Oliver, John Sawbridge, Philip Stanhope (Viscount Mahon), James Townsend; and three "Yankees": William and Arthur Lee, and Stephen Sayre. Broke up in 1771 on the issue of the use of its funds to help William Bingley, an imprisoned printer, or Wilkes, resulting in the formation of the Constitutional Society with Horne, Oliver, Sawbridge, and Townsend. **69**-23, 33, 127, 154, 175, 270, **73**-8, 51, **74**-79, **75**-255
    Robert Morris, **70**-208
    "Verses," **69**-A

Soldiering.
    enlistment, **67**-29
    John Scott's anti-war poem, **82**-23
    a military review, war as false show, **80**-313
    **See also:** Camps.

Soldiers, American. "Faction's coward sons," and British fear of American riflemen and bush fighters. **75**-25, 80, 210, 211, 214, 306, **76**-11, 37, 38, 60, 62, 214, 257
    American way of fighting, **77**-71
    belittled, **75**-53
    better than anticipated, **78**-108, 171, 179, 197
    brave, **76**-40
    cowardly, **75**-249, **76**-400 (print), **77**-134, 137, 216
    fearless, **76**-88
    martial courage of, **76**-79
    "poltroons," **79**-6
    poor quality, **77**-90
Soldiers, Contrasted.
    English and American, **76**-88
    French and British, **78**-172, 173, **82**-172
Soldiers, English. **78**-425, 426
    Americans need peace, **78**-321
    anti-recruiting satire, **75**-320 (print)
    brave and aggressive, **82**-172
    compassion for defeated Americans, **80**-30[4]
    cowardly, **82**-75
    drunken soldiers embarking for America, **76**-246
    effeminate, **76**-21, 37, 38, **78**-134, **79**-13
        and ill with venereal disease, **77**-25
    Germain is cowardly, **77**-148
    honored, **79**-90
    Howes are cowardly, **77**-83
    low pay of common soldier, **76**-151
    "man of fashion" goes to America to escape creditors, **80**-333
    praise of battle heroes, English officers in army and navy, **83**-158
    praise of volunteers, **78**-529, 530
    satire on high-born officers going to America, **81**-172
    soldier pay, **79**-453
    a soldier poet, **79**-32, 263, 315
    support of American War, **77**-274
    taught bush fighting, **78**-98
    timidly surrender, **82**-52
    valorous and humane, **76**-152
    **For more on Soldiers, English, see:** Soldier and Sailor Poets and Poetry.
Soldiers, Scottish. **76**-212, **77**-58, **78**-71, **80**-1, 5, 6
    brave, **78**-271
    ferocious, **78**-108
    with Wolfe at Quebec and Eliott at Gibraltar, **85**-32
    **See also:** William Alexander (Lord Stirling, American), Fraser, Maitland, Colvill's poems.
Soldiers, Veteran. **See:** Veteran Soldiers.
Somerset, Henry, 5th Duke of Beaufort (1744-1803). Tory peer; supported the North ministry. **78**-7, **79**-232
Spain. "Haughty Dons," "our natural foe."
    1761-63, Seven Years' War, **61**-14, 34, 38, **62**-2, 9, 32, 54, **64**-20, **65**-30, **80**-12

1770-71, Falklands Islands dispute, **70**-18, 29, 39, 53, 56, 57, 71, 113, 115, 125, 169, 174, 184, 191, 232, **71**-43, 108, 131, 132, **72**-82, **75**-223

1774-79, and American War, **74**-15, **75**-121, 130, 203, 209, 215, 278, 300, 301, **76**-9, 14, 16, 20, 85, 166, 197, 333, 356, 363, **77**-158, 224, 246, 305, **78**-75, 173, 217, 464, 486, 516

    the real enemy, **75**-321

1779-83, Spain declares war June 21, 1779, **79**-12, 238, 400, **80**-249, 425 (print)

    Fort Omoa, Honduras, **79**-174
    peace, **82**-13
    Spain will pay for the war, **80**-92
    Spanish Manifesto, **79**-328, 385, 424, 425

King of Spain and Washington, **85**-43

**For more on Spain and American War, see**: British Navy, and British Navy and Rodney's Engagements under rubric of American War.

Spencer, Georgiana, Duchess of Devonshire (1757-1806). Married William Cavendish, 5th Duke of Devonshire, 1774. Canvassed for Fox in the difficult Westminster election of 1784. **84**-70, **85**-13, 44

Spies. **80**-44

    **See**: John André, Maria Gibbons, Francis Henry De La Motte, Nathan Hale.

Stamp Act. Passed March 22, 1765; an internal duty on legal transactions for the purpose of collecting funds to support imperial troops stationed in America; after receiving much colonial opposition, repealed March 18, 1766, accompanied by the Declaratory Act (q.v.). **65**-14, 19, 21, 24, 69, 134, 135, 147, **66**-7, 9, 10, 19, 25, 36, 52, 59, 60, 63, 64, 67, 70, 71, 74, 75, 91, 105, 108, 110, 120, 134, 137, 140, **68**-26, **69**-270, **70**-77, 85, **74**-89, 178, 216, **76**-12, 22, 39, 42, **78**-7, **80**-12, 34, 306, **81**-3, **84**-39, 171

    American Nonimportation Agreement, **66**-41

        **See more on Nonimportation under rubric**: America.

    and Receipt Tax, **83**-262
    Ireland, **74**-149, 161
    Pitt and repeal, and its effect, loss of America, **78**-504

Standing Army. One of America's grievances against Britain. The Quartering Act, passed March 24, 1765, permitted quartering of British soldiers on the inhabitants of the colonies.

    and Boston Massacre, **73**-16
    and navy and America, **72**-106

Stanhope, Charles, Viscount Mahon (1753-1816). MP, 1780-86; then House of Lords, when he became 3d Earl Stanhope. A Wilkesite lord; brought into Parliament by Shelburne; opposed North's ministry and continuation of American War; advocated Parliamentary reform.

    his proposed tax on dogs, **84**-100
    leader of reform, **84**-131

Stanhope, Philip Dormer, 4th Earl Chesterfield (1699-1773). Courtier and author of famous letters. Opponent of coercion and punitive legislation against American colonists; urged the creation of a third secretary of state for the colonies. **66**-24

    and repeal of Stamp Act, **66**-75
    and Rockingham ministry, **66**-106

Stanley, Hans (1721-80). MP, 1743-47; 1754-80. A placeman during the North ministry with little political influence; voted against repeal of the Stamp Act, and consistently against concessions to America. **77**-67

Star Spangled Banner: American National Anthem. **83**-238

Tomlinson, **78**-A, **80**-A
  **See also:** John Stafford Smith in Part I of Index.
Stormont, 7th Viscount. **See:** David Murray.
Strafford, Earl of. **See:** Thomas Wentworth.
Strutt, John (1727-1816). MP, 1774-90. Country gentleman, staunch Tory supporter of the North ministry; the only MP to refuse a vote of thanks to Keppel for services rendered, February 12, 1779. **79**-98, 373
The Stuart Dynasty: James I, Charles I and II, James II, and the Young Pretender Prince Charles Edward. **See:** Tory Tradition. The Stuarts.
Stuart, John, 3d Earl of Bute (1713-92). Representative Scottish peer, 1737-41, 1760-80. Tutor to Prince of Wales, later George III; favorite of the King, and PM May 1762-April 1763, the Cider Tax being the cause of his downfall. Satirized as "The Thane," he became the symbol of anti-Tory and anti-Scottish hatred among the English and was thought to be the most influential leader of the King's "secret friends" and advisors in the "secret cabinet," and all English disputes were blamed on him. **61**-3, **62**-5, 6, 10, 11, 16, 18, 20, 21, 28, 33, 57, 62, 64, **63**-2, 3, 4, 9, 10, 11, 13, 16, 21, 26, 29, 31, 34, 45, 63, 71, 77, 78, 80, 82, 102, 108, 120, 132, 140, 144, 148, 152, 156, 158, 159, 160, 173, 175, 181, 182, 183, 184, 187, **64**-1, 5, 8, 9, 10, 17, 18, 20, 24, 26, 29, 31, 33, 35, 40, 48, 50, 51, 56, 64, 72, 73, 84, 95, 98, 100, 104, **65**-1, 5, 6, 8, 17, 18, 28, 33, 36, 38, 41, 45, 49, 65, 71, 76, 78, 79, 95, 100, 104, 105, 109, 121, 130, 136, 141, 143, **66**-7, 13, 14, 28, 35 (and **82**-66 & **83**-64), 45, 47, 50, 58, 66, 84, 96, 97, 103, 106, 107, 111, 116, 119, 122, 130, 139, 140, **67**-7, 10, 26, 32, 33, 41, 48, **68**-3, 6, 9, 10, 20, 21, 22, 23, 25, 35, 40, 43, 75, 91, 93, 99, 115, 122, 123, 124, **69**-3, 6, 10, 12, 13, 14, 19, 28, 45, 60, 69, 79, 80, 86, 101, 106, 108, 109, 119, 121, 129, 165, 182, 188, 196, 216, 222, 225, 240, 245, 261, 262, 263, 268, 269, **70**-9, 11, 15, 17, 22, 23, 24, 26, 32, 36, 37, 40, 41, 53, 54, 56, 77, 95, 116, 144, 150, 152, 170, 176, 179, 182, 185, 186, 197, 222, 244, **71**-4, 6, 42, 51, 61, 64, 69, 76, 85, 125, 128, **72**-23, 95, **73**-1, 7, 8, 18, 21, 26, 36, 71, 83, **74**-7, 9, 36, 58, 72, 76, 78, 93, 113, 120, 128, 152, 172, 173, 174, 193, **75**-13, 33, 34, 40, 55, 66, 69, 101, 118, 168, 184, 190, 194, 218, 223, 225, 227, 239, 259, 270, 285, **76**-16, 19, 21, 22, 25, 27, 39, 73, 98, 167, 184, 225, 287, 298, 311, 362, **77**-15, 23, 33, 56, 66, 67, 130, 178, 183, 215, 237, 294, 313, **78**-8, 12, 15, 16, 25, 27, 44, 56, 127, 131, 237, 258, 286, 290, 292, 296, 345, 414, 415, 416, 479, 498, 501, 519, 523, 550, **79**-5, 28, 31, 37, 44, 45, 108, 372, 457, **80**-7, 40, 62, 64, 69, 90, 91, 123, 233, 237, 321, 378, 386, 404, 405, **81**-39, 259, **82**-66 (and **66**- 35), 161, 290, **83**-3, 19, 77, 151, **84**-19, 39, 69, 149, 171, **85**-33
  alleged conversion to Roman Catholicism, **78**-392
  and Fox-North Coalition, **83**-153, 199
  and freedom of speech, **77**-302
  and Mansfield, **82**-319
  and North, **79**-380
  and "oeconomy," **80**-250
  and Rev. Dr. Dodd, and Peace of 1763, **76**-393
  and Samuel Johnson, **75**-132
  and Shelburne, **78**-43
  and younger Pitt, **86**-3
  blamed for Quebec Act, **74**-52
  blamed for taxing Americans and menacing them with Quebec Act, **74**-64
  the cause of all the troubles and the loss of empire, **81**-7
  character, **78**-82

Churchill's *Candidate* and *Independence,* **64**-A
Churchill's *Conference, Epistle to Hogarth,* and *Prophecy of Famine,* **63**-A
consummate Scotch Tory, **75**-245
corrupt, **83**-20
determines government's leadership, **76**-266
encourages war against America, **76**-93
"Epigram," **64**-A
"guides the King," **79**-354
influences Tory court leaders, **76**-334
intended epitaph, **82**-116
introduces corruption to court, **82**-4
mismanages the war, **80**-430
modern Achitophel, **78**-457
"Mourn, . . ." *Pride,* **66**-A
offer to Pitt rejected, **78**-144
"Parody . . .," **70**-A
political teacher of North, **84**-16
present in all state measures, **81**-105
Quebec Act, **76**-80
the real enemy of the King, **79**-484
resigns as PM, April 8, 1763, **63**-87
responsible for faction, **79**-125
review of career, **78**-298
"secret influence," **66**-35, **82**-66, **83**-64
"Spoken . . .," **70**-A
"The Thane," a Stuart, **82**-372
"Verses Extempore," **65**-A

Subscriptions (public and private). **60**-49
    Horne's trial for assisting American prisoners, **77**-209
Suffolk, 12th Earl. **See:** Henry Howard.
Sullivan, John (1740-95). American general, and member of Congress; served in many engagements of American War: Boston siege, Canada invasion, Long Island (where he was captured and later exchanged for Gen. Prescott, September 1776), Trenton, Brandywine, and Germantown; also at the Franco-American operation at Newport, R.I., July-August 1778.
    cited as a "Whig," **80**-277
    failed in attack on British in R.I., **79**-527
Sumter, Thomas (1734-1832). Partisan leader in South Carolina in American War; took part in the Braddock expedition, 1755, and the Forbes expedition to Ft. Duquesne, 1758. In American War defeated by Tarleton at Camden, S.C., August 16-18, 1780; and by Cornwallis at Black Stocks, S.C., November 9, 1780. **80**-258, **81**-115
Surrey, Earl. **See:** Charles Howard.
Swift, Jonathan (1667-1745). Tory political author in reign of Queen Anne and of George I and II.
    "Battle of the Books," political writing in Swift's day and in 1760's, **63**-A
Talbot, William, Earl (1710-82). MP, 1734-37; then House of Lords. Lord Steward of the Household, 1761. Fought a duel with Wilkes, October 5, 1762. **63**-152, **79**-275
Tar and Feathers. A cruel form of punishment adopted by American lynch mobs, inflicted on alleged enemies of the American community. **74**-91, 222 (print), **75**-11, 24, 53, 165, 190, 194, 227, 243, 287, **76**-22, **78**-70, 533, **83**-19, **84**-16

also riding a pole and blinding, **77**-6
Tarleton, Banastre (1754-1833). MP, 1790-1806, 1807-12. Colonel in British army, with reputation for savage ferocity. Fought in America, from Howe's capture of New York, 1776, to Cornwallis's surrender at Yorktown, 1781. **80**-308, **81**-94, 115, 210, **82**-9, 21, 31, **82**-357, **83**-25, 158
    charged with cruel and brutal behavior in America, **81**-135
    genuine fighter, **80**-164
    victory at Camden, **80**-258
Taxation of American Colonies. An American grievance that eventually led to civil war. **65**-8, 34, 147, **68**-95, **71**-90, **74**-8, 64, 119, 132, **75**-1, 13, 30, 42, 77, 116, 128, 188, 201, 227, 251, 261, **76**-17, 18, 42, 134, 198, 199, 228, 275, 381, **81**-102
    and Barrington, **78**-187
    and consent, **78**-44, 45
    and corruption, **76**-115
    and Odell, **80**-22
    and representation in Parliament, **76**-29
    as cause of American War, **74**-212, **78**-244, **79**-205
    Britain's just right, **80**-34
    causes of American conflict are taxes, smuggling, nonimportation, coercion, **75**-249
    death and taxes, **78**-104
    immediate cause of rebellion, **84**-16
    justified, **76**-11
    on fish and tea, **75**-107
    taxation without consent as cause of war, **78**-19
    tea, **75**-228
    **See also:** Stamp Act, and Tea.
Taxes. After the Peace of Paris, 1763, the need for additional revenue led to new taxes in Britain as well as America, inevitably generating protests. **62**-16, 55, 62, **63**-12, 26, 38, 39, 63, 73, 74, 89, 100, 102, 108, 133, 134, 138, 140, 143, 159, 163, 172, 174, 176, 177, 179, 183, 184, 185, 186, 187, **64**-1, 5, 8, 48, 51, 53, **65**-20, 100, 147, **66**-19, 20, 72, 74, 88, 93, **67**-5, 11, 18, 22, **72**-62, 106, **74**-38, 53, 68, 89, 95, 174, **75**-196, 240, **76**-181, **77**-18, 174, **78**-19, 308, 518, **79**-453, **80**-90, **84**-100
    "Address [and] The Great Man's Reply," **63**-A
    and Fox-North Coalition, **83**-54
    and Pitt, **85**-59 (print)
    and Pitt's budget, **84**-111, 112
    and politics, **82**-191
    and younger Pitt's tax policy, **84**-41
    burdensome, **78**-47
    the cost of the war and the need for more revenue, **77**-131, 138
    debate between "patriot" in Opposition and courtier in government, **81**-40
    high taxes an inducement to end American War, **82**-190
    horse tax, **84**-138
    increase, **76**-278, **78**-214, 215, **79**-166, **81**-182, **83**-32
        objections to, **79**-156, 157
    King wants taxes to continue American War, **82**-150
    need for revenue, **80**-307, 319
        after American War, **84**-47
    new scheme for raising revenue, **84**-168
    North's taxes, **82**-113, 127

　　　　　new, **82**-417
　　　　　on soap, **82**-230
　　　　　on theatre, **82**-266
　　　　　protest at, **82**-304
　　　numerous tax revenues paying for the war, **80**-105
　　　"On the Candle and Window Tax," **84**-A
　　　on coal, "Pit Coal," **84**-174
　　　oppressive taxes and emigration, **85**-51
　　　Pitt's new taxes, **85**-12, 18, 19, 21, 22, 28, 29, 49, 50
　　　Pitt's tax on candles and windows, **84**-145
　　　Pitt's tax policy, **84**-125
　　　protest, **82**-359
　　　protest at excise taxes, especially Cider Tax, passed March 31, 1763, **63**-13
　　　Receipt Tax, **83**-79, 125, 262
　　　　　and emigration, **83**-106
　　　　　and Stamp Tax, **83**-262
　　　reduction of, **79**-284
　　　Scottish complaint, **82**-351
　　　"A Song," **66**-A
　　　taxation the lesser evil, **84**-186
　　　tea and window light tax, **84**-136
　　　Tory Scots and excessive taxation, **79**-384
　　　waste of American War and Fox-North Coalition, **84**-179
　　　window tax, **64**-70
　　　**See also**: Stamp Tax, Taxation of American Colonies, Tea, Townshend Acts.
Tea (and the American Rebellion). **74**-15, 177, 222, 227, **75**-228, **76**-12, 22, **77**-15, **78**-8, 66, 217, 226, 331, **78**-510, **79**-3, 205, **80**-12, 306, **82**-39
　　　and Johnson, **76**-25
　　　Boston Tea Party, December 16, 1773, **74**-31, 40, 46, 55, 89, 114, 183, 195, **78**-170, **80**-12, **81**-3
　　　cause of American War, **82**-328
　　　defense of tea tax, **80**-34
　　　tea tax, "a paltry tax," **77**-22
　　　trifling cause of the rebellion, **77**-48, 84, 117
　　　**See also**: East India Company, Nonimportation, Townshend Acts.
Temple, 1st Earl. **See**: Richard Temple Grenville.
Temple, 2d Earl. **See**: George Nugent-Temple.
Temple Bar. London location of corpses of those executed for treason. **79**-409
Theatre in America. **76**-77, **77**-43, **78**-425, 426
Theodore, "King of Corsica." Theodore-Antoine, Baron de Neuhoff (1694-1756) German adventurer, attempted to lead a Corsican rebellion against Genoa, 1736, provided the Corsicans acknowledged him as their king.
　　　and Paoli, **69**-150
Thomson, James (1700-48). Scottish poet and playwright; with Mallet wrote *Alfred, a Masque* (1740), which included the patriotic lyric "Rule Britannia." Thomas Arne composed the melody.
　　　and Churchill, **64**-13
　　　Mallet and John Home, and *Masque of Alfred*, **78**-522
Thornton, Henry (1760-1815). MP, 1782-1815. Son of John Thornton, banker, supporter of Methodists; partner in father's banking firm and governor of Bank of England; supported Shelburne, 1782; voted for reform and against Fox's India Bill, 1783, and then supported Pitt's administration.

opposed to practice of giving money to electors, **82**-335

Thrale, Henry (1728?-81). MP, 1765-80. Brewer, friend of Samuel Johnson, who wrote for him some of his election literature, 1768 and 1774. Voted to expel Wilkes from House of Commons, 1769; generally supported Ld North. He and Whitbread were government contractors supplying beer during American War.
    Whitbread and Calvert vs Wilkes, **69**-80

Thurlow, Edward (1731-1806). MP, 1765-78; then House of Lords. Solicitor-general, 1770-71; attorney-general, 1771-78; ld chancellor, 1778-83. Voted against repeal of Stamp Act, 1766; argued for aggressive measures against America; critical of North only in 1781-82 when he joined Rockingham; then supported Pitt against Fox-North Coalition, 1784. **72**-1, 6, **75**-120, **77**-67, **78**-16, 274, **79**-38, 292, 302, 310, **80**-10, 123, **81**-124, 175, 186, **82**-4, 9, 197, **83**-29, 151, **84**-19, 40, 71, 112, 125
    allied with Pitt against Fox, **84**-8
    and Mrs. Siddons, **83**-195
    and Pitt, **84**-81, **85**-12
        lead the nation, **84**-16
    in Pitt's ministry, **84**-5
    unity with Richmond, **82**-382

Thynne, Thomas, 3d Viscount Weymouth (1734-96). Peer; member of Duke of Bedford's "Bloomsbury gang" in 1760's; in House of Lords opposed repeal of Stamp Act, 1766; in North's ministry as secretary of state, 1775-79. **67**-5, **68**-121, **69**-59, 214, **70**-110, 112, **71**-64, **73**-4, 10, **79**-33, 275, 284, 310

The Times. Summaries of issues and topics currently debated. **65**-103, 120
    American times, **80**-22
    American view of the year 1769, **69**-268
    are characterized by failures everywhere, **78**-480, 481
    Britain declining and divided, October 1779, **79**-453, 454
    Britain will be victorious over America, France, and Spain, **77**-293
    Cider Bill and "Present Times," **63**-143
    class conflict, **71**-81
    corruption, **70**-92, 153, **72**-53
        politics, and America, **69**-95
    Cowper's "Table Talk," **82**-A
    current state of affairs, end 1779, **79**-271
    destabilizing faction, **69**-162
    Edinburgh riots, **80**-21
    Edward Walpole
        on the anarchy of the times, **69**-18
        on the mob and riots and anarchy, **69**-199
    English freedom and American rebellion, **75**-9
    "Epigram on the Times," and self-interest, **70**-A
    evils of, **72**-85
    failures and Minority committing treason, December 1778, **78**-512
    forecast of year 1772, **72**-107
    "The Genius . . .[and] The Times," evils of, **72**-A
    greed and sedition, **69**-161
    hard times, reprint of Freeth's "The Times," **75**-119
    hostility in the world and Falkland Islands dispute, **70**-174
    immoral and absurd, **72**-10
    in these times failures are rewarded; vs Howe, Burgoyne, and Keppel, **79**-209
    the Irish and the times, **63**-152

liberty and self-interest, **64**-5
May 1783, Shelburne and Fox, **83**-252
nation is being destroyed by fools and knaves, **78**-119
nation is being ruined and the ministry thrives, **78**-437
North's new ministry and Tories, **70**-152
objection to "brutal Game-Acts," **71**-89
"Ode on his Majesty King George III," political situation in 1761, **61**-A
on Bute and corruption and Wilkes from Whig perspective, **68**-123 (print), 124 (print)
on contentious, useless debates in Parliament, **83**-88
"On the Present Times" and the common people, **63**-118
oppression as seen by a Wilkesite partisan, **69**-20
oppressive times because of despotism, **76**-371
party differences and instability, **71**-83
party dissension, February 1784, **84**-187
pathetic state of affairs, **70**-27
the peace, Scots, Bute, and Pitt, **65**-121
Pitt's leadership is needed; others are self-interested, **80**-288
political instability in postwar years, March 1781-December 1783, **83**-202
politics split between Whigs and Tories, **78**-526
present situation, August 1775, **75**-33
present times, Bate's Tory newspaper bias, **80**-35
"Price of Stocks at the Political Exchange," **63**-132
    and a depression, **67**-39
problems of satire in 1780, **80**-37
review of issues of the times, May 1785, and Fox, Pitt, India Bills, Irish trade, reform, and taxation, **85**-51
Samuel Butler comments on abuses of arbitrary government, **70**-30
satire dominates the times, **76**-81
satire
    on state of the nation, **70**-195
    on times, Christmas, 1777, **77**-197
satirized, **64**-53
    from Whig perspective, **65**-139
significant issues of, **70**-23
situation in June 1775, **75**-121
situation in March 1780, the ministry, King, Parliament, and reform, **80**-344
situation in May 1783, and politics of peace, corruption, and Fox, **83**-253
situation in November 1782 and Shelburne, America, and Ireland, **82**-326
situation in September 1780, Britain alone fights the world, **80**-345
state of Britain, March 1778, **78**-450
"State of Political Stocks," 1774, **74**-176
state of politics for the new year 1775, **75**-247
state of the nation, **73**-77
    after Burgoyne's defeat, **77**-126
    being ruined, December 31, 1779, **79**-445
    corrupt and discontented, **72**-78
summary of popular grievances in reign of George III, **79**-384
summary of year 1772, **72**-57
survey of society and professions, **67**-38, **75**-219
sweeping satiric survey of vicious times, including politics, **79**-10
terrible times despite peace and prosperity, **69**-166

"Things as they Are," July 1778, concerning Europe and American War, **78**-A
Tories dominate Whigs, **69**-79
Tory corruption and oppression, **70**-176
Tory politics dominate, **64**-48
totally negative view of present parlous time, **70**-2
venal 1772, **73**-34
war dominates literature of times, **81**-229
warning against civil war, **69**-217
Whig and Tory agree that North must resign, **78**-110
Whitehead's odes and times, **79**-296
Wilkes
    and Horne, **69**-167
    and liberty and Bute, **69**-165
    and political chaos, **68**-110
    and sedition, **69**-164
    is irrelevant, but North is blundering seriously, **71**-109
    Middlesex election and Bute, **69**-216
will bring victory of Tories, papists, and Jacobites over true Whigs, **77**-57
world is turned upside down in these times, February 1779, **79**-491
wretched times after Yorktown, **82**-71
the year 1771, **71**-108
the year 1774 from Irish perspective, **74**-154
year's end, December 1774, **74**-171

Tooke, John Horne. **See**: John Horne.
Tory and Tories, American. **See**: Loyalists, or American Tories.
Tory Court Leaders in 1776.
    North, Germain, Rigby, Weymouth, Suffolk, Mansfield, Jenkinson, Thurlow, Wedderburn, Sandwich, and Bute, **76**-334
    **See also**: Hillsborough, Stormont, Dundas, Dyson, Gower, and North Ministry.
Tory Opinion of Oliver Cromwell. **69**-173, **72**-12, **76**-162
Tory Peer, character of a.
    ambitious, proud, timid, and vain, **84**-101
    careless about the people's rights, **84**-196
Tory Poems and America, 1774-85. **74**-78, 90, 93, **75**-34, 62, 67, 153, 184, 240, 242, 251, 258, **76**-19, 22, 28, 73, 227, 266, 366, **77**-32, 109, 288, **78**-7, 23, 44, 246, 269, 324, 375, 405, 413, 548, 550, **79**-35, 399, 465, **80**-34, 80, **81**-17
    and Quebec Act, **74**-115
    anti-Tory, **80**-40
    C. Wesley damns the Opposition, the heirs of Cromwell, for fomenting rebellion and civil discord, **82**-391
    defense of King George and monarchy, **80**-157
    defense of a strong monarchy, **81**-179
    Hampden, Hancock, Hartley, and hell, **80**-154
    ironic verse by "red hot Tory" who hates Fox, the people, and liberty, and limitations on King's prerogative, **85**-36
    satire on Whig Opposition as seditious republican traitors, **80**-305
    a soldier's view of "puritannic rage" and the American rebellion, **76**-162
    a strong monarch will control destructive party spirit and civil war, **82**-218
    Tory biased news, **80**-35
    Tory court leaders influenced by Bute, **76**-334

Tory plot and the Keppel-Palliser controversy, **79**-518
vs American republican Congress, **80**-78
vs the anti-monarchist and republican "patriot" poets, **79**-31
vs Opposition, **81**-2
vs republican hater of King and Church, favors King and younger Pitt, and "moderate" Tory position, **84**-77
vs Whig republican Keppel and the Opposition, **79**-143
Whigs have been dead since 1688, **82**-306
Whigs of all denominations damned after rebel defeats, 1779-80, **80**-277

Tory Politicians.
    Bute, Mansfield and Sandwich, and Scotch, **73**-7
    Bute, North, Sandwich, **74**-93
    **See also:** Tory Court Leaders, and *passim,* all Tory entries.

Tory Tradition. The Stuarts, and the Origin of the Tory Ideological Tradition. The Stuart Dynasty. James I, Charles I, Charles II, James II (1603-88). Also Prince Charles Edward Stuart, the Young Pretender.
    Charles I (1633-49), **64**-39, 95, **65**-89, 118, 125, 126, 127, **68**-27, **69**-217, 248, **73**-48, 73, **75**-57, 167, 229, **76**-1, 10, 43, 133, 165, 189, 330, **77**-237, **78**-475
        and Bute, **82**-372
        and George III, **75**-216, **81**-161
        anti-Tory verse, **73**-64
        Churchill's *Gotham*, and "On the Calves-Head Club," **64**-A
        execution of, a lesson to tyrants, **73**-21
        George III, tyranny, and American War, **84**-171
        Tory martyr, **65**-86
        tyrant, **81**-138
    Charles II (1660-85), **69**-185, **71**-53, **76**-304, **77**-267, 320, **78**-407, **79**-393, **80**-77, 141
    George III as Stuart and Tory Jacobite, an absolute monarch or an oppressive tyrant, **64**-78, **70**-182, **72**-62, **76**-167, **78**-223
        "The Vine and the Bramble," **70**-A
        **For more, see**: George III, *passim*.
    James I (1603-33), **69**-65
    James II (1685-88), **72**-23, **74**-57, 66, **76**-9, **78**-264
        and Bute, **82**-372
        a tyrant, banished to France, **82**-38
    Prince Charles Edward Stuart, the Young pretender (1720-88), **64**-91, **70**-244, **76**-167
        Protestant fears of, **76**-149

Tory Tradition. The Stuarts. References. **63**-100, **64**-38, **65**-5, 12, 20, 38, 50, 58, **66**-93, **67**-7, **68**-1, **69**-6, 94, 131, **70**-9, 142, **71**-44, 87, 101, 133, **73**-12, 87, **74**-69, 103, **76**-12, 73, 194, 308, 361, **77**-24, 267, **78**-4, **80**-314
    and present monarchy, **80**-384
    and tyranny, **78**-350, 475, 498, **79**-14
        divine right, **79**-37
    a celebration of limited monarchy directed at George III and Tories, **85**-33
    Churchill's *Gotham*, **64**-A
    Restoration of Stuarts in America with French help, **74**-109
    Stuart despotism and Popery, **74**-157, **75**-75, 222, 292
    "Stuart Maxims," **69**-247
    Stuart maxims adopted in reign of George III, **81**-201

"Stuart pride" and loss of Canada, **76**-9
Stuart sentiment and coercion of America, **75**-153, 186
Tory view of politics, **72**-12
Tory Tradition. The Stuarts. Tories, Jacobites, and Scotch Rebels. **68**-27, **73**-71, 82, 83, 84, **77**-33, 292, **78**-15, 246, 286, **86**-3
Tory Writers.
David Hume, David Mallet, John Shebbeare, James Scott, Samuel Johnson, James Macpherson, and Tobias Smollett, **73**-7
Samuel Johnson, James Macpherson, John Shebbeare, Hugh Kelly, **76**-226
Samuel Johnson, William Whitehead, John Shebbeare, **75**-62
**Other Tory authors in this period:** John Dalrymple (4th Bt), John Lind, and poet Thomas Hastings.
Townsend, James (1737-87). MP, 1767-74, 1782-87. London alderman, 1769; sheriff, 1769-70; ld mayor, 1772-73; prominent London Whig adherent of Chatham and Shelburne. Supported Wilkes until break, 1771, when he left the Bill of Rights Society and joined Oliver and Sawbridge to form the Constitutional Society with Horne; opposed the American measures of the North ministry; opposed Fox-North Coalition. **69**-129, 183, 250, **70**-47, 101, 113, 178, 192, 195, **71**-97, **72**-1, 65, 80, 88, 93, **73**-1, 3, **78**-4
Townshend, Charles (1725-67). MP, 1747-67. Member Board of Trade and Plantations, 1749-54, and President Board of Trade, 1763-65; chancellor of the exchequer, 1766-67. Tightened enforcement of colonial customs and excise payments, thereby increasing American resentment; author of the celebrated tea tax as part of the Townshend Acts, June-July 1767, which caused a furor in America. **63**-130, **65**-76, **66**-69, 101, **67**-9, 13, 16, 17, 26, 35, 43
"Epigram. Natural . . .," **63**-A
"Extempore Answer," **64**-A
**See also:** Townshend Acts.
Townshend, Charles (1728-1810). MP, 1756-84, 1790-96. Cousin of the more famous Charles Townshend of the 1760's; close friend of North; had several places and served in the Portland ministry (Fox-North Coalition), 1783.
in the Portland ministry, **83**-265
Townshend, George, 4th Viscount (1724-1807). MP, 1747-64. Elder brother of the famous Charles Townshend; general, second in command to Wolfe at Quebec; Viceroy of Ireland, 1767-72. Supported the North ministry in House of Lords. **59**-4, 16, **60**-6, 11, 23, 48, **62**-2, 7, **67**-28, **68**-14, 67, **69**-5, 17, **70**-186, **71**-46, 130, **72**-58, 81, **73**-35, **75**-58, **79**-232, **90**-1
Townshend, John (1757-1833). MP, 1780-84, 1788-90, 1793-1818. 2d son of George Townshend; close friend of Charles James Fox. Opposed the North ministry, 1780-82, and supported reform of Parliament, 1782; ld of Admiralty Board during Fox-North Coalition; was one of the authors of *The Rolliad* political satires, 1784-85. **79**-41, 54, 59, 100, **83**-21
and Mrs. Siddons, **83**-195
Townshend, Roger (1731-59). Lt-col British army; brother of Charles Townshend; killed while reconnoitring French lines at Ft. Carillon (Ticonderoga), July 25, 1759. His monument is in Westminster Abbey beside that of Major André. **84**-10
"Inscription on a Monument . . .," **59**-A
Townshend, Thomas (1733-1800). MP, 1754-83. Opposed Grenville's Stamp Act and measures concerning Wilkes, 1763-65; supported Rockingham ministry and was leading speaker for repeal of Stamp Act; second only to Fox and Burke as speaker opposing North's measures against America; defended Shelburne's peace against Fox; helped defeat Fox's India bill in House of Lords, 1783. **69**-90,

126, **80**-245, **81**-42, **82**-223

Townshend Acts, passed by Parliament, June 26, 29, July 2, 1767, including Townshend Revenue Act, act establishing a new system of Customs Commissioners, and an act suspending the New York Assembly. The revenue act imposed duties on glass, lead, painters' colors, paper, and tea.

    American objection to, **68**-95
    Grafton and Shelburne responsible for, **80**-34, 306
    repealed except for tea duty, April 12, 1770, **71**-7
    **See also:** Charles Townshend, 1725-67.

Trecothick, Barlow (1718?-75). MP, 1768-74. Reared in Boston, Massachusetts, and Jamaica, and settled in London, c. 1750; wealthy London merchant; alderman, 1764-74; sheriff, 1766; ld mayor, 1770 (after Beckford's death); provincial agent for New Hampshire, 1766-74. Expert on American and West Indian trade; urged conciliatory measures towards America. **69**-198, 202, **73**-3

Trimmers. Political hypocrites. **72**-104, **78**-20, **84**-107, 176

    "Epigram. Natural . . .," **63**-A
    **See also:** "Vicar of Bray" in Part I of index.

Tromp, Martin Harpertzoon (1597-1653), and Cornelius Van Tromp (1629-91). Father and son; famous Dutch admirals of the 17th century.

    spelling in text = "Trump," **81**-206

Tryon, William (1729-88). Royal governor of North Carolina, 1765-70, and of New York, 1770-78; commanded a force of Loyalists, 1777, and engaged in some destructive raids before returning to England, 1780.

    praised, **74**-126

Tucker, Josiah (1712-99). Dean of Gloucester, a Tory. Wrote many essays on the American question. His solution: America should be separate, free, and independent but tied to Britain commercially; allegedly advised prosecution of Minority Opposition for treason, calling them "all republicans." **75**-183, 281, **76**-17, 18, 190, **78**-43, 151, **79**-56, 105, 106, 327, **82**-13

    and Opposition, **79**-281

Turkey.

    as American ally in the American War, **78**-516

Tyler, Wat, Jack Straw, and Jack Cade. Rebels and incendiaries, leaders of revolts in the 14th and 15th centuries. Tyler and Straw (Rackstraw?) leaders of Peasant Revolt, 1381; Cade, leader of an uprising in Kent, 1450.

    Fox, seditious subversive like Catiline, Cade, Tyler, and Straw, **84**-214
    mob of Americans misled by hypocritical demagogues, **75**-92
    Wilkes and Horne, and the seditious followers of Cromwell, Tyler, and Cade, **69**-139
    Wilkes, Tyler and Straw, and America, **76**-28

Tyranny, Tyrant.

    and George III, **81**-37
    and prerogative, **76**-116
    defined, **74**-200
    **For more entries, see:** Tory Tradition, The Stuarts; especially George III as Stuart, Tory, . . . and oppressive tyrant under same rubric.

United States of America. **84**-209, **85**-4, 6. **See:** America.

Unity, Union, Unanimity. The need for national unity, for reduction of faction and divisive party spirit, or for union of Britain and America. **63**-160, **65**-116, **67**-31, **68**-24, **70**-198

    against Minority factionalism, **80**-133
    and movement towards reform, **82**-145
    and new Rockingham ministry, **82**-301

Britain weakened by American rebellion abroad and factious Opposition
    at home, 80-187
British and American unity during the crisis, **68**-98, **74**-34, 121, 151, 219,
    221, **75**-313, **76**-54, 272, **77**-328, 329
        empire now disunited for ever, **76**-199
British disunity helps America, **81**-15
British unity in a just cause, liberty, **81**-108
disunity has lost the war, **81**-174
distinguishes between Whig and Tory unity, **80**-40
England must unite or fall, **80**-389
for end of faction, **82**-26
Fox's supporters bring discord, but unity is needed, **84**-202, 203
more important than reform, **80**-306
        needed to expel faction, support Shelburne, and save the
            empire, **82**-22
need in time of crisis, **82**-347
needed during the peace, **83**-135
of "Loyal Britons," of Britain and America, **82**-30
Parliament needs unity in this critical time, **80**-375
Pitt brings discord, but nation needs unity, **84**-108
requires proper public spirit of Opposition, **80**-41
under George III, **82**-122
under Keppel in Rockingham ministry, **82**-91
under new administration, **80**-9
under Rockingham, **82**-378
under Shelburne, **82**-37, 169
Unity against France, Spain, and world, **77**-2, 146, **78**-19, 65, 198, 211,
    223, 293, 364, 416, **79**-38, 48, 53, 117, 198, 206, 225, 229, 231, 232,
    236, 258, 261, 345, 391, 438, 447, 462, 466, 499, 505, 510, 522, **80**-4,
    20, 205, 249, 360, 401, **81**-123, 132, **83**-190
        against all enemies, **82**-320, 379
        against Bourbon enemies, **82**-382
        against Bourbon nations and Holland, **82**-80, **83**-25
        against France, **82**-374
        Britain must unite against its enemies, **81**-212
        "Britain's Admonition," **79**-A
        "Exert your pow'rs," **79**-A
        "The following Verses," **79**-A
        hope for Anglo-American unity against France, **79**-23
        unanimity theme begins February 1779, and need for union of parties,
            North and Thurlow, with Fox, Burke, and Dunning, **79**-469
        under North, **78**-7, **79**-12, 18, **80**-34
        united Britain vs confederated powers, **81**-31, 85
    war with Bourbon powers, **70**-115
    with America against Bourbon enemies, **82**-11, 14, 20
The Universities, Cambridge vs Oxford, 72-76. **See also**: Encaenia (Oxford); and
    Gray, *Ode Performed in the Senate-House at Cambridge*, Part I of Index.
The Ushant Episode, July 27, 1778, the first fleet action in the war with France,
    1778-83. Not far from Brest, Ushant is a small island about 11 miles off the
    coast of Britanny. **78**-48, 52, 67, 74, 76, 116, 135, 136, 149, 176, 216, 217,
    279, 281, 315, 381, 383, 410, 476, 481, 483, 484, 492, 497, 553, **79**-35, 40,
    177, 241, 252, **80**-285, 422 (print), **82**-341

the Court Martial of Keppel and of Palliser, charges and counter charges, **78**-200, 272, 334, 493, **79**-11
 Keppel vs Palliser, Whig vs Tory, **79**-186
The French Fleet and Ushant, **78**-459, 534, **79**-104
**See also**: Keppel and Ushant Episode and Palliser under rubric of Augustus Keppel.

Van Trowser, _____. Name is an invention derived from the type of breeches worn by sailors, preceded by a generic preposition to denote Dutch origin.
 defeat of Van Trowser by Rodney and Vaughan, February 3, 1781, **81**-183, 250

Vaudreuil. **See**: Pierre-François de Rigaud, Marquis de Vaudreuil-Cavagnal.

Vaughan, John (c. 1731-95). MP, 1774-95. General officer from 1777; served in Germany during Seven Years' War, and at capture of Martinique, 1762; served in America to 1767 and in America and West Indies, 1775-81; second in command to Clinton in expedition to relieve Burgoyne up the Hudson River, 1777, and was with Rodney in the seizure of St. Eustatius, February 3, 1781. **77**-149
 and Burke, St. Eustatius, **81**-146
 defeat of Dutch on St. Eustatius, **81**-183
 French recapture St. Eustatius, November 27, 1781, **82**-110
 praised by Freeth, **82**-143
 St. Eustatius, **81**-130

Vergennes, Charles Gravier, Comte de (1718-87). French foreign minister, negotiated the Franco-American alliance, ratified by Congress, May 4, 1778; helped negotiate the release of Asgill, 1782, and was active in the Peace of Paris, 1783.
 Fletcher on Vergennes and Shelburne and the peace, and on Asgill, **85**-4

Vernon, Edward (1723-94). British admiral; captured Pondicherry, India, from the French, 1779. **79**-182

Vestris, Gaetano Apollino Baldassare (1729-1808). Celebrated French dancer visiting London; his son was principal *ballerino* at the King's Theatre, in the Haymarket, 1780-81.
 and Burke and North, **81**-240

Veteran Soldiers.
 of American War
  an old soldier's history, **85**-14
  Fox and election of 1784, **84**-37
  officers, **79**-429
  petition to increase annuity, **79**-487
  returning, **81**-198, **82**-356, **83**-188, 198, **84**-91
  thoughts about the war, **84**-67
 of French and Indian War, **75**-250
 of Seven Years' War
  neglected, **63**-180 (print)
  petition for increase of half pay, **73**-91
  treated inhumanely, **63**-109

Virginia. **See**: Colonies under rubric of America.

Voltaire (François-Marie Arouet) (1694-1778). Europe's leading man of letters—playwright, poet, historian, philosopher, novelist, critic, etc.
 Pitt, Earl of Chatham, and Voltaire compared, **78**-367

Vredenbergh, Jacob. Patriotic New York barber who refused to complete shaving a captain of a British transport ship, October 1, 1774, achieving thereby a brief notoriety. **75**-180, 319 (print)

Waldegrave, John, 3d Earl (1718-84). MP, 1747-63; then House of lords. Army officer in Seven Years' War; supported every administration, 1767-83, opposed Stamp Act repeal and Fox-North Coalition. **60**-48

Wallace, James (1731-1803). British naval officer in American War. **78**-211, **79**-440

Walpole, Horace (1717-97). MP, 1741-68. Letter writer and historian of the reigns of George II and George III. Son of Sir Robert Walpole, friend of Henry Seymour Conway. Voted against Grenville over Wilkes and general warrants; opposed North ministry and its American War. **63**-2
    poems in Walpole's *Journal . . . George III*, **78**-396, 432
    Sir Robert Walpole's peace policy and North's war policy, **78**-356
    Tickell's *Epistle from Fox to Townshend*, **78**-41
    vs North's American measures, **74**-12
    **See also**: Robert Mackreth for Walpole's nephew, 2d Earl of Orford.

Walpole, Robert, 1st Earl of Orford (1676-1745). Prime Minister, 1721-42, in reigns of George I and George II; noted for the long peace of his administration, the cynical adage that "every man has his price," and the benign neglect afforded American colonies during his administration. **63**-134, **66**-33, 98, **78**-356, **79**-114, **81**-55
    and North, **82**-173

War.
    dominates the literature of the time, **81**-229
    **See**: Seven Years' War, 1755-63; and the American War, 1775-83.

Warburton, William (1698-1779). Bishop of Gloucester, 1759-79; denounced Wilkes' *Essay on Woman* in House of Lords, November 15, 1763.
    in Churchill's *Duellist*, **64**-A
    **See**: Church of England.

Ward, Artemas (1727-1800). American officer, first served under Abercrombie in the unfortunate attack on Ft. Carillon (Ticonderoga), 1758; appointed general, second in command to Washington, June 17, 1775; with Washington and Putnam, led American troops besieging Boston, 1775-76. **75**-110, 238
    siege of Boston, **76**-325

Ward, John, 2d Viscount Dudley (1725-88). MP, 1754-74; then House of Lords. Tory peer; member of the "cabinet" with Basil Feilding, Earl of Denbigh; consistently supported Grafton and North. **75**-51

Warkworth, Lord. **See**: Hugh Percy.

Warren, Joseph (1741-75). American physician, political writer and orator; patriot leader, slain at Bunker Hill, Massachusetts, June 17, 1775. **75**-19, 25, 48, 173, 302, 306, **76**-5, 16, 37, 38, 97, **78**-295, **79**-3, 6, **83**-31, **85**-6, **93**-1

Washington, George (1732-99). May have begun the French and Indian War with the assassination near Ft. Duquesne of the Sieur de Jumonville, May 28, 1754; Braddock's ADC in the Battle of the Wilderness, July 9, 1755; appointed commander-in-chief of American forces, June 17, 1775; first U.S. President, 1789-97.
    above party faction, **84**-124
    America will defeat the Howes and Burgoyne, **77**-285
    American hero, **77**-124
    among the American heroes fighting in a just cause, **76**-27
    and André, **80**-119, **81**-14, 103
        cruel and ignoble death, **84**-9
        cruel to André, **81**-227
    and Battle of Long Island, **76**-200, 263, 306
    and Gage, his antagonist, **75**-30

and King of Spain, **85**-43
and loyal Britons, **76**-202
and Loyalists, Asgill, and André, **83**-12
and Loyalists in peace treaty, **83**-124
and Paine brought about American independence, **83**-38
and rebel defeats at Charleston, S.C., and Penobscot Bay (Maine), **80**-277
and Sandwich in retirement, **82**-376
and siege of Boston, **76**-325
and slavery, **83**-9
and Yorktown disaster, **81**-137
appointed chief of American army, **76**-22
as "dictator," admired by Whigs, **77**-80
Blake on Washington as leader of American rebellion against British tyranny, **93**-1
blames Opposition for disloyalty and exalting Washington, **79**-40
Brackenridge's "Rising Glory of America," **72**-14, **78**-73
Britain's failures in campaigns against Washington, **78**-171
"Britannia's Admonition," objection to British praise of Washington, **79**-A
British merchant asks Washington to punish those responsible for American War, **79**-533 (print)
British unable to defeat Washington, **77**-183
captured Boston and Trenton, **77**-102
Carleton cannot defeat Washington, **77**-202
"famous for retreat," **77**-88
favors America and Washington, **78**-408
a fighting fool, **77**-167
formidable rebel foe, **76**-217
George III will never hunt down Washington, **82**-208
gunboat named for Washington, Champlain fleet, August-September 1776, **76**-396
hope for reconciliation of Washington and Cornwallis to save Britain, **81**-29
Howe and Clinton vs Washington, **77**-132
Howe vs Washington in 1776, **77**-133
hunting dogs are given rebel names including Washington's, **79**-41
hypocritical parson demeans Washington, **78**-20
impartial view of Washington in history of American War, **81**-3
in the American War, a vivid review of events in the war, **85**-6
in boastful American song, **76**-166
in command of a nasty rabble, **75**-154
in a London raree show and Burgoyne's campaign, **77**-66
inability of British government to defeat Washington, **82**-212
leader of American rebellion, **83**-19
letter from General Schuyler to Washington, **77**-242
Mrs. Maria Gibbons, a Loyalist, spies on Washington, **77**-321
negative view of, **76**-11
news of Franco-American alliance evokes American blessings upon Washington, **78**-208
North and general fast, **76**-252
obstinate rebel, **77**-218
often defeated, but never surrenders, **80**-180
panegyric of, **81**-12
praise of, **79**-45

      praise of Loyalist Duché for criticism of Washington, **78**-517
      praise of Washington after Yorktown, **82**-9
      praise of Washington's leadership in struggle for liberty, but criticism of slave-owners, **83**-31
      praised as defender of liberty, **75**-150
      praised by British Whig poet, **75**-29
      radical Whig satire favors America and Washington, **79**-35
      respect but not admiration for "The American Fabius," **80**-57
      satire on Abingdon for adopting Washington's cause, **78**-4
      satirized by Tory Odell, **80**-22
      Tory satire on Opposition poets who favor rebels and Washington, **79**-31
      Tory view of British faction and American rebels, **78**-7
      Washington and Jephson's *Braganza*, the rebel who aspires to be king, **78**-259
      Washington's horse, **76**-374
      wasteful civil war and Washington, **81**-203
      Wesley (John) and Washington, **78**-10
Watson-Wentworth, Charles, 2d Marquess of Rockingham (1730-82). Country gentleman and statesman; after he opposed Bute, 1762, in Opposition to 1765; 1st ld of treasury and prime minister, July 13, 1765-August 2, 1766, when Stamp Act was repealed and Declaratory Act passed; in Opposition to North and coercive American policy, 1770-82; formed ministry with Shelburne March 26, 1782, but died suddenly July 1, 1782. Burke was his secretary. **65**-1, 15, 26, 39, 45, **66**-75, **67**-5, **68**-10, 124, **69**-13, 140, 258, **70**-2, 24, 77, 87, 101, 130, 192, **73**-4, **75**-49, **76**-22, 42, 290, **77**-5, 23, 207, **78**-12, 14, 23, 299, 316, **79**-20, 44, 302, 317, **80**-24, 33, 34, 69, 229, 306, 317, **82**-3, 4, **83**-3, 32, **84**-39, 149
      accused of helping the French, **82**-151
      and Burke, **80**-411, 412
      and Declaratory Act, 1766, **77**-149
      and Fox, **84**-161
      Burke's patron, **81**-251
      death, **82**-53, 88, 89, 115, 178, 211, 249 to 254, 368
          and Fox, **83**-193
          at an "inauspicious hour," **83**-52
          untimely, **82**-25
      gains from Keppel episode, **80**-169
      "On the Report . . .," **65**-A
      praised, **82**-353
      role at end of American War, **84**-16
      soon to be premier, **81**-144
      Stamp Act repeal, **78**-7
      traitor, **80**-185
      **See also**: Rockingham Ministry, July 13, 1765-August 2, 1766; and March 26, 1782-July 1, 1782, below.
Watson-Wentworth, Charles, 2d Marquess of Rockingham. Rockingham Ministry, July 13, 1765-August 2, 1766. Chief members: Rockingham, PM; John Cavendish, Henry Seymour Conway, Dowdeswell, Grafton, Onslow, Pratt (Earl Camden), Richmond, Thomas Townshend, and Charles Yorke. **65**-62, 65, 71, 74, 75, 76, 77, 101, 149, **66**-9, 64, 69, 75, 82, 85, 89, 101, 106, 111, 120, 122, 124, 138
      collapse, **66**-32
      **See also**: Charles Watson-Wentworth, 2d Marquess of Rockingham.
Watson-Wentworth, Charles, 2d Marquess of Rockingham. Rockingham Ministry, March

26, 1782-July 1, 1782. Chief members: Rockingham, PM; Barré, Burke, John Cavendish, Cavendish-Bentinck (Duke of Portland), Conway, Charles James Fox, Charles Howard (Earl Surrey), Keppel, Pratt (Earl Camden), Richmond, Shelburne, R. B. Sheridan, Thurlow. **82**-3, 25, 27, 103, 382, **83**-20
    and end of American War, **82**-174
    and North's resignation, **82**-204
    and Rodney, **82**-399
    and Sheridan, **82**-102
    and unanimity, **82**-301
    appointments recommended, **82**-370
    Burns, **84**-A
    castigated, **82**-349
    change to Rockingham from North ministry, **82**-140 (see also **83**-107)
    change to Rockingham ministry, **82**-260
    comes to power, **82**-227
    guardians of liberty, **82**-362
    initiated peace proceedings, **83**-21
    led by Fox and Burke, **83**-84
    must make the peace, **82**-369
    praised, **82**-197
    protests peace negotiations, **82**-118
    recalls Rodney, **82**-109
    Rockingham Whigs rule the nation, **82**-332
    unity under Rockingham ministry, **82**-378
    Whigs displace Tories, **82**-258
    will bring peace to America, **82**-228
    will save the nation from ruin, **83**-23, 32
    **See also:** Charles Watson-Wentworth, 2d Marquess of Rockingham.

Wayne, Anthony (1745-96). American general, noted for his capture of Stony Point, New York, July 16, 1779.
    Cocking's narrative on Stony Point, **81**-3
    Humphreys on Wayne, **85**-6

Webb, Philip Carteret (1700-70). MP, 1754-68. Solicitor to Treasury, 1756-65. Supported Bute, 1762; took a prominent part in the prosecution of Wilkes under Grenville, 1763; upheld the legality of general warrants, 1764; voted against repeal of the Stamp Act, 1766. **64**-8

Webster, James (d. 1781). Scottish colonel with Cornwallis's army; died in the Battle of Yorktown, 1781.
    Colvill's poem, **82**-8
    Miles Parkin on Webster's death, **83**-25

Wedderburn, Alexander (1733-1805). Scottish solicitor; MP, 1761-80; then House of Lords as Baron Loughborough, 1780. Opposed repeal of Stamp Act, 1766; treated Franklin brutally in House of Commons inquiry into theft of Governor Hutchinson's correspondence, 1774; supported British cause in the conflict with America, but favored conciliation and helped draw up the Howe proposals of 1776 and the North proposals of 1778. **70**-113, 195, **71**-6, 76, 92, 102, **72**-1, **73**-8, **74**-5, 73, **75**-252, 275, **76**-91, **77**-3, 67, 301, **78**-309, **79**-44, 310, 384, **80**-16, 219, **81**-39, 135, **82**-212, **84**-219
    and American prisoners, **81**-205
    and Judge Jeffreys, **80**-384

Wentworth, Thomas, Earl of Strafford (1593-1641). Advisor of Charles I, executed by Parliament for supporting his tyranny. **65**-125

Wesley, John. **See:** Part I of Index.

West, Benjamin (1738-1820). Popular historical painter, noted for "The Death of Wolfe." Born in America, but settled in London, 1763; founding member of Royal Academy, 1769.
 Wolcot, "Peter Pindar," on West and America, **83**-34
West Indies, in Seven Years' War, 1759-63, and in American War, 1775-83, etc. **77**-22
 American War undermines prosperity of, **83**-3
 and American War, **78**-491
 Antigua; objections to slavery in West Indies and America, **83**-9
 Edwards (Bryan), **92**-1
  and slavery, **76**-9
 Fletcher's poem on the peace, **85**-4
 Guadeloupe, **59**-6, 34, 40, **60**-25, 42, **62**-8, **63**-27
  "A Morning Scene in Paris," **60**-A
  "A New Song," **60**-A
 Havana, Cuba, **60**-3, **61**-1, **62**-3, 8, 9, 12, 23, 31, 41, 43, 52, 53, **74**-205, **79**-39, **80**-12
 Jamaica, **79**-314, **82**-199, 213
  and slavery, **77**-14
 Martinique, **60**-3, **62**-3, 8, 26, 34, 36, 50, **63**-27
  "On Gen Monckton's Writing Home," **62**-A
  "Song," **62**-A
 St. Lucia
  Cowper's "Epinikion" and "Present for the Queen of France," defeat of D'Estaing at St. Lucia, **79**-A
 St. Vincent and war against Caribs, 1772-73, **73**-61
 a West Indian opinion of American War, **77**-255
 **See also:** West India Actions under rubric of American War, British Navy, Rodney's Engagements under rubric of American War, British Navy (Martinique, St. Eustatius, Sea Battle of the Saints); William Beckford; Bryan Edwards; Slavery, Slaves, and Slave Trade.
Weymouth, 3d Viscount. **See:** Thomas Thynne.
Whig Americans. **74**-64, **75**-2, 7, 29, **76**-298
 the strange alliance of Saints of the Good Old Cause and Bourbon Papists, **79**-272
Whig and Tory.
 advice to Whigs and Tories to fight tyranny, **70**-241
 agree on responsibility of King and people, **79**-246
 agree that North must go, **78**-110
 American Whigs vs British Tories and their war, **78**-226
 and Ireland, **77**-250
 and new Pitt ministry, **84**-115
 "Answer to an Epigram," **64**-A
 are alike, **84**-84
 are equally corrupt and self-interested, **84**-199
 attack on Presbyterian republican Whigs, **65**-16
 "Battle, . . ." on party factions, Whig and Tory, **63**-A
 both corrupt, **64**-14, **71**-134
 both self-interested, **78**-72
 both to blame for American War, **78**-102
 Burke and Fox vs Stormont, Mansfield, and Bute, **83**-77
 Bute must lead the Tories, **67**-48
 Bute, Pitt, and the peace, Whig vs Tory, **66**-13

cannot unite, **63**-119
Churchill, Whiggish republican vs lawless tyranny, **65**-73
a corrupt Whig, **67**-12
Cumberland, a Whig prince, **65**-94, 99
defense of Charles the Martyr, vs republican sectaries and libertarians, **65**-127
defense of Pitt against Tory criticism, **66**-21, 125
defense of Whigs against Grafton and North, **70**-18
a defense of Whigs and Glorious Revolution against Tory Stuarts, **76**-308
defense of Wilkes' Whig politics, **68**-1
disagree on how to regain American colonies, **79**-131
Eden (William) shifts allegiance from Whigs to Tories, **85**-23
"Fable," on a Tory placeman, **69**-A
faith in King George as a Whig, **70**-142
for Whig principles against Bute and Tories, **66**-5
Fox-North Coalition, **84**-2
    and their opposition to Shelburne, **83**-137, 222
the Fox-North "monstrous" Coalition, **83**-24
Gibbon shifts allegiance to Tories, **79**-291
Heaven is Tory, a monarchy, **65**-138
in conflict, **63**-144, **64**-12, 54, **81**-7
in a fable, **71**-16
in 1784 Parliamentary elections, Fox vs Cecil Wray, **84**-37
Kidgell, a Tory, **64**-71
loyal Tories vs disloyal Whigs and American rebels, **80**-387
a loyal Tory objects to treason by critical Whig poets, **79**-31
lukewarm and dishonest Whigs ally with Tories, **74**-138
a moderate Whig and America, **67**-5
must unite, **79**-232
nation's troubles caused by King's favoring Tories, **75**-231
neither Tory nor Whig, **73**-26
North favors Tories over Whigs, **73**-89
North liked by Whig and Tory, **73**-96
[old?] Whig and Tory allied in the new Pitt ministry, **84**-183
on fraudulent Whigs and impudent Tories and the American War, **77**-7
on King as Jacobite, definition of Whig and Tory, Americans are not Tory although France is their ally, **81**-181
on monarchy, **81**-179
on Scotch Tories and Jacobites, especially Smollett, **63**-146
on the anniversary of Charles I's execution, **77**-238
"On the Calves-Head Club," **64**-A
on trends, **64**-40
party politics in the provinces, **67**-6
Pitt's political career, Tory and Whig, **67**-26
Portland is neither Whig nor Tory, **83**-221
praise of Mrs. Macaulay, a Whig, **66**-16
a pure lyric, neither Whig nor Tory, **75**-175
"a Revolution Whig" advises Tories on Wilkes and liberty, **71**-73
satire need to lash Tory politics, **65**-5
satire on Tories from Whig perspective, **65**-139
satire on Tory Johnson with allusions to America, **77**-25
satire on Tory taste, politics, and writing, **73**-7
the split in the nation's politics between Whig and Tory, **78**-526

the times favor Tories, **69-79**
Tories against seditious Whigs, **70-113**
Tories are favored at court, **81-185**
Tories are in power, Whigs are banished, and the Bourbon enemy rejoices, **80-404**
Tories are responsible for everything that will undermine the Revolution constitution, including the American War, **79-384**
Tories create difficulties even in America, **69-268**
Tories dominate court, **64-48, 69-53, 70-24**
Tories dominate even to America, **69-19**
Tory advice on dealing with Whig Opposition, **69-43**
a Tory attack on Price's Whig political philosophy, **76-284**
Tory bias for prerogative, **66-11**
Tory defense of Charles the Martyr against Whig attack, **73-48**
Tory pleasure at death of Newcastle, "Prince of Whigs," **68-82**
Tory poem against seditious Whigs, **70-8**
Tory politics cannot become worse, **70-176**
Tory rule ruins England, **69-260**
Tory view on freedom of the press, **64-65**
triumph of Tories over Whigs in George III's reign, **77-57**
Trumbull's *McFingal* and America, **75-23**
vs Presbyterian republican Whigs, **65-117**
vs Tories, **64-56**
and arbitrary power, **64-73**
Whig Abingdon vs Tories, Scotch, Johnson, Shebbeare, and J. Wesley, **78-498**
Whig and Tory differences on monarchy, **65-48**
Whig and Tory irreconcilable, **69-106**
Whig attacks on Tories, **81-208, 259**
a Whig awakens the nation to Tory danger, **75-184**
Whig Fox will reform Tory corruption, **82-406**
Whig ideals leave Britain because of Tory war, **78-292**
Whig Keppel vs Tory Sandwich and Palliser, **79-186**
Whig liberty vs Stuart tyranny, **69-6**
a Whig poem on Whig-Tory divisions, **65-12**
Whig Pratt vs Tory Mansfield, **72-95**
Whig Rockingham displaces Tory North, the monarchy now needs protection, **82-258**
Whig vs Tory ideology, **69-21**
Whig vs Tory political concepts, **69-13**
Whigs, American and British, are being attacked by Tories, **76-298**
Whigs are the true patriots, **73-8**
"The Whigs disclaim the [American] War," and Tory Scotch and Jacobites are to blame, **76-73**
Whigs, Old Whigs, and Tories, and the younger Pitt, **84-112**
Whigs vs Tories, **68-103, 78-128**
**See also**: Tory and Tory Tradition; and Whig Tradition.
Whig and Tory. Color metaphor.
Whig orange and Tory blue, **74-138**
Whig Ideals.
doctrine of limited monarchy, James II vs William III, **74-57**
summarized in Middlesex Petition, with American participation, **69-9**
**See also**: Whig Liberty.

Whig(s) in the Cause of Liberty, 1770.
    summary lists of Whigs, including Americans, **70-101, 103, 104**
Whig(s) in the Cause of Liberty, 1773.
    list of Supporters of Bill of Rights Society, includes Americans Sayre and William Lee, **73-51**
Whig Liberty. **69-6, 10, 13**
    American liberty is in the "Old English" spirit of the Whig martyrs Russell and Sidney, **76-264**
    American liberty must be protected, **74-9**
    American struggle for liberty justified, but not for independence, **82-22**
    and force of nature, **71-73**
    and Magna Carta, independence and integrity, **70-196**
    and the people, **69-27**
    anti-liberty poem, **69-18**
    Britain must continue to fight for freedom, as King William did in the past, **78-264**
    Britons must defend their rights, **74-17**
    constitutional liberty and natural rights protected by law, **69-3**
    corruption has undermined liberty, **73-53**
    Cromwell and Sidney must help threatened liberty, **71-110**
    defense of "native rights of human kind," "the unalienable rights of all," and America, **69-21**
    free elections, free press, and free Ireland and America, **74-12**
    a history of the Whig view of liberty up to American War and the need to free slaves in West Indies and America, **83-9**
    "Kings may make LORDS—but cannot make a MAN," **69-8**
    liberty and need for restraint, applied to America, **84-76**
    liberty for Britain and for America, **74-4**
    liberty is being defended in America, **75-9**
    liberty or death, **74-133**
    liberty, virtue or merit, equality, free consent, and "the Rights of Men," **82-184, 185**
    Parliament is hostile to British liberty, **74-28**
    support of America fighting to be free from tyranny, **75-5**
    Whig system of government by consent justifies American resistance to tyranny, **78-44**
    **See also**: Whig Poems.
Whig Opposition to Large Standing Army. **69-3, 34, 184**
Whig Poems.
    Abingdon, a true Whig opponent of the war, **77-215**
    advice to King George to become a Whig, **77-294**
    America admonishes England to beware the Scotch and preserve liberty, **79-61**
    America fights against Britain's unjust war in the spirit of Magna Carta, and Hampden and Sidney, **76-6**
    America is urged to resist clerical and royal tyranny in the Whig republican tradition of Hampden and Sidney, **75-297**
    American rebels in tradition of rebel chiefs of 17th century, **79-14**
    American War is a Tory war against English subjects, English Whigs, **76-339**
    American Whig tradition traced to Glorious Revolution, **76-308**
    Americans are in the "old English" spirit of Russell and Sidney, **76-264**
    an assertion of the rights of man regarding Luttrell's wrongfully taking a

seat in Parliament after losing an election, **69-130**
attacks the American War as unconstitutional and unjust, and urges ministry be cashiered, **76-42**
Bradshaw on the American rebellion, an anti-Whig war, **80-115**
British history from 1688 to 1776 reviewed in a defense of the American patriot cause from Whig perspective, **76-9**
the celebrated Middlesex Petition defends the people against attacks on liberty, **69-9**
Churchill's *Gotham* and the Whig ideal of a patriot king, **64-A**
criticism of Pitt's ministry for Toryism that displaces Fox's defense of people's rights, **84-19**
De Brent on Mrs. Macaulay, a genuine Whig, **70-A**
a defense against Tories, Jacobites, and Scotch, **80-84**
defense of Whig rights and freedom against Scotch, Tories, and Jacobites, **76-323**
defense of Whig tradition against Grafton and North, **70-18**
defines Whig and Tory, and favors Whig principles, **84-2**
England needs a Cato to resist tyranny and defend "the rights of men", **79-517**
for election reforms, for "equal Rights and equal Laws in equal choosing Parliament by ev'ry Briton's free Consent," **83-160**
for Fox, the constitution or limited monarchy and the rights of man, **85-33**
for Whig principles against Bute and Tories, **66-5**
for Wilkes and liberty against illegal general warrants, **68-103**
history, 1755-78, from the Whig perspective, **78-16**
history, 1760-75, from a radical Whig perspective, **75-223**
a history of Whig view of liberty up to American War, and the problem of slavery in America and West Indies, **83-9**
King George hates Whigs, his real friends, **75-231**
Milton's Whig doctrine of government on the people and the king, **80-202**
"old Rome" inspires republican liberty, **79-313**
on Samuel Johnson's Toryism, inability to withstand despotic power, **84-164**
the Opposition must replace the present Tory ministry, end the American War and introduce reforms, **80-9**
people and king under law, **83-229**
the protestant interest and freedom allied to bring peace with America through the spirit of King William, **77-317**
"The Sons of Liberty" commemorate King William's birthday and the Glorious Revolution, **78-511**
a strong Whig poem against Stuart monarchy, **65-12**
a summary of Whig views on government in defense of Wilkes, **69-13**
*The Thistle*, **73-A**
"To the Memory of William Russell," **73-A**
Tory Scots have ruined the country, corrupted government and strengthened the King's power, **80-90**
true patriotism means Whig ideals are fought for in the tradition from Russell to Wilkes, **73-8**
tyranny and civil war in reign of Charles I and of George III, **84-171**
vs monarchy and its prerogatives, and Tory Pitt, **84-115**
a warning to kings, defense of Hampden, Sidney, and Commonwealth republican political principles, **73-64**

a Whig blames Tories for all national troubles, **81-7**
a Whig election lyric, 1780, **80-229**
a Whig king is a constitutional monarch with limited powers derived from the people, **70-160**
Whig liberty and the 18th century constitution "secur'd a Brunswick's reign," i.e. George's throne, **77-320**
Whig lyric invokes the spirit of Hampden and Sidney, **74-125**
   against the "haughty oppressor," **74-153**
Whig patriot prays for end of American War and against Tories, corrupt politicians, Scotch, and the national fast, **78-128**
a Whig poem expressing republican levelling principles, **82-184**
a Whig republican poem directed at ministerial oppression, **79-298**
a Whig review of the situation in January 1776, American and British Whigs are under attack, **76-298**
Whig satire on a politician servile to King, **74-111**
Whig satire on Tories and their American War, **81-259**
a Whig state poem in praise of constitutional liberty, **76-194**
Whig tribute to Magna Carta and its meaning for "the Rights of Men," **82-185**
Whig view of execution of Charles I, **81-138**
Whigs in America and Britain must unite against Tories, purge tyranny from the land and restore freedom and natural rights, **80-40**

Whig Tradition. Cue Words and Phrases, and Concepts. Republic or rule by Parliament; or a compromise, limited or constitutional monarchy; government by free consent of the people governed through freely elected representatives in Parliament, this system identified as constitutional liberty; natural rights or the rights of man; liberty, free press, free election (no bribery); equal rights, equal laws; no hereditary privileges, no arbitrary power or "High Prerogative" (or traditional hereditary royal privileges), no "passive obedience" to authority with hereditary privileges, no standing army (traditionally controlled by the monarch); power is derived from the people.
   The opposite of Whig is Tory.

Whig Tradition. History. The Origin of the Whig Ideological Tradition in the Puritan and Glorious Revolution. **See:** following entries.

Whig Tradition. History. The Puritan Past and the American Revolution.
   American rebels as "Cromwellians," **77-150**
   American rebels as Puritans, **77-314**
   Americans as hypocritical Puritan rebels and French alliance, **78-33**
   Burgoyne on Puritan bigots and theatre during siege of Boston, **76-77, 82-55**
   false patriots support ruinous rebellion of Puritan republicans, **78-7**
   Gordon riots blamed on republicans, Dissenters like old Puritans, and Americans, **81-17**
   Loyalist officer deplores rebellion and "puritannic rage," **76-162**
   New England Whig rebels and Dissenters as Puritan roundheads and republicans, **80-218**
   "republican fanaticks," hypocritical Puritan demagogues, and America, **75-92, 76-11**

Whig Tradition. Invocation of Heroes and Saints in the Whig Pantheon.
   Algernon Sidney
         and attack on North's ministry and American War, **78-44**
         and Brutus, Cromwell, Marvell, and Montgomery, **76-359**
         and Brutus, Wilkes, and criticism of Tory Dalrymple, **73-A**

and Corsican freedom, **69**-21
and Cromwell, **71**-110
and King William, **76**-298
and Locke and Price, **78**-36
defense, **73**-107
    against Tory Dalrymple, **73**-94
his republican leadership needed in North's corrupt Parliament, **74**-28
honors the Whig martyr, vs **76**-366, anti-American verse, **76**-326
Locke, Magna Carta, Minority Opposition, and America, **77**-23
Locke, Somers, and Magna Carta, **72**-95

Hampden, Russell, and Sidney
    and American rebels, **79**-14
    and American War, **76**-339
    and Brass Crosby, **71**-68
    and Cato, Beckford, **70**-95
    and Cromwell, Marvell, and Wilkes, **68**-124
    and Drake, Raleigh, and Wilkes, **69**-120
    and King William, Duke of Cumberland, and America, **76**-9
    and Locke, **77**-294
    and Milton and American Colonies, **74**-4
    and Milton, Locke, Harrington, Pym, **68**-7
    and Pym, Vane, and opposition to American War, **75**-13
    and Raleigh, Joseph Warren, Sam Adams, and Hancock, **76**-97
    and Wilkes and America, **77**-20

John Hampden
    and American War, **75**-204
    and Camden, **76**-336
    and Fox and liberty, **84**-122
    and Gen. Charles Lee and Washington, **76**-218
    and Hancock and Hartley, **80**-154
    and King William, **76**-194
    and Milton, **72**-14 (same as **78**-73)
    and Montgomery, **76**-211
    and Mrs. Macaulay, **77**-24
    and Wilkes, **63**-88, **70**-148
        and Boston and Canada, etc., **74**-6
    and Wolfe and Montgomery, all fought for freedom, **76**-139
    Hampden's freedom lost through corruption, **73**-53
    vs American War, **76**-361
    vs Charles I, **65**-126
    vs Wilkes and Churchill, **64**-6
    Wilkes, Cato, and Robert Morris, **70**-208
    Wolfe, Pitt, Wilkes, Camden, and America, **76**-34

Sidney and Hampden
    Alfred, Magna Carta, and America, **76**-6
    ancient Spartans and Romans, and America, **75**-297
    and Churchill, Wilkes, Camden, **68**-103
    and Cromwell, Bull, Mayor of London, and America, **74**-9
    and Cruger, Wilkes, and America, **76**-39
    and Marvell and Wilkes, **69**-127
    and Milton, Locke, King William, Magna Carta, Price, and America, **83**-9

and Paoli and Wilkes, **69**-13
and Raleigh and Pym, **73**-8
and the rights of Middlesex freeholders, **70**-25
and Whig "Patriots," the Opposition, **74**-125
and Wilkes, **69**-110, **70**-40, 108
Churchill's *Duellist*, and Wilkes, **64**-A
King William and Glorious Revolution vs Stuart tyranny, **85**-34
need for these incorruptible political leaders, **63**-49
"recalled" to fight oppression, **64**-101
vs the "haughty oppressor," **74**-153
Sidney and Russell
and King William and constitutional monarchy, **77**-320
slandered by Dalrymple, **73**-25
tribute to Whig martyrs, **73**-112
Whig martyrs and America, **76**-264
Whig martyrs and Brutus, **82**-184
William Russell
"To the Memory of William Russell," and King William, **73**-A
William III
celebration of the day William of Orange came to England and began the Revolution, **78**-264
vs Tories and Jacobites on "Great Nassau's" birthday, **76**-323
William III and others
and Hampden, **76**-194
and Russell, **73**-A
and Sidney, **76**-298
Hampden and Sidney, and Glorious Revolution, **85**-34
Hampden, Russell, Sidney, Duke of Cumberland, and America, **76**-9
Milton, Locke, Magna Carta, Price, and America, **83**-9
Sidney, Russell, and constitutional monarchy, **77**-320
**For more on King William III, see**: William III.
Whig Tradition. Other Heroes.
Alfred
juries and respect for law by magistrates, **75**-522
symbolizes integrity and prophesies British imperial greatness and disintegration, **89**-3
Ancient Roman republicans, **73**-9, **75**-297
Brutus, **76**-359, **82**-184
*The Thistle*, Brutus, **73**-A
**See also**: Cato.
Lawyers and Political Thinkers
Locke, Coke, Pratt, and Price, **78**-45
Self-sacrificing patriots
Marcus Curtius and John Felton, **69**-52
**See also the following names in this index**: John Bradshaw, Oliver Cromwell, John Hampden, Andrew Marvell, John Milton, William Russell, Algernon Sidney, John Wilkes, William III (King of England).
Whitbread, Samuel (1720-96). MP, 1768-90, 1792-96. Independent in politics; wealthy brewer. Voted for the expulsion of Wilkes, February 3, 1769, and defended it, February 17, 1769; but also voted against the seating of Luttrell, May 8, 1769. Supported North administration over American War.
Calvert and Thrale vs Wilkes, **69**-80
Whitehead, William (1715-85). Poet Laureat. **See**: Index, Part I.

Wilkes, John (1727-97). MP, 1757-64, 1768-February 4, 1769, February 16-17, 1769, 1774-90; alderman of City of London, 1769; sheriff, 1771-72; ld mayor, 1774-75; City chamberlain, December 1779-d. Founded with Churchill the *North Briton*, 1762, ostensibly to attack Tory Scots in government, Bute and the peace, in which they were supported by Richard Grenville, Earl Temple. The 45th number, April 23, 1763, was considered a libel on King George, thereby beginning a series of controversial events lasting about a decade in which Wilkes became the hero of the discontented, reformers and radicals, the champion of the Bill of Rights and the English constitution. His name, joined with the number 45, became a symbol in England and America of the rights of Englishmen, on which the colonists based their cause. Wilkes opposed the coercive measures of the North ministry against America in the 1770's; in the end he supported Pitt against the Fox-North Coalition. **63**-2, 3, 4, 5, 8, 10, 11, 13, 19, 21, 23, 25, 28, 32, 36, 37, 40, 44, 45, 46, 50, 52, 56, 59, 61, 62, 63, 67, 69, 70, 75, 77, 78, 81, 93, 94, 97, 100, 103, 127, 131, 133, 139, 142, 145, 147, 149, 150, 156, 157, 165, 166, 169, 171, 172, 173, 181, 187, 188, 189, **64**-1, 6, 8, 9, 10, 14, 18, 19, 22, 28, 33, 34, 37, 42, 43, 67, 75, 79, 92, 96, 99, 103, 104, **65**-1, 6, 8, 46, 51, 80, 115, 119, 128, 139, 143, **66**-7, 38, 44, 47, 56, 57, 101, 122, **68**-1, 2, 3, 4, 6, 8, 17, 20, 21, 22, 24, 25, 27, 28, 29, 31, 32, 33, 39, 41, 43, 46, 50, 51, 52, 53, 54, 55, 58, 60, 62, 63, 65, 66, 68, 70, 71, 73, 74, 76, 77, 79, 81, 83, 84, 89, 90, 91, 92, 94, 97, 100 to 106, 109 to 116, 118 to 124, **69**-6, 8, 12, 13, 20, 22, 23, 24, 29, 35, 37, 41, 42, 44, 45, 47, 48, 55, 56, 64, 68, 70 to 76, 81, 83, 85, 88, 89, 93, 94, 101, 103 to 106, 110 to 117, 119, 120, 124 to 129, 132, 134, 139, 142, 144 to 148, 152, 153, 155, 158 to 161, 164, 165, 167, 169, 171, 173 to 178, 180, 184, 186, 189, 190, 192, 193, 196, 201, 203 to 206, 208, 209, 212, 214, 215, 216, 223 to 231, 238, 239, 241, 250, 251, 253 to 255, 262 to 264, 266, 268, 269, **70**-2, 3, 6, 7, 8, 11, 16, 22, 23, 34, 40, 42, 44, 45, 47, 60, 64, 68, 69, 72, 77, 87, 90, 101, 103, 104, 105, 108, 119, 127, 140, 141, 148, 157, 158, 170, 172, 173, 185, 188, 192, 224, 230, **71**-3, 4, 5, 9, 11, 18, 22, 25, 29, 45, 47, 49, 56, 57, 60, 61, 64, 66, 70, 72, 80, 82, 83, 84, 88, 93, 97, 99, 100, 101, 109, 111, 113, 114, 116, 123, 131, **72**-6, 7, 12, 19, 22, 57, 62, 64, 70, 73, 77, 80, 82, 87, 88, 93, **73**-1, 3, 6, 7, 8, 10, 24, 33, 38, 43, 61, 67, 83, 102, 111, **74**-6, 7, 30, 43, 44, 50, 75, 76, 79, 81, 97, 100, 123, 124, 134, 135, 136, 177, 182, 184, 203, 214, 215, **75**-1, 57, 88, 92, 94, 102, 133, 161, 188, 223, 240, 271, **76**-80, 129, 141, 179, 194, 204, 337, 391, **77**-169, 198, **80**- 10, 34, 40, 44, 61, 220, **81**-42
    "Addressed to the Two Patriots" and "On the Dispute among the Popular Party," **71**-A
    ally of the younger Pitt, **84**-28, 44
    "Alphabetical," "Dialogue," "Enchantment," "Epigram for . . . ," "Extempore," "If Alderman Squint," "Impromptu," Oakman, "On a Late Repeated Expulsion," "On the Merchants' Address," "The Poetical Wish," "Prophecy," "To Governours," "To the Farringdon Ward," **69**-A
    and America, **66**-138 (print), 139 (print)
    and American rebels, **75**-19, 21, 34, 285, **76**-23, 39, 283, 290, 344, 390, **77**-13, 72, 81, 97, 160, 183, 207, **78**-4, 7, 16, 23, 43, 292, 316, 415
        eulogy of Wilkes, **77**-20
        in list of Opposition, **79**-59
        "Liberty," Wilkes among the Opposition, **89**-2
        praises Hancock and Sam Adams, **76**-130
        summary of Wilkes's political significance, **79**-49
        Tory view of Wilkes and American War, **76**-28

　　　　　Wilkes in Opposition, satirized, **78**-556 (print), 557 (print)
and Churchill, **63**-128
and Fox, the demagogue, **82**-394
and Fox-North Coalition, **83**-281
and Gordon riots, **80**-153, 261, 342
and Hampden, **63**-88
and Luttrell, **84**-139
and Paoli, **69**-96 to 99
and reform, **84**-123
and riots, **79**-222
and Sandwich, **70**-91, **79**-102
Chamberlain, **79**-288
changes politics, **80**-167
　　　sells out the cause of freedom, helps Papists, a hypocrite, **80**-353, 354
character of, **82**-4
Churchill's *Conference, Epistle to Hogarth,* and *Prophecy of Famine,* **63**-A
Churchill's *Duellist,* "A Conference," "Ode to Ambition," "Soliloquy," **64**-A
consistently self-interested, **84**-152
defended, **80**-355
demagogue, **63**-58
elected City Chamberlain, **77**-303
"An Epigram," "Epigrams," **65**-A
evil history of Wilkes, the demagogue, **69**-249
factious and republican, **80**-134
hostile review of Wilkes's career, **73**-18
Junius, **70**-61
no longer "patriot," **82**-331
*Ode to Palinurus* and "Parody," **70**-A
prematurely dead, **76**-137
*Pride,* **66**-A
re-appears in England, **66**-100
reconciled with George III after the peace, **83**-298 (print)
returns from exile in France, **66**-133
review of career, **73**-18, **76**-140
Satanic, seditious and subversive republican, **76**-10
Scottish view of Wilkes, **70**-238
seditious and subversive, **75**-312
supports Pitt against Fox, **85**-13
supports Pitt and "the Prerogative Scale," **84**-54
*The Thistle,* **73**-A
a turncoat, review of Wilkes's career to his political death as a true patriot, **84**-57, 95, 110
Whig Wilkes and Tory government, **63**-66
Wilkes's debts, **70**-193
Wilkes' assassins. **See**: Alexander Dunn, John Forbes, Samuel Martin; also William Talbot, who fought a duel with Wilkes.
Williams, Charles Hanbury (1708-59). MP, 1734-47, 1754-59. Diplomat, satirical author and poet noted for his odes.
　　Williams' poem adapted to Pitt's elevation to peerage, **66**-24
Williams, John (d. after 1774). London publisher, popular hero; sentenced by Judge Mansfield after a trial, July 26, 1764, for reprinting *North Briton,* No.

45, in his *North Briton Complete*, 1763; after Parliament had ordered it burnt, sentenced to spend six months in King's Bench prison, stand in the pillory (February 14, 1765), and pay a fine of £100. **65**-32, 112, 129, 132, 145, 146, 148 (print)

    "Epigrams," **65**-A

William III, King of England (1650-1702). Prince of Orange, son of William II, Prince of Orange, stadtholder of the Dutch republic, and Mary, daughter of Charles I of England; married Mary, eldest daughter of Duke of York, later James II of England; proclaimed joint sovereign in conjunction with his wife February 13, 1689, James escaping to France. "Great Nassau," William became the model of a constitutional monarch and symbol of opposition to Popery and superstition and Stuart tyranny. His birthday, November 4, was often celebrated in connection with the success of the Glorious Revolution. His success as defender of the Revolution at the Battle of the Boyne, July 1, 1690, a critical battle in Ireland that sent James back to France and permanent exile, is celebrated to this day in Northern Ireland.

    American War and protestant interest, **77**-317
    and English liberty, **78**-392
    and Gen. Howe, **77**-90
    and Ireland, **81**-99
    and Mrs. Macaulay, **78**-350
    and Revolution Constitution, **79**-384
    Battle of the Boyne for English liberty against Papists and French, **64**-2
    birth and landing of William and freedom, **74**-80
    birthday celebration and defense of Whig rights and freedom, **76**-323
    commemoration of birth of the savior of England, **82**-38
    commemoration of the Revolution of 1688, **85**-34
    controls faction, **64**-80
    desires peace and freedom, **81**-18
    established freedom for 18th century England, **69**-13
    forced bigot papists from England, **83**-223
    forced Stuart tyranny and superstition from England in the Glorious Revolution, **78**-264
    Glorious Revolution and Brunswick line, **79**-191
    his constitutional monarchy "secur'd a Brunswick's reign," **77**-320
    inspires the fighters for freedom, **71**-44
    praised, **74**-57, 72
    rescued Britain from "a Bigot Tyrant," James II, **83**-9
    song for birthday, **78**-511
    symbol of struggle against tyranny, **76**-9
    vs the Popery of Quebec Act, **75**-69
    vs Stuart maxim of rule by divine right, **65**-55
    vs Tory oppression and corruption, **70**-176

Wilson, Thomas (1703-84). Prebendary of Westminster; member of Society of Supporters of Bill of Rights; a follower of Wilkes and an admirer of Catharine Macaulay. **69**-126

Windham, William (1750-1810). MP, 1784-1810. Friend of Fox and Burke, also Samuel Johnson; member of the Literary Club. Supported Fox-North Coalition and accepted post as chief secretary to Ld Northington, Ld Lt of Ireland, 1783; drifted from reforming opinions to support of status quo.

    praise of Windham, with others of Patriot Opposition, Burke, John Cavendish, George Savile, John Townshend, **79**-100

Witherspoon, John (1723-94). American Presbyterian clergyman; emigrated from

Scotland to become President of the College of New Jersey (Princeton), 1768; signer of Declaration of Independence. Satirized as a seditious Puritan Presbyterian fanatic, king-killing republican. **76**-1, **79**-26, **80**-22

Wolfe, James (1727-59). British general, served on staff in the Battle of Culloden, 1746, ending the Jacobite rebellion and Stuart threats to English political stability; served also in French and Indian War, under Amherst in the successful attack on Louisburg, 1758, and as commander of the brilliantly successful attack on Quebec, 1759, in which he and the opposing French general Montcalm lost their lives. Wolfe, "the conqueror of Quebec," secured the British colonies in North America against French expansion as he "helped win an empire." He became the very model of the noble "British Hero." A monument attesting to his great achievement and his status as Britain's national hero is in Westminster Abbey. **58**-1, **59**-1, 2, 6, 7, 10, 12 to 15, 16, 17 to 23, 26, 27, 30, 32, 34, 35, 38, 39, 41, 42, **60**-3, 5, 6, 11, 13, 17, 25, 30, 31, 35, 36, 39, 41, 47, **62**-7, 17, **63**-17, 24, 51, **64**-1, 3, 7, **66**-67, 75, **68**-14, **69**-5, 7, 17, 19, **71**-46, **72**-3, 11, 51, 55, 56, 58 to 60, 69, 72, 74, 86, 99 to 102

    America should ally with Britain against France as before, **79**-23
    and Admiral Saunders, **73**-5
    and American rebellion, **75**-13
    and American rebels, **76**-166
    and Arnold, **78**-414
    and Burgoyne, **78**-97, 325
    and Carleton and Quebec, **76**-296, 342
    and General Howe, **78**-32
    and General Montgomery, **76**-12, 255
    and Quebec and the siege of 1775, **81**-204
    and the French, **73**-66
    as British heroic warrior, **80**-27
    as inspiration for patriotic British youth, **81**-10
    as symbol of British patriotism and anti-gallican spirit, **79**-2
    Colvill's epitaph on Wolfe, **72**-A
    Cowper's patriotic appreciation of Wolfe's military genius, **85**-2
    critical view of Wolfe, of the violent and destructive military mind, **80**-122
    Delamayne's *Oliviad*, **62**-A
    died at the peak of British glory just before "the Butean system", **81**-7
    enough on Wolfe!, **73**-65
    epitaph(s), **73**-27, 28, 31, 32
        "Epitaph," **72**-A
        on the epitaphs, **73**-75
        satire on, **73**-95
    the epitaph contest
        in year 1772, **72**-15
        passim in year 1772, **72**-26 to 49
    "Epitaph for General Wolfe," **60**-A
    French intervention justifies British war against America, **79**-1
    in Brackenridge's "Rising Glory of America," **72**-14, **78**-72
    in Westminster Abbey, the war against France and the recent loss of America, **84**-10
    inscriptions and epitaph, **73**-44 to 46
    the meaning of Wolfe for America, **72**-17

             memorial inscription, **72-13**
             "A Morning Scene in Paris," **60-A**
             "A New Song," **60-A**
             not yet forgotten, **74-206**
             "A Notable Remark," **72-A**
             "An Ode on . . . George III," **61-A**
             "Ode on the Happy Fate of Canada," **60-A**
             praise of England's national hero, **82-392**
             a valorous warrior, like Tarleton, **82-21**
             Wolfe's sacrifice in vain as France enters war, **80-14**
             Wolfe's spirit berates Hancock for unjustified rebellion, **75-258**
             Wolfe's spirit invoked to give patriotic aid to Britain as it asserts its
                rights, **80-41**
             Wolfe's vision of the future greatness of Britain, **90-1**
Wombwell, George (1734-80). MP, 1774-80. Government contractor and East India
    Company director, and friend and follower of Sandwich, Secretary of the Navy;
    held army contracts to victual 12,000-13,700 men in America; also held
    contract for victualling Gibraltar; supported the North Ministry. **77-315**
Women and the Times. **See**: Feminist, and Feminist Poems in Part II of index;
    also Women Authors in Part I of index.
Woodfall, Henry Sampson (1739-1805). Printer, journalist, and manager of the
    daily *Public Advertiser* of London; with brother William, he was involved in
    controversies with the House of Commons concerning their reports of proceed-
    ings of the House, and was summoned before it for printing the letters of
    Junius. **79-265, 80-382, 82-296**
        **See also**: Newspapers; and Rights: Liberty of the Press.
Woodfall, William (1746-1803). Brother of Henry Sampson Woodfall; editor-
    publisher of the *London Packet*, 1772-74; on staff of the London *Morning
    Chronicle*, 1774-89; like his brother, he was criticized by the House of
    Commons for printing reports of their debates. **82-296**
        **See also**: Newspapers; and Rights: Liberty of the Press.
Wooster, David (1711-77). American general, served in French and Indian War,
    especially Ticonderoga, 1758, and Amherst's operations, 1759-60; fought in
    Battle of Long Island, August 1776. **76-263**
Wray, Cecil (1734-1805). MP, 1768-80, 1782-84. A founder of the Society of
    Supporters of the Bill of Rights, 1769; supported Wilkes; opposed the North
    ministry to the end of the American War; supported reform; but ran against Fox
    in the Westminster election because of his hostility for North. **84-37, 70,
    86-3**
             and "Westminster Scrutiny" of Fox's election victory, **85-12**
             vs Fox, **83-7, 84-215**
Wright, James (1716-85). A friend of Bute; attorney-general of South Carolina,
    1742; governor of Georgia, 1761-66; supported Stamp Act, 1766; defended
    Savannah successfully against D'Estaing and Lincoln, October 1779. **79-9**
Writers for the court, 1763
        according to Churchill's *Author*: Tobias Smollett, Arthur Murphy, John
            Shebbeare, William Guthrie, Philip Francis, and John Kidgell, **63-A**
Wyndham, Charles, 2d Earl of Egremont (1710-63). MP, 1735-50; then House of
    Lords. Tory, but cooperated with the Whig ministries; secretary of state,
    southern department, 1761-63, and participated in peace negotiations at end of
    Seven Years' War, 1761-63; associated with Halifax in prosecution of Wilkes by
    general warrant, 1763. **62-5, 63-2, 65-8**
Wyvill, Christopher (1740-1822). Clergyman; a leading organizer of the reform

movement against the corruption of Parliament; organized the Yorkshire Association, 1779-80, and other reform groups in England; inevitably this movement became an attack on North and his style of securing support. **80**-157, **81**-186, **84**-131

    criticized as rebel, **80**-97
    "Dialogue between a Certain Personage and his Minister," **84**-A
    disloyal republican, **80**-216
    **See**: Yorkshire Association; Reform Movement.

Yankee, and Yankee Doodle. Cant name for colonial Americans. **75**-2, **76**-16, 62, 262, 376, **77**-66, 83, 128, 134, 167, 268, 285, **78**-66, 71, 171, 375, 415, 550, **79**-270, 276, 424, **81**-33

    "cowardly Yankies," depicted ironically, **76**-214
    Germain's "Yankey War," **76**-213
    Lee (General Charles), "A hardy tribune of the Yanky crew," **82**-24
    "The Lexington March," **75**-25
    Loyalist Yankees, **80**-235
    "A New-York Yankee," **76**-385
    "Nick Nankeedoodle," **70**-62
    "the obstinate Yankees" cannot be defeated, **78**-510
    "the Portsmouth Yankey," **65**-8
    privateers of the "Yankies," **78**-268
    Scotch and Tories are "Yank-Hunting," **81**-259
    Scotch vs "stubborn Yankies," **75**-76, **78**-142
    Scotch vs "Yankies," **80**-228
    Tarleton vs "Yankies," **82**-31
    West, "our Yankey painter," **83**-34
    "Yankee-doodle," **75**-7
    "Yankee Doodle," **75**-25, **76**-396, **78**-527
        chorus, **80**-199
        cowardly americans, **76**-400 (print)
    "Yankee Doodle, . . . an ungrateful son," **78**-7
    "Yankee Heroes," **76**-397
    "Yankey war," **82**-155
    "Yankies," **75**-23, **76**-25
    "Yanky" and "Yankee-doodle," **73**-51
    younger Pitt on the "cursed Yankee wars," **85**-12

Yates, Joseph (1722-70). Appointed Judge of the court of King's Bench, 1764; involved with Wilkes when he returned from exile and outlawry in France, 1768.
    Mansfield, Quebec Act, and shade of Judge Yates, **74**-185

Yonge, George (1733-1812). MP, 1754-61, 1763-96, 1799-1801. Admiralty Board, 1766-70; in office during second Rockingham administration, 1782, secretary-at-war and privy councillor, Shelburne ministry, 1782-83; and in War Office of younger Pitt's ministry, 1783-94. Opposed general warrants and later, North and American War.
    praised by Tasker as member of second Rockingham ministry, **83**-32

Yorke, Charles (1722-70). MP, 1747-68; 1768-70. Attorney-general, 1762-63, 1765-66, at time of the Wilkes case; appointed ld chancellor, Jan 1770, after Camden was dismissed, but committed suicide soon after.
    died January 20, 1770, **70**-133

Yorke, Joseph (1724-92). MP, 1751-80. Minister at The Hague, 1751-61; ambassador, 1761-80.
    ambassador to Holland, **79**-454
    lyric addressed to Yorke on enlargement of American War, **81**-125

Yorke, Philip, Baron and 1st Earl of Hardwicke (1690-1764).  MP, 1719-34; then House of Lords.  Opposed Bute's peace, December 9, 1762, and Cider Tax, March 28, 1763; opposed Government on general warrants and restrictions on Parliamentary privilege, although he had no sympathy with Wilkes.  **62**-5
   death, **64**-94

Yorkshire Association.  The first of 25 county reform associations; formed and directed by Christopher Wyvill, 1779, to organize the tendency toward reform of the "Oeconomy" of Parliament and the administration of government.  The association platform was directed at shortening the duration of Parliaments and the equalisation of representation; but it succeeded in having only minor economic reforms adopted.  **See**: Reform Movement and Wyvill.

Yorktown, Virginia.  **See**: Battles and Campaigns, Yorktown, Virginia, under rubric of American War.

Zoutman, Johan Arnold.  Dutch admiral, engaged Admiral Hyde Parker in the inconclusive but bloody Battle of the Dogger Bank, August 5, 1781.  **81**-34, 46
   narrative of the sea battle at Dogger Bank, **81**-77

INDEX

Part III

Verse Forms and Other Forms

Abcedarian poem (also called Alphabet poem). **64**-10, **67**-15, **69**-22, 29, **70**-17, **72**-64, **75**-33, 34, 35, **76**-43, 48, 49, **77**-33, **78**-219, 408, **79**-59, **83**-151
    "Alphabetical Gimcrack," **69**-A
Acrostic poem. **59**-5, 7, 10, **60**-9, **61**-4, **62**-12, **63**-23, 181, **64**-7, 11, **65**-13, **68**-92, **69**-24, 25, **70**-10, 11, **75**-27, **76**-371, **79**-334, **82**-32, 33, 34, **83**-35
Allegory (see also Fable). **63**-83, **69**-141, 269, **70**-34, 226, 231, **71**-16, 133, **74**-89, **75**-1, 22, 240, **76**-34, 36, 58, 74, 230, 295, 314, 316, **77**-290, **78**-22, 275, 292, **79**-26, 392, 431, 443, 446, **80**-20, 199, 201, 272, 417, 418, 419, 420, 425, 427, 430, **81**-29, 87, **82**-5, 16, 39, 138, **83**-3, 19, 150, **84**-16, **85**-13, **93**-1
Alphabet poem. **See**: Abcedarian poem.
Anapest tetrameter couplets. **58**-12, **63**-46, 116, 165, **64**-31, 32, 79, 89, **74**-36, 132, 146, 179, 216, 222, **75**-143, **76**-134, **77**-50, 70, 130, 168, 281, **78**-48, 52, 53, 64, 89, 241, 386, 397, 410, 419, 420, 440, 441, 463, 510, **79**-34, 59, 62, 97, 105, 106, 134, 138, 143, 157, 169, 180, 217, 218, 332, 338, 364, 428, 523, **80**-111, 181, 191, 274, 304, 347, 368, 374, 400, 416, **81**-7, 23, 95, 156, 207, 228, 250, 262, **82**-28, 150, 240, 315, 381, 390, **83**-36, 61, 78, 88, 95, 102, 147, 235, 237, 255, 264, **84**-21, 46, 50, 88, 95, 138, 148, 168, 169, 211, **85**-21, 52
    in quatrains, **83**-114
    "On Gen. Monckton's writing home," **62**-A
    "Poetical Paraphrase," **78**-A
    "A Spurious Speech," **77**-A
Anapest tetrameter quatrains. **70**-214, **82**-114, 255
Anthem. **78**-59
Ballad. **58**-4, 9, **61**-12, **62**-14, 34, 48, **63**-182, 188, 189, **64**-40, **65**-74, 75, 76, 136, **66**-14, 111, 134, 140, **68**-37, 64, 108, **69**-14, 36, 44, 55, 101, 186, 193, 249, 253, 268, **70**-15, 22, 32, 34, 72, 82, 91, 172, 205, **71**-11, 133, **72**-18, **73**-18, 38, 105, **74**-8, 32, 42, 46, 114, 152, **75**-2, 25, 39, 109, 137, 211, 241, **76**-14, 35, 40, 64, 65, 68, 165, 264, 304, 344, **77**-6, 15, 58, 60, 66, 132, 133, 144, 321, **78**-62, 65, 66, 67, 71, 77, 90, 113, 117, 171, 226, 236, 292, 295, 298, 333, 416, 479, **79**-67, 109, 112, 186, 205, 229, 235, 240, 245, 257, 267, 268, 270, 271, 273, 279, 284, 370, 386, 401, 414, 431, 453, 489, 490, 527, 528, **80**-2, 90, 124, 174, 176, 198, 199, 215, 216, 217, 227, 269, 322, 325, 342, **81**-13, 25, 30, 77, 126, 127, 183, **82**-1, 16, 45, 46, 50, 125, 141, 246, 321, 323, 327, 337, 375, **83**-7, **84**-23, 26, 39, 62, 109, 111, 113, 117, 118, 139, 161, 166, 179, 214, **85**-19, 28, 49, **86**-4
    Burns, **84**-A

"Excellent New Ballad," **63-A**
   octaves, **80**-5
   sixains, **79**-272, **80**-392
Blank Verse. **55**-2, **56**-1, **57**-1, **59**-21, **60**-6, **61**-41, 51, **63**-62, 129, **64**-7, 97, **65**-10, 64, **66**-25, 57, 64, 117, **68**-6, 7, **69**-2, 7, 15, 16, 120, 180, 219, 237, **70**-39, 158, 190, **71**-44, 91, 92, **72**-14, 38, 73, 95, **73**-39, 79, 80, 112, **74**-17, 41, 83, 97, 133, 173, 190, **75**-5, 14, 15, 16, 49, 131, 150, 234, **76**-34, 41, 74, 205, 280, 299, 317, **77**-4, 153, 164, 298, **78**-5, 26, 60, 73, 75, 100, 229, 250, 291, 306, 348, 442, 447, 448, 449, **79**-1, 102, 185, 221, 256, 379, 533, **80**-15, 19, 24, 51, 366, **81**-16, 22, 108, **82**-20, 26, 77, 185, 251, 286, 334, 367, 369, **83**-184, 207, 260, 279, **84**-17, **85**-2
   "Ghost of Lord Chatham," **83-A**
   "Hail to the Son of Fame," **79-A**
   "Jaffier's Ghost," **68-A**
   "Real Patriot," **76-A**
   "Soliloquy," **64-A**
Burlesque. **83**-24
   doggerel, **62**-11
   **See also**: Doggerel and Hudibrastic Verse.
Burlesque Dialogue. **76**-390
Burlesque Oratorio. **75**-237, **80**-305
Cantata (recitatives and airs). **62**-44, **63**-174, **64**-75, **70**-31, **72**-87, **73**-62, **76**-66, **77**-40, 189, **78**-3, 213, **79**-39, 89, **80**-221, **82**-194, **83**-70, **84**-68
   "Peace, 1763," **63-A**
   Woods, "Lyric Ode to Public Courage," **79-A**
   **See also**: Oratorio.
Catch. **67**-13, **76**-398, **78**-515, **79**-85, 86, 87, 88, **82**-175, **83**-152
Character (or Portrait). **63**-162, **64**-15, **69**-47, 261, **70**-33, 93, 187, **72**-1, 6, 7, **73**-1, 3, 4, 10, **74**-160, **76**-81, **78**-16, 82, 83, 84, 237, 259, 291, 418, 419, 420, 421, **79**-90 to 93, 378, **80**-10, 22, 23, **81**-37, 38, **82**-59, 285, 333, 366, **83**-52
   "A Character," **65-A**
   "Character of a Good King," **66-A**
Cinquain. **70**-195, **76**-334, **78**-109, 361, **79**-438, **80**-87, 301
   "An Ode," **65-A**
Couplet. **59**-36, 43, **60**-27, 29, **63**-177, 178, 183, 184, **69**-163, 169, **73**-50, 126, **74**-50, 223, **75**-96, 111, 320, **77**-68, 308, 331, **78**-115, 154, 444, 507, 555, 556, **79**-120, 154, 330, 349, **80**-356, 419, 421, 422, 429, 430, **81**-111, 171, 266, **82**-409, 410, 414, 417, 421, **83**-291 (print), 296 (print), 297 (print), 298 (print), **85**-60 (print), 61 (print)
   dimeter, **81**-264
   "Epigram Addressed," **64-A**
   epigraph, **77**-103
   four stress, **83**-30
   in sixains, **70**-176
   irregular c, **77**-37
   irregular meter, **82**-126
   "A Notable Remark," **72-A**
   tetrameter, **78**-557
   "To the Farringdon Ward Without," **69-A**
   trimeter, **85**-47
   **Also passim**: especially Anapest Tetrameter Couplet, Heroic Couplet, Hexameter Couplet, Hudibrastic Couplet, Octosyllabic Couplet.

Dactylic tetrameter. **69**-9, **70**-21, **74**-8, **75**-26
    couplets, **70**-43, **73**-15, **78**-19
Dialogue. **63**-5, 21, 77, **64**-19, 104, **65**-28, 29, 30, 67, **66**-36, 37, 38, 59, 64, 91, **67**-16, **68**-34, **70**-2, 41, 76, 188, 190, **71**-26, **72**-14, 19, 20, **74**-9, 49, 52 to 57, 108, **75**-51, 67, 116, **76**-82, 91, 92, 93, 131, 390, **77**-5, 71, 247, 253, **78**-107 to 110, **79**-102, 105, 106, 107, 388, **80**-14, 20, 23, 37, 49, **81**-40, 51, 244, **82**-13, 41, 76, 306, **83**-44, 67, 112, 113, 127, **84**-2, 38, 41, 44, 71, 75, 154, 160, **86**-4
    "A Conversation," **69**-A
    "A Dialogue," **69**-A
    "Dialogue," **84**-A
    "A Pill," **68**-A
Dimeter couplets. **64**-11, **76**-378, **77**-78, 126, **78**-450, **81**-264
Dimeter quatrains. **67**-41
Dixain. **60**-43, **69**-133, **75**-289, **78**-35, 312, **79**-4, 22, 304, 307, **80**-14, 242, 249, **81**-12, 31, 232, **82**-18, 140, 313, 320, 345, 378, **83**-165
Doggerel. **61**-42, **72**-82, **73**-66, **76**-191, **77**-279, **79**-34, 407, **80**-255, **82**-148, 417, **85**-47
    burlesque, **62**-11
    oc, **77**-137, 162, 517
    single rhyme, **82**-272
    six-stress, **77**-325
    three-stress couplets, **73**-34, **82**-265
    **See also**: Burlesque and Hudibrastic Verse.
Double Quatrain. **See**: Quatrain.
Dream Vision. **68**-7, 120, **70**-231, **71**-90, **77**-73, **78**-115, 327, 438, **79**-380
    "Genius of America," **78**-47
    **See also**: Vision.
Eclogue. **76**-99, **82**-13, **83**-37, **84**-22
Elegy (and Elegiac Quatrains or Stanzas). **59**-13, **60**-12, **63**-24, **64**-18, **66**-3, 40, 41, 42, **69**-1, 19, 56, 66, 115, 128(?), **70**-47, 48, 49, 92, 168, **71**-20, **73**-21, **74**-5, 47, 178, **75**-8, 17, 36, 37, 50, 173, 277, **76**-5, 10, 30, 97, 98, 135(?), 163(?), **77**-9, 10, 76, 289, **78**-121, 123 124, 196, 271, 329, 364, 365, 366, 413, 480, **79**-60, 184, 262, 339, **80**-6, 21, 88, 89, 340, **81**-188, **82**-84 to 88, 89(?), 248, 305, 347, 387, **83**-71, 149, 269, **84**-10, 45, 102, **89**-2
    elegiac epistle in HC, **80**-13, 86
    "Elegy" in HC, **70**-A
    HC, **60**-8, **78**-120, 122
    Irregular Pindaric(!), **77**-75
    "On the Defection of Corsicans," **69**-A
Eleven-line stanzas. **82**-236
Epic. **60**-1, 2, 3, **62**-7, **67**-3, **69**-17, **76**-22, **77**-4, **81**-3, **82**-7, 26, **85**-4, **90**-1
Epigram. **59**-15, **60**-38, **61**-9, 26, 33, 34, **62**-19 to 25, 49, **63**-10, 19, 25 to 48, 53, 70, 78, 82, 94, 96, 100, 102, 103, 112, 114, 115, 128, 136, 137, 154, **64**-12, 20 to 35, 43, 49, 59, 63, 64, 70, 71, 72, 83, 89, 96, 103, 106, **65**-17, 18, 33 to 49, 72, 86, 91, 92, 101, 103, 106, 112, 120, 124, 138, **66**-8, 17, 21, 35, 43 to 52, 78, 79, 81, 82, 83, 86, 92, 94, 99, 107, 123, 124, 129, 130, **67**-18 to 21, 29, 43, 44, 45, **68**-28, 38 to 42, 45, 51, 53, 54, 75, 76, 78, 82, 83, 93, 98, 102, 106, 111, 114, 116, **69**-28, 34, 42, 49, 58, 59 to 65, 74, 75, 76, 98, 100, 104, 144 to 148, 153, 157, 167, 168, 172, 174, 190, 191, 196, 208, 216, 223, 230, 242, 245, 264, 266, **70**-25, 28, 29, 46, 51 to 60, 68, 70, 83, 117, 119, 121, 125, 126, 127, 138, 144, 151, 206, 213, 232, 238, 240, **71**-9, 15, 22 to 29, 39, 40, 47, 49, 50, 52, 55, 57, 75, 78, 80, 93, 100, 108,

114, 123, 126, 128, 132, 134, **72**-21 to 26, 68, 71, 75, 76, **73**-22 to 25, 70, 73, 76, 77, 88, **74**-24, 30, 33, 39, 62, 64 to 72, 94, 96, 130, 135, 136, 139, 162, 169, 199, 215, 217, 220 (and 208), 223, **75**-32, 38, 44, 59, 64, 68, 70 to 87, 93, 96 to 100, 138, 145, 157, 174, 178, 182, 183, 185, 186, 190, 196, 197, 198, 205, 218, 231, 243, 246, 258, 260, 268, 285, 291, 292, 294, 295, 304, 308, 314, **76**-72, 100 to 132, 143, 144, 147, 150, 151, 157, 159, 161, 168, 179, 181, 186, 207, 232 to 234, 237, 238, 241, 242, 249, 251, 261, 263, 267, 268, 272, 286 to 288, 291, 301, 302, 306, 338, 346, 348, 357, 362, 370, 374, 375, 385, 388, 392, **77**-34, 38, 46, 47, 61, 70, 79 to 102, 110, 141, 142, 145, 170, 190 to 193, 195, 196, 200, 201, 203, 205, 213, 219, 221, 226, 232 to 234, 239 to 241, 253, 254, 257, 266, 269 to 272, 280, 283, 295, 302, 303, 305, **78**-70, 93, 104, 106, 111, 119, 130 to 150, 175, 180, 187, 193, 202, 204, 216, 235, 239, 244, 248, 265, 267, 302, 337, 339, 351, 359, 377, 390, 396, 411, 413 to 415, 430, 436, 439, 443, 444, 454, 455, 473, 483, 491, 499, 516, 519, 524, 533, 535, 538, 539, 547, **79**-72, 118 to 141, 159, 166, 169, 176, 199, 204, 216, 246, 265, 266, 322, 328 to 331, 335, 342, 351, 362, 374, 388, 430, 444, 472, 482, 501, 502, 511, 515, **80**-50, 71, 91 to 109, 159, 179, 193, 195, 222, 258, 266, 267, 278, 279, 283, 289, 291, 297, 311, 317, 320, 351, 356, 386, 402, 403, 411, **81**-26, 40, 47, 51, 57 to 61, 64, 66, 67, 68, 73, 80, 81, 90, 105, 106, 124, 148, 150, 161, 162, 170 to 172, 179, 180, 182, 192, 194, 207, 214, 224, 246, **82**-43, 52, 58, 65, 66, 92 to 114, 149, 189, 208, 230, 232, 235, 240, 244, 252, 257, 260, 261, 275, 276, 304, 307, 318, 322, 331, 352, 354, 364, 377, 381, **83**-38, 44, 47, 55, 56, 57, 64, 74 to 90, 102, 119, 121, 125, 179, 195, 206, 210, 221, 229, 247, 252, 279, 283, **84**-42, 43, 46 to 53, 105, 145, 158, 167, 189, **85**-21 to 24, 41

    "Answer to an Epigram on" (Churchill), **64**-A
    "Epigram," **65**-A, **68**-A, **76**-A
    "Epigrams" [2], **63**-A, **69**-A, **70**-A
    "Extempore," **69**-A
    ingredients of, **85**-46
    "Leave prating," **78**-A
    "Minister's Reasoning," **83**-A
    "On Occasion," **68**-A
    "On the Late Riot," **68**-A
    "On the Opinion" [2], **69**-A
    "One Hannibal, **76**-A
    "Political Squibs," **66**-A
    "To Governours," **69**-A
    "To the Farringdon Ward Without," **69**-A

Epigraph. **77**-103, **80**-67, 68, 209, 409
Epilogue. **See**: Prologue and Epilogue.
Epistle. **59**-3, **61**-10, **63**-49, **65**-24, 56, 61, **66**-4, 53, **68**-16, 21, 43, 44, 87, **69**-21, 105, 106, **70**-3, 96, **71**-42, **73**-7, 26, **74**-3, **75**-7, 10, 11, 54, 55, 88, 104, 143, 215, **76**-10, 23, 133 to 135, 156, 176, **77**-18, 104, 105, 106, 107, 168, 279, **77**-18, 104 to 107, 168, 279, **78**-4, 8, 9, 13, 14, 34, 44, 48, 89, 151, 409, **79**-9, 13, 14, 17, 24, 30, 41, 45, 47, 142, **80**-16, 18, 27, 72, 110, 111, 157, 164, 196, 197, 424 (print), **81**-7, 11, 72, 119 to 122, **82**-9, 12, 127, **83**-18, 25, **84**-9, 54, 55, 66, 104, **85**-25, **89**-3
    elegiac epistle in HC, **80**-13, 86
    "Epistle to Hayley," **81**-A
    *Noble Cricketers*, **78**-A
Epitaph. **59**-12, 14, **60**-13, **61**-21, **63**-50, 51, **64**-13, 36, 58, 66, 69, **65**-50, 87,

**66**-8, 11, 34, 54, 55, 63, **67**-35, **69**-37, 66, 67, **70**-102, 136, 187, 218, 229, 233, 239, **71**-30 to 32, **72**-15, 27 to 51, 86, 99, 100, **73**-27 to 32, 44, 45, 95, **74**-73 to 78, **75**-89, 90, 141, 262, **76**-136 to 141, 189, 211, 254, 255, 256, 340, 360, **77**-108, 223, 262, 306, **78**-152 to 169, 504, 505, **79**-135, 143 to 149, **80**-10, 74, 112 to 122, 138, 170, 194, 206, **81**-62, 63, 98, 164, **82**-24, 115 to 117, 137, **83**-13, 60, 91, 92, 192, 193, **84**-4, 56 to 61, 74, 76, 137, 210, **85**-26, 27, **88**-1
  as art form, **73**-31, 95
  Colvill, "Epitaph," **72**-A
  "Counter-Epitaph," **64**-A
  "Epitaph," **64**-A, **80**-A
  "Epitaph at Thebes," **65**-A
  "Epitaph for Wolfe," **60**-A
  "Here rest," **78**-A
Essay. **69**-13, **77**-23, **80**-32, **83**-20, **84**-19
Extempore (including Impromptu). **59**-15, **60**-14, **63**-52, 53, 54, 172, **65**-52, 69, 77, 115, 143 to 146, **66**-8, 56, 94, **68**-45, 46, 53 to 56, 97, **69**-71 to 81, 92, 97 to 99, 103, 208, **70**-59, 61 to 70, 84, **71**-33 to 41, 50, 51, 100, **72**-56, **73**-33, 43, **74**-79 to 81, 103, **75**-58, 93 to 102, 106, 110, 132 to 135, 176, 214, 238, 254, **76**-87, 128, 143 to 154, 179 to 182, 236, 245, 373, **77**-39, 48, 88, 109 to 123, 152, 217, 230, 272, 308, **78**-55, 114, 116, 172 to 193, 202, 203, 241, 242 to 244, 280, 385, 407, 451, 471, 476, 477, 496, 497 to 517, 523, 536, **79**-98, 101, 108, 150 to 183, 215 to 221, 326, 328, 407, 426, 459, 464, 520, 524, **80**-125 to 132, 154, 166, 167, 184, 190, 264, 274, 307, 338, 347, 349, 361, 388, 413, **81**-36, 45, 64 to 70, 83, 89, 95, 149, 173, 202, 206, 211, **82**-119 to 124, 131, 157, 161 to 168, 170, 263, 264, 266, 325, 329, 350, 365, 404, 407, **83**-94 to 99, 120 to 125, 201, 231, 238(!), 254, **84**-58, 63, 64, 83 to 85, 130, 140
  "Exert," **79**-A
  "Extempore," **68**-A (4), **69**-A, **78**-A
  "Extempore Answer," **64**-A
  "French Peace," **79**-A
  "French sail'd," **79**-A
  "Impromptu," **68**-A, **69**-A, **83**-A
  "Occasioned by the Pardon of MacQuirk and Balfe," **69**-A
  "Political Squib," **63**-A
  "Spoken Extempore," **70**-A
  "'Tis true that Keppel pants for fame," **79**-A
  "To the Celebrated Mrs. Macaulay," **69**-A
  "Verses Extempore," **65**-A
Fable (including nature, animal and botanical, and allegorical). **62**-32, **63**-57, 69, 125, 157, **64**-81, **65**-21, 25, 31, 53, 111, **66**-126, 134, 140, **67**-30, **68**-16, 63, 98, **69**-108, 109, **70**-42, 98, 99, 154, 155, **71**-16, 18, 62, 98, 133, **74**-59, 82, 102, 117, 216, 218, **75**-38, 103, 128, 129, 142, 146, 151, 240, **76**-89, 94, 155, 190, 197, 229, 230, 314, 316, 336, 399, **77**-1, 255, 278, 300, 332, **78**-22, 95, 194, 195, 210, 275, 420, 506, 555, **79**-366, 376, **80**-47, 133, 140, 272, 385, **81**-239, 245, **82**-299, 309, 361, **83**-68, 95, 103, 131, 273, **84**-15, 27, 30, 169, 186, **85**-1
  classical fable, **75**-66
  "Fable," **69**-A
  "The Loaded Ass," **68**-15
  Oakman's "Mastiff," **69**-A
  "Snarling Pug," **63**-A

"The State Coach," **68**-A
"Thieves and Butcher," **68**-A
"Vine and Bramble," **70**-A

Fourteeners. **61**-14, 20, **63**-179, **70**-132, 177, **73**-66, **74**-68, 150, **75**-42, 188, 209, **78**-328, 548, **79**-107, 251, **82**-406, **83**-208

Glee. **77**-138, **79**-203

Heptameter Couplets. **78**-556

Heroic Couplets. **55**-A, **56**-A, **57**-2, **58**-2, 7, 8, 10, **59**-5, 10, 11, 14, 22, 28, 29, 30, 34, 37, 38, 40, 41, **59**-A, **60**-5, 8, 9, 11, 13, 15, 24, 30, 35, 36, 37, 39, 41, 45, 47, 49, **61**-5, 11, 13, 22, 25, 27, 28, 30, 38, 46, 48, **62**-1, 4, 5, 7, 8, 16, 17, 32, 39, 41, 42, 45, 57, 58, 60 to 63, 65, 67, **63**-1, 2, 5 to 7, 9, 15, 17, 20, 25, 29, 33, 38, 39, 44, 45, 47, 49, 51, 53, 54, 56, 58, 60, 63, 68, 71, 75, 78, 83, 86, 88, 89, 92 to 95, 97, 98, 101, 105, 106, 108, 109, 111, 112, 114, 115, 117, 119, 121, 123, 124, 136 to 138, 145, 147 to 149, 154, 155, 158, 161, 163, 164, **64**-1, 3, 4, 6 to 9, 15, 19, 21, 26, 27, 30, 37, 38, 42, 44, 46, 48, 50, 53, 58, 62, 65, 66, 68 to 70, 74, 76, 77, 90, 92, 93, 95, 96, 98 to 100, 103 to 107, **65**-4, 5, 8, 10 to 12, 20, 21, 23, 24, 27, 30 to 32, 54 to 58, 72, 79, 83, 96, 97, 104, 108, 110 to 112, 118, 119, 121, 128 to 131, 133, 139, **66**-2, 4, 5, 7 to 9, 12, 22, 26, 27, 32, 37, 41, 42, 58, 60, 65, 67, 77, 80, 87, 89, 96, 104, 106, 114, 116, 119 to 122, 128, 131, 132, 137, **67**-3, 5, 6, 22, 35, 36, 47, 48, **68**-5, 6, 9, 10, 13, 14, 20 to 22, 24 to 27, 31 to 33, 43, 46, 48 to 50, 55, 57, 65, 66, 77 to 79, 86, 87, 89, 91, 92, 99 to 101, 103, 105, 107, 110, 115, 123, **69**-3 to 5, 8, 10, 12, 13, 17, 18, 21, 22, 24, 25, 31, 32, 38, 41, 46, 47, 52, 57, 63, 67 to 70, 72, 77, 81, 82, 88, 93, 94, 96, 97, 102, 111, 112, 116, 121, 142, 144, 147, 149, 152, 155, 156, 158 to 160, 162, 166, 170, 172, 188, 189, 197, 199, 207, 218, 220, 225, 226, 228, 232, 233, 236, 241, 243, 247, 250, 254, 255, 257, 261, 263, 265, 269, **70**-2 to 4, 6 to 9, 13, 23, 24, 26, 33, 35, 36, 58, 59, 75, 76, 79, 80, 84, 86 to 89, 93 to 95, 99, 106, 116, 124, 128, 130, 133, 135, 136, 139, 142, 147 to 150, 153, 160, 163, 170, 171, 175, 180, 183, 186, 188, 189, 200 to 204, 207 to 209, 212, 217, 219, 223, 234 to 236, 239, 243, **71**-1, 3 to 5, 7, 10, 16, 17, 19, 21, 28, 31, 36 to 38, 41, 56, 58, 73, 74, 76, 81, 87, 96, 98, 99, 111, 120 to 122, 126, 136, 137, **72**-1, 6, 7, 9, 12, 15, 17, 20, 26, 30 to 32, 34, 36, 40 to 42, 45, 47 to 51, 53, 55, 56, 58, 61, 64, 74, 83, 84, 90 to 92, 94, 98, 100 to 103, 105, 106, **73**-1 to 8, 10, 11, 14, 17, 19, 32, 35, 41, 42, 44, 46, 56, 59, 68, 78, 82, 83, 88, 90, 97, 98, 100, 104, 107, **74**-1 to 7, 9, 11, 12, 15, 22, 28, 31, 34, 35, 51, 52, 57, 58, 63, 64, 66, 69, 86, 93, 99, 107, 108, 111, 131, 137, 140, 143, 147 to 149, 155, 156, 160, 161, 163 to 168, 170, 172, 175, 180 to 182, 184, 185, 189, 191, 193 to 195, 197, 198, 200, 205, 206, 209, 219, **75**-4, 6, 7, 10, 11, 19, 20, 28 to 31, 40, 45, 54 to 56, 65, 69, 70, 72, 73, 75, 85, 89, 91, 104, 114, 125, 127, 129, 132, 134, 139, 148, 149, 152, 156, 159, 174, 179, 181, 184, 186, 197, 199, 200, 202, 204, 206 to 208, 217, 220, 221, 223, 225, 226, 230, 239, 245, 250, 257, 259, 261 to 263, 266, 269, 271, 275, 276, 280 to 282, 290, 306, 307, 311, 321, **76**-3, 8, 12, 18, 20 to 22, 32, 38, 39, 42, 44, 47, 50, 54, 60, 61, 69 to 71, 75, 77, 78, 80, 81, 93, 97, 99, 114, 116, 120, 128, 133, 136 to 139, 142, 162, 167, 169, 176 to 178, 184, 186, 194, 196, 199, 201, 204, 209, 210, 215, 244, 246, 247, 256, 258, 260, 266, 268, 270, 271, 273, 279, 290, 292, 294 to 297, 312, 328, 335, 342, 343, 345, 347, 349, 350, 354, 358, 359, 361, 367, 369, 382, 385, 392, 394, 395, **77**-3, 5, 7, 8, 10, 12, 14, 16 to 19, 22 to 24, 26, 30, 39, 54, 65, 77, 79, 105, 140, 145, 148, 155, 159, 169, 188, 202, 206, 208, 210, 212, 215, 216, 222, 225, 231, 235, 237, 238, 241, 247, 252, 253, 272, 274, 295, 299, 310, 318, 319, **78**-3, 6 to 12, 14 to 18, 21, 25, 30 to 32, 34, 36, 38,

1710

44, 61, 76, 79, 85, 101, 102, 105, 118, 126, 131, 133, 137, 139, 140, 142, 146, 152, 158, 159, 164, 166, 190, 191, 198, 206, 218, 223, 233, 244, 254, 255, 260 to 262, 269 to 271, 277, 278, 289, 293, 302, 327, 334, 336, 341, 343, 350 to 352, 355, 356, 363, 368, 375, 380, 385, 394, 398, 402, 413, 414, 418, 424 to 427, 438, 443, 468, 469, 473, 477, 478, 482, 485, 487, 488, 492, 495, 496, 498 to 503, 508, 509, 518, 521 to 523, 538, 541, 554, **79**-8 to 11, 13 to 15, 17, 18, 20, 23, 25, 26, 30 to 33, 37, 38, 40 to 42, 44, 45, 48, 49, 51, 53, 61, 64, 66, 72, 76, 77, 79, 84, 111, 117, 119, 123, 127, 130, 136, 144, 155, 156, 158, 164, 171, 172, 181, 201, 222, 226, 231, 232, 246, 249, 250, 253, 255, 265, 289, 290, 318, 321, 324, 327, 341, 343, 353 to 355, 358, 361, 365, 369, 374, 375, 377, 380, 382, 383, 388, 389, 392, 412, 430, 433, 458, 459, 461 to 463, 465, 467, 470, 475, 486, 499, 504, 507, 512, 517, 519, 530, 531, 536, **80**-4, 7 to 9, 11 to 13, 16, 18, 20, 22, 27, 28, 30, 31, 34, 35, 37, 40, 43, 45, 64, 67, 69, 77, 79, 83, 91, 99, 101, 104 to 106, 110, 117, 119, 128, 130, 132, 141, 150, 153, 157, 160, 165, 171, 177, 179, 184 to 187, 195, 202, 204, 207, 209, 210, 212 to 214, 250, 260, 262 to 266, 276, 288, 294, 298, 308, 309, 311, 314, 318, 319, 328, 349, 350, 354, 355, 362, 365, 369, 371, 372, 378, 380, 383, 384, 386, 389, 399, 402, 409, 412, 424, **81**-3 to 5, 14, 15, 19, 28, 29, 32, 35, 37, 38, 47, 54 to 57, 59, 61 to 63, 68, 72, 76, 84, 87, 90, 93, 100, 101, 103, 105, 106, 109, 110, 113 to 115, 118, 123, 129, 147, 148, 150, 152, 154, 155, 158, 161 to 163, 167, 169, 172, 177, 181, 182, 184, 186, 190, 194, 212 to 217, 219, 220, 222, 223, 230, 231, 233, 234, 235, 240, 242 to 244, 248, 257, **82**-3, 4, 7, 8, 19, 22, 24, 32 to 35, 37, 41, 44, 47, 49, 52 to 55, 57 to 60, 69, 78 to 80, 91, 92, 94, 95, 100, 103, 108, 110 to 112, 115, 116, 118, 121, 122, 124, 130, 132 to 134, 147, 149, 158, 159, 167, 169, 170, 174, 176 to 180, 186, 195, 197, 198, 207, 225 to 229, 231, 233 to 235, 241, 242, 244, 245, 247, 250, 252, 254, 257, 258, 260, 262, 263, 268, 270, 273, 279 to 281, 284, 292, 297, 299, 302, 303, 306 to 308, 310, 311, 314, 318, 319, 325, 331 to 333, 349, 353, 354, 357, 358, 361, 362, 366, 368, 372, 374, 380, 382 to 384, 392, 394, 401, 405, 408, 420, **83**-8, 12, 14, 18, 21, 22, 25, 28, 29, 32, 38, 41, 42, 46, 48, 50 to 52, 56 to 58, 62, 65, 66, 72, 74, 75, 77, 80, 82, 85, 89, 92, 94, 98 to 101, 104, 105, 115, 117, 119, 124, 127 to 129, 134, 136, 138, 139, 144, 146, 148, 153, 158, 159, 174, 187, 190, 193, 195 to 197, 199 to 201, 203, 204, 211 to 213, 216, 218, 220, 222 to 225, 229, 234, 239, 240, 245, 247, 251, 256, 258, 263, 266, 273, 274, 276, 280, 282, 286, 288, 294, **84**-1 to 3, 5, 8, 9, 18 to 20, 22, 36, 40, 42, 43, 52, 60, 64, 72, 77, 78, 81, 89, 96, 99, 101, 103, 104, 106, 107, 110, 120, 121, 130, 132, 135, 142, 143, 146, 147, 150, 154, 159, 160, 164, 165, 170, 182, 183, 189 to 191, 193, 194, 196 to 199, 201, 205, 206, 208, 210, 212, 216, 219, **85**-4, 6, 7, 10, 13, 15, 27, 32, 39, 40, 42, 44, 53, 55, 58, 59, **87**-1, **90**-1

"Address," **80**-A
and mixed verse, **79**-28
and triplets, **81**-226
"Answer to the Epitaph," **64**-A
"Attempt," **64**-A
"A Bad Omen," **65**-A
"Battle of the Books," **63**-A
"Britannia to her Sons," **79**-A
"Britannia's Admonition," **79**-A
*British Coffee House*, **64**-A
"A Character," **65**-A
"Character of a Good King," **66**-A
Churchill's *Author, Conference, Epistle to Hogarth, Prophecy of Famine,* and

"Verses Written in Windsor Park," 63-A
Churchill's *Candidate, Gotham, and Independence,* 64-A
Colvill, "For General Wolfe's Monument," 72-A
"A Conference," 64-A
Cowper's "Epinikion," 79-A
Cowper's "On the Victory," 80-A
Cowper's "Table Talk," 82-A
Delamayne, *The Oliviad,* 62-A
"Elegy" in HC, 70-A
"Epigram," 65-A, 70-A, 76-A
"Epilogue," 81-A
"Epistle," 81-A
"Impertinent Curiosity," 77-A
"Impromptu," 69-A
irregular, 75-102, 79-348, 82-237
"Lines," 68-A
"Lines On the Death of Major Sill," 78-A
"Minister's Reasoning," 83-A
"A Morning Scene," 60-A
"Mourn, Albion," 66-A
*Noble Cricketers,* 78-A
"Nonconformists' Nosegay," 82-A
"O Pitt!", 78-A
octaves, 77-11
"On Churchill's Poems," 63-A
"On his Majesty's . . . taking a View from Cooper's Hill," 62-A
"On Political Justice," 67-A
"On the Calves-Head Club," 64-A
"On the Earl of Chatham's Funeral," 78-A
"On the Merchants' Address," 69-A
"On the Opinion . . . relating to the death of Mr. Clarke," 69-A
"On the Reports of a change in the Ministry," 65-A
"Parliamentary Duellists," 81-A
"Patriotism," 64-A
*Pride,* 66-A
"Questions and Answers," 83-A
"Remarks on the Slavery of Negroes," 75-A
"The Ribband," 69-A
rough, 79-346
"The Sequel of Britannia's Address," 79-A
"Shall Pitt," 66-A
"Superiority of England," 70-A
"Survey thy crimes," 62-A
*The Thistle,* 73-A
"To Benjamin Franklin," 65-A
"To E.G.," 64-A
"To Governours," 69-A
"To Mrs. Macaulay," 70-A
"To the Celebrated Mrs. Macaulay," 69-A
"To the Glorious Defenders of Liberty," 63-A
"To the Memory of William Lord Russell," 73-A
"To the Person," 68-A
"Verses," 68-A, 69-A, 78-A, 84-A

"Verses to the Memory," **66**-A
Heroic Quatrains, Heroic Stanzas. **See**: Quatrains.
Hexameter Couplets.  **60**-19, **61**-6, 19, 42, **62**-11, 18, 26, **63**-21, 36, 42, 74,
   130, 159, 172, 180, **64**-17, 20, 29, 59, 64, 76, **65**-67, **66**-6, 85, 97, 102, **67**-
   16, 23, **68**-34, 84, 109, 122, **69**-23, 33, 48, 53, 117, 140, 141, 234, **70**-18,
   71, 96, 122, 182, 184, 194, 221, 224, **71**-8, 24, 71, 117, **72**-62, 96, **73**-25,
   87, 89, 103, **74**-98, 106, **75**-51, 66, 82, 108, 121, 124, 194, 215, 232, 258,
   318, **76**-49, 55, 63, 88, 90, 92, 104, 152, 156, 192, 212, 262, 298, 318, 319,
   337, 372, 376, 377, 384, 397, **77**-45, 46, 72, 73, 161, 209, 218, 229, 258,
   284, 294, **78**-20, 49, 50, 63, 138, 238, 369, 370, 401, 435, 451, **79**-106, 173,
   236, 243, 328, 336, 356, 372, 385, 425, 497, 516, **80**-46, 54, 76, 84, 139,
   172, 196, 197, 254, 255, 303, 312, 324, 351, 381, 394, 401, 420, 426, 427, **81**-
   27, 34, 46, 50, 71, 80, 107, 112, 119 to 122, 153, 238, **82**-65, 67, 76, 93,
   97, 163, 168, 172, 189, 359, **83**-84, 108, 130, 137, 150, 176, 177, 210, 236,
   252, **84**-28, 38, 54, 61, 71, 100, 134, 152, 155
   "A Conversation," **69**-A
   "French Peace," **79**-A
   "The French sail'd to Jersey," **79**-A
   Goldsmith, *Retaliation*, **74**-A
   "If Alderman Squint," **69**-A
   in quatrains, **79**-213, 256
   John Ketch, **70**-A
   "On a Celebrated Female Writer," **70**-A
   "On a late repeated Expulsion," **69**-A
   "On the Late Riot," **68**-A
   "On Two Late Advertisements," **68**-A
   "The Poetical Wish," **69**-A
   "Prophecy of Liberty," **69**-A
   "Teague's Address," **69**-A
   "To a Friend," **70**-A
Hexameter Quatrains.  **66**-112, **68**-119, **78**-213, **80**-420, 426, 427, **82**-256
Hexameter Triplets.  **79**-399, **80**-321
Horatian Ode.  **See**: Ode, Regular Horatian.
Hudibrastic Verse.  Hudibrastic Doggerel.  **59**-31, **62**-10, 11, **63**-4, **64**-5, 81, **65**-
   1, 26, **66**-71, **67**-26, **68**-18, **69**-109, **70**-30, 98, 154, **71**-62, 94, 125, **74**-8,
   **75**-23, 92, 155, 201, 213, **76**-4, 336, 356, **77**-1, 44, 276, **78**-33, 372, 481, **79**-
   5, 424, 534, **80**-73, 284, **81**-176, **82**-73, **83**-3, 19, 20, 143, **84**-11, 16
   "An Addressicle," **68**-A
   epistle, **81**-94
   fable, **65**-53
   mock elegy, **66**-40
   "Snarling Pug," **63**-A
   Wesley, *The American War*, **82**-A
   **See also**: Burlesque and Doggerel.
Hymn.  **75**-60, 305, **76**-52, 158, 235, **77**-243, **78**-382, **79**-513, 514, **80**-39, 42,
   398, **81**-169, **82**-29, 30,
   ode, **71**-48
   prayer, **82**-6, 152
Imitation of.  (**See also**: Parody, with which it has often been identified.)
   Joseph Addison, *Cato*, **66**-25
   Anacreon, **68**-52, **78**-471, **79**-300
       Tomlinson, **78**-A
   Aristotle, "Ode to Virtue," **82**-184

"Ballad of the Battle of La Hogue," **82**-327
The Bible, **68**-17, **73**-101, **74**-85, 196, **84**-162
    diction, **80**-28
    Psalm 72, **77**-243
    Psalm 137, **74**-150
    Psalm 151, **68**-3
Samuel Butler, *Hudibras*, **75**-92, **76**-30, **78**-33, **81**-176, **83**-9, 19, **84**-162
Chevy Chase, a ballad. **See**: Tune, Chevy Chase.
Charles Churchill, **84**-164
Colley Cibber, **79**-296
William Collins, "Ode Written in the Year 1746," **78**-155, **80**-21, 30[2]
Herbert Croft, *Abbey of Kilkhampton*, **80**-114, 118
Dante, **80**-28
Elijah Fenton, "Ode to Lord Gower," **80**-241
John Gay, **80**-242
Thomas Gray, **80**-28
    "The Bard," **76**-6, **79**-3, 35, 302, **82**-287
    "Elegy," **69**-56, **70**-49, 168, **74**-178, **84**-45
    "Progress of Poesy," **82**-218
Horace, **55**-1, **59**-2, 3, **60**-5, 17, **61**-1, **63**-58, 65, **64**-2, 44, **65**-3, **66**-39, **67**-2, **69**-19, 95, **70**-2, **71**-46, **75**-130, **76**-216, 339, 363, **77**-5, 18, 25, 125, 263, **79**-36, 209, 227, 317, **80**-37, 163, 234, 245, 377, 410, **81**-74, 91, 92, **82**-127, 132, 158, 159, 160, 215, 223, 283, 389, **84**-2
    "Dialogue," **84**-A
    "paraphrase," **70**-156, **84**-66
Samuel Johnson, *Idler*, **65**-64
Juvenal, **82**-59, **84**-19
King George III
    the King's Speech, **77**-50, 51
    manner, **74**-207
    an order, **83**-205
    a proclamation, **77**-256
King of Prussia, "Fifth Ode," **77**-11
David Mallet, "Ballad of William and Margaret," **66**-14, **77**-15, **79**-386
Martial, **69**-64, 270, **72**-25, **79**-131
Andrew Marvell, "Royal Resolutions," **79**-399, **80**-321
Medieval poetry, **67**-27, **75**-111, **79**-264, 510
    Chatterton, **77**-116, **80**-28, **82**-12, 16
    **See**: Tune, Chevy Chase, **61**-12.
*Middlesex Petition*, **69**-9 (paraphrased)
John Milton, **80**-28
    blank verse sublime, **60**-6, **77**-4
    Doctrine of Government, **80**-202
    "Lycidas," **75**-8
    Miltonic sublime in HC, **76**-22
    mock epic, **80**-24
    "On the Morning of Christ's Nativity," **77**-53
    *Paradise Lost*, **82**-26, **84**-17
        Battle of the Angels, **65**-1
Frederick, Lord North
    oration on beginning of American War, paraphrased, **75**-209
Bishop Thomas Percy, "O Nancy," song
    "Imitation," **83**-A

Persius, **84**-5
Alexander Pope, **62**-24, **65**-10, **66**-5, **70**-186, **84**-18
    Churchill's *Conference*, **62**-A
Matthew Prior, **81**-219, **83**-219, **84**-12
Punch's Address to Minos, **79**-99
General Philip Schuyler's Letter to Washington, **77**-242
William Shakespeare, **74**-97, **80**-28
    Hamlet's Soliloquy, **61**-41, **64**-A, **73**-39
    *Macbeth*, banquet scene, **75**-122
    **See**: Parody, Shakespeare.
William Shenstone, *Pastoral*, **70**-27
Richard B. Sheridan, song in *School for Scandal*, **79**-202
Edmund Spenser, **75**-22
Sternhold and Hopkins, hymns, **76**-381
The Surrey Address (on Wilkes and Peace of 1763), **63**-147
Jonathan Swift, "The State Coach," **68**-A
Virgil
    *Aeneid*, **76**-182
    *Georgic I*, **78**-223
Charles Hanbury Williams, **66**-24

Impromptu. **See**: Extempore.

Inscription. **59**-19, 20, 23, **60**-13, 18, **61**-13, **62**-31, **63**-50, **66**-8, 65, **67**-25, 37, **68**-2, 59, 60, 61, **69**-37, 69, 70, 87, 194, **70**-61, 85, 88, 89, 101, 102, **71**-10, 32, 53, **72**-13, 27, 28, 43, 46, 58, 59, 60, **73**-31, 44, 45, **74**-73, 74, 75, 76, 77, 78, 95, 110, **75**-141, **76**-3, 140, 141, 188, 189, **77**-108, 153, 154, 262, 306, **78**-23, 88, 153, 156, 157, 160, 161, 162, 163, 165, 167, 168, 169, 246, 247, 248, 249, 250, 251, 252, 504, 505, **79**-15, 145, 146, 147, 149, 223, 228, 460, **80**-10, 29, 56, 57, 74, 112, 113, 114, 115, 116, 118, 120, 122, 138, 168, 169, 170, 171, 206, 364, **81**-96, 97, 98, 99, 104, 164, **82**-74, 117, 173, 185, **83**-91, 116, 133, 230, 248, **84**-4, 56, 76, 90
  "Epitaph," **72**-A, **80**-A
  "Here Rest," **78**-A
  quatrains, **77**-187

Instructions to the Artist. **59**-18, **71**-54, **76**-45, **78**-253, **80**-172
    Cowper's "To Sir Joshua Reynolds," **80**-A

Irregular Pindaric Ode. **See**: Ode, Irregular Pindaric.

Litany. **66**-93

Lyric. **See**: Song.

Metaphor. **71**-30, **74**-16, 50, 176, **76**-190, 192, **77**-87, 310, **78**-275, **79**-275.
  **See**: Simile.

Mini-drama, Mini-play. **See**: Playlet.

Mixed Forms, Irregular Verse. **69**-215, **76**-1, 32, **77**-20, 57, 107, 207, 242, **78**-129, 132, 151, 178, 181, 257, 301, 313, 353, 378, 428, 506, 546, **79**-28, 288, 323, 367, 378, 387, 410, **80**-59, 102, 405, 406, **81**-48, 185, 237, **82**-126, 346, 395, 404, **83**-47, 135, 185, **84**-123, **85**-18
  "A Monody," **64**-A
  "Paulus," **89**-2
  "The Seer," **61**-A

Mock Poem.
  Mock Address, **63**-179, **80**-230
  Mock Elegy, **66**-40, 42
  Mock Epic, **63**-1, 2, **75**-23, 121, **76**-31, **80**-2, 24
  Mock Epitaph, **66**-54, 55, 94

Mock Oratorio, 75-237
Monody. **65**-73, **69**-115, **73**-53, **75**-158, 212, **77**-172, **81**-14, **82**-184, **83**-149
    "A Monody," **64**-A
    "Paulus," **89**-2
Monologue. **73**-2
    **See**: Soliloquy.
Monorhyme. **72**-57
Nine-line Stanzas (*not* Spenserian). **84**-87
Occasional Poems, for public performance on special occasions. **63**-5, **66**-64, **68**-73, **69**-20, 51, **70**-190, **72**-14, **74**-118, **78**-293, **79**-290, **81**-130, **83**-154
    Gray's *Installation Ode*, **69**-A
    "Ode at the Encaenia," **73**-62
    "Ode on the Emancipation of Ireland," **82**-A
    **See also**: Prologues and Epilogues, and Whitehead's laureate odes, 1760-85 in Part I of index.
Octave. **59**-33, **60**-20, **61**-47, **66**-75, **69**-108, 192, **74**-127, **76**-269, **77**-177, 178, 244, 312, 329, **78**-312, 318, 325, **79**-319, 493, **80**-5, 6, 246, 247, 277, 290, 341, 382, **82**-17, 106, 203, **83**-33, 108, 163, **84**-14, 175, **85**-37
    alternating rhymes, **79**-177
    in couplets, **78**-209
    in HC, **77**-11
    occasional rhymes, **79**-227
    "Ode on George III," **61**-A
    *Ode to Palinurus*, **70**-A
    Puddicombe, **84**-A
Octosyllabic Couplets. **61**-3, 10, **62**-1, 29, 30, **63**-14, 16, 22, 26, 31, 32, 34, 35, 40, 55, 57, 65, 66, 69, 72, 77, 87, 99, 102, 107, 113, 125, 128, 134, 135, 139, 150, 151, 157, 167, 168, 171, **64**-49, 56, 57, 60, 63, 78, 80, 86, 102, **65**-25, 61, 63, 93, 123, 126, 132, 135, 137, 142, **66**-11, 71, **67**-7, 11, 31, 42, 46, **68**-1, 29, 36, 63, 120, 124, **69**-20, 90, 95, 105, 106, 113, 183, 184, 217, 248, 260, 267, 271, **70**-38, 40, 152, 155, 156, 167, 173, 174, 178, 181, 197, 199, 210, 211, 216, 222, 226, 228, 242, **71**-18, 43, 54, 70, 77, 83, 84, 90, 115, 130, 131, 132, **72**-35, 70, 77, 79, **73**-12, 48, 108, **74**-29, 33, 54, 81, 82, 105, 116, 129, 138, 142, 158, 192, 202, 213, 214, 220, **75**-12, 21, 24, 46, 103, 110, 146, 151, 154, 157, 193, 195, 214, 222, 227, 236, 240, 278, 288, 312, **76**-2, 24, 56, 59, 89, 94, 155, 197, 229, 230, 277, 293, 314, 315, 336, 352, 365, 383, 399, **77**-18, 56, 63, 83, 87, 94, 97, 107, 143, 156, 157, 197, 232, 234, 240, 242, 254, 255, 256, 264, 268, 275, 276, 300, 307, 314, 317, 332, **78**-22, 33, 43, 45, 81, 86, 95, 130, 136, 141, 182, 192, 194, 195, 216, 217, 228, 256, 268, 274, 275, 319, 335, 381, 384, 393, 395, 409, 434, 471, 483, 489, 512, 517, 528, 534, 558, **79**-36, 71, 91, 94, 131, 133, 163, 175, 178, 188, 200, 224, 234, 252, 254, 285, 295, 337, 350, 367, 371, 384, 390, 403, 405, 413, 446, 457, 481, 484, 487, 491, **80**-3, 23, 33, 47, 65, 72, 81, 82, 96, 135, 136, 137, 140, 190, 194, 200, 256, 259, 261, 268, 270, 272, 310, 315, 317, 338, 346, 353, 358, 359, 361, 382, 385, 393, 395, 396, 418, 423, **81**-11, 17, 49, 67, 74, 94, 102, 117, 151, 159, 168, 179, 208, 211, 229, 237, 239, 245, 247, 249, 256, 265, **82**-8, 10, 13, 39, 42, 43, 71, 75, 96, 102, 148, 181, 239, 243, 259, 294, 301, 309, 312, 324, 328, 350, 365, 371, 399, 411, **83**-47, 54, 90, 97, 103, 123, 131, 143, 157, 160, 180, 182, 198, 219, 226, 249, 268, 271, 272, 291, **84**-7, 24, 57, 73, 79, 93, 94, 140, 184, 186, 204, 209, 213, **85**-22, 26, 51, **89**-3
    "Answer to the Epigrams," **64**-A
    Churchill's *Duellist*, **64**-A

"Congratulatory Address," **79-A**
Cowper's "Address to the Mob," "Present for the Queen of France," **79-A**
Cowper's "To Sir Joshua Reynolds," **80-A**
"A Dialogue," **69-A**
"Epigram," **63-A**
"Epitaph," **64-A**
"Epitaph for Wolfe," **60-A**
"A Fable," **69-A**
"The following Verses," **79-A**
"Hail to the son of Fame," **79-A**
in quatrains, **83**-181
in sixains, **82**-393
Oakman's "Mastiff in Prison," **69-A**
"On Real Slavery," **76-A**
"On the Candle," **84-A**
"On the Opinion," **69-A**
"The Sentence pass'd," **64-A**
"The State Coach," **68-A**
"The Thieves and Butcher," **68-A**
"'Tis true," **79-A**
Underwood on Churchill, **69-A**
"Vine and Bramble," **70-A**
Wesley, "American Independency," **83-A**
Wesley, *American War*, **82-A**
Wilmot, **79-A**

Octosyllabics (other than couplets).
    alternate rhymes, **68**-23
    rhyme on Horne throughout, **69**-103
    triplets, **74**-157

Ode. **66**-64, **67**-1, **74**-204, **76**-217, **78**-315, **79**-295, 296, **80**-14, 17, 21, 30, 238, **82**-146, 371
    "dramatic ode," **85**-9
    irregular in couplets, **70**-109
    irregular lyric ode, **77**-167
    mixed, **78**-307
    mixed verse, **77**-207
    "Order of St. Patrick," **83-A**
    **See:** Ode, Regular Horatian; Ode, Irregular Pindaric; Ode, Regular Pindaric; Imitation of Horace (under rubric Imitation).

Ode, Irregular Pindaric. **58**-3, **59**-6, **60**-32, 34, 50, **61**-7, 39, 50, **62**-66, **63**-170, **65**-82, 140, **68**-71, **69**-6, 125, 134, 229, **70**-90, 114, 198, 237, **71**-64, 65, 68, 69, 135, **72**-3, 107, **73**-57, 61, 62, 63, 109, 110, **74**-119, 120, 122, 123, 124, 128, 151, 186, 210, 211, **75**-9, 16, 126, 144, **76**-36, 57, 170 to 174, 200, 220, 222, 225, 243, 274, 289, 332, 334, 386, 387, **77**-24, 75, 146, 147, 172, 179, 180, 182, 224, 328, **78**-24, 28, 39, 40, 56, 68, 69, 308, 310, 311, 316, 317, 321, 326, 543, 544, 549, **79**-12, 21, 39, 207, 302, 303, 521, 522, **80**-1, 41, 52, 175, 208, 232, 236, 237, 239, 352, 407, 408, 415, **81**-1, 140, 193, 252, 253, **82**-21, 25 (revision of **78**-39), 89, 206, 211, 213, 214, 217, 396, **83**-24, 34, 164, 171, 186, 277, 278, **84**-13, 127, 128, 217, 218, **85**-16, 31, 54, 56, 57, **1800**-1
    Gray's *Installation Ode*, **69-A**
    monody, **65**-73
    "Ode to be performed at the Altar of Discord," **82-A**

        trimeter, **82**-341
Ode, Pindaric. **81**-9(?)
        experimental, **81**-10
Ode, Regular Horatian. **55**-1, **58**-1, **59**-2, 32, **61**-37, **62**-2, 3, 6, 9, 38, 43, **63**-81, 153, **64**-7, 54, 55, **65**-7, 81, 85, **66**-10, 72, 73, 74, 75, 84, **67**-4, 28, 38, 50, **68**-11, 12, 19, 67, 74, **69**-10, 11, 30, 39, 50, 123, 124, 126, 127, 129, 130, 131, 132, 133, 137, 138, 139, 143, 221, 244, **70**-77, 107, 110, 111, 112, 113, 115, 169, **71**-12, 14, 66, 67, 105, 110, 112, 118, **72**-66, **73**-9, 72, 106, **74**-23, 37, 43, 121, 125, 126, 127, 154, 187, 197, **75**-13, 61, 62, 105, 120, 142, 166, 167, 168, 169, 170, 177, 187, 219, 235, 267, 299, 302, 313, 316, **76**-19, 27, 28, 79, 217, 218, 219, 221, 223, 224, 226, 227, 231, 257, 300, 307, 341, 353, 363, 380, 391, **77**-25, 28, 41, 134, 139, 149, 175, 176, 177, 178, 183, 184, 185, 244, 249, 263, 292, 315, 322, 329, **78**-2, 23, 27, 35, 47, 87, 94, 96, 273, 309, 312, 318, 320, 322, 323, 324, 325, 330, 345, 346, 361, 423, 453, 486, 490, 513, **79**-4, 90, 92, 93, 95, 100, 103, 113, 214, 248, 258, 291, 292, 293, 294, 297, 299, 301, 304, 305, 306, 307, 308, 310, 311, 312, 313, 314, 316, 436, 437, 438, 469, 525, **80**-30, 43, 61, 123, 152, 163, 189, 230, 233, 235, 238(?), 242, 243, 245, 246, 247, 248, 249, 252, 271, 273, 290, 302, 376, 377, 391, 410, **81**-12, 31, 42, 92, 136, 138, 139, 142, 143, 144, 145, 166, 218, 232, 241, 251, 255, **82**-14, 17, 18, 23, 31, 56, 127, 156, 209, 210, 212, 215, 216, 219, 220, 221, 222, 223, 236, 295, 313, 320, 326, 330, 343, 345, 370, 376, 391, 397, 400, 402, **83**-5, 11, 14, 16, 17, 31, 33, 53, 140, 161, 162, 163, 165, 166, 167, 168, 169, 170, 172, 173, 227, **84**-14, 29, 35,   82, 119, 122, 123(?) 124, 126, 129, 153, 156, 202, **85**-34, 35, 36, 37, 38
    "Contented Man," **76**-A
    couplets in sixains, **60**-31, 33
    dixains, **60**-43, **75**-289
    double quatrains, **71**-63
    elegiac ode, **80**-87
    except last stanza, **73**-64
    in OC, **78**-319
    octaves, **59**-33, **60**-20, **76**-269
    "An Ode," **63**-A
    "An Ode, Inscribed to Conway," **65**-A
    "Ode on Canada," **60**-A
    "Ode on George III," **61**-A
    "Ode to Alderman Oliver," **71**-A
    "Ode to Ambition," **64**-A
    *Ode to Palinurus*, **70**-A
    Puddicombe, "Ode to William Pitt," **84**-A
    quatrains, **58**-6, **60**-25, 44, **75**-171, 172, 173, 270, **76**-228, 339
    sixains, **59**-26, **60**-40
    slightly irregular, **79**-315
    triplets and tail, **78**-464
    twelves, **76**-281
    unrhymed, **77**-181
Ode, Regular Pindaric. **61**-2, **76**-6, **77**-27, **79**-2(?), 3, 22, 29, 35, 261, **80**-240, 241, **82**-11, 218, **83**-9
    abbreviated ode, **84**-125
    in two parts, **79**-529
    "Ode on Emancipation," **82**-A
Opera. **77**-65, **82**-5

Oratorio. **70**-108, **71**-6, **75**-237, **78**-56, **79**-207, **80**-305, **83**-233, **84**-127
    ode, **79**-309, **80**-208
    **See also**: Cantata; and Ode, Irregular Pindaric.
Panegyric. **59**-1, 30, **60**-23, 27, **61**-13, 35, **62**-3, 59, 67, **63**-3, 85, 117, 162, **65**-70, 94, 97, 108, **66**-8, 131, **67**-17, **68**-13, 102, 105, **69**-11, 17, 88, **70**-114, 124, 141, 185, 200, 202, 204, 207, 208, 210, 218, 219, 234, 236, **71**-5, 14, 31, 69, 99, 111, 118, **72**-3, 46, 95, **73**-3, 29, 97, 98, 100, 104, **74**-17, 41, 126, 182, **75**-207, 271, 273, 275, 302, **76**-218, 277, 331, 340, 342, 343, 359, 360, **77**-10, 20, 21, 169, 172, 190, 319, **78**-2, 24, 34, 61, 122, 124, 126, 159, 166, 167, 229, 249, 272, 274, 278, 326, 348, 350, 389, 394, 402, 418, 505, **79**-39, 49, 51, 301, 341, 519, **80**-23, 123, 129(?), 152, 165, 168, 189, 211, 212, 252, 350, 359, 371, **81**-9, 38, 56, 88, 110, 114, 115, 116, 117, 147, 175, 227, **82**-20, 21, 176, 178, 181, 197, 247, 251, 254, 274, 280, 325, 343, 360, 368, 369, 400, **83**-11, 21, 26, 29, 52, 244, 246, 260, 274, **84**-4, 14, 64, 105, 124, 134, 142, 195, 197, 201, 206, **85**-15, 25, 37, 38, 40, 54, 55
    "Congratulatory Address," **79**-A
    freedom of the press, **72**-61
    ironic, **75**-11
    Puddicombe's "Ode to William Pitt," **84**-A
    "Verses," **84**-A
Paraphrase. **82**-284(?)
    *Middlesex Petition Inversed*, **69**-9
    Ushant in French Gazette, **78**-410
    **See also**: Imitation and Parody.
Parody on
    Addison's *Cato*, **63**-126, **66**-25, 57, **69**-180, **71**-91, **77**-227
    Advertisement
        for election, **80**-181, 368
        for meeting at Bath, **78**-405
    Announcement
        theatrical, **69**-214
    Ballad, **See**: Ballad and Tune, esp. "Chevy Chase" and Mallet's "Margaret's Ghost"
    Bible
        Psalm(?), **84**-162
        Psalm 1, **74**-85
        Psalm 23, **65**-134
    Burgoyne's Proclamation, **77**-44, 45, 136
    "Coachman's Song," **76**-A (parodied by "The Minister's Song")
    Congress's Resolutions. **See**: Declaration by Second Continental Congress.
    Herbert Croft, *Kilkhampton Abbey*, **80**-170, 206, **81**-96, 104
        imitation(?), **80**-114
    Declaration by the Continental Congress of the Causes and Necessity of Taking up Arms, **75**-108
    John Dickinson, "Liberty Song,"
        parody on Garrick's "Heart of Oak," **68**-96
        parody on Dickinson's song, **68**-95
        parody on the parody on Dickinson's song, **68**-85
    John Dryden, "Alexander's Feast," **71**-6, **78**-56, **84**-127
        "Epitaph on Milton," **70**-159, **71**-106, 107, **78**-472, **81**-267, **85**-17
        "Young Statesmen," **82**-77
    Encaenia honoring Ld North's installation as Chancellow at Oxford, **73**-61
    Epitaph on King Charles II, **80**-121

Henry Fielding, *Tom Thumb* (duet between Mr. Noodle and Mr. Doodle), **83-208**
General Thomas Gage, Proclamation, **75-288**
David Garrick, "Heart of Oak," **65-80, 68-95,** 96
    Shakespeare's "Mulberry Tree" (from *Jubilee*), **75-48**
    **See:** Tune, "Heart of Oak."
John Gay, *Beggar's Opera*, **77-288**
Thomas Gray
    "The Bard," **79-302, 82-287**
    "Elegy," **69-66, 70-49, 74-178, 84-45,** 102
    *Installation Ode*, **69-136, 69-A** (see annotation)
    "Lines on Henry Fox, Ld Holland," **84-102**
    "Ode on Death of a Favourite Cat," **70-A, 75-165**
    "Progress of Poesy," **82-218**
    **See:** Gray, Imitation.
Samuel Johnson, "Marmor Norfolciense," **76-32**
King's Speech (George III), **72-82, 74-105, 77-50,** 258, **82-28**
Litany, **66-93, 80-44,** 306, **85-45**
David Mallet, "William and Margaret" ("Margaret's Ghost"), **79-386**
Mary, Queen of Scots' Lamentation, **84-34**
William Mason, "Ode to Naval Officers," **79-29**
*Midas*, first song, **73-81**
John Milton, *Paradise Lost*, **84-17**
    **See:** Imitation, Milton
Frederick, Ld North, speech, **77-51**
Northampton Address, **80-230**
Robert C. Nugent, *Verses*, **75-24**
Thomas Otway, *Venice Preserv'd*, **71-13**
Parody on a Parody, **68-85, 85-16**
Peace Proclamation, 1783, **83-226**
Pollio, an Elegy, **69-181**
Alexander Pope, **66-60, 73-82, 83, 75-220**
    **See:** Imitation, Pope.
Punch's Address to Minos, **79-99**
*The Quaker* (play by Charles Dibdin), "Song," **77-286**
Walter Raleigh, "Go, Soul," **64-73**
Report of a Naval Battle, **80-181**
Nicholas Rowe, *Fair Penitent*, **70-157**
General Arthur St. Clair's "Letter to Congress," **77-137**
William Shakespeare
    *Hamlet*, **69-219, 70-39,** 158, **73-39, 75-210, 76-280, 77-298, 78-404, 79-256,** 411
        "The Ghost," **83-A**
        "Soliloquy," **64-A**
    *Julius Caesar*, **73-79, 74-190**
    *Macbeth*, **76-299, 79-63, 80-134, 83-45,** 69, 207
        "The Enchantment," **69-A**
    Miscellaneous, **75-49, 82-192,** 285
        Garrick's "Mulberry Tree" in his *Jubilee*, **75-48**
    *Othello*, **82-286**
    *Richard III*, **66-98, 73-80, 78-291**
    *Romeo and Juliet*, **63-127**

Songs
- "Chevy Chase," **74**-152, **75**-211, **79**-109, 370, 490, **80**-2, **82**-16
  - **See also**: Ballad, and Tune, "Chevy Chase."
- "Have you been to Abingdon?", **77**-29, 245
- "Hunting Song," in *Thomas and Sally* (farce by Isaac Bickerstaffe, music by Thomas Arne), **69**-176, 177, 178, 179, **79**-68
- "Jolly Young Waterman," **76**-278
- "Maid of the Mill for me," song in Frances Brooke's *Rosina*, **83**-209
- "Moderation," **82**-288
- "Rule, Britannia" (by James Thomson, music by Thomas Arne), **74**-26, **76**-51
  - **See**: Tune, "Rule, Britannia"
- Scotch Song, "The Lass of Peaties Mill," **78**-406
- Song in *The Camp*, **79**-369
- "Vicar of Bray," **71**-45, 129
  - **See**: Tune, "Vicar of Bray."

Spanish Manifesto, **79**-424
Edward Thompson, "The Hyaena," **79**-447
"Three Children Sliding on the Ice," **78**-303
Thomas Wharton, "The Revenge of America," **82**-312
William Whitehead
- "King's Birthday Odes,": **74**-119, 120, 122, 151, 210, **76**-225, 274, **78**-310, 324, **79**-295, 529, **80**-52, 62, 236, **85**-16
- "New Year Odes," **73**-13, 57, **76**-57, 364, **77**-244, **78**-314, 403, **79**-298, 303, **80**-237, 238, **81**-140, **82**-214

Pasquinade. **71**-53, **79**-371, **80**-339
Pastoral. **76**-279, **77**-165, 247, **79**-32
    pastoral elegy in HC, **77**-17
Persona (poems using fictional projections of character). **60**-7, 10, 17, 26, **61**-4, 5, 14, 41, 42, **62**-2, 24, 56, **63**-11, 12, 13, 14, 15, 58, 80, 126, 127, 130, 165, **65**-63, **66**-25, **68**-6, 31, 68, 87, **69**-41, 48, 53, 57, 91, 92, 102, 116, 117, 124, 139, **70**-12, 19, 20, 25, 26, 27, 31, 37, 38, 41, 66, 72, 96, 182, 194, 224, **71**-59, 70, 89, 91, **72**-54, 62, 82, 83, **73**-2, 15, 48, 84, **74**-8, 35, 90, 105, 173, 207, **75**-37, 51, 52, 115, 154, 209, 227, 236, 283, 288, 297, 312, 318, **76**-1, 8, 10, 16, 24, 38, 44, 62, 92, 93, 131, 133, 134, 178, 192, 193, 194, 201, 214, 252, 280, 361, **77**-25, 35, 41, 44, 45, 50, 51, 72, 74, 135, 136, 137, 141, 150, 159, 160, 161, 162, 242, 258, 279, 281, **78**-4, 13, 25, 35, 52, 53, 54, 60, 64, 81, 82, 86, 107, 108, 109, 110, 254, 257, 293, 300, 412, 438, 463, 515, **79**-13, 14, 61, 73, 76, 78, 99, 102, 106, 107, 236, 245, 249, 255, 364, 380, 399, 400, 404, 411, 412, 424, 428, 474, 496, 511, **80**-14, 54, 61, 86, 157, 182, 203, 233, 321, 324, 331, **81**-5, 29, 41, 72, **82**-9, 11, 20, 28, 41, 148, 150, 168, 253, 286, 298, 300, 359, 377, 383, **83**-36, 61, 89, 101, 108, 127, 143, 147, 157, 165, **84**-17, 23, 34, 53, 79, 93, 94, 121, 148, 154, 184, 188, 214
  - A. Marvell, **68**-82, 105, **74**-109
  - "André to Washington," **84**-9
  - "Brest Council," **79**-A
  - Cowper, "Modern Patriot," **82**-A
  - "Ghost of Lord Chatham," **83**-A
  - "Jaffier Ali Cawn's Ghost," **68**-A
  - "Minister's Reasoning," **83**-A
  - "A Morning Scene," **60**-A

"On his Majesty's taking a view from Cooper's Hill," **62**-A
"Sequel of Britannia's Address," **79**-A
"A Spurious Speech," **77**-A
Pindaric Ode.  **See**: Ode, Irregular and Regular Pindaric, and Ode, Pindaric.
Play.
    pantomime, **84**-220
    Shakespeare's *Cymbeline*, a scene, **76**-313
    tragedy, **61**-1, 15, **78**-26
Playlet.
    "From the Massachusetts Spy," Hutchinson and Oliver vs Massachusetts Assembly, **73**-A
    satire on Fox and Burke, **82**-77
    satire on Fox for opposing Shelburne's peace, **83**-45
    satire on Fox-North Coalition, **83**-69
    satire on Opposition for being factious and republican, **80**-134
    satire on Opposition for wanting principle and being republican, **79**-185
    venal Britain vs America, **78**-442
Prayer.  **75**-60, 69, **76**-52, 78, 228, **78**-129, 255, **79**-379, **80**-29, 39, 58, 82, 397, **81**-76, 151, **82**-6, 152
    litany, **78**-128
    **See also**: Hymn.
Prologue and Epilogue.  **66**-65(?), **74**-51, **76**-77, **78**-26, 293, 425, 426, 427, 478, **79**-382, **80**-308, **82**-55, 69, 303, 311, **83**-12, 154
    "Epilogue," **81**-A
Prophecy.  **58**-11, **61**-11, **64**-77, 78, **65**-20, 83, 109, **66**-97, **68**-6, 42, **69**-189, 260, **70**-23, 176, **71**-95, 96, **73**-12, 87, 107, **74**-16, 25, 86, 156, 162, 163, 164, 172, **75**-41, 111, 221 to 225, **76**-1(?), 16, 39, 54, 55, 59, 165, 290 to 294, 309, **77**-57, 173, 246, **78**-63, 73, 100, **79**-3, 28, 37, 264, 383, 384, 510, **80**-14, 15, 19, 33, 200, 298, **82**-11, 14, 16, 173, 188, 304, **83**-189, **89**-3
    fighting for supremacy in the air, **83**-287
    "Prophecy of Liberty," **69**-A
    "The Seer," **61**-A
Prose Poems (other than Inscriptions).  **63**-132, **65**-107, **67**-39, **69**-182, 214, **70**-164, **72**-10, 85, **73**-47, 86, 101, **74**-16, 38, 50, 171, 176, **75**-244, 247, **76**-285, **78**-221, 474, **79**-452, **80**-306
    "Political Genealogy," **69**-A (same as **73**-86)
    "Things as they Are," **78**-A
    unrhymed "free numbers," **82**-184
    **See also**: Inscription.
Punch and Street Theatre.  **77**-258, **78**-64, **79**-99, 387, 409(?)
Quatrain (all varieties).  **59**-17, 32, 35, **60**-7, 26, 44, 48, 52, 53, **61**-1, 29, 35, 40, **62**-3, 15, 27, 33, 47, 55, 56, 59, **63**-3, 12, 23, 28, 30, 43, 44, 48, 64, 67, 70, 81, 84, 90, 96, 103, 120, 122, 133, 146, 166, 169, 173, **64**-7, 12, 13, 23, 24, 25, 33, 34, 36, 39, 41, 43, 47, 51, 59, 61, 67, 71, 72, 82 to 85, 91, 94, 101, 102, **65**-6, 16, 43, 51, 69, 71, 88, 89, 94, 99, 102, 114, 116, 117, 124, 125, 127, 134, 141, 144, 146, 147, **66**-12, 18, 23, 24, 31, 38, 83, 88, 90, 95, 103, 107, 115, 123, 127, 130, 138, **67**-12, 24, 28, 32, 33, 38, **68**-35, 42, 52, 73, 97, 121, **69**-14, 27, 43, 56, 59, 78 to 80, 107, 114, 115, 128, 137, 150, 151, 154, 164, 168, 171, 173, 187, 195, 198, 200, 206, 209, 211, 212, 213, 224, 231, 235, 239, 246, 258, 259, 262, **70**-20, 21, 41, 49, 50, 52, 64, 65, 67, 68, 78, 81, 92, 100, 118, 120, 129, 147, 214, 215, 230, 244, **71**-20, 33 to 35, 39, 48, 52, 72, 79, 82, 88, 89, 95, 97, 100, 103, 108, 113,

114, **72**-11, 22, 37, 39, 54, 59, 67, 78, 98, **73**-36, 43, 49, 50, 52 to 54, 65, 67, 69, 71, 75, 76, 85, 91, 99, 111, **74**-21, 24, 25, 30, 44, 47, 49, 80, 85, 92, 109, 118, 121, 144, 145, 201, 207, 221, **75**-8, 17, 38, 41, 43, 52, 57, 58, 60, 67, 87, 94, 98, 133, 136, 140, 147, 163, 171 to 173, 175, 203, 216, 219, 229, 233, 253, 264, 270, 272 to 274, 277, 279, 283, 284, 293, 295 to 297, 300 to 303, 315, 317, 320, **76**-5, 14, 15, 30, 52, 58, 65, 67, 73, 82, 101, 103, 105, 106, 108, 111, 113, 117, 122, 126, 129 to 131, 135, 145, 146, 149, 153, 154, 158, 163, 181, 183, 190, 193, 195, 198, 203, 208, 228, 233 to 235, 241, 248 to 250, 253, 259, 265, 283, 287, 304, 305, 309, 310, 316, 320, 329 to 331, 333, 351, 355, 379, 381, 389, 393, 396, **77**-9, 34, 36, 42, 48, 55, 62, 69, 74, 82, 84, 88 to 92, 96, 98, 99, 106, 107, 110, 111, 113 to 119, 121 to 123, 151, 158, 165, 185, 187, 190, 191, 194, 198, 199, 201, 203 to 205, 211, 214, 219, 223, 228, 236, 239, 246, 251, 257, 259 to 261, 267, 277, 278, 287, 289, 290 (and **79**-443), 293, 296, 301, 303, 304, 309, 320, 324, 326, 330, **78**-47, 54, 55, 57 to 59, 72, 80, 93, 97, 107, 112, 114, 116, 121, 123 to 125, 127, 134, 135, 145, 147, 149, 170, 172 to 177, 179, 180, 183, 185, 186, 189, 196, 197, 199, 201, 222, 225, 227, 234, 235, 240, 245, 264, 266, 272, 276, 282, 284, 288, 292, 297, 303 to 305, 309, 323, 329, 338, 342, 344, 354, 357, 358, 360, 364, 366, 367, 371, 374, 376, 379, 382, 383, 387 to 389, 391, 392, 399, 431 to 433, 436, 437, 439, 445, 465, 467, 475, 476, 486, 494, 497, 519, 520, 524, 525, 527, 529, 531, 536, 537, 540, 546, 553, **79**-6, 7, 46, 50, 52, 54, 56 to 58, 60, 69, 70, 73 to 75, 81, 83, 90, 92, 93, 116, 122, 124, 125, 137, 142, 148, 150 to 153, 159 to 162, 165 to 168, 174, 176, 182, 190 to 192, 206, 212, 215, 216, 219, 220, 225, 244, 248, 259, 260, 264, 266, 269, 285, 287, 293, 297, 305, 315, 326, 333, 335, 340, 351, 352, 357, 362, 363, 366, 367, 373, 381, 391, 393, 394, 400, 402, 408, 426, 427, 429, 432, 435, 439 to 443, 445, 449, 451, 455, 456, 466, 468, 471, 473, 476, 479, 480, 483, 485, 488, 495, 500, 502, 503, 505, 508, 510, 511, 518, 520, 524, **80**-30, 49, 50, 53, 63, 70, 78, 80, 85, 88, 89, 92, 93, 95, 97, 103, 108, 121, 125, 126, 154, 161, 166, 180, 188, 193, 203, 219, 220, 222, 251, 253, 257, 258, 267, 275, 278, 279, 281, 282, 285 to 287, 292, 296, 300, 307, 316, 320, 329, 330, 363, 373, 375 to 377, 379, 425, **81**-18, 20, 25, 35, 36, 40, 41, 45, 53, 58, 60, 64 to 66, 83, 86, 89, 91, 111, 138, 146, 149, 157, 160, 165, 169, 174, 175, 178, 183, 187 to 189, 196 to 199, 201, 202, 204 to 206, 209, 210, 236, 240, 254, 258, 261, 263, **82**-15, 36, 47, 61, 62, 64, 70, 72, 81, 84, 86 to 88, 98, 99, 101, 104, 105, 107, 119, 120, 123, 128, 131, 151, 152, 224, 230, 248, 249, 256, 261, 264, 267, 271, 274, 276, 277, 283, 291, 296, 298, 324, 329, 340, 342, 344, 348, 356, 363, 379, 386, 387, 400, 409, 413, 415, 416, 418, 419, **83**-10, 44, 49, 59, 71, 76, 79, 83, 96, 114, 118, 120, 126, 141, 142, 149, 152, 159, 161, 162, 166, 167, 169, 175, 178, 181, 183, 188, 189, 202, 214, 221, 228, 231, 241, 257, 259, 262, 265, 269, 270, 275, 283 to 285, 289, **84**-10, 29 to 33, 47 to 49, 63, 65 to 67, 74, 83 to 86, 90, 92, 97, 98, 108, 133, 137, 141, 144, 145, 151, 157, 163, 171, 174, 176, 180, 192, 195, 204, 207, 220, **85**-3, 23, 36, 41

    alternating rhyme, **82**-27
    and sixains, **75**-47
    "Answer to an Epigram," **64**-A
    "Blunt Courtier," **70**-A
    "Comparison," **80**-A
    Cowper, "Modern Patriot," "On the Burning of Mansfield's Library," **82**-A
    Cowper, "On the Trial," **79**-A
    double quatrain, **71**-63, **77**-134, **78**-457, **79**-535, **83**-31, **84**-34, 114
        Burns in, **84**-A
        Freeth in, **82**-A

        "Imitation" in, **83**-A
    "Epigram," **63**-A, **64**-A, **68**-A, **69**-A
    "Epigram on the Times," **70**-A
    "Exert your pow'rs," **79**-A
    "Extempore," **68**-A, **69**-A, **78**-A
    "Extempore Answer," **64**-A
    "Hint," **79**-A
    "Impromptu" [4], **68**-A, **83**-A
    in couplets, **63**-178, 184, **70**-97, 134, **73**-16, **75**-83, **78**-103, 108, 299,
        526, **79**-197, **80**-419 to 421, 430, **82**-421
    in HC, **81**-44, 85, **83**-58, 290, **84**-142
    in OC, **70**-242, **78**-421
    irregular, **80**-370
    "Lead on," **79**-A
    "Liberty," **89**-2
    mixed with couplets, **63**-110
    "On a late Remonstrance," **73**-A
    "On a Ropemaker," **75**-A
    "On Ingratitude," **78**-A
    "On Occasion of the Election at Brentford," **68**-A
    "On Reading Mrs. Macaulay," **69**-A
    "On St. Sepulchre's Bells," **65**-A
    "On the Burning of Mansfield's Library," **82**-A
    "On the Defection of the Corsicans," **69**-A
    "One Hannibal," **76**-A
    "A Pill," **68**-A
    Puddicombe, "Verses on his Majesty's Birth-Day," **73**-A
    rough, **80**-428
    "Stanzas," **70**-A
    "To the Author of Verses (on Churchill)," **64**-A
    unrhymed, **81**-203
    unusual, **69**-175
    "Verses Extempore," **65**-A
Raree Show. **77**-66, **78**-422, **79**-409, **80**-313
Rebus. **63**-134, **83**-288
    in HC, **80**-424
    in OC, **68**-124
Receipt, Recipe. **64**-82, **66**-68, **70**-178, **73**-89, **74**-22, **76**-300, 301, **77**-264, **79**-390, **81**-128, 187, **82**-308
    of an epigram, **85**-46
    prescription, **75**-218, **76**-287
Regular Horatian Ode. **See**: Ode, Regular Horatian.
Regular Pindaric Ode. **See**: Ode, Regular Pindaric.
Rondeau. **75**-214, 238, **79**-395, **85**-48
Satire (nature, function or mission, limits, and techniques). **65**-5, **79**-36, **80**-23
    and censorship of targets, **69**-6
    Churchill's *Conference* and *Epistle to Hogarth*, **63**-A
    Churchill's *Gotham*, **64**-A
    defended, **77**-5
    function of, **79**-91
        in this age, **82**-401
    Horace modernized, political limits on satire, **80**-37

indiscriminate and unmerited abuse by hacks, **74**-202
the public and moral mission of satire, **69**-236
purpose, **69**-156
style and targets, **74**-7
Tory limits on satire, **79**-31
Underwood on nature of Churchillian satire, **67**-8

Septain. **64**-54, **70**-113, **78**-208, **79**-19, 294, **80**-295, **81**-87, **82**-370, **83**-173

Sermon. **76**-71, **81**-248

Simile. **59**-31, **66**-103, **68**-15, **70**-171, 199, **71**-17, 70, **74**-212, **76**-190, 316, **77**-61, 268, 273, 278, 324, **78**-92, 358, **79**-74, 97, **82**-294, **83**-219, 249
   **See also**: Metaphor.

Sixain. **59**-26, 39, **61**-26, **62**-13, **63**-8, 13, 82, 104, 153, 160, **64**-28, 47, 52, 55, 73, 83, 87, **65**-15, 66, 84, 85, 90, 91, 122, **66**-21, 29, 35, 46, 61, 62, 66, 72 to 74, 76, 118, 125, 126, 135, **67**-10, 17, 34, **68**-30, 38, 44, 58, 72, 74, 76, 80, 113, 116, **69**-20, 30, 39, 50, 51, 76, 83, 91, 123, 126, 129 to 132, 138, 140, 161, 165, 174, 210, 240, 244, 252, 256, **70**-12, 18, 42, 62, 69, 73, 107, 110 to 112, 141, 143, 166, 169, 179, 213, 220, 227, **71**-12, 51, 59, 66, 67, 86, 102, 105, 109, 116, 119, **72**-16, 24, 52, 66, 93, **73**-60, 102, **74**-23, 53, 79, 101 to 103, 141, 203, 212, 218, **75**-47, 61, 62, 94, 158, 166, 168 to 170, 177, 180, 187, 192, 249, 267, 313, 319, **76**-14, 16, 28, 35, 85, 86, 102, 132, 147, 160, 180, 213, 217, 218, 221, 223, 226, 227, 231, 300, 303, 306, 307, 334, 341, 353, 373, 380, 391, **77**-41, 80, 85, 86, 95, 101, 104, 152, 163, 170, 175, 177, 183, 184, 193, 213, 220, 233, 248 to 250, 266, 269, 271, 273, 280, 283, 285, 292, 315, 316, 322, 323, 332, 333, **78**-2, 4, 27, 47, 65, 87, 94, 96, 111, 188, 230, 263, 273, 279, 280, 281, 313, 320, 322, 324, 330, 345, 346, 362, 375, 436, 453, 458, 466, 490, 513, 514, 535, **79**-47, 55, 65, 68, 70, 95, 100, 101, 103, 110, 114, 121, 126, 128, 129, 139, 199, 208, 209, 214, 258, 286, 291, 292, 299, 300, 308, 310, 312 to 314, 316, 317, 325, 344, 345, 347, 359, 368, 376, 434, 436, 437, 448, 450, 454, 464, 469, 474, 477, 478, 501, 509, 513, 516, 525, **80**-30, 60, 61, 123, 127, 159, 162, 173, 189, 192, 200, 226, 233 to 235, 248, 252, 271, 273, 279, 327, 331, 357, 390 to 392, 397, 410, 413, **81**-30, 42, 52, 69, 136, 138, 139, 142 to 145, 166, 173, 218, 221, 225, 251, **82**-9, 12, 56, 66, 82, 85, 90, 99, 103, 127, 129, 135, 137, 161, 205, 209, 210, 212, 215, 219, 220, 222, 223, 230, 253, 266, 269, 282, 290, 293, 295, 300, 317, 322, 326, 330, 335, 343, 375, 376, 391, 393, 398, 407, 410, **83**-5, 11, 14, 40, 53, 55, 64, 68, 81, 86, 87, 122, 140, 170, 172, 191, 194, 227, 246, 250, 261, 293, **84**-35, 41, 51, 66, 75, 80, 105, 124, 129, 153, 156, 169, 172, 177, 181, 202, 203, **85**-12, 20, 34 to 36, 38, 43, 46

   "The Address," **63**-A
   "Addressed to the Two Patriots," **71**-A
   "Advertisement from France," **60**-A
   "Brest Council," **79**-A
   "Contented Man," **76**-A
   "Dialogue," **84**-A
   in couplets, **63**-187, **65**-62, **70**-176, **73**-40
   in OC, **67**-31
   "Leave prating," **78**-A
   "An Ode," **63**-A
   "Ode on Canada," **60**-A
   "Ode to Ambition," **64**-A
   "Spoken Extempore," **70**-A

Six-line bob-tail stanza. **84**-136

Sixteen-line stanza. **79**-526, **82**-156

Soliloquy.  **61**-41, **63**-126, **66**-25, **69**-57, **70**-39, 75, **72**-83, **73**-15, 39, **74**-83, 173, **75**-210, 234, **76**-68, 178, 184, 201, 280, **77**-136, 141, 283, 298, **78**-291, 404, **79**-52, 256, 377, 411, **80**-331, 286, **82**-332, 334, **84**-53, 93
   **See also**: Monologue and Persona.
Song.  **58**-5, 13, **59**-9, 16, 24, 27, 42, **60**-21, 22, 28, 42, 46, 51, **61**-15, 16, 17, 45, **62**-34 to 37, 50 to 54, 59, **63**-61, 67, 73, 79, 80, 131, 140 to 143, 152, 175, 176, 186, **64**-45, 88, **65**-14, 29, 59, 60, 68, 80, **66**-1, 15, 19, 20, 28, 30, 33, 36, 59, 69, 70, 100, 101, 108, 110, 113, 133, 134, **67**-30, 40, **68**-2, 17, 47, 62, 70, 85, 88, 90, 94 to 96, 112, 113, 119, **69**-35, 44, 54, 85, 86, 89, 110, 118, 119, 176 to 179, 201 to 206, **70**-31, 37, 44, 45, 73, 74, 91, 103 to 105, 140, 162, 165, 172, 190, 192, 193, 205, 225, 241, **71**-6, 11, 45, 61, 101, 127, 129, **72**-63, 65, 80, 81, 87 to 89, **73**-37, 38, 55, 58, 81, 92, 93, 105, **74**-26, 32, 45, 48, 60, 61, 84, 87 to 91, 113 to 115, 153, 174, 177, **75**-25, 39, 48, 52, 53, 101, 107, 112, 115 to 119, 123, 153, 160 to 164, 242, 251, 252, 255, 256, 286, 309, **76**-11, 13, 25, 40, 46, 51, 64, 73, 91, 95, 96, 160, 164, 166, 175, 185, 202, 206, 214, 217, 264, 275, 276, 282, 308, 320 to 325, **77**-2, 29, 31, 35, 40, 43, 49, 59, 112, 124, 128, 129, 131, 132, 144, 166, 173, 174, 186, 265, 282, 285, 287, 288, 291, 297, 311, 313, **78**-37, 54, 59, 65 to 67, 77, 78, 80, 98, 99, 198, 205, 207, 208, 210 to 215, 224, 231, 232, 281, 283 to 286, 292, 294 to 299, 331, 405, 422, 446, 456 to 460, 511, 513, 530, 532, 542, 550 to 553, **79**-19, 63, 78, 80, 82, 85, 87, 88, 96, 104, 112, 115, 187, 193-198, 200(?), 205, 209 to 211, 229, 230, 233, 237 to 239, 241, 242, 247, 263, 270, 274, 276 to 284, 360, 395, 396, 401, 404, 409, 414 to 423, 447, 453, 488, 494, 498, 535, **80**-26, 48, 55, 75, 90, 142 to 149, 155, 156, 158, 176, 183, 201, 205, 215, 216, 218, 223 to 229, 231, 280, 293, 295, 299, 313, 323, 326, 332 to 336, 342 to 344, 367, 387, 404, 417, **81**-21, 30, 33, 39,  43, 75, 77 to 79, 82, 125, 130, 131, 133 to 135, 137, 141, 191, 198, 259, **82**-5, 10, 38, 40, 45, 46, 50, 51, 63, 136, 138(?), 139, 140, 142 to 145, 146(?), 154, 193, 194, 196, 199 to 205, 238, 278, 288, 289, 316, 317, 321, 323, 327, 335 to 339, 351, 355, 360, 373, 378, 388, 403, 412, **83**-15, 26, 39, 43, 63, 106 to 111, 152, 155, 156, 209, 217, 232, 238, 241 to 243, 253, 267, 281, 295 (print), **84**-26, 37, 39, 69, 70, 111 to 118, 131, 139, 149, 161, 166, 172 to 179, 185, 187, 200, 215, **85**-19, 28 to 30, 33, 49, 50, **86**-2, 3, **89**-2
   "Answer to Paddy's Address," **79**-A
   "Ballad," **68**-30
   carol, **70**-196
   a catch, **67**-13, **78**-515
   election song, **63**-76
   Freeth, **66**-A, **82**-A
   "French Politicks," **60**-A
   Garrick's "Heart of Oak," **60**-16
   glee, **77**-138, **79**-203
   "Lead on," **79**-A
   "Modern Mobbing," **79**-A
   "A New Ballad," **62**-48
   "A New Song," **60**-A
   oratorio, **70**-108
   "Song," **62**-A, **66**-A
   a toast, **65**-22
   Tomlinson, **78**-A, **80**-A
   "Volunteer's Rouse," **79**-A
   "While Byron," **79**-A
   Woods, **79**-A

Sonnet (all Italian or Modified Italian sonnets, with few exceptions). 63-144, 66-109, 69-227, 73-24, 75-5, 224, 76-326, 327, 78-287, 461, 462, 79-15, 80-337, 82-11, 23, 83-5, 244, 84-6
    "Address to Britannia," 70-A
    in couplets, 77-327
    John Scott, 66-16
    non-standard, eccentric, 74-100
Spenserian Stanza (two interlinked quatrains in iambic pentameter with rhyme linked last line in iambic hexameter). 69-123, 75-22, 83-16, 17
Squib. 65-19, 66-94, 76-23, 84-58
    "Political Squib," 63-A, 66-A
    "Verses," 69-A
Tetrameter Couplet. 59-3, 67-49, 68-68, 71-42, 72-82, 73-84, 75-265, 298, 310, 76-62, 191, 284, 77-150, 78-557, 79-424, 80-33, 414
    **See also:** Hudibrastic Verse.
Three-stress Couplets. 73-51, 76-45, 245, 311, 78-243
Toast. 58-133, 74-27, 159, 75-287, 76-84, 264, 368, 77-171
    song, 65-22, 79-202
    verse, 58-12, 79-372, 80-151, 82-255, 84-32
Trimeter Couplets. 65-65, 105, 70-19, 85-47
Triplet. 62-64, 63-118, 66-68, 137, 69-64, 251, 270, 70-191, 74-157, 76-124, 125, 368, 400, 77-127, 135, 78-71, 128, 200, 258, 416, 464, 493, 79-399, 496, 532, 80-178, 348, 81-226, 246
    and octosyllabic couplet, 63-102
    "A New Song," 60-A
    octosyllabic, 79-532
    plus tail, 75-112
    trimeter triplet, 79-235
    with fragmented fourth line rhyme, 63-11
Tune. (The melody of traditional or popular songs adopted for the lyrics recorded in this catalogue.)
    "A Begging we will go," 64-88, 73-38, 75-251, 80-223
    "A Cobler there was," 63-186, 75-163, 78-551, 79-489, 80-227, 84-111, 113, 179
    "A Cruising we will go," 79-447, 80-198
    "All in the Land of Essex," 76-73
    "All shall yield to the Mulberry Tree," 82-139
    "The Anacreontic Song," 83-238
        Tomlinson, 78-A, 80-A
    "And a Cruising we will go," 80-198
        **See:** "A Cruising we will go."
    "As I derrick'd along," 62-53
    "As I was a driving my waggon one day," 74-90, 83-110
    "As I went to Abingdon," 77-29, 82-289
        **See:** "Have you been to Abingdon?" and "I went to Abingdon."
    "The Babes in the Wood," 77-287, 85-50
        **See:** "The Children in the Wood."
    "Ballynamona Oro," 84-178
    "Begging we will go," 64-88
        **See:** "A Begging we will go."
    "The Belleisle March," 68-94, 201
    "Bessy Bell and Mary Gray," 76-325
    "Black Joke," 79-274, 80-147

"Black Sloven," **80**-323
"Blow, blow, thou Winter's Wind," **71**-61
"Britannia rule the waves," **62**-51, **79**-282
    **See**: "Rule, Britannia."
"British Grenadiers," **76**-166, **82**-50
"Bumper, 'Squire Jones," **66**-20, **68**-88
"Caesar and Pompey were both of them horned," **65**-59, **82**-145
"Cassini," **80**-148
"Cease, rude Boreas," **79**-404 (melody same as "Welcome, welcome, brother debtor")
"The Chace of Killruddy," **77**-132
"Chevy Chase," **61**-12, **62**-14, **63**-188, **69**-55, 186, 249, **74**-42, 152, **75**-211, **78**-295, **79**-109, 370, 490, **82**-2, 16
    "Cheviot Chace," **70**-82
    "Excellent New Ballad," **63**-A
"The Children in the Wood," **77**-287, **80**-292, **84**-62
    **See**: "The Babes in the Wood."
"Christ Church Bells," **77**-166
"Come, haste to the Wedding," **74**-87
"Come, jolly Bacchus," **69**-204
"Come, let us prepare," **79**-A ("Modern Mobbing")
"Come then, all ye social powers," **77**-2, **78**-211, **79**-96, **80**-231
    **See**: "Come, ye Lads."
"Come, ye Lads who wish to shine," **80**-231 (same as **78**-211, "Come then, all ye social powers")
"Come, ye party jangling Swains," **83**-111
"Cotillon," **78**-284
"Cupid's Recruiting Serjeant," **72**-87
"The Cutpurse," **71**-11
"The Dargle," **78**-66
"Dearest Jenny," **70**-37
"Death and the Lady," **66**-36
"Derry down," **70**-193, 205, 241, **74**-177, **76**-175, **77**-66, 291, **78**-226, 299, **79**-112, 233, 277, **80**-124, 336, 343, 367, **81**-39, 259, **82**-46, 202, **83**-7, 281, **84**-26, 117, 118, 173, **85**-19, 49
"Deserves to be reckon'd an Ass," **79**-279
"Despairing beside a clear stream," **77**-82
"The Diaboliad"(?), **80**-146
"Doodle, doodle, doo," **63**-80, **66**-69, **69**-206, **79**-409
"Drink and set your hearts at rest," **83**-111
"The Dublin Volunteer Quick-step," **82**-203
"The Dusky Morn," **85**-28
"The Dusky Night," **82**-412
"English Brown Bear," **81**-125
"Fame, let thy Trumpet sound," **78**-511
"Farewell to the Highlands," **74**-84
"(A, The) Free and accepted Mason," **76**-160, **79**-494, **89**-2
"Gee-ho Dobbin," **63**-131, 189, **68**-112 (sp. "Geho Dobbin")
"Get you gone, Raw-head and Bloody-bones," **81**-135
"Gillicrankie," **84**-A (Burns)
"Give Isaac the Nymph," **76**-25
"Give round the Word, dismount, dismount," **82**-141
"God save the King," **81**-141
    "Song," **62**-A

"The Gods of the Greeks," **79-416**
"Green grow the Rushes-O," **69-89**
"Hail England, old England," **77-189**
"Hark Away," **73-93**
"Hark, hark away, away to the Downs!", **83-107**
"Hark! the loud Drum," **82-153**
"Have you been to Abingdon? Heigh Sir! hoa Sir!", **77-245**
  **See:** "As I went to Abingdon."
"He that has the best Wife," **62-48**
"Hear me, gallant Sailor, hear me," **79-78**
"Heart(s) of Oak," **60-16, 63-76, 140, 143, 65-80, 66-108, 68-95, 69-203, 70-192, 71-101, 74-20, 75-242, 76-46, 78-212, 231, 460, 79-82, 238, 81-78, 82-336, 339, 83-242**
"Here we go up, up, up," **83-217**
"Hey, my Kitten." **See:** "Oh my Kitten."
"The Highland March to St. James's," **75-286, 76-321, 78-224, 80-228**
"Hosier's Ghost," **74-114, 77-173(?), 80-404, 81-127**
"The Hounds are all out," **69-86**
"How little do the landsmen know," **80-269**
"I went to Abingdon," **82-200**
  **See:** "As I went to Abingdon," and "Have you been to Abingdon?"
"I winna marry any lad, but Sandy o'er the Lea," **76-282**
"In Charles the Second's Merry Days." **See:** "Vicar of Bray."
"In Stories we're told," **81-131, 82-205**
"In Story we're told," **78-285**
"In the Garb of Old Gaul," **75-164**
"Jolly Mortals, fill your Glasses," **76-95, 79-195, 80-142, 84-174**
"(A) Jolly Parson, that lived at Norton Falgate," **79-273**
"Jolly Young Watermen," **76-278, 79-198**
"King George and Old England Forever!" **79-498**
"King John and the Abbot of Canterbury," **78-405**
"Langolee," **84-114**
"Larry Grogan," **65-75, 80-176, 293, 85-30**
  "Answer to Paddy's Address," **79-A**
"The Lass of Peatie's Mill," **78-406**
"Liberty Hall," **80-149**
"Liberty or Death," (from *The Election*), **74-60**
"Lie down, Laugh, and Tickle," **80-183**
"A light heart and a thin pair of breeches," **75-101**
"Lilliburlero," **74-174**
"The Lillies of France," **63-142, 66-100**
"Lochabar," **73-105**
"Lochiel's Reel, Or The Haughs of Cromdale," **84-175**
"Lumps of Pudding," **76-202**
"Maid of the Mill" (last song), **70-144**
"The Maid of the Mill for me" (in *Rosina*, a comic opera by Frances Brooke, music by William Shield, January 1783), **83-209**
"The Man of Kent," **72-63**
"March in (Handel's) *Rinaldo*," **78-54**
"The Men of Kent," **82-40**
"A Merry Song about Murder," **80-201**
"Merry toned Horn," **61-45**
"The Middlesex Farmer," **70-45**

"The Miller," **69**-205
"Moderation," **82**-288
"Moll Spriggins," **69**-44
"Mrs. Anne, Mrs. Anne, it gives me consarne," **84**-131, 215
"The Muffled Bells of Bow and Bride," **75**-115
"Nancy Dawson," **72**-65, **82**-136, **83**-243
"Nothing at all," **85**-30(?)   See: "Larry Grogan."
"Nottingham Ale," **80**-335
"Now's the Time for Mirth and Glee," **83**-109
"Of Jacobites our Town is full," **78**-550
"Of the famous Ninety two," **79**-239
"Oh (O) my Kitten, my Kitten", **74**-113, **75**-162, **80**-216, **81**-33, 137, **84**-115
"Oh that I ne'er had been married," **75**-52
"Oh the Broom, the bonny bonny Broom," **80**-145
"Oh the days when I was young!", **79**-241
"Old Woman of Grimstone," **63**-176, **66**-30, **75**-118
    "The Old Woman at Grinstead," **68**-90
"O Ponder well, ye Parents dear," **82**-201
"O the Roast Beef of Old England," **80**-229, 387, **83**-43(?) 232, **84**-112, 161
    **See also**: "(The) Roast Beef (of Old England)."
"Over the Hills and far away," **66**-15, **79**-193, 420
"Pretty Sally," **72**-81
"Push about the brisk Bowl," **62**-50, **66**-59, **75**-116, **78**-210, 296, **82**-143, **84**-70
    **Also**: "Push about the Jorum"
"Push about the Jorum," **82**-143, **84**-70
"The Roast Beef of Old England," **63**-59, 175, **74**-115, **75**-117, **79**-283, **83**-295
    "Roast Beef," **82**-204, **83**-295
    "A Song," **66**-A
    **See also**: "O the Roast Beef of Old England."
"Room for Cuckolds, here comes my Lord Mayor," **72**-80
"Rule, Britannia," **62**-51, **63**-79, **69**-118, **70**-104, **72**-88, **73**-58, **74**-26 61, **76**-51, 185, **77**-129, 311, **78**-232, 542, **79**-282, **80**-156, **81**-132, 200, **83**-267
"Rural Felicity," **82**-378, **83**-37
"Scotch Reel," **79**-275
"Shawnbree," **65**-60, **83**-106
"Shiling O'Geary," **77**-313
"Sir John, he got him an ambling nag," **75**-161
"Smile, Smile, Britannia," **63**-141
"Social Powers," **79**-96
    **See**: "Come then, all ye social powers."
"Stick a pin there," **79**-197
"Strange rumours of War," **82**-A (Freeth)
"The Sun was in the Firmament," **66**-133, **80**-144
"Sweet Willy O!", **84**-200
"Teague's Ramble to London," **83**-108
"That's a Jubilee," **80**-215
"That the World is a Lottery," **80**-334
"Then why should we quarrel for riches," **79**-423
"There was a jovial Beggar," **65**-148, **66**-19

"There was a Magpye," **78**-298
"There was an Old Woman, and what do you think," **84**-109
"This bottle's the sun of our table," **76**-25
"'Tis a Twelvemonth ago, nay, perhaps, it is twain," **72**-89
"To all ye Ladies now at Land" (ballad by Ld Germain's grandfather, Charles Sackville, 6th Earl of Dorset), **77**-128, **79**-421
"To Britons I attune the Lyre," **79**-80
"'Twas when the seas were roaring," **81**-134
"'Twas you that kiss'd the pretty Girl," **79**-86
"Two Welchman partners in a Cow," **83**-11
"The Vicar and Moses," **80**-143
"The Vicar of Bray," **71**-45, 129, **79**-281, **82**-388, **84**-139, 149
    "The Revolution Anthem," **76**-308
    **Also entitled**: "In Charles the Second's Merry Days."
"The Warwickshire Lad," **80**-295
"The Wat'ry God," **77**-124, **82**-317
"Welcome, Welcome, Brother Debtor" (Melody is the same as "Cease, rude Boreas"), **79**-404, 535, **80**-90, **81**-77
"Well met, brother Tar," **76**-214
"What cheer, my honest Messmates," **80**-205
"When all the Attic Fire was fled," **68**-113, **78**-513
"When Britain (Britons) first at Heaven's Command," **76**-185, **77**-311
    **See**: "Rule, Britannia."
"When Summer Days were long and fair," **82**-141
"The White Cliffs of Albion," **79**-292, 419
"Who's e'er been at Paris," **74**-88
"The Wooden (Naval) Walls of Britain (England)," **73**-37, **80**-155, **82**-403
"World turned upside-down," **60**-51, **66**-134, 140(?)
"Yankee Doodle," **75**-25
    chorus, **79**-276, 527, **80**-199
"Ye Commons and Peers," **62**-54
"Ye Medley of Mortals," **77**-144, **79**-205
"Ye Warwickshire Lads and ye Lasses," **75**-53, **83**-111
Twelves, **69**-127, **76**-281, **79**-311, **80**-243, 302, **82**-68, 397, **83**-168
Unrhymed "Free numbers," **82**-184
    **See also**: Prose Poems.
Unrhymed verse poems, **77**-181, **93**-1
Vaudeville, **77**-43
Vision, **70**-231, **73**-85, **74**-155, 208, 220, **75**-122, **76**-35, 74, **77**-24, **78**-3, 31, 35, **79**-44, **80**-7, **83**-214
    **See also**: Dream Vision.